CURt W9-BUO-047

MANAGERS AND THE LEGAL ENVIRONMENT

STRATEGIES FOR THE 21ST CENTURY

Second Edition

MANAGERS AND THE LEGAL ENVIRONMENT

STRATEGIES FOR THE 21ST CENTURY

Second Edition

Constance E. Bagley
Graduate School of Business
Stanford University

West Publishing Company
Minneapolis/St. Paul   New York   San Francisco   Los Angeles

Copyeditor: Jan Krygier
Index: Maggie Jarpey
Composition: Parkwood Composition

WEST'S COMMITMENT TO THE ENVIRONMENT

In 1906, West Publishing Company began recycling materials left over from the production of books. This began a tradition of efficient and responsible use of resources. Today, up to 95 percent of our legal books and 70 percent of our college and school texts are printed on recycled, acid-free stock. West also recycles nearly 22 million pounds of scrap paper annually - the equivalent of 181,717 trees. Since the 1960s, West has devised ways to capture and recycle waste inks, solvents, oils, and vapors created in the printing process. We also recycle plastics of all kinds, wood, glass, corrugated cardboard, and batteries, and have eliminated the use of Styrofoam book packaging. We at West are proud of the longevity and the scope of our commitment to the environment.

Production, Prepress, Printing and Binding by West Publishing Company

COPYRIGHT ©1991   By WEST PUBLISHING COMPANY
COPYRIGHT ©1995   By WEST PUBLISHING COMPANY
                   610 Opperman Drive
                   P. O. Box 64526
                   St. Paul, MN 55164-0526

Printed in the United States of America
 02 01 00 99 98 97 96 95   8 7 6 5 4 3 2 1 0

Library of Congress Cataloging in Publication Data

ISBN: 0-314-04391-8 (Hard)

CONTENTS IN BRIEF

TABLE OF CONTENTS

PREFACE

While no business curriculum would be complete without an overview of the legal environment in which business takes place, the comprehensive legal environment of business text must offer more. To achieve maximum effectiveness, such a text should not only prepare students for their future careers in business, but should also serve as a practical reference that enables managers to spot legal issues before they become legal problems. This objective has been foremost in the mind of the author of *Managers and the Legal Environment: Strategies for the 21st Century,* Second Edition. As its title implies, the text is designed as a "hands-on" and transactional guide for current and future business managers, including entrepreneurs. It provides them with both a broad and a detailed understanding of how law impacts on their daily decisions. No manager operating in the complex and everchanging global business environment of the 1990s and the 21st century can compete successfully without such knowledge.

The topics covered in *Managers and the Legal Environment: Strategies for the 21st Century* demonstrate its focus on meeting the needs of business managers. The text covers not only the essential legal topics of contracts, torts, antitrust, labor relations, criminal law and the principles of business organization, but also those of vital concern to business managers, such as consumer protection, intellectual property, lending transactions, and securities offerings, as well as international business transactions. The chapter on real property and land use illustrates the overall approach in the text: It includes not only the key legal concepts of property law and land use,

but also a detailed discussion of the essentials of real estate project financing.

In all instances, the form of presentation is dictated by a desire to convey the dynamic interplay between business decisions and the legal environment. When the most effective method of presenting the material is to demonstrate how actual business conflicts are resolved in the courts, an approach emphasizing judicial cases is used. This approach is employed in a majority of the chapters. When certain material, such as discussions of lending transactions and international trade, is best conveyed with text, this is the approach taken.

In addition, the legal topics discussed in the main body of the text are on the cutting edge of business regulation. Such topics include NAFTA, owner/operator liability under the Comprehensive Environmental Response, Compensation and Liability Act (CERCLA), the look-and-feel debate under copyright law, the fiduciary duties of officers and directors in a corporate takeover, AIDS in the workplace, and enterprise share liability for defective products.

This text is suitable for a class in the legal environment of business at the undergraduate, M.B.A., executive M.B.A., or executive education levels. The objective is to be a comprehensive and challenging, yet approachable and understandable, text that will work for both those with substantial work experience and those that are studying business at the undergraduate level for the first time.

Each chapter of *Managers and the Legal Environment: Strategies for the 21st Century* employs a wide array of effective teaching devices that reinforce the goals of the text. These include:

■ A Case in Point

Each chapter presents cases, set off from the body of the text, as examples of the law in action. These cases represent crucial court decisions that have shaped important business law concepts, or that present key legal conflicts that managers will address in their careers. Included are many modern cases that represent the most current statement of the law. These cases include, for example, the 1994 Delaware Supreme Court decision *Paramount Communications Inc. v. QVC Network* Inc., concerning the fiduciary duty of directors faced with a hostile takeover bid. Other traditional cases, like *Meinhard v. Salmon* and *MacPherson v. Buick Motor* Co., are used to show early developments in the law that remain applicable today. The selection and approach to cases is guided by the author's above-stated goal of teaching students to identify legal issues before they become legal problems.

The format of the Case in Point section is designed to convey a detailed understanding of the cases, while simultaneously covering a large range of material. The case citation and facts are followed by a statement of the issue presented, which reinforces the legal principle being illustrated by the case. Each case discussion then proceeds with a presentation of the court's decision then a description of the result.

The opinions in two out of the five-to-seven cases in each chapter are presented in the language of the court, edited for clarity and brevity. Excerpts from dissenting opinions are used occasionally to demonstrate how reasonable people can come to different conclusions about the same facts. This is important for two reasons. First, today's dissent may be tomorrow's majority opinion. Second, comparing the arguments raised in the opinion with those of the dissent requires, and strengthens the student's ability to engage in, critical analysis. Each edited case is followed by two thought-provoking questions which challenge the student's understanding of the court's language and reasoning.

The opinions in the remaining three-to-five cases in each chapter are summarized, thereby permitting the coverage of more cases and concepts than would be feasible if all cases were in the language of the court. The author believes that students benefit from reading a more rigorous treatment of cases than is provided by the short briefs found in many texts. Thus students are provided with a detailed recitation of the facts, the issues, the court's reasoning, and the result.

Many cases also include comments. The comments place the case in its proper legal perspective and offer commentary on why the case is important, why the court decided it a certain way, or what the ramifications of the decisions are for business actors. Thus cases are not presented in a vacuum. Instead, students are provided with an explanation of the key significance of the case. This helps students understand how an individual case impacts on the legal environment as a whole. In addition, the comments encourage students to develop the ability to think critically about court decisions.

■ Ethical Considerations

This text places great emphasis on ethical concerns, stimulating students to understand how their actions as managers must incorporate considerations of ethics and social responsibility.

Ethical considerations are emphasized in three ways. First, the opening chapter, "Ethics and the Law," includes topics such as racial discrimination in Denny's restaurants, the Tylenol and Perrier recalls, and the Chernobyl, Bhopal, and *Exxon Valdez* disasters. Second, the text includes relevant excerpts from the Dun & Bradstreet Code of Conduct. Finally, ethical considerations are highlighted throughout the text.

These ethical considerations are commentaries on how standards of ethics and social responsibility do (and sometimes do not) inform the process of lawmaking. The text discusses the ethical implications of business decisions made in response to legal rules, as well as the moral boundaries of the legal regime. For example, cases discussing the legal rules regarding the payment of greenmail and hushmail by a target company are followed by a discussion of whether such payments, or antitakeover measures generally, are ethical and socially responsible.

■ International Considerations

Two chapters cover international aspects of the legal environment: One chapter addresses international trade law, including the Uruguay Round of GATT and European Union; the other is a transactional, integrated discussion of international business transactions. International considerations are also highlighted in many chapters. For example, both the Product Liability and the Securities Fraud and Insider Trading chapters describe the relevant European Community Directives. Taiwanese environmental law is discussed in the Environmental Law chapter. The impact of the U.S.-Japan trade imbalance is examined in the International Trade chapter. Labor unions in Europe and Japan are discussed in the Labor-Management Relations chapter.

■ Economic, Historical, and Political Perspectives

Each chapter has a separate "boxed" section that puts the law in that chapter into economic, historical, or political perspective. For example, the Contracts chapter traces the doctrine of unconscionability from Roman law. The Labor-Management Relations chapter describes President Clinton's intervention in the American Airlines flight attendant strike, and the Environmental Law chapter describes the economics of selling the right to pollute.

These Perspectives add a "real world" dimension to the material. Too often law is presented in a vacuum, divorced from the larger political and economic context in which the law is created. The goal of these sections is to heighten students' awareness of these larger forces. In addition, business managers should be made aware of the complicated interplay between economics and the law. That interplay is crucial to the operation of a business, but it is often less than predictable.

■ In Brief

To provide a visual aid for the student, the text includes 21 summaries, under the heading "In Brief," that break down into digestible pieces the key elements of material presented in that chapter. In some cases, this may be represented in the form of a flow chart; in others, it may appear in the form of a decision tree or matrix.

■ At the Top

Ten highlighted sections interspersed throughout the text reflect the importance of corporate governance and vicarious liability in today's business and regulatory environment. These sections reflect matters that concern not only upper management and corporate officers, but also employees generally.

■ Inside Story

Each chapter contains case summaries that present fascinating and detailed descriptions of real-world business conflicts. A strong effort has been made to include up-to-the-minute, cutting-edge business disputes. The Inside Stories cover conflicts between key-industry players, such as the IBM and Fujitsu $800 million arbitration, the Treasury Auction scandal at Salomon Brothers, the Dow Corning breast implants, the Caterpillar strike, the Telemex privatization, and the *Pennzoil v. Texaco* case. These Inside Stories bring the legal conflicts to life and reinforce the students' appreciation for how such conflicts are played out in the real world.

■ Defined Terms, Key Words and Phrases, and Glossary

Throughout the text all crucial legal terms are placed in italics and defined immediately. A list of key terms used in a chapter appears immediately before the end-of-chapter Questions and Case Problems, with a page reference to the place where that term is defined.

In addition to the references to defined terms contained in Key Words and Phrases, there is also a comprehensive glossary at the end of the text. The Glossary defines each term that has been placed in italics anywhere in the text. The definition of terms in both the Glossary and Key Words and Phrases helps convey the concepts and improves the students' legal and business vocabulary.

■ The Responsible Manager

Each chapter concludes with a section entitled The Responsible Manager. This section is an in-depth discussion of the crucial legal considerations that the successful manager must take into account. The Responsible Manager sections serve to summarize each chapter, but they are far more than a mere summary: In a concise yet sophisticated manner, they alert managers to the legal issues they must spot in order to avoid violating the law or plunging the company into expensive, time-consuming litigation. In addition, the sections highlight the ethical concerns managers need to confront to adequately serve their company and community.

These sections play a vital role in establishing this text as a must-have for practicing business managers. By turning to the Responsible Manager section in a particular area of the law, managers will find a wealth of practical information that will bring them up to speed on the key legal issues in that area. In addition, these sections are not merely check-lists—they contain a depth of analysis that is demanded by the complex, real-life nature of the problems at hand.

For example, the Responsible Manager section of the Environmental Law chapter is entitled "Managing Risks of Environmental Liability." The first part alerts managers to the various potential sources of environmental liability. The often dire financial consequences of non-compliance are explained. Tied into this discussion is the observation that non-compliance will also lead to injury to persons and property. The second part outlines, in detail, the importance of conducting due diligence investigations, as well as the manner in which such investigations are carried out. The notions of risk allocation, and liability created inadvertently for lenders, are also discussed. Finally, issues surrounding the potential liability of lessors for environmental damage done by lessees, and those relating to SEC disclosure requirements about potential environmental liability are covered. Thus, the section functions as a guide and reference that will point managers to the crucial legal (and corresponding financial and ethical) concerns in a particular area.

The Responsible Manager section for the Courts, Litigation and Alternative Dispute Resolution chapter provides a step-by-step guide to setting up an effective alternative dispute resolution procedure. The Product Liability chapter section provides a manager's guide to reducing risks of exposure for product liability.

■ Pronouns

The text alternates between feminine and masculine pronouns, to include both genders. This seemed less awkward than the artificial construction that results from repeatedly saying "he or she" and "his or her."

■ End of Chapter Questions and Case Problems and Answer Manual

Each chapter is followed by ten sophisticated and thought-provoking questions that require students to synthesize and review the material. The questions are diverse in nature. Some are imaginative hypotheticals that raise the central legal issues in a creative and humorous fashion. Others are based directly on specific cases, presenting real-world legal conflicts as opportunities for students to apply the appropriate law. In most chapters at least half the questions are based on actual cases, with the citation provided for the enterprising student who wants to look up the case in preparation for class. Often the questions based on actual cases raise issues at the cutting edge of the law.

A complete and separate *Answer Manual*, prepared by the author, identifies the issues presented in each of the questions and provides thorough, cogent model answers.

■ Instructor's Manual

The *Instructor's Manual* was developed by Patricia Billow (University of Akron). This manual includes chapter outlines, case summaries, and teaching suggestions.

■ Test Bank

The *Test Bank* was developed by Arthur Levine (California State University–Long Beach) and Peter Lee. It contains true/false test questions, multiple-choice test questions, and essay test questions. The *Test Bank* also includes multi-subject final exam essay questions, prepared by the author.

WESTEST 3.0 Computerized Testing allows instructors to create edit, store, and print exams.

■ Study Guide

The *Study Guide* was prepared by Patricia Billow (University of Akron). It includes chapter objectives, chapter outlines, study questions (fill-in-the-blank, true/false, multiple choice, and essay). Answers are provided in the *Study Guide* .

■ Other Teaching Aids

Cutting Edge Cases in the Legal Environment of Business A collection of 17 recent legal environment of business edited cases, using the court's own language in an expanded format.

Business Law and Legal Environment Video Library Includes a variety of professionally produced videos, including the complete Drama of the Law I and II series.

CD-ROM Resources for Business Law and the Legal Environment Includes cases, key legislation and regulations, relevant articles of the UCC and more. This CD-ROM utilizes West's PREMISE © software which allows you to search for and retrieve specific items quickly.

Business Law and Legal Environment Videodisc Includes topical and issues-oriented video material and more than 1,000 still-frame images.

Ten Free Hours of WESTLAW West's computerized legal research and Dow Jones News/Retrieval service.

"You Be the Judge" This software program provides case problems for ten topic areas. Students are given the facts and then asked how the case should be decided.

Contracts: An Interactive Guide and UCC Article 2 Sales: An Interactive Guide These are interactive programs designed to aid in teaching contracts and sales.

West's Regional Reporters Gives professors and students updated case decisions from their region throughout the year.

Please ask your West representative for the qualification details for the above listed supplements.

■ *Pennzoil v. Texaco* Case Study and Accompanying Video

The *Pennzoil v. Texaco* case study is the Inside Story for the Contracts chapter. It includes excerpts from the court's opinion and the briefs so that students can have the experience of seeing such material first hand. This particular case study can serve as the basis for discussion or for the staging of a mock trial in which students can play the lawyers, executives, investment bankers, and jury. An edited videotape of the mock trial conducted by students in the author's class at the Graduate School of Business at Stanford University is also available.

■ Changes in the Second Edition

After teaching courses at Stanford using the first edition and reviewing suggestions from other professors using the text, I concluded that it would be more logical to order the chapters differently, and to break the 25 chapters into seven discrete units.

One entirely new chapter has been added—Chapter 19 "Consumer Protection." The chapter formerly entitled "Employees" has been broken into two chapters. Chapter 12 "The Employment Agreement" deals with non-regulatory aspects of the relationship between the employee and the employer. Items discussed include wrongful discharge and at-will employment. Chapter 13 "Civil Rights and Employment Discrimination" addresses the explosion in legislation that has occurred in the last five years as it affects the employment relationship. New topics in this chapter include the Civil Rights Act of 1991, the Americans with Disabilities Act, and the Family and Medical Leave Act.

Several chapters have been shortened and collapsed into other chapters to reflect both the relative importance of the material and lessons learned in using the first edition. In particular, former chapter 20 "Lending Transactions" was combined with former chapter 25 "Business Bankruptcies" to form new chapter 24 "Debtor–Creditor Relations and Bankruptcy." Former chapter 21 "Financing the Start-up Company" was collapsed into former chapter 22 "Public and Private Offerings of Securities," to create new chapter 22 "Public and Private Offerings of Securities." Former chapter 24 "Insider Trading" was combined with former chapter 23 "Securities Fraud" to form new chapter 23 entitled "Securities Fraud and Insider Trading."

■ Acknowledgments

A number of professors reviewed portions of the manuscript and the first edition, and provided guidance, correction and helpful commentary. I thank each of them.

Reviewers who provided insight for this edition include:

Barbara Ahna, Pacific Lutheran University
Rodolfo Camacho, Oregon State University
Kenneth D. Crews, Indiana University
James G. Frierson, East Tennessee State University
John P. Geary, Appalachian State University
David G. Jaeger, Case Western Reserve University

Arthur Levine, California State University–Long
     Beach
Susan L. Martin, Hofstra University
William F. Miller, Stanford University
Alan R. Thiele, University of Houston

Reviewers for the first edition include:

Thomas M. Apke, California State University,
     Fullerton
Dawn Bennett-Alexander, University of Georgia
Robert L. Cherry, Appalachian State University
Frank B. Cross, University of Texas, Austin
Charles J. Cunningham, University of Tampa
Michael Engber, Ball State University
Andrea Giampetro-Meyer, Loyola College, Maryland
James P. Hill, Central Michigan University
Tom Jackson, University of Vermont
Roger J. Johns, Jr., Eastern New Mexico University
Jack E. Karns, East Carolina University
Mary C. Keifer, Ohio University
Nancy Kubasek, Bowling Green University
Paul Lansing, University of Iowa
Nancy R. Mansfield, Georgia State University
Arthur J. Marinelli, Ohio University
John McMahon, Stanford University
Gregory C. Mosier, Oklahoma State University
Patricia H. Nunley, Baylor University
Mark M. Phelps, University of Oregon
Michael W. Pustay, Texas A&M
Roger Richman, University of Hartford
John C. Ruhnka, University of Colorado at Denver
Linda B. Samuels, George Mason University
Susan Samuelson, Boston University
Rudy Sandoval, University of Texas, San Antonio
John E. H. Sherry, Cornell University
S. Jay Sklar, Temple University
Larry D. Strate, University of Nevada, Las Vegas
Gary L. Tidwell, College of Charleston
William V. Vetter, Wayne State University
William H. Walker, Indiana-Purdue University, Ft.
     Wayne
Darryl Webb, University of Alabama

The following practitioners reviewed portions of the
manuscript and provided leading-edge input from the
trenches of business law practice:

Dale E. Barnes, Jr., McCutchen, Doyle, Brown &
     Enersen

John A. Denniston, Brobeck, Phleger & Harrison
Laurie Farrow, Mediation Law Offices
Paul D. Frederick, Ashford & Wriston
Webb B. ("Bill") Morrow III, Cooley Godward Castro
     Huddleson & Tatum
J. Thomas Rosch, Latham & Watkins
Diane Wilkins Savage, Cooley Godward Castro
     Huddleson & Tatum
Edward L. Strohbehn, Jr., McCutchen, Doyle, Brown
     & Enersen

Any mistakes or inadequacies are my own.

Special thanks to the Dean's Office at the Graduate
School of Business at Stanford University for their generous support of this project.

My Faculty Assistant, Marilyn Gildea, provided
invaluable word processing, editing, and research support. Her keen eye for detail and consistency helped
immeasurably to convert the manuscript into a clear,
understandable text. She worked Herculean hours and yet
always kept her sense of humor and perspective. Marilyn,
thanks a million. I could not have done it without you.

The following students at the Stanford Law School
helped as research assistants: Nicole Chang, Christy
Haubegger, Scott Hudson, Cassandra Knight, David
Patron, and Nanci Prado. Charles M. Hurr, a member of
the California and New York bars, also assisted, particularly in the area of consumer protection. I thank each of
them for their hard work and creativity.

I also thank Mikhail Klimenko, Ph.D. student at the
Stanford Graduate School of Business, and Mark
Benning and Janet Yearwood, Stanford M.B.A. students,
for their assistance.

Finally, thanks to Clyde H. Perlee, Jr., Publisher and
Editor-in-Chief of West Educational Publishing, for his
insightful and creative suggestions for this second edition, and to Senior Developmental Editor Jan Lamar, who
helped make it all come together. Thanks also to
Production Editor Carole Balach for a wonderful layout
and for meeting a seemingly impossible production
schedule. Once again it has been a real pleasure having
West Publishing as my publisher. I couldn't be more
pleased.

Constance E. Bagley

TABLE OF CASES

The principal cases are in bold type. Cases cited or dicussed are in roman type. Cases that can also be retreived on West's LEGAL CLERK® Research Software System are indicated by a colored dot in this list and by a computer logo in Questions and Case Problems for each chapter.

About the Author

Constance E. Bagley received her J.D., *magna cum laude,* from the Harvard Law School and her A.B., with distinction and departmental honors, from Stanford University, after being elected Phi Beta Kappa her junior year. Bagley received Honorable Mention for the Stanford University Graduate School of Business Distinguished Teaching Award in 1993. Before joining the faculty at Stanford University's Graduate School of Business, she was a corporate partner at the San Francisco firm of McCutchen, Doyle, Brown & Enersen. She is a member of the Faculty Advisory Board of the *Stanford Journal of Law, Business & Finance* and is a contributing editor of the *California Business Law Reporter,* published by the Board of Regents of the University of California.

Dedication

To Christy and Mercedes

UNIT I

FOUNDATIONS OF THE LEGAL AND REGULATORY ENVIRONMENT

Chapter 1

ETHICS AND THE LAW

■ Introduction

Importance of Ethics in Business

In a Business Roundtable report on company conduct in America, a group of prominent business leaders called ethics in business "one of the most challenging issues confronting the corporate community in this era." Managers can expect to confront difficult ethical decisions about the environment, product marketing and safety, affirmative action, the impact of multinationals on developing countries, corporate restructuring, and white-collar crime.

Chapter Summary

This chapter begins with the definition of business ethics and its relationship to economic performance. It discusses some notable examples of social responsibility and irresponsibility on the part of corporations. The chapter shows how corporate conduct raises ethical as well as legal issues. It then discusses the role of the corporation and its managers in ensuring ethical conduct and the evolving role of the law in this area. The chapter concludes with a discussion of different theories of ethics.

Business Ethics

Definition of Business Ethics

There is more to a successful company than meeting bottom-line financial objectives. A manager concerned with ethics must consider how these financial objectives are met and what the company contributes to the worth of society. Most, if not all, business executives would agree that upholding good business ethics is essential to the success of a company and a strong economy. John Akers, former chairman of IBM, has stated: "Ethics and competitiveness are inseparable . . . the greater the measure of mutual trust and confidence in the ethics of a society, the greater its economic strength."[1]

Despite the consensus on the importance of ethics, however, there is no precise definition of what constitutes good business ethics. Many decisions that may not at first glance appear to involve ethics have subsequent ethical implications.

Ethical conduct goes beyond merely complying with the law; conduct deemed legal can still be unethical. Many people associate ethics with such concepts as integrity, fairness, and honesty. For more than 75 years, the J. C. Penney Company has considered ethical business behavior to be that which conforms to the Golden Rule: Do unto others as you would have them do unto you.

How does a manager decide what is ethical? The chief executive officer (CEO) of a highly successful Scandinavian multinational tells his managers to conjure up the following scenario:

> Assume that the decision you are about to make in Timbuktu becomes public knowledge in our home country, the host country and significant third world countries where our company is operating. Assume further that you, as the decision-maker, are called upon to defend the decision on television both at home and abroad. If you think you can defend it successfully in these public forums, the probability is high that your decision is ethical.[2]

Ethical Scandals

The corporate world has been rocked by a number of ethical scandals involving a variety of activities, including insider trading, tax evasion, overcharging on government contracts, ignoring safety or environmental regulations, shady corporate restructurings, and drug and alcohol abuse while on the job. The savings and loan crisis in the U.S. in the late 1980s and early 1990s revealed a great deal of unethical activity. There is even more unethical activity that has not caught the public eye. A 1988 survey by one of the Big Six accounting firms, Touche Ross, found that 94% of top corporate executives believed the business community was troubled by ethical problems.

Relationship of the Law and Ethics

The following case illustrates how legal liability can depend a great deal on how one views the ethical nature of the situation.

---

1. "Good Takes on Greed," *The Economist*, February 17, 1990, 71.

2. Alden Lank, "The Ethical Criterion in Business Decision Making: Operational or Imperative?," in Touche Ross and Co., *Ethics in American Business: A Special Report* (Touche Ross and Co., 1988), 48 (hereafter cited as *Touche Ross Report*).

■ A Case in Point: In the Language of the Court

Case 1.1
MEINHARD v. SALMON
Court of Appeals of New York
249 N.Y. 458, 164 N.E. 545
(N.Y. 1928).

FACTS In 1902 Louisa Gerry leased the Bristol Hotel in New York City to the defendant, Walter Salmon. The lease was for a term of 20 years, beginning in 1902, and ending in 1922. The lessee, Salmon, was to renovate the hotel building for use as shops and offices at a cost of $200,000.

Salmon needed funds in order to complete his proposed renovations to the building, and he got Meinhard to act as a financial backer. Salmon and Meinhard entered into a joint venture agreement with the following terms: Meinhard agreed to pay to Salmon half of the moneys necessary to recon-

Case 1.1 continued on following page

*Case **1.1** continued*

struct, alter, manage, and operate the property, and Salmon agreed to pay to Meinhard 40% of the net profits for the first five years of the lease and 50% for the years thereafter. If there were losses, each party was to bear them equally. Salmon, however, was to have sole power to "manage, lease, underlet and operate" the building.

In January 1922, with less than four months of the lease to run, Elbridge Gerry, who had become the owner of the property, approached the defendant Salmon. Salmon and Gerry agreed to enter into a new 20-year lease for not only the Bristol Hotel, but also an entire tract of property surrounding it. The new lessor (the entity leasing the property) was the Midpoint Realty Company, which was owned and controlled by Salmon. Under the new lease, the Bristol Hotel would eventually be torn down and new buildings to cost $3 million would be built on the old Bristol site and adjacent lots.

The lease between Gerry and the Midpoint Realty Company was signed and delivered on January 25, 1922. Salmon had not told Meinhard anything about it. Meinhard was not informed even of the existence of a new project. The first that he knew of it was in February, when the new lease was a done deal.

Meinhard demanded to be included in the new lease. The defendants, Salmon and Gerry, refused to do so.

Meinhard sued. A referee found in favor of Meinhard but limited his interest in (and corresponding obligations under) the lease to 25%. Both the plaintiff and the defendant cross-appealed to the Appellate Division of the New York court. On appeal, the plaintiff, Meinhard, was awarded one-half of the interest in (and corresponding obligations under) the lease. The defendant, Salmon, appealed to the New York Court of Appeals, the highest state court in New York.

ISSUE PRESENTED   Did Salmon, as Meinhard's joint venturer, have a relationship of trust (or *fiduciary duty*) to Meinhard which obligated him to give Meinhard the opportunity to be included in a new lease covering property that was originally leased by Salmon on behalf of the joint venture?

OPINION   CARDOZO, C. J. (later a justice of the U.S. Supreme Court), writing for the New York Court of Appeals:

. . . .

Joint adventurers, like copartners, owe to one another, while the enterprise continues, the duty of the finest loyalty. Many forms of conduct permissible in a workaday world for those acting at arm's length, are forbidden to those bound by fiduciary ties. A trustee is held to something stricter than the morals of the market place. Not honesty alone, but the punctilio of an honor the most sensitive, is then the standard of behavior. As to this there has developed a tradition that is unbending and inveterate. Uncompromising rigidity has been the attitude of courts of equity when petitioned to undermine the rule of undivided loyalty by the "disintegrating erosion" of particular exceptions. Only thus has the level of conduct for fiduciaries been kept at a level higher than that trodden by the crowd. It will not consciously be lowered by any judgment of this court.

The owner of the [property], Mr. Gerry, had vainly striven to find a tenant who would favor his ambitious scheme of demolition and construction.

Baffled in the search, he turned to the defendant Salmon [who was] in possession of the Bristol, the keystone of the project. . . . To the eye of an observer, Salmon held the lease as owner in his own right, for himself and no one else. In fact he held it as a fiduciary, for himself and another, sharers in a common venture. If this fact had been proclaimed, if the lease by its terms had run in favor of a partnership, Mr. Gerry, we may fairly assume, would have laid before the partners, and not merely before one of them, his plan of reconstruction. . . . The trouble about [Salmon's] conduct is that he excluded his coadventurer from any chance to compete, from any chance to enjoy the opportunity for benefit that had come to him alone by virtue of his agency. This chance, if nothing more, he was under a duty to concede.

. . . .

We have no thought to hold that Salmon was guilty of a conscious purpose to defraud. Very likely he assumed in all good faith that with the approaching end of the venture he might ignore his coadventurer and take the extension for himself. He had given to the enterprise time and labor as well as money. He had made it a success. Meinhard, who had given money, but neither time nor labor, had already been richly paid. There might seem to be something grasping in his insistence upon more. Such recriminations are not unusual when coadventurers fall out. They are not without their force if conduct is to be judged by the common standards of competitors. That is not to say that they have pertinency here. Salmon had put himself in a position in which thought of self was to be renounced, however hard the abnegation. He was much more than a coadventurer. He was a managing coadventurer. For him and for those like him the rule of undivided loyalty is relentless and supreme. . . .

. . . .

RESULT   The judgment for the plaintiff, Meinhard, was affirmed. He was granted one-half of the interest in (and corresponding obligations under) the new lease between Salmon and Gerry.

COMMENTS   In *Meinhard v. Salmon*, the court seemed to assume without explanation that joint venturers had a fiduciary duty to one another. Judges can disagree on what types of business relations give rise to a standard that is "higher than the morals of the market place," thereby giving rise to a fiduciary duty. Furthermore, there is even disagreement as to what constitutes proper morals of the marketplace. In one recent case, decided by the New York Court of Appeals, the same court that decided *Meinhard v. Salmon*, a majority of the judges concluded that a finder of a buyer for a business did not have a fiduciary duty to disclose to the seller the unsavory reputation of the potential buyer.[3] The dissenting judge disagreed. He argued that there was a fiduciary relationship between the parties, and, that even if there were not, the morals of the marketplace would require disclosure. Fiduciary duty and this case are discussed more fully in chapter 5.

---

3. *Northeast General Corporation v. Wellington Advertising, Inc.,* 624 N.E.2d 129 (N.Y. 1993).

Case **1.1** *continued on following page*

*Case **1.1** continued*

Questions
1. Would the result in this case have been different if Gerry had offered Salmon a lease on property far removed from the Bristol property that was the subject of the Salmon-Meinhard joint venture?
2. Why is it appropriate to hold joint venturers to a legal and ethical standard that is higher than the norms of the market place?

Ethics Are Simply Good Business

Not only is ethical behavior good for business, it can even improve the bottom line. This conclusion has generally been accepted by corporate America, and a number of empirical studies support it. For example, the Touche Ross survey found that 63% of the respondents believed that high ethical standards strengthen a business's competitive position. In another study, the Ethics Resource Center in Washington, D.C., surveyed 21 companies that had a written commitment stating that the public was central to their existence. It found that $30,000 invested in these companies 30 years ago would have outperformed by nearly nine times the same investment in Dow Jones composite-index companies that had no written commitment.

Social Responsibility and Profits

A company has an obligation to be both ethical and socially responsible. But what does it mean to be socially responsible? In his seminal article *The Social Responsibility of Business Is to Increase Its Profits,*[4] Nobel Prize winner in economics Milton Friedman asserts that the only guiding criterion for the corporation should be profitability. He argues that it is not the role of business to promote social ends in and of themselves. Friedman asserts that a corporation is an "artificial person" and therefore has no true responsibilities to any constituent other than its owners, or shareholders. When a company makes a decision to spend money for a social cause, it is in essence making the decision for someone else and spending someone else's money for a general social interest.

Friedman's main argument rests on his view that spending corporate funds on social issues is, in effect, usurping the role of government. Spending money in

ways that are not consistent with shareholder wishes is tantamount to imposing a tax and unilaterally deciding where the money will be spent. Because taxation is a governmental function, and only the government has sufficient legislative and judicial provisions to ensure that taxation and expenditures fairly reflect the desires of the public, a corporation making taxation decisions on its own would render the executive "simultaneously legislator, executive and jurist."

Friedman concludes his landmark article by asserting that "social responsibility" is an inherently collectivist attitude and is a "fundamentally subversive doctrine." In a free society, "there is one and only one social responsibility of business—to use its resources and engage in activities designed to increase its profits so long as it stays within the rules of the game, which is to say, engages in open and free competition without deception or fraud."

Friedman's very polemic viewpoint has not gone uncriticized. For example, Richard Nunan argues that corporations are sometimes better equipped than the government to handle certain social issues. For example, soft drink companies have a much better and more credible forum to promote recycling of bottles than the public sector. Furthermore, sometimes corporations even "have moral obligations to pursue socially desirable goals. Specifically, they have a minimal moral obligation to avoid creating social injury and to correct any past social injuries for which they can be held directly responsible."[5]

Some companies have mandated ethical behavior and social commitment as an integral part of their business. Examples include Ben & Jerry's (ice cream and yogurt), The Body Shop (lotions, soaps and cosmetics), and Odwalla (fresh juices). Giant retailer Dayton Hudson

---

4. Milton Friedman, *An Economist's Protest* (1972), 177-84.

5. Richard Nunan, "The Libertarian Conception of Corporate Property: A Critique of Milton Friedman's View on the Social Responsibility of Business," *Journal of Business Ethics* 7 (Kluwer Academic Publishers, 1988), 891-906.

(owner of Target and other stores) regularly gives a certain percentage of its profits to charitable causes.

The Tension: Stride Rite

Stride Rite shoe company found itself in the uncomfortable position of trying to balance "the demands of two masters—shareholders and society."[6] On the one hand, this nationwide company with $625 million in annual sales can be seen as a paradigm of a company able to help improve the quality of life in the community while maintaining a solid financial bottom line. A favorite on the New York Stock Exchange, having almost doubled its sales within the past seven years, Stride Rite was also recognized for its social commitments. It had received 14 public-service awards within the past three years from renowned institutions such as the National Women's Political Caucus and Harvard University. Among other things, the company has contributed 5% of pretax profits to a certain foundation, donated sneakers, set up scholarships for inner city youths, and pioneered the effort in the corporate world to set up on-site facilities for day care and elder care.

Like other companies, Stride Rite has been forced to face the issue of social responsibility versus profitability. In 1984, Stride Rite laid off 2,500 people as a result of a decision to move certain factories abroad to take advantage of lower labor costs. In May 1993 the company announced the closing of its plant in New Bedford, Massachusetts. Facing an unemployment rate of about 14%, residents of New Bedford did not take well the news of the announced closing, and two suspicious fires caused damage estimated at $750,000. Chairman Ervin Shames spoke in defense of the company's seemingly split personality: "Putting jobs into places where it doesn't make economic sense is a dilution of corporate and community wealth. . . . It was a difficult decision. Our hearts said, 'Stay,' but our heads said 'Move.'"[7] A former chairman of the company, Arnold Hiatt, acknowledges the difficulty in the situation: "To the extent that you can stay in the city, I think you have to [but] if it's at the expense of your business, I think you can't forget that your primary responsibility is to your stockholders."[8]

Others see the world of social responsibility as a variable-sum, win-win game. An act need not hurt to be socially responsible. It can help public relations or employee morale. Ewing Kauffman, owner of the Kansas City Royals baseball team and founder of Marion Laboratories, says:

> And the surprising thing, by doing these things, the company increases their image in the community and the region, but even more important is the fact that it creates a feeling of pride among the people who work at that company. They're proud to work at that company, they're proud that their company does those type of things.[9]

Trade-Off Between Good Ethics and Short-Term Economic Return

The proposition that good ethics is good business suggests that there may never be need for a trade-off between what is the best behavior from an ethical point of view and what might be best for short-term economic results. As the Stride Rite example shows, however, this is not always the case. In today's rapidly changing business world, the success of a business is often measured by short-term earnings. Even though companies may preach ethics, the managers who are promoted are generally the ones who demonstrate profitability in their units. Other employees get the message that the bottom line is really what matters. Particularly when business turns sour or becomes more competitive, companies and individuals will often turn their backs on fairness and honesty.

The decay of cultural and social institutions, and the complexities of conducting business in a multinational environment, have been cited as threats to the ethical conduct of business. Even organizations with institutional codes of ethics have encountered problems. For example, cadets at West Point were found guilty of cheating, despite the strong institutional requirements for honesty and integrity. In 1994, naval officials announced that the U.S. Naval Academy had implicated about 125 midshipmen, or about 15% of the class of 1994, for cheating. The Naval Academy, like West Point, has an honor code that prohibits lying, cheating, or stealing.

The following case illustrates both the trade-off between good ethics and short-term economic performance, as well as the limited role of the law in requiring ethical behavior.

---

6. Joseph Pereira, "Social Responsibility and Need for Low Cost Clash at Stride Rite" *The Wall Street Journal*, May 28, 1993, A1. This discussion of Stride Rite is derived from and based upon this article. Reprinted by permission of *The Wall Street Journal*, ©1993 Dow Jones & Company, Inc. All Rights Reserved Worldwide.
7. *Ibid*, A5.
8. *Ibid*, A5.

9. Casey Gilmore, "Mr. K Looks Back, Looks Ahead: On Business and Civic Duty," *Kansas City Business Journal*, September 25, 1992.

■ **A Case in Point:**   **Summary**

Case 1.2
McGANN v. H & H MUSIC
COMPANY
United States Court of Appeals
for the Fifth Circuit
946 F.2d 401 (5th Cir. 1991),
cert. denied, 113 S.Ct. 482
(1992).

FACTS   John McGann was an employee at H & H Music Company. The company had a medical insurance plan for its employees, including McGann, that covered them for up to $1 million in benefits in case of illness. In 1987 McGann learned that he was afflicted with AIDS. He discussed his condition with the executives of the company. He was the only employee then known to have AIDS.

In early 1988 H & H changed its medical plan to limit benefits to those employees with AIDS-related illnesses to only $5,000. McGann sued, arguing that the company had through this action violated the Employee Retirement Income Security Act of 1974 (ERISA) by discriminating against him for exercising a right to which he was entitled. The trial court granted summary judgment for the defendant, H & H Music Company, thereby deciding as a matter of law that H & H should win.

ISSUE PRESENTED   Does discrimination by an employer in the insurance coverage of certain diseases, like AIDS, violate the Employee Retirement Income Security Act of 1974 (ERISA)?

SUMMARY OF OPINION   The U.S. Court of Appeals affirmed the trial court decision in favor of H & H Music. The court did this even though it was convinced that the reduction in AIDS-related benefits was a direct result of the company's knowledge of McGann's illness and that their decision may have involved some prejudice against persons with AIDS. The court ruled that the defendant's actions were permissible because McGann did not have a right to the continuance of the same medical benefits he had received when he first joined H & H. The plan expressly provided that: "The Plan Sponsor may terminate or amend the Plan at any time or terminate any benefit under the Plan at any time." Such a provision was consistent with ERISA. The court also stated that the company had a right to try to reduce its costs in a manner such as the one it had exercised.

The court noted that a number of courts had held that ERISA does not mandate that employers provide any particular benefits and does not itself proscribe discrimination in the provision of employee benefits. Nonetheless, the court agreed that it would have been a violation of ERISA if H & H had discriminated against McGann as an individual for filing medical claims for his AIDS treatment. However, because all employees with AIDS were treated alike, there was no discrimination within the meaning of ERISA.

RESULT   The Court of Appeals affirmed the lower court decision in favor of the defendant employer, H & H. H & H could legally pay lower benefits for medical treatment of AIDS than it paid for other diseases.

COMMENTS   The court acknowledged that ERISA "does not prohibit an employer from electing not to cover or continue to cover AIDS, while covering or continuing to cover other catastrophic illnesses, even though the employer's decision in this respect may stem from some 'prejudice' against AIDS or its victims generally."

EXHIBIT 1-1   Relationship Between Compensation and Ethics

You are a manager of a company bidding on a contract for the U.S. Navy. Although your price is the same as your competitor's, your engineers have told you that it will take your firm longer to develop and manufacture the product. What would you tell the Navy if the Navy asked about your development and manufacture schedule? Here's how the managers in *Industry Week's* survey responded.

	Salary under $40K	Salary $40K–$80K	Salary $80K–$120K	Salary over $120K
Manager indicates company can match competitor's schedule and hopes to find a solution later.	5%	12%	18%	22%
Manager describes company's production schedule as engineers outlined it.	78%	59%	51%	41%

From "Torn Between Halo & Horns," *Industry Week,* March 15, 1993. *Used by permission.*

Balance Between Economic Performance and Ethics

One possible solution to the tension between economic performance and ethics is to set minimum ethical standards that all employees must meet. Managers must try to demonstrate that high ethical standards lead to business success. For example, Johnson & Johnson CEO Ralph Larsen has said that Johnson & Johnson's high-level executives try hard to ensure that their employees live up to their corporate credo, which stresses honesty and integrity. In the words of Larsen, "The Credo shouldn't be viewed as some kind of social welfare program. It's just plain good business."[10]

On the other hand, in a survey done by *Industry Week*, there is evidence to suggest that the more highly compensated a manager, the more likely he is to compromise business ethics. Thirteen hundred managers were asked how they would handle the following situation: Their company is involved in bidding on a contract for the U.S. Navy. Although their price is equivalent to that of their competitor's, their engineers tell them that it will take several more months than their competitor to develop and

manufacture the same output. When questioned what the manager would tell the Navy when asked about their development schedule, the more highly compensated managers were more willing to be less than frank with the Navy to get the business (see Exhibit 1-1).

■ Promoting Ethical Behavior

The CEO Sets the Ethical Tone of the Corporation

The chief executive officer (CEO) plays the most significant role in instilling a sense of ethics throughout the organization. William F. May, chairman of the Trinity Center for Ethics and Corporate Policy, states: "The CEO has a unique responsibility; he's a role model. What he does, how he lives, and the principles under which he operates become pretty much those the rest of the corporation emulate."[11] John J. Mackowski, chairman and CEO of the Atlantic Mutual Companies, states:

I think the CEO's responsibility is to view ethics within the corporate culture, understand how its values—good or bad—come to bear upon the company, its business, and its

10. Faye Rice, Stratford P. Sherman, Brian O'Reilly, Brian Dumaine, Sarah Smith, and Patricia Sellers, "Leaders of the Most Admired: Corporate Citizenship," *Fortune*, January 29, 1990, 40.

11. *Touche Ross Report*, 28.

"I KNOW THE DIFFERENCE BETWEEN RIGHT AND WRONG, BUT SO FAR I'VE NEVER HAD REASON TO ACT ON THAT INFORMATION."

employees. In well-run corporations, for example, the great thing is the sense the staff has of fairness. And for most things, they know enough so that they really need not go to a supervisor to find out what is right or wrong. It's there in specific statements about how they are supposed to deal with customers or one another. And that direction has to come from the top.[12]

This is not to downplay the role of middle management. It is often an employee's immediate supervisor who has the most direct effect on the employee. Direction from the top, however, makes middle management aware that the CEO is serious about her commitment to ethics. Ethics cannot be made a high priority of

the corporation overnight, but it can be achieved through strong leadership and support from the CEO.

The chairman and chief executive officer of The Dun & Bradstreet Corporation (a global credit rating agency and the preparer and publisher of the Nielsen TV ratings) introduced his company's policy on business conduct with the letter shown in Exhibit 1-2. (All excerpts from The Dun & Bradstreet Corporation Policy on Business Conduct used with permission.)

Treatment of Employees

Typically, corporations with high ethical standards emphasize employee self-esteem. If employees feel that they are being treated fairly, they take pride in both themselves and their company. If not, they may retaliate by

---

12. *Touche Ross Report*, 28.

Historical Perspective
Aquinas on Law and Ethics

Saint Thomas Aquinas (1225?-1274), theologian and philosopher, believed that an unjust law could not properly be considered a law at all. The only true laws were those that followed eternal law—as far as eternal law could be discovered by the use of human reason and revelation. Eternal law is the orderly governance of the acts and movements of all creatures by God as the divine governor of the universe.

Because not every individual follows a natural inclination to do good, that is, to act virtuously in order to achieve happiness and to avoid evil, human laws are framed to train, and sometimes compel, her to right actions, as well as to restrain her from doing harm to others. According to Aquinas, in order for human law to be considered law, that is, binding on human conscience, it must be just. In order to be just, a human law must be: (1) consonant with a reasoned determination of the universal good; (2) within the power of individuals to fulfill; (3) clearly expressed by legitimate authority; (4) approved by custom, that is, the declaration of right reason by a community; and (5) widely promulgated. To the extent that human law is just, it is in concert with eternal law, as discerned through human reason, and is binding on individuals. Human laws that promote private benefit over the common good are unjust, and individuals are bound not to obey them. Instead individuals should "disregard them, oppose them, and do what [they] can to revoke them."[a]

Most modern legal theorists separate the question of a law's status as law from the question of its inherent morality. They argue that a law may help to resolve moral issues, punish immoral action, and serve a moral purpose (as, for example, when laws permit participation in government); but a law need not be inherently moral to be a real law. In this so-called positive-law view, any law counts as a real law if it has been created according to recognized procedures by someone with the recognized authority to do so—a king, for instance, or, in the U.S. system, a legislature, a judge, or an administrative agency. A properly created law may, of course, be criticized as immoral. Persons may even wish to disobey it. But they do so in the full knowledge that they are disobeying a valid law.

In the United States the split between legal and moral debate has always been less clear than positive-law theorists might wish. Americans have always given their moral debates a peculiarly legal flavor, mainly because certain important but ambiguous phrases in the U.S. and state constitutions invite a person to "constitutionalize" moral questions. Moral questions are readily translatable into questions about the meaning and scope of the constitutional doctrines of due process of law, equal protection under the laws, or cruel and unusual punishment.

It has become a national trait of Americans to wish to find their moral convictions embodied in their constitutions. Just as Aquinas believed that unjust laws could not accord with eternal law, so many Americans believe that unjust laws cannot be constitutional. Perhaps it is for this reason that so many of the most controversial American moral debates—such as those on slavery, prohibition, civil rights, equal rights for women, gays in the military, the right to die, and abortion—have focused on the interpretation of constitutions or have been framed in terms of possible constitutional amendments. In some ways the tendency in the United States to look to constitutions for the determining of the just quality of law is akin to the use by theologians of the Judeo Christian Scriptures as supernatural revelation or knowledge of the universal good that is eternal law.

As this comparison of present-day constitutional analysis to thirteenth-century theology indicates, the past is often a valuable pointer to the future. At the same time, one must be able to distinguish differences between doctrines that prevailed in the past and those that should prevail in the future. In this regard it is important to recall the positivists' distinction between law and morals. If a person confuses "what's allowed" with "what's right," he risks cutting his ethical discussions short, and missing opportunities both for the encouragement of morality by law and for the reform of law in the light of society's morals.

a. P. Glenn, *A Tour of the Summa* (1978), 170.

EXHIBIT 1-2   A CEO's Message on Ethics

To All Dun & Bradstreet Associates:

Dun & Bradstreet's strategy is to be number one in the markets we serve, and to serve our customers, ourselves and our shareowners as "One Company"—one company that is a global company. To be one company worldwide, we must share the same values and the same principles of business conduct—principles that govern the way we approach every sale, every contact with a customer, every relationship with a competitor, every business decision. And principles that govern the way we treat each other.

We have developed this Policy on Business Conduct to guide D&B associates in applying ethical practices to their everyday work. Our policy describes not only our standards of integrity, but also some of the specific principles and areas of the law that are most likely to affect us as we do our jobs. Each of us must recognize that unethical actions are often illegal actions, and can subject D&B associates and the Company to serious penalties.

If you have questions about the policy, or are concerned about possible violations, don't hesitate to seek advice; consult your manager, human resources person or Legal Department. You can also contact D&B's Office of Business Practices, where your inquiry will be kept confidential. This booklet includes the phone number for D&B's Vice President–Business Practices and other people who may be able to help.

Values at Dun & Bradstreet are a shared responsibility. And that means each of us is personally accountable for upholding the highest standards of individual and business integrity.

Sincerely,

Charles W. Moritz
Chairman and Chief Executive Officer

Used by permission.

stealing supplies or inventory, padding expense accounts, or calling in sick when they are actually well. They may simply not produce at their optimum level. Thus it is in a corporation's best interest to ensure that its internal corporate culture is ethical. One way that has been used to empower employees to report ethical violations and other problems that could result in legal liability is to provide a forum whereby they can report such matters without fear of retribution from their immediate supervisors or co-workers. Some legal protection is provided to so-called "whistleblowers" by statutes (discussed later in this chapter).

John H. Stookey, president and chairman of Quantum Chemical Corporation, focuses on employee self-esteem:

If people work in an organization which demeans their sense of self-worth, they are humiliated by small amounts every day. But if they work for an organization that enhances their self-esteem, it is enormously valuable to

them. So if by publishing a code of ethics or by setting an example you can reinforce a person's sense that he is part of an upstanding enterprise, you are reaffirming his faith in himself. He becomes prouder of who he is and of where he's working. If you understand that process, it is not difficult to raise the ethical standards of an institution, because you can play to those needs and a lot of people will work with you.[13]

Mission Statements

Corporations sometimes include ethical language in their corporate mission statements. This language may not mention ethics by name, but stresses that the corporation has responsibilities in addition to profit maximization, and that it has obligations to both employees and cus-

---

13. *Touche Ross Report*, 34.

EXHIBIT 1-3   Excerpts from The Dun & Bradstreet Corporation's Policy of Business Conduct

---

Ethical Business Practices

Dun & Bradstreet policy and its *Statement of Values* require that associates conduct themselves according to the highest standards of integrity and business ethics. You must never let any misguided sense of corporate loyalty lead you to disobey the laws of those countries in which we operate.

Besides being the right thing to do, ethical conduct is good business practice. Customers, suppliers and others may not come back if they feel we have mistreated them. Ethical business conduct is also regulated by many laws. These laws deal with fraud, deceptive acts, bribery, consumer protection, competition, unfair trade practices and patents, trademarks and copyrights. Several types of these illegal business practices are discussed below.

Used by permission.

tomers. An example of a mission statement stressing the development of human capital might be: "To utilize professional management and flexible strategies by developing capital and human resources to satisfy investors' reasonable profit expectations."

Codes of Ethics

Codes of ethics are the most widespread means by which companies communicate their ethical standards to their employees. A code of ethics is a written set of rules or standards that states the company's principles and clarifies its expectations of employee conduct in various situations. Although these codes vary from company to company, they govern such areas as selling and marketing practices, conflict of interest, political activities, and product safety and quality.

The Ethics Resource Center reported in 1987 that 74% of all large corporations in America had adopted a code of conduct; 50% of them were written in the post-Watergate era between 1974 and 1979. In 1986, the Center for Business Ethics found that of companies taking steps to institutionalize ethics, 93% had compiled codes of ethics.

Business leaders judge a code of ethics to be one of the most effective measures for encouraging ethical business behavior. James Burke, chairman of Johnson & Johnson, believes that Johnson & Johnson's code of ethics helped the company out of its Tylenol tampering crisis. Johnson & Johnson's code begins: "We believe that our first responsibility is to the doctors, nurses, and patients, to mothers and all others who use our products and services. In meeting their needs, everything we do must be of high quality."[14] When it was discovered that

Tylenol capsules had been tampered with, the company acted swiftly to remove the product from the shelves. "Dozens of people had to make hundreds of decisions on the fly," says Burke. "There was no doubt in their minds that the public was going to come first in this issue because we had spelled it out [in our credo] as their responsibility."[15]

It is important to note that a company code of ethics is ineffective without proper implementation. It is not enough simply to state the rules of the company; the code must give employees an understanding of principles to guide them in making practical decisions. The code should be a living document, reviewed periodically to meet new circumstances. Managers should go over the code with personnel to ensure understanding of the company's values. The company should supplement the written code of ethics with ethics education programs conducted by professional trainers. The company should also pay increased attention to ethical standards in recruiting and hiring.

Exhibit 1-3 contains excerpts from The Dun & Bradstreet Corporation's Policy of Business Conduct.

Oversight

In an effort to enforce ethical standards, some companies have set up oversight committees. According to a 1992 survey by the Center for Business Ethics, nearly half of the respondents (all Fortune 1000 companies) had ethics officers. Nearly all of these officers had been appointed in the previous five years.[16]

---

14. *Touche Ross Report*, 38.

15. Stanley J. Modic, "Corporate Ethics: From Commandments to Commitment," *Industry Week*, December 14, 1987, 33.
16. Rosie Sherman, "Ethicists: Gurus of the '90s," *National Law Journal*, January 24, 1994, 1.

EXHIBIT 1-4   Sample Questions form the Citicorp "Work Ethic" Game

1. An important customer arranges a meeting for you and several of your staff at a private club. The meeting is about to begin when a waiter tells you that a member of your staff has been refused admittance because of his race.

You:
  (a) ask the customer to move the meeting to a local restaurant so your colleague can attend.
  (b) tell the customer that the meeting will have to be rescheduled at a Citicorp facility.
  (c) ask your employee to leave and say you'll talk to him when you get back to the office.
  (d) say an emergency has come up, you have to leave, but you'll reschedule the meeting.

2. You're responsible for purchasing office equipment and supplies for your department. After you've held the job for a year, your husband becomes a salesperson for one of your suppliers and gets assigned to your unit as part of his sales territory.

You:
  (a) do nothing.
  (b) update your conflict of interest disclosure form and ask your supervisor to remove you from decisions concerning that supplier.
  (c) replace equipment from your husband's company with equipment from another supplier.
  (d) ask your husband to request another territory.

Used by permission.

In general, ethics committees are responsible for setting standards or policy and for handling employee complaints or infractions. The membership of these committees often includes executive officers or directors of the company. Ombudsmen investigate employee complaints. Judiciary boards usually decide cases of ethics code violations.

Another method of oversight is the social audit. Increasingly, companies have been performing social audits of their activities in sensitive or controversial areas. For example, a company might conduct an internal audit of its disposal of chemical waste, or a bank might audit the reporting practices of its securities trading division. Oversight committees may also be responsible for looking at ethical considerations in a company's benefits programs.

Ethics Training

Many companies hold workshops and courses in ethics for their employees or hire ethics consultants to run training sessions; 60% of the companies that provide ethics training do so during the orientation process for new employees. Companies cite two primary goals of ethics training: (1) to develop a general awareness of ethics in business and (2) to draw attention to practical ethical issues.

Some companies have developed innovative methods for educating their employees in ethics. Citicorp, the largest bank holding company in the United States, created a board game to instruct its employees in Citicorp policies, laws governing the workplace, and ethical decision making. The game, called "The Work Ethic—An Exercise in Integrity," has been played in company orientation sessions and training programs by more than 40,000 Citicorp employees at all levels of management.[17]

In the game, teams of employees are presented with ethical dilemmas and alternative courses of action. Each team, after discussion, selects one of four courses of action. The teams advance on the gameboard according to the ethical appropriateness of their responses. The questions cover a wide range of subjects, including bribery, customer confidentiality, sexual harassment, and discrimination. Two sample questions are shown in Exhibit 1-4.

Citicorp feels that the game has been successful in communicating to employees the importance of ethics in business and in teaching them the standards and policies of Citicorp. "The Work Ethic" game is just one of several

---

17. Citicorp North America, "Business Ethics: What Is Business's Responsibility?" *Asset-Based Finance Journal* 8, Fall/Winter 1987.

programs at Citicorp to increase awareness of the importance of ethics.

■ Social Responsibility

The public's perception of socially responsible behavior influences the ethical decisions that businesses make. Many companies have faced severe financial setbacks caused by decisions that, in hindsight, were perceived by the public as unethical. Consumer products companies are particularly sensitive to public perception, given their reliance on individual retail sales. As William D. Smithburg, chairman and chief executive officer of the Quaker Oats Company, wrote: "[I] know ethical behavior is sound business practice because every day at the Quaker Oats Company I am reminded that we succeed or fail according to the trust consumers have in us."[18]

Issues of social responsibility arise in the areas of product safety, the environment, investment, advertising campaigns, underpaid foreign workers, and charitable contributions.

Product Safety

Socially responsible businesses place a heavy emphasis on the safety of their products. Huge costs have been associated with failure to meet the public's perception of what is safe.

Tylenol Johnson & Johnson's Tylenol success story is an illustration of socially responsible behavior. In September 1982, some Tylenol capsules were tampered with and laced with cyanide poison. As soon as the first deaths were reported, the company recalled 31 million bottles of Tylenol. This recall cost Johnson & Johnson approximately $100 million. Although the short-term economic costs of such a move were enormous, within a matter of months Johnson & Johnson was able to regain the market share it had lost. By living up to its reputation for integrity and social responsibility, Johnson & Johnson enhanced both its public image and its long-term profitability.

Jack-in-the-Box An incident involving contaminated meat linked to the Jack-in-the-Box fast-food restaurant chain illustrates the complexities of handling an ethically sensitive issue. In January 1993, an outbreak of severe diarrhea and stomach complaints in more than 200 persons in Washington state was linked to beef served in the

Jack-in-the-Box restaurants. The chain immediately took the precaution of suspending sales of all ground beef products in 60 restaurants in western Washington until the arrival of a new shipment of ground beef. Several days later, a two-year-old boy died from a sickness caused by the bacteria-contaminated meat. A toll-free number was set up to answer customer questions. The affected families were contacted, and those who could not be individually reached were told publicly that all of their hospital bills would be paid. Despite the fact that the chain has been in business for more than 40 years and has sold millions of hamburgers, no amount of advertisement or "cleanup" could completely save the Jack-in-the-Box name from being tarnished.

Nestlé's Infant Formula Nestlé's promotion of infant formula in developing countries is an example of ethically questionable behavior, and led to a worldwide boycott of the Swiss company's products in the late 1970s and early 1980s. Critics argued that the marketing of infant formula caused women to abandon breastfeeding for formula, which poor families could not afford. They also argued that the formula could be dangerous when mixed with impure water, when overdiluted, or when prepared in unsanitary bottles—all scenarios that could easily occur in developing countries. This boycott ended in 1984, when Nestlé agreed to comply with the infant formula marketing standards of the World Health Organization (WHO). It has been estimated that Nestlé lost more than $40 million in revenues as a result of the boycott.

In 1988, several groups, including Action for Corporate Accountability (ACA), the successor of groups that led the original boycott, were again calling for a boycott of Nestlé because of its controversial marketing practices in the Third World. Once again, Nestlé was accused of violating WHO's guidelines for marketing infant formula. The International Baby Food Action Network agreed with the ACA's claims and renewed its efforts in the boycott in 1990.

Nestlé responded to these accusations by claiming that it did adhere to the WHO's Code for the Marketing of Breastfeeding Substitutes and individual national codes. In addition, Nestlé attempted to improve infant nutrition by adopting a plan of action developed in collaboration with the Nestlé Infant Formula Audit Commission, an independent body of church leaders, scientists, and academics, chaired by former U.S. Senator and Secretary of State Edmund Muskie. The plan was designed to achieve the objective of improving the health of children during the first two years of life. It had two focuses: (1) indus-

---

18. *Touche Ross Report*, 45.

trywide termination of all donations of infant formula, which discourage breastfeeding; and (2) the development of educational materials and new products to improve maternal and child health. Notwithstanding these efforts, as of 1993, the boycott continued.

The Environment

Closely akin to product safety is environmental safety. Disregard for safety has resulted in some spectacular environmental disasters.

Bhopal The Union Carbide disaster at a pesticide factory outside of Bhopal, India, in 1984 provides a vivid example of the failure to make the right ethical decisions. Union Carbide, prior to the accident, had been warned by a team of experts that the plant had "serious potential for sizable releases of toxic materials."[19] In addition, there were six serious accidents at the Bhopal facility during the six years that preceded the disaster. Clearly, Union Carbide had reason to believe the facility was at risk. On December 3, 1984, in the most lethal industrial accident ever, some 40 tons of methyl isocyanate gas was emitted from the plant. As of 1991, more than 3,800 persons had died as a result of the accident, and 20,000 were left seriously disabled. The Indian government has received more than 650,000 claims from individuals physically and psychologically affected, and as of 1993 had accepted 300,000 claims.

If this disaster had occurred in the United States, Union Carbide would have been financially crippled, if not driven into bankruptcy, by the lawsuits that would have followed. In a settlement with the Indian government, however, Union Carbide—which has $5 billion in equity—agreed to pay $470 million to settle all present and future claims. Although this appears to be a great deal of money at first glance, *The Wall Street Journal* has estimated that the victims are likely to receive less than $1,000 apiece. Alok Pratap Singh, leader of one of the larger victim groups, estimates the needs of Bhopal at $4.5 billion over the next 20 years.[20]

In January 1990, the newly elected Indian government announced that it would review the company's settlement with the Bhopal victims. In October 1991, India's Supreme Court upheld the $470 million settlement. The attorney for one of the biggest groups of victims and

other opponents of the settlement had unsuccessfully argued that Union Carbide should be required to pay "first world" not "third world" rates for deaths and injuries.[21]

The Rhine: Sandoz Company Thirty tons of agricultural chemicals and solvents and 440 pounds of mercury were spilled into the Rhine River in Europe in 1986. Ecologists dubbed it one of the worst environmental disasters of the decade. Drinking water was contaminated, and hundreds of thousands of fish and eels died. The disaster stemmed from a fire that destroyed a Sandoz Company warehouse in Switzerland in November 1986. Sandoz and the Swiss authorities were accused of negligence in failing to follow safety regulations. Sandoz, the third-largest chemical manufacturer in Switzerland at the time, suffered a blow to its public image as protests and demonstrations erupted across western Europe.

Exxon Valdez Another environmental disaster with grave consequences was the Valdez, Alaska, oil spill. On March 24, 1989, 10.1 million gallons of crude oil spilled from the tanker *Exxon Valdez* into the waters of Prince William Sound. More than 36,000 migrating birds were killed, an estimated 1,000 miles of shoreline was affected, and one of the world's richest salmon fisheries was greatly impaired. Exxon estimated that the costs of cleaning up the most disastrous oil spill in North American history was upwards of $2 billion. The spill cut Exxon's earnings for 1989 to $3.81 billion compared with $5.26 billion in 1988.

Questionable ethical decisions by Exxon and unacceptable behavior by certain Exxon employees triggered severe worldwide criticism. The captain of the vessel was not at the helm of the tanker when it went aground. He had left the third mate, who was clearly unqualified under U.S. Coast Guard standards to navigate through the Prince William Sound, to steer the tanker. The Coast Guard was also criticized for not keeping a closer watch on the radar.

In February 1990, a U.S. federal grand jury indicted Exxon and its shipping subsidiary on five criminal charges, two of which were felonies, that carried possible penalties of more than $600 million. In 1991 Exxon reached a $1.025 billion settlement agreement with the federal government and the State of Alaska. The $900 million civil portion of the settlement is to be paid to the

---

19. Robert Sherrill, "Corporate Crime and Violence: Big Business Power and the Abuse of the Public Trust," *Nation*, November 28, 1988, 568.

20. Anthony Spaeth, "Court Settlement Stuns Bhopal Survivors," *The Wall Street Journal*, February 22, 1989, A12.

21. Scott McMurray, "India's High Court Upholds Settlement Paid by Carbide in Bhopal Gas Leak," *The Wall Street Journal*, October 4, 1991, B8.

state over a 10-year period. Exxon also agreed to pay a $125 million criminal fine, including restitution of $100 million to be equally divided between the state and federal governments to pay for restoration in Alaska.

In March 1990, the captain of the tanker was convicted of negligently discharging oil. He was acquitted, however, of criminal mischief, operating the tanker while intoxicated, and reckless endangerment. The captain was sentenced to 1,000 hours of community service, mostly to help clean oil-soaked beaches, and ordered to pay $50,000 in partial restitution.

In August 1994, in a civil suit brought as a class action involving about 10,000 commercial fishermen, a federal court jury in Anchorage awarded compensatory damages against Exxon of $286.8 million. The jury awarded $5 billion in punitive damages in September 1994.

Public outrage at the Valdez oil spill and Exxon's cleanup efforts has not gone unnoticed by some corporations. Exxon appointed one of its top executives to monitor its environmental actions worldwide. It also placed a scientist on its board of directors, and the board formed a public issues committee to respond to shareholder, consumer, and environmental concerns. Some oil companies, such as Chevron, advertise on television their sensitivity to environmental issues.

Individual and institutional investors are also taking steps toward more environmentally responsible behavior. The Social Investment Forum undertook a project called the Coalition for Environmentally Responsible Economies (CERES) to draft investor guidelines. The CERES principles, which were introduced in 1989, have been presented at numerous shareholder meetings Approximately 75 companies had endorsed the principles as of 1994. The largest are Sun Company (an oil marketer), H.B. Fuller (a specialty chemicals manufacturer), and General Motors.[22] The guidelines focus on environmental awareness and corporate activities such as using and preserving natural resources, safely disposing of pollutants, marketing safe products, and reducing environmental risks. Some pension funds and institutional investors have adopted such shareholder proposals and plan to base their investments on corporations' adherence to these principles.

Chernobyl In 1986 an explosion at the Chernobyl nuclear power plant in the former Soviet Union released a radioactive cloud that spread over the Soviet Union and across Europe. Radioactivity was found in reindeer in Norway and cattle producing milk in France. Some Soviet scientists and politicians claim that the accident released at least 20 times more radiation than the Soviet government admitted, that Soviet officials failed to evacuate nearby cities and towns right away, though they knew of the danger, and that the experts knew that the Chernobyl design was unsafe.[23]

Nationalist and environmental groups in the Soviet republic of the Ukraine, where the plant is located, fought hard for the closing of the Chernobyl nuclear plant complex. In March 1990, the Soviet Union announced that it would phase out operation of the plant by 1995. The economic problems faced by the former republics of the Soviet Union caused a reversal of that decision in 1993.

Russian Dumping in the Sea of Japan In October 1993, the Russian government came under sharp criticism for dumping 800 tons of low-level radioactive waste 550 kilometers off the shores of Japan. Russia claimed it could afford no other alternative.

In November 1993, 72 nations approved a total ban on radioactive waste disposal at sea. When the ban became effective in February 1994, Russia was the only country that refused to ratify it. With Japan's help, however, Russia constructed in 1994 land-based facilities to store liquid nuclear waste. Russia thereby averted the need to dump additional radioactive waste in the Sea of Japan.

Love Canal Between 1942 and 1954, the Hooker Chemicals & Plastics Corporation used the Love Canal area (a 16-acre parcel of land located in the city of Niagara Falls, New York) as a landfill for toxic chemical wastes from its Niagara Falls plant. In 1953, the company transferred the site to the city school board, and an elementary school was built in the central section of the parcel. A health emergency was declared in 1978 when chemical residues began seeping into the basements of neighborhood homes. In 1979, the State of New York and the United States brought suit to recover cleanup costs. In 1985, Hooker settled a lawsuit with 1,300 current and former residents of the Love Canal area for $20 million; the residents had originally sought $16 billion for personal injury and property damage claims. As of 1994, the amount of the remedy was undetermined, but a federal

---

22. Michael Parrish,"GM Signs on to Environmental Code of Conduct," *Los Angeles Times*, February 4, 1994, D1.

23. Michael D. Lemonick, "The Chernobyl Cover-Up," *Time*, November 13, 1989, 73. See also Felicity Barringer, "Evolution in Europe: Four Years Later, Soviets Reveal Wider Scope to Chernobyl Horror," *The New York Times*, April 28, 1990.

district court in New York ruled in a 1994 opinion that plaintiffs were not entitled to punitive damages because Hooker's landfill operation did not constitute a reckless and wanton disregard for the health and safety of others.[24] (This case is discussed in greater detail in chapter 16.)

Positive Action

Some companies make socially responsible choices without waiting for a problem to arise. For example, even though Great Britain did not at the time require cars to have catalytic converters to reduce air pollution, in 1990 German carmaker Audi was the first company to put catalytic converters as standard equipment on its cars sold in Great Britain. Audi expected that this move, along with a heavy advertising campaign targeted to the Green environmental movement, would increase its sales by 40% in an otherwise stable market.

Many companies took positive environmental actions to enhance their images before Earth Day on April 22, 1990. For example, the three largest sellers of canned tuna stopped buying tuna caught with nets that kill dolphins in the process. The dolphins were drowning because they could not get to the surface to breathe air. Many companies labeled their products as environmentally sound. Shell Oil announced that it had put a new low-polluting gasoline on the market. Shell President Frank H. Richardson stated, "This new gasoline reflects Shell's ongoing commitment to make environmental considerations a priority in the development of our new products and processes."[25]

In response to the *Exxon Valdez* debacle, Conoco, one of the United States's largest oil companies, announced in April 1990 that it was ordering two new oil tankers with double hulls. Experts believe that double-hull tankers can prevent or limit spills if the tanker runs aground. Conoco President and Chief Executive Officer Constantine S. Nicandros stated, "We are in the business by the public's consent. We are sincere in our concern for the air, water and land of our planet as a matter of enlightened self-interest."[26]

> 66
>
> *"We are in the business by the public's consent. We are sincere in our concern for the air, water and land of our planet as a matter of enlightened self-interest."*

The examples in this section highlight three important needs. Companies must: (1) think critically about the moral aspects of corporate activity; (2) be ethical and be perceived by the public as ethical; and (3) be socially responsible and be perceived as socially responsible and credible throughout the world, given the globalization of the marketplace and of information.

■ Other Manifestations of Ethical Dilemmas

What Shareholders Really Want

In a recent survey, 246 shareholders from across the U.S. were asked what they thought their corporations should spend money on. It turned out that money is not always the first thing on shareholders' minds. Sometimes the environment takes priority.[27] Two areas were targeted: (1) cleaning up plants and stopping environmental pollution, and (2) making safer products. In a list of 10 items, "higher dividends" ranked only third. Falling to the bottom of the list was "spending more money on charitable contributions and programs to benefit women or racial minorities." Concern for ethics per se fell to fifth place. When seen in totality, the study seems to suggest that a corporation should do several things to manage expenditures and social concerns. There should be a corporate awareness of social, ethical, and environmental issues at all levels; methods should be developed to evaluate and report on the social and environmental impacts of corporate activities; and incentives to encourage employees to be responsible should be integrated into the performance evaluation system and corporate culture. The corporate structure should be modified to deal with social, environmental, and ethical crises.

24. *United States v. Hooker Chemicals & Plastics Corp.*, 850 F. Supp. 993 (W.D.N.Y. 1994).
25. J. Michael Kennedy and Patrick Lee, "Shell Selling Low-Polluting Gas in Nine Smoggiest Cities," *Los Angeles Times*, April 12, 1990, A1.
26. "Conoco Says It Will Order Oil Tankers with Double Hulls," *Los Angeles Times*, April 11, 1990, D1.

27. Mark Epstein, "What Shareholders Really Want," *The New York Times*, April 28, 1991, Sec. 3, p.11. The results of the study and the recommendations arising therefrom are based upon this article.

Reprinted with special permission of King Features Syndicate.

Socially Responsible Investment

Besides being concerned about product and environmental safety, the public has begun to put pressure on corporations and institutional investors to invest responsibly, that is, in such a way as not to lend support to unjust, oppressive regimes. For instance, many companies with direct or indirect economic ties to South Africa were the subject of consumer boycotts. In addition, many shareholder groups attempted to pass anti-apartheid resolutions to prohibit investment in South Africa. More than 100 U.S. companies divested, including Citicorp, ITT, Ford Motor Company, and Coca-Cola Company. The divesting companies often sold their holdings to white-controlled local firms, but a few sold their holdings to blacks. Coca-Cola Company, in March 1987, became the first American company to sell its South Africa holdings to blacks. These boycotts and shareholder resolutions were critical in helping end apartheid in South Africa, a result for which Nelson Mandela and F. W. de Klerk won the Nobel Peace Prize in 1993.

More recently, activists have exerted pressure on U.S. companies to divest themselves of investments in China, Burma, and Northern Ireland in order to put pressure on these countries to improve their record on human rights generally and to improve employee working conditions in particular.

Advertising Campaigns

Companies have sometimes canceled advertising campaigns or abandoned certain products when faced with public outrage or a consumer boycott. For example, in December 1989, Pepsi dropped a commercial featuring female singer Madonna's song "Like a Prayer" because some viewers considered it sacrilegious. Religious activists spearheaded a boycott against Pepsi, which cost the company approximately $10 million. This case raises the issue of whether a company should abandon an advertising campaign just because some groups find it offensive. Or should Pepsi have been more morally sensitive in the first place?

In January 1990, R. J. Reynolds Tobacco Company withdrew its new "Uptown" brand of cigarettes after being criticized by the Bush administration for targeting African-American smokers. The new cigarette was condemned for being the first brand to explicitly target minority smokers. Reynolds had made a costly mistake.

Another example of questionable target marketing by a company occurred in 1991. That summer G. Heileman Brewing Co. planned to release a new malt liquor called "Power Master." The name and label were designed to connote the product's high alcohol content of 5.9%, which would have made Power Master the strongest malt liquor on the market. Power Master was also targeted through advertising and design specifically at the African-American community. African Americans and Hispanics are the largest consumers of malt liquors currently on the market. African-American activist groups threatened protests, including billboard whitewashing campaigns, in response to the new product. Michael L. Pfleger, pastor of St. Sabina Catholic Church in Chicago and one of the persons arrested for protesting outside

Heileman headquarters in La Crosse, Wisconsin, stated: "We're not going to tolerate target marketing when the product is death or disease."[28] Heileman decided to withdraw the product before it was even released to the shelves.

Companies such as RJR Nabisco (makers of Camel cigarettes) have faced public outcry to limit their advertising. Groups have particularly attacked the Camel advertisements featuring a cartoon figure, Old Joe Camel.[29] A number of studies showed that ads involving this sharply dressed camel who frequents pool halls and pickup bars were tremendously successful in targeting children. In a study involving 229 children ages three to six, more than half were familiar with the figure, and associated him with cigarettes. Six-year-olds were nearly as familiar with Joe Camel as they were with the Mickey Mouse logo for the Disney Channel.[30] Despite RJR's contentions that such studies are inaccurate and that advertising does not cause people to start smoking, but only to switch brands, the cartoon character's appeal to children continues to raise considerable concern among the community, parents, and some public figures. For example, former surgeon general Antonia Novello, known for having "lashed out" at other cigarette campaigns that aroused children, asked for a voluntary ban of ads involving the camel-like Old Joe. RJR refused to ban the character, which also appeals to teenage males.

The Camel controversy flared up again in 1994 with the introduction of "Josephine Camel." Female and male camels are shown drinking, smoking, shooting pool, and playing darts and cards at "Joe's Place," a multilevel bar. The four-page, full-color ads appeared in magazines such as *People, Us, Glamour, Redbook,* and *Sports Illustrated.* Although the staff of the Federal Trade Commission (FTC) suggested a ban on the Old Joe Camel character in August 1993, as of spring 1994 the FTC had not acted. Former surgeon general Novello said, "It is my hope that the introduction of the female camel will be the straw that breaks the camel's back of public and policy opinion."[31] An RJR representative, citing the duties of the company to its stockholders, stated it would be "wrong to interrupt" an ad campaign solely because of antismoker protests.[32]

Underpaid Foreign Workers

In 1992 the press revealed that some of the products of top U.S. retailer Wal-Mart that were marked "Made in the U.S.A." were actually made by child laborers in Bangladesh working for pennies a day. The head of Wal-Mart's Bangladesh operation denied that they were children, saying, "The workers just look young because they are malnourished adults."[33] Wal-Mart Chief Executive Officer David Glass denied that the retailer misled the public with its "Buy America" campaign, and stated that Wal-Mart was unable to substantiate the fact that children were working in factories in Bangladesh. Rosalene Costa, a human-rights worker in Bangladesh interviewed by NBC "Dateline," said the children working at the factory were about 12 years old. The children told her their real ages when the supervisor was not around.[34]

Maquiladora plants in Mexico, which give U.S. companies access to cheap Mexican labor, raise issues of what is fair pay. As with the Bhopal settlement, one must consider the ethics of having a "first world" and "third world" rate of pay. Much of the opposition to the North American Free Trade Agreement (NAFTA), discussed in chapter 3, related to the feared "export" of U.S. jobs and the exploitation of workers in Mexico.

Charitable Contributions

Although the law clearly permits companies to make charitable contributions, such contributions raise the issues cited by Milton Friedman earlier in this chapter concerning management's giving away of other people's money. Controversial charities include Planned Parenthood (which advocates a woman's right to an abortion) and the Boy Scouts (which refuses to admit homosexuals). One way out is to let shareholders decide, on a pretax basis, where they want the contributions to go. Berkshire Hathaway, headed by lauded investor Warren Buffet, does just that. Each shareholder who holds Berkshire Hathaway stock in her own name (not through a broker) is permitted to designate where her pro rata share of contributions should go. Although Berkshire

28. Thomas Palmer, "A Target-Marketing Ploy Backfires—Malt Liquor Aimed at Blacks Dies Aborning, A Victim of Insensitivity," *Boston Globe,* July 14, 1991, 71.
29. Joanne Lipman, "Surgeon General Says It's High Time Joe Camel Quit," *The Wall Street Journal,* March 10, 1992, B1, B8.
30. Kathleen Deveny, "Joe Camel Is Also Pied Piper, Research Finds," *The Wall Street Journal,* December 11, 1991, B1, B6.
31. Kevin Goldman, "A Stable of Females Has Joined Joe Camel In Controversial Cigarette Ad Campaign," *The Wall Street Journal,* February 18, 1994, B1.

32. *Ibid,* B8.
33. "NBC Questions Wal-Mart's 'Buy America' Campaign," *United Press International,* December 22, 1992.
34. *Ibid.*

International Consideration

In the past, business ethics differed somewhat from culture to culture. However, as the market shifts from a domestic to an international one, and as advances in technology create a greater flow of information, business ethics are becoming more standardized, and some firms are having trouble making this major adjustment. For example, in Japan gift-giving is expected, but in the United States it might be viewed as a bribe. Payment of bribes to foreign officials is prohibited by the Foreign Corrupt Practices Act, discussed in chapter 3.

Hathaway's high share price ($19,005 per share at the New York Stock Exchange close on August 10, 1994) and resultant low number of shareholders make this practice feasible, the concept could be applied elsewhere.

Even charity can be taken to extremes. The directors of oil giant Occidental Petroleum were sued by shareholders irate at the board's decision to build a $100 million art museum carrying chairman Armand Hammer's name to house his art collection (which had been purchased largely with Occidental corporate funds). Although the court held that the business judgment rule (discussed in chapter 21) protected the directors from personal liability, it suggested that the shareholders would be fully justified in throwing out the board through a shareholder vote.

Shareholder Resolutions

Shareholders can influence a company's ethical conduct, just as the CEO, the management, the employees, and the public can. As noted earlier in the case of South Africa, shareholders, through corporate resolutions, can pressure the board of directors to change company policy.

■ Whistleblowing and the Role of the Law

The law—civil as well as criminal—plays an important part in promoting ethical conduct. Ethical behavior often requires a higher standard than that prescribed by the law; an action that is unethical may nonetheless be legal. On the other hand, unethical behavior tends to result in illegal behavior over time.

When a manager breaks a law, he can expect to be punished. The same may not be true for those who demonstrate unethical conduct. However, courts and legislatures continually modify the law to take account of ethical standards. For example, scandals about American companies' payment of bribes to foreign officials led to passage of the Foreign Corrupt Practices Act, which generally makes such payments illegal. When reading the following section, keep in mind that unethical conduct often brings about new laws.

Protection for Whistleblowers

Many employees are reluctant to "blow the whistle"—to report illegal or unethical conduct that they observe at work—for fear of being seen as a troublemaker or being fired. In the 1970s, the legislatures and courts began to provide more protection for whistleblowers. The body of law that has developed provides a good example of how the law can encourage ethical behavior in the workplace.

The Civil Service Reform Act U.S. Senator Patrick Leahy, in a 1977 study entitled "The Whistleblowers," reported that "federal employees are currently afraid to bring problems to the attention of their superiors" and that "the fear of reprisal is so prevalent throughout the bureaucracy that waste and illegality are too often allowed to go unchecked." In response to reports like this one, and with the support of then President Jimmy Carter's campaign for openness in government, in 1978 Congress passed the Civil Service Reform Act to protect the rights of federal employees who report wrongdoing. This law specifically prohibits reprisals against a federal employee who reports an activity that she believes violates a law, rule, or regulation. Nevertheless, many federal employees remain intimidated by a record of retribution.

The False Claims Act and Pentagon Fraud In 1986, the federal government extended its whistleblower protection to nonfederal employees. The False Claims Act allows private citizens to sue government contractors in the name of the U.S. government if they believe that the government is being defrauded. The act offers protection to employees of government contractors who blow the whistle on this type of fraud. It also provides an incentive to report such fraud, by allowing the employee to collect at least 15% of any damages and civil fines awarded to the government; some employees have been

In Brief: Relationship of Ethics to Law

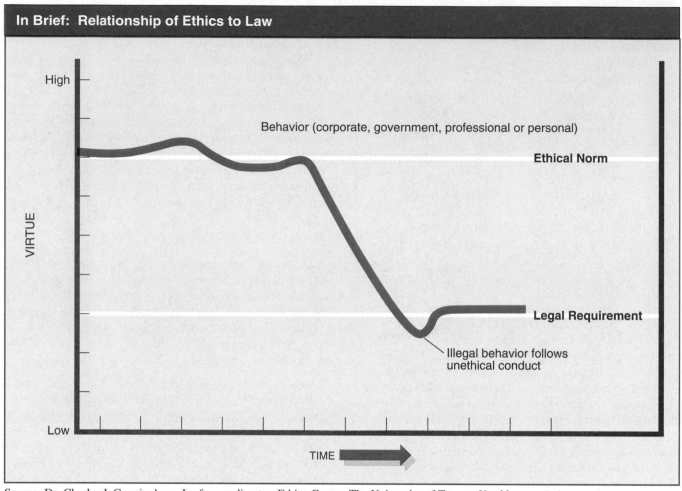

Source: Dr. Charles J. Cunningham, Jr., former director, Ethics Center, The University of Tampa. *Used by permission.*

able to retire with a large bank account as a result of this provision.

The False Claims Act essentially privatizes the government's antifraud function. According to a contributing editor of the *Defense Contract Litigation Reporter:* "Some lawyers suspect that this new class of guerrilla plaintiffs will become the most dangerous foe of the military-industrial complex since the Viet Cong."[35] The defense industry is spending millions of dollars to defend suits filed under the act. As of October 1989, 198 suits had been filed and 13 settled for a total of $26.7 million. Approximately $2.7 million went to private plaintiffs.

The Northrop Corporation, a defense contractor, challenged the right of Congress to enact such a law. Several Northrop employees had filed suit under the act, alleging that the company had overcharged the government at least $2 billion for the B-2 stealth bomber. Northrop sought to dismiss the suit, arguing that the act was unconstitutional. However, a federal district court upheld the act. [36]

Other Federal Legislation   The Whistleblower Protection Act of 1989 provides further protections through the Merit Systems Protection Board. It also increases the authority of the Office of Special Counsel, an independent investigative and prosecutorial agency. Provisions to protect whistleblowers have been included in other legislation, such as the Clean Air Act of 1982,

---

35. France, "The Private War on Pentagon Fraud," *ABA Journal,* March 1990, 46.

36. Catherine Gewertz, "Northrop Loses Bid to Dismiss Stealth Suit," *United Press International,* August 14, 1989.

the National Labor Relations Act, and the Federal Railroad Safety Act. These laws often protect both the disclosure of information (such as reporting to authorities or testimony given in an investigation) and an employee's refusal to participate in illegal activities. The statutes vary on what channels a whistleblower must go through to seek redress for retaliatory action by the employer. Some statutes require federal agencies to hold a hearing before reinstatement of the employee. Others require the employee to bring his case in federal district court. Usually the statutes allow an employee to collect back pay and attorney's fees if reinstated.

By 1993, there were 27 federal laws forbidding retaliation against whistleblowers.

State and Local Protection   State and city governments have also enacted whistleblower legislation. For example, a lawsuit was filed under Pennsylvania's law by a hospital worker who was fired after he reported to the state Department of Environmental Resources the hospital's burning of infectious waste. As of 1991, 25 states had adopted whistleblower statutes protecting public employees, and 14 states had adopted statutes protecting either private sector employees or both public and private sector employees.[37]

Difficulty of Blowing the Whistle   It is easy to forget how difficult it can be for an employee to blow the whistle. In their book *Whistle-Blowers: Exposing Corruption in Government and Industry,* Myron and Penina Glazer report on interviews with 64 whistleblowers. Says one man who reported violations at the Comanche Peak nuclear plant in Glen Rose, Texas: "Be prepared for old friends to suddenly become distant. Be prepared to change your type of job and lifestyle. Be prepared to wait years for blind justice to prevail."[38] A former Senate aide describes how he sacrificed his career when he went public with evidence of his boss's financial misconduct.[39] Whistleblower legislation is designed to provide job protection and legal recourse against this kind of reprisal.

Even with legislative and judicial protections, however, whistleblowers do suffer. For example, on the eve of the space shuttle Challenger's takeoff in January 1986, two senior engineers from Morton Thiokol warned that the shuttle's O-ring gaskets (manufactured by Morton Thiokol) might be affected by the forecasted cold weather. Seven astronauts died in the disaster that followed. According to *The Economist,* even though the two Morton Thiokol employees were praised for their actions, their careers suffered.[40]

This is consistent with a study of 1,700 whistleblowers interviewed by Edna Ottney, a quality assurance engineer who has investigated employee concerns in the nuclear power industry since 1985. She reported that 90% of the respondents experienced negative reactions. A study published in the September 1993 issue of the *British Medical Journal* shows that this is a problem that transcends national borders. Of 35 Australian whistleblowers surveyed, eight lost their jobs as a result of whistleblowing, 10 were demoted, 10 resigned or retired early because of ill health related to victimization, 15 were taking prescribed medication to deal with stress, and 17 had considered suicide.[41]

The Courts' Role

The rationale behind the protection of whistleblowing is that it is in the public interest. However, it would be irresponsible for the law to blindly protect all employee disclosures. Some disclosures may be intended merely to harass the employer. Consequently, the courts have established standards of review by which to judge the actions of both employers and employees. For example, when a dismissed employee seeks reinstatement, the U.S. Court of Appeals for the Federal Circuit requires a showing of a "genuine nexus [or connection]" between the whistleblowing and the employee's dismissal.[42] Proving this connection is often difficult.

Other cases have established a fair process by which to review claims in whistleblower cases. Courts must balance the public interest in the enforcement of laws, the whistleblower's interest in being protected from reprisal, and the employer's interest in managing its work force.

The following case illustrates the impact of the law in protecting certain types of employees from job reprisals if those employees follow the ethical precepts of their profession.

37. Daniel P. Westman, *Whistleblowing—The Law of Retaliatory Discharge* (1991).
38. Quoted in Joel Chineson, "Bureaucrats with Conscience," *Legal Times*, April 17, 1989, 50.
39. *Ibid.*

40. "Good Takes on Greed," *The Economist*, February 17, 1990, 72.
41. Marcy Mason, "The Curse of Whistle-Blowing," *The Wall Street Journal*, March 14, 1994, A14.
42. *Warren v. Department of the Army*, 804 F.2d 654, 656 (Fed. Cir. 1986).

■ **A Case in Point:**   **Summary**

Case 1.3
WIEDER v. SKALA
Court of Appeals of New York
80 N.Y.2d 628, 609 N.E.2d 105,
593 N.Y.S.2d 752 (N.Y. 1992).

FACTS   An attorney, Wieder, sued his law firm after he was fired. Wieder had complained to partners at his firm about the actions of another attorney at the firm, actions that he claimed violated the ethical rules that all attorneys must follow as members of the bar. The partners of the firm did not want Wieder to make a complaint to the bar's ethics committee. The partners told Wieder that they would deal with the matter of the other attorney themselves. They then threatened to fire Wieder if he pursued the matter with the ethics committee any further on his own.

ISSUE PRESENTED   Can an attorney be threatened with discharge if he reports an ethical violation to the bar association in accordance with bar rules?

SUMMARY OF OPINION   The New York Court of Appeals ruled that the firm had breached its contract of employment with Wieder when it threatened to fire him. The court explained that in most cases an employer can fire an employee at any time for virtually any reason. However, this case was distinguishable from most because Wieder had ethical duties as a member of the bar. The firm, by asking him not to report the other attorney's misconduct, had put Wieder in an untenable position by forcing him to choose between his duty as a member of the bar and his duties as an employee of the firm. The firm's action, the court ruled, therefore breached the contract of employment that it had with Wieder.

RESULT   The law firm could not legally fire attorney Wieder for complying with the rules of his profession.

COMMENTS   Note that the court distinguished this case and the employment relationship of a lawyer at a law firm from other more general employment relationships and firings for similar whistleblowing actions. The court explained that in most cases an employer has the right to fire an employee (and the employee has the right to quit) unless those rights have been expressly contracted out of at the time of employment. In most cases employees are working simply in furtherance of their company's primary responsibilities and goals. In contrast, as the court explained, a lawyer's only purpose as an employee and associate with a law firm is to perform professional services as a duly admitted member of the bar. The implied understanding that both the lawyer and the firm will practice within the ethical standards of the profession is so fundamental as to require no expression in the employment contract.

International Focus: OECD Code of Business Conduct

In the past, business ethics differed somewhat from culture to culture. However, as the market shifts from a domestic to an international one, and as advances in technology create a greater flow of information, business ethics are becoming more standardized. A generalized code of business conduct was drawn up by the Organization of Economic Cooperation and Development (OECD) in 1976.[43] The code, which discusses proper behavior and ethical conduct for multinationals, has had a significant impact on international business practice.

---

43. "Transnational Corporations: Issues Involved in the Formulation of a Code of Conduct," *Report of the Secretariat* (July 20, 1976).

The code includes the views of government, business, labor, and consumer groups. It requires multinational corporations: (1) to act in accordance with the economic, commercial, and social goals and priorities of the host country; (2) to abstain from bribery and other corrupt practices seeking favorable treatment from the host government; (3) to abstain from political intervention in the host country; (4) to make a positive contribution to the balance of payments of the host country; (5) to abstain from borrowing from local financial institutions, so that they can reserve their capital for local enterprises; (6) to monitor the multinational's impact on employment, wages, labor standards, working conditions, and industrial relations; (7) to protect the environment of the host country; and (8) to disclose information on the multinational's activities so that the home country and the host country can formulate government policy.

■ The Law and the "Unethical"

Employer's Liability for Acts of Employees

The ethical responsibility of a company is not limited to how it provides a service or manufactures a product. Companies have additional responsibilities to their employees and to society in general. The law enforces this responsibility by imposing liability on employers in certain instances. For example, companies are faced with the ethical decision of whether to serve alcohol at company gatherings. In some states, including New Jersey and Washington, an employer may be held liable for injuries caused by an employee's drunken driving after an office party.

In a 1985 Minnesota case, an employee who became extremely intoxicated at a Christmas party drove his truck across the center line of a highway and struck another car. The employee was killed and the two passengers in the other car were injured. Like other states, Minnesota has a *dram shop act*, a statute that makes a tavern liable for damage or injury caused by a drunk driver who was served drinks even though visibly intoxicated. The Minnesota Supreme Court found that the state's dram shop act did not impose liability on an employer for providing alcohol to an employee. The court held that the statute applied only to commercial vendors, not to employers who serve liquor free at a party.[44]

In response to growing concern about drunken driving, there have been fewer office parties during the holidays and stricter controls on the amount of drinking at the parties that are held. Many companies still have parties but have banned the consumption of alcohol at them. Some smaller companies now throw their parties in hotels and pay for their employees to stay overnight. For example, Advanced Environment Technology Corporation of Flanders, New Jersey, paid for hotel rooms for 68 employees and their guests, and for breakfast the next morning.

An employer may be held liable for sending home an intoxicated employee even if the employee did not become intoxicated at an office party, but instead was found to be drinking on the job, as in the following case.

---

44. *Meany v. Newell*, 367 N.W.2d 472 (Minn. 1985).

■ A Case in Point: In the Language of the Court

Case 1.4
OTIS ENGINEERING
CORPORATION v. CLARK
Supreme Court of Texas
668 S.W.2d 307 (Tex. 1983).

FACTS   Robert Matheson worked the evening shift at the Otis Engineering plant. He had a history of drinking on the job, and was intoxicated on the night of the automobile accident in which he killed himself and the wives of the plaintiffs Larry and Clifford Clark. Some of Matheson's co-workers told Matheson's supervisor, Donald Roy, that Matheson was acting strangely, including bobbing and weaving near his machine, and that he seemed intoxicated. Roy said that he observed Matheson's condition and was aware that other employees believed he should be removed from the machine. When Matheson returned from his dinner break, Roy suggested that he should go home. Roy, as he escorted Matheson to the company's parking lot, asked if Matheson was all right and if he could make it home.

Case 1.4 continued on following page

*Case **1.4** continued*

Matheson answered that he could. Thirty minutes later, some three miles away from the plant, the fatal accident occurred.

The medical examiner testified that Matheson had a blood alcohol content of 0.268%. This indicated he had ingested a substantial quantity of alcohol, an amount representing some 16 to 18 cocktails if consumed over a period of one hour, or 20 to 25 cocktails if consumed over a period of two hours. The doctor stated that persons working around Matheson would undoubtedly have known of his condition.

When some night-shift employees came to work around 10:30 P.M. and remarked there had been an accident on Belt Line Road, Roy immediately suspected Matheson was involved. Upon hearing of the accident, Roy, acting on a hunch and without any further corroborating information, voluntarily went to the police station to see if Matheson was involved.

The Clarks sued Matheson's employer Otis Engineering Corporation for the wrongful death of their wives in the car accident with Matheson. Otis moved for summary judgment, arguing that as a matter of law Otis was not liable for Matheson's conduct. The trial court granted Otis's motion for summary judgment and dismissed the Clarks' claims. The court of appeals reversed and remanded (sent back) the case for trial, holding there were genuine issues of fact for a jury to decide. Otis appealed.

ISSUE PRESENTED   Can an employer who sent an intoxicated employee home be held liable for injuries to third parties caused by the employee's off-the-job drunken driving?

OPINION   KILGARLIN, J., writing for the Texas Supreme Court:

. . . .

Otis' motion for summary judgment was granted on the basis that as a matter of law Otis owed no duty to the Clarks. In order to establish tort liability, a plaintiff must initially prove the existence and breach of a duty owed to him by the defendant. As a general rule, one person is under no duty to control the conduct of another, even if he has the practical ability to exercise such control. . . .

. . . .

What we must decide is if changing social standards and increasing complexities of human relationships in today's society justify imposing a duty upon an employer to act reasonably when he exercises control over his servants. . . .

. . . .

As Dean Prosser [former Dean of the Law School at the University of California, Boalt Hall] has observed, "[C]hanging social conditions lead constantly to the recognition of new duties. No better general statement can be made, than the courts will find a duty where, in general, reasonable men would recognize it and agree that it exists." If . . . we change concepts of duty as changing social conditions occur, then this case presents the Court with the opportunity to conform our conception of duty to what society demands.

. . . .

[T]he standard of duty that we now adopt for this and all other cases currently in the judicial process, is: when, because of an employee's incapacity, an employer exercises control over the employee, the employer has a duty to take such action as a reasonably prudent employer under the same or similar circumstances would take to prevent the employee from causing an unreasonable risk of harm to others. . . .

Therefore, the trier of fact in this case should be left free to decide whether Otis acted as a reasonable and prudent employer considering the following factors: the availability of the nurses' aid station, a possible phone call to Mrs. Matheson, having another employee drive Matheson home, dismissing Matheson early rather than terminating his employment, and the foreseeable consequences of Matheson's driving upon a public street in his stuporous condition. . . .

. . . .

DISSENTING OPINION   McGEE, J.:

. . . .

In my opinion, Otis was under no legal duty to restrain Matheson or to refrain from sending him home before the end of his shift, as the majority holds. The inability of a majority of the court to state why Otis owed a duty to the Clarks' decedents convinces me that the imposition of liability on third parties for the torts of an intoxicated person is not the proper remedy.

To compound the problem, the majority reaches an incorrect result. No court in any jurisdiction has ever suggested that an employer may be held liable for the off-duty, off-premises torts of an intoxicated employee when the employer has not contributed to the employee's state of intoxication. Moreover, and because of the pervasiveness of alcohol-related accidents of all types, today's decision radically increases the potential liability of all Texans without even acknowledging those policies that militate against the recognition of a duty in cases such as this. In my opinion, the bench, the bar, and the public are entitled to know the reasons for and the consequences of expanded liability, matters the majority opinion chooses not to address.

. . . .

. . . [W]hat is the action that a "reasonably prudent employer" must take to avoid liability under this rule? Concededly, the facts of this one case make this appear a simple question since Otis maintained a nurse's station for ill employees. The rule of this case, however, will apply to small and large employers alike, and most small employers have no such facility, nor do they have the practical ability to take the other steps suggested by the majority. . . . In an attempt to do justice in this one case, the majority has placed an impractical and unreasonable duty upon all employers.

. . . .

. . . [T]he majority erodes the concept that an individual is responsible for his or her own actions. I would adhere to the rule that an employee is not acting in the course and scope of his employment while traveling to and

*Case **1.4** continued on following page*

*Case **1.4** continued*

from work and that the employer will not be held liable to one injured by the employee's negligent operation of an automobile during these trips to and from work. It is well settled in Texas that a person is under no duty "to anticipate negligent or unlawful conduct on the part of another." . . .

RESULT   The summary judgment for Otis was reversed, and the case was sent back to the trial court for a jury determination of whether Otis acted as a reasonable and prudent employer in light of the facts of the case. If the jury found that Otis did not act reasonably and prudently, then Otis would be liable to the plaintiffs for damages.

COMMENTS   The employer may also be responsible for an automobile accident caused by an employee on his way home who was not intoxicated but was exhausted from being forced to work 27 consecutive hours.[45]

Questions
1. Should a tavern owner who refused to serve an intoxicated person be liable for a fatal accident involving the intoxicated person if the tavern's employee jump-started the person's car?
2. Should there be an ethical duty to prevent harm to, or even affirmatively help, others even if there is no legal duty?

---

45. *Robertson v. LeMaster*, 301 S.E.2d 563 (W.Va. 1983). This case is discussed in chapter 7.

Criminal Liability of Manager for Acts of Her Subordinates

The law increasingly holds managers responsible for both the misdeeds of their employees and for criminal violations by the employer corporation. This can result in not only civil but also criminal liability for a manager who fails to properly oversee compliance by his company.

Application of this in the environmental law context is discussed in chapter 16. The following case involves the Federal Food, Drug and Cosmetic Act, which makes it a criminal offense to mislabel or adulterate food, drugs, or cosmetics that are part of interstate commerce. A chief executive officer faced criminal charges under that act in this case.

■ **A Case in Point:**   **Summary**

Case 1.5
UNITED STATES v. PARK
Supreme Court of the
United States
421 U.S. 658, 95 S.Ct. 1903
(1975).

FACTS   John Park was the chief executive officer of Acme Markets, Inc., a national retail food chain headquartered in Philadelphia, Pennsylvania. Acme employs 36,000 people and has 874 retail outlets and 16 warehouses. In 1971, the Food and Drug Administration (FDA) informed Park of violations by his company of the Federal Food, Drug and Cosmetic Act, including the presence of rats in one of the warehouses in which food was stored.

Park was told by members of the company that the appropriate vice president was looking into the matter and was taking corrective action. Park did not further investigate the matter. Months later in 1972, the FDA found evidence of rodent infestation in the firm's Baltimore warehouse. A letter to Park, dated January 27, 1972, included the following: "We note with much concern that the old and new warehouse areas used for food storage were actively and extensively inhabited by live rodents. Of even more concern was the observation that such reprehensible conditions obviously existed for a prolonged period of time without any detection, or were completely ignored. . . . We trust this letter will serve to direct your attention to the seriousness of the problem and formally advise you of the urgent need to initiate whatever measures are necessary to prevent recurrence and ensure compliance with the law." A second inspection was done in March. On that occasion the inspectors found that there had been improvement in the sanitary conditions, but that there was still evidence of rodent activity in the building and in the warehouses. The inspectors also found some rodent-contaminated lots of food items.

Acme and Park were charged with five criminal counts of violation of the Federal Food, Drug and Cosmetic Act by storing food shipped in interstate commerce in warehouses where it was exposed to rodent contamination. Acme, but not Park, pled guilty to the charges. At trial, Park was convicted on all five counts. He was found guilty under a theory of vicarious liability for the acts or omissions of other corporate employees. He was also found strictly liable under the statute's strict liability standard. Under strict liability, a defendant can be found guilty even without a showing of criminal intent by the defendant or any other member of the corporation.

ISSUE PRESENTED Can the chief executive officer of a company be held vicariously and strictly criminally liable under the Federal Food Drug, and Cosmetic Act for the introduction of misbranded and adulterated articles into interstate commerce?

SUMMARY OF OPINION The U.S. Supreme Court upheld Park's conviction under both the vicarious liability and the strict liability theories. The Court stated that strict liability was applicable because "the public interest in the purity of its food is so great as to warrant the imposition of the highest standard of care on distributors." The Court reasoned that Acme's employees were in a sense under Park's general direction. By virtue of Park's position, he had authority and responsibility to maintain the physical integrity of Acme's food products. The statute makes individuals, as well as corporations, liable for violations. An individual is liable if it is clear, beyond a reasonable doubt, that the individual had a responsible relation to the situation, even though he may not have participated personally. Thus Park, as CEO, could be found criminally liable even if he did not consciously do wrong.

RESULT The conviction of CEO Park for causing adulteration of food that had traveled in interstate commerce and that was held for sale was upheld.

Employer's Liability for Racial Discrimination by Employees

When the Civil Rights Act of 1964 was promulgated, the laws prohibiting discrimination in public accommodations, such as restaurants, were designed with Birmingham, Alabama, lunch counters in mind. Some 30 years later, in the largest settlement under the federal public-accommodation laws, Denny's Restaurants agreed to pay more than $54 million to settle lawsuits filed by African-American customers. Forty-six million dollars will be paid to customers, and another $8.7 million will go to pay attorney's fees.

Since 1987, more than 4,300 claims of discrimination had been filed by African-American customers of Denny's. These claims converged into two class action

At the Top

Responsibility for ethical behavior and compliance with the law extends from the top of the management hierarchy down. It cannot be delegated away. Managers provide role models—be they good or bad—for their subordinates.

suits based in California and Maryland. Among the claims were those of six African-American Secret Service agents assigned to President Bill Clinton's detail. In a Denny's in Annapolis, Maryland, 15 white Secret Service agents were seated and served, while the African-American agents were refused a table.

Another African-American customer, 15-year-old Rachel Thompson, was refused the free meal that Denny's advertises for a customer's birthday, despite having provided a baptismal certificate and school records containing her birthdate. She recalls the incident: "I felt embarrassed. It was humiliating because other families in there were looking at us, and I guess they thought we were some kind of bad criminals because . . . the staff members there were just gathered around our table, shaking their heads and screaming."[46]

Rachel Thomas, the 33-year-old vice president of a skin care company, recalled the incident in which she, her husband and their three children waited for an hour and twenty minutes after a waitress took their order and never returned. About her children, she said, "Those babies don't have anything to do with this racism, and they were the ones put out by it . . . You can't explain it to them; they don't understand."[47]

An African-American federal judge from Houston and his wife, who had been traveling for 18 hours, were forced to wait for almost an hour at a Denny's in California, while white teenagers taunted them, calling them "niggers."

In all, there were thousands of complaints of unequal treatment to African-American customers that included

not being served, having to pay a cover charge, and having to prepay for meals. The company denied that it had a policy of discrimination. However, during pretrial fact-finding, a former manager testified about training sessions in which managers were told how to deal with "too many blacks in a restaurant at one time," which was referred to as a "blackout."[48]

Jerome J. Richardson, the chairman and chief executive of Flagstar (the company that owns Denny's), said that the "settlements are not an admission that Denny's has had a policy or practice of discrimination against African-Americans." Rather, he sought to portray the incidents as random: "We serve one million customers a day at Denny's and we have 40,000 employees. It would be naïve on my part to say that customers are always satisfied."[49]

John Relman, a lawyer for the Washington Lawyers' Committee for Civil Rights, saw it differently: "We believe that there was, at the company, an attitude that went into the management level, but we don't know exactly how high. This attitude at the company, at the management level and working its way down, had the effect of causing discriminatory attitudes going down to the lowest levels of the company."[50]

As part of the settlement of the class action suits, Denny's agreed to hire Los Angeles civil rights lawyer Sharon Lybeck Hartmann to monitor any discrimination claims that may arise. In addition, African Americans posing as customers will be used to investigate whether Denny's discriminates in the future.

White-Collar Crime

Liability for negligent conduct that results in harm to others may sometimes be debatable. Liability for criminal conduct is not. Unfortunately, the decade of the 1980s saw white-collar crime rise to the forefront of the business agenda. White-collar crime, such as fraud and embezzlement—crimes characterized by deceit and dishonesty on the part of corporate executives and their employees—has proved quite costly. The short-term costs include lost profits. The long-term costs include erosion of the moral base of the organization, a loss of public confidence in business, and a threat to the free enterprise system. To counteract white-collar crime, the corporate community needs to create an ethical business

46. Timothy Ziegler, "Denny's Victims Discuss Harassment," *San Francisco Chronicle*, May 25, 1994, A3.
47. *Ibid.*

48. Stephen Labaton, "Denny's Restaurants to Pay $54 Million in Race Bias Suit," *The New York Times*, May 25, 1994, Al.
49. *Ibid.*
50. *Ibid.*

environment; individual businesses cannot do it alone. White-collar crime is discussed further in chapter 15.

Employee Drug Testing

Sometimes the law has to balance the conflicting interests of different groups in resolving a social issue. Such an issue is employee drug testing, which is expected to increase through the 1990s because of the prevalence of drug usage and its negative effects. The employer's interest in a drug-free workplace must be balanced against the employee's constitutional right to privacy.

Employers are concerned about drug and alcohol abuse because it results in lower productivity, lower quality output, accidents, absenteeism, tardiness, and excessive use of medical facilities. Employees, on the other hand, argue that drug testing is an invasion of their privacy, particularly when there is no objective reason to think that the employee has been using drugs.

In January 1990, former U.S. surgeon general C. Everett Koop stated that studies show that 14% to 25% of the nation's workers have illegal drugs in their systems on any given day. He believes that the American workplace is the proper arena in which to address the nation's drug problem.

Businesses can make and enforce rules against drug use or possession on work premises. They can prohibit employees from being under the influence of drugs while working. They can develop drug education programs. They can provide drug and alcohol rehabilitation programs and counseling. Regardless of how businesses deal with the problem of drug and alcohol abuse, they should not lose sight of their ethical responsibilities to their employees. Drug testing of employees is discussed further in chapter 12.

■ Different Theories of Ethics

It is sometimes difficult to define what constitutes good ethical behavior. This is due in part to the fact that there are several underlying ethical theories. People, consciously or not, employ ethical theories in their decision-making process. The important thing for a manager to remember is that there are different "ethically correct" ways of looking at a decision. Because there are different ways of approaching a given situation, a manager's constituencies may not always reach a similar decision, and

hence may not be as willing to accept the implications and consequences.

The two main schools of ethical thought are *teleological* and *deontological*. Teleological theory is concerned with the *consequences* of something. The good of an action is to be judged by the effect of the action on others. Deontological theory is the other main school. It focuses more on the *motivation* behind an action rather than the consequences of an action.

For example, suppose that a construction company donates materials to build shelters for the homeless. In judging this action within the teleological framework, the fact that some homeless people are given shelters is the important issue. Within a deontological framework, one would want to know why the company was motivated to supply the materials for the shelters. On the other hand, suppose an employer makes a promise to throw a party if the firm reaches profitability, and then breaks it. Under teleological theory, so long as the consequences of breaking the promise are insignificant, then the action of breaking the promise is not in and of itself bad. However, deontological theory would suggest that there is something intrinsically wrong with making a promise and breaking it, no matter what the consequences. Thus a particular action can be evaluated differently depending on the system under which it is examined.

For illustrative purposes, several theories within these two schools are briefly developed. *Utilitarianism* is a major teleological system which stands for the proposition that the ideal is to maximize the total benefit for everyone involved. Under a utilitarian theory, no one person's particular interest is given more weight than another but rather the utility of everyone as a group is maximized.

For example, suppose that a $10,000 bonus pool is to be divided among three executives, and that their marginal benefits from receiving a portion of the money can be quantified. Imagine that the money must be allocated in one of two ways. Under Distribution 1, the three persons benefit 6, 12, and 24 units, respectively. Under Distribution 2, the three persons benefit 8, 12, 16 units, respectively. A utilitarian would want Distribution 1 because the total benefit (6+12+24=42) is greater than under Distribution 2 (8+12+16=36). There is no concern that the other distribution seems more equal and fair; similarly, there is no concern that under the benefit-maximizing utility distribution, the worst-off person has considerably less than the worst-off person in Distribution 2. On the other hand, *Rawlsian moral theory,* a deontological theory, aims to maximize the worst-off person in society. According to that theory, Distribution 2 is better. Under a Rawlsian scheme, the favored distribution is the one preferred by the person who faces the possibility of getting the worst share.

Kantian theory is another main deontological line of thought. Kant advocated maxims that epitomize a morality based on freedom and rationality. Kant's categorical imperative looks to the form of an action, rather than the intended result, in examining the ethical worth. The form of an action can be delineated into the *universalizability* and *reversibility* of an action. Universalizability asks whether one would want everyone to perform in this manner, and reversibility looks to whether one would want such a rule applied to one's self. For example, in deciding how long a break to give the workers on an assembly line, a manager might try to apply this theory. In choosing between a 10-minute break every three hours with bathroom breaks whenever necessary versus a longer lunch break, a manager might ask herself—under universalizability—whether she would like a world in which all companies applied a similar system. Under reversibility, the manager would decide whether he would want to be subjected to a particular break system as an employee.

The consequences of an action motivated by a certain ethical system can often be evaluated within a comparative justice framework. This allows a framework for comparing the rights-based moral theories of Kant or Rawls to, for example, a utilitarian framework. Three main categories within this framework are *distributive, compensatory,* and *retributive theories of justice.*

Distributive justice focuses on how the burden and benefits of a particular situation of a system are distributed. An ideal system maximizes the overall pie by dividing it such that incentives are enough to entice persons to produce more; the system also concerns itself with a fair distribution of these goods—compensating those who contributed while still upholding a certain minimum standard. For example, the U.S. tax system can easily be seen within a distributive justice framework.

Compensatory justice aims at compensating people for the harm done by others. For example, if someone is found responsible for making another person miss five days of work, a compensatory system of justice would ask that the victim be somehow "paid back" for the lost wages.

A *retributive justice* system framework also is appropriately employed when someone does harm to another, yet the focus is more on how to deter another harm from happening. Thus, suppose X steals an idea from Y and makes $100,000. If the idea had not been stolen, Y could have made $500. Under a compensatory framework, one would ask that Y be compensated for X's wrongdoing, and that X pay Y $500. On the other hand, under a retributive framework, X should be taught that stealing an idea is wrong. X should be required to give up any benefit to Y and pay Y closer to $100,000.

■ The Ethics of the Junk Bond Era: Leveraged Buyouts

Definition of an LBO   The law does not only impose restrictions on behavior. Sometimes it can indirectly encourage behavior that is not necessarily ethical. An example is the corporate craze of the 1980s, junk bond financing of leveraged buyouts.

A leveraged buyout (LBO) is a takeover financed with loans secured by the acquired company's assets. Groups of investors, including management, use borrowed money along with some of their own money to buy back the company's stock from its current shareholders. Like most other business trends, leveraged buyouts have both positive and negative implications, involving critical ethical considerations.

Tax reforms and the laissez-faire (let it be) approach of the Reagan administration toward mergers and acquisitions, plus a willingness by managers and financiers to take on huge amounts of debt to buy stock, triggered the popularity of *junk bonds*—forms of high-yield, high-risk, unsecured corporate indebtedness that are not investment grade.

Although fewer LBOs occurred in the first half of the 1990s because of restricted credit, the same issues discussed in this section apply to such vanguard business trends as strategic acquisitions and corporate downsizing.

Benefits from LBOs   In some cases, leveraged buyouts proved favorable for the acquired company, because a more efficient and productive organization resulted. Corporate waste, such as lazy and unproductive management, excess layers of bureaucracy, and unprofitable divisions, triggered many of the early takeovers. By reducing such waste, these takeovers may have contributed to the resurgence in American productivity growth in the 1980s. Without junk bond financing, for example, Ted Turner's cable empire might never have been built. The same holds true for the long-distance telephone carrier MCI Communications.

Greed   The junk bond phenomenon has not been without its faults, however. The main criticism is that it has evolved from an important financial innovation to an extraordinarily abused one. One reason for this is an uncommon focus on greed, manifested as short-term wealth maximization at the expense of the long term.

Those profiting had a rationale for their sudden surge in wealth. As corporate raider Gordon Gekko, in the 1987 movie *Wall Street,* put it: "Greed, for lack of a better word, is good. Greed is right. Greed works. Greed clarifies, cuts through, and captures the essence of the evolutionary spirit. Greed, in all of its forms—greed for life, for money, for love, knowledge—has marked the upward surge of mankind."[51]

Nevertheless, the economy may suffer because of the emphasis on greed. Employees may unexpectedly lose their jobs. Expenditures on research and development and long-range planning may be cut, jeopardizing the competitiveness of U.S. industry in the longer term.

The issue of greed was spotlighted on the cover of *Time* magazine in its December 5, 1988, issue. It pictured F. Ross Johnson, CEO of RJR Nabisco, maker of products ranging from Oreo cookies to Camel cigarettes. He was proposing a leveraged buyout of the company. *Time* characterized this transaction as "a Game of Greed" and wrote: "This man would pocket $100 million from the largest corporate takeover in history. Has the buyout craze gone too far?" Johnson's bid was ultimately rejected by a special committee of RJR Nabisco's board of directors in favor of a $25 billion leveraged buyout sponsored by Kohlberg Kravis Roberts & Co. (KKR), a very active LBO sponsor. The *Time* cover was later described as "the final nail in Johnson's coffin."[52]

The vast amounts of money that are made from these buyouts help to explain why they became so prevalent. Early estimates of potential fees from the RJR Nabisco deal ran as high as $500 million. It was estimated that the buyout fee would total $80 million to $100 million, the junk bond underwriting and bank commitment fees would reach $250 million, and the merger and advisory fees would add another $50 million to $100 million.

Investment banks and law firms received approximately $200 million after the Campeau Corporation bought Federated Department Stores in 1988, after an 11-week battle. Campeau's U.S. retailing giants, Allied Stores Corporation and Federated Department Stores, Inc., declared bankruptcy in early 1990, when they were unable to meet the debt service obligations on the debt incurred in the leveraged buyout. This was the largest retailing bankruptcy in history. Allied Stores and

Federated Department Stores owned such well-known department stores as Bloomingdale's and Abraham & Straus in New York, Rich's in Atlanta, Burdines in Florida, and Bon Marché in Seattle. R. H. Macy & Co., owner of Macy's department stores, also was forced into bankruptcy by LBO debt it could not repay. Ironically, in 1994, Macy was forced by Federated Department Stores into a merger as part of Macy's bankruptcy proceeding.

Conflicts of Interest Leveraged buyouts and acquisitions generally give rise to ethical problems regarding conflict of interest and self-dealing. Management-led buyouts present unique conflicts of interest. When management is doing the buying, it has a strong incentive to make a deal to purchase the company from the existing shareholders for the lowest possible price. This incentive conflicts with management's responsibility as a protector of the interests of the shareholders of the target company to obtain the highest price for the existing shareholders.

The large fees paid advisors in mergers and acquisitions can present conflicts of interest. An example occurred in the $4.2 billion Sterling Drug takeover attempt by the Swiss pharmaceutical house F. Hoffmann-La Roche & Co. in 1988. Sterling hired the investment banking firm Morgan Stanley to defend it and, if possible, to help it maintain its independence. Morgan Stanley and Sterling struck the following deal.

■ If Morgan Stanley put up a successful defense that left Sterling as an independent company, Morgan Stanley could collect fees that would not exceed $10 million.

■ If Sterling was bought out for $72 a share, which is what Hoffmann-La Roche first offered, Morgan Stanley would pocket fees of $10.6 million.

■ If Sterling was sold for $80 a share, Morgan Stanley would be paid fees of $15.2 million.

■ For every dollar over $80 that a successful bidder paid for Sterling, Morgan Stanley could add another $1.4 million to its fee.

There was a conflict between the fee structure and Sterling's goal of remaining independent. If Morgan Stanley met Sterling's goal to fend off the takeover attempt, it would receive the lowest fee offered. In the end Morgan Stanley negotiated a friendly deal with Eastman Kodak, which paid $89.50 a share. Although Sterling lost its independence, its shareholders were richly compensated. Morgan Stanley earned $28.9 million in fees.

These conflicts are not unique to the investment banking industry. Sterling Drug was a longtime client of Morgan Bank of New York, one of the most prestigious

51. Quoted in Joseph Nocera, "The Decade That Got Out of Hand," *Best of Business Quarterly*, Winter 1989-90, 18.
52. Bryan Burrough and John Helyar, *Barbarians at the Gate: The Fall of RJR Nabisco* (1990).

commercial banks in the United States. When Hoffmann-La Roche made its surprise move to take over Sterling, Morgan Bank was not surprised—because it was the financial advisor to Hoffmann-La Roche. John M. Pietruski, Sterling's chairman, stated in a public letter to the chairman of Morgan Bank, Lewis T. Preston: "I am shocked and dismayed by what I consider to be Morgan Bank's unethical conduct in aiding and abetting a surprise raid on one of its longtime clients."[53]

Morgan Guaranty Trust Co. came under fire in March 1988 when it helped one client, SmithKline Beecham Corp., the Philadelphia pharmaceutical giant, buy a firm that another client, Corning Glass Works, had agreed to purchase. Corning officials were surprised by the rival bid and outraged by Morgan Guaranty's role. When asked for a reaction, Stephen Albertalli, director of investor relations of Corning Glass, said: "You can imagine what it might be. I just don't use four-letter words over the phone."[54]

Fairness to Affected Groups   A further ethical consideration is the fairness of a leveraged buyout to affected persons. For example, it has been suggested that the heavy use of debt will put a significant strain on the financial system if the economy weakens. Junk bonds have already played a role in the S&L crisis. Savings and loan institutions that invested heavily in junk bonds have had to write down their junk bond portfolios from cost to market value. This made it impossible for some savings and loans to meet applicable capital and asset requirements, requiring federal regulators to take control as part of the multibillion-dollar S&L bailout.

What about the employee pension funds and insurance companies that provide the capital for many of the buyouts? What about the loss to bondholders when a company takes on additional debt? When RJR Nabisco announced it was considering a leveraged buyout, for example, its outstanding bonds lost an estimated $800 million in value. (The lawsuit by RJR Nabisco's senior debtholders, including Metropolitan Life Insurance Company, whose investment-grade debt was adversely affected by the leveraged buyout, is discussed in chapter 24.)

Finally, the impact on employees is significant. Employees of acquired companies have been laid off, had their wages cut, seen their employee pension funds diminish, and had their collective bargaining or labor union agreements circumvented. Edward Hennessy, Jr., chairman and CEO of Allied-Signal, Inc., acknowledges the employer's role in maintaining a productive quality work force:

> If we choose to deny the larger human and social impact of the corporation, if we try to reduce the company to the bare essentials of a commercial transaction, we will end up with a work force that is less capable and less dedicated over the long run. We will also cause society to be indifferent—if not completely hostile—to the interests of corporations and their shareholders.[55]

Remedial Action   Legislatures, as well as employees and bondholders, have attempted to lessen the detrimental effects of LBOs. In early 1990, Congress considered antitrust, bankruptcy, and tax legislation to help curb leveraged buyouts. Many states amended their corporate law statutes to permit corporations to consider nonshareholder groups, such as employees, when assessing a possible takeover. In fact, Connecticut requires that the impact on all affected groups or constituencies be considered. In addition, many states have passed laws that protect employees from takeover-related disruptions, including surprise plant closings.

Action by Labor Unions   Labor unions have pushed for more protective successorship laws to shield employees from layoffs and from disregard of collective bargaining agreements after a change of control. Unions have also pursued greater restrictions on the use of pension plan funds to finance buyouts; more complete disclosure requirements concerning the effects on employees of proposed acquisitions; representation for labor unions on the board of directors; and a requirement that severance payments benefit the entire work force, not just top executives—who, after a change of control, are often paid large sums under "golden parachute" agreements. Companywide severance plans are called "tin parachutes."

Legal Action by Employees   Employees have also taken legal action. In February 1990, for example, Oakland, California-based Safeway Stores, Inc., settled a class-action suit brought by 210 former employees for $8.2 million. A *class action* is a suit filed on behalf of all persons who have allegedly been harmed by the defendant's conduct—in this case, all the employees who were fired in 1986 as a result of the leveraged buyout of Safeway by Kohlberg Kravis Roberts & Co. The employ-

---

53. Quoted in Leslie Wayne, "How the Morgan Bank Struck Out," *The New York Times*, February 7, 1988, Sec 3, p. 1.
54. Quoted in Jed Horowitz, "Morgan's Role in Merger Pits It Against Client," *American Banker*, March 28, 1988, 1.

55. *Touche Ross Report*, 44.

ees claimed that Safeway breached promises of job security. This suit was the first class action brought by fired employees in connection with an LBO.

Action by Bondholders   Rather than selling their junk bonds at a huge loss, bond-holder groups have formed to challenge leveraged buyouts. For example, the bondholders of SCI Television, Inc. threatened a "fraudulent conveyance" suit, alleging that loading a company with excessive debt cheats its existing creditors. (Fraudulent conveyances are discussed in chapter 24.) The result was that Kohlberg Kravis Roberts & Co. (KKR), which had arranged the SCI Television LBO, and George N. Gillett, Jr., who controlled SCI, kicked in $20 million each to save the company. In addition, KKR canceled a $160 million note it held.[56]

Rise and Fall of Drexel Burnham   The story of Drexel Burnham Lambert, Inc. reflects the rise and fall of the junk bond era. Drexel started the 1980s as a second-tier investment banking firm; junk bond financing started as a second-tier form of investment. When Drexel, through the leadership of Michael Milken, evolved into the premier junk financing firm, junk bonds became the primary investment vehicle of leveraged buyouts.

Drexel's reign was short-lived, however. Drexel was rocked by securities fraud scandals in the late 1980s, and junk bond king Michael Milken was indicted in March 1989 on 98 counts of securities fraud and violations of the Racketeer Influenced and Corrupt Organizations Act. In December 1988, Drexel agreed to plead guilty to six criminal counts of mail, wire, and securities fraud and to pay $650 million in fines and penalties. Milken pled guilty in April 1990 to six felony counts carrying a maximum prison sentence of 28 years and agreed to pay fines of $200 million. He actually served more than two years in prison, with time off for assisting the government in other investigations and prosecutions. He also agreed to pay $400 million into a fund to satisfy claims by investors and others who assert that they were defrauded by Milken. (The Milken case is discussed in the "Inside Story" in chapter 15.)

Facing a severe cash crunch in February 1990, Drexel filed for bankruptcy. The collateral backing its credit lines was so devalued that Drexel could not obtain a loan to meet $100 million in obligations due February 13, 1990. Drexel's proposed collateral—a portfolio of junk bonds, securities issued in private placements, and oil and gas limited partnership interests—was not liquid or readily salable enough to provide adequate security for a loan. Drexel never emerged from bankruptcy and went out of business.

The Responsible Manager

Ensuring Ethical Conduct

Ethical behavior is reinforced when top management exemplifies the company's values and takes a leadership role in programs to promote ethics; when the company creates an atmosphere of openness and trust in which employees feel comfortable in reporting violations; and when activities to enhance and reward ethics are part of every operating level of the company.

At the outset, a business must accept the proposition that high ethical standards and business success go hand in hand. Although ethics alone may not ensure long-term success, unethical behavior leads to illegal behavior and business failure. Members of top management cannot just pay lip service to this notion. Rather, they should show a dedication and commitment to ethics. They should realize that ethical responsibility is not just a component of a successfully run business but in fact is a type of thinking that permeates an entire organization.

The manager should recognize the critical importance of self-esteem, both at the individual and the organizational level. The company should create a proper balance between economic performance and ethics, and demonstrate that a strong ethical culture is a prerequisite to long-term profitability. In doing so, the corporation must look at itself honestly and objectively. It should ask itself what factors, either because of its industry or its internal corporate structure, inhibit it from being ethical.

A corporation needs a clearly written policy, such as a code of ethics. This policy must be legitimized and reinforced through formal and informal interaction with the entire management, beginning with the CEO. It must include procedural steps for reporting violations of the code of ethics and enforcing the code. As discussed in chapter 12, the company should include a code of ethics in its employment agreements.

A corporation should institute ethics training, including setting up a forum to discuss ethical dilemmas. In deciding whether a decision is ethically right, a corporation should ask whether a decision is fair or unfair to its personnel, customers, suppliers, and the communities where it does business. Managers should consider the

---

56. Michele Galen, "Holding a Lot of Junk? Need a Good Lawyer?" *Business Week*, February 12, 1990, 73.

direct and indirect results of a particular decision, including the impact on public image. They should ask themselves how much short-term benefit they are willing to forego for long-term gain.

Ethics is related to laws, but they are not identical. The legal thing to do is usually the "right" thing to do—but managers often have to go beyond their legal obligations to act ethically.

The law acknowledges that in a business deal, misunderstandings may arise, unforeseen events may occur, expected gains may disappear, or dislikes may develop

that tempt one party to act in bad faith. The law, by requiring each party to act in good faith, significantly reduces the risk of a party breaking faith.[57] When reading the chapters that follow, consider whether the courts, in applying the law, are doing anything more than requiring businesspersons to do what they knew or suspected they really should have done all along.

---

57. See Robert S. Summers, " 'Good Faith' in General Contract Law and the Sales Provisions of the Uniform Commercial Code," 54 *Virginia Law Review* 195 (1968).

Inside Story

Treasury Auction Scandal at Salomon Brothers

Salomon Brothers is a major investment banking firm, which specializes in trading securities, corporate finance, and mergers and acquisitions. In 1991 Salomon Brothers purchased U.S. government securities in violation of auction bidding rules. This revelation reduced confidence in the integrity of the Treasury bond market and raised serious questions about the need for greater supervision at securities firms.

In the wake of the notorious insider trading scandals of the 1980s and the negative press surrounding the book *Liar's Poker,* in which Salomon traders are described as betting millions of dollars on the order of serial numbers on a dollar bill, the Salomon bidding scandal received the full attention of the media. Salomon now faces the challenge of changing its aggressive and "macho" culture in order to placate regulators, customers, and the public. Although Salomon's aggressiveness enabled the firm to become a dominant force in the industry, that same characteristic may have been responsible for Salomon's fall from grace. The brash, swashbuckling attitude that has become so identified with Salomon traders is both a product of the firm's history as an outsider and the nature of its core business, trading. Trading is an inherently risky business and, like poker, it involves some deceptive activity (for example, convincing competitors you want to buy when you really want to sell). The Salomon culture was compounded by the fact that Salomon employees were among the most powerful traders in the world, moving around vast sums of money for enormous profit. These elements of risk, deception, and power coalesced to cre-

ate a sense of arrogance aptly described by Tom Wolfe in *Bonfire of the Vanities* as the "Masters of the Universe" phenomenon. In many ways, this arrogance can be viewed as one of the underlying causes of the incredible Wall Street trading scandal that unfolded in the summer of 1991.

The scandal involved the U.S. Treasury bond market—a market that has a daily trading volume of more than $100 billion and is supervised by the Federal Bank of New York, the Securities and Exchange Commission (SEC), and the U.S. Treasury. Traditionally, this market has experienced lax regulation with irregular enforcement. In 1990, however, the Treasury limited the amount any securities firm could buy in an auction to 35%, although companies can submit bids on behalf of their customers above this limit. It is Salomon's disregard of these regulations that form the heart of this Wall Street scandal.

The Treasury Scandal

Paul Mozer, chief of government bond trading at Salomon, was the central figure connected with the illegal bidding. After receiving a letter in late April 1991 from a regulator seeking information about a bid discrepancy, Mozer informed Vice Chairman John Meriwether about illegal bidding in the 1991 Treasury auction. Meriwether immediately informed both the president, Tom Strauss, and the CEO and chairman of the board, John Gutfreund. These three top officials then met to discuss the matter with Donald Feuerstein, Salomon's chief legal officer, who recommended that

Inside Story, continued

the matter be brought to the government's attention as a possible criminal act. At this point, the government was completely unaware of any illegal bidding.

No action was taken by Salomon. Nearly one month later, Salomon effectively bought at least 44% of the May 22 Treasury issue of two-year notes and possibly controlled as much as 85% of them. Shortly after the Treasury auction, prices rose sharply as notes were scarce and short sellers got "squeezed." In late May, the SEC and the Treasury began secret investigations of Salomon's activities after receiving complaints by numerous institutions caught in the "squeeze."

In June 1991 the SEC and the Justice Department issued subpoenas to Salomon and certain clients to investigate possibly illegal trading activities. In response, Salomon launched internal investigations of its government bond trading activities in early July. It soon discovered that it had acted illegally in four auctions over the past eight months by acquiring more than 35% of the auction and submitting bids in the names of customers without the customers' authorization.

The Aftermath

On Friday August 9, 1991, Salomon publicly revealed that its traders violated bidding rules of four different Treasury auctions and suspended four employees, including Paul Mozer. This public announcement was made before the government completed its investigation in an effort to preempt any possibly damaging and misleading information released by the government lawyers to the press. Salomon also hoped that appearance of full disclosure would help avoid the long drawn out publicity that occurred in the Drexel debacle.

On August 16, Salomon publicly revealed that John Gutfreund, Tom Strauss, and John Meriwether knew in April of Paul Mozer's illegal February bids, but did nothing. Despite initial intentions of riding out the unfolding scandal, Gutfreund offered to resign, along with Strauss and Meriwether, at the next Board meeting. Two days later, the Board accepted the three resignations and appointed as interim chairman and CEO Warren Buffet, a Salomon director for the past four years and the head of substantial Salomon shareholder Berkshire Hathaway. The new Salomon leader met for the first time with Salomon employees and gave a pep talk to 100 managing directors. At a subsequent news conference, Buffet declared his intention to come clean with regulators in an aggressive manner.

The matter, however, would not be resolved until many months later. On May 19, 1992, the SEC struck a $290 million settlement with Salomon Brothers. Nearly seven months later, the SEC announced an end to its long investigation of Gutfreund, Meriwether, and Strauss. Accused of failing to supervise Mozer, the men settled the charges without admitting or denying wrongdoing. The punishment appeared commensurate with each man's position of authority at Salomon. Gutfreund, the former CEO and chairman, paid $100,000 in fines and agreed not to become chairman or CEO of a securities firm without SEC approval. Strauss was fined $75,000 and suspended from working in the securities industry for 6 months. Meriwether received the smallest sanction—a $50,000 fine and a 3-month suspension. In 1993 Mozer pled guilty to two felony counts of making false statements to U.S. officials. He was sentenced to four months in prison and fined $30,000.

The Treasury auction scandal at Salomon, in many ways the final chapter of corporate excesses of the 1980s, represents the changing government attitude toward regulating corporate accountability. It was the first case in which the SEC imposed fines in a failure-to-supervise case and is perceived as the benchmark for how supervisors should conduct themselves.[58]

The scandal also demonstrates the principle that unethical conduct leads to more government regulation. In December 1993, President Bill Clinton signed into law the Government Securities Act Amendments of 1993 to further regulate the $4.5 trillion government securities market. According to Rep. Edward Markey (D–Mass.), who introduced the House version of the bill and chairs the House Energy and Commerce Telecommunications and Finance Subcommittee, "This bill directly respond[s] to the lessons of the Salomon Brothers and related scandals by enhancing market surveillance and enforcement and providing new sales practice rules and other important protections for investors."[59]

---

58. This discussion is based in large part on the unpublished paper "Salomon Brothers: The Treasury Auction Scandal," by Sheila Bonini, Henry Davis, Jon Kane, Larry Paul, and Amy Sayre (May 22, 1992). *Used by Permission*

59. Quoted in "Government Securities Reform Bill with Rollup Measure Signed by President," 25 *Securities Regulation & Law Report* 1708-09 (December 24, 1993).

Key Words and Phrases

class action suit **34**
compensatory justice **32**
deontological theory of ethics   **31**
distributive justice **32**
dram shop act **25**

fiduciary duty **4**
junk bonds **32**
Kantian theory **32**
leveraged buyout *(LBO)* **32**
Rawlsian moral theory **31**

retributive justice **32**
reversibility **32**
teleological theory of ethics   **31**
universalizability **32**
utilitarianism **31**

Questions and Case Problems

1. Why are business ethics important to a manager?

2. In 1993 shops began selling a line of clothes and other items depicting Charles Manson, the mass murderer whose followers killed seven persons, including actress Sharon Tate, in two Los Angeles homes in August 1969. Manson has been repeatedly denied parole and remains in prison for the gruesome murders committed by him and members of his cult. In 1993 the rock band "Guns and Roses" included a song written and sung by Manson in its new release.

Cecily Turner is in charge of ordering policies for Mammoth Records, a large national retail chain of stores selling compact disks, tapes, videos, and T-shirts. She has received a flood of letters and faxes from angry parent groups, church leaders, politicians, and others demanding that Mammoth pull the "Guns and Roses" CD and tape, and stop selling the Manson T-shirts. Turner knows that these are very popular items at the retail stores. If Mammoth stops selling them, its competitors will pick up the extra business, thereby reducing Mammoth's profits. What should Turner do?

3. Rose Stern is a manager/buyer in charge of purchasing blue jeans for a large retail store chain. She's also a die-hard football fan. This year the Super Bowl will be played in the Metrodome in Minneapolis, Minnesota, her hometown. Stern's team, the Minnesota Vikings, is expected to reach the Super Bowl.

Currently, the store chain carries four brands of jeans. In an effort to streamline its product line, however, the CEO has decided to cut back to three brands of blue jeans, leaving to Stern the decision of which brand to cut. Assume that all four brands are equally profitable. What if the makers of Brand One send Stern a pair of Super Bowl tickets? Should she accept these tickets? Is this a bribe? What if the maker of Brand One is also a close friend of hers? Or a relative? Is this a bribe? Or is it simply a friendly business gesture?

4. Assume the same facts as in question 3, except that Brand One underperforms the other three brands. How should that affect her decision? What if it is mid-January and the Vikings are definitely in the Super Bowl? Stern has waited her entire life to watch the Vikings play in the Super Bowl. Even if she would not accept the tickets before, should she accept them

now? Can she get out of her dilemma by offering to pay the face value of the tickets? Should she accept the tickets if she has already decided to discontinue Brand One?

5. Juan Gonzales is one of two partners who own a family-style, 24-store restaurant chain in the Northeast. The restaurants have a reputation for serving quality food at bargain prices. Since the opening of the first restaurant 34 years ago, the restaurants have generated a loyal clientele. However, many of these customers are older. Because the restaurant business has recently taken a turn for the worse, Gonzales feels it is time to revamp his restaurant's image so that it appeals to the younger generation. Consequently, Gonzales and his partner have taken on a significant amount of debt in order to remodel and renovate.

Five of the 24 restaurants are in New York City. In the last few days, Gonzales has received 15 phone calls from people who claim that they have gotten sick after eating at his restaurant in the Bronx. After investigation, Gonzales discovers that a shipment of frozen sausage was contaminated with salmonella Ohio, a rare form of food poisoning. How should Gonzales respond to the 15 customers who have already called? How should he respond to any further complaints? If Gonzales denies that the contamination was caused by his restaurants, it is possible that no one will find out. After all, there are thousands of restaurants and grocery stores in New York City that could have poisoned the customers.

Should Gonzales pull all of the shipments of sausage from his freezers? What if he decides to compensate the victims but his partner disagrees? What if both Gonzales and his partner agree to compensate the poisoned victims, but because of the recent debt this is not financially feasible? How should he balance the ethical implications with the economic implications? Should his response vary depending upon whether Gonzales's restaurants are insured?

6. Henry Sherman is the CEO of the nation's leading fur company. In years past, the fur trade has been incredibly lucrative. However, Sherman has recently become quite concerned about the future of the fur industry. A public outcry has erupted regarding the killing of the animals supplying the furs. Animal-rights activists are pressuring state legislatures to pass laws that would limit or prohibit the sale of furs in their jurisdictions. Rather than taking a wait-and-see approach, Sherman decides to monitor the most influential animal-rights group, Save the Animals.

Sherman hires a small public affairs firm to scrutinize the actions of Save the Animals. In addition to keeping a close eye on Save the Animals, the public affairs firm tracks other players in the industry, both groups and individuals.

Sherman is quite satisfied with the information that the public affairs firm provided. He was told that the information was gathered from newsletters, news reports, and other published material available to the public. The information allows Sherman to lobby effectively against antifur legislation, making his shareholders, employees, and customers all quite happy.

Six months later, Sherman learns that most of the crucial information he had received was not collected from public documents. Rather, it was gathered by an informant who had infiltrated Save the Animals. Should Sherman terminate his contract with the public affairs firm? Are the public affairs firm's actions ethical? Are they legal? Is this spying? Assuming that there is no legal protection against private surveillance, and hence the monitoring is legal, is the legal thing to do the right thing to do?

An argument can be made that this is good business, because Sherman's stakeholders are happy. Is good business good ethics?

7. How would a responsible manager of a hostile takeover target react to the following statement? How would a responsible partner of a leveraged buyout firm react?

> Amazing as it may seem, the battle between raiders and companies is sometimes said to be a Darwinian struggle that assists the evolution of business by creating organizations that are ever more efficient, more competitive, and more fit for survival.
>
> Actually, what we're seeing is the reverse of evolution. Our liberating of resources from managerial control has become so indiscriminate that we're undoing the very process of building for the future which business depends on. We're headed back down the Darwinian slope toward lower forms of organization as deal after deal leaves more and more of our operations either reduced to fragments or liquidated into money.
>
> So, business must work to build awareness that dealmaking for fast bucks is wrongheaded and dangerous. We must stress the point that business people cannot contribute to the good of society by concentrating on near-term profits alone. Even more important is the need to increase competitiveness and profitability over the long term. (*Touche Ross Report*, 40.)

8. After years of consulting in the beer business, three MBAs from the University of Houston decided to buy and operate a liquor retailer. When they located a target store, they sat outside to count cars and cases of beer moving out of the door, looked over the seller's purchase records, talked with his major suppliers, and analyzed his prices, inventory turns, and competitive position. After they had agreed to terms, signed a letter of intent, and obtained loans to buy the real estate and inventory, they signed a confidentiality statement designed to prevent them from sharing the retailer's financial information with anyone if the deal fell through. When they went to see the retailer's accountant, she checked to see that they had signed the confidentiality statement, called her client to double-check that they were the buyers, and then gave them the ledger books and tax returns for the past four years, as well as the "real" books for the last four years.

The MBAs discovered that the seller was actually running his business illegally by selling part of his inventory wholesale to competing stores, rather than retail to customers. The retailer did not possess a wholesale liquor license; one cannot have both a wholesale and a retail license in the state in question. The seller was buying huge quantities of beer to gain the highest discounts from the distributors, and then selling part at retail and part at wholesale. He reported his retail revenue as his gross revenue to the IRS, the state tax board, and the liquor board. His wholesale revenue went into the mattress.

The MBAs decided not to complete the transaction, as they had no intention of running the business that way. The store owner received an all-cash offer of $50,000 more than the MBAs had agreed upon, but he liked the "young, enthusiastic guys." The MBAs told him to take the other offer, and they parted on friendly terms.

What should the MBAs have done? Who was hurt by the retailer's illegalities? Could the MBAs have told someone without violating the nondisclosure agreement?

9. Arnita Kim is the CEO of BioDef, a biotechnology company that depends heavily on a year-to-year contract with the Department of Defense to provide antidotes for use in the event of biological warfare. Antidotes are drugs that combat the diseases spread by release of deadly biological agents. The existing product has a shelflife of one year. This creates a current stream of income for BioDef as the government has to replace its supply of antidotes every year. However, the research director for BioDef has just told Kim of a major research breakthrough that makes it possible, at little extra cost, to extend the shelflife of the antidotes from one year to four years.

The current contract with the Department of Defense will expire in two months. What is Kim legally required to tell the government about the breakthrough? What should she tell the government? What factors should Kim consider in making this decision?

10. What can a manager do to prevent retaliation for whistleblowing?

Chapter 2

CONSTITUTIONAL BASES FOR BUSINESS REGULATION

■ Introduction

Effect of United States Constitution on Business

The United States Constitution, including the Bill of Rights, imposes limitations on the way business is conducted in the United States. It gives federal and state governments the power to regulate business activities, and it provides that certain rights cannot be taken away from private persons and businesses. It allocates responsibility for regulating business to the three branches of the federal government: the Congress, the executive branch (which includes the president) and the courts.

The Constitution became effective in 1789. The first ten amendments to the Constitution, called the Bill of Rights, were added in 1791. Seventeen amendments were added subsequent to the Bill of Rights. The most recent, the Twenty-seventh Amendment, was adopted in 1992; it prohibits changes in congressional pay from taking effect until after an intervening election of representatives.

Chapter Summary

This chapter first discusses the structure of the government of the United States as established by the Constitution and the allocation of different tasks to the three branches of government. This allocation is referred to as the separation of powers. The scope of judicial powers of the federal courts and the concept of judicial review are outlined, as is the Supremacy Clause. Next, the chapter details the scope of executive and legislative power. This is followed by an analysis of conflicts that arise among the three branches.

The chapter then discusses the doctrine of federalism, which serves to allocate power between the federal government and the various state governments. The central importance of the Commerce Clause of the Constitution to this doctrine is explored. Finally, the chapter outlines the individual rights established by the

Constitution and the various methods of protecting those rights. Among the various constitutional issues discussed are the rights guaranteed under the Bill of Rights, and the concepts of substantive due process, eminent domain, and equal protection.

Structure of Government

The Constitution divides governmental power between the state and federal governments, giving the federal government certain specified powers. Without a grant of power from the Constitution, the federal government cannot act. All powers not expressly given to the federal government in the Constitution rest with the states. It should be noted that both the state and the federal government can regulate the same business activity. For example, there are both federal and state laws governing protection of the environment. However, if a state law conflicts with a federal law, the federal law takes precedence or *preempts* the state law.

> *Without a grant of power from the Constitution, the federal government cannot act.*

Separation of Powers

Within the federal government, power is divided among the judicial branch (the courts), the executive branch (the president), and the legislative branch (the Congress). This division of power among the three branches is typically referred to as the *separation of powers*.

The Judicial Power

The power of the judiciary is established in various parts of the Constitution. Articles I and III give Congress the authority to establish federal courts. Article III provides the basis for the judicial power of federal courts.

Article III

Article III of the Constitution vests judicial power in the Supreme Court of the United States, and such other lower courts as the Congress may from time to time establish. Federal judicial power extends to all cases or controversies:

- Arising under the Constitution, laws, or treaties of the United States

- Of admiralty and maritime jurisdiction

- In which the United States is a party

- Between two or more states

- Between a state and citizens of another state

- Between citizens of different states

- Between citizens of the same state claiming lands under grants of different states

- Between a state or citizens thereof and foreign states, citizens, or subjects

This provision grants *subject matter jurisdiction* to the federal courts, meaning that federal courts have the power to decide these types of cases.

Article III gives the Supreme Court *appellate jurisdiction* in all such cases; this means that a lower court tries the case and the Supreme Court hears only appeals from the lower court's decision. The Supreme Court also has *original jurisdiction* over cases affecting ambassadors and cases in which a state is a party. This means that these cases are tried in the Supreme Court, not in a lower court. Today, the Supreme Court's original jurisdiction is mainly used to decide controversies between states.

Congress has used its authority under article III to establish federal district courts and courts of appeal. The structure of the federal court system is discussed in chapter 4. All cases that fall under one of the categories listed above, except those in which the Supreme Court has original jurisdiction, are tried in federal district courts, or in some instances in state courts with a right to remove them to federal court.

Article I   Article I allows Congress to establish special courts other than the federal district courts and courts of appeal established under article III. These specialized courts are often granted administrative as well as judicial powers. Examples of such courts are the United States Tax Court, the United States Bankruptcy Court, and the courts of the District of Columbia.

Judicial Review   The federal courts also have the power to review acts of the other two branches of the federal government to determine whether they violate the Constitution. This power of *judicial review* makes the federal judiciary a watchdog over the government.

The Constitution does not explicitly state that the federal courts have this power of review. The power was established by a landmark decision of the Supreme Court in 1803. In *Marbury v. Madison*,[1] the Supreme Court stated that it is the duty of the Supreme Court to determine what the law is. The Supreme Court held that the written Constitution must be the fundamental and paramount law of the land. Any law enacted by Congress that conflicts with the Constitution is void.

The Supremacy Clause   Federal courts also have the power to review the executive, legislative, or judicial acts of the states. The Supremacy Clause of article VI states that the Constitution, laws, and treaties of the United States take precedence over state laws and that the judges of the state courts must follow federal law.

The Executive Power

The executive power of the president is defined in article II, section I, of the Constitution. Various executive functions may be delegated within the executive branch by the president or by Congress.

Article II, section 2, enables the president, with the advice and consent of the Senate, to appoint the justices of the Supreme Court. It also allows the president to appoint all ambassadors and consuls, and all other officers of the United States whose appointments are not provided for elsewhere in the Constitution.

Article II, section 2, also empowers the president to grant reprieves and pardons for offenses against the United States, except in cases of impeachment. President Gerald Ford invoked this section when he pardoned Richard Nixon after Nixon resigned from the presidency following the Watergate burglary scandal in the early 1970s.

Article I, section 7, grants the president the power to either approve or disapprove acts of Congress before they take effect. The president thus has veto power over laws that do not meet her approval. Congress can override a president's veto by a two-thirds vote of both the House of Representatives and the Senate.

The president has extensive power over foreign affairs. The president may not declare war, but he may take other military action through his power as commander-in-chief of the armed forces under article II, section 2. President Ronald Reagan invoked this power to authorize the United States's invasion of Grenada. In 1989, President George Bush used this power to invade Panama.

The president also has the power to make treaties with the advice and consent of the Senate; that is, with two-thirds of the senators voting to ratify the treaty. Ratified treaties, along with the Constitution, are the supreme law of the land. Any laws enacted in violation of either of these are void. The president may also make executive agreements that do not require the advice and consent of the Senate. These agreements are superior to state law but not to federal law. Treaties and executive agreements are discussed further in chapter 3.

The Legislative Power

Article I, section 8, of the Constitution enumerates the powers of the Congress, which consists of the House of Representatives and the Senate. Congress has the power: (1) to regulate commerce with foreign nations and among the states; (2) to spend to provide for the common defense and general welfare; (3) to coin money; (4) to establish post offices; (5) to lay and collect taxes; (6) to issue patents and copyrights; (7) to declare war; and (8) to raise and support armies. The courts have given a broad interpretation to Congress's power to regulate commerce among the states and its power to spend for the common welfare. Congress also has the power to make laws that are "necessary and proper" to carry out any power vested in the government of the United States.

Conflicts Between the Branches

Inherent in the system of checks and balances is a built-in potential for conflict between the three branches of government. At times, the power of one branch of the government must be curbed in order to ensure the autonomy of another branch.

Article I, section 6, states that senators and representatives "shall not be questioned in any other Place" for "any Speech or Debate in either House." This immunity was clarified by the Supreme Court in a case in which a former senator was prosecuted for accepting a bribe relating to his actions on postal rate legislation. The Supreme Court held that the immunity only "protects against inquiry into acts which occur in the regular course of the legislative process and the motivation for those acts." The immunity does not protect all acts "relating to the legislative process." The Supreme Court let the prosecution proceed. Because the issue was whether the senator accepted the bribe, it was not necessary for the prosecu-

---

1. 5 U.S. 137 (1803).

tor to inquire into whether the illegal promise was performed.[2]

The Constitution does not expressly grant immunity to executive officials, but some immunities are implied. It has been inferred from the extensive impeachment proceedings outlined in the Constitution that the president is immune from criminal prosecution prior to impeachment. In addition, it has been held that the president may not be sued for damages resulting from official acts. This immunity is based on the president's unique position in the constitutional scheme.

The president also has a type of immunity known as *executive privilege,* which protects against the forced disclosure of presidential communications made in the exercise of executive power. Yet sometimes the executive privilege must give way to the judicial branch's need to obtain evidence in a criminal trial.

The leading case in this area involved President Richard Nixon and his refusal to comply with a subpoena issued in the trial of seven of his associates for conspiracy to obstruct justice and other offenses related to the burglary of the Democratic National Headquarters in the Watergate Hotel in 1972.[3] President Nixon had been requested to produce tape recordings and documents related to conversations between himself and his aides and advisors. The president released edited transcripts of some of the conversations, and then filed to declare the subpoena invalid. Nixon claimed executive privilege as to the confidential conversations between himself and his advisors. The Supreme Court found that neither the separation of powers doctrine nor the need for confidentiality of high-level communications could justify a presidential privilege at all times because this "unqualified" privilege would upset the constitutional balance of a workable government. In particular, the Court found that where the president's claim of privilege was based only on the generalized interest in confidentiality and not on the need to protect military or diplomatic secrets, the president's interest could not prevail over the fundamental demands of due process of law in the fair administration of criminal justice.

This standard was applied in 1989 to President Ronald Reagan's assertion of presidential privilege in connection with the trial of Admiral John Poindexter for alleged illegal activities involving sales of arms to Iran and diversion of the proceeds to the Contras in Nicaragua. The Contras, called "freedom fighters" by President Reagan, were trying to depose the government in Nicaragua. They were backed by the United States, but Congress later forbade sending money to help them. Admiral Poindexter sought to subpoena President Reagan's diaries and notes for use in Poindexter's defense. The U.S. District Court for the District of Columbia stated that:

History and legal precedent teach that documents from a former or an incumbent President are presumptively privileged. That is so for a variety of interrelated reasons. First, a request for documents in the possession of a President involves the exercise of jurisdiction over the presidency and accordingly implicates the possibility of a conflict between the branches. Second, because of the dignity and stature of the presidency, a court must exercise deference and restraint when asked to issue coercive orders against a President with respect to his person or his papers. Third, executive privilege is fundamental to the operation of government, and it exists "not for the benefit of the President as an individual, but for the benefit of the Republic." Fourth, the kinds of documents demanded by defendant in this case—the President's diary and his own notes—touch the core of the presidency as well as intimate and confidential communications by the President with himself.[4]

The court recognized that executive privilege is not absolute but concluded that it was appropriate to narrow the scope of the subpoenas and let President Reagan respond before deciding the question of executive privilege.

The principle of separation of powers has barred certain legislation. For example, in 1986 the Supreme Court held that the deficit-reduction functions given under the Gramm-Rudman-Hollings Act violated the Constitution. Pursuant to another law, the comptroller general is removable only by Congress, and the Supreme Court concluded that it would be improper for Congress to have the power to remove an officer performing executive duties.[5] This case is discussed in chapter 6.

The Supreme Court has also found the legislative veto provisions in many laws unconstitutional, as in the case that follows. A legislative veto allows Congress to veto the actions of the executive branch.

---

2. *United States v. Brewster,* 408 U.S. 501, 92 S.Ct. 2531 (1972).
3. *United States v. Nixon,* 418 U.S. 683, 94 S.Ct. 3090 (1974).

4. *United States v. Poindexter,* 727 F.Supp. 1501 (D.D.C. 1989). In a subsequent decision, *United States v. Poindexter,* 732 F.Supp. 135 (D.D.C. 1990), the court ordered production of some but not all of the documents requested by Poindexter.
5. *Bowsher v. Synar,* 478 U.S. 714, 106 S.Ct. 3181 (1986).

■ A Case in Point: Summary

Case 2.1
INS v. CHADHA
Supreme Court of the
United States
462 U.S. 919, 103 S.Ct. 2764
(1983).

FACTS   Jagdish Rai Chadha was an East Indian born in Kenya and holding a British passport. He had been lawfully admitted into the United States on a nonimmigrant student visa, but continued to stay in the country after his visa expired. The Immigration and Naturalization Service (INS) asked him to show cause why he should not be deported. Chadha applied for suspension of the deportation under section 244(a)(1) of the Immigration and Nationality Act. This section gives the attorney general the power to suspend deportation if the alien is of good moral character and is a person whose deportation would, in the opinion of the attorney general, result in extreme hardship to the alien or his family. After a hearing, the immigration judge ordered that Chadha's deportation be suspended. As required by the Immigration and Nationality Act, the judge reported the suspension to Congress.

The House of Representatives passed a resolution pursuant to section 244(c)(2) of the act and vetoed the suspension. The section authorized either house of Congress, by resolution, to invalidate the decision of the executive branch to allow a particular deportable alien to remain in the United States. Ordered deported, Chadha sought review of the order of deportation.

ISSUE PRESENTED   Is a legislative veto by the House of Representatives of an executive order constitutional?

SUMMARY OF OPINION   The U.S. Supreme Court held unconstitutional the section of the act that allowed one house of Congress to invalidate a decision by the executive branch. The Court reasoned that action by a house of Congress pursuant to that section is essentially legislative. Thus, as detailed in article I of the Constitution, it was subject to the constitutional requirements of passage by a majority of both houses and presentation of the action to the president for signature or veto. The one-house legislative veto was held unconstitutional because it violated the constitutional requirements of bicameralism (action by both houses of Congress) and presentment of legislation to the president.

RESULT   The attorney general was ordered to stop taking any steps to deport Chadha.

■ Federalism

The federal government's powers are limited to those expressly granted in the Constitution. Its powers are also subject to specific restrictions, such as those in the Bill of Rights. State governments, on the other hand, have general powers not specified in the Constitution. These include the *police power* to protect the health, safety, welfare, or morals of the people of the state.

Some powers are exclusively federal because the Constitution expressly limits the states' exercise of those powers. Exclusive federal powers include the power to make treaties, to coin money, and to impose a duty on imports. Other powers are inherently in the states' domain, such as the power to structure state and local governments. One of the boundaries between federal and state powers is the Constitution's Commerce Clause.

The Commerce Clause

Article I, section 8, gives Congress the power to regulate commerce with other nations, with Indian tribes, and between states. The Commerce Clause is both a restraint on state action and a source of federal authority. The commerce power has been interpreted to allow federal regulation of such areas as interstate travel, labor relations, and discrimination in accommodations.

The first Supreme Court discussion of the Commerce Clause was by Chief Justice John Marshall in the 1824 case *Gibbons v. Ogden*.[6] A steamboat monopoly affecting navigation between New York and New Jersey violated a federal statute regulating interstate commerce. The Court held that under the Supremacy Clause, the federal statute prevailed. In the decision Justice Marshall discussed in detail his view that interstate commerce—which he defined as "commerce which concerns more states than one"—included every activity having any interstate impact. Therefore, Congress could regulate all such activities.

From 1887 to 1937, the Supreme Court developed a view of the Commerce Clause quite different from Marshall's view. The Supreme Court interpreted "commerce" narrowly, holding that activities such as mining and manufacturing were not commerce and therefore could not be regulated by Congress. The Supreme Court was not persuaded by the fact that the products of these activities would later enter interstate commerce. During this period the Supreme Court struck down important New Deal legislation, arguing that the Commerce Clause did not grant Congress the power to regulate such activities.

The turning point in the Supreme Court's attitude came in *NLRB v. Jones & Laughlin Steel Corp.*[7] The Court held that Congress could regulate labor relations in a manufacturing plant because a work stoppage at such a plant would have a serious effect on interstate commerce; the steel manufactured by the plant was shipped across state lines.

Today most federal regulation of commerce is upheld under the Commerce Clause. The Supreme Court usually defers to the findings of Congress. If legislation has a "substantial economic effect" on interstate commerce it is held to be a valid exercise of the commerce power. The Supreme Court will uphold such laws made by Congress so long as there is some rational ground for finding that the items regulated have an effect on interstate commerce.

There are three ways that an item, person, or activity may come under the federal commerce power. Congress may regulate (1) interstate travel or shipments; (2) any activity, including single-state activities, if it has a close and substantial relationship to interstate travel or shipments; or (3) single-state activities, if the regulation is necessary and proper to the regulation of interstate travel or shipments.

Congress has used the broad grant of power in the Commerce Clause to regulate activities only marginally related to interstate commerce. This is demonstrated in the following case.

---

6. 22 U.S. 1 (1824).

7. 301 U.S. 1, 57 S.Ct. 615 (1937).

■ **A Case in Point:**   **Summary**

Case 2.2
HEART OF ATLANTA MOTEL, INC. v. UNITED STATES
Supreme Court of the United States
379 U.S. 241, 85 S.Ct. 348 (1964).

FACTS The Heart of Atlanta Motel was a 216-room motel for transient guests. The motel was easily accessible by a major highway. The operator of the hotel solicited patronage from outside the state of Georgia through various national advertising media, including magazines of national circulation. It maintained more than 50 billboards and highway signs within the state, soliciting patronage for the motel. It accepted convention trade from outside Georgia, and approximately 75% of its registered guests were from out of state.

The operator of the hotel brought an action attacking the constitutionality of title II of the Civil Rights Act of 1964. Among other provisions, the act prohibited discrimination or segregation on the ground of race, color, religion, or national origin in any inn, hotel, motel, or other establishment of more than five rooms that provides lodging to transient guests. Prior to passage of the act the motel had followed a practice of refusing to rent rooms to African Americans, and it alleged that it intended to continue to do so.

*Case **2.2** continued on following page*

*Case **2.2** continued*

A three-judge court sustained the validity of the act, and the plaintiff motel appealed.

ISSUE PRESENTED Are the provisions of the Civil Rights Act of 1964 prohibiting discrimination in public accommodations a valid exercise of Congressional power under the Commerce Clause?

SUMMARY OF OPINION The U.S. Supreme Court noted that people have become increasingly mobile with millions of people of all races traveling from state to state. African Americans in particular have been the subject of discrimination in transient accommodations, having to travel great distances to secure lodging. Often they have been unable to obtain accommodations and have had to call upon friends to put them up overnight. These conditions had become so acute as to require the listing of available lodging for African Americans in a special guidebook which the Court called in itself "dramatic testimony to the difficulties Blacks encounter in travel."

The Court stated that the power of Congress to deal with these obstructions depended on the meaning of the Commerce Clause. The Court reasoned: "The determinative test of the exercise of power by the Congress under the Commerce Clause is simply whether the activity sought to be regulated is 'commerce which concerns more States than one' and has a real and substantial relation to the national interest." The Court concluded that the action of Congress in the adoption of the act as applied here to a motel which concededly served interstate travelers is within the power granted it by the Commerce Clause of the Constitution, as interpreted by the Supreme Court for 140 years. Although it may be argued that Congress could have pursued other methods to eliminate the obstructions it found in interstate commerce caused by racial discrimination, this was a matter of policy that rested entirely with Congress, not with the courts.

RESULT Title II of the Civil Rights Act of 1964 is constitutional. The Heart of Atlanta Motel may not legally refuse provision of accommodations to African Americans.

COMMENTS Even though the main purpose of the act was to legislate against moral wrongs, this did not make the act unconstitutional. Congress, exercising the powers granted by the Commerce Clause, had previously legislated with respect to gambling, fraudulent securities transactions, misbranding of drugs, wages and hours, and crop control. The fact that Congress was legislating against moral wrongs in no way lessened the effect on interstate commerce. Because the activity affected interstate commerce, Congress had the power under the Commerce Clause to pass laws to regulate it. Although the operation of the hotel was local, it affected interstate travel.

In *Katzenbach v. McClung*,[8] a case argued concurrently with *Heart of Atlanta*, the Supreme Court upheld the application of the Civil Rights Act to a restaurant when a substantial portion of the food that it served had moved in interstate commerce. The Court reasoned that the restaurant's discrimination against African Americans, who were potential customers, resulted in its selling less food that had traveled in interstate commerce. Thus, the discrimination had a substantial effect on interstate commerce.

---

8. 379 U.S. 294, 85 S.Ct. 377 (1964).

Limits on State Powers

Federal powers enumerated in the Constitution impose many limits on state action. This chapter discusses only the limits on state power resulting from the commerce power, but the principles apply to other federal powers as well.

Where Congress has indicated a policy by acting, Congress's action preempts state action—the Supremacy Clause makes federal laws supreme over state laws. Where Congress has not taken action, the "dormant" Commerce Clause imposes restrictions on state action. What those restrictions are can be difficult to determine.

Since the mid-1930s, the Supreme Court has tried to clarify when state regulation is valid in the absence of preempting federal regulation. The principle the Court now follows is that state regulation affecting interstate commerce will be upheld if the regulation is (1) rationally related to a legitimate state end, and (2) does not create any undue burden on interstate commerce. A regulation creates an *undue burden* when the regulatory burden on interstate commerce outweighs the state's interest in the legislation.

The Supreme Court is hostile toward state protectionism and discrimination against out-of-state interests. However, not all state regulations found invalid under the Commerce Clause are protectionist or discriminatory. The problem lies in determining the purpose of the legislation. Protectionist regulations may be explicitly discriminatory; they may be enacted for a discriminatory purpose; or they may have the effect of favoring local interests at the expense of out-of-state concerns.

> **66**
>
> *The Supreme Court is hostile toward state protectionism and discrimination against out-of-state interests.*

A Madison, Wisconsin, regulation that barred the sale of pasteurized milk unless it had been processed and bottled within a radius of five miles from Madison was struck down as discriminatory.[9] The city claimed that the

Ethical Consideration

Heart of Atlanta and *Katzenbach v. McClung* demonstrate the Supreme Court's use of its power of judicial review to uphold legislation aimed at curing a social evil such as racial discrimination.

ordinance was a health measure, but the Supreme Court found that it discriminated against milk originating in other states. On the other hand, a Minnesota statute banning plastic, nonreturnable milk containers was upheld in the face of claims that it discriminated against interstate commerce.[10] The statute, stated the Supreme Court, was not "simple protectionism"; it "regulated evenhandedly" by prohibiting all milk retailers from selling their products in the plastic containers. The regulation applied regardless of whether the milk, the containers, or the sellers were from inside or outside the state.

A North Carolina statute prohibited the sale of apples that bore a grade other than the applicable U.S. grade. Washington State apples bore their own state's grade on the container, a grade that was equal to or more stringent than the U.S. grade. The North Carolina statute was held invalid because, although neutral on its face, the effect of the statute was to discriminate against Washington apples.[11]

The Supreme Court struck down a Massachusetts law that required every milk dealer who sold milk in Massachusetts to contribute to a state fund based on the volume of the milk that the dealer had sold within the state, regardless of the price the dealer paid for the milk or its point of origin.[12] Massachusetts dairy farmers received a form of subsidy because they, but not the out-of-state producers, were entitled to disbursements from the fund, based on the volume of milk they produced.

---

9. *Dean Milk Co. v. City of Madison*, 340 U.S. 349, 71 S.Ct. 295 (1951).

10. *Minnesota v. Clover Leaf Creamery Co.*, 449 U.S. 456, 101 S.Ct. 715 (1981).

11. *Hunt v. Washington State Apple Advertising Commission*, 432 U.S. 333, 97 S.Ct. 2434 (1977).

12. *West Lynn Creamery Inc. v. Healy,* 114 S.Ct. 2205 (1994).

"As a matter of fact, I _have_ read the Constitution,
and, frankly, I don't get it."

Drawing by Weber; ©1988 The New Yorker Magazine, Inc. *Used by permission.*

The Court reasoned that the combination of the Massachusetts tax, which was levied on all producers, combined with the subsidy provided to only local Massachusetts dairy farmers, was akin to the kind of tariff that the Commerce Clause was meant to prohibit. In part because most of the milk sold in Massachusetts is produced by out-of-state entities, the Massachusetts law had the effect of enabling higher-cost Massachusetts dairy farmers to compete with lower-cost dairy farmers in other states. This "violates the principle of the unitary national market by handicapping out-of-state competitors, thus artificially encouraging in-state production even when the same goods could be produced at lower cost in other States."[13]

The proper division between state and federal regulation is more obvious when Congress has already enacted laws in an area. State law is preempted when it directly conflicts with federal law or when Congress has manifested an intention to regulate the entire area without state participation.

---

13. *Ibid.*

The issue of preemption is especially important to a corporation that is trying to prevent a *hostile takeover.* In a hostile takeover a third party, called a *raider,* seeks to obtain control of a corporation, called the *target,* over the objections of its management. (Hostile takeovers are discussed further in chapters 20 and 21.) A number of state legislatures, in response to a wave of hostile takeovers that resulted in the loss of jobs and the relocation of corporate headquarters out of state, adopted antitakeover statutes. The constitutionality of these statutes was challenged by corporate raiders, who argued that federal law was exclusive in this area. One of the early forms of state antitakeover legislation was struck down in *Edgar v. MITE Corp.*[14]

MITE Corporation, an Illinois company, initiated a tender offer for all of the outstanding shares of Chicago River and Machine Co. by filing with the Securities and Exchange Commission the schedule required by the Williams Act (part of the federal Securities Exchange Act of 1934 which governs tender offers). In following this procedure, MITE did not comply with legislation in effect at the time in Illinois.

The Illinois Business Take-Over Act required that any person or company intending to make a tender offer (an offer to shareholders to buy their shares) must notify the secretary of state and the target company of the offer 20 days before it was to become effective. During that time the offeror could not communicate its offer to the shareholders, but the target company was free to disseminate information to its shareholders concerning the impending offer. Additionally, any takeover offer had to be registered with the secretary of state, who was authorized to hold a hearing on the fairness of the offer.

A plurality of the Supreme Court found that the act violated the Supremacy Clause. In particular, the Court found that three provisions of the act conflicted with congressional mandates: (1) the precommencement provisions insisting on 20-days' notice frustrated the no notice objectives of the Williams Act, which intended to foil the target company's attempts to repel tender offers beneficial to shareholders; (2) the failure to provide a deadline by which a hearing on a contested takeover must be brought thwarted the Williams Act provision allowing the purchase of shares pursuant to the tender offer to proceed without unreasonable delay; and (3) the requirement that the Illinois secretary of state review the fairness of tender offers contravened the congressional

intent to prevent investor protection from overriding investor authority.

In *CTS Corp. v. Dynamics Corp. of America,*[15] the Supreme Court upheld Indiana's Control Share Acquisition Act. The Indiana act provided that a "control share acquisition" that would otherwise have given the acquiror the power to vote more than specified percentages of the stock of the target (that is, 20%, 33 ⅓%, or 50%) would not in fact result in acquisition of the commensurate voting rights unless they were conferred by a majority of the disinterested shareholders at a meeting to be held within at least 50 days. The Indiana act was one of many post-*MITE,* second-generation antitakeover statutes.

In finding that the Indiana act did not have the three traits of the Illinois statute discussed in *MITE,* the Supreme Court reasoned that the Indiana act did not give either the target company or the offeror an advantage in communicating with shareholders about an impending offer. The act did not impose an indefinite delay, as did the statute in *MITE,* and it did not prevent an offeror from consummating an offer on the 20th business day, the earliest day permitted under applicable federal regulations, because the shareholders could agree to hold a special meeting within this period. Finally, the Court reasoned that, unlike the Illinois statute, which required the state government to interpose its views of fairness, the Indiana act allowed the shareholders collectively to evaluate the fairness of the offer.

The Court then focused on whether the Indiana act frustrated the purpose of the Williams Act. According to the Court, unlike the statute considered in *MITE,* the Indiana act did not operate in favor of management against offerors and to the detriment of shareholders. To the contrary, the Indiana act "protect[ed] the independent shareholder against both of the contending parties," thus furthering a basic purpose of the Williams Act, which is "placing investors on an equal footing with the takeover bidder." The Court further noted that the Indiana act "operated on the assumption, implicit in the Williams Act, that independent shareholders faced with tender offers are at a disadvantage." By providing shareholders with the opportunity to vote as a group to reject the offer, the Court stated, the Indiana act protected individual investors from the coerciveness of having to accept a tender offer for fear of having to sell later at a depressed price.

---

14. 457 U.S. 624, 102 S.Ct. 2629 (1982).

15. 481 U.S. 69, 107 S.Ct. 1637 (1987).

Pennsylvania adopted one of the toughest antitakeover statutes in the United States in 1990. The provisions of the statute are discussed in chapter 20.

The following case addresses the application of these principles to an increasingly problematic area—the disposal of hazardous waste.

■ **A Case in Point:**   **In the Language of the Court**

Case 2.3
CHEMICAL WASTE
MANAGEMENT, INC. v. HUNT
Supreme Court of the
United States
112 S.Ct. 2009 (1992).

FACTS Chemical Waste Management, Inc. owned and operated a hazardous waste treatment, storage, and disposal facility in Emelle, Alabama. Alabama is one of only 16 states that have commercial hazardous waste landfills. The Emelle facility was the largest of 21 landfills of this kind. From 1985 through 1989, the tonnage of hazardous waste received per year more than doubled. Of this, up to 90% of the tonnage permanently buried each year was shipped in from other states.

Alabama responded to this increase by legislating Act No. 90-326, which included a cap that limited the amount of hazardous wastes or substances that may be disposed of in any one-year period. The act also imposed an additional fee "for waste and substances which are generated outside of Alabama and disposed of at a commercial site for the disposal of hazardous waste or hazardous substances in Alabama."

Chemical Waste Management filed suit in state court requesting declaratory relief against the respondents and seeking to enjoin enforcement of the act. In addition to state law claims, Chemical Waste contended that the act violated the Commerce Clause of the United States Constitution. The trial court, finding the only basis to be the origin of the waste, declared the additional fee to be in violation of the Commerce Clause. On appeal, the Alabama Supreme Court reversed, holding that the additional fee at issue advanced legitimate local purposes that could not be adequately served by reasonable nondiscriminatory alternatives and was therefore valid under the Commerce Clause. Chemical Waste Management appealed.

ISSUE PRESENTED Does a state law imposing an additional fee on out-of-state hazardous waste violate the Commerce Clause?

OPINION WHITE, J., writing for the U.S. Supreme Court:

. . . .

II
No State may attempt to isolate itself from a problem common to the several States by raising barriers to the free flow of interstate trade.

The Act's additional fee facially discriminates against hazardous waste generated in States other than Alabama, and the Act overall has plainly discouraged the full operation of petitioner's Emelle facility. Such burdensome taxes imposed on interstate commerce alone are generally forbidden. . . . Once a state tax is found to discriminate against out-of-state commerce, it is typically struck down without further inquiry.

The State, however, argues that the additional fee imposed on out-of-state hazardous waste serves legitimate local purposes related to its citizens' health and safety. Because the additional fee discriminates both on its face and in practical effect, the burden falls on the State "to justify it both in terms of the local benefits flowing from the statute and the unavailability of nondiscriminatory alternatives adequate to preserve the local interests at stake." . . .

The State's argument here does not significantly differ from the Alabama Supreme Court's conclusions on the legitimate local purposes of the additional fee imposed, which were:

> The Additional Fee serves these legitimate local purposes that cannot be adequately served by reasonable nondiscriminatory alternatives: (1) protection of the health and safety of the citizens of Alabama from toxic substances; (2) conservation of the environment and the state's natural resources; (3) provision for compensatory revenue for the costs and burdens that out-of-state waste generators impose by dumping their hazardous waste in Alabama; (4) reduction of the overall flow of wastes traveling on the state's highways, which flow creates a great risk to the health and safety of the state's citizens.

These may all be legitimate local interests, and petitioner has not attacked them. But only rhetoric, and not explanation, emerges as to why Alabama targets only interstate hazardous waste to meet these goals. As found by the Trial Court, "although the Legislature imposed an additional fee of $72.00 per ton on waste generated outside Alabama, there is absolutely no evidence before this Court that waste generated outside Alabama is more dangerous than waste generated in Alabama. The Court finds under the facts of this case that the only basis for the additional fee is the origin of the waste." In the face of such findings, invalidity under the Commerce Clause necessarily follows, for "whatever [Alabama's] ultimate purpose, it may not be accomplished by discriminating against articles of commerce coming from outside the State unless there is some reason, apart from their origin, to treat them differently." The burden is on the State to show that "the discrimination is demonstrably justified by a valid factor unrelated to economic protectionism," and it has not carried this burden.

Ultimately, the State's concern focuses on the volume of the waste entering the Emelle facility. Less discriminatory alternatives, however, are available to alleviate this concern, not the least of which are a generally applicable per-ton additional fee on all hazardous waste disposed of within Alabama, or a per-mile tax on all vehicles transporting hazardous waste across Alabama roads, or an evenhanded cap on the total tonnage landfilled at Emelle which would curtail volume from all sources. To the extent Alabama's concern touches environmental conservation and the health and safety of its citizens, such concern does not vary with the point of origin of the waste, and it remains within the State's power to monitor and regulate more closely the transportation and disposal of all hazardous waste within its borders. . . . In sum, we find the additional fee to be "an obvious effort to saddle those outside the State" with most of the burden of slowing the flow of waste into the Emelle facility. "That legislative effort is clearly impermissible under the Commerce Clause of the Constitution."

. . . .

DISSENTING OPINION   REHNQUIST, C.J.:

Taxes are a recognized and effective means for discouraging the consumption of scarce commodities—in this case the safe environment that attends appropriate disposal of hazardous wastes. I therefore see nothing unconstitutional in Alabama's use of a tax to discourage the export of this commodity to other States, when the commodity is a public good that Alabama has helped to produce. . . .

*Case **2.3** continued on following page*

*Case **2.3** continued*

In short, the Court continues to err by its failure to recognize that waste—in this case admittedly hazardous waste—presents risks to the public health and environment that a State may legitimately wish to avoid, and that the State may pursue such an objective by means less Draconian than an outright ban. Under force of this Court's precedent, though, it increasingly appears that the only avenue by which a State may avoid the importation of hazardous wastes is to ban such waste disposal altogether, regardless of the waste's source of origin. I see little logic in creating, and nothing in the Commerce Clause that requires us to create, such perverse regulatory incentives. . . . The result is that the Court today gets it exactly backward when it suggests that Alabama is attempting to "isolate itself from a problem common to the several States." To the contrary, it is the 34 States that have no hazardous waste facility whatsoever, not to mention the remaining 15 States with facilities all smaller than Emelle, that have isolated themselves.

. . . .

RESULT   The decision of the Alabama Supreme Court was reversed. The Alabama act imposing an additional fee on waste from out-of-state was unconstitutional.

Questions
1. Would the result in this case have been different if the interstate waste posed health hazards not posed by the Alabama waste?
2. Can a state justify a quarantine of plants and animals coming across its borders from out of state? If so, how is a quarantine different from an additional fee?

Federal Fiscal Powers

Two other federal powers, the taxing and spending powers, have been invoked to regulate traditionally local "police problems" as well as purely economic problems. The Constitution grants a broad taxing power to the federal government. The only specific limitations imposed are that (1) direct taxes and capitation (per head) taxes must be allocated among the states in proportion to population; and (2) all custom duties and excise taxes must be uniform throughout the United States. The single prohibition is that no duty shall be levied upon exports from any state. The Fifth Amendment's due process clause is also a general limitation on the taxing power.

Taxes have an economic impact on business. The federal government has imposed taxes in order to affect the behavior of business as well as to raise revenues. The Supreme Court has, however, upheld taxes solely because of the power to tax granted to the government. The Court will not look into the purpose behind the tax in determining its validity.

Congress has the power to spend in order to provide for the common defense and general welfare. An exercise of the spending power will be upheld so long as it does not violate a specific check on the federal power.

■ Protection of Individual Liberties

The Constitution

Although most guarantees of individual liberties are found in the amendments to the Constitution, the Constitution itself contains three specific guarantees of individual rights.

The Contracts Clause   Article I, section 10, of the Constitution specifically prohibits a state legislature from impairing the obligation of existing contracts. The Fifth Amendment imposes a similar bar on federal legislation that would retroactively impair the obligations of a contract.

Historical Perspective
The Unified Internal Market

One of the primary concerns of the framers of the U.S. Constitution in drafting the Commerce Clause was to ensure that the United States would enjoy the economic benefits of a unified internal market. Under the Articles of Confederation, the several states had attempted to maximize their wealth at the expense of their neighbors. They had enacted various trade barriers, including tariffs and bans on imports from and exports to other states.

For example, states such as New York, which controlled major foreign ports, imposed taxes on incoming foreign goods destined for the other states. The other states retaliated by taxing goods brought into the state at such a high rate as to foreclose access to their markets. As a result of these policies, inefficient industries in certain states were protected from competition from more efficient industries in other states. These policies also restricted the economic freedom of citizens to operate their businesses on a nationwide scale. Economic efficiency was impaired.

The framers of the Constitution provided for a strong central government with the sole authority to regulate interstate trade and commerce. Congress would be able to act in the best interests of all citizens of the United States. It would not be subject to political pressure to maximize the welfare of the citizens of one particular state at the expense of those of another. Also, it could enact legislation designed to maximize efficiency on a national scale.

The Commerce Clause has been used time and time again to strike down various types of state legislation that restricted the free movement of goods and services among the states. Thus, the Commerce Clause has both ensured the economic benefits of free trade among the states and guaranteed the right to pursue economic activities on a nationwide scale, unhampered by discriminatory state legislation.

In this regard, it is interesting to contrast the experience of the United States with that of Europe. The establishment of the European Economic Community in the 1950s and its hoped for but unsuccessful expansion into a completely integrated single market by the end of 1992 may be regarded either as the first attempt at international unification of markets, or as a belated attempt to achieve what the United States of America did in 1789. (The factors that impeded the economic unification of Europe in 1992 and the steps that must be accomplished prior to adoption of a single European currency by 1999 are discussed in chapter 3.)

A recent application of the Contracts Clause arose in connection with insurance law changes mandated by California voter-approved Proposition 103, discussed in the case that follows.

■ A Case in Point: Summary

Case 2.4
CALFARM INSURANCE COMPANY v. DEUKMEJIAN
Supreme Court of California
48 Cal. 3d 805, 258 Cal. Rptr. 161, 771 P.2d 1247 (1989).

FACTS   On November 8, 1988, the voters of California approved an initiative, Proposition 103, which made numerous fundamental changes in the regulation of automobile and other types of insurance. Seven insurers and the Association of California Insurance Companies filed suit against Governor George Deukmejian and others, contending that Proposition 103 was unconstitutional on its face, under both the U.S. and California constitutions. Among other challenges, the insurance companies challenged the

*Case **2.4** continued on following page*

*Case **2.4** continued*

part of the initiative that made it illegal for insurance companies to refuse to renew policies for automobile insurance except for (1) nonpayment of premiums; (2) fraud or material misrepresentations affecting the policy or the insured; or (3) a substantial increase in the hazard insured against. Before enactment of Proposition 103, insurers had an unfettered right to refuse to renew policies. Because the new restrictions on renewal applied to policies issued before enactment of Proposition 103, the insurers argued that it violated the constitutional prohibition against a "law impairing the obligation of Contracts." (U.S. Const., art I, § 10.)

ISSUE PRESENTED   Do new restrictions on an insurance company's ability to refuse to renew an automobile insurance policy entered into prior to enactment of the new restrictions violate the Contracts Clause?

SUMMARY OF OPINION   In analyzing the constitutionality of the non-renewal provisions of Proposition 103, the California Supreme Court relied heavily upon the law as set forth by the U.S. Supreme Court in *Exxon Corp. v. Eagerton*.[16]

In that case, the U.S. Supreme Court upheld an Alabama law that imposed a severance tax on oil and gas while prohibiting price increases that would pass on the burden of the tax even though some sellers had contracts that expressly authorized such price increases. The decision explained:

> Although the language of the Contracts Clause is facially absolute, its prohibition must be accommodated to the inherent police power of the State "to safeguard the vital interests of its people." This Court has long recognized that a statute does not violate the Contracts Clause simply because it has the effect of restricting, or even barring altogether, the performance of duties created by contracts entered into prior to its enactment. Thus, a state prohibition law may be applied to contracts for the sale of beer that were valid when entered into, a law barring lotteries may be applied to lottery tickets that were valid when issued, and workmen's compensation law may be applied to employers and employees operating under pre-existing contracts of employment that made no provision for work-related injuries.

Applying these standards and others from other jurisdictions, the California Supreme Court upheld the nonrenewal restrictions. The decision rested in part on the fact that insurance is a highly regulated industry in which further regulation can reasonably be anticipated. Proposition 103 does not prevent an insurer from discontinuing its California business; an insurer can still withdraw from doing business in California. Furthermore, Proposition 103, as interpreted by the California Supreme Court earlier in its opinion, guaranteed that insurers renewing policies would receive fair and reasonable rates. Because the nonrenewal impairment of contract was found by the court to be "relatively moderate and restrained," the constitutional hurdle that the law had to overcome was correspondingly low. The public interest in making insurance available to all Californians and the fear that insurance companies would refuse to renew in California, leaving drivers without the car insurance required by law, was sufficient, when measured against the relatively low degree of impairment of contract rights involved, to justify the non-renewal provision under the U.S. and California constitutions, even as applied to existing policies.

---

16. 462 U.S. 176, 103 S.Ct. 2296 (1983).

RESULT   California can legally change the nonrenewal provisions applicable to existing automobile insurance policies without violating the U.S. or state constitutions.

COMMENTS   The provision of Proposition 103, which rolled back insurance rates by 20%, was upheld under a due process attack because Proposition 103 provided an individualized mechanism whereby insurers could obtain rate increases that would give them a fair and reasonable return. However, the part of Proposition 103 that prohibited rate increases for one year following enactment of Proposition 103 unless the insurer was threatened with insolvency was struck down as unconstitutional on its face. Although price controls and rent controls are often upheld, they cannot be confiscatory. The property owner is entitled to a reasonable return on the owner's investment. Even if profits in the past were excessive, this would not justify an unreasonably low rate of return for the future.

Ex Post Facto Laws   Article I, section 9, and article I, section 10, prohibit *ex post facto* laws. These are laws that punish actions that were not illegal when performed.

Bills of Attainder   Article I, section 9, prohibits the federal government from enacting laws to punish specific individuals. Such laws are termed *bills of attainder.*

The Bill of Rights

The first ten amendments of the Constitution constitute the Bill of Rights. The first eight amendments contain specific guarantees of individual liberties that limit the power of the federal government. The First Amendment guarantees freedom of religion, speech, press, and association. The Second Amendment grants persons the right to bear arms. The Third Amendment provides that no soldier shall be quartered in any house. The Fourth Amendment prohibits unreasonable searches and seizures and requires that warrants shall be issued only upon probable cause. The Fifth Amendment: (1) contains the grand jury requirements; (2) forbids double jeopardy (that is, being tried twice for the same crime); (3) prohibits forcing a person to be a witness against himself; (4) prohibits the deprivation of life, liberty, or property without due process of law; and (5) requires just compensation when private property is taken for public use. The Sixth Amendment guarantees a speedy and public trial in all criminal prosecutions by jury. The Seventh Amendment gives the right to a jury trial in all civil (that is, noncriminal) cases when the value in dispute is greater than $20. The Eighth Amendment prohibits excessive bails or fines as well as cruel and unusual punishment.

Applicability to the States

The Fourteenth Amendment provides that no state shall "deprive any person of life, liberty, or property, without due process of law" (the Due Process Clause) and "[n]o State shall make or enforce any law which shall abridge the privileges or immunities of citizens of the United States" (the Privileges and Immunities Clause). After the Fourteenth Amendment was passed, it was argued that the Due Process Clause and the Privileges and Immunities Clause made the Bill of Rights applicable to state governments.

The Supreme Court has rejected this theory. It has held that the provisions of the Bill of Rights are incorporated into the Fourteenth Amendment only if they are fundamental to the American system of law or are safeguards "essential to liberty in the American scheme of justice."[17]

Many provisions of the Bill of Rights have been held to limit the actions of state governments as well as the federal government. For example, if a state government were to abridge the freedom of speech, it would violate the First Amendment as applied to state governments through the Fourteenth Amendment.

Other provisions have been held not to apply to the states: the Second Amendment right to bear arms, the Fifth Amendment requirement of a grand jury indictment before any criminal prosecution, and the Seventh Amendment guarantee of a jury trial in civil cases.

---

17. *Duncan v. Louisiana*, 391 U.S. 145, 88 S.Ct. 1444 (1968).

In Brief: Outline of the Bill of Rights

Amendment I
Establishment Clause
Free Exercise Clause
Freedom of Speech
Freedom of Press
Right to Assembly and Petition

Amendment II
Right to Keep and Bear Arms

Amendment III
Restrictions on Quartering Soldiers

Amendment IV
No Unreasonable Search and Seizure
Requirements for Warrants

Amendment V
Presentment or Indictment of a Grand Jury for
    Capital or Otherwise Infamous Crime
Double Jeopardy Clause
No Self-Incrimination
Due Process Clause
Takings Clause

Amendment VI
In Criminal Prosecutions:
    Right to a Speedy and Public Trial
    Right to a Jury Trial
    Confrontation Clause
    Right to Counsel

Amendment VII
Right to a Jury Trial in Civil Cases

Amendment VIII
No Excessive Bail
No Excessive Fines
No Cruel and Unusual Punishment

Amendment IX
List of Rights of the People in the Constitution
    Not Exhaustive

Amendment X
Powers Not Delegated by the Constitution to
    the United States nor Prohibited by it to the
    States, Are Reserved to the States or to the
    People

The Eighth Amendment prohibition against the imposition of excessive bail has not been explicitly applied to the states, but in a number of state cases the Supreme Court has assumed that it applied. The Fifth Amendment's prohibition against the taking of property without just compensation has not been incorporated into the Fourteenth Amendment, but the due process guarantee in the Fourteenth Amendment has been interpreted to provide the same protection.

The Supreme Court has not yet determined whether the Third Amendment, which prohibits the quartering of soldiers in private houses, and the excessive fine provision of the Eighth Amendment are applicable to state governments.

Article IV, section 2, of the Constitution and section 1 of the Fourteenth Amendment both guarantee the privileges and immunities of citizens. Article IV provides that citizens of each state shall receive all the privileges and immunities of citizens of other states. This provision prohibits any unreasonable discrimination between the citizens of different states. Any such discrimination must reasonably relate to legitimate state or local purposes. The Fourteenth Amendment prohibits the states from making laws that would abridge the privileges or immu-

nities of citizens of the United States—that is, the rights that go with being a citizen of the federal government, such as the right to vote in a federal election. Only one case has held that a state violated this provision; it was later overruled.

Due Process

The due process clauses of the Fifth Amendment (which applies to the federal government) and the Fourteenth Amendment (which applies to the states) prohibit depriving any person of life, liberty, or property without due process of law. *Procedural due process* focuses on the fairness of the legal proceeding. *Substantive due process* focuses on the fundamental rights protected by the due process clauses.

Procedural Due Process

Whenever a governmental action affects a person's life, liberty, or property, the due process requirement applies and some form of notice and hearing is required. The type of hearing varies depending on the nature of the action. In general, greater procedural protections are afforded to criminal defendants because the possibility of imprisonment and even death in capital cases is at stake.

The Due Process Clause of the Fourteenth Amendment has been interpreted to make virtually all of the procedural requirements in the Bill of Rights applicable to state criminal proceedings. These rights are discussed in chapter 15.

Substantive Due Process

Disputes have raged over the years as to whether people in our society possess certain fundamental rights with which the government may not interfere. It has been argued that such rights are guaranteed by the due process clauses of the Fifth and Fourteenth Amendments. This protection of fundamental rights is known as substantive due process. The notion of substantive due process was not wholeheartedly received by the Supreme Court until the end of the nineteenth century, mainly because substantive due process rights are not specifically listed in the Constitution.

66

Disputes have raged over the years as to whether people in our society possess certain fundamental rights with which the government may not interfere.

Limit on Economic Regulation The Supreme Court first invalidated a state law on substantive due process grounds in 1897.[18] A Louisiana law prohibited anyone from obtaining insurance on Louisiana property from any marine insurance company that had not complied in all respects with Louisiana law. The Court held that the statute violated the fundamental right to make contracts.

Early in the twentieth century the concept was applied to more controversial areas, such as state statutes limiting working hours. In *Lochner v. New York*,[19] the Supreme Court struck down a New York statute that prohibited the employment of bakery employees for more than 10 hours a day or 60 hours a week. The Court held that the statute interfered with the employers' and employees' fundamental right to contract with each other.

Ethical Consideration

The decision in *Lochner v. New York* reflected a very narrow and overly technical view of individual rights in a situation in which a state had enacted legislation to protect the rights of workers. It ignored the fact that the workers could not effectively bargain for a reasonable limit on working hours.

In the period from 1905 to 1937, the Supreme Court invoked the doctrine of substantive due process to invalidate a number of laws relating to regulation of prices, labor relations, and conditions for entry into business.

In 1937, the Supreme Court changed direction. It upheld a minimum wage law for women in Washington, overruling an earlier decision striking down a similar statute.[20] In 1938, the Court upheld a statute that prohibited the interstate shipment of "filled" milk (milk to which any fat or oil other than milk fat has been added).[21] The Court made clear that if any state of facts, either known or reasonably assumed, provides a rational basis for the legislation, it will not be held to violate substantive due process. Under this test, economic regulation is usually upheld.

In certain cases involving torts, or civil wrongs, the jury is entitled to award the plaintiff not only compensatory damages equal to the plaintiff's actual loss but also punitive or exemplary damages, designed to punish and make an example of the defendant. Usually, the size of the punitive damages bears some relationship to the size of the compensatory damages. The following case addressed the issue of whether an award of punitive damages that was 526 times the amount of compensatory damages was so excessive as to violate substantive due process.

---

18. *Allgeyer v. Louisiana*, 165 U.S. 578, 17 S.Ct. 427 (1897).
19. 198 U.S. 45, 25 S.Ct. 539 (1905).

20. *West Coast Hotel Co. v. Parrish*, 300 U.S. 379, 57 S.Ct. 578 (1937).
21. *United States v. Carolene Products Co.*, 304 U.S. 144, 58 S.Ct. 778 (1938).

■ **A Case in Point:**   **In the Language of the Court**

Case 2.5
**TXO PRODUCTION CORP. v.
ALLIANCE RESOURCES
CORP.**
Supreme Court of the
United States
113 S.Ct. 2711 (1993).

FACTS In 1984, geologists employed by TXO Production Corp. concluded that the recovery of oil and gas under the surface of a 1,002.74-acre
tract of land known as the Blevins Tract would be extremely profitable. They
strongly recommended that TXO—a large company that was engaged in oil
and gas production in 25 states—obtain the rights to develop the oil and
gas resources on the Blevins Tract. Those rights were then controlled by
Alliance Resources Corp. Prodded by its geologists, TXO approached
Alliance with what Alliance considered to be a "phenomenal offer." TXO
would pay Alliance $20 per acre in cash, pay 22% of the oil and gas rev-
enues in royalties, and pay all of the development costs. On April 2, 1985,
Alliance accepted TXO's offer, agreeing to assign its interest in the Tract to
TXO. With respect to title to the property, Alliance agreed to return the con-
sideration paid to it if TXO's attorney determined that "title had failed."

Evidence demonstrated that TXO knew that Alliance had good title to the
oil and gas development rights, yet acted in bad faith and advanced a
claim on those rights in an effort to renegotiate its royalty arrangement with
Alliance.

When the negotiations were unsuccessful, TXO commenced this litigation. In particular, in August 1985, TXO brought a declaratory judgment
action to remove a cloud on title relating to certain oil and gas rights. Such
an action is a way to resolve conflicting claims to a piece of or an ownership
interest in real property. Alliance made a counterclaim for slander of title.
Slander of title is a common law cause of action in which a property owner
asserts that another person has maliciously published derogatory false
statements about the property owner's title, or right to the property. Alliance
was awarded $19,000 in compensatory damages and $10 million in punitive damages.

TXO was a large, wealthy company and had engaged in similar nefarious
activities in other parts of the country. The West Virginia Supreme Court of
Appeals, which upheld the punitive damages award, stated that TXO
"knowingly and intentionally brought a frivolous declaratory judgment
action" when its "real intent" was "to reduce the royalty payments under a
1,002.74 acre oil and gas lease," and thereby "increas[e] its interest in the
oil and gas rights." TXO appealed the $10 million punitive damage award.

ISSUE PRESENTED Is a punitive damages award equal to 526 times the
amount of compensatory damages so "grossly excessive" as to violate the
Due Process Clause of the Fourteenth Amendment?

OPINION STEVENS, J., writing for a plurality of the U.S. Supreme Court:
In a common-law action for slander of title, respondents obtained a judgment against petitioner for $19,000 in actual damages and $10 million in
punitive damages. The question we granted certiorari to decide is whether
that punitive damages award violates the Due Process Clause of the
Fourteenth Amendment.

. . . .

TXO first argues that a $10 million punitive damages award—an award
526 times greater than the actual damages awarded by the jury—is so
excessive that it must be deemed an arbitrary deprivation of property without due process of law. TXO correctly points out that several of our opinions

have stated that the Due Process Clause of the Fourteenth Amendment imposes substantive limits "beyond which penalties may not go." . . . .

. . . .

In the end, then, in determining whether a particular award is so "grossly excessive" as to violate the Due Process Clause of the Fourteenth Amendment, we return to what we said two Terms ago in *Haslip*:[22] "We need not, and indeed we cannot, draw a mathematical bright line between the constitutionally acceptable and the constitutionally unacceptable that would fit every case. We can say, however, that [a] general concer[n] of reasonableness . . . properly enter[s] into the constitutional calculus." . . . [I]t is with this concern for reasonableness in mind that we turn to petitioner's argument that the punitive award in this case was so "grossly excessive" as to violate the substantive component of the Due Process Clause.

. . .TXO correctly notes that state courts have long held that "exemplary damages allowed should bear some proportion to the real damage sustained." . . .

That relationship, however, was only one of several factors that the State Court mentioned in its *Garnes*[23] opinion. Earlier in its opinion it gave this example: "For instance, a man wildly fires a gun into a crowd. By sheer chance, no one is injured and the only damage is to a $10 pair of glasses. A jury reasonably could find only $10 in compensatory damages, but thousands of dollars in punitive damages to teach a duty of care. We would allow a jury to impose substantial punitive damages in order to discourage future bad acts." . . .

Taking account of the potential harm that might result from the defendant's conduct in calculating punitive damages was consistent with the views we expressed in *Haslip*, *supra*. In that case we endorsed the standards that the Alabama Supreme Court had previously announced, one of which was "whether there is a reasonable relationship between the punitive damages award and *the harm likely to result from* the defendant's conduct as well as the harm that actually has occurred." Thus, both State Supreme Courts and this Court have eschewed an approach that concentrates entirely on the relationship between actual and punitive damages. It is appropriate to consider the magnitude of the potential harm that the defendant's conduct would have caused to its intended victim if the wrongful plan had succeeded, as well as the possible harm to other victims that might have resulted if similar future behavior were not deterred. In this case the State Supreme Court of Appeals concluded that TXO's pattern of behavior "could potentially cause millions of dollars in damages to other victims." . . .

. . . .

In sum, we do not consider the dramatic disparity between the actual damages and the punitive award controlling in a case of this character. On this record, the jury may reasonably have determined that petitioner set out on a malicious and fraudulent course to win back, either in whole or in part,

---

22. *Pacific Mutual Life Ins. Co. v. Haslip*, 499 U.S. 1, 111 S.Ct. 1032 (1991).
23. *Garnes v. Fleming Landfill, Inc.*, 186 W. Va. 656, 413 S.E.2d 897 (W.Va. 1991).

Case **2.5** continued on following page

*Case **2.5** continued*

the lucrative stream of royalties that it had ceded to Alliance. The punitive damages award in this case is certainly large, but in light of the amount of money potentially at stake, the bad faith of petitioner, the fact that the scheme employed in this case was part of a larger pattern of fraud, trickery and deceit, and petitioner's wealth, we are not persuaded that the award was so "grossly excessive" as to be beyond the power of the State to allow.

RESULT The judgment of the West Virginia State Supreme Court of Appeals in favor of Alliance was affirmed. TXO was required to pay the $10 million in punitive damages.

Questions
1. Justice Kennedy concurred in the result but argued that the standard for deciding whether punitive damages were unconstitutional should focus not on the amount of money a jury awards in a particular case but on its reasons for doing so. He argued: "When a punitive damages award reflects bias, passion or prejudice on the part of the jury, rather than a rational concern for deterrence and retribution, the Constitution has been violated, no matter what the absolute or relative size of the award." Which argument do you find more persuasive, that of Justice Stevens, writing for the plurality, or that of Justice Kennedy?
2. Senior officers of TXO slandered Alliance's title with intent and malice. Should the result be any different if the case had involved negligence or misdeeds by poorly supervised, low-level employees of TXO?

Protection of Fundamental Rights Substantive due process challenges are given more weight when fundamental rights other than the right to make contracts are at issue. Fundamental rights include most of the guarantees of the Bill of Rights, the right to privacy, the right to travel, the right to vote, and the right to associate with other people. Legislation that limits fundamental rights violates substantive due process unless it can be shown to promote a compelling or overriding government interest.

The Supreme Court has made clear that the fundamental rights protected by substantive due process are not limited to those specifically enumerated in the Constitution or the Bill of Rights.

Substantive due process was extended to the right to privacy in *Griswold v. Connecticut*.[24] The executive director of the Planned Parenthood League of Connecticut and a physician who served as medical

director for the league at its center in New Haven were arrested. They were charged with giving birth control advice in violation of a Connecticut statute that prohibited the use of any drug, medicinal article, or instrument for the purpose of preventing conception.

In finding that the Connecticut statute was an unconstitutional invasion of individuals' right to privacy, the Supreme Court discussed the penumbra of rights surrounding each guarantee in the Bill of Rights. The Court defined "penumbra" as the peripheral rights that are implied by the specifically enumerated rights. For example, the Court noted that the First Amendment's freedom of the press necessarily includes the right to distribute, the right to receive, the right to read, freedom of inquiry, freedom of thought, freedom to teach, and freedom of association. The Fourth Amendment, which prohibits unreasonable searches and seizures, similarly includes a "right to privacy, no less important than any other right carefully and particularly reserved to the people." The Supreme Court found that the Connecticut statute encroached on the right to privacy in marriage.

---

24. 381 U.S. 479, 85 S.Ct. 1678 (1965).

This right to privacy is an essential element in the debate between pro-choice and pro-life groups concerning a woman's right to an abortion. It is relevant in other areas as well. For example, in a recent case,[25] a schoolteacher sued a board of education alleging that the non-renewal of her teaching contract was due to the fact that she was an unwed mother, and her pregnancy had been by means of artificial insemination. The district court held that a woman has a constitutional privacy right to become pregnant by means of artificial insemination.

Mandatory drug testing also presents privacy issues. The Supreme Court has upheld certain regulations concerning drug testing for public employees. This issue is discussed in chapter 12.

■ Compensation for Takings

One of the earliest provisions of the Bill of Rights incorporated into the Fourteenth Amendment was the Fifth Amendment provision that private property shall not be taken for public use without just compensation. State and federal governments have the power of *eminent domain*, which is the power to take property for government uses such as building a school, park, or airport. If property is taken from a private owner for such a purpose, the owner is entitled to just compensation. A more complex situation arises when the government does not physically take the property, but imposes regulations that restrict its use. If the regulation amounts to a taking of the property, the owner is entitled to just compensation. The question, of course, is: When does a regulation constitute a taking?

Takings Cases

In one instance, the Supreme Court held that there was a taking when a homeowner was required to grant a public right-of-way through his property in order to obtain a building permit to replace his oceanfront house with a larger one.[26] This case, and land use regulation generally, are discussed in chapter 17.

Another case involved the Federal Communications Commission's regulation of the rates a utility company could charge for the attachment of television cables to the utility company's poles. The Supreme Court held that the regulation was not a taking, as long as the rates were not set so low as to be unjust and confiscatory.[27]

In another case, *Penn Central Transportation Company,* the owner of Grand Central Station in midtown New York City, was prohibited from constructing an office building above Grand Central Station. The prohibition was ordered by the Landmarks Preservation Commission, which had designated the station a landmark. Under New York City law, the commission could prevent any alteration of the fundamental character of such buildings. A high rise would arguably have altered the fundamental character of Grand Central Station. The Supreme Court found that the prohibition was not a taking.[28] This case is discussed in chapter 17.

The disclosure of trade secrets by the government can constitute a taking requiring just compensation.[29] Trade secrets are discussed in chapter 11.

■ Equal Protection

The Equal Protection Clause of the Fourteenth Amendment places another limitation on the power of state governments to regulate; a comparable limitation is imposed on the federal government by the Due Process Clause of the Fifth Amendment. The Equal Protection Clause provides that no state shall "deny to any person within its jurisdiction the equal protection of the laws." The Supreme Court's interpretation of this clause is the subject of much debate.

Establishing Discrimination

In order to challenge a statute on equal protection grounds, it is first necessary to establish that the statute discriminates against a class of persons. Discrimination may be found on the face of the statute, in its application, or in its purpose. The statute may explicitly (on its face) treat different classes of persons differently. Or the statute

25. *Cameron v. Board of Education of the Hillsboro, Ohio, City School District*, 795 F. Supp. 228 (S.D. Ohio 1991).
26. *Nollan v. California Coastal Commission*, 483 U.S. 825, 107 S.Ct. 3141 (1987).

27. *FCC v. Florida Power Corp.*, 480 U.S. 245, 107 S.Ct. 1107 (1987).
28. *Penn Central Transportation Co. v. New York City*, 438 U.S. 104, 98 S.Ct. 2646 (1978).
29. *Ruckelshaus v. Monsanto Co.*, 467 U.S. 986, 104 S.Ct. 2862 (1984).

itself may contain no classification, but government officials may apply it differently to different classes of people. Finally, a statute may be neutral on its face and in its application but have the purpose of creating different burdens for different classes of persons.

In determining whether a facially neutral law is a device to discriminate against certain classes of people, the Supreme Court looks at three things: (1) the practical or statistical impact of the statute on different classes of persons; (2) the history of the problems that the statute seeks to solve; and (3) the legislative history of the statute. The following case demonstrates the application of this approach.

■ **A Case in Point:**   **Summary**

Case 2.6
ARLINGTON HEIGHTS v. METROPOLITAN HOUSING DEVELOPMENT CORP.
Supreme Court of the United States
429 U.S. 252, 97 S.Ct. 555 (1977).

FACTS   A nonprofit developer planned to build town houses in the largely white suburb of Arlington Heights. Of the 64,000 residents, only 27 were African Americans. The purpose of the plan was to allow low- and moderate-income tenants, including members of racial minorities, to live in the units. The village refused to rezone the area to permit the multifamily units.

The federal district court found that the refusal of the village to rezone the property from single-family to multiple-family use did not violate the Equal Protection Clause. In reaching this decision, the court found that the officials who denied the request were motivated by a concern for the integrity of the zoning laws, and not by any discriminatory plan.

The court of appeals reversed the lower court. It observed that the refusal to rezone was racially discriminatory because it would have an disproportionate impact on African Americans. African Americans constituted an overwhelming 40% of those Chicago-area residents who would have been eligible tenants of the development. Given the high degree of racial segregation in the area, the appeals court held that the action must be subjected to strict scrutiny and would only be upheld if it was necessary to promote compelling interests. None were found.

ISSUE PRESENTED   Does the refusal of a village to rezone property from single-family to multiple-family use violate the Equal Protection Clause if the rezoning decision will have a disproportionate impact on African Americans?

SUMMARY OF OPINION   The U.S. Supreme Court reversed the court of appeals. The Court held that despite the fact that the failure to rezone had a clearly disproportionate effect on African Americans, the Court should look to the purpose of the decision not to rezone rather than the effect of the decision. A racially discriminatory purpose must be proved before an act will be held to violate the Equal Protection Clause. A racially disproportionate impact is only one of the factors to be considered in deciding whether there was a discriminatory intent. Other factors are: the historical background of the challenged decision; the specific antecedent events; departures from normal procedures; and contemporary statements of the decision makers.

The Court found that the rezoning request was dealt with in the usual way. The area had always been zoned for single-family residences.

Arlington Heights's apartment policy called for multifamily dwellings only in buffer areas between commercial land and single-family residences. Absent a showing of discriminatory intent, the refusal to rezone did not violate the Equal Protection Clause.

RESULT   Arlington Heights could not be required to rezone the village from a single-family to a multiple-family zone.

Ethical Consideration

Even if it may be legal to refuse to rezone property to promote integration, do communities have a social responsibility to work toward a multiracial and multicultural society?

If a statute is found to be discriminatory on its face, in its administration, or in its purpose, it is then necessary to determine whether the discrimination is permissible.

Validity of Discrimination

The Supreme Court has evolved three tests to determine the constitutionality of various types of discrimination, depending on how the statute classifies the persons concerned.

Rational Basis Test   The rational basis test applies to all classifications that relate to matters of economics or social welfare. Under this test, a classification will be held valid if there is any conceivable basis upon which the classification might relate to a legitimate governmental interest.

Strict Scrutiny Test   A classification that determines who may exercise a fundamental right, or one that is based on a suspect trait such as race, is subject to strict scrutiny. Under the strict scrutiny test, a classification will be held valid only if it is necessary to promote a compelling state interest. The right to privacy, the right to vote, the right to travel, and certain guarantees in the Bill

of Rights are fundamental rights. Rights such as welfare payments, housing, education, and government employment are not fundamental rights.

Substantially Related Test   The Supreme Court occasionally applies a third test, which is stricter than the rational basis test but less strict than strict scrutiny. This intermediate test applies to classifications such as gender and legitimacy of birth. Under this test, a classification will be held valid if it is substantially related to an important governmental interest.

Racial Discrimination

Racial discrimination was the major target of the Fourteenth Amendment, so it is clear that racial classifications are suspect. However, some uncertainties arise over racial classifications that are intended to be benign.

From 1896 to 1954, the "separate but equal" doctrine allowed separate services to exist for minorities as long as they were equal to the services provided for whites. In *Plessy v. Ferguson*,[30] the Supreme Court upheld a law requiring that all railway companies provide separate but equal accommodations for African American and white passengers. Fifty-eight years later, the Supreme Court held in *Brown v. Board of Education*[31] that the doctrine had no place in education. The justices unanimously decided that the "segregation of children in public schools solely on the basis of race, even though the physical facilities and other 'tangible' factors may be equal, deprives the children of the minority group of equal educational opportunities." Supreme Court rulings following

---

30. 163 U.S. 537, 16 S.Ct. 1138 (1896).
31. 347 U.S. 483, 74 S.Ct. 686 (1954).

Brown made it clear that no governmental entity may segregate people because of their race or origin.

> **"**
>
> *"Segregation of children in public schools solely on the basis of race, even though the physical facilities and other 'tangible' factors may be equal, deprives the children of the minority group of equal educational opportunities."*

Complications concerning racial classifications have arisen more recently in the area of affirmative action intended to benefit racial or ethnic minorities. The debate has raged over whether strict scrutiny should be applied only to legislation that discriminates against a minority or also to legislation that favors a minority.

Quota systems setting aside a certain number of positions in schools or housing for minority members are usually struck down by the court. Under a strict quota system, individual circumstances are disregarded, and members of minority races have less of a chance of obtaining a position if a limited number of positions are set aside for them.

When a program gives members of a minority preferential treatment by lowering standards or guaranteeing a minimum share of the benefits, the issue is more difficult. This is because historically the Equal Protection Clause was adopted after the Civil War to protect minorities, in particular, African Americans. The Supreme Court has shown more tolerance for affirmative action plans mandated by Congress than for those prescribed by state and local governments. For example, in *Metro Broadcasting, Inc. v. Federal Communications Commission,*[32] the Supreme Court upheld two minority preference policies adopted by the Federal Communications Commission (FCC) because they were specifically approved—indeed, mandated—by Congress. The Court concluded that these "benign" racial classifications serve the important governmental objective of broadcast diversity and are substantially related to the achievement of that objective. The four dissenting justices argued that " 'benign' racial classification" is a contradiction in terms and that the Court erred in not subjecting the congressionally mandated classifications to strict scrutiny. Justice Kennedy concluded his dissent by stating: "I regret that after a century of judicial opinions we interpret the Constitution to do no more than move us from 'separate but equal' to 'unequal but benign.' "

Private employers are not limited by the Equal Protection Clause, which applies only to governmental actions. However, as explained in chapter 13, private individuals are subject to the Civil Rights Act and other federal and state antidiscrimination statutes.

Other Forms of Discrimination

Three classifications are subject to the intermediate-level (substantially related) test of heightened scrutiny: gender, illegitimacy, and alienage.

Classifications based on gender will be upheld if substantially related to important governmental interests. In this area, the Supreme Court decides on a case-by-case basis. It has invalidated statutory provisions that gave female workers fewer benefits for their families than male workers. It has upheld differential treatment for women when it was compensatory for past discrimination, but not when it unreasonably denied benefits to men. It has upheld a statutory rape law applying only to men; exemption from the draft for women; and the exclusion of insurance benefits for costs relating to pregnancy. (Gender discrimination is discussed further in chapter 13.)

Classifications based on the legitimacy of children will be held invalid unless substantially related to a proper interest of the state. The Supreme Court will usually look at the purpose behind the classification, and will not uphold any law intended to punish illegitimate children.

Aliens do not receive the protection of constitutional guarantees, which apply only to citizens. For example, in 1990 the Supreme Court held that the Fourth Amendment prohibition of search and seizure without a warrant did not apply to a drug raid of an alien's premises in Mexico.[33] Because of Congress's plenary power over aliens, classifications imposed by the federal government based on alienage are valid if they are not arbitrary and unreasonable. State and local laws that classify on the basis of alienage are, however, subject to the strict scrutiny test discussed earlier; except that if a law discriminates against alien participation in state government, the rational basis test will be applied.

---

32. 497 U.S. 547, 110 S.Ct. 2997 (1990). *Compare Richmond v. J. A. Croson Co.,* 488 U.S. 469, 109 S.Ct. 706 (1989) (the setting aside by a local governmental agency of certain contracts for minorities is invalid).

---

33. *United States v. Verdugo-Urquidez,* 494 U.S. 259, 110 S.Ct. 1056 (1990).

■ Freedom of Speech

The First Amendment states that "Congress shall make no law . . . abridging the freedom of speech, or of the press." However, not all speech is protected equally by the First Amendment. The type of speech most clearly protected is political speech, including speech critical of governmental policies and officials. It has been argued that other types of speech, such as defamation, obscenity, advertising, and "fighting words," should be accorded a lesser degree of protection. Still other types of expression—bribery, perjury, and counseling to murder—are considered not to be protected by the First Amendment at all.

Determining whether a type of speech is protected by the First Amendment is only the first step of the analysis. If it is determined that a certain expression is protected, it must then be determined to what extent the expression may be regulated without violating the First Amendment.

"Clear and Present Danger" Test

Prior to World War I, Congress followed the mandate of the First Amendment literally, making no law restricting freedom of speech, assembly, or the press. However, in response to vocal resistance to the war, Congress passed the Espionage Act of 1917 and the Sedition Act of 1918. In 1919, the Supreme Court, in a decision by Justice Oliver Wendell Holmes, first discussed the "clear and present danger" test in affirming a conviction under the Espionage Act.[34]

Schenck was convicted for circulating to men who had been called and accepted for military service a document that stated that the draft violated the Thirteenth Amendment, which prohibits slavery or involuntary servitude. The Supreme Court considered the defendant's actions in the context of a nation at war:

> [T]he character of every act depends upon the circumstances in which it is done. The most stringent protection of free speech would not protect a man in falsely shouting fire in a theatre and causing a panic. [The] question in every case is whether the words used are used in such circumstances and are of such a nature as to create a *clear and present danger* that they will bring about the substantive evils that Congress has a right to prevent. (Emphasis added.)

The Supreme Court held that many things that might be said in peacetime cannot be allowed in time of war. Schenck's conviction under the Espionage Act was upheld as constitutional.

34. *Schenck v. United States*, 249 U.S. 47, 39 S.Ct. 247 (1919).

> 66
>
> *"The most stringent protection of free speech would not protect a man in falsely shouting fire in a theatre and causing a panic."*

Later, during the height of the Cold War, the clear and present danger doctrine was applied in a manner restricting First Amendment freedoms more severely. In the 1960s, the test became stricter and more protective of free speech. In *Brandenburg v. Ohio*,[35] the Supreme Court held that "the constitutional guarantees of free speech and free press do not permit a State to forbid or proscribe advocacy of the use of force or of law violation except where such advocacy is directed to *inciting or producing imminent lawless action* and is likely to incite or produce such action."

Defamation

Defamatory words—words that harm a person's reputation—are protected by the First Amendment even though they are false, if they are made about a public figure without knowledge they were false, that is, without actual malice. Defamation is discussed further in chapter 7.

Obscenity

Obscene material does not enjoy any protection from the First Amendment. Obscene material is defined as material that appeals to a prurient or sordid and perverted interest in sex; has no serious literary, artistic, political, or scientific merit; and is on the whole offensive to the average person.

Commercial Speech

Commercial speech, especially advertising, has always been subject to substantial regulation. It was formerly thought that commercial speech was excluded from the coverage of the First Amendment; under the most recent case law, however, it has full protection. The government cannot suppress commercial speech, but it can make reasonable regulations regarding the time, place, and manner of such speech.

Misleading advertising may be restricted or entirely prohibited. Truthful advertising relating to lawful activities is protected by the First Amendment. However, the

35. 395 U.S. 444, 89 S.Ct. 1827 (1969).

government retains some authority to regulate. The government must have a substantial interest and the interference with speech must be in proportion to the interest served.[36]

For example, restrictions on advertisements of casino gambling were upheld in *Posadas De Puerto Rico Associates v. Tourism Co.*[37] Puerto Rico's Game of Chance Act of 1984 legalized certain forms of gambling in licensed places to promote the development of tourism, but prohibited the advertising of gambling parlors to the public in Puerto Rico. The Supreme Court rejected the argument that the regulations impermissibly suppressed commercial speech. The Court found that although the advertising of gambling was entitled to a limited form of First Amendment protection, Puerto Rico had a substantial government interest in restricting such advertising to reduce the demand for casino gambling by Puerto Rico's residents. The statute's restrictions on advertising directly advanced this interest. Moreover, they were no more extensive than necessary to serve the government's interest, because they applied only to advertising aimed at Puerto Rico residents and not to advertising outside Puerto Rico intended to attract tourists.

There is controversy over the extent of First Amendment protection of liquor and cigarette advertising. The federal district court for the District of Columbia upheld federal legislation forbidding cigarette advertising on radio and television.[38] The Rhode Island Supreme Court upheld a statute prohibiting the advertising of liquor prices by retailers.[39]

Prior Restraints

Prior restraints of speech, such as prohibiting in advance a demonstration in a public area, are considered a more drastic infringement on free speech than permitting the speech to occur but punishing it afterwards. Restrictions concerning the time, place, and manner of speech are usually acceptable under the First Amendment; but regulations that restrict speech in traditional public forums are scrutinized closely, as in the following case.

36. *In re R.M.J.*, 455 U.S. 191, 102 S.Ct. 929 (1982).
37. 478 U.S. 328, 106 S.Ct. 2968 (1986).

38. *Capital Broadcast Co. v. Mitchell*, 333 F.Supp. 582 (D.D.C. 1971).
39. *S&S Liquor Mart, Inc. v. Pastore*, 497 A.2d 729 (R.I. 1985).

■ **A Case in Point:**   **Summary**

Case 2.7
FW/PBS, INC. V. CITY OF DALLAS
Supreme Court of the
United States
493 U.S. 215, 110 S.Ct. 596
(1990).

FACTS   In 1986, the city of Dallas adopted an ordinance regulating sexually oriented businesses. A sexually oriented business was defined as "an adult arcade, adult bookstore or adult video store, adult cabaret, adult motel, adult motion picture theater, adult theater, escort agency, nude model studio, or sexual encounter center." The ordinance regulated such businesses through zoning, licensing, and inspections. The ordinance also banned motels that rented rooms for fewer than ten hours.

The court of appeals upheld the ordinance as a content-neutral regulation of time, place, and manner. The court found that the ordinance was "designed to serve as a substantial government interest" and allowed for "reasonable alternative avenues of communication."

ISSUE PRESENTED   Can a city ban adult bookstores and theatres and motels that rent rooms for less than ten hours?

SUMMARY OF OPINION   The U.S. Supreme Court viewed the ordinance, except for the ban on ten-hour motels, as a prior restraint on speech. Any system of prior restraint comes to the Supreme Court bearing a strong presumption that it may be unconstitutional. The Court held that the ordinance did not comply with the procedural safeguards for that type of regulation. The safeguards necessary are: (1) any prior restraint must be for no longer than necessary to preserve the status quo until a court hearing; (2) the court hearing must be promptly available; and (3) the would-be censor must bear both the burden of going to court and the burden of proof once in court.

However, the Supreme Court upheld the part of the ordinance that prohibited motels from renting rooms for less than ten hours. Such rooms are often used for prostitution. Dismissing the argument that the ordinance unconstitutionally interfered with the right of association, Justice O'Connor stated: "Any 'personal bonds' that are formed from the use of a motel room for less than 10 hours are not those that have 'played a critical role in the culture and traditions of the nation by cultivating and transmitting shared ideals and beliefs.' "

RESULT   The city of Dallas could legally ban motels from renting rooms for less than ten hours but could not ban adult bookstores and theatres.

COMMENTS   It should be noted that no question was presented or decided concerning whether the material regulated by the ordinance was obscene. The regulations were struck down as unconstitutional prior restraints on speech.

> *"Any 'personal bonds' that are formed from the use of a motel room for less than 10 hours are not those that have 'played a critical role in the culture and traditions of the nation by cultivating and transmitting shared ideals and beliefs.' "*

■ Freedom of Religion

Two clauses of the First Amendment deal with religion. The Establishment Clause prohibits the establishment of a religion by the federal government and through the Fourteenth Amendment by state governments. The Free Exercise Clause prohibits certain, but not all, restrictions on the practice of religion. For example, in *Employment Division, Oregon Department of Human Resources v. Smith*,[40] the Supreme Court held that an Oregon statute that made criminal the use of peyote, an hallucinogenic drug, was constitutional. Accordingly, the Court held that it was constitutional to deny unemployment benefits to

persons fired for their ingestion of peyote for sacramental purposes at a ceremony of the Native American Church. In 1993 Congress passed the Religious Freedom Restoration Act, which decriminalizes certain uses of drugs during religious ceremonies.[41]

The government must remain neutral in matters of religion. However, in *Jimmy Swaggart Ministries v. Board of Equalization*,[42] the Supreme Court held that the imposition of sales and use taxes on the sale of religious materials does not contravene the Free Exercise Clause of the First Amendment. The tax was only a small fraction of any sale, and it applied neutrally to all relevant sales regardless of the nature of the seller or purchaser. There was no danger that the seller's religious activity was being singled out for special and burdensome treatment. The Court also held that the tax did not violate the Establishment Clause. There was little evidence of administrative entanglement between religion and the government; the government was not involved in the organization's day-to-day activities. The imposition of the tax did not require the state to inquire into the religious content of the items sold or the religious motivation behind selling or purchasing them. The items were sub-

---

40. 494 U.S. 872, 110 S.Ct. 1595 (1990).

41. 42 U.S.C. § 2000 (1993).
42. 493 U.S. 378, 110 S.Ct. 688 (1990).

ject to the tax regardless of the content or motive for selling/purchasing them.

The Responsible Manager

Preserving Constitutional Rights

Although the Constitution is directed at establishing and limiting the powers of federal and state governments, its provisions have a profound effect on private actors in society. Federal and state governments impose a myriad of regulations on businesses and on individuals. Regulation of activities such as commercial speech, employment practices, admissions policies, securities, and production procedures must comply with the limitations established by the Constitution.

It is important for managers to know the limitations that may constitutionally be imposed on individuals and organizations. Although the costs are usually high, at times it may be worth it for a company to challenge a regulation on constitutional grounds. This was true for the insurance companies in California that successfully challenged Proposition 103's freeze on rate increases for one year.

Managers often have an interest in influencing legislation or other government action, through political action committees or lobbying. When pursuing change, it is useful to know the constitutional limitations placed on different segments of the government.

A manager should be aware of the rights deemed valuable by the Constitution. Although the Constitution addresses only government actions, managers of private organizations should be aware of the societal values reflected in the Constitution.

It may seem at times that constitutional law is far removed from the world of business. This is often a misconception. Constitutional law is as close as the nearest private club that does not admit African Americans, Jews, women, or homosexuals. Such clubs may be important places for conducting business and for networking in general. A manager invited to become a member of such a club or to accompany his boss or client as a guest faces a tough choice.

Cities like New York and San Francisco have enacted ordinances to ban such clubs if they are of a certain size and are used for the conduct of business. Such ordinances must pass constitutional muster. The courts will balance the First Amendment rights of association and free speech against the city's social policy against discrimination.

Such ordinances relate not to political speech (the most protected form of speech) but to commercial speech. Commercial speech is not wholly without protection, however. The Supreme Court has held, for example, that lawyers must be permitted to advertise. But the Court permits greater regulation of commercial speech than political speech. For this reason, ordinances banning discriminatory clubs usually extend just to clubs where business is conducted. It will generally be assumed that business is conducted if the manager's employer pays for club dues, meals, or drinks.

Inside Story
Effect of Politics on Supreme Court Appointments

The nomination process for the United States Supreme Court has grown increasingly politicized and controversial over time. Televised Supreme Court nomination hearings before the Senate Judiciary Committee have riveted the nation's attention as few other internal events in Congress have. Being nominated to the Supreme Court now brings along with it a process of public scrutiny akin to running for national political office.

The 1991 nomination of Clarence Thomas to the "black seat" on the Supreme Court resulted in a public spectacle, the effects of which are still rippling throughout the country. The retirement of Justice Thurgood Marshall, a stalwart advocate of civil rights and liberal causes on the Court, left the Court without an African-American member. President Bush nominated Thomas, a 43-year-old African-American conservative federal judge, to fill that void. Thomas seemed to be a safe bet: His writings and opinions were sparse and generally without controversy. Thomas went so far as to deny ever having engaged in a debate on the issue of abortion:

Senator Leahy: Have you (Judge Thomas) ever had discussion of *Roe v. Wade*[43] other than in this room, in the 17 or 18 years it's has been there?

Judge Thomas: Only, I guess, Senator, in the fact in the most general sense that other individuals express concerns one way or the other, and you listen and you try to be thoughtful. If you are asking me whether or not I have ever debated the contents of it, the answer to that is no, Senator.[44]

Even this denial, preposterous as it seemed to some, could not derail Thomas's quest for a seat on this nation's highest court. Without extensive writings to defend, Thomas gained wide support in the Senate.

However, after completing an initial hearing, Thomas was called back before the Judiciary Committee to face allegations of sexual harassment put forward by African-American law professor and former colleague Anita Hill. The ensuing melee, while shedding fascinating light on the intersection of race, gender, and ideology in the Senate and society in general, resulted in no substantial conclusions as to the truth of the allegations. Rather it became a circus in which actors on both sides paraded before the committee, asserting their versions of the truth.

In the end, only three senators, all Democrats, admitted to changing their votes. Thomas was approved by a vote of 52 to 48. Many members of the Senate sought to avoid the political fallout on both sides of the issue. Responding to allegations during the hearings about Anita Hill's mental stability, Senator Nancy Landon Kassebaum (R-Kansas), who voted to confirm Thomas, attempted to maintain the support of women, as well as that of her political party. Specifically, in response to questions of committee members Arlen Spector and Howell Heflin, suggesting that Professor Hill's accusa-

tions were the product of wild "fantasy and mental instability,"[45] she condemned the tactics employed to discredit the allegations of misconduct, stating that she "found no evidence that Professor Hill was mentally unstable, is inclined to wild fantasy, or is part of a decade-long conspiracy to get Clarence Thomas." However, she also declined to change her vote in favor of Thomas's confirmation, because she "saw no compelling reason to overturn that judgment."[46] Southern Democrats, responding to pressure from their large African-American and conservative constituencies, also refused to change their votes after Thomas, undaunted by the allegations, charged the committee with conducting a "high tech lynching of uppity Blacks." This blatant intimidation tactic dulled the edge on the remaining questioning of the Senate.

Though public opinion polls following the hearings found that more Americans believed Judge Thomas over Professor Hill, the spectacle of 12 white men grilling an African-American woman about her charges of sexual harassment set in motion a political movement which resulted in the election of historic numbers of women and African Americans to both the House and Senate. In 1992, Carol Mosely Braun became the first African-American woman to serve in the United States Senate, and California became the first state in history to send two women, Dianne Feinstein and Barbara Boxer, to the Senate. Partially in an effort to change the image of the Judiciary Committee, both Senators Braun and Feinstein were asked to join the committee.

Ruth Bader Ginsburg was nominated to the Court in 1993. The politics of that nomination swirled around the question of whether the Senate should apply an abortion "litmus test" to her appointment, in light of the changing Supreme Court position on the pivotal issue of whether a woman has a constitutional right to an abortion. President Clinton sought to nominate a person

---

43. 410 U.S. 113, 93 S.Ct. 705 (1973).
44. Nomination of Judge Clarence Thomas to be Associate Justice of the Supreme Court of the United States: Hearings Before the Senate Comm. on the Judiciary, 102nd Cong., 1st. Sess. 147 (1991).

45. Nomination of Judge Clarence Thomas to be Associate Justice of the Supreme Court of the United States: Hearings Before the Senate Comm. on the Judiciary, 102nd Cong., 1st. Sess. 83 (1991).
46. Adam Clymer, "The Thomas Confirmation: The Senate's Futile Search for Safe Ground," *The New York Times*, October 16, 1991.

Inside Story, continued

who would receive widespread support from the Senate Judiciary Committee. Any indication of a controversial hearing was immediately dispelled in Judge Ginsburg's opening remarks. In an effort to preempt potential "litmus test" type questions she hinted at the inappropriateness of deciding a case in advance, but promised to impartially hear each case before the Court "without reaching out to cover cases not yet seen." She continued in her opening remarks:

You are well aware that I come to this proceeding to be judged as a judge not an advocate. Because I am and hope to continue to be a judge it would be wrong for me to say or preview in this legislative chamber how I would cast my vote on questions the Supreme Court may be called upon to decide. Were I to rehearse here what I would say and how I would reason on such questions, I would act injudiciously. Judges in our civil system are bound to decide concrete cases not abstract issues. Each case comes to court based on particular facts and its decisions should turn on those facts and governing law stated and explained in light of the particular arguments the parties or their representatives present. A judge sworn to decide impartially can offer no forecasts, no hints, for that would show not only disregard for the specifics of a particular case; it would display disdain for the entire judicial process.[47]

Judge Ginsburg came to the hearing as a judge on the U.S. Court of Appeals for the District of Columbia, where she had served since being appointed to the bench by President Carter in 1980. Her thirteen years of judicial experience, coupled with impressive credentials, won the judge nearly unanimous support from the public as well as the Judiciary Committee. Justice Ginsburg was easily confirmed by a vote of 96 to 3.

Another pivotal nomination in the recent past was that of Robert Bork, a well-known constitutional scholar, by President Reagan in 1987. Bork was the last nominee to the Supreme Court to have a "paper trail" of opinions and writings on constitutional matters. The nightmare Senate hearings, in which Bork was forced to attempt to explain to the senators and the general public

the reasoning behind some of his more radical statements over the years, of which he had many, were enough to convince any president of the impossibility today of nominating someone with that kind of record. The hearings surrounding Bork's nomination were controversial, as was Bork's constitutional scholarship. The Senate probed deeply and substantively for information central to Bork's constitutional views in an effort to determine if Bork would overturn widely accepted, mainstream constitutional law. In the end, Bork's views and the resultant political uproar across the nation led to his being denied confirmation to the Court.

In response to this more extensive probing by the Senate, recent presidents have attempted to nominate individuals who produce little to no legal opinions on critical issues. The nominations of David Souter, often referred to as a "stealth candidate" due to his anonymity prior to nomination, and Clarence Thomas are illustrative. The nomination and confirmation of Justice Thomas also marked the eighth consecutive appointment to the Supreme Court by a Republican president. The effects of this historic turn may upstage even the massive changes brought about by the reconstruction of the Court during the Roosevelt years.

Franklin Delano Roosevelt was probably the first president in history to attempt explicitly and publicly to use the power of judicial appointment to change the Court's position on the key political issues of the day. Frustrated with the Supreme Court's overturning of much of his New Deal legislation on the basis of strict laissez-faire economic ideology, Roosevelt introduced his now famous Court-packing bill which would have added one justice to the Court for every sitting Justice who had reached the age of 70. The bill would have increased the Court's membership to fifteen and given Roosevelt a clear majority.

The bill was never passed by the Senate. However, the message had been sent, and the Court soon began to soften its position on issues of economic security. One month after the plan was announced, Justice Roberts inexplicably changed his position and voted to overturn *Morehead v. Tipaldo,*[48] which had struck down New York's minimum wage law in 1936. The statute was

---

47. Nomination of Judge Ruth Bader Ginsburg to be Associate Justice of the Supreme Court of the United States: Hearings Before the Senate Comm. on the Judiciary, 103rd Cong., 1st. Sess. 222 (1993).

---

48. 298 U.S. 587, 56 S.Ct. 918 (1936).

Inside Story, continued

subsequently upheld in *West Coast Hotel v. Parrish*.[49] Roosevelt made nine appointments over the next six years. At the time of his death while still in office, Roosevelt had completely revamped the Court and secured passage of his New Deal legislation.

Although Roosevelt's motivations were clearly political, other presidents have made considerations of diversity and representation key to their selection of nominees. Thurgood Marshall was clearly qualified for the nomination, having argued a number of monumental cases before the Court including *Brown v. Board of Education*,[50] the landmark school desegregation case. President Lyndon Johnson's appointment of him also took into consideration the need for African Americans to be represented on the Court for the first time. Similarly, the appointments of Justices Sandra Day O'Connor (the first woman member of the Court) and Clarence Thomas by Presidents Reagan and Bush respectively, served to expand and maintain the gender and racial diversity of the Court.

The power and impact of appointments should not be underestimated. President Eisenhower's appointment of Chief Justice Earl Warren to the Court in 1953 further demonstrates the influence of politics on the nomination process. At the time, Warren was the Republican governor of California and had been a critical factor in Eisenhower's 1952 bid for the presidency. Eisenhower repaid the political debt with the nomination, despite misgivings by powerful Republicans such as Vice President Nixon about Warren's progressive stance on certain issues. Although Warren was believed to be a moderate Republican at the time of the nomination, the Warren Court became the most progressive, activist court in history, leading a constitutional revolution in the application of the Bill of Rights to the states.

The executive office holds the power to identify and nominate individuals to the judiciary. A cursory investigation will reveal that some combination of personal friendship and political compatibility are often the overriding factors for appointment. The nomination of Abe Fortas in 1965 is one example. In 1965, Adlai Stevenson, then U.S. Representative to the United Nations, died of a heart attack while on a visit in London, England. The death of Stevenson sparked a battle over the composition of the Supreme Court. As the nation mourned the death of a great public servant, President Johnson recognized a tremendous opportunity. He was swift and deliberate in his action. A mere six days following the death of Stevenson, Johnson announced that he was nominating the Honorable Arthur Goldberg, then Associate Justice of the Supreme Court, to succeed Stevenson as U.S. Representative to the United Nations. This created a vacancy on the Court.

Certainly, Johnson was not ignorant of the eminent power and prestige of the Court. Johnson had won a seat in the House of Representatives in 1937, about the time that President Roosevelt was threatening to "pack" the Supreme Court. Johnson watched as the Court ruled his party's New Deal legislation unconstitutional.

He had also witnessed, firsthand, the power of the Court. After serving in Washington, Johnson ran for a Texas seat in the Senate. Following a narrow victory in the primary, Johnson's opponent made allegations of vote fraud and obtained a temporary restraining order prohibiting the state's secretary from printing Johnson's name on the ballot for the general elections. Despite an appeal by Johnson, the injunction remained in effect. Immediately thereafter a young lawyer by the name of Abe Fortas took over the case. Fortas argued Johnson's case to Justice Black in the Fifth Circuit Court of Appeals. Fortas won the case, as did Johnson the Senate election. Had Justice Black not signed the order staying the injunction, Johnson would not have been elected to the Senate, possibly ending his political ascendancy to the White House.

Presidents of the past have regarded Supreme Court nominations as the highest appointments they can make. Johnson was no different. Two days after removing Goldberg from the Court, he made another announcement. On July 22, 1965, President Johnson appointed his longtime friend Abe Fortas as Associate Justice of the Supreme Court.

The appointment of Fortas to the bench is a clear example of how friendship, both personal and political, influences the nomination process. President Johnson, in nominating Fortas, not only placed a close friend on the Supreme Court, but in the process repaid an old political debt.

---

49. 300 U.S. 379, 57 S.Ct. 578 (1937).
50. 347 U.S. 483, 74 S.Ct. 686 (1954).

Key Words and Phrases

appellate jurisdiction **41**
bill of attainder **55**
eminent domain **61**
ex post facto **55**
executive privilege **43**
hostile takeover **49**

judicial review **41**
original jurisdiction **41**
police power **44**
preempt **41**
prior restraints **66**
procedural due process **56**

raider **49**
separation of powers **41**
subject matter jurisdiction **41**
substantive due process **56**
target **49**
undue burden **47**

Questions and Case Problems

1. What are the three branches of the U.S. government? What functions does each branch serve?

 2. In the context of a labor dispute affecting the steel industry during the Korean War, President Truman issued an executive order directing the secretary of commerce to take possession of most of the nation's steel mills, to ensure that they continued to run. When the secretary took possession of the companies, the companies sued him on the grounds that the seizure was beyond the constitutional power of the president, and thus invalid. The government argued that presidential authority to effect such a seizure, although not authorized by statute or explicitly granted by the Constitution, should be implied from the aggregate of the president's powers under the Constitution. Can presidential authority to effect such a seizure be fairly implied from the aggregate of presidential powers under the Constitution? Would implying such presidential authority impinge on the autonomy of either of the other branches of government? [*Youngstown Sheet & Tube Co. v. Sawyer*, 343 U.S. 579, 72 S.Ct. 863 (1952)]

 3. In an exercise of its police power Oregon enacted a bottle bill, which required retailers of beer or carbonated beverages to accept empty containers in exchange for a statutory refund value. The bill also prohibited retail sale of beverages in metal containers with detachable pull-top openers. The purpose of the legislation was to reduce litter in Oregon and reduce injuries to people and animals caused by discarded pull-tops. Manufacturers of cans and out-of-state beverage bottlers challenged the legislation on the ground that it imposed an undue burden on interstate commerce and was thus invalid under the Commerce Clause of the Constitution.

(a) What are the grounds on which state legislation may be struck down as violating the Commerce Clause?

(b) Assuming that the manufacturers and canners showed that the bill would have a substantial impact on interstate commerce, how could the state of Oregon justify the legislation? [*American Can Co. v. Oregon Liquor Control Com'n.*, 15 Or.App. 618, 517 P.2d 691 (1973)]

4. Congress enacted legislation making carjacking a federal crime. Its stated justifications included transportation of car-

jacked vehicles across state lines, either in parts or intact, and the effect of car theft on insurance rates.

A Tennessee resident was a victim of a carjacking in Tennessee by another Tennessee resident. The car was later recovered in Tennessee. The car had been transported to Tennessee from a manufacturing site outside of the state. The perpetrator was charged with violation of the federal carjacking statute.

Does Congress have the power, under the Commerce Clause, to make carjacking a federal crime? [*U.S. v. Cortner*, 834 F. Supp. 242 (M.D.Tenn. 1993). *Compare U.S. v. Watson*, 815 F. Supp. 827 (E.D.Pa. 1993)]

 5. The city of San Diego enacted an ordinance regulating billboards. The ordinance permitted billboards for on-site commercial advertising, but not for other commercial advertising or for noncommercial communications. On-site commercial advertising was defined as a sign advertising goods or services available on the property where the sign was located. The city's stated purposes in enacting the ordinance were to reduce traffic hazards caused by distracting sign displays and to preserve and improve the appearance of the city.

(a) Does the portion of the ordinance limiting commercial billboard advertising to on-site billboards violate the Constitution?

(b) Does the portion of the ordinance banning the use of billboards for noncommercial communications violate the Constitution? [*Metromedia, Inc. v. City of San Diego*, 453 U.S. 490, 101 S.Ct. 2882 (1981)]

(c) Can a municipality constitutionally probibit all residential signs except for sale and warning signs in order to prevent visual clutter? [*City of Ladue v. Gilleo*, 114 S.Ct. 2038 (1994)]

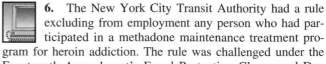 **6.** The New York City Transit Authority had a rule excluding from employment any person who had participated in a methadone maintenance treatment program for heroin addiction. The rule was challenged under the Fourteenth Amendment's Equal Protection Clause and Due Process Clause.

(a) What level of scrutiny should a court use to analyze the classification created by the transit authority's rule?

(b) What arguments might the plaintiffs make for striking down the rule? What arguments might the transit authority make to justify the rule? [*New York City Transit Authority v. Beazer,* 440 U.S. 568, 99 S.Ct. 1355 (1979)]

 7. Mr. Thomas, a Jehovah's Witness, was transferred to a department producing military tanks. He quit his job because his religious beliefs forbade participation in the production of armaments. The Indiana Employment Security Review Board denied Thomas's claim for unemployment benefits, because a statute made benefits unavailable to those who voluntarily leave their employment without good cause. Did Indiana violate Thomas's constitutional rights? Frame the legal and ethical arguments for and against requiring Indiana to pay Thomas unemployment benefits. [*Thomas v. Review Bd. of Indiana Employment Sec.,* 450 U.S. 707, 101 S.Ct. 1425 (1981)]

 8. A Wisconsin law permitted creditors to freeze the wages of a debtor (in legal terms, to garnish the wages) until the completion of a trial to determine the debtor's liability. Under the law, creditors' lawyers could effect a gar-

nishment by requesting a summons from a court and serving it on the debtor's employer. No notice to the debtor was required until ten days after the summons was served. Did the law authorizing garnishment without prior notice and opportunity for a hearing violate the constitutional rights of debtors? Explain why or why not. [*Sniadach v. Family Finance Corporation of Bay View,* 395 U.S. 337, 89 S.Ct. 1820 (1969)]

9. For what purposes may the government take property from a private individual or business? Can restrictions on the use of private property ever amount to a taking of the property? If a taking occurs, is the owner of the property entitled to any compensation?

10. John Doe filed a complaint with New York City's Commission on Human Rights alleging that he was not hired because he was a single gay male suspected of having HIV. His case was settled and the city made public the terms of the conciliation agreement. Did New York City violate John Doe's right to privacy? [*Doe v. New York City,* 15 F.3d. 264 (2d Cir. 1994)]

Chapter 3

INTERNATIONAL TRADE

■ Introduction

High-Priority Concern

Over the course of the past decade, economic and political events such as the U.S.–Japan trade deficit, the emergence of a unified trading block in North America, the formation of the European Community (EC), and the opening to trade of Eastern Europe and the former Soviet Union have made the importance of international trade even more apparent than before. International trade is a high-priority concern not only for industries worldwide and sovereign governments but for individuals as well. The debates surrounding the North American Free Trade Agreement (NAFTA) in 1993 and the Uruguay Round of the General Agreement on Tariffs and Trade (GATT) in 1993 and 1994 signaled to the world and, in particular, the American public, that we are living in a global economy.

The emergence of Japan and other Asian countries as exporting powers and the changes previously mentioned indicate that U.S. industry has become vulnerable to competition from abroad. Several less developed countries (namely Korea, Singapore, Hong Kong, and Taiwan) have become competitive in a widening range of industries. In the meantime, the U.S. has amassed a huge trade deficit, $115.8 billion for 1993.

For American companies, the result is more competition from abroad, new markets overseas, and new opportunities in traditional foreign markets. The changes in the world economic arena, however, also affect smaller domestic firms with no apparent involvement in international transactions.

Because a far greater number of countries are exporting their goods into the United States than ever before, domestic products are faced with increased competition. In addition, because some foreign goods may be sold for less in the U.S. than their domestic equivalents due to fluctuating exchange rates, the American consumer is also affected by the emergence of global markets that result in changes in the selection and price of goods.

These are the issues—dealing with import competition and opening foreign markets for U.S. exports—that are the targets of U.S. international trade policy

74

and trade law. For corporate managers, a basic knowledge of these laws and issues regulating trade is more important than ever.

Chapter Summary

This chapter begins with a discussion of trade law and policy, followed by a summary of how the U.S. government is organized to regulate international trade. The bulk of the chapter addresses the major U.S. laws and international agreements in this field. The final section discusses the European Community and its plan for political and economic integration.

■ Developments in Trade Policy

The U.S. government has given trade policy increasingly higher priority over the last few decades. The office of U.S. Trade Representative, created less than 35 years ago, now has cabinet-level rank. Policymakers have come under increasing pressure to protect U.S. industries from import competition and to press foreign governments to open their markets to U.S. exports.

One attempt to deal with these issues was signed into law by President Reagan in 1988. The Omnibus Trade and Competitiveness Act of 1988 seeks to improve the ability of domestic industries to obtain relief from import competition, but without changing the basically open nature of the U.S. market. At the same time, this law seeks to open foreign markets to U.S. exports by giving the president strong encouragement to negotiate reductions in foreign tariff and nontariff barriers.

Expanding Multilateral Rules

The act authorized the president to press for further reductions in tariffs and nontariff barriers to trade, in the multilateral negotiation known as the Uruguay Round. It also authorized him to seek expansion of the rules of international trade, which previously covered only trade in goods, to cover intellectual property rights, trade in services, and international investment.

The Past as a Warning for the Future

As the following article demonstrates, U.S. trade policy can have a dramatic effect on business.

Economists are Right for a Change, 1930

PRESIDENT HERBERT HOOVER, ignoring the pleas of 1,028 economists to veto it, signed with six gold pens the Smoot-Hawley Tariff Act on June 17, 1930. It was a hollow celebration.

The day before, anticipating the signing, the stock market suffered its worst collapse since November 1929, and the law quickly helped push the Great Depression deeper.

Its tariffs, which by 1932 rose to an all-time high of 59% of the average value of imports (today it's 5%), were designed to protect U.S. farm and textile products from foreign competition. Economists warned that angry nations would retaliate, adding that foreigners would also have fewer dollars to buy U.S. goods as well as to settle their World War I debts.

Within two years, Great Britain and more than 20 other nations raised their tariffs and reduced buying of U.S. imports. Within the U.S., prices and output continued their fast fall.

From 1930 to 1931, U.S. imports dropped 29%, but U.S. exports fell even more, 33%, and continued their collapse to a modern-day low of $2.4 billion in 1933.

One long-lasting effect of the act: The definition of "ornamental apparel," which has braid or lace, has stuck over the years and still adds to the duty paid. But in 1930, it was 90%; now it's 30%. In the 1930s it was another reason for women to use plainer lingerie.

In 1934, Congress passed the Reciprocal Trade Agreements Act to empower the president to reduce tariffs by half the 1930 rates in return for like cuts in foreign duties on U.S. goods. The "beggar thy neighbor" policy was dead.[1]

■ United States Trade Law

U.S. trade laws are enacted by Congress and administered by the federal government and administrative agencies.

---

1. *The Wall Street Journal*, Apr. 28, 1989. Reprinted with permission of *The Wall Street Journal*, ©1989 Dow Jones & Company, Inc. All Rights Reserved Worldwide.

The Role of Congress

Under the U.S. Constitution, Congress has exclusive power to regulate foreign commerce, which includes imports and exports, foreign investment, licensing of technology, and other commercial activities. This chapter deals primarily with trade laws; that is, those laws directed at imports and exports, although some of these laws affect other activities as well.

Trade laws are generally designed either to restrict or to facilitate imports and exports. Imports are restricted primarily by means of tariffs and quantitative limitations; certain imports are facilitated by being exempted from U.S. tariffs. Exports are controlled by means of export licenses; certain exports are facilitated by special federal government financing, certain tax breaks, and section 301 of the Trade Act of 1974, which is discussed later in this chapter.

The Role of the President

The president administers U.S. trade laws pursuant to the authority delegated to him by Congress. In addition, as chief executive, the president has broad power to negotiate trade agreements. However, the president has no power to regulate trade without congressional delegation or approval. Nevertheless, as the case below shows, the president can negotiate nonbinding, voluntary undertakings.

■ **A Case in Point:**   **In the Language of the Court**

Case 3.1
CONSUMERS UNION, INC. v. KISSINGER
United States Court of Appeals for the District of Columbia
506 F.2d 136 (D.C.Cir. 1974), *cert. denied*, 421 U.S. 1004, 95 S.Ct. 2406 (1975).

FACTS   In order to assist the U.S. steel industry, President Nixon, through his secretary of state Henry Kissinger, sought to reduce steel imports from Japan and Europe by convincing foreign producers to limit their exports to the United States. The undertakings to do so were voluntary, and no attempt was made by the U.S. to legally enforce them.

Consumers Union, believing that U.S. consumers were hurt by this restriction on supplies of foreign steel, sued the secretary of state. It argued that the president had in effect regulated foreign commerce without any specific statutory delegation of authority from Congress and thus exceeded his authority.

ISSUE PRESENTED   Did the president act within his powers in negotiating nonbinding, voluntary undertakings by foreign producers to reduce their exports to the United States?

OPINION   McGOWAN, J., writing for the U.S. Court of Appeals:

. . . .

The steel import restraints do not purport to be enforceable, either as contracts or as governmental actions with the force of law; and the executive has no sanctions to invoke in order to compel observance by the foreign producers of their self-denying representations. They are a statement of intent on the part of the foreign producer associations. The signatories' expectations, not unreasonable in light of the reception given their undertakings by the executive, are that the executive will consult with them over mutual concerns about the steel import situation, and that it will not have sudden recourse to the unilateral steps available to it under the Trade Expansion Act to impose legal restrictions on importation. The President is not bound in any way to refrain from taking such steps if he later deems them to be in the national interest, or if consultation proves unavailing to meet unforeseen difficulties: and certainly the Congress is not inhibited from enacting any legislation it desires to regulate by law the importation of steel.

The formality and specificity with which the undertakings are expressed does not alter their essentially precatory nature insofar as the executive branch is concerned. In effect the President has said that he will not initiate steps to limit steel imports by law if the volume of such imports remains within tolerable bounds. Communicating, through the Secretary of State, what levels he considers tolerable merely enables foreign producers to conform their actions accordingly, and to avoid the risk of guessing at what is acceptable. Regardless of whether the producers run afoul of the antitrust laws in the manner of their response, nothing in the process leading up to the voluntary undertakings or the process of consultation under them differentiates what the executive has done here from what all presidents, and to a lesser extent all high executive officers, do when they admonish an industry with the express or implicit warning that action, within either their existing powers or enlarged powers to be sought, will be taken if a desired course is not followed voluntarily.

RESULT The U.S. Court of Appeals upheld the export restraint by the foreign producers. It ruled that the president did not exceed his constitutional authority, because the export restraints were accomplished through an informal, voluntary agreement. The restraints were not legally binding on the foreign exporters, and were not enforced by U.S. authorities.

COMMENTS In order for the U.S. Customs Service to enforce this agreement by excluding imports in excess of the agreed limits, congressional approval would have been required. The effect of the voluntary restraints was perhaps the same as if quotas had been imposed by Congress; but the court did not feel it could interfere with the president's power to conduct foreign relations. Congress later approved the steel restraints. President Reagan negotiated new steel export restraints with foreign governments in 1984, and President Bush extended them in 1988; Congress approved both actions. In 1993, the Clinton administration threatened the major steel exporting nations with sanctions for dumping cut rate steel in the United States.

Questions
1. What incentives do foreign exporters have to voluntarily refrain from exporting their goods to the U.S.?
2. Could the U.S. Customs Service have enforced this agreement by excluding imports in excess of the agreed limits?

Administrative Agencies

The agencies primarily responsible for administration of the trade laws are the U.S. Trade Representative (USTR), the Department of Commerce, the Department of State, the Department of the Treasury, the U.S. International Trade Commission, and the U.S. Customs Service (which is part of the Treasury Department).

The USTR is responsible for the development of U.S. trade policy and the negotiation of trade agreements with other countries, with the assistance of the other agencies.

The USTR makes all policy decisions concerning the operation of these agreements. The Department of Commerce is generally responsible for implementing U.S. trade policy, enforcing certain import relief laws and export controls, and promoting U.S. exports. The Department of State administers controls on munitions exports and defends U.S. economic interests through U.S. embassies abroad.

The Department of the Treasury administers embargoes imposed on U.S. trade with countries such as Cuba and Libya. The embargo on Vietnam was lifted by

President Clinton in 1994, despite protests from some veterans groups that the embargo was necessary to ensure continued cooperation in accounting for U.S. military personnel who were prisoners of war (POWs) or missing in action (MIAs) after the Vietnam War. President Clinton responded that lifting the embargo would actually increase Vietnamese cooperation on this sensitive issue.

The International Trade Commission is an independent agency with a variety of responsibilities, including investigations concerning the effect of imports on U.S. industries. The Customs Service enforces all U.S. customs laws and import restrictions, and collects U.S. tariffs. Other agencies, such as the U.S. Department of Agriculture, administer restrictions on U.S. trade falling in their particular areas of responsibility, with the assistance of the Customs Service.

The Interagency Committee

The president makes trade policy decisions based on the recommendations of an interagency committee, headed by the USTR. Included on the committee are the agencies listed above, in addition to the Department of Labor, the Council of Economic Advisors, and other agencies interested in trade policy. Private interests are typically given the opportunity to express their views to any of these agencies, or to the interagency committee directly. For example, tariffs on a particular product are rarely changed without first consulting the affected industry. Government officials at all of the agencies are generally receptive to requests and comments from U.S. companies. In many cases, public hearings are held before decisions are made.

■ Tariffs

Tariffs are the basic tool for limiting imports to protect domestic industries. Today, most tariffs are *ad valorem* tariffs, meaning that the importer must pay a percentage of the value of the imported merchandise. For instance a 10% tariff on a shipment of imports valued at $10,000 would result in a *duty*, that is, a required payment, of $1,000.

U.S. tariffs are established by federal law. They can only be changed by law, or by administrative action authorized by law. Congress frequently changes U.S. tariffs. However, under the auspices of the Trade Agreement Program begun in 1934, Congress has also periodically delegated to the president the authority to reduce U.S. tar-

iffs in exchange for tariff concessions by other nations. In addition, it has for many years delegated to the president the power to increase tariffs temporarily in order to protect domestic industries in certain specified situations. These import relief laws are discussed later in this chapter.

Beer Dispute With Canada

On August 5, 1993, the United States Trade Representative announced that the United States and Canada had reached an agreement on a dispute over Canadian discrimination against U.S. beer imports sold in Ontario. Under terms of the agreement, the U.S. would lift duties on beer exports from Ontario. In turn, beer imported from the U.S. would be sold in the stores of the Ontario Brewers Retail Incorporated and there would be limits on the amount of fees the Brewers Retail could charge for stocking American beer.

The United States was required to lift the 50% *ad valorem* duties on beer brewed in Ontario; Canada was required to lift its 50% counter-retaliatory duties on some U.S. beer. In addition, other Canadian provinces were required to comply with the agreement. Any new Canadian or provincial practices must be consistent with the GATT.

Despite the agreement, Ontario's environmental levy tax (a ten-cents-a-can levy on cans containing alcoholic beverages) is still in effect. The tax affects U.S. brewers more than Canadian brewers because most U.S. beer is sold in cans while Canadian beer is sold in bottles. U.S. brewers claim that their attempts to export beer in bottles have been thwarted by Ontario restrictions on the numbers and locations of bottle collection centers. The agreement, however, does not require Ontario to change its environmental levy.

The Harmonized Tariff Schedule

The United States has accepted an internationally harmonized tariff system. Current tariffs are found in a document entitled the *Harmonized Tariff Schedule of the United States* (*HTS*).[2] The *HTS* lists the tariffs imposed by Congress and the president on goods, based on their country of origin. Exhibit 3-1 reproduces the first two pages from the General Notes (that is, the general instructions) to the *HTS*. Exhibit 3-2 reproduces a page from the schedule covering beverages.

---

2. Published by the U.S. International Trade Commission in USITC Publication 2232.

EXHIBIT 3-1   Harmonized Tariff Schedule of the United States: General Notes

HARMONIZED TARIFF SCHEDULE of the United States
Annotated for Statistical Reporting Purposes

Page 1

GENERAL NOTES

1. **Tariff Treatment of Imported Goods.** All goods provided for in this schedule and imported into the customs territory of the United States from outside thereof are subject to duty or exempt therefrom as prescribed in general notes 3 and 4.

2. **Customs Territory of the United States.** The term "customs territory of the United States", as used in the tariff schedule, includes only the States, the District of Columbia and Puerto Rico.

3. **Rates of Duty.** The rates of duty in the "Rates of Duty" columns designated 1 ("General" and "Special") and 2 of the tariff schedule apply to goods imported into the customs territory of the United States as hereinafter provided in this note:

    (a) **Rate of Duty Column 1.**

        (i) Except as provided in subparagraph (iv) of this paragraph, the rates of duty in column 1 are rates which are applicable to all products other than those of countries enumerated in paragraph (b) of this note. Column 1 is divided into two subcolumns, "General" and "Special", which are applicable as provided below.

        (ii) The "General" subcolumn sets forth the general most-favored-nation (MFN) rates which are applicable to products of those countries described in subparagraph (i) above which are not entitled to special tariff treatment as set forth below.

        (iii) The "Special" subcolumn reflects rates of duty under one or more special tariff treatment programs described in paragraph (c) of this note and identified in parentheses immediately following the duty rate specified in such subcolumn. These rates apply to those products which are properly classified under a provision for which a special rate is indicated and for which all of the legal requirements for eligibility for such program or programs have been met. Where a product is eligible for special treatment under more than one program, the lowest rate of duty provided for any applicable program shall be imposed. Where no special rate of duty is provided for a provision, or where the country from which a product otherwise eligible for special treatment was imported is not designated as a beneficiary country under a program appearing with the appropriate provision, the rates of duty in the "General" subcolumn of column 1 shall apply.

        (iv) **Products of Insular Possessions.**

            (A) Except as provided in additional U.S. note 5 of chapter 91 and except as provided in additional U.S. note 3 of chapter 96, and except as provided in section 423 of the Tax Reform Act of 1986, goods imported from insular possessions of the United States which are outside the customs territory of the United States are subject to the rates of duty set forth in column 1 of the tariff schedule, except that all such goods the growth or product of any such possession, or manufactured or produced in any such possession from materials the growth, product or manufacture of any such possession or of the customs territory of the United States, or of both, which do not contain foreign materials to the value of more than 70 percent of their total value (or more than 50 percent of their total value with respect to goods described in section 213(b) of the Caribbean Basin Economic Recovery Act), coming to the customs territory of the United States directly from any such possession, and all goods previously imported into the customs territory of the United States with payment of all applicable duties and taxes imposed upon or by reason of importation which were shipped from the United States, without remission, refund or drawback of such duties or taxes, directly to the possession from which they are being returned by direct shipment, are exempt from duty.

            (B) In determining whether goods produced or manufactured in any such insular possession contain foreign materials to the value of more than 70 percent, no material shall be considered foreign which either--

                (1) at the time such goods are entered, or

                (2) at the time such material is imported into the insular possession,

            may be imported into the customs territory from a foreign country, and entered free of duty; except that no goods containing material to which (2) of this subparagraph applies shall be exempt from duty under subparagraph (A) unless adequate documentation is supplied to show that the material has been incorporated into such goods during the 18-month period after the date on which such material is imported into the insular possession.

EXHIBIT 3-1   Harmonized Tariff Schedule of the United States: General Notes, *Continued*

HARMONIZED TARIFF SCHEDULE of the United States
Annotated for Statistical Reporting Purposes

Page 2

General Note 3(a)(iv) (con.):

 (C) Subject to the limitations imposed under sections 503(b) and 504(c) of the Trade Act of 1974, goods designated as eligible under section 503 of such Act which are imported from an insular possession of the United States shall receive duty treatment no less favorable than the treatment afforded such goods imported from a beneficiary developing country under title V of such Act.

 (D) Subject to the provisions in section 213 of the Caribbean Basin Economic Recovery Act, goods which are imported from insular possessions of the United States shall receive duty treatment no less favorable than the treatment afforded such goods when they are imported from a beneficiary country under such Act.

(b) <u>Rate of Duty Column 2</u>. Notwithstanding any of the foregoing provisions of this note, the rates of duty shown in column 2 shall apply to products, whether imported directly or indirectly, of the following countries and areas pursuant to section 401 of the Tariff Classification Act of 1962, to section 231 or 257(e)(2) of the Trade Expansion Act of 1962, to section 404(a) of the Trade Act of 1974 or to any other applicable section of law, or to action taken by the President thereunder:

Afghanistan	German Democratic Republic	Mongolia
Albania	Kampuchea	North Korea
Bulgaria	Laos	Romania
Cuba	Latvia	Union of Soviet Socialist
Czechoslovakia	Lithuania	Republics
Estonia		Vietnam

(c) <u>Products Eligible for Special Tariff Treatment</u>.

 (i) (A) Programs under which special tariff treatment may be provided, and the corresponding symbols for such programs as they are indicated in the "Special" subcolumn, are as follows:

    Generalized System of Preferences . . . . A or A*
    Automotive Products Trade Act . . . . B
    Agreement on Trade in Civil Aircraft C
    United States-Canada Free-Trade Agreement . . . . CA
    Caribbean Basin Economic Recovery Act . . . . E or E*
    United States-Israel Free Trade Area IL

 (B) Articles which are eligible for the special tariff treatment provided for in subdivision (c) of this note and which are subject to temporary modification under any provision of subchapters I and II of chapter 99 shall be subject, for the period indicated in the "Effective Period" column in chapter 99, to rates of duty as follows:

  (1) if a rate of duty for which the article may be eligible is set forth in the "Special" subcolumn in chapter 99 followed by one or more symbols described above, such rate shall apply in lieu of the rate followed by the corresponding symbol(s) set forth for such article in the "Special" subcolumn in chapters 1 to 98; or

  (2) if "No change" appears in the "Special" subcolumn in chapter 99 and subdivision (B)(1) above does not apply, the rate of duty in the "General" subcolumn in chapter 99 or the applicable rate(s) of duty set forth in the "Special" subcolumn in chapters 1 to 98, whichever is lower, shall apply.

 (C) Unless the context requires otherwise, articles which are eligible for the special tariff treatment provided for in subdivision (c) of this note and which are subject to temporary modification under any provision of subchapters III or IV of chapter 99 shall be subject, for the period indicated in chapter 99, to the rates of duty in the "General" subcolumn in such chapter.

 (D) Whenever any rate of duty set forth in the "Special" subcolumn in chapters 1 to 98 is equal to or higher than, the corresponding rate of duty provided in the "General" subcolumn in such chapters, such rate of duty in the "Special" subcolumn shall be deleted; except that, if the rate of duty in the "Special" subcolumn is an intermediate stage in a series of staged rate reductions for that subheading, such rate shall be treated as a suspended rate and shall be set forth in the "Special" subcolumn, followed by one or more symbols described above, and followed by an "s" in parentheses. If no rate of duty for which the article may be eligible is provided in the "Special" subcolumn for a particular subheading in chapters 1 to 98, the rate of duty provided in the "General" subcolumn shall apply.

EXHIBIT 3-2   Sample Page from the Harmonized Tariff Schedule.

HARMONIZED TARIFF SCHEDULE of the United States (1992) -- Supplement 1

IV
22-2

Annotated for Statistical Reporting Purposes

Heading/ Subheading	Stat. Suf. & cd	Article Description	Units of Quantity	Rates of Duty 1 General	Rates of Duty 1 Special	2
2201		Waters, including natural or artificial mineral waters and aerated waters, not containing added sugar or other sweetening matter nor flavored; ice and snow:				
2201.10.00	00 1	Mineral waters and aerated waters............	liters..	0.4¢/liter	Free (A,CA,E,IL,J)	2.6¢/liter
2201.90.00	00 4	Other...........................	t.......	Free		Free
2202		Waters, including mineral waters and aerated waters, containing added sugar or other sweetening matter or flavored, and other nonalcoholic beverages, not including fruit or vegetable juices of heading 2009:				
2202.10.00		Waters, including mineral waters and aerated waters, containing added sugar or other sweetening matter or flavored................	....	0.3¢/liter	Free (A*,E,IL,J) 0.1¢/liter (CA)	4¢/liter
	30 4	Carbonated soft drinks..................	liters			
	60 7	Other................................	liters			
2202.90		Other: Milk-based drinks:				
2202.90.10	00 1	Chocolate milk drink..............	liters..	20%	Free (E,IL,J) 12% (CA)	20%
2202.90.20	00 9	Other 1/..........................	liters.v kg	17.5%	Free (E,IL,,J) 10.5% (CA)	35%
2202.90.90		Other................................	....	0.3¢/liter	Free (A,E,IL,J) 0.1¢/liter (CA)	4¢/liter
	10 2	Nonalcoholic beer..................	liters			
	90 5	Other............................	liters			
2203.00.00		Beer made from malt.............................	....	1.6¢/ liter 2/	Free (A*,E,IL, J) 2/ 0.9¢/liter (CA) 2/	13.2¢/ liter 2/
		In containers each holding not over 4 liters:				
	30 5	In glass containers.....................	liters			
	60 8	Other.................................	liters			
	90 2	In containers each holding over 4 liters......	liters			

1/ See subheading 9904.10.60.
2/ Imports under this subheading are subject to a Federal Excise Tax (26 U.S.C. 5051) of $18 per barrel of 31 gallons and at a like rate for any other quantity or for fractional parts of a barrel.

For each product category, there are two basic rates of duty. There is one column for most countries (column 1) and a second one for most European Community countries (column 2). These columns reflect tariffs imposed by Congress or negotiated by the president under the Trade Agreements Program. Column 1 is subdivided into general and special tariffs. Special tariffs reflect preferential rates for certain countries on certain products; these are described later in this chapter. Temporary increases in U.S. tariffs are listed in chapter 99 of the *HTS*.

Country of Origin

U.S. tariffs vary depending on the country of origin. A good is considered the product of the country from which it was first exported, unless it has been substantially transformed into a new article of commerce. If such a *substantial transformation* occurs, the country of origin is considered to be the country in which the transformation took place.

Tariff Classification

Tariffs also vary depending on the article's *tariff classification*, that is, where it is best described in the *HTS*. Determining an article's classification is often a simple matter because many articles are described exactly in the schedules. For example, on the sample page shown in exhibit 3-2, mineral waters are classified under item 2201.10. However, articles are not always as clearly described, and disagreements may occur. This is especially true of newly developed products. For example, under an earlier tariff schedule optical fibers were not specifically described. Consequently, there was a question whether optical fibers should be classified as an article of glass, or an optical element, or part of a communications system.

Customs Valuation

The duty paid on an imported article depends on the value assigned to it by the Customs Service, that is, on the *customs valuation* of the article. The lower the valuation, the lower the duty.

The basic rule of customs valuation in the United States is that the value of an article for customs purposes is the *transaction value*, which is the price indicated on the sales invoice. Following this rule makes customs valuation for most imports a simple matter. However, there are exceptions to this rule. For example, if the importer and the foreign seller are related, the Customs Service is authorized to determine whether the invoice reflects a price negotiated by two parties at arm's length.

There are further rules to keep in mind. For example, the cost of foreign inland freight is not *dutiable*—subject to duty—if charged separately from the invoice price. If, however, the cost of foreign inland freight is included in the invoice price, then it is included in the valuation and becomes dutiable. Careful customs planning can avoid such needless costs.

Customs Laws

Proper customs planning can not only minimize the import duties paid, but also help to avoid violations of the customs laws. Penalties can be severe and can involve forfeiture of the imported articles, along with heavy fines.

The U.S. customs laws are administered by the Customs Service. Its headquarters are in Washington, D.C., but the service has a district office at every U.S. port. Tariff rulings by the district offices can be appealed to headquarters and then to the U.S. Court of International Trade. Appeals from this court are to the U.S. Court of Appeals for the Federal Circuit and then to the U.S. Supreme Court. The customs laws are found in title 19 of the *U.S. Code*. The regulations of the Customs Service are in title 19 of the *Code of Federal Regulations*.

> 66
>
> *Proper customs planning can not only minimize the import duties paid, but also help to avoid violations of the customs laws. Penalties can be severe and can involve forfeiture of the imported articles, along with heavy fines.*

■ Tariff Preferences

Pursuant to authority delegated by Congress, the president has established preferential tariffs for imports from certain developing countries. The most important of these tariffs is based on the Generalized System of Preferences.

The Generalized System of Preferences

The Generalized System of Preferences (GSP), which was agreed to multilaterally, is a program developed by the industrialized countries to assist developing nations by improving their ability to export. Under the GSP, which was adopted in title V of the Trade Act of 1974,[3] the president has designated certain products as eligible for duty-free treatment if they are produced in developing countries designated as eligible beneficiaries of the program. The eligible countries and products are listed in General Note 3(c)(ii) of the *Harmonized Tariff Schedule*. Products eligible for GSP treatment are indicated by an "A" in the "Special" column of the *HTS*. It is necessary to determine the country of origin of imports on order to

---

3. 9 U.S.C. §§ 2461-2466 (1988).

decide if they are eligible for the preferential tariff. Under the GSP, an eligible product receives duty-free treatment only if 35% or more of the value of the product was added in an eligible country. There are also limitations on the volume of eligible articles that may be imported from a single country. If the volume limitation is exceeded, the product is automatically removed from the category of eligible imports from that country.

If a country is found to be sufficiently competitive, the president can remove it from the program, either entirely or with respect to individual products. This process is referred to as "graduation." In 1989, Hong Kong, Singapore, South Korea, and Taiwan were graduated from the program entirely.

Countries can also be removed from the GSP program for policy reasons, such as failure to protect intellectual property rights. A review of the program is conducted annually to determine which countries and products should be removed from or added to the program. The program is administered for the president by the U.S. Trade Representative.

The Caribbean Basin Initiative

The Caribbean Basin Initiative (CBI), like the GSP, provides duty-free treatment for products from specified developing countries—in this case, the Caribbean nations. Its scope, however, is broader than that of the GSP. All products are eligible, except import-sensitive items such as certain textiles and sugar. The program was established in 1983 by the Caribbean Basin Economic Recovery Act.[4] The Act authorizes the president to designate the countries that will be beneficiaries of the Initiative. Eligible products are designated by an "E" in the "Special" column of the *HTS*.

U.S.–Israel Free Trade Agreement

Under the U.S.–Israel Free Trade Agreement,[5] all tariffs between the United States and Israel are eliminated in 1995. The agreement was negotiated by the president under the authority delegated to him by Congress in title IV of the Trade and Tariff Act of 1984. It is strictly a bilateral agreement. Thus the tariff preferences provided by the two countries apply only to trade between them, and to imports from other countries. Unlike the GSP and the CBI, this is a two-way free trade area, in which both countries have made tariff concessions. Congress

approved the agreement in the United States-Israel Free Trade Area Implementation Act of 1985.[6] Eligible articles are indicated by "IL" in the "Special" column of the *HTS*.

North American Free Trade Agreement

An even more significant agreement is the trilateral North American Free Trade Agreement.[7] The agreement provides for the elimination of all barriers to trade between the U.S., Canada, and Mexico and for the free cross-border movement of goods and services between the territories of the three signatories. It is designed to improve the three countries' economies and to benefit 370 million consumers with lower-priced goods and increased investment opportunities. The agreement established the world's largest free-trade zone.

The pact gradually phases out tariffs between the U.S., Canada, and Mexico, creating a large open regional market, and providing enhanced legal protection to foreign investors. Tariff elimination is addressed in chapter 3 of the pact, entitled "National Treatment and Market Access." Prior to entering into NAFTA, the U.S. and Canada had entered into a bilateral trade agreement which went into effect January 1, 1989.[8] This agreement provided for the elimination of tariffs and trade barriers over a ten-year period. These provisions between the two countries were incorporated into NAFTA.

Under NAFTA, Mexican tariff elimination on U.S. capital goods is staged in three categories: "A," "B," and "C." Tariffs on Category A goods were eliminated in January 1994. Category A goods include automobiles. Category B goods, which include textile and apparel goods, will be duty-free in 1998. Category C goods, which include the majority of capital goods, will be duty-free in 2003. The U.S. eliminated the majority of tariffs on Mexican goods on January 1, 1994.

In addition to eliminating its custom duties, each country is required to accord national treatment to the goods of the other nations in accordance with article 3 of the GATT. The agreement also substantially reduces the barriers to government procurement and effectively results in totally open procurement by the year 2004.

The agreement prohibits new restrictions on investment and on trade in services among the three countries. It includes major provisions on specific industries, such

---

4. 19 U.S.C. §§ 2701-2706 (1988).
5. Free Trade Agreement, April 22, 1985, United States-Israel, _U.S.T._, T.I.A.S. No._, 24 I.L.M. 653 (1985).

6. Pub. Law No. 99-47, 99 Stat. 82 (codified as amended 19 U.S.C. 2112 (1988)).
7. Free Trade Agreement, May 1993, United States-Canada-Mexico, _U.S.T._, T.I.A.S. No._, 32 I.L.M. 605 (1993).
8. Free Trade Agreement, January 2, 1988, United States-Canada, _U.S.T._, T.I.A.S. No._, 27 I.L.M. 281 (1988).

as agriculture, telecommunication, and energy. In addition, special rules of origin are established to ensure that only products originating in the United States, Canada, or Mexico enjoy duty-free treatment. Certificates of origin are required on all goods being exported between the three countries to certify that the good qualifies as an "originating" good.

The pact also provides for the adequate protection and enforcement of intellectual property rights and attempts to ensure that these rights do not become barriers to trade. Each country is required to implement several international agreements regarding intellectual property rights, such as the Berne Convention for the Protection of Literary and Artistic Works and the Paris Convention for the Protection of Industrial Property Rights.

NAFTA explicitly protects U.S. environmental regulations and includes a mechanism for sanctions if Mexico fails to enforce its own environmental laws. In addition, a side agreement set up a three-nation mechanism, the Commission on Environmental Cooperation, to address environmental disputes. Any country or private interest group that believes that a nation is not enforcing its environmental laws may complain. If the commission determines that a violation has occurred, it can impose a fine up to $20 million or impose trade sanctions on the offending country. No prior trade agreement has addressed as many pollution issues; the GATT does not even mention the word "environment."

Fruit, vegetable, and sugarcane growers in Florida were concerned that the pact would leave them open to unfair competition from Mexican growers unburdened by high labor and regulatory costs. They also feared that Mexico, which has the same growing season as Florida, could replace Florida produce in some markets.

Primarily to protect the Florida growers, the treaty phases out U.S. agricultural tariffs over 15 years. In addition, during that period any dramatic increases in Mexican fruit and vegetable imports will trigger temporary "snap-back" tariffs to protect U.S. growers.

Congress approved the agreement on November 17, 1993, and it went into effect on January 1, 1994.

■ Foreign Trade Zones

Foreign trade zones are special areas within or adjacent to a U.S. port of entry, that have been designated as such under the Foreign Zones Act of 1934.[9] Under this act and the implementing regulations, merchandise may be imported into the United States directly to a foreign trade zone. The import duties normally due upon entry into the United States are not due until the merchandise is withdrawn from the zone.

Foreign trade zones provide several advantages. Merchandise may be imported to a foreign trade zone for demonstration purposes only; if it is reexported from the zone, no duties are owed. Merchandise may be imported into a foreign trade zone and manufactured into a new article of commerce. In that case, duties are owed on the new article of commerce when it is withdrawn from the zone for consumption in the United States. This is advantageous to the importer if the rate of duty is lower on the manufactured product than on the imported intermediate product.

Foreign trade zones are created by application to the Foreign Trade Zones Board at the U.S. Department of Commerce and are administered by the Customs Service. Individual companies may lease space in a zone or, in some cases, establish a physically separate zone.

■ The Trade Agreements Program

As noted earlier, Congress has periodically granted the president the authority to negotiate tariff reductions with other countries. Besides negotiating bilateral preferential agreements, the United States participates in the General Agreement on Tariffs and Trade (GATT),[10] which is the principal multilateral mechanism devoted to the regulation of international trade.

■ The GATT

The GATT has had a profound effect on world trade since its creation in 1947. It established the *most favored nation* (MFN) principle, which has been the foundation of the world trading system. This principle is set out in article I of the GATT. It states that each member country must accord to all other GATT members tariff treatment no less favorable than it provides to any other country. In other words, if the United States agrees to lower its tariff on imports of a product from a certain country, it must grant the same treatment to all other member countries of

---

9. 19 U.S.C. §§ 81a-81u (1988).

10. General Agreement on Tariffs and Trade, opened for signature, October 30, 1947, T.I.A.S. No. 1700, 55 U.N.T.S. 194 (entered into force January 1, 1948).

GATT. (The GSP and other preferential agreements discussed above are exceptions to the MFN principle and are authorized by the GATT.) The theory behind the MFN principle is that world trade will be enhanced if countries avoid discriminating among themselves and creating trading blocs that expand trade within the blocs but restrict trade between them.

Under the GATT, there has been a series of multilateral trade negotiations in which the GATT members agreed to tariff reductions. Despite the complexity and length of these negotiations, they have been enormously successful. Tariffs today are a small fraction, on the average, of what they were when the GATT was formed. A second basic principle of the GATT is that of *bound tariffs*. Each time tariffs are reduced, they become bound; that is, they may not be raised again. If any country raises its bound tariffs, it must compensate, normally in the form of other tariff concessions, the other GATT members. This principle is set out in article II of the GATT.

A third basic principle, set out in article III of the GATT, is that of national treatment. GATT members must not discriminate against imported products in favor of domestically produced products. Thus, for example, special taxes on imported goods are illegal, if not applied equally to domestic products.

> **66**
> *Tariffs today are a small fraction, on the average, of what they were when the GATT was formed.*

MFN Status for China

On May 28, 1993, President Clinton renewed China's favorable trade status, which allows it to export its products to the United States at the lowest possible tariffs. The Clinton administration also issued an executive order setting forth the conditions for China's continued favorable trade status. President Clinton threatened to cancel China's preferred trade status in June 1994 if Beijing did not make significant progress on human rights, including at a minimum greater freedom of emigration and less use of prison labor.

China responded to the threat of losing its preferential trade status. In January 1994 it agreed to tighten an agreement to prevent products made by prison labor from being exported to the United States. In addition, China made major concessions to the United States to enact a new textiles agreement, which for the first time permits United States custom inspections on Chinese soil.

Maintaining an economic relationship is in the interest of both countries. Cancellation of China's favorable trade status would undermine the rapid pace of China's continued economic expansion. American businesses eager to invest in China would also be hurt. Many economists argued the key to China's uninterrupted economic expansion is the United States, where China sold more than $40 billion in goods in 1993 compared to only $2.5 billion ten years ago. In 1993, the United States exported to China products with a value of approximately $9 billion.

Opponents of the withdrawal of China's MFN status argued that trade status should not be linked to human rights. They stated that trade with China was so economically important to the United States, and so important for encouraging political reform in China, that the effects of a cancellation would be disastrous for both American business and Chinese reform. This was due to the presumption that if trade preferences were withdrawn, average tariffs on Chinese goods would rise from 8% to 40%, making it very difficult for China to export to the United States.

In June 1994 President Clinton renewed China's MFN status. Clinton made a major policy shift by announcing that the U.S. would no longer use trade as a weapon to bludgeon China into improving its human rights record.

Ethical Consideration

Your company imports electronic parts from China for use in its finished products. If MFN status were revoked, you would have to buy these parts elsewhere, at a much higher price. This would reduce your profits on your most important products by one-fourth. Some, but not all, of your competitors would be similarly affected. Your trade association is considering lobbying the president and Congress to retain China's MFN status. Should you support this effort to resist, for commercial reasons, U.S. attempts to encourage better treatment of the Chinese citizens by their government? Consider whether trade with the U.S. will help or hinder the development of democracy in China.

This shift was sharply criticized by some members of Clinton's own Democratic Party in Congress.

Strains on GATT

Tariffs are not the only barrier to trade. Nontariff barriers in some cases have replaced tariffs as a means of protecting domestic industries threatened by import competition. For example, the preference often given to domestic products in government procurement can reduce the volume of imports.

In the Tokyo Round of the GATT negotiations, several agreements were negotiated in an effort to regulate nontariff barriers. These agreements included new international codes on topics such as government procurement, export subsidies, product standards, and customs valuation—all of which had been used (both inadvertently and otherwise) to restrict imports or artificially stimulate exports. These codes, commonly called the MTN codes, were named after the round of negotiations known as the Tokyo Round of Multilateral Trade Negotiations (MTN). The MTN codes were a positive step; however, many developing countries refused to participate in their negotiation and did not accede to the codes.

Under the most-favored-nation principle, any reduction in nontariff barriers should be applied to all GATT members. The industrialized countries, along with a few developing countries that eventually signed some of the MTN codes, decided that the codes were too important to apply without reciprocal concessions and were also too important to discard for lack of unanimity in GATT. These countries therefore agreed to apply the codes to each other but not to give the same benefits to the countries that did not accede. Most-favored-nation treatment under the codes thus became conditional. It was granted only to those countries that signed the codes rather than to all GATT signatories. This *conditional MFN* was a significant departure from the MFN principle, because benefits were granted to some GATT members and not to others.

The erosion of the MFN principle may continue. The European Community (EC) has negotiated significant preferential agreements with developing countries. The United States has entered into a free trade agreement with Mexico and Canada, as well as Israel. Some influential officials, such as Michael Mansfield, a former senator and former U.S. Ambassador to Japan, have proposed that the United States should enter into free trade agreements with Japan, South Korea, and Taiwan. This is in part a reaction to the EC, which has removed many significant barriers to trade among its member countries. Japan and other Asian countries have also begun to consider the wisdom of a preferential trade pact among

themselves. These developments raise the specter of a world divided into regional trading blocs, which is precisely what the founders of the GATT wished to avoid.

In the United States, frustration at the continued existence of nontariff barriers despite the GATT rules has grown in direct proportion to the U.S. trade deficit. This frustration produced the Omnibus Trade and Competiveness Act of 1988, which strengthened the power of the president to negotiate with and, if necessary, retaliate against countries whose nontariff barriers are hampering U.S. exports. Most other countries have condemned this resort to unilateralism in place of the multilateral approach of the GATT. Nevertheless, it has produced some results.

❝

In the United States, frustration at the continued existence of nontariff barriers despite the GATT rules has grown in direct proportion to the U.S. trade deficit.

Japan   Most notable among countries perceived as being less than open to imports is Japan. Under the Omnibus Trade and Competitiveness Act of 1988 and previous laws, several presidents had negotiated bilateral agreements to open the Japanese market to specific industries. Beyond these sectoral, industry-specific negotiations, the United States and Japan engaged in talks, known as the Structural Impediments Initiative, designed to remedy the perceived structural and macroeconomic causes of the U.S. trade deficit with Japan. The United States includes among these causes the high savings rate in Japan and Japan's failure to apply its antitrust laws to prevent private restraints of trade. Japan has countered with its list of causes on the U.S. side, including the low investment rate by citizens of the United States.

In 1993, the U.S. and Japan entered into a "framework" agreement that committed Japan to reduce its trade surplus and to open its markets to foreign cars and car parts, insurance, and telecommunications. Left unsettled was how to measure whether Japan was living up to its import-creating commitments. That question was supposed to be answered in trade talks.

Unfortunately, trade negotiations broke down in 1994 without the U.S. and Japan reaching agreements to open Japan's markets for automobiles, auto parts, insurance, and telecommunications. The stumbling block was Washington's demand for "objective criteria" to measure progress, which Japan insisted were numerical targets that would contravene free trade.

In 1989, under pressure from Washington, Japan agreed to give Motorola Inc. roughly one-third of the cellular phone market in the Tokyo region. However, Motorola complained that Japanese companies have worked behind the scenes to sabotage the accord, and that as a result, it has less than 4% percent of the Japanese market. The Clinton administration highlighted the closed nature of the Japanese market by focusing on this fight over cellular phones.

The U.S. government determined in 1994 that Tokyo had violated the 1989 cellular telephone agreement with Motorola. That determination was the first step in levying sanctions against Japan equal to the alleged damages suffered by Motorola in lost revenue.

The president can impose a variety of sanctions to force the opening of the Japanese market to American exports. However, almost all of them carry the risk of hurting American companies and consumers or damaging political ties with Tokyo. Options include the renewal of a tough trade provision, namely a trade law known as Super 301 (discussed later in this chapter). Under the law, the president can identify a country that systematically discriminates against American goods. If that country does not remove its trade barriers within 18 months, the president may take action. In mid-1994 President Clinton signed an executive order that reestablished his power to use Super 301, without identifying Japan as the target. If the president later chooses to take a tougher stand, Japan can then be singled out in that executive order.

On the heels of the failed negotiations, then Prime Minister Morihiro Hosokawa warned the United States against imposing trade sanctions on Japan, stating that such action would force Tokyo to retaliate with sanctions on American products. Prime Minister Hosokawa also pointed out that such action on the part of the U.S. would be a contravention of the GATT. He stated that under no conditions would the Japanese government drop its resistance to "numerical targets" for opening Japanese markets, the issue that was the main stumbling block in the negotiations.

The Americans insisted that Japan agree to certain numerical indicators that will prove whether it is opening its markets to autos, telecommunications, insurance, and medical equipment. The Japanese refused to accept such indicators, arguing that it would constitute "managed trade."

American officials said there was no chance that they would compromise on the issue of numerical indicators. They contended that because the 31 previous trade agreements between the U.S. and Japan relied upon Japanese promises instead of quantitative and qualitative measures, the agreements did not make a dent in the Japanese trade surplus with the United States, which stood at $59.3 billion at the end of 1993.

Another possible measure that could be taken against Japan is for the United States to drive up the value of the Japanese yen and therefore make Japanese exports more expensive and American imports to Japan cheaper. Driving up the yen is the preferred weapon of American auto manufacturers. However, pushing the dollar down against the yen raises the cost of living in the United States by making a range of imports, not just Japanese automobiles, more expensive. It also encourages the Japanese to withdraw their funds from the U.S. stock and U.S. Treasury bond markets. The Clinton administration has repeatedly stated that it does not believe in artificially manipulating exchange rates.

A third tool available to the administration is to stop allowing the expansion of so-called foreign trade zones in the United States. These zones allow Japanese manufacturers to import parts from Japan duty-free until the final product is shipped to American customers.

Another option is to have the Justice Department bring antitrust suits against Japanese concerns doing business in the United States that are also part of cartels in Japan that lock out American companies.

The Uruguay Round

The perceived threats to the GATT and to world trade provided the stimulus for the Uruguay Round of GATT negotiations. In this round, the eighth in the history of the GATT, members sought to further reduce tariffs and non-tariff barriers to trade.

The 117 nations agreed to reduce their tariffs by an average of one-third over six years. The U.S. and the EC will reach this average by cutting their tariffs on each other's goods in half, while cutting tariffs on goods from the rest of the world by much less. In addition, agricultural tariffs will be reduced by 36% in industrial nations and 24% in developing nations.

For the first time, agriculture, services, textiles, and investment services were covered by international rules of fair trade. The agreement, also for the first time, protects the right of service-sector companies to operate on foreign soil free of discriminatory laws.

The Uruguay Round was the most ambitious GATT round ever held. It was completed at the end of 1993, three years later than it had been expected to conclude.

During the final days of the Uruguay Round, the United States and the European Community struggled to reach an agreement not on farm subsidies but rather access to American movies and television programs in Europe. A battle raged over demands by the American movie and entertainment industries for the removal of all European restrictions on American television programs and for assurances that new American multimedia technologies—involving interaction among cable, telephone, computers, and entertainment—would not be held back by European restrictions. There was a lot of money at stake. Sales in Europe of American entertainment products totaled $3.7 billion in 1992.

France and other European countries have typically restricted American-made programs to a maximum of 50% of the total television broadcasts and have imposed a series of taxes on movie tickets, television movies, and videocassettes that raised $350 million in 1992. The money generated from the taxes has been used to underwrite French films.

Ethical Consideration

Restrictions on American media imports raise both economic and cultural issues. For years Quebec has been concerned that the U.S. media would turn Canada into a mini-U.S. To what extent should media companies worry about protecting local culture? Should popular tastes prevail, as in the ad "I want my MTV!"?

The president's *fast track authority* (which allowed the president to negotiate trade agreements and submit them for an up or down vote by Congress with no amendments allowed) expired in March 1994. This forced the U.S. and Europe to agree to disagree over issues concerning the entertainment industry, aircraft and shipping, and financial services—including banking and mortgage brokers. As of 1994, the GATT included many industries that were not previously covered in world trade agreements, but it was more limited than had been envisioned at the opening of the Uruguay Round.

A few other details remained to be worked out. These included specific tariff cuts, rules for the occasional copying of patented and copyrighted works without permission from the owner, and the extent to which the developing countries must open fabric and clothing markets in exchange for similar openings by wealthier countries.

In Brief: Topics Not Covered in Uruguay Round

■ Entertainment (including movies, TV, interactive entertainment media)
■ Aircraft
■ Shipping
■ Financial services (including banking and mortgage brokers)
■ Aspects of intellectual property

■ Import Relief Laws

In a series of laws, known collectively as the import relief laws, Congress has authorized the president to raise U.S. tariffs on specified products and to provide other forms of import protection to U.S. industries. These laws vary as to the nature of the unfair practice (if any) to which they are directed, the degree of injury required in order to obtain relief, the nature of the relief authorized, the agencies authorized to provide the relief, and the amount of discretion given to the president in determining whether to grant relief.

Section 201

Section 201 of the Trade Act of 1974,[11] usually referred to simply as section 201, provides for temporary relief to domestic industries seriously injured by increasing imports, regardless of whether unfair practices are involved. It is sometimes called the *fair trade law*. The relief is designed to give the U.S. industry a few years (normally no more than five) to adjust to import competition.

The U.S. International Trade Commission (ITC) investigates petitions filed by U.S. industries. If the ITC makes an affirmative finding of injury from imports, it recommends specific import relief, such as higher duties or quantitative limits on imports. The president must provide the recommended relief unless she finds that it

_____

11. 19 U.S.C. § 2251 (1988).

would not be in the national economic interest as defined in the law. Because import relief always has economic costs, such as inflationary effects, the president in many cases decides not to provide relief.

The Omnibus Trade and Competitiveness Act of 1988 encourages petitioning industries to submit plans illustrating how they will use section 201 relief to adjust to import competition. It further provides that the ITC should recommend relief that not only addresses the injury caused by imports, but that also will facilitate the domestic industry's adjustment to import competition. As a complement to that, the law provides that the president can grant either import relief or other appropriate relief within his legal authority.

Thus, the law encourages making relief conditional on the ability of the domestic industry to meet the competition or to transfer its resources elsewhere. The legislative history suggests that, with this broader authority,

Congress expects that relief will be granted in almost all cases sent to the president.

An excellent example of the use of section 201 is provided by the U.S. steel industry. In 1984, when President Reagan negotiated the new set of voluntary steel export restraints (discussed earlier in this chapter), he did so after the steel industry had filed a section 201 petition. The International Trade Commission recommended relief, but President Reagan decided not to impose higher tariffs or mandatory quotas under this law. Instead, he negotiated bilateral agreements with most of the major steel-producing countries.

In another case, the ITC refused to recommend relief under section 201 for the automobile industry. A majority of the commission found that the injury being suffered by the industry was not primarily caused by imports.

In the following case, the president rejected a recommendation by the ITC for quotas on shoe imports.

■ **A Case in Point:**

Case 3.2
PRESIDENTIAL DECISION UNDER SECTION 201: NONRUBBER FOOTWEAR
Statement by the President, August 28, 1985.

Summary

FACTS Following a request from the U.S. shoe industry, the Senate Finance Committee requested an investigation of imports of nonrubber footwear under section 201 of the Trade Act of 1974. The International Trade Commission (ITC) determined by a 5–0 vote that imports were a substantial cause of serious injury to the domestic industry. The ITC recommended that quotas be established on imports of nonrubber footwear for five years.

ISSUE PRESENTED Would placing quotas on shoe imports be detrimental to the national economic interest?

DECISION President Reagan rejected the recommendation for quotas. He reasoned that, in this case, the cost of protection would be too high. Quotas would cost the American consumer almost $3 billion, and the GATT rules would require the United States to compensate its trading partners with $2 billion in trade. There was no reason to believe that quotas would help the industry become more competitive.

RESULT The recommendation by the International Trade Commission to provide relief was rejected.

COMMENTS Like some other U.S. industries, footwear manufacturers had made several requests for relief from imports and had been granted relief in 1977 and again in 1981. Relief under section 201 is supposed to be temporary in nature. President Reagan in essence decided that the purpose of section 201, which is to give temporary breathing space so that the specific industry has the chance to become competitive, had already been fulfilled.

The ITC recommended relief in approximately 50% of the investigations made under section 201. The presidents in office granted relief in approximately half of those cases. These odds might change dramatically as a result of the amendments to the Omnibus Trade and Competitiveness Act of 1988.

The Antidumping Law

The antidumping law[12] is the most frequently used import relief law. If a U.S. industry is materially injured by imports of a product being *dumped* in the United States—that is, sold below the current selling price in the exporter's home market or below the exporter's cost of production—the law imposes an antidumping duty on such imports. The amount of the duty is equal to the amount of the dumping margin, that is, the difference between the U.S. price and the price in the exporting country. If dumping and material injury are found to exist, relief is mandatory.

The law applies a different standard to nonmarket economy (that is, Socialist) countries in determining what constitutes dumping of imports from those countries, on the theory that prices in such countries do not reflect market forces and are therefore not a reasonable basis for determining whether price discrimination exists.

Flat Panel Dispute With Japan   In 1991 the Advanced Display Manufacturers Association of America and its member companies filed an antidumping petition with the International Trade Commission against Japanese imports of flat panel displays. (Flat panel displays are used in laptop computers.) The commission's preliminary determination stated that Japan was selling high information content flat panel displays in the U.S. at less than fair value.

The decision of the ITC was a blow to some of the largest U.S. computer manufacturers, who claimed that the antidumping duties would force U.S. manufacturers to produce their products offshore because many relied on the Japanese displays.

The U.S. Commerce Department's International Administration revoked the controversial antidumping order on certain flat panel displays imported from Japan in 1993. The order applied retroactively to February 1991.

The revocation was the result of a changed circumstances review initiated by Guardian Industries, the con-

trolling shareholder of Optical Imaging Systems (OIS). Guardian, on behalf of OIS, asked for the revocation of the antidumping order on active matrix liquid crystal high information content flat panel displays (AMLCDs) because it had no interest in maintaining the order.

Under section 751 of the 1930 Tariffs Act, the Commerce Department may revoke an antidumping duty order if it determines that changed circumstances sufficient to warrant revocation exist. A finding that the order under review is no longer of interest to domestic "interested parties" constitutes grounds for revocation. OIS was the only member of the petitioner, the Advanced Display Manufacturers Association of America, known to produce the active matrix flat panel displays and hence was the "interested party."

Several large manufacturers supported OIS, including Apple Computer Inc. and IBM. They argued that the order had injured downstream users of AMLCDs. Their primary argument was that the production of products using AMLCDs had been forced offshore in order to avoid the duty, resulting in a loss of domestic jobs, tax revenue, and competitiveness.

The Countervailing Duty Law

The countervailing duty law[13] provides that, if a U.S. industry is materially injured by imports of a product benefiting from a foreign subsidy, a *countervailing duty* must be imposed on those imports, that is, an import duty that offsets the amount of the benefit conferred by the subsidy. *Countervailable subsidies* are benefits provided by a government to stimulate exports. They can take many forms, including direct grants and loans to industry at below-market interest rates. For certain countries, injury to the U.S. industry is not a prerequisite; the existence of a countervailable subsidy suffices to trigger relief.

As under the antidumping law, if subsidy and (where applicable) injury are found to exist, relief is mandatory.

Section 337

Section 337 of the Tariff Act of 1930[14] provides that, if a U.S. industry is injured (or there is a restraint or monopolization of trade in the United States) by reason of unfair acts in the importation of articles into the United States, an order must be issued requiring the exporters and

---

12. 19 U.S.C. §§ 1673 (1988).

13. 19 U.S.C. § 1303, §§ 1671a-1671h (1988).
14. 19 U.S.C. § 1337 (1988).

importers to cease the unfair acts or, if necessary, excluding imports of the offending articles from all sources. This law, usually referred to simply as section 337, is applicable to unfair competition of all kinds not covered in other import relief laws, but is most commonly used in cases involving patent or trademark infringement. Relief is mandatory unless the president disapproves the ITC decision, which seldom happens.

The Omnibus Trade and Competitiveness Act eliminated the requirement to show economic injury in cases involving intellectual property rights (infringement of patents, trademarks, and copyrights). The act affects most section 337 cases and makes it significantly easier for U.S. companies to obtain relief under this statute. The injury requirement had caused some cases to be lost by the U.S. industry, and undoubtedly caused some companies to postpone filing section 337 complaints until imports of the offending articles reached a significant volume. The theory behind the change was that American intellectual property rights needed better protection, and that infringement of those rights constituted injury in and of itself.

Section 406

Section 406 of the Trade Act of 1974,[15] usually referred to simply as section 406, is similar to section 201. It provides for import relief if a U.S. industry is suffering material injury by reason of rapidly increasing imports from a Communist country. Relief is discretionary.

Section 232

Section 232 of the Trade Expansion Act of 1962,[16] usually referred to simply as section 232, provides for relief from imports threatening to impair U.S. national security. It has been used very rarely. Relief is discretionary.

■ Specific Import Restrictions

As of 1994, there were a number of industry-specific, quantitative limitations on imports of agricultural products, textiles, automobiles, and steel. Imports of dairy and certain other agricultural products are restricted in order to protect federal support programs.

■ The Buy American Act

Under the Buy American Act,[17] federal agencies, in their procurement of supplies and equipment, must give a preference to products made in the United States unless their price is a certain percentage higher than the price of the equivalent foreign product. Products are deemed to be American made, and therefore eligible for the preference, if they are manufactured in the United States and at least 50% of the components are American made.

As noted earlier in this chapter, preferences to domestic industry in procurement by governments are a common form of nontariff barrier to imports that was addressed in one of the GATT MFN codes. Pursuant to that code (the Agreement on Government Procurement), many U.S. agencies have joined foreign agencies in eliminating this preference. However, defense-related articles are not subject to the agreement and hence still receive the Buy American Act preference.

■ Laws Affecting Exports

The law known as section 301 is intended to facilitate exports. The Export Administration Act and the Arms Export Control Act are intended to control exports.

Section 301

Section 301 of the Trade Act of 1974[18] authorizes the president to investigate alleged unfair practices of foreign governments that impede U.S. exports of both goods and services. If the president finds that the practice is unfair, and if it is not withdrawn, he may take any action within his power that he deems appropriate. Section 301 has been used with growing aggressiveness by the U.S. government.

In the Omnibus Trade and Competitiveness Act of 1988, Congress made several changes to force even greater use of this trade weapon. First, it created a program known as *Super 301*. This program requires that a list be drawn up of the foreign governments whose practices pose the most significant barriers to U.S. exports, and that section 301 investigations be commenced immediately with respect to these practices. In 1989, the U.S. Trade Representative placed Japan, Brazil, and India on

---

15. 19 U.S.C. § 2436 (1988).
16. 19 U.S.C. § 1862 (1988).

17. 41 U.S.C. §§ 10a-10d (1982 & Supp. 1987).
18. 19 U.S.C. § 2411 (1988).

this list. Negotiations with all three nations resulted in the removal of significant trade barriers. The Structural Impediments Initiative with Japan, noted earlier in this chapter, was undertaken pursuant to Super 301 authority. Super 301 expired in 1990 but was renewed in 1994.

The Omnibus Trade and Competitiveness Act also made several other significant changes: (1) It transferred the decision-making authority under section 301 from the president to the U.S. Trade Representative; (2) it made U.S. action mandatory with respect to foreign government practices that violate trade agreements with the United States, with some specific exceptions (in particular, where action would have an adverse impact on the U.S. economy that substantially outweighed any benefits); (3) it imposed new time limits for action; and (4) it specified that section 301 applies to export targeting, denial of specified worker rights, and toleration of systematic anticompetitive activities by private firms.

The Semiconductor Dispute with Japan   U.S. semiconductor manufacturers petitioned the government under section 301 for relief from alleged unfair competition by Japanese manufacturers. The petition alleged that Japanese companies were dumping their products at unfairly low prices, not only in the U.S. market but also in other countries. It further alleged that access to the Japanese market by U.S. firms was severely limited. In 1986, an agreement was reached between the U.S. and Japanese governments in an effort to resolve the issues raised in the petition.

Under terms of the agreement, the government of Japan promised that Japanese producers would not dump semiconductors either in the U.S. market or in third-country markets. The United States claimed that there was also an understanding concerning increased U.S. access to the Japanese market for semiconductors, but this was disputed by the Japanese government. The agreement was unusual in that it purported to affect behavior in third countries, which were not party to the agreement.

In 1988, President Reagan determined that Japan had not fully complied with any aspect of the agreement. Under the authority of section 301, he ordered retaliation in the form of increased U.S. tariffs on certain products imported from Japan. This tariff increase affected U.S. companies that were not involved in the original dispute. It was subsequently eliminated for some products, after President Reagan determined that Japan was complying with some aspects of the agreement.

The agreement with Japan was helpful in some ways to the U.S. semiconductor industry, which is perceived as vital to the U.S. economy. At the same time, it arguably hurt the U.S. computer industry by raising the prices of semiconductors used in computer manufacture.

Definition of Restriction on Trade   A country can limit exports by indirect means. It is not always clear what is a disguised restraint on trade, as is demonstrated in the following presidential decision under section 301.

■   **A Case in Point:**   **Summary**

**Case 3.3
PRESIDENTIAL DECISION
UNDER SECTION 301:
LIVESTOCK**
Statement by the President,
December 24, 1987.

FACTS   In 1987, the United States requested that the GATT Committee on Technical Barriers to Trade investigate the European "Council Directive Prohibiting the Use in Livestock Farming of Certain Substances Having a Hormonal Action." The investigation found, due to European Community (EC) insistence and against scientific evidence, that meat produced from animals treated with hormones was dangerous to human health.

ISSUE PRESENTED   Was a directive of the European Community banning the importation of meat produced from animals treated with hormones a disguised restriction on trade?

DECISION   President Reagan determined that the directive restricted United States commerce. He reasoned, however, that an increase in customs duties should be postponed so long as the EC allowed member states to import U.S. meat products. Until the directive was enforced, there was no reason to raise EC customs duties.

RESULT The directive was a disguised restriction on international trade. However, the president postponed an increase in EC customs duties because the EC member states were still allowed by the EC to import U.S. meat products.

COMMENTS Because the directive constituted a disguised restriction on international trade, in violation of the GATT, the president turned to the GATT Committee for assistance rather than the ITC.

The Export Administration Act

The Export Administration Act of 1979[19] is the primary restriction on U.S. exports. It authorizes the secretary of commerce to prohibit exports where necessary to protect national security, carry out U.S. foreign policy, enforce U.S. nuclear nonproliferation policy, and prevent the export of goods that are in short supply. Some controls are imposed unilaterally by the United States. Others are imposed jointly with U.S. allies on exports to Communist countries. These are agreed upon and administered through an informal arrangement known as CoCom.

The Act's most significant restrictions are those that control high technology and its products. The explosion of high-technology industries has resulted in a radical increase in the volume of U.S. exports that are controlled under this law. This restriction has had serious adverse consequences for U.S. exporters competing for business abroad.

The Omnibus Trade and Competitiveness Act of 1988, reflecting the importance attached to the trade deficit and the need to promote U.S. exports, removed many controls on exports, particularly to friendly countries. The United States and its allies are further reducing controls on exports to Eastern Europe and the former Soviet Union in the light of the reduced military threat now posed by those countries.

Export Licenses The export controls are enforced by a system of export licenses. Certain categories of commodities and technical data may not be exported without an export license from the Commerce Department's Bureau of Export Administration. The bureau reviews all applications and determines whether to issue licenses. Its decision in each case is based on a number of factors, including the nature of the item to be exported, the country to which it is to be shipped, the foreign consignee, and the use to which it will be put. The restrictions vary with all of these factors.

Managers should be aware of these controls when they plan export transactions and negotiate with foreign buyers. Moreover, they must ensure that the rules are followed. The rules are complex and easily misunderstood, and the civil and criminal penalties for violations are severe.

Three points are often overlooked by exporters. First, U.S. restrictions apply not only to exports of goods, but also to exports of technology (referred to as technical data). Second, U.S. restrictions apply not only to exports from the United States, but also to many reexports of U.S.-origin goods and technology to third countries by other countries. The restrictions also apply to exports from other countries of certain foreign-made articles that are direct products of U.S. technology. Third, the transfer of technical data to a foreign citizen in the United States is generally considered to be an export, which means that an export license is required. Such transfers include verbal exchanges of technology on U.S. soil and visits by foreign nationals to U.S. plants.

The Arms Export Control Act

The Arms Export Control Act[20] authorizes the secretary of state to prohibit exports of munitions and munitions technology from the United States. The act is administered by the Office of Munitions Control of the State Department, which issues the International Traffic in Arms Regulations (ITARs) and operates a licensing system similar to that of the Commerce Department, based on the United States Munitions List.[21] The Commerce and State Departments both issue advisory opinions to exporters concerning the applicability of export controls to specific transactions.

---

19. 50 U.S.C. App. § 2401 *et seq.* (1982 & Supp. 1987).

20. 22 U.S.C. § 2751-2796 (1988).
21. 22 C.F.R. Part 121 (1990).

■ The Foreign Corrupt Practices Act

Following the discovery that more than 400 American corporations had made bribes or questionable payments abroad, the Foreign Corrupt Practices Act (FCPA)[22] was passed in 1977 as an amendment to the Securities Exchange Act of 1934 (the 1934 Act). The bribes in question were often given to high-ranking foreign officials to secure contracts with the foreign government. Bribes were also given to low-ranking officials to expedite the granting of routine requests such as applications for permission to import or export.

Prohibited Payments

The FCPA prohibits any payment by a company, its employees, or its agents directly or indirectly to a foreign government official or a foreign political party for the purpose of improperly influencing government decisions in order to obtain business abroad, if the payment is made or furthered by means of an instrumentality of U.S. commerce such as the U.S. Mail. The statute is violated even if the bribe is only offered but never paid. It is also violated if the payment is made to a private company with the knowledge that it will be funneled to the government.

An exception is made for payments to low-ranking officials who merely expedite the nondiscretionary granting of a permit or license. However, if any of the allegedly nondiscretionary tasks paid for are in fact discretionary, the American company will be in violation of the FCPA. A second exception is made for payments to foreign businesses, as long as they are not acting as conduits for the money to pass to the foreign government.

A troublesome clause of the FCPA prohibited payments to third persons (such as local agents) with "reason to know" that the payment would be passed on to a government official or political party. This standard was considered by many to be unacceptably vague for a criminal statute. The Omnibus Trade Act amended this clause to prohibit such payments only when they are made with actual knowledge or a willful disregard of the fact that they will be used in violation of the law.

Directors, officers, employees, or agents of the corporation who violate this portion of the FCPA are subject to a $10,000 fine and up to five years in prison; the corporation can be fined up to $1,000,000. The FCPA is administered by both the Department of Justice and the Securities and Exchange Commission.

---

22. 15 U.S.C. §§ 78a-78LLL (1988).

Record-Keeping Requirements

The record-keeping requirements of the FCPA apply to all public companies that file periodic reports with the Securities and Exchange Commission under the 1934 Act. A purely domestic public company that is not engaged in foreign trade must still comply with the FCPA record-keeping requirements.

The FCPA requires each corporation to keep records that accurately reflect the dispositions of the company's assets, and to implement internal controls to ensure that the corporation's transactions are completed as authorized by management. Periodic reports must be filed.

Failure to maintain the appropriate records and procedures is a violation, whether or not there is payment of a bribe. This portion of the FCPA was designed to prevent companies from developing a slush fund and then accounting for questionable payments as legitimate business expenses. The record-keeping provisions of the FCPA do not contain any specific penalties. Violations are punished in accordance with the basic criminal and civil sanctions under the 1934 Act, discussed in chapter 15.

Mergers

Persons working in mergers and acquisitions must pay special attention to the FCPA. All target companies need to be investigated to determine if they are in compliance with the FCPA, particularly those that conduct business abroad or have a foreign subsidiary.

 Ethical Consideration

The FCPA creates an ethical dilemma for the corporation that seeks to engage in commerce in a country where graft is a prerequisite to getting business accomplished. Many in the business community believe it will be difficult to impose American business values in other countries. What should a manager do?

Prosecution

For the most part, prosecutions under the prohibited payments provisions have been few. In one case, Young and

Rubicam, a prominent New York advertising agency, was indicted under the FCPA and the Racketeer Influenced and Corrupt Organizations Act (RICO). (RICO is discussed further in chapter 15.) The government alleged that Young and Rubicam made payments to Jamaican government officials in order to acquire the lucrative Jamaican tourist advertising campaign. Young and Rubicam pled guilty to one count of conspiracy and agreed to pay a $500,000 fine to settle charges of encouraging bribes to foreign officials. All other charges under the FCPA and RICO were dropped.

In June 1994 Lockheed Corp. and two of its officers were indicted under the FCPA for allegedly paying money to a member of the Egyptian parliament who had previously been a consultant for Lockheed. Even after becoming a member of parliament, and thereby a "foreign official" under the act, the consultant allegedly continued to help Lockheed in Egypt with the sale of aircraft to the Egyptian government. To keep the arrangement secret, Lockheed allegedly paid commissions to a company the consultant's husband controlled.[23]

International Initiatives

American companies have complained that the FCPA puts them at a competitive disadvantage compared with foreign companies from countries which permit the payment of bribes. Relief may be in sight due to the backlash in response to the political corruption scandals in Europe, Japan, and the former Soviet Union in the early 1990s. In June 1994, the Council of the OECD (which consists of 25 member states from Europe, Australia, Canada, Japan, Mexico, and the United States) adopted a recommendation that member states take "concrete and meaningful steps" to deter and combat bribery of foreign officials.[24] A similar resolution was adopted at about the same time by the 32 ministers of justice of the Council of Europe. The Organization of American States (OAS) also created a working group to consider model legislation against "foreign aspects of corruption."[25]

---

23. Joseph P. Griffin, "Initiatives Abroad Against Foreign Bribery Raise Prospect of Putting U.S. Firms, Foreign Rivals on Level Playing Field," *BNA's Corporate Counsel Weekly,* August 10, 1994, 8.
24. *Ibid.*
25. *Ibid.*

■ Deferral of Corporate Income Tax

Under the rules of the GATT, exported goods can legally be exempted from sales taxes or value-added taxes. However, exporters may not be exempted from income taxes. Exemptions from corporate income taxes based on export performance are considered to be illegal export subsidies.

Some countries rely heavily on sales or value-added taxes. Exporters in those countries benefit from exemptions from such taxes for exported goods. The United States relies more on corporate income taxes, which are not exempt. Consequently U.S. exporters are at a disadvantage.

The U.S. solution to this was to enact legislation authorizing domestic international sales corporations (DISCs). The law allowed deferral of federal income tax liability on a portion of the export earnings of any subsidiary company that met the criteria for a DISC. However, this benefit was found to be inconsistent with GATT rules.

The U.S. government retained the DISC provisions for small businesses. For other companies, it enacted legislation authorizing the establishment of foreign sales corporations (FSCs). This law exempts from taxation a portion of the export income of any company that meets the criteria for an FSC. To be considered an FSC, a company must conduct a specified amount of its economic activities outside the United States; its management must be located outside the United States; and arm's-length pricing rules must be adhered to along with other requirements. In fact, these criteria are less onerous than they appear. It is relatively simple to set up an FSC in order to handle a company's export sales. Some small companies may elect to be either a DISC or an FSC.

■ Export Trading Companies

Before 1982, there were complaints that efforts by U.S. companies to compete abroad by pooling their resources were hindered by the U.S. antitrust laws. The Export Trading Company Act of 1982[26] sought to address these concerns.

Under this law, the Department of Commerce may certify an export trading company formed by two or more independent companies exclusively for export purposes. If a certificate is issued (with the concurrence of

---

26. 15 U.S.C. §§ 4001 *et seq.* (1988).

the Department of Justice), the participants in the export trading company are protected from private treble damage actions and government criminal and civil suits under federal and state antitrust laws for the export activities specified in the certificate. However, the law does not protect them from private antitrust actions for actual damages. Certification is authorized for export activities that do not restrain competition in the United States and do not constitute unfair competition in the U.S. export trade.

Bank Participation

In addition to the antitrust provisions, the act encourages the formation of export trading companies by allowing banking organizations to participate in the formation of such companies. This is an exception to the general rule against the participation of banks in commercial activities. The intention is to make the banks' resources available to U.S. exporters.

The act also permits the Export-Import Bank of the United States (discussed below) to guarantee loans to export trading companies and other exporters. This provision, however, applies only to short-term loans, generally with a term of 12 months or less. The intention is to make available to exporters loans that would not otherwise be available.

■ The Export-Import Bank

The Export-Import Bank of the United States (Eximbank) was created more than 50 years ago to provide financing for the purchaser of U.S. exports. Eximbank is the U.S. government's response to foreign governments' export subsidies; by offering financing at below-market interest rates, Eximbank allows U.S. exporters to compete with foreign companies.

Major Programs

The major programs of Eximbank have traditionally been direct long-term loans at fixed interest rates to foreign buyers, and financial guarantees. Long-term loans or guarantees are generally reserved for exports of turnkey projects such as manufacturing, electric power, and petrochemical plants. Short-term and medium-term bank guarantees and short-term and medium-term export credit insurance are also provided. Other programs have been introduced over the years, including the I-Match Program, which authorized Eximbank to make interest-subsidy payments to private lenders when necessary to

compete with foreign subsidized financing. Another program is the Tied Aid Credit War Chest, which authorized $300 million to be used to subsidize exports and fight mixed credit financing by foreign governments. This program is part of the Treasury Department's effort to negotiate a comprehensive agreement among the industrialized countries to limit the practice of mixing foreign aid with export credit, which distorts trade.

■ The President's Power to Restrict Trade

Over the years, Congress has authorized the president to regulate or restrict trade and other economic activity when necessary to protect the U.S. national security, foreign policy, or economy. In 1917, Congress passed the Trading With The Enemy Act, which prohibited trade with enemies during time of war. The scope of the authority granted to the president under this law was expanded gradually to include the restriction of domestic and international commercial transactions in response to declared states of emergency.

Congress grew impatient with the practice of presidents in invoking the state of emergency declared during the Korean War to control economic transactions long after the war had ended. Congress therefore redefined the president's economic powers in the International Emergency Economic Powers Act, passed in 1977.[27] This law authorizes the president to restrict trade and other commercial transactions only when a national emergency has been declared in response to an "unusual and extraordinary threat, which has its source in whole or substantial part outside the United States, to the national security, foreign policy or economy of the United States." Successive presidents have imposed total or partial economic embargoes on China (now withdrawn), North Korea, Vietnam (now withdrawn), Cambodia, Cuba, and more recently, on Iran, Libya, and Nicaragua (the last now withdrawn).

The economic sanctions imposed under these laws are administered by the Office of Foreign Assets Control in the Department of the Treasury, which issues appropriate regulations. To varying degrees, the regulations apply not only to transactions in the United States, but also to transactions by foreign affiliates of U.S. companies and to transactions abroad involving U.S. property.

---

27. 50 U.S.C. §§ 1701 *et seq.* (1982 & Supp. 1987).

The application of the regulations to foreign operations of U.S. companies has caused considerable difficulty, particularly for companies subjected to conflicting requirements imposed by foreign governments on their foreign affiliates. U.S. firms operating internationally must be aware of the potential application of these restrictions to all of their operations anywhere in the world, as is demonstrated in the following case.

■ **A Case in Point:** **In the Language of the Court**

Case 3.4
DRESSER INDUSTRIES, INC.
v. BALDRIDGE
United States District Court for
the District of Columbia
549 F.Supp. 108 (D.D.C. 1982).

FACTS In response to the imposition of martial law in Poland in 1982, President Reagan prohibited exports of certain equipment to the Soviet Union that could be used in building a gas pipeline between the Soviet Union and Western Europe. This economic sanction was intended to pressure the Soviet Union into permitting Poland to lift its martial law. The United States failed to convince its European allies to join in the economic sanction. In an attempt to prevent European companies from exporting equipment to the Soviet Union for the pipeline, President Reagan ordered that the U.S. prohibition on exports to the pipeline be extended to all persons subject to U.S. jurisdiction.

Consequently, the U.S. Department of Commerce, in its order prohibiting exports of certain equipment to the Soviet Union, applied the prohibition not only to companies in the United States, but also to foreign subsidiaries of U.S. companies. In addition, it prohibited the export from any country by any company (regardless of whether U.S.-owned) of equipment manufactured from technology obtained from the United States. Subsequently, the Department of Commerce issued orders imposing sanctions against a number of European companies for violation of its order. These sanctions denied the companies all U.S. export privileges.

European governments reacted angrily, claiming that this extraterritorial application of U.S. export controls violated their sovereignty and was contrary to international law. The government of Great Britain acted to prohibit British companies from complying with the U.S. order. The French government, invoking its law, ordered the French subsidiaries to meet their contractual obligations by exporting equipment to the Soviet Union for the pipeline.

Dresser (France), S.A., and its U.S. parent, Dresser Industries, Inc., sought to enjoin the sanctions imposed on Dresser (France) by the U.S. Department of Commerce.

ISSUE PRESENTED Could a foreign subsidiary of a U.S. company obtain a court injunction against sanctions imposed for violation of U.S. export regulations?

OPINION GREEN, J., writing for the Federal District Court:

. . . .

Most acutely evident to all those involved in this case is the potential for profound harm that could injure the United States should injunctive relief issue. The regulations that lie at the heart of this dispute, which prohibit the export of certain goods and technology to the Soviet Union, particularly those goods sought for the construction of the gas pipeline between that

Case *3.4* continued on following page

*Case **3.4** continued*

country and Western Europe, were promulgated as part of a major foreign policy exercise. The purpose of this foreign policy action was to effectuate the response of the United States to certain events which have transpired over the past year in Poland, creating a political situation in that country which this country's leadership has declared unacceptable and which has shown no substantial sign of reversal to previous conditions. Accordingly, the United States has a grave interest in its ability to enforce these regulations which are, in its view, essential to the accomplishment of important foreign policy objectives. As the relief plaintiff seeks would only serve to benefit them and those doing business with them, to the potentially serious detriment of the United States, it cannot be doubted that the public interest does not lie with a grant of the injunction requested by plaintiffs.

. . . .

RESULT   The Federal District Court denied the request for an injunction. The court found that there was still a possibility of an administrative resolution of the dispute and that the plaintiffs had therefore not shown that Dresser (France) would suffer irreparable harm if an injunction were not granted. In addition, such an injunction could potentially harm U.S. foreign policy objectives and would therefore not be in the public interest.

COMMENTS   Like other U.S. government attempts to apply its export controls to foreign subsidiaries of U.S. companies, this effort was unsuccessful, even though the sanctions were upheld in the court. Companies in Great Britain and France had no choice but to follow the orders of their government, despite the U.S. sanctions.

Questions
1. What type of harm would come to the U.S. if Dresser (France) had honored its contractual obligations?
2. Should the U.S. be able to dictate the trade practices of other countries?

■ The European Community

The European Community (EC) is, among other things, a customs union or *common market*. This means that there are no tariffs on trade among its member states, and the member states apply a single set of tariffs (called the common customs tariff) on goods imported from outside the EC. The 12 members of the EC are Belgium, Denmark, France, Germany, Greece, Ireland, Italy, Luxembourg, the Netherlands, Portugal, Spain, and the United Kingdom. Founded with the intention of forming a single internal market free of all barriers to trade among the member states, it has embarked on an ambitious program to achieve complete economic, monetary, and eventually political union.

In furtherance of these goals, the member states have ceded a certain amount of sovereignty to the EC. For instance, the EC negotiates international trade agreements on behalf of the member states. This includes GATT negotiations. The EC has the exclusive power to take action against dumping in the Community by companies in nonmember countries. Agriculture is centrally coordinated through the Common Agricultural Policy, which supports prices of agricultural products and promotes the modernization of agriculture throughout the Community. EC competition law, based on U.S. antitrust principles, has been used by the Community to prevent companies from engaging in private restraints of trade among the member states.

The European Economic Community (EEC) was established in 1957 by the Treaty of Rome.[28] The EEC,

---

28. Treaty establishing the European Economic Community, March 25, 1957 (EEC Treaty), 298 U.N.T.S. 11.

the European Coal and Steel Community (established in 1951), and the European Atomic Energy Commission (Euratom, established in 1957) are three separate legal entities, but they are served by one set of institutions and are collectively referred to as the European Community (EC). The Treaty of Rome created the four institutions that have responsibility for governing the EC: (1) the European Commission; (2) the Council of Ministers; (3) the European Parliament; and (4) the European Court of Justice.

The European Commission

The European Commission is the executive branch of the EC. It is composed of 17 individuals appointed by the governments of the member states. Each commissioner is in charge of one or more of the commission's 22 subdivisions, called directorates general. Commissioners are expected to act independently of their national governments. With a staff of approximately 10,000 civil servants, the commission initiates much of the Community legislation and, in areas in which authority has been delegated to it by the Council of Ministers or the Treaty of Rome, adopts its own legislation. The commission is charged with "the proper functioning and development of the common market."[29] To this end it formulates recommendations, addresses opinions to members, and may bring member states before the European Court of Justice for failure to carry out their obligations under the Treaty of Rome. The commission also represents the EC in international trade negotiations.

The Council of Ministers

The Council of Ministers is the legislative body of the EC. It enacts Community legislation based on proposals referred to it by the commission. The members of the council are appointed by the governments of the member states, and they represent the interests of their respective states.

At one time, the most important decisions required a unanimous vote of the council. However, since the enactment of the Single European Act in 1987 (discussed below), most measures that will promote the establishment of a single internal market need only a qualified majority (54 of 76 votes). Each member state has a certain number of votes, generally in proportion to its population.

EC legislation may be in the form of regulations, which are directly applicable in the Community and are

---

29. EEC Treaty, Art. 155.

enforced by the commission. Legislation may also take two other forms. One is the directive, which is a law directing member states to enact certain laws or regulations. Directives are binding with respect to the results to be achieved, but must be implemented by enactment of national laws in the member states. The third form of legislation is the decision, which is an order directed at a specific person or member state.

The European Parliament

Despite its name, the parliament is not the legislative body. In fact, it acts primarily as a consultative body. The members of the European Parliament are elected directly by the citizens of the member states (it is the only community body directly elected), generally in proportion to the population of each state. The parliament has the power to dismiss the commission and to reject the commission's annual budget.

The parliament's role has become more important with the passage of the Single European Act. The parliament must now be consulted twice on each legislative proposal: It first considers the proposed law at the committee level, and then expresses its opinion by a vote in plenary session. It can reject the proposal, in which case the law can be enacted only by a unanimous council vote. It can also amend commission proposals, whereupon, if the commission supports the amendment, it can be defeated only by a unanimous council vote.

The European Court of Justice

The European Court of Justice (ECJ) is the judicial branch of the EC. Its role is to interpret the treaties establishing the EC. The ECJ has been a major force in affirming the powers of the Community institutions and therefore in the development of the single EC market. (A subsidiary court, the Tribunal of First Instance, was established in late 1988 pursuant to the Single European Act. Its function is to reduce the ECJ's caseload.) In addition to hearing and deciding adversarial proceedings, the ECJ may make *interlocutory* or interim rulings on legal issues raised by national courts. It may also advise other institutions of the EC.

Private persons and companies may bring cases in the ECJ to annul EC measures if they can demonstrate individual harm from such measures. Similarly, they may challenge the commission's or the council's failure to act. Either the commission or a member state may bring infringement proceedings against a member state for violation of its treaty obligation. Although private litigants may not bring infringement proceedings against member states, they may bring an equivalent action in a national court. The national court, in turn, may refer to the ECJ questions that involve interpretations of the EC treaty, statutes adopted by the council, or acts of EC institutions. National courts from which no appeal may be taken are required to refer such questions to the ECJ. ECJ rulings on referred questions are binding on the court from which they were received.

The following case provides an example of how the ECJ interprets the EC treaty and conforms national actions to it.

■ **A Case in Point:**   **Summary**

Case 3.4
DONCKERWOLCKE v.
PROCUREUR
European Court of Justice
Case 41/76 (1976) ECR 1921.

FACTS   Two Belgian merchants imported into France textile products that had originated in Syria and Lebanon. The textiles had cleared customs in Belgium and been sold in Belgium. Under French customs regulations, the merchants were required to complete a form upon entering into France indicating the origins of the products. The merchants stated the country of origin as Belgium.

The merchants were subsequently prosecuted for violating French customs rules. They received suspended prison sentences and were fined an amount equal to three times the value of the goods. The French court referred the case to the European Court of Justice on appeal.

ISSUE PRESENTED   Were the monitoring measures in question—the obligation to declare the origin of the imported goods and to obtain an import license—compatible with the EC treaty?

SUMMARY OF OPINION   The Court of Justice reversed the importers' sentence on the grounds that it was not reasonably related to the crime. The decision was based on article 115 of the EC treaty. Under that article, limitations may only be placed on the free movement within the Community of goods enjoying the right to free circulation by virtue of measures of commercial policy adopted by the importing Member State in accordance with the EC treaty. Because the Community has full responsibility for matters of commercial policy as stated in article 113(1), actions relating to commercial policy taken on a national level are only permissible if authorized by the Community.

The court stated that within this context, Member States may require from an importer a certificate declaring the actual origin of the goods in question even when the goods are put into free circulation in another Member State. Knowledge of the origin of the goods is necessary for both states to determine the scope of the commercial policy measure that they may adopt pursuant to the treaty. However, Member States may only require from the importer an indication of the origin of the goods in so far as he may reasonably be expected to know it.

The court concluded that the fact that the importer did not comply with the obligation to declare the real origin of the goods should not give rise to the application of penalties disproportionate to the nature of the violation. Therefore, the seizure of the goods or a penalty based on the value of the goods would be incompatible with the provisions of the treaty and considered an obstacle to the free movement of goods. The requirement of an import license for the introduction into a Member State of goods put into free circulation in another Member State is incompatible with the EC treaty unless authorized by the Commission in accordance with article 115.

RESULT   The importers' sentence was set aside. The French government had acted in violation of the EC treaty.

COMMENTS   Articles 9 and 10 of the treaty provide that once an imported good has cleared customs in one Member State, it may circulate freely within the Community. However, article 115 permits Member States, subject to Commission approval, to impose restrictions on intra-Community trade of goods originating in third countries. These restrictions apply even if the third-country good has cleared customs in another Member State. Despite the fact that article 115 was intended as an emergency safeguard to prevent circumvention of national quotas, a few Member States have frequently relied on it, and national quotas have persisted for many years.

The Single European Act and 1992

The goal of the Single European Act (SEA) was to remove all barriers to trade among member states by the end of 1992. In fact, much of the implementing legislation necessary for a true single market was enacted before that date. The measures included the elimination of (1) physical barriers to trade (such as immigration and customs controls), (2) technical barriers (that is, national standards and requirements on the provision of goods and services, such as product standards and professional qualifications), and (3) fiscal barriers (such as differing national tax structures). These barriers made it difficult to transfer goods, services, capital, or persons from one member state to another.

Many laws have been enacted in the form of directives ordering member states to harmonize their laws so that companies and individuals can operate on the basis of a single standard or rule. Others have been enacted in order to facilitate mergers and other forms of economic cooperation across member state lines.

The creation of the single EC market will have profound effects on U.S. businesses. It will facilitate the formation of larger European companies with a larger home market and will also facilitate large-scale research and development in Europe. The net result will be—indeed, the primary objective of the EC is—to make European companies more competitive in Europe and in world markets.

At the same time, the single market will create a larger market for American goods and will make the EC a more attractive place in which to invest. For those willing and able to take advantage of the benefits, the EC presents an exciting opportunity.

The Maastricht Treaty on European Union

The Maastricht Treaty on European Union (TEU)[30] is named after the Dutch city in which it was signed. It entered into force on November 1, 1993.

The treaty provides for economic and monetary union as well as political union. The economic provisions resulting from the treaty will commit the member states to converge their economic and monetary policies. The convergence criteria call for the 12 community nations to harmonize their budget deficits, inflation levels, public-sector debt, and other economic indicators at specific target levels.

A European Monetary Institute was to be created in 1994 to coordinate the activities of the central banks and to make recommendations on general monetary policy. The second stage in monetary coordination was also scheduled to begin in 1994. In this stage, member states without central banks had to create them and total monetary union was hoped for by the end of 1994. The European monetary crisis, discussed in the "Economic Perspective" in this chapter, prevented this from occurring.

In 1996, the European Council will determine whether to start the third stage, in which a European System of Central Banks (ESCB) would be created, with a European Central Bank (ECB) at its core. The final stage, the implementation of a single European currency, is set to take place in 1999.

The European Council has allowed Britain to opt out of the monetary control exercised by the European Central Bank and the single currency system for as long

---

30. Treaty on European Union, O.J.C. 224/1 (August 31, 1992).

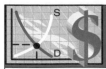

Economic Perspective
The European Currency Crisis

The currency systems of Western Europe were thrown into disarray in 1992, as the result of an underlying crisis afflicting the economies of Europe. The crisis was originally rooted in the high cost of unification of West Germany and East Germany. Reunification drove up German interest rates at a time when other European countries needed lower rates to help them out of the economic slump that had followed the rapid growth in the 1980s. Since 1990, unemployment rates had been on the rise and investment had been down throughout most of Europe.

The European response to this economic situation was complicated by the fact that the major currencies were linked to one another. Under this system, they were allowed to fluctuate only within narrow margins of their basic value, as expressed in European Currency Units, or ECUs. As a result, as German interest rates began drawing investors and increasing the Deutschmark's value, other governments had to bolster their own

currencies to keep them within the permitted margins of the so-called exchange rate mechanism. They did this by raising their own interest rates to make their currencies more competitive in the global money markets. This approach, however, had the unfortunate side effect of hampering domestic growth by limiting new investment. For example, although French inflation was low, high interest rates began driving the French economy into a slump. Britain, which had succeeded in lowering inflation, found that its high interest rates prevented economic growth. Eventually, the political pressure created by high interest rates was sufficient to cause the British government to withdraw from the EC monetary system entirely.

In July 1993, speculators decided that France could no longer defend its currency against Germany's determination to keep its interest rates high. Speculators launched an attack on the French franc, and the European mon-

etary system was once again threatened. Investors rushed to buy gold, pushing prices to new heights. Currency speculators pursued a strategy to force a devaluation of the franc, which would result in enormous profits.

In response, the European Community's finance ministers and central bank chiefs agreed to let their currencies rise as much as 15%. In effect, the decision was to let the markets decide whether the franc and other currencies should be devalued against the mark without any formal decisions by the governments involved.

The European monetary system, created in 1979 to provide for broadly stable rates, had originally been viewed as the forerunner to a single European currency, a development that could have come as early as 1997. Community officials are now estimating that a single European currency will not become possible until, at the earliest, 1999.

---

as it desires. Britain will not be prevented from joining at a later date.

The political component of the TEU will expand the Community sphere to include the following areas: immigration, tourism, health, education, consumer protection, and culture. European political cooperation will also be expanded. The TEU's Protocol on Social Policy enables 11 of the member states to adopt social legislation by a qualified majority vote. Britain chose to opt out of this provision as well.

The TEU represents a significant step toward political and economic integration. It adopted the concept of a European Union which no longer consists of a European Economic Community but rather a European Community.

This concept of integration is furthered by the TEU's new provision on European citizenship, including the right to travel freely within the territory of the European Union.

The Responsible Manager
Engaging in International Trade

It is important to plan in advance for import and export operations. There are many restrictions and other important rules that may affect the operation. Failure to plan can lead to inadvertent violations of law. A common mistake by exporters is to provide technology to foreign persons without obtaining the prerequisite export licenses. Another is to assign an incorrect value to imported goods for customs purposes. Lack of planning can also cause the company to miss such benefits as duty-free treatment under the North American Free Trade Agreement and other international agreements.

Managers need to take account of the rapid changes occurring in world trade. Barriers to trade with Eastern European countries have been removed. Significant reduction of barriers to trade with other countries are being negotiated. New markets and new opportunities are arising with great speed. At the same time, these changes carry new risks for managers. They will cause increased competition not only overseas, but also in the United States. Government regulation of trade will change, but not as rapidly as the world is changing. Managers should keep abreast of regulatory changes and should also be aware of gaps between the new realities of world trade and the government's efforts to regulate.

Inside Story

Passage of NAFTA

An odd alliance formed between organized labor, Ross Perot (independent presidential candidate in 1992), and Pat Buchanan (Republican right-wing presidential candidate in 1992 who lost the Republican nomination to George Bush) to attempt to derail the North American Free Trade Agreement. Organized labor, asserting that NAFTA would steal U.S. jobs and slash wages, lambasted President Clinton for supporting the agreement. Union members swarmed over Capitol Hill, waving signs depicting an oversized monkey labeled "NAFTA" sitting on the shoulders of a frowning worker in a hard hat. President Clinton accused labor leaders of using "musclebound" and "roughshod" tactics to defeat the accord.

The proponents of the pact were also strange bedfellows: Bill Clinton and former presidents George Bush, Ronald Reagan, and Jimmy Carter. The Republicans in Congress, who had opposed the Clinton budget a month before, supported the pact. The Democrats in Congress, however, were mostly opposed.

The debate over NAFTA became far removed from the underlying facts. Labor and environmental issues took a back seat to power and ambition. The debate was filled with rhetoric and one liners, such as Ross Perot's reference to the potential loss of American jobs as one "giant sucking sound."

Despite the cries of betrayal from the unions and Ross Perot's threats that "we'll remember in November," it appears that the electorate soon forgot the NAFTA vote. Following the passage of the agreement, one of its biggest foes put it behind him. The A.F.L.-C.I.O.'s president, Lane Kirkwood, agreed to end his bitter dispute with President Clinton over the pact shortly after the vote. The two men subsequently began to work together on health care reform.

Others, however, were not so quick to forget. Ron Carey, president of the International Brotherhood of Teamsters, made it clear that his union intended to follow through on the warnings of voter retaliation it had given to the president and members of Congress favoring the accord.

The impact of NAFTA on the environment was also a widely disputed topic. Although the U.S. Environmental Protection Agency believed the pact would improve Mexico's environment, many environmental activists believed the trade pact would weaken U.S. environmental laws. Critics claimed that the agreement would cause U.S. companies to flee south to evade tough U.S. enforcement of environmental laws.

Environmentalists were, however, divided over NAFTA. Grassroots organizations such as Friends of the Earth said that NAFTA would create a "polluters' paradise" in Mexico. However, seven major environmental groups endorsed NAFTA after receiving a commitment from the Clinton administration that it would negotiate side deals to settle any remaining environmental disputes. Among those groups claiming that the agreement would all but guarantee a cleaner hemi-

Inside Story continued on following page

Inside Story, continued

sphere were the National Wildlife Federation, World Wildlife Fund, Nature Conservancy, Audubon Society, Environmental Defense Fund, Natural Resources Defense Council, and Defenders of Wildlife.

On Capitol Hill President Clinton made huge concessions to Congress in order to obtain members' votes. In some cases, members of Congress publicly proclaimed they sought concessions for their vote; in other cases, members denied any attempts to barter their support. Clinton was accused by Ralph Nader of having pledged approximately $4.4 billion in pork barrel projects and political favors. One Texas Democrat, J.J. Pickle, is alleged to have secured a pledge for the construction of the $10 million J.J. Pickle Center for the Study of Trade in the Western Hemisphere, to be built in Austin, Texas. The money for the center is included in the NAFTA-implementing bill.

While Clinton was lobbying Capitol Hill, Vice President Al Gore was debating Ross Perot on television. The debate was characterized by political and personal one-upsmanship. Both men failed to address the real issues. Vice President Gore failed to frame the debate around why freer trade opens markets and cre-

ates jobs at home and abroad. Perot, on the other hand, lost the debate due to his boorish behavior, characterized by whining, mean-spiritedness, disrespect for the vice president, and a blatant disdain for the people of Mexico. At one point in the debate, Perot asserted that it was the dream of every Mexican to "someday have an out-house."[31]

Although the debate may have lacked substance, there was plenty of sarcasm. Vice President Gore repeatedly interrupted Perot, challenging his presentation and suggesting that he was more interested in promoting his own political ambitions than finding the truth. Perot, in turn, instructed Vice President Gore to be quiet and stop interrupting him.

The Clinton administration's attempts to lobby Congress were probably more successful than the debate. Although the opinion polls reflected a slight increase in the number of NAFTA proponents after the debate, few people appeared to have been swayed either for or against the agreement.

---

31. Quoted in Maureen Dowd, "The Free Trade Accord: Media-Watch," *The New York Times*, November 10, 1993, B3.

Key Words and Phrases

ad valorem tariff **78**	dumped **90**	most favored nation **84**
bound tariffs **85**	dutiable **82**	substantial transformation **82**
common market **98**	duty **78**	super 301 **91**
conditional MFN **86**	fair trade law **88**	tariff classification **82**
countervailing subsidies **90**	fast track authority **88**	transaction value **82**
countervailing duty **90**	foreign trade zones **84**	
customs valuation **82**	interlocutory **99**	

Questions and Case Problems

1. A fast-growing U.S. beverage company wishes to import mineral water and has asked you, its vice-president for purchasing, to recommend foreign sources. You know that sources exist in France, Canada, and Australia. What U.S. trade laws should you consider in choosing among these sources?

2. Assume you determine that the best source of mineral water for your purposes is France, but the tariff makes imports from that country noncompetitive. How could you seek a reduction in this tariff?

3. You are the vice-president for marketing at a U.S. manufacturer of electric shavers. Imports of electric shavers have been increasing rapidly in the last year, undercutting your prices and taking significant market share from your company. The shavers are coming from five countries. You know that exporters in two of these countries are selling in the United States at prices below their home market prices, and that exporters in two other countries are receiving export subsidies. The single exporter in the fifth country appears to be infringing a patent that your company holds on a particular type of electric shaver, but your lawyers have said it is not a strong patent. Which U.S. import relief laws might be available to you to relieve the competitive pressure from these imports?

4. You are president of a U.S. engineering company. You have made a competitive bid to help design a new airport to be built by the Japanese government, but your bid has not been accepted. You believe that all significant engineering work on this project is being reserved by the government for Japanese companies. You are concerned that future projects will also be reserved for local companies. Does U.S. law provide for any relief?

5. In each of the following situations, name the U.S. government agency to which a request for assistance or petition for relief would be most appropriately addressed.

(a) You believe that your company's domestic sales are being damaged by increasing imports from Country X. No unfair trade practices are being employed by Country X.

(b) You believe that your company's export business to Country Y is limited by unfair practices of that country's government.

(c) Your company specializes in research and development. New technologies developed by your firm often have important military applications. The government of Country Z makes your company a very attractive offer to purchase a recently developed technology. You would like to accept the offer, but are unsure whether export of the technology is prohibited under the Arms Export Control Act.

6. Your company is U.S.-based and has a subsidiary in France. The French government is encouraging companies to do business in Shangri-la, a country with colonial ties to France but with a Marxist dictatorship. The U.S. has imposed an embargo on all U.S. trade with that country. Can your French subsidiary sell its products to Shangri-la? Should it?

7. You are discussing the possibility of licensing know-how to a Vietnamese company for the manufacture of personal computers. A delegation is coming to visit your company in Massachusetts to negotiate the terms of the license, to see your plant, and to discuss your technology. What laws and regulations might be applicable to this meeting?

8. Glenn Levy works for Waks Enterprises, a foreign subsidiary of Curtis Holding Company, a U.S. corporation. His supervisor has in the past asked him to make payments to a low-level government employee of Aldebaron, the foreign country in which Waks Enterprises is located, to "get the paperwork moving." Levy has always made these payments. His supervisor has now asked him to make a payment to Seith Petrylak, who is known to have influence with the Aldebaron minister of finance. Levy does not know what the payment is for.

Should Levy make the payment to Petrylak? Could any of Levy's actions result in criminal penalties? Does Waks Enterprises face any criminal penalties? What about Curtis Holding Company? What is the ethical thing to do?

9. What factors provoked the breakdown in the EC's attempt to create a unified currency? What is the effect on trade and investment when a country must devalue or revalue it currency?

10. After the passage of NAFTA, several members of the Clinton administration suggested that the super 301 program should be reinstated. Do you agree with their proposal? Why?

Chapter 4

COURTS, LITIGATION, AND ALTERNATIVE DISPUTE RESOLUTION

■ Introduction

Equal Justice Under the Law

"Equal justice under the law" is the inscription on the front of the United States Supreme Court building in Washington, D.C. It is a reminder that the judicial system is intended to protect the legal rights of those who come before a court. In a litigation-prone society, managers should understand the judicial system and be prepared to use it to protect the rights of their companies.

Chapter Summary

This chapter explains the court system and litigation process, including discovery, the attorney-client privilege, and various trial strategies for companies involved in a lawsuit. It also discusses alternatives to litigation, such as mediation and arbitration.

The Court System

The United States has two judicial systems: federal and state. Federal and state courts have different subject matter jurisdiction. In general, federal courts are courts of limited subject matter jurisdiction, whereas state courts have general subject matter jurisdiction and can therefore hear any type of dispute. The jurisdiction of the federal courts arises from the U.S. Constitution and the statutes enacted by Congress. The jurisdiction of a state's courts arises from that state's constitution and statutes. The two coexisting judicial systems are a result of the federalism created by the U.S. Constitution, which gives certain powers to the federal government while other powers remain with the states.

The basic structure of the federal and state court systems is diagrammed in Exhibit 4-1. In practice, the structure of the U.S. court system is more complex than the diagram indicates. For example, an applicant may appeal an adverse decision from the U.S. Patent and Trademark Office to the Board of Patent Appeals and Interferences. The person may then appeal an unfavorable ruling from this court to the Court of Appeals for the Federal Circuit. Alternatively, the applicant may appeal the unfavorable ruling of the Board of Patent Appeals and Interferences by filing a civil action, in the U.S. District Court for the

EXHIBIT 4-1   Hierarchy of the Federal and State Court Systems

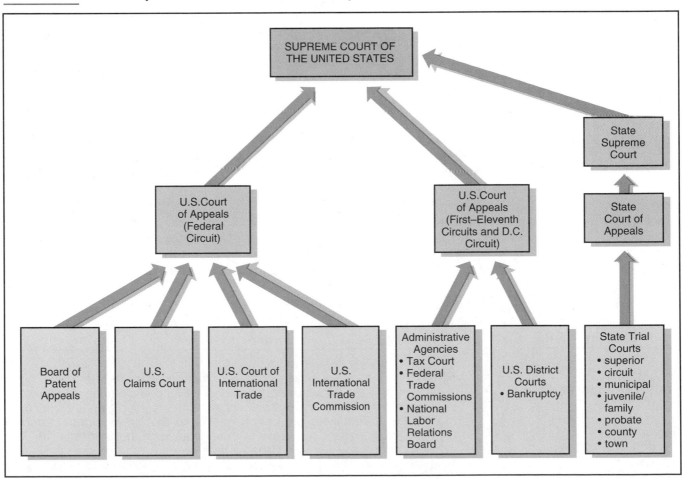

District of Columbia, against the Commissioner of the U.S. Patent and Trademark Office.

How to Read a Case Citation

When an appellate court decides a case, the court writes an opinion, which is published in one or more *reporters*—collections of court opinions. Some trial courts also publish opinions. The citation of a case (the "cite") includes the following information:

1. The plaintiff's name
2. The defendant's name
3. The volume number and title of the reporter in which the case is reported
4. The page number at which the case report begins
5. The court that decided the case (if the court is not indicated, it is understood to be the state or U.S. supreme court, depending on the reporter in which the case appears)
6. The year in which the case was decided.

For example, *Toys "R" Us, Inc. v. R. H. Macy & Co.,* 728 F.Supp. 230 (S.D.N.Y. 1990), indicates that in 1990 an opinion was issued in the case of Toys "R" Us, Inc. (the plaintiff) against R. H. Macy & Co. (the defendant). The case was decided in federal district court, in the Southern District of New York. The case is reported in volume 728 of the *Federal Supplement,* beginning on page 230. *Save the Yaak Committee v. Block,* 840 F.2d 714 (9th Cir. 1988), was decided in the U.S. Court of Appeals for the Ninth Circuit in 1988. It is reported at page 714 of volume 840 of the *Federal Reporter,* second series.

Some cases are reported in more than one reporter. For example, the famous New York taxicab case discussed in chapter 20, *Walkovszky v. Carlton,* is cited as 18 N.Y.2d 414, 276 N.Y.S.2d 585, 223 N.E.2d 6 (N.Y. 1966). One

may locate this case in volume 18 of the second series of *New York Reports,* in volume 276 of the second series of the *New York Supplement,* or in volume 223 of the second series of the *Northeastern Reports.*

When the lawsuit is originally filed, the case name appears as *plaintiff v. defendant.* If the case is appealed, the case name appears as *appellant* or *petitioner* (the person who is appealing the case or seeking a writ of certiorari) v. *appellee* or *respondent* (the other party). So if the defendant lost at the trial level and appealed the decision to a higher court, the name of the defendant (now the appellant) would appear first in the case citation.

Federal Jurisdiction

Federal courts derive their legal power to hear civil cases from three sources, known as diversity jurisdiction, federal question jurisdiction, and jurisdiction when the United States is a party.

Diversity Jurisdiction

Diversity jurisdiction exists when the lawsuit is between citizens of two different states and the amount in controversy, exclusive of interest and all costs, exceeds $50,000. The purpose of the monetary requirement is to keep the federal judicial system from becoming overburdened with trivial cases.

Diversity jurisdiction was traditionally justified by the fear that state courts might be biased against the out-of-state party. In federal district court, all litigants are in a neutral forum, and there should be no local prejudice for the home team.

Most diversity cases are decided under state laws and thus could also be resolved in state court. The following landmark case addressed the question of whether state or federal law should apply to a suit brought in federal court exercising its diversity jurisdiction.

■ A Case in Point: Summary

Case 4.1
ERIE RAILROAD CO. v. TOMPKINS
Supreme Court of the United States
304 U.S. 64, 58 S.Ct. 817 (1938).

FACTS Tompkins, a citizen of Pennsylvania, was injured on a dark night by a passing freight train owned by the Erie Railroad Company. At the time of the accident, Tompkins was walking along the railroad's right of way near Hughestown, Pennsylvania. Tompkins alleged that the accident occurred through the negligent operation or maintenance of the train; that he was rightfully on the premises because he was walking along a commonly used footpath; and that he was struck by something which looked like a door projecting from one of the moving cars. Tompkins filed his lawsuit in federal district court in New York because Erie Railroad was a corporation of that state. Erie Railroad denied liability. The case was tried before a jury.

Pennsylvania had no statute applicable to this case. Cases of this type were decided under common law, that is, the body of law created by court decisions. Erie Railroad contended that the common law of Pennsylvania, and not what was known as federal common law, should apply to this cause of action. Under Pennsylvania common law, as declared by the Pennsylvania Supreme Court, persons who use the pathways alongside railroad tracks, rather than the proper crossways, are trespassers. According to Pennsylvania law, a railroad is not liable for injuries to trespassers resulting from its negligent actions.

The district court judge refused to instruct the jury about the Pennsylvania law; the case went to the jury under federal common law. The jury awarded Tompkins $30,000. Erie Railroad appealed. The court of appeals held that the jury did not need to consider whether the law of Pennsylvania applied in this situation, because the issue at trial concerned "general law" rather than the specific law in Pennsylvania. The court stated that when there is an issue of general law, such as the responsibility of a railroad for injuries caused by its servants, then in the absence of a state statute, a federal court is free to decide what the common law of the state is or should be. Thus, the court of appeals affirmed the jury verdict. Erie Railroad appealed to the Supreme Court.

ISSUE PRESENTED   Should state or federal law govern in cases in federal court sitting in diversity that do not concern matters governed by the U.S. Constitution or acts of Congress?

SUMMARY OF OPINION   The U.S. Supreme Court ruled that in cases where a federal court exercises its diversity jurisdiction, it must apply the relevant state law as declared by either the state's legislature or its highest court. The Court further ruled that a federal court cannot ignore state law unless the lawsuit concerns the U.S. Constitution or a U.S. statute. In essence, the Supreme Court abolished the notion of federal common law in diversity cases.

RESULT   The Supreme Court reversed the decision of the court of appeals. Erie Railroad won the right to have the case tried using Pennsylvania law. Because, under Pennsylvania law, plaintiff Tompkins was considered a trespasser to whom Erie Railroad owed no duty of care, Erie Railroad was not liable to Tompkins.

COMMENTS   The *Erie* doctrine, as the rules established in this case have become known, serves an important purpose. It ensures that the outcome of the case in federal court will be similar to what it would have been in a state court. This prevents litigants (the parties to a lawsuit) from *forum shopping,* that is, from choosing between federal or state court depending upon where the laws are most favorable to their position.

When litigants are in federal court because of diversity jurisdiction, they cannot choose which state's law the court will apply. The court itself makes this decision, applying well-established conflict of law rules which prescribe which state's law should apply to a particular kind of case.

Determining Citizenship A natural person is a citizen of the state wherein she has her legal residence or domicile. A person may have a house or residence in more than one state. She is a citizen, however, only of the state that is considered her home.

A corporation, on the other hand, may have dual citizenship. A corporation is deemed a citizen of the state in which it has been incorporated and of the state where the company has its principal place of business. Federal courts usually apply one of three tests in determining where a company engaged in multistate operations has its principal place of business.

The first is the "nerve center" test. To find the corporation's nerve center, courts consider: (1) where the executive and administrative offices are located; (2) where the income tax return is filed; and (3) where the directors and stockholders meet. The second test focuses on the place of operations. This test requires locating the majority of the corporation's physical operations, such as manufacturing facilities or offices. The "total activity" test, a combination of the first two tests, considers all aspects of the corporate entity, including the nature and scope of the company's activities. The "total activity" test is gaining popularity among the courts.

Federal Question Jurisdiction

A *federal question* exists when the dispute concerns federal law, namely a legal right arising under the U.S. Constitution, a federal statute, an administrative regulation issued by a federal government agency, federal common law, or a treaty of the United States. There is no minimum monetary requirement for lawsuits involving a federal question.

United States Is a Party

Federal courts have jurisdiction over all lawsuits in which the United States government, or an officer or agency thereof, is the plaintiff or defendant. As with federal question jurisdiction, there is no minimum monetary requirement for lawsuits where the United States is a party.

■ Federal Courts

The main function of the federal courts is to interpret the Constitution and laws of the United States. George Washington told the Supreme Court in 1790, "I have always been persuaded that the stability and success of the National Government, and consequently the happiness of the American people, would depend in a considerable degree on the interpretation and execution of its laws."

66

> *"I have always been persuaded that the stability and success of the National Government, and consequently the happiness of the American people, would depend in a considerable degree on the interpretation and execution of its laws."*
>
> – George Washington

President Washington signed into law the Senate's first piece of legislation, entitled "An Act to Establish the Judicial Courts of the United States." This act created federal trial courts. Two years later, Congress created the courts of appeals. The three-tiered system of district courts, courts of appeals, and the Supreme Court remains today. The president of the United States nominates the federal judges who serve on the district courts, the courts of appeals, and the Supreme Court. The United States Senate, pursuant to its "advice and consent" power, then votes to approve or reject the judicial nominee. The Constitution does not impose any age or citizenship requirements on judicial candidates as it does on those seeking presidential or congressional office. Once confirmed by the Senate, federal judges have a lifetime appointment to the bench. They may be removed from office only by legislative impeachment, if they violate the law. The federal judiciary is more independent than either the executive or legislative branches; lifetime tenure protects federal judges from public reprisal for making unpopular or difficult decisions.

U.S. District Courts

The U.S. district courts are the trial courts of the federal system. Currently, the country is divided into 94 judicial districts. Each state has at least one district, and the more populous states have as many as four. Exhibit 4-2 shows various districts. Many districts have two or more divisions. For example, the main location for the U.S. District Court for the Western District of Texas is in San Antonio. However, the Western District of Texas also has courts in Austin, El Paso, Midland, and Waco. Thus, a plaintiff may file his lawsuit with the nearest federal district court, provided, of course, that the court has jurisdiction over the particular controversy.

EXHIBIT 4-2 Geographical Boundaries of the U.S. District Courts and Circuit Courts of Appeals

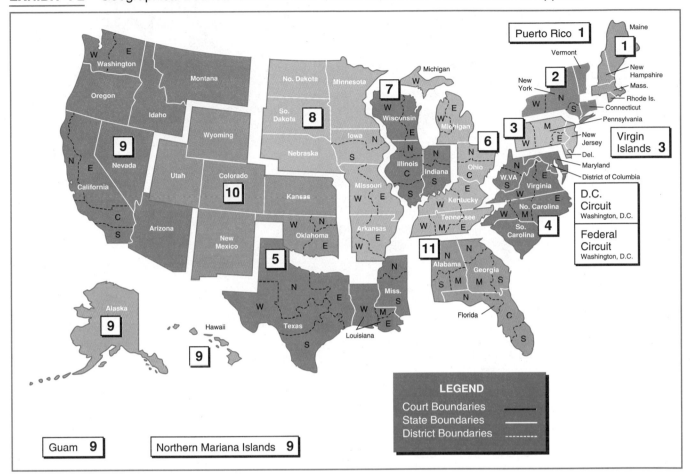

U.S. Courts of Appeals

The primary functions of a court of appeals are: (1) to review decisions of the trial courts within its territory; (2) to review decisions of certain administrative agencies and commissions; and (3) to issue *writs,* or orders, to lower courts or to litigants. Only final decisions of lower courts are appealable. A decision is final if it conclusively resolves an issue in a dispute or the entire dispute.

Cases before the court of appeals are usually presented to a panel of three judges. Occasionally, all the judges of a court of appeals will sit together to hear and decide a particularly important or close case. This is called an *in banc* (or en banc) *hearing.* The court of appeals can either affirm or reverse the decision of the lower court. It may also *vacate,* or nullify, the previous court's ruling and *remand* the case—send it back to the lower court for reconsideration. Frequently, the panel of judges will decide an appeal based upon the legal briefs or written

memoranda submitted to the court, rather than hearing oral arguments presented by the lawyers.

There are 13 courts of appeals, one for each of the 12 regional circuits in the United States and one for the federal circuit. Exhibit 4-2 shows the geographical boundaries of the circuits. The Court of Appeals for the Federal Circuit, created in 1982, does not have any jurisdiction over a specific geographic region, but rather hears appeals from various specialized federal courts, including the Claims Court, the Court of International Trade, and the Internal Trade Commission. Exhibit 4-3 lists the states and territories included within each circuit. The Ninth Circuit, encompassing ten states and Guam, is the largest circuit, with 28 active judges. The Court of Appeals for the First Circuit has only six active judges.

Specialized Federal Courts

The federal system has several specialized courts that resolve legal disputes within particular subject areas.

EXHIBIT 4-3   United States Courts of Appeals

CIRCUIT	REGION
■ *District of Columbia*	District of Columbia
■ *First*	Maine, Massachusetts, New Hampshire, Puerto Rico, Rhode Island
■ *Second*	Connecticut, New York, Vermont
■ *Third*	Delaware, New Jersey, Pennsylvania, Virgin Islands
■ *Fourth*	Maryland, North Carolina, South Carolina, Virginia, West Virginia
■ *Fifth*	Canal Zone, Louisiana, Mississippi, Texas
■ *Sixth*	Kentucky, Michigan, Ohio, Tennessee
■ *Seventh*	Illinois, Indiana, Wisconsin
■ *Eighth*	Arkansas, Iowa, Minnesota, Missouri, Nebraska, North Dakota, South Dakota
■ *Ninth*	Alaska, Arizona, California, Guam, Hawaii, Idaho, Montana, Nevada, Oregon, Washington
■ *Tenth*	Colorado, Kansas, New Mexico, Oklahoma, Utah, Wyoming
■ *Eleventh*	Alabama, Georgia, Florida
■ *Federal*	Based in Washington, D.C., but hears cases from all regions

The bankruptcy courts are units of the federal district courts that hear proceedings involving the bankruptcy laws and regulations of the United States. When companies such as Drexel Burnham Lambert, Eastern Airlines, or Federated Department Stores filed for protection from their creditors under chapter 11 of the bankruptcy laws, they did so in federal bankruptcy court. (The law of bankruptcy is discussed in greater detail in chapter 24.)

The tax courts hear taxpayer petitions or appeals regarding federal income, estate, and gift taxes. The Court of International Trade has jurisdiction over disputes involving tariffs or import taxes and trade laws. This court also hears cases on appeal from the U.S. International Trade Commission, which handles disputes involving unfair practices in import trade. The U.S. Court of Military Appeals hears cases from the lower courts and tribunals within the armed services.

U.S. Supreme Court

The Supreme Court was created directly by article III of the Constitution. The Court consists of one chief justice and eight associate justices. At least six justices must be present to hear a case.

The majority of the cases heard by the Supreme Court are on appeal from the U.S. courts of appeals. A decision by a state supreme court is appealable to the U.S. Supreme Court only when the case concerns the U.S. Constitution or some other federal law. The Supreme Court may hear direct appeals of a federal district court decision if the court declared an act of the U.S. Congress unconstitutional. For example, the Supreme Court heard arguments concerning the Flag Protection Act of 1989 after two federal district courts had declared the act unconstitutional. (The Supreme Court affirmed the district court decisions.)

The Supreme Court has the discretion to decide which of the cases within its jurisdiction it will hear. When it decides to hear a case, the Supreme Court issues a *writ of certiorari* ordering the lower court to certify the record of proceedings below and send it up to the Supreme Court. Four justices must vote to hear a case before a writ can be issued. If a writ was sought but denied by the Supreme Court, the citation for the case will indicate "*cert. denied.*"

The Court will not hear an appeal unless a real and substantial controversy is involved and resolving the lawsuit will provide actual relief to one party. Further, the party pursuing the appeal must have standing to sue. *Standing* means that the party seeking relief is the proper party to advance the litigation, has a personal interest in the outcome of the suit, and will benefit from a favorable ruling.

The Supreme Court will not decide cases in which a political question is involved. A *political question* is defined as a conflict that should be decided by one of the political branches of government or by the electorate. The judicial branch of government respects certain disputes that are more properly within the authority of the legislative or executive branches.

State Courts

The state courts handle the great bulk of legal disputes in the U.S. Each state's constitution creates the judicial branch of government for that state. For example, "the judicial authority of this State shall be vested in one Supreme Court, one Court of Appeals, circuit courts, and such other courts as the General Assembly may later establish."[1] The various sections then provide the details of the state judicial system. These include the number of justices sitting on the state's supreme court, the jurisdiction of the state courts, the geographic districts of the various courts of appeals, the manner in which to select or appoint justices and judges, and the tenure of the justices and judges.

For a state court to hear a civil case, the court must have personal jurisdiction. *Personal jurisdiction* means that the court has legal authority over the parties to the lawsuit. Personal jurisdiction may be based upon the residence or activities of the person being sued (called *in personam* jurisdiction) or upon the location of property at issue in the lawsuit (called *in rem* jurisdiction). For example, if an individual does any business in the state, then she is properly within the jurisdiction of the state courts. Owning property in a state, causing a personal injury or property damage within the state, or even paying alimony or child support to someone living within the state might also put a person within the jurisdiction of that state's courts.

Most states have *long-arm statutes,* which subject an out-of-state defendant to jurisdiction where the defendant is doing business or commits a civil wrong in the state. Long-arm statutes must also comply with due process requirements. As long as the person has sufficient *minimum contacts* with a state, such that it is fair to require him to appear in a court of that state, the state has personal jurisdiction over that person. This doctrine was set forth in the following case.

---

1. Constitution of the State of Indiana, article 7, section 1.

A Case in Point: In the Language of the Court

Case 4.2
INTERNATIONAL SHOE CO. v. WASHINGTON
Supreme Court of the
United States
326 U.S. 310, 66 S.Ct. 154
(1945).

FACTS   International Shoe Co. was a Delaware corporation, having its principal place of business in St. Louis, Missouri. It was engaged in the manufacture and sale of shoes and other footwear. The state of Washington sued International Shoe Co. to recover contributions under the Unemployment Compensation Act. The shoe company insisted that it should not be subject to Washington state courts and law because the company did not maintain a "presence" in the state of Washington.

International Shoe maintained places of business in several states, other than Washington, at which its manufacturing was carried on. Its merchandise was distributed interstate through several sales units or branches located outside the state of Washington.

The shoe company had no office in Washington and made no contracts either for sale or purchase of merchandise there. It maintained no stock of merchandise in that state and made no deliveries of goods in intrastate commerce there. However, during the years in question (1937 to 1940), International Shoe employed eleven to thirteen salesmen under direct supervision and control of sales managers located in St. Louis. These salesmen resided in Washington, their principal activities were confined to that state, and they were compensated by commissions based upon the amount of their sales. They were supplied with samples to show prospective purchasers, and they would sometimes rent rooms to have such showings. The authority of the salesmen was limited to exhibiting their samples and soliciting orders from prospective buyers, at prices and terms set by the shoe company. Orders would be transmitted to the St. Louis office. No salesman in Washington had authority to enter into contracts or to make collections.

Case 4.2 continued on following page

Case **4.2** continued

ISSUE PRESENTED   Under what circumstances may a company that is incorporated under the laws of one state be subjected to the laws and courts of another state?

OPINION   STONE, J., writing for the U.S. Supreme Court:

. . . .

. . . [D]ue process requires only that in order to subject a defendant to a judgment *in personam*, if he be not present within the territory of the forum, he have certain minimum contacts with it such that the maintenance of the suit does not offend "traditional notions of fair play and substantial justice."[2]

. . .

. . . .

It is evident that the criteria by which we mark the boundary line between those activities which justify the subjection of a corporation to suit, and those which do not, cannot be simply mechanical or quantitative. The test is not merely, as has sometimes been suggested, whether the activity, which the corporation has seen fit to procure through its agents in another state, is a little more or a little less. Whether due process is satisfied must depend rather upon the quality and nature of the activity in relation to the fair and orderly administration of the laws which it was the purpose of the due process clause to insure. That clause does not contemplate that a state may make binding a judgment in personam against an individual or corporate defendant with which the state has no contacts, ties, or relations.

But to the extent that a corporation exercises the privilege of conducting activities within a state, it enjoys the benefits and protection of the laws of that state. The exercise of that privilege may give rise to obligations; and, so far as those obligations arise out of or are connected with the activities within the state, a procedure which requires the corporation to respond to a suit brought to enforce them can, in most instances, hardly be said to be undue.

Applying these standards, the activities carried on in behalf of appellant in the State of Washington were neither irregular nor casual. They were systematic and continuous throughout the years in question. They resulted in a large volume of interstate business, in the course of which appellant received the benefits and protection of the laws of the state, including the right to resort to the courts for the enforcement of its rights. The obligation which is here sued upon arose out of those very activities. It is evident that these operations establish sufficient contacts or ties with the state of the forum to make it reasonable and just according to our traditional conception of fair play and substantial justice to permit the state to enforce the obligations which appellant has incurred there. Hence we cannot say that the maintenance of the present suit in the State of Washington involves an unreasonable or undue procedure.

. . . .

RESULT   Because the court concluded that International Shoe had established minimum contacts through its activities in the state of Washington, it ruled that the state could maintain its suit against the company.

---

2. *Milliken v. Meyer*, 311 U.S. 457, 463, 61 S.Ct. 339, 343 (1940).

Questions

1. What legal benefits did International Shoe enjoy by having its salesmen in Washington? Are those benefits related to the burden the state of Washington sought to impose in this case?

2. Suppose an officer of XYZ Corporation, which is incorporated in New York, is in Florida on vacation. XYZ does no business in Florida. Can a plaintiff successfully assert personal jurisdiction over XYZ Corporation by serving a summons on the XYZ officer on the beach in Florida?

Courts have held that negotiating business contracts by means of telephone calls, the mail, or even the telecopier is sufficient to provide the state court with personal jurisdiction over an individual or corporation.

State Trial Courts

At the lowest level of the state trial court system are a few courts of limited jurisdiction. These courts decide minor criminal matters, small civil suits, and other specialized legal disputes. Examples include traffic courts, small claims courts, juvenile courts, and family courts. Within these courts, the procedures can be informal. Parties may appear without lawyers, the court may not keep a complete transcript or recording of the proceedings, and the technical rules of evidence and formal courtroom procedures may not apply. In small claims court, the jurisdiction of the court is usually limited to disputes involving less than, for example, $5,000. Any dispute involving more than this amount must be heard by a higher-level trial court.

The second level of state trial courts consists of courts of general or unlimited jurisdiction. These courts have formal courtroom procedures, apply the standard rules of evidence, and record all proceedings.

State court actions cover a broad spectrum of business activities. For example, in Fort Worth, Texas, the owner of a barbecue restaurant sued a former employee for absconding with a secret barbecue sauce recipe. In Louisiana, a plant worker sued the chemical company Monsanto because she suffered an anxiety attack after a supervisor violently berated her for not working. Shell Oil Company's insurers were sued in state court—unsuccessfully—to provide coverage for the $2.5 billion cleanup of hazardous waste at the U.S. Army facility near Denver, Colorado.

State Appellate Courts

A state appellate court is similar to its counterpart in the federal system. It usually consists of a panel of three judges which reviews the lower court ruling for errors in application of the law or procedures. The court of appeals usually accepts the findings of fact of the trial judge or jury, unless a particular finding is clearly unsupported by the evidence presented at trial. The state appellate court is not required to accept the lower court's conclusions of law. The appellate court will consider legal issues *de novo,* or anew, as if the trial court had not made any conclusions of law at all. A state court of appeals may affirm, reverse, or vacate and remand any final decision of a lower court.

State Supreme Court

Each state has one court acting as the highest judicial authority in that state. Most states call that court the supreme court. (In New York, the highest state court is called the Court of Appeals, and the state trial courts are called supreme courts. The intermediate appellate court is called the supreme court, appellate division.) The number of justices on the court varies from three to nine. The state supreme court usually has discretionary jurisdiction over all decisions of the court of appeals. Further, a state supreme court may have jurisdiction over cases where a statute of the state or the United States has been ruled unconstitutional in whole or in part. A state supreme court also resolves appeals in criminal cases in which a sentence of death has been imposed.

Choice of Law and Choice of Forum

The question of what law to apply comes up not only in the context of diversity cases heard in federal court but also in state court actions involving the citizens of more than one state. This question is governed by a complicated set of *conflict of law rules.* In general, the state that has the greatest governmental interest in a case will provide the governing law. Another way to put this is that governing law is selected by looking at a grouping of contacts: The state with the greatest contacts with the litigants and the dispute has the greatest interest in having its law applied.

Sometimes a state will use formalistic rules. For example, some states apply the law of the state where a contract was entered into in deciding which state's contract law to apply. For example, because the contract between Pennzoil and Getty Oil Co. with which Texaco intentionally interfered was entered into in New York, New York contracts law governed the issue of whether there was a binding contract. (This case is discussed in chapter 8.)

The parties to a contract can agree in advance which law should govern their dispute in the event that one develops. This is done in a section usually entitled "Governing Law." Parties can also agree in advance where their dispute is to be litigated. This is done by using a *choice of forum clause*.

A contract can also provide that disputes will be decided by a method other than litigation in court. A common choice is arbitration, which is discussed later in this chapter.

In 1970 the U.S. ratified the Convention on the Recognition and Enforcement of Foreign Arbitral Awards[3] for differences arising out of commercial legal

International Consideration

The same issues of choice of law and choice of forum arise in cases involving parties from different countries. It is customary for a contract involving parties from different jurisdictions to specify which country's law will govern and where the dispute will be tried.

relationships. The convention became part of the supreme law of the U.S., as enforceable as congressional enactments, by reason of article VI, clause 2 of the U.S. Constitution. The convention provides that signatories will honor agreements to arbitrate unless the agreement is "null and void, inoperative or incapable of being performed."[4] The following case addresses the issues of when a choice of law, choice of forum, and arbitration clause will be enforced by a U.S. court in a case involving claims of violations of the U.S. securities laws.

---

3. 9 U.S.C. § 201 *et seq.* (1970).

4. 9 U.S.C. § 201 art. II (3) (1970).

■ A Case in Point: Summary

Case 4.3
RILEY v. KINGSLEY UNDER-WRITING AGENCIES, LTD.
United States Court of Appeals for the Tenth Circuit
969 F.2d 953 (10th Cir. 1992),
cert. denied, 113 S.Ct. 658 (1992).

FACTS   Ronald Riley was interested in becoming a member of Lloyd's of London. Lloyd's has functioned as a market for writing insurance policies for 300 years. Its "members" have personal liability for losses in excess of premiums paid by the insured. Riley traveled to England on several occasions to pursue this quest. In 1980 Riley entered into a General Undertaking with Lloyd's and a Members' Agent's Agreement with the underwriters. Both of these agreements provided that the courts of England would have exclusive jurisdiction over any dispute and that the laws of England would apply. Additionally, the Member's Agent's Agreement provided for arbitration in the event of any dispute.

Riley remained a member of Lloyd's through 1990, and each year he increased the amount of premium income underwritten. In connection with his underwriting, he was required to meet Lloyd's deposit requirements. Therefore, he obtained letters of credit. In the event a member fails or refuses to cover his pro rata share of underwriting liability, Lloyd's may draw on the letter of credit.

The syndicates in which Riley participated experienced large losses, resulting in calls in excess of £300,000. Riley was notified that if he did not satisfy the calls, Lloyd's would draw against the letters of credit.

Proceeding apparently on the theory that the best defense is a good offense, Riley filed action in U.S. District Court against multiple defendants, including Kingsley Underwriting Agencies, Ltd., a registered underwriting agency with Lloyd's. Riley alleged that the defendants had engaged in the offer and sale of unregistered securities and made untrue statements of material fact and material omissions in connection with the sale of securities, violating the U.S. Securities Act of 1933, the U.S. Securities Exchange Act of 1934, and Colorado state securities law. He also alleged common law fraud. The defendants in turn sought to enforce the forum selection and choice of law clauses, and thus dismiss any U.S. action.

The district court held that the arbitration and choice of forum and law provisions in the contracts were valid and enforceable. Therefore, it dismissed all of Riley's claims. Riley appealed.

ISSUE PRESENTED   Are the choice of forum and law provisions and arbitration clauses in the contracts between an English company and a U.S. citizen valid and enforceable?

SUMMARY OF OPINION   The U.S. Court of Appeals affirmed the district court's holding that the parties had to abide by their agreement to resolve any disputes in England using English law. The court listed three primary reasons for its decision: (1) the parties' undertaking was truly international in character; (2) all parties other than Riley and FirstBank (a bank which issued some of Riley's letters of credit) were British; and (3) virtually all activities giving rise to the suggested claims occurred in England.

The court further explained that recent U.S. Supreme Court decisions upheld the enforcement of choice of law and choice of forum clauses. The main reason for upholding these agreements, the courts have stated, is that American businesses are rapidly expanding into global markets; this expansion would be greatly hindered if Americans and the American judicial system maintain the parochial notion that all disputes must be settled in U.S. courts using U.S. law. These agreements must be enforced to achieve the orderliness and predictability necessary for an international business transaction.

Riley suggested that enforcement of these provisions would deprive him of his day in court. The court ruled that he would not be deprived of his day in court, his day simply may be more difficult in England using English law. As long as the law of the chosen forum is not inherently unfair, U.S. courts will uphold agreements enforcing those foreign jurisdictions.

The court also upheld the arbitration agreement, relying heavily on *Scherk v. Alberto-Culver Co.*,[5] in which the Supreme Court reasoned: "A parochial refusal by the courts of one country to enforce an international arbitration agreement . . . would invite unseemly and mutually destructive jockeying by the parties to secure tactical litigation advantages. . . . [T]he dicey atmosphere of such a legal no-man's land would surely damage the fabric of international commerce and trade, and imperil the willingness and ability of businessmen to enter into international commercial agreements."[6] The court found no public policy that would invoke the "null and void" exception to the Convention on the Recognition and Enforcement of Foreign Arbitral Awards. Accordingly, the agreement to arbitrate arbitration was honored by the U.S. court.

---

5. 417 U.S. 506, 94 S.Ct. 2449 (1974).
6. 417 U.S. 506, 516-17, 94 S.Ct. 2449, 2455-56 (footnote omitted).

*Case **4.3** continued on following page*

Case 4.3 continued

RESULT   The appellate court dismissed Riley's claims, holding that his case was subject to the choice of forum, law, and arbitration agreements he had entered into.

■ Sources of the Law

In applying the law, federal and state courts look to constitutions, statutes, regulations, and common (or case) law.

Constitutions

Courts may be called on to interpret the U.S. or state constitution. For example, the First Amendment provides that Congress shall make no law abridging the freedom of speech. Incidents of flag burning have required courts to interpret just what type of conduct constitutes speech protected by the First Amendment. Lawsuits concerning random drug testing of employees have centered on whether this testing violates the Fourth Amendment ban on unreasonable searches or the right to privacy.

The U.S. Constitution does not expressly set forth a right to privacy. As explained in chapter 2, such a right is found in the "penumbra" of other express rights. Some state constitutions do expressly grant a right to privacy, however. The following case addresses the issue of whether the National Collegiate Athletic Association (NCAA) violates the right to privacy guaranteed by the California State Constitution by requiring random drug tests of student athletes.

■ A Case in Point: Summary

Case 4.4
HILL V. NATIONAL COLLEGIATE ATHLETIC ASSOCIATION
Supreme Court of California
26 Cal.Rptr.2d 834,
865 P.2d 633 (Cal. 1994).

FACTS   The National Collegiate Athletic Association (NCAA) sponsors and regulates intercollegiate athletic competition throughout the United States. Under the NCAA's drug testing program, randomly selected college student athletes competing in postseason championships and football bowl games are required to provide samples of their urine under closely monitored conditions. Urine samples are chemically analyzed for proscribed substances. Athletes testing "positive" are subject to disqualification.

Plaintiffs, who were student athletes attending Stanford University at the time of trial, sued the NCAA, contending its drug testing program violated their right to privacy secured by article I, section I of the California state constitution. That section provides: "All people are by nature free and independent and have inalienable rights. Among these are enjoying and defending life and liberty, acquiring, possessing, and protecting property, and pursuing and obtaining safety, happiness, and privacy." Stanford intervened in the suit and adopted plaintiffs' position.

ISSUE PRESENTED   Does the NCAA's drug testing program violate athletes' right to privacy under the California state constitution?

SUMMARY OF OPINION   The California Supreme Court set forth the elements of the cause of action for violation of the state constitutional right to privacy: (1) a legally protected privacy interest; (2) a reasonable expectation of privacy; and (3) serious invasion of a privacy interest.

The court then outlined possible defenses to each of the above elements. Invasion of a privacy interest is not a violation of the state constitutional right to privacy if the invasion is justified by a competing interest.

The court also stated that because the NCAA is a private organization and not a governmental agency, it may be subject to a lesser standard in showing the strength of its competing interest. Invasions of the right to privacy are thought to be potentially more dangerous when committed by the government than when committed by private actors.

The court applied the above guidelines as follows:

Plaintiffs correctly asserted that the NCAA's drug testing program impacts legally protected privacy interests. First, by monitoring an athlete's urination, the NCAA's program intrudes on a human bodily function that by law and social custom is generally performed in private and without observers. Second, by collecting and testing an athlete's urine and inquiring about the ingestion of medications and other substances, the NCAA obtains information about the internal medical state of an athlete's body that is regarded as personal and confidential.

In terms of the reasonable expectation of privacy, the court stated that the observation of urination obviously implicates privacy interests. However, in the case of the plaintiffs and other student athletes, the reasonable expectations of privacy must be viewed within the context of intercollegiate athletic activity and the normal conditions under which it is undertaken.

By its nature, the court stated, participation in intercollegiate athletics, particularly in highly competitive postseason championship events, involves close regulation and scrutiny of the physical fitness and bodily condition of student athletes. Required physical examination (including urinalysis) and special regulation of sleep habits, diet, fitness, and other activities that intrude significantly on privacy interests are routine aspects of a college athlete's life not shared by other students or the population at large. Athletes frequently disrobe in the presence of one another and their athletic mentors and assistants in locker room settings where private bodily parts are readily observable by others of the same sex. They also exchange information about their physical condition and medical treatment with coaches, trainers, and others who have a "need to know."

As a result of its unique set of demands, athletic participation carries with it social norms that effectively diminish the athlete's reasonable expectation of personal privacy in regarding bodily condition, both internal and external. Drug testing has become a highly visible, pervasive, and well-accepted part of athletic competition, particularly on intercollegiate and professional levels. It is a reasonably expected part of the life of an athlete, especially one engaged in advanced levels of competition, where the stakes and corresponding temptations are high.

Finally, in terms of the competing interests, the NCAA asserted that it had two: (a) safeguarding the integrity of intercollegiate athletic competition; and (b) protecting the health and safety of student athletes. The central purpose of the NCAA is to promote competitive athletic events conducted pursuant to "rules of the game" enacted by its own membership. In this way, the NCAA creates and preserves the "level playing field" necessary to promote vigorous, high-level, and nationwide competition in intercollegiate sports.

The court found that in light of the NCAA's history, its decision to enforce a ban on the use of drugs by means of a drug testing program was reasonably calculated to further its legitimate interest in maintaining the integrity of intercollegiate athletic competition. The court also noted that before beginning its testing program, the NCAA commissioned a study that showed significant and widespread use of drugs by student athletes.

*Case **4.4** continued on following page*

*Case **4.4** continued*

RESULT The California Supreme Court held that the NCAA's drug testing program did not violate the student athletes' state constitutional right to privacy.

COMMENTS The court noted that the closest question presented in this case concerned the method used by the NCAA to monitor athletes as they provided urine samples. The method included observation by an NCAA official (of the same sex as the athlete) standing five to seven feet away as the athlete urinated. The court stated that there may indeed be less intrusive alternatives to direct monitoring that could nonetheless fully satisfy the tester's objective of ensuring a valid sample. However, the court found that it was limited to the record before it, and necessarily left any further consideration of less intrusive alternatives to direct monitoring initially to the judgment and discretion of the NCAA, and then to future litigation, if any.

Statutes

Congress enacts statutes in such areas as public assistance, food and drugs, patents and copyrights, labor relations, and civil rights. For example, title 42 of the United States Code, section 2000(a), provides that "all persons shall be entitled to the full and equal enjoyment of the goods, services, facilities, privileges, advantages, and accommodations of any place of public accommodation . . . without discrimination or segregation on the ground of race, color, religion or national origin."

Regulations

Courts sometimes hear cases arising under regulations issued by administrative agencies and executive departments. Federal regulations and rules are printed in the multi-volume *Code of Federal Regulations (CFR)*, which is revised and updated every year.

The *CFR* covers such varied topics as the regulations applying to the federal highways, issued by the Department of Transportation; the Internal Revenue Service regulations, issued by the Department of the Treasury; and the immigration and naturalization rules and procedures, issued by the Department of Justice. Administrative rules and regulations, and the various agencies, are discussed in chapter 6.

Common Law

Common law is case law—the legal rules made by judges when they decide a case in which no constitution, statute, or regulation exists to resolve the dispute. Common law originated in England and includes all of the case law of England and the American colonies before the Revolution, as well as American case law since the colonial period.

Stare Decisis

Common law developed through the doctrine of *stare decisis,* which translates as "to abide by decided cases." Once a court resolves a particular issue, other courts addressing a similar legal problem will generally follow that court's decision.

> *Once a court resolves a particular issue, other courts addressing a similar legal problem will generally follow that court's decision.*

A legal rule established by a court's decision may be either persuasive or authoritative. A decision is *persuasive* if it reasonably and fairly resolved the dispute. Another court confronting a similar dispute will probably choose to apply the same reasoning.

An *authoritative decision*, by contrast, is one that must be followed, regardless of its persuasive power. The U.S. Court of Appeals for the Seventh Circuit explained:

Whether a decision is authoritative depends on a variety of factors, of which the most important is the relationship between the court that decided it and the court to which it is cited later as a precedent. *The simplest relationship is hierarchical: the decisions of a superior court in a unitary system bind the inferior courts.* The most complex relationship is between a court and its own previous decisions.

Political Perspective

Should the U.S. Adopt the British Rule That the Loser Pays the Winner's Attorney's Fees?

The costs of litigation are spiraling, and policymakers are scrambling to find the cause. With greater frequency, informed legal commentators have fingered plaintiffs who file lawsuits to extort a settlement, even when they know that the expected return from the trial will be negative. To deter such "nuisance" lawsuits and lessen the tide of excessive litigation in general, scholars, politicians, and ordinary citizens have called for an adoption of the British rule whereby the loser of a trial must provide for the legal expenses, including attorney's fees, of the victor. The American system, by contrast, requires each litigant to bear his own attorney's fees regardless of the trial's outcome, unless there is a contract providing that the loser must pay the attorney's fees for the winner.

In the early 1990s, these calls for legal reform entered mainstream politics. To address the problems of excessive litigation, competitive disadvantage, and frivolous lawsuits, President Bush's Council on Competitiveness established a working group on Federal Civil Justice Reform in January 1991. The working group, led by Solicitor General Kenneth W. Starr, was asked to recommend reforms to the federal civil justice process in order to decrease the costs and time required to resolve legal disputes.

In August 1991, the council released a report entitled "Agenda for Civil Justice Reform in America" to overhaul what was considered an overburdened civil justice system in the world's most litigious society. The council made 50 recommendations for legal reform which represented the Bush administration's extensive blueprint to streamline the American civil justice system and thereby curb the multibillion-dollar expenditures for litigation costs which were thwarting American business in the world economy. The proposals were primarily aimed at achieving swifter justice, reducing the costs of litigation, and expanding opportunities to protect rights.

Of the five areas targeted for major reform,[a] the Bush administration's proposal to adopt the British rule was by far the most controversial in political and legal circles. The British rule—also known as the

"loser pays" rule—simply states that the losing party at trial must pay the legal costs of the winner. Although the "loser pays" rule is commonly referred to as the British rule, such a rule is applied in virtually every Western European country.

Under the council's recommendation, a modified "loser pays" rule would be adopted in cases involving state law brought under the federal court's diversity jurisdiction. The loser would pay the winner's costs of vindicating its prevailing position, but fee shifting would be limited to the amount in fees that the loser incurred, which could be further limited by judicial discretion. The Council suggested the rule as one of the quickest ways to get a handle on the litigation explosion. The report stated:

> Adopting a "loser pays" rule for payment of attorney's fees will provide those bringing suit with a choice of methods to finance their litigation. The rule would help fund meritorious claims not currently initiated because the cost of pursuing the claim would have exceeded the expected recovery. . . . Because the losing party will be obligated to pay the winner's fees, this approach will encourage litigants to evaluate carefully the merits of their cases before initiating a frivolous claim or adopting a spurious defense.[b]

The report went on to state that the rule is also grounded in fairness—in the equitable principle that a party who suffers should be made whole.

The Legal Community Reacts

Former American Bar Association President John Curtin maintained that the proposal for a modified British rule was rejected by the ABA because of the "chilling effect" such a rule would have on the legal rights of certain individuals. He explained that execution of the "loser pays" rule would discourage potential litigants with bona fide claims from bringing suit due to trepidation over monetary ruin.[c]

Both consumer groups and civil libertarians attacked the proposals. Public Citizen, a consumer advocate organization led by Ralph Nader, criticized the council's recommendations in an August 13, 1991,

---

a. The five main areas targeted for major reforms were discovery, punitive damages, expert evidence, alternative dispute resolution, and cost shifting. *Federal News Service*, August 13, 1991, 1.

b. *Agenda for Civil Justice Reform in America*, 24.

c. "Judiciary, ABA President Challenges Quayle Council Recommendations for Civil Justice Reforms," *Daily Report for Executives* BNA), August 14, 1991, A-3.

Political Perspective
Should the U.S. Adopt the British Rule That the Loser Pays the Winner's Attorney's Fees?—*Continued*

news release, calling the report an "anti-worker, anti-consumer, pro-corporate-wrongdoer blueprint for undermining America's system of common law."[d] Nader vehemently denounced the fee-shifting proposal, asserting that the rule would be exploited by "corporate goliaths" to "intimidate victims" with the prospect of defeat at trial "no matter how serious the injury or how egregious the wrongdoing."[e]

Critics of the proposal such as the Association of Trial Lawyers contended that the fee-shifting rule would limit access to the judiciary for the indigent and would inhibit the bringing of novel or untested legal theories. Bob Gibbins, president of the Association of Trial Lawyers of America, set forth a scathing attack of the proposed "loser pay" rule, stating that "[i]f in force, it could deny justice to those who cannot afford to pay their opponent's lawyer in addition to their own. The American rule stands for a vital American principle of providing access to justice for people of all means. Again, do we really want to change that?"[f]

In practice, the British rule is not as detrimental to plaintiffs as might appear at first glance. As the *ABA Journal* reported,[g] only about 40% of British plaintiffs in court actions involving personal injury are subject to the "loser pays" risk of the British rule.[h] Most plaintiffs avoid the risk by one of three methods.

---

d. *Ibid.*

e. *Ibid.*

f. Bob Gibbins, "Propositions Built on Myth," *The National Law Journal*, October 7, 1991, 17.

g. Herbert M. Kritzer, "The English Rule," *ABA Journal* (November 1992), 55.

h. *Ibid.*, based on a 1986 study conducted for the Lord Chancellor's Department, which is the management arm of the English judiciary.

The first method is that of a legal aid program. For those plaintiffs financially eligible for legal aid, the British government pays their legal costs. Some legal aid plaintiffs have their costs only partially subsidized, but most pay little or nothing. About 28% of British personal injury plaintiffs receive legal aid.

The second method of avoiding the "loser pays" risk is through trade unions. Most unions provide legal representation for their members and absorb litigation costs. Usually unions limit such funding to litigation related to members' accident claims. These are typically work-related claims, but many unions also fund nonwork-related claims. About 29% of British accident cases are handled by union-funded solicitors.

The third method for avoiding the risk is through legal expense insurance. Currently only about 2% of all British cases are pursued under this method. It should be noted, however, that insurance makes a significant difference in how solicitors handle cases, mainly because their clients do not have to be concerned about costs.

Methods of allocating legal costs cut deeply into the issue of distributive justice. When a litigant receives a favorable verdict at trial, is it unfair that he should have to bear the loss of his legal expenses? A claim of fairness can be linked to the idea that a trial's outcome authenticates the moral supremacy of the victor and the culpability of the loser. Proponents of this view argue that the winning side should therefore be restored fully to her position before the suit was brought or the injury was sustained.

A court must give considerable weight to its own decisions unless and until they have been overruled or undermined by the decisions of a higher court, or other supervening developments, such as a statutory overruling. But [a court] is not absolutely bound by [its previous rulings], and must give fair consideration to any substantial argument that a litigant makes for overruling a previous decision.[7]

---

7. *Colby v. J. C. Penney Co.*, 811 F. 2d 1119, 1123 (7th Cir. 1987).

Federal courts interpreting state law must follow that state's courts—this was the principle established in *Erie Railroad Co. v. Tompkins,* discussed earlier in this chapter. Every court must follow a decision of the U.S. Supreme Court, unless powerfully convinced that the Supreme Court itself would change its decision at the first possible opportunity.

It is not often that the Supreme Court reverses its opinion, but it does happen. For example the Supreme Court rejected in 1954, in the *Brown v. Board of Education*[8] school desegregation case, the "separate but equal" test it had adopted in 1896 in *Plessy v. Ferguson.*[9] More recently, the Supreme Court has been called upon to reverse the

1973 holding in *Roe v. Wade*[10] that a woman has a constitutionally protected right to an abortion. The importance of the doctrine of *stare decisis* was underscored in the following case.

8. 347 U.S. 483, 74 S.Ct. 686 (1954).
9. 163 U.S. 537, 16 S.Ct. 1138 (1896).

10. 410 U.S. 113, 93 S.Ct. 705 (1973).

■ **A Case in Point:** **In the Language of the Court**

Case 4.5
PLANNED PARENTHOOD OF S.E. PENNSYLVANIA v. CASEY
Supreme Court of the
United States
112 S.Ct. 2791 (1992).

FACTS The Pennsylvania Abortion Control Act of 1982 (as amended in 1988 and 1989) requires that a woman seeking an abortion give her informed consent prior to the abortion procedure, and that she be provided with certain information at least 24 hours before the abortion is performed. For a minor to obtain an abortion, the act requires the informed consent of one of her parents, but provides for a judicial bypass option if the minor does not wish to or cannot obtain a parent's consent. Another provision of the act requires that, unless certain exceptions apply, a married woman seeking an abortion must sign a statement indicating that she has notified her husband of her intended abortion. The act exempts compliance with these three requirements in the event of a "medical emergency," and imposes reporting requirements on facilities that provide abortion services.

Five abortion clinics and one physician, representing himself as well as a class of physicians who provide abortion services, brought suit seeking declaratory and injunctive relief. Each provision was challenged as unconstitutional on its face. Relying on *Roe v. Wade*, the District Court entered a preliminary injunction, held all the provisions at issue unconstitutional, and entered a permanent injunction against enforcing them. The Court of Appeals for the Third Circuit upheld as constitutional all of the regulations except for the husband notification requirement.

ISSUE PRESENTED In light of *Roe v. Wade* and the doctrine of *stare decisis*, should the Pennsylvania abortion regulations be upheld as constitutional?

OPINION O'CONNOR, KENNEDY, and SOUTER, J.J., writing for a plurality of the U.S. Supreme Court:

I

Liberty finds no refuge in a jurisprudence of doubt. Yet 19 years after our holding that the Constitution protects a woman's right to terminate her pregnancy in its early stages, *Roe v. Wade*, that definition of liberty is still questioned. Joining the respondents . . . the United States, as it has done in five other cases in the last decade, again asks us to overrule *Roe*.

. . . .

After considering the fundamental constitutional questions resolved by *Roe*, principles of institutional integrity, and the rule of *stare decisis*, we are led to conclude this: the essential holding of *Roe v. Wade* should be retained and once again reaffirmed.

Case **4.5** continued on following page

*Case **4.5** continued*

[The Court then gave a brief synopsis of the *Roe v. Wade* holding and its trimester approach to abortion regulation. Under *Roe* a woman's right to an abortion is virtually absolute in the first trimester of pregnancy. Regulations designed to protect the woman's health but not to further the state's interest in potential life are permissible in the second trimester. In the third trimester, when the fetus is viable, prohibitions are permitted provided the life or health of the mother is not at stake. The Court rejected the trimester framework which it did not consider to be part of the "essential holding" of *Roe*. Instead, the Court concluded that a woman has a right to terminate her pregnancy prior to the time the fetus is viable regardless of when that occurs.]

. . . .

III
A

The obligation to follow precedent begins with necessity, and a contrary necessity marks its outer limit. . . . Indeed, the very concept of the rule of law underlying our own Constitution requires such continuity over time that a respect for precedent is, by definition, indispensable. At the other extreme, a different necessity would make itself felt if a prior judicial ruling should come to be seen so clearly as error that its enforcement was for that very reason doomed.

Even when the decision to overrule a prior case is not, as in the rare, latter instance, virtually foreordained, it is common wisdom that the rule of *stare decisis* is not an "inexorable command," and certainly it is not such in every constitutional case. Rather, when this Court reexamines a prior holding, its judgment is customarily informed by a series of prudential and pragmatic considerations designed to test the consistency of overruling a prior decision with the ideal of the rule of law, and to gauge the respective costs of reaffirming and overruling a prior case. . . .

So in this case we may inquire whether *Roe's* central rule has been found unworkable; whether the rule's limitation on state power could be removed without serious inequity to those who have relied upon it or significant damage to the stability of the society governed by the rule in question; whether the law's growth in the intervening years has left *Roe's* central rule a doctrinal anachronism discounted by society; and whether *Roe's* premises of fact have so far changed in the ensuing two decades as to render its central holding somehow irrelevant or unjustifiable in dealing with the issue it addressed.

[One] comparison that 20th century history invites is with the cases employing the separate-but-equal rule for applying the Fourteenth Amendment's equal protection guarantee. They began with *Plessy v. Ferguson* holding that legislatively mandated racial segregation in public transportation works no denial of equal protection, rejecting the argument that racial separation enforced by the legal machinery of American society treats the black race as inferior. The *Plessy* Court considered "the underlying fallacy of the plaintiff's argument to consist in the assumption that the enforced separation of the two races stamps the colored race with a badge of inferiority. If this be so, it is not by reason of anything found in the act, but solely because the colored race chooses to put that construction upon it." Whether, as a matter of historical fact, the Justices in the *Plessy* majority believed this or not, this understanding of the implication of segregation was the stated justification for the Court's opinion. But this understanding of the facts and the rule it was stated to justify were repudiated in *Brown v. Board of Education.* . . .

The Court in *Brown* addressed these facts of life by observing that whatever may have been the understanding in *Plessy's* time of the power of segregation to stigmatize those who were segregated with a "badge of inferiority," it was clear by 1954 that legally sanctioned segregation had just such an effect, to the point that racially separate public educational facilities were deemed inherently unequal. Society's understanding of the facts upon which a constitutional ruling was sought in 1954 was thus fundamentally different from the basis claimed for the decision in 1896. While we think *Plessy* was wrong the day it was decided, . . . we must also recognize that the *Plessy* Court's explanation for its decision was so clearly at odds with the facts apparent to the Court in 1954 that the decision to reexamine *Plessy* was on this ground alone not only justified but required.

. . . .

. . . In constitutional adjudication as elsewhere in life, changed circumstances may impose new obligations, and the thoughtful part of the Nation could accept each decision to overrule a prior case as a response to the Court's constitutional duty.

Because the case before us presents no such occasion it could be seen as no such response. Because neither the factual underpinnings of *Roe's* central holding nor our understanding of it has changed (and because no other indication of weakened precedent has been shown) the Court could not pretend to be reexamining the prior law with any justification beyond a present doctrinal disposition to come out differently from the Court of 1973. . . .

. . . .

RESULT   The Court upheld what it considered to be the central holding of *Roe v. Wade* under the doctrine of *stare decisis*. At the same time, the Court upheld the Pennsylvania abortion regulations, except for the spousal notification requirement, as constitutional. The regulations imposed procedural requirements that the Court did not consider central to the holding of *Roe*.

COMMENTS   Chief Justice Rehnquist explicitly stated in his dissent that *Roe* was wrongly decided and could be overturned consistently with the traditional approach to *stare decisis* in constitutional cases. Justice Blackmun, author of the *Roe* opinion, strongly disagreed and argued that under the test of strict scrutiny that he believed should be applied, all provisions of the Pennsylvania law should be struck down. He noted the slim margin behind the Court's decision to uphold *Roe*:

In one sense, the Court's approach is worlds apart from that of the Chief Justice and Justice Scalia. And yet, in another sense, the distance between the two approaches is short—the distance is but a single vote.

I am 83 years old. I cannot remain on this Court forever, and when I do step down, the confirmation process for my successor well may focus on the issue before us today. That, I regret, may be exactly where the choice between the two worlds will be made.

Case **4.5** *continued on following page*

*Case **4.5** continued*

As discussed in the "Inside Story" for chapter 2, Justice Ruth Bader Ginsburg refused to have applied an abortion litmus test to her nomination to the Court in 1993.

Questions
1. What factors did the Court consider in deciding whether to overturn *Roe v. Wade*?
2. Why did the Court conclude that overturning *Plessy* in *Brown v. Board of Education* was appropriate but that overturning *Roe v. Wade* would not be?

A court of appeals does not have to follow another court of appeals. A trial court does not have to follow another trial court. It must follow the court of appeals above it, but need not follow other appellate courts. Thus, if the U.S. Court of Appeals for the Tenth Circuit (based in Denver) interprets a federal air pollution regulation in a certain way, the U.S. Court of Appeals for the Sixth Circuit (based in Cincinnati) may follow that interpretation, but is not compelled to do so. The authority of the Tenth Circuit does not reach beyond its own geographical boundaries. However, a federal district court in Tulsa, which is within the Tenth Circuit, would be compelled to interpret the regulation in accordance with the decision of the Court of Appeals for the Tenth Circuit.

Restatements   Today, many rules that originated as common law have been collected into *restatements* compiled by legal scholars, practicing attorneys, and judges. There are restatements of various areas of the law, such as torts, contracts, property, and trusts. The restatements do not compel a judge to make a particular decision unless the rule has been adopted by the state's legislature. They are persuasive rather than authoritative.

■ Civil Procedure

Civil procedure refers to the methods, procedures, and practices that govern the processing of a civil lawsuit from start to finish. The Federal Rules of Civil Procedure (FRCP) control the trial practices in all of the U.S. district courts. Each federal district court may also adopt its own local rules, applicable only within that district, to supplement the federal rules. Individual judges may even have particular rules as to how certain procedures operate in their own courts.

Each state has a set of rules governing the procedures in the state trial court system. Often, the state rules will be similar in many respects to the federal rules. There is also a separate set of rules for practicing before the various courts of appeals and supreme courts. These rules address every requirement, from the time deadline for filing an appeal, to the contents of the notice of appeal, to the paper size, line spacing, and type style for briefs filed with the court. Each court system has its own rules or guidelines to ensure the orderly processing of the lawsuit.

Filing a Claim

Complaint   The *complaint* briefly states a grievance and makes allegations of: (1) the particular facts giving rise to the dispute; (2) the legal reason why the plaintiff is entitled to a remedy; and (3) the "prayer," or request for relief. The complaint should also explain why this particular court has jurisdiction over the alleged dispute and whether the plaintiff requests a jury trial. If the plaintiff does not request a jury trial within the time limit, that right is deemed to be waived.

Summons   After the plaintiff files the complaint, the clerk of the court prepares a summons. The summons officially notifies the defendant that a lawsuit is pending against her in a particular court and that she must file a response to the complaint within a certain number of days. The clerk then stamps the official seal of the court on the summons. Next, the plaintiff or the clerk will serve the official summons and complaint on the defendant. Service is usually completed by sending the documents to the defendant by mail. After a defendant receives the summons and complaint, she will have from 20 to 30 days to file an answer.

Answer   The defendant's *answer* may admit or deny the various allegations in the complaint. If the defendant believes that she lacks sufficient information to assess the truth of an allegation, she should state this. Such a statement has the effect of a denial. The answer may also deny that the law provides relief for the plaintiff's claim regardless of whether the plaintiff's factual allegations are true.

The answer may put forth affirmative defenses to the allegations in the complaint. An *affirmative defense* admits that the defendant has acted in a certain way, but claims that the defendant's conduct was not the real or legal cause of harm to the plaintiff. An example of an affirmative defense in a contract case is the requirement under the statute of frauds (discussed in chapter 8) that certain agreements are not enforceable unless they are in writing.

An answer may also include a *counterclaim,* a legal claim by the defendant against the plaintiff. The counterclaim need not be related to the plaintiff's claim.

If the defendant does not file an answer within the time required, a *default judgment* may be entered in favor of the plaintiff. The defendant, however, may ask the court to set aside the default judgment if there were extenuating circumstances for not filing the answer to the complaint on time.

The complaint, the answer, and any reply to the answer filed by the plaintiff are referred to as the *pleadings.*

Discovery

Before a trial is held, the parties collect evidence to support their claims, through a process called *discovery.* In general, parties may obtain discovery regarding any matter relevant to the lawsuit. Discovery includes *depositions,* which are written or oral questioning of any person who may have helpful information about the facts of the case; *interrogatories,* which are written questions to the parties in the case and their attorneys; and *requests for production of documents* such as medical records and personal files.

The basic purpose of discovery is to eliminate the "game" elements in a trial. If all the parties to the lawsuit have all the evidence before trial, everyone benefits. By revealing the strengths and weaknesses of the various claims, discovery frequently allows the lawsuit to be *settled*—resolved by agreement without a trial. At the least, discovery helps prevent any major surprises from occurring at trial because each side already has learned about the other's case.

Discovery serves other useful functions. First, it can preserve evidence. For example, depositions preserve the testimony of important witnesses who may otherwise be unavailable at trial. Second, discovery reduces the number of legal issues to be presented at trial, because the parties can see beforehand which claims they have evidence to support and which ones are not worth pursuing.

Discovery has its drawbacks, however. The process is very expensive, because discovery is labor intensive. Frequently, hours and days of depositions and hundreds of interrogatories will be undertaken. The strategy behind such a plan can be twofold: to wear down the opposing party by making the lawsuit more expensive than a victory would be worth; or to keep the papers flowing at such a rate that the other side cannot discern what all the documents really state. Such tactics often lead to discovery disputes that end up before the court.

Ethical Consideration

Abuse of the discovery process can result in the imposition of sanctions or penalties, including fines. Less flagrant behavior may not be punished, but it still may be unethical. Abuses happen most often when a well-funded corporation is sued by an individual or a company with limited resources. A manager should ensure that his lawyers do not use hundreds of interrogatories and weeks of depositions just to wear down the other side and exhaust their resources.

Not all relevant information is subject to discovery. For example, the *work-product rule* protects information that an attorney prepares in the course of her work. This information includes the private memoranda and personal thoughts of the attorney created while she is preparing a case for trial. The rationale behind the work-product rule is that a lawyer, while performing her duties, must "work with a certain degree of privacy, free from unnecessary intrusion by opposing parties and their counsel."[11] Work-product materials may be obtained only with a showing of extreme necessity, such that the failure to obtain the materials would unduly prejudice an attorney's case or create hardship and injustice.

---

11. *Hickman v. Taylor,* 329 U.S. 495, 510, 67 S.Ct. 385, 393 (1947).

Attorney-Client Privilege

An even more important limitation on discovery and testimony at trial is the *attorney-client privilege,* which dates back to the sixteenth century and provides that a court cannot force the disclosure of confidential communications between a client and his attorney.

The rationale of the attorney-client privilege is to promote the administration of justice. Clients are more likely to make a full and frank disclosure of the facts to an attorney if they know that the attorney cannot be compelled to pass the information on to adversary parties. An attorney is better able to advise and represent a client if the client discloses the complete facts. The privilege may also help to prevent unnecessary litigation, because an attorney who knows all the facts should be better able to assess whether litigation is justified.

The attorney-client privilege is an exception to the general rule of evidence that any person with knowledge of a case may be called to testify in depositions or at trial. Thus, by protecting certain communications, the attorney-client privilege does limit the amount of evidence that can be produced at trial. As a result, courts will place certain limitations on the scope of the privilege.

To be protected by the privilege, a communication must occur between the attorney and the client. The communication must also be intended as confidential. If the client plans to relay the information to others, or makes the communication in the presence of other individuals not involved in the lawsuit, there is no confidentiality.

The attorney-client privilege belongs to the client alone. The attorney, however, has an obligation to alert the client to the existence of the privilege and, if necessary, to invoke it on the client's behalf. The client can waive the privilege over the attorney's objection if the client so desires.

Limitations The attorney to whom the communication is made must be a practicing attorney at the time of the communication, and the person making the communication must be a current or prospective client seeking legal advice. If the client were conversing with the attorney about nonlegal matters, the conversation would not be protected.

The attorney-client privilege does not protect client communications that are made to further a crime or other illegal act. If an executive were to ask his attorney about the best way to embezzle money, that conversation would not be privileged.

> **"**
> *If an executive were to ask his attorney about the best way to embezzle money, that conversation would not be privileged.*

Corporate Clients With communications between a corporate client and an attorney, it is often difficult to define what element of the corporation can be considered the client. The corporation does not fit the common definition of a client, because a company itself is unable to communicate with the attorney except through its officers, directors, agents, or employees. The case below is a key decision defining who is the client for purposes of applying the attorney-client privilege in a corporate setting.

■ A Case in Point: Summary

Case 4.6
UPJOHN CO. v. UNITED STATES
Supreme Court of the United States
449 U.S. 383, 101 S.Ct. 677 (1981).

FACTS In January 1976, independent accountants conducted an audit of one of the foreign subsidiaries of Upjohn, an international pharmaceuticals company. The accountants discovered that the subsidiary made payments to, or for the benefit of, foreign government officials in order to secure government business. The accountants informed Upjohn's vice president and general counsel. In response to the accountants' information, the general counsel conducted an internal investigation of Upjohn's foreign subsidiaries. In conjunction with outside attorneys, Upjohn's general counsel distributed a questionnaire to foreign managers concerning these alleged practices. Upjohn's attorneys also interviewed 33 other company employees and officers. Upjohn voluntarily submitted a report to the Securities and

Exchange Commission disclosing certain questionable payments. A copy of the report was submitted to the Internal Revenue Service (IRS), which immediately began an investigation to determine the tax consequences of the payments. The IRS issued a summons to Upjohn demanding to see the results of the questionnaires, files related to the questionnaires, and copies of the employee interviews. Upjohn refused to turn over these documents, on the ground that the information was protected by the attorney-client and work-product privileges.

The IRS filed a lawsuit in federal district court, seeking to enforce the summons. The district court ruled that Upjohn must comply with the IRS summons. Upjohn appealed the decision to the Court of Appeals for the Sixth Circuit. The court of appeals ruled that Upjohn did not waive its attorney-client privilege. This privilege, however, only covered communications made by officers and agents responsible for directing Upjohn's response to the lawsuit. Thus, only the communications of the company personnel who were within a "control group"—the senior level of officers and managers guiding the corporation—were considered confidential. According to the Sixth Circuit, the communications of the regular employees to Upjohn's attorneys were not confidential, because these individuals were not identified with the corporation as a whole. Upjohn appealed the Sixth Circuit's decision to the U.S. Supreme Court.

ISSUE PRESENTED   Are the communications by a company's employees to corporate counsel protected by the attorney-client privilege when the employee responses to counsel were confidential communications made while the company was seeking legal advice?

SUMMARY OF OPINION   The U.S. Supreme Court rejected the "control group" test, on the ground that it would frustrate the very purpose of attorney-client privilege, which is to encourage communication of relevant information by all employees to the corporation's attorneys. Further, the middle- and lower level employees, rather than the senior officers, will normally be the ones whose actions embroil the corporation in serious legal difficulties. Accordingly, these same employees will be the ones possessing relevant information needed by corporate counsel to advise as to actual or potential legal problems.

The Supreme Court adopted a "subject matter" test to determine when the attorney-client privilege is available to a corporation. Under this test, the privilege protects the communications or discussions of any company employee with counsel so long as the subject matter of the communication relates to that employee's duties and the communication is made at the direction of a corporate superior. The Court also ruled that the attorney-client privilege extends to communications made to both in-house and outside counsel as long as the attorneys are acting in a legal capacity. Previously, courts addressing this issue had been reluctant to protect communications with in-house counsel.

RESULT   The Supreme Court reversed the ruling of the court of appeals. Communications between Upjohn's attorneys and all of its employees, not just a small, upper-level group, were deemed protected under the attorney-client privilege as long as those communications passed the "subject matter" test.

COMMENTS   The decision in *Upjohn* did not resolve all of the uncertainties regarding the application of attorney-client privilege to corporations.

Case **4.6** *continued on following page*

*Case **4.6** continued*

The Supreme Court did not decide whether the attorney-client privilege applies to communications with former employees. Nor did it resolve the issue of what exactly constitutes a voluntary waiver of the attorney-client privilege by a corporation. Finally, there is still uncertainty about the protection that the privilege gives corporations in suits brought against them by shareholders.

In *In re Bieter Co.*,[12] the U.S. Court of Appeals for the Eighth Circuit held that the attorney-client privilege extends to communications between a partnership's attorney and a consultant to the partnership who was the functional equivalent of an employee. Even though the consultant was an independent contractor, not an employee, he was still a representative of the client partnership. Factors pointing to this included the fact that he had daily contact with the partnership's principals, he had acted as the partnership's sole representative in critical meetings, and he had worked with the partnership's attorneys on the lawsuit.

Guidelines Following the Supreme Court's decision in *Upjohn,* there are a few guidelines for attorneys and corporations concerning the best method by which to keep communications within the scope of the attorney-client privilege.[13]

1. Communication between an attorney and a corporation is only protected when a client is seeking or receiving legal advice—not business advice. Thus, corporations should request legal advice in writing and assign communication with the attorney to a specific employee who has responsibility over the subject matter at issue.

2. Companies should make sure that all communication between employees and corporate counsel is directed by senior management and that the employees know they must keep all communications confidential.

3. Corporations should demonstrate the confidentiality of attorney-client communications by dealing directly with counsel (not through intermediaries) and by maintaining confidential files and documentation.

4. When a company gives a governmental agency access to its communications or files, the company should negotiate a written agreement of confidentiality with the agency, or an agreement that the agency will not take physical possession of the documents. The corporation should also investigate the possibility of statutory protection in this situation.

Pretrial Activity

Before the trial begins, the attorneys and the judge usually meet to discuss certain issues.

Motion to Dismiss The lawsuit may be resolved before trial by the judge granting a motion to dismiss. A motion formally requests the court to take some action. A *motion to dismiss* seeks to terminate the lawsuit on the ground that the plaintiff's claim is technically inadequate. A judge will grant a motion to dismiss if the court lacks jurisdiction over the subject matter or the parties involved; if the plaintiff failed to properly serve the complaint on the defendant; or if the plaintiff has failed to state a claim upon which relief can be granted.

A party may file a motion to dismiss immediately after the complaint and answer have been filed. This is known as a motion for judgment on the pleadings. One party, usually the defendant, argues that the complaint alone demonstrates that the action is futile.

The moving party may file affidavits, that is, sworn statements, or other written evidence in an attempt to show that the cause of action is without merit. When information or documents other than the pleadings are involved, the motion becomes a motion for summary judgment.

Summary Judgment A judge will grant *summary judgment* only if all of the written evidence before the court clearly establishes that there are no disputed issues of material fact and the party who requested the summary judgment is entitled to recover as a matter of law. If there is even a scintilla, that is, even the slightest bit, of evidence that casts doubt on an important fact in the lawsuit,

12. 16 F.3d 929 (8th Cir. 1994).
13. Based on Block and Remz, "After 'Upjohn': The Uncertain Confidentiality of Corporate Internal Investigative Files," in American Bar Association Section of Litigation, *Recent Developments in Attorney-Client Privilege, Work Product Doctrine and Confidentiality of Communications Between Counsel and Client* (1983).

the judge must not grant summary judgment. However, a judge may grant summary judgment on some issues of the case and let the other issues proceed to trial. This is called a partial summary judgment.

Pretrial Conference Pretrial or status conferences may be held either in open court or in the judge's chambers. During these conferences, the attorneys for the litigants meet with the judge to discuss the progress of their case. Topics discussed may include: (1) the issues as stated in the pleadings; (2) any amendments to the pleadings; (3) the scheduling of future discovery and a plan for the timely completion of discovery; (4) the status of pending motions or prospective motions that a party may file; (5) a schedule of the disclosure of witnesses or exhibits; and most important, (6) the prospects for a settlement of the dispute. The main goal of a pretrial conference is to formulate an efficient plan for the trial.

Trial

A trial usually goes through the following stages.

1. Selection of the jury (if the trial is before a jury). The judge or attorneys may question the potential jurors.
2. Opening statements, first by the plaintiff's attorney and then by the defendant's attorney.
3. Presentation of evidence and witnesses by the plaintiff's attorney. This consists of:
   a. Direct examination of witnesses by the plaintiff's attorney
   b. Cross-examination of witnesses by the defendant's attorney
   c. Redirect examination by the plaintiff's attorney
   d. Recross-examination by the defendant's attorney
   e. Redirect and recross-examination repeated until both sides have no further questions to ask.
4. Presentation of evidence and witnesses by the defendant's attorney. This consists of:
   a. Direct examination of witnesses by the defendant's attorney
   b. Cross-examination of witnesses by the plaintiff's attorney
   c. Redirect and recross-examination until both sides have no further questions to ask.
5. Motion for a directed verdict by either attorney.
6. Closing arguments, first by the defendant's attorney and then by the plaintiff's attorney.
7. The judge's instructions to the jury.
8. Jury deliberations.
9. Announcement of the jury verdict.

"*Not another change of venue, Counsellor!*"

Drawing by Ed Fisher; © 1971 The New Yorker Magazine, Inc.

Selection of Jury   Each side can challenge any number of jurors for cause during a process of questioning the potential jurors called *voir dire*. Cause includes any relationship between the juror and any of the parties or their counsel. Most jurisdictions also permit a limited number of preemptory challenges. These can be used by counsel to remove potential jurors who counsel thinks might be inclined to decide for the other side. The U.S. Supreme Court has held that it is unconstitutional to use a preemptory challenge to remove a potential juror due to race or gender.[14]

Motion for a Directed Verdict   At the close of the presentation of all of the evidence, either attorney may ask the judge to grant a motion for a *directed verdict*. The moving party asserts that the other side has not produced enough evidence to support the legal claim or defense alleged. The motion requests that the judge take the case away from the jury and direct that a verdict be entered in favor of the party making the motion. Should the judge agree that there is not even an iota of evidence to support one party's claim or defense, the judge will issue a directed verdict. This does not happen very frequently.

Jury Verdict   After both sides have presented the closing arguments, the judge instructs the jury on applicable rules of law. After deliberating in private, the jury delivers its verdict, specifying both the prevailing party and the relief to which that party is entitled. In federal court, the six-person jury verdict must be unanimous. In state courts, a unanimous jury verdict is not always required. Frequently, 9 out of 12 votes is sufficient.

Posttrial Motions

The announcement of the jury verdict does not necessarily conclude the case. Either party may make a motion to set aside the verdict or to have the case retried.

Judgment Notwithstanding the Verdict   Immediately after the jury has rendered its verdict and the jury has been excused from the courtroom, the attorney for the losing party may make a motion for judgment notwithstanding the verdict. Such a judgment, also known as a judgment *n.o.v.*, from the Latin *non obstante veredicto*, reverses the jury verdict on the ground that the evidence of the prevailing party was so weak that no reasonable jury could have resolved the dispute in that party's favor.

However, if there is any reasonable possibility that the evidence could support the jury verdict, the judge will deny a motion for a judgment n.o.v., or j.n.o.v.

New Trial   The judge may order a new trial if there were serious errors in the trial process—such as misconduct on the part of the attorneys or the jurors, or the improper admission of evidence that severely prejudiced one party's chances for a fair trial.

Appeal

If the trial judge does not grant the motion for a j.n.o.v. or a new trial, the losing party can appeal the decision. The appellate court will review the manner in which the trial judge applied the law to the case and conducted the trial. The court of appeals can review the presentation of evidence at trial, the denial of a motion for a directed verdict, the jury instructions, and even the jury award of damages.

    If the appellant loses before the court of appeals, she may want to have the supreme court consider the decision. However, appeals are expensive. The losing party should seriously consider the likelihood of success at the higher court before pursuing an appeal.

■ Class Actions

If the conduct of the defendant affected numerous persons in a common way, the case may be brought by a representative of the class of persons affected as a *class action*. This was done in the asbestos personal injury cases brought against asbestos manufacturers such as GAF Corp. and Pfizer Inc., and the silicone breast implant cases involving Dow Corning and others. (The Dow Corning settlement is discussed in the "Inside Story" in chapter 10.) Class actions are the norm in actions alleging securities fraud.

    Written notice of the formation of the class must be mailed to all potential class members. Anyone who wants to litigate separately can opt out of the class. *Business Week* estimates that 260,000 out of millions of potential claimants for asbestos-related injury elected to opt out of a $1 billion settlement reached in 1993 involving 20 of the largest asbestos manufacturers.[15] If a person does not opt out, he is a member of the class and will be bound by any decision or settlement reached in the class action.

---

14. *See Batson v. Kentucky,* 476 U.S. 79, 106 S.Ct. 1712 (1986) (race); *J.E.B. v. Alabama ex rel. T.B.,* 114 S.Ct. 1419 (1994) (gender).

15. Catherine Yang, "Look Who's Talking Settlement," *Business Week,* July 18, 1994, 72.

Although historically corporate defendants have condemned class actions as an easy way for an eager plaintiff and her lawyer to get to court, this is changing. *Business Week* reports that some defendants see class actions as an efficient way to end a "litigation nightmare."[16]

A class action can have the following advantages in a major product liability case: (1) the settlement can bind not only present class members but also future claimants; (2) standardized payment schedules avoid the risk of widely divergent jury awards; (3) some claimants who suffered less harm than others can be excluded from the settlement; and (4) the filing of suits and the settlement can occur on the same day.[17] Any settlement of a class action requires approval by the court hearing the case. Even if the trial court approves of a settlement, a person excluded from compensation can still challenge it as a violation of due process under the U.S. Constitution. It is unclear how the U.S. Supreme Court might rule on such a claim.

Ethical Consideration

Is it ethical for a manufacturer of a product that caused harm to persons who will not discover it until a future date to enter into a class action settlement that provides limited funds for future claimants?

■ Litigation Strategies for Plaintiffs

When planning to file a lawsuit, the plaintiff must decide which legal claim is most likely to succeed. The plaintiff must also decide in which court to pursue the lawsuit.

The Decision to Sue

Parties frequently file a lawsuit without giving sufficient thought to the various consequences. Before filing a lawsuit, anyone in business should consider: (1) whether the

16. *Ibid.*
17. *Ibid.*

likelihood of recovery and the amount of recovery are enough to justify the cost and disruption of litigation; (2) whether the defendant will be able to satisfy a judgment against him; (3) whether the defendant is likely to raise a counterclaim; (4) whether suing will cause any ill will among customers, suppliers, or other sources of corporate financing; (5) whether any publicity accompanying the suit will be harmful; and (6) the impact of the litigation on the company's relationship with the defendant. For example, a company may be advised not to sue the manufacturer of its multimillion-dollar computer over a $50,000 software problem if the company must rely on this manufacturer for support, service, and parts for the next few years.

If a lawsuit appears inevitable, there may be some advantage to filing a claim first. The plaintiff's claim determines in what court the case will be heard. The defendant, however, may be able to remove an action from state court to federal court if there is diversity of citizenship or a federal question. Alternatively, she may be able to remove the action to a more appropriate *venue,* or location.

Parties should always consider settling the suit. Recent figures show that more than 90% of cases settle out of court, saving all parties the time, cost, and ill will of a trial. Filing a lawsuit can be a tactic to encourage settlement of a dispute that neither party really wishes to bring to trial. Settlement discussions usually occur during the pretrial stages.

Parties should also consider alternatives to litigation, such as arbitration and mediation. Alternative dispute resolution techniques are discussed later in this chapter.

Some attorneys recommend that companies construct a prelitigation "decision tree" which determines at each step of the proceeding the chances of prevailing or losing, the costs of going forward, and the potential amount of recovery. Developing a decision tree forces a company to conduct a substantial factual and legal analysis of its claim. This is in everyone's interest; courts are inclined to impose monetary penalties or "sanctions" on companies, individuals, and attorneys who file lawsuits without sufficient facts or the legal basis to support their claims.

The Decision to Settle

Some lawsuits are unlikely to settle, for example: (1) cases presenting legal questions—such as the meaning of an ambiguous term in a contract—that the court should clarify to avoid future disputes between the same parties; (2) cases that could bring a large recovery if the plaintiff wins and no great harm if it loses; and (3) cases where one side has acted so unreasonably that settlement is impossible.

Sometimes a lawsuit is worth pursuing simply to establish a company's credibility as one that will fight to support a legitimate business position. Such a philosophy, however, if applied too rigidly, can be expensive and may do more harm than good.

Settlement is likely in a case where pursuing the lawsuit all the way to trial is not cost efficient. For example, if a plaintiff alleges that a product is defective and caused him a loss of $4,500, the legal expenses will far exceed the original loss. Discovery alone is likely to cost more than $4,500. In such a case, it is in both parties' interest to settle the dispute if at all possible. However, if the plaintiff's claim is similar to many other identical claims that may be brought against the company, settling the first claim could appear to commit the defendant to paying all the other claims too.

Pretrial Preparation

Having decided to file a lawsuit, the company should carefully select the personnel who will act as the contacts for the attorneys. These individuals should make sure that the necessary information and documents are gathered for the attorneys. The contact persons should have substantial authority in the company.

Executives or senior management who will be involved in the lawsuit or with the corporate attorneys should not handle public relations. This could lead to disputes regarding the waiver of the attorney-client privilege.

At the Top

It is important for members of higher management and in some cases the full board of directors to become involved in the decisions of when to sue, when to settle or dismiss, and how vigorously to defend. Sometimes the managers or employees intimately involved in the case lack the perspective and objectivity to determine the merits and the full impact a particular litigation decision will have on the company as a whole.

The company should instruct all employees not to destroy any documents that may be relevant to the lawsuit. Destruction of these documents, particularly after the claim is filed, can be harmful and even illegal. Document retention policies are discussed in greater detail later in this chapter.

The company should instruct employees not to discuss the lawsuit with anyone, including family or close friends. Casual comments about bankrupting the opposing party or teaching an opponent a lesson may turn up as testimony at trial, with undesirable consequences.

The company and its attorney should develop a budget for the lawsuit. Then at each step of the case, strategic options can be discussed on the basis of cost-benefit analysis. The budget should include not only the lawyer's fees but also: (1) the cost of employee time; (2) damage to company morale; (3) disruption of business; and (4) other hidden expenses. A budget will help the company manager and lawyer decide whether to pursue the lawsuit or attempt to settle.

The attorney and client should then select a court in which to file the lawsuit. Federal courts may be more accustomed to handling complex business litigation, such as that involving federal securities law or employment discrimination laws. State courts are usually skilled in handling business disputes ranging from contract matters to personal injury lawsuits. Other considerations about where to file include: (1) the convenience and location of necessary witnesses and documents; (2) the location of trial counsel; (3) the reputation and size of the company and its opponent in a particular area; and (4) the possibility of favorable or unfavorable publicity.

All courts urge the parties to confer and settle the case if possible. The judge will act as a settlement mediator and objectively assist counsel in recognizing the strengths and weaknesses of their cases. Some state courts require a settlement conference before a specially designated settlement judge. The parties may also hire retired judges, professional mediators, law school professors, or mediators who are part of a bar association settlement program.

■ Litigation Strategies for Defendants

A defendant receiving a complaint and summons should never let the lawsuit go unattended. An answer is required usually within 20 to 30 days. The defendant should also plan a defense strategy and follow it step by step. Factual and legal preparation should be done promptly, so that important evidence—such as the memory of key witnesses—is not lost.

When a company receives the complaint, efforts should be made to determine why the plaintiff felt it necessary to sue. Some of the factors may include:

■ Whether prior bargaining or negotiations with the plaintiff broke down, and why

■ Whether the company's negotiator was pursuing the wrong tactics or following an agenda inconsistent with the company's best interests

■ Whether the lawsuit resulted from bad personnel practices that the company still needs to correct.

Senior executives should also get together and decide whether it would be beneficial to discuss the lawsuit with the plaintiff.

A defendant should also promptly consider the possibility of a settlement, and review the ways in which amicable negotiations could be commenced or resumed. The defendant may also want to consider mediation or arbitration as alternatives to an expensive trial.

If the lawsuit cannot be settled, then the defendant should proceed with the same steps required of the plaintiff—plan a strategy, prepare a budget for the action, and so on. If the suit was filed in a state court, the defendant must decide whether it is possible, and desirable, to move the action to federal court.

If the plaintiff has sued in a place that is greatly inconvenient for the defendant and its witnesses, the defendant may file a motion for a change of venue. A federal district court may transfer the case to a federal district court in another state. A state court, however, can only transfer the case to another location within the state.

Ethical Consideration

Defendants are faced with ethical dilemmas when they know they did something wrong yet don't think the other parties can prove it. Ethical issues also arise when a company uses its superior economic resources to wear down an individual plaintiff through excess use of pretrial motions and discovery requests. The tobacco companies have been accused of employing these tactics in litigation arising out of disease or deaths attributed to cigarette smoking.

■ Document Retention

When a company is a defendant in a lawsuit, company documents may be used to prove liability in court. According to *The Wall Street Journal,* some companies are destroying three times as many documents as they did a decade ago. Companies have learned that nearly any corporate document can become a powerful weapon in court in the hands of opposing counsel. A well-designed and well-executed document management program can: (1) reduce corporate liability; (2) protect trade secrets and other confidential information; and, most important, (3) save on litigation costs.[18] Time and money are wasted when corporate staff and lawyers are forced to search for documents during discovery. With an organized document management program, a company knows exactly what documents are in its possession and where these documents are located.

> 66
>
> *A well-designed and well-executed document management program can: (1) reduce corporate liability; (2) protect trade secrets and other confidential information; and, most important, (3) save on litigation costs.*

Most companies do not have established policies regarding document retention and destruction. They practice what some professionals call the "search and destroy" technique of file management: arbitrarily cleaning out file cabinets when storage space is running low.

However, federal and state regulations require companies to retain certain records. The *Code of Federal Regulations* contains more than 2,400 regulations requiring that certain types of business records be maintained for specific periods of time. Many regulatory agencies have increased their retention requirements, forcing some companies to increase their file capacities by more than 15% a year.

---

18. Much of the discussion of document retention that follows is based on the work of John Ruhnka, associate professor at the Graduate School of Business Administration, University of Colorado at Denver, and Robert B. Austin, CRM, CSP, of Austin Associates, Denver; including John Ruhnka and Robert Austin, "Design Considerations for Document Retention/Destruction Programs," 1 *Corporate Confidentiality and Disclosure Letter* 2 (1988).

Designing a Policy

In general, documents that a company is not required to retain for any business or legal purpose should be eliminated from company files. Documents that are kept may be obtained by opposing counsel during discovery, and they may be harmful to the company in court. For example, an interoffice memorandum that described company strategy toward a competitor as "target and exploit their weak points to eliminate them from the market" could be produced in court as evidence of intent to engage in an illegal and unfair business practice.

Documents containing elements of a company's decision-making process can sometimes be used out of context. A well-known example is the memorandum that was found in the files of Ford Motor Company during discovery for a trial in 1972 arising out of a death caused by a Ford Pinto's allegedly defectively designed fuel tank. The memo, prepared in compliance with the regulations of a federal agency, compared the cost of design modifications to the Pinto fuel tank with the potential loss of life that might be caused by the existing design. During the trial, the plaintiff's counsel convinced the jury that the memo was proof that Ford decided to defer redesign of the fuel tanks on the basis of this cost study. The jury awarded compensatory damages of $3.5 million and punitive damages of $125 million against Ford. (Compensatory damages compensate the injured party for the harm suffered; punitive damages are intended to punish the wrongdoer for conduct that is outrageous, willful, or malicious.)

Even when a company has been careful to destroy records, duplicates may exist in an employee's personal files, where they are still subject to discovery. For example, in the mid-1970s, the Weyerhauser Company paid $200 million in a case when company documents were found through discovery in personal files in the home of a retired company administrative assistant.

An employee's private diaries or notebooks are also subject to discovery. Opposing counsel could glean from them a great deal about a company's operations. Companies should therefore include this type of record in its document management program.

Corporate Privacy

Besides protecting a company in the event of litigation, a document management program protects corporate privacy and trade secrets. A company should destroy confidential or proprietary materials as soon as possible. It should also preserve the confidentiality of employee records and destroy these records when they are no longer necessary. If an employee sues a company for wrongful termination, the employee's file is subject to discovery, and careless or unsubstantiated information in the file may be persuasive evidence at trial. Further, corporations can be liable for damages if confidential information in an employee's file, such as a medical record indicating past drug use, is made public.

Necessary Elements of a Document Retention Program

Well-Planned and Systematic   To stand up in court, a document retention program must be well planned and systematic. Companies usually appoint a senior officer of the organization to be responsible for the supervision and auditing of the document management program. Policies should be established as to the types of documents to be destroyed, including documents stored on computer or word processing disks. The documents should then be systematically destroyed according to an established time frame (for example, when they reach a certain age).

No Destruction in the Face of a Potential Lawsuit
It is illegal to destroy documents when the company has notice of a potential lawsuit. A company cannot wait until a suit is formally filed against it to stop destroying relevant documents. A company must halt destruction as soon as it has good reason to believe that a suit is likely to be filed or an investigation started. Companies that did not halt destruction of documents have been forced to pay damages even when they acted accidentally. For example, in *Carlucci v. Piper Aircraft*,[19] flight data information essential to the case was missing. The judge did not believe Piper's claim that it had not deliberately destroyed the relevant document. The judge issued a directed verdict for the plaintiff and rendered a $10 million judgment against Piper.

 Ethical Consideration

If a company may legally destroy incriminating documents because there is no likelihood of a lawsuit, is it ethical to do so?

---

19. 102 F.R.D. 472 (S.D.Fla. 1984).

No Selective Destruction   The importance of a systematic document management program cannot be emphasized enough. The court will scrutinize whether document destruction was done in the ordinary course of business. Any hint of selective destruction jeopardizes the defensibility of a document management program.

■ Alternative Dispute Resolution

Litigation is expensive and takes a toll on management and employees. To avoid the cost and disruption of litigation, companies increasingly use alternative methods to resolve legal disputes. For example, General Mills has estimated that it saved hundreds of thousands of dollars through the use of alternative procedures. Alternatives to litigation include negotiation, mediation, minitrials, and arbitration.

66

"The first thing we do, let's kill all the lawyers."

—*William Shakespeare*, Henry VI,
Part 2, Act IV,
Scene ii, Line 75.

Negotiation

The legal system itself encourages negotiated settlements to legal disputes. For example, 27 utility companies sued Westinghouse Corporation in 1975. Westinghouse had breached its contracts to deliver about 70 million pounds of uranium because the price of uranium had more than doubled. The district court judge assigned to ten of the suits encouraged the utility customers to negotiate out-of-court settlements with Westinghouse. The judge thought that a business solution to the lawsuits, rather than a legal one, might be more advantageous to all parties. If the court forced Westinghouse to pay damages, Westinghouse would be crippled financially. It might not be able to complete the construction of certain nuclear-power plants that it was building for the same utility companies. Inventive and mutually beneficial settlements were reached in many of the cases. (The Westinghouse uranium cases are discussed in the "Inside Story" in chapter 9.)

Mediation

Litigation can turn business colleagues into bitter enemies. Mediation can be a less hostile alternative.

In mediation, the parties agree that they will try to reach a solution themselves, with the assistance of a mediator. The mediator guides the parties in a structured set of discussions. She confers with both parties, pointing out the elements of their dispute and the areas of agreement. Sometimes the mediator helps the parties to identify their goals. A mediator's role is to suggest ways to resolve the dispute fairly. A mediator cannot enforce any solution; the parties must come to a reconciliation themselves and then agree to abide by it.

One insurance company, Travelers, noted that more than 85% of the cases it submitted to mediation were settled. Even in the cases where a settlement could not be reached, the mediation process helped the litigants focus on the most important issues, which allowed for a quicker resolution at trial. The corporation still saved money, time, and other resources.

Minitrial

In a minitrial, the lawyers conduct discovery for a condensed period, usually a few weeks. They then exchange legal briefs or memoranda of law. At this point, the top management of the two businesses hears the lawyers from each side present their case in a trial format. The presentations are moderated by a neutral third party, often an attorney or a judge.

After the minitrial, the managers of the two businesses meet to settle the case. If they are unable to reach a settlement, the presiding third party can issue a nonbinding opinion. The managers can then meet again to try to settle on the basis of the third-party opinion.

Minitrials have several advantages. Like litigation, they allow a thorough investigation and presentation of the parties' claims; but they give the managers the opportunity to work out their differences directly rather than through their attorneys. By shortening the time for discovery and presentation of the case, minitrials can reduce the possibility of the two sides becoming locked into opposing positions. The presence of a neutral third party gives the process an added element of discipline. Should the managers come to an impasse in their discussions, the third party can offer suggestions about a settlement. Finally, minitrials have the advantage of remaining relatively private. This is important to parties in disputes over confidential information or trade secrets.

An example of a successful minitrial is the 1986 settlement of the dispute between the companies Telecredit and TRW. This minitrial took place in a hotel conference room. After brief presentations by both sides, Telecredit's cofounder conferred with a vice president of TRW. Within half an hour, the two parties had agreed on the outlines of a settlement, which was negotiated over the following 11 weeks. The two companies estimated that the minitrial saved them at least $1 million in combined legal fees.

However, because minitrials involve discovery, the production of briefs, oral argument, and the hiring of a third party, they can still be fairly expensive. Only when disputes are expected to involve large damage awards or protracted litigation do minitrials make economic sense.

Arbitration

Arbitration is the resolution of a dispute by a neutral third party, called an arbitrator. The arbitrator is usually chosen by the parties to the dispute or a third party like the American Arbitration Association (AAA). Unlike mediation or a minitrial, arbitration results in a binding decision. A common way by which parties enter into arbitration is through an arbitration clause in a contract. When writing a contract, the parties often include an arbitration clause that specifies that in the event of dispute, they will arbitrate specific issues in a stated manner. Arbitration clauses are especially important in international contracts.

Unfortunately, arbitration clauses often do not include details of how arbitration will proceed, when and where it will take place, and who will preside. Most arbitration clauses simply state that the parties will arbitrate all disputes relating to or arising out of their contract—leaving the parties to fight over the specifics of arbitration after a dispute arises.

International Consideration

When parties to a contract are from nations with different legal regimes, it is often helpful to include arbitration clauses. Many Europeans and Japanese are uncomfortable with the U.S. legal system, particularly its discovery procedures for obtaining evidence prior to trial through depositions, written interrogatories, and document production.

Choice of Arbitrator The choice of an arbitrator is crucial. Unlike a judge's decision, which can be set aside if erroneous, an arbitrator's ruling generally is binding.

An arbitration clause can list the names of potential arbitrators; the parties should check the availability of these candidates before listing them. Alternatively, the arbitration clause can refer the selection of an arbitrator to the AAA. American Arbitration Association arbitrators are skilled, and the AAA makes special efforts to identify arbitrators experienced in handling particular types of disputes. The AAA decides how many arbitrators to appoint (usually from one to three) and may include arbitrators from different professions—unless the arbitration clause specifies the number and kind of arbitrators desired. Arbitration clauses often provide that each party will choose its own arbitrator, and that these two will pick a third.

Parties to Arbitration Usually, the parties to the contract are the parties to the arbitration. Sometimes, however, a dispute arises between parties to several different contracts, for example, between a construction subcontractor and an architect. The parties should ensure that there is an arbitration clause in each contract and that each party agrees to a consolidated arbitration with other parties on related issues.

Scope of Arbitration Foreseeing which disputes are better arbitrated is difficult. A broad arbitration clause, which may apply to tort as well as contract claims, is preferable. Parties should also agree upon a location close to their businesses and a reasonable timetable by which to settle their disputes. The arbitration clause may make provisions for starting the arbitration, for example, by means of a prehearing conference.

Arbitration Versus Litigation The following case illustrates the Supreme Court's tendency to favor arbitration over litigation, even when the rights at issue are protected by federal law.

In Brief: Models of Alternative Dispute Resolution

Mediation Model

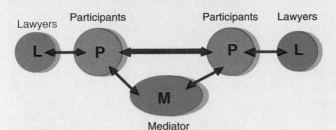

1. Introduces, structures, gains rapport
2. Finds out facts, isolates issues
3. Helps identify alternatives
4. Guides negotiation and decision making
5. Clarifies/writes an agreement or plan
6. Provides for legal review and processing
7. Available for follow-up, review, revision

Information Flow

Negotiation Model

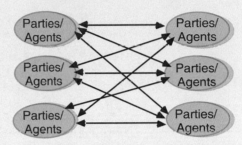

1. Parties or Party decide they want to settle a dispute.
2. Orientation and positioning are very important.
3. Discussion and arguing of Issues begins between a few designated participants or all the parties can participate.
4. Either an agreement or final impasse is reached

Information Flow

Adjudication Model
(Litigation & Arbitration)

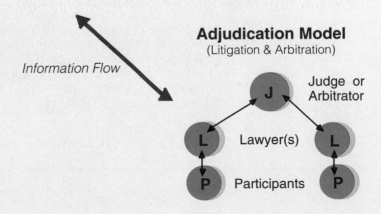

1. Listens to each side's presentation.
2. Decides option based on predetermined criteria (legislation, precedent, fairness, etc.).

■ **A Case in Point:**   **Summary**

Case 4.7
RODRIGUEZ DE QUIJAS v.
SHEARSON/AMERICAN
EXPRESS, INC.
Supreme Court of the
United States
490 U.S. 477, 109 S.Ct. 1917
(1989).

FACTS Ofelia Rodriguez de Quijas and four other individuals invested $400,000 in securities with Shearson/American Express, Inc. They signed a standard customer agreement with Shearson. The agreement included a clause stating that the parties would settle through arbitration any controversy relating to the account.

The investment eventually turned sour, and Rodriguez de Quijas and the other investors sued Shearson and its broker-agent in charge of the account. Plaintiffs alleged that Shearson lost their money in unauthorized fraudulent transactions. In the complaint, plaintiffs alleged that Shearson violated section 12(2) of the Securities Act of 1933, which prohibits the sale of securities by means of misleading statements.

Shearson argued that the plaintiff's claims were subject to mandatory arbitration. The plaintiffs argued that the agreement to arbitrate was unenforceable and that they were entitled to a jury trial.

ISSUE PRESENTED Is a predispute agreement to submit to compulsory arbitration any controversy relating to a securities investment enforceable?

SUMMARY OF OPINION The U.S. Supreme Court held that agreements to arbitrate claims under section 12(2) of the Securities Act of 1933 were enforceable. The Court noted that in recent years it had upheld agreements to arbitrate claims under the Securities Exchange Act of 1934, the Racketeer Influenced and Corrupt Organizations Act, and the antitrust laws. By agreeing to arbitrate a statutory claim, a party does not forego the substantive rights afforded by the statute. The agreement only means that the resolution of the dispute will be in an arbitral, rather than judicial, forum. The Supreme Court strongly endorsed statutes, such as the Federal Arbitration Act, that favor this method of resolving disputes.

RESULT Shearson/American Express, Inc. was entitled to have this dispute resolved by arbitration.

COMMENTS In *Shearson Lehman/American Express v. Bird*,[20] the Supreme Court vacated a decision by the Court of Appeals for the Second Circuit. The court of appeals had ruled that a predispute agreement to arbitrate statutory claims under the Employee Retirement Income Security Act (ERISA), which governs pensions and other employee benefit plans, was not enforceable. The Supreme Court's action seems to indicate that predispute agreements to arbitrate claims under ERISA are enforceable. ERISA is discussed further in chapter 14.

---

20. 493 U.S. 884, 110 S.Ct. 225 (1989).

The Responsible Manager

Staying Out of Court

Legal problems or disputes often arise in business, and an amicable solution to them is not always possible. Some form of dispute resolution then becomes the next step.

The courts are there to assist litigants in working out a fair solution to their dispute. But litigation is expensive, time consuming, and disruptive to everyone involved. Consequently, all parties benefit when the courts are used as the last step in the legal process rather than as the starting point.

A manager should decide when litigation, as opposed to a settlement or other method of resolving the dispute, is the company's best strategic move. If the problem is a recurring one, or if the opposing party is clearly making a frivolous claim or attempting to use the lawsuit as a way to extort money from the company, then the courtroom becomes the most practical alternative. In many cases, however, negotiation, mediation, a minitrial, or arbitration will enable the parties to conclude their dispute more quickly and with less expense and hardship.

The first step in implementing an alternative dispute resolution (ADR) program is generating enthusiasm within the company for the program.[21] The general counsel or other appropriate person should explain to company officers and executives the benefits of an ADR program, including the savings of time and money, the decrease in disruption to employees or management, and the fact that solutions generally are more business-oriented in nature. High-level management should demonstrate its commitment to an ADR program and explain its benefits to other executives, who may be unfamiliar with such a program. The company needs to involve: (1) in-house counsel; (2) the executives and corporate managers; (3) outside counsel; (4) the company's adversaries; and (5) certain field personnel, such as insurance industry claims personnel. Training of these various players is also essential.

Once a company establishes a formal program, the next step is for the general counsel and company manager to see that the alternative dispute resolution procedures are employed. Some companies negotiate ADR clauses into all of their standard business agreements or contracts. Other companies leave it to their attorneys to decide which disputes are best resolved by alternative dispute resolution rather than litigation.

After deciding that an alternative dispute resolution method will be the best way to achieve its goal, the company must persuade the opposing party to participate in the procedure. Certain forms of ADR, such as mediation, are usually accepted readily—the proceeding is informal and can be terminated at any time, and a mediator can also protect the confidentiality of sensitive data, which might be made public during litigation.

Once a company has developed an ADR program, continuous feedback from all participants is required in order to monitor, refine, and improve the program. Constructive criticism is vital. Frequently, corporate managers or executives will be in a position to discover a weakness in a particular ADR procedure that could harm the company. The company may wish to designate one employee as the ADR "point person" who monitors the program to ensure that flaws are corrected and strengths are further refined.

Establishing an alternative dispute resolution program has cost-benefit advantages. Valuable management time is saved by avoiding litigation. Equally important, alternative dispute resolution procedures allow flexibility in resolving legal disputes.

---

21. This discussion is based on *Mainstreaming: Corporate Strategies for Systematic ADR Use* (Center for Public Resources, Inc., 1989).

Inside Story

The $800 Million Arbitration: IBM/Fujitsu

In the past, companies usually did not submit legal disputes to arbitration when there were significant sums of money or assets at stake. This has changed. IBM Corporation set a precedent in 1985 when it turned to arbitration to resolve its dispute with Fujitsu Ltd., a Japanese electronics firm that was trying to gain access to IBM programming materials.

The dispute began in 1982, when IBM accused Fujitsu of copying IBM software to use as a base to develop its own operating system software. IBM claimed that Fujitsu was violating IBM's software copyrights. An agreement was reached in 1983, but the agreement fell through. IBM initiated arbitration with the American Arbitration Association in 1985. Two arbitrators were chosen to arbitrate the dispute: Robert Mnookin, then a professor at Stanford Law School and an authority in dispute settlement; and John Jones, a retired executive and expert in computer systems.

Two years later, the arbitrators issued the first of two decisions resolving the dispute. They held that Fujitsu had the right to obtain access to IBM programs in order to develop and market imitations of IBM mainframe software products. The arbitrators' order left unresolved the dollar amount that Fujitsu would pay IBM for access to the IBM programs. The order was perceived,

however, as a major breakthrough for companies trying to compete with IBM, the traditionally dominant force in the software market. Observers of this market thought that the arbitrators' decision could help to shape new trends in the mainframe industry worldwide.

A second order, issued in 1988, set dollar amounts for the payments that Fujitsu would make to IBM for access to the IBM software. The license for future use alone was valued at close to $400 million, bringing the total amount Fujitsu could conceivably pay to approximately $800 million.

In these two orders, the arbitrators set out a complex arrangement to govern the relationship between the two companies through the year 2002. The orders included provisions for mutual access to each company's programming material, a complex payout plan, and strict rules for governing the exchanges of information and software between the two companies.

This arbitration is unprecedented not only for the magnitude of the assets involved but also for its potential impact on the level of competition in the international market for computer software. The IBM/Fujitsu arbitration signaled an increased use of arbitration to resolve disputes in the international business environment.

Key Words and Phrases

Questions and Case Problems

1. Answer the following questions with regard to the case cite *Southwest Engineering Co. v. United States*, 341 F.2d 998 (8th Cir. 1965).

(a) In what year was the case decided?

(b) What court decided the case?

(c) Can you tell from the cite which party originally brought the lawsuit?

(d) Can you tell from the cite which party brought the appeal?

2. One method of obtaining personal jurisdiction over an absent corporation is to attempt to gain jurisdiction over the parent through jurisdiction over the subsidiary. If a foreign corporation has no contact with a particular state except that it owns a subsidiary doing business in that state, should that be a significant contact that would allow the state to claim jurisdiction over the parent? [*Newport Components, Inc. v. NEC Home Electronics (U.S.A.), Inc.*, 671 F. Supp 1525 (C.D. Cal. 1987)]

3. Stig Slosh, a native of Albany, New York, was touring the U.S. with his band De Minimis Fringe. While playing a concert in the state of Nowhere, Slosh was struck in the head by the band's giant fiberglass armadillo, a prop suspended by ropes that glided across the stage during the opening song. The accident occurred because the stagehands assigned to manipulate the prop miscalculated its position in the air. Slosh and the band were forced to cancel the show, but they finished the remainder of the tour. The armadillo was damaged beyond repair and had to be discarded. However, the band was not too upset about this. They were already leaning toward dropping the prop from their act, as it didn't seem to add much. However, the band did not make this fact public. Instead, Slosh sued the local concert promoter, Graham Bell, a resident of Nowhere, in federal district court.

(a) Bell tries to have Slosh's suit thrown out of federal court. Bell claims that a federal court has no subject matter jurisdiction over this lawsuit. What arguments can Slosh make to keep the suit in federal court? (If any additional facts are needed to make this argument, state what they are.) What is Bell's best argument for keeping this suit out of federal court? How might Bell get the information needed to make this argument?

(b) Assume that Slosh succeeds in keeping the lawsuit in federal court. Slosh bases his suit against Bell on the general common-law principle that employers are financially liable for the actions of their employees. The stagehands were in fact employed by Bell. Bell counters that the laws of the state of Nowhere should apply. (Under Nowhere common law, performers assume full financial responsibility for any damage caused by props they use in their acts.) Which law should govern? Why?

4. Employee sued Employer for denying her the authority, salary, and other privileges associated with her position because of her race. The complaint filed by Employee's attorney did not set forth any facts supporting the allegation that Employee was denied the perquisites of her position on the basis of race. Employee never served Employer with the summons and complaint, but Employer was aware of the lawsuit.

(a) Employer moves to dismiss the complaint for failure to state a claim. Should the judge grant the motion?

(b) Employer moves to dismiss the lawsuit for failure of service of process. Should the judge grant the motion? Should the fact that Employer appeared in court to contest the sufficiency of service of process affect the outcome? [*Martin v. New York State Department of Mental Hygiene*, 588 F.2d 371 (2d Cir. 1978)]

5. Whatawad, Inc. was a major producer of bubble gum. In the last year, Whatawad lost a significant portion of its market share to Humungo Bubble, Inc., its main competitor in the field. Humungo ads boasted that in a test conducted by independent researchers, Humungo gum blew larger bubbles than Whatawad. In fact, the test was conducted by Humungo's own research team. Before he quit the company, Ian Ventor, head of research at Humungo, told his supervisor that he wanted to inform Humungo's in-house counsel about the false statement in the ad. The supervisor told Ventor that it was his own choice whether to take such action. Ventor went ahead and told the in-house counsel.

Lotta D. Kay, the vice president of sales for Whatawad, was determined to prevent further erosion of her company's business. In a written memo, Kay instructed her sales representatives to offer kickbacks to the wholesalers who purchased bubble gum from Whatawad if they would increase orders by 10%. Although Kay instructed the sales representatives to destroy her memo, Kay's own secretary forgot to delete the memo from the company's computer system.

(a) Suspecting the use of kickbacks, the district attorney's office brings charges against Whatawad. When these charges are brought, the CEO of Whatawad instructs both Kay and her sales representatives to reveal all the details of their activity to trial lawyers hired specifically to defend the firm in this suit. They do that. The district attorney demands to see the notes describing their discussions. Will he be successful in obtaining the notes covering either Kay's or the sales representatives' conversations? What policies shape the law in this area?

(b) Immediately after the charges are brought, Kay finds out about the undeleted memo and deletes it herself from the system. Kay's secretary believes this is an unethical act and reports it to the district attorney. Does Kay have any liability for this action? What procedures should Whatawad have followed to ensure that this document did not remain in the system? Should a company use a document retention system to destroy documents that clearly demonstrate wrongdoing on the part of the company?

(c) The district attorney decides to prosecute Humungo for false advertising. He demands to see the notes of the conversation between Ian Ventor and the in-house counsel. What arguments can the district attorney make to obtain these notes? How should the company respond?

6. DuLac Corporation, a leading U.S. manufacturer of chemicals and synthetic fabrics, is incorporated in the state of Blue Waters. All of DuLac's business is conducted within Blue Waters and all of its offices are located within the state. Blue Waters is under the federal jurisdiction of the Court of Appeals for the Fourth Circuit. The Environmental Protection Agency (EPA) commenced an investigation of DuLac's disposal procedures for DRT, a mixture of the toxic compound DNGR and the neutralizing agent HRMLS. Upon discovering that DuLac had disposed of DRT in dump sites not approved for toxic waste disposal, the EPA filed suit against DuLac for cleanup costs and punitive damages, under a federal statute forbidding the disposal of DNGR or any derivative thereof except in approved toxic-waste dump sites. The action was brought in a federal district court sitting in Blue Waters. DuLac's only defense to the action is that, as the DNGR in DRT is fully neutralized, DRT should not be considered a derivative of DNGR for purposes of the statute. A month later, the lawyer for the EPA offers to settle the case for cleanup costs only.

(a) Assume that the Court of Appeals for the Sixth Circuit recently interpreted the statute literally, upholding an award of punitive damages against a company that had disposed of fully neutralized DNGR. As DuLac's lawyer, would you advise the company to accept the settlement offer? Explain your answer with reference to the principle of *stare decisis.*

(b) Assume that another district court within the Fourth Circuit recently reached the same result as the Sixth Circuit. How would you advise DuLac regarding the settlement offer?

(c) Assume that the U.S. Supreme Court recently reached the same result as the Sixth Circuit. Would your advice to DuLac remain the same?

7. A Minnesota component parts manufacturer placed its products into the stream of interstate commerce by delivering them to a shipper FOB (Free on Board) Waseca, Minnesota, for delivery to an address in Houston, Texas. By shipping the goods "FOB Waseca, Minnesota," title to the goods and the risk of loss shifted to the buyer when the goods were delivered to the shipper in Waseca, Minnesota. Can the Minnesota company be sued in the courts of Texas for product defects and breach of warranty? [*Ruston Gas Turbines, Inc. v. Donaldson Company, Inc.*, 9 F.3d 415 (5th Cir. 1993)]

8. Sterling, Inc. is a manufacturer of state-of-the-art computers. For the past ten years, Sterling has acquired all of its microchips from NoBugs Corporation, the only producer of chips meeting Sterling's high specifications. The relationship has been mutually profitable. Sterling could not have built its reputation as an industry leader without NoBugs's reliability and consistently high-quality products; and Sterling's business enabled NoBugs to grow rapidly while providing its investors with an attractive rate of return. Some months ago, several of Sterling's computers exploded shortly after installation. Upon investigation, Sterling discovered that tiny imperfections in NoBugs's microchips had aggravated a dormant design defect in the computers, causing the explosions. Analysis of the chips indicated that they were indeed below specification and that the imperfections were caused by a slight miscalibration of NoBugs's encoding equipment. NoBugs recalibrated the equipment and promptly resumed production of perfect chips. Sterling's losses from the explosions—lost profits, out-of-pocket costs associated with compensating customers for the explosions, and injury to business reputation—are estimated to exceed $20 million. Sterling and NoBugs disagree on the amount of the loss for which NoBugs should be responsible. Sterling's CEO is considering a lawsuit. She asks you, her assistant, to prepare a memo outlining the advantages and disadvantages of various methods of resolving the dispute. Draft that memo.

9. A former shareholder of Texas International which, prior to reorganization, provided airline service to Houston and Dallas, Texas, filed a lawsuit arising out of the share-for-share merger between Texas International and Texas Air Corporation, a holding company formed for the purpose of effectuating the proposed reorganization (Texas Air). In the reorganization, the shareholders of Texas International were eliminated as such and received in exchange for their stock of Texas International an equal number of shares of Texas Air. The plaintiff challenged a part of the transaction which called for a loan of more than $3 million at a favorable interest rate to a substantial shareholder of Texas International. Does the plaintiff have standing to bring a derivative suit on behalf of the former shareholders of Texas International for activities that occurred prior to the reorganization? [*Schreiber v. Carney*, 447 A.2d 17 (Del.Ch. 1982)]

10. As a manager, how would you design and implement a policy to limit litigation costs by taking advantage of alternative dispute resolution mechanisms? Be specific in your answer.

Chapter 5

AGENCY AND FORMS OF BUSINESS ORGANIZATIONS

■ Introduction

Joining With Others to Achieve Business Goals

Business organizations allow individuals to work together. If an individual could achieve his business goals on his own, there would be no need for him to join with others. However, this is rarely the case. Even when a single person runs a small business, the chances are good that at some point she will hire others to work with her.

Joining with others to further a business goal raises two types of legal issues. The first set of issues concerns when a person is responsible for the actions of another, and when one person has the power to bind another to a contract. The rules governing these issues are largely provided by agency law, which has developed over several centuries. The second set of legal issues concerns the forms that business organizations may take. These issues are governed by a combination of agency law and statutory law.

Chapter Summary

This chapter defines and discusses the central principles of agency law. Next, it describes the three forms in which most businesses are organized: the sole proprietorship, the partnership (general or limited), and the corporation. It discusses examples of how agency law is applied to these forms. Finally, the chapter discusses the tax treatment of each form of business organization, with examples. The business organization most commonly used for large-scale enterprises, the corporation, is discussed further in chapter 18.

Relationship of Agent to Principal

In an *agency* relationship, one person, the *agent,* acts for or represents another person, the *principal.* The principal delegates a portion of his power to the agent. The agent then manages the assigned task and exercises whatever discretion is given to her by the principal. The agency relationship is created by an express or implied contract or by law.

Fiduciary Responsibility

In agreeing to act on behalf of the principal, the agent becomes a *fiduciary,* that is, a person having a duty to act primarily for the benefit of another in matters connected with his undertaking. Loyalty and obedience are the hallmarks of the fiduciary relationship. An agent has a duty to act solely for the benefit of her principal in all matters directly connected with the agency undertaking. This is the *duty of loyalty.* For example, an agent entrusted with the power to buy a piece of land for his principal cannot buy the land for himself instead.

An agent also has a duty to act with due care. This *duty of care* includes a duty to avoid mistakes, whether through negligence, recklessness, or intentional misconduct. Some states require an agent to use the same level of care a person would use in the conduct of her own affairs. Others use a comparative approach: An agent is to use the same level of care a reasonable person in a like situation would use. Application of these duties to officers, directors, and controlling shareholders is discussed in chapter 21.

As the following case demonstrates, an agent who breaches a fiduciary duty may be liable to the principal for any resulting losses.

■ A Case in Point: Summary

Case 5.1
TARNOWSKI v. RESOP
Supreme Court of Minnesota
236 Minn. 33, 51 N.W.2d 801
(Minn. 1952).

FACTS Resop wanted to invest in jukeboxes, the coin-operated music machines that are found in restaurants, diners, and soda fountains. He engaged Tarnowski as his agent and gave him the job of researching and negotiating for the purchase of a string of such machines along a certain route in Wisconsin.

Tarnowski was dishonest in reporting the extent and nature of his research. Tarnowski told Resop that he had made a thorough investigation of the route; that it had 75 locations in operation; that each location had one or more machines; that these machines were not more than six months old; and that the gross income from all the locations amounted to more than $3,000 per month.

In reality, Tarnowski made only a superficial investigation of five locations, and he knowingly adopted as his own the sellers' false claims regarding the other locations. The route actually had only 47 locations, and not every location had a jukebox. Some of the jukeboxes were seven years old. The gross income on all the machines was far less than $3,000 per month. Moreover, Tarnowski collected a secret commission of $2,000 from the sellers for consummating the sale.

When Resop found out about the fraudulent representations of Tarnowski and the sellers, he tried to rescind (undo) the sale. The sellers refused to comply, and he sued them for return of the $10,000 he had invested in the business. That claim was settled for $9,500.

Resop then initiated two causes of action against Tarnowski. The first sought to recover the secret $2,000 commission. The second sought to recover damages for: (1) the loss suffered in operating the route prior to rescission; (2) the loss of time devoted to the operation; (3) expenses in connection with rescission of the sale; (4) expenses in connection with the suit against the sellers; and (5) attorney's fees in connection with the present suit. A jury awarded Resop $5,200. Tarnowski appealed.

ISSUE PRESENTED   If an agent breaches his fiduciary duty of loyalty to his principal, can he be held liable for any losses the principal incurs as a result of the breach, and be required to give to the principal any gains the agent received because of the breach?

SUMMARY OF OPINION   The Minnesota Supreme Court first considered the claim for the secret commission. It held that the principal, Resop, had an absolute right to the $2,000, regardless of whether he had recovered any or all of his money from the sellers. An agent is bound by a pledge of fidelity to his principal. He is barred from placing his own interests in conflict with those of the principal, even if the principal cannot show any damages have occurred as a result. By accepting money from the sellers, Tarnowski had in essence taken a bribe to perform his duties in the manner desired by them. Such an act violates an agent's fiduciary duty to his principal. Because any gain an agent receives while acting on behalf of a principal belongs to the principal, the money was rightfully Resop's.

As to the second claim, the court found that Tarnowski was liable for every category of damages sought by Resop. As an agent, Tarnowski had a special duty of loyalty to his principal which exceeded the duty of the average person to act reasonably in regard to other persons. By violating that duty, Tarnowski had committed an intentional tort against Resop. (Intentional torts are discussed further in chapter 7.)

RESULT   An agent can be held liable for losses incurred if he breaches his fiduciary duty of loyalty to his principal. In this case Tarnowski was ordered to repay Resop for his losses and to pay Resop the $2,000 secret commission he received.

 Ethical Consideration

Because all the expenses the principal incurred could be directly traced to the misdeeds of his agent, law and ethics demanded that the agent be held financially responsible. This principle still has vitality today and can be used whenever an agent of a business organization violates her fiduciary duty to that organization.

Sometimes it is not clear whether a person acting on behalf of another does or does not have a fiduciary duty to the other person. This was the issue in the following case dealing with a person hired to "find" a buyer for a company.

■ **A Case in Point:**   **In the Language of the Court**

Case 5.2
NORTHEAST GENERAL
CORPORATION
v. WELLINGTON
ADVERTISING, INC.
Court of Appeals of New York
82 N.Y.2d 158, 624 N.E.2d 129
(N.Y. 1993).

FACTS In 1988 plaintiff Northeast General Corporation, through its agents Dunton and Margolis, entered into an agreement with defendant Wellington Advertising, Inc. relating to the sale of Wellington Advertising. Northeast was to act "as a non-exclusive independent investment banker and business consultant for the purposes of finding and presenting candidates for purchase, sale, merger or other business combination." The agreement further provided that Northeast General would be entitled to a finder's fee, based on the size of the transaction, if a transaction was completed within three years of when Wellington was introduced to the "found" buying party.

Margolis, one of Northeast General Corporation's agents, after consultation with Northeast's new president, Dunton, introduced Sternau to Wellington's president, Arpadi, as a potential purchaser of Wellington. Ultimately, Sternau and Wellington entered into a purchase agreement.

Before introducing Sternau to Wellington, Dunton was informed by an unidentified investment banker that Sternau had a reputation for buying companies, removing assets, rendering the companies borderline insolvent, and leaving minority investors unprotected. Dunton did not, prior to the closing of the Wellington-Sternau deal, disclose this information to Wellington.

After Northeast's introduction of Sternau to Wellington, but prior to signing the merger agreement, Dunton called Arpadi and offered further help with the transaction. Arpadi declined that help and discouraged Dunton from any further involvement. After the merger agreement was signed, companies controlled by Sternau purchased the controlling stock of Wellington, leaving Wellington's principals, including Arpadi, as minority investors. Ultimately, Wellington was rendered insolvent, and Arpadi and other minority investors suffered financial losses.

Wellington delivered a check for Northeast's finder services, but before the check could be negotiated, payment was stopped.

Northeast sued Wellington to recover its finder's fee. After a trial, the jury found in favor of Northeast and awarded it the agreed-upon finder's fee. The trial court judge set aside the jury's verdict. The judge's decision, which rested on arguments of public policy, imposed a fiduciary-like duty on finders to disclose adverse information to their clients. The Appellate Division court upheld the trial court judge's action. Northeast General appealed.

ISSUE PRESENTED Does a finder-seller agreement create a relationship of trust with a "fiduciary-like" obligation on the finder to share information with the seller regarding the potential buyer's bad reputation?

OPINION BELLACOSA, J., writing for the New York Court of Appeals:

. . . .

Before courts can infer and superimpose a duty of the finest loyalty, the contract and relationship of the parties must be plumbed. We recognize that "[m]any forms of conduct permissible in a workaday world for those acting at arm's length, are forbidden to those bound by fiduciary ties" (*Meinhard v. Salmon*, 249 N.Y. 458, 464). Chief Judge Cardozo's oft quoted maxim is a timeless reminder that "[a] trustee is held to something stricter than the moral of the market place. Not honesty alone, but the punctilio of an honor the most sensitive" (id.). If the parties find themselves or place themselves in the milieu of the "workaday" mundane market place, and if they do not create their own relationship of higher trust, courts should not ordinarily transport them to the higher realm of relationship and fashion the stricter duty for them.

The Northeast-Wellington agreement contains no cognizable fiduciary terms or relationship. The dissent ascribes inordinate weight to the titles non-exclusive "independent investment banker and business consultant." These terms in the context of this agreement are not controlling, since Dunton did not perform the services of an investment banker or consultant. Instead, Dunton's sole function was "for purposes of finding and presenting candidates." That drives the analysis of this case because he was a traditional finder functioning under a finder's agreement, and his role ceased when he found and presented someone. The finder was not described or given the function of an agent, partner or co-venturer.

. . . Probing our precedents and equitable principles unearths no supportable justification for such a judicial interposition, however highly motivated and idealistic. Indeed, responding to this fine instinct would inappropriately propel the courts into reformation of service agreements between commercially knowledgeable parties in this and perhaps countless other situations and transactions as well.

This Court may sense a sympathetic impulse to balance what it may view as the equities of a situation such as this. The hard judicial obligation, however, is to be intellectually disciplined against that tug. Instead, courts must focus on the precise law function reposed in them in such circumstances, which is to construe and enforce the meaning and thrust of the contract of the parties, not to purify their efforts.

. . . The character of the Northeast-Wellington agreement was not one of trust importing duties beyond finding a prospect. The fact that Wellington did not employ its own independent, traditional methods to check out the reputation of the prospect and accepted what turned out to be a bad prospect does not warrant this Court rescuing it from its soured deal by any post-agreement fiduciary lifeline.

. . . .

The commonplace mores of the market place suffice and are appropriate to govern relationships established by contract of the type involved here, which contemplates and asks nothing more of the parties than performance of a simple service. In sum, defendants' financial losses from their market mishap with Sternau is not reason enough to propel a sweeping new fiduciary-like doctrine into finders' agreements.

. . . .

DISSENTING OPINION   HANCOCK, J.:

A fiduciary relationship is one founded on trust or confidence reposed by one person in the integrity and fidelity of another. The term is a very broad one. It is said that the relation exists, and that relief is granted, in all cases in which influence has been acquired and abused, in which confidence has been reposed and betrayed. The origin of the confidence and the source of the influence are immaterial. The rule embraces both technical fiduciary relations and those informal relations which exist whenever one man trusts in and relies upon another. Out of such a relation, the law raises the rules that neither party may exert influence or pressure upon the other.

. . . .

*Case **5.2** continued on following page*

*Case **5.2** continued*

The narrow question applying the above rules is whether Arpadi's and Dunton's relationship exhibits sufficient trust and de facto control upon which to ground Dunton's duty to disclose negative information regarding the very deal he was promoting. The record reveals more than enough evidence to demonstrate both elements. By imparting confidential business details as well as his personal plans and intentions [which included Arpadi's statement that he was "terrified" he "would lose everything" in a bad merger], Arpadi reposed trust in Dunton as a business counselor to find candidates likely to conform to Arpadi's investment goals. Arpadi expected Dunton to perform as a finder with Arpadi's interests at heart, i.e., not to remain silent as Wellington was being circled by a corporate predator. Dunton exerted de facto control and influence over Arpadi by fostering Arpadi's false belief that there was no reason not to accept Sternau as a suitable candidate. Dunton's review of the intimate details of Arpadi's business marked Dunton's acceptance of that trust. There is no doubt that as regards the proposed merger with [Sternau's company], Dunton and Arpadi stood in a fiduciary relation to each other.

. . . .

There is a final point. Even if only the agreement between Northeast and Arpadi were to be considered, the law would, I submit, imply a duty on the part of Dunton to disclose critical adverse information in these circumstances. . . .

. . . .

. . . Indeed, I believe that many would agree that even the "morals of the market place" would require it. Surely [Dunton] should not be rewarded for his failure.

. . . .

RESULT   The judgment for Wellington was reversed by the New York Court of Appeals notwithstanding the dissent because a majority of the judges on the court voted for reversal. Accordingly, Wellington was ordered to pay the finder's fee to Northeast General.

Questions
1. Which arguments do you find more persuasive, those of the majority or the dissent?
2. The court stated that a broker, who helps negotiate a deal and thereby brings the parties to an agreement, would have a fiduciary duty to act in the best interests of the person who hired him. Should a finder, who merely introduces the parties, be governed by a lesser ethical standard? If not, is it the role of the law to enforce that standard?

■ Agent's Ability to Bind the Principal

An agent has the ability to bind the principal in legal relations with third parties if the agent has actual or apparent authority to do so. Even in the absence of such authority, the principal may be bound by the unauthorized acts of her agent if she subsequently ratifies those acts. A principal can be bound even if his identity is undisclosed to the third party.

Actual Authority

The principal may give the agent *actual authority* to enter into agreements on her behalf, that is, the principal may give consent for the agent to act for and bind the principal. This consent (or authority) may be express or implied.

Express Authority   Express authority may be given by the principal's actual words, for example, a request that the agent submit a budget for a proposed plan of action. Express authority may also be given by an action that indicates the principal's consent, for example, sending the agent a check in partial payment for the purchase of materials necessary to execute the plan. An agent has express authority if he has a justifiable belief that the principal has authorized him to do what he is doing.

Implied Authority   Once the agent is given express authority, she also has implied authority to do whatever is reasonable to complete the task she has been instructed to undertake. For example, if an agent is instructed to purchase a truck costing up to $20,000 for his principal, the agent has implied authority to select the appropriate make and model, negotiate the purchase price, and finalize the sale.

Persons in certain positions or offices have implied authority to do what is reasonable for someone in that position. For example, the vice president of purchases for a trucking business, because of her position, would have the implied authority to engage in the activities described in the preceding paragraph. However, there are limits to such implied authority. For example, the vice president of purchases for a trucking division would not have the implied authority to buy an office building. Similarly, an officer of a corporation does not have the authority to bind the corporation to sell or grant shares of its stock. (A case addressing this matter is discussed in chapter 18.)

Apparent Authority

Apparent authority is created if a third party reasonably believes that the agent has authority to act for and bind the principal. This belief may be based on the words or acts of the principal, or on knowledge that the principal has allowed his agent to engage in certain activities on his behalf over an extended period of time.

Ratification

The principal can bind herself to an agent's unauthorized acts through *ratification,* that is, affirmation, of the prior act. When an act has been ratified, it is then treated as if the principal had originally authorized it.

Ratification, like authorization, can be either express or implied. Express ratification occurs when the principal, through words or behavior, manifests an intent to be bound by the agent's act. For example, a principal could ratify his agent's unauthorized purchase of a truck either by saying okay or simply by paying the bill for the vehicle. Implied ratification occurs when the principal, by her silence or failure to repudiate the agent's act, acquiesces in it.

Undisclosed Principal

An agent may lawfully conceal his principal's identity, or even his existence. This may be desirable if, for instance, the principal is trying to buy up adjacent properties in one area before news of a business venture is made public, or if her wealth would cause the seller to demand a higher price. If there is an *undisclosed principal,* that is, if the third party does not know the agent is acting for the principal, the principal will nonetheless be bound by any contract the agent enters into with actual authority. (If the agent acts without authority, the principal will not be bound; however, the agent himself may be liable on such a contract.)

> **"**
> *An agent may lawfully conceal his principal's identity, or even his existence.*

Ethical Consideration

It is lawful, but may be unethical, to use an agent to enter into a contract with a third party who has made it clear that she is unwilling to enter into a deal with the undisclosed principal.

■ Types of Agency Relationships

An agent may be either an employee of the principal or an independent contractor.

"*We—your agents, successors, licensees, and assigns—would like to share a few thoughts with you.*"

Drawing by Koren; © 1980 The New Yorker Magazine, Inc. *Used by permission.*

Employee

The most common form of agency relationship is the employer-employee relationship, sometimes still referred to as the master-servant relationship. The basic characteristic of this relationship is that the employer has the right to control the conduct of the employee. The employee may have the authority to bind the employer to a contract under theories of actual or apparent authority. Under the doctrine of respondeat superior, the employer will be liable for the torts that the employee commits while acting within the scope of his employment, as discussed in chapter 7.

Independent Contractor

An independent contractor, such as a lawyer working for a client or a plumber working for a house builder, is not an employee of the person paying for her services, because her conduct is not fully subject to that person's control. However, if the person hiring the independent contractor has the right to some control over how the independent contractor performs her work, or if she gives the independent contractor the power to enter into contracts on her behalf, an agency relationship may exist.

For example, suppose a builder contracts for $100,000 to build a house for Ken. Ken has no control over the builder's manner of doing the work, because the house is one of a large group of houses that the builder is constructing in a housing subdivision. The builder is not Ken's agent.

On the other hand, suppose Ken retained control over the builder's manner of doing work or authorized the builder to enter into a transaction with a third party on his behalf. Under either of these two circumstances, the independent contractor could become Ken's agent.

If an independent contractor is an agent, the person hiring the independent contractor is bound by any authorized contract the independent contractor enters into on that person's behalf. However, the person hiring the independent contractor is not liable to third persons for torts committed by the independent contractor (unless the agency agreement gave the hirer control over the contractor's conduct).

It is not always clear who is an employee and who is an independent contractor. Some of the relevant factors include: (1) who supplies the necessary tools; (2) where the work takes place; (3) to what degree the conduct of the person performing the work is dictated by another; (4) who selects the manner in which the work is to be performed; and (5) how long the person performing the work has worked for the other party.

◼ Liability for Torts of Agents

A principal may be liable for not only the contracts but also the torts of her agents. According to the doctrine of *respondeat superior*, if an agent is acting within the scope of his employment, the agent's employer will be liable for any injuries or damage to the property of another that the agent causes. As stated in *Jones v. Hart*, decided in England in 1798:

If the servants of A with his cart run against another cart, wherein is a pipe of wine, and overturn the cart and spoil the wine, an action lieth against A. For whoever employs another, is answerable for him, and undertakes for his care to all that make use of him.

The act of the servant is the act of his master, where he acts by authority of the master.

If the principal is required to pay damages to a third party because of an agent's negligence, the principal has the right to demand reimbursement from the agent.

Scope of Employment

As the following case illustrates, it is not always clear whether an employee who commits a tort against a third party is acting within the scope of his employment.

◼ **A Case in Point:** **Summary**

Case 5.3
RILEY v. STANDARD OIL CO. OF NEW YORK
Court of Appeals of New York
231 N.Y. 301, 132 N.E. 97
(N.Y. 1921).

FACTS Arthur Riley, a child, was hit and severely injured by a truck driver named Million. Million was an employee of the Standard Oil Company of New York, a large corporation even in the 1920s. Riley's mother, acting as a *guardian ad litem* (a person authorized to bring suit on behalf of a minor), sued Standard Oil. She sought to recover damages for personal injury from Standard Oil, on the ground that the company was responsible for the tortious act of its agent, the truck driver.

Million had been instructed by his supervisor to drive a company truck from a Standard Oil mill to the freight yard of the Long Island Railroad, which was about two and a half miles away. Million was supposed to pick up several barrels of paint at the freight yard and bring them back to the mill. Before leaving the mill, Million found some pieces of scrap wood and loaded them in the truck. As he pulled out of the mill, he did not turn in the direction of the freight yard. Instead, he drove to his sister's house, which was about four blocks in the opposite direction. After unloading the wood for his sister, he headed back toward the mill on his way to the freight yard. En route to the freight yard, but before he passed the mill, Million hit Arthur Riley.

The only issue on appeal was whether Million was in fact acting as an agent for the company—that is, whether he was in the scope of his employment—when he hit Arthur Riley.

*Case **5.3** continued on following page*

*Case **5.3** continued*

Standard Oil claimed that at the moment Million hit Riley, he was not acting as an authorized agent of the company. His supervisor had told him to go to the freight yard, and he had no express actual authority to go in the opposite direction to deliver the wood to his sister. Nothing in his task indicated that Million had the implied actual authority to do so. Hence, the defendant argued that this personal errand was done without any authority and was outside the scope of employment. The defendant argued that, at least until Million returned to his initial point of departure (the entrance to the mill), he was not acting as an agent for Standard Oil, and therefore the company could not be held liable for his actions.

ISSUE PRESENTED   For the purpose of determining a principal's liability for the conduct of its agent, does the scope of employment include returning to work after a deviation for a personal errand?

SUMMARY OF OPINION   The New York Court of Appeals rejected Standard Oil's argument. It held that if Million had hit Riley while on the way to his sister's house, it would have been up to the jury to decide whether this side trip was a separate journey on his own business, distinct from that of his master, or a mere deviation from the general route. If the jury found it to be a new journey, Million would not have been acting as Standard Oil's agent, and the company would not be liable for his negligence. However, the accident occurred when Million had already completed his personal errand and was headed back in the direction of his assigned destination. The court concluded, "At some point in the route Million again engaged in the defendant's business. That point, in view of all the circumstances, we think he had reached."

RESULT   Standard Oil was liable for employee Million's negligence. Million was deemed to be acting in the scope of employment when returning from his errand.

COMMENTS   Courts apply various standards in determining whether an agent is acting within the scope of her employment for purposes of tort liability. However, most courts consider such factors as when and where the tort occurred, what the employee was doing when the tort occurred, and why the employee was doing what she was doing.

Ethical Consideration

Before the *Riley* case, there was much precedent for not holding an employer responsible for accidents caused by a driver-employee when he was using the employer's vehicle for his own purposes. The three out of seven judges who dissented in *Riley* were able to cite a long list of such cases. The court could have held that Million, like the drivers in the previous cases, was still on his errand and not an agent when he hit Riley.

However, several of the judges were concerned with improving the tort system for victims of accidents. The facts of the *Riley* case allowed them to arrive at a more equitable result. Standard Oil, as a large company, was in the best financial position to pay the damages for the serious injury caused by one of its drivers. To decide this close call the other way would have placed the financial burden on those least able to cover the loss.

■ Liability of Principal for Violations of Law by Agent

Under the theory of *vicarious liability* the manager of a company can be held liable for violations of law by a lower-level employee even if the manager told the employee not to violate the law. This is demonstrated in the following case involving violations of federal housing and civil rights laws.

■ A Case in Point: In the Language of the Court

Case 5.4
CHICAGO v. MATCHMAKER REAL ESTATE SALES CENTER, INC.
United States Court of Appeals for the Seventh Circuit
982 F.2d 1086 (7th Cir. 1992).

FACTS   In 1987 the Leadership Council, a nonprofit fair housing corporation in the city of Chicago, suspected that the agents of Matchmaker Real Estate Sales Center were engaging in the illegal practice of racial steering. "Racial steering" is a practice by which real estate brokers and agents preserve and encourage patterns of racial segregation in available housing. This is done by steering members of racial and ethnic groups to buildings and neighborhoods already predominantly inhabited by members of that same racial and ethnic group, and away from buildings and neighborhoods inhabited primarily by members of other races or groups. Racial steering violates section 1982 of the Civil Rights Act of 1866 and the Fair Housing Act of 1968.

The Leadership Council, beginning in July 1987, conducted a series of tests of Matchmaker's activities. Pairs of African-American and white "testers"—individuals who posed as home seekers—went to Matchmaker and inquired about buying homes in Chicago and its suburbs. The Leadership Council closely matched the African-American and white teams for financial qualifications (including income and possible down payments) and housing needs (such as family size and preferences).

In each test the Matchmaker agents engaged in blatant acts of racial steering. For example the African-American testers and white testers were, in the same time period with very similar housing qualifications and requirements, given very different housing listings that included only houses in neighborhoods already dominated by the testers' own racial groups. One Matchmaker agent, Carol Scarpiniti, even went so far as to tell one of the white tester couples behind closed doors that she knew she was "not supposed to steer," but because the white testers were unfamiliar with the area, she would give them "boundaries" to tell them "where not to live."

Matchmaker's sole shareholder and chief executive officer, Erwin Ernst, exercised day-to-day control over Matchmaker and its real estate agents. However, he did not engage in nor did he condone racial steering practices. He had created written office policies and procedures requiring that his agents comply with fair housing laws. He was also a signator of an agreement by a national realtors organization ordering full compliance with fair housing laws, and actively worked to get other Chicago brokers to sign the agreement. He required all of his real estate agents to attend fair housing training courses sponsored by local real estate boards.

The City of Chicago, the Leadership Council and the individual testers sued the realty corporation; its sole shareholder, Ernst; and its sales agents. The agents were found liable for compensatory and punitive damages, as were Ernst and the realty company. The defendants appealed.

Case 5.4 continued on following page

*Case **5.4** continued*

ISSUE PRESENTED   Should a realty firm and its sole owner and chief executive officer owner be held liable for the illegal acts of racial steering committed by the firms real estate agents?

OPINION   BAUER, J., writing for the U.S. Court of Appeals:

. . . .

The doctrine of respondeat superior "enables the imposition of liability on a principal for the tortious acts of his agent and, in the more common case, on the master for the wrongful acts of his servant."[1] "As a matter of well-settled agency law, a principal may be held liable for the discriminatory acts of his agent if such acts are within the scope of the agent's apparent authority, even if the principal neither authorized nor ratified the acts."[2] . . . A principal cannot free itself of liability by delegating to an agent the duty not to discriminate. [The court noted that the discriminatory acts of Matchmaker's agents were within the scope of their employment even though Matchmaker's policy prohibited discrimination.]

Federal courts have routinely applied these principles in fair housing cases and held principals liable for the discriminatory acts of their agents. For example, in *Walker v. Crigler,*[3] the plaintiff brought suit under the Fair Housing Act against the owner of rental property and his agent, a professional realtor. The plaintiff, a single mother, alleged that the realtor had discriminated against her because of her sex. A jury found the realtor liable, but ruled in favor of the owner. On appeal, the Fourth Circuit held that the evidence was sufficient "to support the conclusion that [the owner] specifically intended that [the realtor] not discriminate." Given this finding, the court noted that "[t]he central question to be decided . . . is which innocent party, the owner whose agent acted contrary to instruction, or the potential renter who felt the direct harm of the agent's discriminatory failure to offer the residence for rent, will ultimately bear the burden of the harm caused." The court concluded that the Fair Housing Act's "overriding societal priority" requires that "the one innocent party with the power to control the acts of the agent, the owner of the property or other responsible superior, must act to compensate the injured party for the harm, and to insure that similar harm will not occur in the future." . . .

Here, Matchmaker (through Ernst), like the owner in *Walker*, specifically instructed its agents not to discriminate. As in *Walker*, the question we must decide is who among the innocent parties—the plaintiffs or Matchmaker and Ernst—should bear the responsibility for the discriminatory acts of Matchmaker's agents. We agree with the Fourth Circuit that "we must hold those who benefit from the sale and rental of property to the public to the specific mandates of anti-discrimination law if the goal of equal housing opportunity is to be reached."

. . . .

RESULT   The court affirmed the magistrate judge's decision holding Matchmaker and Ernst vicariously liable for compensatory damages due to

---

1. *General Building Contractors Association v. Pennsylvania*, 458 U.S. 375, 392, 102 S.Ct. 3141, 3151 (1982).
2. *Coates v. Bechtel*, 811 F.2d 1045, 1051 (7th Cir. 1987).
3. 976 F.2d 900 (4th Cir. 1992).

the illegal acts of its agents, even though the principal had specifically instructed his agents not to act in such an illegal way. However, the court reversed the magistrate judge's order for punitive damages to be paid by Matchmaker and Ernst. A principal is liable for punitive damages for the discriminatory acts of his agent only if he knew of or ratified the acts.

Questions
1. Is it fair to hold Ernst liable for the illegal acts he did not condone?
2. Why were punitive damages against Matchmaker and Ernst inappropriate?

At the Top

Although having a policy against illegal practices may not insulate the employer and its owner from civil liability for criminal acts of its lower-level employees, it reduces the chance the employees will break the law to begin with and it reduces the likelihood of the assessment of punitive damages against the employer and its owner.

Forms of Business Organization

Individuals or groups contemplating the formation of an organization must consider two key areas in determining which form the business will take.

First, statutes and common law determine such crucial features as whether there is limited liability for the organization's members, whether one person is an agent of another with power to bind the other person or the entity, whether an interest or membership in the organization is transferable, how the structure of management and ownership is designed, and the ease with which the organization can be created or sustained. The following sections discuss how these and other features can be combined and varied to create the three major types of business organizations: the sole proprietorship, the partnership (including general partnership, joint venture, limited partnership, and master limited partnership), and the corporation. A fourth form of business organization which is authorized in only certain states is the *limited liability company*.

Second, each type of organization receives different federal income tax treatment. Income tax considerations are dealt with in the last section of this chapter.

Sole Proprietorship

The sole proprietorship is the simplest and most prevalent form of business enterprise in the United States. In a *sole proprietorship* one person owns all of the assets of the business and is solely liable for all of the debts of the business. That individual has complete control of the business; other people may be hired as employees or independent contractors.

There are no formal requirements for forming a sole proprietorship. However, if the business operates under a *fictitious business name*—that is, a name other than the name of the owner—that name must be registered with the state. A sole proprietorship ends upon either the discontinuation of the business or the death of the proprietor.

Introduction to Partnerships

Partnerships can take a variety of forms. In a general partnership the partners have unlimited liability; in limited partnerships (discussed later in this chapter) certain of the partners may be able to limit their liability. Other partnerships discussed in this chapter are the joint venture (a partnership created for a specific, temporary purpose) and the master limited partnership.

General Partnership

A *general partnership* is created when two or more persons agree to place their money, efforts, labor, or skills in a business and to share the profits and losses. Real profits, not just wages or compensation, must be shared. A partnership is like a marriage or a family. Its members work for each other's benefit, sharing not only the benefits of the relationship but the burdens as well.

> 66
> *A partnership is like a marriage or a family. Its members work for each other's benefit, sharing not only the benefits of the relationship but the burdens as well.*

Each partner has control over the business. Each partner may have the authority to bind the others with respect to third parties. Thus a partnership is, in effect, a mutual agency relationship.

The Uniform Partnership Act, which has been adopted by most states, defines a partnership as "an association of two or more persons to carry on as co-owners of a business for profit." The word "persons" includes individuals, corporations, other partnerships, and other associations. The word "co-owners" indicates that the most basic characteristic of a partnership is joint ownership. Whereas a single individual can own a corporation or a sole proprietorship, a partnership by definition requires two or more persons doing business together.

Each co-owner may contribute either capital or services. For example, suppose Pro and Ron decide to form a partnership, called Rad Waves, to manufacture windsurfing equipment. Ron contributes the start-up and operating capital, and Pro contributes only his management services. Even though Pro has not contributed capital to the partnership, he is (unless agreed otherwise) an equal partner with Ron in Rad Waves.

The Uniform Partnership Act's definition of partnership mentions profits but not losses. However, some courts have held that a person who shares in the profits of the business but not in its losses is not a partner.

Under the Uniform Partnership Act, which is based upon common law, a partnership is not an entity distinct from the members composing it. Under certain modern statutes, however, a partnership may be treated as a separate entity for various purposes. For instance, a partnership may own property in the partnership name, it may keep its own financial records, and it may file informational tax returns with the Internal Revenue Service. In addition, creditors of the partnership have priority over creditors of the individual partners in receiving payment out of the partnership's assets. This assignment of priorities is called *marshaling assets.*

Formation of a General Partnership

A general partnership can be created with nothing more than a handshake and a general understanding between the partners. For example, students agree to work together on a business plan; a baker and a chef agree to open a restaurant together; an engineer and a mechanic agree to design bicycles together. In each case, a partnership of sorts is formed. However, the intention of one party alone cannot create a partnership. There must be a meeting of the minds. Hence, in the Rad Waves example, if Ron viewed his agreement with Pro as forming a partnership, while Pro contemplated a mere employee-employer relationship, a partnership would not be formed.

A partnership does not require a minimum of capital in order to be formed. However, partners usually contribute cash or property, or agree to provide personal services to the partnership. In some instances, a partnership interest may be received as a gift. There need not be a partnership name. There may or may not be a written partnership agreement.

Without a Written Agreement   If there is no written partnership agreement, the state laws will determine whether the relationship is to be treated as a partnership or some other relationship, such as an agency. Even if the relationship is recognized as a partnership, if there is no written agreement, the state partnership laws will govern the partnership. Some provisions of those laws could lead to undesirable business results.

In the Rad Waves example, Pro and Ron could form a partnership with a simple oral agreement. However, without a written agreement, state partnership law will impose certain rules on the partnership. For example, Pro and Ron will be required to share the profits and losses equally. Furthermore, until the partnership is terminated, neither partner may withdraw capital without the consent of the other. If there were a third partner, her death would terminate the partnership even if Pro and Ron would have preferred to continue it. These are just a few examples of the dangers of forming a partnership without a written partnership agreement.

With a Written Agreement   A written partnership agreement can prevent future misunderstandings. It can provide for a dispute-resolution mechanism, such as arbitration. It can also override those provisions of partnership statutes that could turn out to be undesirable to the partnership.

A partnership agreement usually includes the term of the partnership's existence, the capital characteristics of the partnership, the division of profits and losses between the partners, partnership salaries or withdrawals, the duties of the partners, and the consequences to the partnership if a partner decides to sell his interest in the partnership or becomes incapacitated or dies. Also included are the name of the partnership, the names and addresses of the partners, the type of business to be conducted, and the location of the business.

Drafting a partnership agreement focuses the partners' attention on matters that might not be considered if less formal partnership arrangements were made. For example, will all partners have an equal voice in management? What limits will be placed on the managing partners? How will disputes be settled? May a partner be expelled? May new partners be admitted? If so, by what process?

Operation of a General Partnership

The operation of a general partnership may be informal. Decisions may be made by consensus rather than by formal votes. However, lack of formality should not be equated with lack of responsibility for the fortunes, or misfortunes, of the partnership. For example, if Pro and Ron form Rad Waves as a general partnership, they will each be responsible for the full amount of any liabilities incurred by the partnership or by either partner acting within the scope of his authority as a partner. Hence, Ron's personal assets could be seized if Rad Waves's partnership assets were insufficient to satisfy a judgment against Rad Waves. Ron's personal assets might also be seized if Rad Waves breached a contract entered into by Pro on behalf of the partnership.

A partnership is a form of mutual agency. Each partner has authority to act on behalf of the other in the conduct of the partnership's business. Each partner in a general partnership is liable for the debts incurred by another partner acting in the name of the partnership if that partner had express authority to assume the debt or was carrying on the business of the partnership in the usual way.

Decision Making in a General Partnership

Unlike a corporation, which has a centralized board of directors and a staff of hired executives for decision making, a general partnership is characterized by direct owner management and control of the business. Each partner's assets are vulnerable to the poor business decisions of her fellow partners. It is therefore important that each partner have a voice in the business decisions of the partnership.

66

Each partner's assets are vulnerable to the poor business decisions of her fellow partners.

A partner may choose to cede managerial control of the business to one or more of the other partners. However, unless the parties expressly agree otherwise, partnership law requires unanimous agreement of all partners on all but the most ordinary matters. If the partners in an informal partnership cannot agree on a decision, they may disband the partnership, distribute its assets, and terminate it.

Dissolution of a General Partnership

Dissolution of the general partnership occurs when the partners no longer carry on the business together. There are many reasons for dissolving a partnership. The agreed term for the partnership may expire, or the partners may decide to dissolve the partnership prior to the expiration of the agreed term. A particular undertaking in the agreement may be completed. A partner may desire to dissolve the partnership. (Absent an agreement to the contrary, withdrawal of a general partner results in the dissolution of the partnership.) A partner may be expelled, with the remaining partners agreeing to terminate the partnership. A partner may die, with the agreement not providing for continuation of the partnership thereafter. A partner or the partnership may go bankrupt.

The business for which the partnership was formed may become unlawful, for example, if there is a war between the countries of two or more of the partners. In such a case the partnership will be dissolved regardless of the wishes of the partners. In other situations, a court may issue a decree of dissolution when a partner becomes disabled, insane, or otherwise unable to perform as a partner, or when a partner willfully breaches the agreement or conducts herself in partnership matters in such a manner as to make it impractical to carry on the partnership. Because the purpose of partnerships is to make a profit, a partnership may be dissolved by court decree if it becomes apparent that it is unprofitable and lacks any real prospect of success. However, if the partnership has reasonable prospects of earning money in the future, it may not be dissolved by court decree despite recent losses.

Winding Up the General Partnership

Upon dissolution, all of the partners' authority ceases except their authority to complete transactions begun but not yet finished, and to wind up the partnership. *Winding up* involves settling the accounts and liquidating the assets of the partnership for the purpose of making distributions and terminating the concern. The liabilities and obligations of the partners do not end at dissolution; the partnership continues throughout the winding-up period.

During the winding-up process, the partners' fiduciary duties to one another continue. The winding-up partners may not run the business for their own benefit, but must account as trustees to the withdrawing partners or to the estate of a deceased partner.

Termination of the General Partnership

Termination occurs when all the partnership affairs are wound up and the partners' authority to act for the partnership is completely extinguished. A dissolved partnership may terminate or may be continued by a new partnership formed by the remaining partners (including perhaps the estate or heirs of a deceased partner).

■ Joint Venture

A *joint venture* is a one-time partnership of two or more persons for a specific purpose, such as the construction of a hydroelectric dam or cogeneration plant. Like a general partnership, a joint venture requires that the parties share a community of interest, have the mutual right to direct and govern; share the partnership's profits and losses; and combine their property, money, efforts, skill, or knowledge in the undertaking. Unlike a general partnership, a joint venture is not a continuing relationship. It terminates when the project terminates.

In a joint venture there is no mutual agency of the partners unless specifically provided for. Thus, the authority of one member to bind the others is more limited than in a general partnership. To avoid inadvertently conferring apparent authority to bind the other members, a joint venture should make it clear in its dealings with third parties that it is a joint venture and not a partnership. This distinction should be reflected in the entity's name and in its recitation of its legal status in its contracts.

■ Limited Partnership

A *limited partnership* is similar to a general partnership except that one or more members may be designated as limited partners. *Limited partners* are liable for the partnership's debts only up to the amount they personally contributed to the partnership. Hence, their personal assets are protected. However, the general partners of a limited partnership remain jointly and severally liable for partnership contracts, debts, and torts just like partners in a general partnership.

Limited partnerships are often used to raise capital, as the limited liability of these partnerships makes them attractive to investors. In the Rad Waves example, the general partners might desire to raise capital to finance a sportswear line to promote their other products. To do so, they could restructure their partnership as a limited partnership with Ron and Pro remaining as general partners. They could then offer an investor a limited partnership interest in the renamed Rad Waves, L.P. If Ernestine contributed $1,000 to the partnership (assuming the relevant statute was complied with) she would then be a limited partner in Rad Waves, with her personal liability for any obligations limited to her $1,000 original investment.

Limited Participation

A partner's liability is limited unless, in the words of the Uniform Limited Partnership Act, he "takes part in the control of the business." Thus, if a limited partner had a voice in the business decisions of the partnership, she would be opening herself up to the possibility of liability beyond her original capital investment. Furthermore, a limited partner may contribute money or property to the partnership, but generally not services. Hence, in the Rad Wave example, if Ernestine assisted with the design of the sportswear line, in most states her liability could exceed her original $1,000 capital contribution. Therefore, limited partners should not take part in any partnership activity beyond monitoring the progress of their investment and exercising such statutory rights as the right to vote on the removal of a general partner. Moreover, the limited partner's name cannot appear in the name of the partnership without incurring unlimited liability.

Formal Requirements

Unlike a general partnership, a limited partnership is not generally recognized under state law until a certificate of limited partnership is filed, often with the county recorder or the secretary of state. Requirements for the certificate vary from state to state, but generally the certificate identifies the limited and general partners, details essential facts, and defines the rights and duties of the partners.

Under most state's statutes, in order to create a limited partnership, the partnership agreement must clearly designate the limited partners as such. Any partnership that does not substantially meet this and other statutory requirements will be treated as a general partnership, with mutual liability and apparent authority of each partner.

Although it is prudent and usually necessary to follow the formal requirements for formation of a limited part-nership, the would-be limited partners cannot escape lia-bility for the partnership's obligations by claiming that a formality was not followed. This is demonstrated in the following case, which is equally applicable to the forma-tion of informal limited and general partnerships.

■ **A Case in Point:**   **Summary**

Case 5.5
SHINDLER v. MARR & ASSOCIATES
Court of Appeals of Texas
695 S.W.2d 699
(Ct.App.Tex. 1986).

FACTS Theodore C. Bentley was acting as managing partner of Eaglewood Associates, Ltd. (Eaglewood). "Eaglewood" included James C. Shindler, Ralph E. Reamer, and Bentley. As managing partner Bentley signed a letter confirming a brokerage commission agreement in July 1977 with Marr & Associates. Subsequently, Brant Matz, an employee/broker of Marr & Associates, successfully negotiated certain financing for the con-struction of an apartment project. At the closing, defendants refused to pay Matz the $60,000 finder's fee, claiming that they were not operating as a limited partnership in July 1977 when Bentley signed the agreement, and that Bentley was not authorized to act for them. The jury found that the par-ties were operating as a limited partnership in July 1977 even though the certificate of limited partnership was not filed with the Secretary of State until December 1977. Defendants Shindler, Reamer, and Eaglewood appealed.

ISSUE PRESENTED Were the members of "Eaglewood" operating as a limited partnership in July of 1977 and thus liable for the actions of their partner, Bentley?

SUMMARY OF OPINION Shindler, Reamer, and Eaglewood Associates, Ltd. contended that they could not have operated as a limited partnership in July 1977 because the certificate of limited partnership was not filed with the secretary of state until December 1977. The Texas Court of Appeals responded that strict compliance with the applicable statutes was not required for the formation of a limited partnership. The Texas statute provid-ed that a limited partnership is formed if there is substantial compliance in good faith with the requirements.

The court emphasized that the primary purpose of filing requirements under the Texas Uniform Limited Partnership Act is to provide notice to third parties dealing with the partnership of the essential features of the partner-ship arrangement. The nature and legal existence of the partnership, how-ever, did not depend on the filing. In fact, neither a written nor an oral agreement is essential in order to establish a partnership. The partnership relation may be implied from the facts and circumstances surrounding the transaction and the conduct of the parties. It is the common intention to do the thing that constitutes a partnership that determines the relationship existing between the parties. If they intend to do a thing that constitutes a partnership, they are partners whether their express purpose was to create or avoid partnership.

The facts of this case supported the contention that the partnership rela-tion had indeed been formed as of July 1977. For example, Bentley signed the $60,000 commission agreement as "General Partner" on behalf of Eaglewood Associates, Ltd. Neither Shindler nor Reamer ever repudiated the contract, or indicated opposition (before the closing) to the payment of

Case 5.5 continued on following page

*Case **5.5** continued*

a finder's commission. Shindler admitted that they operated as a partnership before the certificate had been filed. Shindler and Reamer each expressly acknowledged that they accepted the benefits of the commission agreement.

RESULT   Eaglewood Associates, Ltd. and its partners Shindler and Reamer were held liable, along with Bentley, to pay the commission agreement Bentley had signed on behalf of the partnership.

Ethical Consideration

Evaluate the conduct of Shindler and Reamer in case 5.5.

■ Master Limited Partnership

In the early 1980s, the oil and gas and real estate industries spurred the creation of a hybrid entity, the master limited partnership (MLP). A *master limited partnership* is similar to other partnerships except that it offers the advantage of liquidity—ownership interests are publicly traded on the New York and American stock exchanges and in the over-the-counter market. The use of the MLP has been extended to areas as diverse as films, restaurants, and aircraft leasing. MLP units are sold in publicly registered offerings and attract individual investors who desire liquid investments with income tax advantages and capital security. However, many of the tax advantages of MLPs ended with the Revenue Act of 1987, which requires MLPs to be taxed like corporations.

■ Corporations

A *corporation* is an organization authorized by state law to act as a legal entity distinct from its owners. As a separate legal entity, the corporation has its own name and operates with limited powers to achieve specific purposes.

Limited Liability

A corporation has the very attractive feature of limited liability for its shareholders. Because the corporation is a separate entity, only the corporation itself is responsible for its liabilities. Entrepreneurs or investors can undertake risky ventures using the corporate form without having to worry about losing their personal assets if things go badly. (An exception to this general rule, "piercing the corporate veil," is discussed in chapter 20.)

> **"**
>
> *Entrepreneurs or investors can undertake risky ventures using the corporate form without having to worry about losing their personal assets if things go badly.*

Perpetual Life

Corporations have the advantage of perpetual life. Thus, if a key investor dies, or decides to sell his interest in the business, the corporation as an entity continues to exist and to conduct business.

Decision-Making Structure

Corporations have a distinctive decision-making structure. The center of authority is the board of directors. Although the managers and officers of the corporation run the day-to-day business affairs, and the shareholders have a statutory right to affirm or reject certain actions by the board, the board of directors is responsible for making most major corporate decisions. This centralization of authority is a key feature of corporations and should be kept in mind when comparing the corporation to the partnership.

The directors are not the principals of the corporation; they are its agents. If they fail to act with proper authority their principal, the corporation, will not be bound by their action. For example, there is a general common-law rule that the directors are agents of the corporation only in their combined capacity as a board and not individually. One nineteenth-century case found that even though all of the directors of a corporation individually signed a document to convey title to land owned by the corporation to a third party, that sale was void because the approval was not given by the board of directors as a body.[4]

It would be difficult for a corporation to function if it had to hold a board meeting every time it needed board approval for an action. Therefore, modern statutes provide that actions requiring board approval can be approved either at a board meeting or by the written consent of every board member.

■ Professional Corporation

Groups of doctors, lawyers, architects, or other professionals may join together to form a *professional corporation,* which is similar to a business corporation except that the shareholders still have personal liability for such actions as malpractice. In the past, the tax law made it advantageous for individuals to form a professional corporation because it allowed them to set aside more pretax money in retirement plans. However, this advantage does not exist under current tax law.

■ Limited Liability Company

The *limited liability company* is taxed like a limited partnership, and its members have limited liability. However, like a corporation, its members can participate in management without incurring unlimited liability. Characteristics of the limited liability company (LLC) are discussed in this chapter's "Inside Story."

■ Income Tax Considerations

The federal and state income tax laws treat different types of organizations differently. Because provisions in the tax laws often change, it is more important to understand the general issues than to strive for a detailed knowledge of the tax laws for any given year.

The analysis that follows is concerned solely with federal income tax consequences under the Internal

Revenue Code of 1986, as amended and in force as of January 1, 1994. Many state income tax provisions follow the federal rules.

Separate Taxable Entities and Pass-Through Entities

For income tax purposes there are two basic kinds of business organizations: (1) those that are taxed at both the entity level and the owner level; and (2) those that are taxed only at the owner level.

Corporations generally fall into the first category and are treated as taxable entities separate from their owners. Such corporations are governed by the tax rules in subchapter C of the Internal Revenue Code, and are sometimes called *C corporations.* A C corporation can have any kind and any number of shareholders, without limitation.

Certain closely held corporations may elect to be taxed under subchapter S of the Internal Revenue Code. Such an *S corporation* is not treated as a separately taxable entity. An election to be taxed under subchapter S does not affect the status of the organization as a corporation for state corporate law purposes.

Partnerships and joint ventures (other than master limited partnerships), S corporations, and limited liability companies are known as *pass-through entities* because they are not separate taxpayers and all of their income and losses generally are passed through and taxed to their owners.

Certain trusts, cooperatives, and other organizations that are noncorporate entities under state law are taxed in part as separate taxable entities and in part as pass-through entities.

C Corporations

The tax treatment of a C corporation is different from that of pass-through entities in several respects. Each may have favorable or unfavorable tax consequences, depending upon the circumstances.

Property Transfers   Because a C corporation is a separate taxable entity, a transfer of cash or any other kind of property between the corporation and its owners is a taxable transaction unless it comes within one of the statutory exceptions in subchapter C.

It is easier to transfer property to and from a partnership on a tax-free basis than it is with either a C corporation or an S corporation. For example, a transfer of property to either type of corporation in exchange for stock is tax-free only if the persons transferring the property

---

4. *Baldwin v. Canfield*, 26 Minn. 43, 1 N.W. 261 (Minn. 1879).

own 80% or more of the stock of the corporation immediately after the transaction. In contrast, an exchange of property for a share in a partnership is tax-free, without regard to the percentage share in the partnership.

Similarly, property that has appreciated in value may be more easily distributed on a tax-free basis from a partnership than from a corporation. The partnership is not subject to tax on the appreciated property. The partner receiving the property is not taxed until he subsequently sells the property. In contrast, a corporation will be taxed on the appreciation in value just as if it had sold the property for cash, and the shareholders will be taxed on the fair market value of the property they have received. Thus in the case of a C corporation there will be both a corporate-level tax and a shareholder-level tax on the distribution. For an S corporation, the taxable income is passed through and will be taxed only at the shareholder level.

Cash Distribution   The income of a C corporation is taxed at the corporate level, and taxed again at the individual level when it is distributed. This double taxation does not occur with the other forms of business organizations. This difference may make a pass-through entity preferable to a C corporation as the chosen form of business organization.

Double taxation can be reduced in two ways. First, the tax liability of the corporation can be reduced to the extent that corporate income can be offset by tax-deductible payments to shareholders. For example, if personal services are a major source of the corporation's income, payment of compensation to shareholders will reduce the corporation's taxable income. If capital investment is a major source of income, payment of interest or rent to shareholders may provide similar relief.

Second, the tax liability of the shareholders can be reduced to the extent that the business income is retained by the corporation. However, the accumulated earnings of a corporation may be taxed if they are not being retained for a legitimate business purpose of the corporation.

Cash distributions from partnerships and S corporations are tax-free to the recipients, up to the amount of their previous capital contributions less any income previously passed through to them. Distributions from C corporations, on the other hand, generally result in taxable dividend income to the shareholders.

Operating Losses   If the business operations of a C corporation produce a loss, as is frequently the case with start-up companies and real estate investments in their early years, the operating loss will be recognized at the

corporate level. This means that the shareholders receive no tax benefits from the operating loss, and the corporation receives no benefit until it has operating income against which its prior losses can be deducted.

On the other hand, if the same business is operated by a partnership or S corporation, the operating loss each year will be passed through to the individual partners or shareholders. They may, if certain tax law requirements are satisfied, deduct the operating loss from their other income. However, passive-loss limitations allow only owners who materially participate in the business to deduct its losses from other income. Passive investors may not deduct such losses from ordinary income, but can use passive losses to offset passive gains.

Capitalization   A C corporation has no tax-law restrictions as to its capitalization. As business needs require, the corporation may issue common stock, preferred stock, bonds, notes, warrants, options, and other instruments. These instruments may confer the right to varying degrees of control, and varying shares of earnings, and may be convertible, redeemable, or callable. However, the tax treatment of each kind of capital instrument is not always the same as its classification by the corporation. For example, shareholder debt may be treated as stock if the corporation has too little *equity capital,* that is, capital received in exchange for shares in the ownership of the corporation. As a consequence, tax-deductible "interest" payments may be recast as nondeductible "dividends."

S Corporations   If a domestic corporation has no more than 35 shareholders, all of whom are individuals who are U.S. citizens or U.S. residents (with a limited exception for certain trusts and estates), and has only one class of stock, it may elect to be taxed under subchapter S of the Internal Revenue Code. Because an S corporation can have only one class of stock, it is not permissible to have preferred stock and common stock. If the requirements for designation as an S corporation are not met, the corporation is classified as a C corporation.

Corporations and partnerships may not be shareholders—otherwise it would be possible to circumvent the ceiling on the number of shareholders. An S corporation is also prohibited from owning 80% or more of the stock of any other corporation.

Although the tax law allows an S corporation to have only one class of stock, it does permit differences in voting rights among its holders. In addition, S-corporation debt may avoid being treated as a second class of stock if it meets the requirements of a tax law safe harbor (that is, a clearly defined exception to adverse tax treatment).

In Brief: Choice of Business Entity: Pros and Cons

The following chart lists the principal considerations in selecting the form of business entity and applies them to the C corporation, S corporation, general partnership, limited partnership, and limited liability company. The considerations are listed in no particular order, in part because their importance will vary with each business formation depending on the nature of the business, sources of financing and the plan for providing financial returns to the owners (e.g., distributions of operating income, a public offering, or a sale of the business). Other factors that are not listed will also influence choice of entity. In addition, the "yes or no" format oversimplifies the applicability of certain attributes.

	C Corporation	S Corporation	General Partnership	Limited Partnership	Limited Liability Company
Limited Liability	Yes	Yes	No	Yes [A]	Yes
Flow-through Taxation	No	Yes	Yes	Yes	Yes
Simplicity/Low Cost	Yes	Yes	No	No	No
Limitations on Eligibility	No	Yes	No	No	No
Limitations on Capital Structure	No	Yes	No	No	No
Ability to Take Public	Yes	Yes [B]	No [C]	No [C]	No [C]
Flexible Charter Documents	No	No	Yes	Yes	Yes
Ability to Change Structure Without Tax	No	No	Yes	Yes	Yes
Favorable Employee Incentives (including incentive stock options)	Yes	Yes/No [D]	No [E]	No [E]	No [E]
Qualified Small Business Stock Exclusion for Gains	Yes [F]	No	No	No	No
Special Allocations	No	No	Yes	Yes	Yes
Tax-Free In-Kind Distributions	No	No	Yes	Yes	Yes

[A] Limited liability for limited partners only; a limited partnership must have at least one general partner with unlimited liability.

[B] S Corporation would convert to C Corporation upon a public offering because of the number of shareholders.

[C] Although the public markets are generally not available for partnership offerings, a partnership or LLC can be incorporated without tax and then taken public.

[D] Although an S Corporation can issue incentive stock options (ISOs), the inability to have two classes of stock limits favorable pricing of the common stock offered to employees.

[E] Although partnership and LLC interests can be provided to employees, they are poorly understood by most employees. Moreover, ISOs are not available.

[F] Special low capital gains rate for stock of U.S. C corporations with not more than $50 million in gross assets at the time stock is issued if the corporation is engaged in an active business and the taxpayer holds his stock for at least five years.

Source: Bill Morrow of Cooley, Godward, Castro, Huddleson & Tatum. *Used by permission.*

The election to be treated as an S corporation must be made with the consent of all of the shareholders, and must be made within specified time periods. It remains in effect until revoked or terminated. Once the election is terminated, a new election cannot be made for five years.

An S corporation pays no income tax but is required to file an informational return. The shareholders pay taxes on their share of the income or loss shown on the informational return, whether or not the income is actually distributed.

Partnerships

The capitalization of a partnership is generally limited to equity and debt, but the partnership agreement or loan agreements may provide a large degree of flexibility in this regard.

A partnership can have any kind and any number of partners. However, as the number of partners increases, there may be a greater risk of being taxed as a corporation. For example, certain publicly traded master limited partnerships are taxed as C corporations.

A partnership pays no taxes but must file an informational return. Individual partners are taxed on their share of the partnership income even if no cash is actually distributed to the partners.

It is possible for a business entity to be classified differently for tax purposes than for state law purposes. For example, a limited partnership may be taxed as a corporation if it has corporate attributes such as continuity of life, centralized management, limited liability for all owners, and free transferability of interests. A limited partnership may be considered to have limited liability if the general partner is a corporation with insufficient net worth to meet possible liabilities. A "limited partnership" whose ownership interests are freely transferable and traded on public exchanges (referred to as a master limited partnership) will be taxed as though it is a corporation.

Items of partnership income or loss generally can be allocated to specific partners at specific times so long as these allocations have a substantial economic effect apart from tax considerations. Thus a partnership can allocate a disproportionate amount of losses or depreciation to a particular partner in the early years, and allocate a disproportionate amount of later income to the same partner until the loss is recovered. This form of allocation may generate a valuable tax deferral for that partner.

No comparable allocation can be made by a C corporation, except to a limited extent by capitalizing the corporation with different classes of stock and debt. An S corporation is even more limited in this respect. It

may have only one class of stock, and all income and losses must be allocated strictly in proportion to stock ownership.

The Responsible Manager

Choosing the Appropriate Business Organization

The individuals who participate in the creation of a business organization will often go on to become its managers. These managers have a strong incentive to maximize the new enterprise's potential for success. To do this, several concerns must be addressed during the entity-selection process.

First, a manager should define and clarify the business goals of the enterprise in a business plan. For example, if the enterprise will need capital from a large number of individuals, it will be necessary to ensure limited liability for some or all of these investors. A general partnership would not be suitable, as there would be no limited liability for passive investors.

A related concern is clarifying the goals of the individual participants in the enterprise. For example, experienced managers who have developed a new product that requires little capital outlay would probably want exclusive control of the new business. A general partnership might be best suited to their needs.

If a general partnership is chosen, there are additional concerns. For example, it is important to put the partnership agreement in writing. A written partnership agreement forces people to think through their business objectives and relationships before they begin working together. It also avoids the imposition of certain statutory partnership rules that apply when there is no written agreement.

If several persons work together on an informal basis with a common business objective, and then one leaves, there can be the problem of *forgotten founder*. The person who left may have ownership rights in the enterprise. Such rights can be based on the laws of intellectual property if the person leaving created a protectable piece of property, such as a patentable invention, or computer software that is protected by copyright law. (Intellectual property is discussed in chapter 11.) Even if the founder created no protectable intellectual property before leaving, she may have been a partner in an informal oral general partnership if the parties had been sharing profits and losses. As such, she would be entitled to a share of the partnership assets.

One way to mitigate the forgotten founder problem is to incorporate early and issue shares that are subject to vesting over time. A common vesting schedule provides that if a person leaves in the first year, he forfeits all his rights to any stock. This is called *cliff vesting*. One-quarter of the stock is often vested at the end of the first year. The rest is vested monthly over the next three to four years.

If early incorporation is either infeasible or otherwise undesirable, it is important to spell out in writing at the beginning of a joint project what will happen if someone leaves. Otherwise, those who remain could find themselves sued years down the road for a share of the company that finally is formed or for a partnership interest or for royalties for use of intellectual property.

Tax considerations play a major role in the choice of a business entity. Because tax law is constantly changing, its impact on a particular business form cannot be predicted with certainty. Nonetheless, the larger issues, such as whether taxation would be at both the entity and owner level or only at the owner level, must be considered.

Optimal tax planning does not necessarily mean tax minimization. When deciding how to organize a business, the company must weigh the tax advantages against the agency costs.

To help her in this crucial decision, a manager will often need advice from specialists in business taxation and business entity formation. Ownership issues, in both partnerships and corporations, can be extremely compli-

cated. The manager should also understand the various agency relationships that are created by each of the organizations. Legal specialists can help managers to evaluate the different alternatives, as no one specific business form will meet every need and goal.

Once a business form has been selected and a new enterprise created, managers are presented with new and sometimes more complex considerations. Even in the simplest form of enterprise, the sole proprietorship, the manager has a broad range of concerns. For example, he will probably hire employees or others to act on his behalf, so he must consider the impact of agency law. He may be liable for any tort committed by his employees, so he has a strong interest in properly monitoring their performance. By clearly defining the scope of employment, managers can decrease the risk of vicarious liability for employees' torts. The manager should ensure that the work environment and the machines and other equipment used in the business are safe. She should also stress to the employees the importance of not only complying with the law but also being ethical and safety conscious.

A manager must be careful, in dealing with employees, that she leaves little doubt as to the boundaries of their actual authority. Similarly, in dealings with third parties, the manager should make explicit, unambiguous statements as to the scope and limit of an employee's authority to enter into contracts. If she does not do this, she may find that, for example, a purchasing agent has inadvertently been given the apparent authority to bind the business to a large purchase of supplies, above the actual needs of the business. A manager should aim at clarity in all her dealings with third parties, no matter what type of business enterprise she manages.

Inside Story

Limited Liability Companies

The limited liability company is one of the newest types of business organization that can be organized under state law in the U.S. It combines the limited liability of a corporation with the pass-through tax benefits associated with a partnership. A variation of the limited liability company has been in existence in Germany, France and Brazil for a number of years. In Germany, for example, it is called a "GmbH"; in France an "SNC."

The first states to enact limited liability company (LLC) statutes were Wyoming, in 1977, and Florida, in 1982. Due to the uncertainty surrounding the treatment by the Internal Revenue Service (IRS) of the LLC, there

Inside Story continued on following page

Inside Story, continued

was little interest among other states for several years. The LLC was designed to provide flow-through tax advantages as in a partnership, but it was unclear whether the IRS would honor such status. In 1988, the IRS issued a ruling classifying a Wyoming LLC as a partnership for tax purposes. In the period 1993–1994 the IRS issued additional favorable revenue rulings covering another 13 states' LLC legislation.

Typically two or more persons are needed to form an LLC. In some states, only one person over the age of eighteen is required to organize it. All states require that articles of organization be filed with the secretary of state that include the name of the company and period of duration. Many states require that the duration only be for 30 years, in order to ensure that the firm does not have an endless continuity of life.

The statutes permit the formation of LLCs for any lawful purpose except the business of banking and insurance. Once an LLC has filed its articles of organization with the secretary of state, it secures a notice to third parties that the individual members of the company are not personally liable for debt, obligations, acts, or liability of the company. In addition to limited liability, the LLC statutes have four basic characteristics. First, LLC laws require the LLCs to conform their names to specific guidelines. All of the state statutes require the words "limited liability company," "limited company," or "L.C." to appear in the company's name. The rule is designed to ensure that parties dealing with the LLC are notified of its limited liability feature. Second, the company is given full *juristic personality*, meaning it is treated as a separate legal entity. Third, a member is permitted to control the admission of new members to the LLC. Membership is not freely transferable and members generally have to be given the right to withdraw from the company. Fourth, limited liability firms have to be dissolved upon the death of a member and provide for probate or sale of a deceased's share.

In order to retain the tax advantages of being classified as a noncorporate entity for tax treatment, the LLC must avoid at least two of the following four corporate characteristics identified by the IRS: (1) continuity of life; (2) centralized management; (3) limited liability; and (4) free transferability of ownership interest.

Two corporate characteristics present in the LLC are centralized management and limited liability. Under the statutes, an LLC is managed by designated managers, constituting less than all of the members and therefore creating centralized management. The IRS also determined that in LLCs, the individual members are not personally liable for the organization's debts and obligations, thus the corporate characteristic of limited liability exists.

Although the LLC has often been compared to the subchapter S corporation, it has some advantages over the S corporation. For example, the LLC has no citizenship requirements, which allows it to attract capital from international markets. The LLC has no maximum limit on the number of shareholders, whereas the S corporation is limited to 35 shareholders.

Also, the S corporation allows for only one class of stock. The LLC has no such limits, providing the LLC with greater flexibility in planning distributions and special allocations. Finally, there is no limitation on the ownership of other corporations, and there are usually no tax penalties upon liquidation.

The LLC also has advantages over the limited partnership, because it provides limited liability to all its members, including those who participate in management. In the limited partnership, too much participation in the management and control of the partnership can result in the partner's forfeiture of limited liability. LLC members can manage the company directly, whereas corporate general partners in limited partnerships must control indirectly through the corporation.

The number of states providing for creation of LLCs has increased tremendously in recent years. In mid-1994 there were 36 states with LLC statutes, up from eight states in 1991. This number will probably increase as the IRS continues to issue favorable tax classification rulings.

Even if the IRS continues to issue favorable rulings, Congress could decide to change the Internal Revenue Code to provide that LLCs will be taxed as corporations. This happened with master limited partnerships when Congress decided their taxation as limited partnerships was too big a drain on federal revenues.

Key Words and Phrases

actual authority **151**	fiduciary **146**	principal **146**
agency **146**	forgotten founder **166**	professional corporation **163**
agent **146**	general partnership **157**	ratification **151**
apparent authority **151**	*guardian ad litem* **153**	*respondeat superior* **153**
C corporation **163**	joint venture **160**	S corporation **163**
cliff vesting **167**	juristic personality **168**	sole proprietorship **157**
corporation **162**	limited liability company **157**	termination **160**
dissolution **159**	limited partner **160**	undisclosed principal **151**
duty of care **146**	limited partnership **160**	vicarious liability **155**
duty of loyalty **146**	marshaling assets **158**	winding up **160**
equity capital **164**	master limited partnership **162**	
fictitious business name **157**	pass-through entity **163**	

Questions and Case Problems

1. What are the duties of an agent to her principal?

2. Han Delbar was the sole proprietor of a bicycle shop called We Deal Wheels. He had two employees, Sandy Gear and Jebb Sprocket. Gear had the title of salesperson. She sold bikes and accessories to the public, and also bought items from wholesalers. Sprocket had the title of repairperson; he did the repairs. Both employees sometimes did business-related errands outside the shop. At 10:00 A.M. one Monday, business was slow, so Delbar and Gear decided to test ride a new mountain bike that the shop had just started selling. They left Sprocket to tend the store. At 10:30 A.M. a salesperson from R Tools R Jools, Inc., a wholesale tool supplier, walked into the shop. She found Sprocket there alone. She showed him a new line of high-priced bicycle repair tools. Sprocket was impressed and felt that the store should carry the tools. He said to the R Tools salesperson: "I'm in charge of repairs here, and so it makes sense for me to order these tools. You can bill us for $1,000 worth." The salesperson had done business with Gear in the past. Also, she had been told by Delbar that Sprocket was in charge of repairs and that We Deal Wheels would make good on any order purchased on credit. She was only too happy to make the sale by leaving the requested tools.

At 10:45 A.M. Delbar and Gear made it to a wooded area at the edge of town. Gear told Delbar that a true test of the bike's performance would require taking the long way back to the shop, across a rocky stretch of terrain. Delbar said that he himself wanted to go straight back, but that Gear could go the long way so long as she returned to the shop with all due haste. On her ride back, Gear stopped to buy a soda at the local grocery store. Rushing out of the store, Gear accidentally knocked over an old man, who broke his leg and arm in the fall.

At 11:30 A.M. Delbar returned to the store and saw the tools. He immediately called R Tools R Jools to cancel the order, believing they were too high-priced. He told Sprocket that he should not order tools in the future.

(a) R Tools R Jools refuses to take back the order and Delbar refuses to pay for it. R Tools R Jools sues Delbar to collect the money. What arguments will each make in an attempt to win this suit? Who should win? How could Delbar have ensured his success on this issue?

(b) The injured old man sues Delbar, as Gear's employer, for his injuries. What arguments will Delbar make to avoid liability? Will he be successful? Assume that Delbar can succeed on his legal arguments. Does he have any ethical duty to pay?

3. Art D. Lers ran a small but prosperous rare print shop. To keep the shop stocked with the finest prints, Lers needed to make purchases at trade shows throughout the world. When he was too busy to attend, Lers sometimes sent his employee, Rembrandt. On other occasions he paid for the services of an independent buyer named Rubens.

On March 14, Lers sent Rembrandt to Tokyo to buy ten nineteenth-century Japanese prints. Lers told Rembrandt that he should use his own best judgment and buy the ten prints that he considered to be of the finest quality. Price was no concern. While at the show, Rembrandt made a written list of the finest prints. The total came to eleven. Rembrandt was unable to eliminate any from the list on the basis of quality. He closed his eyes and brought his finger down on the paper, and it landed on print #4. Rembrandt purchased that print for himself and bought the other ten for Lers.

On April 14, Rubens, who had his own business buying prints for himself and other dealers, called Lers. Rubens said he would be attending a show in Munich and asked if Lers wished him to purchase a few prints on Lers's behalf. Lers replied that he was interested, but only if Rubens agreed to fax him photocopies of all prints for sale, then let Lers select five before

Rubens bought any. Rubens did not usually make such concessions, but he agreed to do it. Rubens and Lers signed Rubens's standard contract, with a typed-in clause for the faxing arrangement. Once at the show, Rubens faxed the copies. Lers selected five prints. One of the five was a forgery, but Lers could not detect it in a fax. Rubens spotted the forgery and discreetly mentioned it to the show's organizer. Not wanting to create a scandal, the organizer offered Rubens $5,000 to remain silent. Rubens accepted the bribe.

(a) Lers believes that the print Rembrandt purchased for himself is the best of the Tokyo lot. Rembrandt refuses to sell it to Lers. (After he returned, Rembrandt decided his print was the finest.) The dealer sues his employee to obtain possession. What arguments could Rembrandt's lawyers make? How would Lers's lawyers counter? Has Rembrandt violated a fiduciary duty to Lers?

(b) Lers finds out about the Munich forgery. Lers's lawyer advises him that he cannot sue Rubens under contract law because Rubens's standard contract explicitly denies any liability for forged artwork. Does Lers have any other way to force Rubens to reimburse him for the loss? What can Lers recover in damages if he is successful?

4. Mary Webster and David Taylor agreed orally to write and publish together four books on model railroading. One year later Taylor terminated the partnership unilaterally and published two of the books on his own. Webster wishes to sue Taylor. What information should you obtain from Webster, and is there any way she can state a valid claim against Taylor?

5. Ernie Jameson is a design engineer with a proven track record in the field of electronic musical instruments. He has recently designed a new VLSI (very large scale integrated) chip. This chip is meant to be the heart and soul of a digital sampling keyboard to be called Echo. Jameson believes the Echo will set a new industry standard. He wishes to organize a business enterprise to build and market it. He has a meeting with his lawyer, at which he conveys to her the following bits of information:

■ It will take approximately two years to turn the VLSI chip into a marketable product.

■ Jameson has more than $200,000 in savings from previous ventures. He does not want any of that money at risk in this new venture. However, he wants a part of the ownership but is unsure what percentage he wants.

■ There are five private investors currently willing to put up money in this venture. Only two out of the five want to play an active role in the enterprise. Jameson is willing to give these two some limited control.

■ Jameson knows that he is not qualified to manage the new endeavor. Nonetheless, he wants a significant say in how it proceeds.

■ Five more investors could be attracted to this project, but only if they could be guaranteed some fixed return on their money, or could realize immediate tax benefits from investing.

■ Jameson would like Bernie Lord, a manager much in demand in the electronics field, to be his CEO. To attract him to the enterprise would take significant incentives.

Jameson is not committed to using any particular type of business organization; he is interested in weighing the alternatives. What possible types of business organizations could accommodate the needs of the various players? What are the advantages and disadvantages of each alternative? Which one should Jameson choose?

6. An individual was acting as the president and chairman of the board of a charitable organization. In that capacity he was authorized as a signer to the organization's five bank accounts, with the power to withdraw funds. He also sometimes handled transfers of funds. Do the above facts necessarily support the contention that he had the apparent authority to make withdrawals of any amount on the accounts, including unusually large sums that were transferred to private accounts? [*Calabrese Foundation, Inc. v. Investment Advisors, Inc.*, 831 F.Supp. 1507 (D.Col. 1993)]

7. A construction company contracted with a partnership to build two homes. The partnership then breached the contract by not paying the full balance due on the homes. The construction company tried to sue the partnership for its assets, as well as the individual partners for their personal assets. Are the partners personally liable for the debts of their partnership? [*Wayne Smith Construction Company, Inc. v. Wolman, Duberstein & Thompson*, 604 N.E.2d 157 (Ohio 1992)]

8. An individual was the sole general partner of a large office building in Austin, Texas, along with several limited partners. The limited partners were also lessees of space in the office building. Each tenant of the building (including the limited partners/lessees) was responsible for the "finish-out" construction of that tenant's office space. Most of these tenants hired one of two contractors to finish out their office spaces. On most of these finish-out jobs the contractors paid Johnson, the sole general partner, a 15% fee. Each contractor simply added this fee to the sum charged to the tenant. Some tenants knew about the fee and others did not. Did Johnson owe a fiduciary duty to his limited partners (who were also his tenants) to disclose the fee? [*Johnson v. J. Hiram Moore, Ltd.*, 763 S.W.2d 496 (Ct.App.Tex. 1989)]

9. The plaintiffs were models in a "fitness fashion show," featured as part of a "Working Women's Survival Show" exhibition at a convention center in St. Louis. B.P.S., doing business as Wells Fargo Guard Service, had contracted with the city to provide guards at the center.

Security at the convention center included a number of television surveillance cameras scattered around the center, which were monitored on small screens in a central control room. The direction in which the cameras were pointing could be adjusted manually or automatically in the control room. The control room also had a large screen that the guards could use to view the image from the cameras or to monitor what was being taped on the VCR. The purpose of having the VCR was to enable the guards to videotape suspicious activities. The Wells Fargo guards were told to practice taping on the VCR.

Promoters for the Working Women's Survival Show had a makeshift curtained dressing area set up near the stage for the models in the fashion shows. Unbeknown to the models, the dressing area was in a location that could be monitored by one of the surveillance cameras. That fortuity was discovered by two Wells Fargo guards, Rook and Smith. Rook had the rank of "Captain" within Wells Fargo, denoting supervisory capacity, though there was testimony that when he worked in the control room, he had no supervisory authority. Another supervisor with disputed supervisory authority, Ramey, walked by the control room and saw the guards using the large screen to view women in a state of undress. Ramey said that he thought the guards were watching pornographic tapes that they had brought to work. (There was testimony that the guards watched their own pornographic tapes in the control room.)

Either Smith or Rook (each accuses the other) focused the camera on the plaintiffs and taped them as they were changing clothes for the fashion show. Another guard, Sonntag, took the tape home, leaving a decoy in its place. Sonntag decided to report the incident to Wells Fargo management. When he phoned Wells Fargo he asked for a particular individual to accompany him in taking the tape to the police. Wells Fargo insisted that he turn the tape over to them. He decided to take it to the police station anyway, but stopped when he was frightened by a Wells Fargo car with men in it parked outside the station. He then noticed a television anchorman also outside the police station. He gave the tape to the anchorman, who aired a redacted (edited) version of it on the local television news.

Can Wells Fargo Guard Service be held liable for the unauthorized actions of its agents, even if those actions are done for reasons of personal pleasure rather than for work? [*Does v. B.P.S. Guard Services, Inc. d/b/a Wells Fargo Guard Service*, 945 F.2d 1422 (8th Cir. 1991)]

10. Must all partnership receivables be received by a partnership before it can be terminated by a court? What if termination is sought in 1992 but certain payments to which the partnership is entitled will not be payable until 1997 at the earliest and 2001 at the latest? [*Doting v. Trunk*, 856 P.2d 536 (Mont. 1993)]

Chapter 6

ADMINISTRATIVE LAW

■ Introduction

Importance of Administrative Agencies

Administrative law concerns the powers and procedures of administrative agencies, such as the Internal Revenue Service, which collects taxes, and the Securities and Exchange Commission, which regulates securities markets. The activities of administrative agencies affect nearly everyone, frequently on a daily basis. Administrative agencies set limits on pollution and emissions and regulate disposal of hazardous waste. They regulate radio and television, food and drugs, and health and safety. Although the number of federal court trials in all cases is probably less than 10,000 annually, agencies such as the Social Security Administration act annually on millions of applications for benefits. Federal and state administrative agencies solve practical problems that cannot be handled effectively by the courts or legislatures.

Administrative agencies date back to the country's earliest days. The first Congress established three administrative agencies, including one for the payment of benefits to Revolutionary War veterans. The Patent Office was created in 1790, and ten other federal administrative agencies were created before the Civil War.

At three critical junctures in United States history, Congress made extensive use of administrative agencies. During the Progressive Era, from 1885 until 1914, Congress turned to agencies such as the Interstate Commerce Commission, the Federal Reserve Board, the Federal Trade Commission, and the Food and Drug Administration to solve problems concerning railroads, shipping, banks, trade, and food and drugs. In response to the stock market crash in 1929 and the subsequent Depression, Congress created many agencies to deal with the crisis and delegated broad authority to them. Finally, during the dawn of the environmental era in the 1970s, Congress turned extensively to federal administrative agencies to regulate health and restrict pollution. The Environmental Protection Agency, which did not even exist in 1960, today administers a budget of more than $4.5 billion and has nearly 15,000 employees.

Since 1985,[1] the management of agencies has come under close scrutiny. Partly as a response to what was perceived as a strategy of the Republican administrations to "deregulate by inaction," Congress resorted to a more micromanagement approach of agency action and enacted very detailed amendments to regulatory statutes. In some cases these amendments required the agencies to produce rules or standards by a certain deadline; in others prohibitory amendments forbade the agency to spend money on a specific program.

As well, there was a general push by the executive branch to centralize and coordinate supervision of regulation in the White House. President Reagan's executive orders 12,291 and 12,498 required agencies to subject every "major rule" to cost-benefit analysis and to review for conformity with a program supervised by the Office of Management and Budget (OMB). Vice President Al Gore's 1993 report on increasing government efficiency, *From Red Tape to Results: Creating a Government that Works Better and Costs Less,* suggested that the Clinton administration will step up reliance on technocratic controls to "reinvent government."

Some critics see this micromanagement as having made a bad situation worse. Agencies are compelled to work under unreasonable utopian directives instructing them, for example, to regulate all carcinogens in food or to protect the safety of all workers, while at the same time their ability to act is limited by their budgets and formalized procedures. Furthermore, the regulatory calendar is further cluttered up by forced concentration of limited resources on arbitrary deadlines.

Chapter Summary

This chapter discusses the various ways in which administrative agencies operate. Agencies make rules to effectuate legislative enactments; they resolve conflicts by formal adjudication, a courtlike proceeding; they carry out informal discretionary actions; and they conduct investigations regarding compliance with specific laws and regulations.

This chapter also addresses the key principles of administrative law. Constitutional issues include the separation of powers, the delegation of authority, and the protections afforded by the Bill of Rights. Issues arising from the judicial review of agency actions include the doctrines of ripeness and exhaustion of administrative remedies. Doctrines that limit the decision-making power of agencies include the principle that agencies are bound by their own rules, and that they must explain the basis for their decisions.

Finally, the chapter describes how to find the rules of a particular agency and how to obtain documents from the government.

---

1. Appreciation goes to Professor Robert W. Gordon, Stanford Law School, for his valuable insights on recent developments in the area of administrative law.

■ How Administrative Agencies Act

The Fourth Branch of Government

Courts adjudicate legal disputes, the legislature adopts laws, and the executive branch administers the laws. Although usually part of the executive branch, administrative agencies can rightly be called a fourth branch of government. This fourth branch performs some of the functions of each of the other three branches, with quasi-legislative and quasi-judicial as well as executive roles. An administrative agency functions in four primary ways: making rules, conducting formal adjudications, taking informal discretionary actions, and conducting investigations.

Making Rules

A state legislature or Congress frequently lacks the time, human resources, and expertise to enact detailed regulations. Sometimes issues are so politically sensitive that elected officials lack the will to make the tough decisions. In such cases, the legislature will pass a law presenting general principles and guidelines and will delegate authority to an administrative agency to carry out this legislative intent. The agency will then adopt appropriate rules or regulations.

The process that administrative agencies use to adopt rules is similar, but not identical, to the legislative process. The basic procedure involves three steps.

Notice to the Public   First, the administrative agency gives notice to the public of its intent to propose a rule. Generally, the agency will publish the proposed rule and give the public an opportunity to submit written comments. Exhibit 6-1 shows a proposed rule published by an administrative agency. Exhibit 6-2 is a fictitious example of a written comment on the proposed rule. The letter: (1) identifies the company that is concerned; (2) describes why it is concerned; (3) suggests a specific change in the language of the proposed rule; and (4) provides factual information to support its position. These kinds of comments are very helpful to an agency and can influence the final rule.

Agencies may, but are not always required to, hold a formal public hearing. They always allow people to comment on proposed rules by meeting informally or telephoning the agency personnel. If a company is particularly concerned about a proposed rule, it would be wise to both call and meet with the proposing agency about its concerns.

Evaluation   Second, the administrative agency evaluates the comments, responds to them, and decides on the scope and extent of the final rule.

Adoption   Third, the agency will formally adopt the rule by publishing it in the *Federal Register* along with an explanation of changes. The final rule will also be *codified,* that is, added to the *Code of Federal Regulations.* (These two publications are discussed later in the chapter.)

Federal agency officials who decide what rules are to be adopted are not elected. The president appoints some; others are hired through civil service procedures. In either instance, the rules they adopt are as binding as the laws passed by the legislative branch, and, like statutes, rules can be challenged in court. Such challenges are discussed later in this chapter.

In concluding this discussion of rule making, it should be noted that the federal government has attempted to make the regulatory process less cumbersome and time-consuming, more informal, and less vulnerable to judicial review by applying the Japanese-style of seeking consensus of the major affected groups on the substance of new regulations. This process is known as *regulatory negotiations* or "reg. neg." Representatives of major groups convene and work out a compromise through negotiation. Congress has facilitated this process by adopting amendments to the Administrative Procedures Act (APA) entitled "Negotiated Rulemaking Procedure."[2]

Conducting Formal Adjudications

Courts do not have the time, money, and personnel to hear all of the cases that might arise in the course of regulating individual and corporate behavior. Consequently, the legislatures frequently give administrative agencies the responsibility for solving specific types of legal disputes, such as who is entitled to government benefits, or the imposition of civil penalties on regulated industries.

Formal agency adjudications are courtlike proceedings which can be presided over by one or more members of the agency or by an *administrative law judge.* The presiding official is entitled to administer oaths, issue subpoenas, rule on offers of proof and relevant evidence, authorize depositions, and decide the case at hand.

These formal adjudications typically include a prehearing discovery phase. The hearing itself is conducted like a trial. Each side presents its evidence under oath, and testimony is subject to cross-examination. The main difference between administrative adjudications and courtroom trials is that there is never a jury at the administrative level.

An administrative agency's decision in a formal adjudication can be appealed to a court. Agency actions that set rates for natural gas prices or that provide licenses for dams are examples of the kinds of cases that regularly go to court. In most instances, judicial review of an agency action is based on the *record,* that is, the oral and written evidence presented at the administrative hearing. The court's review is limited to determining whether the administrative agency acted properly on the evidence

---

2. 5 U.S.C. 561 *et seq.* (1993).

EXHIBIT 6-1 A Proposed Rule Published by an Administrative Agency

DEPARTMENT OF HEALTH AND HUMAN SERVICES

Food and Drug Administration

21 CFR Part 330

[Docket No. 92N–0454]

RIN 0905–AA06

Labeling of Drug Products for Over-the-Counter Human Use

AGENCY: Food and Drug Administration, HHS.

ACTION: Proposed rule.

SUMMARY: The Food and Drug Administration (FDA) is proposing to amend its general labeling policy for over-the-counter (OTC) drug products to allow for the interchangeable use of certain words in labeling required by an OTC drug monograph. Examples include "doctor" and "physician," and "consult" and "ask." Thus, the phrase "consult a doctor" could be used interchangeably with the phrases "ask a doctor," "consult a physician," and "ask a physician." This proposal provides alternate terminology in the labeling of OTC drug products.

DATES: Written comments by June 4, 1993. The agency is proposing that the final rule based on this proposal be effective 30 days after the date of its publication in the **Federal Register**.

ADDRESSES: Written comments to the Dockets Management Branch (HFA–305), Food and Drug Administration, rm. 1–23, 12420 Parklawn Dr., Rockville, MD 20857.

FOR FURTHER INFORMATION CONTACT: William E. Gilbertson, Center for Drug Evaluation and Research (HFD–810), Food and Drug Administration, 5600 Fishers Lane, Rockville, MD 20857, 301–295–8000.

SUPPLEMENTARY INFORMATION: The agency has proposed in a number of tentative final monographs and has included in a number of final monographs a provision that the words "doctor" and "physician" may be used interchangeably in the labeling of OTC drug products. (See, for example, §§ 333.150(e), 333.350(e), and 336.50(e); 21 CFR 333.150(e), 333.350(e), and 336.50(e).) Instead of including this provision in each OTC drug monograph, the agency is proposing to include such a provision in § 330.1 (21 CFR 330.1) as part of the general conditions under which an OTC drug is generally recognized as safe, effective, and not misbranded.

The agency believes that there are other monograph terms for which substitutes could be used, at

Hourly Demand Data By Specified Week, are proposed to be replaced by the following:

Part III Schedule 2: Planning Area Hourly Demand and Forecast Summer and Winter Peak Demand and Annual Net Energy For Load

Respondents, which participate in a national, regional or subregional process for consolidating and ensuring the consistency and accuracy of actual and forecast demand information are required to authorize the national, regional or subregional organization to release that information to the public without conditions and in an easily accessible electronic format.

If the respondent does not participate in the development of national, regional or subregional actual and forecast demand information, it is required to submit its own, equivalent, demand information directly to the Commission along with this report, as follows.

Respondents must submit on a 3.5 inch diskette formatted for the DOS operating system the following data file in ASCII format: the planning area's actual hourly demand, in megawatts, for each hour of the year starting with 12 midnight, January 1, 1993, central standard time. The file should have 8760 records (8784 for leap years).

Also provide on the diskette a file containing the planning area's forecast summer and winter peak demand, in megawatts, and annual net energy for load, in megawatthours, for the next ten years.

[FR Doc. 93–7825 Filed 4–2–93; 8:45 am]
BILLING CODE 6717–01–M

TENNESSEE VALLEY AUTHORITY

18 CFR Part 1301

Freedom of Information Act

AGENCY: Tennessee Valley Authority (TVA).

ACTION: Proposed Rule.

SUMMARY: The Tennessee Valley Authority is proposing to amend its Freedom of Information Act regulations to more accurately reflect its direct reasonable operating costs in searching for and reviewing records requested under the Freedom of Information Act.

DATES: Comments must be received by May 5, 1993.

ADDRESSES: Comments regarding this proposed rule should be sent to Mark R. Winter, TVA, 1101 Market Street (MR 2F), Chattanooga, TN 37402–2801. As a convenience to commenters, TVA will accept public comments transmitted by facsimile ("FAX") machine. The telephone number of the FAX receiver is (615) 751–2902. Receipt of FAX transmittals will not be acknowledged.

FOR FURTHER INFORMATION CONTACT: Mark R. Winter, (615) 751–2523.

SUPPLEMENTARY INFORMATION: TVA is proposing to amend 18 CFR 1301.2(c)(1)

to more accurately reflect its direct reasonable operating costs in searching for and reviewing records requested under the Freedom of Information Act. The rates proposed reflect an average rate for the range of TVA pay grades typically involved in responding to Freedom of Information Act requests. For time spent by clerical employees, the charge is currently $8.35 per hour. For time spent by supervisory and professional employees, the charge is currently $19.75 per hour. TVA is proposing to amend the charges to $10.10 per hour and $32.20 per hour, respectively. In conformance with section (a)(4)(A)(iv) of the Freedom of Information Act, as amended, TVA is also proposing to amend 18 CFR 1301.2(d)(2) by reducing the amount of search time that will be provided without charge from 4 hours to 2 hours.

List of Subjects in 18 CFR Part 1301

Administrative practice and procedure, Freedom of Information, Privacy Act, Sunshine Act.

For the reasons set forth in the preamble, title 18, chapter XIII of the Code of Federal Regulations is proposed to be amended as follows:

PART 1301—PROCEDURES

1. The authority citation for part 1301 continues to read as follows:

Authority: 16 U.S.C. 831–831dd, 5 U.S.C. 552.

2. Section 1301.2 is amended by revising paragraph (c)(1) and the first sentence of paragraph (d)(2) to read as follows:

§ 1301.2 Schedule of fees.

*   *   *   *   *

(c) * * *

(1) *Search time charges for other than computer searches.* For time spent by clerical employees in searching files, the charge is $10.10 per hour. For time spent by supervisory and professional employees, the charge is $32.20 per hour.

*   *   *   *   *

(d) * * *

(2) Except for documents provided in response to a commercial use request, the first 100 pages and the first 2 hours of search time will be provided without charge. * * *

*   *   *   *   *

William S. Moore,
Manager, Information Support Services.
[FR Doc. 93–7610 Filed 4–2–93; 8:45 am]
BILLING CODE 8120–08–M

EXHIBIT 6-2   Comment on a Proposed Administrative Rule

SUTHERLAND-SPIERS PHARMACEUTICALS
ONE SUTHERLAND CIRCLE
MINNEAPOLIS, MN 55402
(612) 203-1234

May 3, 1993

Dockets Management Branch (HFA-305)
Food and Drug Administration
12420 Parklawn Drive, Room 1-23
Rockville, MD 20857

Dear Sir or Madam:

On April 5, 1993, the Food and Drug Administration proposed an amendment to its general labeling policy for over-the-counter (OTC) drugs to allow for the interchangeable use of certain required words. 58 Fed. Reg. 17553. The goal of the proposed rule 21 CFR § 330.1 is to streamline labeling requirements and permit the use of simpler, shorter terms that may be better understood by consumers. We write in support of the agency's proposed change and offer several additional alternative terms which might be included in the final rule.

We are a major drug manufacturer subject to the rules and regulations of the Food and Drug Administration. Like the Food and Drug Administration, we are concerned about the safe and effective use of OTC drugs. Any change in existing rules which might make OTC drug labeling simpler and easier to understand for consumers deserves our support. While we agree with the proposed changes, we believe that the inclusion of additional alternative terms will better achieve the stated goal of the proposed rule.

The agency has proposed that, at the manufacturers' discretion, the word "ask" could be substituted for the word "consult" and that the words "doctor" and "physician" may be used interchangeably in the labeling of OTC drug products. We suggest that several additional interchangeable terms be included in the final rule: (1) "clean" or "cleanse," (2) "persist" or "continue," (3) "chronic" or "persistent," (4) "assistance" or "help," (5) "pulmonary" or "lung," and (6) "indication" or "use." Each of these pairings already appears in several existing OTC drug labeling regulations.

We understand that the proposed rule is intended only to provide a glossary of comparable terms that may be used interchangeably, not to make substantive changes in the underlying required label statements. For example, the final rule should not permit the term "health professional" as an alternative to the terms "doctor" or "physician," because a "health professional" may include pharmacists, nurses, midwives, and others who are not licensed to practice medicine.

Please call us if we can provide any additional information.

Sincerely,

Johanna A. Washington, President

reflected in the record. In some cases, the laws governing the administrative adjudication provide for a *de novo* (that is, new) proceeding in court, where the entire matter is litigated from the beginning.

Taking Informal Discretionary Actions

The basic role of administrative agencies is to provide a practical decision-making process for repetitive, frequent actions that are inappropriate to litigate in courts. These *informal discretionary actions* have been called the lifeblood of administrative agencies. Common examples are: the awarding of governmental grants and loans; workers' compensation cases; the administration of welfare benefits; the informal resolution of tax disputes; and determination of Social Security claims. Informal discretionary action also governs most applications to government agencies for licenses, leases, and permits, such as driver's licenses, leases of federal lands, and the registration of securities offerings.

Informal discretionary actions also include matters such as contracting, planning, and negotiation. Thus, the process of negotiating a contract with a government agency to supply military parts or to build bridges or highways is within the realm of administrative law. In fact, most of what the governmental agencies do falls within the category of informal discretionary action.

The most noteworthy aspect of these informal actions is their lack of clear procedural rules. In court, there is a strict set of rules and procedures to be followed, and a specific person is assigned to hear the case. In informal discretionary actions, the agency frequently has no formal procedures, such as notice to the public, opportunity to file briefs, or opportunity to submit oral testimony. Informal agency actions can lead to quick and practical problem resolution, but they can also lead to seemingly endless administrative paper shuffling.

> 66
>
> *Informal agency actions can lead to quick and practical problem resolution, but they can also lead to seemingly endless administrative paper shuffling.*

Conducting Investigations

Many administrative agencies have the responsibility to determine whether a regulated company or person is complying with the laws and regulations. They can use their subpoena power to make mandatory requests for information, conduct interviews, and perform searches. Based on these investigations, the agencies may file administrative suits seeking civil penalty assessments, or they may go to court and seek civil and criminal penalties.

Since 1970, governmental agencies have increasingly relied on their investigatory and prosecutorial powers. The indictment and conviction of the arbitrageur Ivan Boesky and numerous other financial figures for insider trading resulted from administrative investigations and the exercise of administrative prosecutorial powers. These cases are discussed in chapter 23.

The investigatory powers possessed by administrative agencies can lead to fines ranging from thousands of dollars to hundreds of millions of dollars. For example, the Securities and Exchange Commission (SEC) settled its three-year securities fraud investigation of junk-bond king Michael Milken in 1990 for $600 million. (This case is discussed further in the "Inside Story" in chapter 15.) It should be noted that administrative agencies, such as the Occupational Safety and Health Administration, sometimes fail to collect the whole fine.

■ Administrative Agencies and the Constitution

Constitutional issues raised by the creation of administrative agencies concern the separation of powers, the proper delegation of authority, and the limits imposed on agency actions by the Bill of Rights.

Separation of Powers

The Constitution of the United States provides for a legislature, an executive, and a judiciary. It does not specifically provide for administrative agencies, thus raising the question of whether the delegation of legislative and judicial powers to an administrative agency is constitutional.

The few cases addressing this issue have upheld the constitutionality of this "fourth branch" of government. In 1855, a court decision allowed the Department of the Treasury to audit accounts for money owed to the United States by customs collectors, and to issue a warrant for the money owed. The Supreme Court rejected the position that such activity was a judicial action that only the courts of the United States were empowered to carry out.[3]

---

3. *Den ex dem. Murray v. Hoboken Land & Improvement Co.*, 59 U.S. 272 (1856).

Historical Perspective
Deregulation of the Airline Industry

Practically since its birth, interstate commercial aviation in the United States was regulated by the Civil Aeronautics Board (CAB). The CAB, established in 1938, had authority to set fares for each route, and it controlled the allocation of routes to airlines. It was not possible for a carrier to serve an interstate market without CAB authorization. Because airlines were not free to enter a given market, there was no mechanism to ensure: (1) that the lowest-cost providers of airline service in a given market replaced less efficient producers; and (2) that prices were related to the costs of providing airline service in a particular market and to the demand for the service. Such a mechanism is a necessary condition for the efficient allocation or distribution of scarce resources among competitors. Through regulation of fares and allocation of routes, the CAB, rather than the market, was charged with ensuring that the airline industry operated efficiently.

The 1981 inauguration of President Reagan marked the beginning of an era of deregulation of industries, accompanied by the demise of many administrative agencies formerly charged with their regulation. The Reagan administration cited the inefficiency of regulated industries as a reason to let free market forces prevail. This inefficiency was partially caused by the "capture" of the agencies by the very industries they were supposedly controlling. Capture theorists argued that the concerns of the administrative agencies became so linked to those of the industries that the agencies became, in effect, mechanisms to enforce oligopolistic pricing and to prevent competitors from entering the regulated industry.

Deregulation of the airline industry, the beginnings of which predate the Reagan administration, has been widely touted as one of the free-market theorists' greatest successes. Critics of the CAB argued that its system of regulation did not work to ensure the efficient operation of the airline industry. First, they identified a pattern in which the CAB assigned more profitable routes to carriers in financial trouble—carriers that were probably less efficient. Second, they charged the CAB with blocking the entry of would-be carriers into the industry as a whole, and also with blocking the entry of already operating carriers into specific markets, through its system of route allocation. Third, they alleged that by prohibiting fare competition among airlines and by setting fares well above costs, the CAB was spurring nonprice competition among airlines. Nonprice competition included more comfortable seating, more convenient flight schedules, and more direct routing. Such competition drove up costs, which were then validated by the CAB's granting fare increases, creating an endless spiral of increasing costs and rising fares. A significant group of fare-conscious potential customers, who would prefer more basic service at a lower fare, was thus being denied access to air travel.

The critics bolstered their arguments by pointing to the intrastate air travel industries which had sprung up in several of the larger states. Purely intrastate flights were not subject to the CAB's authority. Thus, intrastate carriers were free to set fares at competitive levels and serve the routes they wished to serve. The prices charged by these intrastate carriers, notably Pacific Southwest Airlines in California and Southwest Airlines Company in Texas, were a fraction of those charged for interstate flights of comparable distance.

In response to such criticism, in 1978 deregulation of the airline industry was begun and the CAB was stripped of its authority to set fares and allocate routes among carriers. Almost immediately, a host of new carriers entered the airline industry, and existing carriers began to compete in routes to which they had previously been denied access. People Express Airlines, Inc., which began to fly in 1981, epitomized the new breed of carriers. The new entrants emphasized their low fares made possible by no-frills service, in stark contrast to the industry pattern of nonprice competition.

The immediate result of deregulation was drastically lower fares and great expansion of the airline industry. People who could not afford to fly before became enthusiastic customers of the new entrants. The established carriers, faced with dropping market shares, began cutting costs and switching to more efficient, bigger planes to enable them to slash fares as well. It seemed that deregulation was an unqualified success.

In recent years, however, several trends in the airline industry indicate that deregulation's benefits may have been short-lived. Most of the discount carriers disappeared in the wave of airline mergers in the mid-1980s, which left the airline industry more concentrated than before. For example, Texas Air Corp. acquired People

Historical Perspective
Deregulation of the Airline Industry–*continued*

Express Airlines in December 1986, making Texas Air the largest airline holding company in the U.S. as of that date. Decreased competition and the lack of further cost-cutting opportunities combined to stop the decline in inflation-adjusted fares. From 1986 to 1988, real fares declined only 1% to 3%. Since 1988, real fares have once again begun to climb upward.

An additional concern of critics of deregulation is the uneven distribution of benefits from reduced fares. In the wake of the airline merger wave, some cities were left with only a few major carriers. Sizable fare increases in these markets resulted from the lack of competition. According to a study published by the General Accounting Office in June 1989, 1988 fares were 27% higher in markets dominated by one or two major carriers than in other markets.

Also, fare cuts have benefited vacation travelers far more than business travelers. Business travelers generally use unrestricted coach fares. Some researchers estimate that these fares rose approximately 45% in the 1980s, after taking account of inflation. Deregulation has also resulted in the expansion of "hub and spoke" systems that bring passengers from different cities to a central airport and then transfer them to flights to their final destinations. The Economic Policy Institute, a nonprofit organization, maintains that travelers now fly 5% to 30% farther than before deregulation, when there were more direct flights. Thus, as passengers are flying more miles to get from place to place, it is possible that they are actually paying more for transportation, although the price per mile has declined.

Of course, the airline industry underwent many changes in addition to deregulation in the 1980s. Lower fuel prices and more efficient aircraft contributed to lower costs and lower fares. Also, capacity limits have been reached at several major airports. This external constraint on competition may be responsible for some of the fare increases in these markets in the past few years.

In general, commentators agree that real fares today are still lower than they were when the airline industry was regulated. According to a Department of Transportation study, real fares in 1988 were 20% lower than they were in 1978. Also, the average profit margins of the airline industry in 1988 and 1989 remained at 1.8 and 0.4%, respectively, which is below the average for most industries. However, recent trends toward higher fares indicate that these gains for the consumer may be eroded in the years ahead. The data also indicate that attention to preventing further market concentration and alleviating capacity constraints at certain airports might provide a means of securing the benefits of lower fares in the future.[a]

---

a. This discussion is based in part on and derived from A. Nomani, Sr., "One Sure Result of Airline Deregulation: Controversy About Its Impact on Fares," *The Wall Street Journal*, April 19, 1990, B1. Reprinted by permission of *The Wall Street Journal*, © 1990 Dow Jones & Company, Inc. All Rights Reserved Worldwide.

In 1935, in a case involving the Federal Trade Commission (FTC), the Supreme Court explained with approval that the FTC was an administrative body created by Congress to carry out legislative policies in accordance with a prescribed legislative standard and to act as a legislative or judicial aid by performing rule-making and adjudicatory functions. The Supreme Court said the FTC exercised power in the effectuation of "quasi-legislative" or "quasi-judicial" powers, or as an agency of the legislative or judicial departments of the government. It found no constitutional violation in allowing an administrative agency to perform judicial and legislative functions. It did not, however, provide much explanation as to why this was permissible.[4] Justice Jackson subsequently said:

> [Administrative bodies] have become a veritable fourth branch of the Government which has deranged our three-branch legal theories as much as the concept of a fourth

---

4. *Humphrey's Executor v. United States*, 295 U.S. 602, 55 S.Ct. 869 (1935).

dimension unsettles our three dimensional thinking. . . . Administrative agencies have been called quasi-legislative, quasi-executive and quasi-judicial, as the occasion required. . . . The mere retreat to the qualifying "quasi" . . . is a smooth cover which we draw over our confusion as we might use a counterpane to conceal a disordered bed.[5]

> 66
>
> *"[Administrative bodies] have become a veritable fourth branch of the Government which has deranged our three-branch legal theories as much as the concept of a fourth dimension unsettles our three dimensional thinking. . . ."*

5. *FTC v. Ruberoid Co.*, 343 U.S. 470, 487–88, 72 S.Ct. 800, 810 (1952).

A more recent separation-of-powers case arose from the Gramm-Rudman-Hollings Deficit Reduction Act. This case, together with the legislative veto case *INS v. Chadha*[6] (case 2.1), shows that the concept of separation of powers retains some viability.

6. *INS v. Chadha*, 462 U.S. 919, 103 S.Ct. 2764 (1983).

■ **A Case in Point:** **Summary**

Case 6.1
BOWSHER v. SYNAR
Supreme Court of the
United States
478 U.S. 714, 106 S.Ct. 3181
(1986).

FACTS In 1985, President Reagan signed into law a bill to reduce the budget deficit. This law is popularly known as the Gramm-Rudman-Hollings Act. The purpose of the act was to reduce the federal deficit by setting a maximum deficit amount for fiscal years 1986 to 1991, progressively reducing the budget deficit to zero by 1991.

If the federal budget deficit were not reduced as the act required, an automatic budget process took effect. The comptroller general would calculate, on a program-by-program basis, the amount of reductions needed to meet the target. He would then report that amount to the president, who was required to issue a sequestration order mandating these reductions. A *sequestration order* directs spending levels to be reduced below the levels authorized in the original budget. Unless Congress then acted to modify the budget to reduce the deficit to the required level, the sequestrations would go into effect.

The comptroller general, unlike the employees of the executive branch and agency officials, does not serve at the pleasure of the president. He can be removed from office only by Congress. This removal authority became the focus of litigation. Congressman Synar and others opposed to the act claimed that it violated the separation-of-powers clause in the United States Constitution, because the comptroller general was exercising executive powers but was not controlled by the executive branch.

ISSUE PRESENTED Does the comptroller general's exercise of executive functions under the deficit reduction process of the Gramm-Rudman-Hollings Act violate the Constitution's requirement of separation of powers?

SUMMARY OF OPINION The U.S. Supreme Court noted that the Constitution divided the powers of the federal government into three broad categories: legislative, executive, and judicial. The declared purpose of the separation was to diffuse power to preserve liberty. This fundamental principle of constitutional law reflects the principle that a system of checks and balances between these coordinate branches will promote liberty.

The Court reviewed the early history of the Constitution. It found that the Constitution did not contemplate an active role for Congress in the supervision of officials charged with the execution of laws.

The Court concluded by finding unconstitutional the comptroller general's role in the budget reduction process. The Court stated that because only Congress could remove the comptroller general, the act had the effect of giving Congress a direct role in the execution of the law. This violated the United States Constitution's requirement of separation of powers.

RESULT The Supreme Court agreed with Congressman Synar and held that the comptroller general's role under the "reporting provisions" of the deficit reduction process of the Gramm-Rudman-Hollings Act was unconstitutional because it is not within the Constitution for Congress to have a direct role in the execution of laws. The court allowed a period of not more than 60 days for Congress to implement fallback provisions.

COMMENTS The members of the cabinet, such as the secretary of commerce, the secretary of the treasury, and the secretary of state, are appointed by the president, as are many other heads of administrative agencies, such as the Federal Reserve Board and the Securities and Exchange Commission. One of the few clear constitutional limits that have evolved regarding administrative agencies is that the removal of such officials may not be controlled by the legislative branch.

Nonetheless, the separation-of-powers doctrine has not generally been an impediment to the exercise of authority by administrative agencies. The courts have held that the Constitution contemplates a practice that will integrate the separate powers of the three branches into a workable government. Administrative agencies are an essential part of such a government.

Delegation of Authority

The delegation of authority issue concerns the nature and degree of direction the legislature must give to administrative agencies. There are only two cases in which the Supreme Court has refused to uphold the delegation of power to administrative agencies. One case concerned delegation of power regarding shipments of oil between states in excess of government-set quotas.[7] The second case concerned the delegation of authority to the president to determine codes of fair competition for various trades and industries.[8] In both cases, the Supreme Court held that while Congress was free to allow agencies to make rules within prescribed limits, Congress itself must lay down the policies and establish the standards.

Both before and after these two cases, however, the Supreme Court upheld vague standards, such as those requiring rules to be set "in the public interest," "for the public convenience, interest or necessity," or "to prevent unfair methods of competition." As a practical matter, it is necessary to allow such broad delegations to administrative agencies. There is virtually no way Congress or

---

7. *Panama Refining Co. v. Ryan*, 293 U.S. 388, 55 S.Ct. 241 (1935).

8. *Schechter Poultry Corp. v. United States*, 295 U.S. 495, 55 S.Ct. 837 (1935).

the state legislative bodies can draft detailed legislation that anticipates all conceivable situations. The limitations imposed by these two Depression-era cases remain on the books, however, as a protection against overreaching legislative delegations that would place arbitrary and uncontrolled power in the hands of unelected officials.

Limits Imposed by the Bill of Rights

There is very little limit to the investigatory powers of administrative agencies. They must, of course, comply with constitutional principles protecting freedom from self-incrimination, and from unreasonable search and seizure. However, over the years, these principles have been severely eroded.

Self-Incrimination   The Fifth Amendment's protection against self-incrimination does not apply to records that the government requires to be kept. Specifically, the Fifth Amendment protections do not apply to records that are regulatory in nature, are of a kind that the party has customarily kept, and have at least some public aspect to them. In addition, the Fifth Amendment's protection against self-incrimination does not apply to corporations.

Probable Cause   Administrative agencies in carrying out their investigatory power are not required to have *probable cause*—that is, reason to suspect a violation—before beginning an investigation. The agencies may inquire into regulated behavior merely to satisfy themselves that the law is being upheld. For example, the Internal Revenue Service needs no specific cause to order an audit of a company's tax records.

Search and Seizure   In the administrative arena, the courts have largely obliterated the protection of the Fourth Amendment against unreasonable searches and seizures. Particularly for industries like liquor and firearms, which are highly regulated, the government can conduct full inspections of property and records almost without restriction.

Right to Jury Trial

A formal adjudication before an administrative agency resembles a court trial before a judge. This resemblance raises the question whether the administrative adjudication violates the constitutional right to a trial by jury. In two Supreme Court cases, one decided in 1927 and one in 1937, the Supreme Court decided there was no such constitutional right. One case upheld the system for collection of taxes without a jury trial[9]; the other upheld the right of the National Labor Relations Board to require reinstatement of discharged employees and payment of back wages based solely on an administrative hearing.[10] These cases held that the Seventh Amendment right to a jury trial extends only to cases for which a right to trial by jury existed in common law before the enactment of the Seventh Amendment. Because administrative agencies adjudicate statutory rights that were unknown at the time the Seventh Amendment was enacted, the Court held that the right to a jury trial did not apply.

■ Principles of Administrative Law

Choice of Approach

Because, theoretically, an administrative agency can exercise legislative-type functions through its rule-making authority and judicial-type functions through its adjudicatory authority, the question quickly arose of how administrative agencies were to choose between the two processes. There are competing considerations.

On one hand, it is simple and efficient to set forth a general rule that applies to unknown parties in future activities. On the other hand, until the agency has had experience with the subject matter and has dealt with a number of individual cases, it may lack sufficient information to proceed with rule making.

In 1947, the Supreme Court held that administrative agencies have a fundamental right to decide whether to proceed on a case-by-case basis or by rule.[11] Such a right is necessary because an administrative agency cannot anticipate every problem it might encounter; problems could arise that were so specialized and varying in nature as to be impossible to capture within the boundaries of a general rule.

Over the years, the agency's choice on how to proceed has frequently been limited by Congress. Typically, legislation requires the agency to enact a regulatory program and provides a deadline for the issuance of final regulations. This congressional direction shows the interaction between Congress, the judiciary, and the administrative

---

9. *Wickwire v. Reinecke*, 275 U.S 101, 48 S.Ct. 43 (1927).

10. *NLRB v. Jones & Laughlin Steel Corp.*, 301 U.S. 1, 57 S.Ct. 615 (1937).

11. *Securities and Exchange Commission v. Chenery Corp.*, 332 U.S. 194, 67 S.Ct. 1575 (1947).

agencies. Although the courts will not interfere with the authority of administrative agencies to act, Congress, which is the source of the agencies' authority, may fill the gap left when the agency fails to adopt final regulations.

Authority to Act

Administrative agencies can be compared to large corporations in size, structure, and, to some extent, function. Agencies provide benefits, sign contracts, and produce products. In the private arena, a person acting on behalf of an organization may bind the organization in accordance with the person's actual authority and also in accordance with the person's apparent authority (concepts discussed in chapter 5). Under the rules for government agencies, there is only actual authority.

The issue of apparent governmental authority is particularly important in the western states, where the United States owns up to 90% of the land. These lands are administered by the United States Forest Service and the Bureau of Land Management. Local citizens have a great deal of contact with these agencies. Not surprisingly, one of the first cases deciding the scope of a government official's authority was a case involving these public lands.

In 1917, the Supreme Court held that the United States was not bound by acts of its officials who, on behalf of the government, entered into an agreement that was not permitted by law.[12] The Court rejected the argument that the neglect of duty by officers of the government was a defense to the suit by the United States to enforce a public right to protect a public interest. The Court has repeatedly upheld this fundamental principle that government employees acting beyond their authority cannot bind the government. The basic purpose of this rule is to prevent personal actions from circumventing Congress and the formal process of law. The negative effect of the rule, however, is to take away incentive for the government to make sure that its officials know the law and administer it properly.

The uninitiated naturally rely on the word of a government employee who explains the scope of his authority. This is a mistake. In fact, it is incumbent upon anyone dealing with government agencies to make sure that the person she is dealing with is authorized to act and that the proposed actions are permitted by law.

---

12. *Utah Power Light Co. v. United States*, 243 U.S. 389, 37 S.Ct. 387 (1917).

> 66
>
> *The uninitiated naturally rely on the word of a government employee who explains the scope of his authority. This is a mistake.*

■ Judicial Review of Agency Actions

If the courts control agency action with too heavy a hand, an agency can grind to a halt. If too little oversight is exercised, agencies can run roughshod over individual rights.

Congress or the appropriate state legislature sets the standards for judicial review of agency actions. Some agency actions are not reviewable because they are committed at the discretion of the agency. Most agency actions are, however, reviewable by the courts, but the basic standard of review is highly deferential to the agency.

Review of Rule Making and Informal Discretionary Actions

The basic standard for judicial review of agency rule making and informal discretionary actions is that the court will uphold the agency's action unless it is arbitrary and capricious. Under the "arbitrary and capricious" standard, if the agency has a choice between several courses of action, the court will presume that the chosen course is valid. It will uphold the action unless the person challenging it shows that it lacks any rational basis.

For example, under some laws, agencies must determine the reasonableness of rates set by regulated industries such as the electrical power and the radio and television industries. Under general accounting principles, depreciation could be calculated on a straight-line basis, by dividing the total cost of the asset by the years it will be in use, or on an accelerated basis that results in more depreciation in the earlier years. In those kinds of cases the courts have deferred to the agency's choice of what method of accounting produced a reasonable cost, even when the company proposed an equally reasonable alternative. So long as the agency had a rational basis for its action, the courts defer to the agency's decision.

It is more difficult for an agency to persuade a court to uphold a rule when Congress has not expressly granted rule-making authority. In a case decided in early 1994, the U.S. Court of Appeals for the District of Columbia concluded that the Environmental Protection Agency

(EPA) had the power to adopt some rules but not others.[13] The statute at issue was the Comprehensive Environmental Response, Compensation and Liability Act (CERCLA). CERCLA, discussed further in chapter 16, generally imposes strict liability (liability without fault) on all past and present owners of sites with hazardous waste. However, CERCLA contains an exception for secured creditors, that is, persons who lend money secured by a security interest, mortgage, or deed of trust on the property. The EPA adopted a lender liability rule designed to "interpret" this provision of CERCLA. The court concluded that there was no evidence that Congress intended the EPA to have the power to define who is liable under CERCLA. The EPA can bring prosecutions, but so can private parties seeking reimbursement of cleanup costs from those "liable" under section 106(b)(2)

of CERCLA. Thus, it is up to the courts, not the EPA, to decide who is liable. The lender liability rule was not due judicial defense as an "interpretation" under *Chevron USA Inc. v. Natural Resources Defense Council Inc.*[14] (see case 6.3) because there was no evidence that Congress expressly or implicitly gave the EPA authority to reconcile in a reasonable manner statutory ambiguities or to fill statutory interstices.

An administrative agency cannot adopt rules that go beyond the grant of authority provided by Congress. The power of the Securities and Exchange Commission to adopt a rule relating to tender offers was at issue in the following case. In a *tender offer*, a company makes a public offer to buy securities at a price that is usually higher than the market price of the securities prior to the announcement of the tender offer.

---

13. *Kelley v. Environmental Protection Agency*, 15 F.3d 1100 (D.C.Cir. 1994).

14. 467 U.S. 837, 104 S.Ct. 2778 (1984).

■ A Case in Point: In the Language of the Court

Case 6.2
UNITED STATES OF AMERICA v. CHESTMAN
United States Court of Appeals for the Second Circuit
947 F.2d 551 (2d Cir. 1991), *cert. denied*, 112 S.Ct. 1759 (1992).

FACTS   In 1986, Ira Waldbaum, the controlling shareholder of the Waldbaum supermarket chain, agreed to sell Waldbaum to the Great Atlantic and Pacific Tea Company (A&P) for a tender price of $50 per share. Ira told his three children of the pending sale, as well as his sister, Shirley, instructing all of them to keep quiet about the news. Despite Ira's warning, Shirley told her daughter, Susan Loeb, who told her husband, Keith. Susan also told Keith not to tell anyone, because it might ruin the pending sale.

The next day, Keith Loeb called his stockbroker, Robert Chestman. When he was not able to reach Chestman, he left a message for Chestman to call him "ASAP." When he spoke with Chestman later that morning, he informed Chestman that he had some definite information that Waldbaum was about to be sold at a "substantially higher" price than its market value and asked Chestman for advice. Chestman responded that he could not advise Loeb what to do "in a situation like this."

That morning, Chestman executed several purchases of Waldbaum stock, for his own as well as his clients' discretionary accounts (including Loeb's). The shares ranged in price from $24.65 per share to $26.00 per share.

Loeb alleged that he spoke to Chestman again that afternoon. Chestman denied that he ever spoke with Loeb on the day of the trading, asserting that he purchased the stock based on his own research.

Waldbaum stock rose to $49 per share the next business day after the tender offer was announced. A grand jury returned an indictment on July

---

15. The other counts are discussed in chapter 23.

20, 1988, charging Chestman with, among other counts,[15] violation of rule 14e-3(a). Rule 14e-3(a), adopted by the Securities and Exchange Commission pursuant to section 14(e) of the Securities Exchange Act of 1934, makes it a crime to trade on nonpublic information about an upcoming tender offer if that information was obtained from the issuer, the offeror, or someone working on their behalf. Chestman was convicted by a jury of violating this rule. He appealed.

A panel of the Second Circuit reversed Chestman's conviction on all counts. A majority of the active judges of the Second Circuit voted to rehear in banc (with all judges sitting) the panel's decision with respect to several issues, including the Rule 14e-3(a) conviction.

ISSUE PRESENTED   Did the SEC have the authority to enact rule 14e-3(a), which made it a crime to trade on the basis of material nonpublic information concerning an upcoming tender offer that one knows or has reason to know has been acquired "directly or indirectly" from an insider of the offeror or issuer, or someone working on their behalf?

OPINION   MESKILL, J., writing on behalf of the U.S. Court of Appeals:

In this rehearing in banc, we consider for the first time the validity of Rule 14e-3(a) which was promulgated by the Securities and Exchange Commission (SEC) under section 14(e) of the 1934 Act. . . .

. . . .

A. Rule 14e-3(a)

. . . .

1. Validity of Rule 14e-3(a)

Chestman's first challenge concerns the validity of a rule prescribed by the SEC pursuant to a congressional delegation of rulemaking authority. The question presented is whether Rule 14e-3(a) represents a proper exercise of the SEC's statutory authority. . . .

. . . .

One violates Rule 14e-3(a) if he trades on the basis of material nonpublic information concerning a pending tender offer that he knows or has reason to know has been acquired "directly or indirectly" from an insider of the offeror or issuer, or someone working on their behalf. Rule 14e-3(a) is a disclosure provision. It creates a duty in those traders who fall within its ambit to abstain or disclose, without regard to whether the trader owes a pre-existing fiduciary duty to respect the confidentiality of the information. Chestman claims that the SEC exceeded its authority in drafting Rule 14e-3(a)—more specifically, in drafting a rule that dispenses with one of the common law elements of fraud, breach of a fiduciary duty.

In reviewing this claim, our scope of review is limited. "If Congress has explicitly left a gap for the agency to fill, there is an express delegation of authority to the agency to elucidate a specific provision of the statute by regulation. Such legislative regulations are given controlling weight unless they are arbitrary, capricious, or manifestly contrary to the statute."

*Case **6.2** continued on following page*

Case **6.2** *continued*

. . . Keeping these principles in mind, we consider whether Congress authorized the SEC to enact Rule 14e-3(a).

The plain language of section 14(e) represents a broad delegation of rulemaking authority. The statute explicitly directs the SEC to "define" fraudulent practices and to "prescribe means reasonably designed to prevent" such practices. It is difficult to see how the power to "define" fraud could mean anything less than the power to "set forth the meaning of" fraud in the tender offer context. This delegation of rulemaking responsibility becomes a hollow gesture if we cabin the SEC's rulemaking authority, as Chestman urges we should, by common law definitions of fraud. Under Chestman's construction of the statute, the separate grant of rulemaking power would be rendered superfluous because the SEC could never define as fraud anything not already prohibited by the self-operative provision. Such a narrow construction of the congressional grant of authority would cramp the SEC's ability to define fraud flexibility in the context of the discrete and highly sensitive area of tender offers. And such a delegation of "power," paradoxically, would allow the SEC to limit, but not extend, a trader's duty to disclose.

Even if we were to accept the argument that the SEC's definitional authority is circumscribed by common law fraud, which we do not, the SEC's power to "prescribe means reasonably designed to prevent" fraud extends the agency's rulemaking authority further. The language of this portion of section 14(e) is clear. The verb "prevent" has a plain meaning: "To keep from happening or existing especially by precautionary measures." A delegation of authority to enact rules "reasonably designed to prevent" fraud, then, necessarily encompasses the power to proscribe conduct outside the purview of fraud, be it common law or SEC-defined fraud. Because the operative words of the statute, "define" and "prevent," have clear connotations, the language of the statute is sufficiently clear to be dispositive here. We note, however, other factors that bolster our interpretation.

. . . .

. . . All told, the legislative history indicates that Congress intended to grant broad rulemaking power to the SEC under section 14(e). This delegation or authority was aimed at promoting full disclosure in the tender offer context and, in so doing, contributing to informed decisionmaking by shareholders.

In promulgating Rule 14e-3(a), the SEC acted well within the letter and spirit of section 14(e). Recognizing the highly sensitive nature of tender offer information, its susceptibility to misuse, and the often difficult task of ferreting out and proving fraud, Congress sensibly delegated to the SEC broad authority to delineate a penumbra around the fuzzy subject of tender offer fraud. To be certain, the SEC's rulemaking power under this broad grant of authority is not unlimited. The rule must still be "reasonably related to the purposes of the enabling legislation." The SEC, however, in adopting Rule 14e-3(a), acted consistently with the authority. While dispensing with the subtle problems of proof associated with demonstrating fiduciary breach in the problematic area of tender offer insider trading, the Rule retains a close nexus between the prohibited conduct and the statutory aims.

. . . .

In sum, the language and legislative history of section 14(e), as well as congressional inactivity toward it since the SEC promulgated Rule 14e-3(a), all support the view that Congress empowered the SEC to prescribe a rule that extends beyond the common law.

. . . .

RESULT   The court concluded that Rule 14e-3(a) did not exceed the SEC's authority. Chestman's Rule 14e-3(a) convictions were affirmed.

Questions
1. How much weight should a court give to the fact that Congress had not amended section 14(e) since rule 14e-3(a) was adopted?
2. Rule 10b-5 is an SEC antifraud rule that the U.S. Supreme Court has held requires a showing of *scienter*, that is, intent to defraud or breach of fiduciary duty (discussed further in chapter 23). Scienter is not required under rule 14e-3. Why should the SEC have greater authority to regulate fraud in connection with tender offers than it has in garden-variety cases of insider trading in violation of rule 10b-5?

Review of Factual Findings

The courts use a *substantial evidence standard* to review factual findings that the agencies make in formal adjudications. Under this standard, the courts defer to agency factual determinations even if the record would support other factual conclusions. By contrast, in court trials, courts make factual determinations based on the "preponderance of evidence" standard in civil cases or the "beyond a reasonable doubt" standard in criminal cases.

Review of Statutory Interpretations

The earliest cases held that courts would decide the law but would defer to an agency's *construction* (that is,

interpretation) of a statute within its area of expertise. This rule makes sense, because it allows those with the practical experience to have the greatest influence in deciding how to implement a particular law. Although the Supreme Court's position on this issue has varied somewhat, its most recent cases have reinforced the rule of deference to administrative interpretation of law. This is demonstrated in the following case.

■ **A Case in Point:**   **Summary**

Case 6.3
CHEVRON USA, INC. v. NATURAL RESOURCES DEFENSE COUNCIL INC.
Supreme Court of the United States
467 U.S. 837, 104 S.Ct. 2778 (1984).

FACTS   In 1977, Congress passed a law that required states that had not achieved national air quality standards to set up a permit program regulating new or modified air pollution sources. The law required the state program to be consistent with the rules of the Environmental Protection Agency (EPA) governing air pollution.

The EPA had two basic choices in adopting its rules. It could have (1) defined an air pollution source as a piece of equipment in a plant, or (2) applied what became known as the "bubble concept" and treated all pollution-emitting devices within the same industrial grouping as though they were encased within the same "bubble." The difference in the two interpretations

*Case **6.3** continued on following page*

*Case **6.3** continued*

had significant practical consequences. The bubble concept gave operators flexibility by allowing them to offset pollution increases elsewhere in the facility by halting use of a particular dirty piece of equipment. The environmentalists charged that the bubble rule was inconsistent with the Clean Air Act, because it allowed higher overall levels of pollution.

The EPA had tried for several years to adopt a rule incorporating the bubble concept. It had flip-flopped from one position to another. Its final rule was neither a contemporaneous interpretation of the law nor a particularly uniform interpretation. It was not a contemporaneous interpretation because it was not the EPA's initial interpretation of the law after it was passed. It was not a uniform interpretation because the EPA took one position in its original interpretation and another in its subsequent interpretation.

The Natural Resources Defense Council Inc. (a public interest group) challenged the EPA's final rule. The court of appeals vacated the regulations and certiorari was granted for review of the EPA's interpretation of the Clean Air Amendments.

ISSUE PRESENTED   In reviewing an agency's construction of a statute that it administers, if Congress has not directly spoken to the precise question at issue, should the court defer to the agency's construction?

SUMMARY OF OPINION   First, the U.S. Supreme Court found that Congress had not clearly addressed the issue either in the text of the law or in the legislative history. Second, the Court said that in the absence of such guidance from Congress, the proper course for the Court was to defer to the agency's resolution of the issue left undecided by Congress.

The Court explained that of the three branches of government, the federal judiciary is the least accountable to the voters. The members of Congress and the leader of the executive branch are subject to periodic elections. Federal judges are appointed by the president and must be confirmed by the Senate, but once appointed, they serve for life. In the Supreme Court's opinion, it was, therefore, inappropriate for the judiciary to substitute their policy choices for those of the agency officials. In such situations, federal judges have a duty to respect the policy choices of those who are accountable to the voters. As a result, the Supreme Court upheld the agency's interpretation of the law.

RESULT   The Supreme Court reversed the judgment of the court of appeals and upheld the EPA's final rule. The bubble concept was a permissible interpretation of the Clean Air Amendments.

Review of Procedures   For a number of years, the courts have endeavored to bring greater fairness to the administrative process. Some courts began to require agencies to follow procedures not specified by statutes or required by the Due Process Clause of the Fifth Amendment of the Constitution. This occurred most frequently in the rule-making area, where rule-making proceedings were often challenged as being fundamentally unfair and in need of greater public participation. These challenges were most often made by public-interest groups battling large corporations with entrenched positions of influence with the agency.

In 1978, in a case involving a challenge by an environmental advocacy group to the licensing of a nuclear power plant, the Supreme Court held that the courts may not impose additional procedural requirements on agencies.[16] Absent extremely compelling circumstances,

---

16. *Vermont Yankee Nuclear Power Corp. v. NRDC*, 435 U.S. 519, 98 S.Ct. 1197 (1978).

administrative agencies are free to fashion their own rules of procedure and to pursue their own methods of inquiry to discharge their broad and varied duties. A court is not free to impose on an agency its view as to what procedures the agency must follow; the court may only require the agency to comply with its own procedural rules and to conform to the requirements of the Due Process Clause of the Fifth Amendment.

The reason for these highly deferential review standards is evident: The role of administrative agencies is to relieve the burden on the courts by having the agencies make their own adjudications. If the courts were to engage in searching inquiry on all factual questions and exercise their own judgment on policy or procedural issues, the function of administrative agencies would be greatly diminished.

The scope of judicial review of a decision not to take an enforcement action is explored in the following case.

■ A Case in Point: Summary

Case 6.4
HECKLER v. CHANEY
Supreme Court of the
United States
470 U.S. 821, 105 S.Ct. 1649
(1985).

FACTS   Prison inmates were convicted of capital offenses and sentenced to death by lethal injection of drugs under the state laws of Oklahoma and Texas. The inmates claimed that the drugs used were approved by the FDA for the medical purposes stated on their labels, but were not approved for use in human executions. Furthermore, the drugs had not been tested for the purpose of execution, and given that the drugs would likely be administered by untrained personnel, it was likely that the drugs would not induce the quick and painless death intended. The inmates argued that the use of these drugs for human execution was an "unapproved use of an approved drug."

The inmates petitioned the Food and Drug Administration (FDA), alleging that use of the drugs for such a purpose violated the Federal Food, Drug and Cosmetic Act (FDCA). Specifically, they requested the FDA to take various investigatory and enforcement actions to prevent these perceived violations. They asked the FDA to affix warnings to the labels stating that they were unapproved and unsafe for human execution, to send statements to the drug manufacturers and prison administrators stating that the drugs should not be so used, and to adopt procedures for seizing the drugs from state prisons and to recommend the prosecution of those involved in the chain of distribution who knowingly distributed or purchased the drugs with the intent to use them for human execution. The FDA refused the request.

The federal district court for the District of Columbia denied the inmates relief and the inmates appealed. The U.S. Court of Appeals for the District of Columbia reversed and held that the FDA's refusal to take enforcement actions was both an abuse of discretion and reviewable; the court remanded the case with directions that the agency be required to "fulfill its statutory function."

ISSUE PRESENTED   Is the decision of the Food and Drug Administration not to take enforcement actions under the Federal Food, Drug and Cosmetic Act with respect to drugs used to carry out the death penalty subject to judicial review?

SUMMARY OF OPINION   The U.S. Supreme Court focused on the extent to which determinations by the FDA not to exercise its enforcement authority over the use of drugs in interstate commerce may be judicially reviewed.

The Court reviewed the Administrative Procedures Act's comprehensive provisions for judicial review of agency actions. The Court recognized that there are many factors that make judicial review of agency decisions to

Case **6.4** continued on following page

*Case **6.4** continued*

enforce something unsuitable. An agency decision not to enforce often involves a complicated balancing of a number of factors that are peculiarly within its expertise. The agency must not only assess whether a violation has occurred, but whether agency resources are best spent on this violation or another; whether the agency is likely to succeed if it acts; whether the particular enforcement action requested best fits the agency's overall policies; and whether the agency has enough resources to undertake the action at all. An agency generally cannot act against each technical violation of the statute it is charged with enforcing. As well, the agency is far better equipped than the courts to deal with the many variables involved in the proper ordering of its priorities. In conclusion, the Court found that an agency's decision not to take enforcement action should be presumed immune from judicial review.

The Court concluded by noting that the fact that the drugs involved in this case are ultimately to be used in imposing the death penalty "must not lead this Court or other courts to import profound differences of opinion over the meaning of the Eighth Amendment to the United States Constitution into the domain of administrative law."

RESULT   The Supreme Court reversed the lower court's ruling and held that there is a presumption of unreviewability of decisions of an agency not to undertake enforcement action. The inmates could not force the FDA to act.

The Supreme Court has also significantly restricted *standing* to sue to obtain judicial review of federal agency action. In the following case, the court held that members of an environmental organization could not challenge a federal action arguably violating the Endangered Species Act unless they could show a certain personal connection with the species.

■ **A Case in Point:**   **In the Language of the Court**

Case 6.5
LUJAN v. DEFENDERS OF WILDLIFE
Supreme Court of the
United States
112 S.Ct. 2130 (1992).

FACTS   Section 7 of the Endangered Species Act of 1973 (ESA) was intended to protect species of animals against threats to their continuing existence caused by humans. The ESA instructs the secretary of the interior to promulgate by regulation a list of those species which are either endangered or threatened under enumerated criteria, and to define the critical habitat of these species. Section 7(a)(2) of the act then provides, in pertinent part:

> Each Federal agency shall, in consultation with and with the assistance of the Secretary [of the Interior], insure that any action authorized, funded, or carried out by such agency . . . is not likely to jeopardize the continued existence of any endangered species or threatened species or result in the destruction or adverse modification of habitat of such species which is determined by the Secretary, after consultation as appropriate with affected States, to be critical.

In 1978, the Fish and Wildlife Service (FWS) and the National Marine Fisheries Service (NMFS), on behalf of the secretary of the interior and the secretary of commerce respectively, promulgated a joint regulation stating that the obligations imposed by section 7(a)(2) extend to actions taken in foreign nations. The next year, however, the Interior Department began to reexamine its position. A revised joint regulation was proposed in 1983 and reinterpreted the section to require consultation only for actions taken in the United States or on the high seas.

Shortly thereafter, organizations dedicated to wildlife conservation and other environmental causes filed this action against Manuel Lujan, the secretary of the interior. Plaintiffs sought a declaratory judgment that the new regulation, which required other agencies to confer with the Secretary of the Interior under section 7 of the Endangered Species Act (ESA) only with respect to federally funded projects within the United States and on the high seas, was in error, and an injunction requiring the Secretary to promulgate a new regulation restoring the initial interpretation of the geographic scope.

The federal district court dismissed the case for lack of standing and the Court of Appeals reversed.

OPINION   SCALIA, J., writing for the U.S. Supreme Court:
. . . The preliminary issue, and the only one we reach, is whether the respondents here, plaintiffs below, have standing to seek judicial review of the rule.

. . . .

Over the years, our cases have established that the irreducible constitutional minimum of standing contains three elements: First, the plaintiff must have suffered an "injury in fact"—an invasion of a legally-protected interest which is (a) concrete and particularized, and (b) "actual or imminent, not 'conjectural' or 'hypothetical,' " Second, there must be a causal connection between the injury and the conduct complained of—the injury has to be "fairly . . . trace[able] to the challenged action of the defendant, and not . . . th[e] result [of] the independent action of some third party not before the court." Third, it must be "likely," as opposed to merely "speculative," that the injury will be "redressed by a favorable decision."

The party invoking federal jurisdiction bears the burden of establishing these elements. . . .

. . . .

[W]hen the plaintiff is not himself the object of the government action or inaction he challenges, standing is not precluded, but it is ordinarily "substantially more difficult" to establish.

We think the Court of Appeals failed to apply the foregoing principles in denying the Secretary's motion for summary judgment. Respondents had not made the requisite demonstration of (at least) injury and redressability.

. . . .

. . . "But the 'injury in fact' test requires more than an injury to a cognizable interest. It requires that the party seeking review be himself among the injured." . . .

With respect to this aspect of the case, the Court of Appeals focused on the affidavits of two Defenders' members—Joyce Kelly and Amy Skilbred. Ms. Kelly stated that she traveled to Egypt in 1986 and "observed the traditional habitat of the endangered Nile crocodile there and intend[s] to do so

*Case **6.5** continued on following page*

*Case **6.5** continued*

again, and hope[s] to observe the crocodile directly," and that she "will suffer harm in fact as a result of [the] American . . . role . . . in overseeing the rehabilitation of the Aswan High Dam on the Nile . . . and [in] develop[ing] . . . Egypt's . . . Master Water Plan." Ms. Skilbred averred that she traveled to Sri Lanka in 1981 and "observed th[e] habitat" of "endangered species such as the Asian elephant and the leopard" at what is now the site of the Mahaweli Project funded by the Agency for International Development (AID), although she "was unable to see any of the endangered species;" "this development project," she continued, "will seriously reduce endangered, threatened, and endemic species habitat including areas that I visited . . . [, which] may severely shorten the future of these species;" that threat, she concluded, harmed her because she "intend[s] to return to Sri Lanka in the future and hope[s] to be more fortunate in spotting at least the endangered elephant and leopard." When Ms. Skilbred was asked at a subsequent deposition if and when she had any plans to return to Sri Lanka, she reiterated that "I intend to go back to Sri Lanka," but confessed that she had no current plans: "I don't know [when]. There is a civil war going on right now. I don't know. Not next year, I will say. In the future."

We shall assume for the sake of argument that these affidavits contain facts showing that certain agency-funded projects threaten listed species—though that is questionable. They plainly contain no facts, however, showing how damage to the species will produce "imminent" injury to Mss. Kelly and Skilbred. That the women "had visited" the areas of the projects before the projects commenced proves nothing. As we have said in a related context, " '[p]ast exposure to illegal conduct does not in itself show a present case or controversy regarding injunctive relief . . . if unaccompanied by any continuing, present adverse effects.' " And the [women's] profession of an "inten[t]" to return to the places they had visited before—where they will presumably, this time, be deprived of the opportunity to observe animals of the endangered species—is simply not enough. Such "some day" intentions—without any description of concrete plans, or indeed even any specification of when the some day will be—do not support a finding of the "actual or imminent" injury that our cases require.

. . . .

. . . To say that the Act protects ecosystems is not to say that the Act creates (if it were possible) rights of action in persons who have not been injured in fact, that is, persons who use portions of an ecosystem not perceptibly affected by the unlawful action in question.

Respondents' other theories are called, alas, the "animal nexus" approach, whereby anyone who has an interest in studying or seeing the endangered animals anywhere on the globe has standing; and the "vocational nexus" approach, under which anyone with a professional interest in such animals can sue. Under these theories, anyone who goes to see Asian elephants in the Bronx Zoo, and anyone who is a keeper of Asian elephants in the Bronx Zoo, has standing to sue because the Director of AID did not consult with the Secretary regarding the AID-funded project in Sri Lanka. This is beyond all reason. Standing is not "an ingenious academic exercise in the conceivable." . . .

. . . .

RESULT The Supreme Court reversed the appeals court's ruling and held that the plaintiffs did not assert sufficiently imminent injury to have standing. Their claimed injury was not redressable.

COMMENT This case along with others is believed to have had a hampering effect on environmental organizations' access to court.

■ Limits of Review

No Right to Probe the Mental Processes of the Agency

One of the most critical points of administrative law concerns the extent to which a court can inquire into the process by which an administrative agency makes its decision. This issue was one of the first decided in the administrative law arena. It was resolved in a case making headline news at the end of the New Deal era involving a decision of the secretary of agriculture.[17] The Packers and Stockyards Act authorized the secretary of agriculture to determine reasonable rates for services rendered by cattle marketing agencies, and the marketing agencies of the Kansas Stockyards wanted to challenge the ultimate price set as being too low. The federal district court had allowed the marketing agents to require the secretary to appear in person at the trial. He was questioned at length regarding the process by which he reached his decision about the rates. The interrogation included questions as to what documents had been studied and the nature of consultations with his subordinates. The Supreme Court held that it was improper to permit this questioning relating to the mental processes of the Secretary.

Today, formal federal review procedures limit judicial review of agency actions to the record compiled before the agency. Thus, once an administrative process is complete, there is generally no judicial opportunity to inquire into the whys and wherefores of the decision-making process. Without this shield from judicial review, agency actions would be tied up in court and would lose their efficacy.

Nevertheless, the system of checks and balances is maintained in this area. Although a court may not inquire into the decision-making process, the legislature may. Congress regularly holds oversight hearings on how agencies are administering the law. Criticism from a key member of Congress or a congressional committee can lead to newspaper headlines and changed agency policies. Congress can also use the appropriation process to withhold funds from disfavored programs and to fund favored ones.

Timing of Review

Two judicial doctrines are intended to prevent premature transfer of cases from the administrative arena to the courts: the doctrines of exhaustion of administrative remedies and of ripeness.

Exhaustion *Exhaustion of administrative remedies* concerns the timing and substance of the administrative review process. The general rule is that a court will not entertain an appeal to review the administrative process until the agency has had the chance to act and all possible avenues of relief before the agency have been fully pursued. The purpose is to conserve judicial resources. However, a party is not required to exhaust all administrative avenues where that would be futile.

The exhaustion doctrine can also be understood to require a party to present his arguments to the administrative agency and to give the agency the chance to rule on them in the first instance. In reviewing an administrative agency's action, the courts will not rule on issues that the party failed to present to the agency.

Ripeness The *ripeness* doctrine helps ensure that courts are not forced to decide hypothetical questions. Courts will not hear cases until they are "ripe" for deci-

---

17. *United States v. Morgan*, 313 U.S. 409, 61 S.Ct. 999 (1941).

sion. The issue of ripeness most frequently arises in preenforcement review of statutes and ordinances, that is, where review is sought after a rule is adopted but before the agency seeks to apply the rule in a particular case. The general rule is that agency action is ripe for judicial review where the impact of the action is sufficiently direct and immediate as to make review appropriate.[18]

■ Decision-Making Power of Agencies

There are a number of doctrines that limit administrative agencies' decision-making powers.

Only Delegated Powers

The general rule is that an administrative agency may only do what Congress or the state legislature has authorized it to do. Agency action contrary to or in excess of its delegated authority is void.

The Iran-Contra controversy, to some extent, involved the question of whether Oliver North, a government official, exceeded the authority delegated to the National Security Agency (NSA) or contravened a congressional enactment. Congress had placed limits on the ability of specified government agencies to raise funds to supply the efforts of rebels seeking to overthrow the government of Nicaragua. For many years, the NSA and the Central Intelligence Agency—two administrative agencies in the national security area—had been authorized to aid the rebels. When Congress withdrew this authority, Oliver North's alleged transgression was to continue providing such aid without proper authority. The drama of the Oliver North case is repeated daily on a smaller scale as administrative agencies seek to determine the scope of their authority to act.

> ❝
> *The drama of the Oliver North case is repeated daily on a smaller scale as administrative agencies seek to determine the scope of their authority to act.*

---

18. *Abbott Laboratories v. Gardner*, 387 U.S. 136, 87 S.Ct. 1507 (1967) (preenforcement review of FDA generic drug labeling rule was appropriate because the issue was purely legal, the regulations represented final agency action, and the impact of the rules was direct and immediate).

Obligation to Follow Own Rules

Not only are agencies required to act within the authority delegated to them, they are also required to follow their own rules and regulations. When an administrative agency adopts a regulation, it becomes binding on the public. It also binds the agency. For example, in *Service v. Dulles,*[19] the Supreme Court held that a State Department employee could not be discharged without being provided reasons, contrary to the agency's regulations regarding discharges under the State Department's Loyalty Security Program.

At the federal level, one of the most prominent procedural obligations is the requirement to prepare an environmental impact statement before approving major federal actions. The National Environmental Policy Act (NEPA), passed in 1969, dramatically changed how all federal agencies conduct their business.

Before 1969, an agency could focus exclusively on its *substantive legal obligations* (the legal rules that define the rights and duties of the agency and of persons dealing with it) and on its own duly adopted *procedural obligations* (the rules that define the manner in which these rights and duties are enforced). With NEPA's passage, each federal agency assumed a new procedural obligation to consider the environmental impacts of its proposed actions and the alternatives to those impacts. Each of the hundreds of thousands of federal actions must comply with NEPA. As a result, each agency attempts to document its compliance as a routine part of its procedures. The agencies have not found it easy to meet these procedural requirements. There are hundreds of cases invalidating agency action as a result of the failure to meet this obligation.

Explanation of Decisions

As discussed earlier, courts will not inquire into the mental processes of the decision maker. The corollary to this principle is that the agencies must explain the basis for their decisions and must show that they have taken into account all relevant considerations as required by the statute. If an agency makes a decision and fails to provide an adequate explanation of why it acted, the courts will invalidate the agency's action. In some instances, however, the court may permit the agency to explain deficiencies in the record and add supplementary explanations of why it acted.

As the next case shows, agencies can fail to take the simple action required, even in the most critical cases.

---

19. 354 U.S. 363, 77 S.Ct. 1152 (1957).

| ■ A Case in Point: | Summary |

Case 6.6
**MOTOR VEHICLE MANUFAC-
TURERS ASSOCIATION v.
STATE FARM MUTUAL
AUTOMOBILE INSURANCE
COMPANY**
Supreme Court of the
United States
463 U.S. 29, 103 S.Ct. 2856
(1983).

FACTS   Since 1929, motor vehicles have been the leading cause of accidental deaths and injuries in the United States. The National Highway Traffic
Safety Administration (NHTSA) was created within the Department of
Transportation to reduce traffic accidents and deaths and injuries resulting
from traffic accidents. NHTSA was authorized to set motor vehicle safety
standards.

In 1967, NHTSA began to require the installation of seatbelts in autos.
When it became apparent that seatbelts were often not used, NHTSA
began to consider passive restraint systems such as air bags and automatic seat belts. Against considerable pressure by automobile makers, the
agency decided to adopt a rule requiring passive restraints.

In 1978, NHTSA finally adopted such a rule, initially for large cars in the
model year 1982. The auto makers geared up to meet the standard. But
after the 1980 election of President Reagan, the new Secretary of
Transportation rescinded the rule on the ground that there were no benefits
to the rule.

ISSUE PRESENTED   Is an agency's decision to rescind a rule proper if
the agency fails to consider all relevant statutory criteria and fails to explain
why it made its decision?

SUMMARY OF OPINION   The U.S. Supreme Court acknowledged its policy of deferring to agency actions and restated that it will uphold even a
decision of less than ideal clarity if the agency's path may reasonably be
discerned. The Court, however, found that the agency's decision making
was flawed on procedural grounds.

The Court invalidated the agency's action in rescinding the rule. The
agency failed to present an adequate explanation for the rescission, and
the record did not show that the rescission was the product of "reasoned
decision making." The Court found that the agency had failed to consider all
the relevant factors.

The Supreme Court thus invalidated the agency's action because it had
failed to conduct procedurally proper rule making, not because it had
reached the wrong conclusion.

RESULT   The Supreme Court held that the agency had improperly
rescinded the rule and remanded the case to the lower court with the direction to remand the matter to the NHTSA for further consideration consistent
with the opinion.

COMMENTS   The judiciary's insistence that an agency make a reasoned
decision, supported by an explanation of why it acted, is a major restraint
on improper agency action.

■ Finding an Agency's Rules

The most important publication in dealing with federal agencies is the *Federal Register,* published daily by the Government Printing Office. Agencies are required by law to use the *Federal Register* to provide notice to the public of proposed and final rules. Rules that are not properly published in the *Federal Register* are void.

Once a rule is finally adopted by an agency, it is codified in the *Code of Federal Regulations (CFR).* The *CFR* contains more than 50 titles and includes the regulations of approximately 400 federal agencies and bureaus.

In addition to these officially published documents, federal agencies maintain internal guidance documents. For example, the United States Forest Service controls millions of acres of timber lands. Its formal rules are sparse, but it publishes a manual and a handbook, which contain thousands of pages of guidance on such topics as how to conduct timber sales. The Forest Service's manual and handbook are not generally available and may be difficult to find, but they are an important source of law, agency practice, and policy. Reports of court cases provide equivalent information. Cases decided by agency adjudication are usually not reported.

■ Obtaining Documents From an Agency

In court proceedings and in formal agency adjudications, documents may be obtained by discovery. In other situations, individuals are entitled to obtain copies of government records pursuant to federal and state statutes. The federal statute authorizing this procedure is the Freedom of Information Act (FOIA).[20] Under the FOIA any citizen may request records of the government on any subject that is of interest. Unlike discovery, an FOIA request need not show the relevance of the documents to any particular legal proceeding, or that the requester has any specific interest in the documents. It is sufficient that the requester seeks the documents.

In theory, the Freedom of Information Act provides an easy way to obtain documents from a government agency. The agency is required to respond to a document request within ten days. In practice, months, weeks, or even years may pass before the government responds to an FOIA request. Moreover, requesters are required to

20. 5 U.S.C. § 552 (1988).

pay the cost of locating and copying the records. However, these costs are waived for public interest groups, newspaper reporters, and certain other requesters.

> 66
>
> *In theory, the Freedom of Information Act provides an easy way to obtain documents from a government agency. In practice, months, weeks, or even years may pass before the government responds to an FOIA request.*

Not all documents in the government's possession are available for public inspection. FOIA exempts:

1. Records required by an executive order to be kept secret in the interest of national defense or foreign policy

2. Records related solely to the internal personnel rules and practice of an agency

3. Records exempted from disclosure by another statute

4. Trade secrets or confidential commercial and financial information

5. Interagency memorandums or decisions that reflect the deliberative process

6. Personnel files and other files the disclosure of which would constitute a clearly unwarranted invasion of personal privacy

7. Information compiled for law enforcement purposes

8. Reports prepared on behalf of an agency responsible for the regulation of financial institutions

9. Geological information concerning wells

The government is not required to withhold information under any of these exemptions. It may do so or not in its discretion.

Frequently, regulated companies are required to submit confidential information to the government. From the perspective of a company submitting such information, the Freedom of Information Act presents a danger of disclosure to competitors. To protect information from disclosure, it should be marked as privileged and confidential, so that government officials reviewing FOIA requests will not inadvertently disclose it.

From the perspective of those doing business with the government, the Freedom of Information Act provides an excellent opportunity to learn who is communicating with the agency and what the agency is thinking about a particular matter. The FOIA can also be useful in obtaining government studies and learning generally about government activities.

Each federal agency has its own set of regulations relating to FOIA requests. These regulations must be complied with strictly or the consideration of the request can be greatly delayed.

In Brief: Seven Basic Steps in Working with an Administrative Agency

STEP 1

Investigate applicable standards which will govern agency's actions

STEP 2

Identify and evaluate agency's formal structure

STEP 3

Determine what facts are before the agency

STEP 4

Identify the interests of others who may be involved in decision-making process

STEP 5

Adopt a strategy to achieve the desired goal

STEP 6

Eliminate adverse impact on other interested parties

STEP 7

Get involved in the administrative process early

The Responsible Manager

Working with Administrative Agencies

Administrative agencies are intended to be practical problem-solving entities. It is therefore easier for a non-lawyer to work with an administrative agency than to represent herself in court. Most simple administrative matters do not require an attorney, but one may be necessary to handle more complicated matters.

There are seven basic steps in working with an administrative agency as shown in the "In Brief" in this chapter.

As specified in step 1, a manager working with an agency should investigate the basic legal standards that will govern the agency's actions in the matter at hand. These include the agency's laws, its regulations, and its internal manuals and procedures. It is also important to investigate how the agency's administration of its laws and regulations is affected by its past history and by current political influences. Agencies, like any other bureaucracy, tend to have biases in how they carry out their laws and regulations.

These investigations are important for three reasons. First, a manager needs to know what facts must be presented in order to prevail in a claim. Second, it is possible that the agency personnel may not know the applicable legal standard. Many administrative agencies have little access to legal advice and find it helpful to have a clear presentation of the law under which a person is proceeding. Third, it is important to know the law at the outset of an administrative proceeding, because under the doctrine of exhaustion of administrative remedies, issues not raised before the agency are deemed to be waived if the matter is later brought before a court.

The second step is to identify and evaluate the agency's formal structure, to understand how the agency operates. Administrative agencies can have complicated structures. Because the power to make decisions may be vested in more than one official, it is important to know all of the decision maker's options before proceeding. A person can start at the top, the middle, or the bottom. The important point is to start at the right place. Finding out where that is takes some effort.

A manager needs to determine what facts the agency already has (step 3). In a judicial proceeding, the parties create the record by filing documents with the court. All parties have access to those documents and share the same factual record. The same is not true in an administrative agency proceeding. The factual record may be scattered about the agency in different files and offices. In order to function effectively before the agency, a manager must identify and locate this record.

Step 4 recommends that a manager identify the interests of other agencies or parties who may be involved in the decision-making process. In a court proceeding, all of the parties to a case are known; in an administrative matter, the parties may not be formally designated. It helps to identify at the outset the people concerned, and to determine how the proposed action will affect those people.

Upon completing this background information, the manager should move on to step 5 and adopt a strategy to achieve the desired goal. Investigation of an administrative matter could show that the agency lacks the authority to do what is proposed. In that case, the manager must persuade the agency to adopt new rules, or to go to the legislature to have new laws adopted. The most significant task, however, is to decide whether additional factual information should be gathered and presented to the agency. The record before the agency will normally be the record in court. The use of experts during the administrative process and the submission of key documents are important.

In reviewing a proposed action, a manager may find that it will have undesirable impacts on other interested parties (step 6). Elimination of those impacts is an effective way to avoid costly disputes.

Finally, as indicated in step 7, a manager needs to participate in the administrative process at the earliest possible time and to continue participating throughout the proceedings. Once set in motion, agencies tend to stay in motion unless they are deflected by an outside force. The greater the momentum that has gathered, the harder it is to move the agency off the path it is pursuing. It is therefore important to participate early in the process, and to try to influence the agency before it makes up its mind rather than after.

Inside Story

Environmentalism Meets Politics in Rio

In June 1992 national leaders from more than 150 countries came together at the United Nations Earth Summit in Rio de Janeiro, Brazil, to discuss serious global challenges confronting the planet's environment. The centerpiece of this unprecedented gathering of world leaders was the biodiversity treaty, which provides for the protection of endangered species and their surroundings. The United States refused to sign the treaty. While many environmentalists focused on the United States's refusal to sign the treaty, astute commentators in Washington realized that the Earth Summit in Brazil was also a political battleground for different camps in the Bush administration.

At the summit, William K. Reilly—then head of the Environmental Protection Agency (EPA) and consummate Republican administration outsider—underwent a test of political agility and failed bitterly. As leader of the U.S. delegation in Rio, Reilly was placed in the unenviable position of representing the pro-business ideology of the Bush administration—an ideology he had frequently opposed in his job as chief of the EPA. But as the environmental ambassador to Earth Summit, Reilly was once again cast as the outsider—this time, however, not of his own choosing. Unknown White House officials intercepted and leaked a confidential memorandum that Reilly sent to George Bush during the summit, thereby publicizing Reilly's secret efforts to reach a compromise on the biodiversity treaty.

In addition to infuriating Reilly and foreclosing any possibility of the U.S. signing the treaty, the leak highlighted the deep divisions within the Bush administration over environmental policy. On one side of the debate stood Reilly, the former president of the World Wildlife Federation and the first professional conservationist to head the EPA. In a Republican administration that was ideologically suspicious of business regulation, Reilly was accustomed to swimming against the tide. Nonetheless, Reilly fought single-handedly for environmental causes, often publicizing reports to focus attention and even requesting Republican politicians and foreign leaders to lobby President Bush. Reilly's perseverance in spite of his political isolation allowed him to hold the president to his campaign promises—strengthening clean air laws and accelerating the phaseout of ozone-depleting chemicals. But each success was hard-won and sharpened his rivalry with conservative White House aides, who considered him self-serving and too liberal.

Although Reilly publicly supported the biodiversity treaty's adoption by the United States and considered the treaty's goals consistent with his agency's purpose and mandate, the EPA chief was well aware of the issue's complexity as well as his difficulties in leading the U.S. delegation. In the midst of the 1992 election campaign, the White House was swept up in an antiregulatory crusade that was inspired by fears of political fallout from the recession and by the early primary success of GOP challenger Patrick Buchanan. Consistent with his isolationist philosophy, Buchanan demanded that President Bush boycott the Earth Summit entirely.

In Rio, Reilly clearly saw his mission as damage control. One month prior to the summit, the United States opposed scheduled limits on "greenhouse" gases—the only industrialized nation to do so. President Bush delayed his travel plans to attend the Summit meeting until U.S. negotiators were able to water down the treaty on global warming controls. President Bush then decided not to sign the biodiversity treaty one weekend prior to the Earth Summit's opening. Even though Washington was isolated before the summit's opening ceremony, Reilly was nevertheless determined to go. Dapper, well-traveled, and fluent in four languages, the Yale-educated lawyer was a man at home in the world of diplomacy. Reilly was widely considered a rare celebrity among government officials, having been invited to dine with both the King of Sweden and Bianca Jagger on his trip.

However, the EPA chief did have serious objectives to accomplish at the summit. Secretly meeting with his Brazilian hosts the day of his arrival, Reilly sought to hammer out differences with other countries in order to allow President Bush to sign the treaty before its unveiling at the end of the Earth Summit. These overtures were a diplomatic gamble for both Brazil and Reilly.

Inside Story continued on following page

Inside Story, continued

Reilly had previously denied to reporters that the United States was interested in reopening negotiations on the treaty. From Brazil's perspective, it wanted to make the summit as successful as possible, but not at the expense of appearing to be a pawn of the United States. Reilly discreetly offered the Brazilians a list of changes he considered necessary for U.S. acceptance of the treaty. He then sent a classified diplomatic cable to the White House reporting the role of the Brazilians and requesting clearance for the proposed revisions.

In an unplanned turn of events, Reilly's memorandum was leaked to *The New York Times*, creating a furor in the U.S. and Brazilian delegations and becoming a major topic of discussion on the third day of the Earth Summit. The leak foreclosed any possibility that the United States would sign a modified version of the biodiversity treaty and avoid isolation at the summit. Although it was never discovered who leaked the classified information, many insiders viewed the episode as Reilly's latest skirmish with Vice President Dan Quayle's Council on Competitiveness. Reilly was often in conflict with the Council, a group established to undo onerous business regulation and which often sought to temper environmental policies advocated by the EPA director. The council's top officials were well known within the administration for their outspoken opposition to the biodiversity treaty. Council Director David McIntosh and John Cohrssen, staff member and biotechnology expert, authored a memo outlining their objections one month prior to the treaty's final negotiations in Nairobi. That memorandum was also leaked and widely circulated.

Ultimately, the leaked message was a source of great embarrassment for the United States and the Bush administration. As Jamsheed Marker, Pakistan's ambassador to the United Nations, said, "People are wondering what the hell is going on in Washington. The perception of the U.S. is not one of leadership, but that of blocking" the summit's progress. Indeed, the U.S. refusal to sign the treaty despite otherwise unanimous acceptance contributed to the image of the United States as a summit spoiler—a perverse twist given that the U.S. supported early on the need for a biodiversity convention.

U.S. prestige was not the only casualty of the leaked memorandum, however. The leak also humiliated Reilly and undermined his authority as the director of the EPA. The incident clearly illustrates how an otherwise powerful administrative agency can be inhibited by outside political forces opposed to the agency's agenda. The effect of such unfriendly forces can be both swift and unexpected. As Reilly described in a memorandum one month following the fiasco, "[f]or me personally, it was like a bungee jump. You dive into space secured by a line on your leg. . . . It doesn't typically occur to you that someone might cut your line."[22]

---

21. Michael Weisskopf, " 'Outsider' EPA Chief Being Tested," *The Washington Post*, June 8, 1992, A1.
22. "Environment, U.S. Likely to Near Stabilization of CO_2 Emissions by 2000, Reilly Says," *Daily Report for Executives* (BNA), July 29, 1992, 146.

Key Words and Phrases

Questions and Case Problems

1. Why are administrative agencies called the "fourth branch" of the U.S. government?

2. A statute gives the Department of the Interior the power to allow or to curtail mining within the national forests "as the best interests of all users of the national forest shall dictate." Is this a valid delegation of legislative power to the agency, or is it too broad a delegation of power?

3. Assume that on June 29, 1994, Congress enacted a statute to deal with the problem of toxic-waste dump sites. These dump sites, in use for many years, leak toxic chemicals and thereby endanger people and poison groundwater. The statute created a "superfund" to which all companies producing toxic waste must contribute. This superfund will pay for cleaning up the most dangerous toxic-waste dump sites.

The statute also created the Toxic Waste Agency (TWA) to administer the superfund and cleanup operations. The TWA has adopted rules to determine how much each company must contribute to reach the $10 billion amount needed to clean up the waste sites. The contributions will depend on the toxicity of the chemical wastes that the company produces, the length of time the company has been in operation, and its ability to pay.

To help determine each company's required contribution, the TWA developed a list of all sources of toxic waste. Included on the list is the chemical XYZ, the manufacture of which produces toxic waste. However, the chemical ABC is not on the list. Nagel Corporation makes XYZ and concedes that it produces toxic wastes. Nagel also believes that the manufacture of ABC produces toxic wastes. ABC is manufactured exclusively by Seith Cooper Chemical Company.

Nagel appeals to the correct court concerning the absence of ABC on the list of toxic chemicals. The commissioner of the TWA asks the court to dismiss the appeal because Nagel lacks standing. What is the result?

 4. The Occupational Health and Safety Act of 1970 (OSHA) created new statutory duties for employers. It permitted the federal government, in proceedings before an administrative agency, to impose civil penalties on employers violating the OSHA. A jury trial was not available in the administrative proceedings. Did the penalty provisions of the OSHA violate the Seventh Amendment rights of employers? Explain why or why not. [*Atlas Roofing Company, Inc. v. Occupational Safety and Health Review Commission*, 430 U.S. 442, 97 S.Ct. 1261 (1977)]

5. Section 102(c) of the National Security Act of 1947 provides that "the Director of Central Intelligence may, in his discretion, terminate the employment of any officer or employee of the Agency whenever he shall deem such termination necessary or advisable in the interests of the United States" [50 U.S.C. § 5403(c)]. The director of the CIA terminated a homosexual CIA employee without stating any reason for the dismissal. The employee sought judicial review of his termination on the ground that it was arbitrary, capricious, or an abuse of discretion. Is judicial review of the director's actions proper? [*Webster v. Doe*, 486 U.S. 592, 108 S.Ct. 2047 (1988), *aff'd in part, rev'd in part* by *Doe v. Gates*, 981 F.2d 1316 (D.C.Cir. 1993)]

6. The Food and Drug Administration (FDA), charged with implementation of the Federal Food, Drug and Cosmetic Act, refused to approve the cancer treatment drug Laetrile on the ground that it failed to meet the statute's safety and effectiveness standards. Terminally ill cancer patients sued, claiming that the safety and effectiveness standards implemented by the FDA could have no reasonable application to drugs used by the terminally ill. The statute contained no explicit exemption for drugs used by the terminally ill. The case reached the court of appeals, which agreed with the plaintiffs and approved intravenous injections of Laetrile for terminally ill cancer patients. The United States appealed to the Supreme Court. Under what standard should the Supreme Court review the FDA's determination that an exemption from the Federal Food, Drug and Cosmetic Act should not be implied for drugs used by the terminally ill? [*United States v. Rutherford*, 442 U.S. 544, 99 S.Ct. 2470 (1979)]

7. The Occupational Safety and Health Act authorized the promulgation of regulatory standards governing workplace safety and health. It provided that the standards should, to the extent possible, ensure that no employee will suffer material health consequences even from a lifetime of exposure to an occupational hazard.

In 1978, the Occupational Safety and Health Administration created a strict standard limiting occupational exposure to cotton dust. This standard set the permissible concentrations of cotton dust at the lowest feasible level for then existing technology. The American Textile Manufacturers Institute, an organization representing the cotton industry, challenged the validity of the standard, arguing that the act required the agency to demonstrate a reasonable relationship between the costs and the benefits associated with the standard. Should the strict standard set by the Occupational Safety and Health Administration be upheld? [*American Textile Manufacturers Institute v. Donovan*, 452 U.S. 490, 101 S.Ct. 2478 (1981)]

8. It is not always clear whether an administrative agency is required to have a search warrant to pursue an investigation. Is a warrant required to conduct an investigation in the following cases?

(a) An Occupational Safety and Health Administration inspector entered Joy and Barry's, an electrical and plumbing installation business, to conduct a search of the working areas of the business that were not open to the public. Joy and Barry's was selected for inspection at random by the agency. Ron, the general manager of the business, refused to allow the inspector to enter without a warrant. Must the inspector get a warrant to conduct the investigation, which is authorized under the Occupational Safety and Health Act? [*Marshall v. Barlow's, Inc.,* 436 U.S. 307, 98 S.Ct. 1816 (1978)]

(b) Jon is a liquor dealer holding a federal retail liquor dealer's occupational tax stamp. He refused to allow tax agents to inspect his locked storeroom. May they inspect the storeroom without a search warrant? [*Colonnade Catering Corp. v. United States*, 397 U.S. 72, 90 S.Ct. 774 (1970)]

(c) Wendy, president of Tom and Barb's Silver Mines, refused to allow a government agent to conduct a warrantless search of the mine, even though the Federal Mine Safety and Health Act of 1977 authorized the secretary of labor to make warrantless inspections of mines. Additionally, the Mine Act specifies that underground mines must be inspected four times a year. Should the Supreme Court uphold Wendy's refusal to allow the inspector to enter? [*Donovan v. Dewey*, 452 U.S. 594, 101 S.Ct. 2534 (1981)]

9. In 1977, Michael Pertschuk was appointed chairman of the Federal Trade Commission (FTC). On his accession to the chairmanship, Pertschuk sought to transform the agency into an efficient organization for advancing the interests of the consumer. The first major policy initiative undertaken by Pertschuk focused on the effects of television advertising on children.

Pertschuk began speaking frequently on the subject of children's television. On the October 31, 1977, broadcast of the "Today" show, he expressed his view that no advertising directed at preschoolers should be allowed to be broadcast. He also sent letters to the Federal Communications Commission chairman and the Food and Drug Administration commissioner, describing his objections to advertising aimed at children.

On April 27, 1978, a Notice of Proposed Rule-Making was released by the FTC which included three options. One of the options would have banned all television advertising for "any product which is directed to audiences composed of a significant proportion of children who are too young to understand the selling purpose of or otherwise comprehend or evaluate the advertising." In response to this notice, on May 8, 1978, the national trade associations of advertisers, advertising agencies, and toy manufacturers petitioned Pertschuk to remove himself from participation in the rule-making proceeding. They alleged that his public statements on the issue evidenced prejudgment and bias. Should Pertschuk remove himself from participating in the rule-making proceedings? [*Association of National Advertisers, Inc. v. Federal Trade Commission*, 627 F.2d 1151 (D.C.Cir. 1979), *cert. denied*, 447 U.S. 921, 100 S.Ct. 3011 (1980)]

10. Maria Reilly is the executive vice president of DNA in Combat, Inc., a genetic engineering company based in Cambridge, Massachusetts. Eighteen months ago she filed an application for FDA approval of a promising anticancer drug, DBL. Two months ago she met Gene Splice at an après-ski party and invited him to her room to listen to her CD collection. After that night, Splice returned to his job as a senior specialist in the division of the FDA responsible for approving new drugs based on recombinant DNA, and Reilly returned to Cambridge. Two weeks after her return, Splice wrote Reilly a letter on FDA letterhead, saying, "It was nice to see your name cross my desk on your company's petition for approval of DBL. I'd really like to see you again—why don't you fly down this weekend?"

Reilly considered requesting that the petition be referred to another specialist at the FDA. However, she is concerned that that would delay the approval process by at least 18 months. Her chief scientist has advised her that a key competitor is expected to have a similar drug on the market in four months. What should she do?

UNIT II

THE LEGAL ENVIRONMENT

Chapter 7

TORTS

■ Introduction

What Is a Tort?

A *tort* is a civil wrong resulting in injury to a person or her property. A tort case is brought by the injured party to seek compensation for the wrong done. A crime, by contrast, is a wrong to society which is prosecuted by the state (see chapter 15). Even though a crime may be perpetrated against an individual, the victim is not a party to a criminal action. Criminal law generally is not concerned with compensating the victim, but with protecting society and punishing the criminal.

However, the distinctions between tort and criminal law are not always as clear as they first appear. A criminal statute might call for the criminal to compensate the victim. The victim might sue the perpetrator of the crime in tort, using the violation of a criminal statute as a basis for the tort claim. In some cases tort law purports, like criminal law, to protect society through the award of punitive damages.

Chapter Summary

This chapter discusses intentional torts first, then negligence, and then strict liability. Tortious activity by more than one individual or entity raises the issues of vicarious liability and apportioned responsibility. The chapter applies these various theories to the evolving law of toxic torts.

Elements of an Intentional Tort

In order for a party to prevail in a tort action, the plaintiff must prove all elements of a claim. Intentional torts require the plaintiff to prove: (1) actual or implied intent; (2) a voluntary act by the defendant; (3) causation; and (4) injury or harm. The act must be the actual and legal cause of the injury. The act required depends upon the specific intentional tort.

Intent

Intent is the subjective desire to cause the consequences of an act. *Actual intent* can be shown by evidence that the defendant intended a specific consequence to a particular individual. Intent is implied if the defendant knew that the consequences of the act were certain or substantially certain even if he did not actually intend any consequence at all.

As the degree of certainty of the result decreases, the defendant's conduct loses the character of intent and becomes recklessness. As the result becomes even less certain, the act becomes negligence, which is treated later in this chapter. For example, if Metro Corporation's custodian, Hal Burnet, dumped garbage out of Metro's third-floor office window onto a busy sidewalk and hit Alexis Douglas, the law would likely imply intent to hit Douglas. Even though Burnet may have had no subjective intention of hitting Douglas with the garbage, throwing it onto a busy sidewalk was substantially certain to result in at least one pedestrian being hit. However, if late one night Burnet put garbage in the middle of the sidewalk in front of the office building for morning pickup and Douglas tripped over it, the intent to cause harm is not so clear. If intent is not established, Burnet will not be liable for the intentional tort of battery which requires intent to bring about a harmful contact. However, Douglas might be able to establish negligence if she can show that a reasonable person would not have left the garbage on the sidewalk.

Intent may be transferred. If the defendant intended to hit one person, but instead hit the plaintiff, the intent requirement is met as to the plaintiff.

Defenses

Even if a plaintiff has proved all elements of a tort, the defendant may raise a legal defense to absolve himself of liability. The most frequently raised defense is consent. If the plaintiff consented to the act of the defendant, there is no tort. Even if the plaintiff did not explicitly consent, the law may imply consent. For example, a professional athlete injured during practice is deemed to have consented to the physical contact attendant to practice.

The defendant may also be absolved of liability by a claim of self-defense or defense of others.

Types of Intentional Torts

The intentional torts of battery, assault, false imprisonment, intentional infliction of emotional distress, trespass to land, nuisance, conversion, trespass to personal property, defamation, invasion of privacy, disparagement, injurious falsehood, fraudulent misrepresentation, interference with contractual relations, and interference with prospective business advantage are discussed below. A single set of facts may give rise to claims under more than one theory.

Battery

Tort law recognizes a basic right to have one's body free from harmful or offensive contact. Battery is the violation of that right.

Battery is the intentional, nonconsensual, harmful, or offensive contact with the plaintiff's body or with something in contact with it. Offensive contact, such as dousing a person with water or spitting in her face, may be a battery, even though the plaintiff has suffered no physical harm. The contact may be by the defendant directly or by something the defendant has set in motion. For example, putting poison in someone's food is a battery.

Another example of battery occurred after a New York Mets-Los Angeles Dodgers baseball game in July 1993. Amanda Santos, a two-year-old girl, was injured by an explosive device tossed in the parking lot by Vince Coleman, then a Mets outfielder. The young girl's family filed suit against Coleman and a number of other parties alleging battery, infliction of emotional distress (discussed later in this chapter), conspiracy to commit battery and inflict emotional distress, negligence, and negligent infliction of emotional distress.[1] The suit requested unspecified general, special, and punitive damages.

---

1. "Coleman is Sued, And So Is Davis," *The New York Times,* October 19, 1993, B13.

An example of a controversial case of battery occurred when a San Francisco cab driver used his taxicab to apprehend an escaping mugger by pinning him to a wall. The escaping mugger sued the cabbie for use of excessive force and the jury rendered a verdict of more than $24,000. The judge ordered a new trial, stating: "It is not now, nor was it ever the law, that before submitting to a lawful arrest, a fleeing felon is entitled to a fair fistfight."[2]

Assault

Assault also protects the right to have one's body left alone. Unlike battery, however, it does not require contact. It is an intentional, nonconsensual act that gives rise to the apprehension (though not necessarily fear) that a harmful or offensive contact is imminent.

Generally, assault requires some act, such as a threatening gesture, and the ability to follow through immediately with a battery. A punch thrown from close range that misses its target may be an assault, but a threat to punch someone is not. If a defendant makes a threatening gesture and says, "I would hit you if I weren't behind this desk," and she is in fact behind the desk, there is no assault. The immediacy requirement has not been met. Similarly, the threat "I'll beat you up if you come to class next week" is not immediate enough to be an assault.

False Imprisonment

False imprisonment protects the right to be free from restraint of movement. It is intentional, nonconsensual confinement by physical barriers or by physical force or threats of force. It requires that the plaintiff either knew he was confined or suffered harm as a result of the confinement.

False imprisonment has been found when the plaintiff's freedom of movement was restricted because of force applied to the plaintiff's valuable property. For example, if a store clerk grabs a package from a customer walking out the door, this is false imprisonment because the customer cannot be expected to abandon her package to leave the store.

Shopkeepers who detain and later release a person mistakenly suspected of shoplifting are sometimes sued for false imprisonment. Most states have legislation

---

2. Harriet Chiang, "Taxi Driver Must Pay $24,595 to Mugger He Captured," *San Francisco Chronicle,* February 7, 1992, A1; Associated Press, "New Trial Set for Cabby Who Has To Pay Mugger," *The Record, Northern New Jersey,* March 29, 1992, A14.

exempting shopkeepers from such claims if the shopkeeper has acted in good faith and the detention is made in a reasonable manner, for a reasonable time, and is based upon reasonable cause.

Intentional Infliction of Emotional Distress

The tort of *intentional infliction of emotional distress* protects the right to peace of mind. The law has been slow to redress purely mental injuries, and is still evolving in this area. Jurisdictions differ sharply in their acceptance of this tort. In most jurisdictions, in order to prove intentional infliction of emotional distress, a plaintiff must show: (1) outrageous conduct by the defendant; (2) intent to cause, or reckless disregard of the probability of causing, emotional distress; (3) severe emotional suffering; and (4) actual and proximate (or legal) causation of the emotional distress. The reluctance of the courts to accept intentional infliction of emotional distress as an independent tort most likely stems from the fear that plaintiffs will file false claims. Therefore, some jurisdictions also require a physical manifestation of the emotional distress.

> 66
> *Insulting, abusive, threatening, profane, or annoying conduct is not in itself a tort. Everyone is expected to be hardened to a certain amount of abuse.*

The mental distress must be foreseeable. The defendant is only liable to the extent that the plaintiff's response is reasonably within the range of normal human emotions.

The acts of the defendant must be outrageous or intolerable. Insulting, abusive, threatening, profane, or annoying conduct is not in itself a tort. Everyone is expected to be hardened to a certain amount of abuse. In determining outrageousness, courts will consider the context of the tort, as well as the relationship of the parties. For example, in the workplace, the plaintiff can expect to be subjected to evaluation and criticism, and neither criticism nor discharge is in itself outrageous. On the other hand, sexual harassment by a supervisor in the workplace is less tolerated than it might be, for example, if done by a patron in a nightclub. The following case concerns an employer's liability for sexual harassment in the workplace.

■ **A Case in Point:**   **In the Language of the Court**

Case 7.1
FORD v. REVLON, INC.
Supreme Court of Arizona
734 P.2d 580 (Ariz. 1987).

FACTS   Plaintiff Leta Fay Ford was an employee of Revlon in the Phoenix office's purchasing department. In 1979 Revlon hired Karl Braun as the new manager for the purchasing department, which made him Ford's supervisor.

In April 1980 Braun invited Ford to dinner, supposedly to discuss business. However, at the end of the evening when Ford tried to leave, Braun told her to stay because he planned to spend the night with her. When she rejected his advances, he told her "you will regret this." This was only the first of several incidents in which Braun harassed Ford, including one a month later at a company picnic at which Braun held Ford in a chokehold, fondled her, and made lewd comments to her. Ford testified at trial that after the initial incident of harassment, her working relationship with Braun was strained and uncomfortable.

Ford had not reported the first incident to Revlon management. After the picnic incident, however, she began a series of meetings with several members of Revlon management in order to report her complaints. She contacted managers at both her Phoenix office and at Revlon headquarters in New Jersey. She told them that she was afraid of Braun, she wanted help, and that the strain was making her sick.

The harassment continued throughout 1980. Braun threatened that he would destroy Ford and said that so long as she worked for him she was never going to go anywhere. When no action had been taken by December 1980, Ford called the manager at the New Jersey office to whom she had complained earlier. That person, Marie Kane, told Ford that the situation was too hot for her to handle and that she did not want to be involved. Kane suggested that Ford put the matter in the back of her mind and try to forget the situation.

During the time of the harassment, Ford developed high blood pressure, a nervous tic in her left eye, chest pains, rapid breathing, and other symptoms of emotional stress. Ford felt weak, dizzy, and generally fatigued. She consulted a physician about her condition.

In February 1981 Ford submitted a written request for transfer out of the purchasing department. Finally in late February a meeting was held in personnel at Ford's demand so she could have something done about her situation with Braun. She again gave the details of her complaint and submitted a handwritten complaint which read in part:

> I am asking for protection from Karl Braun. I have a right to be protected.
> I am collapsing emotionally and physically and I can't go on.

Not until three months later did the representative from personnel submit a report on Ford's complaint to a Revlon vice president. The report confirmed Ford's charge of sexual assault and recommended that Braun be censured. In May 1981, a full year and one month after Braun's initial act of harassment, Braun was issued a letter of censure from Revlon.

In October 1981 Ford attempted suicide. Later that month Revlon fired Braun.

In April 1982 Ford sued both Braun and Revlon for assault and battery, and for intentional infliction of emotional distress. At trial two written personnel policies were admitted as evidence. The policies stated in part that "any employee who has a complaint about any aspect of his or her employment is entitled to have the complaint heard, investigated and, if possible,

*Case **7.1** continued on following page*

*Case **7.1** continued*

resolved" and that "legitimate complaints are to be satisfied as promptly and as fully as possible."

The trial court jury found both Braun and Revlon liable for assault and battery, and found intentional infliction of emotional distress by Revlon. Revlon appealed. The court of appeals reversed the judgment of the trial court, holding that because Braun was not found liable for intentional infliction of emotional distress, Revlon could not be found liable. Ford appealed.

ISSUE PRESENTED   Can an employer's failure to take appropriate action in response to an employee's complaint of sexual harassment constitute the tort of intentional infliction of emotional distress?

OPINION   CAMERON, J., writing for the Arizona Supreme Court:

. . . .

INDEPENDENT TORT LIABILITY OF THE EMPLOYER
[The court began by stating that even if employee Braun were not liable for intentional infliction of emotional distress, employer Revlon could be found liable due to Revlon's failure to investigate Ford's complaint.]

. . . We believe that Revlon's failure to investigate Ford's complaint was independent of Braun's abusive treatment of Ford.

IS REVLON LIABLE FOR INTENTIONAL INFLICTION OF EMOTIONAL DISTRESS?

. . . .

Elements of the tort of intentional infliction of emotional distress have been set out by this court. . . . The three required elements are: first, the conduct by the defendant must be "extreme" and "outrageous"; second, the defendant must either intend to cause emotional distress or recklessly disregard the near certainty that such distress will result from his conduct; and third, severe emotional distress must indeed occur as a result of defendant's conduct.

We believe that the conduct of Revlon met these requirements. First, Revlon's conduct can be classified as extreme or outrageous. Ford made numerous Revlon managers aware of Braun's activities at company functions. Ford did everything that could be done, both within the announced policies of Revlon and without, to bring this matter to Revlon's attention. Revlon ignored her and the situation she faced, dragging the matter out for months and leaving Ford without redress. Here is sufficient evidence that Revlon acted outrageously.

Second, even if Revlon did not intend to cause emotional distress, Revlon's reckless disregard of Braun's conduct made it nearly certain that such emotional distress would in fact occur. Revlon knew that Braun had subjected Ford to physical assaults and vulgar remarks, that Ford continued to feel threatened by Braun, and that Ford was emotionally distraught, all of which led to a manifestation of physical problems. Despite Ford's complaints, Braun was not confronted for nine months, and then only upon Ford's demand for a group meeting. Another three months elapsed before Braun was censured. Revlon not only had actual knowledge of the situation but it also failed to conduct promptly any investigation of Ford's complaint.

Third, it is obvious that emotional distress did occur. Ample evidence, both medical and otherwise, was presented describing Ford's emotional distress. Ford testified about her emotional distress and her development of physical complications caused by her stressful work environment. The evidence convinced the jury, which found that emotional distress had occurred.

We also note that Revlon had set forth a specific policy and several guidelines for the handling of sexual harassment claims and other employee complaints, yet Revlon recklessly disregarded these policies and guidelines. Ford was entitled to rely on the policy statements made by Revlon. . . . We hold that Revlon's failure to take appropriate action in response to Ford's complaint of sexual harassment by Braun constituted the tort of intentional infliction of emotional distress.

. . . .

RESULT   The decision of the court of appeals was vacated. The judgment of the trial court was reinstated. Therefore, Ford received the monetary award for damages that she had been granted by the jury.

Questions

1. Would Revlon still have been held liable in this case if it did not have a specific policy, which it failed to follow, for handling sexual harassment claims? How important a factor should that policy be in the court's decision? Is it possible that this court's decision would discourage other companies from instituting their own sexual harassment policies and guidelines?

2. What qualifies as the "severe emotional distress" necessary to prove that the defendant is liable for the intentional infliction of emotional distress? What if Ford had only felt very uncomfortable and inhibited in her work environment as opposed to attempting suicide and suffering from other physical ailments?

Ethical Consideration

Although the court held the company liable for the intentional infliction of emotional distress in the preceding case, sexual harassment in the workplace often occurs without tort liability. A company has an ethical duty to prevent such harassment. To this end, managers should establish administrative guidelines that deal with allegations of sexual harassment in an effective and fair manner. The motivation to address this problem should come not merely from concern about tort liability, but also from the recognition that it is in the best interests of both the employees and the company to respond to such concerns.

Sexual harassment in the workplace and title VII of the Civil Rights Act of 1964, which prohibits it, are discussed further in chapter 13.

Trespass to Land

The previously described torts have involved interference with personal rights. *Trespass to land* is an interference with a property right. It is an invasion of property without consent of the owner. The land need not be injured by the trespass. The intent required is the intent to enter the property, not the intent to trespass. Thus, a mistake as to ownership is irrelevant.

Trespass may occur both below the surface and in the airspace above the land. Throwing something, such as trash, on the land, or shooting bullets over it, may be trespasses, even though the perpetrator was not standing on the plaintiff's land.

Refusing to move something that at one time the plaintiff permitted the defendant to place on the land may be a trespass. For example, if the plaintiff gave the defendant permission to leave a forklift on the plaintiff's land for one month, and it was left for two, the defendant may be liable for trespass.

Nuisance

Nuisance is a nontrespassory interference with the use and enjoyment of property, for example, by an annoying odor or noise.

Public nuisance is unreasonable and substantial interference with the public health, safety, peace, comfort, convenience, or utilization of land. A public nuisance action is usually brought by the government. It may also be brought by a private citizen who experiences special harm different from that of the general public.

Private nuisance is interference with an individual's use and enjoyment of his land. Destruction of crops by flooding, the pollution of a stream, or playing loud music late at night in a residential neighborhood can constitute a private nuisance.

The focus of both public and private nuisance claims is on the plaintiff's harm, not on the degree of the defendant's fault. Therefore, even innocent behavior on the part of the defendant is actionable—that is, it may be the basis for a claim—if that behavior resulted in unreasonable and substantial interference with the use and enjoyment of the plaintiff's property. To determine whether the defendant's conduct is unreasonable, the court will balance the utility of the activity creating the harm and the burden of preventing it against the nature and the gravity of the harm. For example, hammering noise during the remodeling of a house may be easier to justify than playing loud music purely for recreation.

Conversion

Conversion is the exercise of dominion and control over the personal property, rather than the real property (that is, land), of another. This tort protects the right to have personal property left alone. It prevents the defendant from treating the plaintiff's property as if it were her own. It is the tort claim a plaintiff would assert to recover the value of property stolen, destroyed, or substantially altered by the defendant.

The intent element for conversion does not include a wrongful motive. It merely requires the intent to exercise dominion or control over goods, inconsistent with the plaintiff's rights. The defendant need not know that the goods belonged to the plaintiff.

Trespass to Personal Property

Where personal property is interfered with but not converted—that is, taken, destroyed, or substantially altered—there is a *trespass to personal property* (sometimes referred to as *trespass to chattels*). No wrongful motive need be shown. The intent required is the intent to exercise control over the plaintiff's personal property. For example, an employer who took an employee's car on a short errand without the employee's permission would be liable for trespass to personal property. However, if the employer damaged the car or drove it for several thousand miles, thereby lowering its value, he would be liable for conversion.

The tort of trespass to chattels can include demonstrations that involve private property on private land. For example, in an Oregon case[3] a logging company sued six members of an environmental group who climbed on and chained themselves to the company's logging equipment. The members of the environmental group had to pay punitive damages for demonstrating against government policies while on private property. The court ruled that the enforcement of these tort punitive damages did not violate the protesters' First Amendment rights.

Defamation

Defamation is the communication (often termed *publication*) to a third party of an untrue statement of fact that injures the plaintiff's reputation, by exposing her to "hatred, ridicule or contempt."

Libel is written defamation, and *slander* is spoken defamation. The distinction between libel and slander is sometimes blurred with respect to modern communications.

Special rules apply to the requirement of injury to reputation. In an action for slander (spoken defamation), the plaintiff must prove he has suffered actual harm, such as the loss of credit, a job, or customers, unless the statement is so obviously damaging that it falls into the category of *slander per se*. Slander per se means that the words are slanderous in and of themselves, for example a statement that a person has committed a serious crime, is guilty of sexual misconduct, or is not fit to conduct business. In an action for libel (written defamation), the law presumes injury; that is, no actual harm need be shown (unless the statement on its face is not damaging).

---

3. *Huffman and Wright Logging Co. v. Wade,* 317 Or. 445, 857 P.2d 101 (Or. 1993).

Ethical Consideration

The damage done to a person's reputation by defamation can be instantaneous, because the false statements frequently receive attention in the electronic and print media. The public, quick to latch on to the initial defamatory statements, is less likely to notice a court decision some years later that holds that the statements were in fact false.

Because of this phenomenon, someone determined to cast doubt on another person's reputation has a good chance for success. Once the damage is done, it is largely irreversible. Therefore, ethical restraint must sometimes take the place of legal restraint.

Defenses Defenses to defamation actions are framed in terms of privilege and may be asserted in a number of circumstances. An *absolute privilege* cannot be lost. A *qualified privilege* can be lost under certain conditions. If the defendant has an absolute privilege, she can publish with impunity a statement she knows to be false. She can even do it with the most evil intention. Absolute privilege is limited to situations in which: (1) the defendant has consented to the publication; (2) the statement is a political broadcast made under the federal "equal time" statute; (3) the statement is made by a government official in the performance of governmental duties; (4) the statement is made by participants in judicial proceedings; or (5) the statement is made between spouses.

In most jurisdictions, truth is an absolute defense to a defamation claim. The law will not protect a reputation the plaintiff does not deserve. However, the burden is on the defendant to prove that the derogatory statements are true. The law in most jurisdictions presumes that the plaintiff has a pristine reputation unless the defendant proves otherwise.

> **❝**
>
> *In most jurisdictions, truth is an absolute defense to a defamation claim. The law will not protect a reputation the plaintiff does not deserve.*

There is a qualified privilege to make statements to protect one's own personal interests, including statements to a peer review committee. There is a qualified privilege to make statements to protect legitimate business interests, such as statements to a prospective employer, or to provide information for the public interest, such as credit reports. Qualified privileges can be lost if the person making the statement abuses the privilege.

Media Defendants The media, such as newspapers, television, or radio, when they are commenting upon a public official or public figure, have a qualified privilege that is almost absolute. Public officials include legislators, judges, and police officers. The definition of a public figure is addressed below.

The U.S. Supreme Court, in applying the First Amendment right of freedom of the press, has held that in order for a public official or public figure to recover damages for defamation by a media defendant, there must be a showing of *actual malice*. That means the statement must have been made with the knowledge that it was false or with a reckless disregard as to whether it was false. (Other aspects of the First Amendment are discussed in chapter 2.)

Public figures are those who, by reason of the notoriety of their achievements or the vigor and success with which they seek the public's attention, are injected into the public eye. In *Time, Inc. v. Firestone*[4] the U.S. Supreme Court made it clear that social prominence does not automatically indicate public-figure status sufficient to trigger the actual malice requirement. Mary Alice Firestone had married into the famous and wealthy industrial family of Russell Firestone. When she and her husband divorced, Time, Inc. falsely reported the basis of her divorce. Mrs. Firestone sued Time, Inc. for defamation. The Supreme Court rejected the argument that Mrs. Firestone was a public figure. The Court stated that although Mrs. Firestone was prominent in the social circle of Palm Beach, Florida, this did not make her a public figure. It further stated that not all controversies of interest to the public are "public controversies" of the type that triggers the actual malice requirement. The Court concluded that Mrs. Firestone did not have to prove actual malice to prevail.

Misquotations in some circumstances can constitute evidence of malice. The following case sets forth the standard to follow in analyzing this issue.

---

4. *Time, Inc. v. Firestone*, 424 U.S. 448, 96 S.Ct. 958 (1976).

■ **A Case in Point:**   **In the Language of the Court**

Case 7.2
MASSON v. THE NEW
YORKER MAGAZINE, INC.
Supreme Court of the
United States
501 U.S. 496, 111 S. Ct. 2419
(1991).

FACTS   The Sigmund Freud Archives are located at Maresfield Gardens outside of London, and serve as a repository for materials about Freud, including his own writings, letters, and personal library. In 1980, Dr. Kurt Eissler and Anna Freud hired Jeffrey Masson as Projects Director of the Sigmund Freud Archives. After assuming his post, Masson became disillusioned with Freudian psychology. In a 1981 lecture, Masson advanced his theories of Freud. Soon after, the Board of the Archives terminated him as Projects Director.

Janet Malcolm, an author and a contributor to *The New Yorker*, interviewed Masson in person and on the telephone, often taping the interviews. Based on the interviews and other sources, Malcolm wrote a lengthy article about the archives. One of Malcolm's narrative devices consisted of enclosing lengthy passages in quotation marks, reporting statements of Masson, Eissler, and other subjects. According to Masson, although he expressed concern at the number of errors in passages of the article that fact-checkers for *The New Yorker* discussed with him, he was not allowed to see portions that he wished to review before publication.

The New Yorker published the piece in December 1983, as a two-part series. In 1984, with knowledge of at least Masson's general allegation that the article contained defamatory material, respondent Alfred A. Knopf, Inc., published the entire work as a book, entitled *In the Freud Archives*. Although the work received complimentary reviews, the book portrays Masson in a most unflattering light.

Masson filed a libel suit in California, claiming that a number of statements (which do not appear in any similar form on Malcolm's tapes) were defamatory. The following is one of the examples Masson presented in the suit.

"Intellectual Gigolo." Malcolm quoted a description by Masson of his relationship with Eissler and Anna Freud as follows:

> Then I met a rather attractive older graduate student and I had an affair with her. One day, she took me to some art event, and she was sorry afterward. She said, "Well, it is very nice sleeping with you in your room, but you're the kind of person who should never leave the room—you're just a social embarrassment anywhere else, though you do fine in your own room." And you know, in their way, if not in so many words, Eissler and Anna Freud told me the same thing. They like me well enough "in my own room." They loved to hear from me what creeps and dolts analysts are. I was like an intellectual gigolo—you get your pleasure from him, but you don't take him out in public. . . .

The tape recordings contain the substance of Masson's reference to the graduate student but no suggestion that Eissler or Anna Freud considered him, or that he considered himself, an "intellectual gigolo." Instead, Masson said, on the tapes:

> They felt, in a sense, I was a private asset but a public liability. . . . They liked me when I was alone in their living room, and I could talk and chat and tell them the truth about things and they would tell me. But that I was, in a sense, much too junior within the hierarchy of analysts, for these important training analysts to be caught dead with me.

Malcolm argued that not all of the conversations were recorded. She explained that at times her tape recorder was broken. In addition, she claimed to have taken notes that she later typed up from conversations between the two of them while walking or traveling by car. Masson denied that Malcolm took notes during these conversations or that she ever claimed her tape recorder to be broken.

The New Yorker Magazine, Inc. and Malcolm moved for summary judgment. All parties agreed that Masson was a public figure and so could escape summary judgment only if the evidence in the record would permit a reasonable finder of fact, by clear and convincing evidence, to conclude that the respondents published a defamatory statement with actual malice.

The federal district court held that these passages did not raise a question of fact for the jury. The court of appeals affirmed, and Masson appealed to the U.S. Supreme Court.

ISSUE PRESENTED Does a deliberate alteration of a person's words put in quotation marks equate with the knowledge of falsity necessary for a finding of actual malice?

OPINION

KENNEDY, J., writing for the U.S. Supreme Court:

In this libel case, a public figure claims he was defamed by an author who, with full knowledge of the inaccuracy, used quotation marks to attribute to him comments he had not made. The First Amendment protects authors and journalists who write about public figures by requiring a plaintiff to prove that the defamatory statements were made with what we have called "actual malice," a term of art denoting deliberate or reckless falsification. We consider in this opinion whether the attributed quotations had the degree of falsity required to prove this state of mind, so that the public figure can defeat a motion for summary judgment and proceed to a trial on the merits of the defamation claim.

. . . .

II

A

Under California law, "libel is a false and unprivileged publication by writing . . . which exposes any person to hatred, contempt, ridicule, or obloquy, or which causes him to be shunned or avoided, or which has a tendency to injure him in his occupation." . . .

The First Amendment limits California's libel law in various respects. When, as here, the plaintiff is a public figure, he cannot recover unless he proves by clear and convincing evidence that the defendant published the defamatory statement with actual malice, i.e., with "knowledge that it was false or with reckless disregard of whether it was false or not." Mere negligence does not suffice. Rather, the plaintiff must demonstrate that the author "in fact entertained serious doubts as to the truth of his publication," or acted with a "high degree of awareness of . . . probable falsity."

Actual malice under the *New York Times*[5] standard should not be confused with the concept of malice as an evil intent or a motive arising from spite or ill will. . . . In place of the term actual malice, it is better practice that jury instructions refer to publication of a statement with knowledge of falsity or reckless disregard as to truth or falsity. This definitional principle must be remembered in the case before us.

---

5. *New York Times Co. v. Sullivan*, 376 U.S. 254, 84 S.Ct. 710 (1964).

Case **7.2** continued on following page

*Case **7.2** continued*

B

In general, quotation marks around a passage indicate to the reader that the passage reproduces the speaker's words verbatim. . . .

. . . .

Of course, quotations do not always convey that the speaker actually said or wrote the quoted material. . . . Writers often use quotations . . . and a reader will not reasonably understand the quotations to indicate reproduction of a conversation that took place. In other instances, an acknowledgment that the work is so-called docudrama or historical fiction, or that it recreates conversations from memory, not from recordings, might indicate that the quotations should not be interpreted as the actual statements of the speaker to whom they are attributed.

The work at issue here, however, as with much journalistic writing, provides the reader no clue that the quotations are being used as a rhetorical device or to paraphrase the speaker's actual statements. To the contrary, the work purports to be nonfiction, the result of numerous interviews. At least a trier of fact could so conclude. The work contains lengthy quotations attributed to petitioner, and neither Malcolm nor her publishers indicate to the reader that the quotations are anything but the reproduction of actual conversations. Further, the work was published in *The New Yorker,* a magazine which at the relevant time seemed to enjoy a reputation for scrupulous factual accuracy. These factors would, or at least could, lead a reader to take the quotations at face value. . . .

C

The constitutional question we must consider here is whether, in the framework of a summary judgment motion, the evidence suffices to show that respondents acted with the requisite knowledge of falsity or reckless disregard as to truth or falsity. This inquiry in turn requires us to consider the concept of falsity; for we cannot discuss the standards for knowledge or reckless disregard without some understanding of the acts required for liability. We must consider whether the requisite falsity inheres in the attribution of words to the petitioner which he did not speak.

In some sense, any alteration of a verbatim quotation is false. But writers and reporters by necessity alter what people say, at the very least to eliminate grammatical and syntactical infelicities. If every alteration constituted the falsity required to prove actual malice, the practice of journalism, which the First Amendment standard is designed to protect, would require a radical change, one inconsistent with our precedents and First Amendment principles. Petitioner concedes this absolute definition of falsity in the quotation context is too stringent. . . . We agree, and must determine what, in addition to this technical falsity, proves falsity for purposes of the actual malice inquiry.

Petitioner argues that, excepting correction of grammar or syntax, publication of a quotation with knowledge that it does not contain the words the public figure used demonstrates actual malice. . . .

We reject the idea that any alteration beyond correction of grammar or syntax by itself proves falsity in the sense relevant to determining actual malice under the First Amendment. An interviewer who writes from notes often will engage in the task of attempting a reconstruction of the speaker's statement. That author would, we may assume, act with knowledge that at times she has attributed to her subject words other than those actually used. Under petitioner's proposed standard, an author in this situation would lack First Amendment protection if she reported as quotations the substance of a subject's derogatory statements about himself.

Even if a journalist has tape recorded the spoken statement of a public figure, the full and exact statement will be reported in only rare circumstances. . . .

. . . .

We conclude that a deliberate alteration of the words uttered by a plaintiff does not equate with knowledge of falsity for purposes of *New York Times Co. v. Sullivan* . . . unless the alteration results in a material change in the meaning conveyed by the statement. The use of quotations to attribute words not in fact spoken bears in a most important way on that inquiry, but it is not dispositive in every case.

. . . .

The judgment of the Court of Appeals is reversed, and the case is remanded for further proceedings consistent with this opinion.

RESULT   The evidence presented a jury question whether Malcolm acted with the requisite knowledge of falsity or reckless disregard as to the truth or falsity of five of the passages. The case was, therefore, remanded for trial.

COMMENTS   In the summer of 1993, a San Francisco jury ruled that Masson had been defamed by all five quotations but that Malcolm knew only two were false. The first was the quote that Masson would turn Freud's house in London into a place of "sex, women, fun," and the second was that if the head of the archives who fired him thought that Masson would keep quiet about it, "he had the wrong man." The jury exonerated The New Yorker Magazine, Inc. The jury deadlocked on damages due from Malcolm and a mistrial was declared. On September 9, 1993, the court ordered a new trial with Malcolm as the sole defendant on the issues of both liability and damages.[6] The court dismissed the claims against The New Yorker Magazine, Inc., however, after finding, based on a review of the evidence, that the editors "neither knew the quotations were false, nor acted with a reckless disregard as to falsity."

Questions
1. Do you agree with the Court that "the use of quotations to attribute words not in fact spoken" is not dispositive of whether the journalist acted with knowledge of falsity?
2. Did Malcolm violate journalistic ethics by her actions in this case?

---

6. *Masson v. The New Yorker Magazine, Inc.* 832 F.Supp. 1350 (N.D.Cal. 1993).

If the plaintiff is not a public figure, he need not prove malice. A private plaintiff may raise a defamation claim if the defendant acted with knowledge, or acted in reckless disregard of the facts, or was negligent in failing to ascertain the facts. If the plaintiff proceeds on a negligence theory, he must prove actual damages, such as loss of business or out-of-pocket costs. If the plaintiff proves malice, damages are presumed, meaning no proof of damages is required.

Invasion of Privacy

Invasion of privacy is a violation of the right to keep personal matters to oneself. It can take several forms.

Intrusion is objectionable prying, such as eavesdropping or unauthorized rifling through files. Injunctions or court orders are usually available to prevent further intrusion. There must be a reasonable expectation of privacy in the thing into which there is intrusion. For example, courts have held there is no legitimate expectation of privacy in conversations in a public restaurant. The tort of intrusion does not require publication of the information obtained.

Public disclosure of private facts does require publication, for example, stating in a newspaper that the plaintiff does not pay debts or posting such a notice in a public place. The matter made public must not be newsworthy. The matter must be private, such that a reasonable person would find publication objectionable. Unlike in a defamation case, truth is not a defense.

Appropriation of a person's name or likeness may be an invasion of privacy. Often this tort is committed for financial gain. For example, using a fictitious testimonial in an advertisement, or using a person's picture in an advertisement or article with which he has no connection, would be a tort.

Disparagement

Disparagement is the publication of statements derogatory to the quality of the plaintiff's business, to the business in general, or even to her personal affairs, in order to discourage others from dealing with her.

To prove disparagement, the plaintiff must show that the defendant made false statements about the quality or ownership of the plaintiff's goods or services, knowing that they were false, or with conscious indifference as to their truth. The plaintiff must also prove that the statements caused him actual harm; damages will not be presumed.

One interesting case of business and product disparagement involved a rare painting and the disparaging remarks of an art expert regarding the painting.[7] After the expert's remarks regarding the quality and authenticity of the painting were made, the painting failed to sell at an auction. However, the court refused to award damages on this basis because the painting's owner had failed to prove that he suffered a specific pecuniary loss (i.e., did not sell the painting) due to the disparaging remarks. The owner did not name any specific buyers who did not purchase the painting because of the remarks. The owner also did not show a decline in "general business" or a solid basis for the damage he sought. The sale price of a

similar painting was not enough to show that his painting would have sold for the same amount.

Injurious Falsehood

False statements that are knowingly made, although they may not be disparaging of the plaintiff's business, may nevertheless give rise to an *injurious falsehood* claim. For example, a false statement that the plaintiff has gone out of business or does not carry certain goods, if it results in economic loss to the plaintiff, is a tort.

The range of damages for injurious falsehood is more restricted than for defamation. Injurious falsehood permits recovery only of pecuniary (that is, monetary) losses related to business operations, whereas defamation permits recovery for loss of reputation, including emotional damages, as well as pecuniary losses.

Defenses   The defenses available to the defendant in a defamation action apply to injurious falsehood. In the case of comparison of goods, the privilege is even broader than the privilege available in defamation. For example, a defendant who favorably compares her own goods to those of a competitor is privileged, even though she may not honestly believe in the superiority of her own goods.

Ethical Consideration

A comparison of goods may not be actionable under the law, but it raises ethical issues. If a person knows that his goods are inferior, is claiming that they are better than a competitor's a form of lying?

Fraudulent Misrepresentation

The tort of *fraudulent misrepresentation,* also called fraud or deceit, protects economic interests and the right to be treated fairly and honestly. Fraud requires proof that the defendant intentionally misled the plaintiff by making a material misrepresentation of fact upon which the plaintiff relied. It also requires that the plaintiff suffer injury as a result of the reliance. For example, a third party who has relied to his detriment upon an accoun-

---

7. *Kirby v. Wildenstein*, 784 F.Supp. 1112 (S.D.N.Y. 1992).

tant's misleading opinion regarding a company's financial statement might sue the accountant for fraud. The following case addressed the issue of what state of mind is required to meet the intent requirement for fraud.

■ A Case in Point: Summary

Case 7.3
CITIZENS NATIONAL BANK OF WISNER v. KENNEDY AND COE
Supreme Court of Nebraska
232 Neb. 477, 441 N.W.2d 180 (Neb. 1989).

FACTS   Three Nebraska banks entered into a loan agreement with Duncan Feeders, Inc. (DFI) to provide DFI with a $500,000 line of credit. In deciding to grant the line of credit, the banks reviewed financial compilations prepared by accountants Kennedy and Coe. The banks advanced moneys on the line of credit. DFI defaulted on the loan. The banks sued Kennedy and Coe, claiming that they fraudulently misrepresented the financial condition of DFI and were negligent in their preparation of documents in connection with the loan.

Following trial, the judge ruled that the accountants did not act fraudulently, because they had no intent to deceive. The judge also ruled that the accountants were not negligent. The banks appealed.

ISSUE PRESENTED   Can recklessness in making an assertion or representation to a client constitute fraud?

SUMMARY OF OPINION   The Nebraska Supreme Court held that the trial court applied the wrong elements to determine whether there was fraudulent misrepresentation. The court held that intent to deceive is not required. Instead, it set forth the following test. There is fraudulent misrepresentation if: (1) at the time a false representation was made, the representation was known to be false, or was made recklessly, "without knowledge of its truth and as a positive assertion"; (2) the representation was made with the intention that it be relied upon; (3) the plaintiff relied upon the representation; and (4) damage occurred as a result.

Therefore, to recover under a theory of fraudulent misrepresentation, the plaintiff need not prove intent to deceive. It is enough if the defendant made the representation recklessly.

RESULT   The decisions of the trial and appellate courts were reversed and the case was remanded for trial. A showing of recklessness was sufficient to prove a fraudulent misrepresentation claim.

COMMENTS   Several states have chosen not to follow Nebraska's example of allowing recklessness to be sufficient to prove fraud. They include New Jersey, New York, North Carolina, Oklahoma, and Virginia.

Fraud can also be based upon the defendant's omission of a material fact when the defendant has a duty to speak because of a special relationship with the plaintiff.

For example, in a California case[8] Williams, the plaintiff owner of a Buick dealership, had relied on a bank for several years for financial advice. The plaintiff was 25 years old and had worked his way up from lot boy. When Williams wanted to purchase a new dealership, Security Pacific, the bank, suggested he purchase Viking. Viking was losing money, and owed Security Pacific money. In the meantime, Security Pacific was seeking a bailout from its financial obligations. The bank withheld all of this information from Williams. Williams then suffered

---

8. *Security Pacific National Bank v. Williams*, 213 Cal.App. 3d 927, 262 Cal.Rptr. 260 (1989).

great financial hardship and eventually lost both dealerships after the bank refused to extend financing.

The California Court of Appeal upheld a jury verdict of $4.5 million, including $2.5 million in punitive damages. The court held that the bank owed Williams a *fiduciary duty*, that is, a duty to act with integrity.

The court also held that although statements as to future actions are generally deemed opinions and therefore not actionable, an exception is found where: (1) the defendant held itself out to be specially qualified and the plaintiff acted reasonably in relying upon the defendant's superior knowledge; (2) the opinion is that of a fiduciary or other trusted person; and (3) the defendant stated its opinion as an existing fact or as implying facts that justify a belief in its truth.

Interference with Contractual Relations

The tort of *interference with contractual relations* protects the right to enjoy the benefits of legally binding agreements. It provides a remedy when the defendant intentionally induces another person to breach a contract with the plaintiff. The basis of interference with contractual relations is intent to interfere. Thus, courts usually require that the defendant induce the contracting party to breach, rather than merely create the opportunity for the breach. The defendant must know of the existence of the contract or interest between the plaintiff and the other person, or there must be sufficient facts that would lead a reasonable person to believe there was such a contract or interest.

Perhaps the most famous case involving tortious interference with contract was *Pennzoil v. Texaco*, discussed in the "Inside Story" in chapter 8. A jury decided against Texaco for interfering with Pennzoil's contract to buy Getty Oil, awarding $10.5 billion to Pennzoil. The case was ultimately settled for $3 billion.

Defenses   As in defamation, truth is a defense to a claim for interference with contractual relations. There is no liability where a true statement was made to induce another to break relations with the plaintiff.

Interference with contractual relations also requires an unacceptable purpose in some jurisdictions. If good grounds exist for the interference, the defendant is not liable. For example, if a manager of a corporation is incompetent, a stockholder of a corporation may be able to induce breach of the employment agreement between the manager and the corporation. The stockholder's motive would be to protect her investment. On the other hand, a defendant may not interfere with another person's contract in order to attract customers or employees away from that person.

Interference with Prospective Business Advantage

Courts are less willing to award damages for interference with prospective contracts than they are to protect existing contracts. A party still engaged in negotiating a contract has fewer rights not to have his deal disturbed than a party that has already entered into a contract.

To prove *interference with prospective business advantage,* the plaintiff must prove that the defendant interfered with a relationship the plaintiff sought to develop and that the interference caused the plaintiff's loss. The interference must be intentional. However, in rare cases courts have permitted recovery where the defendant was merely negligent.

Defense   Most jurisdictions recognize a privilege to act for one's own financial gain. In some jurisdictions, the plaintiff has the burden of showing that the defendant acted from a motive other than her own financial gain, such as revenge. In others, the defendant has the burden of proving that she acted only for financial gain. Any purpose sufficient to create a privilege to disturb existing contractual relations will also justify interference with prospective business advantage.

As in defamation and interference with contractual relations, truth is a defense. Some jurisdictions have applied the First Amendment defenses available in defamation cases.

Interference with prospective business advantage is usually done by a competitor, or at least by one who stands to benefit from the interference. However, it is not a tort to compete fairly. For the purposes of competition, a defendant may attempt to increase his business by cutting prices, allowing rebates, refusing to deal with the plaintiff, secretly negotiating with the defendant's customers, or refusing to deal with third parties unless they agree not to deal with the plaintiff.

 Ethical Consideration

Are practices such as refusing to deal with the plaintiff, secretly negotiating with the defendant's customers, or refusing to deal with third parties unless they agree to refuse to deal with the plaintiff ethical?

■ Elements of Negligence

An essential element of every intentional tort is the mental element of intent. Negligence does not include a mental element. Rather, the focus is on the conduct of the defendant. The law of negligence requires that all people must act as reasonable persons, taking appropriate care in any given situation. It does not require that the defendant intended, or even knew, that her actions would harm the plaintiff. In fact, even if the defendant was full of concern for the safety of the plaintiff, his conduct may still be negligent. It is enough that he acted carelessly or, in other words, that his conduct created an unreasonable risk of harm.

Negligence is defined as conduct that involves an unreasonably great risk of causing injury to another person or damage to property. In order to establish liability under a negligence theory, the plaintiff must show: (1) the defendant owed a duty to the plaintiff to act in conformity with a certain standard of conduct, that is, to act reasonably under the circumstances; (2) the defendant breached that duty by failing to conform to the standard; (3) a reasonably close causal connection exists between the plaintiff's injury and the defendant's breach; and (4) the plaintiff suffered an actual loss or injury.

Duty

A person with a legal *duty* to another is required to act reasonably under the circumstances to avoid harming the other person. The required standard of care is what a reasonable person of ordinary prudence would do in the circumstances. It is not graduated to include the reasonably slow person, the reasonably forgetful person, or the reasonable person of low intelligence.

> 66
>
> *The required standard of care is what a reasonable person of ordinary prudence would do in the circumstances. It is not graduated to include the reasonably slow person, the reasonably forgetful person, or the reasonable person of low intelligence.*

Duty of Accountants and Other Professionals to Third Parties The issue of duty takes on special significance where the plaintiff asserts a claim of professional negligence, or malpractice, against a lawyer, an architect, or an accountant. Although a professional clearly owes a duty to her client, she may not have a duty to a third party, with whom she does not have a contractual relationship. In the case of *Citizens National Bank of Wisner v. Kennedy and Coe,*[9] discussed earlier, the Nebraska Supreme Court held that an accountant's duty of reasonable care is to his clients and generally does not extend to third parties. In that case, even though the plaintiff banks could show that their debtor's accountant knew the banks would rely on its audit and that the audit was grossly misleading, the Nebraska Supreme Court held that the accountant was not liable to the banks for negligence (though it could be liable for intentional misrepresentation). Other courts have disagreed, holding that an accountant owes a duty to all persons he knows will rely on his opinion in the audited financial statements.[10]

In *Bily v. Arthur Young & Co.,*[11] the California Supreme Court held that a claim against an auditor for general negligence, or malpractice, cannot be asserted by any person other than the client. However, a claim for negligent misrepresentation of a material fact can be asserted by any "intended beneficiary" of the auditor's report. The court suggested the following jury instruction on negligent misrepresentation in auditor liability cases:

> The representation must have been made with the intent to induce plaintiff, or a particular class of persons to which plaintiff belongs, to act in reliance upon the representation in a specific transaction, or a specific type of transaction, that defendant intended to influence. Defendant is deemed to have intended to influence [its client's] transaction with plaintiff whenever defendant knows with substantial certainty that plaintiff, or the particular class of person to which plaintiff belongs, will rely on the representation in the course of the transaction. If others become aware of the representation and act upon it, there is no liability even though defendant should reasonably have foreseen such a possibility.

In a case of intentional misrepresentation or fraud, if an accountant intends that a person or class of persons will rely on her opinion, then the accountant is liable to any such person. In addition, suit can also be brought by any person whom the accountant reasonably should have foreseen would rely upon the intentional misrepresentation. Thus, the greater the defendant's degree of fault, the wider the scope of potential plaintiffs.

---

9. 232 Neb. 477, 441 N.W.2d 180 (Neb. 1989).
10. *First Florida Bank, N.A. v. Max Mitchell & Co.,* 558 So.2d 9 (Fla. 1990).
11. 3 Cal. 4th 370, 11 Cal.Rptr. 2d 51, 834 P.2d 745 (Cal. 1992).

Duty in Other Contexts

Duty of Landowner or Tenant   A possessor of land (such as a tenant) or its owner has a legal duty to keep the property reasonably safe. Such a person can be liable for injury that occurs outside, as well as on, his premises. For example, he may be liable for harm caused when water from his cooling tower covers the highway; or when sparks from his railroad engine, which is not properly maintained, start a fire on adjacent property; or when his roof sheds snow onto the highway.

A landowner must exercise care in the demolition or construction of buildings on her property and in the excavation of her land. The landowner has been held liable when a pole on his property collapsed after it was hit by a car and injured a pedestrian; and when the landowner erected a sign that obstructed the view and caused an accident.

Generally, landowners are not liable for harm caused by natural conditions on their property, such as uncut weeds that obstruct a driver's view, the natural flow of surface water, or falling rocks. However, the landowner may be liable if she has altered the natural state of the land, for example, by erecting a dam which flooded a highway, by erecting a canopy so that water dripped from it to freeze on the sidewalk, or by planting a row of trees that obstructed the view of motorists.

In a few jurisdictions, landowners have a duty to maintain sidewalks that abut, that is, are right next to, their property. In all jurisdictions, a landowner has a general duty to inspect his land and keep it in repair, and he may be liable if a showroom window, a downspout, a screen, or a loose sign falls and injures someone.

Duty to Trespassers   In general, a landowner owes no duty to an undiscovered trespasser. Occasionally a landowner may be liable even to a trespasser who is on her property without permission. One such case was brought by a burglar who was hurt when he fell through a skylight while trying to break into a house.

If a substantial number of trespassers are in the habit of entering at a particular place, the possessor has a duty to take reasonable care to discover and to protect the trespassers from activities carried on by her. Some courts have also established a duty to protect such trespassers from dangerous conditions, such as concealed high-tension wires, that do not result from the possessor's activities. Some jurisdictions require the possessor to exercise reasonable care once he knows of the trespasser's presence.

Trespassing children are owed a higher level of duty. The *attractive nuisance* doctrine imposes liability for physical injury to children trespassers caused by artificial conditions on the land if: (1) the landowner knew or should have known that children were likely to trespass; (2) the condition is one she would reasonably know involved an unreasonable risk of injury to such children; (3) the children because of their youth did not discover the condition or realize the risk involved; (4) the utility to the possessor of maintaining the condition is not great; (5) the burden of eliminating the risk is slight compared with the magnitude of the risk to the children; and (6) the possessor fails to exercise reasonable care to protect the children.

Duty to Licensees   A *licensee* is anyone who is on the land of another person with the possessor's express or implied consent. The licensee enters for his own purposes, not for those of the possessor. Social guests and uninvited sales representatives are licensees.

The possessor must exercise reasonable care for the protection of the licensee. This duty differs from that to a trespasser because the possessor is required to look out for licensees before they enter the land. However, she is not required to inspect for unknown dangers. The duty arises only when the possessor has actual knowledge of a risk.

Duty to Invitees   An *invitee*, or business visitor, is someone who enters the premises for the purposes of the possessor's business. The possessor owes a higher duty to an invitee than to a licensee. The possessor must protect invitees against known dangers and also against those dangers that he might discover with reasonable care.

The invitee is of particular importance to a manager. There are thousands of "slip and fall" cases each year due to wet floors, icy sidewalks, or broken steps. A customer is clearly an invitee, and is accordingly owed a higher duty of care than a licensee such as a social guest.

Emergencies   In determining duty, the law allows reasonable mistakes of judgment in some circumstances. In emergency situations, the duty is to act as a reasonable person would act in the circumstances.

The defendant is expected to anticipate emergencies. Drivers must drive defensively. Innkeepers must anticipate fires and install smoke alarms, and in some cases sprinkler systems, and must provide fire escapes and other fire safety features. Owners of swimming pools in subdivisions with children must fence their property.

Duty to Rescue The law does not impose a general duty to rescue. However, once one undertakes a rescue, the law imposes a duty to act as a reasonable person and not to abandon the rescue effort unreasonably. Thus, if Ciril Wyatt sat on a river shore and watched Edward Donnelly drown, she would not be liable in negligence for Donnelly's death. However, if Wyatt saw Donnelly drowning, jumped in her boat, sped to him, tried to pull him into the boat and then changed her mind and let him drown, she would be liable.

A special relationship between two people may create a duty to rescue. If Donnelly were Wyatt's husband or child or parent, Wyatt would have a duty to rescue him. Other relationships that create a duty to rescue are employer and employee; innkeeper and guest; teacher and student; bus, train, or other common carrier and passenger; and possibly team members, hunting partners, or hiking partners.

There is a duty to rescue those whom one has placed in peril. For example, if Wyatt had been driving her boat in a negligent manner, thereby causing Donnelly to fall overboard, she would have a duty to rescue him.

Ethical Consideration

Some jurisdictions do impose a general duty to rescue. In France, for example, a bystander has a duty to attempt a rescue if it is clear that such an attempt can be made without any risk to the rescuer. Whether or not the law requires it, an adult watching a child drowning in a two-foot pool of water (for example) should make the effort to rescue the child. Society has a moral expectation that people should protect persons, particularly children, who are unable to protect themselves.

Breach of Duty

Once it is determined that the defendant owed the plaintiff a duty, the next issue is whether the defendant breached the duty.

Standard of Conduct In many cases, the required standard of conduct will be that of the reasonable person. However, a person who is specially trained to participate in a profession or trade will be held to the higher standard of care of a reasonably skilled member of that profession or trade. For example, the professional conduct of a doctor, architect, pilot, attorney, or accountant will be measured against the standard of the profession. A specialist within a profession will be held to the standard of specialists.

The court will also look to statutes and regulations to determine whether the defendant's conduct amounted to a breach of duty. Some jurisdictions merely allow the statute to be introduced into evidence to establish the standard of care. Others shift the burden to the defendant to prove he was not negligent once the plaintiff shows the defendant violated a statute and the violation caused the injury. This is often an impossible burden to satisfy. This rule, sometimes referred to as *negligence per se,* applies only if the statute or regulation was designed to protect a class of persons from the type of harm suffered by the plaintiff and if the plaintiff is a member of the class to be protected.

Courts will also look to the custom or the practice of others under similar circumstances to determine the standard of care. Although the custom in the industry may be given great weight, it is not ordinarily dispositive or conclusive.

Res Ipsa Loquitur The doctrine of *res ipsa loquitur* ("the thing speaks for itself") allows the plaintiff to prove breach of duty and causation (discussed below) indirectly. Res ipsa loquitur applies when an accident has occurred and it is obvious, although there is no direct proof, that the accident would not have happened absent someone's negligence. For example, if a postoperative X-ray showed a surgical clamp in the plaintiff's abdomen, even if no one testifies as to how the clamp got there, it can reasonably be inferred that the surgeon negligently left it there.

Res ipsa loquitur has three requirements. First, the plaintiff's injury must have been caused by a condition or instrumentality that was within the exclusive control of the defendant. This requirement eliminates the possibility that other persons, not named as defendants, were responsible for the condition that gave rise to the injury. Second, the accident must be of such a nature that it ordinarily would not occur in the absence of negligence by the defendant. Third, the accident must not be due to the plaintiff's own negligence.

Once res ipsa loquitur is established, jurisdictions vary as to its effect. In some jurisdictions it creates a presumption of negligence, and the plaintiff is entitled to a directed verdict (whereby the judge directs the jury to find in favor of the plaintiff) unless the defendant can prove he was not responsible. This rule has the effect of shifting the burden of proof, normally with the plaintiff, to the defendant. Other jurisdictions leave the burden of proof with the plaintiff, requiring the jury to weigh the inference of negligence and to find the defendant negligent only if the preponderance of the evidence (including the res ipsa inference) favors such a finding.

Causal Connection

In addition to establishing duty and breach, the plaintiff must prove that the defendant's breach of duty caused the injury. The causation requirement has two parts: actual cause and proximate (or legal) cause.

Actual Cause   The plaintiff establishes *actual cause* if she proves that but for the defendant's negligent conduct, the plaintiff would not have been harmed. The defendant is not liable if the plaintiff's injury would have occurred in the absence of the defendant's conduct. For example, if George Broussard put a garbage can out on the sidewalk for morning pickup and Anna Chang came along and broke her ankle, Broussard's conduct would not be the actual cause of Chang's injury if it were established that Chang had caught her heel in the sidewalk, turned her ankle, and then bumped into Broussard's garbage can.

When the plaintiff names more than one defendant, the actual-cause test may become a substantial-factor test: Was the defendant's conduct a substantial factor in bringing about the plaintiff's injury?

A further problem may arise if more than one individual could possibly have been the negligent party. A classic case involved two hunters shooting quail on an open range.[12] Both shot at exactly the same time, using identical shotguns. A shot from one of the guns accidentally hit another hunter. Clearly only one of the two defendants caused the injury, but there was no way to determine which one it was. The court imposed the burden on each defendant to prove that he had not caused the injury. Because neither could do so, both were held liable for the whole injury.

Proximate Cause   Once the plaintiff has proved that the defendant's conduct is an actual cause of the plaintiff's injury, he must also prove that it is the *proximate* cause, that is, that the defendant had a duty to protect the particular plaintiff against the particular conduct that injured him. Through the requirement of proximate cause, the law places limits on the defendant's liability. A defendant may not be liable for all of the injuries for which actual cause is established, as is demonstrated in the following leading case.

---

12. *Summers v. Tice,* 33 Cal.2d 80, 199 P.2d 1 (Cal. 1948).

■ **A Case in Point:**   **Summary**

Case 7.4
PALSGRAF v. LONG ISLAND RAILROAD CO.
Court of Appeals of
New York
162 N.E. 99 (N.Y. 1928).

FACTS   Mrs. Palsgraf, the plaintiff, was standing on a platform of the defendant's railroad. A train stopped at the station. Two men ran forward to catch it. The train began moving. Although it was moving, one of the men was able to reach the train without a problem. The other man, who was carrying a package, jumped aboard the train but seemed unsteady and about to fall. A guard on the train, who had held the door open, reached forward to help him in. Another guard who was on the platform pushed the man from behind. Because of the guard's pushing, the package that the man was carrying was dislodged and fell upon the railroad tracks.

The package was small and covered by a newspaper. It contained fireworks, but there was no way to tell what the contents were just from observing the outside of the package. The fireworks exploded when they fell. The shock of the explosion made some scales many feet away at the end of the platform fall. The scales struck Mrs. Palsgraf, causing her injury.

Mrs. Palsgraf sued the railroad. The trial court jury entered a verdict in favor of Mrs. Palsgraf. This judgment was affirmed by the appellate court. The railroad appealed again.

ISSUE PRESENTED   Can the act of one person that results in harm to another person be considered negligence although the harm was unintentional and unforeseeable to the person acting?

SUMMARY OF OPINION The New York Court of Appeals reversed the trial and appellate courts' decisions and dismissed Mrs. Palsgraf's complaint. The court based its decision on its finding that the railroad's guard had not acted negligently in relation to Mrs. Palsgraf. The court explained that negligence must be considered in relation to the surrounding circumstances and factors of a given situation. In this case, the railroad guard could not have possibly known that the falling package would pose a danger to persons standing far away from it.

In order to sustain a claim of negligence, Mrs. Palsgraf needed to show that the defendant's guard had acted negligently and had exposed her to an unreasonable hazard. This claim could be sustained even if it were shown that he had done so unintentionally. However, Mrs. Palsgraf would need to show that the hazard would have been apparent to the reasonable person. Thus, she would have to argue that the guard had acted unreasonably, without the level of care that the typical reasonable person would have used in a similar situation.

Because the hazard of the exploding package was impossible for anyone, even the most reasonable and careful person to detect, the court held that the defendant could not be held liable. Even if the defendant's guard had deliberately thrown the package down to the ground, the defendant would not have been held liable because there was nothing to indicate that this activity could pose a danger to anyone, especially someone standing as far away as Mrs. Palsgraf.

RESULT The decisions of the trial and appellate courts were reversed. Mrs. Palsgraf's complaint was dismissed.

COMMENTS Note that if the railroad guard had, for instance, stumbled over a package that appeared to be a bundle of newspapers on the platform, but the package was instead a bundle of dynamite, the railroad still would not be liable for negligence to a person standing at the other end of the platform because the harm would have been similarly unforeseeable as in the above case. However, a person who was, for example, driving at a reckless speed through a crowded street would be liable for negligence regardless of the consequences because the act involves a foreseeable risk of harm to others.

The defendant is not required to compensate the plaintiff for injuries that were unforeseeable, even if the defendant's conduct was careless. Courts apply the foreseeability requirement in two different ways. Some courts limit the defendant's liability to those consequences that were foreseeable. Others look to whether the plaintiff was a foreseeable plaintiff, that is, whether the plaintiff was within the *zone of danger* caused by the defendant's careless conduct.

Injury Finally, the plaintiff must prove injury to the plaintiff or the plaintiff's property. Even if a defendant is negligent, the plaintiff cannot recover if he can show no harm suffered as a result of the defendant's conduct.

■ Defenses to Negligence

In some jurisdictions, the defendant may absolve herself of part or all of the liability for negligence by proving that the plaintiff was also negligent.

Contributory Negligence

Under the doctrine of *contributory negligence*, if the plaintiff was also negligent in any manner, he cannot recover any damages from the defendant. Thus, if a plaintiff was 5% negligent and the defendant was 95% negligent, the plaintiff's injury would go unredressed. To address this inequity, most courts have replaced the doctrine of contributory negligence with that of comparative negligence.

Comparative Negligence

Under the doctrine of *comparative negligence,* the plaintiff may recover the proportion of her loss attributable to the defendant's negligence. For example, if the plaintiff was 5% negligent and the defendant 95%, the plaintiff can recover 95% of her loss. Comparative negligence may take two forms: ordinary and pure. In an *ordinary comparative negligence* jurisdiction, the plaintiff may recover only if she is less culpable than the defendant. Thus, if the plaintiff is found 51% negligent and the defendant 49% negligent, the plaintiff cannot recover. In a *pure comparative negligence* state, the plaintiff may recover for any amount of the defendant's negligence, even if the plaintiff was the more negligent party. For example, if the plaintiff was 80% negligent and the defendant was 20% negligent, the plaintiff may recover 20% of her loss.

Assumption of Risk

The *assumption of risk* defense requires that the plaintiff: (1) knew the risk was present and understood its nature; and (2) voluntarily chose to incur the risk. It applies when the plaintiff, in advance of the defendant's wrongdoing, expressly or impliedly consented to take his chances of injury from the defendant's actions. Such consent, like consent to an intentional tort, relieves the defendant of any liability. For example, the plaintiff assumes the risk if she consents to take the chance of injury by riding in a car she knows had faulty brakes, or if she voluntarily chooses to walk where the defendant has negligently scattered broken glass.

In those jurisdictions that have adopted the comparative negligence doctrine, there is a strong trend to abolish assumption of the risk as a defense. Sometimes courts use duty to determine the viability of the defense of assumption of risk in a comparative negligence state, as in the following case.

■ **A Case in Point:**   **Summary**

Case 7.5
HARROLD v. ROLLING "J"
RANCH
California Court of Appeal
23 Cal.Rptr.2d 671,
19 Cal.App.4th 578 (1993).

FACTS   In September 1983 Charlene and John Harrold became members of a resort, and in November of that same year they took a vacation there. As part of the resort's membership package, it offered horseback riding at the nearby stables of Rolling "J" Ranch. Charlene Harrold, along with two of her friends and two young girls, decided to go horseback riding.

The five riders were escorted by two wranglers. Before starting the ride, the riders were instructed on certain basics of horseback riding, such as how to signal and command the horse. The riders were also warned not to run the horses.

About 20 to 30 minutes into the ride, one of the young girls complained she was cold. Ms. Harrold decided to give the jacket she was wearing to the young girl. Having experienced no problems with the horse during the ride, Ms. Harrold wrapped the reins around the saddle horn. She then started to remove her jacket from her shoulders.

While both of her arms were still in the sleeves and caught behind her, the horse suddenly spooked. Ms. Harrold tried, but was unable, to remain on the panicked horse. When the horse bucked for the second time, Ms. Harrold was thrown to the ground, landing on her tailbone.

Unbeknown to Ms. Harrold, on a previous ride, this same horse had spooked and thrown a rider when that rider took off and waved a hat. Rolling "J" Ranch neither warned Ms. Harrold of this prior incident nor did they retrain the horse to avoid the recurrence of a similar incident.

The trial court granted summary judgment in favor of the riding stable. Ms. Harrold appealed.

ISSUE PRESENTED   Did Rolling "J" Ranch have a duty to warn Ms. Harrold of the horse's prior "spooking" incident, or did she assume the risk of such an occurrence?

SUMMARY OF OPINION   The California Court of Appeal first had to decide whether Rolling "J" Ranch owed a duty to Ms. Harrold in the context of the horseback riding activity. If the court found that there was no duty owed, then under the California Supreme Court's decision *Knight v. Jewett*,[13] it also had to find that Ms. Harrold "assumed the risk" of the activity.

The court found that a riding stable and other similar commercial operators of recreational activities do owe a limited duty of care to their patrons. Generally this duty is to maintain the facilities in a proper and safe working condition, and to ensure that the facilities and related services do not create a greater risk of injury than that inherent in the sport or activity itself.

The court concluded that there is definitely some inherent risk of injury in horseback riding, even if the horses are walking on a guided trail. The commercial operator's duty is to not increase this inherent risk. The duty according to the court is, therefore, to supply horses which are not unduly dangerous. In addition, the operator has a duty to warn riders if a given horse has shown a predisposition to act in ways that increase the risk beyond that usually found in horseback riding.

In this case the court concluded that it was unreasonable to impose a duty on a riding stable operator to provide "ideal" horses that never bite, buck, or spook. The court stated that the stable did have a duty to warn customers if a certain horse had a dangerous propensity or predisposition. However, one prior spooking incident does not qualify as showing an overall dangerous propensity. The horse was simply acting as a horse, with the inherent risks of any horse.

RESULT   The appellate court affirmed the trial court's ruling of summary judgment in favor of the defendant riding stable. The court concluded that Ms. Harrold had assumed the risk inherent in the activity of horseback riding.

COMMENTS   The fact that Ms. Harrold was an experienced horseback rider seemed to factor into the court's decision in this case. Courts have reached similar decisions in cases in which, for example, experienced skiers assume the risk of skiing over moguls. The ski resort has a duty to maintain properly groomed trails and to operate the lifts safely, but skiers do assume a certain amount of risk in an inherently dangerous sport.

---

13. 3 Cal.4th 296, 11 Cal.Rptr.2d 2, 834 P.2d 696 (Cal. 1992).

■ Vicarious Liability and Respondeat Superior

It is possible for one person to be held vicariously liable for the negligent, or in some cases the intentional, conduct of another.

Under the doctrine of *respondeat superior*—"let the master answer"—a "master" or employer is vicariously liable for the torts of the "servant" or employee if the employee was acting within the scope of his employment. The doctrine of respondeat superior may also apply where the person is not paid but acts on behalf of another person out of friendship or loyalty.

Ethical Consideration

Underlying the doctrine of respondeat superior is the policy of allocating the risk of doing business to those who stand to profit from the undertaking. Because the employer benefits from the business, it is more appropriate for the employer to bear the risk of loss than for the innocent customer. The employer is in a better position to absorb such losses or shift them, through liability insurance or price increases, to customers and insurers and, thus, to the community in general.

An employer is liable for her own negligence in supervising or hiring an employee. She may also be vicariously liable for her employee's wrongful acts, even if she had no knowledge of them and in no way directed them, provided they were committed while the employee was acting within the scope of his employment.

Activities within the scope of employment are activities closely connected to what the employee is employed to do, or reasonably incidental to it. Courts will consider numerous factors in determining the scope of employment, such as the time, place, and manner of the act; the degree of deviation from normal methods of carrying out the employment; whether the act is generally done by such employees; or whether the employer could reasonably expect that the employee would do the act. Generally, an employee's conduct is considered within

At the Top

Some courts, like the Supreme Court of Texas in *Otis* (case 1.4), have held that under certain circumstances employers have a legal duty to protect strangers from injuries caused by their employees. *Otis* concerned an automobile accident involving an intoxicated employee sent home by his employer.

The employer may also be responsible for the safe passage home of an employee who was not intoxicated but was tired from working too many consecutive hours. In *Robertson v. LeMaster*,[14] LeMaster was an employee of the Norfolk and Western Railway Company. He was doing heavy manual labor, including lifting railroad ties and shoveling coal. After 13 hours at work he told his supervisor that he was tired and wanted to go home. The supervisor told him to continue working. This happened several times, until finally LeMaster said that he could no longer work because he was too tired. His supervisor told him that if he would not work, he should get his bucket and go

home. He had been at work a total of 27 consecutive hours. On his way home, he fell asleep at the wheel and was involved in an accident, causing injuries to Robertson. Robertson sued the railroad.

The Supreme Court of Appeals of West Virginia concluded that requiring LeMaster to work such long hours and then setting him loose upon the highway in an obviously exhausted condition was sufficient to sustain a claim against the railroad. The court regarded the issue in this case as not the railway's failure to control LeMaster while he was driving on the highway, but rather whether the railroad's conduct prior to the accident created a foreseeable risk of harm. The court concluded that the railway's actions created such a foreseeable risk.

As in *Otis* the accident occurred off-site and outside of regular working hours. But in this case the accident was caused by fatigue and not intoxication. Because it was the employer's fault that LeMaster was so tired, this decision seems even more compelling than that of *Otis* from both an ethical and legal standpoint.

14. 171 W.Va. 607, 301 S.E.2d 563 (W.Va. 1983).

the scope of her employment if it: (1) is of the nature that she was employed to perform; (2) is within the time and space limitations normally authorized by the employer; and (3) furthers, at least in part, the purpose of the employer.

In determining scope of employment, courts will consider evidence that the employer has forbidden the act, or forbidden doing it in a certain manner. However, the giving of such orders does not in itself absolve the employer. An employer cannot avoid vicarious liability simply by instructing the employee to act carefully.

> **❝**
>
> *An employer cannot avoid vicarious liability simply by instructing the employee to act carefully.*

If the wrongful act occurs while the employee has interrupted her employment to engage in an activity for her own benefit, the employer is not vicariously liable. However, it is often unclear whether the employee's act was entirely outside the employer's purpose (called a *frolic*) or only a *detour*. Jurisdictions differ in their treatment of such cases.

Some courts look solely to the employee's purpose. So long as the employee is fulfilling his own objectives, he is outside the scope of employment. However, when any part of his purpose is to accomplish his employer's objectives, then he is acting within the scope of employment.

The majority of jurisdictions focus on foreseeability. The employer is liable if the employee's deviation might reasonably be expected, even if the deviation was for her own ends.

If intentional conduct caused the plaintiff's injury, courts will look to the nexus, or connection, between the conduct and the employment. They will first examine whether the employee was acting within the scope of employment. Usually, intentional torts exceed the scope of employment. For example, a security company was found not liable when one of its security guards raped a worker in a client's building, even though the guard used his position to create the circumstances for the rape.[15] Some courts may look beyond the scope of employment to determine whether the employee exercised authority conferred by her employer. Thus, one court held a county vicariously liable for battery, among other things, when one of its law enforcement officers stopped a woman, placed her in his patrol car, drove to an isolated place, and threatened to rape and murder her.[16]

In general, an employer is liable for his employee's intentional torts if the wrongful act in any way furthered the employer's purpose, however misguided the manner of furthering that purpose. Whether an act was in the scope of employment is an issue for the jury to decide.

■ Successor Liability

Under the doctrine of *successor liability*, individuals or entities who purchase a business or real property may be held liable for the tortious acts of the previous owner. For example, if a company buys the assets of a ladder manufacturer and continues in the same line of business, the acquiring company can be held liable for defective ladders manufactured and sold before the acquisition. Successor liability may also apply in the area of toxic torts, discussed later in this chapter.

■ Liability of Multiple Defendants

The plaintiff may name numerous defendants. In some cases, the defendants may ask the court to *join,* or add, other defendants. As a result, when a court determines what liability exists, it must grapple with the problem of allocating the losses among multiple defendants.

Joint and Several Liability

Under the doctrine of *joint and several liability,* multiple defendants are jointly (that is, collectively) liable and also severally (that is, individually) liable. This means that once the court determines that multiple defendants are at fault, the plaintiff may collect the entire judgment from any one of them, regardless of the degree of that defendant's fault. Thus, it is possible that a defendant who played a minor role in causing the plaintiff's injury must pay for all the damages. This is particularly likely when only one defendant is solvent, that is, when only one has money to pay the damages.

Some states have adopted statutes to limit the doctrine of joint and several liability.

---

15. *Rabon v. Guardsmark, Inc.,* 571 F.2d 1277 (4th Cir. 1978), *cert. denied,* 439 U.S. 866, 99 S.Ct. 191 (1978).

16. *White v. County of Orange,* 166 Cal.App. 3d 566, 212 Cal.Rptr. 493 (1985).

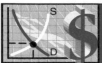

Economic Perspective
The Cost of Tort Litigation and Calls for Reform

EXHIBIT 7-a   Ratio of Tort Costs to Gross Domestic Product[a]

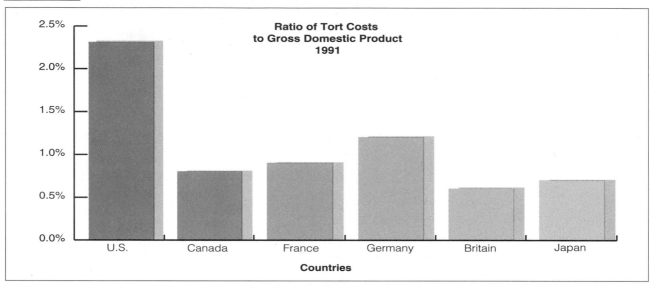

a.   Ratios in other countries were: Australia (0.9%), Belgium (1.2%), Denmark (0.4%), Italy (1.3%), Spain (1.0%), and Switzerland (1.0%).

Note: Tort costs include the costs of personal injury, property damage, product liability, and malpractice. Data from *Tort Cost Trends: An International Perspective*, distributed by Tillinghast, a Towers Perrin Company (1992). *Used by permission.*

The U.S. tort system covers all personal injury and property damage litigation other than cases concerning contracts. Examples of tort litigation are malpractice cases, product liability suits, and lawsuits resulting from automobile accidents. The United States has always devoted a much higher percentage of national output to the tort system than other nations (see Exhibit 7-a).

In the period from 1965 to 1975, tort costs in the United States averaged 1% to 1.3% of gross domestic product (GDP), while the average for 12 other industrial nations was 0.5%. By 1985 U.S. tort costs represented 1.7% of GDP. In 1986 the figure

Contribution and Indemnification

The doctrines of contribution and indemnification can mitigate the harsh effects of joint and several liability. *Contribution* distributes the loss among several defendants by requiring each to pay its proportionate share to one defendant that discharges their joint liability. *Indemnification* allows a defendant to shift its individual loss to other defendants whose relative blame is greater. These other defendants can be ordered to reimburse the one that has discharged a joint liability.

However, the right to contribution and the right to indemnification are worthless to a defendant if all the other defendants are insolvent or lack sufficient assets to contribute their share.

Economic Perspective
The Cost of Tort Litigation and Calls for Reform

reached 2.6%. By the year 2000, U.S. tort costs may reach $300 billion or 3.5% of GDP.[b]

The high percentage of GDP devoted to tort litigation is not in itself a cause for concern. For example, it is possible that the United States spends more money on its tort system than do other nations because the United States has a less comprehensive social welfare system. Injured parties who would be compensated through government programs in other nations must seek redress in the United States through the tort system.

The inefficiency of tort litigation as a substitute for government social welfare programs is, however, of concern to economists. The costs of the tort system include legal and administrative expenses as well as the payment of jury awards and settlements. Approximately 57% of tort costs are swallowed up by

administrative costs (24%), defense costs (18%), and claimants' legal costs (15%). As a result, only 43 cents of every dollar spent on the tort system reaches the injured parties the system was designed to protect. By contrast, the U.S. workers' compensation system remits 70% of its costs to its beneficiaries; the health insurance system remits 85%; and the Social Security system 99%. These more efficient systems grew at annual inflation-adjusted rates of approximately 8.5% from 1980 to 1991, compared with the 12% growth rate of the tort system. GDP increased 7.4%.

Of additional concern to economists is the fact that only half of the amount tort claimants actually receive is reimbursement for economic losses, such as property damage, medical expenses, and lost wages. The other half represents compensation for pain and suffering. Some commentators have questioned the economic validity of awarding damages for pain and suffering, and certain states have passed legislation limiting the size of such awards. If one subscribes to the view that pain and suffering awards are not economically justifiable, the efficiency of the tort system in returning costs

to injured parties drops to below 25%.

In 1994 a number of the largest companies in the U.S. joined forces to push for tort-reform legislation. Companies including General Motors, Ford Motor Co., AT&T, Pfizer, Johnson & Johnson, Exxon, and Texaco formed the Civil Justice Reform Group. Each member contributed up to $100,000 to the group's war chest. Funds, as well as research and lobbying support, are channeled to other civil-reform groups that are working to limit punitive damages, reduce exposure for large product-liability awards, deter frivolous lawsuits, and cap awards for pain and suffering. Not surprisingly, the 60,000-member Association of Trial Lawyers of America decried the formation of the group. Association President Barry J. Nace stated: "This is how corporations are trying to subvert the only means that the consumer has of getting any kind of justice."[c]

---

b. Data in this "Economic Perspective" are based in part on information contained in Gene Koretz, "Economic Trends: Litigation's Cost Is Rocketing—Its Efficiency Isn't," *Business Week*, November 6, 1989, 34; and Robert Sturgis, *Tort Cost Trends: An International Perspective*, 1992.

---

c. Richard B. Schmitt, "Powerful Companies Unite to Push for Legal Reform," *The Wall Street Journal*, March 10, 1994, B1. This description of the Civil Justice Reform Group is based on this article.

66

The right to contribution and the right to indemnification are worthless to a defendant if all the other defendants are insolvent or lack sufficient assets to contribute their share.

■ Strict Liability

Strict liability is liability without fault, that is, without either intent or negligence. Strict liability is imposed in two circumstances: (1) in product liability cases (the subject of chapter 10), and (2) in cases revolving around abnormally dangerous activities.

In Brief: Business Torts

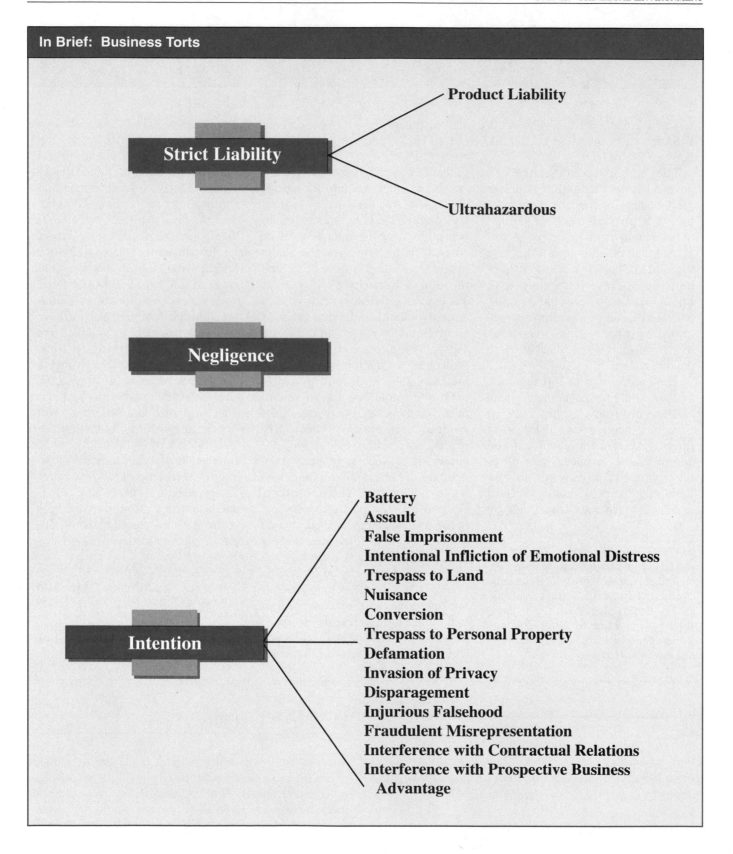

Strict Liability
- Product Liability
- Ultrahazardous

Negligence

Intention
- Battery
- Assault
- False Imprisonment
- Intentional Infliction of Emotional Distress
- Trespass to Land
- Nuisance
- Conversion
- Trespass to Personal Property
- Defamation
- Invasion of Privacy
- Disparagement
- Injurious Falsehood
- Fraudulent Misrepresentation
- Interference with Contractual Relations
- Interference with Prospective Business Advantage

Ultrahazardous Activities

If the defendant's activity is *ultrahazardous,* that is, so dangerous that no amount of care could protect others from the risk of harm, the defendant is strictly liable for any injuries that result from his act. An activity is ultrahazardous if it: (1) necessarily involves a risk of serious harm to persons or property that cannot be eliminated by the exercise of utmost care; and (2) is not a matter of common usage.

Courts have found the following activities ultrahazardous: (1) storing flammable liquids in quantity in an urban area; (2) pile driving; (3) blasting; (4) crop dusting; (5) fumigating with cyanide gas; (6) constructing of a roof so as to shed snow onto the highway; (7) emission of noxious fumes by a manufacturing plant located in a settled area; (8) locating oil wells or refineries in populated communities; and (9) test-firing solid-fuel rocket motors. However, courts have considered parachuting, drunk driving, maintaining power lines, and letting water escape from an irrigation ditch not to be ultrahazardous. Discharging fireworks is not ultrahazardous because the risk of serious harm could be eliminated by proper manufacture. In most jurisdictions, liability does not attach until the court determines that the dangerous activity is inappropriate to the particular location.

Under strict liability, once the court determines that the activity is abnormally dangerous, it is irrelevant that the defendant observed a high standard of care. For example, if the defendant's blasting injured the plaintiff, it is irrelevant that the defendant took every precaution available. Although evidence of such precautions might prevent the plaintiff from recovering under a theory of negligence, it does not affect strict liability. If a business involves an ultrahazardous activity, the managers should realize that in the event of injury they may have no defense to a claim of strict liability. The role of insurance for ultrahazardous activities is therefore particularly important.

■ Damages

Tort damages generally attempt to restore the plaintiff to the same position he was in before the tort occurred. (In contrast, contract damages try to place the plaintiff in the position he would have been in had the contract been performed. See chapter 8.) Tort damages may include punitive as well as compensatory damages.

Actual Damages

Actual damages, also known as *compensatory damages,* measure the cost to repair or replace an item, or the decrease in market value caused by the tortious conduct. Actual damages may also include compensation for medical expenses, lost wages, and pain and suffering.

Punitive Damages

Punitive damages, also known as *exemplary damages,* may be awarded to punish the defendant and deter others from engaging in similar conduct. Punitive damages are only awarded in cases of outrageous misconduct, such as that of the bank in the *Security Pacific* case discussed earlier in this chapter. The amount of punitive damages may properly be based on the defendant's wealth and, in most jurisdictions, must be proportional to the actual damages. Several states have limited punitive damage awards to situations in which the plaintiff can prove by clear and convincing evidence that the defendant was guilty of oppression, fraud, or malice.

■ Equitable Relief

If a monetary award cannot adequately compensate for the plaintiff's loss, courts may apply *equitable relief.* For example, the court may issue an *injunction,* that is, a court order, to prohibit the defendant from continuing a certain course of activity. This remedy is particularly appropriate to torts such as trespass or nuisance, when the plaintiff does not want the defendant's conduct to continue. The court may issue an injunction ordering the defendant to perform a certain activity. For example, a newspaper could be ordered to publish a retraction. In determining whether to apply injunctive relief, the courts will balance the hardship to the plaintiff against the benefit to the defendant.

■ Toxic Torts

Since the 1970s tort law has been evolving in response to sustained social and political concern over toxic substances and their potential for personal injury and environmental and property damage. These concerns are evident almost daily in the media. When courts have been asked to adjudicate the disputes arising from the widespread use of toxic substances, the traditional tort rules for determining liability, measuring damages, and allocating them among the parties have not always provided for ready answers. The resulting pressure for change has caused some courts to modify these rules and even to recognize new categories of damages. The prudent manager should keep abreast of developments in this emerging area of tort law and strive to reduce the risk of liability for toxic substances used or distributed in her enterprise. However, even the best managers cannot eliminate the risk of toxic tort liability. For example, a company may find itself liable for toxic exposures that have not yet caused any injury.

Definition

A *toxic tort* is a wrongful act that causes injury by exposure to a harmful, hazardous, or poisonous substance. Modern industrial and consumer society utilizes these substances in a variety of ways, creating countless opportunities for toxic tort claims.

Potential toxic tort defendants include those manufacturers: (1) that utilize substances that may injure an employee, a consumer, or a bystander; (2) whose processes emit hazardous by-products into the air or discharge them into a river; (3) whose waste material goes to a disposal site where it may migrate to the groundwater and contaminate nearby wells; or (4) whose product itself contains or creates substances that can injure. However, liability is not limited to manufacturers. Everyday activities of governmental agencies, distribution services, and consumers may provide a basis for toxic tort claims. Some substances once thought safe,

such as asbestos, have resulted in ruinous litigation when it was later established that they were harmful. Even financial institutions can be caught in the toxic tort net, by becoming involved in the operations of a business handling hazardous materials or by taking contaminated land as collateral.

Expensive to Defend

Toxic tort claims are among the most difficult and expensive of lawsuits to defend or prosecute. Expert witness costs alone can run into the millions for a single case. Toxic tort claims are also difficult to evaluate and, as a consequence, often cannot be insured against at a reasonable cost. Cause and effect relationships are difficult to establish because of disagreement within the medical and scientific community. When illness or injury does occur, it is often years after exposure began. Because exposures causing the injury can accumulate from a multitude of sources, including food, air, water, and skin contact, it is difficult to allocate blame among the various possible sources.

Open-ended claims for punitive damages are commonplace in toxic tort cases. Thus, plaintiffs typically allege intentional torts such as trespass, battery, intentional infliction of emotional distress, and outrageous or despicable conduct.

Strict Liability

Some courts, as in the following case, have held hazardous waste disposal to be an ultrahazardous activity and have imposed strict liability for injuries resulting from it.

■ **A Case in Point:**   **Summary**

Case 7.6
STERLING v. VELSICOL CHEMICAL CORPORATION
United States Court of Appeals for the Sixth Circuit
855 F.2d 1188 (6th Cir. 1988).

FACTS   In 1964 Velsicol Chemical Corporation bought and operated a landfill for disposal of waste from its pesticide production facility. In 1967 a government study raised concerns over potential migration of contaminated groundwater from the landfill, but residential wells were not believed to be threatened. In 1978, more complete studies disclosed that residential wells had in fact been contaminated. The plaintiffs, who represented 128 persons who consumed water from the contaminated wells, sued for damages under theories of strict liability, negligence, trespass, and nuisance.

The federal district court held that the operation of a waste burial site for toxic materials made Velsicol strictly liable for all resulting contamination under the doctrine of strict liability for ultrahazardous activities. It awarded compensatory damages of $5,273,492.50 to five representatives of the class and punitive damages of $7.5 million to the entire class. The district court concluded that punitive damages were warranted because Velsicol's actions in creating, maintaining, and operating its chemical waste burial site, and especially its failure to heed warnings from several state and federal agencies, "constituted gross, willful and wanton disregard for the health and well-being of the plaintiffs."

Velsicol appealed the lower court's decision.

ISSUE PRESENTED   Can a company that owns a landfill used for burial of waste from its pesticide production facility be held strictly liable to area residents whose well water was contaminated?

SUMMARY OF OPINION   The U.S. Court of Appeals upheld the finding of liability by the lower court but ordered a recalculation of damages to limit the compensatory damages to injury that could be proved by medical evidence. It ordered that the punitive damages award be reduced by the amount (which was unstated) attributable to the defendant's conduct at trial that the trial court had considered outrageous. (Misconduct during the trial is not subject to punitive damages, though it may be punished in other ways.)

RESULT   The Court of Appeals found Velsicol strictly liable to area residents whose well water was contaminated. Velsicol was ordered to pay damages according to the court's ruling.

COMMENT   Claimants have asked courts to extend this type of strict liability to more commonplace businesses, such as a manufacturer of consumer goods that sends its waste containing some hazardous material to the local dump. The strict liability doctrine, if applied, would impose liability even if the manufacturer had no idea the waste was hazardous at the time.

New Theories of Damages

Under traditional tort principles, toxic tort plaintiffs who prove exposure to a toxic substance and a defendant's liability for that exposure may still not receive a damage award because the rules require proof of an actual injury. The plaintiffs may be at risk of developing cancer or some other disease in the future, but tort law generally has not allowed recovery for risk of future disease unless some precursor symptom is present, or unless the plaintiff proves he is more likely than not to get the disease. In the face of these limitations on damages, courts are being asked to allow awards for emotional distress in the absence of either physical symptoms or an intentional tort.

In *Sterling v. Velsicol Chemical Corporation* (case 7.6),[17] the trial judge who found Velsicol strictly liable also awarded compensatory damages to individuals who had consumed contaminated well water. The trial court awarded damages for physical symptoms caused by drinking the well water and also gave awards for

increased risk of cancer, fear of increased risk of cancer, impairment of the immune system, and for a psychological ailment known as posttraumatic stress disorder. The trial judge also awarded damages for impairment of the residents' quality of life, under the traditional tort of nuisance, and punitive damages.

Applying Tennessee law, the Sixth Circuit on appeal disallowed the award for increased risk of cancer, because no expert had testified that there was more than a 50% chance the plaintiffs would develop cancer. The awards for impairment of the immune system and for posttraumatic stress disorder were also thrown out, on the ground that the medical evidence was insufficient. The award for fear of increased risk of cancer was allowed, but was reduced to a fixed annual sum multiplied by the number of years of exposure. This limited measure of damages for fear of future cancer is unusual and may not be applied in other states.

Another novel remedy that is being urged is the award of damages to cover the future cost of medical monitoring in order to detect the disease at the onset, when treatment may be more effective.

---

17. 855 F.2d 1188 (6th Cir. 1988).

The Responsible Manager

Reducing Tort Risks

Managers should implement ongoing programs of education and monitoring to reduce the risks of tort liability. Because torts can be committed in numerous ways, the programs should cover all possible sources of liability. For example, the management of a company that does not respond satisfactorily to an allegation of sexual harassment may be liable for intentional infliction of emotional distress. Statements made by representatives of a company about some individual or product can constitute defamation.

In addition to preventing intentional torts such as these, managers should work to prevent their employees from committing acts of negligence, which can lead to large damage awards against the company. Any tort prevention program must recognize that under the principle of respondeat superior, employers will be held liable for any torts their employees commit in the scope of their employment. It is crucial, therefore, to define the scope of employment clearly.

Managers should use care to avoid committing torts that are related to contractual relations and competition with other firms. For example, a company may be held liable for interference with contractual relations if a court finds that the company intentionally tried to induce a party to breach a contract. Also, although competition itself is permissible, intentionally seeking to sabotage the efforts of another firm is not. Managers may need to consult counsel when they are unsure whether their activity has crossed the line from permissible competition to tortious interference with a prospective business advantage.

In the toxic torts area, managers should adopt a long-term policy to protect employees, customers, and the environment from excess toxic exposure. They should identify any hazardous toxic substances used in their business activities or products, or released into the environment. Where appropriate, managers should test and monitor to determine levels of exposure. Often, it is necessary to obtain an expert assessment of the hazards of toxicity of these substances.

Managers should develop a plan to control and reduce toxic exposure. This can be done by reducing the quantity of toxic substances used, by recycling, by seeking less toxic alternatives, and by educating and training employees. Managers should implement a plan by assigning responsibilities, allocating resources, and auditing compliance. The waste management plan should include criteria for choosing third-party contractors. Insurance should be obtained, if available, and coverage should be reviewed periodically. Management should adopt a contingency plan for responding to toxic accidents and develop a public relations plan both for routine (that is, safe) use of toxic substances and for possible toxic accidents.

A program of overall risk management and reduction is essential to limit the potential of tort liability. It is often desirable to designate one person to be in charge of risk management. That person would keep track of all claims and determine what areas of the business merit special attention. The head of risk management should be free to report incidents and problems to the chief executive officer and the board of directors, in much the same way as an internal auditor reports directly to the independent directors on the audit committee. This enhances independence and reduces the fear of reprisals if the risk manager blows the whistle on high-ranking managers.

Inside Story

EMF Litigation

A new area of tort litigation is emerging that may prove to be more widespread and costly than the asbestos litigation that consumed millions of dollars in the 1980s. The area is that of electromagnetic fields, commonly known as EMFs.

EMFs are found virtually everywhere in modern life, from microwave ovens to TVs, electric blankets, cellular phones, computers, and the power lines that run above houses. Although scientists are certain that EMFs exist and can measure their levels to a high degree of

Inside Story, continued

accuracy, no one really knows the effects of EMF exposure. Some studies link it to cancer, particularly cancer in children. Other studies find that there is no link at all. Although there has been a large number of studies, the results have been contradictory and inconclusive.

The lack of conclusive evidence has not stopped an emergence of EMF litigation. In *Zuidema v. San Diego Gas & Electric* a family sued its local utilities company alleging that their daughter's rare kidney cancer was caused by her exposure to EMFs from the power lines. The family lost its claim, but the case is still a landmark one because it is the first EMF personal injury lawsuit to be decided by a jury.[18]

The loss in the *Zuidema* case has not deterred other plaintiffs. At least nine other EMF cases were pending in 1994. Similar to asbestos litigation, cases are being brought while the scientific debate continues, but "[p]resently, more studies exist that appear to link EMF exposure to an increased risk of cancer than existed linking asbestos exposure to an increased risk of cancer at a similar embryonic stage of asbestos litigation."[19] Because EMFs are virtually everywhere, almost anyone of any class or age could be a plaintiff, as opposed to the shipyard workers, insulation installers, and others who were typically exposed to asbestos in World War II.

Litigants sue under a number of theories including negligence and failure to warn. The greatest bar to recovery thus far has been the inability to prove a strong enough linkage between EMFs and cancer in order to show causation.

In July 1994 Washington state's Department of Labor and Industries ruled that a 50-year-old aluminum worker was entitled to worker's compensation for cancer he claimed was caused by exposure to EMF on the job. According to attorneys in the case, this is the first time a government body has acknowledged such a link.[20] An official of the state agency indicated that under its guidelines, the agency had to accept the claim, because the worker's physician stated it was "more probable than not" that his cancer was caused by EMF exposure at the workplace.[21]

Another basis of litigation has been the loss of property value. Using this ground it is unnecessary to prove actual EMF danger; one only has to prove that public fear of EMF led to a loss of one's property value. This area of EMF litigation is probably the one utilities companies have to fear the most in the immediate future. For example, in *San Diego Gas & Electric v. Daley*,[22] the California Court of Appeal held that fear of EMF could lead to recovery of damages for diminution of property value. In that case, the plaintiff was awarded more than $2 million in damages and fees.

However the scientific debate comes out, the battle in the courtroom one is sure to be interesting . . . and costly.

---

18. Mary Lou Pickel, "Tower of Power," *Los Angeles Times*, December 16, 1993, BB1. See also "Power Struggles," 13 *California Lawyer* 20 (June 1993).
19. Roy W. Kreiger, "On the Line," 80 *ABA Journal* 40, 44 (January 1994).

20. Bill Richards, "Cancer Link to Electromagnetic Fields Recognized in Washington State Ruling," *The Wall Street Journal*, July 14, 1994, B6.
21. *Ibid.*
22. 205 Cal.App.3d 1334, 253 Cal.Rptr.144 (1988).

Key Words and Phrases

Questions and Case Problems

1. Francoise de Clercq is at the beach swimming. Somebody is drowning. She sees a rope next to her. She decides not to help the person, and the person drowns. Can the person's family successfully sue her? What if somebody else wanted to save the person, but de Clercq hid the rope and the swimmer drowned? What if de Clercq is the swimmer's mother? Lawyer? Business competitor? What if, instead, Tim Garcia saw a baby fall into a bathtub while the baby's parents were away. If Garcia does not help the baby and the baby drowns, is he liable?

2. Linda Stein owned Clowntown USA, a successful amusement park. The main attraction of the amusement park was a very steep and fast roller coaster. Although Stein maintained the roller coaster meticulously, she knew that it was unsafe for riders under four feet tall. Accordingly, she instructed her employee, Oliver Operator, not to permit anyone under four feet tall to get on the roller coaster. On a particularly busy day in June, Operator forgot his instructions and allowed several children below four feet tall to ride on the roller coaster. The children were thrown from the ride and suffered serious bodily injury.

(a) Under what doctrine could the children's parents sue Stein for damages? What would Stein's lawyer assert as a defense? Who would be likely to prevail?

(b) Would your answer change if Stein had merely told Operator to be careful in operating the roller coaster, without specifically telling him not to permit anyone under four feet tall to ride it?

(c) What additional defense could Stein assert if she could prove that the children's parents had read and understood a conspicuous sign posted at the roller coaster ticket booth stating that the ride was dangerous for those under four feet tall and that anyone under that height rode at their own risk?

3. Joe and Alice Washington, and their baby, Pearl, live in a house next to a closed city dump. Since they moved in five years ago the only source of water for drinking, cooking, and bathing has been a well under the house. Last month Joe discovered that the well was contaminated by small amounts of waste solvents leaking from the dump. Joe and Alice show no symptoms, but worry that the contamination will eventually make them sick. Baby Pearl has a condition that may become leukemia, and Joe and Alice are concerned that future children may be harmed as well. As a result of stress caused by worrying about the effects of the contamination on themselves and their family, Joe and Alice begin to smoke, and do so even while Alice is nursing Pearl.

Joe and Alice learn that 5% of the solvents were sent to the dump by Big Corporation, and 10% of the solvents came to the dump from Small Company. Big has $10 million in insurance. Last year Big shut down the local plant, laying off 2,000 employees. Small dissolved last year. Its former owner, Bill Small, is worth $3 million. The other 85% of the solvents come from thousands of separate households and small businesses throughout the city, all of which pay the city trash collection fees.

(a) What torts can Joe and Alice claim against the city? Big Corporation? Small Company? Bill Small? The local dry cleaner?

(b) If the city condemns the home, paying full market value, what types of damages can Joe and Alice still claim?

(c) What torts can Pearl claim if she develops leukemia and lung cancer 30 years later? Against whom?

4. Assume the facts in question 3. Joe and Alice's lawyer discovers that ten years ago Big Corporation and Small Company received copies of federal regulations classifying the solvent wastes as hazardous. No one at Small Company bothered to read the regulations, and the company continued to dispose of the solvents at the city dump. However, Big Corporation's environmental engineer issued orders that the solvents be sent to a hazardous waste site instead of the city dump. However, no one was assigned to police the order, and about once a month some solvent went to the city dump by mistake. The environmental engineer reissued the orders twice after hearing of the mistakes, but occasional violations continued until the plant closed.

(a) Can Joe and his family recover punitive damages against Big Corporation? Small Company? Bill Small?

(b) What additional facts would improve the chances of securing a large punitive damages award?

5. A patient with a large tumor consented to have a particular physician remove it. The patient later discovered that the physician was HIV-infected. Can that patient recover for damages of emotional distress based on her fear that she may have contracted AIDS from her physician, even if she did not actually contract the disease? Does it matter if the patient discussed with her physician her fear of contracting AIDS during surgery, and if she asked him about his health? Does it matter how low the risk of transmission in this manner is? [*Kerins v. Hartley,* 17 Cal.App. 4th 713, 17 Cal.App. 4th 1699A, 21 Cal.Rptr.2d 621 (1993), *review granted and opinion superseded by* 24 Cal.Rptr.2d 236, 860 P.2d 1182 (Cal. 1993)]

6. A water skier was skiing barefoot and backward in a channel of the Sacramento River Delta. He was severely injured when the back of his head struck a tree limb that extended over the channel from one of the riverbanks. The water skier sued his friend who was operating the boat that towed him. The skier's theory was that the boat operator drove negligently and was too close to the riverbank. Should the water skier be able to recover damages in such an accident? Did he assume the risk inherent in water skiing? Does it matter that the driver of the boat was not a professional boat operator, but just a friend and co-participant in the activity? [*Ford v. Gouin,* 3 Cal.4th 339, 11 Cal.Rptr.2d 30, 834 P.2d 724 (Cal. 1992)]

7. During one of his typical end-of-the-show presentations on "60 Minutes," Andy Rooney discussed the many products that manufacturers send to him in the mail. While Rooney was lamenting the vast amount of junk mail he receives, he mentioned "Rain-X," a product that was sent to Rooney by its inventor and manufacturer. The product was sent after Rooney had complained in an earlier episode that he thought cars needed larger windshield wipers. Rooney then, on the air, said that he had tried the sample of "Rain-X" on his windshield and that it didn't work. Should the inventor/manufacturer be able to sue Andy Rooney for business disparagement? How about defamation? [*Unelko Corp. v. Rooney,* 912 F.2d 1049 (9th Cir. 1990), *cert. denied,* 499 U.S. 961, 111 S.Ct. 1586 (1991)]

8. A K-Mart shopper, Burrow, wanted to purchase two lamps. A salesperson placed the two lamps into two cardboard boxes that were not the original cartons. The salesperson then carried the boxes to the cashier and told the cashier the price of the lamps. The cashier rang up the purchase and gave Burrow a receipt. Burrow placed the receipt in her purse and waited for her daughters to pay for their purchases before leaving the store. When she was leaving the store an employee approached her and insisted on searching her boxes. According to Burrow, the employee then snatched the boxes from her hands and, after searching the boxes, told her she could go. A jury awarded Burrow $2,000 based on her false imprisonment claim. Should the jury award stand? [*Burrow v. K-Mart Corp.,* 166 Ga.App. 284, 304 S.E.2d 460 (1983)]

9. One manufacturer of firearms equipment wrote a booklet to persuade potential customers to buy its products as opposed to those of an upstart competitor whose owner was a former employee of the first manufacturer. In a second version of the booklet it was asserted that the upstart competitor had inferior equipment and that the upstart's owner had organized his company while still working for the first manufacturer. The manufacturer continued the attacks, although toned down, in a third booklet, and its president made other attacking statements in a book he published. A jury awarded $1 million in damages to the upstart competitor based on its disparagement claim. Should the jury award stand even if there was no proof of damages in the form of monetary loss directly attributable to the defendant's false statements? What if the business simply failed to grow at the expected rate, as opposed to having lost money, and it is believed that failure is due to the defendant's attacks? [*Advanced Training Systems, Inc. v. Caswell Equipment Co., Inc.,* 352 N.W.2d 1 (Minn. 1984)]

10. Chris Beck, an employee of Henrietta Marlow, attended a Christmas party that Marlow sponsored for her employees. The party was held on Marlow's business premises. Nobody was required to attend the party, which started late in the afternoon and continued into the early evening. Beck was served many drinks by Marlow's secretary and became intoxicated. One hour later Beck left the party, ran a red traffic light, and struck another car. The driver of the other car, who was speeding, was killed in the accident. The other car had a broken headlight.

Whom can the wife of the other car's driver sue? Under what theory? What should the attorney for Beck try to show the jury? What should the attorney for Marlow try to prove to the jury?

Chapter 8

CONTRACTS

■ Introduction

Why Contract Law Is Important

Contract law defines which agreements will be enforced by the courts and which will not. Contracts are central to the conduct of business both in the United States and internationally. Without contract law, a seller could not ship goods to a buyer knowing that he has an enforceable right to be paid for the goods. Similarly, a buyer could not order goods knowing that the seller must deliver or pay damages for nondelivery. Leases of real property, loan agreements, employment agreements, settlement agreements, and joint venture agreements are all based on the parties' expectation that the promises made will be enforceable.

Contract law comes from statutes, case law, and tradition. It varies slightly from state to state. Many states follow the Restatement (Second) of the Law of Contracts, which is the basis for much of the discussion in this chapter. Common-law contracts include contracts involving services and real property. Commercial transactions involving the sale of goods, that is, movable personal property, are governed by article 2 of the Uniform Commercial Code (UCC), which has been adopted, with variations, in every state. Article 2 is discussed in more detail in chapter 9.

Chapter Summary

This chapter discusses the elements necessary for a valid contract: offer, acceptance, and consideration. It addresses the issues of misunderstanding or mistake about the meaning of a contract, the requirements that some contracts be in writing, and the rules for looking beyond the written terms of an agreement to discern the parties' intentions. Fraud and duress are discussed, as well as the duty of good faith and fair dealing, the right to rely on a noncontractual promise in certain situations, and the enforceability of agreements to negotiate. The chapter

238

discusses damages for breach of contract. It ends with a look at the conflicts that may arise between a party's contractual obligations and her obligations to others, and liability for interference with a contract.

Contract Formation

A contract is a legally enforceable promise. If the promise is broken, the person to whom the promise was made—the *promisee*—has certain legal rights against the person who made the promise, the *promisor*. If the promisor fails to carry out his promise, the promisee may be able to recover money damages, or she may be able to get an injunction or a court order forcing the promisor to perform the promise. The remedies for breach of contract are discussed later in this chapter.

Formulation of a contract requires offer, acceptance, and consideration. Each is discussed below.

Offer and Acceptance

An *offer* is a manifestation of willingness to enter into a bargain that justifies another person in understanding that his assent to that bargain is invited and will conclude it. *Acceptance* is a response by the person receiving the offer that indicates willingness to enter into the agreement proposed in the offer. A typical example of offer and acceptance is: Nanci Anthony says to Jim Levy, "I'll give you $100 for your new computer software package," and Levy says "OK." A contract has been made. Anthony is now legally obliged to give Levy the money, and Levy is obliged to give Anthony the software.

Offer and acceptance can be verbal, written, or implied by conduct. For example, a manager offers a consultant $5,000 to develop a business plan for her company. The consultant begins interviewing key executives and drafting a business plan. By starting work on the business plan, he has accepted the offer. The acceptance is implied by his action, even though he did not actually say "I accept your offer."

The person making the offer is the *offeror*. The person to whom the offer is made is the *offeree*. The offeror can revoke the offer—that is, cancel it—at any time before the offeree accepts. However, once the offeree has accepted, verbally or by conduct, the offeror cannot take the offer back.

An offer is effective upon receipt. The offeror can specify authorized and unauthorized means of accep-

tance. For example, the offeror could specify that the offer can be accepted only by a facsimile to a stated facsimile number and that the acceptance is not effective until actually received. In the absence of such a provision, acceptance is effective upon dispatch. Thus, if a person drops a letter accepting an offer in the mailbox, a contract is formed when the letter is put in the mailbox, and the offeror cannot thereafter revoke the offer.

Most advertisements are not offers because they are not specific enough. Although an advertisement that offers specified goods or services at a specific price, leaving nothing to be negotiated, can be an offer that needs only acceptance to create a contract, courts rarely consider an advertisement specific enough to be an offer.

Option Contracts

Sometimes an offeror agrees to hold an offer open for a certain amount of time in exchange for some consideration from the other party. Such an agreement is known as an *option contract*. Under such an agreement, the offeror cannot revoke the offer until the time has expired for acceptance.

Under the UCC, a merchant's firm offer, in writing, to buy or sell goods is equivalent to an option contract and is enforceable even if the other party gave no consideration for the firm offer. The merchant cannot revoke until the time has elapsed; if no time is stated, the offer must be held open for a reasonable amount of time, which cannot exceed three months.

Termination of Offer

An offer terminates when the time of acceptance has elapsed, or if the offeror dies or becomes incapacitated. Death or incapacity of the offeree can also terminate the offer if the offer is intended only for the offeree. An offer is also terminated when it is rejected by the offeree, or when the offeree makes a counteroffer.

Meeting of the Minds

The traditional concept of contract formation requires a "meeting of the minds": what the offeree accepts must be a mirror image of what the offeror has offered. For example, Gaye Hale offers to rent to Victor Lee 6,000 square feet of office space in New York City for $2 per square foot. Lee accepts the offer of office space and says he wants ten free underground parking spaces included as well. Under traditional contract law there is no meeting of the minds. Lee's request for the parking spaces is considered a counteroffer rather than an acceptance. Accordingly, there is no contract.

Counteroffer

A *counteroffer* is a new offer by the offeree. By modifying the terms of the original offer, the offeree has rejected it and made a counterproposal instead. If the original offeror accepts the counteroffer, a contract is formed. If not, there is no contract. Once a counteroffer has been made, the original offer is terminated unless the offeror agrees to keep the offer open under an option contract. Without such an agreement, the original offeree cannot revive the original offer by accepting it after the offeror has rejected the counteroffer.

If an offeree expressly withholds a decision on the offer, and merely inquires into terms, the original offer is still open. For example, Cassandra Heartsong offers a managerial position at $105,000 per year to Misha Samms, and Samms responds, "Does that include a five-week paid vacation?" This is an inquiry into terms, as distinguished from a counteroffer, and does not terminate the original offer.

Intent to Be Bound

The difficulty with this narrow concept of contract formation is that it does not recognize the realities of how businesses enter into agreements. A joint venture agreement between contractors to build a nuclear power plant, for example, can involve months of negotiations and a whole series of letters, memorandums, and draft contracts.

Rarely will there be a single piece of paper that both parties sign to make a contract. As a result, it is sometimes difficult to determine exactly at what point the parties have entered into a valid legally binding contract.

At some point in negotiations the parties will usually manifest an intention, either orally or in writing, to enter into a contract. Such an *intent to be bound* can create an enforceable contract. The courts will look at the specific facts of each case when determining whether the parties regarded themselves as having completed a bargain.

Expression of Intent   Generally a court will look not to the parties' secret intentions but rather to their outward expressions of intent. Intention is determined objectively by observable behavior, not subjectively by what the party says she was thinking. This objective standard of contract interpretation makes it possible to plan one's business based on reasonable expectations of what the other party's words mean.

Definiteness   One indication of intent to be bound is the definiteness of the agreement. If a number of essential terms are left open, such as price, subject matter, duration of the contract, and manner of payment, there is no contract. However, courts are showing an increasing willingness to fill in missing terms of a contract, including price, if they are convinced that the parties intended to bind themselves. The UCC supplies specific rules for filling in a variety of terms in contracts for the sale of goods, as discussed in chapter 9.

A preliminary agreement that is subject to approval by a higher authority, such as the board of directors, may not be considered an expression of intent to be bound. This was a key issue in the following case.

■ **A Case in Point:**   **Summary**

Case 8.1
APOTHEKERNES
LABORATORIUM FOR
SPECIALPRAEPARATER
v.
IMC CHEMICAL GROUP, INC.
United States Court of Appeals
for the Seventh Circuit
873 F.2d 155 (7th Cir. 1989).

FACTS   Apothekernes negotiated to buy a biochemical division of IMC and had been assured by the person negotiating for IMC that the IMC board of directors would approve the purchase contract. All of the substantial terms of the purchase agreement were agreed upon and a letter of intent was signed. The letter of intent stipulated that the terms were "subject to our concluding an Agreement of Sale which shall be acceptable to the Boards of Directors of our respective corporations, whose discretion shall in no way be limited by this letter." The IMC board rejected the deal and Apothekernes sued on two grounds. The first was that when the negotiators had agreed to all of the terms, a binding contract had been formed.

Second, the letter of intent imposed a duty to negotiate in good faith which was violated when the IMC board rejected the deal.

ISSUE PRESENTED   Does rejection of a letter of intent by the board of directors constitute a breach of contract or a breach of the duty to negotiate in good faith when the negotiators had a meeting of the minds but the letter of intent explicitly provided that the board of directors had unlimited discretion to accept or reject the letter of intent?

SUMMARY OF OPINION   The U.S. Court of Appeals held that there was no contract. Even though there was a meeting of the minds, the fact that the letter of intent explicitly stated that the deal was subject to board approval should have put the buyer "on notice" that any promises of rubber-stamp board approval were not to be taken seriously. The court recognized IMC's duty to negotiate in good faith, but held that good faith does not guarantee that such negotiations would result in a binding contract.

RESULT   The IMC board had the right to reject the letter of intent negotiated by a subordinate.

COMMENTS   This is one of the first cases to recognize that there can be an enforceable agreement to negotiate in good faith. The meaning of good faith is discussed later in this chapter.

Battle of the Forms

The rule that there is no contract until there is a meeting of the minds is difficult to apply to standardized or form contracts. For example, ABC Company sends a purchase order to XYZ Company. The purchase order is a preprinted form with the terms of the agreement printed on the back, in very small type. XYZ sends back a sales agreement on its own preprinted form with different terms printed on the back. Under traditional contract law, the second form is a counteroffer, and there is no contract unless ABC accepts the goods. If ABC accepts the goods, it accepts them on the terms of the second form, that is, on the terms set forth in XYZ's sales agreement.

The UCC, which applies only to sales of goods, offers two alternatives to the traditional rule. Depending upon the circumstances, the terms agreed to will be either: (1) the areas of agreement between the two forms, plus standard terms supplied by the UCC; or (2) the first form plus any nonessential changes in the second form. This is discussed more fully in chapter 9.

Many contracts are a mixture of individually negotiated terms and standard, preprinted terms. Where there is a conflict, the negotiated term will prevail. For example, in *Steiner v. Mobil Oil Corp.*,[1] Steiner, a gas station owner,

told Mobil Oil Corporation that he only wanted a Mobil franchise if Mobil would guarantee a specific gas discount for the next ten years. Steiner's condition was stated verbally in the negotiations and again in a letter to Mobil. Mobil sent back a thick packet of documents in which was buried a form limiting the discount to the first year of the franchise. The station owner stowed the packet in a drawer without reading all of the forms. A year later, when Mobil discontinued the discount, the station owner sued. The California Supreme Court held that since Mobil had verbally agreed to the discount term, it was obligated to notify the station owner (with a cover letter, for example) of any change in the final printed documents. Although this case should not be read as an excuse for not reading documents before signing them, the court was probably influenced by the fact that a gas station owner was fighting a major corporation like Mobil, and that the disputed form was buried in a thick packet of documents.

Capacity

To enter a contract, a party must have *capacity*, that is, the requisite presence of mind for a meeting of the minds. Generally, a minor or an insane person does not have capacity to enter into a contract that is binding on the incapacitated person. However, if a person without capacity, such as a minor, chooses to enforce the contract

---

1. 20 Cal.3d 90, 141 Cal. Rptr. 157, 569 P.2d 751 (Cal. 1977).

against a party with capacity, she may do so. In effect, the law gives the person without capacity an option: Enforce the contract if it is favorable; avoid the contract if it is not. Thus, a contract with a person lacking capacity is not void but rather voidable by the person lacking capacity. A minor or other person who lacks capacity is often appointed a guardian or conservator who can enter into contracts on his behalf; such contracts are enforceable against both the otherwise incapacitated party and the other party.

Third-Party Beneficiary

A person who is not a party to a contract can sometimes enforce the contract between the contracting parties. For example, Sheila Tanner agrees to sell to Fernando Acosta a piece of real property in exchange for a $100,000 payment by Acosta to Jack Reynolds. Acosta is the promisor, Tanner is the promisee, and Reynolds is the *third-party beneficiary* or intended beneficiary. A person is not a third-party beneficiary with legal rights to enforce the contract unless the contracting parties intended to benefit that party.

Creditor Beneficiary   If the promisee entered into the contract in order to discharge a duty she owed the third party, then the third party is a *creditor beneficiary* and has the right to enforce the contract between the promisor and promisee. However, the third party must prove that the promisee intended the contract to satisfy her obligation to him. For example, if Tanner owed Reynolds $100,000, and agreed to sell the land to Acosta in order to pay off that debt, Reynolds has enforceable rights under the contract. Reynolds can sue Acosta directly to compel performance. If the contract is not carried out, Reynolds also has the option of suing Tanner for the $100,000 she owes him.

Donee Beneficiary   A *donee beneficiary* is created when the promisee does not owe an obligation to the third party, but rather wishes to confer a gift. For example, if Tanner agreed to sell her property to Acosta in order to make a $100,000 gift to Reynolds, Reynolds would be a donee beneficiary and could enforce the contract in most jurisdictions, but only against Acosta. Some jurisdictions, such as New York, require a family relationship between the donee beneficiary and the promisee.

■ Consideration

A promise does not always constitute a valid contract. Each side must provide something of value. The thing of value, known as *consideration*, can be money, an object, a promise, a service, or a giving up of the right to do something. An act or promise will constitute consideration if it precludes a person from doing something he was otherwise legally entitled to do or if it requires a person to do something she was otherwise not legally required to do. A promise to take property off the market for 30 days constitutes consideration. So does a promise to do a mid-year audit. A promise to do something illegal, such as payment for sexual favors in states where prostitution is illegal, is not valid consideration; as a result, the promise is unenforceable.

Peppercorn Theory

Generally, courts will not look at the value of the consideration. Even nominal or token consideration can be adequate. All that is necessary is that something be provided on each side, thus the adage that even a peppercorn is sufficient consideration for a contract.

Any promised benefit to which the promisor is not otherwise entitled is adequate consideration. Similarly, any legal detriment that the promisee agrees to sustain is good consideration so long as the promisee was not already legally bound to suffer the detriment. For example, a promise to quit smoking in the workplace may or may not be a consideration, depending on whether it is legal in the relevant locale to smoke in the workplace. If it is legal, the promise constitutes consideration. If it is illegal, the promise is worthless and does not constitute consideration.

Bilateral and Unilateral Contracts

Consideration can be either a promise to do a certain act or the performance of the act itself.

A *bilateral contract* is a promise given in exchange for another promise. One party agrees to do one thing and the other party agrees to do something in return. For example, Ibrahim Todd promises to give Maria Holbrook $10 if Holbrook promises to drive Todd to business school. The exchange of promises represents consideration and makes the promises binding.

A *unilateral contract* is a promise given in exchange for an act. A unilateral contract is accepted by performing the specified act. For example, Todd promises to give Holbrook $10 if Holbrook drives him to business school. Holbrook can only accept the contract by driving Ibrahim to business school.

Mutuality of Obligation

The corollary of consideration is the concept of *mutuality of obligation*. Unless both parties are obligated to perform their side of the bargain, neither will be. Mutuality of obligation only applies to bilateral contracts. In the case of a unilateral contract, the promisor becomes bound only after the promisee has performed the required act. Thus, in the example above, once Holbrook has driven Todd to school, Todd has an obligation to pay her $10.

Another way to look at mutuality of obligation is to say that to be enforceable, a bilateral contract must limit the behavior of both parties in some fashion. If one party has full freedom of action, there is no contract.

Illusory Promise

Although a peppercorn can be sufficient consideration, a promise that does not in fact confer any benefit on the promisor or subject the promisee to any detriment is an *illusory promise*. Because there is no mutuality of obligation in such a case, the resulting agreement is unenforceable. The following case provides an example of an illusory promise.

■ A Case in Point: Summary

Case 8.2
WICKHAM & BURTON COAL CO. v. FARMERS' LUMBER CO.
Supreme Court of Iowa
189 Iowa 1183, 179 N.W. 417
(Iowa 1920).

FACTS   Wickham & Burton Coal Co. had agreed to sell coal to Farmers' Lumber Co. for a certain price. Under the agreement, Wickham was to sell all of the coal Farmers' Lumber wanted to purchase from them. Thus, Wickham was bound to fill every order from Farmers' Lumber, but Farmers' Lumber was not bound at all.

ISSUE PRESENTED   Is a promise to buy as much coal as you want to purchase from a particular vendor an enforceable promise?

SUMMARY OF OPINION   The Iowa Supreme Court held that Farmers' Lumber's promise to purchase only what it wanted to purchase, which could be nothing at all, was illusory. Because there was no consideration flowing from Farmers' Lumber to Wickham, there was no contract.

RESULT   There was no enforceable contract between Wickham and Farmers' Lumber.

COMMENTS   How could Wickham have avoided the finding of an illusory contract? One way would be to have required Farmers' Lumber to purchase all the coal it needed from Wickham. Such an agreement is called a *requirements contract*. If the parties had entered into such a contract, the promise to buy coal would not have been found to be illusory because Farmers' Lumber would have agreed to forego buying any coal from any seller but Wickham.

Requirements and Output Contracts

In a *requirements contract*, the buyer agrees to buy all its requirements of a specified commodity, such as steel, from the seller, and the seller agrees to meet those requirements. The parties do not know how much steel the buyer will actually need, but whatever that amount is, the buyer will buy it all from that seller. The buyer is constrained from buying steel from another supplier.

In an *output contract*, the buyer promises to buy all of the output that the seller produces. Again, the parties do not how know many units that will be, but the seller must sell all its output to that buyer. The seller cannot sell any of its product to another buyer.

These types of contracts are not enforceable if the requirement or output is unreasonable or out of proportion to prior requirements or outputs. For example, the buyer cannot take advantage of the seller by increasing his requirement to triple the usual amount. The seller will not be required to sell anything over the reasonable or usual amount required by the buyer.

Conditional Promise

Conditional promises often look illusory, but they are enforceable as long as the promisor is bound by conditions beyond her control. For example, Xerox promises to hire Diane Hall as an inventor on condition that the Patent and Trademark Office issues a patent on her new photocopying process. Although the likelihood of obtaining a patent may be remote, the decision is out of the parties' hands. If the patent is issued, there will be a binding contract, and Xerox will be obligated to hire the inventor. The contract is valid at the time it is agreed, but performance is not required until the condition is satisfied.

If the condition is not satisfied, either party can cancel the contract. For example, a partner might agree to sell his share of the partnership for ten times the partnership's earnings on condition that an audit of the partnership's books shows earnings of at least $5 million. The partner will not be obligated to sell his share if the earnings of the partnership are less than $5 million.

There are three types of conditions. A *condition precedent* is a condition that must be satisfied before there is even a binding contract. A *condition concurrent* is satisfied at the same time the binding contract is formed. A *condition subsequent*, as in the Hall-Xerox example, must be satisfied before performance is required. A binding contract exists prior to satisfaction of a condition subsequent but performance is not required unless and until the condition is satisfied.

■ Misunderstanding and Mistake

Misunderstandings may arise from ambiguous language in the contract, or from a mistake as to the facts.

Ambiguity

If the terms of a contract are subject to differing interpretations, the following rule applies. The party that would be adversely affected by a particular interpretation can void, or undo, a contract when: (1) both interpretations are reasonable, and (2) the parties either both knew or both did not know of the different interpretations. If only one party knew or had reason to know of the other's interpretation, the court will find for the party who did not know or did not have reason to know of the difference.

Mistake of Fact

Like misunderstanding due to ambiguity, a mistake of fact can make a contract *voidable,* that is, subject to being undone by one or more parties. A court's willingness to undo a contract based upon a mistaken assumption of fact depends heavily on the particular circumstances. The court will look at three factors to determine if a mistake has been made: (1) the substantiality of the mistake; (2) whether the risks were allocated; and (3) timing.

Substantiality of the Mistake   A court is more likely to void the contract when the mistake has a material effect on one of the parties. For example, in *Raffles v. Wichelhaus,* [2] two parties had signed a contract in which Wichelhaus agreed to buy 125 bales of cotton to be brought by Raffles from India on a ship named *Peerless.* There were, however, two ships named *Peerless,* both sailing out of Bombay during the same year. Raffles meant the *Peerless* that was sailing in December, Wichelhaus meant the *Peerless* that was sailing in October. When the cotton arrived in the later ship, Wichelhaus refused to complete the purchase and Raffles sued for breach of contract. The English court held that the contract was voidable due to the mutual mistake of fact. The court described the situation as one of "latent ambiguity" and declared that there was no meeting of the minds and therefore no contract.

Note that the three-month delay made the cotton worthless to the buyer and thus the mistake was substantial. What if the delay had been only a few days? In that case, the court would probably have enforced the contract. On the other hand, even if the delay had only been a few days, if the buyer had planned to resell the cotton on the open market and the price of cotton had dropped sharply between the arrival of the first and the arrival of the second ship, then the mistake would probably have been substantial enough to make the contract voidable.

Allocation of the Risks   If one party accepts a risk, then this allocation of risk becomes part of the bargain even if it is doubtful the risk will materialize, and that party must bear the consequences. For example, Jennifer Gerald wants to sell Antonio Cameron her house. She says she is uncertain whether the house needs a retaining wall to bolster the foundation. Cameron does not want to pay for a report by a structural engineer. He says he doesn't think the house needs a retaining wall. He is willing to take

---

2. 159 Eng. Rep. 375 (Exch. 1864).

the risk of being wrong about that, if Gerald will lower the selling price. They sign a contract to this effect. Structural damage is subsequently discovered. The parties have allocated the risk of a mistake about the need for a retaining wall, and the contract is valid.

If the parties have not expressly allocated a risk, sometimes a court will place the risk on the party that had access to the most information. In other cases, it might be imposed on the party better able to bear the risk.

Timing The party alleging a mistake of fact must give prompt notice when the mistake is discovered. If too much time passes before the other party is notified, undoing the contract might create more problems than letting it stand.

Mistake of Judgment

A mistake of judgment occurs when the parties make an erroneous assessment about some aspect of what is bargained for. For example, in a futures contract Seller agrees to sell Buyer his crop of sugar in three months at a price of 50 cents per pound. Seller is betting that the market price in three months will be less than 50 cents. Buyer is betting that the market price will be higher. One of them will be mistaken, but the futures contract will still be valid. This is a mistake of judgment. Such a mistake is not a valid defense to enforcement of the contract. (The UCC doctrine of commercial impracticability does allow a contract to be voided if there is too great a price shift. This doctrine was at issue in the Westinghouse uranium supply cases, discussed in chapter 9.)

The line between judgment and fact is unclear, and cases with similar circumstances can have different outcomes. In one case, the Wisconsin Supreme Court held that a contract to sell a stone for $1.00 was enforceable when neither party knew at the time that the stone was in fact a diamond.[3]

Under seemingly similar facts, the Michigan Supreme Court held that a contract for the sale of a cow thought to be barren, but later found to be with calf, was a mistake of fact which made the contract unenforceable.[4] The court reasoned:

> If there is a difference or misapprehension as to the substance of the thing bargained for; if the thing actually delivered or received is different in substance from the thing bargained for, and intended to be sold,—then there is no contract. . . . A barren cow is substantially a different creature than a breeding one.

A dissenting judge pointed out that the buyer had believed the cow could be made to breed, in spite of the seller's statements to the contrary, and had decided to take a chance on the purchase. He reasoned:

> There was no mistake of any material fact by either of the parties in the case as would license the vendors to rescind. . . . As to the quality of the animal, subsequently developed, both parties were equally ignorant, and as to this each party took his chances. If this were not the law, there would be no safety in purchasing this kind of stock.

It is unclear whether the assumption that a stone is worth only a dollar or a cow is barren is an assumption of fact or of judgment. As the majority and dissenting opinions in the Michigan case demonstrate, different judges reach different conclusions. One judge might consider the distinction to be merely semantic, while another might consider it significant.

Much of contract law comes down to the expectations of the parties involved. In the diamond case, both parties agreed that the value of the stone was unknown. The transaction was thus a conscious allocation of the risks involved. In the cow case, however, the seller did not consider the possibility that the cow was not barren. The buyer did not make known his secret belief that the cow could be made to breed. From the seller's point of view, the transaction was for a barren cow with no chance of breeding. However, the buyer did not see the transaction that way. The case might have come out differently if the buyer had explicitly said to the seller, "I know you believe the cow is barren, but I believe she can be made to breed and I'm willing to take the risk in buying her."

Disclosing all expectations may make for firm contracts, but it is not the most effective negotiating technique. If the seller believes a cow can be made to breed, she will demand a higher selling price. Why pay the higher price when the vast majority of business transactions are completed without any need to do battle in the courtroom? One of the challenges of business is balancing the slim (but expensive) chances of litigation against the desire to make an advantageous deal.

■ Statute of Frauds

Although most oral contracts are enforceable, many states have statutes requiring certain types of contracts to be evidenced at the minimum by some form of written communication. Such a statute is called a *statute of frauds*. If a contract covered by the statute is oral, it is a

---

3. *Wood v. Boynton,* 64 Wis. 265, 25 N.W. 42 (Wis. 1885).
4. *Sherwood v. Walker,* 66 Mich. 568, 33 N.W. 919 (Mich. 1887).

Ethical Consideration

The possibility that only one party may know the true value of an item being sold raises ethical issues. For example, an antique dealer at a garage sale might see a desk for sale for $50 that he recognizes as a Louis XV desk worth $15,000. Does he have an obligation to disclose the true value to the person holding the garage sale?

Under current law, he probably is not required to disclose the desk's true value unless he has some special relationship to the seller, such as family ties or a business connection in which the other party is relying on him to protect her interest (see chapter 1 for a discussion of such a fiduciary duty). From an ethical point of view, it seems unfair of him to take advantage of the ignorance of the homeowner, particularly if financial circumstances made it necessary for the homeowner to sell the desk. On the other hand, it seems fair for the antique dealer to get some reward for the effort he has spent in becoming an expert in antiques, and for the time he may have spent pawing through junk at countless garage sales.

Both the stone/diamond case and the barren cow case were decided in the nineteenth century. Similar mistakes about value occur today. A person recently sold a map for $3 that later turned out to be worth more than $19 million. This case appears to be similar to the stone/diamond case, in that the parties knew what they were dealing with, namely a map. If a court decided that it should be governed by the stone/diamond case, then the purchaser of the map would have no legal duty to pay the seller any part of the $19 million. Is there a moral duty to share the windfall with the seller?

What if a framed picture sold for $25 turned out to have an original copy of the U.S. Constitution behind the picture? Is this a mistake of judgment or of fact? What, if anything, is the buyer's ethical responsibility to the seller in such a case?

valid contract, but the courts will not be able to enforce it if the statute of frauds is raised as a defense.

There are four traditional justifications for requiring certain contracts to be evidenced by some writing. First, requiring a written document avoids fraudulent claims that an oral contract was made. Second, the existence of a written document avoids fraudulent claims as to the terms of the contract. Third, the statute encourages persons to put their agreements in writing, thereby reducing the risk of future misunderstandings. Fourth, the writing required by the statute has the psychological effect of reinforcing the importance of the parties' decision to enter into a contract.

Transactions Subject to the Statute of Frauds

Contracts that must be evidenced by some writing include: (1) a contract for the transfer of any interest in real property; (2) a promise to pay the debt of another person; (3) an agreement that by its terms can not be performed within a year; (4) and a *prenuptial agreement* (that is, an agreement entered into before marriage that sets forth the manner in which the parties' assets will be distributed and the support to which each party will be entitled in the event the parties divorce).

The agreement does not have to be embodied in a formal, legal-looking document to satisfy the statute of frauds. An agreement can be represented by an exchange of letters that refer to each other, even if no single letter is sufficient to reflect all essential terms. Details or particulars can be omitted; only the essential terms must be stated. What is essential depends on the agreement, its context, and the subsequent conduct of the parties. The UCC has its own statute of frauds, discussed in chapter 9.

Under the *equal dignities rule,* if an agent acts on behalf of another (her principal) in signing an agreement of the type that must under the statute of frauds be in writing, the authority of the agent to act on behalf of the principal must also be in writing. Thus, an individual uses a written *power of attorney* to authorize a person, called an attorney-in-fact (who need not be a lawyer), to sign documents on the individual's behalf. Corporations authorize officers to sign through a combination of written authority specified in the bylaws of the corporation and the minutes of the governing body, the board of directors.

If there is clear evidence that a person made an oral promise, a court will strain to recharacterize the nature of the agreement so that it does not come within the statute of frauds.[5] One cannot count on such leniency, however, so the prudent manager will put any and all agreements that *might* fall within the statute of frauds in writing.

The Parol Evidence Rule

If a contract is in writing, when will a court go beyond the words of the contract and look to other evidence to ascertain the intent of the parties? Under the *parol evidence rule,* when there is a written contract that the parties intended would encompass their entire agreement, parol (that is, oral) evidence of prior or contemporaneous statements will not be permitted to alter the terms of the contract. Such extrinsic evidence is inadmissible in court and cannot be used to interpret, vary, or add to the terms of an unambiguous written contract that purports to be the entire agreement of the parties. A court will usually not look beyond the "four corners" of the document to discern the intentions of the parties.

> ❝ *A court will usually not look beyond the "four corners" of the document to discern the intentions of the parties.*

Clarifying Intentions

The parol evidence rule does not prohibit showing what the contract means. For example, if the contract stated a party was to purchase a carload of tomatoes, it would not violate the parol evidence rule to give evidence showing that "carload" in the relevant commercial setting means a train carload, not a Chevy truckload. This evidence merely explains the ambiguous term "carload"; it does not vary the term. Parol evidence is also admissible to show mistake (discussed above) or fraud or duress (discussed below).

Courts are willing to look beyond the written agreement if its language is ambiguous. Sometimes a court will find ambiguity in language that seems to have a plain meaning. One case involved a transaction for

financing an office building.[6] The lender was a major life insurance company and the borrowers were a partnership consisting of an insurance company and two prestigious law firms. The financing documents specifically provided that the $56.5 million loan at 12¼% interest for 15 years could not be prepaid before 12 years had elapsed. After interest rates came down, the partnership tried to refinance and take advantage of the lower rates despite the provision in the contract. Notwithstanding the clear language of the contract, the court permitted the partnership to admit oral testimony to attempt to prove the true intentions of the parties.

Modern courts make a particular effort to discern the parties' intentions, notwithstanding the words that are written in the contract. In the landmark case of *Pennzoil v. Texaco,* discussed in the "Inside Story" in this chapter, the court held that the jury had reasonable evidence before it to conclude that the parties had intended to enter into a binding agreement. This was the case even though the document that was signed by two of the three parties was entitled a "memorandum of agreement" and the transaction was expressly made subject to the signing of other documents.

■ Voidable and Unenforceable Contracts

Contract cases often come before the courts when one party refuses to perform its side of the bargain. The usual defense is that, for one reason or another, the contract is voidable or is unenforceable. A contract is *voidable* if it was: (1) fraudulently induced; (2) related to activities requiring a license when no license is obtained; (3) entered into under duress; (4) involved a party lacking capacity (discussed earlier); or (5) affected by mistake (discussed earlier). A contract is *unenforceable* if it was: (1) illegal or (2) unconscionable. A contract is unenforceable when some public policy interest dictates that the agreement should not be upheld, regardless of the desire of one or more of the parties. A voidable contract, such as a contract with a minor, can be upheld if both parties agree to honor it, but can be avoided (not honored) by the minor if he so chooses. Similarly, a contract with a corporation can be avoided by the corporation if the officer signing it did not have actual or apparent authority.

---

5. See, e.g., *Wilson Floors Co. v. Sciota Park, Ltd.*, 54 Ohio St. 2d 451, 377 N.E.2d 514 (Ohio 1978) (oral promise by construction lender to pay subcontractor if he returned to work served lender's own pecuniary interest so the agreement did not have to be in writing to be enforceable).

---

6. *Trident Center v. Connecticut General Life Insurance Co.*, 847 F.2d 564 (9th Cir. 1988).

At the Top

Although one purpose of board minutes is mere formality, another purpose is to answer agency questions that may arise from corporate transactions. Board minutes are one way in which lawyers can determine that an officer has actual authority to engage in a particular activity or to take certain actions on behalf of the corporation.

In addition (and discussed later in this chapter), performance will be excused if changed circumstances make enforcement of the contract inappropriate.

Fraud

A contract is voidable if it is tainted with fraud. There are two types of fraud: fraud in the factum and fraud in the inducement. *Fraud in the factum* occurs when a party is persuaded to sign one document thinking that it is another. For example, if a person were given a deed to sign for the transfer of real property, after being told he was signing an employment agreement, the deed could be avoided by the defrauded party.

The second type of fraud, *fraud in the inducement*, occurs when a party makes a false statement to persuade the other party to enter into an agreement. For example, if a jeweler told a customer that the stone in a ring was a diamond, when the jeweler knew it was zirconium, an agreement to purchase the ring would be fraudulent, and the purchaser would have the right to rescind, that is, cancel, the contract. A contract is not voidable due to fraudulent misrepresentations unless the misrepresentation is material to the bargain and relied upon by the party seeking to void the contract.

A variation of the second type of fraud occurs when a party has a duty to disclose information to the other party but fails to do so. For example, a partner who knows the true value of a piece of property cannot sell it to a fellow partner without disclosing the true value. Often a duty to disclose arises out of a special relationship between the parties (i.e., a fiduciary relationship), such as a trustee and beneficiary.

Failure to Possess Required License

Many states require licenses for the conduct of particular kinds of business. These range from real estate and securities broker licenses to chauffeur licenses to contractor licenses. Many statutes provide that if a party fails to have a required license, the other party to the contract does not have to fulfill its side of the bargain, usually payment. This is true even if the unlicensed party performed the work perfectly.

What happens if a party falsely promises to provide a licensed contractor to work with an unlicensed firm? It is clear that the unlicensed firm cannot sue for breach of contract. But, can it sue for fraud? That was the issue in the following case.

■ A Case In Point: Summary

Case 8.3
HYDROTECH SYSTEMS, LTD. v. OASIS WATERPARK
Supreme Court of California
52 Cal.3d 988, 277 Cal.Rptr. 517, 803 P.2d 370 (Cal. 1991).

FACTS Hydrotech, Inc. is a New York corporation that manufactures and installs equipment that creates ocean-like "waves" in pools. It is not licensed to do this work in California. Oasis Waterpark is a water-oriented amusement park located in Palm Springs, California. Desiring the unique patented device and installation of Hydrotech's wave-creating equipment, Oasis's contractor, Wessman, contracted with Hydrotech to sell and install the equipment at the Oasis Waterpark for a total contract price of $850,000. The contract provided that Wessman was to hold a specified portion of the price pending satisfactory operation of the pool.

Wessman withheld the price for the equipment once the pool was fully operative. Hydrotech sued for the price of the equipment. Hydrotech also made a fraud claim against Oasis, asserting that it had originally hoped to only sell and deliver equipment for the wave pool, not install it, due to licensing concerns. Hydrotech further alleged that Oasis, in order to persuade

Hydrotech to install the equipment, promised that it would arrange for a California-licensed contractor to "work with" Hydrotech on any construction. Hydrotech asserted that had it known that Oasis's promises were false when made, it would not have relied to its detriment in performing the work.

Section 7031 of the Business and Professions Code states that one may not sue in a California court to recover "compensation" for "any act or contract" that requires a California contractor's license, unless one "alleges and proves" he was duly licensed at all times during the performance. Hydrotech argued that section 7031 should not be applied because it possessed unique expertise in the field and performed only at the customer's insistence. In addition, Hydrotech asserted that section 7031 does not apply to the sale of equipment, only services, and does not bar tort actions for fraud.

ISSUE PRESENTED   Does the contractor licensing statute preclude a claim for fraud?

SUMMARY OF OPINION   The California Supreme Court held that the licensing statute bars an unlicensed contractor's claim for fraud when the primary deceit alleged is a false promise to pay, and the damages primarily consist of, or are measured by, the price or value of the work and materials furnished. The court reasoned that any other result would circumvent the clear statutory policy of deterring unlicensed contract work.

The statutory disallowance of claims for payment by unlicensed subcontractors is intended to deter such persons from offering their services, or accepting solicitations of their work. The policy applies regardless of whether the other party's promise to pay for the work was honest or deceitful and even if the other party knew the subcontractor was not licensed.

RESULT   Contractor Wessman was not obligated to pay subcontractor Hydrotech because Hydrotech did not have a California contractor's license.

COMMENTS   The dissenting judge noted that the complaint clearly alleged a fraudulent scheme whereby the defendants, with the intent of avoiding payment under their contract, insisted that Hydrotech, known to be unlicensed, engage in contracting work for which a license was required. The dissent argued that allowing fraudulent wrongdoers to obtain the substantial penalties and forfeitures and be unjustly enriched can only encourage owners and contractors to engage in fraudulent schemes to hire unlicensed persons in anticipation that, when the debts come due, they can turn their backs and refuse to pay in reliance on the licensing statute. On the other hand, he argued, the legislative policy of deterrence is not furthered by denying recovery for fraud. Unlicensed contractors are not encouraged to undertake the unlawful activity by the remote possibility that, if unpaid, they might be able to prove fraud.

 Ethical Consideration

What role does the law have in preventing the fraudulent promise to pay for work done by an unlicensed contractor? Did Hydrotech, in case 8.3, only get its due for violating the licensing law or should the defendant have been required—legally or ethically—to honor its promise of payment?

Duress

A contract is also voidable if one party was forced to enter into the agreement through coercion or duress, such as a threat of physical harm if the party does not sign the contract. There can be more subtle forms of duress, such as an implied threat that an employee will lose her job unless she signs an agreement waiving certain rights to employee benefits.

Economic duress is usually not enough to invalidate a contract. Thus, many courts would uphold an agreement to sell a farm even if the owner had to sell it at a bargain price to avoid bankruptcy.

 Ethical Consideration

It can be unfair, though not necessarily illegal, to take advantage of someone's financial hardship to drive a hard bargain.

Illegality

A contract with an illegal purpose or result is unenforceable as an *illegal contract*. Sometimes, a statute will expressly make a contract illegal. For example, *usury statutes,* which limit the interest rate on loans, usually provide that any loan agreement in violation of the statute is unenforceable. In some jurisdictions, this means that no amount of interest can be collected; in some states, the principal amount of the loan is not collectable. Loans that violate the usury statutes also violate criminal law.

Other examples of illegal contracts include price-fixing agreements in violation of the antitrust laws; bribes; wagering contracts or bets in violation of applicable gambling laws; and unreasonable *covenants not to compete.* To be reasonable, a covenant not to compete must be reasonable as to scope of activities, length of time, and geographic area and must be necessary to protect goodwill.

Unconscionability

A contract term is *unconscionable* if it is oppressive or fundamentally unfair. This concept is applied most often to consumer contracts, where the consumer may have little or no bargaining power. The purchase terms are dictat-ed by the seller, and the buyer can take it or leave it. For example, an exorbitantly high price, such as $900 for an item valued at $350, can be considered unconscionable if the item is a necessity and the consumer has no other options but to buy from that particular seller.

Courts usually refuse to enforce contract terms that they find unconscionable. When the term is central to the contract, the court can either rewrite the term (for example, by substituting a fair market price) or void the contract. As further described in the "Historical Perspective" in this chapter, the doctrine of unconscionability had its origins in Roman law.

Unconscionability has both a procedural and a substantive element.

Procedural Element   The procedural element focuses on two factors: oppression and surprise. *Oppression* arises from an inequality of bargaining power that results in no real negotiation and an absence of meaningful choice for one party to the contract. *Surprise* arises when the terms of the contract are hidden in a densely printed form drafted by the party seeking to enforce these terms. Form contracts are usually drafted by the party with the superior bargaining position.

Substantive Element   No precise definition of substantive unconscionability can be set forth. Courts have talked in terms of "overly harsh" or "one-sided" results. One commentator has pointed out that unconscionability turns not only on a "one-sided" result but also on an absence of justification for it. The most detailed and specific commentaries observe that a contract is largely an allocation of risk between the parties, and therefore a contractual term is substantively suspect if it reallocates the risk of the bargain in an objectively unreasonable or unexpected manner. But not all unreasonable risk allocations are unconscionable. The enforceability of a suspect term often depends on whether there is also unconscionability. The greater the unfair surprise or inequality of bargaining power, the less the courts will tolerate an unreasonable risk allocation.

Persons are sometimes asked to sign a general release, especially before embarking on a dangerous activity such as skydiving or race car driving. A *general release* purports to relieve the owner of the facility of any liability for injuries suffered by the person using the facility, including liability for negligence. A number of earlier cases have held that the exculpatory language in a general release agreement was invalid because the agreement was unconscionable. However, there appears to be a trend toward honoring these releases, as demonstrated in the following case.

Ethical Consideration

The law prevents the party with greater bargaining power from taking unfair advantage of the weaker party. Even if driving a hard bargain may not rise to the level of unconscionability, it may still be unethical.

■ **A Case in Point:**   **In the Language of the Court**

Case 8.4
KURASHIGE v. INDIAN DUNES, INC.
California Court of Appeal
200 Cal. App. 3d 606, 246 Cal. Rptr. 310 (1988).

FACTS   Indian Dunes Park, owned by Indian Dunes, Inc., was used by the general public for motorcycle dirt-bike riding. On December 21, 1982, Kurashige was injured while riding his motorcycle on the park's trails. Before using the park, Kurashige had signed a general release agreement, which was printed in red ink with ten-point bold type and capital letters saying: "SINCE ALL MOTORBIKE RIDING IS DANGEROUS WE REQUIRE ALL RIDERS AND VISITORS TO ASSUME ALL RISK BY SIGNING THIS GENERAL RELEASE." At the bottom of the agreement, the words, "MOTORCYCLING IS DANGEROUS" were printed in red in seventeen-point bold type. Below the agreement were three columns of 28 lines each for the riders to sign. Printed on each of the 84 lines were the words "THIS IS A RELEASE" in capital letters.

The agreement provided in pertinent part that each of the undersigned "Hereby Releases, Waives, Discharges and Covenants not to sue [defendants], all for purposes herein referred to as Releasees, from all liability to the Undersigned . . . for all loss or damage and any claim or demands therefor, on account of injury to the person or property or resulting in death of the Undersigned, whether caused by the negligence of Releasees or otherwise while the Undersigned is upon the Park premises. . . ."

Kurashige suffered injury and sued the owner of Indian Dunes. The trial court granted summary judgment in favor of Indian Dunes, and Kurashige appealed. By granting the motion for summary judgment, the court took the issue of liability away from the jury and decided as a matter of law that the defendant should prevail. Kurashige appealed

ISSUE PRESENTED   Is the exculpatory language in a general release agreement enforceable as a general matter, and more specifically, as against a claim of unconscionability?

OPINION   SPENCER, J., writing for the California Court of Appeal:
[The court began by considering whether any general release, regardless of terms, was valid. Relying on *Tunkl v. Regents of the University of California*,[7] the court held that an exculpatory provision may stand only if it does not involve "the public interest."]

. . . .

---

7. 60 Cal.2d 92, 32 Cal.Rptr. 33, 383 P.2d 441 (Cal. 1963).

*Case **8.4** continued on following page*

*Case **8.4** continued*

. . . [T]he "General Release" agreement used here was printed legibly, contained adequate, clear and explicit exculpatory language and indicated defendants were to be absolved from the consequences of their own negligence. Furthermore, it did not involve the public interest: defendants' business was not generally thought to be suitable for public regulation; defendants did not perform a service of great importance to the public, and the business was not a matter of practical necessity for members of the public; and defendants' customers did not place their persons under defendants' control.

. . . .

[The court then addressed the plaintiff's contention that the general release was unconscionable.] Turning to the procedural element of unconscionability, the first question is whether the "General Release" agreement was oppressive, whether there was "an inequality in bargaining power which result[ed] in no real negotiation and 'an absence of meaningful choice.' "[8] The record shows there was no real negotiation; the "General Release" agreement was preprinted and all users of Indian Dunes Park were required to sign it before using the park. However, the record does not show plaintiff had no meaningful choice in deciding to sign the agreement. . . . There is no evidence plaintiff could not have ridden his motorcycle elsewhere without the constraints imposed upon him by defendants.

The next question is whether plaintiff was surprised by supposedly agreed-upon terms hidden within a printed form drafted by defendants. The entire release agreement was printed at the top of the form signed by plaintiff. Warnings as to the dangers of motorcycling, the rider's assumption of the risk and the release and waiver of all liability stood out and the exculpatory provisions of the agreement were clearly set forth. Thus, the agreement was not procedurally unconscionable.

In examining the issue of substantive unconscionability, one question to be asked is whether the agreement was one-sided and, if so, whether the one-sidedness was justified. A further question is whether the agreement reallocated the risks of the bargain in an objectively unreasonable or unexpected manner. Risk reallocation which will be subjected to special scrutiny is that in which the risk shifted to a party is one that only the other party can avoid. Clearly, the agreement here was one-sided; all of the risk was reallocated to the Park's user, plaintiff. As previously discussed, the risk reallocation was not unexpected; the agreement clearly indicated the user assumed all risk of his use of the Park's facilities.

Was the risk reallocation objectively unreasonable? One signing the agreement warrants he knows "the present condition [of the Park and] that said condition may become more hazardous and dangerous during the time [he is] upon said premises." The agreement warned the user motorcycling is dangerous; implicit in the knowledge of the danger of motorcycling "is the knowledge that riding over rough, uneven terrain in an outdoor park poses a risk of injury from a fall" or other accident.[9] Moreover, to a certain extent, the risk of injury is conditioned upon the user's skill and experience

---

8. *A & M Produce Co. v. FMC Corp.*, 135 Cal.App.3d 473, 486, 186 Cal.Rptr. 114 (Cal. Ct. App. 1982).

9. *Coates v. Newhall Land & Farming, Inc.*, 191 Cal.App.3d 1, 9, 236 Cal.Rptr. 181 (Cal. Ct. App. 1987).

as a motorcycle rider, factors over which the Park's owners and operators have no control. In view of the foregoing, the risk reallocation was not unreasonable and the "General Release" agreement was not substantively unconscionable.

. . . .

RESULT   The general release was upheld and the court affirmed the trial court's grant of summary judgment for the defendant Indian Dunes.

COMMENTS   It would appear that the court would limit the use of general releases in a county hospital. Would it matter if the hospital were private?

Questions

1. Would the result in this case have been any different if the plaintiff had been thrown off his bike after riding into a barbed-wire fence not visible from the hill he had just crested? What about a big hole on the other side of the hill?

2. What would the court consider a practical necessity for members of the public? A bus? A cosmetic surgery clinic? A public park for camping that charges a small fee?

 Ethical Consideration

Envelopes for the processing of photographic film typically contain printed language on the outside of the envelope stating that in the event of loss, defect, or negligence in the processing, the purchaser's damages are limited to the replacement of the film and processing. Shortly before Mr. Sam Smoke died of a heart attack, his wife, Sara Smoke, took pictures of him playing with his new granddaughter. After his death, Mrs. Smoke took the film to Photo-Finish for processing. She gave the company her name but did not sign anything. Photo-Finish lost the film. Mrs. Smoke sued for negligence and claimed damages to compensate her for the emotional distress caused by the loss of the invaluable pictures. What is Photo-Finish legally required to do? What should it do?

■ Changed Circumstances

Contracts often contain provisions for a variety of future events so that the parties involved can allocate the risks

of different outcomes. It is not always possible, however, to anticipate every occurrence. There are three theories used to address this situation: impossibility, impracticability, and frustration of purpose.

Impossibility

If Julian Sanchez signs a contract to sell Trevor Brown computer chips of a special type manufactured only in Sanchez's factory, which later burns down through no fault of his own before he can manufacture the computer chips, it becomes impossible to perform the contract. The destruction of Sanchez's factory is a changed circumstance that neither party contemplated when they made the contract.

Is Brown entitled to money damages for Sanchez's nonperformance? No; as Sanchez's performance has become impossible, he is discharged from his obligations under the contract, and Brown is not entitled to damages. If, however, the computer chips could be manufactured in another factory, Sanchez would have an obligation to have them manufactured there when his factory burned down. This is the case even if it cost Sanchez more money to manufacture them at another facility.

Impracticability

Closely related to impossibility is the concept of impracticability, where performance is possible but is commercially impractical. As a rule, impracticability is difficult to prove.

EXHIBIT 8-1   Charlie Brown Looks at Contracts

PEANUTS reprinted by permission of UFS, Inc.

Historical Perspective
Unconscionability and Freedom of Contract

The principle of freedom of contract embodies the idea that the judicial system should give effect to the expressed intention of parties to an agreement. This has always been a fundamental precept of Western legal systems. It is based on the belief that the terms of a contract express the free will of the contracting parties. Parties should be able to dispose of their property and services in any manner they see fit.

It is difficult for a court to evaluate the fairness of a contract and to figure out the relative values of a business deal to the parties. Accordingly, courts observe the general principle that they should not substitute their judgment about the fairness of a contract for that of the parties.

Freedom of contract ensures that the law does not unduly restrict the ability of the competitive market to bring about productive and allocative efficiency. Productive efficiency exists where competition among parties seeking to earn profits results in survival of only the lowest-cost producers of a good. Allocative efficiency exists where goods and services are produced up to the point where the cost of production of goods equals their price, which results in efficient allocation of scarce societal resources to the production of various goods.

Leaving the parties to define the contract terms as they see fit will result in greater maximization of profitability, provided the following three conditions are met: First, that the parties to the contract are better informed than the courts about the conditions under which the benefits of the deal can be maximized; second, that the parties are equally well informed and enjoy roughly equal bargaining power; and third, that the legislature is unable to provide rules detailed enough to govern the particular business situations in which the contract was agreed.

Naturally, these conditions are met more fully in some contexts than in others. Also, public policy concerns must be respected; contracts that produce results contrary to public policy should not be enforced, even if they enhance economic efficiency. Courts have therefore created exceptions to the principle of freedom of contract, voiding contracts in two types of cases: (1) when the three conditions mentioned above are not met; and (2) when the purpose or the result of the contract violates public policy.

The first type of case, in which the conditions necessary for freedom of contract to maximize economic efficiency are not met, may be characterized as involving procedural unconscionability. The second type of case, in which the contract leads to a result that is against public policy, may be characterized as involving substantive unconscionability.

These concepts date back to Aristotelian theory and Roman law. Under Roman law, each party to an exchange had to give something equal in value to what he received. Unequal exchanges were considered fundamentally unjust. The law remedied the injustice in extreme cases through the doctrine of *laesio enormis*. This doctrine developed from language in the Code of Justinian that provided a remedy for those who sold land at less than half its "just price." *Laesio enormis* expanded this provision to cover contracts for goods whose contract price deviated by at least half from the just price. Under the Roman system, the just price was the market price for similar goods under similar circumstances. The German and French laws that relieve a party from its obligations under a contract that is not for the just price have their roots in the Roman doctrine of *laesio enormis*.

In the United States and England, the general principle of freedom of contract, embodied in the common-law rule that the judiciary would not examine the fairness of an exchange, has always been limited by the doctrine of unconscionability. In the eighteenth century, unequal exchanges were considered evidence of fraud in the making of the contract. Courts would refuse to enforce unconscionable contracts, which were generally defined as those involving harsh or oppressive terms of exchange.

The coming of the Industrial Revolution and the emergence of large corporations in the mid-1800s brought about fundamental changes in the mode of analysis of contract law. As goods became more complex, the seller typically had greater knowledge of them than the buyer, and the bargaining power of large corporations often greatly exceeded that of the individuals with whom they contracted. Thus, a greater number of contracts failed to satisfy the "equal footing" condition necessary to make freedom of contract efficiency-enhancing. Consequently, courts became less hesitant to intervene to protect the party to a contract who was perceived to be weaker. The doctrine of unconscionability was expanded to cover situations where the parties were not on an equal footing.

Historical Perspective
Unconscionability and Freedom of Contract, *continued*

Modern courts have also been willing to void contracts on grounds of substantive unconscionability. For example, in *American Home Improvement, Inc. v. MacIver,*[a] the New Hampshire Supreme Court held that a contract for the payment of $1,750 plus $800 in credit charges for the purchase and installation of 14 windows, a door, and a coating for the sidewalks of a house was unconscionable because the goods and services were worth far less than the price. The court focused not on the

a.   105 N.H. 435, 201 A.2d 886 (N.H. 1964).

process by which the contract was formed but on the unjust result of the bargain struck. (Other cases applying the doctrine of unconscionability to the sale of goods under article 2 of the Uniform Commercial Code are discussed in chapter 9.)

[The discussion of Roman, French, German, and English law and certain aspects of the discussion of U.S. law set forth above are based upon James Gordley, "Equality in Exchange," 69 *California Law Review* 1587 (1981), and the authorities cited therein.]

Impracticability was invoked by several shipping companies when political turmoil in the Middle East shut down the Suez Canal in June 1967. A number of merchant ships had to detour around the Cape of Good Hope. The detour increased the shipping costs so much that the shipping companies suffered substantial losses. Several of these companies sued to nullify the contracts they had entered into before the Suez Canal was closed. They claimed performance was impractical, and sought to recover the full costs of sailing the longer route around the Cape of Good Hope. In only one case did the court grant relief. The other courts found that the added costs were not so great as to make performance impracticable.

Frustration of Purpose

Frustration of purpose occurs when performance is possible, but changed circumstances have made the contract useless to one or both of the parties. A famous example is the King Edward VII coronation case.[10] Henry contracted to rent a room in London from Krell for the acknowledged purpose of viewing King Edward VII's coronation procession. Krell had advertised the room as one that would be good for viewing the coronation. When the King became ill with appendicitis and the coronation was postponed, Henry refused to pay for the apartment. Krell sued. The English court ruled that Henry did not have to

10. *Krell v. Henry,* 2 K.B. 740 (C.A. 1903).

pay because the entire reason for the contract had been "frustrated."

Note that performance of the contract was not impossible: Henry still could have rented the room. The outcome of the case would have been different if the room had not been rented for the express purpose of viewing the coronation. In that case Krell would have won because the purpose of the contract would have just been for the rental of the room, not for the viewing of the coronation.

The contract defense of frustration requires that: (1) the parties' principal purpose in making the contract is frustrated; (2) without that party's fault; (3) by the occurrence of an event, the nonoccurrence of which was a basic assumption on which the contract was made. For performance to be excused, this frustration of purpose must have occurred without the defendant's fault. The defense of frustration is unavailable if the defendant helped cause the frustrating event or if the parties were aware of the possibility of the frustrating event when the contract was entered into.

■ Duty of Good Faith and Fair Dealing

Every contract contains an implied covenant of good faith and fair dealing in its performance. This implied covenant imposes on each party a duty not to do anything that will deprive the other party of the benefits of the agreement. One court defined a lack of good faith as "some type of affirmative action consisting of at least . . . a design to mislead or to deceive another."[11] The covenant has been implied and enforced in a variety of contexts, including insurance contracts, agreements to make mutual wills, agreements to sell real property, employment agreements, and leases. (Its application in the employment context is discussed in chapter 12.)

For example, suppose Shirley Reese was looking for an apartment. She came upon Tara Ropley's apartment building and proceeded up the stairs to speak with the manager. Reese tripped on a broken step, falling and breaking her arm and leg. It was clear that the steps had not been maintained very well. Ropley had insurance of $25,000 to cover this type of liability claim. Reese's lawyer originally demanded $200,000, which included a claim for punitive damages. Ropley's insurance company refused to pay the claim. Reese's lawyer then lowered Shirley's claim to $20,000. Ropley's insurance company did not believe that Ropley was negligent and took the case to trial. The jury awarded Reese $180,000. Ropley is liable for the full amount, although she was insured for only $25,000. Ropley then brings an action against her insurance company for not settling the claim within the policy limits. Under the implied covenant of good faith and fair dealing, the insurance company will have the obligation to pay the full $180,000 judgment. An insurance company can refuse to settle within the policy limits. But once an insurance company refuses an offer to settle within the policy limits and instead goes to trial, the insurance company becomes contractually responsible under the implied covenant of good faith and fair dealing for paying whatever amount is awarded at trial.

The precise meanings of "good faith" and "fair dealing" are the subject of extended debate among legal scholars. The terms themselves are ambiguous, and the practical meanings may vary over time. What was considered fair dealing 20 years ago may be considered unfair today, and vice versa.

Two commonly used rules of thumb, while not precise, do offer some guidance. The businesswoman in doubt can ask herself if her actions would embarrass her or her company if they should become public. She can also ask herself if she would follow the same course of action if she were dealing with a friend or relative.

Ethical Consideration

The implied covenant of good faith and fair dealing prevents certain unethical practices. For example, a businessperson purchases a 40-foot-wide strip of land from a home owner for a small sum of money. He then sells most of the land to the county, which lays down a road on the land. The businessperson keeps a two-foot-wide strip of the land between the home owner's property and the new road. When the home owner crosses over this two-foot strip to get to the road, the businessperson threatens to sue for trespass. He then offers to sell back the two-foot strip for an extravagant sum. Technically, all of the facts support the businessperson's position, because he has legal title to the two-foot strip. However, most courts would rescind the contract because the purchase of the land was not in good faith.

> *The precise meanings of "good faith" and "fair dealing" have been the subject of extended debate among legal scholars.*

Although these questions address moral rather than legal issues, they can be useful in evaluating whether a contemplated action would meet the legal test of good faith. (Good faith in the context of negotiations is discussed more fully later in this chapter.)

■ Contract Modification

Traditional contract law does not allow a contract to be modified if the modification would change the obligations of only one party. Under this view, no consideration has been given for the change. Over time, lawyers developed a variety of techniques to meet the formal requirements of consideration. One technique was *novation,* by which the original contract is canceled by mutual agreement, and a new one is written with the desired change. Another technique was formal change, where the consideration for the desired modification is a formal but meaningless change, such as making the payment in cash rather than with a bank check.

---

11. *Bunge Corp. v. Recker,* 519 F.2d 449, 452 (8th Cir. 1975).

In the modern business environment, modifications to contracts are often necessary. The UCC allows modification of contracts for the sale of goods without consideration as long as the change meets the test of good faith.

■ Damages

If one party breaches a contract, the other party is entitled to monetary damages. The purpose is to give the plaintiff the benefit of the bargain he contracted for, that is, to put the plaintiff in the position he would have been in had the contract been performed. A secondary purpose of damages is to discourage breaches of contract.

Over the years a variety of methods have developed to measure appropriate monetary damages. The three standard measures are: (1) expectation, (2) reliance, and (3) restitution. These measures may seem similar, but the resulting damage awards can be very different. In addition, a party who breaches a contract may have to pay punitive damages if that party seeks to shield itself from liability by denying, in bad faith, that the contract exists at all. However, recognizing that it is sometimes economically efficient to breach a contract, the legal system generally does not punish a party for breach of contract alone. Punitive damages, traditionally a tort remedy, are also awarded where the court finds oppressive, malicious, or fraudulent conduct.

Types of Damages

Expectation Damages   *Expectation damages* give the plaintiff the benefit of her bargain, putting her into the cash position she would have been in if the contract had been fulfilled. For example, Seller contracts to sell Buyer ten bales of cotton at $20 per bale. When the time comes to deliver the cotton, Seller reneges. Buyer can buy cotton elsewhere, but the market price is now $25 per bale. This extra cost will cut into the profit margin on the cloth Buyer had planned to make out of the cotton. Instead of spending $200 for ten bales of cotton, Buyer now has to pay $250 for ten bales of cotton. Buyer's expectation damages are the difference between the two expenditures, that is, $50.

Consequential Damages   In addition to damages that compensate for the breach itself, the plaintiff is entitled to *consequential damages,* that is, compensation for losses that occur as a foreseeable result of the breach. For example, Buyer buys the cotton elsewhere, but the transportation costs from this other location are $10 higher. This $10 is added to the $50 in damages. If the delay in finding a new vendor causes Buyer to be late in delivering cloth to one of its customers, any late fees Buyer pays will also be added to the damages.

Consequential damages must be reasonably foreseeable. They will be awarded only if the breaching party knew, or should have known, that the loss would result from a breach of the contract.

For example, in *Hadley v. Baxendale,*[12] the plaintiff owned a mill in which the crankshaft broke. The crankshaft was sent by carrier to be repaired. Because this was the only crankshaft the mill owned, the mill was completely shut down until the carrier returned with the crankshaft. The carrier did not deliver the shaft as quickly as promised. The plaintiff/owner sued the carrier for lost profits for the time for which the mill was closed. The English appellate court did not award damages for lost profits because the carrier had no way of knowing that the non-delivery of the crankshaft would mean the closure of the mill, as most mills had more than one crankshaft. In order for lost profits to have been awarded, the loss of profits had to be reasonably foreseeable or a natural consequence of the breach. Neither was the case here.

A similar example is the case of the stove manufacturer who paid a carrier $50 to ship a new model of stove to a major exhibition. The stove did not arrive until the exhibition was over. The manufacturer sued for the value of all the lost business he had expected to get at the exhibition.[13] The court found that the $50 was too small an amount to serve as insurance for the entire business. Moreover, the value of the lost business was too speculative to calculate with any certainty. Damages were limited to the shipping expenses of $50.

Uncertainty of Damages   In the stove case just described, it was impossible to measure the consequential damages (the stove manufacturer's lost business). Sometimes it is not possible to know even what the benefit of the bargain would have been. For example, Publisher & Sons signs a contract to publish a book Rachel Author has written. Publisher decides not to publish the book. What damages is Author entitled to? The benefit of her bargain would be the royalties from a published book, but the parties have no way to measure how much those royalties would have been. Because Rachel has the burden of proving the amount of her loss, she may collect very little in damages.

---

12. *Hadley v. Baxendale,* 9 Ex. 341, 156 Eng. Rep. 145 (1854).
13. *Security Stove & Manufacturing Co. v. American Railways Express Co.,* 227 Mo.App. 175, 51 S.W.2d 572 (Mo.App.Ct. 1932).

Similarly, new businesses have no record of past profits by which to estimate the loss caused by a breach. Traditionally, the new-business rule prevented new businesses from collecting anything. This rule is changing as more sophisticated methods are developed for projecting future profits.

Reliance Damages   *Reliance damages* compensate the plaintiff for any expenditures she made in reliance on the contract that was subsequently breached. Instead of giving her the benefit of the bargain, reliance damages return her to the position she was in before the contract was formed. For example, Seller agrees to sell Buyer a heavy drill press. Buyer invests in renovation work to strengthen the floor where the drill press will be placed. Buyer tells Seller of this work. Seller then sells the drill press to someone else. Reliance damages will require Seller to reimburse Buyer for the renovation expenses.

Restitution and *Quantum Meruit*   *Restitution* is similar to reliance damages; but while reliance damages look at what the plaintiff has lost, restitution looks at what the other party has gained from the transaction. The usual measure of restitution is the amount it would cost the receiver of the benefit to buy that benefit elsewhere.

A court will order restitution under the doctrine of *quantum meruit* if one party has received a benefit for which he has not paid, when there was no contract between the parties. The obligation to give restitution is implied as a matter of law. For example, a doctor provides medical service to an unconscious accident victim. The doctor normally charges $200 for the care rendered. The patient could have gotten the same care from another doctor for $100. The value of the care to the patient is therefore $100. Because the patient was unconscious, he was unable to bargain for the services and enter into a contract. In a situation like this, a court will act as if there were a contract in order to prevent the patient from benefiting unfairly. The court will order the patient to make restitution by paying the doctor $100 for her services.

Mitigation of Damages

When one party breaches a contract, the other party has a duty to avoid increasing the amount of damages, and even to take reasonable action to *mitigate,* or lessen, the amount of the damages. In the cotton example discussed above, suppose that cotton is available on the open market at $24 and $25 per bale. If the quality is the same at either price, the buyer is required to buy at the lower price.

Liquidated Damages

The parties to a contract may include a clause that specifies the amount of money to be paid if one of them should later breach the agreement. Such *liquidated damages* clauses are frequently used in real estate and construction contracts. The amount of the liquidated damages should be the parties' best estimate of what the expectation damages would be. Courts will not permit liquidated damages that are substantially higher than the losses. The effect of such a large amount would be to punish the party for breaching, and this is contrary to the purpose of contract damages.

■ Specific Performance

Instead of awarding monetary damages, a court may order the breaching party to complete the contract as promised. Specific performance is ordered only when the goods are unique, when the subject of the contract is real property, or when the amount of the loss is so uncertain that there is no fair way to calculate damages.

Courts never force an employee to provide services under an employment contract. It would constitute involuntary servitude in violation of the Thirteenth Amendment of the U.S. Constitution. For example, a chief executive officer agrees to work for a corporation for five years. If he walks out after three years, the court will not force him to continue his employment. The court may, however, issue an injunction barring him from working for someone else. Similarly, if a professional baseball player with a seven-year contract with the Chicago Cubs breaches his contract and starts playing for the Houston Astros, an injunction can be granted to prevent him from playing for the Astros.

■ Promissory Estoppel

If one party fails to perform its contractual obligations, a court may award damages or, in some cases, order specific performance. But if there is no contract—only a promise—can a court enforce the promise? Traditionally, a promise is enforceable only if it is exchanged for consideration. Because a promise to make a gift is not a contract, it will not usually be enforced. For example, if Aunt Leila promises to give her niece $1,000 for a trip to Europe on the first Christmas after she turns 21, Aunt Leila is not bound by that promise. She is free to change her mind because she has not received any consideration in return for the promise.

But suppose the niece relies on this promise and purchases a nonrefundable plane ticket to Europe. Has the niece's action changed the nature of Aunt Leila's promise? Traditional contract law says no, because the niece's action was not part of a bargain with the aunt. The modern view is quite different. If the niece acts, to her detriment, in reliance on the promise, and if the aunt should reasonably have known that she would do so, the promise is enforceable under the doctrine of *promissory estoppel.*

The modern form of promissory estoppel is defined as follows:

> A promise which the promisor should reasonably expect to induce action or forbearance on the part of the promisee or a third person and which does induce such action or forbearance is binding if injustice can be avoided only by enforcement of the promise. The remedy granted for breach may be limited as justice requires.

Requirements

Promissory estoppel does not make all promises enforceable. The general rule is that gratuitous promises—that is, promises not supported by consideration—are not binding. Promissory estoppel allows an exception to this rule only if the following four requirements are met.

Promise   There must be a promise. A statement of future intent is not sufficient, nor is an estimate or a misstatement of fact. For example, Hank Delane asks Bart Andrews the time and Andrews mistakenly tells Delane it is two o'clock when it is really three o'clock. As a result Delane misses an important appointment. Delane has relied on the information to his detriment, but there was no promise.

Justifiable Reliance   The promise must cause the promisee to take an action that she would not have otherwise taken. When the niece buys the plane ticket to Europe, she is relying on her aunt's promise. If she had not bought the ticket there would be no reliance, and her aunt would be free to take back her promise.

Foreseeability   The action taken in reliance on the promise must be reasonably foreseeable to the promisor. It is foreseeable that the niece would buy a plane ticket as a result of her aunt's promise. It is not foreseeable that she would quit her job to take a six-month vacation in Europe. Therefore, the aunt would probably have to pay for the plane ticket but not for the niece's lost wages.

Injustice   A promise that has been reasonably relied upon will be enforced only if the failure to do so would cause injustice. The exact meaning of "injustice" has been debated in a variety of legal tracts, but a good rule of thumb is whether or not the promisee has been harmed by her reliance on the promise. If the niece had made a plane reservation that could be canceled without penalty, there would be no injustice in letting the aunt take back her promise, and promissory estoppel would not apply.

Business Applications

Textbook examples of promissory estoppel may seem of minor importance to a businessperson, but recent applications in this area to contract negotiation, especially negotiation of employment contracts, are changing longstanding norms of business transactions.

The original interpretation of promissory estoppel was that it applied only to gifts, not to bilateral exchanges. However, a series of cases in the mid-1960s used promissory estoppel to enforce promises made in the course of contract negotiations. The leading case is set forth below.

■   **A Case in Point:**   **In the Language of the Court**

Case 8.5
HOFFMAN v. RED OWL STORES, INC.
Supreme Court of Wisconsin
26 Wis. 2d 683, 133 N.W.2d 267 (Wis. 1965).

FACTS   Hoffman negotiated with Red Owl Stores, Inc. to open a Red Owl grocery store. The negotiations went through several stages and continued for more than two years before they broke down.

When Hoffman first approached Red Owl about buying a franchise, he said he only had $18,000 to invest. Red Owl assured him that this amount would be sufficient. Hoffman already owned a bakery, and with Red Owl's encouragement, he bought a small grocery store to get more experience. The store was profitable, but Red Owl advised Hoffman to sell it because he would have a larger Red Owl store within a few months. A site in Chilton was soon found for the new store, and Hoffman paid the $1,000 deposit.

Meanwhile, Hoffman had also rented a residence for himself and his family by the new site.

Red Owl then told Hoffman that he had to sell his bakery before the franchise deal could go through. He sold it, and negotiations proceeded regarding the details of financing and leasing the new store. At this stage, Red Owl increased Hoffman's required investment from $18,000 to $24,100, and a few weeks later to $26,100. Hoffman requested money from his father-in-law, who agreed to put money into the business provided he could come in as a partner. Negotiations broke down when Red Owl insisted that the father-in-law sign an agreement stating that the money he was advancing was an outright gift. Hoffman sued Red Owl for damages based on the defendant's failure to keep promises which had induced the plaintiff to act to his detriment.

ISSUE PRESENTED   Can a party to failed negotiations successfully assert a claim for promissory estoppel based on the precontractual negotiations and agreements and his acts taken in reliance thereon?

OPINION   CURRIE, C.J., writing for the Wisconsin Supreme Court:

. . . .

Many courts of other jurisdictions have seen fit over the years to adopt the principle of promissory estoppel, and the tendency in that direction continues. As Mr. Justice McFADDIN, speaking in behalf of the Arkansas court, well stated, that the development of the law of promissory estoppel "is an attempt by the courts to keep remedies abreast of increased moral consciousness of honesty and fair representations in all business dealings."[14]

. . . .

The record here discloses a number of promises and assurances given to Hoffman by Lukowitz on behalf of Red Owl upon which plaintiffs relied and acted upon to their detriment.

Foremost were the promises that for the sum of $18,000 Red Owl would establish Hoffman in a store. After Hoffman had sold his grocery store and paid the $1,000 on the Chilton lot, the $18,000 figure was changed to $24,100. Then in November, 1961, Hoffman was assured that if the $24,100 figure were increased by $2,000 the deal would go through. Hoffman was induced to sell his grocery store fixtures and inventory in June, 1961, on the promise that he would be in his new store by fall. In November, plaintiffs sold their bakery building on the urging of defendants and on the assurance that this was the last step necessary to have the deal with Red Owl go through.

. . . .

There remains for consideration the question of law raised by defendants that agreement was never reached on essential factors necessary to establish a contract between Hoffman and Red Owl. Among these were the size, cost, design, and layout of the store building; and the terms of the lease

---

14. *Peoples National Bank of Little Rock v. Linebarger Construction Company*, 219 Ark. 11, 17, 240 S.W.2d 12, 16 (Ark. 1951).

*Case **8.5** continued on following page*

Case *8.5* continued

with respect to rent, maintenance, renewal, and purchase options. This poses the question of whether the promise necessary to sustain a cause of action for promissory estoppel must embrace all essential details of a proposed transaction between promisor and promisee so as to be the equivalent of an offer that would result in a binding contract between the parties if the promisee were to accept the same.

Originally the doctrine of promissory estoppel was invoked as a substitute for consideration rendering a gratuitous promise enforceable as a contract. In other words, the acts of reliance by the promisee to his detriment provided a substitute for consideration. If promissory estoppel were to be limited to only those situations where the promise giving rise to the cause of action must be so definite with respect to all details that a contract would result were the promise supported by consideration, then the defendants' instant promises to Hoffman would not meet this test. However, . . . [it is not necessary that] the requirement that the promise giving rise to the cause of action must be so comprehensive in scope as to meet the requirements of an offer that would ripen into a contract if accepted by the promisee.

Rather the conditions imposed are:
(1) Was the promise one which the promisor should reasonably expect to induce action or forbearance of a definite and substantial character on the part of the promisee?
(2) Did the promise induce such action or forbearance?
(3) Can injustice be avoided only by enforcement of the promise?

We deem it would be a mistake to regard an action grounded on promissory estoppel as the equivalent of a breach of contract action. As Dean Boyer points out, it is desirable that fluidity in the application of the concept be maintained.[15]

. . . .

We conclude that injustice would result here if plaintiffs were not granted some relief because of the failure of defendants to keep their promises which induced plaintiffs to act to their detriment.

. . . .

"The wrong is not primarily in depriving the plaintiff of the promised reward but in causing the plaintiff to change position to his detriment. It would follow that the damages should not exceed the loss caused by the change of position, which would never be more in amount, but might be less, than the promised reward."[16]

. . . .

RESULT   The court awarded damages to the plaintiffs for all items except for one—damages for loss, if any, on the sale of the grocery store, fixtures, and inventory—as to which a new trial was ordered to determine appropriate damages.

---

15. Benjamin F. Boyer, "Promissory Estoppel: Requirements and Limitations of the Doctrine," 98 *University of Pennsylvania Law Review* 459, 497 (1950).
16. Warren Seavey, "Reliance on Gratuitous Promises or Other Conduct," 64 *Harvard Law Review* 913, 926 (1951).

Questions

1. Assuming that Hoffman relocated his family to be near the new store site, should the personal moving expenses of Hoffman's family be reimbursed?

2. Suppose that Hoffman made less money at his new job at the grocery store than he had previously made at the bakery. Given that Hoffman had only taken on this job at the grocery store to gain experience before owning a Red Owl, should he be compensated for his lost wages?

Parties to a business negotiation will say many things in order to move discussions along and get the best bargain possible. Often it is necessary to agree on one issue before the next one can be discussed. Promissory estoppel forbids the retraction of a bargaining concession if the other party has acted in reliance on it. For example, in *Arcadian Phosphates, Inc. v. Arcadian Corp.*,[17] the parties were engaged in negotiations for the sale of Arcadian's phosphate fertilizer facility to API. A four-page memorandum of understanding, which made the deal subject to the approval of Arcadian's board, was signed. It outlined the assets to be purchased, the purchase price, and an option for Arcadian to purchase up to 20% of API. It further provided that both parties would "cooperate fully and work judiciously in order to expedite the closing date and consummate the sale of the business."

While final negotiations were continuing, the market for phosphates changed dramatically. Market prices for diammonium phosphate, the bellwether of the industry, went up 25% in five weeks. The consensus at the next board meeting of Arcadian was that the joint venture could not proceed as originally contemplated. When Arcadian informed API of its change in position, API sued Arcadian claiming breach of contract or, in the alternative, promissory estoppel.

The U.S. Court of Appeals for the Second Circuit upheld dismissal of API's breach of contract claim, but reversed the lower court's dismissal of the promissory estoppel claim. The court stated that it was unclear whether Arcadian made an unambiguous promise to negotiate in good faith. If it did, and if API sustained an injury when it relied on the promise, a finding of promissory estoppel would be appropriate. In that event, the appropriate measurement of damages would be API's out-of-pocket expenses, not the profits API could expect to make through the joint venture.

---

17. 884 F.2d 69 (2d Cir. 1989).

■ Precontractual Liability

Cases such as *Arcadian* and *Hoffman* have extended promissory estoppel to provide compensation for losses incurred when business negotiations fail. Liability for such losses, when negotiations fail to ripen into a contract, is now known as *precontractual liability*. This doctrine deserves considerable attention because of its importance to complex business negotiations and its evolving nature. In addition, although the law may not always require fair dealing in negotiations, ethical considerations may. E. Allan Farnsworth, professor of law at Columbia University, has written an insightful summary of the current state of the law concerning precontractual liability and the likely direction of future developments. His article, "Precontractual Liability and Preliminary Agreements: Fair Dealing and Failed Negotiations" is excerpted and summarized below.[18]

Introduction

Business contracts today are often formed through complex negotiations, often involving many parties. These negotiations are a far cry from the simple bargaining envisioned by the traditional rules of offer and acceptance. During negotiations, there is often no actual offer or counteroffer, but rather a series of agreements reached through a gradual process.

If negotiations fail before a contract has been signed, a number of questions of law can arise that the classic rules of offer and acceptance do not address: Does the disappointed party have a claim against the other for expenses or opportunity costs? Do parties in negotiation have to conform to a standard of fair dealing?

---

18. Copyright © 1987 by the Directors of the Columbia Law Review Association, Inc. All Rights Reserved. This article originally appeared at 87 *Columbia Law Review* 217 (1987). Reprinted by permission.

The principles of existing contract law can be applied to all three stages of the process of contract formation. These are: (1) negotiation, (2) preliminary agreements, and (3) the ultimate agreement.

> *Business contracts today are often formed through complex negotiations, often involving many parties. These negotiations are a far cry from the simple bargaining envisioned by the traditional rules of offer and acceptance.*

Negotiation

Under traditional contract law, the offeror is free to back out and revoke the offer at any time before a contract is made. Under this doctrine a party entering negotiations does so at the risk of their being broken off.

In recent decades, however, courts have shown increasing willingness to impose precontractual liability on grounds of unjust enrichment, misrepresentation, or specific promise.

Unjust Enrichment   *Unjust enrichment* occurs when a negotiating party unfairly appropriates the benefits of negotiation for her own use. For example, if one party discloses a trade secret in the interest of the negotiation, it would be unfair for the other party to use that secret for its own benefit if negotiations fail.

The normal time and effort put into a negotiation is considered part of the risk of negotiating. However, if an architect, for example, renders a service to a developer, such as drawing plans, the developer cannot then use the plans to award the contract to another party.

If a court finds that there was unjust enrichment, it may order the unjustly enriched party to pay for the benefits it has received. In practice, restitution has been ordered in only a few cases, where ideas were misappropriated during negotiations.

Misrepresentation   Misrepresentation occurs when a party: (1) enters into a negotiation without serious intent to reach agreement; (2) fails to give prompt notice of a change in mind or intent; (3) alleges more authority to negotiate than it actually has; or (4) fails to disclose something it has a duty to disclose. For example, the Supreme Court of Washington found misrepresentation when the owner of a warehouse told the lessee that he intended to renew the lease for three years, when he was actually negotiating the sale of the facility. The owner was entering into negotiations without serious intent to reach agreement. The court held that the owner must carry out his promise to renew the lease. In practice, courts have rarely applied the law of misrepresentation to failed negotiations.

Specific Promise   A negotiating party who breaks a promise made during negotiations may be liable if the other party acted in reliance on that promise. This application of promissory estoppel was used in *Hoffman v. Red Owl Stores* [case 8.5].

Preliminary Agreements

Preliminary agreements are made during negotiations in anticipation of some later, final agreement. Examples from business include letters of intent between a buyer and a seller of a business, commitment letters by a bank to lend money, and memorandums of understanding between two companies that plan to merge.

Two common types of preliminary agreements are agreements with open terms and agreements to negotiate.

Agreements with Open Terms   In a preliminary agreement with open terms, the parties leave some terms to be negotiated later. If those terms remain unresolved because one party did not fulfill its obligation to negotiate, a court will hold that party liable.

If the parties fail to agree on the open terms despite continued negotiation, they are bound by the terms of their original agreement, and the courts are left to supply the missing terms as they see fit. For example, some agreements for the sale of goods leave the price open for later determination. Should later negotiations on the price fail, a court will supply the missing price.

The important point here is that preliminary agreements with open terms are binding even if the parties cannot later agree on the missing terms.

An agreement with open terms imposes on the parties a duty of fair dealing. A breach of this duty entitles the injured party to out-of-pocket damages, and it also entitles the injured party to refuse to perform under the agreement. In some cases, it may be regarded as a breach of the contract, entitling the injured party to benefit-of-the-bargain damages.

To determine the enforceability of preliminary agreements, courts examine: (1) the intent of the parties to be bound, and (2) the definiteness of the terms of the agreement. The great bulk of litigation concerning the enforceability of preliminary agreements with open terms has involved the problem of intent, as in the case of *Pennzoil v. Texaco* [discussed in the "Inside Story" for this chapter].

The parties can make a preliminary agreement non-binding by stating their intent not to be bound. However, courts will honor such an intent only if it is expressed in the clearest language. For example, titling an agreement a "letter of intent," or using the phrase "formal agreement to follow" might not be enough to prove to a court that the parties did not intend to be bound.

In deciding whether the parties to a preliminary agreement intended to be bound, courts look to a variety of factors, including: (1) the degree to which the terms of the agreement are spelled out; (2) the circumstances of the parties (for example, the importance of the deal to them); (3) the parties' prior course of dealing with each other, if any; and (4) the parties' behavior subsequent to the execution of the agreement (for example, issuing a press release may demonstrate intent).

Agreements to Negotiate   In a preliminary agreement to negotiate, the parties do not agree to be bound by the terms of the agreement. They are simply agreeing to continue the process of negotiations, with the aim of reaching an ultimate agreement. For example, in mergers and acquisitions, a letter of intent between the acquiring company and the target does not bind the two parties if, after continued negotiations, the parties are unable to agree on the formal or definitive documents.

The parties to an agreement to negotiate should deal fairly. However, courts have refused to enforce agreements to negotiate even when there has been a breach of the duty of fair dealing. The courts have argued that: (1) a court cannot fashion an appropriate remedy for breach of the duty because there is no way to know what the ultimate agreement would have been; and (2) a court cannot properly determine the scope of the duty of fair dealing under such agreements. [Note that this was written before the Seventh Circuit decision in *Apothekernes* (case 8.1).]

The Ultimate Agreement

Even when parties agree to and sign an ultimate agreement, it may not become final until certain conditions are met. If the conditions are not met, the contract terminates automatically. For example, a contract can be drafted as binding subject to obtaining financing or government approval. A buyer of real estate may condition her purchase on a pending government ruling on zoning. Courts have even allowed the parties to leave open the precise nature of a financing.

Conditional clauses must not be illusory promises. For example, courts usually disallow clauses that condition an agreement on the approval of a party's own lawyer.

The Meaning of Fair Dealing

Parties to a negotiation should describe as specifically as possible the duty of fair dealing to which they have agreed. Instead of simply pledging to use "best efforts" to negotiate fairly, the parties should specify whether the negotiations are to be exclusive, how long they must continue, what must be disclosed, and what must be held in confidence. Given the uncertain state of the law on these matters, no drafter should leave these items to a court to fill in.

Courts will go beyond the language of a preliminary agreement and look at the circumstances surrounding the negotiation to determine whether the dealings were fair. For example, courts will examine trade practices and the previous relationship of the parties.

Unfair Dealing   Unfair dealing can be broadly grouped under seven headings: (1) refusal to negotiate, (2) improper tactics, (3) unreasonable proposals, (4) nondisclosure, (5) negotiation with others, (6) reneging, and (7) breaking off negotiations.

A refusal to negotiate can take several forms, besides an outright refusal to talk about terms. Delay tactics can be tantamount to outright refusal. Refusal to negotiate except on certain terms can also be considered a breach. For example, a party cannot condition its willingness to bargain on a change in the composition of the other party's bargaining team.

Stubborn and unyielding bargaining alone does not constitute unfair dealing, but it can be evidence of it. For example, an employer who consistently rejects out of hand all of a union's proposals would likely be found to be bargaining in bad faith, that is, dealing unfairly.

Although it is difficult for courts to judge the reasonableness of a proposal made in a negotiation, some cases are clear. For example, a proposal to renew a franchise on terms significantly less favorable to the franchisee, when there has been no change in circumstances, would most likely be considered unreasonable.

Successful negotiation often requires skillful judgment about what to communicate to the other party. However, in some instances, failure to disclose facts amounts to a misrepresentation. In general, parties are under an obligation not to misstate facts or intentions. There is a heavier burden of disclosure when the parties are not on equal footing, for example, when a fiduciary (such as a trustee) negotiates with a beneficiary.

Fairness does not generally require a party to negotiate with one party to the exclusion of all others. However, it seems reasonable, although perhaps not legally required, for each party to keep the other apprised of relevant proposals from third parties and to give an opportunity to respond to counteroffers. The agreement to negotiate may contain an exclusive-negotiation clause which obligates one party to refrain from negotiating with others. Courts have not always upheld these clauses, but they are more inclined to do so if the clause specifies a time limit on the exclusivity.

Reneging on an agreement to negotiate can be considered a breach of the duty of fair dealing, particularly if the negotiations are well advanced. Reneging can amount to a refusal to negotiate.

There are some situations in which a party is justified in breaking off negotiations, such as changed circumstances, mistake, unfair dealing by the other party, or an impasse in the negotiations that makes it clear that the negotiations have no chance of success. However, a party cannot arbitrarily break off negotiations without making a reasonable effort to reach an agreement.

Fair Dealing   The standard of fair dealing ordinarily requires at least three things. First, each party must actually negotiate and refrain from imposing improper conditions on the negotiation. Second, each party must disclose enough about parallel negotiations to allow the other party to make a counterproposal. Third, each party

must continue to negotiate until an impasse—or an agreement—has been reached. The standard does not require a party to bargain exclusively, to bargain for a specific length of time, or to disclose the basis of its proposals.

■ Conflicting Duties

Sometimes there is a conflict between the duties owed under a contract and a duty owed to other parties. This comes up frequently in the context of mergers and acquisitions.

Merger Agreements

A *merger agreement* is an agreement between two companies to combine into one. A merger cannot generally be completed until it is approved by the shareholders of both companies.

A merger agreement will frequently require the board of directors of the target company—that is, the company being acquired—to recommend the deal to the shareholders and to use their best efforts to consummate the transaction. Such a provision is called a best-efforts clause. What happens if a third party comes along and offers a higher price to the target company? May the board of directors of the target company negotiate with the third party? May it recommend the new deal to the shareholders? Has the third party incurred any liability by interfering with the previously signed merger agreement? Or is the third party just being competitive by offering a better price?

As was explained in the discussion in chapter 7 on torts, the elements required to be proven in a suit for tortious interference with a contract are as follows: (1) a contract must exist between the plaintiff and another; (2) the defendant must have knowledge of the contract between the plaintiff and the other party; (3) the defendant's actions must cause the other party to breach the contract with the plaintiff; (4) the plaintiff must be damaged in some way; and (5) the defendant must intentionally and wrongfully induce the other party to breach the contract with the plaintiff.

Different courts have disagreed on what actions the target company's board of directors may or must take with regard to best-efforts clauses and what liability a competing bidder has if it succeeds in persuading the board of directors of the target company to breach the agreement with the first suitor and recommend the second deal to the shareholders.

International Consideration

When doing business with companies in other nations, it is important to remember that although the law in the United States stems from a common law tradition, many non-English-speaking countries follow the civil law tradition. This system of jurisprudence was originally used in the Roman Empire, where it included Institutes, Codes, Digests, and Novels. Civil law countries rely primarily on codes (such as the Napoleonic Code in France) rather than case-by-case common law to develop rules for behavior. Therefore, it is prudent to include in multinational contracts a provision stating which country's law will apply (a choice of law provision) and in which jurisdiction a dispute must be brought (a choice of forum provision).

In Brief: Decision Tree for Contract Analysis

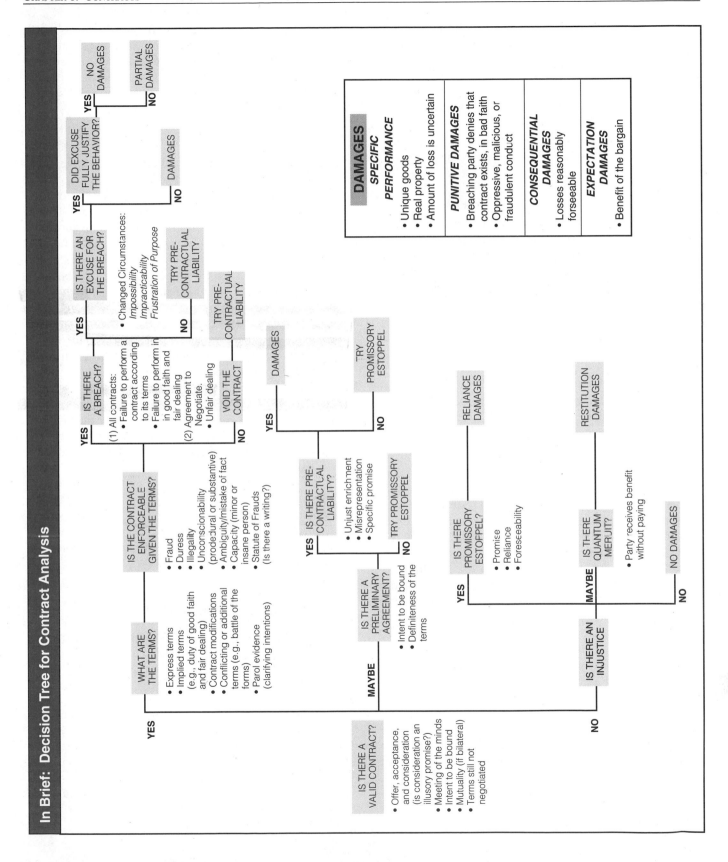

IS THERE A VALID CONTRACT?
- Offer, acceptance, and consideration (is consideration an illusory promise?)
- Meeting of the minds
- Intent to be bound
- Mutuality (if bilateral)
- Terms still not negotiated

IS THERE A PRELIMINARY AGREEMENT?
- Intent to be bound
- Definiteness of the terms

IS THERE PRE-CONTRACTUAL LIABILITY?
- Unjust enrichment
- Misrepresentation
- Specific promise

IS THERE PROMISSORY ESTOPPEL?
- Promise
- Reliance
- Foreseeability

IS THERE AN INJUSTICE

IS THERE QUANTUM MERUIT?
- Party receives benefit without paying

WHAT ARE THE TERMS?
- Express terms
- Implied terms (e.g., duty of good faith and fair dealing)
- Contract modifications
- Conflicting or additional terms (e.g., battle of the forms)
- Parol evidence (clarifying intentions)

IS THE CONTRACT ENFORCEABLE GIVEN THE TERMS?
- Fraud
- Duress
- Illegality
- Unconscionability (procedural or substantive)
- Ambiguity/mistake of fact
- Capacity (minor or insane person)
- Statute of Frauds (Is there a writing?)

IS THERE A BREACH?
(1) All contracts:
- Failure to perform a contract according to its terms
- Failure to perform in good faith and fair dealing
(2) Agreement to Negotiate.
- Unfair dealing

IS THERE AN EXCUSE FOR THE BREACH?
- Changed Circumstances:
  Impossibility
  Impracticability
  Frustration of Purpose

DID EXCUSE FULLY JUSTIFY THE BEHAVIOR?

NO DAMAGES

PARTIAL DAMAGES

DAMAGES

TRY PRE-CONTRACTUAL LIABILITY

VOID THE CONTRACT

TRY PRE-CONTRACTUAL LIABILITY

DAMAGES

TRY PROMISSORY ESTOPPEL

RELIANCE DAMAGES

RESTITUTION DAMAGES

NO DAMAGES

DAMAGES

SPECIFIC PERFORMANCE
- Unique goods
- Real property
- Amount of loss is uncertain

PUNITIVE DAMAGES
- Breaching party denies that contract exists, in bad faith
- Oppressive, malicious, or fraudulent conduct

CONSEQUENTIAL DAMAGES
- Losses reasonably forseeable

EXPECTATION DAMAGES
- Benefit of the bargain

In *Jewel Companies, Inc. v. Pay Less Drug Stores Northwest, Inc.,*[19] the U.S. Court of Appeals for the Ninth Circuit held that the board of directors of a target company that had signed a merger agreement with one suitor could bind itself to refrain from negotiating or accepting a second merger proposal prior to the shareholder vote on the first proposal. The court stated:

> It is nowhere written in stone that the law of the jungle must be the exclusive doctrine governing parties within the world of corporate mergers. The legitimate exercise of the right to contract by responsible boards of directors can help bring some degree of much needed order to these transactions.

The court held that the third party, which offered a higher price, could be liable for tortious interference with contract if the target company and the first suitor intended an agreement not to deal with any other party until the first deal was put to the target company's shareholders for a vote.

❝

"It is nowhere written in stone that the law of the jungle must be the exclusive doctrine governing parties within the world of corporate mergers."

In *ConAgra, Inc. v. Cargill, Inc.,*[20] the merger agreement between the target company and the first suitor stated that "nothing herein contained shall relieve either Board of Directors of their continuing duties to their respective shareholders." The Nebraska Supreme Court interpreted this clause to mean that the parties agreed that the target company was not contracting out of its duty to recommend the deal that would be best for its shareholders. The court held that the third party, which offered a higher price, could disrupt the merger with the first suitor without facing liability for tortious interference with contract.

The Delaware Supreme Court cited *ConAgra* with approval in *Paramount Communications Inc. v. QVC Network Inc.*[21] Paramount had entered into a friendly merger agreement with Viacom. As part of the deal, Paramount granted Viacom an option to buy Paramount shares at a favorable price (a *lock-up option*) together with a termination fee payable if the merger did not go through. QVC made a hostile bid for Paramount and

sought to invalidate the lock-up option, which was worth about $500 million. The Delaware Supreme Court held that because the directors of Paramount had violated their fiduciary duties by granting the option, Viacom had no enforceable contractual right to the option. This case is discussed in the "Inside Story" in chapter 21.

Fiduciary Outs

A merger agreement can be drafted to prevent the target company from soliciting other offers yet allow it to consider unsolicited offers. For example, Lucky Stores, Inc. and a management buyout group led by Gibbons, Green, van Amerongen entered into a merger agreement while Lucky was facing a hostile takeover bid by American Stores. The American bid was for $45 a share; the Gibbons bid was for $61 a share. The agreement between Lucky and Gibbons gave the Lucky directors a *fiduciary out*, which allows the target company's directors to remain faithful to their fiduciary duties to their shareholders even after signing an agreement with a suitor. In this case, the fiduciary out allowed the directors of Lucky to recommend to their shareholders unsolicited offers other than the Gibbons offer. In return for this privilege, Lucky agreed to pay Gibbons a $20 million break-up fee if Lucky's directors recommended a deal other than the one with Gibbons. A *break-up fee* is an agreed-upon payment to a suitor if, through no fault of the suitor, the merger is not consummated.

After hearing of the Gibbons bid and receiving access to certain confidential information concerning Lucky, American raised its bid to $65 a share. Lucky's board of directors recommended the higher American bid. American eventually acquired Lucky, and Gibbons was paid the $20 million break-up fee.

The Responsible Manager

Acting in Good Faith and Dealing Fairly

A contract requires a meeting of the minds. It is rarely to a manager's advantage to try to slip a provision by the other party that the manager knows would be unacceptable if it were pointed out. It is far preferable to hash out any ambiguities at the negotiation stage while the parties are on good terms and in the mood to make a deal. Positions tend to polarize once the agreement is signed and a dispute arises.

---

741 F.2d 1555 (9th Cir. 1984).
222 Neb. 136, 382 N.W.2d 576 (Neb. 1986).
637 A.2d. 34 (Del. 1994).

Similarly, it is inappropriate and often unethical to bury offensive terms in a preprinted form contract in the hope that the other party will not spot them. Courts will sometimes refuse to enforce such terms, especially when they conflict with the position taken in the negotiations or are contrary to the spirit of the deal.

It makes both legal and ethical sense to abide by the covenant of good faith and fair dealing in negotiating a contract. It is also good business. Contract litigation is expensive and time consuming.

A manager should carefully consider whether there will be a conflict between the acts required by a contract and his fiduciary duties to the corporation and its share-holders. In general, a manager should not bind herself to recommend a particular deal to the shareholders, because it is always possible that a better offer will come along. She should reserve the right to recommend the best deal, even if to do so requires paying a break-up fee to the first bidder.

A manager should ensure that he is not tortiously interfering with the contract of another. As *Pennzoil v. Texaco,* discussed below, demonstrates, even a very large company can be driven into bankruptcy if its executives guess wrong either on the question of whether there is a contract or on the question of whether their deal tortiously interferes with it.

Inside Story

Pennzoil v. Texaco

In 1983, Pennzoil Company and Getty Oil Company negotiated a memorandum of agreement for a merger. Their cadres of lawyers were in the process of drafting the final documents when Texaco, Inc. came along and offered a better price for Getty. Getty accepted Texaco's offer, and Pennzoil subsequently sued Texaco for tortious interference with contract. Texaco asserted that Pennzoil never had a contract, because the parties had not yet agreed on every essential term of the deal. A Texas jury disagreed and awarded Pennzoil $10.5 billion in compensatory and punitive damages.

It took the two parties four and a half months to present all the facts and arguments to the jury. The published opinion of the Texas Court of Appeals summarizes the events in question.[22]

Excerpts From the Opinion of the Court of Appeals: The Facts

For several months in late 1983, Pennzoil had followed with interest the well-publicized dissension between the board of directors of Getty Oil Company and Gordon Getty, who was a director of Getty Oil and also the owner, as trustee, of approximately 40.2% of the outstanding shares of Getty Oil. On December 28, 1983, Pennzoil announced an unsolicited, public tender offer for 16 million shares of Getty Oil at $100 each.

Soon afterwards, Pennzoil contacted both Gordon Getty and a representative of the J. Paul Getty Museum, which held approximately 11.8% of the shares of Getty Oil, to discuss the tender offer and the possible purchase of Getty Oil. In the first two days of January 1984, a "Memorandum of Agreement" was drafted to reflect the terms that had been reached in conversations between representatives of Pennzoil, Gordon Getty, and the Museum.

Under the plan set out in the Memorandum of Agreement, Pennzoil and the Trust (with Gordon Getty as trustee) were to become partners on a 3/7ths to 4/7ths basis respectively, in owning and operating Getty Oil. Gordon Getty was to become chairman of the board, and Hugh Liedtke, the chief executive officer of Pennzoil, was to become chief executive officer of the new company. The plan also provided that Pennzoil and the Trust were to try in good faith to agree upon a plan to restructure Getty Oil within a year, but if they could not reach an agreement, the assets of Getty Oil were to be divided between them, 3/7ths to Pennzoil and 4/7ths to the Trust.

The Memorandum of Agreement stated that it was subject to approval of the board of Getty Oil, and it was to expire by its own terms if not approved at the board meeting that was to begin on January 2. Pennzoil's CEO, Liedtke, and Gordon Getty, for the Trust, signed the Memorandum of Agreement before the Getty Oil board meeting on January 2, and Harold Williams, the president of the Museum, signed it shortly after the board meeting began. Thus, before it was submitted to the Getty Oil board, the Memorandum of Agreement had been executed by parties who together controlled a majority of the outstanding shares of Getty Oil.

22. *Texaco, Inc. v. Pennzoil Co.,* 729 S.W.2d 768 (Tex.Ct.App. 1987).

Inside Story continued on following page

Inside Story, *continued*

The Memorandum of Agreement was then presented to the Getty Oil board, which had previously held discussions on how the company should respond to Pennzoil's public tender offer.

The board voted to reject recommending Pennzoil's tender offer to Getty's shareholders, then later also rejected the Memorandum of Agreement price of $110 per share as too low. On the morning of January 3, Getty Oil's investment banker, Geoffrey Boisi, began calling other companies, seeking a higher bid than Pennzoil's for the Getty Oil shares.

When the board reconvened at 3 P.M. on January 3, a revised Pennzoil proposal was presented, offering $110 per share plus a $3 "stub" that was to be paid after the sale of a Getty Oil subsidiary ("ERC"), from the excess proceeds over $1 billion. Each shareholder was to receive a pro rata share of these excess proceeds, but in any case, a minimum of $3 per share at the end of five years. During the meeting, Boisi briefly informed the board of the status of his inquiries of other companies that might be interested in bidding for the company. He reported some preliminary indications of interest, but no definite bid yet.

The Museum's lawyer told the board that, based on his discussions with Pennzoil, he believed that if the board went back "firm" with an offer of $110 plus a $5 stub, Pennzoil would accept it. After a recess, the Museum's president (also a director of Getty Oil) moved that the Getty board should accept Pennzoil's proposal provided that the stub be raised to $5, and the board voted 15 to 1 to approve this counterproposal to Pennzoil. The board then voted themselves and Getty's officers and advisors indemnity for any liability arising from the events of the past few months. There was evidence that during another brief recess of the board meeting, the counteroffer of $110 plus a $5 stub was presented to and accepted by Pennzoil. After Pennzoil's acceptance was conveyed to the Getty board, the meeting was adjourned, and most board members left town for their respective homes.

That evening, the lawyers and public relations staff of Getty Oil and the Museum drafted a press release describing the transaction between Pennzoil and the Getty entities. The press release, announcing an agreement in principle on the terms of the Memorandum of Agreement but with a price of $110 plus a $5 stub, was issued on Getty Oil letterhead the next morning, January 4, and later that day, Pennzoil issued an identical press release.

On January 4, Boisi continued to contact other companies, looking for a higher price than Pennzoil had offered. After talking briefly with Boisi, Texaco management called several meetings with its in-house financial planning group, which over the course of the day studied and reported to management on the value of Getty Oil, the Pennzoil offer terms, and a feasible price range at which Getty might be acquired. Later in the day, Texaco hired an investment banker, First Boston, to represent it with respect to a possible acquisition of Getty Oil. Meanwhile, also on

January 4, Pennzoil's lawyers were working on a draft of a formal "transaction agreement" that described the transaction in more detail than the outline of terms contained in the Memorandum of Agreement and press release.

On January 5, *The Wall Street Journal* reported on an agreement reached between Pennzoil and the Getty entities, describing essentially the terms contained in the Memorandum of Agreement. The Pennzoil board met to ratify the actions of its officers in negotiating an agreement with the Getty entities, and Pennzoil's attorneys periodically attempted to contact the other parties' advisors and attorneys to continue work on the transaction agreement.

The board of Texaco also met on January 5, authorizing its officers to make an offer for 100% of Getty Oil and to take any necessary action in connection therewith. Texaco first contacted the Museum's lawyer, Marty Lipton, and arranged a meeting to discuss the sale of the Museum's shares of Getty Oil to Texaco. Lipton instructed his associate, on her way to the meeting in progress of the lawyers drafting merger documents for the Pennzoil/Getty transaction, not to attend that meeting, because he needed her at his meeting with Texaco. At the meeting with Texaco, the Museum outlined various issues it wanted resolved in any transaction with Texaco, and then agreed to sell its 11.8% ownership in Getty Oil.

At noon on January 6, Getty Oil held a telephone board meeting to discuss the Texaco offer. The board voted to withdraw its previous counterproposal to Pennzoil and unanimously voted to accept Texaco's offer. Texaco immediately issued a press release announcing that Getty Oil and Texaco would merge.

Soon after the Texaco press release appeared, Pennzoil telexed the Getty entities, demanding that they honor their agreement with Pennzoil. Later that day, prompted by the telex, Getty Oil filed a suit in Delaware for declaratory judgment that it was not bound to any contract with Pennzoil. The merger agreement between Texaco and Getty Oil was signed on January 6; the stock purchase agreement with the Museum was signed on January 6; and the stock exchange agreement with the Trust was signed on January 8, 1984.

In addition to the facts described in the Excerpts from the Opinion of the Court of Appeals set forth immediately above, the Pennzoil lawyers emphasized several other events as evidence that both Pennzoil and Getty intended to be bound by the five-page memorandum of agreement.

On January 4, the day after the board meeting, Goldman Sachs sent Getty Oil a bill of $6 million for financial advisory services. Pennzoil subsequently argued that because it was customary to send a bill only after a deal had been concluded, Getty's banker must have considered the board approval at the end of the January 3 meeting as completing the deal.

Inside Story, continued

At the conclusion of the Getty board meeting on January 3, during which the board voted 15 to 1 to approve the Pennzoil merger, congratulations were exchanged and many of the individuals present, including several Pennzoil representatives, shook hands. Exactly who shook hands with whom could never be clearly established. At trial, Texaco pointed out that, handshakes notwithstanding, the Getty board of directors left the meeting without signing the memorandum of agreement.

That evening Hugh Liedtke called Gordon Getty's hotel suite and spoke to Gordon's wife, Ann. Ann was enthusiastic about the events of the day and asked, "Would you care to come up and join us in some champagne to celebrate the occasion?"[23] Liedtke declined, saying that he had dinner plans; but the following day, January 4, he and Gordon Getty made plans to visit Getty Oil headquarters together as a symbolic statement of the change of leadership.

At trial, Pennzoil made this an issue of honor and the value of a man's word, asserting that a handshake and a toast were actions that could and often did seal a bargain. For its part, Texaco pointed to the fact that it had not made an offer until it was invited to do so by Getty. John McKinley, chairman of Texaco, repeatedly asked if Getty Oil was free to deal and was assured by Gordon Getty and by the Getty Museum that there was no contract with Pennzoil. In addition, under the law of New York, where the deals were all made, a contract does not exist until the parties have agreed on all of the essential terms of the deal. Texaco argued that in a $5 billion deal involving four parties (Pennzoil, Getty Oil Company, the Sarah Getty Trust, and the Getty Museum) a five-page memorandum cannot possibly cover all the essential terms. Why else were upwards of 30 lawyers working around the clock to draw up the merger documents?

In contract cases, the meaning of a person's actions is often interpreted in light of the prevailing norms in the community or the industry. In this case the norms of Wall Street bankers were very different from the norms of Texas oil companies. *The Wall Street Journal* reporter Thomas Petzinger, Jr., contrasts the two groups:

> Amid the differences in corporate strategies, a collision of ethical values would erupt in the Houston courtroom. That was because every important event in the fracas—from the midnight dealmaking on the Upper East Side of New York to the trial itself less than two years later in Houston—involved a battle between two groups: the Old Good-Ol'-Boys of the oil fields and the New Good-Ol'-Boys of Wall Street.
>
> Under the Old Good-Ol'-Boys rules, you always dealt honorably with your friends; as for everyone else, well, they had better watch their step. No industry honored personal friendship more highly than the 20th-century oil industry, and no industry permitted such ruthless treatment of outsiders. You dealt with comrades on a handshake—"my word is my bond," went the motto of the All-American Wildcatters Association, of which Pennzoil's Liedtke was a prominent member—but with outsiders on a contract. "If I give my word, no one can break it," an oilman once told J. Paul Getty, "but if I sign this contract, my lawyers can break it."
>
> The New Good-Ol'-Boys of the 1980's lived by a much more modern code. Until the dotted line was signed, you remained free to stick it to anyone, even your friends if you had to. In fact, your friends expected it, and sometimes they even respected you for it. Wall Street permitted such anything-goes behavior for a perfectly good reason: The person who outmaneuvered everyone else—whether to sell at the highest price or buy at the lowest—got the best deal for whichever pension funds, insurance companies, widows, orphans, small-time speculators and big-money investors he happened to represent. In this culture, nothing was final until the last whereas and wherefore and thereupon had been recorded. There were "deals," and then there were "done deals."[24]

Before going further into the many legal arguments involved, it will be useful to look more closely at the memorandum of agreement reproduced in Exhibit 8-2.

As soon as the board meeting adjourned on the evening of January 3, work began on the legal documents and on the press release to announce the deal. Both were supposed to be completed by the next morning, but only the press release was ready. Typed on Getty Oil letterhead and dated January 4, 1984, it announced that Getty Oil and Pennzoil had "agreed in principle" to a merger. It further stated: "The transaction is subject to execution of a definitive merger agreement, approval by the stockholders of Getty Oil and completion of various governmental filing and waiting period requirements."

Getty and Pennzoil had an agreement in principle, but did they have a contract? Just what was it that the board of directors had approved? At the time that the press release went out, the lawyers were still working out the details of the merger

---

23. Reprinted by permission of The Putnam Publishing Group from Thomas Petzinger, Jr., *Oil and Honor: The Texaco-Pennzoil Wars.* Copyright © 1987 by Thomas Petzinger, Jr. [All excerpts from *Oil and Honor: The Texaco-Pennzoil Wars* (hereinafter referred to as *Oil and Honor*) reprinted by permission.]

24. *Oil and Honor*, 18.

Inside Story continued on following page

Inside Story, continued

EXHIBIT 8-2   The Pennzoil–Getty Memorandum of Agreement

Memorandum of Agreement
January 2, 1984

The following plan (the "Plan") has been developed and approved by (i) Gordon P. Getty, as Trustee (the "Trustee") of the Sarah C. Getty Trust dated December 31, 1934 (the "Trust"), which Trustee owns 31,805,800 shares (40.2% of the total outstanding shares) of Common Stock, without par value, of Getty Oil Company (the "Company"), which shares as well as all other outstanding shares of such Common Stock are hereinafter referred to as the "Shares", (ii) The J. Paul Getty Museum (the "Museum"), which Museum owns 9,320,340 Shares (11.8% of the total outstanding Shares) and (iii) Pennzoil Company ("Pennzoil"), which owns 593,900 Shares through a subsidiary, Holdings Incorporated, a Delaware corporation (the "Purchaser"). The Plan is intended to assure that the public shareholders of the Company and the Museum will receive $110 per Share for all their Shares, a price which is approximately 40% above the price at which the Company's Shares were trading before Pennzoil's subsidiary announced its Offer (hereinafer described) and 10% more than the price which Pennzoil's subsidiary offered in its Offer for 20% of the Shares. The Trustee recommends that the Board of Directors of the Company approve the Plan. The Museum desires that the Plan be considered by the Board of Directors and has executed the Plan for that purpose.

1. Pennzoil agreement. Subject to the approval of the Plan by the Board of Directors of the Company as provided in paragraph 6 hereof, Pennzoil agrees to cause the Purchaser promptly to amend its Offer to Purchase dated December 28, 1983 (the "Offer") for up to 16,000,000 Shares so as:
(a) to increase the Offer price to $110 per Share, net to the Seller in cash and
(b) to increase the number of Shares subject to the Offer to 23,406,100 (being 24,000,000 Shares less 593,900 now owned by the Purchaser).

2. Company agreement. Subject to approval of the Plan by the Board of Directors of the Company as provided in paragraph 6 hereof, the Company agrees:
(a) to purchase forthwith all 9,320,340 Shares owned by the Museum at a purchase price of $110 per Share (subject to adjustment before or after closing in the event of any increase in the Offer price or in the event any higher price is paid by any person who hereafter acquires 10 percent or more of the outstanding Shares) payable either (at the election of the Company) in cash or by means of a promissory note of the Company, dated as of the closing date, payable to the order of the Museum, due on or before thirty days from the date of issuance, bearing interest at a rate equivalent to the prime rate as in effect at Citibank, N.A. and backed by an irrevocable letter of credit (the "Company Note")
(b) To proceed promptly upon completion of the Offer by the Purchaser with a cash merger transaction whereby all remaining holders of Shares (other than the Trustee and Pennzoil and its subsidiaries) will receive $110 per Share in cash, and
(c) in consideration of Pennzoil's agreement provided for in paragraph 1 hereof and in order to provide additional assurance that the Plan will be consummated in accordance with its terms, to grant to Pennzoil hereby the option, exercisable at Pennzoil's election at any time on or before the later of consummation of the Offer referred to in paragraph 1 and the purchase referred to in (a) of this paragraph 2, to purchase from the Company up to 8,000,000 Shares of Common Stock of the Company held in the treasury of the Company at a purchase price of $110 per share in cash.

3. Museum agreement. Subject to approval of the Plan by the Board of Directors of the Company as provided in paragraph 6 hereof, the Museum agrees to sell to the Company forthwith all 9,320,340 Shares owned by the Museum at a purchase price of $110 per Share (subject to adjustment before or after closing as provided in paragraph 2(a)) payable either (at the election of the Company) in cash or by means of the Company Note referred to in paragraph 2(c).

4. Trustee and Pennzoil agreement. The Trustee and Pennzoil hereby agree with each other as follows:
(a) Ratio of Ownership of Shares. The Trustee may increase its holdings to up to 32,000,000 Shares and Pennzoil may increase its holdings to up to 24,000,000 Shares of the approximately 79,132,000 outstanding Shares. Neither the Trustee nor Pennzoil will acquire in excess of such respective amounts without the prior written agreement of the other, it being the agreement between the Trustee and Pennzoil to maintain a relative Share ratio of 4 (for the Trustee) to 3 (for Pennzoil). In connection with the Offer in the event that more than 23,406,100 Shares are duly tendered to the Purchaser, the Purchaser may (if it chooses) purchase any excess over 23,406,000; provided, however, (i) the Purchaser agrees to sell any such excess Shares to the Company (and the company shall agree to purchase) forthwith at $110 per Share and (ii) pending consummation of such sale to the Company the Purchaser shall grant to the

Inside Story, continued

EXHIBIT 8-2 *continued*

Trustee the irrevocable proxy to vote such excess Shares.

(b) Restructuring plan. Upon completion of the transactions provided for in paragraphs 1, 2 and 3 hereof, the Trustee and Pennzoil shall endeavor in good faith to agree upon a plan for the restructuring of the Company. In the event that for any reason the Trustee and Pennzoil are unable to agree upon a mutually acceptable plan on or before December 31, 1984, then the Trustee and Pennzoil hereby agree to cause the Company to adopt a plan of complete liquidation of the Company pursuant to which (i) any assets which are mutually agreed to be sold shall be sold and the net proceeds therefrom shall be used to reduce liabilities of the Company and (ii) individual interests in all remaining assets and liabilities shall be distributed to the shareholders pro rata in accordance with their actual ownership interest in the Company. In connection with the plan of distribution, Pennzoil agrees (if requested by the Trustee) that it will enter into customary joint operating agreements to operate any properties so distributed and otherwise to agree to provide operating management for any business and operations requested by the Trustee on customary terms and conditions.

(c) Board of Directors and Management. Upon completion of the transactions provided for in paragraphs 1, 2 and 3 hereof, the Trustee and Pennzoil agree that the Board of Directors of the Company shall be composed of approximately fourteen Directors who shall be mutually agreeable to the Trustee and Pennzoil (which Directors may include certain present Directors) and who shall be nominated by the Trustee and Pennzoil, respectively, in the ratio of 4 to 3. The Trustee and Pennzoil agree that the senior management of the Company shall include Gordon P. Getty as Chairman of the Board, J. Hugh Liedtke as President and Chief Executive Officer and Blaine P. Kerr as Chairman of the Executive Committee.

(d) Access to Information. Pennzoil, the Trustee and their representatives will have access to all information concerning the Company necessary or pertinent to accomplish the transactions contemplated by the Plan.

(e) Press releases. The Trustee and Pennzoil (and the Company upon approval of the Plan) will coordinate any press releases or public announcements concerning the Plan and any transactions contemplated hereby.

5. Compliance with regulatory requirements. The Plan shall be implemented in compliance with applicable regulatory requirements.

6. Approval by the Board of Directors. This Plan is subject to approval by the Board of Directors of the Company at the meeting of the Board being held on January 2, 1984, and will expire if not approved by the Board. Upon such approval the Company shall execute three or more counterparts of the "Joinder by the Company" attached to the Plan and deliver one such counterpart to each of the Trustee, the Museum and Pennzoil.

IN WITNESS WHEREOF, this Plan, or a counterpart hereof, has been signed by the following officials thereunto duly authorized this January 2, 1984.

/s/ GORDON P. GETTY
_____
Gordon P. Getty as Trustee of the Sarah C. Getty Trust

The J. Paul Getty Museum

By /s/ HAROLD WILLIAMS
_____
Harold Williams, President

Pennzoil Company
By _____
J. Hugh Liedtke Chairman of the Board and
Chief Executive Officer

Joinder by the Company

The foregoing Plan has been approved by the Board of Directors.

Getty Oil Company

By _____

January 2, 1984

Inside Story, continued

documents. How would the $5 stub be paid? What were the tax implications? Could the museum get its money right away even though Pennzoil itself could not buy the shares until the government had approved the merger?

Details like these kept the Pennzoil lawyers at work on the first draft through the night of January 3 and all of the following day. The Getty and museum lawyers started reviewing the documents on January 5. By this time, however, Texaco and Getty were deep in negotiations.

The lawyers from both sides gathered to review the final draft on the evening of January 5. Work proceeded slowly, as one by one the Getty lawyers left the session. By 1 A.M. all of the Getty lawyers were gone. They were all at the offices of the museum's lawyer, Marty Lipton, drafting documents for a deal with Texaco.

Marty Lipton, the museum's lawyer, was concerned that Liedtke would try to sue everyone involved. Lipton asked for and got an indemnity clause, whereby Texaco agreed to cover the cost of legal fees or court judgments obtained in any lawsuit against the museum. Gordon Getty also demanded and received an indemnity. The museum got one thing more. In the standard representations and warranties section the museum affirmed that it owned the shares it inherited from J. Paul Getty, but would not warrant that a contract had not been made with Pennzoil: "[N]o representation is made with respect to the standstill agreement, the consent, the stockholders' agreement or the Pennzoil agreement."[25]

The Texaco deal was much simpler than the Pennzoil deal. Texaco simply bought out everyone at $125 a share. By 7 A.M. on January 6, 1984, the drafts of the contracts between Texaco and Getty Oil and between Texaco and the Sarah Getty Trust were close to completion. The contract with the museum had been completed and signed. By 8 A.M. a news release on Texaco letterhead had gone out. At 9 A.M. the Getty board of directors held another board meeting. This time they discussed and approved the deal with Texaco. As Sid Petersen, Getty's chairman said the next day, "The fat lady has sung."[26]

All the deal making was done. Texaco acquired Getty Oil and Pennzoil was left out in the cold. No one on Wall Street saw anything wrong with the deal, but the attitude in the Texas oil business was different.

At the 1984 Pennzoil stockholder meeting, Hugh Liedtke discussed the decision to sue Texaco.

There is perhaps a greater question involved. It turns on the crucial point of integrity in our industry.

It's one thing to play hardball. It's quite another thing to play foul ball.

Conduct such as Texaco's is not made legal simply by protestations that the acts involved were, in fact, legal. All too often such assertions go unchallenged, and so slip into some sort of legal limbo, and become accepted as the norm by default. In this way, actions previously considered amoral somehow become clothed in respectability.

Pennzoil's litigation challenges this mindless slip into acceptability. We seek to test the acceptable standards of behavior in our industry.

A contract is a contract. We used to say that in the oil industry, business was done on a handshake. Should it now require handcuffs?

. . . We believe that integrity is more than just a word. It is a standard of conduct in a world perhaps gone slipshod. Our industry was built on that standard, and Pennzoil will continue to make every effort to see to it that this standard is upheld.[27]

On January 10, 1984, Pennzoil filed suit in Delaware against Getty Oil, Gordon Getty, the Getty Museum, and Texaco. Pennzoil wanted specific performance, that is, a court order that would give them back their deal with Getty. A few days later Pennzoil discovered the indemnity clauses and added tortious interference with contract to its claims against Texaco.

The Delaware case was to be tried before a judge, not a jury. Through some legal maneuvering on Pennzoil's part and Texaco's failure to file an answer in the Delaware case right away, the case against Texaco ended up in a Texas court before a jury. (The suits against Getty, the trust, and the museum continued in Delaware.) For four and a half months the two sides presented their evidence. Before the jury retired to the jury room, the judge instructed them how to apply the law to the facts they had heard. The word "contract" never appeared in the jury instructions. Instead the judge used the word "agreement." Did this confuse the jury?

The jury deliberated and then returned a verdict in favor of Pennzoil. For Texaco's interference with contract, the jury awarded Pennzoil $7.53 billion compensatory damages and $3 billion punitive damages. (The punitive damages were eventually reduced to $1 billion. The compensatory damages were not changed.)

Pennzoil v. Texaco is on the books now and can be cited as precedent in similar cases. In legal circles the arguments still continue as to whether or not this was a correct verdict.

Defining New York contract law is no easy task when the cases, statute books, and commentaries fill literally hundreds

---

25. *Oil and Honor*, 231.
26. *Oil and Honor*, 234.

---

27. *Oil and Honor*, 275–76.

Inside Story, continued

of volumes. It is no surprise that parties to a lawsuit will come up with different interpretations of the law. Even when parties do agree on a particular rule of law, they will often disagree as to the application of that rule.

For example, Pennzoil's brief characterized Texaco's arguments as follows:

Texaco seeks to create the illusion of error by depicting New York law as a creature from a strange planet. According to Texaco's muddled presentation, this alien body of law encourages commercial piracy and discourages the formation of commercial contracts. Not surprisingly, New York law is just the opposite.

What did the judges for the Court of Appeals for the First Supreme Judicial District of Texas think of all this? In a lengthy opinion, excerpted below, they upheld the jury's verdict.

_____

Excerpts From the Opinion of the Court of Appeals: Legal Analysis

Under New York law, if parties do not intend to be bound to an agreement until it is reduced to writing and signed by both parties, then there is no contract until that event occurs. If there is no understanding that a signed writing is necessary before the parties will be bound, and the parties have agreed upon all substantial terms, then an informal agreement can be binding, even though the parties contemplate evidencing their agreement in a formal document later.

Thus, under New York law, the parties are given the power to obligate themselves informally or only by a formal signed writing, as they wish. The emphasis in deciding when a binding contract exists is on intent rather than on form.

To determine intent, a court must examine the words and deeds of the parties, because these constitute the objective signs of such intent. Only the outward expressions of intent are considered— secret or subjective intent is immaterial to the question of whether the parties were bound.

Several factors have been articulated to help determine whether the parties intended to be bound only by a formal, signed writing: (1) whether a party expressly reserved the right to be bound only when a written agreement is signed; (2) whether there was any partial performance by one party that the party disclaiming the contract accepted; (3) whether all essential terms of the alleged contract had been agreed upon; and (4) whether the complexity or magnitude of the transaction was such that a formal, executed writing would normally be expected.

Although the magnitude of the transaction here was such that normally a signed writing would be expected, there was sufficient evidence to support an inference by the jury that the expectation was satisfied here initially by the Memorandum of Agreement,

signed by a majority of shareholders of Getty Oil and approved by the board with a higher price, and by the transaction agreement in progress that had been intended to memorialize the agreement previously reached.

The record as a whole demonstrates that there was legally and factually sufficient evidence to support the jury's finding in Special Issue No. 1 that the Trust, the Museum, and the Company intended to bind themselves to an agreement with Pennzoil at the end of the Getty Oil board meeting on January 3, 1984.

Texaco next claims that even if the parties intended to bind themselves before a definitive document was signed, no binding contract could result because the terms that they intended to include in their agreement were too vague and incomplete to be enforceable as a matter of law.

For a contract to be enforceable, the terms of the agreement must be ascertainable to a reasonable degree of certainty. The question of whether the agreement is sufficiently definite to be enforceable is a difficult one. The facts of the individual case are decisively important. The agreement need not be so definite that all the possibilities that might occur to a party in bad faith are explicitly provided for, but it must be sufficiently complete so that parties in good faith can find in the agreement words that will fairly define their respective duties and liabilities. On review, the agreement must be sufficiently definite for the court to be able to recognize a breach and to fashion a remedy for that breach.

Texaco's attempts to create additional "essential" terms from the mechanics of implementing the agreement's existing provisions are unpersuasive. The terms of the agreement found by the jury are supported by the evidence, and the promises of the parties are clear enough for a court to recognize a breach and to determine the damages resulting from that breach.

_____

The *Pennzoil v. Texaco* decision attracted a great deal of media attention. Not only was the damages award the largest in U.S. history, it was also a surprise to large sectors of the business community, which had been handling mergers and acquisitions in much the same way that Texaco had done. *The Wall Street Journal* and *The New York Times,* as well as many other business publications, ran a number of articles condemning the jury verdict and the Texas appellate court that upheld it.

Both sides used the media to build support in the business community and to try to influence the outcome of the appeal. There were rumors that Pennzoil tried to use its political influence also. Pennzoil went so far as to publish public relations pamphlets and hold symposia on the case. An example of Pennzoil's use of the press is shown in Exhibit 8-3. Texaco

Inside Story continued on following page

Inside Story, continued

EXHIBIT 8-3   Pennzoil Comment on Texaco Bankruptcy

© 1987 Margulies, The Houston Post. *Reprinted by permission.*

claimed that the Texas judges were biased because of campaign contributions made by Pennzoil's lawyer Joe Jamail.

Texaco filed for bankruptcy in 1987 under chapter 11 of the Bankruptcy Code after its appeals in the Texas courts failed. As part of the plan of reorganization, Texaco agreed in 1988 to settle the case with Pennzoil for $3 billion.

This case has had a tremendous impact on Wall Street. Thomas Petzinger, Jr., describes what has been referred to as the "Texaco chill":

Did corporate America hear the jury's message? Did the Pennzoil case put the honor back in a handshake?

If anything, it began to render the handshake obsolete.

Some time after the verdict, Michel Zaleski, a New York investment banker, was winding up a day and a half of tough negotiations. At that moment of achieving an agreement in principle, he would recall, "I looked the guy in the eye, stuck out my hand and said, 'let's shake on it.'"

"We can't do that," the lawyer on the other side replied sternly.

"I never thought a handshake was anything more than a moral commitment," Zaleski says. "But now people are afraid to make even a moral commitment for fear someone will use it against them."

The Wall Street Journal would dub the phenomenon "the Texaco chill." It crept into a news conference at which Frank Borman, the chairman of Eastern Airlines, was trying to justify the company's sale to Texas Air Corporation at what many considered to be an unfairly low price. A rival takeover offer would probably never succeed, Borman said—"even if someone offered more."

Why was that? "You probably have heard of Texaco and Pennzoil," he said. There was talk that Borman's comment helped convince Chicago's Pritzker family, which controlled Braniff Incorporated, to back off from an interloping bid for Eastern—one that presumably would have more handsomely rewarded that company's shareholders.

Lawyer Klaus Eppler was advising several directors of Sperry

Inside Story, continued

Corporation when they agreed not to oppose a tender offer by Burroughs Corporation, a transaction that created a new computer company second in size only to IBM. When Sperry issued a public announcement about its assent to the takeover, "I warned my clients that by doing so they had probably created an enforceable contract," Eppler would recall.

The Texaco chill began ranging beyond the takeover game and into more prosaic corporate transactions. Pratt & Whitney reportedly had a handshake agreement to supply United Parcel Service with $400 million of the engines for twenty UPS jets. Then Rolls-Royce Ltd. slipped in with a bid of $25 million less. The resourceful negotiators from Pratt & Whitney breathed a mention of the Texaco case, one source said, whereupon UPS told Rolls-Royce to take their less expensive engines and fly home.

Where deals have fallen through, the Texaco case has emboldened the losers to seek the same redress that Hugh Liedtke did—even in cases beyond the borders of the U.S. In June 1986, Allied-Lyons PLC of London sued Hiram Walker Resources Ltd. in Canada for $6.49 billion (U.S.), claiming that it had a deal to buy Hiram Walker's liquor business. Hiram Walker made the deal while resisting a takeover by Gulf Canada Ltd. But when Gulf Canada ultimately succeeded in gaining control of Hiram Walker, it canceled whatever arrangements Hiram Walker had made with Allied-Lyons.

"Our lawyers have seen similarities in the Texaco-Pennzoil decision and this situation," said Sir Derrick Holden-Brown, chairman of Allied. Allied's damages demand was believed the largest ever filed in a Canadian court.

The Texaco chill certainly didn't freeze out competition, nor did it make the New Good Ol' Boys of Wall Street begin acting like the Old Good Ol' Boys of the oil patch. Nevertheless, investment bankers everywhere began treading more lightly—if only to become more diligent in determining the extent of their target's freedom to deal.

"No longer can we say, 'We stole a deal fair and square,' " said the investment banker Alan Rothenberg. And that was reform enough.[28]

---

28. *Oil and Honor*, 459–60.

Key Words and Phrases

acceptance **239**
bilateral contract **242**
break-up fee **268**
capacity **241**
condition concurrent **244**
condition precedent **244**
condition subsequent **244**
consequential damages **258**
consideration **242**
counteroffer **240**
covenant not to compete **250**
creditor beneficiary **242**
donee beneficiary **242**
equal dignities rule **246**
expectation damages **258**
fiduciary out **268**
fraud in the factum **248**
fraud in the inducement **248**
general release **250**

illegal contract **250**
illusory promise **243**
intent to be bound **240**
laesio enormis **255**
liquidated damages **259**
lock-up option **268**
merger agreement **266**
mitigate **259**
mutuality of obligation **243**
novation **257**
offer **239**
offeree **239**
offeror **239**
oppression **250**
option contract **239**
output contract **243**
parol evidence rule **247**
power of attorney **246**
precontractual liability **263**

prenuptial agreement **246**
promisee **239**
promisor **239**
promissory estoppel **260**
quantum meruit **259**
reliance damages **259**
requirements contract **243**
restitution **259**
statute of frauds **244**
surprise **250**
third-party beneficiary **242**
unconscionable **250**
unenforceable **247**
unilateral contract **242**
unjust enrichment **264**
usury statutes **250**
voidable **244**

Questions and Case Problems

1. New medicines go through several phases of clinical evaluation before general release onto the market. HEM Pharmaceuticals Corp. conducted a clinical trial with 92 patients designed to evaluate the effectiveness, side effects, and risks of Ampligen. Ampligen was classified by the FDA as an "investigational new drug" not yet permitted to be sold freely as a prescription medication for chronic fatigue syndrome. HEM sought to have the patients participate in its study so HEM could obtain FDA approval for its new drug.

All of the patients signed consent forms warning of the experimental status of Ampligen and possible side effects. Although the patients were free to withdraw from the clinical trial at any time, if they remained in the study they were required to accept the risks of treatment, to forego other drugs, to not become pregnant, and to submit to intrusive and necessarily uncomfortable testing for one year. After the testing ended, they would be entitled to receive Ampligen for a full year at no charge.

At the end of the one-year study, HEM refused to supply the free year's supply of the drug to the patients. HEM argued that because the patients participated voluntarily and were free to withdraw, they had no binding obligation and so gave no consideration. Is HEM correct? Was HEM's conduct ethical? [*Dahl v. HEM Pharmaceuticals Corp.*, 7 F.3d 1399 (9th Cir. 1993)]

2.   Landlord agreed to rent Tenant an office for $2,000 per month for three years. Tenant encountered financial difficulties. Landlord agreed to reduce the rent to $1,200 per month, and Tenant agreed not to file for bankruptcy. Tenant had no plans to file for bankruptcy. Unbeknownst to both Landlord and Tenant, a promise not to file for bankruptcy is unenforceable under the Bankruptcy Code. Was the agreement to reduce the rent binding? Would it make a difference if Tenant had planned to file for bankruptcy if he couldn't get the rent reduction? Was Tenant's conduct ethical?

3.   Jane Murcello, contract administrator for Tommy's Restaurants, contacted the Fresh Bread Company and made an agreement with the bread company that it would supply Tommy's with all of the hamburger buns that it needed. The Fresh Bread Company began supplying Tommy's with the hamburger buns. Murcello then contacted the Fresh Bread Company, stating that Tommy's was going to produce a fish sandwich and would need a special type of bun. She gave the dimensions of the new fish bun and the projected quantities. She stated, "I look forward to increasing our business with you." The Fresh Bread Company made several changes to its kitchen in preparation for baking the buns. Murcello called back two months later saying that she had decided to give the contract to Bake'm Company. The Fresh Bread Company sues Tommy's for breach of contract. Who should prevail?

4.   Andy Barstow, owner of a store, entered into a detailed letter of intent to negotiate in good faith the lease of a store with Zandra Ingalls, a prospective tenant. The letter included an outline of what terms needed to be negotiated, including price. Barstow promised to withdraw the store from the marketplace during the negotiations. Ingalls, during the time of the negotiations, spent money developing a marketing plan for her business. She also brought in a carpenter, who started building some furniture and cabinets specially designed for the new

store. Barstow called Ingalls the following week, saying that he had decided to lease the store to his friend, Marsh Burke. What damages, if any, can Ingalls recover?

5.   Lanci was involved in an automobile accident with an uninsured motorist. Lanci and Metropolitan Insurance Co. entered settlement negotiations and ultimately agreed to settle all claims for $15,000. Lanci's correspondence accepting the settlement offer clearly indicated his belief that his policy limit was $15,000. However, Lanci did not have a copy of his policy and, in fact, Lanci's policy limit was $250,000. When Lanci learned the correct policy limit, he refused to accept the settlement proceeds of $15,000. Should Lanci be able to void the contract? On what basis? [*Lanci v. Metropolitan Insurance Co.*, 564 A.2d 972 (Pa. Super. Ct. 1989)]

6.   Tenant Whitehead entered into a lease with landowner Williams with the purpose of using the three ponds on Williams's property for a "fish-out" facility. A "fish-out" facility is an operation where members of the public pay a fee, catch fish on the property, have the fish cleaned for them, and then take them home to eat. The premises were in a total state of disrepair, and Whitehead was given immediate access to get the property ready for his business. However, soon after Whitehead began readying the system necessary for pond maintenance, it became clear that he would be unable to maintain the water level in the ponds. The primary lake water level fell, but Whitehead was unwilling to pump water from a nearby creek because of the fact that a waste treatment facility was located a short distance upstream from the intake point. The main lake also sprang a leak. A number of remedies were tried, but Whitehead was never able to get the planned catfish operation up and running successfully.

Can Whitehead be excused from paying the rent? Should Williams pay for the improvements to the pond? [*Williams v. Whitehead*, 854 S.W. 2d 895 (App. Ct. Tenn. 1993)]

7.   Contractor agreed to build a house for $150,000. Contractor began work on the agreed-upon site and unexpectedly hit a layer of rock when digging the foundation. Contractor demanded another $10,000 from Owner to finish the job. Owner refused to pay and ordered Contractor to finish the job. Contractor refused. What remedies, if any, are available to Owner?

8.   In 1965 the plaintiff, Chicago, Milwaukee, St. Paul and Pacific Railroad Company, and the defendant, Chicago and North Western Transportation Company, entered into a ten-year agreement for the defendant's joint use of the plaintiff's depot and 11.1 miles of track in the city of Milwaukee. The defendant agreed to pay for the partial use of the plaintiff's new passenger depot and the right to use the plaintiff's tracks. The National Rail Passenger Corporation, Amtrak, was created in 1970 by Congress. Under the statute that resulted in its creation, Amtrak could contract with railroads to release them from their entire responsibilities for providing intercity passenger service. Although railroads were not required to join Amtrak, both the plaintiff and the defendant did join. On April 30, 1971, the defendant notified the plaintiff that Amtrak had

relieved the defendant of its responsibilities as a passenger carrier and that the defendant was terminating the depot and track leasing agreement, effective May 1, 1971.

The plaintiff sued the defendant for $2,245,876.45 for breach of the depot and track leasing agreement. Who should prevail? [*Chicago, Milwaukee, St. Paul and Pacific Railroad Co. v. Chicago and North Western Transportation Co.*, 82 Wis.2d 514, 263 N.W.2d 189 (Wis. 1978)]

9. Employer called Sally Denoco and offered her a two-year employment contract. Denoco said, "Great, I accept," and quit her present job, forfeiting unvested stock options. After six months Employer fired Denoco, and she sued. Who should win? Does it matter if Employer made a note to himself after the phone call: "Sally Denoco—two-year contract. Salary to be negotiated."? If Denoco were to win, what would be her damages?

10. In October 1984, the majority stockholder of the Pittsburgh Athletic Company, Inc., which then held the Pittsburgh Pirates baseball team franchise, announced that he intended to sell his family's interest in the team. After unsuccessfully attempting to sell the team to local investors, the majority stockholder announced, in June 1985, that he was seeking out-of-town purchasers, even if those purchasers intended to move the Pirates to another city.

In response to this announcement, Mayor Caliguiri and other city representatives began searching for local investors to purchase the team. In pursuit of this objective, Caliguiri publicly indicated that the city would provide substantial financial support to the purchasers. In reliance upon Caliguiri's commitment of financial assistance, in November 1985 a group of local companies formed Pittsburgh Associates for the purpose of purchasing the team and keeping the Pirates in Pittsburgh.

It was alleged that in negotiations both before and after the formation of Pittsburgh Associates, Caliguiri firmly promised that the city would provide the partnership with $25 million toward the purchase and operation of the Pirates. In return, Pittsburgh Associates would contribute $26 million.

In reliance upon Caliguiri's express promise to provide $25 million in capital, Pittsburgh Associates entered into an asset purchase agreement with the Pittsburgh Athletic Company on December 13, 1985. On December 24, 1985, the Urban Redevelopment Authority of Pittsburgh (URA) and Pittsburgh Associates entered into an equity participation loan agreement. Immediately before the closing, the city indicated that it would present Pittsburgh Associates with the sum of only $20 million at the closing, $5 million less than the original $25 million commitment made by Caliguiri.

Prior to the scheduled closing of the Purchase Agreement, the limited partners of Pittsburgh Associates met with Caliguiri. At that meeting, the limited partners informed him that the Pirates's operating expenses were continuing to rise at a substantial rate and that the economic viability of the team required the city to provide the full $25 million originally committed. The limited partners expressly explained that Pittsburgh Associates could not and would not close the Purchase Agreement without the city's commitment to provide the remaining $5 million on an unconditional basis.

In response, Caliguiri promised Pittsburgh Associates that if it agreed to close the Purchase Agreement and purchase the Pirates, the city would unconditionally provide Pittsburgh Associates with additional capital of $5 million. In reliance upon that commitment, Pittsburgh Associates purchased the Pittsburgh Pirates. Thereafter, in connection with the subsequent buyout of several limited partners and associated financial transactions, the obligation of the city was reduced from $5 million to $4.2 million. Despite Pittsburgh Associates' numerous requests over six years to obtain those funds so as to make the Pittsburgh Pirates a viable, competitive baseball club, the city failed to provide Pittsburgh Associates with the promised $4.2 million.

Assuming for the sake of analysis that Mayor Caliguiri had the authority to make the promises he did on behalf of the city of Pittsburgh, did such promises constitute a contract? If so, what are the plaintiff's damages? If not, is promissory estoppel relevant? If so, what are the plaintiff's damages? [*Pittsburgh Associates v. The City of Pittsburgh*, 630 A.2d 505 (Comm. Ct. Pa. 1993)]

Chapter 9

SALES

■ Introduction

When Does Article 2 of the UCC Apply?

Article 2 of the Uniform Commercial Code (UCC) governs the sale of goods. UCC section 2-105 defines *goods* as "all things (including specially manufactured goods) which are movable at the time of identification to the contract for sale." *Identification to the contract* means the designation—by marking, setting aside, or other means—of the particular goods that are to be supplied under the contract. The UCC has attempted to eliminate some of the legal formalities of traditional contract law, to be in greater accord with the needs and realities of the business world. Many provisions of the UCC can be changed by the express agreement of the parties. To the extent that the UCC is silent on a subject, the common-law contract provisions described in chapter 8 will apply.

The UCC does not govern the rendering of services or the sale of land. Contracts for selling services or land are governed by common-law contract principles.

Sometimes the characterization of an activity as a sale of goods or of services is not clear. For example, is a hospital performing a blood transfusion selling blood or rendering medical services? This distinction can be critical for purposes of both the UCC warranties and product liability in tort (discussed in chapter 10).

Similarly, there can be an issue as to whether something attached to land is considered goods or land. This gray area includes *fixtures,* which are items of personal property that are attached to real property and cannot be removed without substantial damage. Fixtures are not considered goods under article 2. They are generally subject to the rules governing real property.

The UCC regulates sales of goods by both merchants and nonmerchants, to whom different rules may apply. Thus, for example, if Sam Jacoby were to sell a car to Jay Malone, the UCC would dictate both parties' rights and obligations under the sales contract, whether Jacoby was employed as a car dealer or whether he was simply selling his personal possessions on his own behalf. UCC section 2-104 defines a *merchant* as "a person who deals in goods of the kind or otherwise by his occupation holds himself out as having knowledge or skill peculiar to the practices or goods involved in the transaction."

Chapter Summary

This chapter addresses contract formation under the UCC and the UCC approach to the "battle of the forms," where the form accepting an offer contains terms different from those on the form that constitutes the offer. The special warranty provisions of the UCC are discussed, including express warranties and implied warranties of merchantability and fitness for a particular purpose. The chapter then reviews excuses for nonperformance and remedies for unexcused nonperformance.

■ Contract Formation

Under common law, a contract was enforceable only if all necessary terms were expressed at the time of contracting. The UCC departs from this approach and permits a contract to be enforced if the parties intended a binding contract, even though important terms may have been left open for later agreement. If a dispute later arises over a missing term, the court may simply use a "gap filler" as provided by the UCC. The court will only fill in missing terms, however, if the party attempting to enforce the contract can prove there was a genuine agreement, not a mere proposal or intention to continue negotiations. It must be apparent that there has been an offer, an acceptance, and consideration.

Offer

"Offer" is not defined by the UCC, although it is used in several important sections. Therefore, traditional common-law principles (discussed in chapter 8) determine whether an offer has been made. Under the UCC, as in common law, neither an invitation for bids nor a price quotation is an offer. Similarly, a proposal by a sales representative that is subject to approval by the home office is not an offer.

Acceptance

The UCC does not define "acceptance" either, except to state that an acceptance may contain terms additional to or different from those in the offer. This is different from the common-law "mirror-image" rule, which required the acceptance to contain the same terms as the offer.

Unless the offeror indicates unambiguously that her offer can only be accepted in a particular way, an offer may be accepted in any manner and by any medium that is reasonable in the circumstances.

Consideration

As with other contracts, contracts for the sale of goods ordinarily must have consideration to be enforceable. However, a *firm offer*, that is, a signed offer by a merchant that indicates that the offer will be kept open, is not revocable for lack of consideration. The offer must be kept open during the time stated, or for a reasonable period of time if none is stated, up to a maximum of three months. This rule is just one example of how the UCC provides more stringent standards for merchants than for nonmerchants. Under common law, an agreement to modify a contract is binding only if there is consideration for the modification. However, under the UCC an agreement to modify a contract is binding even if there is no consideration for the modification. However, if the original contract was required to be in writing to satisfy the statute of frauds (discussed later in this chapter), then the agreement to modify the contract must be in writing also.

■ Battle of the Forms

In a battle of the forms, the parties negotiate on the essential terms of the contract (for example, quantity, quality, and delivery date) but neglect to bargain over items that are less immediately important (for example, whether disputes will be subject to arbitration, for how long a period the buyer may complain of defects, or on whom the risk of loss during shipment falls). The parties then exchange standard printed forms, each of which is filled with fine print listing all kinds of terms advantageous to the party that drew up the form. As a result of these exchanges, two questions arise: (1) Is there a contract? and if so, (2) what are its terms?

> " *The parties then exchange standard printed forms, each of which is filled with fine print listing all kinds of terms advantageous to the party that drew up the form.*

Section 2-207 of the UCC calls a truce in the battle of the forms by effectively abolishing the mirror-image rule. It is not necessary for an offer and acceptance to match exactly in order for a contract for the sale of goods to exist. Adding to or modifying terms in the offer does not make the acceptance a counteroffer, as is true under common law.

Definite Response

A definite and timely assent to an offer constitutes an acceptance. The presence of additional or different terms is not a bar to contract formation. The crucial inquiry is whether the parties intended to close a deal. If the offeree's response manifests the intent to enter into a deal, the offer has been accepted. For example, if additional or different terms merely appear in the standard printed language of a form contract, it is likely that the offeree intended to close a deal.

If, however, the response indicates only a willingness to continue negotiations, it is not an acceptance but a counteroffer. For example, an additional or different term that directly pertains to one of the negotiated terms, such as price or quantity, is evidence that the parties are still negotiating and have not reached an agreement.

Conditional Response

If the offeree wants to make a counteroffer rather than an acceptance, he should state clearly that his acceptance is conditioned on the offeror's agreement to the additional or different terms. The safest course is to use UCC language, for example: "This acceptance is expressly made conditional on offeror's assent to all additional or different terms contained herein. Should offeror not give assent to said terms, there is no contract between the parties." Less direct language (such as "The acceptance of your order is subject to the conditions set forth herein," and "Acceptance of this order is expressly limited to the condition of purchase printed on the reverse side") has been held an acceptance rather than a counteroffer.

Acceptance With Additional Terms

What is the effect of additional or different terms in an acceptance when the contract is not expressly made subject to the offeror's agreeing to those terms? The answer depends on whether the parties are merchants. If even one of the parties is not a merchant, additional terms are construed as proposals for additions to the contract that the acceptance has created. Unless the offeror expressly agrees to the added provisions, they do not become part of the contract. If both parties are merchants, on the other hand, the additional provisions in the acceptance automatically become part of the contract, unless: (1) the offer expressly limits acceptance to the terms of the offer; (2) the new terms materially alter the original offer; or (3) the party making the original offer notifies the other party within a reasonable time that she objects to the new terms. If one of these exceptions applies, the additional or different terms serve as proposals requiring the express consent of the offeror to become part of the contract.

No Acceptance

Section 2-207(3) addresses those situations where goods are shipped, received, and paid for, even though the writings between the parties do not establish a contract under traditional contract law. Under this section, a contract exists whenever the parties act as if there is a contract between them. It is not necessary to determine which document constitutes the offer and which the acceptance. The only issue to be decided is what the terms of the con-

"You have a pretty good case, Mr. Pitkin. How much justice can you afford?"

Drawing by J.B. Handelsman; © The New Yorker Magazine, Inc.

tract will be. Section 2-207(3) provides that the terms of the contract will be those on which the writings agree, supplemented by the UCC's gap-fillers where needed.

The following case addresses a battle of the forms under section 2-207.

■ A Case in Point: In the Language of the Court

Case 9.1
DAITOM, INC. v.
PENNWALT CORP.
United States Court of Appeals
for the Tenth Circuit
741 F.2d 1569 (10th Cir. 1984).

FACTS   In 1976, Daitom, Inc. planned the construction of a dextro calcium pantothenate producing plant. As part of that project, Daitom solicited bids for two rotary vacuum dryers, which would be used to dry the calcium pantothenate. In September 1976, Pennwalt Corporation submitted a typewritten proposal to supply the dryers, specifying the equipment, the price, and the terms of delivery and payment. Pennwalt attached to this typewritten sheet a preprinted form that specified the conditions of the sale. A reference in the sheet made the preprinted form an integral part of the proposal.

In response, Daitom issued a purchase order to Pennwalt in October 1976. The purchase order was a preprinted form that included lengthy standard terms and conditions. In an appropriate column, Daitom typed a description of the dryers and referenced the Pennwalt proposal of September.

In May 1977, Pennwalt delivered the dryers to Daitom. Daitom did not install the dryers until construction of the building was completed in June 1978. Upon installation, the dryers did not function properly. Two days after installation, Daitom notified Pennwalt of the problems. Although representatives from Pennwalt visited the plant, they failed to repair the dryers.

Daitom then filed suit, alleging that Pennwalt had breached a contractual warranty. In response, Pennwalt claimed that under the contract, no warranty claims could be asserted more than one year after delivery of the dryers. Pennwalt pointed to language in the September proposal that conditioned Pennwalt's offer on Daitom's agreeing to a one-year limit on warranty claims.

Pennwalt argued that the September proposal was an offer, which was accepted by Daitom's October purchase order. According to Pennwalt, these writings established a contract that included a one-year limit for warranty claims. The one-year period started upon delivery of the dryers, even though Daitom did not have an opportunity to test them until over a year after they were delivered.

Daitom contended that its purchase order was not an acceptance of the one-year warranty limitation, because the purchase order contained standard language preserving all of Daitom's rights and remedies available at law. Among these legal rights was the right to make warranty claims up to four years after delivery—the standard limitation period specified by the UCC. Daitom's acceptance of the deal was expressly conditioned upon Pennwalt's assenting to the different terms contained in the purchase order. Daitom further contended that because Pennwalt did not agree to the new terms, the parties' writings did not constitute a contract. Instead, a contract was established through the conduct of the parties. Because the UCC fills in terms that are not agreed upon by the parties, its four-year rule should apply.

Alternatively, Daitom argued that if the purchase order constituted an acceptance, so that there was a written contract, conflicting terms should

*Case **9.1** continued on following page*

Case **9.1** continued

be "knocked out" and supplemented by the UCC. Because the parties' writings were in conflict as to the time limit for asserting warranty claims, the UCC's four-year period would apply.

The federal district court held that the one-year period of limitations specified in Pennwalt's proposal and the shortening of the typical four-year period of limitations available under the UCC became part of the contract of sale and governed the claims for breach of warranties. Diatom appealed.

ISSUE PRESENTED   If there has been an acceptance of an offer, and if the offer and the acceptance are on printed forms that contain differing terms, is there a contract? If so, what are its terms?

OPINION   DOYLE, J., writing for the U.S. Court of Appeals:

. . . .

Section 2-207 has been commented on in one case as a "murky bit of prose," and as "one of the most important, subtle, and difficult in the entire code, and well it may be said that the product as it finally reads is not altogether satisfactory." . . .

. . . .

. . . Here the additional or different terms in Daitom's purchase order were, to be sure, boilerplate terms. And though important in themselves, they do not come out and state an unwillingness to proceed with the purchase of the rotary dryers if the terms were not assented to by Pennwalt. . . . Having found an offer and an acceptance which was not made expressly conditional on assent to additional or different terms, we must now decide the effect of those additional or different terms on the resulting contract and what terms became part of it. . . .

. . . .

The difficulty in determining the effect of different terms in the acceptance is the imprecision of drafting evident in section 2-207. The language of the provision is silent on how different terms in the acceptance are to be treated once a contract is formed pursuant to section 2-207(1). That section provides that a contract may be formed by exchanged writings despite the existence of additional or different terms in the acceptance. Therefore, an offeree's response is treated as an acceptance while it may differ substantially from the offer. This section of the provision, then, reformed the mirror-image rule; that common law legal formality that prohibited the formation of a contract if the exchanged writings of offer and acceptance differed in any term. . . .

. . . Between merchants, such additional terms become part of the resulting contract unless 1) the offer expressly limited acceptance to its terms, 2) the additional terms materially alter the contract obligations, or 3) the offeror gives notice of his or her objection to the additional terms within a reasonable time. Should any one of these three possibilities occur, the additional terms are treated merely as proposals for incorporation in the contract and absent assent by the offeror the terms of the offer control. In any event, the existence of the additional terms does not prevent a contract from being formed.

Section 2-207(2) is silent on the treatment of terms stated in the acceptance that are different, rather than merely additional, from those stated in the offer. It is unclear whether "different" terms in the acceptance are intended to be included under the aegis of "additional" terms in section 2-207(2) and, therefore, fail to become part of the agreement if they materially alter the contract. . . . However, Comment 6 suggests that different terms in exchanged writings must be assumed to constitute mutual objections by each party to the other's conflicting terms and result in a mutual "knockout" of both parties' conflicting terms; the missing terms to be supplied by the UCC's "gap-filler" provisions. . . .

Despite all this, the cases and commentators have suggested three possible approaches. The first of these is to treat "different" terms as included under the aegis of "additional" terms in section 2-207(2). Consequently, different terms in the acceptance would never become part of the contract, because, by definition, they would materially alter the contract (i.e., the offeror's terms). . . .

The second approach, which leads to the same result as the first, is that the offeror's terms control because the offeree's different terms merely fall out; section 2-207(2) cannot rescue the different terms since that subsection applies only to additional terms. . . .

The third, and preferable approach, which is commonly called the "knock-out" rule, is that the conflicting terms cancel one another. Under this view the offeree's form is treated only as an acceptance of the terms in the offeror's form which did not conflict. The ultimate contract, then, includes those non-conflicting terms and any other terms supplied by the UCC, including terms incorporated by course of performance (§2-208), course of dealing (§1-205), usage of trade (§1-205), and other "gap fillers" or "off-the-rack" terms (e.g., implied warranty of fitness for particular purpose, §2-315). . . .

We are of the opinion that this is the more reasonable approach, particularly when dealing with a case such as this where from the beginning the offeror's specified period of limitations would expire before the equipment was even installed. The approaches other than the "knock-out" approach would be inequitable and unjust because they invited the very kind of treatment which the defendant attempted to provide [by delivery of equipment in boxes even though the purchaser had no plant].

. . . .

This particular approach and result are supported persuasively by the underlying rationale and purpose behind the adoption of section 2-207 [which was] drafted to reform the infamous common law mirror-image rule and associated last-shot doctrine that enshrined the fortuitous positions of senders of forms and accorded undue advantages based on such fortuitous positions. To refuse to adopt the "knock-out" rule and instead adopt one of the remaining two approaches would serve to re-enshrine the undue advantages derived solely from the fortuitous positions of when a party sent a form. . . . While it is laudable for business persons to read the fine print and boilerplate provisions in exchanged forms, there is nothing in section 2-207 mandating such careful consideration. The provision seems drafted with a recognition of the reality that merchants seldom review exchanged forms with the scrutiny of lawyers. . . .

. . . .

RESULT There was a contract—Daitom's purchase order constituted acceptance of Pennwalt's offer despite the differing terms. A four-year,

Case 9.1 continued on following page

*Case **9.1** continued*

rather than a one-year, limitation applied to warranty claims. Because the parties were still within the four-year period, the court remanded the case to the district court for consideration of the merits of the warranty claim.

Questions

1. Would the result in the case have been different if the machines had been installed immediately and then only after one year of use broke down?

2. Why is it appropriate that the court not mandate that merchants carefully scrutinize the language in their contracts? Would the result have been different if, instead of boilerplate forms, specific, custom contracts had been written?

■ Statute of Frauds

UCC section 2-201 is a statute of frauds. It provides that a contract for the sale of goods for $500 or more is unenforceable unless it is at least partly in writing. Section 2-201 states:

1. There must be some writing evidencing the sale of goods.

2. The writing must be signed by the party against whom enforcement is sought.

3. The writing must specify the quantity of the goods sold.

"Some Writing"

Statutes of frauds generally require all the essential terms of the contract to be in writing; the UCC's requirement for "some writing" is relatively lenient. The official comments to section 2-201 state: "All that is required is that the writing afford a basis for believing that the offered oral evidence rests on a real transaction. It may be written in lead pencil on a scratch pad." The comments go on to state: "The price, time and place of payment or delivery, the general quality of the goods, or any particular warranties may all be omitted." (It should be noted that the official comments to the UCC help courts to understand the drafters' intentions, but they are not binding. If a judge believes there is a conflict between the statute and the comment, the judge will follow the statute.)

> 66
> *"All that is required is that the writing afford a basis for believing that the offered oral evidence rests on a real transaction. It may be written in lead pencil on a scratch pad."*

Signature

The writing must be signed by the party against whom enforcement is sought, unless the sale is between merchants and (1) a confirmation of the contract has been received, (2) the party receiving it has reason to know its contents, and (3) that party has not made a written objection within ten days after the confirmation was received. For example, an invoice that a seller sent to a buyer would be a contract enforceable against the buyer if there was no response from the buyer within ten days after receiving the invoice.

Quantity of Goods

The only term that must appear in the writing is that which designates the quantity of goods. This term is necessary to provide a basis for awarding monetary damages in the case of a breach. The contract is not enforceable beyond the quantity of goods shown in the writing. If no quantity is specified, the contract is unenforceable unless: (1) the goods were specially manufactured for the buyer and are not suitable for resale to others in the ordinary course of the seller's business; (2) the defendant admits in a judicial proceeding that there was an agreement; or (3) payment for the goods was made and accepted or the goods were received and accepted.

■ Warranties

Goods delivered pursuant to a contract may not live up to the buyer's expectations. In many such cases the buyer can sue the seller for breaching an express or implied warranty that the goods sold would have certain qualities or would perform in a certain way.

The UCC's warranty provisions attempt to determine what attributes of the goods the parties have agreed upon. The UCC allows a great deal of flexibility in this regard, permitting consideration of the description of the goods, the seller's words, common uses in the trade, the price paid, and the extent to which the buyer has communicated particular needs to the seller. The seller of goods may find himself bound, perhaps unintentionally, by one of the three warranties provided by the UCC.

Types of Warranties

An express warranty becomes part of the contract as a result of some statement by the seller. An implied warranty of merchantability automatically applies to every sale of goods by a merchant. An implied warranty of fitness for a particular purpose arises in certain transactions in which the buyer has relied on the seller's expertise in selecting the goods.

Limiting Liability

The seller can avoid responsibility for the quality of the goods under any of these warranties. First, the seller need not make any express warranties. This may be difficult to do, however, because even a simple description of the goods may constitute a warranty. Second, a seller may disclaim any warranties of quality if she follows specifically delineated rules in the UCC that are designed to ensure that the buyer is aware of, and assents to, the disclaimers. For example, section 2-316 allows a seller to exclude all implied warranties by using "expressions like 'AS IS,' 'WITH ALL FAULTS' or other language which in common understanding calls the buyer's attention to the exclusion of warranties and makes plain that there is no implied warranty." This language means that the buyer takes the entire risk as to the quality of the goods involved. Third, the seller can refrain from professing expertise with respect to the goods, and can leave the selection to the buyer.

More commonly, the seller limits his responsibility for the quality of the goods by limiting the remedies available to the buyer in the event of breach. A typical method is the inclusion of a provision limiting the seller's responsibility for defective goods to repair or replacement.

Under the UCC, a seller is not an absolute insurer of the quality of goods sold. In order to recover for breach of warranty, a buyer must prove that: (1) the seller made an express or implied warranty under the UCC; (2) the goods were defective at the time of the sale; (3) the loss or injury was caused by the defect rather than the buyer's negligent or inappropriate use of the goods; and (4) the seller has no affirmative defenses such as a disclaimer of warranty.

As an alternative to suing for breach of warranty, the plaintiff may sue in tort for strict product liability. A product liability claim may succeed where a breach-of-warranty claim would not. For example, the plaintiff's negligence will not defeat a claim for product liability (but it may reduce the damages, under a theory of comparative fault). Chapter 10 discusses this issue.

■ Express Warranty

An *express warranty* is an explicit guarantee by the seller that the goods will have certain qualities. UCC section 2-313 has two requirements for the creation of an express warranty. First, the seller must either make a statement or promise relating to the goods, provide a description of the goods, or furnish a sample or model of the goods. Second, this statement, promise, description, sample, or model must become a "part of the basis of the bargain" between the seller and the buyer. This second requirement is intended to ensure that the buyer actually relied on the seller's statement when making a purchasing decision. For example, if a car dealer asserts that a car will reach 130 MPH, and the buyer's response is "I'm never going to take it above 55," it is unlikely that the buyer could claim breach of warranty if the car failed to go over 70 MPH.

Puffing

Section 2-313(2) provides that a warranty may be found even though the seller never uses the word "warranty" or "guarantee" and has no intention of making a warranty. The seller has the burden of proving that the buyer did not rely on her representations. However, if a seller is merely *puffing*—that is, expressing an opinion about the quality of the goods—he has not made a warranty. For example, a car salesperson's statement that "this is a top-notch car" is puffing, whereas a factual statement such as "it will get 25 miles to the gallon" is an express warranty.

Unfortunately, the line between opinion and fact is not always easy to draw. Much turns on the circumstances surrounding the representation, including the identities and relative knowledge of the parties involved.

A number of courts employ a two-prong test to distinguish warranty language from opinion. The first prong is whether the seller asserted a fact of which the buyer was ignorant. If so, the assertion may be a warranty. The second prong is whether the seller merely stated a view on something about which the buyer could be expected to have formed her own opinion and could judge the validity of the seller's statement. In this second instance, the seller's statement is an opinion, not a warranty. The following case illustrates the difficulty of making these distinctions.

■ **A Case in Point:**   **Summary**

Case 9.2
ROYAL BUSINESS MACHINES, INC. v. LORRAINE CORP.
United States Court of Appeals for the Seventh Circuit
633 F.2d 34 (7th Cir. 1980).

FACTS   Over an 18-month period, Royal sold a number of copying machines to Michael L. Booher, a businessman affiliated with Lorraine Corporation. The machines required extensive maintenance, and Booher sued Royal for breach of express warranties. The trial court found that the following statements made by Royal prior to the sale constituted express warranties:

1.   The copying machines and their component parts are of high quality.

2.   Experience and testing show that the frequency of repairs is very low on such machines and will remain so.

3.   Replacement parts are readily available.

4.   The cost of maintenance for each machine is and will remain low.

5.   The cost of supplies for each machine is and will remain low.

6.   The machines have been extensively tested and are ready to be marketed.

7.   Experience and reasonable projections show that Booher's purchase of the machines and subsequent leasing to other customers will return substantial profits to Booher.

8.   The machines are safe and cannot cause fires.

9.   Service calls, including preventative maintenance calls, are and will be required for the machines every 7,000 to 9,000 copies on average.

ISSUE PRESENTED   When do statements about an expensive product such as a copying machine made by a salesperson in a sales pitch within a business transaction constitute express warranties?

SUMMARY OF OPINION   The U.S. Court of Appeals began by stating that an express warranty: (a) is an affirmation of fact or promise; (b) that relates to the goods; and (c) becomes a part of the basis of the bargain between the parties. It then examined each of Royal's statements.

The court found that Royal's affirmation that the machines and their component parts were of high quality (statement number 1) was a statement of the seller's opinion. It was the kind of puffing to be expected in any sales transaction. It was not a positive statement of fact describing a product's capabilities. Royal's representation about the frequency of repair (statement number 2) also lacked the specificity of an affirmation of fact and merely reflected the seller's opinion.

The assertions that replacement parts were readily available (statement number 3) and that the cost of supplies was low (statement number 5) were statements of fact, but they did not relate to the goods being sold—that is, the machines themselves—as required by UCC section 2-313(1)(a). Royal's representation that Booher would realize substantial profits (statement number 7) was not an affirmation of fact relating to the goods under section 2-313(1)(a), and it did not describe the goods as required by section 2-313(1)(b).

On the other hand, the statements about maintenance costs (statement number 4) and frequency of service calls (statement number 9) were assertions of fact directly related to the goods. The assertions that the machines were fully tested and ready to be marketed (statement number 6) and that they would not cause fires (statement number 8) were also held to be assertions of fact relating to the goods.

RESULT Statements numbered 4, 6, 8, and 9 were express warranties.

COMMENTS Whether a statement about a product is an express warranty or merely an opinion depends on the context in which it is made, the degree to which the buyer is ignorant of the subject matter of the statement, the extent to which the seller was merely puffing, the time when the statement was made, and other factors concerning the relationship between the two parties.

This case was complicated by the fact that the sales extended over an 18-month period. Booher's expectations were likely to change during the extended course of dealing. As the court stated:

> Booher's expanding knowledge of the capacities of the copying machines would have to be considered in deciding whether Royal's representations were part of the basis of the bargain. The same representations that could have constituted an express warranty early in the series of transactions might not have qualified as an express warranty in a later transaction if the buyer had acquired independent knowledge as to the fact asserted.

The court's reasoning highlights the fact that course of dealing can affect a buyer's ability to rely on representations by a seller.

■ Implied Warranty of Merchantability

The *implied warranty of merchantability* guarantees that the goods are reasonably fit for the general purpose for which they are sold, and that they are properly packaged and labeled. The warranty applies to all goods sold by merchants in the normal course of business. It does not depend on the seller's statements or use of a sample or model. Rather, it depends on the identity of the seller as a merchant who deals in goods of a certain kind.

To be merchantable under UCC section 2-314(2), goods must:

1. Pass without objection in the trade under the contract description

2. Be fit for the ordinary purposes for which such goods are used

3. Be within the variations permitted by the agreement and be of even kind, quality, and quantity within each unit and among all units involved

4. Be adequately contained, packaged, and labeled as the agreement may require

5. Conform to the promises or affirmations of fact made on the container or label, if any.

Fungible goods, like grain, must be of average quality within the contract description.

Reasonable Expectations

The key issue in determining merchantability is whether the goods do what a reasonable person would expect of them. The contract description is crucial. Goods considered merchantable under one contract may be considered not to be merchantable in another. A bicycle with a cracked frame and bent wheels is not fit for the ordinary purpose for which bicycles are used, but it will pass under a contract for the sale of scrap metal.

> "
> *A bicycle with a cracked frame and bent wheels is not fit for the ordinary purpose for which bicycles are used, but it will pass under a contract for the sale of scrap metal.*

When no contract description exists, the most frequent claim upon which breach is based is that the goods are not fit "for the ordinary purposes for which such goods are used." Proof that the goods are imperfect or flawed is often insufficient to succeed on this claim. Even imperfect goods can be fit for their ordinary purposes.

Ethical Consideration

This case raises the ethical question of what investigations a seller should make before putting goods on the market. It is hardly reasonable to require a bookstore to test every recipe in every cookbook it sells, but it might well be reasonable for bookstores to consider buying cookbooks only from well-regarded publishers like Sunset Publishing that have test kitchens.

The courts will not uphold all claims by dissatisfied buyers against sellers. In *Cardozo v. True*,[1] Ingrid Cardozo purchased a cookbook from True's bookstore. Several days later, Cardozo followed a recipe in the book for the preparation of the dasheen plant commonly known as "elephant ears." While preparing the roots for cooking, she ate a small slice and immediately experienced a burning of the mouth area, coughing, gasping, and intense stomach cramps. She sued the bookstore for breach of implied warranty of merchantability. The Florida District Court of Appeals held that a bookstore is not liable under the implied warranty of merchantability

---

1. 342 So.2d 1053 (Fla. App. 1977), *cert. denied*, 353 So.2d 674 (Fla. 1977).

for the content of the books the store sells, but only for the physical characteristics of the books, such as printing and binding. The implied warranty of merchantability does not include the thought processes or suggestions conveyed by the authors of the book.

■ Implied Warranty of Fitness for a Particular Purpose

The *implied warranty of fitness for a particular purpose* is set forth in UCC section 2-315. It guarantees that the goods are fit for the particular purpose for which the seller recommended them. Unlike the implied warranty of merchantability, this warranty does not arise in every sale of goods by a merchant. It will be implied only if four elements are present: (1) the buyer had a particular purpose for the goods; (2) the seller knew or had reason to know of that purpose; (3) the buyer relied on the seller's expertise; and (4) the seller knew or had reason to know of the buyer's reliance.

Reliance

In order to prove that the buyer did not in fact rely on the seller's expertise, the seller may try to show that: (1) the buyer's expertise was equal to or superior to the seller's; (2) the buyer relied on the skill and judgment of persons hired by the buyer; or (3) the buyer supplied the seller with detailed specifications or designs which the seller was to follow.

In the following case, a court found that there was an implied warranty of fitness for a particular purpose.

■ A Case in Point: Summary

Case 9.3
LEWIS v. MOBIL OIL CORP.
United States Court of Appeals
for the Eighth Circuit
438 F.2d 500 (8th Cir. 1971).

FACTS Paul Lewis, a sawmill operator, requested from Frank Rowe, a local Mobil Oil dealer, the proper hydraulic fluid to operate his new hydraulic pump. Lewis told Rowe only that the machinery was operated by a gear-type pump. Rowe requested no further information. After contacting a Mobil representative for a recommendation, Rowe sold Lewis straight mineral oil with no chemical additives. Within a few days Lewis began experiencing difficulty. After several months it was discovered that the oil was not proper for the pump Lewis used. Lewis sued Mobil for breach of the implied warranty of fitness for a particular purpose. At trial Lewis testified that he had been a longtime customer of Mobil Oil and that his only source of contact with the company was through Rowe. It was common knowledge in the community that Lewis was converting his operation into a hydraulic system. Rowe knew this, and in fact had visited Lewis's mill on business matters several times during the course of the changeover. Neither Lewis nor Rowe knew what the oil requirements for the system were. Lewis testified that when his difficulties began, oil was the suspected source of trouble. He therefore asked Rowe on several occasions to be sure that the oil he furnished was the appropriate type.

ISSUE PRESENTED   Under what circumstances is a seller liable for breach of the implied warranty of fitness for a particular purpose?

SUMMARY OF OPINION   The U.S. Court of Appeals held that the evidence adequately established an implied warranty of fitness for a particular purpose. Mobil contended that no warranty of fitness should apply because: (1) Lewis did not specify that he needed an oil with additives; and (2) Lewis did not provide enough information for Mobil to determine that an additive oil was required. In response to this contention, the court cited Comment 1 to UCC section 2-315:

> Whether or not this warranty arises in any individual case is basically a question of fact to be determined by the circumstances of the contracting. Under this section the buyer need not bring home to the seller actual knowledge of the particular purpose for which the goods are intended or of his reliance on the seller's skill and judgment, if the circumstances are such that the seller has reason to realize the purpose intended or that the reliance exists.

> The court added, "Here Lewis made it clear that the oil was purchased for his system, that he didn't know what oil should be used, and that he was relying on Mobil to supply the proper product. If any further information was needed, it was incumbent upon Mobil to get it before making its recommendation."

RESULT   Mobil Oil was liable to the buyer Lewis for breach of the implied warranty of fitness for a particular purpose. A seller is liable under the implied warranty of fitness for a particular purpose if the seller had reason to know the purpose intended for the product by the buyer and that the buyer was relying on the seller's expertise.

COMMENTS   This case demonstrates the importance for managers of providing adequate instruction and training to salespersons and agents about express and implied warranties. A company can be held liable under an implied warranty of fitness for a particular purpose even if it did not intend to make any warranty.

■ Magnuson-Moss Warranty Act

The Magnuson-Moss Warranty Act[2] is a federal law that protects consumers against deception in warranties. It requires that express warranties be made easy to understand.

No seller is required to make a written warranty under this act. However, if the seller does make a written promise or affirmation of fact, then it must also state whether, for example, the warranty is a full or a limited warranty. A *full warranty* gives the consumer the right to free repair or replacement of a defective product. A *limited warranty* might restrict the availability of free repair or replacement. This act is discussed further in chapter 19.

---

2. 15 U.S.C. §§ 2301-12 (1982).

Acceptance of Goods and Risk of Loss

The following case deals with the question of when is a buyer considered to have accepted goods from the seller.

This is an important issue because under the UCC risk of loss passes with acceptance.

A Case in Point: Summary

Case 9.4
LYNCH IMPORTS, LTD. v. FREY
Appellate Court of Illinois
200 Ill.App.3d 781, 558 N.E.2d 484 (1990).

FACTS   On October 22, 1987, the buyers agreed to purchase a 1987 Volkswagen automobile from the seller for the price of $8,706. The agreement was set forth in a purchase order in which the following phrases were handwritten on the purchase contract: "car to be in totally acceptable condition or money will be refunded to the customer," and "acceptance subject to inspection."

On October 24, the buyers took possession of the vehicle and paid the seller $4,706, as part payment on the purchase price. The balance of the purchase price was to be financed. It was understood that the car was to come with air conditioning, but at the time did not have it yet installed. One of two riders attached to the purchase contract provided that the buyer was responsible to have the vehicle fully covered under liability and collision automobile insurance from the instant that buyer takes possession. As well, the rider stated that the buyer was not authorized to return the vehicle without the seller's authorization and no vehicle is to be sold with the condition that the buyer may later return it. About two to three days thereafter, the buyers brought the vehicle to the seller so that the air conditioner could be installed. When they returned in the evening to pick up the vehicle, they were informed that the air conditioner had been installed, but that the vehicle sustained body damage in an accident. The buyers refused to take delivery of the automobile because of the damage and demanded that a new and undamaged be substituted. When the seller refused, the buyers stopped payment on the check and canceled their application for financing the balance of the purchase price.

The car dealership sued the automobile purchaser for damages of $8,706 for breaching the sales contract and for $4,706 for wrongfully stopping the check. The buyers filed a counterclaim for the seller's breach of contract in failing to deliver an acceptable car and sought damages of $1,330.35, representing the difference between the price paid by the buyers when they subsequently purchased a similar automobile and the contract price of the Volkswagen. The circuit court granted summary judgment to the seller. The buyers appealed.

ISSUE PRESENTED   When a buyer takes possession of a car, but it is understood that the buyer will return with the car to have air conditioning installed per the purchase order, has the buyer fully accepted the car and complete responsibility for it?

SUMMARY OF OPINION   The Illinois Appellate Court stated that there existed an issue of material fact as to whether the buyers "accepted" the vehicle on October 24. Buyers argued that they did not "accept" the vehicle and therefore had the right to reject it, which they properly did, when it was damaged upon its return to the seller to install the air conditioner.

Under the provisions of section 2-606 of the Uniform Commercial Code, acceptance is deemed to have occurred when the buyer either signifies that the vehicle was conforming or "takes or retains" the vehicle in spite of its non-conformity. It is unclear as to what the agreement was on October 24, 1987, just prior to the buyer's taking the vehicle. The uncertainty as to what transpired between the parties when the buyers took possession of the vehicle is of particular significance in view of the fact that the original purchase order contained the handwritten phrases: "car to be in totally acceptable condition or money will be refunded to customer" and "acceptance subject to inspection." Section 1-202 of the Uniform Commercial Code provides that the effect of the provisions of the Uniform Commercial Code may be varied by agreement. As presently postured, the handwritten notations in the purchase agreement are sufficient to raise an inference that buyers did not intend to waive their right to defer acceptance until the vehicle was brought to full conformity, even though they took interim possession of the vehicle.

Under section 2-509 of the Uniform Commercial Code, the risk of loss does not pass to the buyer until the buyer accepts the goods, even though the buyer obtains an insurable interest under section 2-501 after the goods are identified to the purchase contract. Thus Rider 2 which provides for the buyer to obtain insurance is not conclusive on its face to pass the risk of loss of the buyer.

RESULT The Appellate Court reversed the lower court's holding because material issues of fact existed, precluding summary judgment. The case was remanded to determine whether the buyers accepted the vehicle and whether they had the right to reject it when it was later discovered to be damaged upon its return to the seller to install air conditioning.

■ Unconscionability

A party is normally bound by the terms of a contract she signs. However, if the contract is so unfair as to shock the conscience of the court, the judge may decline to enforce the offending terms or the entire contract.

UCC section 2-302(1) provides procedural guidelines for judicial review of unconscionable clauses in contracts for the sale of goods, but it does not define "unconscionable." The official comments, however, provide some guidance. For example, comment I to section 2-302 states:

> The basic test is whether, in the light of the general background and the commercial needs of the particular trade or case, the clauses involved are so one sided as to be unconscionable under the circumstances existing at the time of the making of the contract. . . . The principle is one of the prevention of oppression and unfair surprise . . . and not of disturbance of allocation of risks because of superior bargaining power.

In deciding whether a contract is unconscionable, the court considers evidence in addition to the contractual

International Consideration

The international mercantile community, acting through the International Chamber of Commerce, has elaborated a set of definitions of the most important trade terms now in use. The latest edition of these terms is INCOTERMS 1980. There is a widespread practice among traders of all countries to incorporate INCOTERMS into their international sales contracts.

INCOTERMS 1980 contains fourteen trade terms, including FAS, FOB, CTF, and CIF. The CIF term, for example, states that "the seller is required to procure, at his own cost and in a transferable form, a policy of marine insurance against the risk of carriage involved in the contract."

Historical Perspective
Allocation of the Risk of Loss

Goods can be lost in transit due to such events as fire, earthquake, flood, or theft. Prior to the introduction of the UCC in 1954, risk of loss was allocated between buyer and seller under the Uniform Sales Act. In general, the Uniform Sales Act provided that the party that held title to the goods at the time the loss or damage occurred bore the loss. Thus, if title had passed to the buyer before the loss occurred, the buyer was liable to the seller for the price of the goods even though they were never received. If the seller still had title to the goods at the time of the loss, the seller was liable to the buyer for nondelivery unless the seller tendered a replacement for the goods.

These provisions spawned much complex litigation. Because it was unclear exactly what caused title to pass from seller to buyer, it was difficult to determine who held title at a particular time. The passing of title usually did not depend on which party possessed the goods. In situations where title passed to the buyer while the goods were in the seller's possession, the Uniform Sales Act approach could lead to inefficient outcomes, because it is the party in possession of the goods who is most likely to insure against possible loss and is best able to take precautions to minimize the risk of loss.

For example, under the Uniform Sales Act, title passed to the buyer as soon as goods were identified to the contract, that is, designated as the goods to be supplied under the contract. As identification to the contract often occurred well before the goods were shipped to the buyer, the buyer bore the risk of loss or damage to goods over which he had no control. In addition, buyers rarely carried insurance covering goods not yet in their possession.

In the view of Karl Llewellyn, a key drafter of the UCC, the elimination of the passing of title as a determinant of the rights and liabilities of the parties was one of the UCC's greatest contributions to U.S. commercial law. Under the UCC, the passing of title is generally irrelevant to the allocation of the risk of loss. In general, the UCC places the risk of loss on the party controlling the goods at the time loss occurs, as that party may be expected to insure against possible loss and is in a better position to take precautions to protect the goods. The UCC expressly authorizes the buyer and seller to allocate risk of loss between them as they see fit, and provides shorthand symbols such as "F.O.B." (free on board) with defined meanings to facilitate the expression of such an agreement between the parties.

Goods Shipped by Carrier If a sales contract requires or authorizes the seller to ship the goods by carrier, the risk of loss passes to the buyer: (1) at the time the goods are properly delivered to the carrier, if the contract does not require delivery at a particular destination; or (2) at the time the carrier tenders the goods to the buyer at the specified destination, if the contract specifies one.

If the parties indicate that shipment is to be made "F.O.B. seller's place of business," delivery at a particular place is not required, so the risk of loss shifts to the buyer once the goods are properly placed in the possession of the carrier. An indication in the contract that shipment is to be made "F.O.B. buyer's place of business" means that delivery at a particular place is required, so the risk of loss will not shift to the buyer until the goods are tendered to the buyer at her place of business. The parties' selection of an F.O.B. term in a sales contract controls the allocation of the risk of loss even if contrary language exists elsewhere in the contract.

Goods Held by Independent Warehouse When the goods are in the possession of an independent warehouse and the seller provides the buyer with a document enabling him to pick up the goods at the warehouse, the risk of loss passes to the buyer at the warehouse when the buyer receives the document entitling him to pick up the goods.

All Other Cases When the goods are neither to be shipped by carrier nor held by an independent warehouse, the allocation of the risk of loss in transit depends on whether the seller is a merchant. A seller is a merchant if she possesses experience and special knowledge relating to the goods in question. If the seller is a merchant, the risk of loss passes to the buyer only when he receives physical possession of the goods. If the seller is not a merchant, the risk passes to the buyer when tender of delivery is made. Tender of delivery is made when the seller notifies the buyer that she has the goods ready for delivery.[a]

---

a. The discussion in this Historical Perspective is based on James J. White and Robert S. Summers, *Uniform Commercial Code*, 233-71 (3rd ed., 1988).

language, particularly: (1) whether the contractual obligation was bargained for, and (2) whether the parties understood and accepted the obligation.

As under common law (discussed in chapter 8), unconscionability can be either procedural—relating to the bargaining process—or substantive—relating to the provisions of the contract.

Procedural Unconscionability

A contract is procedurally unconscionable when one party is induced to enter a contract without having any meaningful choice. For example, in highly concentrated industries with few competitors, all of the sellers may offer the same unfair contracts on a "take it or leave it" basis. Such contracts are known as *adhesion contracts*. They are most prevalent in consumer transactions where bargaining power is unequal.

It is also procedurally unconscionable for a seller to tuck oppressive clauses into the fine print, or for high-pressure salespersons to mislead illiterate consumers. In commercial transactions, however, it is presumed that the parties have the sophistication to bargain knowledgeably. Procedural unconscionability in the commercial setting is, therefore, more difficult to prove.

> "
> *It is also procedurally unconscionable for a seller to tuck oppressive clauses into the fine print, or for high-pressure salespersons to mislead illiterate consumers.*

Substantive Unconscionability

A contract is substantively unconscionable if its terms are unduly harsh or oppressive or unreasonably favorable to one side, such as in the case of an excessive price or a limitation of one party's rights and remedies.

The courts have not agreed on any well-defined test for determining when a price is so excessive as to be unconscionable. However, prices that were two to three times the price of similar goods sold in the same area have been held unconscionable.

In another example, parties to a contract are allowed to limit the remedies available for breach, but only to a certain extent. If, for example, consumer goods are involved, a provision that limits the purchaser's ability to recover monetary damages for personal injury is *prima facie* (or on its face) evidence of unconscionability.

The following case illustrates how one court handled an unconscionable contract.

Ethical Consideration

Some businesspeople suggest that because low-income persons are statistically more likely to default on loans, creditors must charge a higher interest rate to cover themselves for the increased risk of default. They conclude that if the sellers are not allowed to charge these higher interest rates or prices, low-income buyers will not be able to buy goods on credit. How should a manager balance the need for low-income persons to have credit to buy goods with the need for businesses to make a profit?

■ A Case in Point: In the Language of the Court

Case 9.5
WILLIAMS v. WALKER-THOMAS FURNITURE CO.
United States Court of Appeals
for the District of Columbia
350 F.2d 445 (D.C. Cir. 1965).

FACTS   Ova Lee Williams, a welfare mother of limited education, purchased household items from Walker-Thomas Furniture Company on credit over the course of several years. An obscurely worded provision in the purchase agreement form provided that all installment payments would be credited pro rata to all then outstanding purchases. The effect of this *cross-collateralization clause* was to keep a balance due on all items purchased

*Case **9.5** continued on following page*

*Case **9.5** continued*

until all of the buyer's accounts were reduced to zero. Each new item purchased increased the balance due, giving the seller a continued security interest in all previously purchased items. When Williams's balance was down to $164, she bought a stereo costing $514. This brought her balance up to $678. When she defaulted on a payment, the furniture store tried to repossess all the goods she had previously purchased on credit over the years. She claimed that repossession of all of the goods under the contract was unconscionable.

The trial court decided in favor of Walker-Thomas Furniture Company. Williams appealed.

ISSUE PRESENTED   Is a cross-collaterization clause in a sales contract between a store and a buyer unconscionable if one party has limited bargaining power and lacks specific knowledge to understand the terms if all of the terms are clearly spelled out and the buyer has the option to not buy or to go elsewhere?

OPINION   WRIGHT, J., writing for the U.S. Court of Appeals:

. . . .

We cannot condemn too strongly appellee's [Walker-Thomas Furniture's] conduct. It raises serious questions of sharp practice and irresponsible business dealings. A review of the legislation in the District of Columbia affecting retail sales and the pertinent decisions of the highest court in this jurisdiction disclose, however, no ground upon which this court can declare the contracts in question contrary to public policy. . . .

. . . .

Congress has recently enacted the Uniform Commercial Code, which specifically provides that the court may refuse to enforce a contract which it finds to be unconscionable at the time it was made. . . . Accordingly, we hold that where the element of unconscionability is present at the time a contract is made, the contract should not be enforced.

Unconscionability has generally been recognized to include an absence of meaningful choice on the part of one of the parties together with contract terms which are unreasonably favorable to the other party. Whether a meaningful choice is present in a particular case can only be determined by consideration of all the circumstances surrounding the transaction. In many cases the meaningfulness of the choice is negated by a gross inequality of bargaining power. The manner in which the contract was entered is also relevant to this consideration. Did each party to the contract, considering his obvious education or lack of it, have a reasonable opportunity to understand the terms of the contract, or were the important terms hidden in a maze of fine print and minimized by deceptive sales practices? Ordinarily, one who signs an agreement without full knowledge of its terms might be held to assume the risk that he has entered a one-sided bargain. But when a party of little bargaining power, and hence little real choice, signs a commercially unreasonable contract with little or no knowledge of its terms, it is hardly likely that his consent, or even an objective manifestation of his consent, was ever given to all the terms. In such a case the usual rule that the terms of the agreement are not to be questioned should be abandoned and the court should consider whether the terms of the contract are so unfair that enforcement should be withheld.

In determining reasonableness or fairness, the primary concern must be with the terms of the contract considered in light of the circumstances existing when the contract was made. The test is not simple, nor can it be mechanically applied. The terms are to be considered "in the light of the general commercial background and the commercial needs of the particular trade or case." Corbin suggests the test as being whether the terms are "so extreme as to appear unconscionable according to the mores and business practices of the time and place." . . .

. . . .

RESULT The Court of Appeals held that where the element of unconscionability is present at time the contract is made, the contract should not be enforced. Because the lower trial court which had granted judgment to the furniture company had not recognized that contracts could be unenforceable on that basis and the record was not sufficient for the Court of Appeals to decide the issue as matter of law, the case was remanded to the trial court for further proceedings.

COMMENTS The New York Supreme Court (the state trial court in New York) applied the same logic in *Jones v. Star Credit Corp.*[3] The plaintiff was a welfare recipient who purchased a freezer on credit for $900. With the addition of time credit charges, credit life insurance, credit property insurance, and sales tax, the purchase price totaled $1,234.80. At trial it was established that the freezer's value was only $300. In holding the freezer contract unconscionable, the New York court noted the fundamental tension underlying cases like *Williams:* "On the one hand it is necessary to recognize the importance of preserving the integrity of agreements and the fundamental right of parties to deal, trade, bargain and contract. On the other hand there is the concern for the uneducated and often illiterate individual who is the victim of gross inequality of bargaining power."

Questions
1. Would the result have been any different if instead the items in question were not furniture and other things of "necessity" but rather luxury items such as fur coats and diamond watches?
2. Was the court focusing more on the woman's lack of money or the possibility of her inability to fully comprehend the terms? What if she had a Ph.D. in economics, but was on welfare? What if she were of moderate wealth but had a learning disability that limited her capacity to understand the implications of the terms of the contract?

---

3. 298 N.Y.S.2d 264, 6 UCC Rep. 76 (N.Y. Sup. 1969).

■ Commercial Impracticability

Under the common-law doctrine of impossibility, discussed in chapter 8, a person may be excused from performing his contractual obligation if it is rendered impossible by the occurrence of unforeseen events.

In applying the doctrine of impossibility to a business context, the common law developed the doctrine of *commercial impossibility*. This doctrine allows the risk of nonperformance, under certain circumstances, to shift from the promisor to the promisee.

Application Under the UCC

The UCC has adopted the doctrine of commercial impracticability rather than that of strict impossibility. Section 2-615 states that unless the contract provides otherwise, a failure to perform is not a breach if performance is made impractical by an event unforeseen by the contract. Section 2-615, the associated official comments, and the cases that have arisen under section 2-615 establish certain criteria that a party seeking discharge from performance must show.

Underlying Condition There must be a failure of an underlying condition of the contract, that is, a condition that was not included in the parties' bargain. Certain occurrences are provided for fully in contracts, and the seller is assumed to have figured an appropriate "insurance premium" into the contract price. Other risks are deemed too remote and uncertain to be included in the contract price. The function of the court in applying the doctrine of commercial impracticability is to determine which risks were, or properly should have been, allocated to the buyer, and which to the seller.

Unforeseen Contingency In addition to showing that a condition was not reflected in the contract price, a seller seeking discharge must prove that the contingency that prevents performance was both unforeseen and unforeseeable. To some extent every occurrence is foreseeable—there is always some probability that a fire will destroy the anticipated source of supply, that a key person will die, or that various acts of God will occur. Legally, however, a foreseeable contingency is one that the parties should have contemplated in the circumstances surrounding the contracting. If there is a standard trade custom for allocating the risk, it is assumed that a particular contract follows that custom, unless it specifies differently.

Official comment 4 provides an illustrative, but not exhaustive, list of contingencies that are considered unforeseeable. Wars and embargoes are considered unforeseeable; market fluctuations are not.

Impracticable Performance Even if a seller is able to show that there was a failure of an underlying condition of the contract, and that she did not implicitly assume the risk of this occurrence, she still must prove that the performance was impracticable. Increased cost alone is not sufficient reason to excuse performance, unless it is a marked increase. In one case a ten- to twelve fold increase was considered sufficient. In another case the court observed: "We are not aware of any cases where something less than a 100% cost increase has been held to make a seller's performance impracticable."[4]

---

4. *Publicker Industries, Inc. v. Union Carbide Corp.*, 17 UCC Rep. Serv. 989 (E.D. Pa. 1975).

Transactions that have merely become unprofitable will not be excused. Sellers cannot rely on UCC section 2-615 to get them out of a bad bargain.

> 66
>
> *Transactions that have merely become unprofitable will not be excused. Sellers cannot rely on UCC section 2-615 to get them out of a bad bargain.*

The Westinghouse Uranium Cases

The article excerpted as the "Inside Story" at the end of this chapter discusses the Westinghouse Electric Corporation uranium cases, which dealt with the doctrines of impracticability and impossibility.

■ Damages

The UCC, like the common law of contracts, generally tries to put the nonbreaching party in the same position it would have been in if the contract had been performed. This is usually done through the award of monetary damages.

Sellers' Remedies

If a buyer wrongfully cancels a contract or refuses to accept delivery of the goods covered by the contract, the seller is entitled under UCC section 2-708 to damages. The measure of damages is the difference between the market price at the time and place for delivery and the unpaid contract price, less expenses saved because of the buyer's breach. If this measure of damages is inadequate to put the seller in as good a position as performance would have done, then the seller is entitled to recover the profit (including reasonable overhead) that he would have made from full performance by the buyer. Such a seller is called a *lost volume seller*.

Buyers' Remedies

If a seller wrongfully fails to deliver the goods or repudiates the contract, or if the buyer justifiably rejects the tendered goods, then under UCC section 2-711 the buyer has several choices. She may cancel the contract and recover as much of the price as has been paid and then either: (1) cover, that is, buy the goods elsewhere and be reimbursed for the extra cost of the substitute goods; or (2) recover damages for nondelivery.

If the buyer elects to cover under UCC section 2-712, he must make, in good faith and without reasonable delay, a reasonable purchase of substitute goods. The buyer may then recover from the seller the difference between the cost of cover and the contract price.

If the buyer elects not to cover, under UCC section 2-713 she is entitled to damages. The measure of damages is the difference between the market price at the time the buyer learned of the breach and the contract price. The buyer may also recover consequential damages, which are defined in UCC section 2-715 as:

a. Any loss resulting from general or particular requirements and needs of which the seller at the time of contracting had reason to know and which could not reasonably be prevented by cover or otherwise; and

b. Injury to person or property proximately resulting from any breach of warranty.

■ Specific Performance

If the promised goods are unique, then under UCC section 2-716 a court may order the seller to deliver them.

For example, if there is only one antique Mercedes-Benz of a certain vintage, then damages alone will not be adequate to remedy the loss suffered by the disappointed buyer. Only delivery of the promised car will suffice. On the other hand, if the car is one of thousands, monetary damages will suffice, because an equivalent car can be purchased elsewhere.

The Responsible Manager

Operating Under UCC Contract Law

Any manager who enters into contracts in his own name or in the name of his business should know which body of contract law will govern the transaction. Because every state has adopted the UCC in some form, a central question is whether the transaction is analyzed under article 2 of the UCC or under the common-law rules concerning contracts. Article 2 applies only to the sale of goods, not services or land. Although some things are clearly designated as goods, others may be more difficult to categorize. A manager should obtain legal advice if there is any doubt as to which body of law controls in a particular situation.

Once a manager has determined that article 2 of the UCC controls, she should be aware of the requirements that must be met for the valid formation of a contract. This knowledge is crucial to ensuring that the company can enforce the contracts it has entered into and wishes to uphold. In addition, a manager may have a valid reason to attempt to avoid an agreement that was not formed in the correct manner. Only if he knows the rules of contract formation can he assess whether a contract was validly created.

Managers should also focus on one of the key elements in creating a valid contract: the process of offer and acceptance. The manner of making an appropriate offer is the same under the UCC as it is under common law. However, a manager should note that article 2 allows an offeree to accept an offer even if the offeree's acceptance contains terms additional to or different from those in the offer. The UCC rules in this area and the corresponding case law are both complex and fact specific. Nonetheless, it is crucial that managers understand these rules before they engage in negotiations. Failure to develop this understanding can lead to adverse results. A manager or company may be legally bound to a contract even when there was no intention to be bound.

Article 2 of the UCC also establishes three types of warranties that buyers may rely upon when purchasing goods. Managers of companies that produce goods should be aware of how each warranty is created, how they are applied, and how liability for products can be limited under the UCC framework. It is essential that managers obtain legal advice in this area, as lawsuits under the UCC warranties can lead to large awards of damages. These warranties also provide guidelines for managers regarding what is expected from a product in terms of quality and suitability for its intended use.

Managers should also be familiar with the legal doctrines that allow parties legally to back out of contracts. The doctrine of impracticability can protect a party when unexpected changes in circumstances make performance not literally impossible but commercially ruinous. The doctrine of unconscionability provides managers with guidelines on the legal and ethical limits to one-sided contracts.

Inside Story

The Westinghouse Uranium Contracts

THE WESTINGHOUSE URANIUM CONTRACTS: COMMERCIAL
IMPRACTICABILITY AND RELATED MATTERS*

Westinghouse Electric Corporation surprised and
shocked the business and legal communities when, on
September 8, 1975, it announced that it would not
deliver about 70 million pounds of uranium under fixed
price contracts to 27 utility companies.

Westinghouse supported its position by relying on a
relatively obscure and little used provision of the
Uniform Commercial Code, section 2-615, which provides that a party may be excused from performing contractual obligations on the basis of "commercial
impracticability." It claimed that the potential loss of $2
billion made it "commercially impractical" to meet its
obligations.

The utilities responded predictably enough, by filing
civil suits in thirteen different federal jurisdictions. All
thirteen cases were combined and sent to the U.S.
District Court for the Eastern District of Virginia on the
basis that the commonality was greater than the differences, particularly Westinghouse's defense of commercial impracticability and the problem of how to distribute the uranium that Westinghouse had on hand. Three
utilities brought suit in a Pennsylvania state court and
three Swedish utilities took action in Stockholm.

This is only part of the picture as ripples from this
bombshell spread out. In an effort to protect its interests, in 1976 Westinghouse brought suit against its suppliers of uranium claiming that an international cartel
had caused an unforeseen and precipitous increase in
the price of uranium. Preliminary maneuvers resulted in
a decision from the Supreme Court of Ontario and one
from the British House of Lords that prevented
Westinghouse from getting documents and testimony
relating to their case from foreign corporations. Similar
action was taken in South Africa and Australia.

The suits against Westinghouse were delayed until
September 1981 by Federal District Judge Prentice

---

* Excerpted from William Eagan. "The Westinghouse Uranium
Contracts: Commercial Impracticability and Related Matters."
Reprinted and excerpted by permission of the *American
Business Law Journal,* vol. 18, at 281, 1980.

Marshall because "he was afraid people just weren't
going to be ready in time." As of August 1979, more
than seven million pages of documents had been submitted during the discovery proceedings. This may be
one of the factors that led the judge to observe that this
was "the lawyers' full employment case." The direct
and indirect costs to the various participants in the uranium dispute are considerable. Westinghouse alone
spent $25 million for out-of-house legal expenses in
1976.

On June 18, 1978, Westinghouse named Douglas D.
Danforth to the new No. 2 post of vice chairman and
chief operating officer so that the chairman, Robert E.
Kirby, would have more time to spend trying to solve
the company's uranium problem.

Westinghouse Position

When Westinghouse announced in September 1975
that it would not honor its contractual obligations to
deliver 70 million pounds of uranium under fixed price
agreements, it claimed that dramatic, unprecedented
and unforeseeable events occurred that raised the price
of uranium from about $6.50 to $9.00 per pound to $26
per pound in September 1975. This could lead to a
potential loss to Westinghouse of about $2 billion. By
July 1978 the price had risen to about $44 per pound
and the potential loss escalated to approximately $3
billion.

Westinghouse contended that the unexpected Arab
Oil Embargo of 1973-1974 was one of the factors that
resulted in a major increase in the price of all energy
resources including uranium. Later it argued that an
international cartel was establishing prices for uranium
and thus artificially increasing the price. For these reasons, Westinghouse sought refuge under section 2-615
of the Uniform Commercial Code arguing that it would
be "commercially impracticable" to complete a contract
that could result in bankruptcy.

On October 27, 1978, after having arrived at several
out-of-court settlements, Westinghouse contended that
section 2-712 of the Uniform Commercial Code
requires that if the injured party is to cover [that is, to
buy substitute goods] they must do it "without unrea-

Inside Story, continued

sonable delay." Although the plaintiffs could have covered for $26 to $30 per pound for the first four months after the announcement of default, many still had not covered and were seeking damages of $43 per pound. Thus, Westinghouse argued that if they were to be assessed damages, or if out-of-court settlements should be arrived at, it should be on the basis of the cost of uranium at the date of rescission and not the current $43 per pound.

International Ramifications

Westinghouse's apparently weak case was unexpectedly bolstered when, in the summer of 1976, Friends of the Earth, an environmentally oriented group based in San Francisco and interested primarily in energy, discovered evidence in Australia of the possibility of the existence of an international cartel that was established to control the price of uranium. They immediately took action to take advantage of this windfall on October 15, 1976, by filing suits against 29 foreign and domestic suppliers of uranium including Gulf Oil Corporation and Rio Algom Corporation.

Westinghouse's efforts were somewhat frustrated by the fact that some of the potential suppliers of uranium were foreign corporations, or U.S. subsidiaries of a foreign corporation, or foreign subsidiaries of American corporations. So, when they attempted to acquire pertinent documents from Rio Algom Corporation, for example, they were not successful. Rio Algom is a Delaware corporation operating a uranium mine in Utah but is a wholly owned subsidiary of Rio Algom Limited, a Canadian corporation with Toronto as its principal place of business. The two corporations have common officers, directors, and marketing vice-presidents and all records are kept in Toronto. Rio Tinto Zinc Corporation Limited, a British Corporation based in London, owns the majority of the stock in Rio Algom, Ltd.

Out-of-Court Settlements

Where does this leave Westinghouse in its attempt to chart new applications to the concept of impossibility and specifically to commercial impracticability as contained in Uniform Commercial Code section 2-615? It seems very doubtful that all of this activity will result in a decision that could be used as a precedent in further defining the application of Uniform Commercial Code section 2-615. After all, who would relish the idea of rendering a decision involving a potential award of $2.6 billion against the 36th largest corporation in the U.S. with a net worth of $2.29 billion at the end of 1977? Rarely have judges worked so diligently to avoid handing down decisions. For instance, Judge I. Martin Wickselman of the Court of Common Pleas for Allegheny County, Pennsylvania, Civil Division, was quoted as saying on February 10, 1977:

> I am tired of pussyfooting and, more than that, I am tired of talking to lawyers when other, more powerful men, who have the ultimate power of decision, have not been here. The fiscal well-being, possibly the survival of one of the world's corporate giants is in jeopardy. Any decision I hand down will hurt someone and, because of the potential damage, I want to make it clear that it will happen only because certain captains of industry could not together work out their problems so that the hurt might have been held to a minimum.

> 66 *"Any decision I hand down will hurt someone and, because of the potential damage, I want to make it clear that it will happen only because certain captains of industry could not together work out their problems so that the hurt might have been held to a minimum."*

Judge Wickselman then ordered the chief executives concerned to meet in his office on February 15. On February 16 the Judge stated "Solomon-like as I want to be, I can't cut this baby in half." He also indicated that, in any event, he would hand down a decision in the first week April. Then on March 31, 1977, after several months of trial, Westinghouse and the three utilities, Duquesne Light Co., Ohio Edison Co., and the Pennsylvania Power Co., announced a settlement in which the utilities claimed they were to receive cash, equipment, and services worth up to $11.5 million and Westinghouse contended that the package would cost

Inside Story continued on following page

Inside Story, continued

them about $6 million before taxes because the value of the settlement to the utilities exceeded the actual cost to Westinghouse. (This type of discrepancy occurred in every settlement and still remains unexplained.) Westinghouse also agreed to share with the utilities any proceeds it might receive from its conspiracy suits against its suppliers of uranium.

On another front, Judge Robert Merhige, Jr. of the U.S. District Court for the Eastern District of Virginia was doing what he could to have the seventeen suits before him settled out of court. On the day the trial opened, October 17, 1977, Judge Merhige stated "I don't ever expect to finish these cases. I expect [them] to get settled." At least partially as a result of the urging of the judge, cases involving four utilities were settled within two months. Westinghouse settled with Alabama Power Co. for about $5 million and with Texas Utilities Services, Inc. for $70 million. These settlements included a supply of uranium, future services, and equipment as well as cash. Westinghouse claimed that its cost to settle the Texas Utilities claim was $27 million.

During the final arguments of the case in early June 1978, Judge Merhige ordered, as he had on November 10, 1977, all of the utilities to outline proposals they would accept and present them to a special master appointed to oversee the negotiations. He also warned that he would summon all of the companies' boards of directors to a meeting before he ruled. This action apparently did not have the desired result because no additional agreements were forthcoming as the adversaries continued to maneuver to improve their position until Judge Merhige ruled on October 27, 1978, that:

Westinghouse did not meet its burden of establishing that it is entitled to excuse from the contractual obligations

which the court finds exists with Plaintiffs, either by reason of section 2-615 of the Uniform Commercial Code, or the force majeure clauses in its contracts with Plaintiffs.

The court's reluctance to issue a final and binding decision is indicated by the following:

Having thus announced the Court's decisions on these basic points, the Court believes that there are sound reasons for not issuing its supporting findings of facts and conclusions of law at this time. I know that, if they are filed, they may well result in standing in the way of these cases ending, as I think they ought to end, in settlement. The Plaintiffs should not be misled by today's holding to the effect that Westinghouse is not excused from its contractual obligations. If anything, the Court is disposed to believe that, just as Westinghouse is not entitled to excuse from its contractual obligations, the Plaintiffs are not entitled to anything near the full measure of their prayer for relief.

[T]hese are cases which I think everybody admits should be settled if at all possible, in the public interest, and they are really business problems, and should be settled as business problems by businessmen, as I have been urging from the very first.

It appears that these admonitions had some effect because as of 1980, 14 out of the original 17 lawsuits representing about 85% of the claims against Westinghouse have been settled in out of court agreements. It would seem that Westinghouse has been successful in its endeavor to minimize its losses and shift much of the economic costs of its managerial decisions from its shareholders, employees, and distributors to a broader base consisting of the utility companies and their customers and then on to the ultimate consumer.

Key Words and Phrases

adhesion contracts   **295**
commercial impossibility   **297**
cross-collateralization clause   **295**
express warranty   **287**
firm offer   **281**
fixtures   **280**

full warranty   **291**
goods   **280**
identification to the contract   **280**
implied warranty of fitness for a
     particular purpose   **290**
implied warranty of merchantability   **289**

limited warranty   **291**
lost volume seller   **298**
merchant   **281**
prima facie   **295**
puffing   **287**

Questions and Case Problems

1. What is the definition of "goods"?

2. When does the UCC statute of frauds apply? What does it require?

3. Using its preprinted order forms, Loosier Furniture Company ordered from Barker Furniture Manufacturing Company twelve yew wood dressers at $2,500 each. The order form indicated that it wanted the furniture immediately and that it would pay Barker within sixty days of receipt of the furniture.

Upon receipt of Loosier's order, Barker typed the relevant information on its own preprinted form. Barker's preprinted terms required payment within thirty days of delivery. Moreover, the clerk who typed the form included a note that said the furniture would be shipped immediately after the next "cutting," estimated to be about four months from the order date. Loosier received Barker's form and filed it under "Acknowledgments."

Two weeks later, a fire destroyed the furniture industry's major supplier of yew wood. As a result, the price of yew wood skyrocketed. Is Barker obligated to supply Loosier the twelve dressers at $2,500 each?

4. In September 1988, Arnold Milk Company agreed over the telephone with Fleming that Fleming would be the exclusive distributor of Arnold's milk for as long as Arnold sells milk in the Twin Cities area. In April 1990, Arnold designated Syrio to be Arnold's milk distributor in the Twin Cities area. Fleming sues Arnold for breach of contract. Does Fleming have a valid claim? What damages, if any, can Fleming recover?

5. The City Electric Company transmitted 135 or more volts of electricity to Joe Mama's household appliances, which could handle only 110 volts or less. Mama was injured when his hair dryer blew up in his hand because of the electrical overload. The hair dryer was destroyed. Mama sues City Electric Company for breach of implied and express warranties, claiming damages for his injuries as well as the destruction of his hair dryer. Does Mama have any rights against City Electric Company under article 2 of the UCC? [*Helvey v. Wabash County REMC*, 151 Ind. App. 176, 278 N.E.2d 608 (1972); *Navarro County Electric Cooperative, Inc. v. Prince*, 640 S.W.2d 398 (Tex. App. 1982)]

6. Fanny and Fred Farmer constructed a grain storage shed on some property they owned. Before the Farmers constructed this shed, they took out a first and second mortgage on the land. A few years after they constructed the shed, the Farmers decided to sell their farming business. According to the purchase agreement between the Farmers and the buyer, the shed was not to become a part of the land on which it sat until the realty was paid for in full. Is the shed a fixture, as defined by the UCC? If so, is it covered by the UCC? [*Metropolitan Life Insurance Company v. Reeves*, 223 Neb. 299, 389 N.W.2d 295 (1986)]

7. Dalton Department Store sold Mary Walsh a television set made by Dalton. With the television, Walsh received a warranty which covers all electric and electronic parts for two years and all other metal parts for one year. Walsh had the television set for six weeks and then took it out of the box. She noticed that one of the four legs was shorter than the others; the screen had several big scratches on it; and the remote control did not work. Walsh brought the television set back and demanded that Dalton repair all of the problems at no charge. Dalton refused to do so. What rights does Walsh have? What if Mary had the television for six months and then the glass screen suddenly shattered and the picture tube burned out?

8. Sandy Singlefather has two children and lives in a subsidized housing development in NewCity. He receives federal assistance to help raise his two children. Singlefather recently read an advertisement for household appliances. The advertisement stated that he could "rent to own" his appliances with no credit. Singlefather was in need of a washing machine so he answered the advertisement. The appliance store was more than delighted to accommodate him. Singlefather now pays $30 a week for his washing machine and will own it after he makes 78 payments. A washing machine usually sells for $350. Has Singlefather entered into an unconscionable bargain? What are the standards to establish unconscionability? [*Murphy v. McNamara*, 36 Conn.Supp. 183, 416 A.2d 170 (1979)]

9. Larry Lumberjack had a profitable lumber business. He sold his lumber to most of the major construction companies and contractors around the state. Lumberjack usually shipped his lumber by either freight car or truck, depending upon the location of the customer. Cameron Contractor, one of Lumberjack's best customers, recently ordered three trainloads of lumber from him. Lumberjack was to deliver the lumber to the rail yard and inform Contractor when it arrived. Lumberjack delivered Contractor's lumber, but before he had informed him of the delivery, a fire devastated the rail yard and destroyed Contractor's lumber. However, a number of Contractor's employees had observed the lumber being delivered. Lumberjack is now trying to secure payment from Contractor for the lumber, but Contractor is refusing to pay. Who should prevail? [*Lumber Sales, Inc. v. Brown*, 63 Tenn. App. 189, 469 S.W.2d 888 (1971)]

10. A Ferrari originally commissioned by King Leopold III of Belgium was bought in 1969 by an American, Wayne. Another Ferrari fan, Lee, made Wayne a series of offers for the car, culminating in an offer of $275,000. This was a price previously set by Wayne to discourage offers. Lee, at Wayne's request, produced four checks, one of which was endorsed by Wayne's girlfriend. Wayne then wrote Lee, as he had told him before, that the sale required Wayne's parents' consent. The letter from Wayne to Lee recited that, after talking with his parents, Wayne decided the car would not be sold. Lee sued for breach of contract. Who should prevail? [*Lee v. Voyles*, 898 F.2d 76 (7th Cir. 1990)]

Chapter 10

PRODUCT LIABILITY

■ Introduction

Definition of Product Liability

Product liability is the legal liability of the manufacturer or seller of a product that, because of a defect, causes injury to the purchaser, user, or bystander. Liability extends to anyone in the business of selling the goods or in the chain of distribution.

Today, most states in the United States have adopted strict product liability, whereby an injured person does not need to show that the manufacturer was negligent or otherwise at fault. No contractual relationship is necessary between the manufacturer and the injured person. The injured person merely needs to show that the product was sold in a defective or dangerous condition, and that the defect caused his injury.

Chapter Summary

This chapter discusses the evolution of the strict liability doctrine, beginning with its origin in negligence and warranty theories. It then focuses on the bases for strict liability, including manufacturing defect, design defect, and failure to warn. It examines who may be held liable for defective products, and the allocation of liability among multiple defendants. Defenses to a product liability claim are discussed together with legislative reforms designed to correct perceived abuses in the system. Finally, the law of product liability in the European Community is described.

■ Theories of Recovery

The primary theories on which a product liability claim can be brought are negligence, breach of warranty, and strict liability.

Negligence

To prove negligence in a products case, the injured party must show that the defendant did not use reasonable care in designing or manufacturing its product or in providing adequate warnings (see chapter 7). This can be quite difficult to prove. Moreover, injured persons are often negligent themselves in their use or misuse of the product. This will preclude recovery in a contributory-negligence state and reduce recovery in a comparative-negligence state.

The following case addressed the issue of whether the manufacturer had a duty to a plaintiff who bought the product from a retailer or middleman.

■ A Case in Point: Summary

Case 10.1
MACPHERSON v. BUICK MOTOR CO.
Court of Appeals of New York
217 N.Y. 382,111 N.E. 1050
(N.Y. 1916).

FACTS   MacPherson purchased a new Buick car with wooden wheels from a Buick Motor Company dealer who had previously purchased the car from Buick Motor Company, the manufacturer of the car. MacPherson was injured when the car ran into a ditch. The accident was caused by the collapse of one of the car's wheels because the spokes were made from defective wood. The wheel had been made by a manufacturer other than Buick.

MacPherson sued Buick Motor Company directly. He proved that Buick could have discovered the defects by reasonable inspection, and that such an inspection had not been conducted. No claim was made that the manufacturer knew of the defect and willfully concealed it. After the trial court found in favor of MacPherson, Buick appealed. Buick argued that MacPherson could not sue Buick because there was no contract between Buick and MacPherson. The sale contract was between the dealer and MacPherson.

ISSUE PRESENTED   Can a consumer who purchases a product from a retailer sue directly the manufacturer for negligent manufacture of the product even though there is no contract per se between the consumer and the manufacturer?

SUMMARY OF OPINION   The New York Court of Appeals held that Buick could be held liable for negligence. As a manufacturer, it owed a duty to any person who could foreseeably be injured as a result of a defect in an automobile it manufactured. A manufacturer's duty to inspect was held to vary with the nature of the thing to be inspected. The more probable the danger, the greater the need for caution. Because the action was one in tort for negligence, no contract between the plaintiff and the defendant was required.

RESULT   The Court of Appeals affirmed the lower court's finding that the manufacturer was liable for the injuries sustained by the plaintiff. The manufacturer was found to be negligent in not inspecting the wheels and was responsible for the finished product. Buick Motor Company was liable to the plaintiff.

Case **10.1** continued on following page

*Case **10.1** continued*

COMMENTS   This case established the rule, still applicable today, that a manufacturer can be liable for failure to exercise reasonable care in the manufacture of a product where such failure involves an unreasonable risk of bodily harm to users of the product. This rule is embodied in section 395 of the Restatement (Second) of Torts. The foundations of the law discussed in this case were laid down in *Thomas v. Winchester,*[1] in which the manufacturer of a drug who accidentally mislabeled a poison was held responsible to the customer who ultimately bought the drug from the pharmacist.

---

1. 6 N.Y. 397 (N.Y. 1852).

Breach of Warranty

In a warranty action, the reasonableness of the manufacturer's actions is not at issue. Rather, the question is whether the quality, characteristics, and safety of the product were consistent with the implied or express representations made by the seller (see chapter 9). A buyer may bring a warranty action whenever the product fails to meet the standards that the seller represents to the buyer at the time of purchase.

UCC Warranties   As explained in chapter 9, a warranty may be either express or implied. An express warranty is an affirmation made by the seller relating to the quality of the goods sold. An implied warranty is created by law and guarantees the merchantability and, in some circumstances, the fitness for a particular purpose of the goods sold.

Privity of Contract   A breach-of-warranty action is based on principles of contract law. In order for an injured person to recover, she must be in a contractual relationship with the seller. This requirement is known as *privity of contract.* It necessarily precludes recovery by those persons, such as bystanders, who are not in privity with the seller. In the *MacPherson* case discussed above, MacPherson was not in privity of contract with Buick and could not sue for breach of warranty, only for negligence.

Strict Liability in Tort

Strict liability in tort allows a person injured by an unreasonably dangerous product to recover damages from the manufacturer or seller of the product. Negligent conduct

on the part of the manufacturer or seller is not required. Because the safety of the product is the basis for liability, the injured person may recover damages even if the seller has exercised all possible care in the manufacture and sale of the product.

For a defendant to be held strictly liable, the plaintiff must prove that: (1) he, or his property, was harmed by the product; (2) the injury was caused by a defect in the product; and (3) the defect existed at the time it left the defendant and did not substantially change along the way. Most states follow the formulation of the Restatement (Second) of Torts, which states:

1. One who sells any product in a defective condition unreasonably dangerous to the user or consumer or to his property is subject to liability for physical harm thereby caused to the ultimate user or consumer, or to his property, if
    a. the seller is engaged in the business of selling such a product, and
    b. it is expected to and does reach the user or consumer without substantial change in the condition in which it is sold.

2. The rule stated in Subsection (1) applies although
    a. the seller has exercised all possible care in the preparation and sale of his product, and
    b. the user or consumer has not bought the product from or entered into any contractual relation with the seller.[2]

The first state supreme court to adopt strict product liability was that of California in 1963, in the following case.

---

2. *Restatement (Second) of Torts* § 402A (1977).

■ **A Case in Point:**

In the Language of the Court

Case 10.2
GREENMAN v. YUBA POWER PRODUCTS, INC.
Supreme Court of California
59 Cal.2d 57, 27 Cal.Rptr. 697,
377 P.2d 897 (Cal. 1963).

FACTS William Greenman's wife purchased for her husband's Christmas present a Shopsmith combination power tool that could be used as a saw, drill, and wood lathe. The power tool was manufactured by Yuba Power Products. Mr. Greenman had seen a Shopsmith demonstrated by the retailer and had studied a brochure prepared by the manufacturer. After Mr. Greenman secured an attachment to the tool to make it more useful as a lathe for turning a large piece of wood, he was injured when the wood flew from the machine and hit him in the forehead, causing serious injuries.

Mr. Greenman claimed that the tool was defective and not suitable to perform the work for which it was intended. He sued the manufacturer and retailer for breach of express and implied warranties and for negligent construction of the tool. At trial, evidence was introduced showing that "inadequate set screws" held together the part of the tool that injured Mr. Greenman. The jury returned a verdict for Mr. Greenman and against the manufacturer, based upon negligence and the express warranties.

ISSUE PRESENTED Can a manufacturer be held strictly liable in tort when, knowing that its product would be used without inspection for defects, it places on the market a defective product that causes injury to a person?

OPINION TRAYNOR, J., writing for the California Supreme Court:

. . . .

. . . The jury could therefore reasonably have concluded that the manufacturer negligently constructed the Shopsmith. The jury could also reasonably have concluded that statements in the manufacturer's brochure were untrue, that they constituted express warranties, and that plaintiff's injuries were caused by their breach.

. . . .

. . . A manufacturer is strictly liable in tort when an article he places on the market, knowing that it is to be used without inspection for defects, proves to have a defect that causes injury to a human being. Recognized first in the case of unwholesome food products, such liability has now been extended to a variety of other products that create as great or greater hazards if defective.

Although . . . strict liability has usually been based on the theory of an express or implied warranty running from the manufacturer to the plaintiff, the abandonment of the requirement of a contract between them, the recognition that the liability is not assumed by agreement but imposed by law, and the refusal to permit the manufacturer to define the scope of its own responsibility for defective products make clear that the liability is not one governed by the law of contract warranties but by the law of strict liability in tort. . . .

We need not recanvass the reasons for imposing strict liability on the manufacturer. . . . The purpose of such liability is to insure that the costs of

Case 10.2 continued on following page

*Case **10.2** continued*

injuries resulting from defective products are borne by the manufacturers that put such products on the market rather than by the injured persons who are powerless to protect themselves. Sales warranties serve this purpose fitfully at best. In the present case, for example, plaintiff was able to plead and prove an express warranty only because he read and relied on the representations of the Shopsmith's ruggedness contained in the manufacturer's brochure. Implicit in the machine's presence on the market, however, was a representation that it would safely do the jobs for which it was built. Under these circumstances, it should not be controlling whether plaintiff selected the machine because of the statements in the brochure, or because of the machine's own appearance of excellence that belied the defect lurking beneath the surface, or because he merely assumed that it would safely do the jobs it was built to do. It should not be controlling whether the details of the sales from manufacturer to retailer and from retailer to plaintiff's wife were such that one or more of the implied warranties of the sales act arose. . . . To establish the manufacturer's liability it was sufficient that plaintiff proved that he was injured while using the Shopsmith in a way it was intended to be used as a result of a defect in design and manufacture of which plaintiff was not aware that made the Shopsmith unsafe for its intended use.

. . . .

RESULT   The California Supreme Court affirmed the trial court's finding that the manufacturer was liable to the plaintiff and the monetary award of $65,000. It held that a manufacturer is strictly liable in tort when an article he places on the market, knowing that it is to be used without inspection for defects, proves to have a defect that causes injury to a human being.

Questions
1. What are the policy reasons in favor of imposing strict liability?
2. Suppose Mrs. Greenman had never read the brochure, yet had seen her husband use the tool successfully several times as a lathe. How would the court have decided the claim for breach of express warranties if she had been the one who had been injured and asserted the claim?

Rationale   There are a number of public-policy and legal justifications for the strict liability doctrine. The rule requires the manufacturer to anticipate hazards, to guard against them, and to insure against the risk of injury—and to spread these business costs to the public. The rule also has a deterrent effect. It is more efficient to permit a plaintiff to sue the manufacturer directly, rather than having to sue the retailer, who in turn would sue the manufacturer in an indemnity action on a warranty theory. Finally, the rule extends the warranty of safety to all foreseeable persons, not just the purchaser of the product.

Strategy   Although negligence and breach of warranty are alleged in most product liability cases, they play a secondary role compared to strict liability. Under strict liability, the injured person does not have the burden of proving negligence and does not have to be in privity with the seller. Thus, strict liability is easier to prove than either negligence or breach of warranty.

It should be noted, however, that plaintiffs' attorneys usually try to prove negligence as well as strict liability. Proof of negligence will often stir the jury's emotions, leading to higher damages awards and, in some cases, punitive damages. On the other hand, once the plaintiff has raised the issue of negligence, the defense can introduce evidence that its products were "state of the art" and manufactured with due care. Such evidence would be irrelevant to the issue of strict liability, and hence inadmissible.

> *Proof of negligence will often stir the jury's emotions, leading to higher damages awards and, in some cases, punitive damages.*

■ Definition of Product

Strict liability in tort applies only to products, not services. As is the case with the definition of "goods" under article 2 of the Uniform Commercial Code, it is sometimes not clear what is a product. This was the issue in the following case.

■ A Case in Point: Summary

Case 10.3
WINTER v. PUTNAM'S SONS
United States Court of Appeals
for the Ninth Circuit
938 F.2d 1033 (9th Cir. 1991).

FACTS   The plaintiffs were mushroom enthusiasts who purchased a reference book entitled *The Encyclopedia of Mushrooms* published by the defendant. They relied on the descriptions in the book to help them determine which wild mushrooms were safe to eat. Relying upon the book, the plaintiffs picked and ate some deadly species of mushrooms, became critically ill, and required liver transplants. They alleged that the book contained erroneous and misleading information.

The plaintiffs sued the publisher under, among other things, a theory of product liability and negligence. The defendant publisher argued that information in a book is not a "product" for the purposes of product liability, and that a publisher does not have a duty to investigate the accuracy of the text it publishes.

ISSUE PRESENTED   Is a book publisher responsible under a theory of product liability for erroneous and misleading information printed in one of its books that causes customers to become seriously ill?

SUMMARY OF OPINION   The U.S. Court of Appeals held that product liability law focuses on and is limited to tangible items and does not take into consideration ideas and expressions.

The court used a cost-benefit analysis to justify this holding. It emphasized the fact that the cases in which strict liability is imposed in product liability cases are those in which the costs of damages are best borne by the enterprisers who make and sell the products. In the case of ideas and expressions, a high value is placed on their "unfettered exchange." The threat of liability without fault imposed on the contents of a book could seriously inhibit those who wanted to share thoughts and theories.

The court was not persuaded by the plaintiffs' argument that the mushroom book was comparable to aeronautical charts, depicting geographic features, which were held by several jurisdictions to be products for strict liability purposes. The court found that the mushroom book was not a graphic depiction of technical data, but more a product of pure thought and expression, and would be better likened to a book on how to use an aeronautical chart.

The court held that the publisher had no duty to investigate the accuracy of the books it publishes. Furthermore, a publisher has no duty to give a warning to the consumer that the information in the book is not complete and the consumer may not fully rely on it.

*Case **10.3** continued on following page*

*Case **10.3** continued*

RESULT   The Court of Appeals affirmed the lower court's ruling in favor of the book publisher. The court held that the plaintiffs could not recover against the publisher under a product liability theory and that a negligence claim would fail as well since the publisher had no duty to investigate the accuracy of the book that it published.

Ethical Consideration

Should publishers have an ethical obligation to warn readers that information in a book is not complete and should not be relied upon?

■ Defective Product

An essential element for recovery in strict liability is proof of a defect in the product. The injured party must show that the product was defective when it left the hands of the manufacturer or seller, and that the defect made the product unreasonably dangerous. Typically, it is dangerous if it does not meet the consumer's expectations as to its characteristics. For example, a consumer expects a stepladder not to break when someone stands on the bottom step. A product may be dangerous because of a manufacturing defect, a design defect, or inadequate warnings, labeling, or instructions. It may also be an unavoidably unsafe product.

Manufacturing Defect

A *manufacturing defect* is a flaw in the product that occurs during production, such as a failure to meet the design specifications. A product with a manufacturing defect is not like the others rolling off the production line. For example, suppose the driver's seat in an automobile was designed to be bolted to the frame. If the worker forgot to tighten the bolts, the loose seat would be a manufacturing defect.

Design Defect

A *design defect* occurs when, even though the product is manufactured according to specifications, its inadequate design or poor choice of materials makes it dangerous to

users. Typically, there is a finding of defective design if the product is not safe for its intended or reasonably foreseeable use. A highly publicized example was the Ford Pinto, which a jury found to be defectively designed because the car's fuel tank was too close to the rear axle, causing the tank to rupture when the car was struck from behind.

Inadequate Warnings, Labeling, or Instructions

To avoid charges of *failure to warn*, a product must carry adequate warnings of the risks involved in the normal use of the product. For example, the manufacturer of a ladder must warn the user not to stand on the top step. A product must also be accompanied by instructions on the safe use of the product. For example, sellers have been found liable for failing to provide adequate instructions about the proper use and capacity of a hook, and the assembly and use of a telescope and sun filter.

It should be noted that although a warning can shield a manufacturer from liability for a properly manufactured and designed product, it cannot shield the manufacturer from liability for a defectively manufactured or designed product. For example, an automobile manufacturer cannot escape liability for defectively designed brakes merely by warning that "under certain conditions this car's brakes may fail." However, as will be explained later, some products, such as certain prescription drugs, are unavoidably unsafe. In cases involving such products, the adequacy of the warning determines whether the product, known to be dangerous, is also "defective."

The United States is a heterogeneous country. Diversity is one of its great strengths. With diversity can come challenges, however. Misunderstandings may arise due to differences in culture or language. Legislatures in states with a substantial non-English-speaking population have recognized the need for bilingual or multilingual documents in such areas as voting and public services. The following case addresses the need for bilingual warnings on nonprescription drugs. In particular, it considered whether a bottle of children's aspirin without warnings in Spanish concerning the possible risk of children developing Reye's syndrome was defective.

■ **A Case in Point:**   **Summary**

Case 10.4
RAMIREZ v. PLOUGH, INC.
Supreme Court of California
6 Cal.4th 539, 25 Cal.Rptr.2d
97, 863 P.2d 167 (Cal. 1993).

FACTS In March 1986, when he was less than four months old, plaintiff Jorge Ramirez exhibited symptoms of a cold or similar upper respiratory infection. To relieve these symptoms, the plaintiff's mother gave him St. Joseph's Aspirin for Children (SJAC). Although the product label stated that the dosage for a child under two years old was "as directed by doctor," the plaintiff's mother did not consult a doctor before using SJAC to treat the plaintiff's condition. Over a two-day period, the plaintiff's mother gave him three SJAC tablets. On March 15, the plaintiff's mother took him to a hospital. There, the doctor advised her to administer Dimetapp or Pedialyte (nonprescription medications that do not contain aspirin), but she disregarded the advice and continued to treat the plaintiff with SJAC. Jorge thereafter developed the potentially fatal Reye's syndrome, resulting in severe neurological damage, including cortical blindness, spastic quadriplegia, and mental retardation.

Reye's syndrome occurs in children and teenagers during or while recovering from a mild respiratory tract infection, flu, chicken pox, or other viral illness. The disease is fatal in 20% to 30% of cases, with many of the survivors sustaining permanent brain damage. Several studies showing an association between the ingestion of aspirin during a viral illness, such as chicken pox or influenza, and the subsequent development of Reye's syndrome prompted the United States Food and Drug Administration (FDA) to impose a labeling requirement for aspirin products warning of the dangers of Reye's syndrome. Yet, even before the federal regulation became mandatory, packages of SJAC displayed this warning: "Warning: Reye Syndrome is a rare but serious disease which can follow flu or chicken pox in children and teenagers. While the cause of Reye Syndrome is unknown, some reports claim aspirin may increase the risk of developing this disease. Consult doctor before use in children or teenagers with flu or chicken pox." The package insert contained a similar warning.

The medication purchased by the plaintiff's mother had such warnings in only English, despite the fact that the defendant was aware that Hispanics were purchasing the medication. Because the plaintiff's mother could not read English, she was unable to read the warnings on the SJAC label and package insert. Yet she did not ask anyone to translate the label or package insert into Spanish, even though other members of her household could have done so.

The plaintiff sued defendant Plough, Inc., alleging that he contracted Reye's syndrome as a result of ingesting a nonprescription drug, St. Joseph's Aspirin for Children (SJAC), that was manufactured and distributed by the defendant. The plaintiff sought compensatory and punitive damages on, among other things, a theory of product liability. The complaint alleged that the SJAC plaintiff ingested was defective when it left the defendant's control and that the product's reasonably foreseeable use involved a substantial and not readily apparent danger of which the defendant failed to adequately warn.

In finding no duty to warn and no causal relation between the defendant's actions and the plaintiff's illness, the trial court granted summary judgment for the defendant. On appeal, the court of appeal reversed because it found a duty to warn and felt that a jury question existed as to the adequacy of the necessary warning.

*Case **10.4** continued on following page*

*Case **10.4** continued*

The Supreme Court of California granted review of the lower court's decision.

ISSUE PRESENTED   May a manufacturer of nonprescription drugs that can lead to a deadly illness when taken as "normally expected" incur tort liability for distributing its products with warnings in English only despite the fact that the manufacturer knows that there are non-English-reading users?

SUMMARY OF OPINION   The California Supreme Court began by noting that the defendant conceded that a manufacturer of nonprescription drugs has a duty to warn purchasers about dangers in its products. The issue was whether the defendant's duty to warn required it to provide label or package warnings in Spanish.

Courts have generally not looked with favor upon the use of statutory compliance as a defense to tort liability. But there is some room in tort law for a defense of statutory compliance. Where the evidence shows no unusual circumstances, but only the ordinary situation contemplated by the statute or administrative rule, then the minimum standard prescribed by the legislation or regulation may be accepted by the triers of fact, or by the court as a matter of law, as sufficient for the occasion.

The defendant manufacturer argued that the standard of care for packaging and labeling nonprescription drugs, and in particular the necessity or propriety of foreign-language label and package warnings, has been appropriately fixed by the dense layer of state and federal statutes and regulations that control virtually all aspects of the marketing of its products. The federal government regulates the labeling of nonprescription drugs through section 502 of the Food, Drug and Cosmetic Act.[3]

The Food and Drug Administration (FDA) regulations specify both the subject matter of required warnings and the actual words to be used. For example, the labeling for aspirin, and for most other over-the-counter drugs, must contain a general warning on use by pregnant or nursing women . . . and a warning about Reye's syndrome.

The FDA has stated that it "encourages the preparation of labeling to meet the needs of non-English speaking or special user populations so long as such labeling fully complies with agency regulations." But the controlling regulation requires only that manufacturers provide full English labeling for all nonprescription drugs except those "distributed solely in the Commonwealth of Puerto Rico or in a Territory where the predominant language is one other than English. . . ." The regulation further states that if the label or packaging of any drug distributed in the 50 states contains "any representation in a foreign language," then all required "words, statements, and other information" must appear in the foreign language as well as in English.

The court reasoned that defining the circumstances under which warnings or other information should be provided in a language other than English is a task for which legislative and administrative bodies are particularly well suited. The California Legislature has already performed this task in a variety of different contexts, enacting laws to ensure that California residents are not denied important services or exploited because they lack proficiency in English.

These statutes demonstrate that the Legislature is able and willing to define the circumstances in which foreign-language communications should be mandated. Given the existence of a statute expressly requiring that

---

3. 21 U.S.C. § 352 et seq.

package warnings on nonprescription drugs be in English, the court stated that it was reasonable to infer that the Legislature has deliberately chosen not to require that manufacturers also include warnings in foreign languages. The same inference was considered warranted on the federal level. The court concluded that the prudent course was to adopt for tort purposes the existing legislative and administrative standard of care on this issue.

RESULT Because both state and federal law require warnings in English but not in any other language, a manufacturer is not liable in tort for failing to label a nonprescription drug with warnings in a language other than English. Plaintiff Ramirez's case was dismissed as a matter of law.

COMMENTS The California Supreme Court was influenced by the experience of FDA-mandated Spanish inserts for prescription drugs. Recognizing that "the United States is too heterogeneous to enable manufacturers, at reasonable cost and with reasonable simplicity, to determine exactly where to provide alternative language inserts," the FDA for a time required manufacturers, as an alternative to multilingual or bilingual inserts, to provide Spanish-language translations of their patient package inserts on request to doctors and pharmacists. But the FDA later noted that manufacturers were having difficulty obtaining accurate translations and eventually it abandoned altogether the patient package insert requirement for prescription drugs.

Political Perspective

GM Side-Saddle Gas-Tank Trucks and "Dateline" Simulation

In 1992, the Center for Auto Safety alerted the public to an alleged defect in five million General Motors (GM) pickup trucks built between 1973 and 1987. The trucks are prone to catching fire in accidents due to the "side-saddle" location of their fuel tanks over the rear wheels. The Washington, D.C.-based group asked the National Highway Traffic Safety Administration to investigate and order a recall for safety modifications.

Although GM denied that the trucks were prone to catch fire, and accused the plaintiffs' lawyers of sensationalizing the accidents, certain GM documents suggested that the truck manufacturer realized as early as 1983 that the fuel tanks could have been made less vulnerable to side-impact collisions. In 1988, GM switched to conventional single tanks within the main frame. GM was hit with more than 100 product-liability lawsuits in connection with the fuel tanks during 1992 and 1993.

GM won somewhat of a reprieve later in 1993 when it successfully forced NBC to recant a television report on "Dateline" concerning the danger of its side-saddle trucks. GM discovered that NBC had faked the explosions in the gas tanks; the network had placed miniature rockets beneath the truck to ensure an explosion of the gas tanks. NBC settled out of court and agreed to pay GM $2 million.

In 1993, GM offered owners of the trucks made between 1973 and 1987 $1,000 discounts on new GM trucks or vans. Many consumers, however, felt that the offer was not enough. They wanted GM to either give them cash or modify their gas tanks, at a cost to the company of up to $400 each. Because there are approximately five million of the trucks on the roads, the cost to GM could be upwards of $1.2 billion.

In 1994, General Motor's side-saddle gas-tank pickup trucks came under legal assault once again when the company was charged with covering up alleged design flaws. Nine people claiming to have suffered injuries as a result of the design flaw filed a $100 million lawsuit in Washington accusing GM of conspiracy. GM has denied all charges and has stated that it intends to defend itself vigorously.

In October 1994, the Department of Transportation found that the side-saddle gas-tank trucks were defective. Transportation Secretary Federico Pena said GM "appears to have made a decision favoring sales over safety." GM called Mr. Pena's decision "an unjustified politicalization of the regulatory process."

Ethical Consideration

Should the result be different if the nonprescription medicine is for an illness particular to a certain non-English-speaking group residing in the United States? What if there are advertisements for a particular medicine in a language other than English?

To prevail in a failure-to-warn case, the plaintiff must prove that the failure to provide an adequate warning caused the injury. The issue of causation was central in the following case.

■ **A Case in Point:**   **In the Language of the Court**

Case 10.5
GENERAL MOTORS CORP. v. SAENZ
Supreme Court of Texas
37 Tex. Sup. J. 176, 873 S.W. 2d 353 (Tex. 1993).

FACTS   Ricardo Saenz was driving his employer's water-tank truck down the highway when a rear tire blew out, causing him to lose control of the vehicle. The vehicle overturned, killing Saenz and his passenger, co-worker Josue Ramirez. The decedents' beneficiaries, plaintiffs in this case, contended that the accident occurred because the truck was overloaded, due to the failure of the manufacturers to provide adequate warnings against overloading.

The water-tank truck was built in two stages. The bare truck—the cab and chassis, without the water tank—was a Model C-50 Chevrolet manufactured by General Motors Corporation in 1972. The Model C-50 was designed and built so that it could be modified for a wide variety of uses. The original owner used it as a tow truck. Fifteen years later the bare truck was sold to Sascon, Inc., a paving and utility contractor. Sascon added a 2,000-gallon water tank to the truck so that it could be used to haul water around construction sites, usually at no more than 3 to 5 miles per hour. A few weeks later Sascon sold the water-tank truck to Cantu Lease, Inc., a construction company and decedents' employer.

When the water tank was full, the truck greatly exceeded its gross vehicle weight rating, or GVWR—the maximum safe weight for the entire vehicle: bare truck, added equipment, load, and passengers. The truck's GVWR was imprinted on a metal plate which GM had attached to the doorjamb, in conformity with federal regulations, on the driver's side at eye level. The plate stated that overloading could void the warranty and referenced the owner's manual for additional information. The manual said essentially that overloading can create serious potential safety hazards and can also shorten the service life of the vehicle. The doorplate was still fixed in its place and the owner's manual was in the glove compartment when Sascon purchased the bare truck. Although the owner of Sascon testified that he would not have had so large a tank installed on the truck if he had known that it would hold more water than the truck could safely carry, he also testified that no one at Sascon had ever checked either the doorplate or the owner's manual to ascertain the vehicle's GVWR.

The doorplate and owner's manual remained in place when Cantu purchased the truck. One of Cantu's owners noticed that when the truck was driven with a full tank on a bumpy road, it was so heavy that the fenders hit the tires. In an attempt to correct this problem, a Cantu employee welded spacers to the truck's frame. However, no one at Cantu endeavored to determine whether the load on the truck when the tank was full was too heavy. The day of the accident, Saenz and Ramirez were directed to drive the truck to a job site more than 100 miles away. Saenz drove, although he had no license, and Ramirez rode in the passenger seat. The accident occurred while the truck was traveling at highway speeds.

The plaintiffs sued GM and five other defendants for the wrongful death of Saenz and Ramirez. The plaintiffs claimed damages for themselves and the decedents' estates, alleging negligence and strict liability. The plaintiffs settled with three of the six defendants before trial and with Sascon during trial, receiving a total of $1,605,000. At the time the case was submitted to the jury, GM was the only remaining defendant. The jury found that the accident was caused by GM's inadequate warnings and instructions for the safe use of the truck, and by Sascon's defective design and construction of the completed water-tank truck, as well as its inadequate warnings and instructions for the safe use of the truck. The jury apportioned responsibility for the accident, 70% to GM, and 30% to Sascon, and found plaintiffs' damages to be $3,115,000. The jury also found that GM was grossly negligent, and assessed punitive damages of $2,500,000. The trial court rendered judgment on the verdict against GM for 70% of plaintiffs' actual damages and all punitive damages, court fees and costs, and interest, for a total exceeding $4.8 million.

A divided court of appeals affirmed. The court concluded that GM had a duty to warn of the dangers of overloading its vehicles because it knew of those dangers and could foresee that they would arise in the use of the Model C-50. By referring in the doorplate and owner's manual to the dangers of overloading, GM acknowledged its duty to warn all users of those dangers. But those warnings were inadequate in four respects: (1) GM provided no information concerning "the truck's maximum safe center of gravity for a particular load," (2) the doorplate "did not clearly state how much payload the truck could carry," (3) the risk of the truck overturning was not specifically disclosed, and (4) cautionary language was not set apart from "boilerplate." GM appealed.

ISSUE PRESENTED Can a manufacturer's failure to give adequate instructions for the safe use of its product be the cause of an injury that would not have occurred if the instructions the manufacturer did give had not been ignored?

OPINION HECHT, J., writing for the Texas Supreme Court:

. . . .

We first consider whether the court of appeals correctly held that GM violated a duty to warn against overloading its truck. . . . Generally, a manufacturer has a duty to warn if it "knows or should know of potential harm to a user because of the nature of its product." . . . GM does not dispute that it had a duty to warn all users of its truck against overloading but argues that its doorplate and owner's manual satisfied that duty. . . . [The court concluded that the warnings GM gave were inadequate.]

. . . .

We next consider whether GM's failure to provide warnings and instructions concerning the maximum loading of the Model C-50, different from

*Case **10.5** continued on following page*

*Case **10.5** continued*

those contained on the doorplate and in the owner's manual, caused the accident in this case. . . . [T]o recover on either of their claims plaintiffs must show that but for GM's omission the accident would not have occurred. GM argues that its failure to give a different warning could not have caused the accident when no one paid any attention to the warnings it did give. Plaintiffs respond that the law presumes adequate warnings will be heeded, absent contrary evidence which GM did not offer. From this presumption, plaintiffs contend, it follows that if GM had given adequate warnings, they would have been heeded and the accident would have been prevented. Thus, plaintiffs conclude, GM's failure to give adequate warnings was at least one cause of the accident. GM replies that no presumption can substitute for the proven fact that its warnings went unheeded.

. . . Proving causation in a failure-to-warn case has peculiar difficulties. Proof that a collision between two cars would not have happened had defendant swerved or braked or driven within the speed limit is mostly a matter of physics. Proof that an accident would not have occurred if defendant had provided adequate warnings concerning the use of a product is more psychology and does not admit of the same degree of certainty. A plaintiff must show that adequate warnings would have made a difference in the outcome, that is, that they would have been followed. In the best case a plaintiff can offer evidence of his habitual, careful adherence to all warnings and instructions. . . .

. . . .

. . . In the present case, GM warned against overloading its truck, but the jury found the warning to be inadequate. If despite the inadequacy of GM's instructions, following them would have prevented the accident, then their inadequacy could not have caused the accident. There is no presumption that a plaintiff who ignored instructions that would have kept him from injury would have followed better instructions.

To determine whether the presumption arises in this case, we must look at the inadequacies found in GM's instructions. GM does not contest that its instructions were inadequate, and we therefore assume that they were.

. . . .

The issue is not whether GM could have placed its warning against overloading in a more prominent position, such as a sticker near the gear shift lever as plaintiffs argue; rather, the issue is whether the warning where it was actually placed was sufficient to give reasonable notice against overloading. GM's warning was posted where gross vehicle weights are customarily placed in compliance with federal regulations. It was at eye level on the driver's doorjamb. The owner's manual was in the glovebox. . . . There is no evidence that anyone at Sascon or Cantu would have read a warning free from the inadequacies determined by the court of appeals. Indeed, given that they did not read the warnings GM provided, there is no reason why they would have read the warnings which the court of appeals held should have been provided. While GM could have made the warning inescapably obvious, more than it was, it had no duty to do so. Thus, there is no evidence that the inadequacies in GM's warning caused the accident.

. . . .

RESULT   The Texas Supreme Court reversed the lower court's decision and held that General Motors was not liable to the plaintiffs.

Questions

1. Were the inadequacies of the warnings truly all due to the unsatisfactory language, or would the duty have been satisfied if the warnings were made more conspicuous (e.g., in bright red)?

2. What would the court have found if GM had placed adequate warnings on a removable sticker on the windshield, so that the first owner of the truck would be compelled to notice, and remove, the warnings before she could drive?

Unavoidably Unsafe Product

If the societal value of using an inherently dangerous product outweighs the risk of harm from its use, the manufacturer may be exonerated from liability. For example, certain drugs are generally beneficial but are known to have harmful side effects in some cases. The authors of the *Restatement (Second) of Torts* recognized that there should be a separate concept of product liability for manufacturers of prescription drugs:

> Comment k: There are some products which, in the present state of human knowledge, are quite incapable of being made safe for their intended and ordinary use. These are especially common in the field of drugs. An outstanding example is the vaccine for the Pasteur treatment of rabies. . . . Since the disease itself invariably leads to a dreadful death, both the marketing and the use of the vaccine are fully justified, notwithstanding the unavoidable high degree of risk which they involve. Such a product, properly prepared, and accompanied by proper directions and warning, is not defective, nor is it *unreasonably* dangerous. . . . The seller of such products . . . is not to be held to strict liability . . . merely because he has undertaken to supply the public with an apparently useful and desirable product, attended with a known but apparently reasonable risk.[4]

Nearly every jurisdiction in the United States has followed the reasoning of comment k in some form or another. For example, in a 1986 case, the plaintiff had contracted polio from the Sabin oral polio vaccine. The odds of contracting polio from the vaccine are one in a million. The Kansas Supreme Court held that harm resulting from the use of a drug would not give rise to strict liability if it was "unavoidably unsafe," if its benefits outweighed its dangers, and if proper warnings were given.[5] The California legislature went beyond the pre-

scription drug area to bar consumers from suing manufacturers of tobacco and alcohol under the failure-to-warn theory. The statute does not, however, bar suits alleging a manufacturing defect or a breach of warranty.[6]

■ Who May Be Liable

In theory, each party in the chain of distribution may be liable: manufacturers, distributors, wholesalers, and retailers. Manufacturers of component parts are frequently sued as well.

A manufacturer will be held strictly liable for its defective products regardless of how remote the manufacturer is from the final user of the product; the only requirement for strict liability in this instance is that the manufacturer be in the business of selling the injury-causing product. Thus, occasional sellers, such as people who host garage sales, are not strictly liable. The manufacturer may be held liable even when the distributor makes final inspections, corrections, and adjustments of the product. Wholesalers are usually held strictly liable for defects in the products they sell. However, in some jurisdictions a wholesaler is not liable for latent or hidden defects if the wholesaler sells the products in exactly the same condition that he received them.

A retailer may also be held strictly liable. For example, in the automobile industry, retailers have a duty to inspect and care for the products. There are several jurisdictions, however, where a retailer will not be liable if she did not contribute to the defect and played no part in the manufacturing process.

Sellers of used goods are usually not held strictly liable, because they are not within the original chain of distribution of the product. In addition, the custom in the used-goods market is for there to be no warranties or

---

4. *Restatement (Second) of Torts* § 402A (1977).
5. *Johnson v. American Cyanamid Co.,* 239 Kan. 279, 718 P.2d 1318 (Kan.1986).

6. Cal. Civ. Code § 1714.45 (1994).

expectations relating to the quality of the products (although some jurisdictions have adopted rules requiring warranties for used cars). However, a seller of used goods is strictly liable for any defective repairs or replacements that he makes.

A maker of component parts to manufacturers' specifications is not liable if the specifications for the entire product are questioned, because such a shortcoming is considered a design defect. For example, the maker of a car's fuel injection system would not be liable if the automaker's specifications for the fuel injection system turn out to be defective because the engine provides insufficient power to change lanes safely on a freeway. However, makers of component parts are liable for manufacturing defects.

There is no strict liability in the service industries, only liability for negligence. In some cases it is unclear whether an injury was caused by a defective product or a negligently performed service. For example, a person may be injured by a needle used by a dentist, or the hair solution used by a beautician. Some courts apply strict liability in these situations. Other courts will not go so far down the chain of distribution.

Successor Liability

A corporation purchasing or acquiring the assets of another is liable for its debts if there is: (1) a consolidation or merger of the two corporations; or (2) an express or implied agreement to assume such obligations. There is also successor liability in situations where: (1) the purchasing corporation is merely a continuation of the selling corporation; or (2) the transaction was entered into to escape liability.[7]

Thus, the acquiring corporation can be liable to a party injured by a defect in the transferor corporation's product. For example, a corporation that acquired all of a truck manufacturing company's assets was held liable for an injury caused by a defect in one of that company's trucks. The court reasoned that the new company was essentially a continuation of the predecessor corporation, and that the acquiring corporation was in a better position to bear and allocate the risk than the consumer.[8]

Market-Share Liability

When there are multiple defendants, the injured party may not be able to prove which one of the defendant manufacturers caused the injury. In certain cases, particularly those involving prescription drugs, the court may allocate liability on the basis of each defendant's share of the market. This doctrine of *market-share liability* was applied in the following case.

---

7. *Conway ex rel. Roadway Express, Inc. v. White Trucks,* 639 F.Supp. 160 (M.D. Pa. 1986).
8. *Ibid.*

■ **A Case in Point:**   **Summary**

Case 10.6
HYMOWITZ v. ELI LILLY & CO.
Court of Appeals of New York
73 N.Y.2d 487, 541 N.Y.S.2d 941, 539 N.E.2d 1069 (N.Y. 1989), *cert. denied,* 493 U.S. 944, 110 S.Ct. 350 (1989).

FACTS   Persons whose mothers took the drug diethylstilbestrol (DES) during pregnancy alleged that they were injured by the DES, which, among other things, increased the likelihood of their developing cancer. They sought damages from a number of DES manufacturers. Many of the plaintiffs could not pinpoint which manufacturer was directly responsible for their injuries.

There were a number of factors making it difficult to identify particular DES manufacturers. All manufacturers made DES from an identical chemical formula. Druggists typically filled prescriptions from whatever stock they had on hand. During the 24 years that DES was sold for pregnancy use, more than 300 companies had entered and left the market. The harmful effects of DES were not discovered until many years after the plaintiffs' mothers had used the drug. By the time the lawsuit was filed, memories had faded, records had been lost, and witnesses had died.

The trial courts raised the question of how best to allocate the damages among the different defendants.

ISSUE PRESENTED   Can drug manufacturers that marketed DES for pregnancy use, even those that could prove that their product did not cause the plaintiff's injury, be held liable in proportion to their share of the national market?

SUMMARY OF OPINION Given the difficulty of pinpointing the defendant responsible for each plaintiff, the New York Court of Appeals held that fairest way was to apportion liability based upon each manufacturer's national market share. There were no exceptions for manufacturers who could prove that their particular product did not harm a certain DES victim. The court chose to apportion liability according to the overall culpability of each manufacturer, measured by the amount of risk of injury to which that manufacturer exposed the public.

The court stressed that "the DES situation is a singular case, with manufacturers acting in a parallel manner to produce an identical, generally marketed product, which causes injury many years later." Given this unusual scenario, the court reasoned, it was more appropriate that the loss be borne by those who produced the drug, rather than those injured by it.

RESULT Noting that there were nearly 500 cases pending in the courts of New York, the New York Court of Appeals stated that it was seeking to find a way to achieve justice in an administratively feasible manner. On certified question from the lower courts, the court held: (1) a market share theory using national market for determining liability was an appropriate method, and (2) revival for one year of actions for injuries caused by DES which were previously barred by statute of limitations was constitutional.

COMMENTS New York was one of a few jurisdictions to adopt market-share liability after it was set out in 1980 in *Sindell* v. *Abbott Laboratories*.[9] Judith Sindell had alleged that she contracted cancer as a result of her mother's ingestion of DES while pregnant with Judith. The California Supreme Court formulated the doctrine of market-share liability, reasoning that the manufacturers were in a better position to discover the drug's defects and prevent the resulting injuries, and were better able to bear the costs of such injuries as were not prevented.

Market share liability in DES cases was expressly rejected by the Illinois Supreme Court[10] and the Missouri Supreme Court.[11]

---

9. 26 Cal.3d 588, 163 Cal. Rptr. 132, 607 P.2d 924 (Cal. 1980), *cert. denied*, 449 U.S. 912, 101 S.Ct. 285 (1980).
10. *Smith v. Eli Lilly & Co.*, 137 Ill.2d 222, 560 N.E. 2d 324 (Ill. 1990).
11. *Zafft v. Eli Lilly & Co.*, 676 S.W.2d 241 (Mo. 1984).

Market-share liability has been rejected in many jurisdictions. It has been criticized for being a simplistic response to a complex problem, and for implying that manufacturers must be the insurers of all of their industry's products.

Market-share liability has also been challenged on the constitutional ground that it violates the defendant's right to due process of law because it denies them the opportunity to prove that their individual products did not cause the plaintiff's injury.

■ Defenses

The defendant in a product liability case may raise the traditional tort defenses of *assumption of risk* and, in some jurisdictions, a variation of comparative negligence known as *comparative fault*. In addition, there are defenses that apply only to product liability cases, such as obvious risk, unforseeable misuse of the product, the statute of limitations, the government-contractor defense, and the state-of-the-art defense. Finally, in certain circumstances state product liability law is preempted by federal law. Acceptance of the following defenses varies from state to state.

Comparative Fault

Contributory negligence by the plaintiff is not a defense in a strict liability action. However, his damages may be reduced by the degree to which his own negligence contributed to his injury. This doctrine is known as *comparative fault.*

Assumption of Risk

When a person voluntarily and unreasonably assumes the risk of a known danger, the manufacturer is not liable for any resulting injury under the doctrine of *assumption of risk.* For example, if a ladder bears a conspicuous warning not to stand on the top step, yet a person steps on it anyway and falls, the ladder manufacturer will not be liable for any injuries caused by the fall.

In a leading case in this area, a Washington appellate court found no assumption of risk when a grinding disc exploded and hit a person in the eye.[12] The court reasoned that although the injured person should have been wearing goggles, he could not have anticipated that a hidden defect in the disc would cause it to explode. By not wearing goggles, the injured person assumed only the risk of dust or small particles of wood or metal lodging in his eyes.

Obvious Risk

If the use of a product carries an *obvious risk*, the manufacturer will not be held liable for injuries that result from ignoring the risk. For example, a Volkswagen microbus was held not defective even though the shortened front-end resulted in more serious injuries in a collision.

Unforseeable Misuse of the Product

A manufacturer or seller is entitled to assume that its product will be used in a normal manner. The manufacturer or seller will not be held liable for injuries resulting from abnormal use of its product. However, an unusual use that is reasonably foreseeable may be considered a normal use. For example, operating a lawn mower with the grass bag removed was held to be a foreseeable use,

and the manufacturer was liable to a bystander injured by an object that shot out of the unguarded mower.[13]

> 66
>
> *Operating a lawn mower with the grass bag removed was held to be a foreseeable use, and the manufacturer was liable to a bystander injured by an object that shot out of the unguarded mower.*

Statute of Limitations

A *statute of limitations* is a time limit, defined by the statute, within which a lawsuit must be brought. Ordinarily, the statute of limitations starts to run at the time a person is injured. There are, however, exceptions. In many cases of injuries caused by exposure to asbestos, for example, the plaintiff did not become aware of the injury until after the statute of limitations had run out. This led to the adoption of *discovery of injury statutes,* which generally provide that the statute of limitations for asbestos cases does not begin to run until the person discovers the injury from exposure to asbestos.

For prenatal injuries caused by the drug DES, *revival statutes* have been enacted that allow plaintiffs to file lawsuits which had been previously barred by the running of the statute of limitations. DES manufacturers have argued that the revival statutes violate their right to due process of law. The manufacturers have also argued that their right to equal protection of the laws has been violated because the revival statutes typically designate only a few substances, such as DES or asbestos, but not other dangerous chemical substances. They claimed that this categorization was without sufficient basis, and that it was the result of political compromise. Nevertheless, most courts hold that state revival statutes have a rational basis, and that legislatures enacting such statutes are acting within their broad discretion.[14]

Many statutes of limitations have been amended to define more precisely when a cause of action arises. For example, the Ohio statute provides:

■ An asbestos cause of action arises when the claimant learns or should have realized that he was injured by exposure to asbestos, whichever is earlier.

---

12. *Haugen v. Minnesota Mining and Mfg. Co.*, 15 Wash. App. 379, 550 P.2d 71 (1976).

13. *LaPaglia v. Sears Roebuck & Co.*, 143 A.D.2d 173, 531 N.Y.S.2d 623 (N.Y. App. Div. 1988).

14. See, e.g., *Hymowitz v. Eli Lilly & Co.*, 73 N.Y. 2d 487, 539 N.E.2d 1069 (1989), *cert. denied*, 493 U.S. 944, 110 S.Ct. 350 (1989).

■ An Agent Orange type cause of action involving exposure of a veteran to chemical defoliants or herbicides arises when the claimant learns that he was injured by the exposure.

■ A DES cause of action arises when the claimant learns from a physician that her injury might be related to DES exposures or when she should have realized she had such an injury, whichever is earlier.[15]

Government-Contractor Defense

Under the *government-contractor defense,* a manufacturer of products under contract to the government can avoid product liability if: (1) the product was produced according to government specifications; (2) the manufacturer possessed less knowledge about the specifications than did the government agency; (3) the manufacturer

exercised proper skill and care in production; and (4) the manufacturer did not deviate from the specifications. The rationale for this immunity is that the manufacturer is acting merely as an agent of the government, and to hold the manufacturer liable would unfairly shift the insurance burden from the government to the manufacturer.

Preemption Defense

Certain laws and regulations set minimum safety standards for products. When manufacturers meet those standards, they will sometimes be granted immunity from product liability on the ground that the regulatory scheme preempts state product liability law. For example, automobile manufacturers which did not install air bags claimed that they were not liable for any resulting injuries because air bags were not required by federal law. The *preemption defense* is discussed in the following case.

---

15. Ohio Rev. Code Ann. § 2305.10 (Anderson 1981 & Supp. 1989).

■ **A Case in Point:**   **Summary**

Case 10.7
CIPOLLONE v. LIGGETT GROUP, INC.
Supreme Court of the United States
112 S.Ct. 2608 (1992).

FACTS   Rose Cipollone smoked cigarettes from 1942 until her death in 1984. She smoked brands made by the defendant Liggett Group until 1968. She wanted to be "glamorous" and to imitate the "pretty girls and movie stars" depicted in Liggett advertisements. She was allegedly comforted by advertisements such as "Play Safe, Smoke [Liggett's] Chesterfield" or "Nose, Throat, and Accessory Organs not Adversely Affected by Smoking Chesterfields." In 1968, Mrs. Cipollone switched to the Virginia Slims brand, manufactured by the defendant Phillip Morris. She stated that she switched "because it was very glamorous, [it had] very attractive ads and it was a nice looking cigarette." She switched to the True brand in 1974, a cigarette manufactured by the defendant Lorillard, Inc. In 1981, Mrs. Cipollone was diagnosed as having lung cancer.

Mrs. Cipollone and her husband, Antonio, filed a 14-count complaint alleging that Mrs. Cipollone developed cancer as a result of her use of the defendants' products over a 40-year period. The complaint sought compensation under several legal theories, including strict liability, negligence, breach of warranty, intentional tort, and conspiracy. Before trial, Mrs. Cipollone died of complications resulting from lung cancer.

The jury found that prior to 1966, Liggett failed to warn its consumers of the known health risks of smoking, and that this failure caused Mrs. Cipollone's lung cancer and subsequent death. The jury also found that Mrs. Cipollone partially caused her cancer by voluntarily and unreasonably smoking cigarettes while knowing their danger. The jury assigned 80% of the responsibility to Mrs. Cipollone, and the remainder to Liggett. Liggett was thus not liable for failure to warn, because under New Jersey law the defendant has no liability if more than half of the fault is attributable to the

Case 10.7 continued on following page

*Case **10.7** continued*

plaintiff. The other two manufacturers, Phillip Morris and Lorillard, were not held liable because they had warnings on their packaging, as required by the Federal Cigarette Labeling and Advertising Act of 1966.

The jury also found that Liggett breached express warranties found in its advertisements. They awarded $400,000 to Mr. Cipollone for Liggett's breach of warranty.

The U.S. Court of Appeals for the Third Circuit overturned the $400,000 jury verdict. Mr. Cipollone unexpectedly died on January 10, 1990, a few days after the Third Circuit's decision. His son, executor of Mrs. Cipollone's estate, appealed.

ISSUE PRESENTED   Did the Federal Cigarette Labeling and Advertising Act of 1965 (the 1965 act) or its successor, the Public Health Cigarette Smoking Act of 1969 (the 1969 act), preempt the plaintiff's claims for strict liability for failure to warn, breach of express warranty, neutralization of the federal warnings by positive advertising, intentional fraud and misrepresentation, and conspiracy?

SUMMARY OF OPINION   The U. S. Supreme Court stated that this was a narrow preemption issue under the Supremacy Clause of the U.S. Constitution. Section 5(b) of the 1965 act provided: "No statement relating to smoking and health shall be required in the advertising of [properly labeled] cigarettes." The Court concluded that this barred the states from mandating particular cautionary statements but did not preempt state common-law damage actions.

The 1969 act contained much broader preemption language: It barred requirements or prohibitions imposed under state law; and barred obligations with respect to the advertising or promotion of cigarettes. The Court concluded that Congress intended to preempt all state law, not just statutory law, providing additional requirements for warnings and labeling. This did not, however, extend to state law regarding manufacturing defects or the requirement to use a demonstrably safer alternative design for cigarettes.

Addressing each claim, the Court concluded: (1) federal law preempted claims concerning failure to warn (but not claims based solely on the cigarette manufacturers' testing or research practices or other actions unrelated to advertising or promotion); (2) federal law did not preempt claims of breach of express warranty; (3) federal law preempted the fraudulent misrepresentation claim based on alleged neutralization of the federally mandated warning labels by advertising and promotions that minimized the hazards of smoking, but did not preempt the claims for intentional fraud for allegedly false statements of material fact made in advertisements; and (4) federal law did not preempt claims for conspiracy among the cigarette manufacturers to misrepresent or conceal material facts concerning the health hazards of smoking.

RESULT   All of the plaintiff's claims are preempted by the 1969 act except for claims based on express warranty, intentional fraud and misrepresentation, and conspiracy.

COMMENTS   Although Mrs. Cipollone's son ultimately dismissed his case, this case is important for two reasons. First, it was the first case in which a jury found cigarette manufacturers liable for the health hazards of smoking, thus ending (until the appeal) the tobacco companies' no-loss record.

Second, the Supreme Court opinion leaves open at least some bases for liability in future cases.

In 1994, the California Supreme Court applied the *Cipollone* opinion to decide whether federal law preempted California state law prohibiting unfair advertising.[16]

The plaintiff alleged that R. J. Reynolds Tobacco Co.'s Old Joe Camel ads (discussed in chapter 1) were targeted at teenagers and encouraged them to smoke Camel cigarettes. Under California law it is a crime to sell cigarettes to minors or for minors to smoke them. The California Supreme Court held that the suit was not preempted by federal law because the predicate duty—not to engage in unfair competition by inducing violations of law or advertising illegal conduct—was not based on "smoking and health." Rather, it was a duty not to deceive.

Compliance with a regulatory scheme is not an automatic defense. The regulatory standards are often considered minimal requirements, and compliance with them will not shield a manufacturer from liability in all circumstances.

---

16. *Mangini v. R. J. Reynolds Tobacco Co.,* 7 Cal. 4th 1057, 31 Cal. Rptr. 2d 358, 875 P. 2d 73 (Cal. 1994).

"Love it! 'People of smoke' instead of 'Smokers.'"

Drawing by Mankoff; © 1993 The New Yorker Magazine, Inc.

In Brief: Bases for Product Liability and Defenses

Theory of Liability	Defenses
Negligence	Defendant used reasonable care
	Contributory or comparative negligence
Breach of Warranty	No privity of contract
Strict Liability in Tort	Unavoidably unsafe product
	Comparative fault
	Assumption of risk
	Obvious risk
	Abnormal misuse
	Government contractor
	Preemption
	State of the art

State-of-the-Art Defense

A defense has developed based upon a manufacturer's compliance with the best available technology (which may or may not be synonymous with the custom and practice of the industry). This *state-of-the-art defense* shields a manufacturer from liability if no safer product design is generally recognized as being possible. For example, an Indiana statute provides: "It is a defense that the design, manufacture, inspection, packaging, warning, or labeling of the product was in conformity with the generally recognized state of the art at the time the product was designed, manufactured, packaged, and labeled."[17] A Missouri statute provides that, if the defendant can prove that the dangerous nature of the product was not known and could not reasonably be discovered at the time the product was placed in the stream of commerce, the defendant will not be held liable for failure to warn.[18]

■ Legislative Developments

Legislative reforms are developing in response to larger jury awards, perceived inconsistent treatment of litigants, and the insurance crisis of the 1980s, which made it prohibitively expensive or impossible to obtain product liability insurance in some industries.

17. Ind. Code Ann. § 33-1-1.5-4 (Burns 1985).
18. Mo. Rev. Stat. § 537.764 (1993).

Statutes of Repose

A *statute of repose* cuts off the right to assert a cause of action after a specified period of time from the delivery of the product or the completion of the work. The statute of repose is different from a statute of limitations, in which the time period is measured from the time when the injury occurred. Thus, in a statute of repose, if the repose period is 10 years, a person injured 11 years after the product was delivered would be time-barred from suing by the statute of repose, though not by the statute of limitations.

Statutes of repose have usually been upheld on the ground that they serve some legitimate state purpose, such as encouraging manufacturers to upgrade their products. Absent a statute of repose, a manufacturer might not upgrade, out of fear that upgrading might be seen as an admission that the earlier version was inadequate.

 Ethical Consideration

Given that an upgrade of a product can be construed as an admission of a prior defect, what is the ethical responsibility of a manager contemplating an upgrade needed for improved safety?

Limitations on Punitive Damages

Large awards of punitive damage have been criticized for providing windfalls to injured parties far in excess of their actual losses, and for motivating plaintiffs and their lawyers to engage in expensive and wasteful litigation rather than settling the case.

In response to this criticism, between 1986 and 1989, 25 states enacted legislation limiting punitive damages awards. By 1994, the number of states with such legislation had increased to 36. Although these reforms vary, they typically prevent punitive damages or prohibit punitive awards from exceeding compensatory awards. For example, in 1988 Kansas capped punitive damages awards at the lesser of the defendant's annual gross income or $5 million. New Hampshire prohibited punitive damages altogether in 1986.

Codification of Defenses

As discussed in the previous section, an injured person's conduct can be the basis for a defense to a strict liability action. Several states have enacted statutes to codify such defenses, that is, to add them to the code of laws, which the courts must follow.

Plaintiff's Negligence Michigan law provides that the negligence of the plaintiff does not bar recovery, but damages are reduced by his degree of fault—that is, the negligence attributed to the plaintiff.[19] Under Illinois law, if the jury finds that the degree of the plaintiff's fault exceeds 50%, then the plaintiff cannot recover damages. If the jury finds that the degree of the plaintiff's fault is less than 50%, the plaintiff can recover damages, but the damages will be reduced in proportion to the plaintiff's fault.[20]

Assumption of Risk Under Ohio law, if the claimant's express or implied assumption of risk is the direct and proximate cause of harm, recovery is completely barred.[21]

Misuse of Product Unforeseeable misuse or modification is a defense under Indiana law if it is the proximate cause of the harm and is not reasonably expected by the seller at the time the seller conveyed the product to another party.[22]

Limitations on Nonmanufacturers' Liability

Rather than holding all companies in the chain of distribution liable, many states are limiting the liability of nonmanufacturers. For example, a Minnesota statute provides that once an injured person files a claim against the manufacturer of the product, the court must dismiss the strict liability claim against any other defendants. A nonmanufacturer can be held strictly liable, however, if it was involved in the design or manufacture of the product or provided instructions or warnings about the defect, or if it knew of or created the defect. The nonmanufacturer may also be held strictly liable if the manufacturer is no longer in business or if it cannot satisfy a judgment against it.[23]

An Illinois statute provides that an action against a defendant other than the manufacturer will be dismissed unless the plaintiff can show that: (1) the defendant had some control over the design or manufacture of the product, or instructed or warned the manufacturer about the alleged defect; (2) the defendant actually knew of the defect; or (3) the defendant created the defect.[24]

Limitations on Joint Liability

Traditionally, all defendants in a strict liability action are jointly and severally liable. Each defendant can be held liable not only for the injuries it severally—that is, individually—caused, but also for all of the injuries caused by all of the defendants jointly, that is, collectively.

Some states are beginning to limit joint and several liability in certain situations. For example, an Oregon statute provides:

> Liability of each defendant for non-economic damages is several, not joint. Liability of a defendant who is less than 15% at fault for economic damages is several only. Liability of a defendant who is 15% or more at fault for the economic damages is joint and several, except that a defendant whose fault is less than the plaintiff's is liable only for that percentage of the recoverable economic damages.[25]

An Illinois statute provides:

> Product liability defendants found liable are jointly and severally liable for plaintiff's past and future medical expenses. Any defendant whose fault is less than 25% of the total fault attributable to the plaintiff, the defendants sued by the plain-

---

19. Mich. Comp. Laws § 600.2949 (1992).
20. 735 Ill. Comp. Stat. Ann. 5/2-1116 (Michie 1994).
21. Ohio Rev. Code Ann. § 2315.20 (Baldwin 1994).
22. Ind. Code Ann. § 33-1-1.5-4 (Burns 1994).

23. Minn. Stat. § 544.41 (1993).
24. 735 Ill. Comp. Stat. Ann. 5/2-621 (Michie 1994).
25. Or. Rev. Stat. § 18.485 (1993).

tiff and any third party defendant who could have been sued by the plaintiff, is severally liable for all other damages. A defendant whose fault is 25% or greater than the total fault of the plaintiff, the defendants sued by the plaintiff and any third party defendant who could have been sued by the plaintiff, is jointly and severally liable for all other damages.[26]

Penalties for Frivolous Suits

Some states have enacted penalties to deter frivolous lawsuits. For example, a Michigan statute provides that if a claim or defense is found to be frivolous, the prevailing party can be awarded its legal costs and attorneys' fees.[27]

■ Problems With the System

The product liability scheme that has evolved has increasingly been criticized because of the financial burden it imposes on industry. The cornerstone of the scheme is the assumption that manufacturers are in the best position to insure against loss or to spread the risk of loss among their customers. Nevertheless, the costs to manufacturers—huge jury awards and high insurance premiums—have been enormous. Moreover, manufacturers often find it difficult to obtain insurance without a substantial deductible which must be paid by the manufacturer. Sometimes insurance is not available at all, and companies have to pay all claims themselves. This leads to higher manufacturing costs.

The product liability scheme also takes its toll on industry efficiency and competitiveness. Companies have become unwilling to invest in product creation or modification because this is seen as an admission of guilt. In most jurisdictions, a modification of a product is admissible as evidence of the product's prior defective condition. Companies find themselves in catch-22 situations: Failure to remedy a defect may expose the company to punitive damages, but remedying the defect may expose the company to compensatory damages in subsequent suits.

Federal Product Liability Reform

Senate Bill S687, the Product Liability Fairness Act, was proposed by the Senate Committee on Commerce,

Science, and Transportation in 1992. The bill, sponsored by Senator Robert Kasten (R-Wis.), was a slimmed-down version of federal product liability legislation proposed earlier. The chairman of the Senate Commerce Committee, Ernest Hollings (D-S.C.), led a filibuster against product liability legislation in 1986, and opposed S687. A similar bill in the House of Representatives (HR 1910) had 140 co-sponsors and was the subject of House hearings in February 1994. Although proponents of the Senate bill failed to end a filibuster in June 1994, its proponents plan to try again.[28]

⤷ Ethical Consideration

Even though it is an admission of a defect, a company has an ethical obligation to issue a warning about any defect that is discovered after a product is sold. A recall program, although expensive, may be necessary.

President Bush supported the Senate bill, and the Clinton administration repeatedly promised to review the issue of tort reform. However, as of 1994, the administration had not fulfilled its promises.

The Senate bill represents an attempt to legislate a federal standard for certain aspects of product liability law. It would not put a cap on punitive damages, which many proponents of tort reform had wanted. It would, however, provide certain manufacturers with a defense against punitive damages if their product had received Food and Drug Administration (FDA) approval or Federal Aviation Administration (FAA) certification. The Pharmaceutical Manufacturers Association testified that the cap on punitive damages for FDA-approved products would encourage innovation and ultimately save lives; however, consumer groups released a study showing that 1,300 deaths and thousands of life-threatening illnesses and permanent injuries had been caused by products approved by the FDA. Critics of the bill also argue that the provision is unacceptable to consumers,

---

26. 735 Ill. Comp. Stat. Ann. 5/2-1117 (Michie 1994).
27. Mich. Comp. Laws Ann. § 600.2949 (1992).

28. Catherine Yang, "Snatching Defeat from the Jaws of Victory," *Business Week,* August 1, 1994, 76.

particularly those concerned with women's health and aircraft safety, because it would weaken their rights to challenge the manufacturers who market defective products. Their argument is that punitive damages serve as a necessary check when federal agencies fail.

The Senate bill would eliminate strict liability for nonmanufacturers unless the manufacturer could not be sued or was unable to pay damages. The bill would provide incentives for expedited settlements and methods of alternative dispute resolution procedures. The bill would bar punitive damage awards against drug and medical device manufacturers and light aircraft manufacturers if they complied with federal standards. The bill also would bar lawsuits when the injured party's use of drugs or alcohol was the primary cause of the accident. The House of Representatives version, HR2700, would also provide for a state-of-the-art defense. Such a defense is not included in the Senate bill.[29]

International Consideration

Differences between the products liability laws within the European Community (EC) created two major problems. First, there was uncertainty as to what the applicable law was. This uncertainty was harmful to both the consumer and the manufacturer of the product. Second, competition was distorted within the EC because liability and the severity of the financial repercussions varied from one nation to another. The need for a uniform products liability directive was recognized.[31]

Ethical Consideration

Although there is a movement toward reducing companies' strict liability for injuries caused by their products, one commentator has warned that the movement may be reversed if companies do not act responsibly:

> The law can be said always to be moving toward some point of equilibrium. Perhaps it is at that point now for products. However, should it become apparent in the future that corporations are abusing their current degree of protection or that more persons are being injured by hazardous substances than society can justify, then one may expect to see a return to the trend of increasing the liability of the suppliers of such substances.[30]

Companies can help prevent an adverse shift in the law by monitoring and regulating their own behavior to ensure product safety.

■ The European Community Product Liability Directive

The Council of Ministers of the EC adopted a product liability directive on July 25, 1985, after nearly a decade of debate. The directive was intended to provide increased consumer protection and to harmonize competitive conditions within the EC.[32]

The directive's basic purpose is to hold manufacturers or producers strictly liable for injuries caused by defects in their products. This purpose represents a fundamental change for manufacturers of products marketed in Europe. Traditionally, in most of the 12 member states, an injured consumer had to prove both negligence and privity of contract in order to recover damages from the producer of a defective product. Only France had previously imposed strict product liability.

Comparison with U.S. Strict Liability

The directive is quite similar to the strict liability doctrine prevalent in the United States. In order to recover damages, an injured party has to prove that there was a defect, an injury, and a causal relationship between the

29. See, generally, Roberts, "New Product Liability Law Stirs Debate," *San Francisco Banner Daily Journal*, May 18, 1990, 1.
30. Paul D. Rheingold, "The Future of Product Liability: The Plaintiff's Perspective," *Product Safety and Liability Reporter* 17 (July 21, 1989), 711.

31. P. Wautier, *Products Liability—An International Manual of Practice: European Community* (1988).
32. *Official Journal of the European Community* (No. L 210) 29 (1985).

defect and the injury. (Plaintiffs may also sue under the traditional negligence and contract laws of the EC member states.) In determining whether a product is defective, the courts in the EC countries, like those in the United States, will consider such factors as the product's foreseeable uses and the instructions and warnings provided by the manufacturer. The directive does not apply to services, which remain governed solely by national law.

The available defenses are similar to those available in the United States. For example, a manufacturer will not be liable if: (1) the manufacturer did not put the product into circulation; (2) the defect did not exist when the product went into circulation; (3) the product was neither manufactured nor distributed by the manufacturer; and (4) the defect was due to compliance of the product with mandatory regulations. The manufacturer of a component part will not be liable if the defect was attributable to the design of the product into which the component was fitted.

The directive includes a statute of limitations and a statute of repose. An injured person must sue within three years of when she knew, or should have known, of the injury, the defect, and the manufacturer's identity. A manufacturer's liability will be extinguished ten years after the product was put into circulation, unless the injured party has commenced proceedings in the meantime. Thus, as in some states in the United States, a defect that does not become apparent until 11 years after the product went into circulation may leave the injured person without a remedy. Most EC member states previously had statutes of repose with a 30-year period.

> 66
>
> *Thus, as in some states in the United States, a defect that does not become apparent until 11 years after the product went into circulation may leave the injured person without a remedy.*

Unlike in the United States, a supplier or wholesaler is not strictly liable unless the injured party is unable to identify the manufacturer. In such an instance, the supplier can escape liability by informing the injured person of the manufacturer's identity.

The directive provides for a "development risks" or state-of-the-art defense. A producer can escape liability by proving that the state of scientific knowledge when the product went into circulation was insufficient to allow it to discover the defect. This provision is controversial

because it introduces an element of fault, which is precisely what the strict liability doctrine attempts to exclude. Because the defense is controversial, the directive gives member states a choice of whether to adopt it. Currently, France and Luxembourg have not adopted the defense, the United Kingdom allows it in a modified form, and Germany and Spain have rejected it for pharmaceutical products. Article 15 requires the Council to consider whether or not to repeal the state-of-the-art defense in 1995.

It should be noted that importers of products into the EC are strictly liable under the directive. Thus, U.S. exporters may be required to indemnify overseas importers. They should carry product liability insurance and follow EC safety standards.

Implementation

Member states were required to implement the provisions of the directive by July 1988. There have been problems and delays, however. For example, when the United Kingdom adopted the directive, it modified the directive's state-of-the-art defense. Rather than allowing the producer to escape liability only if it used the best scientific knowledge available, the United Kingdom's provision exonerates producers if they conformed to the generally accepted standards in the industry. The authors of the directive complained that this standard reinstituted the traditional negligence factor in place of strict liability so that as long as the manufacturer took reasonable care in attempting to discover the defect, it would not be liable.

The Responsible Manager

Reducing Product Liability Risk

Managers have the responsibility to minimize their company's exposure to liability in the design, manufacture, assembly, and sale of its products. They should implement a product safety program in order to ensure that products are sold in a legally safe condition. They also have an obligation to discover and correct any defects in the product. The goal should be to prevent accidents. If an accident does occur, evidence of a product safety program is crucial for limiting the manufacturer's liability for punitive damages.

To protect against potential liabilities, managers should implement internal loss-control procedures, obtain insurance protection, and seek the advice of products-liability counsel from the earliest stages of product development.

Managers should check the safety of their products both in their intended use and in reasonably foreseeable misuse. Managers should develop adequate instructions and comprehensive warnings. They should consider the reasonably foreseeable risks of using the product, ways to avoid those risks, and the consequences of ignoring the risks. Managers may find it helpful to follow industry standards, but sometimes a company must break new ground and go beyond what the industry has done in the past.

Managers should have a thorough understanding of all statutes, regulations, and administrative rulings to which a product must conform. Failure of the product to comply with any of these rules will typically be deemed a product defect. However, mere conformance with these rules is considered a minimum requirement, and does not automatically release a manufacturer from liability.

Managers should keep internal records of their product engineering and manufacturing decisions. These records should include design specifications, design failure tests, and safety reviews. Managers should monitor the product at every stage of the production. The records must indicate that the design process was carefully considered; the records must include more than the mere suggestions or ruminations of employees.

Managers should be careful how they advertise and warrant their products. In product liability litigation, the overall impression of such representations may be criticized by opposing counsel. Careless advertising may even lead to product misuse, resulting in an injury for which the manufacturer will be liable.

Managers should continuously monitor field reports of injuries caused by both use and misuse of their company's products. Appropriate reaction to such information may bear on the issue of punitive damages.

Managers have a postsale duty to warn of any hazards of which they have become aware, even if the product was initially thought to be safe. This duty may simply require sending a letter to purchasers of the product. Or it may require providing the purchaser with a corrective device. In addition to updating consumers on product safety concerns, some jurisdictions require management to inform its consumers of technological advances or safety improvements. Section 15 of the Consumer Product Safety Act[33] imposes substantial product-safety reporting requirements. This section requires management to notify an administrative agency if a product does not comply with applicable product safety rules, or if it contains a defect that could create a "substantial risk of injury to the public."

Managers should ensure that their products are performing as intended over the lives of the products, and that the products have as little adverse effect on the environment as possible under current technology. It is helpful to establish a product safety committee, and to conduct regular safety audits in order to identify and correct problems. The advice of experienced counsel can be helpful in this area.

---

33. 15 U.S.C. § 2064 (1988).

Inside Story

Dow Corning Breast Implants

In the early 1960s breast implants began to be used in the United States. Since then, Dow Corning has marketed and sold more than 600,000 silicone breast implants, accounting for roughly 26% of the 2.3 million women who have undergone breast implant surgery. In 1991, more than 150,000 women underwent this type of surgery, with about 20% doing it for reconstructive purposes and 80% for purely cosmetic purposes.

In 1992 Dow Corning, a joint venture between Dow Chemical Company and Corning Corporation, faced serious charges of improper conduct and social irresponsibility concerning the safety of its silicone breast implants. The allegations made by the FDA, women with breast implants, and several consumer and health

Inside Story continued on following page

Inside Story, continued

advocacy groups severely tarnished the reputation of all three companies with the potential of costing billions of dollars. As one *Wall Street Journal* reporter wrote, "[t]his breast implant debacle is shaping up to be the biggest potential litigation and public relations nightmare [in Dow's] and Corning's . . . histories."[34]

The FDA did not regulate medical devices until 1976. By this time, breast implants had been on the market for more than 10 years and were thus "grandfathered" without having to prove their safety or effectiveness. By 1977, however, concern over the safety of breast implants had surfaced. Several scientists and physicians approached the FDA, which then spent the next five years debating the appropriate regulation for these devices. In 1982, the agency announced its intention to categorize breast implants as Class III products under the Medical Device Amendments of 1976. New Class III devices must file a Premarket Approval Application (PMA). Dow Corning, as a manufacturer of preamendment Class III devices, would have had 30 months after their classification to file a PMA.

It was not until 1988, however, that the FDA published its final ruling that breast implants were to be considered Class III products. PMAs had to be filed with the FDA by July 1991. At this time, the FDA also expressed its two primary concerns with breast implants: the adverse consequences that can occur at the site of the implant and the unknown long-term risks of having a foreign substance implanted in the patient's body for a lifetime. The FDA specifically expressed concern regarding capsular contracture, implant failure, microleakage, macroleakage and rupture, interference with the accuracy of mammograms, calcification of the fibrous capsule, immune disorders, and cancer.

In July 1991, the FDA began its preliminary review of the safety and efficacy data submitted by four of the five breast implant manufacturers; the fifth, Surgitek, soon removed its product from the market after the results demonstrating the potential carcinogenic effects of its implant's polyurethane coating were released to the public. The FDA's initial remarks focused on the fact that the

research itself was lacking in quality; it involved too few women, too few adverse effects, and did not focus enough on the long-term effects of the implants. During the next six months, through January 1992, the FDA investigated the validity of the companies' PMAs by conducting its own scientific research and interviewing different parties who would be affected.

In November 1991, following its ruling that implant manufacturers must report the risks of the device in a clear and simple manner so as to easily inform patients of potential health risks, the FDA announced that it had rejected the safety and efficacy studies completed by Dow Corning and three other manufacturers. Although the FDA allowed the products to remain on the market while further studies were completed, the FDA commissioner, Dr. David Kessler, issued a strict warning reminding the industry of its responsibilities:

> . . . [the] FDA is not required to prove that breast implants are unsafe. On the contrary, manufacturers have the responsibility of showing, by presenting valid scientific evidence, that their breast implants are safe and effective—that is, that the risks are acceptable in light of the benefits. . . . The burden of proving safety rests with the manufacturer.[35]

This clear statement by the FDA regarding the industry's burden of proof set the tone for future regulation of Dow Corning.

The statement also attracted the attention of the public. Women were becoming increasingly frustrated by the fact that they had not been informed about the various risks inherent in breast implants. Hundreds of women were expected to file suit, and a few had already been extremely successful in court. Marianne Hopkins, for example, sued Dow Corning alleging that its implants were defective and had caused her to develop an autoimmune disease, and that the company had known of this risk but did not reveal it to her. On December 16, 1992, using evidence from a 1984 liability case involving similar issues, a California jury awarded Hopkins $7.3 million in damages. While Dow Corning appealed that decision, the existence of internal memos cited in both cases—and rumored to prove the

---

34. Joan E. Rigdon, "Corporate Focus: Corning Is Feeling the Heat in Breast Implant Debacle," *The Wall Street Journal*, January 29, 1992, B4.

---

35. *Ibid.*

Inside Story, continued

company's prior knowledge of its products' problems—was disclosed to the media.

On January 6, 1992—the day the FDA's decision was due—the agency called for a 45-day moratorium on breast implants. Simultaneously, it demanded that Dow Corning submit certain internal documents that had been used in previous liability suits to illustrate Dow Corning's knowledge of certain health risks. These documents had been conspicuously omitted from materials submitted in July 1991. The following month, the agency unanimously voted to recommend limited access to implants for only those women who needed the devices for medical reasons. In March, the FDA extended the ban on silicone breast implant production so that further research could be completed.

March 19, 1992, marked Dow Corning's exit from the breast implant market. In a public statement, Keith McKennon, Dow Corning's newly elected chairman of the board, stressed that this decision was not due to alleged safety concerns.

> Let me make it very clear that Dow Corning remains satisfied that Dow Corning implants produced over the years have filled an important medical need for thousands of women, and do not represent an unreasonable risk. Based on past experience, we believe the vast majority of women who have our implants will remain satisfied with the device. Our reasons for not resuming production and sales, therefore, are not related to issues of science or safety but to the existing conditions of the marketplace. Dow Corning has remained in the silicone breast implants business . . . even though it represents less than 1% of our revenues [totaling $1.8 billion] and has not been profitable over its history. Given the continued controversial environment surrounding this product, I see no prospect for business improving.[36]

On April 14, Dow Corning established a recall program so that it could remove all of its implants from the marketplace.

Although Dow Corning recalled the silicone gel implants from the market in April 1992, this action does not signify the end of the story. Dow Corning's actions

and statements over the past several years have raised many concerns about its corporate irresponsibility in dealing with the silicone breast implant controversy. Even though the company has sought a reputation for high ethical standards and a commitment to public safety, its activities during the past two decades have cast uncertainty as to whether the company did indeed behave in a socially responsible manner. Questions of ethics linger which only time and future litigation may answer.[37]

In 1993, breast implant manufacturers and materials suppliers, including Dow Corning, made a $4.75 billion settlement offer, intended to satisfy breast implant claims worldwide. However, the terms of the offer were denounced by some plaintiff lawyers. In particular, some lawyers believed that the money was insufficient to adequately compensate an anticipated 50,000 claimants.[38] In April 1994 Judge Sam C. Pointer, federal district judge in Birmingham, Alabama, accepted the $4.25 billion settlement offer by Dow, B-M Squibb, and Baxter Healthcare. The sole hold-out was General Electric, supplier of raw silicone.

The settlement has been attacked because future victims may find the fund depleted by the time they become ill.[39] In addition, foreign women, who purchased half of all U.S.-made implants, receive only about 3% of the monies set aside for persons who get sick.[40] This settlement demonstrates the difficulty of balancing the needs of yet unknown victims against the manufacturer's need for an efficient settlement.[41]

---

36. Scott S. Seeburger of Dow Corning, quoting remarks made by Keith McKennon on March 19, 1992.

37. The discussion in this Inside Story is based in large part on the unpublished paper "Social Responsibility at Dow Corning Corporation: The Case of Breast Implants," by Lisa Bael, Bettina Shapiro, Dave Tompkins, and Ed Zschau (May 22, 1992). *Used by permission.*

38. "Implant Doubts," *California Lawyer*, Dec. 1993, 22.

39. Catherine Yang, "Look Who's Talking Settlement," *Business Week,* July 18, 1994, 72, 73.

40. *Ibid.*

41. *Ibid.*

Key Words and Phrases

assumption of risk **319**	manufacturing defect **310**	revival statutes **320**
comparative fault **319**	market-share liability **318**	state-of-the-art defense **324**
design defect **310**	obvious risk **320**	statute of limitations **320**
discovery of injury statutes **320**	preemption defense **321**	statute of repose **324**
failure to warn **310**	privity of contract **306**	unavoidably unsafe product **317**
government-contractor defense **321**	product liability **304**	

Questions and Case Problems

1. A product may be deemed unreasonably dangerous as a result of a manufacturing defect, a design defect, or a failure to warn. Explain the differences between the three types of defects.

2. How many times does it take for a misuse of a product to become a hazard about which a warning must be given? When does the obligation to warn actually stop?

3. SemiCorp manufactures electronic components, including a pressure sensor. SemiCorp publishes a catalog that gives the specifications of the sensor and suggests uses ranging from automobile emission systems to medical instruments. SemiCorp sells the sensors through an independent distributor.

SureBeat Company buys sensors from the distributor and uses them in pacemaker devices. Dr. Art Cardi implanted a SureBeat pacemaker in one of his patients, Ed Goodheart. The pacemaker sensor failed while Goodheart was water-skiing, and he drowned.

    a. Who is subject to liability for Goodheart's death?

    b. Does the plaintiff's attorney need an expert to prove the pacemaker is defective?

    c. What arguments can the defense raise to avoid liability? To reduce damages?

    d. As risk manager of SemiCorp, do you recommend the issuance of a warning to customers? A product recall? Both?

4. Assume the facts of question 3. Breath Company, a medical start-up company, tested a few of the sensors manufactured by SemiCorp as a component to control an alarm in a new product: a life-support respirator for use on patients in intensive-care and cardiac-care units of hospitals. Breath Company's business plan projected profits of $10 million from sales of the respirator over the next three years. Breath Company bought 500 sensors at $20 each from the distributor and built 100 respirators.

Just before Breath Company began selling respirators, SemiCorp was sued by Ed Goodheart's widow. SemiCorp also learned that an automobile manufacturer had tested the sensors for use in emission control systems and rejected them as too unreliable. An internal audit of SemiCorp reported that the sen-sor production facility did not follow all of the company's internal quality control standards.

While SemiCorp's management evaluated the economics of the medical market for sensors, Breath Company delivered the 100 respirators to hospitals at $20,000 each. These were soon hooked up to patients as life-support systems. It had orders for 100 more. After two months, SemiCorp issued a warning that its sensors were not suitable for medical life-support systems. After delivering 50 more respirators, Breath Company actually received the warning from the distributor.

Breath Company recalled all 150 respirators, tested and selected a reliable $100 sensor from another source, and began to reintroduce the respirator six months later. Meanwhile, Life Company, a competitor, introduced a similar respirator. Breath Company's efforts to reintroduce the respirator fell short of its business plan and, after a loss of $5 million, the company shut its doors.

    a. As attorney for Breath Company, what warranty and tort theories of liability would you plead against SemiCorp?

    b. What torts would allow Breath Company recovery of damages for the following?

        1. The cost of the sensors—$10,000

        2. The loss of the $5 million investment

        3. The current value of the $10 million profit projected by the business plan

        4. Punitive damages

    c. As counsel for SemiCorp, what arguments would you advance to avoid liability altogether? To limit damages?

5. You are an attorney in the legal department of Beak, Inc., a company that manufactures construction equipment. The head of your department, Kimura Kim, recently received a visit from the company's CEO, who described for Kim a problem with the performance of Beak's Titan cranes. Apparently, the hook portion of the crane has broken off on several occasions, resulting in the release of the object being moved. As yet, no serious injuries have resulted from the accidents. Research by the company's engineering department indicates that the problem occurs only when the cranes are used at full capacity on windy days, and could be eliminated by reinforcing certain joints on the crane. The CEO is considering various alternatives, including: doing nothing; sending a letter to all owners of the crane warning them not to use the crane at full capacity on windy days; recalling the cranes to make the adjustment; and changing the design of the cranes to incorporate the reinforcements. Recalling the cranes would involve a cost to Beak of approximately $100 million. Changing the design of the cranes would require retooling a significant portion of the company's equipment at a cost of $50 million.

Kim asks you to draft a memo outlining Beak's possible liability for injuries resulting from the cranes and recommending a course of action designed to minimize that liability. Draft that memo, paying particular attention to the liability implications of each alternative course of action and the company's ethical responsibilities to its customers.

6. What factors should a court consider in deciding whether a common-law tort action for failure to install anti-lock brakes in a tractor-trailer truck is preempted by the National Traffic and Motor Vehicle Safety Act? [*Taylor v. General Motors Corp.*, 875 F.2d 816 (11th Cir. 1989), *as modified by Myrick v. Freuhauf Corp.*, 13 F.3d 1516 (11th Cir. 1994)]

7. Terrell Redman, senior vice president of Alligator Corporation, is evaluating a potential acquisition for the company. The entity he wishes to acquire has several divisions, two of which manufacture chemicals and industrial tools.

   a. What risks does the acquisition present to Alligator Corporation under products liability law?

   b. Are there ways to limit the company's exposure?

   c. To the extent that products liability law will expose the company to liability for the acquired company's prior conduct, what steps must be taken at the time of the acquisition to ensure the ability to defend potential claims?

[*Tolo v. Wexco*, 993 F.2d 884 (9th Cir. 1993)]

8. Many states have laws regulating sales that impose an implied warranty of merchantability to the effect that the merchandise is fit for consumer use. Should the same durational limit that is provided buyers by express warranties by the manufacturer be applied to implied warranties? [*Carlson v. General Motors Corp.*, 883 F.2d 287 (4th Cir. 1989), *cert. denied*, 495 U.S. 910, 110 S.Ct. 1936 (1990)]

9. Richard Welge loves to sprinkle peanuts on his ice cream sundaes. One day Karen Godfrey, with whom Welge boards, bought a 24-ounce vacuum-sealed plastic-capped jar of peanuts at a convenience store in Chicago. In order to obtain a $2 rebate that the manufacturer was offering to anyone who bought a "party" item, such as peanuts, Godfrey needed proof of her purchase from the jar of peanuts. Using an Exacto knife, she removed the part of the label that contained the bar code. She then placed the jar on top of the refrigerator. About a week later, Welge removed the plastic seal from the jar, uncapped it, took some peanuts, replaced the cap, and returned the jar to the top of the refrigerator, all without incident.

A week later, Welge took down the jar, removed the plastic cap, spilled some peanuts into his left hand to put on his sundae, and replaced the cap with his right hand. But as he pushed the cap down on the open jar, the jar shattered. His hand was severely cut and is now, he claims, permanently impaired.

Welge has brought suit and has named three defendants: the convenience store, the manufacturer of the peanuts, and the manufacturer of the jar itself.

   a. From whom will Welge be able to recover?

   b. What defenses, if any, are available to the defendants?

[*Welge v. Planters Lifesavers Co.*, 17 F.3d 209 (7th Cir. 1994)]

10. Darleen Johnson was driving her Ford car under rainy conditions on a two-lane highway through Missouri. The car's front tires had a reasonable amount of tread remaining on them, but the back tires were nearly bald. For an undetermined reason, Johnson lost control of the car, spun into the other lane, and collided with a pickup truck driven by Kathyleen Sammons. Johnson was killed instantly.

Johnson's father claimed that the inboard C.V. joint boot on the front axle was torn, which allowed debris to contaminate the joint. (The boot is a covering that contains the grease that lubricates the joint.) This contamination allegedly made the joint act like a brake on the left front wheel and caused Johnson's car to pivot around that wheel and into the path of the oncoming pickup truck.

Ford admits that the joint boot can become torn, which will allow contamination of the joint. In its manuals, Ford recommends periodic inspection of the boots. However, Ford contends that the joint on Johnson's car was contaminated during or after the accident. Ford also contends that contamination of the joint could not result in the joint seizing and creating a loss of steering control, and that the worst that could result from contamination would be some vibration and noise. According to Ford, Johnson's accident was caused by road conditions and driving error.

The case is submitted to the jury on theories of strict liability and negligent design and manufacture.

   a. Is Ford liable for Johnson's death?

   b. Are there any additional arguments that Ford can raise in its defense?

   c. Who will prevail in this case?

[*Johnson v. Ford Motor Co.*, 988 F.2d 573 (9th Cir. 1993)]

Chapter 11

INTELLECTUAL PROPERTY

■ Introduction

Types of Intellectual Property

Intellectual property is any product or result of a mental process that is given legal protection against unauthorized use. Different types of intellectual property are protected in different ways. A *patent* is a government-granted right to exclude others from making, using, or selling an invention. The patent holder need not himself make use of the invention. After a period of time (17 years for utility patents and 14 years for design patents in the United States), the patent expires and the invention is dedicated to the public.

A *copyright* is the legal right to prevent others from copying the expression embodied in a literary work, musical work, sound recording, audiovisual work, sculptural work, pictorial work, computer program, or any other form of expression fixed in a tangible medium. The protection also extends to derivative works, that is, works based upon the protected work. It is the expression that is protected, not the ideas underlying the expression. The owner also has exclusive rights to distribute, display, and perform the work. Protection is provided for at least 50 years.

Trademarks—that is, words or symbols that identify brands of goods or services—are also given legal protection. Because trademarks tend to embody or represent the goodwill of the business, they are not legally transferable without that goodwill. Trademarks are protected for an indefinite time. They can be valuable marketing and business assets.

Trade secrets are another valuable form of intellectual property in today's world economy. A *trade secret* is information that gives a business an advantage over its competitors who do not know the information. The classic example of a trade secret is the formula for Coca-Cola. Trade secrets are protected for an indefinite time.

Know-how—that is, detailed information on how to make or do something—can be a trade secret or it can be show-how. Show-how is nonsecret information used to teach someone how to make or do something. It is generally not legally protectable.

Chapter Summary

This chapter describes the law of patents, copyrights, trademarks, and trade secrets in detail. It also discusses technology licensing, that is, the selling of permission to use a patented, copyrighted, or trade secret design, invention, or process.

■ Patents

Patents are one of the oldest recognized forms of intellectual property. Their importance has increased as our society has become more technologically advanced. Texas Instruments, for example, received $391 million from patent royalties in 1992 on net revenues of $7.4 billion. Patents have formed the basis for whole businesses, such as the production of instant cameras, and industries, such as high-engineering plastics and biotechnology. Patent disputes have become one of the battlegrounds on which high-technology battles are fought.

Patent protection is specifically authorized by article I of the United States Constitution. The Constitution grants Congress the power "to promote the Progress of Science and useful Arts, by securing for limited times to . . . Inventors the exclusive Right to their . . . Discoveries." The United States patent law provides for three types of patents: utility patents, design patents, and plant patents.

Utility Patents

Utility patents are the most frequently issued type of patent. A *utility patent* protects any novel, useful, and nonobvious process, machine, manufacture, or composition of matter, or any novel, useful, and nonobvious improvement thereof. If the United States Patent and Trademark Office (PTO) issues a patent, the patent owner has the exclusive right to make, use, and sell the invention for a nonrenewable period of 17 years.

An invention is novel if it was not anticipated, that is, if it was not previously known or used by others in the United States and was not previously patented or described in a printed publication in any country. Even where the invention is novel, it will be denied patent protection if its novelty merely represents an obvious development over *prior art*, that is, existing technology.

The inventor must be diligent in her effort to file for patent protection. A *statutory bar* precludes protection in the United States if, prior to one year before the inventor's filing, her invention was described in a printed publication in the United States or a foreign country, or if it was publicly used or sold in the United States. In most other countries, a patent application must be filed *before* the invention is described in a publication, publicly used, or sold.

Even when the inventor files promptly for protection of a novel, useful, and nonobvious invention, he may still be denied a patent. There is no protection for nonstatutory subject matter, such as abstract ideas (rather than specific applications of ideas), methods for doing business, mental processes, naturally occurring substances, arrangements of printed matter, scientific principles, or laws of nature.

Biotechnology   One of the most controversial applications of the patent law has been championed by the biotechnology industry. As the following Supreme Court case demonstrates, living organisms, if they are humanmade, can be patented.

■ A Case in Point: Summary

Case 11.1
DIAMOND v. CHAKRABARTY
Supreme Court of the
United States
447 U.S. 303, 100 S.Ct. 2204
(1980).

FACTS   In 1972, Ananda Chakrabarty, a microbiologist, filed a patent application related to his invention of a humanmade, genetically engineered bacterium that is capable of breaking down crude oil. Because no naturally occurring bacteria possess this property, Chakrabarty's invention was believed to have significant value for the treatment of oil spills.

The patent examiner rejected the patent application for the bacterium. The Patent Office Board of Appeals affirmed the examiner's decision on the

Case 11.1 continued on following page

*Case **11.1** continued*

ground that living things are not patentable. After various appeals, the U.S. Supreme Court agreed to hear the case.

ISSUE PRESENTED   Is a live, humanmade microorganism patentable subject matter under the United States patent laws?

SUMMARY OF OPINION   The issue before the U.S. Supreme Court was whether Chakrabarty's bacterium constituted a "manufacture" or "composition of matter" within the meaning of section 101 of title 35 of the United States Code. That section provides that the types of inventions that are patentable include "any new and useful process, machine, manufacture, or composition of matter, or any new and useful improvement thereof." In its decision, the Supreme Court did not attempt to determine into which of the categories the new bacterium fell.

   The Court concluded that, though a previously unknown natural organism that is merely discovered cannot be patented, an organism that is created by a person can be. Chakrabarty's bacterium is markedly different from any organism found in nature. It does not fall into the nonpatentable categories of a law of nature, a physical phenomenon, or an abstract idea. It is the result of human ingenuity and research into a wholly new technology. Stating that the patent statutes should include "anything under the sun that is made by man," the Supreme Court extended patent protection to Chakrabarty's new organism.

RESULT   The Supreme Court held that a live, humanmade microorganism is patentable subject matter.

COMMENTS   This case demonstrates the dramatic economic effects that can occur because of developments in the law. The Supreme Court prophetically noted that its decision to allow the patent of Chakrabarty's bacterium could determine whether research efforts would be accelerated by the hope of reward or slowed by the want of incentives. In fact, the *Chakrabarty* decision spawned a whole new industry. It allowed small biotechnology firms to attract venture capitalists and other investors. It spurred investment in commercial genetic-engineering research. The very existence of some biotechnology firms can be traced to the *Chakrabarty* decision.

Computer Software   During the late 1960s and early 1970s, the PTO took the view that computer programs were not patentable subject matter. Software was seen as equivalent to an algorithm and thus not patentable because it constituted a mathematical formula or a scientific principle. This view changed in 1981, when the Supreme Court held that:

[if a] claim containing a mathematical formula implements or applies that formula in a structure or process, which when considered as a whole, is performing a function which the patent laws were designed to protect (e.g., transforming or reducing an article to a dif-

ferent state or thing), then the claim [may be patentable].[1]

   Since then, software patents have been sought by developers and granted by the PTO at a quickening pace. The PTO fielded 6,600 applications for software patents in 1991 and 8,300 in 1993. Many experts believe the PTO is issuing software patents too readily. Most soft-

---

1. *Diamond v. Diehr*, 450 U.S. 175, 176, 101 S.Ct. 1048, 1051 (1981).

ware code is not published, so much of the relevant prior art is not accessible to the PTO examiners. In addition, patent applications are not published until and unless a patent is issued. As a result, the PTO has been issuing patents for computer programs that many believe are not novel or are merely obvious improvements of existing programs. This has created a great deal of concern in the software industry, and spawned a movement to publish patent applications immediately upon filing so that industry experts have the opportunity to introduce evidence of prior art to limit or prevent the issuance of an overbroad or invalid patent.

In March 1994, in part in response to attacks from intellectual-property lawyers that the patent was overly broad, the PTO took the unusual step of reversing a patent granted to Compton's New Media and Encyclopedia Britannica. The patent, which covered virtually all ways of storing and retrieving text, sound, and images stored on compact discs, appeared to give Compton's a dominant position in the fast-growing multimedia market. The fact that the patent was issued in the first place was cited by the interactive Multimedia Association as evidence of the need to improve the training of the PTO's software examiners.

Design Patents

A *design patent* protects any novel, original (rather than nonobvious), and ornamental (rather than useful) design for an article of manufacture. Design patents protect against the copying of the appearance or shape of an article such as a computer terminal cabinet, a perfume bottle, typeface, or the icons and screen displays used in computer programs. A design dictated by function rather than aesthetic concerns cannot be protected by a design patent, but it may be protectable by a utility patent. A design patent has a duration of 14 years, compared to 17 years for utility and plant patents.

Design patents traditionally have been rarely used in the United States; other forms of protection, such as unfair competition law, have been relied upon instead. However, the use of design patents has been increasing recently.

Plant Patents

Plant patents protect any distinct and new variety of plant that is asexually reproduced (that is, not reproduced by means of seeds). The variety must not exist naturally. Thus, a plant patent will not be issued to someone who merely discovers a wild plant not previously known to exist. Once a plant patent is granted, the patent owner will have the exclusive right to exclude others from asexually reproducing or using the plant.

■ Filing for Patent Protection

In order to obtain patent protection, the inventor must file a patent application with the Patent and Trademark Office (PTO). Each patent application contains four parts: the specifications, the claims, the drawings, and a declaration by the inventor. After filing the patent application with the PTO, the applicant is required to make a full disclosure of relevant prior art about which she is aware.

The *specifications* must describe the invention (as defined by the claims) in its *best mode* and the manner and process of making and using the invention so that a person skilled in the relevant field could make and use it. The description of the best mode must be the best way the inventor knows of making the invention at the time of filing the application. All descriptions must be clear, concise, and exact.

The *claims* (the numbered paragraphs at the end of the patent) describe those elements of the invention that will be protected by the patent. Any invention not specifically set forth in the claims is unprotected by the patent. Thus the drafting of the claims is crucial in obtaining adequate protection.

The drawings (except in chemical cases) must show the claimed invention. The declaration by the inventor must state that the inventor has reviewed the application and that he believes that he is the first inventor of the invention. The inventor is also required to make a full disclosure of any known relevant prior art, that is, of developments that relate to the claimed invention. Knowing the prior developments assists the patent attorney in drafting the claims to avoid the prior art, and the patent examiner to determine whether the patent is novel or whether it would have been obvious to those familiar with the relevant field. Once the examiner agrees that a patent should be issued, and the examiner and applicant agree on the precise language of the claims, a patent may be issued.

The patent examiner may initially reject the application as being precluded by prior inventions or otherwise lacking the statutory requirements (99% of all patent applications are initially rejected by the PTO). The inventor may then present arguments (and in extreme cases, evidence) to contest the examiner's rejection or may seek to amend her application to overcome the examiner's rejection. If the application is finally rejected, the inventor can either refile the application as a continuation application, or appeal to the Patent Office's Board of Appeals and subsequently to either the United States District Court for the District of Columbia or the United States Court of Appeals for the Federal Circuit.

Patent Infringement

There are three ways in which a patent may be infringed: directly, indirectly, or contributorily. The patent law defines *direct infringement* as the making, use, or sale of any patented invention within the United States during the term of the patent. When an accused device or process does not have precisely each element of a particular claim of a patent (that is, the patent is not literally infringed), but the patented invention is replicated in a product or process that works in substantially the same way and accomplishes substantially the same result, a direct infringement can be found under the *doctrine of equivalents*. *Indirect infringement* is defined as the active inducement of another party to infringe a patent. *Contributory infringement* occurs when one party knowingly sells an item that has one specific use that will result in the infringement of another's patent. For example, if a company sells a computer add-on card for a specific use that will infringe another's patent, the sale is a contributory infringement even though the add-on card itself does not violate any patent. Direct infringement can be committed innocently and unintentionally; indirect and contributory infringement require some knowledge or intent that a patent will be infringed.

Defenses

A defendant to a patent infringement action may claim a variety of defenses to a patent infringement claim, including: (1) noninfringement of the patent; (2) invalidity of the patent; or (3) misuse of the patent.

Noninfringement

The defense of noninfringement asserts that the allegedly infringing matter does not fall within the claims of the issued patent. This defense compares the specific language of the patent claims with the allegedly infringing matter. If the allegedly infringing matter is not described by the patent claims, then the defense of noninfringement is successful. The patent owner may not assert any claim interpretation at odds with his application on file with the

PTO. This doctrine is known as *file-wrapper estoppel.* Because the patent holder has previously negotiated the scope of his invention with the PTO, he may not renegotiate that scope in a subsequent court proceeding.

Invalidity

A patent is presumed to be valid, but a court may find it invalid if: (1) the invention was not novel, useful, or nonobvious when the patent was issued; (2) the patent covers nonstatutory subject matter such as an abstract idea, a scientific principle, a mental process, or a method of doing business; (3) there was a statutory bar created by a publication or sale of the invention more than one year prior to the filing of the patent application; or (4) any other requirement of the patent law was not met.

The defense of invalidity has historically been very effective in infringement actions. Between 1980 and 1981, for example, approximately 60% of challenged patents were invalidated. In 1982 however, Congress created the United States Court of Appeals for the Federal Circuit (CAFC), which was given exclusive appellate jurisdiction for patent cases. The percentage of invalidated patents has subsequently decreased to less than 50%, but is still substantial.

Patent Misuse

A defense based on patent misuse asserts that although the defendant has infringed a valid patent, the patent holder has abused her patent rights and therefore has lost, at least temporarily, her right to enforce them. Patent misuse is not statutorily defined, but courts have found misuse where a patent holder has conditioned the granting of a patent license upon the purchase of other, unrelated goods or technologies. The patent holder will be barred from recovering for any infringement of her patent during the period of misuse. If the patent holder later "purges" herself of the misuse, however, she may recover for any subsequent infringement.

Remedies

If a valid patent has been infringed, the patent holder has a variety of remedies: (1) preliminary and permanent injunctive relief; (2) damages; (3) court costs; and (4) attorney's fees.

A preliminary injunction may be used to prevent any further infringement of the patent pending the court's ultimate decision. Most courts, however, are reluctant to grant injunctive relief before they have determined that a valid patent has actually been infringed. Once such a determination has been made, the patent holder is entitled to permanent injunctive relief.

Damages may also be awarded, based on a reasonable royalty for the infringer's use of the invention. Court costs, as fixed by the court, may be added. The court also has discretion to increase the award of damages by up to three times for intentional or willful infringement, and to award attorney's fees in exceptional cases.

Since the creation of the CAFC in 1982, courts have become more willing to award substantial damages in patent infringement suits. The more frequent finding of patent validity and the increase in damages awards have dramatically increased the importance of patents.

Previously, patents were so infrequently upheld or found infringed that most businesses ignored any threat of a patent infringement action. More often than not, the court would either invalidate the patent or find that it was not infringed. Moreover, even if the court found an infringement, it would usually award the plaintiff no more than a reasonable royalty. Thus a would-be infringer had little to lose, and in fact had an economic incentive to flout the plaintiff's patent rights.

The CAFC has not only upheld more patents and found more infringements, it has also begun to find intentional or willful infringements. Previously, it was safe to assume that no court would ever find a patent willfully infringed. Now, however, courts will look to the defendant's knowledge or good-faith belief as to its possible violation of the plaintiff's patent rights. Parties that in the past casually ignored the threat of patent infringement actions are now facing the possibility of huge damages awards.

The instant camera litigation between Polaroid Corporation and Eastman Kodak Company, discussed below, illustrates recent trends regarding the enforceability of patents and the potential for large damages awards for patent infringement.

■ A Case in Point: Summary

Case 11.2
POLAROID CORP. v.
EASTMAN KODAK CO.
United States Court of Appeals for the Federal Circuit
789 F.2d 1556 (Fed. Cir. 1986), *cert. denied*, 479 U.S. 850, 107 S.Ct. 178 (1986).

FACTS In 1976, Polaroid sued Kodak for infringement of ten Polaroid patents relating to its instant camera and film system. The suit was brought in response to Kodak's introduction of a new line of instant cameras designed to compete with Polaroid's existing instant cameras.

Prior to the suit, Kodak and Polaroid had a long history of cooperation. During the 1950s the parties had entered into a research agreement under which Polaroid disclosed certain of its color film technology to Kodak, and Kodak supplied Polaroid with film material. Kodak also manufactured the color film used in Polaroid's Instamatic color camera developed in 1963. In the late 1960s Polaroid asked Kodak to produce a new type of film to be used for a new one-step camera (the SX-70) that Polaroid was developing. In return for its agreement to develop and manufacture the new film, Kodak apparently wanted Polaroid to license it to produce its own instant cameras and film. The parties were unable to reach an agreement. Polaroid began to manufacture its own film, and Kodak began a project to develop an instant camera and film. This development effort resulted in the introduction of Kodak's instant camera and film in 1976, which caused Polaroid to file suit against Kodak.

The litigation was a mammoth effort. During pretrial discovery, which lasted from 1976 until 1981, Kodak produced 268,000 pages of documents and Polaroid produced 40,000 pages. The 75-day trial was spread over five months. Seven years after the introduction of Kodak's instant cameras, the Federal District Court for the District of Massachusetts held that Kodak had infringed 20 claims of seven Polaroid patents and enjoined Kodak from any further infringements.

The injunction terminated Kodak's instant camera business and left it with $200 million worth of useless manufacturing equipment and losses of $600

*Case **11.2** continued on following page*

Case 11.2 continued

million. Kodak had to pay more than $150 million to 28 million customers who had purchased a Kodak camera that was now unusable because the injunction also prohibited Kodak from manufacturing or selling film for the cameras.

Kodak appealed the district court judgment in favor of Polaroid.

ISSUE PRESENTED   Were Polaroid's patents invalid or unenforceable because the claimed inventions would have been obvious at the time they were made to one of ordinary skill in the art?

SUMMARY OF OPINION   The U.S. Court of Appeals first looked at Kodak's claim that some of Polaroid's image processing-related patents were invalid because the claimed inventions would have been obvious at the time they were made to one of ordinary skill in the art. In making this assertion of obviousness, Kodak relied solely upon the prior art that was considered by the United States Patent and Trademark Office official who examined the Polaroid patents. This put an added burden on Kodak to overcome the deference due to a qualified government agency presumed to have done its job. Kodak failed to meet this burden.

The court then looked at the alleged infringement. The court rejected Kodak's argument that the injunction was invalid because the district court failed to consider the claimed invention in view of the prior art taken as a whole. The court disagreed, saying that Kodak had not met its burden of finding error in the lower court's conclusion that nothing in the prior art, taken singly or in combination, rendered obvious the inventions claimed in the patent.

RESULT   The Court of Appeals affirmed the lower court decision and held that Polaroid's patents on cameras, film units, and photographic processes were valid, and that Kodak had infringed those patents.

COMMENTS   The parties litigated the issue of damages separately. Kodak claimed that Polaroid was entitled to damages of $177 million, representing a reasonable royalty of 5% for all instant cameras and film sold by Kodak from 1976 until 1985. Polaroid, however, claimed that it was entitled to $12 billion, comprising $4 billion in profits that Polaroid claimed it would have made if Kodak had not entered the instant photography business in 1976, to be tripled because Kodak willfully infringed Polaroid's parents.

Many securities analysts had predicted an eventual award to Polaroid of $1 billion to $1.5 billion. In 1990 Kodak was ordered to pay $909.5 million to Polaroid for infringing its patents. This included $454.2 million in lost profits and royalties and $455.3 million in interest. This is the largest award ever granted in a patent infringement suit. Yet according to *The Wall Street Journal* the award "disappointed Polaroid and heartened Kodak."[2]

Judge A. David Mazzone rejected Polaroid's request that damages be trebled, finding that Polaroid had not proved willful infringement.[3]

---

2. Lawrence Ingrassia and James S. Hirsch, "Polaroid's Patent-Case Award, Smaller than Anticipated, Is a Relief for Kodak," *The Wall Street Journal,* October 15, 1990, A3.
3. *Ibid.*

International Consideration

Given the international scope of manufacturing and distribution, many inventors file for patent protection in a number of countries. There are 179 countries in the world that grant patents, and in each country, an issued patent provides the patent holder with the exclusive right to make, use, and sell the patented invention in that country. International patent protection for United States nationals is governed by the patent laws of the foreign country and any treaty that the United States may have with that country. The laws regarding statutory bars in foreign jurisdictions are radically different than U.S. patent law. A rule of thumb is that any public disclosure of an invention prior to filing the patent application will bar an inventor's ability to obtain foreign patent protection.

The patent practice of other countries is often different from that of the United States. Some jurisdictions are more receptive to certain types of patents than others. In 1989, 30 years after its application was filed, Texas Instruments was granted a patent in Japan on an invention related to integrated circuits. The delay helped Japan's then fledgling computer-chip companies by allowing them to make, use, and sell the U.S. patented integrated circuits in Japan without infringing Japanese patent laws. A patent had been granted on the same invention in the United States in 1964. Securities analysts estimate that the Japanese patent could bring Texas Instruments $100 million to $700 million annually until it expires in 2004.

A number of other countries do not permit invention patents for pharmaceuticals, although they may be entitled to some protection under process patents. Given the differences in patent practice, it is important to discuss with an attorney the rules that apply in the foreign country, prior to disclosure or sale of any patentable subject matter.

■ Copyrights

Best-selling novels, award-winning films, off-the-shelf software packages, and compact discs are all copyrightable works. So are restaurant menus, laser discs, designer linens, plush toy animals, and cereal boxes. The United States Copyright Act of 1976 requires that the material for which copyright protection is sought be original (not copied) and fall within one of the following categories: (1) literary works; (2) musical works; (3) dramatic works; (4) pantomimes and choreographic works; (5) pictorial, graphic, and sculptural works; (6) motion pictures and other audiovisual works; and (7) sound recordings.

The act further requires that the works be fixed in a durable medium from which they can be perceived, reproduced, or communicated. For example, stories may be fixed in written manuscripts, computer software on floppy disks, and recordings of songs on compact discs. Protection is automatic. Neither registration nor the use of a copyright notice is required.

Protected Expression

The act prohibits unauthorized copying of the *protected expression* of a work, but the underlying ideas embodied in the work remain freely usable by others. Section 102 of the act excludes from copyright protection any "idea, procedure, process, system, method of operation, concept, principle or discovery, regardless of the form in which it is described, explained, illustrated, or embodied."

Where an idea and its expression are inseparable, the *merger doctrine* dictates that the expression is not copyrightable. If it were, this would confer a monopoly over the idea. Thus, a manufacturer of a karate video game cannot keep a competitor from producing another video game based on standard karate moves and rules. The idea of a karate game (including game procedures, karate moves, background scenes, a referee, and the use of computer graphics) is not protected expression. The manufacturer can, however, keep her competitor from copying any original graphics she has used in the game so long as they are not inseparable from the idea of karate or of a karate video game.

Useful Articles Doctrine

Under the *useful articles doctrine,* copyright protection does not extend to a useful article, that is, the useful application of an idea. The application of ideas is considered to be within the province of patent law. The act defines pictorial, graphic, and sculptural works to include "works of artistic craftsmanship insofar as their form but

EXHIBIT 11-1   The Strongest Patent Portfolios

Company/ Headquarters Country	Number of U.S. Patents 1992	Current Impact Index 1992	Technological Strength 1992	Technological Strength 1991 (Rank)
1. CANON Japan	1118	1.76	1971	3
2. HITACHI Japan	1165	1.45	1688	2
3. TOSHIBA Japan	1176	1.29	1514	1
4. IBM U.S.	842	1.77	1488	6
5. GENERAL ELECTRIC U.S.	995	1.24	1236	8
6. MITSUBISHI ELECTRIC Japan	976	1.18	1147	4
7. MOTOROLA U.S.	671	1.68	1126	10
8. EASTMAN KODAK U.S.	804	1.25	1005	5
9. XEROX U.S.	477	2.08	990	18
10. AT&T U.S.	528	1.81	955	11
11. MATSUSHITA ELECTRIC Japan	732	1.27	931	16
12. GENERAL MOTORS U.S.*	790	1.17	925	7
13. FUJI PHOTO FILM Japan	652	1.10	719	9
14. NISSAN MOTOR Japan	395	1.80	709	13
15. NEC Japan	502	1.41	709	15
16. TEXAS INSTRUMENTS U.S.	401	1.76	707	14
17. FUJITSU Japan	443	1.57	697	19
18. DUPONT U.S.	684	0.94	644	17
19. PHILIPS Netherlands	607	0.97	589	12
20. SONY Japan	446	1.26	560	29
21. RICOH Japan	366	1.53	559	30
22. 3M U.S. 395	395	1.40	555	21
23. BAYER Germany	692	0.73	507	28
24. SHARP Japan	394	1.21	477	25
25. SIEMENS Germany	550	0.85	468	20

Including GM Hughes Electronics

GLOSSARY:

Number of Patents: The number of patents granted by the U.S. Patent Office. The number excludes design patents and other special cases.

Current Impact Index: A measure of how important a company's patents are, based on how often they are cited in other patents, which shows how frequently they are used as the foundation for other inventions. For example, a company's 1992 index is computed by first calculating the average number of times the patents it was granted in each of the previous five years were cited in new patents granted in 1992. Those figures are divided by the average number of 1992 citations for all U.S. patents in each of the previous five years. That yields a citation rate for each year. A rating of 1.0 means that the company's patents were cited as often as the overall average. A rating of 1.2 means that the company's patents were cited 20% more often than average. Finally, the citation rate for each of the five years is averaged to get the 1992 rating.

Technological Strength: The Number of Patents times the Current Impact Index.

not their mechanical or utilitarian aspects are concerned." For example, blank forms, which are used to record information rather than convey information, are considered articles of use and are not copyrightable.

If the expression of a pictorial, graphic, or sculptural work cannot be identified separately from and exist independently of such utilitarian aspects, copyright protection will be denied to the whole work. An example of an article whose expression is separable from its utilitarian aspects would be a lamp that incorporates a statue of a woman in its base. An example of an article whose expression is not separable from its utilitarian aspects is the layout of an integrated circuit. Although a drawing of the circuit is copyrightable, the actual circuitry is not copyrightable because it is impossible to separate the utilitarian aspect of the circuit from its expression or layout. It is the layout of the circuit that enables the circuit to operate correctly. A drawing of the circuit is copyrightable, but the circuit itself is not. However, it may be patentable, and the layout or topography of the circuit is protected by the Semiconductor Chip Protection Act of 1984.

> 66
>
> *A drawing of the circuit is copyrightable, but the circuit itself is not. However, it may be patentable, and the layout or topography of the circuit is protected by the Semiconductor Chip Protection Act of 1984.*

Exclusive Rights

To encourage the production of new works, copyright owners are given exclusive economic rights in the work. These rights can be conveyed to others. The copyright owner has the exclusive right to make copies of his work and to create derivative new works based upon it. He also has the exclusive right to distribute, publicly perform, and display the work and to import into the United States copies of the work made overseas.

Copyright Ownership

The author of a work is the original owner of the copyright. The author is either the creator of the work or, in the case of a work made for hire, the party for whom the work was prepared. A work made for hire is either: (1) a work created by an employee within the scope of her employment, or (2) a work in one of nine listed categories that is specially commissioned through a signed writing which states that the work is a "work made for hire."

The author can transfer ownership by an assignment of copyright. Assignments are often sought by parties that commission independent contractors to produce works—such as computer programs—that fall outside the nine categories of the act. Thus, if a company is either commissioning a work or preparing a work as an independent contractor, the company should consult with an experienced copyright attorney to make sure that the desired party obtains copyright ownership.

Term

The duration of copyright ownership depends upon the identity of the author. If the author is a known individual, the term is the life of the author plus 50 years. For a work made for hire, or for anonymous, or pseudonymous work, the term is the lesser of 75 years after first publication or 100 years after creation of the work.

■ Copyright Formalities

Using proper copyright notices and registering works for which copyright protection is desired affords the copyright owner substantial benefits.

Copyright Notice

Although copyright notices are not mandatory for works first published after March 1, 1989, the use of a notice is advisable because it prevents an infringer from claiming innocent infringement. For works first published prior to March 1, 1989, most copyright authorities agree that notices should still be used, to avoid the risk of releasing the work into the public domain. A proper copyright notice for works distributed within the United States includes these elements: "Copyright" or "Copr." or "©"; the year of first publication; and the name of the copyright owner.

Registration

Registration with the United States Copyright Office is a prerequisite for filing an infringement suit for a work of U.S. origin. Statutory damages and attorney's fees are available only to owners of registered works. In addition, registration creates a legal presumption of ownership and copyright validity, which can be extremely helpful to a plaintiff in a copyright infringement suit. Because the timing of registration is critical to obtaining some of the related benefits, it is important to consult with a copyright attorney before beginning to publicly distribute a work.

Economic Perspective
Intellectual Property Rights and Incentives to Innovate

A basic tenet of neoclassical economic theory is that productive efficiency and allocative efficiency will be achieved through free competition by private parties interested in maximizing their own welfare. Productive efficiency exists when competition among individual producers drives all but the lowest-cost producers of goods or services out of the market. Allocative efficiency exists when scarce societal resources are allocated to the production of various goods and services up to the point at which the cost of producing each good or service equals the benefit society reaps from its use.

In general, the economic policy of the United States is to foster the functioning of free markets in which individuals may compete. For example, the antitrust laws, discussed in chapter 18, are designed to protect competition by prohibiting any individual entity or group of entities from monopolizing an industry.

An exception to the general free-market orientation of the U.S. economy is the area of intellectual property. The patent laws provide inventors with the opportunity to gain a legally enforceable monopoly over the use and sale of their inventions for a limited time.

The economic rationale for granting monopolies to inventors is based on the high value of innovation to society and the need to give inventors an incentive. Free competition cannot lead to productive and allocative efficiency in an economy as a whole unless an efficient market exists for each product. Innovation may be regarded as a product. Allocative efficiency for innovation

will exist only if it is produced up to the point where the benefit to society from innovation equals the cost of its production.

Technological advances are crucial to a growing economy. Development of new techniques increases productive efficiency, thereby expanding the quantity of goods and services that can be produced with a given level of societal resources. Development of new products meeting previously unfulfilled needs increases the welfare of society as a whole. In the past decade, such innovation has taken on increasing importance for the United States in the international context. Although countries with lower-cost labor have a competitive advantage in the manufacture of goods with established production techniques, the United States's competitive advantage lies in its ability to develop new technologies.

The immense benefits society gains through innovation are difficult for individual innovators to capture. Absent legal rules protecting the ownership of inventions, once a valuable new product or cost-saving technique is introduced, others will immediately copy it and profit from it.

Individuals will only produce innovation up to the point where the rewards they reap equal their costs. To ensure that innovation is produced fully up to the point at which its social cost equals its social benefit, the law must guarantee to innovators a significant part of the benefit from their innovations. The U.S. solution to this problem is to provide inventors, if their inventions meet the requirements for a patent, with a lim-

ited monopoly over the use and sale of their inventions. This system ensures that inventors will be able to capture the full benefit of their inventions during the period of their monopoly, and that the innovation will be freely available to others after that period. The stringent requirements for patents prevent unnecessary restrictions on free competition.

An important secondary objective of providing inventors with patent protection is allowing the scientific community access to knowledge about state-of-the-art technology. Absent a legal monopoly, innovators would keep their advances secret to prevent others from copying them. Such secrecy would result in waste of scarce societal resources, as other researchers would struggle to discover what is already known.

In practice, the granting of a legal monopoly does not often interfere with the condition necessary for productive efficiency, namely, production of goods and services only by the lowest-cost producers. Although a patent holder has the legal right to exclusive use and sale of his invention, if another can use the invention more efficiently, it will be more profitable for the patent holder to sell or license his rights than to retain them for his exclusive use.

For example, assume that a patent holder can reap profits of $10 million per year by producing and selling her patented product. Suppose another company with better production facilities can produce the product at a lower cost, resulting in profits of $12 million per year. The other company would (theoretically) be willing to pay up to $11,999,999 per

Economic Perspective
Intellectual Property Rights and Incentives (cont'd)

year in license fees for the right to produce the product. The patent holder would be willing (at least in theory) to license her rights for any amount in excess of $10 million per year. Thus, the legal monopoly in practice provides the inventor with a means of ensuring that others who profit from his creativity pay him for his contribution.

For example, Jack Kilby of Texas Instruments and Robert Noyce of Fairchild Semiconductor, inventors of the microchip, engaged in a lengthy legal battle to determine which of them would obtain a patent for the chip. Although the patent issue dragged on from 1959 to 1970, the two companies agreed in 1966 to cross-license each other and to joint-

ly license other companies to produce the microchip.

Exhibit 11-1, on page 342, shows the corporations with the strongest U.S. patent portfolios in 1992. As the table indicates, the Japanese and the Europeans take full advantage of the protection provided by U.S. patent laws.

■ Copyright Infringement

Copyright infringement is the copying, display, performance, or distribution of a work without the permission of the copyright owner. A plaintiff in a copyright infringement suit must show substantial similarity of the protected expression, not merely substantial similarity of the ideas contained in the work. In addition, the plaintiff must prove that the alleged infringer had access to the plaintiff's work.

Remedies

A plaintiff is entitled to recover her actual damages and the defendant's profits attributable to the infringement, to the extent that these are not duplicative of each other, as well as attorney's fees under certain circumstances. Alternatively, a plaintiff may elect to recover statutory damages, which can be up to $100,000 for willful infringement, and attorney's fees under certain circum-

stances. Injunctive relief, seizure of the infringing copies, criminal penalties, and exclusion of infringing copies from import into the United States are also available under certain circumstances.

Fair Use Doctrine

Under the *fair use doctrine,* a person may infringe the copyright owner's exclusive rights without liability in the course of such activities as literary criticism, social comment, news reporting, education, scholarship, or research. In deciding what constitutes fair use, the courts balance the public benefit of the defendant's use against the effect on the copyright owner's interests. The factors they consider are the purpose of the use (including whether it was for profit); the economic effect of the use on the copyright owner; the nature of the work used; and the amount of the work that is used. In the following case, publishers of copyrighted articles and books questioned the availability of the fair use doctrine for reproductions used in the classroom.

■ A Case In Point: **In the Language of the Court**

Case 11.3
BASIC BOOKS, INC. v.
KINKO'S GRAPHICS INC.
United States District Court
for the Southern District of
New York
758 F. Supp. 1522 (S.D.N.Y.
1991).

FACTS   Kinko's is a chain of duplication stores that was in the business of preparing course packets as part of its "Professor Publishing" program for its 200 shops around the country located near colleges or universities. The program allowed teachers and professors to select excerpts from works that they wished to assign for the semester. Kinko's would then copy and

Case 11.3 continued on following page

*Case **11.3** continued*

bind the excerpts, often entire chapters or essays, in "anthologies" and sell them directly to the students in preparation for the course.

The major publishing houses of New York sued Kinko's, alleging copyright infringement. Kinko's conceded that they indeed copied the excerpts without obtaining permissions, compiled them, and sold them to students. However, Kinko's asserted among other defenses the fair use doctrine.

ISSUE PRESENTED   Did Kinko's copying of excerpts from works for academic use violate the Copyright Act or was such copying within the reach of the fair use doctrine?

OPINION   MOTLEY, J., writing for the Federal District Court:

Coined as an "equitable rule of reason," the fair use doctrine has existed for as long as the copyright law. It was codified in Section 107 of the Copyright Act of 1976. . . .

. . . .

This case is distinctive in many respects from those which have come before it. It involves multiple copying. The copying was conducted by a commercial enterprise which claims an educational purpose for the materials. The copying was just that—copying—and did not "transform" the works in suit, that is, interpret them or add any value to the material copied, as would a biographer's or critic's use of a copyrighted quotation or excerpt. . . .

A. The 4 Factors of Fair Use.

1. Purpose and Character of the Use.

Section 107 specifically provides that under this factor we consider "whether [the] use is of a commercial nature or is for nonprofit educational purposes." . . .

Transformative use.

. . . .

Most contested instances of copyright infringement are those in which the infringer has copied small portions, quotations or excerpts of works and represents them in another form, for example, a biography, criticism, news article or other commentary. In this case, there was absolutely no literary effort made by Kinko's to expand upon or contextualize the materials copied. The excerpts in suit were merely copied, bound into a new form, and sold. The plaintiffs refer to this process as "anthologizing." The copying . . . had productive value only to the extent that it put an entire semester's resources in one bound volume for students. It required the judgment of the professors to compile it, though none of Kinko's.

Commercial use.

The use of the Kinko's packets, in the hands of the students, was no doubt educational. However, the use in the hands of Kinko's employees is commercial. Kinko's claims that its copying was educational and, therefore, qualifies as a fair use. Kinko's fails to persuade us of this distinction.

. . . Its Professor Publishing promotional materials clearly indicate that Kinko's recognized and sought a segment of a profitable market, admitting that "tremendous sales and profit potential arise from this program."

. . . .

While financial gain "will not preclude [the] use from being a fair use," consideration of the commercial use is an important one.

. . . .

2. The Nature of the Copyrighted Work.

The second factor concerns the nature of the copyrighted work. Courts generally hold that "the scope of fair use is greater with respect to factual than non-factual works." Factual works, such as biographies, reviews, criticism and commentary, are believed to have a greater public value and, therefore, uses of them may be better tolerated by the copyright law. . . . Fictional works, on the other hand, are often based closely on the author's subjective impressions and, therefore, require more protection. These are general rules of thumb. The books infringed in suit were factual in nature. This factor weighs in favor of defendant.

3. The Amount and Substantiality of the Portion Used.

. . . [The] third factor considers not only the percentage of the original used but also the "substantiality" of that portion to the whole of the work; that is, courts must evaluate the qualitative aspects as well as the quantity of material copied. A short piece which is "the heart of" a work may not be fair use and a longer piece which is pedestrian in nature may be fair use. . . .

. . . .

This factor, amount and substantiality of the portions appropriated, weighs against defendant. . . .

In almost every case, defendant copied at least an entire chapter of a plaintiff's book. . . . [T]he excerpts, in addition to being quantitatively substantial, are qualitatively significant.

4. The Effect of the Use on Potential Markets for or Value of the Copyrighted Work.

The fourth factor, market effect, also fails the defendant. This factor has been held to be "undoubtedly the single most important element of fair use." . . .

. . . While it is possible that reading the packets whets the appetite of students for more information from the authors, it is more likely that purchase of the packets obviates purchase of the full texts. This court has found that plaintiffs derive a significant part of their income from textbook sales and permissions. This court further finds that Kinko's copying unfavorably impacts upon plaintiffs' sales of their books and collections of permissions fees. This impact is more powerfully felt by authors and copyright owners of the out-of-print books, for whom permissions fees constitute a significant source of income. This factor weighs heavily against defendant.

5. Other Factors.

In this case an important additional factor is the fact that defendant has effectively created a new nationwide business allied to the publishing industry by usurping plaintiffs' copyrights and profits. This cannot be sustained by this court as its result is complete frustration of the intent of the copyright law which has been the protection of intellectual property and, more importantly, the encouragement of creative expression. . . .

*Case **11.3** continued on following page*

Case 11.3 continued

RESULT The excerpts copied by Kinko's were not a fair use of plaintiffs' copyrights and, therefore, constituted infringement. The court granted the plaintiffs statutory damages of $510,000, injunctive relief, and attorney's fees and costs. The court found that there was a strong possibility that Kinko's would continue its practice without an injunction and enjoined Kinko's from future anthologizing and copying of the works without permission and prepayment of fees.

COMMENTS Application by the courts of the fair use doctrine is not always predictable. In a New York case,[4] internal copying of scientific articles from periodicals purchased by a profit-seeking firm was found not to be a fair use under the Copyright Act. In this case, publishers of copyrighted scientific and technical journals brought an infringement action against Texaco for making unauthorized copies of copyrighted articles for use by the company's scientific research employees. Texaco scientists were in the practice of making copies of helpful articles from the circulating library copy of the scientific and technical journals to keep in their personal files or in the laboratory. The court was not persuaded by the task Texaco confronted in subscribing to a large number of journals in an effort to keep 400 to 500 employees in six U.S. research centers abreast of new scientific findings.

However, the U.S. Supreme Court found that the commercial use of a copyrighted song "Pretty Woman" in a parody by rap group 2 Live Crew did not presumptively constitute unfair use with respect to either character and purpose of use of the copyrighted work or the harm caused by that use to the potential market for the copyrighted work.[5] The Court held that a parody that uses no more than necessary of the lyrics and music of the original work to make it recognizable does not de facto copy an unreasonable part of the copyrighted work, even if the copied part is the heart of the original work.

Questions

1. Does a student's copying of several chapters of a book on reserve at the library constitute an infringement?

2. May an entrepreneur doing research for a business she's starting legally copy complete articles from a magazine and include them in her business plan? Does it matter if the business later becomes successful?

---

4. *American Geophysical Union v. Texaco Inc.*, 802 F.Supp. 1 (S.D.N.Y. 1992), *aff'd,* _ F.3d _(2d cir. 1994).
5. *Campbell v. Acuff-Rose Music, Inc.*, 114 S.Ct. 1164 (1994).

■ The Look and Feel Debate

The courts have come out strongly in favor of copyright protection for computer code, regardless of the medium. Source code, object code, and microcode can all be copyrighted. A more controversial issue is whether copyright protection should extend to the nonliteral aspects of a computer program that comprise its user interface. These nonliteral aspects have frequently been referred to in the media as the software's "look and feel." There are only a handful of federal appellate and district court decisions dealing with this issue. It is too early to tell how the courts will ultimately balance the need to encourage innovation and the need to preserve the free exchange of ideas.

International Consideration

The United States is a party to a number of international copyright treaties, including the Berne Convention for the Protection of Literary and Artistic Works and the Universal Copyright Convention. American works receive the same protection that is afforded to the works of a national in foreign countries that are signatories of the same treaties. If a company decides to distribute a copyrightable work outside the United States, it is important to discuss with an attorney what, if any, copyright protection is available for the work and what steps are necessary to obtain such protection.

User Interface

User interfaces are those commands, menu screens, instructions, icons, video images, and other screen displays that function as a communication link between a computer program and the computer user. Because users

like to minimize the time needed to learn a computer program, those programs whose interfaces are easy to use are often more successful than competing programs. A successful program may also become the standard in the market because users resist having to learn to use a new interface. The economic value of user interfaces has led software developers to claim copyright protection for them. Competitors of successful programs argue that user interfaces should not be copyrightable. The scope of the protection that might be given to user interfaces is unclear, because they are different from the traditional forms of copyrightable subject matter.

Arguments Against Protection   Opponents of copyright protection for user interfaces argue that industry standards should be allowed to develop so that users will not have to learn different interfaces for different programs. They further argue that because interface developments are incremental and are made by merely refining already existing interfaces, no company should have the right to claim exclusive ownership.

Many of the elements of a user interface can be analyzed as uncopyrightable ideas, useful articles, or as blank forms for recording information. Opponents of copyright protection argue that interfaces such as the desktop metaphor (at issue in the *Apple v. Microsoft* case discussed in the "Inside Story" for this chapter) or a spreadsheet are simply ideas for communicating computer commands. They also argue that a user interface is a useful article, analogous to the instruments in an automobile such as a standard "H" pattern gearshift knob. Finally, they argue that where interfaces are used to input data or commands, they are simply uncopyrightable blank forms.

Arguments for Protection   The proponents of copyright protection for user interfaces argue that many elements of an interface can be analyzed under traditional copyright law, which protects nonliteral elements of literary works. The proponents also argue that nonliteral imitation of user interfaces should be considered copyright infringement under the "total concept and feel" test, initially applied to works unrelated to computer software.

Total Concept and Feel

Under "total concept and feel," a copyright is infringed if an ordinary observer would regard the subsequent work as a copy of the original work's total concept and feel, even if the subsequent work does not copy any individual element of the original work. This test is useful to software developers wishing to protect their user interfaces from competitors who use similar interfaces without directly copying any particular element. Many copyright purists, however, argue that the total concept and feel test of infringement should be applied only after the subject matter has been found copyrightable. If a user interface is not copyrightable subject matter because it is an idea or a useful article, such purists argue that a total concept and feel analysis is inappropriate.

A leading total concept and feel case, in which Apple Computer, Inc. sued Microsoft Corporation and Hewlett-Packard Company, was filed in 1988.[6] Apple claimed that the graphic interfaces of Microsoft's Windows 2.03 program and Hewlett-Packard's New Wave program imitated the look and feel of the user interface of the Macintosh computer. This computer features a visual desktop metaphor with pull-down menus and easy-to-understand icons representing computer commands. Many in the industry speculated that the suit was really aimed at discouraging the development by Apple's biggest rival, IBM, of a user-friendly graphic interface. Microsoft Windows would be a critical element of such a development. Rejection by the Federal District Court in California of Apple's claims is discussed in the "Inside Story" for this chapter.

---

6. *Apple Computer, Inc. v. Microsoft Corp.*, 799 F.Supp. 1006 (N.D. Cal. 1992).

> " *Many in the industry speculated that the suit was really aimed at discouraging the development by Apple's biggest rival, IBM, of a user-friendly graphic interface.*

In a 1990 case[7] involving Lotus Development Corp., the court rejected the traditional total concept and feel analysis used in computer software cases in favor of a test that focused on the user interface used in the computer program. The court held that the menu command structure of a computer program, taken as a whole—including the choice of command terms, the structure, sequence and organization of these terms, their presentation on the screen, and the long prompts—is entitled to copyright protection. The following Lotus 1-2-3 case is a further refinement of the 1990 Lotus case and looks at the protectability of the functional relationship of the commands.

---

7. *Lotus Development Corp. v. Paperback Software International*, 740 F.Supp. 37 (D.Mass. 1990).

■ **A Case in Point:**   **Summary**

Case 11. 4
LOTUS DEVELOPMENT CORP. v. BORLAND INTERNATIONAL, INC.
United States District Court for the District of Massachusetts 799 F.Supp. 203 (D. Mass. 1992).

FACTS Lotus Development Corp. sued Borland International, Inc. for alleged infringement of its computer software spreadsheet program Lotus 1-2-3. Lotus contended that Borland's Quattro and Quattro Programs involved copies of the Lotus user interface and as such infringed the Lotus copyright. The trial court found that Lotus had failed to adequately frame its contentions. Lotus subsequently renewed its motion for summary judgment with more specific contentions.

Lotus asserted that Borland copied expressive elements of the Lotus 1-2-3 interface, including menu commands, menu structures, long prompts, and keystroke sequences.

ISSUE PRESENTED Does the replication of the functional relationships found in the menu command hierarchy of a computer software program constitute copyright infringement?

SUMMARY OF OPINION In determining whether to grant summary judgment, the Federal District Court found that although Lotus continued to argue that its entire user interface was copied, a reasonable jury could find that less than the entire user interface was copied. However, in determining whether to grant partial summary judgment, the court did find that express elements of the menu command hierarchy were without dispute copied.

First, the court established that the menu command hierarchy was copyrightable subject material. Although the court recognized that Borland did not directly copy the Lotus 1-2-3 menu command hierarchy, it found that Borland had "copied" the hierarchy in the sense that Borland implemented into its own product the functional relationships found in Lotus 1-2-3. In response to Borland's contention that the duplication of functional relationships does not equal copying, the court held that Borland's definition of copying was idiosyncratic and fundamentally wrong.

RESULT   In finding that express elements of the menu command hierarchy had been copied by Borland, the court granted Lotus summary judgment in part but then ordered further proceedings to determine the extent of copying and appropriate relief.

COMMENTS   It is difficult to reconcile under the total concept and feel test the results in the *Apple* and *Lotus* cases. The issue may eventually be resolved by a U.S. circuit court or the U.S. Supreme Court.

■ Registered Mask Work

The Semiconductor Chip Protection Act of 1984 created a highly specialized form of intellectual property, the *registered mask work*. This is the first significant new intellectual property right in the U.S. in nearly 100 years. Semiconductor masks are detailed transparencies that represent the topological layout of semiconductor chips. The act gives the owner exclusive rights in the mask for a period of 10 years and proscribes copying or use by others. Because this law is relatively new, the legal protections afforded to mask owners are still developing. The law was aimed primarily at counterfeiters who would replicate the semiconductor masks for a chip already on the market and produce the chips without having to spend money on development. The remedies for infringement are an injunction, damages, and the impoundment of the infringing mask and chips.

The following case is the first case litigated under the Semiconductor Chip Protection Act.

■ A Case in Point: Summary

Case 11.5
BROOKTREE CORP. v. ADVANCED MICRO DEVICES, INC.
United States Court of Appeals for the Federal Circuit
977 F.2d 1555 (Fed. Cir. 1992).

FACTS   Brooktree Corporation, a manufacturer of semiconductor chips, sued competitor Advanced Micro Devices, Inc. (AMD) under the Semiconductor Chip Protection Act for patent infringement and infringement of mask work registration in connection with some semiconductor chips used in color video displays. The questionable chips involved a design in which 80% of the circuitry was "similar" to Brooktree's design; two of the three patents that were allegedly infringed related to portions of the registered mask works. The Federal District Court held that the patents were valid and infringed, and also that the registered mask works were infringed. AMD appealed. AMD did not challenge the validity of the mask work registrations or the fact that the chips are protected property, yet asserted that its chips are not infringements.

*Case **11.5** continued on following page*

*Case **11.5** continued*

ISSUE PRESENTED   If a semiconductor chip does not contain a duplication of a registered mask work, can it still be so similar as to constitute an infringement?

SUMMARY OF OPINION   The Semiconductor Chip Protection Act defines an infringing semiconductor to be one that is "made, imported, or distributed in violation of the exclusive rights" of the mask work owner. The U.S. Court of Appeals stated that in order for Brooktree to establish infringement, it must show that AMD's mask works are substantially similar to a material portion of the mask works in Brooktree's chips. No hard and fast rule governs what constitutes substantial similarity.

In affirming that the mask works were infringed, the court was not swayed by AMD's attempted defense of reverse engineering—AMD produced voluminous amounts of paper attempting to show that it had conducted extensive research to reverse engineer the chip, and even though the end product looked like Brooktree's, the path in arriving there was not by copying. After a rather technical analysis involving a close look at the circuitry involved in the individual patents, the court affirmed the validity and infringement of the patents. The court concluded that Brooktree was entitled to actual damages suffered as a result of the infringement, plus any profits made by AMD that were attributable to the infringement.

RESULT   The Court of Appeals affirmed the lower court's decision and held that the patent and mask works were infringed.

COMMENTS   AMD is potentially liable for significant monetary damages based on this infringement. Brooktree presented evidence that it was forced to reduce its prices when AMD announced the sale of its chips at lower prices, and but for the infringement, Brooktree would have continued to sell its chips at the higher prices. A witness for Brooktree predicted that Brooktree would have only reduced prices 10% in the absence of infringement, as compared to the actual 30% reduction.

■ Trademarks

Most people associate a particular trademark with the product to which it is applied without considering how this association has been generated. For example, when consumers purchase Apple computers, they usually do not think about how the word for a type of fruit has become representative of that particular brand of personal computer. Trademark law concerns itself with just such questions: how trademarks are created, how trademark rights arise, how such rights can be preserved, and why certain marks are given greater protection than others.

Statutory Definition

The federal trademark act, otherwise known as the Lanham Act, and the 1988 Trademark Law Revision Act[8] define a trademark as "any word, name, symbol, or device or any combination thereof adopted and used by a manufacturer or merchant to identify and distinguish his goods, including a unique product, from those manufactured or sold by others, and to indicate the source of the goods, even if that source is unknown."

This definition has been interpreted as recognizing four different purposes of a trademark: (1) to provide an identification symbol for a particular merchant's goods; (2) to indicate that the goods to which the trademark has been applied are from a single source; (3) to guarantee that all goods to which the trademark has been applied are of a constant quality; and (4) to advertise the goods.

Basically, a trademark tells a consumer what a product is called, where it comes from, and who is responsible for

---

8. 15 U.S.C. §§ 1051-1072 (1994).

its creation. The trademark does not necessarily reveal the product's manufacturer. For example, the trademark Sanka identifies a brand of decaffeinated coffee. We may not know whether the manufacturer is a company called Sanka, but we know that all coffee products bearing the Sanka mark are sponsored by a single company.

A trademark also implies that all goods sold under the mark are of a consistent level of quality. A consumer purchasing an Apple computer can reasonably expect it to perform as well as other Apple computers.

Benefits

Trademarks benefit both consumers and producers. For consumers, trademarks reduce the cost of finding information about products by dividing the many available products into a few brand types. Without such reference points, a buyer would have to gather information about each individual item she purchased. Trademarks also encourage the production of quality goods, because consumers can trace goods, especially low-quality goods, to their source through their mark.

For producers, a trademark represents the goodwill of a business, that is, an accumulation of satisfied customers who will continue buying from that business. Trademark rights are determined predominantly by the perceptions and associations in the minds of the buying public, so maintaining a strong trademark is essential to preserving the success of a business.

Other Marks

Trademarks should not be confused with other forms of legally protected identifying marks, such as service marks, trade names, and certification marks.

Service Marks   A trademark is used in connection with a tangible product; a *service mark* is used in connection with services. The law concerning service marks is almost identical to that of trademarks.

Trade Names   While a trademark is used to identify and distinguish products, a *trade name* or a corporate name identifies a company, partnership, or business. Trade names cannot be registered under federal law, unless they are also used as trademarks or service marks. However, trade names are protectable under some of the same common-law principles that apply to trademarks. The use of a trade name—evidenced by the filing of articles of incorporation or a fictitious business name statement— gives the company using the name certain common-law rights.

Certification Marks   A *certification mark* placed on a product indicates that the product has met the certifier's standards of safety or quality. An example is the "Good Housekeeping" seal of approval placed on certain consumer goods.

■ Choosing a Trademark

To get a sense of how one chooses a trademark, consider a hypothetical entrepreneur who has developed a new form of computer software. This entrepreneur's program takes personal information—such as place and date of birth and daily biorhythms—and processes it to give the user predictions as to what may happen in the future (on the basis of "the past," that is, on the basis of the inserted information). He has chosen three possible names for his software: Viron, Gypsy in a Disc, and Venus.

The entrepreneur wants to be certain that the trademark he chooses for his software is protectable. Under trademark law, the degree of protection is determined by where a trademark can be classified on a scale of distinctiveness. The more distinctive a mark is, the less likelihood of confusion with other marks. Hence marks that are the most distinctive are given, at least initially, the greatest legal protection. The policy is to reward originality in the creation of a mark.

Inherently Distinctive

Inherently distinctive marks are marks that need no proof of distinctiveness. They are often called strong marks, because they are immediately protectable. Fanciful, arbitrary, or suggestive marks are all inherently distinctive.

Fanciful Marks   A fanciful mark is a coined term having no prior meaning until used as a trademark in connection with a particular product. Fanciful marks are usually made-up words, such as Kodak for camera products and Clorox for bleach. In the preceding hypothetical, Viron is an example of a fanciful, made-up mark.

Arbitrary Marks   Arbitrary marks are real words whose ordinary meaning has nothing to do with the trademarked product, for example, Apple for computers, Camel for cigarettes, and Shell for gasoline.

Suggestive Marks   A suggestive mark suggests something about the product without directly describing it. After seeing the mark, a consumer must use her imagination to determine the nature of the goods. For instance,

In Brief: Distinctiveness of Marks	
Classification of Mark	**Level of Protection**
Inherently Distinctive Fanciful marks Arbitrary marks Suggestive Marks	Protected immediately upon use
Not Inherently Distinctive	Protected only when distinctive secondary measuring is acquired
Nondistinctive Generic terms	Not protected

This material originally appeared in *McCarthy on Trademarks and Unfair Competition*, Third Edition, by J. Thomas McCarthy, available

Chicken of the Sea does not immediately create an association with tuna fish; it merely suggests some kind of seafood. In the hypothetical, Gypsy in a Disc would be an example of a suggestive mark. It merely suggests a future-predicting software program.

Not Inherently Distinctive

Marks that are not inherently distinctive are not immediately protectable. Granting trademark rights for a description of a product that may apply equally to different products would frustrate the fundamental distinguishing purpose of a trademark.

Secondary Meaning   However, marks that are initially unprotectable can become protectable by acquiring *secondary meaning,* that is, a mental association by the buyer that links the mark with a single source of the product. Through secondary meaning, a mark obtains distinctiveness. Once this occurs, the mark is granted trademark protection.

Establishment of secondary meaning depends on a number of factors, such as the amount of advertising, the type of the market, the number of sales, and consumer recognition and response. The testimony of random buyers or of product dealers may be required in order to prove that a mark has acquired secondary meaning.

Secondary meaning is necessary to establish trademark protection for descriptive marks, geographic terms, and personal names.

Descriptive Marks   *Descriptive marks* specify certain characteristics of the goods, such as size or color; proposed uses; the intended consumers for the goods; or the effect of using the goods. Laudatory terms, such as First Rate or Gold Medal, are also considered descriptive marks.

Geographic Terms   Geographic descriptive terms are usually considered nondistinctive unless secondary meaning has been established. However, geographic terms used in an arbitrary manner are inherently distinctive, for example, Salem for cigarettes and North Pole for bananas. In the earlier hypothetical example, Venus would be an example of a geographic term, which would not be distinctive until secondary meaning is established.

Personal Names   Personal first names and surnames are not inherently distinctive. However, an arbitrary use of a historical name, such as Lincoln for a savings bank, does not require secondary meaning.

Nondistinctive

No protection is given to generic terms, such as "spoon" or "software," because doing so would permit a producer to monopolize a term that all producers should be able to use equally. It would be ridiculous to permit one manufacturer to obtain the exclusive right to use the word "computer," for example, and force all competitors to come up with a new word, rather than a brand name, for the same type of product. Generic terms are not protected even when they acquire secondary meaning.

Many terms that were once enforceable trademarks have become generic. "Escalator" was once the brand name of a moving staircase, and "cellophane," a plastic wrap developed by DuPont. Due to misuse or negligence by the owners, these marks lost their connection with particular brands and became ordinary words (see Exhibit 11-2). Xerox Corp. spends more than $100,000 a year explaining that you don't "Xerox" a document, you "copy" it.[9]

For terms that describe products made by only one company, the problem of genericism—the use of the product name as a generic name—is acute. Without competitive products, buyers may begin to think of the trademark as indicative of what the product is rather than where the product comes from. Manufacturers can try to avoid this problem by always using the trademark as an adjective in conjunction with a generic noun. It is all right to say "Sanka decaffeinated coffee" or "an Apple computer," but not "a cup of Sanka" or "an Apple." Once the buying public starts using the mark as a synonym for the product, rather than as a means of distinguishing its source, loss of the trademark is imminent.

> " *It is all right to say "Sanka decaffeinated coffee" or "an Apple computer," but not "a cup of Sanka" or "an Apple."*

■ Creating Rights in a Trademark

Trademark rights initially are obtained in the U.S. through use of the mark in commerce. Following use in interstate commerce, additional rights may be obtained by federal registration. State registration requires only intrastate use.

Use

A trademark is used in commerce if it is physically attached to the goods and advertising, and then sold or distributed. Each subsequent use of a trademark creates greater rights, because increased sales and advertising generate greater customer awareness of the mark as representing the product.

For marks that are not inherently distinctive, use is also necessary to establish secondary meaning. For inherently distinctive marks, ownership is governed by priority of use. The first seller to sell the goods under a mark becomes the owner and senior user of the mark. The mark is protected immediately, provided the adoption and use of the mark are done in good faith and without knowledge, actual or constructive, of any superior rights in the mark. Thus, when an entrepreneur first attempts to acquire trademark rights, he should check whether he is the first user of his proposed mark or any confusingly similar mark for similar products. If this is not done, his use of the mark may be seen as infringing the trademark of a senior user, and he will not obtain any rights in the mark.

There is an exception to the rule of first use. If a subsequent, or junior, user establishes a strong consumer identification with its mark in a separate geographic area, the junior user may be granted superior rights for that area. The senior user, by failing to expand her business to other parts of the country, takes the risk that a junior user may be permitted to use the same or confusingly similar mark in a distant area. The junior user's use must be in good faith, that is, the junior user must take reasonable steps to determine whether any preexisting mark is confusingly similar to the one he plans to use.

This geographic rule is inapplicable, however, if the senior user has applied for or obtained federal registration. Once the senior user has filed an application or has obtained federal registration, she is permitted to claim nationwide constructive notice of the mark. This precludes any use—even a good faith use—of the mark by a junior user. However, the senior user may not take any action against the junior user in a geographically removed area until the senior user is likely to expand into that area.

Federal Registration

Although not a requirement for obtaining U.S. rights in a mark, registration on the federal Principal Register provides many legal advantages. Such registration provides constructive notice of a claim of ownership in all 50

9. Weigel, "Whatever You Do With This Article, Don't 'Xerox' It," *Chicago Sun-Times*, October 7, 1990, 57.

EXHIBIT 11-2   An Attempt to Preserve a Trademark

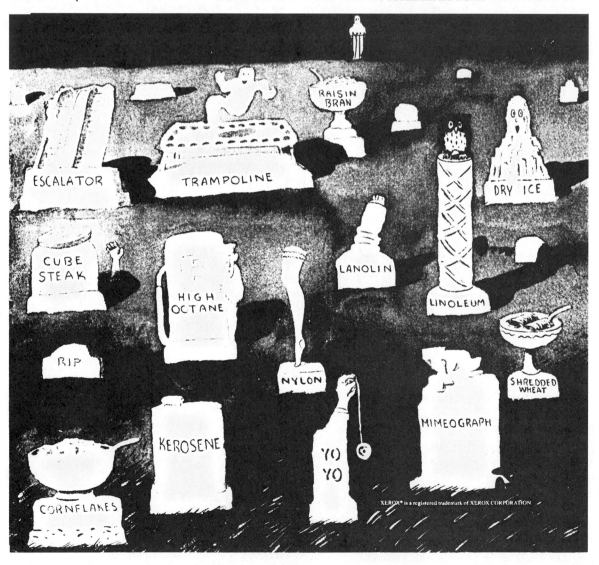

XEROX

Once a trademark, not always a trademark.

They were once proud trademarks, now they're just names. They failed to take precautions that would have helped them have a long and prosperous life.

We need your help to stay out of there. Whenever you use our name, please use it as a proper adjective in conjunction with our products and services: e.g., Xerox copiers or Xerox financial services. And never as a

verb: "to Xerox" in place of "to copy," or as a noun: "Xeroxes" in place of "copies."

With your help and a precaution or two on our part, it's "Once the Xerox trademark, always the Xerox trademark."

Team Xerox. We document the world.

XEROX® is a registered trademark of XEROX CORPORATION

states. This makes it easier to enjoin subsequent users, because unauthorized use of a federally registered mark cannot be in good faith. Other benefits of registration on the Principal Register include: (1) prima facie evidence of ownership; (2) the "incontestable" right (subject to certain defenses) to use the mark, obtainable after five years of continuous use following registration; and (3) the right to prevent importation into the United States of articles bearing an infringing mark.

Registration on the Principal Register makes strategic sense. It deters others from using the mark, as they are on constructive notice of the mark's ownership. It also gives the owner the right to preempt junior users if the owner expands into their territories.

Certain marks that do not qualify for registration on the Principal Register may be registered on the Supplemental Register. However, such registration does not afford the owner any of the above benefits. This type of registration should be pursued only upon the advice of counsel.

Federal registration of trademarks is conducted by the United States Patent and Trademark Office (PTO). The 1988 Trademark Law Revision Act dramatically changed the character of federal trademark law and the registration process. Whereas the prior system required use of the mark before an application could be filed, under the 1988 act an applicant may file either an "actual use" application or an "intent to use" application. For the latter, the applicant must state a bona fide intent to use the mark, must then commence use, and must provide the PTO with a statement of use within six months of receiving notice that its application is entitled to registration. The six-month period can be extended for up to 30 months, giving applicants a total of three years from the date of the notice of allowance in which to file the statement of use. Registration is postponed until the applicant actually uses the mark. However, the applicant has priority rights against any party who, before the application filing date, neither used the same mark nor filed an application for it.

The "intent to use" provision of the 1988 act is aimed at preventing the loss of time, money, and effort that previously occurred when a company developed and marketed a new product under a proposed trademark, only to find that the PTO did not agree that the trademark was registrable.

The registration process can be complex and confusing, and consultation with legal counsel is strongly advised before proceeding. It is also time consuming. It can take up to 18 months after an application is filed for a federal registration to be issued. Most state registrations

take less time. Consequently, a company waiting on federal registration may simultaneously register the mark on the state level to ensure more immediate protection.

State Registration

State registration does not provide as much protection as federal registration. However, it does offer certain benefits. In most states, registration can be obtained within a few weeks of filing and is proof of ownership of the mark. For marks that are not eligible for federal registration, state registration usually provides at the least a modicum of protection, as long as there has been sufficient use of the mark. The degree of protection is determined by the relevant state statute.

State registration cannot preempt or narrow the rights granted by federal registration. For example, a junior user with a state registration predating a senior user's federal registration gains exclusive rights in the mark only in the geographic area of continuous usage preceding the federal registration, and not the entire state. A state trademark law that purported to reserve the entire state for the junior user would be preempted by the Lanham Act.

Trademark Searches

A company about to use a new trademark needs first to conduct a trademark search. Without conducting a search, the company has no way of knowing whether use of the proposed mark will constitute an infringement. The time, money, and effort spent on promotion and advertising will be wasted if use of the mark is ultimately prohibited.

There are various ways of searching a mark. The records of the PTO provide information on federally registered marks; the office of the secretary of state usually can provide relevant data for state marks. Both state and federal registrations describe the mark and the goods it identifies, the owners of the mark, the date of registration, and the date on which the mark was first used. Most of this registration material has been computerized, and can be accessed by an attorney.

Searching for unregistered marks is more difficult. Trade and telephone directories are often a good source of common-law uses of marks. There are also several professional trademark search firms that search databases for customers. Although there is always the risk that a new mark or a common-law user may be untraceable, any search is better than no search. Searching is evidence of a good-faith effort to determine whether any other entity has preexisting rights in a mark.

■ Loss of Trademark Rights

Failure to use one's mark—known as *abandonment*—may result in the loss of rights. A federally registered mark that has been abandoned can be used by a junior user. A trademark search can reveal whether a previously registered trademark has lost its enforceability. There are two types of abandonment: actual and constructive.

Actual Abandonment

Actual abandonment occurs when an owner discontinues use of the mark with the intent not to resume use. Mere nonuse for a limited period does not result in loss of protection. However, there is a presumption of abandonment after two years of nonuse. Because protection for federally registered marks is nationwide, the abandonment must be nationwide for loss of rights to result.

Constructive Abandonment

Constructive abandonment results when the owner does something, or fails to do something, that causes the mark to lose its distinctiveness. Constructive abandonment can result from a mark lapsing into genericism through improper use, such as using "thermos" as a noun rather than a brand name. It can also result from the failure of an owner to adequately control companies licensed to use its mark. Thus, a licensor should carefully exercise quality controls and approval procedures for its licensees' products in order to ensure a consistent quality level.

■ Trademark Infringement

Every trademark owner runs the risk either of having a mark infringed or of being the infringer of someone else's mark. A trademark can be infringed whether or not it is registered; the test for determining infringement in both cases is similar. To establish infringement, a trademark owner must prove: (1) the validity of the mark (note that a federally registered mark is prima facie valid); (2) priority of usage of the mark; and (3) a likelihood of confusion in the minds of the purchasers of the products in question.

Proving validity and priority of usage is fairly straightforward if the mark is registered, and even if the mark is not, proof is a factual matter. The likelihood-of-confusion standard, on the other hand, while a factual test, involves subjectively weighing a variety of factors. These include: (1) the similarity of the two marks with respect to appearance, sound, connotation, and commercial impression;

(2) the similarity of the goods; (3) the similarity of the channels of trade in which the goods are sold; (4) the strength of the marks, as evidenced by the amount of sales and advertising and the length of use; (5) the use of similar marks by third parties with respect to related goods and services; (6) the length of time of concurrent use without actual confusion; and (7) the extent and nature of any actual confusion of the two marks in the marketplace.

Remedies

The remedies for trademark infringement include injunctive relief, an accounting for lost profits due to customer confusion, and damages. The type of relief granted is determined on a case-by-case basis.

International Consideration

Every country has its own methods for determining what is a protectable trademark, how to obtain and maintain trademarks, and the scope of protection available for trademarks. In most countries, unlike the U.S., use of a mark confers no rights, and registration is essential. In addition, registration of a trademark in the U.S. confers no rights in foreign countries, although a U.S. registration can provide an easy basis for registration of corresponding trademarks in countries that participate in multilateral trademark conventions with the United States.

There are people who watch for popular trademarks in the United States and register these marks in foreign jurisdictions in order to establish rights to them that will preclude use by the owner of the mark in the United States. For example, Timberland Co., a U.S. manufacturer of rugged outdoor premium quality shoes, apparel, and accessories, discovered when it decided to export its shoes to Brazil that a large generic shoe manufacturer had already registered the Timberland trademark in Brazil. Timberland sued the shoe manufacturer and was able to overcome its trademark protection based on prior use of its trade name and copyright protection of the Timberland logo. However, as of mid-1994 the verdict was on appeal.

■ Trade Secrets

In our free-market system, the value of information decreases with availability. With a highly mobile work force, the demand for modern technologies and innovation may lead to unauthorized disclosure of sensitive information. Trade-secret law is necessary to protect the owners of such information. As social theorist Alvin Toffler noted in his 1990 analysis, *Powershift,*

> No one buys a share of [Apple Computer Inc.] or IBM stock because of the firm's material assets. What counts are not the company's buildings or machines, but the contacts and power of its marketing and sales force, the organizational capacity of its management and the ideas crackling in the heads of its employees.[10]

This increased emphasis on the value of trade secret information has fueled a growing trend of litigation in this area. For example, during 1993, Procter & Gamble Co. filed suit to prevent one of its top executives, Neil P. DeFeo, from joining Clorox Company, claiming that the executive's knowledge of laundry and cleaning products would harm Procter & Gamble if shared with bleach maker Clorox.[11] Federated Department Stores sued the former chief executive officer of its merchandising division to prevent him from accepting employment as president and chief operating officer of Macy's. General Motors sued its former head of worldwide purchasing, Ignacio Lopez de Arriortua, and Volkswagen, his new employer, claiming that he took trade secret documents, including plans for future GM models and car-building techniques.

The term *trade secret* is difficult to define due to the fact-specific nature of the case law. Trade secrets can take almost any form. Plans, formulas, customer lists, research and development results, sales data, pricing information, computer programs, marketing techniques, and production techniques all can qualify as trade secrets. This list is by no means exhaustive. Anything that makes a company unique, or that a competitor would like to know because the information gives a competitive advantage, may be a trade secret.

The Supreme Court has held that trade-secret law is the province of the states. Until recently, the law of trade secrets was developed by the courts on a case-by-case basis, applying the laws of the relevant state. The decisions were based on tort theories in cases involving theft or misappropriation of trade secrets, and on contract theories when a special relationship or duty was present. Many trade-secret cases involved a combination of the two theories.

Common Law

Under the common law, which is still in effect in most states, the definition most widely accepted by the courts is that contained in the Restatement of Torts. Section 757(b) provides:

> A trade secret may consist of any formula, pattern, device, or compilation of information which is used in one's business, and which gives him an opportunity to obtain an advantage over competitors who do not know or use it. It may be a formula for a chemical compound, a process of manufacturing, treating or preserving materials, a pattern for a machine or other device, or a list of customers.

The courts have developed a number of factors to determine whether specific information qualifies as a trade secret. These factors include: (1) the extent to which the information is known outside the business; (2) the extent to which measures are taken to protect the information; (3) the value of the information; (4) the amount of money or time spent to develop the information; and (5) the ease of duplicating the information.

Unfortunately, even with this formal definition and set of factors, a certain amount of guesswork still is required to determine whether a particular type of information qualifies as a trade secret under the common law. The courts have classified identical types of information differently when the factual settings were only slightly different.

The Uniform Trade Secrets Act

In 1979, the Uniform Trade Secrets Act (UTSA) was promulgated in an attempt to provide a coherent framework for trade-secret protection. The drafters of the UTSA hoped to eliminate the unpredictability of the common law by providing a more comprehensive definition of trade secrets. In particular, the drafters expanded the common-law definition by adding the terms

---

10. Alvin Toffler, *Powershift* (1990).

11. The settlement of this dispute in October 1993 illustrates possible ways to resolve such disputes in the future. The Procter & Gamble executive, DeFeo, agreed not to assume responsibilities for Clorox's hard-surface cleaners, such as Pinesol and Formula 409, until March 1, 1994. These two products compete with Procter & Gamble's Spic & Span, Top Job, and Mr. Clean. DeFeo agreed not to assume oversight for Clorox's powdered bleach until September 1, 1994, and for liquid bleach products until January 1, 1995. The parties agreed that DeFeo could manage the rest of Clorox's U.S. operations immediately. Ann Wozencraft, "Procter & Gamble Co. Settles with Former Exec Hired by Clorox," *Contra Costa Times,* October 27, 1993, C1.

"method," "program," and "technique" to the Restatement's list of types of information that are protected. The intention was to specifically include know-how, that is, technical knowledge, methods, and experience. In addition, the common-law definition was broadened by deleting the requirement that the secret be continuously used in a business. Accordingly, the UTSA defines a trade secret as:

> Information, including a formula, pattern, compilation, program, device, method, technique, or process, that: (1) derives independent economic value, actual or potential, from not being generally known to, and not being readily ascertainable by proper means by, other persons who can obtain economic value from its disclosure or use, and (2) is the subject of efforts that are reasonable under the circumstances to maintain its secrecy.

While the common law did not protect information unless it was in use, the UTSA definition is broad enough to include information that has potential value from being secret; information regarding one-time events; and negative information, such as test results showing what will not work for a particular process or product.

The most significant difference, however, between the UTSA and the common-law definitions is in the overall approach to determining whether information is protectable as a trade secret. As discussed above, at common law a fairly objective five- or six-part test was developed. Although many courts adopted a reasonableness standard when interpreting the individual factors of the test, the focus was on objectivity, as delineated in this test. The UTSA, on the other hand, uses a more flexible test indicating that the steps taken to preserve the information as a trade secret must be reasonable, and the owner must derive independent economic value from secrecy. The latter is a somewhat subjective determination; there are not yet enough cases interpreting the "independent economic value" factor to indicate whether it will become significant over time.

Adopted, at least in part, in 38 states, the UTSA has only partially fulfilled its goal of standardizing trade-secret law. States have tended to incorporate only those parts of the UTSA that embody the existing common law of the particular state. Consequently, in states that have adopted the UTSA, the courts rely on a combination of common law and the UTSA.

Although the UTSA seems to have fallen short of its goal of establishing consistent protection for trade secrets, it may provide broader protection to owners of trade secrets in the states where it has been adopted. Its definition of the term *trade secret* is broader than the common-law definition, so that the burden of proof on the owner is reduced. In addition, the UTSA provides more effective remedies.

However, the UTSA did not improve on the common law definition in all areas. For example, the UTSA adopted separate definitions of the terms *trade secret* and *misappropriation,* but because the definitions overlap it is almost impossible to apply them separately. In addition, the protection of unique trade secrets, such as customer lists, may have been undermined because the UTSA does not directly address this controversial type of trade secret.

Comparison With Other Forms of Protection

Unlike the more formal procedures for patent and copyright protection, there are no lengthy application and filing procedures for trade secret protection. No review or approval by a governmental agency is required. To create and protect a trade secret, one need only develop and maintain a trade secret protection program. Where the information being protected has a short shelf life, trade secret protection may be a more practical solution than copyright or patent protection.

Trade secrets are immediately protectable, and unlike patents or copyrights, there is no fixed length of time for ownership. As long as the protected information remains confidential and is not developed independently by someone else, a trade secret will continue to be protectable under the law.

Another advantage of trade secret protection is that material that would not qualify for patent or copyright protection is often protectable as a trade secret. A trade secret need not be as unique as a patentable invention, or as original as a copyrightable work. It need only provide a competitive advantage. It may be merely an idea that has been kept secret, such as a way to organize common machines in an efficient manner, a marketing plan, or a formula for mixing the ingredients of a product.

Finally, patent and copyright protection usually require disclosure of trade secret information. The patent law requires the disclosure of the best method of making the invention, and the copyright law requires a deposit of the copyrightable work, with certain exceptions. There is always a risk that the protection will not be granted by the reviewing agency after the sensitive information has been revealed. To avoid this risk, trade secret protection may be the safest course of action.

There are two disadvantages to utilizing trade secret protection. First, the confidentiality procedures must be continuously and rigidly followed in order to preserve trade secret status. The cost of a full-fledged program to protect trade secrets can be substantial. Second, trade secret protection provides no protection against reverse engineering or independent discovery. The uncertainty of protection may limit the productive uses of the trade secret.

Protecting a Trade Secret

To properly protect trade secret information, the owner must develop a program to preserve its confidentiality. In almost every jurisdiction, the test of a trade-secret program's adequacy may be reduced to the question of whether the owner has taken reasonable precautions to preserve the confidentiality of his trade secrets.

The most common forms of misappropriation of trade secrets are inadvertent disclosure and disclosure by employees. A program to protect against such disclosures should contain the elements discussed below. This outline, however, should not be relied upon to develop an actual policy. An attorney knowledgeable in the area should always be consulted.

A trade-secret program should be in writing, with a statement explaining its purpose. It should cover in detail four areas: (1) notification; (2) identification; (3) security; and (4) exit interviews. The program must then be properly implemented and maintained.

Notification

A written indication that all employees are aware of the trade-secret program is critical; at a minimum, a written notice should be posted. Ideally, the company's trade-secret policy should be explained to each new employee during orientation, and each new employee should sign a confidentiality agreement. The agreement should specify how long confidentiality will be required. The duration of the agreement should not be so long, however, that a court would view it as overly restrictive and thus unreasonable.

Labeling is another means of notification. A rubber stamp denoting confidential material and the posting of signs in areas containing sensitive materials will in most cases satisfy the reasonableness requirement. However, because in practice it is difficult to ensure consistent and continuous labeling procedures, some authorities believe labeling may actually hurt the trade-secret status of the information. These authorities claim that failure to label some of the documents may be seen as evidence that the information in those documents should not be afforded trade-secret status. More advanced kinds of labeling, such as passwords, lend additional support for a finding of reasonableness.

The company should also provide written notice to any consultant, vendor, joint venturer, or other party to whom a trade secret must be revealed. The notice should take the form of a confidentiality agreement that describes the protected information and limits the receiving party's rights to use it. Without such notice, the receiving party may be unaware of the nature of the information and unwittingly release it into the public domain.

Identification

There is some controversy concerning the appropriate method of identifying trade secrets. One view is that everything within the workplace, or pertaining to the business, is a trade secret. The problem with this umbrella approach is that a court may find it overly restrictive of commerce and therefore against public policy. Such a finding could undermine the company's trade-secret program, exposing all of its trade secrets to unrecoverable misappropriation.

At the other extreme is a program that attempts to specify each trade secret of the company. This approach may be too narrow, because any legitimate trade secrets that are not specified will not be protected. Also, it is often difficult to pinpoint all of a company's potential trade secrets. For example, although it may be easy to designate all research and development projects as trade secrets, gray areas such as sales data, customer lists, or marketing surveys may cause problems.

The best solution may be a program that specifies as much information as possible while also including a limited number of catchall categories.

Security

Measures must be taken to ensure that trade secret information remains secret, at least from the public. The disclosure of a trade secret, whether intentional (for example, as part of a sale) or by mistake, destroys any legal protection.

> **"**
> *The disclosure of a trade secret, whether intentional (for example, as part of a sale) or by mistake, destroys any legal protection.*

A common cause of this disastrous result is the unintentional disclosure of a trade secret during a public tour of the facility. An offhand remark in the hall overheard by a visitor, or a formula left written on a chalkboard in plain view of a tour group, is all that is needed. The best way to avoid this situation is to keep all trade secrets in areas restricted from public access. If such physical barriers are not possible, visitors' access should be controlled through a system that logs in all visitors, identifies them with badges, and keeps track of them while they are on the premises.

Trade secrets may also be inadvertently disclosed by employees participating in trade groups, conferences, and conventions, and through publication of articles in trade journals and other periodicals. To avoid this problem, an employer should consistently and continuously, as part of its trade-secret program, remind its employees and contractors of when and how to talk about the company's business activities.

Exit Interviews

When an employee who has had access to trade secrets leaves the company, she should be given an exit interview. The exit interview provides an opportunity to reinforce the confidentiality agreement that the employee signed on joining the company. If no confidentiality agreement exists, the exit interview is even more important. It will provide the notice and possibly the identification necessary to legally protect a trade secret. The exit interview also lets the former employee know that the company is serious about protecting its trade secrets, and that any breach of confidentiality could result in legal proceedings against the employee. After such a warning, any misappropriation would be deliberate and could therefore result in punitive damages.

In some states, post-termination obligations imposed on a departing employee may be unenforceable. In California, for example, a provision in an employment contract that prohibits an employee from later working for a competitor is void as an unlawful business restraint, except to the extent necessary to prevent the misappropriation of trade secrets. It is therefore important to consult with legal counsel concerning the scope of posttermination restrictions.

The following case highlights the importance of taking precautions to keep information secret because proving infringement is often burdensome.

■ A Case in Point: Summary

Case 11.6
GENERAL ELECTRIC COMPANY v. ILJIN CORP.
United States District Court for the District of Massachusetts
27 U.S.P.Q.2d (BNA) 1372
(D. Mass. 1993).

FACTS In 1984, Chien-Min Sung, a geochemistry Ph.D., ended a seven-year employment with GE Superabrasives and began working for Norton Company's Diamond Technology Center. Upon leaving GE, Sung took an abundance of documents, including drawings and process instructions, related to the production of saw-grade industrial synthetic diamonds. In 1988, Sung and the co-defendants Iljin Corp. and Iljin Diamond Manufacturing Co. entered into several agreements that obligated Sung to transfer technology related to the production of the diamonds. In 1989, GE and Norton sued Sung, alleging that the technology transferred constituted a GE trade secret. The Iljin entities were also named as defendants on the theory that they knew or should have known that the transferred technology constituted a trade secret. The Iljin defendants made a counterclaim, alleging that GE instigated this action in bad faith as part of a continuing effort to monopolize and restrain trade and commerce in the high-quality synthetic diamond market.

ISSUE PRESENTED Is the technology transfer of the process of making synthetic diamonds a trade secret? Can the recipient of the information be liable as well as the grantor of information?

SUMMARY OF OPINION To grant summary judgment for GE, the Federal District Court needed to determine that there was no genuine issue as to any material fact. With respect to GE's claim of misappropriation of a trade secret, the court found that GE had the fact-intensive burden of proving: (1) the information transferred was in fact a GE trade secret, and (2) the Iljin defendants knew or should have known that the information was a GE trade secret. The court also found that Iljin's assertion that GE had made the trade secret claims in bad faith, no matter how difficult to prove, was a question of fact that should go before a jury at trial.

RESULT GE's motion for summary judgment as to the misappropriation of a trade secret was denied. Iljin Corp.'s counterclaims were also denied. Because there were genuine issues as to the material facts in the case, a trial was necessary.

COMMENTS The jury rendered a verdict in favor of GE and against Iljin for misappropriation of GE trade secrets. The court enjoined Iljin from manufacturing saw-grade diamonds for seven years, which was the amount of time, the court concluded, it would have taken Iljin to develop or reverse engineer a technology for commercial production of high-grade saw diamonds.

■ Misappropriation of Trade Secrets

The UTSA defines *misappropriation* by listing the various permutations of when an individual uses the trade secret of another, or learns of a trade secret through improper means. The UTSA defines "improper means" by a list of deceitful actions. The list, however, is not exclusive, and anything that strikes a court as improper would probably qualify as an improper means.

Remedies

Once a trade secret has been misappropriated, the law provides a choice of remedies. These are not mutually exclusive, and the typical trade-secret case involves more than one form of relief.

Injunction A court may issue an injunction ordering the misappropriator to refrain from disclosing or using the stolen trade secret. An injunction is desirable because it preserves the confidentiality of the trade secret.

An injunction is available only to prevent irreparable harm, however. If the secret has already been disclosed, an injunction is usually no longer proper, unless the disclosure was limited, or all of those to whom the secret was disclosed knew of the misappropriation.

Even if the trade secret has been disclosed, however, an injunction may still be appropriate. The court may enjoin the misappropriator from using the information, even though his disclosure has made it no longer a trade secret. The purpose of such an injunction is to deny the misappropriator the benefits of his misappropriation. In this situation, the injunction is often combined with an award of damages.

The owner may also be able to seek an injunction or damages from anyone receiving the misappropriated trade secret, or anyone hiring the individual who misappropriated it.

Finally, an injunction would be appropriate when an individual threatens to use or disclose a trade secret. In that situation, the real damage has yet to occur. In reality, however, very few cases involve threatened disclosure. The owner of a trade secret usually discovers the misappropriation only after the secret has been disclosed.

Damages Monetary damages are often awarded when the owner of the trade secret has suffered financial harm. The situations in which monetary damages are received are fact-specific. Damages may be awarded based upon either a contract theory or a tort theory. The technical differences between the two measures of damages make little practical difference. Most courts will attempt to fairly compensate the owner of a misappropriated trade secret regardless of how the case is characterized.

Under the tort theory of trade secrets, the purpose of the damages is not only to make the owner whole, but to disgorge any profits the misappropriator may have made due to her wrongful act. The key to the tort measure of damages is that there was either a harm, or an unjust gain, or both.

The contract theory of trade secrets, on the other hand, measures damages by the loss of value of the trade secret to the owner as a result of a breach of contract. The loss of value is determined by adding the general loss to any special losses resulting from the breach, and subtracting any costs avoided by the owner as a result of the breach.

Punitive Damages   Punitive damages are available where the misappropriation was willful and wanton. A misappropriation that can be characterized only as a breach of contract does not warrant punitive damages. In some states, attorney's fees are also recoverable by the prevailing party if the misappropriation was willful and malicious.

Criminal Action

Although most cases of trade secret misappropriation are settled through civil actions, a number of states have little-used penal statutes making such conduct a felony. In a California case that startled the computer software industry in 1992, Borland International, Inc. filed a criminal complaint, in addition to a civil suit, against Eugene Wang and Symantec claiming that Wang, a former Borland employee, stole Borland trade secrets for Symantec. The criminal complaint resulted in an indictment of Wang and of Symantec president Gordon Eubanks on 32 counts of conspiracy and trade secret misappropriation. If convicted, each executive faces fines of up to $10,000 per count and up to six years in state prison. The criminal case revolves around electronic mail messages sent by Wang to Eubanks while Wang was still a Borland employee. On the day he announced his resignation, Wang allegedly sent 12 e-mail messages containing Borland trade secrets to Eubanks. The case sent shock waves through the Silicon Valley, where employees frequently move between companies, and has led to speculation that it may inhibit employees from changing jobs as freely as they have in the past.

■   Technology Licensing

Technology licensing is big business worldwide. The volume of commercial technology transfers has increased dramatically since World War II and is accelerating. For many modern business enterprises, intellectual property makes up some of their most significant productive assets.

One way for a technology owner to benefit from its technology is to use it. Another way is to license others to use it. Conversely, a potential acquirer of technology may choose either to develop the technology itself or to obtain it under license from another. Depending upon the circumstances of the parties and the market, a commonality of interest may develop that leads to a license transaction.

International Consideration

Most foreign countries will enforce reasonable nondisclosure restrictions in contracts, at least against parties to the contract. Although such contract restrictions against nondisclosure are generally enforceable, most countries do not recognize the tort law aspect of trade secrets that is recognized in the United States. In some countries, the judicial process itself may destroy the confidential character of the misappropriated information. For example, the Japanese judicial system does not have a procedure equivalent to the America "in camera" (confidentiality) procedure for review of trade secret information.

Advantages to the Licensor

From a licensor's perspective, there are a variety of reasons to license technology.

Corporate Revenue   One obvious reason is to generate revenue. License transactions constitute a substantial source of income for many technology-based companies.

Market Presence   Licensing is often an inexpensive way to gain a presence in a target market. In essence, through the mechanism of a license, a licensor may be able to push many of the costs of market development onto the licensee in exchange for a share of the profits from the venture.

Inexpensive Source   A license transaction may give the licensor an inexpensive source of supply of the licensed product. Where the licensee is operating in a low-cost labor market, such product-purchase rights may be highly valued by the licensor.

Technology Exchange   A licensor seeking new technology may condition its license upon a cross-license of the licensee's existing technology or may require a grant-back of any future technology developed by the licensee.

Dated Technology   Licensing may be a way for a licensor to exploit its older technology. Often a somewhat dated technology is what a licensee can best use.

Advantages to the Licensee

There are also several reasons why a licensee might wish to license technology.

Access to Technology   By taking a license, a licensee can obtain immediate access to new technology, and can avoid the research and development costs that would be necessary to duplicate the technology.

Market Penetration   A license may enable the licensee to penetrate its target market sooner. Without having to independently develop the necessary technology, the licensee may be able to get a head start on its competitors.

Long-Term Relationship   A licensee may be seeking a long-term relationship with its licensor, which will enable it to graduate to higher and higher levels of the licensor's technology (including future developments).

Goodwill   A licensee may seek to share in the goodwill of its licensor through the license transaction. If the licensor has strong trademarks or is otherwise the beneficiary of substantial goodwill, the licensee may be able to benefit in its local market.

Disadvantages to the Licensor

There are a variety of reasons why a licensor may choose not to license its technology.

Future Competition   By far the greatest risk for a licensor is that its licensee may become its future competitor. Numerous examples abound of this phenomenon.

Loss of Skills   A licensor that relies exclusively upon its licensee for the manufacture of the licensed product may find that it loses the ability to manufacture the product efficiently itself.

Service Obligations   Licensors may be reluctant to undertake the service obligations that often arise in license transactions. A licensee may require a lot of training and assistance for the license transaction to be successful. The licensor may not be able ultimately to recoup such costs.

Differences of Approach   The managements of the licensor and licensee may differ on fundamental aspects of the license transaction such as commitment, strategy, and marketing, thereby making success improbable. If

language and cultural differences are added, the licensor may well decide that a proposed transaction is not worth its while.

Disadvantages to the Licensee

A licensee, too, may decide that its differences with the licensor make the transaction not worthwhile. There are several other reasons why a potential licensee may choose not to carry through a license transaction.

Transfer Problems   A licensee may decide not to enter into a license transaction because of concerns about technology transfer problems. Just because a licensor can operate its technology at a certain level does not necessarily mean it can effectively teach the licensee to use it at the same level. Licensees are often bitterly disappointed by the technology they have paid so dearly to acquire.

> 66
> *Licensees are often bitterly disappointed by the technology they have paid so dearly to acquire.*

Royalty Expense   Continuing royalty payments can become burdensome to a licensee, particularly if competitors enter the market who are not paying a comparable royalty.

Intellectual Property Dispute Settlement

A license may be utilized as a means of settling an intellectual property dispute. Patent litigation, for example, is risky both for the defendant, who may face a treble damages award, and for the plaintiff, who may find her patent

International Consideration

If either the licensee or the licensor is located outside the United States, the export control laws of the United States must be carefully complied with to avoid potential liability. Unfortunately, such compliance may result in undue expense or delay. Also, it should be borne in mind that other countries may not offer the same intellectual property protection as the United States.

EXHIBIT 11-3   Extract from American Express Company's Code of Conduct. *Used by permission.*

PROPRIETARY INFORMATION AND TRADE SECRETS

All persons who work for the Company learn, to a greater or lesser degree, facts about the Company's business methods or "secrets of success" which are not known to the general public or competitors. For example, customer lists, the terms or fees offered to a particular customer, or marketing or strategic plans, may give the Company an advantage and must not be disclosed. In addition, such things as internal processing arrangements or proprietary systems developments must not be disclosed. These are just a few examples.

Because these trade practices or methods are developed by employees in the course of their jobs for which the Company pays them a salary, these matters are the property of the Company, and it is important to the continued success of the Company that they remain known only to the Company.

Therefore, except as your duties during your employment may require or as a duly authorized senior officer of the Company may otherwise consent in writing, you shall not at any time disclose or use, either during or subsequent to your employment by the Company, any information, knowledge or data you receive or develop during your employment which is considered proprietary by the Company. This includes, but is not limited to, information stored for business purposes on any computer system (e.g., mainframes, individual terminals and personal computers) and software used by the Company.

In addition, no employee shall disclose information which relates to the Company's secrets as contained in business processes, methods, compositions, improvements, inventions, discoveries or otherwise, or which the Company has received in confidence from others. On the other hand, the Company will not ask you to reveal, and no employee shall disclose to the Company, the proprietary information or trade secrets of others.

---

invalidated. To minimize such risks, the parties may enter into a license agreement. Two biotechnology companies, Cetus Corporation and Amgen, Inc., took such an approach. Amgen had brought an action against Cetus claiming that certain of Cetus's patents relating to Interleukin-2 were invalid; Cetus had counterclaimed that Amgen was infringing Cetus's patents. Rather than letting a court determine their fate, the parties settled the suit through an agreement whereby certain of Amgen's patent rights were assigned to Cetus and Cetus granted Amgen a license to use Cetus's patents.

The Responsible Manager

Protecting Intellectual Property Rights

Some of a company's most important assets may be intangible forms of intellectual property. Consider the formula for Coke, never registered as a patent but kept as a trade secret by generations of executives at the Coca-Cola Company. An effective trade-secret policy is essen-

tial to almost all forms of businesses today. This chapter has provided suggestions for how to implement such a policy. Exhibit 11-3 shows one company's code of conduct on this subject.

Problems can arise when a manager leaves the employment of one company to assume a position at another. It is critical that the manager and the new employer ensure that no confidential information, including trade secrets, is conveyed to the new employer, either in the form of documents or information in the manager's head. Misappropriation of trade secrets is a civil and criminal offense.

If the manager cannot fulfill all the duties of her new job without using trade secrets, it is necessary to scale back her activities and responsibilities. Sometimes, this can be accomplished by having the former employer and the new employer agree that the manager will not assume responsibility for certain product lines that compete until a date when the strategic and other confidential information known by the manager is stale. If at all possible, the departing manager should address this issue up front, and negotiate this as part of her severance arrangements, rather than wait for a costly lawsuit to be brought by the former employer.

In addition to trade secrets, intellectual property is given legal protection through patents, copyrights, and trademarks. Patents, which last 17 or 14 years, depending on type, are extremely important to high-technology companies. In fact, patents have formed the basis for whole businesses, such as biotechnology. A manager should strive to protect his company's patents from infringement by others. Royalties from patents can add tens or even hundreds of millions of dollars to a company's revenues.

Copyrights prevent others from copying literary work, musical work, sound recordings, computer software, and other forms of expression fixed in a tangible medium. A manager should be aware that copyright registration with the U.S. Copyright Office is a prerequisite for filing an infringement suit for a work of U.S. origin. Statutory damages and attorney's fees are available only to owners of registered works.

Trademarks that identify brands of goods or services are protected for an indefinite time. Managers must work to preserve trademarks, however. Once the buying public starts using the trademark as a synonym for the product, rather than as a means of distinguishing its source, loss of the trademark is imminent.

A manager and her company may benefit from technology licensing. Such arrangements offer advantages and disadvantages for both the licensor and licensee.

A manager should not only protect his company's own intellectual property, he should also ensure that the company does not infringe the intellectual property rights of others, whether they be patents, copyrights, trademarks, trade names, or trade secrets.

Inside Story

Microsoft Takes a Bite Out of Apple

Although known as a global mainspring of creativity and innovation, the personal computer business is equally recognized as a highly profitable market for copyright and patent lawyers. Over the past ten years, many of the giant computer software firms have been embroiled in lawsuits—often against each other—to safeguard their copyrighted products. In the mid-1990s, heavyweight legal actions were underway across America, pitting the industry's spirit of free-wheeling creativity against sometimes outdated copyright and patent laws.

The most publicized of these cases is the lawsuit by Apple Computer against Microsoft and Hewlett-Packard (HP). The legal dispute concerned an alleged infringement of a 1985 licensing agreement allowing Microsoft to produce software that would enable IBM-compatible personal computers to more closely emulate Apple's Macintosh. Apple's $5.5 billion complaint, filed in 1988, argued that its competitors, in creating icon-based user interfaces for their systems, had illegitimately expropriated the "look and feel" of the well-liked Macintosh computer.

Apple's lawsuit is the most consequential software copyright case yet heard by a court. As one commentator has written,

Where computer litigation is concerned, the "look and feel" case is the big daddy of all court suits. We're talking the World Series, Super Bowl, even the Wrestlemania of computer cases. Think about it. The mere idea of these three giants wrapped up in mortal combat over the right to fill a computer screen with its bitsy, cartoonish symbols inside hairline-rule windows.[12]

The "Look and Feel" Litigation

In 1989, California Federal District Judge Walker granted several motions in a pretrial hearing which substantially narrowed the areas of dispute. Although ruling that the 1985 agreement between Microsoft and Apple covered 179 of Apple's list of 189 allegedly infringing visual displays in Microsoft's Windows 2.0, Judge Walker declined at that time to resolve the issue of whether copyright law protected certain features of Apple's user interface not covered by the license.

In early spring of 1992, Microsoft moved for summary judgment to answer this remaining question. In the American legal system, when there are no relevant

---

12. Robert Green, "Apple's Look-and-Feel Legal Blues Make You Want to Twist and Shout," *Government Computer News,* May 11, 1992, 61.

Inside Story continued on following page

Inside Story, continued

facts in dispute, an attorney may submit a motion for summary judgment to avoid needless litigation. If the court concurs that the only remaining issue is how the law should be applied to the undisputed facts, it will grant the motion and the case will end without a trial.

In support of its summary judgment motion, Microsoft and HP argued that there was only one or a very limited number of ways to perform the function of some features of the Macintosh interface such as its overlapping windows and pull-down menus. The underpinning of this legal argument was copyright law's merger doctrine, which disallows copyright protection for any material that has no "expression" separable from its "idea." From Microsoft and HP's perspective, the idea behind Macintosh's user interface was indistinguishable from its expression, and the two companies persuasively argued that Apple was improperly construing copyright law so as to protect ideas. As to other features of the Macintosh interface (such as having a title beneath the icon), Microsoft and HP contended that these aspects were covered by the licensing agreement, were not original to Apple, and were not copyright infringements under specific sections of the copyright laws.

Instead of specifically rebutting each of these arguments, Apple generally asserted that the basis of its copyright infringement complaint was on Microsoft's and HP's cloning of the gestalt—or overall look and feel—of the Macintosh interface and the original amalgam of components it operates, rather than on the isolated elements on which Microsoft and HP were focusing. Apple attacked Microsoft's technique of splitting the Macintosh interface into discrete items and then claiming the entire system was not protected due to the unprotectability of its dissected pieces. Apple pointed out that any company may choose and organize geometric shapes in an artistic manner in designing a product. Even if copyright law failed to protect those individual shapes, the end product is nonetheless protected by copyright law. Apple argued that the same principle should apply to software user interfaces.

Two issues seem to have influenced Judge Walker's decision to grant Microsoft and HP's motions for summary judgment at the April 14, 1992, hearing. First, Apple did not respond in a particularized manner to the motions. Generally, the opposing litigant to a motion for summary judgment must respond to the other party's assertion that there are no material facts in dispute to be resolved by trial. Traditionally, lawyers will respond by cataloging specific details that are disputed and require a trial to resolve. In rendering his opinion orally at the April 14 hearing, Judge Walker declared that Apple was in procedural default for failing to specifically respond to the summary judgment motions. But the other and probably more influential factor in the judge's decision was the *Brown Bag Software* decision, which the U.S. Court of Appeals for the Ninth Circuit had decided approximately one week prior to the April 14th decision.

Brown Bag Software v. Symantec

In the spring of 1989, a trial court judge granted Symantec's motion for summary judgment and dismissed the copyright infringement complaint filed by Brown Bag Software. Brown Bag appealed the trial court's ruling because it was quite rare at that time for a trial judge to grant summary judgment in a copyright suit. It was even rarer for an appellate court to affirm such a ruling because almost any factual dispute, no matter how small, would normally be sufficient to allow the case to proceed to trial.[13] Because the *Brown Bag* case represented a judicial departure from business as usual, those who closely follow developments in copyright law awaited the appellate court's ruling on Brown Bag's appeal with great anticipation. One of those watching and waiting was Judge Walker.

The facts of the *Brown Bag* case were relatively straightforward. Software developer John Friend sold an outlining program called PC-Outline to Brown Bag. Although Friend declared in the purchase agreement that he was not designing any program that would infringe the copyright that Brown Bag was acquiring, he developed another outlining program, called Grandview, later that year, which he then sold to Symantec. Symantec, in turn, sold this new program as an updated version of outlining programs it had developed and sold some years before. Brown Bag then sued both Symantec and Friend, seeking restitution for their violations of the copyright laws, and alleging, among

---

13. *Brown Bag Software v. Symantec,* 960 F.2d 1465 (1992), *cert. denied,* 113 S.Ct. 198 (1992).

Inside Story, continued

other things, that Grandview's user interface was substantially similar to that of PC-Outline and had been illegally duplicated from it.

In response to Friend and Symantec's motions for summary judgment, Brown Bag submitted a sworn written statement by a computer expert who identified 17 specific features of PC-Outline and Grandview that were substantially similar. Although substantial similarity is generally a factual question, not a legal one, the trial court ruled that none of these 17 items could be the basis for a finding of copyright infringement. In its appeal, Brown Bag objected to the trial court's method of classifying the programs' similar aspects into a number of different categories and then finding that each category cannot form the basis of a copyright infringement. Foreshadowing Apple's claims against Microsoft and HP, Brown Bag argued that the trial court had erred by engaging in excessive analytical segregation. Brown Bag maintained that by dissecting the user interface similarities into discrete units and then deciding each unit was unprotectable under copyright law, the trial court committed reversible error. Brown Bag asserted that the trial court improperly disregarded the reasonable possibility that a jury could find copyrighted expressiveness in the look and feel of the interface.

Ultimately, the Ninth Circuit appellate court rejected these arguments and affirmed the grant of summary judgment to Symantec and Friend. In agreeing with the trial court's reasoning, the appellate court declared that analytical dissection was appropriate to determine the parameters of protection that copyright law grants to a certain product. If the expression cannot be distinguished from the idea it represents, no copyright infringement exists and summary judgment should be granted.

Apple Trapped in the Brown Bag

Judge Walker granted Microsoft's and HP's summary judgment motions shortly after the Ninth Circuit's ruling on Brown Bag's appeal.[14] The influence of the *Brown Bag* decision is conspicuous not only from the mention Judge Walker made of that appellate ruling, but also from the way he structured his opinion on April 14. Essentially, Judge Walker grouped the items into categories and ruled that infringement cannot be based on the use of items not protected by copyright law. To the extent that the look and feel of the Macintosh user interface necessarily follows from the use of either licensed or unprotected elements, Judge Walker decided that there was no cause of action for copyright infringement.

The crux of the legal struggle between these three corporate giants was whether the "look and feel" of a product is protected by copyright laws, notwithstanding that its constituent parts are unprotected. As sincere as Apple may have been in characterizing its user interface as artistic and aesthetically pleasing, copyright law has doctrines that limit the extent of protection available to a work with both artistic and functional aspects. Unless the artistic aspect of the work is separable from its functional aspect, copyright law says no protection is available to it.

While Microsoft prevailed against Apple in a California trial court, the battle continues in other parts of the country. For instance, three thousand miles across the country in Boston, Massachusetts, Federal District Judge Robert Keeton (the judge who wrote the opinion in the Lotus-Borland litigation (case 11.4)) rejected arguments that he should follow the Ninth Circuit Court of Appeals decision in *Brown Bag*. Both the Apple-Microsoft and the Lotus-Borland federal district court decisions have been appealed to the respective U.S. Courts of Appeals. Final resolution of the look-and-feel controversy may require a decision from the U.S. Supreme Court.

---

14. *Apple Computer, Inc. v. Microsoft Corp.*, 821 F.Supp. 616 (N.D. Cal. 1993).

Key Words and Phrases

Questions and Case Problems

1. Rural Telephone Service Co. published a telephone directory for the Chicago area and distributed it to businesses and residents that use its telephone services. Feist Publications, Inc. published "city directories."

The white pages of this "city directory" list residents, as does the Rural Telephone Service's directory, but they also describe the businesses, state the occupations of the residents, and provide other information. To identify the residents and businesses in the area, Feist used, and later published, the information listed in the Rural Telephone Service's directory. Feist sold the city directory for $10. Does Rural Telephone Service Co. have an actionable claim against Feist for copyright infringement?

[*Feist Publications, Inc. v. Rural Telephone Service Co.*, 499 U.S. 340, 111 S.Ct. 1282 (1991)]

2. Donald Frederick Evans & Assocs. designs, builds, and sells houses. Evans hired an architect to draw plans for its developments. To help market the homes, Evans distributed to buyers a brochure which included the architect's plans. The following month Donald Evans, the president of the firm, received a tip that homes just like those shown in the brochure were being built 20 miles away. Evans drove to the site and saw that homes virtually identical to those designed by Evans's architect were being built there by Continental Homes. Apparently, Continental had obtained a brochure and built the homes from the plans. Can Evans do anything about this? If Continental sold ten homes, what damages, if any, are recoverable?

[*Donald Frederick Evans & Assocs., Inc. v. Continental Homes, Inc.*, 785 F.2d 897 (11th Cir. 1986)]

3. Cecil Hudson worked for Cataphote Corp. Hudson did not know anything about making glass when he joined the company. However, during his employment and with the help of Cataphote, Hudson developed a way to produce glass beads by the vertical updraft furnace method. This process is not patent protected; it employs principles that are in the public domain. Nevertheless, the combination of public-domain techniques employed is novel, and has been kept secret by Cataphote.

Hudson left Cataphote and started his own glass company. After six months of construction, he was ready to begin manufacturing. Cataphote management then called Hudson and stated that they would sue Hudson if he did not stop using the Cataphote updraft furnace method.

Hudson comes to you, his attorney, for help. He asks you, "How can Cataphote sue me, if the method is not patentable, and will Cataphote win?"

What do you tell Hudson, and what questions should you ask him to determine whether Cataphote's claim is actionable?

[*Cataphote Corp. v. Hudson*, 422 F.2d 1290 (5th Cir. 1970)]

4. E.I. duPont de Nemours & Co., Inc. developed a new and very efficient process for manufacturing automobiles. You work for McKivex Company and are writing a consultant's report for a competitor about the manufacturing processes of its competitors. DuPont has a new plant, but the roof has not yet been built over it. You want to learn about the process without getting sued.

Can you take aerial photographs of the plant? Can you go through the garbage cans on the company's grounds looking for information that would describe the process? What if the garbage was already at the city dump?

Can you interview the manufacturing manager on the telephone and write in your report whatever she says?

What if you did consulting for duPont and knew the process—could you then include it in your report for their competitor?

What is ethical?

[*E. I. duPont de Nemours & Co. v. Christopher*, 431 F.2d 1012 (5th Cir. 1970), *cert. denied*, 400 U.S. 1024, 91 S.Ct. 581 (1971)]

5. Virgil Richards conceived a way to regulate the translation of heterologous DNA in bacteria. He worked on this invention with three other people. Richards conceived of the idea in May 1992, reduced it to practice on May 14, 1993, and filed a patent application on June 1, 1994. Richards is being sued by the coinventors for not including their names on the application.

On May 3, 1993, Richards published an article that explained in detail his idea. Clyde Taylor reduced this idea to practice, on May 14, 1993, making only minor changes to the procedure disclosed in the article. He applied for a patent on June 1, 1993.

Can Richards or Taylor obtain a patent for the technology? The process includes some basic scientific principles. Does that mean that both patent applications will be rejected?

[*In Re O'Farrell*, 853 F.2d 894 (Fed. Cir. 1988)]

6. Kristin Diamond enters your office. She has figured out a way to use basic mathematical formulae in a computer program to control the temperature during the molding process of synthetic rubber. She tells you that this new process will revolutionize the industry.

What questions should you ask her, and how can she protect her idea? What are the advantages and disadvantages of filing a patent application? What type of intellectual property protection should she seek?

7. A hypothetical new software product is described below. After reading the product description, think up three trademarks for this product: one that is inherently distinctive; one that is potentially, but not inherently, distinctive; and one that is nondistinctive.

New Product Description

This new software programming language is suited for systems programming, as well as general application programming. Whether you are currently programming in C or Pascal, you will find this new language appropriate for your project. Not only does the system offer high reliability and fast compilation, it also produces code that outperforms all other compilers on the market today. Specific attributes of the system are described in detail below.

The system is easy to learn. If you already know another programming language, then you already know enough of our software to get started.

The system is fast and incorporates the most up-to-date compiler technology. In addition, modules (collections of related procedures and data that implement a well-defined section of a total program) may be compiled separately and saved as object code and later integrated into a complete program.

The system has built-in support for multitasking. It includes a stopwatch, which makes it easy to implement concurrent processes. It also features multiwindowing and multifile editing, resizing and recoloring of windows at any time, program output screen review, pick list for recently used files, personalized commands, hot restart, and interactive or batch operation.

8. Plato Systems designs, manufactures, and sells computer software. In February 1994, Plato received a letter from Titan Computers, a major computer hardware and software manufacturer. In the letter, Titan notified Plato that Titan had begun licensing certain patents relating to computer graphics, attached a list of ten patents, and stated that Titan believed one or more of these patents might be of interest to Plato. Titan's letter offered a patent license at a royalty rate of 1% of Plato's revenues for covered products per patent used, up to a maximum of 3%, plus payment at the same rates for any past infringements of the patents.

Upon review of the ten listed patents, Plato discovered that its Platonic Frames 1.01 program uses a method for manipulating multiple, overlapping windows on a computer display that is substantially the same as a method claimed in one of the patents (the Slick patent). The remaining patents listed in Titan's letter do not appear to cover Plato's current products. The Slick patent was issued on May 1, 1990, based upon an application filed on July 1, 1987. Plato began commercial shipment of Platonic Frames 1.01 in March 1993. However, the same windowing method used in Platonic Frames 1.01 had been used in Plato's earliest product, which was first shipped in September 1989. One of Plato's engineers recalls that the windowing method claimed in the Slick patent was used in an experimental system developed in the mid-1980s by Digilog Corporation, and was described in a technical article by one of Digilog's engineers, published in December 1986.

How should Plato respond to Titan's letter?

9. Sega manufactures video game consoles and cartridges for home entertainment use. Accolade is a competitor in the video cartridge market, but does not manufacture its own consoles. Sega developed a system to protect its trademark rights—the Licensed Trademark Security System (TMSS)—by which the Sega console "reads" a video cartridge for specific computer code. If the video cartridge includes the computer code, it prompts a visual display on the television screen before the game commences, which states "PRODUCED BY OR UNDER LICENSE FROM SEGA." Accolade analyzed Sega's game cartridges using a process known as reverse engineering to figure out which pieces of code were required for compatibility with the Sega console, and developed several video cartridges that include the Sega code necessary for the video game cartridges to be compatible with the Sega console. Because Accolade also copied the TMSS code, however, Accolade's video cartridges prompt the message that the Accolade games are "PRODUCED BY OR UNDER LICENSE FROM SEGA," even though Accolade has no license from Sega to produce compatible video cartridges.

Does Sega have actionable claims against Accolade for the Accolade video game cartridges? What are the claims? Does Accolade have any defense to Sega's claims? If so, what are the defenses? [*Sega Enterprises Ltd. v. Accolade, Inc.*, 977 F.2d 1510 (9th Cir. 1992)]

10. Lewis Galoob Toys developed Game Genie, an add-on product consisting of an application-specific integrated circuit, a ROM, and connectors that attach to the video game cartridge and the control deck for the Nintendo video game console. With the Game Genie, a user can make up to three "wishes" by entering a series of alphabetic codes that will alter the play of the video game cartridge to which it is attached. The effects of the Game Genie are temporary. Once the Game Genie is removed, the video game cartridge plays exactly the way it did before the Game Genie was attached.

Does Nintendo have actionable claims against Lewis Galoob Toys for the Game Genie? What are the claims? Does Lewis Galoob Toys have any defense to Nintendo's claims? If so, what are the defenses? [*Lewis Galoob Toys v. Nintendo of America*, 964 F.2d 965 (9th Cir. 1992)]

UNIT III

HUMAN RESOURCES IN THE LEGAL AND REGULATORY ENVIRONMENT

Chapter 12

THE EMPLOYMENT AGREEMENT

■ Introduction

Employee Rights, Powers, and Protection

The past sixty years have seen an explosion in the number and variety of laws regulating the employment relationship. As a result of the union movement, employees acquired economic and political power in their dealings with employers. With the emergence of the civil rights movement and the antidiscrimination legislation of the 1960s, employers began to examine their hiring and other employment practices more closely with respect to the treatment of women, minorities, and other protected groups.

The courts have developed new doctrines that limit the employer's traditional right to discharge an employee. These judicial decisions have recognized implied contractual obligations to show just cause for a discharge. Indeed, under the current state of the law, an employer may be bound by contracts with its employees without even knowing it.

At the same time, both Congress and state legislatures have enacted legislation protecting all employees in the workplace and regulating the right to discharge employees. With the increasing concern over toxic wastes, for example, many environmental statutes contain provisions prohibiting retaliation against employees who raise concerns about the use of dangerous substances in the workplace. Many states now have whistleblower statutes, which prohibit discharging an employee who has complained to a government agency about working conditions that she believes violate the law. Employers must devote an ever-increasing amount of attention and resources to complying with the sometimes bewildering array of statutes, regulations, and common-law principles that bear upon their relations with their employees.

Chapter Summary

This chapter discusses the traditional rule that employees can be terminated at will, and the exceptions to that rule that have developed in recent years. Drug testing, lie detector tests, and certain hiring practices are also discussed. Chapter 13 describes the major pieces of civil rights legislation that prohibit discrimination. Unionized employees and management-labor relations are discussed in chapter 14.

■ At-Will Employment

Most nonunionized American workers have no written employment contract. They are hired for a job without any express agreement about how long the job will last. For at least the last 100 years, the American rule has been that an employment agreement of indefinite duration is an *at-will contract*; that is, the employee can quit at any time, and the employer can discharge the employee at any time with or without notice. Whether by statute or judicial decision, all states originally followed this rule. The courts reasoned that denying the employer the right to discharge its employee, while the employee was at liberty to quit at any time for any reason, would deprive the employer of property without due process of law. Today, however, the at-will rule has been largely buried under its exceptions.

Employees Not Subject to the Rule

Two groups of employees who generally have not been subject to the at-will rule are public employees and employees who have negotiated express contracts with their employers.

Public Employees Most employees of federal, state, and local government agencies have long worked under civil service or merit systems that provide for tenure, require just cause for discharge, and guarantee administrative procedures to determine whether there is just cause for discharge.

Employees with Contracts A private-sector employee can avoid at-will status by negotiating a contract that provides for a specific term of employment and defines how the contract can be terminated. Persons in professional or managerial positions are more likely to be able to negotiate individual contracts. Other employees must rely on union contracts, which almost universally require just cause for termination and establish arbitration procedures whereby an employee can challenge his discharge.

Statutory Exceptions to the Rule

As the laissez-faire economic philosophy that was the foundation for the at-will rule began to crumble, so did the rule. Civil rights and other federal statutes have limited bad-cause terminations and, with the noteworthy exceptions of New York and several southern states, most states now recognize a variety of circumstances in which an employee may be terminated only for good cause. The sections that follow deal with some of these statutory exceptions to the at-will rule.

> 66
>
> *As the laissez-faire economic philosophy that was the foundation for the at-will rule began to crumble, so did the rule.*

Judicially Created Exceptions

Beginning in the early 1970s, courts in a number of states began to recognize new causes of action for *wrongful discharge,* that is, termination of employment without good cause. These causes of action are based on both contract and tort law. Although some state courts have declined to recognize these exceptions to the at-will doctrine, the trend is toward some level of protection against discharge in certain circumstances. These judicially created exceptions to the at-will rule are discussed in the "Wrongful Discharge" section of this chapter.

■ The National Labor Relations Act

The first and most significant exception to the at-will rule came with the passage of the National Labor Relations Act (NLRA) in 1935. (The NLRA is discussed in detail in chapter 14.) The NLRA made it unlawful for an employer to discharge an employee solely for participating in union activities, complaining about violations of the NLRA, or seeking to exercise any other right guaranteed by the NLRA. In 1937, the United States Supreme Court upheld the constitutionality of that provision. The court held that, although the statute limited the employer's right to discharge while leaving employees free to resign at any time, it nonetheless did not deprive employers of property without due process of law.

Thus, the NLRA substantially altered the traditional right to discharge an employee at will. If an employer discharges a union employee for union activities, the employee has a remedy under the NLRA whereby he can be reinstated and receive back pay for his time off work.

The NLRA also compelled employers to negotiate with unions chosen by their employees, so the employment-at-will relationship was further altered. If the employees chose representation, the employer was required to negotiate with the union about salary and other terms of employment affecting all employees who were eligible to join the union, including those who chose not to join. The employer thus was precluded from negotiating directly with individual employees, whether or not they were union members.

The Employment Act of 1946

Although the Employment Act of 1946 was not, strictly speaking, a statutory exception to at-will employment, it did reflect the interrelationship between economics, politics, and employment law, as described in the following article.[1]

Politicians Cement Ties to Economy, 1946
Even before 1776, economics and politics were the warp and woof of American life. After World War II had ended the Great Depression, Congress decided to formalize the relationship by spelling out Washington's role in running the economy. The Employment Act of 1946 did the spelling out in a masterpiece of sweeping generalities.

In one nonstop sentence, Congress committed the government to use "all practicable means . . . to foster and promote free competitive enterprise and the general welfare." Echoing the spirit, if not the precepts of British economist John Maynard Keynes, the law pledged "useful employment opportunities, including self-employment, production and purchasing power."

Leaving future politicians a free hand with phrases such as "all practicable means," the legislators did make professional economists an integral part of government. The White House got a Council of Economic Advisors and the President was required to submit an annual Economic Report to Congress telling them what he was doing to promote the noble ends of the act. (President Harry Truman named Edwin Nourse, an economist at the Brookings Institution, to head the first three-member council.) Congress itself created a Joint Economic Committee to provide its own expertise.

A generation later, Congress elaborated on the 1946 law with the Full Employment and Balanced Growth Act of 1978. The generalities of the original, however, were left untouched. Just as war was too important to be left to the generals, so the economy was too much to leave to the economists. Economic historian Arthur Menzies Johnson summed up the result when he wrote, presumably with a straight face: "Much depended on the use that an incumbent president chose to make of these new tools."

Wrongful Discharge

Significant inroads on the traditional doctrine of at-will employment have come from judicial decisions as well as legislation. Efforts are underway to draft model, uniform state legislation that would require good cause for any termination and establish an alternative dispute resolution procedure, such as arbitration, to determine whether a termination is justified. Employers would be well advised to consider whether the reasons for any termination will pass muster as "good cause."

The Public-Policy Exception

One of the earliest exceptions to the at-will rule was the *public-policy exception*. Even if an individual is an at-will employee, the employer is prohibited from discharging the employee for a reason that violates public policy. The greatest protection is given to an employee discharged due to a refusal to commit an unlawful act, such as perjury, at the employer's request. Indeed, an employer's request that an employee violate either a criminal statute or a legislative enactment, or even statutes that are not criminal, is almost always deemed against public policy and thus not a valid ground for discharge. The following case provides an example of the public-policy exception, and also illustrates what remedies may be available to an employee discharged contrary to public policy.

---

1. *The Wall Street Journal*, June 28, 1990. Reprinted by permission of *The Wall Street Journal*, © 1990 Dow Jones & Company, Inc. All Rights Reserved Worldwide.

■ **A Case in Point:**   **Summary**

Case 12.1
TAMENY v. ATLANTIC
RICHFIELD COMPANY
Supreme Court of California
27 Cal.3d 167, 164 Cal.Rptr.
839, 610 P.2d 1330 (Cal. 1980).

FACTS   Gordon Tameny sued his former employer, the oil company Atlantic Richfield, claiming that he was discharged after 15 years because he refused to participate in an illegal scheme to fix retail gasoline prices. He contended that his discharge was tortious, not merely a breach of contract, and that he was therefore entitled to punitive damages. The employer conceded that an individual who had been fired for refusing to perform an illegal act could recover from his former employer for wrongful discharge. However, it argued that, because of the contractual nature of the employer-employee relationship, an injury imposed by improper termination of the relationship gives rise only to a breach-of-contract action. (This distinction is critical. Damages for breach of a contract are limited to economic or property losses such as lost salary and benefits. However, if the wrongful act is found to be a tort—that is, a wrong committed against the person—the plaintiff is also entitled to damages for pain and suffering and perhaps punitive damages.) The trial court agreed with the employer and dismissed Tameny's tort claims. Tameny appealed.

ISSUE PRESENTED   May an employee maintain both tort and contract actions if the employee's discharge violates fundamental principles of public policy?

SUMMARY OF OPINION   The California Supreme Court stated that there had never been an "absolute or totally unfettered right to discharge even an at-will employee." Public policy prohibits discharging someone because he refuses to perform an unlawful act.

The court rejected Atlantic Richfield's argument that Tameny's claim was one solely for breach of contract. It found that the obligation not to discharge an employee for refusal to commit a crime does not depend upon promises set forth in an employment contract, "but rather reflects a duty imposed by law upon all employers in order to implement the fundamental public policies embodied in the state's penal statutes. As such, a wrongful discharge suit exhibits the classic elements of a tort cause of action," and entitles the successful plaintiff to tort remedies.

RESULT   Employee Tameny could sue under both contract and tort theories. As a result, damages for pain and suffering and possibly punitive damages would be available.

Many other state courts have recognized public-policy exceptions to the doctrine of at-will employment. For example, in Michigan, the discharge of an employee for refusal to manipulate the sampling results for state pollution reports was held to give rise to a tort cause of action because it violated public policy.[2]

However, the courts also have shown restraint in defining what constitutes a public policy. The Colorado Court of Appeals found no cause of action for a nurse discharged for refusing to follow an order to reduce overtime in an intensive care ward.[3] The nurse had relied on a licensing statute that required nurses to act in a manner consistent with public health and safety. The court found this statute was not sufficient to constitute a clear statement of a public policy which would justify refusal to obey the order.

---

2. *Trombetta v. Detroit, Toledo and Ironton Railroad Co.*, 81 Mich.App. 489, 265 N.W.2d 385 (1978).

3. *Lampe v. Presbyterian Medical Center*, 41 Colo.App. 465, 590 P.2d 513 (1978).

Similarly, in the case that follows, the California Supreme Court held that an employee could be fired for reporting to his superior that his incoming supervisor was under investigation by the Federal Bureau of Investigation for embezzlement from a former employer.

■ **A Case in Point:**   **In the Language of the Court**

Case 12.2
FOLEY v. INTERACTIVE DATA CORP.
Supreme Court of California
47 Cal.3d 654, 254 Cal.Rptr.
211, 765 P.2d 373 (Cal. 1988).

FACTS Daniel D. Foley, the plaintiff, was a former employee of Interactive Data Corp., a company that markets computer-based decision-support services. When Foley was hired by Interactive Data Corp. in 1976, there was no written agreement putting any limitation on the grounds for which he could be terminated.

For the next nearly seven years Foley received a steady series of salary increases, promotions, bonuses, awards, and superior performance evaluations. Foley said that Interactive's officers made repeated oral assurances of job security so long as his performance remained adequate.

Foley also contended that during his employment, Interactive maintained written "Termination Guidelines" that set forth express grounds for discharge and a mandatory seven-step pretermination procedure. Foley understood that these guidelines applied not only to employees under his supervision, but to him as well. On the basis of these representations, Foley alleged that he reasonably believed Interactive would not discharge him except for good cause, and therefore he refrained from accepting or pursuing other job opportunities.

The event that led to Foley's discharge was a private conversation with his former supervisor, vice president Richard Earnest. During the previous year the defendant had hired Robert Kuhne and subsequently named Kuhne to replace Earnest as Foley's immediate supervisor. Foley learned that Kuhne was at the time under investigation by the Federal Bureau of Investigation for embezzlement from his former employer, Bank of America. (Kuhne later, after Foley's discharge, pleaded guilty in federal court to a felony count of embezzlement.) Foley reported what he knew about Kuhne to Earnest, because he was "worried about working for Kuhne and having him in a supervisory position . . ., in view of Kuhne's suspected criminal conduct." Foley asserted he "made this disclosure in the interest and for the benefit of his employer," allegedly because he believed that because Interactive and its parent company, Chase Manhattan Bank, do business with the financial community on a confidential basis, the company would have a legitimate interest in knowing about a high executive's alleged prior criminal conduct.

In response, Earnest reportedly told Foley not to discuss "rumors" and to "forget what he heard" about Kuhne's past. Two months later Kuhne informed Foley that Interactive had decided to replace him for "performance reasons", and that he could transfer to a position in another division in another city, Waltham, Massachusetts. Foley was told that if he did not accept a transfer, he might be demoted but not fired. One week later, in Waltham, Earnest informed Foley he was not doing a good job, and six days later, he notified Foley he could continue as branch manager if he "agreed to go on a 'performance plan.'" Foley asserted he agreed to consider such an arrangement. The next day, when Kuhne met with Foley, purportedly to present him with a written "performance plan" proposal, Kuhne instead informed Foley he had the choice of resigning or being fired. Kuhne offered neither a performance plan nor an option to transfer to another position.

ISSUE PRESENTED   May an employee who was fired after reporting another employee's alleged criminal conduct successfully sue his former employer under a tort theory, arguing that his firing was against public policy?

OPINION   LUCAS, C.J., writing for the California Supreme Court:

. . . .

. . . [T]he employer's right to discharge an "at will" employee is . . . subject to limits imposed by public policy, since otherwise the threat of discharge could be used to coerce employees into committing crimes, wrongdoing, or taking other action harmful to the public weal.

. . . .

In the present case, plaintiff alleges that defendant discharged him in "sharp derogation" of a substantial public policy that imposes a legal duty on employees to report relevant business information to management. An employee is an agent, and as such "is required to disclose to [his] principal all information he has relevant to the subject matter of his agency."[4] Thus, plaintiff asserts, if he discovered information that might lead his employer to conclude that an employee was an embezzler, and should not be retained, plaintiff had a duty to communicate that information to his principal.

. . . .

Whether or not there is a statutory duty requiring an employee to report information relevant to his employer's interest, we do not find a substantial public policy prohibiting an employer from discharging an employee for performing that duty. Past decisions recognizing a tort action for discharge in violation of public policy seek to protect the public, by protecting the employee who refuses to commit a crime, who reports criminal activity to proper authorities, or who discloses other illegal, unethical, or unsafe practices. No equivalent public interest bars the discharge of the present plaintiff. When the duty of an employee to disclose information to his employer serves only the private interest of the employer, the rationale underlying the *Tameny*[5] cause of action is not implicated.

. . . .

RESULT   The court held that Foley's cause of action for a breach of public policy pursuant to *Tameny* was properly dismissed by the appellate court because the facts alleged, even if proven, would not establish a discharge in violation of public policy. However, the court held that Foley could proceed with his cause of action alleging a breach of an implied contract promise to discharge him only for good cause. (Implied contracts are discussed later in this chapter.)

COMMENTS   In *Gantt v. Sentry Insurance*,[6] the California Supreme Court went one step further and held that the *Tameny* cause of action for retaliatory discharge giving rise to tort remedies applied only to claims predicated on public policy expressed in a statute or constitutional provision.

---

4. 2 Witkin, Summary of Cal. Law Agency & Employment, § 41, 53 (9th ed. 1987).
5. *Tameny v. Atlantic Richfield Co.,* 27 Cal.3d 167, 178, 164 Cal.Rptr. 839, 610 P.2d 1330 (Cal. 1980).
6. 1 Cal.4th 1083, 4 Cal.Rptr. 2d 874, 824 P.2d 680 (Cal. 1992).

*Case **12.2** continued on following page*

Case 12.2 continued

Questions
1. Would the court have decided this case differently if Foley had reported to a supervisor that Kuhne was embezzling from Interactive Data?
2. Was the conduct of employer Interactive Data ethical?

A body of law related to that governing retaliation for refusing to commit an illegal act recognizes a tort cause of action for discharge in retaliation for exercising a statutory right or privilege. For example, an employee claimed he was discharged by the Central Indiana Gas Company for filing a worker's compensation claim.[7] Although there was no state statute that prohibited such a discharge, the Indiana Supreme Court recognized a tort cause of action for retaliatory discharge. In another case, an employee of Firestone Tire and Rubber Company was discharged for refusing to take a lie detector test; a Pennsylvania statute prohibited employers from requiring such tests.[8] The U.S. Court of Appeals for the Third Circuit found that the termination gave rise to a tort claim—not just a claim under the statute—because the statute represented a public policy.

Employees who are discharged for carrying out important civic duties are also usually protected by the courts under the public-policy doctrine. An example of a case involving a civic duty is one in which an employee was fired for participation in jury duty activities.[9] In *Nees v. Hocks* the Oregon Supreme Court reasoned that jury duty was an important civic duty and that the will of the community and the effectiveness of the jury system would be thwarted if employers were allowed to discharge employees for fulfilling such an obligation.

This judicially created cause of action for discharge contrary to public policy exists alongside specific statutory provisions that prohibit retaliatory discharge. For example, the National Labor Relations Act prohibits discharge for union activities or for filing charges under the act.[10] The Fair Labor Standards Act of 1938 prohibits discharge for exercising rights guaranteed by the minimum-wage and overtime provisions of that act.[11] The Occupational Health and Safety Act prohibits discharge of employees in retaliation for exercising rights under the act, such as complaining about work procedures or about health and safety violations in the workplace.[12] Many state acts contain similar provisions.[13]

A more recent development has been the adoption of whistleblower statutes (discussed in chapter 1), which prohibit employers from discharging or retaliating against an employee who has exercised the right to complain to a supervisor or government agency.

An example of a state statute protecting private-sector whistleblowers is that of New York.[14] The pertinent portion of the statute reads:

An employer shall not take any retaliatory personnel action against an employee because such employee does any of the following:

(a) discloses, or threatens to disclose to a supervisor or to a public body an activity, policy or practice of the employer that is in violation of law, rule or regulation which violation creates and presents a substantial and specific danger to the public health or safety;

(b) provides information to, or testifies before, any public body conducting an investigation, hearing or inquiry into any such violation of a law, rule or regulation by such employer; or

(c) objects to, or refuses to participate in any such activity, policy or practice in violation of a law, rule or regulation.

Implied Contracts

The second judicial exception to the at-will rule arises from the willingness of courts to interpret the parties' conduct as implying a contract limiting the employer's right to discharge, even though no written or express oral contract exists. Such a contract is known as an *implied*

---

7. *Frampton v. Central Indiana Gas Co.,* 260 Ind. 249, 297 N.E.2d 425 (Ind. 1973).
8. *Perks v. Firestone Tire and Rubber Co.,* 611 F.2d 1363 (3d Cir. 1979).
9. *Nees v. Hocks*, 272 Or. 210, 536 P.2d 512 (Or. 1975).
10. 29 U.S.C. § 158(a)(1), (3), and (4) (1994).
11. 29 U.S.C. § 215(a)(3), § 216(b) (1994).

12. 29 U.S.C. § 660(c) (1988).
13. *See generally* Daniel P. Westman, *Whistleblowing: The Law of Retaliatory Discharge* (1991).
14. N.Y. Labor Law § 740 (McKinney 1989).

contract. Some of the factors that can give rise to an implied obligation to discharge the employee only for good cause are that: (1) she had been a long-term employee; (2) she had received raises, bonuses, and promotions throughout her career; (3) she was assured that her employment would continue if she did a good job; (4) she had been assured before by the company's management that she was doing a good job; (5) the company had stated that it did not terminate employees at her level except for good cause; and (6) she had never been formally criticized or warned about her conduct. Other relevant factors include the personnel policies or practices of the employer and the practices of the industry in which the employee is engaged.

A personnel manual, together with oral assurances, can give rise to a reasonable expectation that an employee will not be terminated except for good cause, as was demonstrated in the following case.

■ **A Case in Point:**   **Summary**

Case 12.3
TOUSSAINT v. BLUE CROSS & BLUE SHIELD OF MICHIGAN
Supreme Court of Michigan
408 Mich. 579, 292 N.W.2d 880 (Mich. 1980).

FACTS   Charles Toussaint was discharged from a middle management position after five years with the medical insurer Blue Cross and Blue Shield of Michigan. He sued his former employer, claiming that his firing violated his employment agreement, which permitted discharge only for cause. Blue Cross contended that Toussaint was hired for an indefinite time and could therefore be discharged at will.

Toussaint testified that he had been told that he would be with the company as long as he did his job properly. Moreover, he had been given a personnel manual which stated that it was the policy of the company to release employees "for just cause only."

ISSUE PRESENTED   Does a provision in a personnel manual that an employee shall not be discharged except for cause, together with statements that the employee will be retained as long as he did his job properly, prevent termination at will?

SUMMARY OF OPINION   The Michigan Supreme Court found for Toussaint. It held that there could be a contractual obligation binding on the employer without negotiations or any meeting of the minds, or even any communication of the policies to the employee. The court stated:

> No pre-employment negotiations need take place and the parties' minds need not meet on the subject; nor does it matter that the employee knows nothing of the particulars of the employer's policies and practices or that the employer may change them unilaterally. It is enough that the employer chooses, presumably in its own interest, to create an environment in which the employee believes that, whatever the personnel policies and practices, they are established and official at any given time, purport to be fair, and are applied consistently and uniformly to each employee. The employer has then created a situation "instinct with an obligation."

RESULT   Employee Toussaint could not be terminated without just cause since he had, due to the personnel manual and statements of his employer, a legitimate expectation that he would not be fired except for just cause.

COMMENTS   Although few courts have been willing to go as far as the Supreme Court of Michigan went in *Toussaint,* some courts have agreed that a personnel manual given to employees may give rise to contract obligations. The Oklahoma Court of Appeals held that the manual constitutes an

*Case **12.3** continued on the following page*

*Case **12.3** continued*

offer of terms and conditions, and the employee's continuing to work is deemed an acceptance of the offer.[15]

---

15. *Langdon v. Saga Corp.*, 569 P.2d 524 (Okla. Ct. App. 1976).

Other courts have been unwilling to treat written personnel policies as contracts. For example, an employee of Citibank claimed the right not to be discharged except for cause, basing this claim on provisions of a personnel manual. A New York appellate court rejected this claim and held that the manual did not create any legal obligation upon the employer because the employee was still free to terminate the relationship at will.[16] Likewise, in a case involving Westinghouse Electrical Corporation, the North Carolina Court of Appeals held that unilaterally

implemented employment policies are not part of the employment contract unless expressly included in it.[17]

Implied Covenant of Good Faith

The third prong in the developing law of wrongful discharge is the recognition of an *implied covenant of good faith and fair dealing* in the employment relationship. This covenant is discussed generally in chapter 8; the following case demonstrates its application in the employment context.

---

16. *Edwards v. Citibank, N.A.*, 74 A.D.2d 553, 425 N.Y. S.2d 327, *appeal dismissed*, 51 N.Y.2d 875, 433 N.Y.S.2d 1020, 414 N.E.2d 400 (1980).

17. *Walker v. Westinghouse Electrical Corp.*, 77 N.C.App. 253, 335 S.E.2d 79 (N.C. Ct. App. 1985).

■   **A Case in Point:**   **Summary**

Case 12.4
FORTUNE v. NATIONAL CASH REGISTER CO.
Supreme Judicial Court of Massachusetts
373 Mass. 96, 364 N.E.2d 1251 (Mass. 1977).

FACTS   Orville Fortune was discharged by the National Cash Register Company after 25 years of service. He sued for wrongful discharge. A jury found that the real reason for the discharge was to deprive Fortune of nearly $46,000 in commissions.

ISSUE PRESENTED   Does termination of an employee to deprive him of a commission violate the implied covenant of good faith and fair dealing?

SUMMARY OF OPINION   The Massachusetts Supreme Judicial Court found that, even though Fortune's written contract stated that his employment was at will, the contract contained an implied good-faith requirement. Termination that was not in good faith constituted a breach of contract. The court limited Fortune to contract remedies. It declined to decide whether all at-will employment contracts contain such an implied covenant.

RESULT   Employee Fortune could recover for breach of contract.

Courts in Texas, New Mexico, Florida, and Wisconsin have expressly declined to recognize an implied covenant of good faith and fair dealing in employment cases. California, like Massachusetts, recognizes such an implied covenant but provides only contract remedies for

breach of the implied covenant; tort remedies like pain and suffering and punitive damages are not available.[18]

---

18. *Foley v. Interactive Data Corp.*, 47 Cal.3d 654, 254 Cal.Rptr. 211, 765 P.2d 373 (Cal. 1988).

■ Fraudulent Inducement

During difficult economic times, a business may engage in puffery and exaggeration to keep and attract highly qualified personnel. The following case serves as a warning that a company may be held liable for overzealous sales pitches under a theory of fraudulent inducement.

■ A Case in Point: In the Language of the Court

Case 12.5
STEWART v. JACKSON & NASH
United States Court of Appeals for the Second Circuit
976 F.2d 86 (2d Cir. 1992).

FACTS   Victoria A. Stewart was an attorney who was employed in the environmental law department of a New York law firm. In October 1988, Ronald Herzog, a partner of the law firm Jackson & Nash, contacted Stewart regarding employment at his firm. Herzog allegedly represented to Stewart that Jackson had recently secured a large environmental law client, that Jackson was in the process of establishing an environmental law department, and that Stewart would head the environmental law department and be expected to service the firm's substantial existing environmental law client.

Stewart accepted employment at Jackson and, upon her arrival, was primarily assigned general litigation matters. Herzog repeatedly assured her that the promised environmental work would be forthcoming and consistently advised her that she would be promoted to a position as head of Jackson's environmental law department. Finally, in May 1990, a Jackson & Nash partner allegedly informed Stewart that Jackson never had environmental work, nor had it secured an environmental law client. Jackson & Nash dismissed Stewart on December 31, 1990.

Stewart filed suit on April 11, 1991, alleging that Jackson & Nash fraudulently induced her to enter into and remain in its employment. The district court dismissed Stewart's claim for failure to state a claim upon which relief could be granted. Stewart appealed.

OPINION   WALKER, J., on behalf of the U.S. Court of Appeals:

. . . .

The district court found that Stewart's fraud claim arose from her termination from the firm and dismissed [the fraudulent inducement claim] on the authority of *Murphy v. American Home Prod. Corp.*[19] *Murphy* held that because at-will employees "may be freely terminated . . . at any time for any reason or even for no reason," they can neither challenge their termination in a contract action nor "bootstrap" themselves around this bar by alleging that the firing was in some way tortious. Following *Murphy,* the court concluded that Stewart, an at-will employee, could not state a fraud claim based on facts arising out of her termination.

We find *Murphy* distinguishable. In *Murphy,* the plaintiff, an at-will employee of the defendant, claimed that he had been fired in a tortious manner. He alleged his firing was deliberately and viciously insulting, was designed to and did embarrass and humiliate the plaintiff and was intended to and did cause plaintiff severe mental and emotional distress thereby damaging

---

19. *Murphy v. American Home Products Corp.*, 58 N.Y.2d 293, 461 N.Y.S.2d 232, 448 N.E.2d 86 (N.Y. 1983).

Case 12.5 continued on the following page

*Case **12.5** continued*

plaintiff. These tort allegations, springing as they do directly from the termination itself, are a transparent attempt to restate the forbidden contractual challenge in the guise of tort.

Stewart's alleged injuries, on the other hand, commenced well before her termination and were, in several important respects, unrelated to it. According to the complaint, Jackson & Nash's misrepresentations caused Stewart, a budding environmental lawyer, to leave a firm with an environmental practice and spend two years in one in which she was largely unable to work in her chosen specialty. The resulting damage to her career development was independent of her later termination from Jackson & Nash and began while she was still at the firm. As she stated in her complaint, Stewart's "career objectives—continuing to specialize in environmental law—was thwarted and grossly undermined during her employment with Jackson." Although *Murphy* precludes an award of damages for injuries caused by her termination, it does not prevent her from recovering for injuries that resulted from her reliance on false statements.

. . . .

In this case Jackson & Nash's declarations that it "had recently secured a large environmental law client" and "was in the process of establishing an environmental law department" were not future promises but representations of present fact. . . . [T]hese representations support a claim for fraudulent inducement which is distinct and separable from any contract action.

. . . [Stewart] asserts that Jackson & Nash informed her that she "would be promoted to a position as head of Jackson's environmental law department . . . [although], upon information and belief, at the time Jackson made the aforesaid representations to Stewart, it knew that it did not intend to make her the head of the environmental law department." While [this] representation . . . appears, initially, to be a future promise (Stewart would be made head of the department), the New York Court of Appeals has explained that while mere promissory statements as to what will be done in the future are not actionable, . . . it is settled that, if a promise was actually made with a preconceived and undisclosed intention of not performing it, it constitutes a misrepresentation of material existing fact upon which an action for recission [based on fraudulent inducement] may be predicated. Stewart's assertion that Jackson & Nash, at the time it made the promise, "knew that it did not intend" to fulfill it, makes [the] representation . . . an allegation of present fact which gives rise to a claim of fraudulent inducement.

. . . .

RESULT Stewart may sue for fraudulent inducement. Jackson & Nash's motion to dismiss was denied.

COMMENTS *Stewart* is notable in that it allows certain plaintiffs to proceed with their case even though fired employees in most states are permitted to sue their employers for wrongful termination only under limited circumstances such as breach of a public policy or discrimination. This anomalous result weakens the protection typically afforded employers by the at-will doctrine, which prohibits most suits against employers filed by employees without contracts.

Although *Stewart* involved the hiring practices of a New York law firm, its legal principle is not easily limited to the specific facts of the case. Neal

Brickman, Stewart's lawyer, suggests that the holding may prompt suits by fired employees from several different professions who claim hiring companies deceived them about working conditions. Because many similar claims have been dismissed by courts viewing them as wrongful termination suits in disguise, Brickman sees newfound potential for claims based not on promises about the future but about the circumstances at the firm when the employee was hired.

Questions
1. What is the difference between breach of contract and fraud in the inducement?
2. Why was it necessary for the plaintiff to couch her claim in terms of the tort of fraudulent inducement?

The line between wrongful discharge—which gives rise only to contract damages—and fraud—which is a tort—is not always clear. In *Hunter v. Up-Right, Inc.*[20] the California Supreme Court held in a 4–3 decision that an employee who was induced to resign because he had been falsely told that his job was being eliminated could not state a valid tort claim for fraud. Instead, he was entitled only to contractual damages of $38,013 for constructive wrongful termination. In essence the majority reasoned that because it was not a tort to terminate the employee for no reason, it was not a tort to employ a falsehood to get him to resign. One of the dissenting judges argued that when the employer circumvents the requirement that the employee be discharged only for good cause (by misleading the employee into resigning and concealing its hostility to the employee's contractual rights), then the employer crosses the line from bad faith to outright fraud, and tort liability should attach.

Ethical Consideration

What role should the law play in penalizing an employer who lies to its employee about the reason for termination in order to persuade the employee to resign? What role do ethics play in this situation?

---

20. 6 Cal. 4th 1174, 26 Cal.Rptr. 2d 8, 864 P.2d 88 (Cal. 1993).

■ At-Will Employment and Preemployment Practices

Employers seeking to preserve at-will employment need to consider not only their practices once an employee is hired, but also their preemployment practices.

In some states, it may be difficult to maintain an at-will relationship except by an express contract or by a disclaimer in the employment application or the personnel manual stating that nothing in the employment relationship and no personnel policy or benefit shall create a right to continued employment. However, if such a disclaimer is plainly contrary to the company's stated policy, it may be rejected by a court. For example, a statement on an application form that employment is at will probably will not be upheld if the company's written personnel policy expressly provides that employees will be given progressive discipline and will not be fired without just cause.

Second, if an employer chooses to have a written personnel policy, care should be taken to see that the language expressly reserves those rights that the employer wishes to maintain, especially with respect to discharge. Also, if employees are given handbooks that purport to summarize the official personnel manuals, the handbook and the manuals must be consistent. Otherwise, courts and juries are likely to uphold that policy that is most favorable to the employee.

Third, if an employer chooses to have a policy of progressive discipline, it is essential that supervisors and managers, as well as the human-resources staff, are trained to administer the policy. In particular, they should be trained to document performance problems and to counsel employees about the need to improve.

Fourth, an employer can enter into an agreement with the employee that any dispute shall be subject to arbitration.

Political Perspective

Illegal Immigrant Workers

In the early 1990s, anti-immigrant sentiment in California rose in tandem with the state's unemployment rate. California was not alone; other states, notably Texas and Florida, as well as many counties and localities, claimed to bear a disproportionate share of illegal immigration's burden, because these levels of government provided undocumented workers with many of the public services they received, while the federal government collected their taxes. The states therefore asked the federal government to pay a larger share of the costs and demanded tough measures to stem the flow of illegal immigration into the United States.

Governor Pete Wilson of California lobbied Congress to reimburse California $2.5 billion for the cost of providing education, medical care, and jailing of illegal immigrants.

Wilson also supported the passage of a constitutional amendment to deny U.S. citizenship to children of illegal immigrants. Supporters of the amendment believed it would thwart the thousands of pregnant women who cross over the border to deliver their babies on U.S. soil, where they receive free health care and their children automatically receive U.S. citizenship. The governor also supported the denial of public school education to children of illegal aliens, and the issuance of a tamper-proof identity card to legal residents, so only they can seek jobs and social services.

The California Senate overrode Wilson's veto of a bill to deport illegal immigrant felons from California prisons. The Assembly declined to follow suit. However, on March 1, 1994, a law was enacted that required applicants for California driver's licenses to prove their U.S. citizenship or legal residency.

Critics of Governor Wilson's platform accused him of "immigrant bashing" by refusing to acknowledge the contributions of illegal immigrants. They argue that many illegal immigrants take low-wage service jobs as maids, nannies, and gardeners, and that those who work for companies provide a flexible low-cost labor pool that may keep U.S. firms from relocating overseas.

Governor Wilson argued that state taxes paid by illegal immigrants should not be counted to offset any portion of aid provided by Congress to reimburse California for delivering federally required services to undocumented residents. The Clinton administration disagreed, arguing that the federal government should count revenues generated by illegal immigrants through property, sales, and income taxes to offset the costs of delivering such services.

The Clinton administration's $1.5 trillion budget granted virtually no funds to pay for services to illegal immigrants. The budget did, however, include nearly $3 billion to the state to provide health care and education to indigent Californians, many of whom were illegal immigrants. Wilson and his proponents continued to lobby the federal government for more money. They felt that the government had inadequately addressed the problem. The only issue on which Wilson and the Clinton administration agreed regarding the federal government's role in assisting state governments occurred after the devastating 1994 Los Angeles earthquake, when Congress passed and President Clinton signed an earthquake-aid bill that restricted illegal immigrants to short-term assistance.

An arbitration clause in a fairly negotiated written contract will withstand judicial scrutiny; however, a *boilerplate* clause—that is, standardized, nonnegotiable language—in an employment application form may be found invalid.

Fifth, an employer should decide whether to establish an internal grievance procedure. Such a procedure can result in fewer lawsuits. However, if the employer establishes a grievance procedure, it must be sure to follow it.

Otherwise, the employer may find itself facing claims for failure to follow its own procedure, especially where the procedure is an elaborate one.

The bottom line is that the employer should have in place a system of checks and balances to ensure that the company's policies are properly communicated and followed. Discharges should be well documented and handled in accordance with these policies. Employees should be treated in a fair and consistent manner.

In deciding whether there is an express or implied contractual right not to be fired except for cause, a court may consider statements made during preemployment interviews and on application forms. Consequently, if an employer wants to preserve the traditional legal right to discharge employees at will, it should see that limitations on this right are not inadvertently created.

To illustrate, an application form might include the following language above the employee signature line: "I understand that, if hired, my employment can be terminated with or without cause, at either my employer's or my option." Inclusion of such language reminds the employee that his employment is at will—and verifies that he was so informed—and lessens the likelihood that the employee will be able to establish an implied contractual right to be discharged only for cause. Additionally, no statements should be made during interviews that could create an impression that the applicant would not be fired without good cause. "Employees are never fired from here without good reason," "Your job will be secure, as long as you do your work" and "We treat our employees like family" are examples of such statements. In short, the employer should not mislead an applicant about the security of the job offered.

Recommendations for Former Employees and Self-Publication

Employers are very often asked to give references regarding former employees to prospective employers. An employee always hopes that such a reference will be favorable, but such is not always the case. At any rate, the employee at least hopes that the reference will be fair. If the reference is not fair and an employer defames the reputation of a former employee, the former employee can sue the employer for defamation.

Traditionally, defamation law requires publication, meaning that the communicator of the defamatory information tells the information to a third party, such as a prospective employer. However, some jurisdictions have an interesting exception to this rule in the employment context. Under the *doctrine of self-publication*, a defamatory communication by an employer to an employee may constitute publication when the employer could foresee that the employee would be required to repeat the communication, for instance, to a prospective employer. The doctrine is designed to provide a cause of action to the job-seeking employee who is forced to "self-publicize" the former employer's defamatory statement. So that dis-

International Consideration

Before making a decision to move abroad, a company should check to see that it will have flexibility in its hiring. Many countries have quotas requiring that a certain percentage of a foreign companies' labor force be nationals of the host country. A business should also make sure that its workers can get visas to work abroad.

gruntled former employees will not overuse the doctrine, most jurisdictions require a showing of abuse on the part of the former employer, and some reasonable degree of foreseeability of a compelled future self-publication.

Employee Drug Testing

In the past ten years, there has been increasing public discussion about the abuse of drugs and alcohol in our society and particularly in the workplace. There is a widespread belief that drug and alcohol abuse lead to decreased productivity, quality control problems, absenteeism on the job, accidents, and employee theft. Many employers are adopting drug-screening programs for their employees and applicants. Some employers are using drug testing in conjunction with a comprehensive drug program that includes employee education and assistance to the employee with a drug or alcohol problem.

Even apart from the legal implications, the practical usefulness of drug testing is limited. First, even the most sophisticated tests (which usually involve a urine or blood sample) cannot establish whether the employee was using drugs at any particular time. The tests can detect certain substances in the employee's body, but they do not tell how long the substance has been present. Second, depending on the level of sophistication of the test and the quality of the testing program, the test may produce erroneous results.

"

Even apart from the legal implications, the practical usefulness of drug testing is limited.

The issue of drug testing generally comes before the courts in the context of discipline or discharge of an employee for refusing to take a test. Although there seems to be great public support for drug testing, there is wide divergence in judicial opinions on the subject. Nonetheless, certain trends emerge. Whether testing will be deemed permissible in a particular situation depends on four factors: (1) whether the employer is a public or private employer; (2) any state constitutional guarantees of right to privacy; (3) any state statutes regulating drug testing; and (4) the scope of the testing program.

Because public employees are protected by the U.S. Constitution's Fourth Amendment prohibition against unreasonable searches and seizures, there are greater limitations on testing. It has long been recognized that urine tests and blood tests are a substantial intrusion upon bodily privacy and are therefore searches subject to regulation. With some exceptions, there is no U.S. constitutional limitation on drug testing in the private sector. However, such testing can raise state constitutional issues discussed further below.

As of 1991, 14 states had adopted legislation regarding drug testing by private employers.[21] Such legislation often sets forth the notice procedures an employer must follow before asking an employee to submit to a drug test. For example, in Vermont, the employer must, before administering the test, give the employee a copy of a written policy setting forth the circumstances under which persons may be tested, the drugs that will be

screened, the procedures involved, and the consequences of a positive result. A Vermont employer must also tell the employee that a false positive result can be caused by medications and other substances.

The fourth major factor, scope, concerns who is being tested: all employees (random testing); only employees in a specific job where it is felt there is a legitimate job-related need (for example, nuclear power plant employees); groups of employees (for example, all employees in one facility because there is a general suspicion of drug use within that group); or specific individuals who are believed to be using drugs. The smaller the group to be tested and the more specific the reason for testing, the more likely a court will uphold the test. Random testing is the most difficult to defend.

An employee may challenge the test in many ways. He may claim the test breached his employment contract; that there was no justification for the test; that it violated the public policy that protects privacy; that he was defamed by false accusations of drug use based on an erroneous test; that he suffered emotional distress, especially if the test result was in error; or that the testing disproportionately affects employees of one race or sex and therefore is discriminatory.

Public Employees

The Supreme Court decided two cases in 1989 that provided some guidance regarding the appropriate balance between the need for safety and a public employee's right to be free from an unreasonable search. Both decisions upheld employee drug-testing programs against Fourth Amendment challenges. The first of these cases concerned railroad employees.

---

21. *See generally* Philip E. Berlin, "More State Laws Now Regulate Drug Testing in the Workplace," *The National Law Journal*, July 8, 1991, 19.

■   **A Case in Point:**   **Summary**

Case 12.6
SKINNER v. RAILWAY LABOR EXECUTIVES' ASSOCIATION
Supreme Court of the United States
489 U.S. 602, 109 S.Ct. 1402 (1989).

FACTS   Railway labor organizations brought suit to enjoin Federal Railroad Administration regulations requiring railroads to conduct blood and urine tests on crew members and other covered employees following major train accidents and authorizing railroads to administer breath and urine tests to employees who violate certain safety rules. The regulations, based upon evidence that alcohol and drug abuse by railroad employees had caused or contributed to a number of significant accidents, allow rail employers to test employees even though no reasonable suspicion of drug use exists prior to testing.

ISSUE PRESENTED   Does mandatory drug testing of railroad employees after an accident, and authorized testing of employees who violate certain safety rules, violate the Fourth Amendment?

SUMMARY OF OPINION   The U.S. Supreme Court held that any intrusion upon individual privacy rights in this context is outweighed by the government's compelling interest in ensuring "the safety of the traveling public and of the employees themselves." According to the Supreme Court, a substance-impaired railroad employee in a safety-sensitive job can cause great human loss before any signs of the impairment become noticeable. The regulations provide an effective means of deterring employees from using drugs or alcohol by putting them on notice that they are likely to be discovered if an accident occurs.

An individualized suspicion requirement would impede railroads' ability to obtain valuable information about the causes of accidents and how to protect the public, because it is impracticable to obtain evidence that a particular employee may be impaired. In the chaotic aftermath of an accident it is difficult to determine which employees contributed to the occurrence, and objective indicia of impairment are absent.

The Court also found that rail employees have a diminished expectation of privacy because they are in a pervasively regulated industry.

RESULT   Railroads can be required to test public employees involved in a major train accident and have the authority to test employees who violate certain safety rules.

The second Supreme Court case held that mandatory drug testing of U.S. Customs Service employees in line for transfer or promotion to certain sensitive positions involving drug interdiction or the handling of firearms does not violate their constitutional rights.[22] Although there was no perceived drug problem among customs employees, the Supreme Court held that the program was justified by the need for national security and by the extraordinary safety hazards attendant to the positions involved.

In the wake of these two decisions, the Supreme Court denied review of, and thereby left intact, lower court rulings upholding a variety of employee drug-testing programs. In one case, the Washington Supreme Court had held preemployment drug testing of applicants for repair jobs at nuclear power plants constitutional, on the grounds that the employer had a compelling interest in maintaining safety and the employees had a diminished expectation of privacy in the pervasively regulated field of nuclear power. In another case the lower court had held that mandatory and random drug testing of a police force, as well as other municipal employees, was constitutionally justified by the need for public confidence in

and respect for police officers. In a third case, the lower court had upheld random urinalysis of civilian drug counselors in the Army.

Private Employees

The private employer must also respect employees' right to privacy. In some states there is a right to privacy under tort law or the state constitution. For example, in California, article 1, section 1 of the state constitution specifically guarantees a right to privacy. That right extends to employees of private as well as public entities.

The right to privacy is the right to be left alone. The courts balance this individual right with the competing public interest in public safety and welfare. Because of the nature of drug testing, which usually involves a blood or urine sample and therefore deals with private functions or requires a bodily intrusion, there is little doubt that drug testing raises privacy issues under state law, as it does under federal constitutional law. Therefore, to justify the test, an employer will have to establish a compelling interest, such as a reasonable belief that the individual was using drugs on the job. Even if the employer has good grounds to believe that the employee is using drugs, a court might require the employer to use impairment tests (such as walking a straight line) to determine whether the

---

22. *National Treasury Employees Union v. Von Raab,* 489 U.S. 656, 109 S.Ct. 1384 (1989).

employee is actually impaired on the job, rather than blood or urine tests, which determine only whether a substance has been ingested at some recent time.

A state constitution's guarantee of privacy was applied to the drug testing of a private employee in the following case.

■ **A Case in Point:**   **Summary of Opinion**

Case 12.7
LUEDTKE v. NABORS ALASKA DRILLING, INC.
Supreme Court of Alaska
768 P.2d 1123 (Alaska 1989).

FACTS   Clarence and Paul Luedtke were both employees for Nabors Alaska Drilling, Inc., a private employer. Both were fired after refusing to submit to urinalysis screenings for drug use.

During Paul's employment with Nabors, he was accused twice of violating the company's drug and alcohol policies. Once he was suspended for 90 days for taking alcohol to one of the drilling rig sites. The other incident involved a search of the rig on which Paul worked. Aided by dogs trained to sniff out marijuana, the searchers found traces of marijuana on Paul's suitcase. Paul was allowed to continue working on the rig only after assuring his supervisors he did not use marijuana.

In October 1982 Paul scheduled a two-week vacation. Because his work schedule was that of two weeks on followed by one week off, Paul's vacation amounted to 28 consecutive days away from work. Just prior to his vacation Paul was instructed to arrange for a physical examination. He arranged for it to take place during his vacation. It was at this examination that Nabors first tested Paul's urine for signs of drug use. The purpose of the physical, as understood by Paul, was to enable him to work on offshore rigs should Nabors receive such contracts. He had no idea a urinalysis screening test for drug use would be performed. Nabors's policy of testing for drug use was not announced until the next month, November.

In November a Nabors representative told Paul he was suspended for "the use of alcohol or other illicit substances." Later he was told he had tested positive for cannabinoids. Paul received a letter in mid-November informing him that he would be required to pass two subsequent urinalysis tests, one on November 30 and one on December 30, before he would be allowed to return to work. Paul sent Nabors a letter drafted by his attorney explaining why he felt the testing and suspension were unfair. Paul did not take the urinalysis test on November 30. Nabors then informed Paul that he was discharged for refusal to take the test.

In November 1982 Clarence Luedtke became subject to the Nabors drug use and testing policy. His name appeared on a list of persons scheduled for drug screening. The people listed were required to complete the test during their next "R & R" period. During that next "R & R" period Clarence decided he would not submit to the testing and informed Nabors of his decision.

Nabors offered to allow Clarence time to "clean up" but Clarence refused. He insisted that he thought he could pass the test, but was refusing as "a matter of principle." Nabors then fired Clarence.

ISSUE PRESENTED   Under what circumstances does a state constitution protect citizens from a drug test by a private employer?

SUMMARY OF OPINION   The Alaska Constitution, article I, section 22, contains Alaska's state constitutional right to privacy.

The Alaska Supreme Court first concluded that because there was no state or governmental action involved in this case, the constitutional privacy guarantees did not apply. The court reasoned that the fundamental right to be free from *governmental* intrusions into one's privacy was the basis for the state constitutional guarantee. The court distinguished the Alaska state constitution's right to privacy from that of California, because the history of the adoption of the California guarantee showed a clear intent by the voters that the clause apply to private as well as governmental action.

In considering the Luedtkes' wrongful termination claim, the court reasoned that there must be a balancing between the Luedtkes' and Nabors's interests. The court determined that where the public policy supporting the Luedtkes' privacy in off-duty activities conflicts with the public policy supporting the protection of the health and safety of other workers, as well as the Luedtkes themselves, the health and safety concerns are paramount. Therefore, Nabors was justified in determining whether the Luedtkes are possibly impaired on the job by drug usage off the job.

RESULT   The Alaska state constitution's right to privacy does not apply to private employers and their use of drug testing. Employer Nabors did not wrongfully terminate Clarence and Paul Luedtke.

COMMENTS   In 1994, the California Supreme Court grappled with the issue of drug testing in a private context.[23] A group of Stanford University student athletes sued the National Collegiate Athletic Association (NCAA), claiming that their right to privacy under the California constitution was being violated. The court held that the right to privacy in the California constitution applied to private as well as government action. Nonetheless, the court upheld the NCAA's drug testing program based primarily on the athletes' lack of a reasonable expectation of privacy within the context of collegiate athletics, and on the NCAA's interests in maintaining a drug-free environment. The court left open the question, however, as to whether the NCAA should use a less intrusive method of testing. (Currently NCAA officials view athletes as the athletes urinate.)

In 1990, the California Court of Appeal had held that a nonintrusive pupillary-reaction test given to all employees of Kerr-McGee Corporation at its chemical plant in Trono, California, might violate the California constitution's right to privacy, depending on the intrusiveness of the test and the employer's safety needs.[24] The test consisted of shining a light in the person's eye and observing how much the pupil contracts. Although the court acknowledged that the pupillary test was less intrusive than urine, blood, or breath tests, it held that the trial court needed more facts to determine just how intrusive the test was.

Compared to the NCAA test at issue in *Hill v. NCAA*, the pupillary-reaction test is obviously far less intrusive. What is less clear is how the courts will apply *Hill v. NCAA* in the employment context.

The result in *Hill v. NCAA* may mean that, at least in California, private actors will be given more leeway with drug tests (i.e., the state constitutional privacy right will not be deemed violated) if the persons being tested do not have a reasonable expectation of privacy.

(*Hill v. NCAA* is discussed further in chapter 4.)

23. *Hill v. NCAA*, 7 Cal.4th 1, 26 Cal.Rptr. 2d 834, 865 P.2d 633 (Cal. 1994).
24. *Semore v. Pool,* 217 Cal.App. 3d 1087, 266 Cal.Rptr. 280 (1990).

A number of states have comprehensive drug and alcohol-testing laws that require reasonable suspicion or probable cause before an employer may test. The requirements for establishing reasonable suspicion or probable cause vary from state to state. For instance, Connecticut's law permits testing when "the employer has reasonable suspicion that the employee is under the influence of drugs or alcohol which adversely affects or could adversely affect such employee's job performance."[25] In addition, Connecticut's law prohibits determination of employment status or promotion based on drug testing.[26] Minnesota permits testing when there exists reasonable suspicion that the employee is under the influence, possesses drugs or alcohol on the employer's premises, or has sustained a personal injury or caused a workplace accident.[27] Congress has been reviewing proposed legislation that could set federal standards for drug testing by private businesses. However, as of 1994 no federal standards had been set.

Although it appears that there may be some limit on implementing a drug-testing program for private as well as public employees, it should be noted that employers have the right to make and enforce rules prohibiting drug use or possession of drugs on work premises, as well as rules prohibiting employees from being under the influence of drugs while at work. Where there are visible signs of intoxication or impairment, or inadequate performance, the employer may take disciplinary action. Because of the inadequacy of drug tests and the uncertainty about the scope of employees' rights, the employer may wish to instead focus upon and develop drug-assistance and drug-education programs, and identify and counsel employees about performance problems that may be caused by drug abuse.

Polygraph Testing of Employees

Another area in which employees' right to privacy may limit an employers' investigative rights is that of polygraph testing. The federal Employee Polygraph Protection Act of 1988[28] makes it unlawful for employers to: (1) request an applicant or employee to take a polygraph exam or other lie detector test; (2) rely upon or inquire about the results of a lie detector test that an applicant or employee has taken; (3) take or threaten to take any adverse action against an applicant or employee

because of a refusal to take, or on the basis of the results of, any lie detector test; or (4) take or threaten to take any adverse action against an employee or applicant who has filed a complaint or participated in a proceeding relating to the polygraph law.

The statute does not completely ban the use of polygraph exams. Employers may test employees who are reasonably suspected of workplace theft, as well as applicants or employees in certain businesses involving security services or the handling of drugs. The act does not restrict federal, state, or local government employers from administering polygraph exams.

The Responsible Manager

Avoiding Wrongful Discharge Suits

Many courts appear to be moving toward providing all employees the protection against discharge without good cause that traditionally was offered only by union contracts or by individually negotiated contracts. As a result employers often find themselves in costly litigation, attempting to convince a jury that a discharge was justified. In the light of these developments, an employer needs to develop a human-resource approach that takes into account the statutory rights of employees, its own business needs, and the evolving common law of the state.[29]

An employer can do many things to limit its exposure to unwanted contractual obligations. First, the employer should articulate the kind of contractual relationship it wishes to have with its employees. That relationship may not be the same for every employee or job classification. In some instances it may be appropriate to maintain an at-will relationship. In other cases, the employer may prefer to have a written contract that specifies the terms and conditions of employment, including the circumstances under which the employment relationship may be terminated by either party. If the company has a code of conduct (as discussed in chapter 1), violations of the code may be good cause for termination, particularly if the employee has signed an agreement to comply with it. For example, American Express Company requires each of its approximately 15,000 managers to sign an agreement to abide by the policies set forth in the company's code of conduct (see Exhibit 12-1).

25. Conn. Gen. Stat. Ann. § 31-51x (West Supp. 1993).
26. Conn. Gen. Stat. Ann. § 31-51u(a) (West Supp. 1993).
27. Minn. Stat. Ann. § 181.951 (West 1993).
28. 29 U.S.C. §§ 2001-2009 (1988).

29. *See* Jeffrey Pfeffer, *Competitive Advantage Through People* (1994), 137–48.

EXHIBIT 12-1   Excerpt from American Express Company's Code of Conduct. *Used by permission.*

AGREEMENT

In consideration of my employment by American Express Company or one of its subsidiary corporations (hereinafter the "Company"), I understand that my conduct as an employee is expected to comply at all times with the highest ethical business standards. I have read the Code of Conduct as set forth in the appendix hereto, and I agree to abide by the terms of the policies set forth herein. In addition, I hereby specifically agree that:

   (A) I will comply with the Company's policies set forth in the Business Ethics section of the Code of Conduct.

   (B) Except as set forth below, I have no agreements with, or obligations to, others in violation of the Company's policy on Conflicts of Interest as set forth in the Code of Conduct.

   (C) Except as my duties during my employment may require or as a duly authorized senior officer of the Company may otherwise consent in writing, I will abide by the Company's policy on Proprietary Information and Trade Secrets that appears in the Code of Conduct.

   (D) I have read the Company's policy regarding Compliance with Laws and Regulations and I agree to abide by it.

   (E) I have read the Company's policy on Improper Payments and I agree to abide by it.

   (F) I have read the Company's policy on Trading in Company Securities and I agree to abide by it.

My obligations to abide by these policies may not be changed or modified, released, discharged, abandoned or terminated, in whole or in part, except by an instrument in writing signed by a duly authorized senior officer of the Company. I further understand that my obligation to abide by these policies is an ongoing one and I agree to promptly disclose to the Secretary any exceptions to or potential conflicts with this Agreement that may arise subsequent to signing this Agreement. Neither this Agreement nor the Code of Conduct is meant to vary or supersede the regular terms and conditions of my employment by the Company or to constitute an employment contract.

Inside Story

Employer Mandate for Health Care

The 1,324-page Clinton administration health plan submitted to Congress in 1994 provided a mandate that employers provide health care coverage for their employees, a mandate built on some of the elements of our existing system.

The relationship between health care and employment in the United States began during World War II. Although the War Labor Board placed a cap on salaries, it allowed wartime employers to attract workers through fringe benefits, one of which was health care. The number of Americans in group hospital plans increased from less than 5 million in 1941 to 26 million by the end of the war. Over the next two decades, many companies began to provide health insurance for their employees.

Since then, three presidents—Nixon, Carter and Clinton—have advocated a national scheme of universal coverage based on the existing American system, in which more than 50% of Americans have received health insurance through their employers. Each plan would require employers to provide a basic package of benefits for their employees.

However, some smaller companies and those that pay low wages protested that they cannot afford to provide such coverage. It is at these companies where the majority of the nation's uninsured people work.

Inside Story continued on following page

Inside Story, continued

According to the Clinton administration, most of the costs of the new plan would be covered by savings generated from the revamping of the current system. However, the administration also considered raising taxes on cigarettes and liquor to generate $10 billion to pay for long-term care for the elderly. President Clinton also stated that the mandate requiring all employers to pay 80% of employees' health insurance costs would be phased in over five to seven years. All employers would be given several years notice before the legislation took effect, and a government subsidy would limit the health care cost for businesses employing four workers or fewer to no more than 3.6% of their payrolls. The payment for larger firms would rise to a maximum of 7%.

Small-business lobbyists opposed an employer health insurance mandate. They argued that an insurance mandate would be a "job-buster" for firms that could least afford it. Because small employers often struggle on thin profit margins, having to pay for health care might force them to reduce salaries.

Critics of the Clinton plan also claimed that it would have a devastating effect on mom-and-pop businesses, which often provide low-paying jobs without health benefits. Economists for and against the Clinton plan argued that low-paid workers would be the most at risk because employers would find it particularly uneconomical to pay $5,000 in annual health care costs for a worker who makes $10,000 a year.

Proponents of the plan claimed that the plan could increase jobs by delivering financial relief to employers. For instance, companies employing high-wage workers and currently providing health care for their employees could gain broader coverage or see a reduction in their health care costs.

The American Medical Association (AMA) dropped its support for the employer mandate after pressure was applied by the National Federation of Independent Business (NFIB). Although the AMA embraced mandates as a way of ensuring coverage for every American, many doctors were uneasy because of their own role as employers. According to the AMA, only two-thirds of its members insure their employees.

A further blow to the Clinton plan occurred when the Business Roundtable chose to support the Managed Competition Act, sponsored by Rep. Jim Cooper (D-Tenn). This act required employers to offer insurance to their employees, but not necessarily to pay for any portion of it. The act excluded two controversial elements of the Clinton plan: price controls on insurance premiums and the employer mandate. Instead, it relied on insurance purchasing pools for small businesses and individuals, and subsidies for the low-income uninsured.

The key to the Managed Competition Act was that it would offer universal access to everyone, even for the unemployed and those whose employers did not provide coverage. The Cooper bill was not as all-encompassing as the Clinton plan, however. In particular, participation would be mandatory only for companies with fewer than 100 employees; under the Clinton plan, participation would be mandatory for companies with fewer than 5,000 employees. Also, companies were required under the Clinton plan to pay 80% of the cost of their employees' coverage; under Cooper's proposal, companies were not required to contribute, only to make coverage available through the alliances. The drawback of Cooper's plan was that although coverage was made more accessible and affordable, it would not cover everyone because it would be up to the individual to buy it.

The Clinton plan also raised questions regarding the definition of an employee. Under the plan, businesses would have to provide at least two-thirds of the health insurance premiums for their employees. However, they would not have to pay the premiums for independent contractors, who would have to pay their own health insurance premiums. The plan did, however, provide independent contractors with federal subsidies to reduce their costs and allow them to deduct the costs from their taxes. In addition, independent contractors would pay premiums to a regional health alliance, just as they would pay taxes to the IRS. Such payments would be easier to collect than individual checks for independent contractors.

Congress recessed for the November 1994 elections without acting on Clinton's plan.

Key Words and Phrases

Questions and Case Problems

1. Dr. Grace Pierce, a medical researcher at Ortho Pharmaceutical Corporation, was an at-will employee. She was the only medical doctor on a team working on the development of the therapeutic drug loperamide. The Ortho formulation of loperamide contained saccharin. Eventually, the development process would require human testing. Human testing would not begin, however, until the Food and Drug Administration (FDA) approved the formulation of the drug.

Pierce objected to Ortho's continuing efforts to develop loperamide using a formulation containing saccharin. She argued that because saccharin might be harmful, the drug should not be tested on humans. After informing her supervisor that she felt she would be violating the Hippocratic oath by continuing to work on the loperamide project, she was reassigned to a different project. Shortly thereafter, Pierce resigned, believing that her unwillingness to work on loperamide had resulted in her effective demotion. She then sued Ortho for wrongful discharge.

Assuming that Ortho induced Pierce's resignation, should she prevail? Discuss the merits of her claim with reference to the public-policy exception to the doctrine of at-will employment. [*Pierce v. Ortho Pharmaceutical Corp.*, 84 N.J. 58, 417 A.2d 505 (N.J. 1980)]

2. In March 1983, 43-year-old Peter Barnes read an ad in the *Chicago Tribune* that Pentrix was seeking experienced word processors to work in its Chicago office. Pentrix is a national corporation specializing in the design and manufacture of hand-held computers. The ad stated that Pentrix was looking for "experienced word processors seeking a career in a stable and growing company." On March 8, 1983, Barnes interviewed with Renee Thompson, the head of Pentrix's word processing department in Chicago. Thompson was impressed with Barnes's prior experience and reassured him that although Pentrix is a national corporation, the employees in Pentrix are like a family and look after one another. Thompson offered Barnes a job at the end of the interview, and Barnes began work on March 15, 1983.

Barnes received an updated policy manual from the personnel department every year that he worked for Pentrix. In addition to discussing such things as vacation, salary, and benefits, the policy manual described Pentrix's progressive discipline system.

Pentrix's progressive discipline system consisted of three basic steps. First, an employee's supervisor must discuss the employee's deficiencies with the employee and suggest ways for the employee to improve his work performance. Second, the employee must receive written notice of his poor performance with suggestions of how the employee's performance can improve. Third, the employee must receive a written warning that if the employee does not improve his performance he will be terminated.

The manual provides that in cases of "material misconduct" a supervisor has the discretion to decide whether to follow the progressive discipline procedures. The policy manual also provided that Pentrix has complete discretion to decide who will be discharged in the event of a company layoff. In 1985, the following language was added to the policy manual:

> These policies are simply guidelines to management. Pentrix reserves the right to terminate or change them at any time or to elect not to follow them in any case. Nothing in these policies is intended or should be understood as creating a contract of employment or a guarantee of continued employment with Pentrix. Employment at Pentrix remains terminable at the will of either the employee or Pentrix at any time for any reason or for no reason.

Barnes signed an acknowledgment of receipt of the 1985 policy manual.

Barnes received several good performance reviews during the time he worked at Pentrix. On a few occasions, Thompson discussed with Barnes the importance of arriving at work on time, but no record was kept of the times that Barnes was late. Thompson noted in Barnes's 1991 and 1992 performance evaluations that Barnes should proofread his work more carefully.

In 1992, Barnes received an offer to work as a word processor for Lintog, another computer manufacturing corporation in Chicago. Barnes discussed this offer with Thompson. Thompson persuaded Barnes to remain at Pentrix by suggesting that Barnes might be promoted to day-shift word processing supervisor when the current day-shift supervisor resigned. The day-shift supervisor has yet to resign from Pentrix.

Barnes was discharged from Pentrix on September 1, 1994. Thompson told Barnes that he was being fired because Pentrix was experiencing a slowdown and that two word processors were being let go in each of Pentrix's 20 offices across the country. Thompson wrote on the separation notice placed in Barnes's personnel file that Barnes was being discharged as a result of a work force reduction. Before leaving Pentrix on September 1, Barnes saw David George, Pentrix's vice president of computer design, getting into his car. George said to Barnes, "Too bad about your job, but maybe this will teach you to stop leaking our computer designs to other companies."

Barnes had trouble sleeping and felt depressed after being fired from Pentrix. He waited three weeks before he began looking for another job. He then submitted an application to Lintog Corporation, the company that had offered him a job in 1992. Rob Grey, the head of the word processing department at Lintog, called Renee Thompson at Pentrix to find out why Barnes had left. Thompson responded that Barnes worked in Pentrix's word processing department for more than ten years and was discharged as a result of a slowdown. Barnes interviewed with Grey on September 28, 1994. During the interview, Grey asked Barnes why he had left his job at Pentrix. Barnes responded that although he was officially told that he was being discharged because of a reduction in force, he was fired because he was wrongly suspected of leaking the corporation's computer designs. Barnes was not hired by Lintog.

What claims might Barnes bring against Pentrix, Inc.?

3. Assume the same facts as in question 2. If you were investigating whether Barnes could sue Pentrix, what information would you want to know?

4. Assume the same facts as in question 2. What damages might Barnes be entitled to recover?

5. Frank Deus was an agent for Allstate Insurance Co. in its Jackson, Mississippi, region from 1968 until August 1987, when he suffered a nervous breakdown which rendered him unable to work. He now suffers from severe tinnitus (ringing in the ears) and depression. He claims that Allstate intentionally inflicted emotional distress upon him, causing his breakdown.

Throughout his nineteen years with Allstate, Deus was a Company Office Agent (COA). His status as a COA was established through an employment agreement with Allstate. The agreement stated that Allstate could not terminate Deus for unsatisfactory work unless it first gave him notice, pursuant to a multi-phase procedure to determine that his work was unsatisfactory and that his job was in jeopardy.

In 1984 Allstate fired 20% of the managers in Deus's office and brought in a number of new people. There was evidence that these changes increased tension for everyone in that office. But there was no indication that Deus was the only agent affected or that the changes were made with the intent of causing anyone emotional distress. Three years later, after his work performance declined due to his tinnitus, and after being placed on probation, Deus was fired.

Deus claims that he was wrongfully terminated. Does he have a valid claim? What will be Allstate's defense? [*Deus v. Allstate Insurance Co.*, 15 F.3d 506 (5th Cir. 1994)]

6. On October 15, 1984, George Anderson was hired by Electronic Data Systems Corp. (EDS) for a managerial position in the Domestic Treasury Department of EDS. From October 1984 to October 1985, Anderson served as the cash manager in the Domestic Treasury Department, where his responsibilities included management of all cash operations, short-term invest-

ments, cash forecasting, and related information systems, plus consulting with various groups within the EDS system.

In October 1985, Anderson was promoted to the position of Manager of Investments and Debt in the Domestic Treasury Department. In that position, Anderson had responsibilities for all domestic short- and long-term investments and for all pension portfolios, corporate portfolios, and Title IX portfolios. In this position, Anderson was charged with the responsibility of administering investment assets totaling approximately $1.3 billion. The petition alleges that he was demoted and discharged for his refusal to commit illegal acts and for reporting the activities of another employee, Douglas Crow. It asserts that Anderson was asked by Crow to commit certain illegal acts.

Anderson refused to commit these acts and reported these incidents and other improper conduct by Crow to management. Anderson asserts a cause of action for wrongful discharge, on the theory that under Texas law employment-at-will contracts cannot be terminated because of an employee's refusal to commit illegal acts. Will Anderson prevail? [*Anderson v. Electronic Data Systems Corp.*, 11 F.3d 1311 (5th Cir. 1994)]

7. Robinson was the branch manager of one of Smith Barney's brokerage offices. One of his most important duties was to recruit experienced brokers. He contracted annually with Smith Barney in 1991, 1992 and 1993 under three separate but identical agreements, each of which was entitled "Branch Managers' Incentive Compensation Plan Agreement." The 1993 agreement provided that:

[I]n consideration of payment of the 1993 Incentive Compensation to me, I agree that should my employment with Smith Barney terminate for any reason and I become employed at a competitor organization, I will not for a one-year period directly or indirectly solicit or induce any Smith Barney employee to resign from either (a) the Smith Barney branch office at which I worked; or (b) any other Smith Barney office within a 50-mile radius of the competitor organization's office at which I work in order for that employee to accept employment at the competitor organization at which I work.

Robinson made this promise in return for a promise from Smith Barney to allow him to participate in the firm's 1993 incentive compensation program. The exact amount of Robinson's incentive compensation was to be calculated after Smith Barney's 1993 profits were determined. He was to receive quarterly advances toward the compensation that he would ultimately be paid. In the event that Robinson were to resign or were to be terminated for cause during 1993, he would be required to return any advances received in that year. In April 1993, Robinson received a $7,000 advance which he did not repay after he voluntarily left Smith Barney's employ on June 17, 1993.

Robinson conceded that during 1993 he left Smith Barney's employ, began to work for a competitor organization, and, having been advised that the agreement was unenforceable, knowingly breached the agreement not to solicit Smith Barney's employees by actively recruiting them.

Did Robinson breach the noncompetition agreement? Will Robinson succeed in challenging the validity of the noncompetition agreement? [*Smith, Barney, Harris Upham & Co. Inc. v. Robinson*, 12 F.3d 515 (5th Cir. 1994)]

8. In 1976, Leonard Linton was a 17-year-old high school student in Dearborn Heights, Michigan. Linton and a companion were arrested by Dearborn police in a field near the high school. Police searched them and found marijuana on Linton's companion. Linton claims that he was not aware that his companion had the marijuana. Linton pled guilty to loitering in a field. He was released upon his parents' payment of a $50 fine. Linton claims that he was not told that he was charged with a crime, that he was not offered the assistance of counsel, and that he did not know that pleading guilty to loitering would give him a criminal record.

After finishing high school, Linton filled out an application for employment with United Parcel Service (UPS). On that application, Linton was asked, "Have you ever been convicted of a crime?" to which he answered, "No." Linton was hired as a part-time loader-unloader and he continued to work there from 1979 to 1988. UPS admits that during these nine years Linton was a hard-working employee.

In September 1988, Linton applied for a full-time position as a next-day specialist air driver. UPS required a second employment application for this position. This application also asked whether he had ever been convicted of a crime, and Linton again answered, "No." UPS conducted a criminal-history check in connection with Linton's application. On October 7, 1988, Linton was discharged on the basis of a report from the state police stating that he had committed a "violation of controlled substance laws." The discharge letter claimed that "employment applications submitted to UPS on August 7, 1979, and September 20, 1988 were falsified." The discharge was pursuant to article 17 of the UPS-union collective bargaining agreement which sets forth the grounds for discharge or suspension.

Pursuant to the collective bargaining agreement, Linton filed a grievance with the union. On the advice of his union steward Linton refused to take a "voluntary quit" deal and expressed his desire to take his grievance to the state committee. This claim was denied.

Did UPS have just cause for terminating Linton because the employment application he signed unequivocally stated that misrepresentation or omission of facts constituted grounds for termination? Should the fact that Linton had no intent to deceive UPS affect the outcome of the case? [*Linton v. UPS*, 15 F.3d 1365 (6th Cir. 1994)]

9. The plaintiffs worked as floor hands on Rig 191, one of several rigs owned by Parker Drilling Co. As floor hands, their job was to connect 90-foot segments of steel pipe, each weighing 1,500 pounds, and place them in the drilling hole in the floor of the rig. This is demanding work. In addition, the drilling hole is often overflowing with mud, making the rig floor slick and treacherous. The work is performed at temperatures as low as -30°F, using heavy tools. Injuries are frequent, ranging from severed fingers to death.

Parker, in the interest of safety, enforced strict discipline aboard the rigs. This included a ban on the use or possession of drugs on the rigs. The drug ban extended to the company-provided sleeping areas, but it did not address employees' drug use during their off-time, so long as they were off the drilling site. The plaintiffs testified that they were aware of Parker's drug policy.

During a routine safety inspection of the North Slope rigs, Parker's safety director, John Haynes, was told by two employees, Bill Reynolds and Joe Watkins, that the plaintiffs were routinely smoking marijuana on the rig and during their breaks.

Based on the written allegations of Reynolds and Watkins, Parker suspended the plaintiffs pending an investigation. At the time of the suspension, the plaintiffs were off the rig on their normal two-week rotation.

After confronting the plaintiffs, who denied using drugs, and based on the information above, Parker fired the plaintiffs. They then brought a wrongful termination action in the Federal District Court for the District of Alaska.

Did Parker have adequate cause for terminating the plaintiffs' employment? [*Sanders v. Parker Drilling Co.*, 911 F.2d 191 (9th Cir. 1990)]

10. Duerr was employed by Delco Products (a division of General Motors) for ten years. For the last three years, prior to leaving on March 31, 1988, Duerr was a salaried employee in a supervisory position. In early 1988, Delco initiated a Voluntary Termination of Employment Plan (VTEP) for certain hourly employees. Under this plan, hourly employees could voluntarily terminate their employment in return for a VTEP benefit payment. In late January 1988, Duerr accepted a future position with a McDonnell Douglas office in California. Duerr alleges that on or about February 1, 1988, he requested that his supervisor and his manager at Delco allow him to return to an hourly position to take advantage of the VTEP. Duerr maintains that on February 15, 1988, he was promised that he could return to an hourly position on February 24, 1988. According to Duerr, in reliance upon this promise, he made a down payment on a house in California.

If Duerr's request to return to an hourly position to take advantage of the VTEP had not been granted, would Duerr have had a claim against Delco? What if Delco, after having promised that Duerr could return to an hourly position, changed its mind? Would Duerr have a cause of action? [*Duerr v. Delco*, 911 F.2d 732 (6th Cir. 1990)]

Chapter 13

CIVIL RIGHTS AND EMPLOYMENT DISCRIMINATION

■ Introduction

Laws Designed to Eliminate Employment Discrimination

The abolition of slavery and the civil rights movement of the 1960s were two of the greatest forces behind all of the civil rights legislation in America today. From the Civil Rights Act of 1866 to that of 1991, the law has been moving in a direction to eliminate discrimination based on race, sex, color, religion, or national origin.

These laws address many areas of discrimination including housing and education. One of the most interesting areas is employment discrimination. Under title VII of the Civil Rights Act of 1964 and, more recently, the Americans With Disabilities Act and the Family and Medical Leave Act, the law is being used to protect those who historically have suffered discrimination in various contexts, including employment.

Chapter Summary

This chapter provides an overview of historic and current civil rights legislation. It also illustrates the various legal theories pursued under each piece of legislation, and how those theories relate to legal and appropriate behavior by managers in a business environment.

■ Overview of Civil Rights Legislation

The federal statutes that forbid various kinds of discrimination in employment are summarized in this section.

Additionally, many states have passed their own fair-employment acts which prohibit discrimination on many of the same bases that the federal legislation does. In some instances, state statutes provide greater protection.

Section 1981

The earliest piece of legislation in the area of employment and civil rights is the Civil Rights Act of 1866.[1] This statute (referred to as section 1981) forbids racial discrimination by employers of any size in the making and enforcement of contracts, including employment contracts. Under section 1981, as amended by the Civil Rights Act of 1991,[2] the bar against racial discrimination applies not only to hiring, promotion, and termination but also to working conditions such as racial harassment and to breaches of contract occurring during the term of the contract.[3]

Section 1981 applies to cases involving state or private conduct. Employees suing under section 1981 are entitled to a jury trial of their claims and may be awarded greater monetary sanctions than are available under title VII, discussed below.

The civil rights movement in the 1960s led to the next wave of legislation limiting the right of employers to establish the terms and conditions of employment.

Equal Pay Act

In 1963, Congress passed the Equal Pay Act,[4] which mandates equal pay for equal work without regard to gender. The act covers all public and private employers with 20 or more employees, including federal, state, and local governments. It is enforced by the Equal Employment Opportunity Commission (EEOC).

Title VII

The most significant piece of employment legislation is title VII of the Civil Rights Act of 1964.[5] This statute, which is enforced by the EEOC, prohibits discrimination in employment on the basis of race, color, religion, national origin, or sex. Congress later amended title VII to provide that discrimination on the basis of sex includes discrimination on the basis of pregnancy, childbirth, or related medical conditions. Title VII covers all public and private employers with 15 or more employees, including federal, state, and local governments.

Age Discrimination in Employment Act

In 1967, Congress passed the Age Discrimination in Employment Act,[6] which protects persons 40 years and older from discrimination on the basis of age. The ADEA is discussed later in this chapter.

Vietnam Era Veterans' Readjustment Assistance Acts

The Vietnam Era Veterans' Readjustment Assistance Acts of 1972 and 1974,[7] enforced by the Department of Labor, require affirmative action to employ disabled Vietnam-era veterans. They apply only to employers holding federal contracts of $10,000 or more.

Vocational Rehabilitation Act

The Vocational Rehabilitation Act of 1973,[8] enforced by the U.S. Department of Labor, prohibits discrimination against the physically and mentally disabled. Section 503 of the act imposes affirmative-action obligations on employers having contracts with the federal government in excess of $2,500, and makes the act applicable to employers receiving federal financial assistance of any amount.

Veterans Re-Employment Act

The Veterans Re-Employment Act of 1974[9] gives employees who served in the military at any time the right to be reinstated in employment without loss of benefits

---

1. 42 U.S.C. § 1981 (1988 & Supp. 1992).
2. 42 U.S.C. § 1981 note (1988 & Supp. 1992).
3. The decision in *Patterson v. McLean Credit Union*, 491 U.S. 164, 109 S.Ct. 2363 (1989), which reached a contrary result, was overturned by the Civil Rights Act of 1991. In *Patterson*, an African-American employee had claimed that she had been discriminated against due to her race because her employer had racially harassed her, had failed to promote her, and discharged her because of race. Such conduct is illegal under section 1981, as amended.
4. 29 U.S.C. § 206 (1988 & Supp. 1992).

5. 42 U.S.C. §§ 2000e-2000e-17 (1988 & Supp. 1992).
6. 29 U.S.C. §§ 621-634 (1988 & Supp. 1992).
7. 38 U.S.C. §§ 4100 *et seq.* (1994).
8. 29 U.S.C. §§ 701-794 (1988 & Supp. 1992).
9. 38 U.S.C. §§ 2021-2026 (1988).

and the right not to be discharged without cause for one year following such reinstatement.

Americans with Disabilities Act

The Americans with Disabilities Act,[10] which became law in 1990, provides millions of disabled Americans with access to employment, transportation, public accommodations, and telecommunications services. The ADA is the most sweeping civil rights measure since the Civil Rights Act of 1964.

The ADA enlarged the definition of "disability" to include any physical or mental impairment that substantially limits one or more major life activities such as walking, talking, or working. Under this definition, persons who have recovered from cancer, alcoholism, or drug abuse, persons with AIDS or who have tested positive for the human immunodeficiency virus (HIV), and persons with disfiguring injuries would all be considered disabled.

The act requires all businesses to provide "reasonable accommodations" to the disabled, unless such an accommodation would result in "undue hardship" on business operations. It also prohibits discrimination in employment on the basis of a person's disability.

The employment provisions of the ADA, which apply to all private employers with 15 or more employees, are discussed later in this chapter.

Civil Rights Act of 1991

After two years of debate, the Civil Rights Act of 1991 was adopted in November 1991. The act serves to amend section 1981 of the Civil Rights Act of 1866, the Civil Rights Act of 1964, the Age Discrimination in Employment Act of 1967, the Attorney's Fees Awards Act of 1976, and the Americans with Disabilities Act of 1990. Perhaps most importantly, the act legislatively overrules several parts of recent Supreme Court rulings that were unfavorable to the rights of plaintiffs in employment discrimination cases. The act also extends coverage of the major civil rights statutes to the staffs of the president and the Senate. In addition, the act provides for the establishment of a "glass ceiling" commission, and requires the Equal Employment Opportunity Commission (EEOC) to engage in educational/outreach activities and to create a Technical Assistance Training Institute.

Certain provisions of the Civil Rights Act of 1991 are discussed, in context throughout this chapter, as part of

Family and Medical Leave Act of 1993

After it had been vetoed twice by former President George Bush, President Clinton signed the Family and Medical Leave Act of 1993[11] into law on February 5, 1993. The act is designed to allow employees to take time off from work to handle domestic responsibilities, such as the birth or adoption of a child or the care of an elderly parent. The act is applicable to both men and women, but seems to have special significance for women, who often are forced into the tenuous position of choosing between job security and caregiving.

The act's overall goal is to promote stability along with the economic security of American families. Employees can, under the act, be assured of a job to return to after familial responsibilities subside. The specific provisions of the act are discussed in detail later in this chapter.

■ Legal Theories Under Title VII

Of all the civil rights legislation, title VII has had the greatest impact on the recruitment, hiring, and other employment practices of American businesses. Remedies available under title VII include compensation for lost salary and benefits, reinstatement or "front pay" equal to what the employee would have received had he not been discharged, and injunctive relief to stop prohibited discriminatory actions.

Litigation under title VII has produced two distinct legal theories of discrimination: (1) disparate treatment and (2) disparate impact.

Disparate Treatment

A plaintiff claiming *disparate treatment* must prove that his employer intentionally discriminated against him by denying him employment or a benefit or privilege of employment because of his race, religion, sex, or national origin. The Supreme Court has established a systematic approach toward proof of these claims. First, the employee must prove a prima facie case. This means she must prove: (1) she is a member of a class of persons protected by title VII; and (2) she was denied a position or benefit she sought, for which she was qualified, and which was

---

10. 42 U.S.C. § 12101-12213 (1988 & Supp. 1992).

11. 29 U.S.C. § 2601-2654 (1993).

available. If the employee proves her prima facie case, the employer then must present evidence (but need not prove) that it had legitimate, nondiscriminatory grounds for its decision. If the employer meets this burden of producing evidence, the employee then must prove that the grounds offered by the employer were only a pretext for unlawful discrimination.

However, the Supreme Court in *St. Mary's Honor Center v. Hicks*[12] determined that a showing of pretext is insufficient to compel judgment for the employee. This holding went against the bulk of prior case law that held that an employee could win his case if he showed that the employer's reasons were without merit. Therefore, after *St. Mary's*, an employer may be able to give a false justification or reason for how it treated an employee, and unless the employee can show that the given reason was false *and* that the employer's real reason for its action was discrimination, then the employee loses his case. Some employment law commentators believe that such a showing may be very difficult for employees to make and anticipate that Congress may legislatively overrule the *St. Mary's* holding.

In a disparate treatment case, for example, an African-American employee may claim that he was fired because of his race. He would show in the first instance that he is an African American, he was fired, and he possessed at least the minimum qualifications for the job. Some courts may require that he also show that his job was not eliminated but was filled by someone else after his termination. Once he proves this, his employer might present evidence that the employee was terminated for excessive absenteeism. The employer might produce the employee's attendance records and a supervisor's testimony that his attendance was unacceptable. The employee may attempt to prove pretext in a number of ways. He may show that his supervisor uttered racial slurs from time to time. He may show that his employer's attendance policy requires a written warning about poor attendance before the employee can be terminated on that ground, and that he received no such warning. He may show that white employees with similar attendance records were not fired. In any event, the employee has the burden of proving that his employer fired him because of his race.

Where an employee proves that the employer's decision was motivated in part by impermissible discrimination, the employer has engaged in an illegal employment practice. However, no damages can be awarded and reinstatement, hiring, or promotion cannot be ordered if the employer demonstrates that it would have taken the same action in the absence of the impermissible motivating factor. In such a case, declaratory relief is still available, as is an award of attorney's fees and costs.[13]

Disparate Impact

The *disparate impact* theory arose out of title VII class actions brought in the 1970s against large employers. These suits challenged testing and other selection procedures, claiming that they systematically excluded women or particular ethnic groups from certain types of jobs. It is not necessary to prove intentional discrimination to prevail in a disparate impact case. Discrimination can be established by proving that an employment practice, although neutral on its face, had a disparate impact on a protected group.

For example, suppose an employer has a policy that it will only hire persons for security guard positions who are at least 5 feet 8 inches tall, weigh at least 150 pounds, and can pass certain agility tests. This would seem like a neutral policy, in that it does not expressly exclude women or Asian males. However, if the number of women or Asian males who are refused employment is proportionately greater than the number of white males refused employment, then that policy has a disparate impact.

To prove disparate impact, the plaintiff must demonstrate that the specific employment practice, policy, or rule being challenged has caused a statistically significant disproportion between the effects on different groups. The employer then has the burden to demonstrate that the challenged practice is job related for the position in question and consistent with business necessity.[14]

---

13. Prior to the Civil Rights Act of 1991, the Supreme Court had held in *Price Waterhouse v. Hopkins*, 490 U.S. 228, 109 S.Ct. 1775 (1989), that in a mixed motives case, the employer has not violated the law and is not liable for damages if the employer could prove by a preponderance of the evidence that it would have made the same decision even if it had not taken the plaintiff's gender into account. Although the Civil Rights Act of 1991 overturned this aspect of *Price Waterhouse v. Hopkins,* the case remains good law for the proposition that sexual stereotyping is an impermissible practice. It is for that proposition that this case is discussed later in this chapter.

14. This standard was set forth in the Civil Rights Act of 1991, which had as one of its stated purposes, "to codify the concepts of 'business necessity' and 'job related' enunciated by the Supreme Court in *Griggs v. Duke Power Co.*, 401 U.S. 424, 91 S.Ct. 849 (1971), and in the other Supreme Court decisions prior to *Wards Cove Packing Co. v. Atonio*, 490 U.S. 642, 109 S.Ct. 2115 (1989)."

---

12. 113 S.Ct. 2742 (1993).

The business justification must relate to job performance. Inconvenience, annoyance, or expense to the employer will not suffice. For example, an Asian applicant who is denied employment because she failed an English language test may challenge the language requirement. If she has applied for a sales job, the employer may justify the requirement on the ground that ability to communicate with customers is an indispensable qualification. On the other hand, if she has applied for a job on the production line, that justification may not suffice. As under disparate treatment analysis, the ultimate burden of persuasion rests with the plaintiff.

In proving that there is disparate impact, the plaintiffs introduce statistical evidence. Such evidence must compare the racial composition of the *qualified* persons in the labor market with the persons holding the jobs in question. Prior to the Supreme Court decision in *Wards Cove Packing Co. v. Atonio*,[15] those challenging racial or other types of discrimination had argued that the relevant comparison was between the total number of minorities in the geographic labor market and the number of jobs in question. The Civil Rights Act of 1991 overturned the part of *Wards Cove* that let employers off the hook if they proved mere evidence of a business justification, not business necessity, but apparently the statistical standard imposed by *Wards Cove* is still good law. According to the Supreme Court, this must be the rule because "the only practical option for many employers" would otherwise be to adopt racial and other quotas. Since President Bush originally vetoed the proposed civil rights legislation in 1990 due to a claim it would require quotas,[16] the silence on this aspect of *Wards Cove* in the act he signed—the Civil Rights Act of 1991—may have been politically necessary.

To get a sense of the fact patterns in which disparate impact claims arise, it is useful to review the facts of *Wards Cove*. Although aspects of the holding in that case were overturned by the Civil Rights Act of 1991, the fact pattern is indicative of the problem.

---

15. 490 U.S. 642, 109 S.Ct. 2115 (1989).

16. "Disapproval of S.2104–The Civil Rights Act of 1990," *Congressional Record–Senate*, S16418 (October 22, 1990).

■ A Case in Point: Summary

Case 13.1
WARDS COVE PACKING CO. v. ATONIO
Supreme Court of the United States
490 U.S. 642, 109 S.Ct. 2115 (1989).

FACTS The employers in this case were two companies that operated salmon canneries in remote areas of Alaska. The canneries operated only during the salmon runs in the summer months. In May or June of each year, a few weeks before the salmon runs began, workers arrived and prepared the equipment and facilities for the canning operation.

The length and size of salmon runs varied from year to year, and hence the number of employees needed at each cannery also varied. Estimates were made as early in the winter as possible. The necessary employees were hired, and when the time came, they were transported to the canneries. Because of the intense work in the canning season and the remote locations of the canneries, all workers were housed at the canneries and had their meals in company-owned mess halls.

Jobs at the canneries were of two general types: "cannery jobs" on the cannery line, which were unskilled positions; and "noncannery jobs," which fell into a variety of classifications. Most noncannery jobs were classified as skilled positions. Cannery jobs were filled predominantly by nonwhites: Filipinos and Alaska Natives. Noncannery jobs were filled with predominantly white workers, who were hired during the winter months from the companies' offices in Washington and Oregon. Almost all of the noncannery jobs paid more than cannery positions. The predominantly white noncannery workers and the predominantly nonwhite cannery employees lived in separate dormitories and ate in separate mess halls.

A group of past and present nonwhite cannery workers brought a title VII action against the companies. They claimed that the companies' hiring and promotion practices were responsible for the racial stratification of the work force and had denied them and other nonwhites employment as noncannery workers on the basis of race. They also complained of the racially segregated housing and dining facilities.

The court of appeals held that the cannery workers had made out a prima facie case of disparate impact. That court relied solely on the workers' statistics showing a high percentage of nonwhite workers in the cannery jobs and a low percentage of nonwhite workers in the noncannery position. The employees appealed.

ISSUE PRESENTED   In proving a disparate impact case, is it sufficient to show that the racial composition of persons holding a particular job is very different from the racial composition of the general population in the labor market?

SUMMARY OF OPINION   The U.S. Supreme Court reversed the court of appeals, ruling that statistical proof can alone make out a prima facie case, but that it had not done so here. A proper statistical analysis, the Court held, would have compared the racial composition of the jobs at issue to the racial composition of the *qualified* population in the relevant labor market. The Court reasoned that it was not an employer's fault if a labor market lacked qualified nonwhites to fill its positions.

The Court further noted that plaintiffs, in establishing a prima facie disparate-impact case, must show more than statistical disparities in the employer's work force. The plaintiff must identify the specific employment practice, such as a method of testing, that is being challenged.

The Court then ruled that if a plaintiff makes a prima facie case, an employer can then show a business justification, which is not necessarily a business necessity, to rebut the plaintiff's contention of discrimination.

A plaintiff could then try to show that other devices, without a similarly undesirable racial effect, would also serve the employer's business interest or justification. The plaintiff's alternative, in order to be acceptable, would have to be equally as effective as the employer's device in achieving the employer's goal, including in terms of cost.

The Court did not rule specifically on the separate housing and dining facilities.

RESULT   The case was remanded to the lower courts for reconsideration in light of the Supreme Court's opinion.

COMMENTS   As noted in text, the first part of the Court's holding regarding business justification versus business necessity was overturned by the Civil Rights Act of 1991. However, that act does not apply to the *Wards Cove* case itself.

Historically, disparate impact analysis has been limited to objective selection criteria, such as tests and degree requirements. However, the Supreme Court has held that this analysis may also apply to subjective bases for decisions, such as interviews and supervisor evaluations. Thus, if an employer makes hiring decisions on the basis of interviews alone, and if the percentage of women or African Americans hired differs significantly from the percentage of women or African Americans in the relevant labor pool, a claim may be made that this process is unlawful under title VII. The issue then will be whether the process is justified by business necessity.

■ Statutory Defenses Under Title VII

Title VII sets forth several statutory defenses to claims of discriminatory treatment. Of these defenses, the one most frequently cited is the defense of bona fide occupational qualification.

"The bunny did not get the job because the bunny is cute. The bunny got the job because the bunny knows WordPerfect."

Drawing by C. Barsotti; © 1994 The New Yorker Magazine, Inc.

Bona Fide Occupational Qualification

Title VII provides that an employer may lawfully hire an individual on the basis of religion, sex, or national origin if religion, sex, or national origin is a bona fide occupational qualification (BFOQ) reasonably necessary to the normal operation of that particular business. This is known as the *BFOQ defense*. Because BFOQ is an affirmative defense, the employer has the burden of showing a reasonable basis for believing that the category of persons (for example, women) excluded from a particular job were unable to perform that job.

The BFOQ defense has been narrowly construed. For example, regulations promulgated by the Equal Employment Opportunity Commission provide that gender will not qualify as a BFOQ where a gender-based restriction is based on: (1) assumptions of the comparative employment characteristics of women in general (such as the assumption that women have a higher turnover rate than men); (2) stereotyped characterizations of the sexes (for example, that men are less capable of assembling intricate equipment than women); or (3) the preferences of co-workers, employers, or customers for one sex or the other.[17] Gender will be considered a BFOQ,

for example, where physical attributes are important for authenticity (as with actors) or where a gender-based restriction is necessary to protect the rights of others to privacy (as with rest room attendants).

The BFOQ defense is not available where discriminatory treatment is based on a person's race or color.

Seniority and Merit Systems

Bona fide seniority and merit systems are not covered by title VII, as long as such systems do not result from intentional discrimination. This is considered an exemption rather than an affirmative defense. Consequently, the plaintiff has the burden of proving a discriminatory intent or illegal purpose. Moreover, although a disproportionate impact may be some evidence of a discriminatory intent, such an impact is not in itself sufficient to establish discriminatory intent.

■ Special Applications of the Laws

The civil rights legislation was founded on the fundamental premise that people ought not be denied a job or opportunity on the job because of their race, religion, or sex. The law has expanded beyond that basic premise to reach more subtle forms of discrimination.

---

17. 29 C.F.R. § 1604.2(a)(1)(i)-(iii) (1988).

Ethical Consideration

As a result of developments in title VII law, employers have been required to examine more closely their rationales for selection criteria. Many longstanding stereotypes held by employers and society in general have been challenged, sometimes by litigation and sometimes by policy makers within the employer's organization. Civil rights legislation did more than prohibit intentional discrimination against minority groups and women. It fostered a major shift in public attitudes about the capabilities of individuals, and contributed to the breakdown of stereotypes regarding ethnic and gender groups.

Pregnancy Discrimination

Female employees for many years have been at a disadvantage in the workplace because of their role as childbearers. In the past, for example, many employers did not provide for pregnancy leave although other medical leaves were permitted.

In 1976, the Supreme Court held that denying a woman disability insurance benefits for a temporary disability caused by pregnancy was not sex discrimination. The Supreme Court reasoned that the denial of benefits was not based on being female but on being pregnant, and that a distinction between pregnant persons (albeit all female) and nonpregnant persons was not sex discrimination.

> **"** *The Supreme Court reasoned that the denial of benefits was not based on being female but on being pregnant, and that a distinction between pregnant persons (albeit all female) and nonpregnant persons was not sex discrimination.*

Congress, recognizing the increasing number of women in the work force and the widespread need for medical insurance and medical leave for pregnancies, responded by passing the Pregnancy Discrimination Act, a portion of title VII that provides that discrimination on the basis of pregnancy is a form of sex discrimination and therefore prohibited.[18] Employers must provide the same compensation for disabilities related to pregnancy and childbirth as they provide for any other disability. Many states have followed suit and, as in other areas of discrimination law, some provide greater protection than does the federal statute.

Fetal Protection Policies

Certain substances used in manufacturing are harmful to the fetus being carried by a pregnant woman. In an effort to avoid such harm (and attendant lawsuits for unsafe working environments) some companies adopted what are called "fetal protection policies." A *fetal protection policy* bars a woman from certain jobs unless her inability to bear children is medically documented. Such a plan was challenged under title VII in the case that follows.

---

18. 42 U.S.C. § 2000e(k) (1988).

■ A Case in Point: **In the Language of the Court**

Case 13.2
AUTOMOBILE WORKERS v. JOHNSON CONTROLS
Supreme Court of the
United States
499 U.S. 187, 111 S. Ct. 1196
(1991).

FACTS Since 1982, Johnson Controls, Inc., a manufacturer of batteries, has maintained a fetal-protection policy designed to prevent unborn children and their mothers from suffering the adverse effects of lead exposure. Lead attacks the fetus's central nervous system and retards cognitive development. Under the policy, women with childbearing capacity will neither be hired for nor be allowed to transfer into those jobs in which lead levels are defined as excessive. The United Automobile, Aerospace and

*Case **13.2** continued on following page*

*Case **13.2** continued*

Agricultural Implement Workers of America, several UAW local unions, and a group of individual employees brought suit alleging that this policy violated title VII. The plaintiffs included a woman who had chosen to be sterilized in order to keep her job as well as women who had suffered losses in compensation when transferred out of jobs that exposed them to lead.

The federal district court and the court of appeals found in favor of Johnson Controls.

The United States Supreme Court granted certiorari "to resolve the obvious conflict between [sic] the Fourth, Seventh, and Eleventh Circuits on this issue, and to address the important and difficult issue of whether an employer, seeking to protect potential fetuses, may discriminate against women just because of their ability to become pregnant."

OPINION   BLACKMUN, J., writing for the U.S. Supreme Court:

. . . .

The bias in Johnson Controls' policy is obvious. Fertile men, but not fertile women, are given a choice as to whether they wish to risk their reproductive health for a particular job. . . .

. . . .

. . . Johnson Controls' policy classifies on the basis of gender and child-bearing capacity, rather than fertility alone. Respondent does not seek to protect the unconceived children of all its employees. Despite evidence in the record about the debilitating effect of lead exposure on the male reproductive system, Johnson Controls is concerned only with the harms that may befall the unborn offspring of its female employees. . . . Johnson Controls' policy is facially discriminatory because it requires only a female employee to produce proof that she is not capable of reproducing.

. . . .

. . . [T]he absence of a malevolent motive does not convert a facially discriminatory policy into a neutral policy with a discriminatory effect. Whether an employment practice involves disparate treatment through explicit facial discrimination does not depend on why the employer discriminates but rather on the explicit terms of the discrimination. . . .

. . . We hold that Johnson Controls' fetal-protection policy is sex-discrimination forbidden under Title VII unless respondent can establish that sex is a "bona fide occupational qualification."

. . . .

The BFOQ defense is written narrowly and this Court has read it narrowly. . . .

Johnson Controls argues that its fetal-protection policy falls within the so-called safety exception to the BFOQ. Our cases have stressed that discrimination on the basis of sex because of safety concerns is allowed only in narrow circumstances. . . .

. . . .

Our case law, therefore, makes it clear that the safety exception is limited to instances in which sex or pregnancy actually interferes with the employee's ability to perform the job. This approach is consistent with the language of the BFOQ provision itself, for it suggests that permissible distinctions based on sex must relate to ability to perform the duties of the job. Johnson Controls suggests, however, that we expand the exception to allow fetal-protection policies that mandate particular standards for pregnant or fertile women. We decline to do so. Such an expansion contradicts not only the language of the BFOQ and the narrowness of its exception but the plain language and history of the Pregnancy Discrimination Act [PDA].

. . . . [W]omen as capable of doing their job as their male counterparts may not be forced to choose between having a child and having a job.

. . . .

We have no difficulty concluding that Johnson Controls cannot establish a BFOQ. Fertile women, as far as appears in the record, participate in the manufacture of batteries as efficiently as anyone else. Johnson Controls' professed moral and ethical concerns about the welfare of the next generation do not suffice to establish a BFOQ of female sterility. Decisions about the welfare of future children must be left to the parents who conceive, bear, support, and raise them rather than to the employers who hire those parents. Congress has mandated this choice through Title VII, as amended by the Pregnancy Discrimination Act. Johnson Controls has attempted to exclude women because of their reproductive capacity. Title VII and the PDA simply do not allow a woman's dismissal because of her failure to submit to sterilization.

Nor can concerns about the welfare of the next generation be considered part of the "essence" of Johnson Controls' business. Judge Easterbrook in this case pertinently observed: "It is word play to say that 'the job' at Johnson [Controls] is to make batteries without risk to fetuses in the same way 'the job' at Western Airlines is to fly planes without crashing."

. . . . Johnson Controls' fear of prenatal injury, no matter how sincere, does not begin to show that substantially all of its fertile women employees are incapable of doing their jobs.

A word about tort liability and the increased cost of fertile women in the workplace is perhaps necessary. . . . More than 40 states currently recognize a right to recover for a prenatal injury based either on negligence or on wrongful death. . . . It is worth noting that OSHA gave the problem of lead lengthy consideration and concluded that "there is no basis whatsoever for the claim that women of childbearing age should be excluded from the workplace in order to protect the fetus or the course of pregnancy." Instead, OSHA established a series of mandatory protection which, taken together, "should effectively minimize any risk to the fetus and newborn child." Without negligence, it would be difficult for a court to find liability on the part of the employer. If, under general tort principles, Title VII bans sex-specific fetal-protection policies, the employer fully informs the woman of the risk, and the employer has not acted negligently, the basis for holding an employer liable seems remote at best.

. . . .

Case **13.2** *continued on following page*

*Case **13.2** continued*

The tort-liability argument reduces to two equally unpersuasive propositions. First, Johnson Controls attempts to solve the problem of reproductive health hazards by resorting to an exclusionary policy. Title VII plainly forbids illegal sex discrimination as a method of diverting attention from an employer's obligation to police the workplace. Second, the spectre of an award of damages reflects a fear that hiring fertile women will cost more. The extra cost of employing members of one sex, however, does not provide an affirmative Title VII defense for a discriminatory refusal to hire members of that gender.

Our holding today that Title VII, as so amended, forbids sex-specific fetal-protection policies is neither remarkable nor unprecedented. Concern for a woman's existing or potential offspring historically has been the excuse for denying women equal employment opportunities. Congress in the PDA prohibited discrimination on the basis of a woman's ability to become pregnant. We do no more than hold that the Pregnancy Discrimination Act means what it says. It is no more appropriate for the courts than it is for individual employers to decide whether a woman's reproductive role is more important to herself and her family than her economic role. Congress has left that choice to the woman as hers to make.

RESULT The judgment of the court of appeals was reversed and the case was remanded for further proceedings consistent with this opinion. Women cannot be excluded from certain jobs because of their childbearing capacity.

Questions
1. Would the Court have decided the case differently if all fertile employees, male and female alike, were banned from jobs involving lead?
2. What must Johnson Controls do now to avoid suits for prenatal injury based on negligence or wrongful death?

Sexual Harassment

With more women in the work force, and more women in positions and workplaces previously dominated by men, the courts also began to recognize sexual harassment as a form of sexual discrimination. Sexual harassment has emerged as one of the more complex and emotional issues in antidiscrimination law.

Early on, the courts recognized that a specific, job-related adverse action—such as denial of promotion—in retaliation for a woman's refusal to respond to her supervisor's sexual advances was a violation of title VII. Such retaliation is referred to as *quid pro quo harassment.*

The courts had also long recognized that creation of a hostile working environment for an employee because of his race was prohibited. An example of such *hostile environment harassment* would be continually subjecting an African-American employee to ridicule and racial slurs. In the following case, the Supreme Court ruled that the creation of a hostile environment by sexual harassment is likewise a form of discrimination under title VII. The facts illustrate the troubled and emotion-laden aspects of these cases.

■ **A Case in Point:**   **Summary**

Case 13.3
MERITOR SAVINGS BANK v. VINSON
Supreme Court of the
United States
477 U.S. 57, 106 S.Ct. 2399
(1986).

FACTS   Mechelle Vinson had been hired by a branch office manager as a teller trainee and was promoted over the years to branch manager. In September 1978, she took an indefinite sick leave and was fired in November for excessive use of that leave. She then brought an action against the bank officer who had hired her and the bank, claiming that for four years she had been constantly subjected to sexual harassment. Vinson testified at trial that during her probationary period the manager had treated her in a familiar manner, and that shortly thereafter he had requested that she engage in a sexual relationship with him. Out of fear of losing her job, she eventually agreed and had a sexual relationship with him over the next four years. She also testified to his explicit sexual conduct in front of other employees, and that he had assaulted her on several occasions. Because she was afraid of the manager, she never reported this harassment to any of his supervisors and never used the bank's complaint procedure because it required an employee to report any grievances first to one's superior—who in Vinson's case was the cause of the grievance. The manager denied all of these allegations. The bank took the position that it was not liable because it had no notice of this alleged misconduct and because Vinson had failed to use the internal grievance procedure to protest.

After hearing 11 days of testimony, the trial court concluded that there was no sexual harassment or discrimination, noting that, if there had been a sexual relationship, it was voluntary. The trial court went on to find that, in any event, the bank could not be liable because no one had put it on notice regarding the manager's alleged actions. The court of appeals reversed this decision, recognizing that there are two kinds of impermissible sexual harassment under title VII: harassment consisting of demands for sexual favors as a condition for employment advancement, and harassment resulting from a hostile working environment. It remanded the case to the trial court to consider if there had been sexual harassment of the second type. The court of appeals also ruled that an employer is absolutely liable for sexual harassment practiced by a supervisor, regardless of whether the employer knew about the misconduct. The bank appealed.

ISSUE PRESENTED   Does the creation of a sexually hostile environment constitute illegal sex discrimination under title VII?

SUMMARY OF OPINION   The U.S. Supreme Court held that there can be sexual harassment solely by the creation of a hostile work environment, even if there is no retaliatory employment action against the employee. It is not necessary for the employee to show a concrete economic effect on employment, such as discharge or denial of a raise or promotion, to establish a violation. It therefore affirmed the decision of the court of appeals to remand the case.

The Supreme Court disagreed with the court of appeals on certain points, however. First, it noted that there is a continuum of conduct and that not every sexually offensive comment or act constitutes actionable sexual harassment. There must be sufficient offensive conduct to give rise to a pervasively hostile atmosphere. The Supreme Court indicated that an employee's voluntary sexual relationship with the accused manager is not a complete defense to a sexual harassment claim, although it may be relevant evidence for understanding the circumstances. "The correct inquiry

*Case **13.3** continued on following page*

*Case **13.3** continued*

is whether respondent by her conduct indicated that the alleged sexual advances were unwelcome, not whether or not her actual participation in sexual intercourse was voluntary."

Second, the Supreme Court held that evidence of a plaintiff's behavior and attire, allegedly inviting sexual conduct, may be admissible as to whether she found particular advances unwelcome. In other words, sexual harassment depends on the totality of the circumstances.

RESULT   Employee Vinson may prevail in her claim of sex harassment if she can show a hostile work environment, even if she cannot show a concrete economic effect on employment.

COMMENTS   Unfortunately, the Supreme Court left unanswered a significant question about the doctrine of *respondeat superior* in sexual harassment cases. (As explained in chapter 7, this doctrine makes an employer, such as a corporation, liable for acts of individual managers and supervisors done in the course and scope of their job.) The question presented in *Meritor* was whether the bank could be held strictly liable for sexual harassment by the manager even if it had no knowledge of that conduct, particularly where the employer had a grievance procedure and the employee failed to use it to bring the matter to the employer's attention. The Supreme Court refused to rule on this issue, but noted that an employer will not always be liable for hostile-environment sexual harassment by a supervisor. On the other hand, absence of notice by the employee to the employer is not an absolute defense for the employer, even where there is some form of grievance procedure.

It should be noted that the law clearly provides that the employer is absolutely liable for a supervisor's *quid pro quo* harassment. The employer is also clearly liable for hostile-environment harassment where it knew of the harassment but failed to take appropriate correction action.

The Supreme Court in *Meritor* placed heavy reliance on the EEOC's guidelines defining sexual harassment. They are a useful guide to the employer in developing an anti-sexual-harassment policy or in educating its supervisors. They state:

Harassment on the basis of sex is a violation of Sec. 703 of Title VII. Unwelcome sexual advances, requests for sexual favors, and other verbal or physical conduct of a sexual nature constitute sexual harassment when (1) submission to such conduct is made either explicitly or implicitly a term or condition of an individual's employment, (2) submission to or rejection of such conduct by an individual is used as the basis of employment decisions affecting such individual, or (3) such conduct has the purpose or effect of unreasonably interfering with the individual's work performance or creating an intimidating, hostile, or offensive working environment.[19]

Since the *Meritor* decision, lower courts have struggled with defining when workplace incidents are sufficiently offensive to create a hostile work environment. They have construed *Meritor* broadly in finding that sexual conduct in the workplace, even when not directed at the plaintiff, may violate the plaintiff's title VII rights. For example, in a case involving a female attorney for the SEC, the court held that open sexual activity in exchange for tangible employment benefits creates a hostile working environment.[20] The plaintiff had testified that she had rebuffed sexual overtures and that the sexually permissive atmosphere made it impossible for her to work as a professional or have a good working relationship with those managers. The Federal District Court for the District of Columbia found that these facts established sexual harassment, as defined by the Supreme Court in *Meritor*. The defendant had violated title VII.

---

19. 29 C.F.R. § 1064.11(a) (1989).

20. *Broderick v. Ruder*, 715 F.Supp. 1 (D.D.C. 1989).

The second area of uncertainty after *Meritor* is the employer's liability for the supervisor's acts. Lower federal courts have held that when a supervisor has authority over the plaintiff, such as authority to promote or discharge, and uses that authority to create a hostile environment or to assist in the harassment, the employer is liable, even without notice of the conduct. It is less clear whether an employer is liable for harassment by co-workers or by a supervisor who has no authority over the plaintiff. The following case illustrates the Supreme Court's interpretation of a situation involving the president of a company harassing one of the company's managers.

■ **A Case in Point:**   **Summary**

Case 13.4
HARRIS v. FORKLIFT SYSTEMS, INC.
Supreme Court of the United States
114 S.Ct. 367 (1993).

FACTS   Teresa Harris worked as a manager at Forklift Systems, Inc., an equipment rental company, from 1985 until 1987. Charles Hardy was Forklift's president.

Throughout Harris's time at Forklift, Hardy often insulted her because of her gender and often made her the target of unwanted sexual innuendoes. Hardy told Harris on several occasions, in the presence of other employees, "You're a woman, what do you know?" and "We need a man as the rental manager." He also told her she was "a dumb-ass woman." Again in front of others, he suggested that the two of them "go to the Holiday Inn to negotiate her raise." Hardy occasionally asked Harris and other female employees to get coins from his front pants pocket. He threw objects on the ground in front of Harris and other women, and asked them to pick the objects up. He made sexual innuendoes about Harris's and other women's clothing.

In August 1987, Harris complained to Hardy about his conduct. Hardy said he was surprised that Harris was offended, claimed he was only joking, and apologized. He also promised he would stop, and based on this assurance, Harris stayed on the job. But a few weeks later Hardy began making more sexual comments to Harris. In October 1987, Harris collected her paycheck and quit.

Harris then sued Forklift, claiming that Hardy's conduct had created an abusive work environment for her because of her gender.

ISSUE PRESENTED   Is a showing of a serious effect on an employee's psychological well-being or other injury necessary for an action for abusive or hostile work environment under title VII?

SUMMARY OF OPINION   The Supreme Court reaffirmed its holding in *Meritor Savings Bank v. Vinson*,[21] that the language of title VII is not limited to "economic" or "tangible" discrimination. The phrase "terms, conditions, or privileges of employment" shows a congressional intent to strike at the entire spectrum of disparate treatment of men and women in employment. Thus, the Court reasoned, people should not be required to work in a discriminatorily hostile or abusive environment. Any conduct that is merely offensive is not actionable under this standard, but requiring the conduct to cause a tangible psychological injury is also not necessary.

The Court further stated:

---

21. 477 U.S. 57, 106 S.Ct. 2399 (1986).

Case 13.4 continued on following page

*Case **13.4** continued*

. . . Title VII comes into play before the harassing conduct leads to a nervous breakdown. A discriminatorily abusive work environment, even one that does not seriously affect employees' psychological well-being, can and often will detract from employees' job performance, discourage employees from remaining on the job, or keep them from advancing in their careers. Moreover, even without regard to these tangible effects, the very fact that the discriminatory conduct was so severe or pervasive that it created a work environment abusive to employees because of their race, gender, religion, or national origin offends Title VII's broad rule of workplace equality.

The Court found that the district court erred when it relied on whether the conduct seriously affected the plaintiff's psychological well-being or led her to suffer injury. That inquiry needlessly focused attention on the existence of concrete psychological harm, an element not required by title VII. The statute is, according to the Court, not limited to such conduct. If the environment would reasonably be perceived, and is perceived, as hostile or abusive, there is no need for it also to be psychologically injurious.

The Court said that in order to determine whether an environment is hostile or abusive, courts must look at all the circumstances. Factors to consider include: (1) the frequency and severity of the discriminatory conduct; (2) whether it is physically threatening, or a mere offensive utterance; and (3) whether it unreasonably interferes with an employee's work performance. Psychological harm may be taken into account to determine whether the plaintiff actually found the environment abusive, but no single factor is required for a determination that an abusive or hostile work environment exists.

RESULT   The Supreme Court ruled that no showing of a serious effect on an employee's psychological well-being or other injury is necessary for an action for abusive or hostile work environment under title VII.

Supervisors and nonsupervising employees should be taught that all forms of sexual conduct and sexual talk in the workplace are inappropriate. To what extent this should be stated in a written policy depends on the culture of the workplace. It is also important to develop an atmosphere in which the employee feels free to bring a complaint. Because the harasser is often the employee's supervisor, a procedure that requires as a first step that the person complain to his supervisor will not be effective. The procedure should provide more than one resource person to whom the employee can complain, and there should be persons of both genders so that the employee has a choice. (Sexual harassment is not a problem which faces only female employees.) The company should ensure that all complaints are thoroughly investigated. Most importantly, the management of a company, whether through its human resource staff or otherwise, must be familiar with the atmosphere of its workplace and be vigilant in maintaining an appropriate environment in which employees can work comfortably.

66

Since the harasser is often the employee's supervisor, a procedure that requires as a first step that the person complain to his supervisor will not be effective.

Baker & McKenzie, the world's largest law firm with 1,670 lawyers in 30 countries, learned the hard way in September 1994 about an employer's liability for sexual harassment by a manager. A California jury awarded legal secretary Rena Weeks $50,000 compensatory damages and $6.9 million punitive damages from Baker & McKenzie for its failure to provide an harassment-free

Ethical Consideration

It is important that an employer protect itself against claims of sexual harassment, not only to meet legal obligations, but also to maintain a workplace conducive to the physical and mental well-being of all employees. Many commentators recommend that a company have a written policy that clearly prohibits sexual harassment and provides a procedure for employees to bring a claim of sexual harassment without intimidation. Such a policy is required by some states such as California. Moreover, a company should provide for nondiscriminatory behavior in its corporate code of ethics.

A rule that no employee should be subjected to requests for sexual favors is not sufficient. Sexual harassment may include overt or subtle sexual advances, even if there is no retaliation when such advances are rebuffed; sexual joking; leering; or any unwelcome touching. The difficult situation is the workplace where physical familiarity has come to be accepted, or where sexual comments are laughed at or tolerated. If management appears to condone such conduct, the employee may feel compelled to go along with it, even if he finds it intimidating or if it interferes with his ability to work.

On the other hand, excessive fear of sexual harassment claims can result in a dehumanized work environment in which supervisors and employees are afraid to make compliments or engage in mentoring for fear their conduct will be misconstrued. How should a manager balance these considerations?

In Brief: Elements of a Sexual Harassment Claim

Unwelcome sexual advances, requests for sexual favors, and other verbal or physical conduct of a sexual nature constitute sexual harassment when:

1) An individual's employment depends on the submission to such conduct;

2) Submission to or rejection of such conduct is used as the basis of employment decisions; or

3) Such conduct unreasonably interferes with the individual's work performance or creates an intimidating, hostile or offensive working environment.

In order to establish a prima facie claim of sexual harassment under title VII, it must be shown that:

1) the employee belongs to a protected group;

2) the employee faced unwelcome harassment;

3) the harassment was based upon sex;

4) the harassment affected a term, condition or privilege of employment; and

5) the harassment's severity or pervasiveness implied employer responsibility.

workplace. The former Baker & McKenzie partner, Martin Greenstein, who allegedly grabbed her breasts and buttocks and dropped M&M candies in her blouse pocket, was ordered to pay $225,000 in punitive damages. In assessing punitive damages equal to 10% of Baker & McKenzie's net worth, jurors were, according to juror Frank Lewis, "highly cognizant of the fact that we were sending a message not only to Baker & McKenzie but to corporate America."[22]

Sexual Stereotyping

In *Price Waterhouse v. Hopkins*,[23] Ann Hopkins had been denied partnership in the Big Six accounting firm Price Waterhouse. She claimed that the firm had discriminated against her on the basis of sex. She produced evidence that the policy board had advised her that, in order to improve her chances for partnership, she should "walk more femininely, talk more femininely, dress more femininely, wear make-up, have her hair styled, and wear jewelry."

The Supreme Court concluded that the evidence produced by Hopkins was sufficient to establish that sexual stereotyping played a part in the firm's decision not to promote her. With respect to sexual stereotyping, the Supreme Court stated: "An employer who objects to aggressiveness in women but whose positions require this trait places women in an intolerable and impermissible Catch-22: out of a job if they behave aggressively and out of a job if they don't. Title VII lifts women out of this bind." In addition, although the case dealt with gender discrimination, the Supreme Court expressly stated that all references to gender and all principles announced in the opinion "apply with equal force to discrimination based on race, religion, or national origin."

---

22. Rachel Gordon, "Amount of Award Split Harassment Jury," *The San Francisco Examiner*, September 3, 1994, A-1.
23. 490 U.S. 228, 109 S.Ct. 1775 (1989).

> *"An employer who objects to aggressiveness in women but whose positions require this trait places women in an intolerable and impermissible Catch-22: out of a job if they behave aggressively and out of a job if they don't. Title VII lifts women out of this bind."*

■ Age Discrimination

The principal federal law prohibiting discrimination in employment on the basis of age is the Age Discrimination in Employment Act (ADEA). As amended, the ADEA prohibits age discrimination in employment with respect to individuals aged 40 years or older. (Prior to its amendment, the ADEA did not offer protection to individuals aged 70 or above.) The ADEA applies to all employers that affect interstate commerce and have at least 20 employees.

The substantive provisions of the ADEA are similar to those of title VII. For example, the ADEA generally prohibits age discrimination with respect to hiring, firing, and compensation, and the terms, conditions, and privileges of employment. Moreover, the ADEA prohibits retaliation against an individual aged 40 or older because of the individual's opposition to unlawful age discrimination or because he has made a charge, testified, or assisted in an investigation, proceeding, or litigation under the ADEA.

The following case illustrates the difficult decision often faced by companies trying to find the right balance between promoting ethical behavior and the financial bottom line.

■ A Case in Point: In the Language of the Court

Case 13.5
HENN v. NATIONAL GEOGRAPHIC SOCIETY
United States Court of Appeals for the Seventh Circuit
819 F.2d 824 (7th Cir. 1987), *cert. denied*, 484 U.S. 964, 108 S.Ct. 454 (1987).

FACTS Experiencing a decline in advertising, the National Geographic Society, publishers of *National Geographic*, decided to reduce the number of employees selling ads. In reducing their work force, the Society targeted employees near retirement age because they felt that they needed to make room for younger employees who might be more likely to cultivate new clients and target new industries. The Society offered every ad salesperson over age 55 the option of early retirement. The Society made the offer in June 1983; the recipients had more than two months to think it over. The

Society offered several benefits as part of the early retirement plan, including retirement benefits calculated as if the retiree had quit at 65 and medical coverage as if the employee were still on the payroll. The letter extending the offer stated that this was a one-time opportunity. Twelve of the fifteen recipients of the letter took the offer; the three who declined are still employed by the Society. All twelve have received the promised benefits.

Four of the twelve retirees filed suit, contending that their separation violated the Age Discrimination in Employment Act (ADEA). The district court granted summary judgment to the Society, thereby deciding as a matter of law that the Society should win. The plaintiff retirees appealed.

ISSUE PRESENTED   Is offering older employees a beneficial early retirement plan, coupled with pressure to work harder if they do not accept the package, age discrimination under the Age Discrimination in Employment Act?

OPINION   EASTERBROOK, J., writing for the U.S. Court of Appeals:

. . . .

To determine the proper treatment of early retirement, we start by assuming that the employer is complying with the ADEA. (Whether the Society was doing so is a question to which we return.) Now the employer adds an offer of early retirement. Provided the employee may decline the offer and keep working under lawful conditions, the offer makes him better off. He has an additional option, one that may be (as it was here) worth a good deal of money. He may retire, receive the value of the package, and either take a new job (increasing his income) or enjoy new leisure. He also may elect to keep working and forfeit the package. This may put him to a hard choice; he may think the offer too good to refuse; but it is not Don Corleone's "Make him an offer he can't refuse." "Your money or your life?" calls for a choice, but each option makes the recipient of the offer worse off. When one option makes the recipient better off, and the other is the status quo, then the offer is beneficial. That the benefits may overwhelm the recipient and dictate the choice cannot be dispositive. The question "Would you prefer $100,000 to $50,000?" will elicit the same answer from everyone, but it does not on that account produce an "involuntary" response.

. . . .

. . . Retirement is an innocuous event, coming once to many employees and more than once to some. Retirement is not itself a prima facie case of age discrimination, not unless all separations from employment are. And as we have explained, an offer of incentives to retire early is a benefit to the recipient, not a sign of discrimination. Taken together, these two events—one neutral, one beneficial to the older employee—do not support an inference of age discrimination.

. . . .

The plaintiffs in this case do not say that they lacked information about the terms of the offer. All had time to discuss the offer with families and financial advisers. They complain that they felt pressure and perceived the choice to be excruciating, but that is not important. They could prevail

Case 13.5 continued on following page

*Case **13.5** continued*

only by showing that the Society manipulated the options so that they were driven to early retirement not by its attractions but by the terror of the alternative.

The plaintiffs complain of two things that made their positions untenable: the "silent treatment" and threats (real and implied) of unpleasant consequences if they did not start selling more ads. The "silent treatment" was principally that no one in the Society would tell them whether they ought to take the offer of early retirement; the Society says this was caused by its policy of sticking to the facts (doubtless to avoid charges of placing undue pressure on the employees), while the plaintiffs say that their inability to get straight answers about whether they should take the offer led them to fear the worst. The threats came about because all four plaintiffs had experienced bad years, and their supervisors told them they needed to sell more ads; this led them to fear for their jobs.

The record contains extensive admissions by the plaintiffs tending to support the district judge's conclusion that any threats made to these plaintiffs while they were considering the offer were no greater than justified by their lack of sales. Selling is a risky profession, and it does not make a salesman's job unbearable to remind him that he must produce and that there are penalties for failure. [Ed.—For a graphic illustration of this, see Glengarry Glen Ross (New Line Cinema 1992).] The plaintiffs say, however, that the Society's warnings were not justified on a more complete review of their performance. They also believe that the Society hassled them more than their sluggish sales performance warranted. To support this belief [plaintiff] Henn states that Bill Hughes, his supervisor, said to him early in 1983: "[s]ome of you older guys will not be around at the end of the year." All four plaintiffs rely on a passage in a memorandum that was part of the bureaucratic process that ended in the offer of early retirement: "Of the total twenty sales members one out of two are over 55 years, six are over age 62 and four are presently over age 65. [sic: actually 5 under 55; 5 between 55-61; 6 from 62-65; 4 over 65] Only one sales person over 65 plans to retire this year and an undetermined number desire to continue toward age 70. If an age balance is not struck soon our average age will obviously increase. Serious repercussions will result if younger sales personnel are not available to cultivate clients in new growth industries and insure future sales. To attract youthful qualified sales personnel we must be cognizant of industry practices and offer required incentives." The author of the memo recommended that salesmen be fired; the Society did not take that advice. It maintains that neither comment supports an inference that it acted or would have acted improperly to any person on the payroll.

The district court concluded that neither these nor other comments and incidents added up to constructive discharge or supported a reasonable belief by the plaintiffs that, had they remained at the Society, they would have been fired unlawfully. They were at risk of discipline or discharge for their performance (or lack of performance), and all four were producing less than their quota. The Society turned down the recommendation that it fire people, so the author of the memorandum did not speak for the Society. And although the record may well support an inference that the Society wanted to reduce the average age of its sales staff, this does not show that it used illegal means. Any early retirement program reduces average age, because only older employees are eligible to retire. That the Society favored the results of its program does not condemn the program. We passed that point when we accepted the conclusion of the EEOC [Equal

Employment Opportunity Commission] . . . that early retirement programs do not violate the ADEA.

RESULT   The Court of Appeals held that the offer of early retirement in this case did not violate the ADEA and, therefore, it affirmed the summary judgment for the employer National Geographic Society. The case was never tried before a jury because the court concluded the defendant should win as a matter of law.

Questions
1. How do you balance the business considerations cited in the memorandum relating to the need to attract qualified young sales personnel with the interests of the older workers?
2. In another case dealing with early retirement programs decided by the U.S. Court of Appeals for the Second Circuit (which includes New York City), *Paolillo v. Dresser Industries, Inc.*, 865 F.2d 37 (2d Cir. 1987), *modified,* 884 F.2d 707 (2d Cir. 1989), the court held that every retirement under an early retirement plan creates a prima facie (on its face) case of age discrimination, and that the employer must show both that the details of the plan have solid business justification and that each decision to retire is "voluntary," that is, "without undue strain." Judge Easterbrook, writing for the Seventh Circuit (which includes Chicago), stated that if *Paolillo* correctly interprets the ADEA, then the grant of summary judgment for the defendant-employer in *Henn* would have been improper. Which legal standard, that of the Second Circuit, or that of the Seventh Circuit, is better from a business point of view? From an ethical point of view?

Interestingly, the ADEA also prohibits unlawful age discrimination among persons within the protected age group. Thus, for example, if two individuals aged 41 and 53 apply for the same position, the employer may not lawfully reject either applicant on the basis of age. Moreover, because the ADEA only protects persons aged 40 or above, individuals under age 40 have no protection from discrimination based on age.

An employer faced with an age-discrimination claim may assert in its defense that: (1) age is a BFOQ reasonably necessary to the normal operation of the business (extremely difficult to prove); (2) the differential treatment is based on reasonable factors other than age; (3) the employer's action is based on a bona fide seniority system or employee benefit plan—such as a retirement, pension, or insurance plan—which is not invoked as a subterfuge to evade the purposes of the ADEA; or (4) the discharge of or discipline of a protected individual was for good cause.[24] Although these defenses are set forth in the ADEA itself, employers should proceed with caution, because the courts construe them strictly.

Older Workers' Benefit Protection Act

The Older Workers' Benefit Protection Act[25] (OWBPA) was signed in 1990 by President Bush. The act was an amendment to the Age Discrimination in Employment Act (ADEA). It prohibits age discrimination in providing employee benefits.[26] The OWBPA also establishes minimum standards for employees who waive their rights under the ADEA. In order to meet minimum standards, the waiver must be made "knowingly and voluntarily" by the employee.

Many states also have enacted laws designed to protect the employment rights of older individuals. There appears to be increasing support for expanding protection against discrimination on the basis of age.

---

24. 29 U.S.C. § 623(f) (1988 & Supp. 1992).

---

25. 29 U.S.C. § 623 (1988 & Supp. 1992).
26. Congress enacted the OWBPA in direct response to a case that held that the ADEA provided a broad exemption to employee benefit plans. The OWBPA overrules the holding in that case, *Public Employees Retirement System of Ohio v. Betts*, 492 U.S. 158, 109 S.Ct. 2854 (1989).

Economic Perspective
Effect of Downsizing on Older Workers

Companies that have attempted to decrease operating costs by restructuring and downsizing their work forces have primarily used two approaches: voluntary retirement programs and involuntary layoffs. Other companies have encouraged the retirement of older employees to make way for younger, less expensive workers.

Older workers have borne the brunt of corporate downsizing. Although the companies allege that severance and retirement packages are more humane than layoffs, there is a monetary motive behind them as well. Older workers generally receive higher paychecks, and even if only a few of them opt for early retirement, the company payroll may be greatly decreased.

The Federal Age Discrimination in Employment Act, enacted in 1967 and amended several times, prohibits any form of discrimination in the workplace because of age. The law eliminated mandatory retirement ages for all but a very few select positions, although it does permit the setting of mandatory retirement ages for executives.

Many workers between the ages of 45 and 65 accept severance packages even though the pension offered is smaller than that they would receive if they were employed until retirement. They do so because they would otherwise have to pay for health insurance, and the prospects of finding another job at their age are slim. It is of little consequence that the severance packages typically require that the recipient forfeit any right to legal remedies for age or other types of discrimination because the benefits they provide are often greater than those obtained from filing a lawsuit; age discrimination cases are difficult to prove and jury awards are typically small.

One Wall Street firm has been attacked for implementing "Operation Fresh Meat," a campaign that is allegedly designed to replace older workers with younger workers who can be paid much less.[a] Former middle-aged employees of the company claim that the firm was laying off older workers while simultaneously hiring college graduates. None of the employees filed a complaint against the company, however; they waived their right to sue for age discrimination in return for severance packages.

Many companies dispute the fact that older employees are bearing the brunt of corporate downsizings. The Commonwealth Fund, a New York nonprofit organization, conducted a survey among 400 companies in 1991 in which managers stated that older workers were not disproportionately affected by downsizing. They did acknowledge, however, that workers over 55 were often encouraged to accept early retirement.

The American work force is getting older. More than one in eight Americans is over 65, and it is predicted that by 2030 one in five will be in that age bracket. In anticipation of this trend in the work force, the federal government eliminated mandatory retirement to allow employees to work as long as they desire. The enactment of the Older Workers' Benefit Program in 1990 amended the Age Discrimination in Employment Act (ADEA) to: (1) prohibit discrimination on the basis of age with regard to employee fringe benefits; (2) establish standards governing the validity of early retirement programs and the eligibility of early retirees for severance pay; and (3) establish specific requirements for the execution of a valid release and waiver of claims under the ADEA.

Downsizing is quickly becoming a constant in the nineties. If companies choose to eliminate older workers and hire only younger employees, they will be losing the experience and knowledge gained over decades. Currently, companies undergoing a restructuring or downsizing offer all employees an opportunity to leave, either with a severance package or an early-retirement package. This differs from the approach they take when hiring new employees, which focuses on the qualifications of each applicant. A more sensible approach to downsizing might be to examine the performance of each employee and determine which employees are best qualified to assist the company after the downsizing is complete. However, steps must also be taken to eliminate age stereotypes.

Some of the myths about older workers are that they are set in their

---

a. Bruce Caldwell, "Old Before Your Time," *InformationWeek*, September 20, 1993, 30.

Economic Perspective
Effect of Downsizing on Older Workers (continued)

ways, cannot adapt to new situations, and rely on outdated information to make business decisions. Companies are often reluctant to promote people over 45 because they feel it is a waste to promote someone with only seven to ten employment years left.

The focus on downsizing and cost reduction may, however, obscure the loss of skills caused by the growing number of retirees. The aging of the labor force and the trend toward early retirement represent a potentially large loss of experienced workers.

An argument can be made that in a world that emphasizes the possession of critical knowledge and information, many companies are throwing away valuable resources in discarding workers with experience, knowledge, and skill.

■ Disability Discrimination

Title I of the Americans with Disabilities Act (ADA) prohibits employers from discriminating against a qualified individual because of a disability in regard to job application procedures, hiring, advancement, discharge, compensation, job training, and other terms, conditions, and privileges of employment. Such discrimination includes the use of selection criteria to screen out individuals with disabilities unless the criteria are job related and consistent with business necessity. Even in that event, the employer may not exclude a disabled individual if that individual, with some "reasonable accommodation," could perform the job, unless the needed accommodation would constitute an "undue hardship" for the employer.

Impermissible Discrimination

The ADA codifies existing judicial analysis of what constitutes impermissible discrimination. Under the ADA, employers are prohibited from intentionally discriminating against disabled persons and from engaging in employment practices that are not intentionally discriminatory, but have the effect of discriminating against disabled persons or perpetuating the past effects of such discrimination. The term "discriminate" as construed by the ADA includes the following prohibited practices:

1. Limiting, segregating, or classifying an applicant or employee because of her disability so as to adversely affect her opportunities or status;

2. Entering into a contractual relationship with an employment or referral agency, union, or other organization that has the effect of subjecting employees or applicants with a disability to prohibited discrimination;

3. Utilizing standards, criteria, or methods of administration that have the effect of discriminating or perpetuating the effects of discrimination because of disability;

4. Denying equal job benefits to a qualified individual because of the known disability of a person with whom the qualified individual is known to have a relationship or association;

5. Not making reasonable accommodations to the known physical or mental limitations of an otherwise qualified employee or applicant with a disability unless to do so would impose undue hardship on the employer;

6. Denying job opportunities to an otherwise qualified employee or applicant with a disability in order to avoid having to make reasonable accommodations for that disability;

7. Using qualification standards or employment tests that tend to screen out individuals with disabilities, unless the qualification standards or employment tests are shown to be job related and are consistent with business necessity; and

8. Failing to select and conduct job testing in such a way as to ensure that when the test is administered to an applicant or employee with a disability that impairs his sensory, manual, or speaking skills, the results of the test accurately reflect the skills or aptitude that test is designed to measure, rather than reflecting the sensory, manual, or speaking impairment.

Definition of Disability

The ADA codifies existing law developed under the Vocational Rehabilitation Act of 1973 by defining a "person with a disability" as: (1) a person with a physical or mental impairment that substantially limits one or more of that person's major life activities; (2) a person with a record of a physical or mental impairment that substantially limits one or more of that person's major life activities; or (3) a person who is regarded as having such an impairment. Because "working" is included among the "major life activities," any impairment that limits the individual's ability to work, or that the employer perceives as limiting those abilities, will be considered a disability. The ADA specifically excludes the following from the definition of disability: homosexuality, bisexuality, sexual behavior disorders, compulsive gambling, kleptomania, and pyromania.

> **"**
>
> *Because "working" is included among the "major life activities," any impairment that limits the individual's ability to work, or that the employer perceives as limiting those abilities, will be considered a disability.*

Psychoactive substance use disorders resulting from current illegal use of drugs, including the use of alcohol in the workplace against the employer's policies, are also excluded from the ADA's definition of a disability. (In addition, the ADA amends the Vocational Rehabilitation Act of 1973 to be consistent with the ADA's exclusion from coverage of current drug users.) However, an employee or applicant who is no longer engaged in the illegal use of drugs or alcohol on the work site, but who is involved in or has completed a supervised rehabilitation program, may be regarded as a disabled person.

Permissible Exclusion

If an applicant or employee is disabled, he may only be excluded from the employment opportunity if, by reason of his disability, he cannot perform the essential functions of the job, or if the employment of the individual poses a significant risk of health or safety to others. In determining whether a job function is essential, the ADA requires that consideration be given to the employer's judgment as to what functions are essential, but also looks to any written job description prepared *before* advertising or interviewing for the job commenced.

EEOC regulations issued in 1991 state that the risk of injury applies if there is risk to others or the disabled employee. However, the risk of injury must be a probability of substantial harm under the person's current con-

dition for it to be used to deny a job due to risk of future injury. Also, employers cannot rely on their own physician's opinion; risk of injury must be based upon generally accepted medical opinion.

Reasonable Accommodation

The ADA requires that employers make reasonable accommodations to an employee's disability, so long as doing so does not cause the employer "undue hardship." Thus, even if a disability precluded an individual from performing the essential functions of the position, or presented a safety risk, the employer is required to assess whether there is a reasonable accommodation that will permit the individual to be employed despite his disability. Title I sets forth a nonexhaustive list of what might constitute "reasonable accommodation" including the following: (1) making work facilities accessible; (2) restructuring jobs or modifying work schedules; (3) acquiring or modifying equipment or devices; (4) modifying examinations, training materials, or policies; and (5) providing qualified readers or interpreters or other similar accommodations for individuals with disabilities.

Undue Hardship

"Reasonable accommodation" is not required if it would impose an "undue hardship" on the employer. The ADA defines "undue hardship" to mean an activity requiring "significant difficulty or expense" when considered in light of: (1) the nature and cost of the accommodation needed; (2) the overall financial resources of the facility, the number of persons employed at the facility, the effect on expenses and resources, or any other impact of the accommodation on the facility; (3) the overall financial resources of the employer and the overall size of the business with respect to the number of employees and the type, number, and location of its facilities; and (4) the type of operation of the employer including the composition, structure, and functions of the workforce, the geographic separateness, and administrative or fiscal relationship of the facility in question to the employer.

Enforcement

Title I of the ADA is enforced in the same manner as title VII of the Civil Rights Act of 1964. Thus, the Equal Employment Opportunity Commission will initially investigate claims of discrimination and may sue to enforce title I's provisions. In addition, the complaining applicant or employee may sue in court and obtain the same remedies as are available under title VII, including back pay, reinstatement or hiring, and attorney's fees and costs.

Obesity as a Disability

A current topic of debate for several courts, both state and federal, is whether obesity should be considered a disability and thus protected from discrimination by employers. The Americans with Disabilities Act protects obese people if the obesity severely limits them and is caused by a physical disorder. It also protects those who are not limited but are regarded as disabled by obesity. It is this second provision that is the hot topic of debate among the courts in determining what is allowable by employers who appear to discriminate against obese applicants and/or employees.

■ AIDS Discrimination

A major issue today is the employer's relationship with an employee who has been diagnosed as having Acquired Immune Deficiency Syndrome (AIDS) or has tested positive for the human immunodeficiency virus (HIV). Because of the increasing number of persons receiving these diagnoses, the incurable nature of the disease, and public unfamiliarity with the facts about the disease, the presence in the workplace of someone diagnosed with AIDS causes concern among employers and employees alike. (Unless otherwise indicated, for purposes of this discussion, the term "AIDS" will be used to indicate anyone who has been diagnosed with AIDS or has tested positive for HIV.)

Although the Americans with Disabilities Act does not specifically list AIDS as a disability, courts would, based on cases defining "handicap" under the Vocational Rehabilitation Act of 1973, include AIDS as a protected disability. Although the case that follows did not directly address AIDS, employers and employment lawyers look to it for guidance. Because the Vocational Rehabilitation Act defines "handicap" in the same manner as the ADA defines "disability," this case is relevant to both acts.

■ A Case in Point: Summary

Case 13.6
SCHOOL BOARD OF
NASSAU COUNTY v. ARLINE
Supreme Court of the
United States
480 U.S. 273, 107 S.Ct. 1123
(1987).

FACTS   The School Board of Nassau County discharged Gene Arline, a teacher with tuberculosis, for fear she would infect students and co-workers. The board agreed that the Vocational Rehabilitation Act prohibits discrimination based on an individual's real or perceived physical or mental inability. However, the board argued that the act does not prohibit employment decisions based on an employer's reluctance to expose its other employees or its clientele to the threat of infection. The board further argued that the contagious nature of Arline's condition excluded it from the act's definition of "handicap."

ISSUE PRESENTED   Is a person with a contagious disease a handicapped person under the Vocational Rehabilitation Act?

SUMMARY OF OPINION   The U.S. Supreme Court held that, in determining whether there is a physical handicap, an employer cannot distinguish between the contagious effects of the disease and its physical impairment of the employee. If a disease is a physical condition that substantially limits one or more of the employee's major life activities, then it is a protected physical handicap as defined by the act. Tuberculosis is such a disease.

Once it was determined that Arline was handicapped, section 504 of the Vocational Rehabilitation Act prohibited her discharge so long as she was "otherwise qualified" to teach. The Supreme Court remanded the case for that determination and indicated that the trial court should consider these factors: how the disease is transmitted; how long the employee is contagious; the potential harm to third persons; and the probability that the dis-

Case 13.6 continued on following page

*Case **13.6** continued*

ease will be transmitted and cause harm to others. The Supreme Court explained that the trial court should defer to the reasonable medical judgments of public health officials and not be swayed by emotional public fears. Further, if the employee was found not able to perform the job because of her handicap, the trial court must then consider whether the school board could have made a reasonable accommodation rather than discharge her.

RESULT   Employee Arline cannot be fired as long as she is otherwise qualified for her position.

COMMENTS   Applying the same otherwise-qualified-to-teach test, the United States Court of Appeals for the Ninth Circuit ordered the Orange County Department of Education to restore a teacher diagnosed with AIDS to his duties.[27] However, an HIV-positive surgical technician in Houston, Texas, was found not "otherwise qualified" to continue his employment.[28] The United States Court of Appeals for the Fifth Circuit determined that although the risk of transmission from health care worker to patient is quite small, it cannot "nullify the catastrophic consequences of an accident." Thus, the surgical technician was not "otherwise qualified" under section 504 of the Vocational Rehabilitation Act.

---

27. *Chalk v. United States District Court*, 832 F.2d 1158 (9th Cir. 1987).
28. *Bradley v. University of Texas M.D. Anderson Cancer Ctr.*, 3 F.3d 922 (5th Cir. 1993).

Despite medical evidence that AIDS cannot be transmitted through casual contact not involving bodily fluids, the version of the ADA passed by the House of Representatives would have allowed employers to transfer employees infected with the HIV virus from food handling positions. Under the final bill, as adopted by Congress and signed by the president, the secretary of health and human services is directed to publish a list of infectious and communicable diseases that may be transmitted through the handling of food. Employers may refuse to assign an individual with such an infectious or communicable disease to a job involving food handling. The secretary of health and human services did not include AIDS or HIV in the food handling infectious disease list.

Duty to Accommodate

Under section 504 of the Vocational Rehabilitation Act and state handicap laws, there is a duty to accommodate the disabled person. Although there are differences among the various statutes, an employer is generally required to make a reasonable accommodation, but not one that results in undue hardship or financial burden.

With passage of the Americans with Disabilities Act an employer's only legal ground for terminating such an employee may be that the employee cannot perform on the job even with a reasonable accommodation.

Dealing With AIDS

An employer cannot justify discrimination against a person with AIDS on the basis of co-worker or customer preference. Likewise, the fact that the employment of someone with AIDS will increase group health insurance costs or cause absenteeism does not make discrimination permissible. However, as was demonstrated in case 1.2, it was once possible for an employer to modify an employer health plan to reduce benefits for employees with AIDS without violating the Employee Retirement Income Security Act of 1974 (ERISA). After passage of the ADA, however, modification of an employer health plan to reduce or eliminate coverage for employees with AIDS would probably be illegal. In 1993, the EEOC issued guidelines suggesting that disability-based distinctions in employer-provided health insurance programs (as was the issue in case 1.2) do violate the ADA except under extremely narrow circumstances. A legal test may emerge from a lawsuit filed by the EEOC based on the 1993 guidelines.[29]

Additionally, many states recognize a common-law right to privacy, and some states have a constitutional right to privacy. This right can protect individuals from improper circulation of information, such as an AIDS diagnosis, even though it is true and properly obtained for a specific purpose. Communication of such personal information might be protected by the qualified-privilege defense as long as it is confined only to those people who have a legitimate need to know. Circulation of an AIDS diagnosis among co-workers, however, would probably not be protected by the privilege. The employer also must be aware of any statutes that prohibit the disclosure of medical information. Some of these statutes specifically prohibit disclosure of AIDS blood-test results.

The employer also runs the risk of being sued for libel or slander if careless statements are made about employees. For example, falsely accusing an employee of being gay or of having AIDS could be grounds for a slander action (if the accusation is oral) or a libel action (if the accusation is in writing). Truth, however, is a complete defense to a libel or slander action.

When an employer learns that an employee has AIDS, the management must also consider its obligation to the employee's co-workers. This is an emerging area of law, where there has been little litigation. Under the federal Occupational Safety and Health Act (OSHA)[30] and similar state statutes, employees are entitled to work in an environment free of hazards that are likely to cause death or serious physical harm. OSHA prohibits an employer from discharging or discriminating against an employee who makes a bona fide complaint about what that employee regards as a safety hazard.[31] Therefore, if co-workers have a good-faith, though erroneous, belief that working with an AIDS patient is hazardous to their health, an employer takes a significant risk in penalizing them for refusal to work.

An increasingly popular means of protecting against such a dilemma is to have an AIDS education program for all employees. Several employers, especially larger corporations, have aggressively developed and utilized such programs. They show videotapes, circulate pamphlets and articles in employee newsletters, and invite medical professionals to give presentations. They strive to give employees accurate medical information about how AIDS is transmitted, to assure employees that the employer is not going to discriminate against an employee having AIDS, and to assure all employees that attention will be given to their health needs.

Ethical Consideration

Individuals with AIDS have been given protection against discrimination under various state and federal statutes. Employers should keep abreast of the federal, state, and local laws as they relate to AIDS, not only for the purpose of educating themselves about their rights, liabilities, and obligations under the law, but also to decide how to deal ethically with the AIDS epidemic.

■ Sexual Orientation Discrimination

Discrimination in employment based on sexual orientation is not barred by title VII or other federal laws, but is prohibited by many local and several state statutes. Legislation to amend title VII to include sexual orientation has been introduced in every term of Congress since 1975, but has yet to gather sufficient support for passage.

In 1992 presidential candidate Bill Clinton openly campaigned for the gay and lesbian vote, and promised to lift the military ban on homosexuals, as well as eliminate other forms of discrimination against gays and lesbians. Thus, many gay and lesbian activists were understandably disappointed with the "don't ask, don't tell" rule that emerged from the military debate. A second setback came with passage of Amendment 2, a Colorado voter initiative, that would have added an anti-gay-rights provision to the Colorado constitution. The effect of the Colorado initiative would have been to repeal the existing gay-rights ordinances of three Colorado cities, and to prevent the state from enacting any future legislation protecting individuals from discrimination on the basis of sexual orientation. The Colorado Supreme Court in 1993 enjoined enforcement of Amendment 2.[32] Oregon voters

---

29. *EEOC v. Mason Tenders District Council Welfare Fund*, No. 93-3865 (S.D.N.Y. June 9, 1993) (complaint filed).

30. 29 U.S.C. §§ 651-678 (1988 & Supp. 1992).

31. 29 U.S.C. § 660(c)(l) (1988).

32. *Evans v. Romer*, 854 P.2d 1270 (Colo. 1993). Amendment 2 was declared unconstitutional in 1994.

rejected a similar statewide anti-gay proposition, and in 1994, the Florida Supreme Court refused to permit a similar anti-gay-rights amendment to appear on that state's ballot.[33] Nonetheless, anti-gay ballot measures continue to appear in many state and local elections.

Another recent example of the debate surrounding the rights of gays and lesbians came in Williamson County, Texas. In December 1993, the Williamson County commissioners voted 3-2 to deny tax breaks worth $750,000 to Apple Computer because of Apple's domestic-partners policy, which provides gay employees and their domestic partners the same health benefits as married couples. The commissioners cited high moral and family values as their reasons for their vote. The debate prior to the vote included much anti-gay sentiment and suggestions that a yes vote would bring homosexuals and AIDS to Williamson County. However, one week later the commission reversed its decision in another 3-2 vote. Political, economic, and public pressure, rather than a change of heart, seemed to have a great deal to do with the change in decision. As of April 1994, nearly 100 private and public employers offered similar domestic-partner benefits.

Gay and lesbian employees who are fired because of their sexual orientation may bring wrongful termination suits under state law in several states. In a 1991 California case, Shell Oil Company and its subsidiary Triton Biosciences were ordered to pay $5.3 million in back pay and damages to a gay executive who was fired solely because he was homosexual.[34] The executive had been with Shell for 19 years and had received consistently high work performance evaluations. However, when Shell accidentally became aware of the executive's sexual orientation, it fired him and refused to pay earned bonuses and other benefits. In addition, Shell shared confidential information concerning the executive's homosexuality with prospective employers and agencies after the firing.

A California court found Shell and Triton guilty of outrageous conduct and intentional infliction of emotional distress. They were ordered to pay $2.5 million for economic loss under the contract causes of action, $800,000 for noneconomic tort damages, and $2 million in punitive damages for intent to inflict emotional distress.

Following this 1991 decision, the California Supreme Court ruled in an unrelated case in 1993 that a tort cause of action is not appropriate in wrongful termination cases except those involving violations of public policy. In other cases, contract damages alone are the appropriate remedy for wrongful termination. To recover on tort claims, plaintiffs' damages cannot be said to result from the termination itself.[35]

At the Top

An employee tends to take her cue from the conduct of her employer. For example, if the employer discriminates in its hiring, retention, and promotion policies, the employee may be more likely to believe that like conduct is acceptable. The employee may take this as an indication of not only how she can but how she should act in a workplace.

■ Affirmative Action

Affirmative action programs are generally viewed as a means to remedy past acts of discrimination. Such programs are usually established pursuant to court orders, court-approved consent decrees, or federal and state laws that impose affirmative action obligations on government contractors.

Executive Order 11246 requires federal government contractors to include in every government contract not exempted by the order a provision that states that the contractor will not discriminate in employment on the basis of race, color, religion, sex, or national origin, and that the contractor agrees to take affirmative steps to prevent discrimination.[36] In some cases, a contractor's affirmative action plan must be put in writing. Although individuals have no private right of action based on an alleged violation of the order, the Department of Labor, through its Office of Federal Contract Compliance Programs, has a wide range of sanctions available to it. These sanctions include, for example, suspending or ter-

---

33. *In re: Advisory Opinion to the Attorney General*, 19 Fla. L. Weekly § 109 (Fla. 1994).
34. *Collins v. Shell Oil Co.*, 56 Fair Empl. Prac. Cas. (BNA) 440 (Cal. App. Dep't Super. Ct. 1991).

35. *Hunter v. Up-Right, Inc.*, 6 Cal 4th 1174, 26 Cal. Rptr. 2d 8, 864 P.2d 88 (Cal. 1993).
36. Executive Order No. 11246, 3 C.F.R. § 339 (1964-1965), reprinted in 42 U.S.C. § 2000e (1982).

minating a government contract and disqualifying the contractor from entering any future government contracts.

Government contractors are subject to affirmative action obligations under other federal laws as well. For example, section 503 of the Vocational Rehabilitation Act of 1973 requires employers with government contracts or subcontracts of more than $2,500 to employ qualified disabled persons and to take affirmative action with respect to such individuals. Similarly, the Vietnam Era Veterans' Readjustment Assistance Act of 1972 requires employers with federal contracts or subcontracts of $10,000 or more to take affirmative action to employ and to advance in employment disabled Vietnam-era veterans.

An employer may also voluntarily establish an affirmative action plan. For example, the United States Supreme Court upheld a collective bargaining agreement between a union and a company that contained an affirmative action plan giving preference to African-American employees entering into a skilled-craft training position.[37] The lawsuit was brought by a white worker who alleged that because the plan resulted in junior African-American employees receiving preference to senior white employees, he and other white employees were being discriminated against in violation of title VII. Concluding that title VII did not preclude all private, voluntary, race-conscious affirmative action programs, the Court noted that the plan: (1) was, like title VII, designed to break down patterns of racial segregation and hierarchy; (2) "did not unnecessarily trammel the interests of white employees"; and (3) was a temporary measure intended to attain rather than maintain racial balance. The EEOC has promulgated regulations regarding voluntary affirmative action plans.[38]

In a case decided in 1989, the United States Supreme Court made it somewhat easier for individuals to bring reverse-discrimination lawsuits based on affirmative action plans.[39] The Court held that federal procedural rules did not preclude white firefighters from challenging the validity of an affirmative action plan that was adopted with federal court approval several years earlier to settle lawsuits by African Americans alleging discrimination in hiring and promotion. The white firefighters argued that the plan violated title VII by denying them promotions based on their race. The Court ruled in a 5–4 decision that the white firefighters were not precluded from challenging employment decisions taken pursuant to the affirmative action plan. The Court stated: "A voluntary settlement . . . between one group of employees and their employer cannot possibly 'settle,' voluntarily or otherwise, the conflicting claims of another group of employees who do not join in the agreement."

In response to this decision, the Civil Rights Act of 1991 limited the ability of persons to challenge affirmative action litigated judgments and consent decrees. A person cannot challenge a judgment or consent decree if any of the following three conditions is applicable: (1) the person had actual notice of the proposed judgment or order sufficient to let that person know that the judgment or decree might adversely affect the interests and legal rights of that person, and had an opportunity to present objections; (2) the person had a reasonable opportunity to present objections to the judgment or order; or (3) the person's interests were adequately represented by another person who had previously challenged the judgment or order on the same legal grounds and with a similar factual situation.

■ Civil Rights Act of 1991

This chapter describes, in context, many of the provisions and effects of the Civil Rights Act of 1991. Other provisions not yet covered include the following. The act overturns *Lorance v. AT&T Technologies*[40] by providing that a seniority system adopted for an intentionally discriminatory purpose can be challenged under title VII when the seniority system is adopted, when an individual becomes subject to the system, or when a person aggrieved is injured by the application of the seniority system.

The act provides that title VII and the Americans with Disabilities Act, like the Age Discrimination in Employment Act, apply to U.S. citizens employed in foreign countries by American-owned or controlled companies unless compliance with title VII or the ADA would cause the employer to violate the law of the foreign country in which it is located.[41]

---

37. *United Steelworkers of America v. Weber,* 443 U.S. 193, 99 S.Ct. 2721 (1979).
38. *See* 29 C.F.R. § 1608.1-12 (1992).
39. *Martin v. Wilks,* 490 U.S. 755, 109 S.Ct. 2180 (1989).

---

40. 490 U.S. 900, 109 S.Ct. 2261 (1989). In *Lorance* the Supreme Court held that the period for filing a challenge began with the date the system was adopted.
41. This effectively overturned *EEOC v. Arabian American Oil Co.,* 499 U.S. 244, 111 S.Ct. 1227 (1991), which had held that title VII did not apply to a U.S. citizen working in Saudi Arabia for a corporation incorporated in Delaware.

The act expanded the categories for which compensatory and punitive damages could be recovered to include intentional religious, disability, and sex discrimination. Under prior law, recovery of damages was limited to victims of intentional racial or ethnic bias. The compensatory and punitive damages available under the act for discrimination based on sex, religion, and disability are capped at $50,000 for employers of 100 or fewer employees; $100,000 for employers with 101 to 200 employees; $200,000 for employers with 201 to 500 employees; and $500,000 for employers with more than 500 employees. The compensatory caps do not apply to intentional racial or ethnic discrimination, however. Punitive damages are available only when the employer acted with "malice or with reckless indifference to" an employee's rights. Any party to a case for damages can demand a jury trial, but the court may not inform the jury of the caps on damage awards.

The act banned so-called *race norming of employment tests,* which is a device designed to ensure that a minimum number of minorities and women are in the application pool. The act prohibits an employer, in connection with the selection or referral of applicants or candidates for employment or promotion, from adjusting the scores of, using different cutoff scores for, or otherwise altering the results of, employment-related tests on the basis of race, color, religion, sex, or national origin.

The act includes as title II the Glass Ceiling Act of 1991. This act states, in its findings and purposes section, that "(1) despite a dramatically growing presence in the workplace, women and minorities remain underrepresented in management and decision-making positions in business; (2) artificial barriers exist to the advancement of women and minorities in the workplace." The act established a Glass Ceiling Commission to study and make recommendations concerning elimination of artificial barriers to advancement and increasing opportunities and development experiences of women and minorities to foster advancement to management and decision-making positions in business.

■ Family and Medical Leave Act of 1993

The Family and Medical Leave Act of 1993[42] has a number of specific and rather straightforward guidelines regarding employee eligibility and employer obligations.

42. Pub. L. No. 103-3, 107 Stat. 6 (1993).

The employee must have worked at the place of employment for at least 12 months, and have completed at least 1,250 hours of service to the employer during that 12-month period to be eligible for a family leave.

For an employer to be covered by the act she must employ 50 or more employees at work sites within 75 miles of each other. Part-time employees are excluded from the act's coverage and may not be counted in calculating the 50 employees necessary for an employer to be covered by the act.

Eligible employees are entitled to 12 weeks of unpaid leave per year. There are four situations in which an employee may use his leave under the act: (1) the birth of a child; (2) the placement of an adopted or foster care child with the employee; (3) care of a child, a parent, or a spouse; or (4) a serious health condition that renders the employee unable to do her job.

An employee cannot contract out of his right to leave time under this act. However, the employer may require, or an employee may choose, to substitute any or all accrued paid leave for the leave time that is now provided for under this act. The act should be considered a floor, not a ceiling, to what employers can provide their employees in terms of a leave option.

Finally, an important aspect of the act is that it requires the employer to restore the employee to the same position, or one with equivalent benefits, pay and other terms and conditions of employment, following the expiration of the leave.

■ Preemployment Practices

From both a legal and a practical standpoint, the employer-employee relationship begins at the start of the application process. Recent years have seen an increase in litigation concerning preemployment practices, such as job advertising, employment applications, job interviewing, and testing. Employers must take care to avoid unlawful discrimination in these activities.

Obviously, a policy or a particular decision not to hire an applicant because she is a woman or is an African American would be subject to challenge under disparate treatment analysis. A policy or decision must not treat some applicants differently from others simply because of their gender or race.

A more common problem in today's business environment concerns hiring practices and policies that appear to be race- or gender-neutral but that have a disparate impact on one race or gender. Where a hiring practice or policy is found to have a disparate impact on a protected class of persons, the employer must show that the policy is a business necessity. The business necessity must be related to job performance and not to inconvenience, annoyance, or expense.

Job Advertisements

Many employers begin the recruitment process by posting or publishing a "Help Wanted" notice. Title VII and the ADEA prohibit employers from publishing or printing job notices that express a preference or limitation based on race, color, religion, sex, national origin, or age, unless such specifications are based on good-faith occupational qualifications. For example, an advertisement for a "waitress" implies that the employer is seeking a woman for the job. If there is no bona fide reason why the job should be filled by a woman rather than a man the advertisement might be considered discriminatory. Similarly, terms such as "young woman" or "girl" should never be used because they discourage job candidates from applying for positions because of their sex or age.

Many state laws also prohibit discriminatory advertisements. For example, Massachusetts and Ohio prohibit notices that express, directly or indirectly, any limitations or specifications concerning race, color, religion, national origin, sex, age, ancestry, or disability

Word-of-mouth recruitment practices, which normally involve current employees informing their family and friends of job openings, also can be discriminatory. When information is disseminated in this way, it may tend to reach a disproportionate number of persons of the same ethnicity as the employer's current employees. Thus, reliance on word-of-mouth recruiting practices may perpetuate past discrimination. Where word-of-mouth is used, it should be supplemented with other recruiting activities that are designed to reach a broader spectrum of people.

Employers advertising for jobs should avoid placing advertisements in publications with sex-segregated help-wanted columns. They should indicate that the employer is an equal opportunity employer, and should use media designed to reach people in both minority and nonminority communities.

Employers use the application and interview process to gain information about an individual's personal, educational, and employment background. Unless it has a valid defense, an employer should avoid making inquiries on an application form, during a preemployment interview, or in some other manner, that identify the protected characteristics of a job candidate. Although federal laws do not expressly prohibit preemployment

inquiries concerning an applicant's race, color, national origin, sex, marital status, religion, or age, such inquiries are disfavored because they create an inference that these factors will be used as selection criteria. These inquiries may be expressly prohibited under state law.

Often the line between permissible and impermissible areas of inquiry is not clear. Because the actions of recruiters, interviewers, and supervisors can expose an employer to legal liability, it is crucial that they understand which questions should and should not be asked. As a general rule, recruitment personnel should ask themselves, "What information do I really need to decide whether an applicant is qualified to perform this job?"

Sex and Marital/Family Status Any preemployment inquiry that explicitly or implicitly indicates a preference or limitation based on an applicant's sex is unlawful unless the inquiry is justified by a bona fide occupational qualification. In rare cases a candidate's sex may be a valid criterion for a job, as in the case of actors or actresses or fashion models. However, questions concerning an applicant's sex, as well as marital/family status should be avoided. For example, application forms and interviewers should not ask:

1. Whether an applicant is male or female
2. The number or ages of an applicant's children
3. How an applicant will arrange for child care
4. An applicant's views on birth control
5. Whether an applicant is pregnant or plans to become pregnant
6. Whether a female applicant prefers to be addressed as Mrs., Miss, or Ms.
7. The applicant's maiden name

In addition, an interviewer should not direct a particular question, such as whether the applicant can type, only to female or only to male applicants.

Some of the above information eventually will be needed for benefits, tax, and EEOC profile purposes, but it can be collected after the applicant is employed.

There are exceptions to this general rule. For example, state law may require employers to collect data regarding the race, sex, and national origin of each applicant, and the job for which she has applied. Certain government contractors are also obligated to collect applicant-flow data. Such data are collected for statistical and record-keeping purposes only and cannot be considered by the employer in its hiring decision. In general, if an employer is required to collect such data, the employer should ask applicants to provide self-identification information on a form that is separate or detachable from the application form.

Age   Application forms and interviewers should not try to identify applicants aged 40 and older. Accordingly, job candidates generally should not be asked their age, their birth date, or the date that they completed elementary or secondary school. An employer can inquire about age only if: (1) age is a bona fide job requirement, as for a child actor; or (2) the employer is trying to comply with special laws, such as those applying to the employment of minors. That it may cost more to employ older workers as a group does not justify differentiation among applicants based on age.

Race   Employers should not ask about an applicant's race. Questions concerning complexion, skin color, eye color or hair color should be avoided, and applicants should not be asked to submit photographs.

National Origin   An applicant should not be asked about his nationality or ancestry, as title VII prohibits discrimination on the basis of national origin. The Immigration Reform and Control Act of 1986 (IRCA)[43] makes it unlawful for an employer with four or more employees to discriminate against applicants or employees on the basis of either their national origin or their citizenship status. (If the employer has 15 or more employees and therefore is covered by title VII, charges of national-origin discrimination must be filed under title VII, not IRCA.)

IRCA also makes it unlawful for an employer of any size to hire knowingly an individual who is not authorized to work in the United States. Violators can be subject to civil and criminal penalties. However, employers must not discriminate against persons solely because they have a foreign appearance or speak a foreign language. The act specifies the correct procedure for determining whether an applicant is authorized to work.

Under the act, any newly hired employee is required to complete a form I-9 certifying that she is authorized to work in the United States and has presented documentation of work authorization and identification to the employer. After examining the documents presented, the employer must complete the remainder of the form, certifying that the documents appear genuine, relate to the employee, and establish work authorization. The form I-9 must be completed within a prescribed period of time.

Religion   An employer generally should not ask questions about an applicant's religion. An employer can tell an applicant what the normal work schedule is, but should not ask which religious holidays the applicant observes or whether the applicant's religion will interfere with his job performance. Title VII's ban on religious discrimination encompasses more than Sabbath observance. It applies to all conduct motivated by religion, such as dress or maintenance of a particular physical appearance. Title VII imposes a duty upon employers to make reasonable accommodation to their employees' religious practices as long as such accommodation will not cause undue hardship to the employer's business.

An employer can ask about a candidate's religious beliefs if they are a bona fide occupational qualification. For example, a school that is owned, supported, or controlled by persons of a particular religion can require that its employees have a specific religious belief. In an extreme case, a federal district court ruled that a helicopter pilot could be required to convert to the Moslem religion in order to fly over certain areas of Saudi Arabia that are closed to non-Moslems.[44] The court ruled that the requirement was a bona fide occupational qualification justified by safety considerations, because Saudi Arabian law prohibits non-Moslems from entry into Mecca, and non-Moslems risk being beheaded if caught entering this area.

> **"**
>
> *In an extreme case, a federal district court ruled that a helicopter pilot could be required to convert to the Moslem religion in order to fly over certain areas of Saudi Arabia that are closed to non-Moslems.*

Disabilities and Physical Traits   Applicants should not be questioned about their general medical condition. Although title VII does not prohibit discrimination on the basis of disability, the Americans with Disabilities Act prohibits all discrimination on the basis of disability. In addition, several states prohibit such discrimination, and the federal Vocational Rehabilitation Act of 1973 forbids discrimination against disabled persons by certain government contractors and by employers receiving federal financial assistance. After an employer has described a job's requirements, the employer can ask the applicant if she can perform the job. If the applicant answers no, the

---

43. Pub. L. No. 99-603, 100 Stat. 3359 (codified as amended in scattered sections of the U.S.C.).

44. *Kern v. Dynalectron Corp.*, 577 F.Supp. 1196 (N.D. Tex. 1983), *aff'd*, 746 F.2d 810 (5th Cir. 1984).

employer should ask if there is any way to accommodate the applicant's limitation. An applicant also can be told that her offer is contingent on passing a job-related medical exam (discussed further below).

Applicants generally should not be asked questions about their height or weight. Height and weight requirements have been deemed unlawful where such standards disqualify physically disabled persons, women, and members of certain ethnic or national origin groups and the employer could not establish that such requirements were directly related to job performance.

Conviction Record   Although an employer can ask applicants if they have ever been criminally convicted, this question should be followed by a statement that the existence of a criminal record will not automatically bar employment. Because in many geographical areas a disproportionate number of minorities are convicted of crimes, the use of conviction records as an automatic exclusion may have a disparate effect on minorities and therefore may be unlawful.

Consideration of a criminal record generally will be lawful only if the conviction relates to the requirements of the particular job. For example, an employer may be justified in rejecting an applicant convicted of theft for a hotel security position. Where a job applicant has been convicted of a crime involving physical violence, the employer may be faced with a delicate problem. Some courts have held the employer liable where an employee with a record of violent behavior later assaulted another employee or a third party. Liability is based on the theory that the employer was negligent in its duties to protect the health and safety of the injured person by hiring such an employee. If the employee is operating in a jurisdiction that recognizes this *negligent-hiring theory,* a policy against hiring any person with a criminal conviction for a violent act is justified. This is an increasingly difficult area for employers, given recent instances of violence in the workplace.

Employers should not ask applicants if they have ever been arrested. Some states, such as Washington and Illinois, prohibit or restrict employers from asking applicants about arrests or detentions that did not result in conviction.

Education   Employers can ask applicants questions regarding their education and work experience, but all requirements, such as possession of a high school diploma, must be job related. Inflated standards of academic achievement, language proficiency, or employment experience may be viewed as a pretext for unlawful discrimination against women and members of minority groups.

Credit References   Rejection of an applicant because of a poor credit rating may be unlawful unless the employer can show that the decision not to hire the applicant was due to business necessity. Because the percentage of minority-group members with poor credit ratings generally is higher than that of nonminority-group members, rejection of applicants on this basis can have a disparate impact upon minority groups.

Preemployment Tests

Many employers use preemployment tests as a screening mechanism. Title VII prohibits employers from using any test that is designed, intended, or used to disqualify applicants in one of the protected groups. In addition, there are restrictions on the use of tests that have the effect of screening out protected-group members. An employer considering a test as a means to select employees must: (1) determine if the test will have an adverse effect on a protected group of applicants; and (2) have the test validated in accordance with procedures specified by the EEOC.

A test has an adverse effect on members of a protected group if the pass rate of any sex, race, or ethnic group is less than 80% of the pass rate for the highest group passing the test. For example, if 100% of whites and only 79% of African Americans pass a particular test, the test is presumed to be unlawful because it has an adverse effect on African Americans.

A test that has an adverse impact on a protected group must be validated under the Uniform Guidelines on Employee Selection Procedures, published by the EEOC. Validation is expensive and complicated. Even if a test is job related, it may still be challenged if alternative, less discriminatory selection procedures would equally aid the employer in making hiring decisions.

Physical Examinations

The Americans with Disabilities Act prohibits preemployment medical examinations or inquiries concerning the existence, nature, or extent of the disability of an applicant unless the inquiries relate directly to that individual's general ability to perform job-related functions and a tentative offer of employment has been made. Medical examinations may only be required after a definite employment offer has been made and before the employee begins her employment duties. The offer of employment may be conditioned on the job-related results of the medical examination only if all entering employees are subject to such an examination. Moreover, the results of such an examination must be treated as confidential medical records and kept separate from other personnel information.

Polygraph Testing

The Employee Polygraph Protection Act of 1988 prohibits most private employers from using polygraph exams or other lie detector tests not only on current employees but also on job applicants. The act does not apply to federal, state, and local governments, although several states do have laws restricting or prohibiting the use of polygraph examinations. For example, in Massachusetts, an employer cannot request that an applicant or employee take a lie detector test as a condition of employment. Rhode Island, Delaware, and Pennsylvania have similar statutes.

Where lie detector tests are permitted, no question should be asked during the test that could not lawfully be asked on an application form or during an interview.

The Responsible Manager
Honoring Employees' Civil Rights

Managers must be aware that there are federal, state, and local statutes forbidding certain types of discrimination, such as discrimination on the basis of race, color, religion, national origin, sex, sexual orientation, age, or disability. They should therefore familiarize themselves with these statutes and notify their employees of their exis-

tence. Managers must prevent unlawful discrimination in both the preemployment and employment process.

In order to prevent unlawful discrimination, management should develop a written policy, clearly outlining discriminatory acts prohibited by federal, state, and local statutes. Employees should be advised that any form of discrimination is inappropriate. The policy should have an enforcement mechanism and should clearly state that violations of the policy will result in poor performance reviews or termination. Such a policy would not only curb discriminatory acts but would demonstrate that management diligently attempted to prevent such behavior in the event that litigation should arise.

The firm should also create a working environment in which employees feel comfortable in bringing complaints against fellow workers and supervisors. Each complaint should be thoroughly investigated and, if necessary, the violator should be punished. In addition, provisions should be made so that there is an individual or two in the company, a male and a female, to whom such suits may be brought. Because supervisors are often the discriminators, this system would have an advantage over one in which an employee must first complain to his supervisor before an investigation could take place.

Although the establishment of such a policy is one way to prevent unlawful discriminatory practices, it is not sufficient in itself. Managers must also abide by the policy and federal, state, and local statutes prohibiting unlawful discrimination. If management participates in discriminatory acts, its employees will have little incentive to abide by the firm's policy against discrimination, and employees will hesitate to bring a claim for discriminatory treatment.

Inside Story
American Stores Settles Sex-Bias Suit for up to $107.3 Million

In the settlement of a sex discrimination case that may alter personnel practices throughout the grocery store industry, Lucky Stores agreed to pay almost $75 million in damages to women who were denied promotions, and to invest an additional $20 million in affirmative-action programs for its female employees.

The class-action settlement was one of the largest ever in a sex discrimination case. It brought to a close a

decade-long battle between the grocery chain, which has 188 stores in its Northern California division and is a division of American Stores, and a group of female employees who were denied desirable assignments, management training, and movement into full-time positions that would have improved their chances for promotions.

The lawsuit had been vigorously contested by the

Inside Story, continued

Lucky Stores chain, which claimed that its female employees were not promoted to better jobs because the women were not interested in the better jobs. The women who brought the suit against the chain contended that they were assigned to dead-end jobs such as working at cash registers or in bakery or delicatessen departments, rather than the main grocery and produce sections, where jobs are generally better paid and can lead to promotions.

One of the plaintiffs was working as a cashier when her son began working in the same position. He was soon offered training and promotion opportunities that were not available to her.

Federal District Judge Marilyn Patel found that from 1984 to 1989, women accounted for 46.6% of the new employees at the Northern California Lucky Stores, but made up 84% of the new employees assigned to low-paying jobs, and that these women were offered few chances to move into management positions.

The Lucky Stores litigation continued for 10 months until the summer of 1992. At that time, Judge Patel ruled against the supermarket chain and ordered it to institute new personnel policies on a trial basis. Under the consent decree filed in federal court, Lucky Stores will provide an entry-level management training program and allow employees to bid for promotions to management positions. It has also set goals for increasing the number of female managers. Since the new policy was instituted, Lucky has filled 58% of new management jobs with women.

The settlement also requires Lucky Stores to revise personnel practices under the supervision of the court and to pay additional damages of up to $13 million if specific targets for hiring and promotions are not met. If the additional damages are necessary, the settlement could reach $107.25 million.

Attorneys for Lucky and the women who brought the class-action lawsuit spent 15 months trying to reach a settlement after Judge Patel ruled on the case. The settlement covers approximately 14,000 women employed at Lucky Stores from 1983 to 1992. The women were expected to receive an average of $5,000 each in damages, depending on seniority, with payments ranging from $100 to $50,000, beginning in January 1995.

Key Words and Phrases

BFOQ defense **404**	fetal protection policy **405**	*quid pro quo* harassment **408**
disparate impact **401**	hostile environment harassment **408**	race norming of employment tests **426**
disparate treatment **400**	negligent-hiring theory **429**	

Questions and Case Problems

1. What are the elements of a claim of hostile environment?

2. Sheila Prescott is an employee at Ladet, Inc. in Miami, Florida. Ladet manufactures tennis clothes for men and women, and has more than 600 employees. Prescott has worked for Ladet since 1988. She is employed in the personnel department and reports directly to the director of personnel, Frank Allen. In May 1993, Prescott and Allen traveled together to the University of Wisconsin on a recruiting trip. While in Wisconsin, Prescott and Allen had sexual intercourse.

In June 1994, Prescott was passed over for a position as head of the personnel department in Ladet's newly opened Denver branch office. This job would have provided Prescott with higher pay. Another woman at Ladet was offered the job.

Prescott has brought a sexual harassment claim against Allen and Ladet. Although Allen and Prescott had sexual intercourse only on that one occasion in Wisconsin, Prescott contends that Allen refused to recommend her for the Denver position because he wanted to keep her in the Miami office. Prescott has not been demoted and has not received a cut in pay.

If you were investigating Prescott's sexual harassment claim, what information would you want to know?

What relief might Prescott be granted?

3. Tony Sadler is a production supervisor for Zydos, Inc., a Nevada manufacturer of printed circuit boards. Several years ago, Sadler worked in Ohio for Axion, Inc. When Zydos was just starting up, it recruited Sadler by offering him better money and a ground-floor role in Zydos's development. Sadler was persuaded to quit his job at Axion and move to Nevada. He has been a successful supervisor at Zydos ever since, receiving several raises, good performance reviews, and a recent promotion.

In his new position, Sadler supervises the Zydos Quality Assurance and Test Department, which comprises 12 employees who test A and B units before sealing and shipping them. The department is made up of one Caucasian, six Hispanics, and five Vietnamese. Most of the employees know how to test both A and B units, but a few have been trained on only one unit. Because Zydos is experiencing significant financial difficulties, the human resources manager has instructed Sadler to prepare a list of potential layoff candidates from his department. He is to examine his employees' flexibility and the importance of their skills to the work at hand. Sadler's layoff candidate list reads:

Name	Reason
Tran Trinh	Elimination of lead position
Yen Chi Pham	Not trained to test A units
Quyen Lam	Not trained to test A units
Dung Tien	Not trained to test A units

The human resources manager of Zydos has contacted you for advice. In addition to providing you with the above information, he tells you that he was contacted this morning by Raul Lopez, a quality assurance tester who had recently received a poor performance review. He complained that he was "getting a raw deal" because Sadler "spends all his time with those geeks." When pressed for details, Lopez complained that Tony favored the Vietnamese, often went to lunch with them, and spent long periods of time talking to them (and especially to a young Vietnamese woman named Hai Nguyen) to the exclusion of others in his department. He confided that everyone thinks Hai and Tony are having an affair.

The human resources manager also tells you that the Vietnamese people are a tightly knit group; that Hai is a very good tester; that she is very shy and submissive; and that, when she came to work at Zydos several months before, destitute and helpless after leaving an abusive Vietnamese boyfriend, Sadler befriended her and helped her get on her feet. He also tells you that the lead tester, Tran Trinh, is a 54-year-old "Vietnamese godfather type" who "rules the roost for the Vietnamese" in Sadler's department and has wide connections with the Vietnamese community. Tran disapproves of Hai's association with Sadler and is a family friend of Hai's ex-boyfriend. Sadler has received a couple of threatening phone calls from Hai's ex-boyfriend regarding things that have occurred at work.

The human resources manager has asked both Hai and Sadler whether they are having a romantic relationship. Both have denied anything but a warm friendship.

What legal liabilities could result from the situation in Sadler's department and what advice would you give Sadler to help avoid each potential liability?

4. Assume the facts in question 3. Further assume that a week has passed and Hai has told the human relations manager that she and Sadler have been having a romantic relationship, that initially it was what she wanted, but that now she wants it to stop. She says that she has told Sadler that it is over, and he is angry. She is afraid that he will fire her or keep "talking like a lover" to her. The human relations manager tells you he fired Sadler immediately.

What legal liability might Zydos have toward Sadler? If either of Hai's worries had come to fruition before Sadler was fired, what legal liabilities might have resulted to Zydos?

5. In 1987, McDonnell Douglas responded to declining business by consolidating its Astronautics, Electronics, and Microelectronics subsidiaries. The company determined that approximately 120 jobs would be eliminated as a result. A voluntary severance program fell short of its goal, resulting in the need to lay off 19 individuals.

Joseph Barbeau, the person in charge of the newly consolidated accounting department, was told that he had to select three people to be laid off. In February 1988 Barbeau selected three employees, including William Glover. He was 59 years old and had worked for the Astronautics subsidiary for more than 20 years. Glover had a B.A. degree and an associate degree but did not have a degree in accounting. His job was that of a "processor" in the Accounts Payable Section; his duties consisted primarily of reviewing invoices to ensure that they complied with the company's purchase orders. Glover sued McDonnell Douglas, alleging that he had been selected for termination based on his age, and was denied consideration for reassignment to another subsidiary based on his age.

What will Glover need to prove in order to prevail? What arguments will McDonnell Douglas make in order to defend itself? [*Glover v. McDonnell Douglas Corp.*, 12 F.3d 845 (8th Cir. 1994)]

6. Plaintiff Candelaria Cuello-Suarez, a United States citizen who was born in the Dominican Republic and was a seventeen-year veteran employee of the Puerto Rico Electric Power Authority (PREPA), held various positions as clerk and typist. She possessed a B.A. degree in business administration with a major in accounting and a minor in management and, shortly after commencement of her lawsuit, obtained her license as a certified public accountant. Over the years, she successfully passed at least ten different tests required for promotion, and always received above-average evaluations in her performance reviews. She never received a reprimand. Prior to filing her lawsuit, the plaintiff filed applications for promotions to supervisory positions, with no success. Subsequent to the filing of her suit in 1988, she applied for the position of Supervisor of Consumer Services. The position was filled by a native Puerto Rican who had been employed by PREPA for seven months and had a B.S. degree in marine biology.

The plaintiff claims that she was denied a promotion on many occasions because of her national origin. What must she prove in order to make a prima facie case of discrimination? What type of a nondiscriminatory justification for its actions will the Puerto Rico Electric Power Authority present? [*Cuello-Suarez v. Puerto Rico Electric Power Authority*, 988 F.2d 275 (1st Cir. 1993)]

7. In March 1988, Ellie Grizzle was hired at age 42 as a general ledger accountant by Travelers, a health maintenance organization (HMO) "umbrella" company in Las Colinas, Texas. Although she did not have a bachelor's degree in accounting, Grizzle had ten years of experience working as an accountant. For the initial period of her employment, March 1988 through March 1989, Grizzle achieved an above average rating of "2" only because the highest rating "1" was reserved for a perfect performance. Grizzle also won an "Outstanding Achievement" award during this period.

In September 1988, Ellie Grizzle applied for but did not receive a supervisory position. According to Grizzle, during an interview with finance director Glen Marconcini she was informed by him that, although she was qualified for the promotion, she would not receive it because she rubbed him the wrong way, she smoked, and also, he was not wild about her age. Thereafter, Grizzle complained to her immediate supervisor, Leon Nary, who interceded on her behalf. As a result of her complaint to Nary, Grizzle received a $2,000 a year raise and was given supervisory authority within her department. No formal complaint was made with respect to Marconcini's alleged comment and, in fact, favorable employment action followed her informal complaint to Nary.

In March 1989, the Travelers Las Colinas and Atlanta offices merged. The following month, Kent Latiolais, a transferee from the Travelers Atlanta office, was made Grizzle's supervisor. The appointment of Latiolais was in effect a demotion for Grizzle. Grizzle testified that she met with Travelers's regional vice-president and comptroller Dave Goltz and expressed concern that she had been passed over for Latiolais's job because of her age and that Goltz "kind of lost his composure for a second," then assured her that he would never discriminate against anyone, including Grizzle, on the basis of age.

From approximately April 1989, Grizzle, Latiolais, and Loretta Scott, a younger co-worker who performed the same function at Travelers as Grizzle, all shared the same small office. In July 1989, Travelers switched to a new computer system on which the plaintiff lacked proficiency, with the result that she made many ledger errors. In the summer of 1989, Grizzle complained to Travelers's director of Internal Accounting, Beverly Snyder, that she was being subjected to increased surveillance and scrutiny of her work by Latiolais, while Scott was not, and that she was being given insufficient computer training. According to Grizzle, Snyder responded that there was nothing that Grizzle could do about it because she was not over the age of 55. Snyder later denied making that statement and also testified that she did not know that the ADEA prohibits age discrimination against people aged 40 and above. In July and December 1989, Grizzle received two warnings by Latiolais regarding her lack of productivity and her ledger entry mistakes. In January 1990 she was placed on "final warning." Documentation of her errors continued during this

period. On February 16, 1990, Latiolais told Grizzle that her performance had not improved and that she was being discharged. Grizzle was only 44 years old on the date of her discharge and only two years older than she was at the time Travelers made the decision to hire her.

Latiolais, Goltz, and Snyder, each of whom was approximately ten years younger than Grizzle, participated in making the decision to fire her. She was replaced by a 23-year-old recent college graduate. On March 16, 1990, Grizzle filed a complaint with the Equal Employment Opportunity Commission (EEOC).

Does Grizzle have a valid claim against Travelers? Should the age of the supervisors who chose to discharge her factor into the court's decision? [*Grizzle v. Travelers Health Network*, 14 F.3d 261 (5th Cir. 1994)]

8. Pam Armstrong was employed by Flowers Hospital as a nurse in the Home Care Services division. Her employment in this position required her to visit and treat patients in their homes. Armstrong was assigned patients in the Headland, Midland, and Dothan areas, and worked during the day, Monday through Friday. When Armstrong was initially hired, she was required to attend a one-day orientation, and following that orientation, she spent the first two weeks riding with another nurse. Upon completion of that two-week period, Armstrong was assigned a number of patients with varying conditions.

On December 12, 1990, Armstrong was informed that she had been assigned a patient who was diagnosed as HIV positive. He was further diagnosed as having cryptococcal meningitis, which is an infectious disease common among AIDS patients.

On the same day, Armstrong informed Cheryl Wynn, her supervisor at Home Care Services, that she did not believe that she should treat this patient because she was in the first trimester of her pregnancy. She expressed concern that if she were required to treat this patient, she might jeopardize her baby. Armstrong stated that it was not the presence of AIDS that concerned her as much as the opportunistic infections commonly present with AIDS patients. She further stated that it was not her own health that she was concerned about, because she, as a healthy adult, would be capable of recovering from most of these infections. Her primary concern was the health of her unborn baby.

Wynn informed Armstrong that the policy of Home Care Services was to not make exceptions and not allow reassignment of patients to other nurses. Home Care's policy on the treatment of AIDS patients stated that the "Universal Precautions" provided by the Centers for Disease Control (CDC) were to be followed by all nurses in treating patients with infectious diseases. Any nurse who refused to treat a patient was subject to termination. After discussing the situation with her supervisor, Wynn informed Armstrong that she would be given two days in which to reconsider her decision. If Armstrong still refused to treat the AIDS patient, she would be given the option of resigning or facing termination. On December 14, 1990, Armstrong had not changed her mind about treating the patient, and refused to resign. She was terminated.

After her termination, Armstrong filed a title VII claim with the Equal Employment Opportunity Commission. The EEOC investigated the matter and returned a finding that there was no reasonable determination of a title VII violation. Do you agree? [*Armstrong v. Flowers Hospital*, 812 F.Supp. 1183 (M.D.Ala. 1993)]

9. Oak Rubber Co. was a manufacturer of industrial vinyl gloves. The company operated six production machines around the clock with three shifts of workers. Each machine was required to be staffed with six glove strippers and one packer. The machines operated continuously through the employees' breaks and lunch periods. Oak scheduled extra workers to substitute for the employees on break, and also to cover for employees who were absent or on vacation. The list of "excused" absences included a number of reasons why an employee might occasionally miss work, but did not include observance of the Sabbath. If Oak did not have enough workers for each machine, it was forced to shut down the affected machine, suffering a loss of production.

The Saturday work schedule was either full or partial production. For those Saturdays scheduled for full production, Oak gave all of its employees 48 hours notice, and made it mandatory for all employees on all shifts to report to work. If, after the employees reported to work, Oak determined that extra workers were available, employees could exercise "work options" to go home without pay.

Cooper was hired by Oak in 1975 as a glove stripper/packer, and worked the night shift from 11:00 P.M. to 7:00 A.M. In January 1984, Cooper attended her first Seventh Day Adventist service and attended regularly thereafter. Cooper knew that the church prohibited all work from sundown on Friday until sundown on Saturday. Cooper nonetheless worked numerous Saturdays in 1984, but was able to attend church services after ending her shift at 7 A.M. She worked a total of nine Saturday shifts in 1985, and reported for work on seven other occasions, but exercised work options to leave early on those occasions. Oak did not schedule any full production Saturdays between July 1985 and November 1986.

In November 1986, Cooper exercised her seniority right to transfer to the day shift. Coincidentally, one day later, Oak announced that the following Saturday was scheduled for full production. Cooper informed her supervisor that she could not work because of her religious beliefs.

Cooper did not work that Saturday or the remaining full production Saturdays in 1986. She received a verbal warning. In January 1987, Cooper talked to her new supervisor about her religion's prohibition against working on Saturdays. The supervisor suggested that Cooper use her seventeen accrued vacation days to avoid working Saturdays, but Cooper was unwilling to use them in this manner. Cooper's supervisor also suggested that she trade back to the night shift so that she could attend

services on Saturday mornings. This alternative was also unacceptable to Cooper because it would still require her to work on the Sabbath. Cooper testified that although she had been willing to work the Friday night shift prior to July 1985, her commitment to the church had grown since that time and prevented her from continuing to do so.

Cooper resigned to avoid disciplinary suspension and what she claimed would be her inevitable termination from employment. One month after Cooper's resignation, Oak hired an additional 18 glove strippers/packers, enhancing its ability to maintain production despite work absences.

Cooper filed suit under title VII, claiming that she was disciplined and constructively discharged because she adhered to her sincere religious beliefs against working on the Sabbath. Was Cooper constructively discharged from her employment, even though she could have used her accrued vacation days rather than resign? Did Oak reasonably accommodate Cooper's religious beliefs when it offered her the option of trading shifts? What type of relief should be granted to Cooper if she wins her suit? [*Cooper v. Oak Rubber Co.*, 15 F.3d 1375 (6th Cir. 1994)]

10. Kenneth Notari, a white male, began his employment with the Denver Water Department in June 1974. During that time, Notari was employed as a seasonal laborer, a customer serviceman, a water serviceman, and an assistant valve operator. On five different occasions, Notari applied for the position of safety and security coordinator. In June 1988, Denver Water selected a woman over him for the position.

The process of applying for a position at Denver Water includes an oral board examination. The board ranks the candidates and refers the top three for interviews with the head of the department that has the vacancy. In this case, after the oral examination, the candidates were interviewed by Gilbert Archuleta, head of the Safety and Security Department, and his superior, James Crockett. After the interviews, Archuleta and Crockett determined that Notari was the applicant best qualified for the position. They then placed Notari's name on a selection sheet and submitted it to the director of personnel, a woman named Rogene Hill. Hill rejected Archuleta and Crockett's selection of Notari and told them that the focus of the position should shift from "safety" to "security." Despite this change in job description, Archuleta and Crockett continued to believe that Notari was the best qualified for the position. However, a reevaluation occurred and a woman was selected for the position over Notari.

After Denver Water denied Notari the position of safety and security coordinator, he filed a charge of discrimination with the EEOC alleging discrimination due to his sex. Is there a probability that but for his gender, Notari would have been promoted? Should Denver Water be permitted to articulate a nondiscriminatory justification for its promotion decision? [*Notari v. Denver Water Department*, 971 F.2d 585 (10th Cir. 1992)]

Chapter 14

LABOR RELATIONS LAW

■ Introduction

National Labor Relations Act

Congress has comprehensively regulated labor-management relations in an attempt to balance equitably the economic power of employers, unions, and individual employees. Through the Wagner Act in 1935 and the Taft-Hartley Act in 1947, Congress sought to provide employees with sufficient economic power by allowing them to organize, but also sought to curb perceived union excesses. The Landrum-Griffin Act was enacted in 1959 primarily to address problems created by corruption within union leadership. Also known as the Labor-Management Reporting and Disclosure Act, the Landrum-Griffin Act established extensive reporting requirements for unions and a "bill of rights" for union members in matters such as union meetings and elections, union disciplinary procedures, and eligibility for union office. These laws are known collectively as the National Labor Relations Act (NLRA).

Chapter Summary

This chapter reviews the origins of the Wagner Act and discusses the coverage and operation of the National Labor Relations Act. It outlines the procedure for employees to vote on whether they wish to be represented by a union; the types of employer conduct that are unlawful under the NLRA; strikes and the rights of strikers; and unlawful union conduct. Labor-management relations in selected countries are briefly reviewed. The chapter concludes with a discussion of other statutes regulating the employer-employee relationship: the Employee Retirement Income Security Act of 1974 (ERISA), the Consolidated Omnibus Budget Reconciliation Act of 1985 (COBRA), the Occupational Safety and Health Act (OSHA), the Worker Adjustment and Retraining Notification Act of 1988 (WARN Act), and the Fair Labor Standards Act (FLSA).

■ History of Labor-Relations Statutes

Prior to Mid-1930s

Before the mid-1930s, attempts by employees to band together and demand better wages and working conditions were largely ineffective. Organized economic action, such as strikes and picketing, were enjoined as unlawful conspiracies. In addition, employers effectively squelched attempts of employees to organize by lawfully discharging union organizers. Because the attempts of employees to organize for improved wages and working conditions were ineffectual, many observers concluded that federal regulation would be required to correct the imbalance in bargaining power between employers and employees.

Norris-LaGuardia Act

In 1932, Congress enacted the Norris-LaGuardia Act,[1] which regulated and largely prohibited the issuance of injunctions or court orders in labor disputes. This statute significantly enhanced the economic position of employees by limiting judicial interference with labor activities.

The following article illustrates the use of injunctions prior to the Norris-LaGuardia Act.

Pullman Strike Strikes Blow to Labor, 1894[2]

Organized labor suffered a body blow in Chicago in 1894. That spring, in the depths of a depression caused by the panic of '93, union members at the Pullman Company's car works struck against a wage cut. To support the walkout, the American Railway Union refused to handle Pullman cars. The General Managers Association, a management group representing 22 railroads serving Chicago, refused to arbitrate the dispute. A federal judge in Chicago then issued a "blanket injunction" forbidding the Pullman strikers to block the railroads or delay the mails.

Violence erupted when strikers wrecked a mail train and seized key points in the switching yards. At this point, and despite the protests of Illinois Gov. John P. Atgeld, President Grover Cleveland ordered a regiment of U.S. Army regulars into Chicago.

Eugene V. Debs, head of the striking Pullman union (and later an unsuccessful Socialist Party candidate for president of the U.S.), defied the Chicago Circuit Court's injunction. He was promptly arrested and sentenced for contempt of court. Debs's appeal to the Supreme Court was rejected, the justices holding that the government had the dormant right, even without a specific law, to remove barriers to interstate commerce. Thus, says historian Samuel Eliot Morison, the legal injunction became a new weapon against strikes.

Samuel Gompers, president of the American Federation of Labor, notified Debs's union that summer that it was beaten. By August, barely five months after it had begun, the Pullman strike was broken.

Wagner Act

With the onset of the Great Depression, Congress perceived the need for further statutory regulation of labor-management relations so that employees could negotiate better wages and working conditions. In 1935, Congress enacted the Wagner Act,[3] which for the first time provided for secret-ballot elections for employees to elect a labor organization to represent them for collective bargaining.

Section 7 of the Wagner Act declared that employees have the right to "self-organization, to form, join, or assist labor organizations, to bargain collectively through representatives of their own choosing and to engage in other concerted activities for the purpose of collective bargaining or other mutual aid or protection." Section 8 made it unlawful for an employer: (1) to interfere with employees' exercise of their section 7 rights; (2) to dominate or interfere with the formation of a labor organization; (3) to discriminate against employees to encourage or discourage membership in a labor organization; (4) to discharge or otherwise discriminate against an employee for filing charges or giving testimony under the NLRA; and (5) to refuse to engage in collective bargaining with a properly selected labor organization.

Growth then Decline in Union Membership

In the years following the passage of the Wagner Act, membership in labor organizations grew from 3 million in 1935 to 14 million in 1947. By 1965, more than 28% of the U.S. nonagricultural work force was organized, down from a peak of 35.5% in 1945. By 1993, only 15.8% of the U.S. work force was organized (see Exhibit 14-1).

As union representation expanded, so did the number of strikes, work stoppages, and disputes among unions

---

1. Pub. L. No. 64, 47 Stat. 70 (codified as amended at 29 U.S.C. §§ 101-115 (1988)).

2. *The Wall Street Journal,* January 23, 1989. Reprinted by permission of *The Wall Street Journal,* © 1989 Dow Jones & Company, Inc. All Rights Reserved Worldwide.

3. Pub. L. No. 74-198, 49 Stat. 449 (codified at 29 U.S.C. § 151-169 (1988 & Supp. 1992)).

EXHIBIT 14-1 U.S. Union Membership, 1921-1993

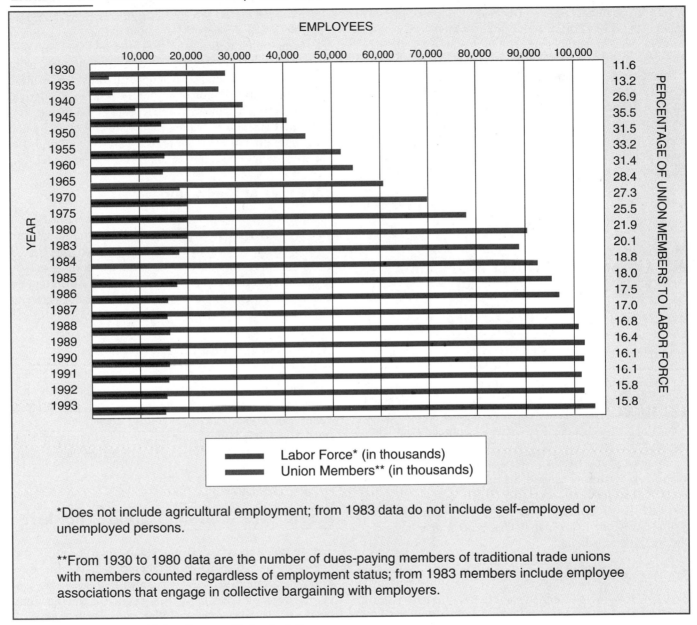

*Does not include agricultural employment; from 1983 data do not include self-employed or unemployed persons.

**From 1930 to 1980 data are the number of dues-paying members of traditional trade unions with members counted regardless of employment status; from 1983 members include employee associations that engage in collective bargaining with employers.

Source: U.S. Department of Labor, Bureau of Labor Statistics.

over what work each union's members were entitled to perform. Many strikes were viewed unfavorably, particularly those that became violent or those that were *secondary boycotts*, that is, strikes against employers with whom the union had no quarrel, designed to encourage such employers to stop doing business with an employ-er with whom it did have a dispute. Many people also felt that the Wagner Act was one-sided, and that the National Labor Relations Board (NLRB), which was given the responsibility of administering the Wagner Act, had become too zealous in its prosecution of employers.

Taft-Hartley Act

Largely because of these concerns, Congress in 1947 passed the Taft-Hartley Act,[4] under which section 7 of the Wagner Act was amended to give employees the right to refrain from forming, joining, or assisting labor organizations. Congress also made it illegal for a labor organization: (1) to restrain or coerce employees in the exercise of their section 7 rights; (2) to cause or attempt to cause an employer to discriminate against an employee on the basis of union membership or lack thereof; (3) to refuse to bargain collectively; (4) to engage in certain secondary boycotts or picketing, that is, boycotting or picketing a company that is not the employer (for example, a customer of the employer); and (5) to threaten to picket an employer to force it to recognize the union.

■ Coverage of the National Labor Relations Act

The National Labor Relations Act (NLRA)[5] covers all enterprises whose operations affect interstate or foreign commerce. However, the NLRB, which administers the act, has, with court approval, limited its jurisdiction to enterprises having a substantial effect on commerce. The dollar volume of an employer's revenues or purchases determines whether that employer's impact on commerce is sufficiently substantial to bring it within the NLRB's jurisdiction.

In general, the NLRA covers only employees located within the territorial United States, not U.S. employees located elsewhere. However, the NLRB has ruled that its jurisdiction extends to foreign employers doing business within the United States that would otherwise be under the NLRB's jurisdiction.

Employees of Nonprofit Institutions

In 1974, Congress extended the NLRB's jurisdiction to employees of all health care institutions, including nonprofit hospitals. Before 1974, the NLRB had taken the position that it would not assert jurisdiction over nonprofit organizations except in exceptional circumstances. However, in recent years the NLRB has shown increasing willingness to take jurisdiction over such organizations.

---

4. Pub. L. No. 80-101, 61 Stat. 136 (codified as amended at 29 U.S.C. § 141-144 (1988)).
5. Pub. L. No. 198, 49 Stat. 449 (1935) (codified as amended at 29 U.S.C. §§ 151-169 (1988 & Supp. 1992)).

Supervisors

Section 7 of the NLRA grants rights only to "employees," not to supervisors. The statute defines a *supervisor* as anyone with authority to hire, suspend, lay off, promote, discharge, discipline, or direct employees, or to effectively recommend such action, provided the exercise of that authority is not of a merely routine or clerical nature but requires the use of independent judgment.

The NLRB will not allow supervisors to vote in union elections; nor, in most cases, may the NLRB find that supervisors have been treated unlawfully under the NLRA.

Independent Contractors

Independent contractors are not covered by the NLRA because they are not employees. In determining whether an individual is an independent contractor, the NLRB invokes the common-law right-to-control test. A person is deemed to be an *independent contractor* if the employer exercises no control either over the means of performing the work or over the end result of the work.

Agricultural Laborers

The NLRA specifically excludes from its coverage any individual employed as an agricultural laborer. An agricultural laborer is one who performs work primarily in connection with: (1) an agricultural operation, or (2) an operation that is both an integral part of ordinary agricultural production and an essential step before the products can be marketed in normal outlets.

■ Representation Election Procedure

The five-member NLRB has established a number of regional offices throughout the country to handle the day-to-day tasks of overseeing *representation elections,* that is, elections among employees to decide whether they want a union to represent them for collective bargaining.

Filing a Petition

The procedure for conducting a representation election is initiated by the filing of a petition with a regional office of the NLRB. The vast majority of those petitions are filed by labor organizations.

In order to obtain an election, a union must make a *showing of interest,* that is, it must prove to the NLRB that a sufficient number of employees have an interest in an election. This is nearly always done by submitting to

"*Actually, Tommy, we're just about full-blooded management, except for your grandfather on your mom's side, who was one-quarter labor.*"

Drawing by Leo Cullum; © 1993 The New Yorker Magazine, Inc.

the NLRB *union authorization cards* from at least 30% of the employees in an appropriate collective-bargaining unit. Generally, these cards contain a statement that the individual signing it wishes to be represented for purposes of collective bargaining by a certain union. If the union cannot provide a showing of interest, the NLRB will dismiss the petition.

An individual employee may file a petition to decertify an incumbent union if at least 30% of the employees in the bargaining unit sign a statement that they no longer wish to be represented for collective bargaining by their union.

Petitions may also be filed by employers at certain intervals to test the union's continuing support. To do so, an employer must show objectively that the majority of employees in the collective bargaining unit no longer wish to be represented by the union.

Appropriate Unit

Regardless of whether the union, the employer, or an employee files the petition for election, the election pro-

cedures are essentially the same, except that, in the case of an initial organizing campaign, the parties or the NLRB may have to determine which employees should be allowed to vote in an election. The NLRB will only hold elections in appropriate collective bargaining units. An appropriate unit is one in which the employees share a community of interest; that is, they have similar compensation, working conditions, and supervision, and they work under the same general employer policies. In determining whether a unit is an appropriate collective baragining unit, the NLRB also looks at: (1) the kind of work performed, (2) similarity in the qualifications and skills of employees, (3) frequency of contact among employees, (4) geographic proximity of employees, and (5) the wishes of affected employees.

Scope of Unit

With certain limitations, the union and the employer are free to agree on the scope of the unit in which an election should be conducted. However, if the proposed unit will include both professional and nonprofessional employees, the consent of the professional employees must be obtained. In addition, section 9(b)(3) of the NLRA prohibits a labor organization from representing security guards if that organization admits nonguards to membership or is affiliated with a labor organization that admits nonguards to membership. As a result, the NLRB will refuse to hold an election among a unit of guards if the petitioning labor organization represents nonguards or is affiliated with a union which represents nonguards. These special rules for security guards are necessary to prevent guards from having conflicts during strikes between their responsiblity as employees and their loyalty as union members.

If the employer and the union cannot agree on the scope of the unit, the NLRB will conduct a hearing to resolve the issue. A common issue at a representation hearing is whether a certain position is supervisory as defined by the NLRA. If it is, that position will be excluded from the unit. If it is not, the individual in that position will be included in the unit and allowed to vote. The director of the regional office in which the petition is filed makes such determinations, which are appealable to the NLRB.

Conduct of Election

Following an agreement between the parties for an election or a decision from the regional director over disputed unit issues, the regional office will conduct an election. The NLRB agent travels to the employer's location, erects a portable voting booth, and oversees the election process. The specific place and time for the election are agreed upon between the employer and union.

The NLRB agent makes sure that no irregularities occur during the election and hands out ballots to the employees. Each employee enters the place of voting and indicates by placing a mark in an appropriate square on the ballot whether she wishes to be represented for collective bargaining by the specified union. The employee then deposits the marked ballot into a ballot box, which is opened at the close of the election by the NLRB agent. The NLRB agent then tallies the election results and signs a ballot count. With a unit of previously unrepresented employees, the union needs 50% plus one of the valid votes cast in the election to win.

Objections

The party losing the election may file objections to it. Objections typically allege misconduct either by the other party before or during the election or by the NLRB agent at the election. For example, a union that has lost an elec-

tion may allege that, just before the election, the employer unlawfully threatened employees with reprisals if they voted for the union. If the objections are deemed without merit, the election will be certified by the NLRB. If they are deemed meritorious, the NLRB will conduct a new election. If an employer's misconduct was so serious that a free and fair election is impossible, the NLRB will order the employer to bargain with the union, even without an election.

> 66
>
> *If an employer's misconduct was so serious that a free and fair election is impossible, the NLRB will order the employer to bargain with the union, even without an election.*

■ Unfair Labor Practices by Employers

Section 8(a) of the NLRA prohibits employers from engaging in specified activities against employees or their unions. Such activities, known as *unfair labor practices,* are investigated and prosecuted by the general counsel of the NLRB and his representatives.

Unfair labor practice charges may be filed in the NLRB's regional offices. Ordinarily, the time limit for filing a charge is six months. A charge is usually investigated by a field examiner or a field attorney of the local office. The regional director then decides whether, based on evidence disclosed by the investigation, the charge has merit.

If the charge is meritorious, the local office will attempt to arrange a settlement. If the matter cannot be settled at the local level, it will be tried before an administrative law judge (ALJ). The decision of the ALJ is reviewable by the NLRB, which may adopt, modify, or reverse the decision. The NLRB's decision is in turn appealable to a federal appellate court and, ultimately, to the Supreme Court of the United States.

Interference with Protected Activities

Section 8(a)(1) of the NLRA makes it illegal for an employer to interfere with, restrain, or coerce employees in the exercise of their section 7 rights to organize and bargain collectively and to engage in other protected, concerted activities. This prohibition covers a wide range of employer conduct, including: (1) threatening employ-

Ethical Consideration

It is unlawful and unethical to tell employees that they will somehow be punished or treated adversely if they support a union, or try to organize their fellow employees, or vote for a union at a representation election. An employer may not rescind a planned wage increase for an employee upon learning that she signed a union authorization card.

ees with any adverse action for organizing or supporting a union; (2) promising employees any benefits if they abandon support for a union; (3) interrogating employees about union sentiment or activity; and (4) engaging in surveillance of employees' union activities. Such conduct is generally thought to chill employees' exercise of their section 7 rights. For example, an employer may not threaten to shut down its business or to take away benefits if the union wins a representation election. Similarly, an employer may not interrogate employees about whether they have signed a union representation card or about the union activities of other employees.

Section 8(a)(1) also prohibits an employer from enforcing an overly broad rule against soliciting other employees (perhaps for union support) or distributing literature on company premises. In general, an employer may only prohibit solicitation or distribution of literature on company property and during work time.

However, nonemployee union organizers do not have the same rights as employees for solicitation and the distribution of literature, as is demonstrated in the following case.

■ A Case in Point: In the Language of the Court

Case 14.1
LECHMERE, INC. v.
NATIONAL LABOR
RELATIONS BOARD
Supreme Court of the
United States
112 S. Ct. 841 (1992).

FACTS   Section 7 of the National Labor Relations Act (NLRA) guarantees employees "the right to self-organization, to form, join, or assist labor organizations," . . . and makes it an unfair labor practice for an employer "to interfere with, restrain, or coerce employees" in the exercise of their section 7 rights. Lechmere, Inc. owns and operates a retail store located in a shopping plaza in the large metropolitan area of Hartford and has some 200 employees who were not organized under any labor union. The United Food and Commercial Workers Union, AFL-CIO began a campaign to organize the employees at a retail store in Newington, Connecticut, owned and operated by Lechmere, Inc.

The union's first attempt to organize was through a full-page advertisement in a local newspaper which drew little response. The union organizers then began a practice of placing handbills on the windshields of cars in the parking lot used by employees of Lechmere. The parking lot is partly owned by Lechmere. Each time the union organizers tried to distribute handbills in the parking lot, they were asked to leave by the management of Lechmere, and the handbills were removed by Lechmere personnel. The organizers then relocated to the grassy strip of public land near the lot where they tried to pass out handbills to cars entering the lot. They began picketing the grassy strip as well as contacting approximately 20% of the employees through direct mail, phone calls, and home visits. These efforts resulted in only one signed union authorization card.

The union filed an unfair labor practice charge with the National Labor Relations Board alleging that Lechmere, Inc. had violated the National Labor Relations Act. The Administrative Law Judge who heard the case ruled in favor of the union and recommended that Lechmere be ordered to

*Case **14.1** continued on following page*

*Case **14.1** continued*

stop barring the union organizers from the parking lot. The National Labor Relations Board affirmed the judgment of the ALJ and the court of appeals enforced the Board's order. The U.S. Supreme Court granted certiorari.

ISSUE PRESENTED   Do nonemployee union organizers have a right to use an employer's private property in order to communicate with employees for purposes of organizing under section 7 of the NLRA?

OPINION   THOMAS, J., writing for the U.S. Supreme Court:

. . . .

This case requires us to clarify the relationship between the rights of employees under §7 of the National Labor Relations Act and the property rights of their employers.

. . . .

Section 7 of the NLRA provides in relevant part that "[e]mployees shall have the right to self-organization, to form, join, or assist labor organizations." Section 8(a)(1) of the Act, in turn, makes it an unfair labor practice for an employer "to interfere with, restrain, or coerce employees in the exercise of rights guaranteed in [§7]. By its plain terms, thus, the NLRA confers rights only on *employees*, not on unions or their nonemployee organizers. In [the case of] *NLRB v. Babcock & Wilcox Co.*,[6] however, we recognized that insofar as the employees' "right of self-organization depends in some measure on [their] ability . . . to learn from the advantages of self-organization from others," §7 of the NLRA may, in certain limited circumstances, restrict an employer's right to exclude nonemployee union organizers from his property. It is the nature of those circumstances that we explore today.

. . . .

. . . [In *Babcock,* the Board noted that] "the right to distribute [organizational union information] is not absolute but must be accommodated to the circumstances. Where it is impossible or unreasonably difficult for a union to distribute organizational literature to employees entirely off of the employer's premises, distribution on a nonworking area, such as the parking lot and the walkways between the parking lot and the gate, may be warranted. [In the same case, the Court] explained that the Board had erred by failing to make the critical distinction between the organizing activities of employees (to whom §7 guarantees the right of self-organization) and nonemployees (to whom §7 applies only derivatively). Thus while "[n]o restriction can be placed on the employees' right to discuss self-organization among themselves, unless the employer can demonstrate that a restriction is necessary to maintain production or discipline, no such obligation is owed nonemployee organizers." As a rule, then, an employer cannot be compelled to allow distribution of union literature by nonemployee organizers on his property. As with many other rules, however, we recognized an exception. Where "the location of a plant and the living quarters of the employees place the employees beyond the reach of reasonable union efforts to communicate with them, employers' property rights may be "required to yield to the extent needed to permit communication of information on the right to organize."

---

6. 351 U.S. 105, 76 S.Ct. 679 (1956).

. . . .

The threshold inquiry in this case, then, is whether the facts here justify application of *Babcock's* inaccessibility exception. . . .

. . . As we have explained, the exception to *Babcock's* rule is a narrow one. It does not apply wherever nontrespassory access may be cumbersome or less-than-ideally effective, but only where "the *location of a plant and the living quarters of the employees* place the employees *beyond the reach* of reasonable union efforts to communicate with them." . . . *Babcock's* exception was crafted precisely to protect the §7 rights of those employees who, by virtue of their employment, are isolated from the ordinary flow of information that characterizes our society. The union's burden of establishing such isolation is, as we have explained, "a heavy one," and not satisfied by mere conjecture or the expression of doubts concerning the effectiveness of nontrespassory means of communication.

The Board's conclusion in this case that the union had no reasonable means short of trespass to make Lechmere employees aware of its organizational efforts is based on a misunderstanding of the limited scope of this exception. Because the employees do not reside on Lechmere's property, they are presumptively not "beyond the reach" of the union's message. Although the employees live in a large metropolitan area (Greater Hartford), that fact does not in itself render them "inaccessible" in the sense contemplated by *Babcock*. Their inaccessibility is suggested by the union's success in contacting a substantial percentage of them directly, via mailings, phone calls, and home visits. . . . [O]ther alternative means of communication were readily available. . . . *Access* to employees, not *success* in winning them over, is the critical issue—although success, or lack thereof, may be relevant in determining whether reasonable access exists. Because the union failed to establish the existence of any "unique obstacles," that frustrated access to Lechmere's employees, the Board erred in concluding that Lechmere committed an unfair labor practice by barring the nonemployee organizers from its property.

. . . .

RESULT Nonemployee union organizers do not have a right to trespass on an employer's private property for the purpose of communicating with and organizing employees, except in very limited circumstances which did not apply in this case. The Court reversed the judgment of the court of affeals, and denied the enforcement of the National Labor Relations Board's order.

Questions
1. Why should nonemployee union organizers have fewer rights than employee organizers?
2. Under what circumstances are nonemployees entitled to trespass on

Section 8(a)(1) also protects employees who engage in concerted activities for mutual aid and protection. For example, an employer may not retaliate against a group of employees who approach it and complain about some aspect of their working conditions, such as poor lighting or uncomfortable temperatures in the workplace. For an activity to be *concerted,* it must be "engaged in with or on the authority of other employees, and not solely by and on behalf of the employee himself."[7] The NLRB will find a violation of the National Labor Relations Act only where: (1) the employer knows of the concerted nature of the employee's activity; (2) the concerted activity is protected by the NLRA; and (3) the discipline at issue is in retaliation for the employee's protected, concerted activity. The following case explores one aspect of the right to engage in concerted activities for the purpose of mutual aid and protection.

---

7. *Meyers Industries, Inc.,* 268 NLRB 493, 497 (1984), remanded sub nom. *Prill v. NLRB,* 755 F.2d 941 (D.C. Cir.), *cert. denied,* 474 U.S. 971 (1985).

Ethical Consideration

It is an unfair labor practice to punish employees who cooperate to bring complaints of wages, hours, working conditions, or the like to management. Managers should encourage, not discourage, such behavior.

■ **A Case in Point:**   **Summary**

Case 14.2
NATIONAL LABOR RELATIONS BOARD v. J. WEINGARTEN, INC.
Supreme Court of the United States
420 U.S. 251, 95 S.Ct. 959 (1975).

FACTS   The employer J. Weingarten, Inc. operated a chain of retail stores which contained food operations. Leura Collins, a salesperson, was represented by the Retail Clerks Union. The employer suspected that she had taken some merchandise without properly purchasing it. Collins was summoned to an interview with an investigator and the store manager. During the questioning, she asked the store manager several times to call the union shop steward or some other union representative, but those requests were denied. The employer also questioned Collins about her disclosure that she had not been paying for her lunches. During this part of the questioning, Collins repeated her request for a shop steward, which was again denied. The employer then terminated the questioning and asked Collins not to discuss the matter with anyone else because it was a private matter.

ISSUE PRESENTED   May an employer deny an employee's request that a union representative be present at an investigatory interview which the employee reasonably believes might result in disciplinary action?

SUMMARY OF OPINION   The U.S. Supreme Court observed that an employee's seeking the assistance of a union representative at a confrontation with the employer clearly falls within the literal wording of section 7 that employees have the right to engage in concerted activities for the purpose of mutual aid and protection. The employee sought "aid or protection" against a perceived threat to her employment security. The union representative, whose participation was sought, safeguards not only the particular employee's interest, but also the interests of the entire bargaining unit by making sure that the employer does not initiate or continue a practice of imposing punishment unjustly. Further, the Supreme Court said, requiring a lone employee to attend an investigatory interview that she reasonably believes may result in the imposition of discipline perpetuates the inequality in bargaining power between employees and employers that the National Labor Relations Act was designed to eliminate.

RESULT   An employer may not deny a union employee's request that a union representative be present at an investigatory interview.

COMMENTS   It is important to keep in mind the limitations of the *Weingarten* decision. It applies only to situations where an employee who is a union member asks for the assistance of a union representative at an investigatory interview that the employee reasonably believes might result in discipline. So far, the *Weingarten* right has not been extended to requests by nonunion employees to have another individual present at such a meeting.

Ethical Consideration

Does fairness dictate that a request by a nonunion employee to have another individual present at an investigatory interview be honored?

Domination of a Labor Organization

Under section 8(a)(2) of the NLRA, an employer may not dominate or assist a labor organization. This provision was enacted to cure the abuse of employers assisting compliant organizations to represent their employees and then imposing "sweetheart" collective bargaining contracts—that is, contracts unduly favorable to the employer. Under this provision, a company may not give financial support to a labor organization. It may not instigate, encourage, or directly participate in the formation of a labor organization. It may not attempt to influence the making of union policy. For example, supervisors may not serve as union officials or on a union bargaining team. An employer may not recognize a union as the bargaining representative of a unit of employees when a majority of its employees do not support the union.

Discrimination Against Union Supporters

Section 8(a)(3) prohibits employers from discriminating against any employee to encourage or discourage membership in any labor organization. A common section 8(a)(3) allegation is a worker being discharged for attempting to organize fellow employees. To prove a violation of section 8(a)(3), it must be shown that the employee's conduct which was protected by section 7 was a substantial or a motivating factor in the discharge. In such a case, the employer may allege a legitimate business reason for the termination, but the alleged business reason may be a pretext, intended to cover up an unlawful discharge. In some cases, such as the one that follows, there may be evidence of both a proper and an improper reason for termination.

A Case in Point: Summary

Case 14.3
NATIONAL LABOR RELATIONS BOARD v. TRANSPORTATION MANAGEMENT CORP.
Supreme Court of the United States
462 U.S. 393, 103 S.Ct. 2469 (1983).

FACTS   Sam Santillo was a bus driver for Transportation Management Corporation. He was discharged by the company shortly after he began organizing other bus drivers to support the Teamsters Union. Santillo filed a complaint with the NLRB alleging that he had been discharged in violation of section 8(a)(3) because of his union activities. The employer's defense was that Santillo had been fired, not for union activities, but because he had left his keys in the bus and had taken unauthorized breaks.

The NLRB decided that the discharge was unlawful, and that the reasons offered by the employer for the discharge were merely pretextual. The NLRB noted that Santillo's practice of leaving his keys in the bus was not known to the employer until after his discharge. It further noted that taking breaks was normal practice, tolerated by the employer, and that the company had not taken action against any other employee for taking breaks.

*Case **14.3** continued on following page*

*Case **14.3** continued*

ISSUE PRESENTED   May an employer avoid liability for dismissing a union organizer by proving by a preponderance of the evidence that the employee would have lost his job in any event for unprotected conduct?

SUMMARY OF OPINION   The U.S. Supreme Court held that the NLRB's test for determining the propriety of a mixed-motive discharge was proper. Thus, where there is some evidence of both lawful and unlawful reasons for discharge, the NLRB must prove that the employee's protected conduct was a substantial motivating factor in the discharge. To then escape liability, the employer must show by a preponderance of the evidence that the employee would have been discharged for legitimate reasons regardless of the protected activity.

RESULT   The Supreme Court upheld the NLRB's decision that Santillo's discharge was unlawful.

COMMENTS   If an employee has been unlawfully discharged, the NLRB may order that the employee be reinstated and given full back pay.

Ethical Consideration

It is an unfair labor practice for an employer to discipline or otherwise take action against a union-represented employee because that person has invoked the provisions of the collective bargaining contract. For example, it is unlawful and unethical to penalize an employee for filing a grievance under a collective bargaining contract.

Section 8(a)(3) permits a union and employer to incorporate a *union security clause* into a collective bargaining contract. Such a clause requires, as a condition of employment, that employees in the collective bargaining unit either become members of the union after a certain period of time or pay fees to the union equivalent to the periodic union dues. The laws of a number of states forbid union security clauses.

In the following case, the Supreme Court considered whether employees who were not union members could object to paying to the union that part of their fees that was not related to collective bargaining or the administration of the contract or grievance procedures.

■ **A Case in Point:**   **Summary**

Case 14.4
COMMUNICATIONS WORKERS OF AMERICA v. BECK
Supreme Court of the
United States
487 U.S 735, 108 S.Ct. 2641
(1988).

FACTS   The Communications Workers of America (CWA) represented certain employees of the American Telephone and Telegraph Company (AT&T). The CWA had negotiated a collective bargaining agreement containing a union security clause. That clause required all represented employees, including those who did not wish to become union members, to pay to the union fees equivalent to union dues. Failure to pay the required fees was grounds for discharge.

Certain employees of AT&T who were not union members objected to paying fees to the union for anything other than collective bargaining, contract administration, or grievance adjustment. They alleged that the union expended some of their fees on other activities, such as organizing employees of other employers, lobbying for labor legislation, and participating in social, charitable, and political events.

ISSUE PRESENTED Does the National Labor Relations Act permit a union, over the objections of dues-paying nonmember employees, to expend funds collected from them on activities unrelated to collective bargaining, contract administration, and grievance adjustment?

SUMMARY OF OPINION The U.S. Supreme Court reasoned that section 8(a)(3) of the NLRA was intended to correct abuses of compulsory unionism, and that union security clauses require nonmember employees to pay only their share of the cost of benefits secured by the union through collective bargaining. The legislative history of section 8(a)(3) showed that Congress was concerned with the dues and rights of union members, not the fees and rights of nonmembers. The absence of such concern indicated that Congress understood section 8(a)(3) to afford nonmembers adequate protection by authorizing the collection of only those fees necessary to finance activities related to collective bargaining.

RESULT Employees in a represented unit who are not union members need pay only those fees necessary for the union to perform activities related to collective bargaining, contract administration, and grievance adjustment.

COMMENTS Under *Beck* it is clear that employees who are union members may be required to pay the entire dues amount. Only nonmembers may object to paying that portion of their fee that will be expended on activities not related to collective bargaining. Because of the uncertainties in accounting, it may be difficult for unions to calculate what percentage of their costs are expended on such activities.

Discrimination Against Employees Who File Charges

Under section 8(a)(4) of the NLRA it is an unfair labor practice for an employer to discharge or otherwise discriminate against an employee because she has filed charges or given testimony to the NLRB, either in a representation proceeding or pursuant to an unfair labor practice charge.

Failure to Bargain in Good Faith

Section 8(a)(5) of the NLRA imposes upon unionized employers a duty to bargain collectively. For example, the employer must be willing to meet union representatives at reasonable times to bargain over the conditions of employment. A related provision, section 8(d), requires employers to bargain in good faith, that is, to approach negotiations with an honest and serious intent to engage in give-and-take bargaining in an attempt to reach an agreement. However, the obligation to bargain in good faith does not compel either party to agree to a proposal

or to make concessions. The examination of whether an employer has bargained in good faith is difficult because it involves determining the employer's subjective frame of mind. The NLRB will look at all of the surrounding circumstances, including the employer's willingness to negotiate and its conduct at the bargaining table.

> "
> *However, the obligation to bargain in good faith does not compel either party to agree to a proposal or to make concessions.*

In *National Labor Relations Board v. General Electric Company*,[8] the court found that an employer did not bargain in good faith when it adopted a take-it-or-leave-it posture and then publicized that position to establish the

---

8. 418 F.2d 736 (2d Cir. 1969), *cert. denied,* 397 U.S. 965 (1970).

idea that the union was powerless. In 1960, many of the employees of General Electric (GE), one of the best-known manufacturers of electrical equipment and appliances in the United States, were represented by the International Union of Electrical, Radio and Machine Workers. Having suffered a crippling strike and having agreed to a contract settlement that it viewed as excessive, GE adopted a new approach in its 1960 collective bargaining negotiations. It announced to the union that it would hold nothing back when it made its offer to the union. GE stated that, though it was willing to accept any suggestions based on facts that the company might have overlooked, it would not engage in give-and-take bargaining but would hold firmly to its offer. GE then advertised that position extensively to employees. Through a "veritable avalanche of publicity," GE described its proposal as both fair and firm.

The U.S. Court of Appeals, affirming a decision of the NLRB, held that the company's collective bargaining posture violated section 8(a)(5). Its well-publicized policy of firmness tended to back the company into an inflexible position and to establish in the minds of employees the idea that the union was unnecessary.

The duty to bargain collectively in good faith prohibits an employer from unilaterally changing some term or condition of employment unless, after bargaining with the union to an impasse, the employer's unilateral changes are consistent with the union's pre-impasse proposal. The duty to bargain in good faith also requires

Ethical Consideration

An employer is required to approach collective bargaining with an honest and serious intent to conclude a collective bargaining agreement. It is an unfair labor practice for an employer to embark on a course of collective bargaining designed to frustrate agreement on the terms of a contract.

employers to bargain over certain subjects. The NLRB and courts have held that there are three categories of bargaining subjects: mandatory, permissible, and illegal. Employers must bargain over mandatory subjects—those that vitally affect the terms and conditions of employment, such as wages and work hours. Employers may, but are not obligated to, bargain over permissible subjects. Employers must not bargain over illegal subjects.

There has been much litigation over what subjects are mandatory. In the following case, the Supreme Court examined whether an employer must bargain over a decision to close part of its operation.

■ **A Case in Point:**   **Summary**

Case 14.5
FIRST NATIONAL MAINTENANCE CORP. v. NATIONAL LABOR RELATIONS BOARD
Supreme Court of the United States
452 U.S. 666, 101 S.Ct. 2573 (1981).

FACTS First National Maintenance Corporation was engaged in the business of providing housekeeping, cleaning, maintenance, and related services for commercial customers. Following a dispute with a nursing home over fees, First National terminated its contract with that customer and discharged its employees who worked there. The union representing those employees requested bargaining over the decision to terminate the contract. First National refused. The union alleged that the employer's refusal breached its duty to bargain in good faith.

ISSUE PRESENTED Does an employer need to bargain over a decision to shut down part of its business purely for economic reasons?

SUMMARY OF OPINION Congress did not intend that the union would become an equal partner with the employer in the running of the business enterprise. An employer must bargain over a decision, the U.S. Supreme Court ruled, only if bargaining would "promote the fundamental purpose of the Act by bringing a problem of vital concern to labor and management within the framework established by Congress as most conducive to industrial peace." The Court also noted that an employer needs to make certain decisions fundamental to its operation without the encumbrance of the collective-bargaining obligation. The Court concluded that bargaining over management decisions that have a substantial impact on the continued availability of employment should be required only if the benefit, for labor-management relations and the collective bargaining process, outweighs the burden placed on the conduct of the business.

RESULT   The Supreme Court ruled that an employer is not required to bargain over every decision that it makes.

COMMENTS   Even though an employer may not be required to bargain over a decision to close part of its operations for economic reasons, the employer will be required to bargain with the union over the effects of such a decision on employees represented by the union. Moreover, the Supreme Court in *First National Maintenance* explicitly limited its holding to "partial closings" accomplished for economic reasons and stated that it was not expressing a view as to other management decisions, including plant relocations, sales, or other kinds of subcontracting or automation. Finally, bargaining over a management decision to close or modify its operations may be required where the decision hinges on labor costs over which the union has some control.

 Ethical Consideration

The law prevents an employer from attempting to escape its collective bargaining obligation by shutting down a unionized operation and moving the functions of that former operation to a nearby site. This violation, known as a *runaway shop*, is to be distinguished from an employer's decision to close permanently a unionized facility and not transfer its functions elsewhere. Is this a fair distinction?

"

An employer must bargain over a decision, the U.S. Supreme Court ruled, only if bargaining would "promote the fundamental purpose of the Act by bringing a problem of vital concern to labor and management within the framework established by Congress as most conducive to industrial peace."

In 1989, the NLRB decided that drug testing is a mandatory subject of bargaining.[9] Johnson-Bateman Company, a manufacturer of concrete pipe, announced a new policy that any employee suffering a work-related injury would be required to take a drug and alcohol test. The union, which had not been given advance notice of this policy or an opportunity to bargain over it, demanded that the company rescind the policy. Johnson-Bateman refused, and proceeded as it had announced.

The NLRB held that the company's proposed drug and alcohol testing was a mandatory subject of bargaining. The testing of employees who require medical treatment for work injuries is germane to the working environment. By requiring testing, the employer had changed the method by which it would investigate possible employee responsibility for accidents and the character of proof on which an employee's job security might depend.

In a companion case, *Star Tribune*,[10] the NLRB ruled that the employer, a daily newspaper, did not violate the NLRA by failing to bargain over the implementation of a mandatory drug and alcohol testing policy for job applicants. The NLRB noted that such testing would not vitally affect either workplace safety or the terms and conditions of employment for current employees represented

9. *Johnson-Bateman Company*, 295 NLRB 26 (1989).
10. 295 NLRB 63 (1989).

by the union. Thus, preemployment testing of applicants was not a mandatory subject of bargaining.

Presumption of Majority Support

A union that is certified by the NLRB as the bargaining agent for a unit of employees enjoys an *irrebuttable presumption* of majority support for one year. Its support may not be questioned during that time, and the employer may not refuse to bargain with the union. Such a refusal is a *per se violation* of the National Labor Relations Act, that is, a violation in itself, without the need for proof of

any further misconduct. After the first year, the employer may rebut the presumption of majority support by showing either: (1) that the union does not in fact have majority support; or (2) that the employer has a good-faith doubt of the union's majority support.

When an employer replaces striking employees, the question arises whether the replacements support or oppose the incumbent union. The NLRB has followed a no-presumption approach and ruled that the replacements' union sentiments should be decided on a case-by-case basis. The Supreme Court approved that approach in the following case.

■ **A Case in Point:**   **Summary**

Case 14.6
NATIONAL LABOR RELATIONS BOARD v. CURTIN MATHESON SCIENTIFIC, INC.
Supreme Court of the United States
494 U.S. 775, 110 S.Ct 1542 (1990).

FACTS   On May 21, 1979, the collective bargaining agreement between Teamsters Local 960 and Curtin Matheson Scientific expired. Curtin Matheson is a company engaged in the purchase and sale of laboratory equipment and supplies. The collective bargaining agreement covered production and maintenance employees.

After the union rejected the company's final offer for a new agreement, Curtin locked out the 27 union employees. The union called for an economic strike, that is, a strike based not on unfair labor practices but on the economics of the offer made by the employer. Curtin hired 29 workers to replace the 22 striking employees. Two months later, the union ended the strike and offered to accept Curtin's final offer. Curtin revoked this offer and withdrew recognition of the union, stating that it doubted that the union had majority support. The union filed an unfair labor practice charge, alleging that the employer lacked good-faith doubt of majority status.

The NLRB held that, although replacements often will not favor the incumbent union, the likelihood of such opposition is insufficient to justify an anti-union presumption.

ISSUE PRESENTED   Should the NLRB assume that workers who replace striking employees are anti-union in determining whether an employer is justified in doubting the union's majority support?

SUMMARY OF OPINION   The U.S. Supreme Court agreed with the NLRB, finding that the circumstances of each strike, and the replacements' reasons for crossing the picket line, may vary. For example, a replacement who otherwise supports the union may be forced to work for a struck employer for financial reasons. A replacement also may desire union representation even though he refuses to support a particular strike. The Court noted that an anti-union presumption could allow an employer to eliminate the union entirely merely by hiring a sufficient number of replacement employees. The Court concluded that the NLRB's adoption of a case-by-case approach was rational, was consistent with the NLRA's policy of maintaining industrial peace, protected the bargaining process, and preserved employees' rights to engage in protected activity.

RESULT The NLRB need not assume that workers who replace striking workers are anti-union. The NLRB may determine the union sentiments of striker replacements on a case-by-case basis.

■ Strikes

Lawful strikes are of two kinds: economic strikes and unfair labor practice strikes. Other kinds of strikes violate the NLRA.

Economic Strikes

Unions often strike employers when they are unable to extract acceptable terms and conditions of employment through collective bargaining. An employer that suffers such an *economic strike* is permitted to hire permanent replacements for the striking employees. If it does so, and the striking employees offer to return to work, the employer need not rehire them unless the departure of the replacements creates vacancies. The following case addressed the right of strikers to reinstatement.

■ A Case in Point:　　　　　**In the Language of the Court**

Case 14.7
LAIDLAW CORP. v. NATIONAL LABOR RELATIONS BOARD
United States Court of Appeals for the Seventh Circuit
414 F.2d 99 (7th Cir. 1969), *cert. denied*, 397 U.S. 920 (1970).

FACTS Following a breakdown in contract negotiations, the International Brotherhood of Pulp, Sulphite, and Papermill Workers struck the Laidlaw Corporation, a manufacturer of wire and related products. During the strike, the employer hired workers to replace the striking employees. Thereafter, a large number of striking employees requested reinstatement, and the company put back to work those employees for whom it had vacancies. The company then terminated the employment of the remaining strikers despite their unconditional offer to return to work. The company refused to reinstate them, even though vacancies were later created by the departure of some strike replacements.

The NLRB held that terminating the strikers following their request for reinstatement and not offering them jobs as vacancies occurred violated section 8(a)(3) and (1) of the National Labor Relations Act.

ISSUE PRESENTED Need an employer reinstate an economic striker if a permanent replacement holds the striker's position at the time the striker requests reinstatement? Must the employer give striking workers hiring preference for any comparable job created by the departure of replacements?

OPINION SWYGERT, J., writing for the U.S. Court of Appeals:

. . . .

In its decision, the Board held that economic strikers "who unconditionally apply for reinstatement at a time when their positions are filled by permanent replacements" not only remain employees, but are entitled to full reinstatement upon the departure of replacements unless they have in the meantime acquired regular and substantially equivalent employment or unless the employer has sustained his burden of proof that the failure to offer full reinstatement was for legitimate and substantial business reasons.

Case 14.7 continued on following page

*Case **14.7** continued*

In so holding, the Board said that it was following the underlying principle enunciated in both *NLRB v. Fleetwood Trailer Co.*,[11] and *NLRB v. Great Dane Trailers*.[12] It noted that the Supreme Court in *Fleetwood* had held that the hiring of new employees at a time when there are outstanding applications for reinstatement from striking employees is presumptively a violation of the Act, regardless of intent, unless the employer demonstrates a "legitimate and substantial business reason" for his failure to hire the strikers. The Board concluded that the situation in *Fleetwood* and the present case are parallel and that the *Fleetwood* rule should be applied against Laidlaw. The Board said: "when job vacancies arose as a result of the departure of permanent replacements, Respondent [Laidlaw] could not lawfully ignore outstanding applications for reinstatement from strikers and hire new applicants. . . ." We agree with the Board's view and its holding.

. . . .

In defense of its position, Laidlaw contends that permanent replacement of economic strikers constitutes a legitimate and substantial justification for not offering the strikers reinstatement. Once jobs are filled by "permanent" employees during an economic strike, the company maintains that the strikers have no right to reinstatement even though the replacements depart from their jobs. For support of this proposition, the company relies on the *Fleetwood* decision and *NLRB v. Mackay Radio & Tel. Co.*[13] Its reliance is misplaced.

. . . .

The justification for not discharging replacements in order to reinstate strikers, found in *Mackay* and mentioned in *Fleetwood*, is the need of the employer to assure permanent employment to the replacements so that the necessary labor force can be obtained to maintain operations during a strike. But such a justification is not present in the instant case. There is no question about the retention of the replacements who were hired during the strike on a permanent basis. The only question is whether the strikers are to be considered employees after the strike, having rights to reinstatement if the replacements depart from their jobs. The legitimate business reason for not discharging replacements in order to reinstate strikers, mentioned in *Mackay* and *Fleetwood*, did not authorize denying the Laidlaw strikers reinstatement after the replacements had for one reason or another departed from their jobs subsequent to the strike's termination. Although there is a "legitimate and substantial business justification" for requiring replaced economic strikers to wait for reinstatement until a vacancy occurs in the labor force, no justification was advanced by Laidlaw for its decision to consider the employment status of striker-applicants terminated if, on the day they applied for reinstatement, their former positions were still occupied by permanent replacements.

. . . .

In the case before us, we believe that the importance of protecting the statutory rights of Laidlaw's employees outweighs the fact that the company

---

11. 389 U.S. 375, 88 S.Ct. 543 (1967).
12. 388 U.S. 26, 87 S.Ct. 1792 (1967).
13. 304 U.S. 333, 58 S.Ct. 904 (1938).

may have relied on prior Board rule or policy. We are in agreement with the statement made by the General Counsel in his brief: "Unless the disadvantaged strikers are compensated, they will have been penalized for exercising statutorily protected rights and the effect of discouraging future such exercises will not be completely dissipated. In these circumstances, it was not arbitrary or capricious for the Board to conclude that complete vindication of employee rights should take precedence over the employer's reliance on prior Board law."

. . . .

RESULT   The U.S. Court of Appeals agreed with the NLRB, holding that the employer's action penalized employees for participating in the strike. The court ruled that strikers are to be considered employees after the strike, with rights to reinstatement if the replacements depart from their jobs.

COMMENTS   An employer may not be required to reinstate a striking employee, even when a vacancy occurs, if: (1) the former striker has secured regular and equivalent employment elsewhere; (2) the employer has legitimate and substantial business reasons, such as a striker's lack of necessary skills; or (3) the striker has committed sufficiently serious misconduct during the strike.

Questions
1. Under what circumstances can an employer faced with a strike hire permanent replacement workers?
2. Why is it good public policy to rehire striking employees to fill vacancies left by replacement workers?

Unfair Labor Practice Strikes

Workers sometimes strike an employer wholly or partly to protest an unfair labor practice. For example, a union may strike because it believes that the employer is not bargaining in good faith. Workers who engage in such an *unfair labor practice strike* have a right to be reinstated to their former positions if they make an unconditional offer to return to work. If the employer refuses to rehire them, the NLRB may award them reinstatement plus back pay. This difference between the rights of economic strikers and those of unfair labor practice strikers may cause debate as to whether the employer committed an unfair labor practice and whether the strike was called to protest that practice.

Unlawful Strikes

The NLRA prohibits certain kinds of *organizational strikes* or picketing, whose purpose is to organize employees, and certain kinds of *recognitional strikes,* whose purpose is to force the employer to recognize the union as a collective bargaining agent for its employees. It also outlaws certain *secondary boycotts,* which are strikes called against an outside company to induce it to put pressure (usually by withholding business) on the employer with whom the union has a dispute.

Organizational Strikes   Section 8(b)(7) of the NLRA prohibits organizational or recognitional strikes or picketing when: (1) the employer has already lawfully recognized another labor organization as the representative of its employees and the union may not properly raise a question concerning that representation; (2) the NLRB has conducted a representation election under the NLRA within the preceding 12 months; or (3) the union has not filed a petition for a representation election within a reasonable period of time, not to exceed 30 days, from the date picketing commenced.

Recognitional Strikes   Section 8(b)(4)(i)(C) of the NLRA makes it unlawful for a labor organization to induce employees (for example, through picketing) to engage in a work stoppage to force the employer to recognize a labor organization if another labor organization has been certified as the employees' representative.

Secondary Boycotts   Section 8(b)(4) of the NLRA was enacted primarily to address the problem of a union unfairly involving neutral employers, with whom the

Political Perspective

Clinton Intervenes in American Airlines Flight Attendant Strike

After failing to reach an agreement despite a year of talks, the American Airlines flight attendants called an 11-day strike against the Dallas-based carrier several days before the Thanksgiving holiday in 1993. Both sides were deadlocked over salary demands, changes in work rules, and concessions sought by management. The airline offered pay raises of up to $36,430 for attendants with 14 years or more of experience, but the flight attendants said the increases would be offset by employee contributions for health and retiree benefits. The company also wanted to reduce the number of attendants on flights that were only partially full. Current contracts require four attendants on a Boeing 727, regardless of the number of passengers on board. American wanted to be able to decrease the number to three in accordance with government requirements.

The flight attendants' union asked American to join them in requesting the National Mediation Board to form an emergency panel to review and recommend a settlement. The airline declined, stating that the process would produce a settlement that would not be in the long-term interest of the carrier.

The flight attendants decided to end their walkout after President Clinton took the unusual step of brokering an agreement between the union and the airline to submit the labor dispute to binding arbitration.

Clinton's actions, including personal telephone calls to the chairman of American Airlines and the president of the flight attendants' union, were the most direct steps taken by a president to influence the outcome of a work stoppage since President Reagan dismissed striking air traffic controllers in 1981. President Bush refused to intervene in an Eastern Airlines strike in 1989 and gave his approval to federal intervention in a freight-rail strike in 1992 only after Congress passed a law calling for such action.

Clinton's intervention differed from Reagan's actions in one significant way. The controllers were striking against a government agency, the Federal Aviation Administration, which is illegal, and the flight attendants were striking against a private company.

Although the White House stated that Clinton had not taken sides in the dispute, airline officials stated that he had, through the nature of his position, persuaded them to agree to binding arbitration, an approach that had been favored by the union.

After Clinton's successful attempt to persuade American Airlines flight attendants and management to accept binding arbitration, resulting in the avoidance of a transportation tie-up over the Thanksgiving holiday, it is more likely that the White House will intervene in future labor disputes that "pose a threat" to the public.

The five-day strike had virtually shut down the world's largest airline. Robert Crandall, American Airlines chairman, estimated that American was losing at least $10 million per day.

Clinton's phone call opened avenues, even if they were not Crandall's preferred route. "I think when he's the elected leader of the country, for any citizen, company or union to say no . . . would require an awfully good reason. . . . When the President said it is important to get this dispute behind us . . . I felt it was incumbent on me to accept his suggestion and I did," Crandall said.[a]

Experts say that presidential pressure can be effective, but that such efforts may prove more dangerous than beneficial. Rather than using existing dispute resolution mechanisms, companies and unions might be tempted to pressure their congressional representatives to use their position to involve the White House in the resolution of the dispute.

Although members of Congress and labor experts view Clinton's actions as precedent setting, White House officials have stated that management and unions should not expect the president to intervene regularly in such matters. Rather, the administration will only mediate such conflicts in extreme situations.

Earlier presidents were hesitant to intercede in labor-management conditions, and when they took such action it was under the guise of a national emergency. As Harley Shaken, a professor at University of California, Berkeley, stated: "Here it was a single carrier and the issue was whether people would get home for Thanksgiving." The Clinton administration has not stated what constitutes an "extreme situation." It can be assumed, however, that it will be a less extreme situation than under past administrations, which acted only in times of war or to break up illegal strikes.

---

a. Richard M. Weintraub and Ann Devroy, "Union Ends Walkout at American; Both Sides Accept Arbitration After Clinton Intervenes," *Washington Post*, November 23, 1993, A1.

union has no quarrel, in a labor dispute. Section 8(b)(4)(B) makes it illegal for a union to engage in or encourage a strike with the object of forcing any person to cease handling the products of an employer or to cease doing business with that employer.

> **"** *Section 8(b)(4) of the NLRA was enacted primarily to address the problem of a union unfairly involving neutral employers, with whom the union has no quarrel, in a labor dispute.*

Section 8(b)(4)(B) allegations arise quite commonly in the construction industry, where, typically, a number of employers work on a single construction site. A union that has a dispute with one of those employers may picket the entire job site, thereby hoping to shut down the work completely and put maximum pressure on that employer. Employers have countered this tactic by directing the employees and vendors of the *primary employer,* that is, the employer with whom the union has a dispute, to use a gate that is physically separated from the gate to be used by all other persons. Under this arrangement, known as the *neutral gate system,* the union may only picket at the gate reserved for the employees and vendors of the primary employer.

■ Unfair Labor Practices by Unions

Section 8(b) of the NLRA specifies several activities, besides unlawful strikes, in which unions may not engage.

Coercion of Employees

Section 8(b)(1)(A) of the NLRA prohibits unions from coercing employees to join the union or to support its activities. For example, a union may not attempt to intimidate employees into voting for it in a representation election. A union is also prohibited from coercing employees to join, or refrain from abandoning, a strike.

Section 8(b)(1) has also been held to obligate a union to represent fairly and honestly all of the employees in the collective bargaining unit, without regard to their union affiliation. The Supreme Court in *Vaca v. Sipes*[14]

held that, as the exclusive bargaining representative of the employees, the union has a statutory duty to represent fairly all of the employees in collective bargaining and in enforcement of the collective bargaining agreement. Under this doctrine, the union has an obligation to represent all members of a designated unit without hostility or discrimination toward any employees. It must exercise its discretion with complete good faith and honesty and avoid arbitrary conduct.

Inducing Employer Discrimination Against Nonunion Workers

Under section 8(b)(2) of the NLRA, a union may not cause or attempt to cause an employer to discriminate against an employee on the basis of union affiliation or activities. For example, a union may not encourage an employer to discharge someone because he does not belong to the union. In addition, a union may not cause or attempt to cause an employer to discriminate against an employee who has been denied union membership for any reason other than failure to pay union dues.

Failure to Bargain in Good Faith

Section 8(b)(3) requires the union to bargain in good faith with the employer. This section requires the union to meet with the employer at reasonable times, and section 8(d) requires it to approach bargaining with a serious and honest intent to conclude a collective bargaining contract. It is rarely alleged that a union has failed to bargain in good faith.

International Consideration

Managers with operations outside the United States need to consider the labor relations laws of the foreign countries in which they have employees. Trade unions, often more active than in the U.S., commonly work more closely with management. For example, at Germany's Volkswagen plants, trade unions sit on special "work councils" which approve or reject company changes in production. Work councils typically represent all workers in an establishment, whether or not they are unionized.

---

14. 386 U.S. 171, 37 S.Ct. 903 (1967).

■ Labor Relations in Selected Countries

The labor relations laws of certain European countries and Japan are discussed below.

United Kingdom

Workers in the United Kingdom are free to organize and join labor unions. A trade union that has been recognized by the employer for collective bargaining purposes enjoys certain rights, including: (1) the right of time off for union officials and members; (2) the right to appoint a representative to handle safety matters; (3) the right to be consulted prior to the transferring of the place of business; and (4) the right to receive certain information related to collective bargaining issues.

Although collective bargaining agreements are commonplace, they are not generally enforceable as contracts unless incorporated into an individual employment contract.

Germany

German workers are allowed to form unions, known under German law as associations. There are three main national unions: (1) the DGB, representing tradespersons; (2) the DAG, representing salaried employees; and (3) the DBB, representing civil service workers. Approximately one-third of the German work force is represented by unions.

A single collective bargaining agreement applies to all unionized workers within a particular trade or industry. In some cases, upon approval by the federal minister of labor, a collective bargaining agreement may bind all workers in an industry, whether unionized or not. A German statute establishes the right to strike.

France

French labor relations are governed primarily by laws and regulations rather than by collective bargaining agreements.[15] These laws and regulations establish wages, the work week, health and safety conditions, legal holidays, and paid vacations. They also prohibit certain types of discrimination.

French workers are free to organize and join unions if they so choose. Workers may elect employee representatives or, in larger companies, a personnel committee to express their concerns to management. The Code du tra-

vail (Employment Code) provides for the negotiation of collective agreements between workers and employers, and the right to strike is fundamental.[16]

Italy

The Italian Constitution grants workers the right to unionize and strike. Organized labor in Italy is dominated by a number of national labor unions. The Statuto dei lavoratori, known as the Workers' Bill of Rights, regulates most aspects of working conditions and union activities. Collective bargaining agreements negotiated between representatives of management and labor unions legally bind only those who belong to the organizations who signed the agreements and those who have elected to adopt them.

Spain

Spanish workers are represented by works councils which voice their concerns to and bargain with management. Collective bargaining agreements are negotiated by a maximum of 24 representatives, half from management and half from labor. An agreement is reached when 60% of each side votes in favor of adopting an agreement. In 1991, slightly more than 4,000 collective bargaining contracts were negotiated, covering more than five million workers.

The Netherlands

The Netherlands Civil Code, which regulates workers' rights, permits unionization and strikes. Approximately 25% of the employed work force is unionized, and nearly 76% of those workers are covered by about 500 collective bargaining agreements. The government has the right to include certain provisions in the agreements.[17]

Belgium

Article 20 of the Belgian Constitution and section 1 of the Law of May 24, 1921, give workers in Belgium the right to unionize or refrain from doing so. Belgian unions not only participate in collective bargaining but also influence the enactment of government regulations and participate in the management of public organizations in the labor field.

---

15. C. Trav., arts. L 131-1 to L 136-4, R 132-1 to R 136-11.

16. Declaration of Rights of the Constitution of October 27, 1946, Preamble ¶ 6, confirmed by the Preamble of the Constitution of October 4, 1958; C. Trav., art. L 521-1.
17. National Trade Data Bank, Market Reports, March 1992.

Approximately 70% of employees are represented by unions. Bargaining is conducted by approximately 20 employer federations. Most collective bargaining agreements concluded at the national level bind all employers, even if they are not members of the employers' organization that signed the agreement. Similarly, the majority of collective bargaining agreements concluded at the industry level bind all employers in the industry at issue, even if they do not belong to the employers' organization that signed the agreement.

Switzerland

The Swiss Constitution does not give workers the right to unionize and strike. However, federal legislation has established the right of workers to join or refrain from joining a union. The six major labor unions in Switzerland, organized along trade or industry lines, represent approximately 789,000 workers. Collective bargaining agreements are common, and nonunion workers may enjoy the benefits of such agreements with the consent of the parties to the agreement.

Japan

Three major statutes govern labor conditions and relations in Japan. The Labor Standards Law regulates matters such as labor contracts, wages, and discrimination; the Labor Union Law and the Labor Relations Adjustment Law regulate unionization, strikes, and related matters. Collective bargaining occurs only during April and May of each year. Labor-management councils assist in collective bargaining. In 1994, more than 33% of the Japanese work force was represented by unions. Of Japan's approximately 72,700 unions, Rengo (Private-Sector Trade Union Confederation) is the largest, with about eight million members.[18]

■ Other Laws Affecting Labor Relations

Federal legislation concerning employee benefits, workplace health and safety, layoffs, and minimum wages indirectly affects labor relations. These laws, which apply regardless of whether employees belong to a union, are discussed below.

■ Employee Retirement Income Security Act

For several decades before 1974, the number of pension plans, the number of employees covered by those plans, and the annual benefits paid to retirees from these plans grew tremendously. Despite these increases, however, many employees who expected to receive pension plan payments upon retirement received either no benefits or far fewer benefits than they had anticipated. Plan officials made ill-advised investments; employees quit or were discharged with few or no vested benefits; or the employer terminated an underfunded plan with insufficient assets to cover its obligations.

To help avoid these problems, Congress enacted the Employee Retirement Income Security Act of 1974 (ERISA).[19] With few exceptions, ERISA applies to all pension plans, and many other types of employee benefit plans, established by employers engaged in interstate commerce. Section 2(b) of Title I of ERISA states that its purpose is to "protect interstate commerce and the interests of participants in employee benefit plans. . . ."[20] With regard to pension plans, ERISA, among other things: (1) establishes minimum funding requirements and participation and vesting standards; (2) imposes fiduciary obligations; (3) requires detailed disclosure and reporting of certain pension plan information; (4) restricts substantially the investment of pension plan assets; and (5) calls for pension plan administrators to provide annual, audited financial statements to the government and participants.

ERISA requires fiduciaries to discharge their duties: (1) solely in the interest of the participants and beneficiaries of the plan and the plan itself; (2) for the exclusive purpose of providing benefits and defraying expenses; (3) with the care, skill, prudence, and diligence that a prudent person acting in a like capacity would exercise; and (4) in accordance with the document and instruments governing the plan.[21]

Employee benefit plans other than pension plans are covered by ERISA if a reasonable person could determine from the surrounding circumstances the existence of intended benefits, beneficiaries, financing for the benefits, and procedures for receiving the benefits. For example, many types of group severance pay plans are deemed to be either pension plans or welfare plans and

18. Investing, Licensing and Trading Conditions Abroad 2:21 (Business International Corp., 1989); "Hosokawa to Canvass Coalition Heads on Cabinet Reshuffle," *Japan Economic Newswire*, February 25, 1994.

19. 29 U.S.C. §§ 1001-1461 (1988 & Supp. 1992).
20. 29 U.S.C. §§ 1001b (1988).
21. 29 U.S.C. §§ 1104 *et seq.* (1988 & Supp. 1992).

thus regulated by ERISA. However, individually negotiated severance agreements are not.

Nonpension benefit plans do not invoke ERISA's vesting, participation, and funding obligations, but they are subject to ERISA's reporting, disclosure, and fiduciary-responsibility rules. For example, employees must be provided with documents such as a summary plan description, a summary annual report, and a summary of any material modifications to the plan. If a severance plan is deemed to be a pension plan, it will be subject to ERISA's vesting, participation, and funding rules.

Under ERISA, an employer must maintain records of each employee's years of service and vesting percentage. Further, the employer or plan administrator must maintain sufficient records, usually including age, hours worked, salary, and employee contributions, to calculate each employee's benefits.

ERISA imposes various penalties for failure to conform to its participation, vesting, funding, and other requirements. Plan participants or beneficiaries may sue for lost benefits and for loss of the plan's tax benefits. Any fiduciary of a plan who breaches a duty is personally liable to make good to the plan losses that resulted from the breach. ERISA also provides for civil penalties for breach of its prohibited transaction rules (which bar many transactions between an ERISA plan and a fiduciary of that plan) of up to 100% of the amount of the prohibited transaction.[22]

To minimize costs and maximize benefit levels, many employers belong to multiemployer pension plans. However, under the Multiemployer Pension Plan Amendments Act of 1980, withdrawal from such a plan may result in stiff penalties.

■ Consolidated Omnibus Budget Reconciliation Act

The Consolidated Omnibus Budget Reconciliation Act of 1985 (COBRA)[23] was established in 1986 to allow group health, dental, and visual benefits to continue for: (1) employees who are terminated voluntarily or involuntarily, unless the discharge was for gross misconduct; and (2) employees whose hours are reduced to the point that coverage would normally cease. COBRA applies to employers of 20 or more workers that sponsor a group health plan. Churches and federal government agencies are exempt from the requirements of COBRA.

Employers must notify employees of their rights when they begin participation in a group health plan or when coverage has been threatened by some event such as termination or reduced hours.

Under COBRA, eligible employees must be given at least 60 days from the date their coverage ceases to elect to have their coverage continued. If coverage continuation is elected, the employer is required to extend, for up to 18 months, coverage identical to that provided under the plan for similarly situated employees or spouses. The eligible employee may be required to pay all or part of the premium, including a 2% charge for administrative services for continued coverage. Disabled employees are eligible for continued coverage for up to 29 months. If the employee declines to continue coverage, the employer has no further coverage obligations.

An employer may discontinue coverage for one of five reasons: (1) the employer ceases to provide group health coverage to any of its employees; (2) the premium for the coverage is not paid; (3) the employee, or former employee, becomes insured under another group plan; (4) the employee, or former employee, becomes eligible for Medicare; or (5) a spouse of the employee, or former employee, becomes divorced, remarries, and becomes covered under her new spouse's plan.

Under the Technical and Miscellaneous Revenue Act of 1988,[24] employers who fail to comply with COBRA's requirements will be subject to adverse tax consequences, including a nondeductible excise tax of $100 per day for each qualified beneficiary. However, the tax will not exceed $200 per day if more than one qualified beneficiary is affected by the same event (such as termination or reduction of hours). The tax will also not be imposed for failures to comply due to reasonable cause that are remedied within the first 30 days of the noncompliance. An employer will not be required to pay an annual tax total in excess of 10% of the total amount paid for its group health plan during the preceding taxable year, or $500,000, whichever is less. These monetary limitations do not apply, however, if noncompliance was caused by willful neglect.

■ Occupational Safety and Health Act

The Occupational Safety and Health Act of 1970 (OSHA)[25] was enacted to require employers to establish

---

22. 29 U.S.C. §§ 1106, 1132 (1988 & Supp. 1992).
23. Pub. L. No. 99-272, 100 Stat. 82 (1986) (codified as amended in scattered sections of 29 U.S.C.).

24. Pub. L. No. 100-647, 102 Stat. 3342 (1989) (codified as amended in scattered sections of 26 U.S.C.).
25. Pub. L. No. 91-596, 84 Stat. 1590 (1970) (codified as amended at 29 U.S.C. §§ 651-678 (1988 & Supp 1992)).

safe and healthy working environments. The federal agency responsible for enforcing the provisions of OSHA is the Occupational Safety and Health Administration (also called OSHA).

Employers are required to provide a workplace free from *recognized hazards,* that is, conditions that are obviously dangerous or are considered by the employer or other employers in the industry to be dangerous.

OSHA also requires employers to maintain certain records, including the OSHA Form 200, which lists and summarizes all work-related injuries and illnesses. (Certain industries, such as retail, finance, and insurance, are exempt from this record-keeping requirement.) A summary of these records must be posted annually at the job site. In addition, employers must post in a conspicuous place: (1) OSHA's official Job Safety Poster; (2) any OSHA citations for violations; and (3) notices of imminent danger to employees, including exposure to toxic substances.

OSHA inspectors are allowed to conduct surprise inspections at work sites where OSHA believes an imminent danger is present, where an employee has filed a complaint, or where a fatality or catastrophe has occurred. During the inspection, the OSHA investigator may review company records, check for compliance with the relevant OSHA standards, inspect fire-protection and other safety equipment, examine the company's safety and health-management program, interview employees, and walk through the facility.

> *OSHA inspectors are allowed to conduct surprise inspections at work sites where OSHA believes an imminent danger is present, where an employee has filed a complaint, or where a fatality or catastrophe has occurred.*

When the inspection has been completed, the inspector will hold a meeting with the employer and the employee representative, if any. The inspector will discuss the results of the inspection, and, if appropriate, issue a written citation for any violations. There are five different types of violations: (1) de minimis (that is, unimportant) violations, for which no notice is posted and no penalty is imposed; (2) nonserious violations, which present hazards that are not likely to cause death or serious bodily harm, and for which a fine may be imposed of up to $7,000 for each violation; (3) serious violations, which have a substantial likelihood of resulting in death or serious bodily harm, and for which a fine may be imposed of up to $7,000 for each violation, (4) willful violations, which are deliberate or intentional, and for which a fine of at least $5,000 and up to $70,000 may be imposed for each violation; and (5) repeated violations, which occur within three years of a previously cited violation, and for which a fine may be imposed of up to $70,000 for each violation. Courts may also impose criminal sanctions for health and safety infractions (see chapter 15).

If OSHA finds a violation, the employer is required to remedy the problem immediately. If remedial action is not taken, OSHA will seek a court order to ensure compliance. The employer may either settle the violation, or seek review of the OSHA decision by the Occupational Safety and Health Review Commission. Beginning in 1986, and more frequently in recent years, OSHA has penalized egregious violations by imposing a separate fine for each violation rather than an overall fine for a group of violations.[26]

There has also been a trend toward increasing the number of criminal prosecutions of employers for OSHA violations. Although the word *employer* has not been defined, it appears to include those corporate officers who are responsible for ensuring compliance with OSHA standards. A number of managers and officers of corporations have been criminally prosecuted for serious violations that led to the deaths of employees. These prosecutions

At the Top

A manager can be held criminally responsible for serious violations of OSHA. Diligent oversight of health and safety aspects of the workplace serves both to reduce the chance of employee serious injury or death in the first place, and to reduce the likelihood that an individual manager will be found criminally liable if, despite his diligence, a fatal accident does occur.

---

26. Anne Lange et al., "Special Report: New Approaches to Safety, Heightened Expectations in Safety and Health Community as 1990s Open," 19 O.S.H.Rep. (BNA) 1355 (January 10, 1990).

have had mixed results. For example, the Michigan Court of Appeals found that a supervisor was not guilty of involuntary manslaughter as he did not own the equipment that caused the accident.[27]

■ Worker Adjustment and Retraining Notification Act

The Worker Adjustment and Retraining Notification Act of 1988 (WARN Act)[28] requires an employer to provide timely notice to its employees of a proposal to close a plant or to reduce its work force permanently. The WARN Act attempts to strike a balance between the employer's interest in maintaining employee productivity and efficiency, and the employee's interest in being forewarned of a mass layoff or plant closing.

The essential features of the WARN Act are as follows. The act applies to employers with 100 or more employees, either all working full time or working an aggregate of at least 4,000 hours per week. The act requires employers to give employees 60 days' advance notice of any plant closing that will result in a loss of employment during any 30-day period for 50 or more employees. A shutdown of a product line or operation within a plant is included within the act's definition of a plant closing. The act also requires 60 days' notice for layoffs during any 30-day period that affect at least 500 employees, or at least 50 employees if they comprise one-third of the work force. Employers are required to give written notice of the plant closing or layoff to each representative of the affected employees or, if there is no representative, to each affected employee. Employers are also required to give written notice to the state and local governments in which the layoff or plant closing will occur.

The WARN Act permits an employer to order the shutdown of a plant before the conclusion of the 60-day notice period if: (1) at the time notice would have been required, the employer was actively seeking capital or business that would enable it to avoid or postpone the shutdown, and the employer reasonably and in good faith believed that giving the required notice would preclude it from obtaining the needed business or capital; or (2) the plant closing or mass layoff was caused by a natural disaster or by business circumstances that were not reasonably foreseeable at the time notice would have been

required. The terms "actively seeking capital" and "business circumstances that were not reasonably foreseeable" remain largely undefined.

The WARN Act does not apply to the closing of a temporary facility. It does not apply to a closing or mass layoff that results from the completion of a particular project if the affected employees were hired with the understanding that their employment would not continue beyond the duration of the project. Finally, it does not apply to a closing or layoff that results from a strike or lockout that is not intended to evade the requirements of the act.

The WARN Act includes several enforcement provisions. Aggrieved employees are entitled to receive back wages and benefits for each day that the employer is in violation. In addition, an employer who violates the act may be subject to a civil penalty of up to $30,000, to be paid to affected communities. A person can bring an action under the WARN Act in federal district court in any district in which the violation is alleged to have occurred, or in any district in which the employer transacts business. The court has discretion to award the prevailing party reasonable attorney's fees.

■ Fair Labor Standards Act

The federal Fair Labor Standards Act (FLSA),[29] enacted in 1938 and amended many times thereafter, was established primarily to regulate the minimum wage, overtime pay, and the use of child labor. Many, if not all, states have established wage and hour regulations as well. In general, where the federal and state laws vary, employers must abide by the stricter law. For example, if an employee works more than eight hours in a day, under federal law the employer need not pay any overtime premium, but under California law, the employer must pay time and one-half; California employers are required to adhere to the California law in that situation.

Because of the wide variance in state laws, this discussion focuses on the federal law.

Who Is Covered The FLSA applies to employees who individually are engaged in interstate commerce or in the production of goods for interstate commerce, or who are employed by employers who engage in interstate commerce. As a practical matter, employers of any size who participate in interstate commerce or in the production of goods for interstate commerce will be covered by the FLSA.

---

27. *Michigan v. Hegedus*, 182 Mich.App. 21, 451 N.W.2d 861 (1990).
28. Pub. L. No. 100-379, 102 Stat. 890 (1988) (codified at 29 U.S.C. §§ 2101-2109 (1988)).

29. 29 U.S.C. §§ 201-219 (1988 & Supp. 1992).

Hours Worked   The FLSA does not limit the number of hours that an employee may work in a workweek or workday, so long as the employee is paid appropriate overtime. (But if an employer forces an employee to work too many hours, the employer may be liable under common law for injury to a third party resulting from the employee's fatigue; see chapter 7.)

Compensation   The FLSA requires that employees be compensated for all hours worked. In the case of professional or off-site employees, the number of hours worked may be hotly contested. In general, the hours that an employer knows or has reason to know that an employee has worked, even though the employee has not been requested to work, are deemed hours worked. Where an employee is asked to be on standby—that is, available to return to work while off duty—the hours spent on standby will not be counted as hours worked if the employee is free to use the time for her own purposes.

> **"**
>
> *In the case of professional or off-site employees, the number of hours worked may be hotly contested.*

Minimum Wage and Overtime   In 1938, the FLSA first established the minimum wage at 25 cents per hour; the federal minimum wage in October 1994 was $4.25 per hour. The FLSA also requires that, with some exceptions, every nonexempt employee be paid one and one-half times the regular rate of pay for hours worked in excess of 40 in a workweek.

Certain types of employees are exempt from the minimum-wage and overtime requirements of the FLSA, for example, salespersons and executive, administrative, and professional employees. The regulations of the Wage and Hour Division of the Department of Labor define the characteristics of executive, administrative, and professional employees in terms of salary and work duties.

For a person to qualify as an executive, his primary duty must consist of the management of the enterprise in which he is employed or of a customarily recognized department or subdivision of the enterprise. The person must also: (1) customarily and regularly direct the work of two or more other full-time employees; (2) have the authority to hire or fire other employees; (3) customarily or regularly exercise discretion; and (4) not devote more than 20% of his time to other types of duties.

To qualify as an administrative employee, a person's primary duty must consist of nonmanual work directly related either to management policies or to the general business operations of her employer or her employer's customers. Her primary duty must require the exercise of discretion and independent judgment.

For a person to qualify as a professional employee, he must have a position requiring advance knowledge in a field of science or learning customarily acquired by a prolonged course of specialized intellectual instruction and study.

Child Labor   The FLSA child-labor provisions were enacted to cure the early twentieth-century abuses of many employers who employed child labor at minimal wages. Under federal law, it is illegal to employ anyone under 14, except in specified agricultural occupations. Children aged 14 or 15 may work in some occupations, but only if the employment occurs outside of school hours and does not exceed daily and weekly hour limits. Individuals aged 16 to 18 may work in manufacturing occupations, but they may not work in jobs that the secretary of labor has declared to be particularly hazardous, such as operating a power-driven woodworking machine, a hoisting apparatus, a metal-forming machine, or a circular or band saw. Jobs entailing exposure to radioactive materials are also deemed to be hazardous.

The Responsible Manager

Building Good Labor Relations

A manager should, at a minimum, observe the restrictions that the National Labor Relations Act places upon employer activity. He should not: threaten adverse treatment if employees support a union; interrogate employees about their union activities; promise employees benefits if they abandon the union; or spy on union activities.

However, a manager is permitted by law to discuss certain matters with employees. She may tell employees that the company opposes a union. She may review with employees the disadvantages of unionism, such as the possibility of strikes and the payment of union dues and initiation fees. Managers may also discuss with employees their current benefits and the company's history of favorable treatment of employees, which has occurred without a union. She may tell employees that it is unlaw-

In Brief: Unfair Labor Practices

By Employers:
1) Interfering with employees' rights to organize and bargain collectively.
- Threatening employees with any adverse action for organizing or supporting a union.
- Promising employees any benefits if they fail to support a union.
- Questioning employees regarding union activity.
- Engaging in surveillance of employees' union activities.
2) Enforcing an overly broad rule against soliciting other employees for union support or distributing union literature.
3) Punishing employees for engaging in concerted activities for mutual aid and protection.
4) Dominating or assisting a labor organization.
5) Discriminating against any employee to encourage or discourage membership in any labor organization.
6) Discharging or otherwise discriminating against an employee because he has filed charges to the NLRB.
7) Failing to bargain collectively and in good faith.
- Changing some term or condition of employment, unless bargaining with the union comes to an impasse, the changes are consistent with the union's pre-impasse proposal.
- Failing to bargain over mandatory subjects.
8) Refusing to reinstate workers who engage in an unfair labor practice strike.

By Unions:
1) Unlawful Strikes.
2) Coercing employees to join the union or support its activities.
3) Failing to fairly and honestly represent all of the employees in a collective bargaining unit, without regard to their union affiliation.
4) Inducing employer discrimination against nonunion workers.
5) Failing to bargain in good faith.

ful for the union to attempt to harass or intimidate them into supporting it.

When a union lawfully represents a unit of employees, management is required by the NLRA to meet at reasonable times with the union and confer in good faith with respect to wages, hours, and other terms and conditions of employment. The law does not specify how many times or for how long the employer must meet with the union. At a minimum, the employer cannot refuse to meet with the union at all, or meet on so few occasions that it is almost impossible to attain an agreement. If a union accuses an employer of unlawfully attempting to delay bargaining, the NLRB will look at all of the surrounding circumstances, including the number and length of meetings, the reasons given by the employer for any delays, and any conditions placed upon bargaining by the employer. Some courts have held that an employer must approach collective bargaining with the same seriousness with which it would approach the negotiation of a commercial contract. In this regard, it may be useful for the manager to review the suggestions for good-faith negotiations described in chapter 8.

The NLRA also requires management to give the union the information it needs to discharge its collective bargaining duties adequately. The general rule is that management must disclose relevant information, such as employees' wages, overtime hours, surveys leading to changes in working conditions, layoffs resulting from subcontracting, and seniority lists. However, some courts hold that the employer need disclose only information that is both relevant and necessary. Thus, management may not be required to disclose particularly sensitive employee data, such as the results of employee aptitude or intelligence tests.

Management must be careful about withdrawing any proposals it has made during bargaining. An employer's reneging upon such proposals may be evidence of bad faith, though it is not normally a per se violation of the law. In determining whether the withdrawal of collective bargaining offers amounts to bad faith, the NLRB looks at such factors as the subjects on which the offer was withdrawn, the number of times the employer reneged, and the reasons offered by the employer for reneging.

Inside Story

The Caterpillar Strike

On November 4, 1991, when negotiations on a new employment contract broke down with Caterpillar Inc. (the world's largest maker of earth-moving equipment), the United Auto Workers union (UAW) announced a strike involving 2,400 Caterpillar workers. The company retaliated on November 7 by locking out an additional 6,000 workers. Observers predicted that the strike would not be quickly resolved. Their predictions were based on the 206-day strike against Caterpillar in 1982, which was the longest in the history of the UAW.

At issue was the concept of *pattern bargaining*. The union insisted that Caterpillar, based in Peoria, Illinois, agree to a settlement similar to one negotiated with Deere & Co., another Illinois firm. The UAW had successfully used this technique of matching agreements within an industry for many years.

Although the pattern agreements do not take into account the relative strengths and weaknesses of different companies, the union argued that it is more fair to pay the same pay and benefits to workers performing the same job for different companies. The UAW also claimed that pattern agreements avoid the need to negotiate a new deal with every company and therefore reduce the number of strikes.

Caterpillar claimed that its operations are more international than those of Deere, and that the union's demands would reduce its ability to compete with foreign rivals. The agreement with Deere was said to be too expensive for Caterpillar, which had recently announced the layoff of 2,100 workers.

Not only did Caterpillar not want to grant parity with Deere, it did not want to agree to a single settlement with the UAW for all of its own factories. It wanted separate, locally negotiated agreements for different plants and divisions, which would have severely limited the union's power.

Caterpillar clearly succeeded in breaking the strike. More than 1,000 workers crossed the picket lines, and more threatened to do so 163 days after the walkout began, effectively forcing the UAW to send it members back to work. The UAW's decision to send its members back came just eight days after Caterpillar had threat-

ened to replace any union worker who failed to return. The threat was not an idle one: Caterpillar had taken job applications and had promised to start hiring new workers in May. The strikers came back to work in April 1992 after a five-and-one-half-month strike, and without a contract.

The UAW insisted that it had not lost the strike. It announced that workers would move the struggle into Caterpillar factories by slowing production and creating product shortages. It was felt that such action would force the company to negotiate a contract along union lines.

The economic differences between the union and the company were not insurmountable. The UAW was seeking a maximum wage of $40,458. The company was offering $39,915. The union wanted to keep an existing health care plan which did not require any contributions from workers. Caterpillar wanted workers to pay a small monthly premium and use specific providers.

The real dispute, in the words of Caterpillar's CEO, was over "the right to manage." Caterpillar claimed that the UAW, by using the old practice of pattern bargaining, was trying to control the company by demanding that it accept the terms of the Deere contract. If Caterpillar had agreed to these terms, it would have had to remain neutral if the union tried to organize the company's 3,000 nonunion employees, guarantee a specific number of union jobs, and give the union input on which jobs should be performed by outside suppliers.

The contract offered by Caterpillar, under which union members continued to work after the strike, guaranteed a two-tier wage system. It gave the company the power to put workers on a flexible schedule, which made weekend work and ten-hour days routine. The contract also offered six-year job security for current workers, but did not make any commitments to the size of the Caterpillar's work force thereafter. The UAW was in a precarious position. If forced to accept Caterpillar's offer, it would have had less bargaining power when it next faced the Big Three auto companies.

Inside Story continued on following page

Inside Story, continued

Legislation supported by President Clinton that would have forbidden companies from hiring permanent strike replacements was defeated in 1994 by Republicans in Congress. Such legislation would have strengthened UAW's position and perhaps forced Caterpillar back to the bargaining table.

Workers in Caterpillar plants employing 13,300 persons in three states went on strike again in June 1994, this time alleging unfair labor practices. This followed 14 wildcat strikes since September 1993. As of the 100th anniversary of Labor Day in September 1994, at least 8,000 Caterpillar workers were out on strike.[31]

---

31. Patricia Moore, "Labor Looks Ahead," *Chicago Sun-Times*, September 4, 1994.

Key Words and Phrases

concerted   443
economic strike   451
employer   459
independent contractor   438
irrebuttable presumption   450
neutral gate system   455
organizational strikes   453

pattern bargaining   463
per se violation   450
primary employer   455
recognitional strikes   453
recognized hazards   459
representation elections   438
runaway shop   449

secondary boycotts   437
showing of interest   438
supervisor   438
unfair labor practice strike   453
unfair labor practices   440
union authorization cards   439
union security clause   446

Questions and Case Problems

1. Electra Price, a machinist, approached her supervisor, John Davidson, and told him that it was too cold for her and others in the plant. She said that she could not work properly and that she was afraid she might hurt herself because her hands were sometimes numb. Davidson asked her whether any of the other employees felt that way, and Price said that a number of them had complained to her. Davidson asked Price whether any of the other employees had asked her to speak for them, and Price said no. Davidson said he would talk to his boss and get back to Price about what they could do. When Davidson told his boss of Price's complaint, the boss became upset at what he felt to be her impertinence and decided to fire her. In light of the above facts, would discharging Price violate the National Labor Relations Act? Would it make a difference if Price had told Davidson that others in her department had asked her to speak to him about the cold conditions?

2. After lengthy collective bargaining negotiations, the parties reached an impasse and the union called a strike. During the strike, the employer hired a permanent replacement for Sam Perkins, a long-term employee. After several weeks of the strike, the nerves of the strikers become frayed and some of them became violent. One day, Perkins battered the car of a replacement worker as he crossed the picket line to work. When the strike was over, the company told Perkins that he could not return to work, both because the company had hired a permanent replacement for him and because he had been discharged for his picket-line violence.

Can the company lawfully refuse to reinstate Perkins to his position because it had hired a permanent replacement for him? Under the National Labor Relations Act, could the company properly discharge Perkins for his picket-line misconduct? [*Local 833, International Union, United Automobile Workers of America v. NLRB*, 300 F.2d 699 (D.C. Cir. 1962), *cert. denied*, 370 U.S. 911, 82 S.Ct. 1258 (1962)]

3. For some time, the Acme Dye Company suspected that a union was attempting to organize its production and maintenance workers. The employer's suspicions were confirmed when Local 123 of the Teamsters Union filed a petition with the National Labor Relations Board asking it to hold a union representation election. Because Acme believed that its employees were unhappy with their relatively low wage levels, Acme sent out a memorandum to all employees immediately after the filing of the petition, thanking them for their hard work and announcing an immediate 5% pay increase for all employees.

Does the announcement of the pay increase, which came as a complete surprise to the employees, violate the National Labor Relations Act? Would it make any difference if the employer could demonstrate that it had planned for several weeks before the filing of the petition to grant a wage increase, and it was merely coincidence that the announcement came on the heels of the union petition? Would the answer be the same if the employer made the announcement just before the filing of the petition? [*NLRB v. Exchange Parts Co.,* 375 U.S. 405, 84 S.Ct. 457 (1964)]

4. Richard Lauren had a long history of poor performance and inappropriate behavior in the workplace. Lauren occasionally reported to work under the influence of liquor, and arrived at and left the workplace as he pleased. Although some supervisors felt that Lauren should be disciplined or discharged, higher level officials decided not to take any action because Lauren was a longtime employee and was well acquainted with the company president. The company then learned that Lauren had assisted the local Butchers' Union in trying to organize some of its employees. Shortly after that, the company discharged Lauren, citing his long history of poor performance and inappropriate conduct, for which there was overwhelming evidence.

Would Lauren's discharge, in the face of undisputed evidence of misconduct, violate the National Labor Relations Act? What would the arguments be for finding his discharge unlawful? [*Edward C. Budd Mfg. Co. v. NLRB,* 138 F.2d 86 (3d Cir. 1943), *cert. denied,* 321 U.S. 778, 64 S.Ct. 619 (1944)]

5. After a successful union organizing attempt at one of its facilities, the Hastings Rug Company decided that it would not be able to afford the substantial increases in labor costs that it believed would result from unionization. It decided to shut down that plant and go out of business altogether. This closure of its entire business resulted in the layoff of all of its employees, many of whom had voted for the union.

Would the closure of the business, with the resultant layoff of union supporters, violate the National Labor Relations Act? Would it make any difference if the company had simply shut down that facility and transferred its work to its other, nonunion, plants rather than closing the entire business? What would the result be if the company simply closed the nonunionized facility and opened an entirely new facility in a nearby town? [*Local 57, ILGWU v. NLRB,* 374 F.2d 295 (D.C. Cir. 1967), *cert. denied,* 387 U.S. 942, 87 S.Ct. 2074 (1967)]

6. The International Brotherhood of Electrical Workers petitioned the NLRB to hold an election among clerical employees of the Phoenix Tire Company. Forty-two of the 100 employees in the appropriate collective bargaining unit signed cards stating that they wished the union to represent them for collective bargaining. During the course of the election campaign, the company committed many unfair labor practices, such as interrogating employees about their union activities, threatening employees with loss of benefits if they voted for the union, and

promising them increased wages and free vacations to Hawaii if the union were voted down. In addition, the three employees who were believed to be the principal union supporters were discharged, ostensibly for legitimate business reasons, but actually because of their union activity. In the union representation election, of the 96 employees who cast ballots, only 10 voted for the union.

Following the election, the union filed objections based upon the employer's conduct. Is the NLRB likely to set aside the results of the first election and order a second one?

The union then filed charges alleging that the employer's actions were illegal. It requested the NLRB to order the company to bargain with the union even without a second election because the employer's illegal acts were so pervasive that there was no reasonable chance for a free and fair election. Should the NLRB order the employer to bargain with the union, even without a second election? Should it make any difference in the analysis if more than half of the employees in the collective bargaining unit had signed cards requesting the union to represent them? [*NLRB v. Gissel Packing Company,* 395 U.S. 575, 89 S.Ct. 1918 (1969)]

7. The Armstrong Rubber Company provides rubber to a nearby tire manufacturer, Steelbelt Tire. The Rubber Workers of America (RWA), which represents the production and maintenance workers of Steelbelt, recently struck Steelbelt after the breakdown of collective bargaining negotiations. Ordinarily Armstrong drivers deliver the rubber to Steelbelt, but they now refuse to cross the picket line established by the RWA. Steelbelt sent one of its replacement workers over to Armstrong to pick up a load of rubber. A group of strikers followed that driver and picketed Armstrong's facility while the driver from Steelbelt was on Armstrong's premises collecting the rubber. When that driver left, the picketers left as well.

Is the RWA's picketing of Armstrong unlawful under these circumstances? Would it make any difference if the pickets remained at Armstrong long after they knew that the driver from Steelbelt had left? Would it be a violation of the National Labor Relations Act for the RWA to picket Armstrong at all times, simply because Armstrong did business with the tire manufacturer? [*IBEW, Local 861 (Plauche Elec., Inc.),* 135 NLRB 250 (1962)]

 8. The production and maintenance employees of the Capston Kettle Company are represented by the United Steelworkers of America. Many of those employees are, however, dissatisfied with the passivity of the union's representation of them. They are particularly unhappy with the company's practice of scheduling overtime with little or no notice, although that scheduling does not violate the collective bargaining agreement. Despite employee dissatisfaction, the union has declined to present their concerns to management, so the dissident employees decide that they will do so themselves. They confront management, demanding changes in the system of scheduling overtime. Management tells the employees that it will not listen to them because they are represented by the union, and it is the union's job to negotiate such matters as overtime scheduling. The employees walk off the job for the rest of the day in protest, but then report to work at the start of the following day.

Is the employer entitled to refuse to discuss the overtime scheduling with the dissident group of employees? Would it make any difference if the union told those employees that it gave its consent to their discussing their concerns with management?

Is the employer entitled to discipline the dissident employees for walking off the job to protest the employer's refusal to listen to them? [*Emporium Capwell Co. v. Western Addition Community Org.*, 420 U.S. 50, 95 S.Ct. 977 (1975)]

9. In the course of collective bargaining negotiations, the union and the employer are far apart on the question of proposed wage increases. The union has demanded a wage increase of $1.00 per hour; the employer has offered three increases of 25 cents per hour over the next three years. The employer tells the union that it simply cannot afford the union's wage demands and that, if it grants them, it will no longer be competitive. The union believes that the employer can easily afford its requested wage increases. The union asks to inspect the company's financial records so that it can determine for itself whether or not the employer is in a position to afford its wage demands. The employer refuses, telling the union that those records are highly confidential and that their disclosure to competitors would be extremely damaging.

May the company lawfully refuse to disclose the requested records? Would it make any difference if the union agreed to keep the records confidential? Should it make a difference if the company refused to accede to the union's wage demands, not on the ground that it cannot afford them, but on the ground that those demands are out of line with the collective bargaining agreements that have been reached recently with its competitors? [*NLRB v. Truitt Mfg. Co.*, 351 U.S. 149, 76 S.Ct. 753 (1956)]

10. The Jonestown Metal Company manufactures metal rods for construction. The 200 or so members of the production and maintenance unit are represented by the Teamsters Union. The collective bargaining contract contains a provision that there will be no strikes or work stoppages of any kind during the term of the contract. With the employer's agreement, the union has designated four employees to act as shop stewards to represent it in day-to-day matters with the employer. On a hot summer day, the employer's air conditioning system breaks down, but the employer refuses to allow employees to go home because of the critical need to fill an order immediately. Nearly all the represented workers then walk out of the plant, without obtaining the union's approval. The shop stewards walk out, too, but neither encourage nor discourage other employees to do the same. When the workers return the next day, the employer informs them that all regular employees will be suspended for one day for their walkout. The shop stewards are discharged because they failed to take any action to halt the strike, which violated the collective bargaining agreement.

Is the employer entitled to impose more severe discipline on the union shop stewards than on the other employees? Would it make a difference if the collective bargaining contract stated that shop stewards would use their best efforts to prevent employees from engaging in strikes that violate the collective bargaining contract? [*Metropolitan Edison Co. v. NLRB*, 460 U.S. 693, 103 S.Ct. 1467 (1983)]

UNIT IV

THE REGULATORY ENVIRONMENT

Chapter 15

CRIMINAL LAW

■ Introduction

Impact on Corporate Behavior

Criminal law is a powerful tool for controlling corporate behavior and ensuring ethical conduct. In the corporate setting, significant resources are devoted to preventing and defending criminal law violations. For instance, Motorola, Inc., a Fortune 100 electronics company that specializes in such products as semiconductors and cellular telephones, has an 80-attorney in-house legal staff. Rich Weise, the general counsel, recalls that in 1984 no one on his legal staff worked full-time on criminal law issues. In 1994, Weise estimated that six attorneys at Motorola, including a former federal prosecutor, work full-time on criminal law issues. These attorneys counsel managers on how to avoid criminal liability in such areas as defense procurement contracts, antitrust law compliance, securities trading by officers and directors, and toxic substances restrictions as spelled out in the Occupational Safety and Health Act and in the environmental laws. Motorola has also assembled a multidisciplinary investigations team, comprised of attorneys, accountants, and other personnel, which is deployed if a crisis arises.

Criminal liability may be imposed in several ways. Individuals are always responsible for their criminal acts, even if working under orders from top management. Individuals may also be responsible for the acts of their subordinates. A corporation itself may also be found guilty of a criminal act, even though the corporation's employees committed the criminal act.

Chapter Summary

This chapter defines the elements necessary to create criminal liability. It discusses the statutory sources of criminal law and describes criminal procedure—the mechanics of a criminal action, the plea options, and the trial. Constitutional issues include search warrant requirements and restrictions on police interrogation. The chapter concludes with a discussion of white-collar and computer crime, the Racketeer Influenced and Corrupt Organizations Act (RICO), and other federal criminal statutes.

Definition of a Crime

A *crime* is an offense against the public at large. It may be defined as any act that violates the duties owed to the community, for which the offender must make satisfaction to the public. An act is criminal only if it is defined as criminal in a federal or state statute or in a local ordinance enacted by a city or county.

Two elements are necessary to create criminal liability: (1) an act that violates an existing criminal statute, and (2) the requisite state of mind.

The Criminal Act

The term *actus reus* (guilty act or wrongful deed) is often used to describe the act in question. A crime is not committed unless some overt act has occurred. Merely thinking about a criminal activity is not criminal.

The State of Mind

Generally a crime is not committed unless the criminal act named in the statute is performed with the requisite state of mind, known as *mens rea* (guilty mind).

The three forms of mens rea are intention to do wrong, recklessness, and negligence. A person has an *intention to do wrong* when he consciously intends to cause the harm prohibited by the statute, or when he knows such harm is substantially certain to result from his conduct. *Recklessness* in the criminal context is conscious disregard of a substantial risk that the individual's actions would result in the harm prohibited by the statute. Recklessness is found when the individual knew of the possible harm of her act, but ignored the risk. *Negligence* is the failure to see the possible negative consequences that a reasonable person would have seen. An individual may be negligent even if he did not know of the possible harm of his act. All that is necessary is that a reasonable person would have known of the possible harm. A reasonable person is often thought of as a rational person using ordinary care under the circumstances. The statute that defines the criminal act also defines the requisite state of mind.

Strict Liability

Under some statutes, a person can be guilty regardless of her state of mind. This is known as *strict liability*.

Strict liability statutes are generally disfavored. Most courts will require clear legislative intent before they will construe a statute as imposing strict liability. The Supreme Court has stated that the requirement of "a relation between some mental element and punishment for a harmful act is almost as instinctive as the child's familiar exculpatory 'But I didn't mean to.' "[1] In the following case, the Court refused to impose strict liability.

---

1. *Morissette v. United States,* 342 U.S. 246, 250-51, 72 S.Ct. 240, 243 (1952).

A Case In Point: Summary

Case 15.1
UNITED STATES v. UNITED STATES GYPSUM CO.
Supreme Court of the United States
438 U.S. 422, 98 S.Ct. 2864 (1978).

FACTS   The United States Gypsum Company was, among other gypsum board manufacturers, charged with price fixing in violation of the Sherman Act. Gypsum board is a laminated type of wall-board composed of paper, vinyl, or other specially treated coverings over a gypsum core and has in the last 30 years substantially replaced wet plaster as the primary component of interior walls and ceilings in residential and commercial construction.

Beginning in 1966, the Justice Department, as well as the Federal Trade Commission, became involved in investigations into possible antitrust vio-

Case 15.1 continued on the following page

*Case **15.1** continued*

lations in the gypsum board industry. In 1971, a grand jury was impaneled and the investigation continued for an additional 28 months. In late 1973, an indictment was filed in the Federal District Court for the Western District of Pennsylvania charging six major manufacturers and various of their corporate officials with violations of section 1 of the Sherman Act. The alleged charges included: "[A] continuing agreement, understanding and concerted action among the defendants and co-conspirators to (a) raise, fix, maintain and stabilize the prices of gypsum board; (b) fix, maintain and stabilize the terms and conditions of sale thereof; and (c) adopt and maintain uniform methods of packaging and handling such gypsum board."

It was further alleged that the defendants "telephoned or otherwise contacted one another to exchange and discuss current and future published or market prices and published or standard terms and conditions of sale and to ascertain alleged deviations therefrom." The bill of particulars provided additional details about the continuing nature of the alleged exchanges of competitive information and the role played by such exchanges in policing adherence to the various other illegal agreements charged.

ISSUE PRESENTED   May the United States Gypsum Company be found guilty of criminal price fixing under the Sherman Act if there is no showing of intent?

SUMMARY OF OPINION   The U.S. Supreme Court began by saying that the case presented several questions, including whether intent is an element of a criminal antitrust offense. The Court first focused on the Government's argument that the price-fixing case at trial was interseller price verification—the practice allegedly followed by the gypsum board manufacturers of telephoning a competing producer to determine the price currently being offered on gypsum board to a specific customer. The Government contended that these price exchanges were part of an agreement among the defendants, had the effect of stabilizing prices and policing agreed-upon price increases, and were undertaken on a frequent basis until sometime in 1973.

The Court then focused on instructions given by the trial judge who stated that intent to fix prices was essentially irrelevant if the jury found that the effect of verification was to raise, fix, maintain, or stabilize prices: "The law presumes that a person intends the necessary and natural consequences of his acts. Therefore, if the effect of the exchanges of pricing information was to raise, fix, maintain, and stabilize prices, then the parties to them are presumed, as a matter of law, to have intended that result."

The Supreme Court held that an effect on prices, without more, would not support a criminal conviction under the Sherman Act. The Court held that a defendant's state of mind or intent is an element of a criminal antitrust offense which must be established by evidence and inferences drawn therefrom and cannot be taken from the trier of fact through reliance on a legal presumption of wrongful intent from proof of an effect on prices.

In explaining its reasoning, the Court quoted a much-cited passage from *Morissette v. United States*.[2] In that case, Mr. Justice Jackson had observed:

"The contention that an injury can amount to a crime only when inflicted by intention is no provincial or transient notion. It is as universal and persistent in mature

---

2. 342 U.S. 246, 250-251, 72 S.Ct. 240, 243 (1952).

systems of law as belief in freedom of the human will and a consequent ability and duty of the normal individual to choose between good and evil. A relation between some mental element and punishment for a harmful act is almost as instinctive as the child's familiar exculpatory "But I didn't mean to," and has afforded the rational basis for a tardy and unfinished substitution of deterrence and reformation in place of retaliation and vengeance as the motivation for public prosecution.

The Court then noted that although strict-liability offenses are not unknown to the criminal law and do not invariably offend constitutional requirements, this generally inhospitable attitude to non-mens rea offenses is reinforced by an array of considerations arguing against treating antitrust violations as strict-liability crimes. The Sherman Act, unlike most traditional criminal statutes, does not precisely identify the conduct that it proscribes, and modern business patterns are so complex that market effects of proposed conduct are only imprecisely predictable. For these reasons, the Court noted that it may be difficult for today's businessperson to tell in advance whether projected actions will run afoul of the Sherman Act's criminal strictures. With this hazard in mind, the Court held that the criminal process should be used only where the law is clear and the facts reveal a flagrant offense and plain intent to restrain trade unreasonably.

RESULT The criminal conviction of the gypsum board manufacturers for violation of the Sherman Act was overturned.

■ Sources of Criminal Law

Conviction of a crime can lead to a substantial fine, a jail sentence, or even the death penalty. Because the results of a criminal conviction can be so serious, all criminal liability is specifically defined in statutes, which are binding on a court. In contrast, much of civil law was developed by the courts without applicable statutes.

A criminal charge and prosecution are brought by either the state or federal government. Under most federal and state laws, crimes are divided into two categories. A *felony* is a crime punishable by death or by imprisonment for more than one year. A *misdemeanor* is a less serious crime, punishable by a fine or a jail sentence of one year or less.

The Model Penal Code

The criminal statutes of the individual states and the federal government are similar, but not exactly the same. This is because most states have adopted the Model Penal Code but have modified it to meet their own needs. The Model Penal Code is a set of criminal-law statutes that were proposed by the National Conference of Commissioners of Uniform State Laws for adoption by the states.

■ Criminal Penalties and the Federal Sentencing Guidelines

State and federal criminal statutes normally specify penalties that include both jail time and monetary fines. The length of a jail sentence is usually within a specified range. In a state court, if the defendant is found guilty, the judge generally has sentencing discretion within that range. In a federal court, the judge has considerably less discretion and must follow the Federal Sentencing Guidelines.

Federal Sentencing Guidelines

Individuals In 1984 Congress passed the Sentencing Reform Act of 1984, which created the United States Sentencing Commission as an independent agency in the judicial branch.[3] The commission, composed of seven voting and two nonvoting members, was established as a permanent agency to monitor criminal sentencing practices in the federal courts. To that end, the

---

3. Pub. L. No. 98-473 §§ 211-239, 98 Stat. 1837, 1976, 1987-2040 (codified principally at 18 U.S.C. §§ 3551-3625, 3673, 3742, and 28 U.S.C. § 991-998).

commission established sentencing guidelines, which took effect November 1, 1987, and apply to all federal crimes committed on or after that date. The guidelines create categories of "offense behavior" and "offender characteristics." A sentencing court must select a sentence (up to the maximum authorized by statute for each federal crime) from within the guideline ranges specified by the combined categories. In unusual cases, a court may depart from the guidelines but must specify reasons for the departure.

The Sentencing Reform Act also abolished federal parole. Rather than permit a parole commission to decide how much of a sentence an offender actually serves, an offender serves the full sentence imposed by the court under the sentencing guidelines, less approximately 15% for good behavior.

In general, Congress sought in enacting the Sentencing Reform Act to create an honest, fair, and effective federal sentencing system, with reasonable uniformity in the sentences imposed for similar criminal offenses committed by similar offenders.

The average length of prison sentences imposed for offenders in federal district courts in 1991 were 156.5 months for murder, 70.8 months for rape, 25.2 months for tax law violations, 24.2 months for bribery, 22.2 months for fraud, 17.2 months for antitrust offenses, and 5.5 months for traffic offenses.[4]

Organizations   In 1991, guidelines were added to cover the sentencing of organizations, including corporations, for the violation of federal law. According to introductory comments, the guidelines for organizations reflect the following principles. First, the court should order the organization to remedy the harm created by the offense if possible. Second, if the organization operated for a criminal purpose or primarily by criminal means, the fines should divest the organization of all of its assets. Third, the range of fines for any organization not operated for a criminal purpose or primarily by criminal means should be based on the seriousness (pecuniary gain or loss) of the offense and the culpability of the organization. Organizations can minimize culpability by taking steps to prevent and detect criminal conduct. An organization's actions after an offense has been committed are also important. Lastly, probation may be an appropriate organizational sentence when necessary to ensure that other sanctions are implemented. Community service

may also be ordered as a condition of probation where community service might repair the harm caused by the offense.

At the Top

Organizations can minimize culpability under the Federal Sentencing Guidelines. For example, organizational culpability is mitigated by the presence of "an effective program to prevent and detect violations of law" by corporate agents. Cooperation with law enforcement officials and acceptance of responsibility for criminal conduct will also mitigate culpability.

■ Criminal Versus Civil Liability

Many regulatory statutes provide for both criminal and civil sanctions if they are violated. An individual or a corporation may therefore be sued under both criminal and civil law for a single act.

Civil law, and in particular tort law (discussed in chapter 7), compensates the victim for legal wrongs committed against the person or his property. Criminal law protects society by punishing the criminal. It does not compensate the victim. However, the victim of a crime may bring a civil suit for damages against the perpetrator. Violation of a criminal statute is *negligence per se;* this means that in a subsequent civil suit, the court will accept the criminal conviction as sufficient proof that the accused was negligent, that is, that the defendant did not act with the care a reasonable person would have used in the same circumstances. Consequently, defendants must carefully review their criminal defense strategy in light of possible future civil litigation.

Burden of Proof

Criminal trials differ from civil trials in imposing a much heavier *burden of proof.* Generally, the plaintiff in a civil trial need only establish the facts by a *preponderance of the evidence.* If the evidence tips the scales only slightly in favor of the plaintiff, she wins. In a criminal case, the

---

4. Source: U.S. Dept. of Justice, Bureau of Justice Statistics.

In Brief: Calculating Corporate Fines Under the Federal Sentencing Guidelines

Determining the Fine for Non-Criminal-Purpose Organizations

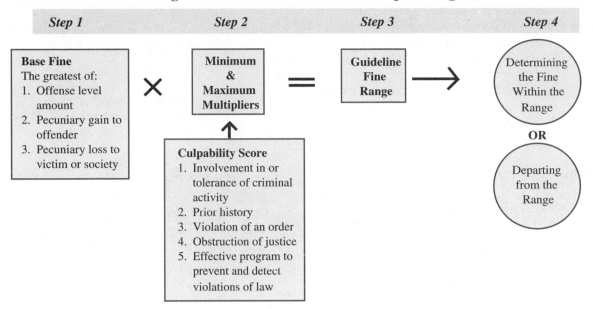

"Offense levels" in Step 1 are determined by referring to specific offenses listed in the Federal Sentencing Guidelines. Offense levels range from one to 43, depending on the severity of the crime. Offense level fines are determined by the following chart:

Offense Level	Fine	Offense Level	Fine
6 or less	$5,000	23	$1,600,000
7	7,500	24	2,100,000
8	10,000	25	2,800,000
9	15,000	26	3,700,000
10	20,000	27	4,800,000
11	30,000	28	6,300,000
12	40,000	29	8,100,000
13	60,000	30	10,500,000
14	85,000	31	13,500,000
15	125,000	32	17,500,000
16	175,000	33	22,000,000
17	250,000	34	28,500,000
18	350,000	35	36,000,000
19	500,000	36	45,500,000
20	650,000	37	57,500,000
21	910,000	38 or more	72,500,500
22	1,200,000		

Pecuniary loss may be used to determine the base fine only "to the extent the loss was caused intentionally, knowingly, or recklessly." The "culpability score" in Step 2 is based on the four aggravating and one mitigating factors listed. The minimum multiplier ranges from .05 to 2.0, and the maximum multiplier is from .20 to 4.0. Thus, the "Base Fine" is multiplied by the maximum and minimum multiplier to arrive at the "Guideline Fine Range." The court then has discretion to set the fine within that range, or in unusual cases, may depart from the range.

---

5. Jennifer Moore, "Corporate Culpability Under the Federal Sentencing Guidelines," 34 *Arizona Law Review* 743, 783 (1992).

accused is presumed innocent until proven guilty beyond a reasonable doubt.

This difference in the degree of proof required is typical of the procedural and constitutional safeguards protecting defendants' rights throughout criminal proceedings. In a criminal case the formidable resources of the state are focused on an individual. In this contest of unequal strength, it seems only fair to require the state to meet a higher standard of proof. Moreover, the deprivation of personal liberty and the lifelong stigma of criminal conviction are at stake in a criminal prosecution, whereas in a civil lawsuit only monetary damages are at stake.

■ Criminal Procedure

A criminal action begins with the arrest of the person suspected of a crime and proceeds through a preliminary hearing to plea bargaining and trial.

Arrest

After a person is arrested, he is taken to the police station and booked; that is, the charges against him are written in a register. The arresting police officer must then file a report with the prosecutor. Based on this report the prosecutor must decide whether to press charges against the arrested person. If charges are to be pressed, many states require that the accused be taken before a public judicial official, usually a justice of the peace or magistrate, to be informed of the charges against him. Bail is often determined during this initial appearance before the public official.

Plea

If the accused is only charged with a misdemeanor, she will be asked at this initial appearance whether she pleads guilty or not guilty. In the case of a felony, the next step in many states is a preliminary hearing, where the prosecutor must present evidence demonstrating probable cause that the defendant committed the felony. Following this hearing, formal charges are usually filed either by the prosecutor through an *information,* a document filed with the court, or by a grand jury through an *indictment.* The accused will then be arraigned before a trial court judge. At the arraignment she will be informed of the charges against her and asked to enter a *plea* of guilty or not guilty.

The accused can also plead *nolo contendere,* which means that he does not contest the charges. For the pur-

pose of the criminal proceedings, this plea is equivalent to a guilty plea. However, a plea of nolo contendere, unlike a guilty plea, cannot be introduced at a subsequent civil trial. Therefore, a nolo contendere plea may be used by corporate defendants who anticipate civil suits based on the same activity for which they face criminal charges.

If the defendant enters a plea of not guilty, the case is set for trial.

⤵ *Ethical Consideration*

A plea of nolo contendere is appropriate if the cost of defending a long-drawn-out criminal trial is significantly higher than any fines to which the corporation is liable. A nolo contendere plea is also appropriate to avoid the emotional costs of defending at a criminal trial. But is it ethical for a corporation to plead nolo contendere when its management knows the corporation is guilty of the wrong? Is the corporation responsible to its shareholders and employees, or to society in general? Does a corporation have an ethical duty to confess guilt even if it will result in stiffer economic penalties and civil damages?

Plea Bargaining

Very few cases ever reach trial. Most cases are resolved through plea bargaining between the accused and the prosecutor. *Plea bargaining* is the process whereby the prosecutor agrees to reduce the charges in exchange for a guilty plea from the accused.

Frequently a lower ranking member of a criminal conspiracy will "cop a plea," that is, provide the prosecutor with testimony incriminating her criminal superiors, in exchange for a reduced sentence or immunity from prosecution. The immunity granted may be either use immunity or transactional immunity. *Use immunity* prohibits the testimony of the witness from being used against her in any way. *Transactional immunity,* which is broader, prohibits any criminal prosecution of the witness that relates to any matter discussed in her testimony.

Consent decrees are common in the corporate context. A *consent decree* is a court order based on an agreement by the defendant corporation to take measures to remedy the problem that led to criminal charges. Like a plea of nolo contendere, a consent decree cannot be introduced as evidence of guilt in a subsequent civil trial, and it raises the same ethical considerations for corporations.

Trial

A criminal trial proceeds in much the same way as civil trials, which were discussed in chapter 4. There are opening statements, direct examination and cross examination of witnesses, and closing arguments. The jury then deliberates to reach a verdict of guilty or not guilty.

■ Fourth Amendment Protections

The Fourth Amendment to the United States Constitution provides:

> The right of the people to be secure in their persons, houses, papers, and effects, against unreasonable searches and seizures, shall not be violated, and no Warrants shall issue, but upon probable cause, supported by Oath or affirmation, and particularly describing the place to be searched, and the persons or things to be seized.

This provision was intended to prevent the arbitrary and intrusive searches which had characterized British rule during the colonial period. Courts have struggled, however, to strike the appropriate balance between the individual's expectation of privacy and the government's legitimate need to secure evidence of wrongdoing to prevent criminal acts and apprehend criminals. The Fourth Amendment applies only to actions by government officials, unless a private person is acting on behalf of the government. The following case illustrates how the Supreme Court has struck the balance in defining a "seizure."

■ A Case in Point: In the Language of the Court

Case 15.2
FLORIDA v. BOSTICK
Supreme Court of the
United States
501 U.S. 429, 111 S.Ct. 2382
(1991).

FACTS   As part of a routine known as "sweeping the buses," two armed police officers wearing badges boarded an interstate bus during a stop in Fort Lauderdale, Florida. The officers conceded that without any articulable suspicion, they requested consent from a passenger to search his luggage and advised him that he had the right to refuse consent. After the passenger indicated consent, and the subsequent search of his luggage revealed cocaine, he was charged in a Florida state court with trafficking in cocaine. He moved to suppress the cocaine evidence on the ground that it had been found in violation of the Fourth Amendment of the Constitution. The appeal eventually came to the Florida Supreme Court, which held that the passenger had been seized for the purposes of the Fourth Amendment because a reasonable person would not have felt free to leave in the situation to avoid questioning. The court further held that an impermissible seizure results when police board a bus during a scheduled stop and question passengers and seek their consent without any articulable suspicion.

ISSUE PRESENTED   Did the police encounter with Bostick on the bus constitute a "seizure" within the meaning of the Fourth Amendment?

OPINION   O'CONNOR, J., writing for the U.S. Supreme Court:

. . . .

. . . [T]he Fourth Amendment permits police officers to approach individuals at random in airport lobbies and other public places to ask them questions and to request consent to search their luggage, so long as a reasonable person would understand that he or she could refuse to cooperate. This case

*Case **15.2** continued on following page*

Case 15.2 continued

requires us to determine whether the same rule applies to police encounters that take place on a bus.

. . . .

. . . The [Florida] Supreme Court reasoned that Bostick had been seized because a reasonable passenger would not have felt free to leave the bus to avoid questioning by the police. . . . The Florida Supreme Court thus adopted a per se rule that the Broward County Sheriff's practice of "working the buses" is unconstitutional. . . .

. . . .

. . . [O]ur review is whether a police encounter on a bus of the type described above necessarily constitutes a "seizure" within the meaning of the Fourth Amendment. . . .
. . . The encounter will not trigger Fourth Amendment scrutiny unless it loses its consensual nature. . . . "Obviously, not all personal intercourse between policemen and citizens involves 'seizures' of persons. Only when the officer, by means of physical force or show of authority, has in some way restrained the liberty of a citizen may we conclude that a 'seizure' has occurred."

. . . .

Bostick insists that this case is different because it took place in the cramped confines of a bus. . . . Bostick maintains that a reasonable bus passenger would not have felt free to leave under the circumstances of this case because there is nowhere to go on a bus. Also, the bus was about to depart. Had Bostick disembarked, he would have risked being stranded and losing whatever baggage he had locked away in the luggage compartment.

. . . .

. . . [T]he mere fact that Bostick did not feel free to leave the bus did not mean that the police seized him. . . . Bostick's movements were 'confined' in a sense, but this was the natural result of his decision to take the bus; it says nothing about whether or not the police conduct at issue was coercive. . . .

. . . .

. . . [T]he "free to leave" analysis on which Bostick relies is inapplicable. In such a situation, the appropriate inquiry is whether a reasonable person would feel free to decline the officers' requests or otherwise terminate the encounter. . . .

. . . .

We adhere to the rule that, in order to determine whether a particular encounter constitutes a seizure, a court must consider all the circumstances surrounding the encounter to determine whether the police conduct would have communicated to a reasonable person that the person was not free to decline the officers' requests or otherwise terminate the encounter. That rule applies equally to encounters that take place on a city street or in an airport lobby, and it applies equally to encounters on a bus. . . .

The judgment of the Florida Supreme Court is reversed, and the case remanded for further proceedings not inconsistent with this opinion.

DISSENTING OPINION   MARSHALL, J.:

. . . .

. . . The majority suggests that this latest tactic in the drug war is perfectly compatible with the Constitution. I disagree. . . .

. . . I agree that the appropriate question is whether a passenger who is approached during such a sweep "would feel free to decline the officers' requests or otherwise terminate the encounter". . . . What I cannot understand is how the majority can possibly suggest an affirmative answer to this question. . . .

. . . .

. . . Two officers boarded the Greyhound bus on which respondent was a passenger while the bus . . . was on a brief stop to pick up passengers in Fort Lauderdale. The officers made a visible display of their badges and wore bright green 'raid' jackets bearing the insignia of the Broward County Sheriff's Department; one held a gun in a recognizable weapons pouch. . . . These facts alone constitute an intimidating "show of authority". . . .

. . . .

. . . Apart from trying to accommodate the officers, respondent has only two options. First, he could have remained seated while obstinately refusing to respond to the officers' questioning. But in light of the intimidating show of authority that the officers made upon boarding the bus, respondent reasonably could have believed that such behavior would only arouse the officers' suspicions and intensify their interrogation. Indeed, officers who carry out bus sweeps like the one at issue here frequently admit that this is the effect of a passenger's refusal to cooperate. . . .

Second, the respondent could have tried to escape the officers' presence by leaving the bus altogether. But because doing so would have required respondent to squeeze past the gun-wielding inquisitor who was blocking the aisle of the bus, this hardly seems like a course that respondent reasonably would have viewed as available to him. . . . We have never suggested that the police must go so far as to put a citizen in immediate apprehension of *being shot* before a court can take account of the intimidating effect of being questioned by an officer with weapon in hand.

. . . .

RESULT   The Court held that no seizure occurred. As a result, the cocaine evidence was admissible.

Questions
1. Would it have mattered if Bostick had been diagnosed with a phobia of strangers and confrontations?
2. Would a different result have been reached if Bostick had asked to leave the bus but had been refused permission by the police?

The Arrest Warrant Requirement

An *arrest* is a Fourth Amendment seizure in which police take a person into custody against his will for purposes of criminal prosecution or interrogation. No arrest is valid unless there is probable cause. *Probable cause* for arrest is defined as a reasonable belief that the suspect has committed a crime or is about to commit a crime. The Fourth Amendment does not require that a warrant be obtained prior to an arrest in a public place so long as there is probable cause. Thus an officer may make a warrantless arrest when she has reasonable grounds to believe a felony has been committed by the suspect or when a misdemeanor has been committed in her presence. In general, an arrest warrant is required only for arrests in the suspect's own home or in another person's home.

Some limited stops and detentions may be justified without a showing of probable cause (e.g., brief questioning when police observe unusual conduct that leads to a reasonable suspicion of criminal activity).

The Search Warrant Requirement

Before conducting a search, a law enforcement agent must obtain a warrant. To be valid, a warrant must be based on probable cause, supported by an oath or affirmation, and describe in specific detail (with particularity) what is to be searched or seized.

To secure a search warrant, a law enforcement agent must persuade a "neutral and detached" magistrate that a search is justified. The rights of private citizens are protected by the requirement that a magistrate, rather than a law enforcement agent, determines whether probable cause exists for a search.

The Supreme Court has indicated that probable cause is to be determined by the totality of the circumstances, balancing the privacy rights of the individual against the government's law enforcement needs. Warrantless searches that do not fall within one of six exceptions (discussed below) therefore violate the Fourth Amendment, and the evidence obtained by such a search is excluded and cannot be used against the defendant at trial. This *exclusionary rule*, and the exceptions to it, are discussed in more detail below.

Exceptions to the Search Warrant Requirement

Most police searches are not pursuant to a warrant, but fall within one of six established exceptions. The six exceptions are: (1) search incident to a lawful arrest; (2) search of an automobile if there is probable cause to believe evidence of crime will be found; (3) anything discovered by police in plain view if the officers are legitimately on the premises; (4) stop and frisk of a suspect if the officer reasonably believes the suspect is dangerous; (5) search where the owner or person who appears to have authority voluntarily and intelligently consents to the search; and (6) instances where the police are in "hot pursuit" or where the evidence may disappear before a warrant can be obtained (e.g., blood samples containing alcohol). Thus, if a person is validly arrested (pursuant to an arrest warrant or following a criminal act observed by a police officer), the officer has the authority to search the arrestee and the area immediately within the arrestee's control, to protect the safety of the officer.

The touchstone of the Supreme Court's analysis in Fourth Amendment cases has been the individual citizen's reasonable expectation of privacy in the circumstances of the case. A citizen's interest in freedom from governmental intrusions is stronger in some locations, such as his home, than in others, such as a business office into which the public is invited. The Supreme Court has permitted warrantless searches of business offices in which the government agent enters during business hours and observes whatever is visible to customers or the public from the public areas of the business establishment.

The following case addressed the issue of what constitutes a "search" and whether the plaintiff had standing to raise a Fourth Amendment claim (that is, whether the plaintiff had a reasonable expectation of privacy).

■ **A Case in Point:**   **Summary**

Case 15.3
DOW CHEMICAL CO. v. UNITED STATES
Supreme Court of the United States
476 U.S. 227, 106 S.Ct. 1819 (1986).

FACTS Dow Chemical Company operates a 2,000-acre chemical manufacturing facility with numerous covered buildings in Midland, Michigan. Dow maintained extensive security around the facility. Security measures around the perimeter bar ground-level public viewing, and Dow also investigates any low-level aircraft flights over the facility. In early 1978, Dow had consented to an inspection by the Environmental Protection Agency (EPA) of two of its power plants in the facility for violations of federal air quality standards. However, when the EPA subsequently sought to inspect the plant, Dow refused. Without obtaining a search warrant to enter the property and despite Dow's refusal to voluntarily agree to a search, the EPA employed a commercial airplane with precision aerial camera mapping equipment to photograph Dow's large manufacturing and research facilities from the air. The powerful equipment allowed power lines as small as 0.5 inches in diameter to be observed. Yet, at all times, the aircraft stayed within navigable airspace.

Dow somehow became aware of the EPA's actions and claimed that its Fourth Amendment rights had been violated. In making this contention, however, Dow conceded that a simple flyover with naked-eye observation, or the taking of a photograph from a nearby hillside overlooking such a facility, would give rise to no Fourth Amendment problem.

ISSUE PRESENTED   Do photographs taken from a commercial plane staying within navigable airspace constitute a "search" prohibited by the Fourth Amendment?

SUMMARY OF OPINION   The U.S. Supreme Court held that this was not a search governed by the Fourth Amendment because what was seen by the plane would have been observable to the public without a warrant. The mere fact that human vision was enhanced somewhat, at least to the degree here, did not give rise to constitutional problems. The Court then alluded to the kinds of intrusions that would give rise to constitutional scrutiny: "An electronic device to penetrate walls or windows so as to hear and record confidential discussions of chemical formulae or other trade secrets would raise very different and far more serious questions; other protections such as trade secret laws are available to protect commercial activities from private surveillance by competitors."

RESULT   The taking of aerial photographs of Dow's industrial plant complex from navigable airspace did not constitute a search prohibited by the Fourth Amendment. Accordingly, the aerial photographs were admissible in evidence.

COMMENTS   There can be no reasonable expectation of privacy in items held out to the public. For example, as illustrated by the case above, items that can be viewed from legal airspace are subject to warrantless searches (flyovers). Similarly, searches of open fields, an individual's handwriting and voice, and the location of her car on public streets are items held out to the public. Also, there can be no legitimate expectation of privacy in contraband. Thus, no warrant is required for a narcotics-detection dog to sniff luggage.

The Supreme Court has held that no search warrant is required for government officials to search an individual's bank deposit records. This is because an individual's expectation of privacy is lessened when the individual reveals his affairs to the bank. The individual assumes the risk that the information will be revealed to the government.

No search warrant is required for a search of the phone numbers a person has called. A search warrant is required to listen to or record conversations conducted on traditional telephones (wiretapping), but not on cordless telephones.[6] A man named Tyler was convicted of stealing $35,000 in merchandise from his employer. His conviction was in part based on intercepted telephone conversations Tyler had made from his cordless telephone. The U.S. Court of Appeals for the Eighth Circuit rejected

---

6. *Tyler v. Berodt*, 877 F.2d 705 (8th Cir. 1989), *cert. denied*, 493 U.S. 1022, 110 S.Ct. 723 (1990).

Tyler's argument that the recording, which would have required judicial approval if the conversation had taken place on a regular phone, violated his Fourth Amendment rights. The court held that Tyler had no reasonable expectation of privacy. The owner's manual stated that the cordless phone operates by broadcasting radio signals between a base unit and a mobile handset, and that communications on the unit could be overheard by other cordless units. The *Tyler* court also stated that persons using a standard telephone to speak to a cordless telephone user are generally thought to be protected, because such a person has no reason to know her words are being broadcast from the cordless phone user's base unit to a handset.

Cellular phones have been treated by courts as similar to cordless phones in that the person initiating the cellular conversation has no justifiable expectation of privacy.[7]

No search warrant or probable cause is required for border searches (including customs agents at an international airport) in order to enforce national boundaries.

Administrative Searches

Where the purpose of government action is regulatory and not prosecutorial, a search warrant may not be required for entry onto private property, usually a business. The probable cause standard is relaxed and is satisfied by the showing of a general and neutral enforcement plan. Thus a government agency (for example, the Occupational Safety and Health Administration) may conduct administrative searches if it demonstrates that its inspections can only be effective if they are a complete surprise and the agency statute prescribes some schedule of inspections. Likewise, no warrant is required to search airline passengers before boarding, to seize contaminated food, or for school officials to conduct searches in the school (school officials need only a reasonable suspicion). A warrant is also not required when the government performs or requires drug testing of employees.

> 66
> *Where the purpose of government action is regulatory and not prosecutorial, a search warrant may not be required for entry onto private property, usually a business.*

The Exclusionary Rule

The exclusionary rule is virtually unique to the U.S. legal system. It prohibits, in many circumstances, the introduction in a criminal trial of evidence offered as proof of guilt that is obtained by an illegal search or seizure in violation of the Fourth Amendment. Illegal evidence includes evidence found when the search went beyond the scope of the warrant, evidence gathered without a warrant when a warrant was required, and evidence acquired directly or indirectly as a result of an illegal search or arrest (called *fruit of the poisonous tree*).

The exclusionary rule is often criticized in the media as simply a device to set guilty criminals free on a technicality. Supporters of the rule argue that the exclusionary rule is necessary to protect personal freedom.

Exceptions to the Exclusionary Rule

With the shift in the composition of the Supreme Court during the 1980s, a number of decisions have restricted the use of the exclusionary rule. For example, a 1984 case[8] addressed the question of whether a court should exclude evidence obtained in violation of the defendant's constitutional rights if the evidence would inevitably have been discovered through legal means. The "inevitable discovery" exception to the exclusionary rule was created, and the Court held that illegally obtained evidence could lawfully be introduced at trial if it could be shown that the evidence would have inevitably been found by other legal means. The defendant was accused of the abduction and brutal murder of a 10-year-old girl on Christmas Eve. The defendant was arrested and he requested counsel. However, before counsel was provided, the police coerced him into showing them where he had buried the girl's body. The police's behavior of "questioning" the defendant before adequate counsel was provided violated the accused's Sixth Amendment right to counsel. Prior to this case, the fact that the body had been found in violation of the accused's rights would have prevented the introduction at trial of any evidence discovered at the location of the body. However, in this particular case, hundreds of volunteers were systematically searching the area where the body was buried and it was concluded that the police would have found the body even if the defendant had not led them to it.

But in a later case,[9] the "inevitable discovery" rule was shown to be limited in its application. Bleichford

---

7. *See, e.g., Edwards v. State Farm Ins. Co.*, 833 F.2d 535 (5th Cir. 1987).

8. *Nix v. Williams*, 467 U.S. 431, 104 S.Ct. 2501 (1984).
9. *United States v. $639,558 in United States Currency*, 955 F.2d 712 (D.C. Cir. 1992).

was a passenger on an Amtrak train traveling from Florida to New York. An Amtrak officer began to suspect him of drug dealings because, among other things, he purchased his ticket with cash moments before departure and then proceeded to change rooms on the train several times.

The train stopped in Washington for a twenty-minute layover and a dog trained to sniff out drugs did a "sweep" around Bleichford's compartment; the dog exhibited some indication of the presence of drugs, but did not aggressively alert the officers to their presence. After the dog left, an Amtrak officer knocked on Bleichford's door and asked for identification. Bleichford subsequently refused to have his bags searched. However, he finally agreed to allow a dog to sniff them. Upon close contact with the bags, the dog gave a positive indication that there were drugs present. When Bleichford again refused to consent to a search of his bags, he was arrested, handcuffed, and removed from the train.

Although the officers had intended to get a search warrant, they were improperly advised by the Assistant U.S. Attorney that they did not need one, so they searched the luggage without it. Upon searching the luggage, no drugs were found, only $635,000 in cash and keys to safety deposit boxes. The prosecution argued that the cash was admissible under the inevitable discovery doctrine because the bags would have inevitably been opened when they were later inventoried. The court found that the inevitable discovery doctrine did not apply.

Although Bleichford was under arrest, absent discovery of more evidence, his luggage would not have been taken to the police station to be inventoried and the cash would never have been discovered.

The Supreme Court has allowed other exceptions to the exclusionary rule. For example, the "good faith" exception allows the prosecution to use evidence seized by police officers who reasonably believed they were acting under a lawful search warrant, even if the search warrant later proves unlawful.

■ Fifth Amendment Protections

The Fifth Amendment prohibits forced self-incrimination, double jeopardy, and criminal conviction without due process of law.

Self-Incrimination

The Fifth Amendment provides that no person "shall be compelled in any criminal case to be a witness against himself." The Supreme Court has held that the protection against self-incrimination includes the preliminary stages in the criminal process as well as the trial itself.

The Supreme Court broke new constitutional ground in the following case concerning confessions given to the police. It is considered a watershed case because it established a new constitutional principle.

■ A Case in Point: In the Language of the Court

Case 15.4
MIRANDA v. ARIZONA
Supreme Court of the
United States
384 U.S. 436, 86 S.Ct. 1602
(1966).

FACTS   The Miranda decision consisted of four separate cases involving suspects' confessions to the police. In each case, the defendant was questioned by police officers, detectives, or a prosecuting attorney in a room in which he was isolated from the outside world. In none of these cases was the defendant given a full and effective warning of his rights at the outset of the interrogation process.

One of the four cases involved Ernesto Miranda, an indigent Mexican defendant; another involved an indigent Los Angeles African American who had dropped out of school in the sixth grade. Miranda was arrested and brought to the police station and interrogated by two officers. The officers admitted at trial that Miranda was not advised that he had a right to have an attorney present. Two hours later, the officers emerged from the interrogation room with a written confession signed by Miranda. At the top of the statement was a typed paragraph stating that the confession was made voluntarily, without threats or promises of immunity and "with full knowledge of my legal rights, understanding any statement I make may be used against

*Case **15.4** continued on following page*

*Case **15.4** continued*

me." Although there was no physical abuse, there was the appearance of mental abuse by the police.

ISSUE PRESENTED   Are statements obtained from a defendant during incommunicado interrogation in a police-dominated atmosphere, without full warning of constitutional rights, admissible?

OPINION   WARREN, C.J., writing for the U.S. Supreme Court:

. . . .

The cases before us raise questions which go to the roots of our concepts of American criminal jurisprudence: the restraints society must observe consistent with the Federal Constitution in prosecuting individuals for crime. More specifically, we deal with the admissibility of statements obtained from an individual who is subjected to custodial police interrogation and the necessity for procedures which accrue that the individual is accorded his privilege under the Fifth Amendment to the Constitution not to be compelled to incriminate himself.

. . . .

Our holding will be spelled out with some specificity in the pages which follow but briefly stated it is this: the prosecution may not use statements, whether exculpatory or inculpatory, stemming from custodial interrogation of the defendant unless it demonstrates the use of procedural safeguards effective to secure the privilege against self-incrimination. By custodial interrogation, we mean questioning initiated by law enforcement officers after a person has been taken into custody or otherwise deprived of his freedom of action in any significant way. As for the procedural safeguards to be employed, unless other fully effective means are devised to inform accused persons of their right of silence and to assure a continuous opportunity to exercise it, the following measures are required. Prior to any questioning, the person must be warned that he has a right to remain silent, that any statement he does make may be used as evidence against him, and that he has a right to the presence of an attorney, either retained or appointed [by the court if defendant cannot afford to retain one himself]. The defendant may waive effectuation of these rights, provided the waiver is made voluntarily, knowingly and intelligently. If, however, he indicates in any manner and at any stage of the process that he wishes to consult with an attorney before speaking there can be no questioning. Likewise, if the individual is alone and indicates in any manner that he does not wish to be interrogated, the police may not question him. The mere fact that he may have answered some questions or volunteered some statements on his own does not deprive him of the right to refrain from answering any further inquiries until he has consulted with an attorney and thereafter consents to be questioned.

. . . .

Again we stress that the modern practice of in-custody interrogation is psychologically rather than physically oriented. . . .

. . . .

The officers are told by the manuals that the "principal psychological factor contributing to a successful interrogation is privacy—being alone with the person under interrogation." . . . To highlight the isolation and unfamiliar surroundings, the manuals instruct the police to display an air of confidence in the suspect's guilt and from outward appearance to maintain only an interest in confirming certain details. . . .

. . . .

When the techniques described above prove unavailing, the texts recommend they be alternated with a show of some hostility. . . .

. . . .

. . . It is obvious that such an interrogation environment is created for no purpose other than to subjugate the individual to the will of his examiner. This atmosphere carries its own badge of intimidation. To be sure, this is not physical intimidation, but it is equally destructive of human dignity. . . .

. . . .

. . . As a practical matter, the compulsion to speak in the isolated setting of the police station may well be greater than in courts or other official investigations, where there are often impartial observers to guard against intimidation or trickery. . . .

. . . .

The warning of the right to remain silent must be accompanied by the explanation that anything said can and will be used against the individual in court. This warning is needed in order to make him aware not only of the privilege, but also of the consequences of forgoing it. It is only through an awareness of these consequences that there can be any assurance of real understanding and intelligent exercise of the privilege. . . .

. . . .

DISSENTING OPINION HARLAN, J.:

. . . .

. . . The new rules are not designed to guard against police brutality or other unmistakably banned forms of coercion. Those who use third-degree tactics and deny them in court are equally able and destined to lie as skillfully about warnings and waivers. Rather, the thrust of the new rules is to negate all pressures, to reinforce the nervous or ignorant suspect, and ultimately to discourage any confession at all.

. . . .

. . . The Court's opinion in my view reveals no adequate basis for extending the Fifth Amendment's privilege against self-incrimination to the police station. Far more important, it fails to show that the Court's new rules are well supported, let alone compelled, by Fifth Amendment precedents. Instead, the new rules actually derive from quotation and analogy drawn from precedents under the Sixth Amendment, which should properly have no bearing on police interrogation. . .

*Case **15.4** continued on following page*

*Case **15.4** continued*

. . . The Court's new rules aim to offset these minor pressures and disadvantages intrinsic to any kind of police interrogation. The rules do not serve due process interests in preventing blatant coercion since, as I noted earlier, they do nothing to contain the policeman who is prepared to lie from the start. . . .

DISSENTING OPINION   WHITE, J.:

. . . .

In some unknown number of cases the Court's rule will return a killer, a rapist or other criminal to the streets and to the environment which produced him, to repeat his crime whenever it pleases him. As a consequence, there will not be a gain, but a loss, in human dignity. The real concern is not the unfortunate consequences of this new decision on the criminal law as an abstract, disembodied series of authoritative proscriptions, but the impact on those who rely on the public authority for protection and who without it can only engage in violent self-help with guns, knives and the help of their neighbors similarly inclined. . . .

. . . .

RESULT   The statements obtained from the defendants during incommunicado interrogation in police-dominated atmosphere, without full warning of constitutional rights, were inadmissible as having been obtained in violation of Fifth Amendment privilege against self-incrimination.

COMMENTS   These warnings, often repeated in television police shows, are known as the *Miranda* warnings.

Questions
1. Would a "police-dominated" atmosphere be found if four Spanish-speaking defendants, who could talk among themselves, were questioned by a non-Spanish-speaking policeman?
2. Would the results have been different if the defendant had been told of his constitutional rights in an intimidating manner?

The Fifth Amendment privilege against self-incrimination applies only to compelled testimonial evidence. The Supreme Court has determined that forcing defendants to provide real evidence such as fingerprints, body fluids (urine and blood), or voice or handwriting samples does not violate the Fifth Amendment prohibition against self-incrimination. Requiring appearance in a lineup also does not violate the privilege.

The Fifth Amendment protection for business records and papers is very limited. The contents of subpoenaed documents are almost never protected by the Fifth Amendment. The act of producing the documents, however, may constitute self-incrimination when the government cannot authenticate the documents without the testimony of the possessor. In the case of corporate documents, whoever has custody of them must generally produce them during a criminal inquiry, even if to do so would incriminate her; producing the records is not considered a personal act, but rather an act of the corporation, which possesses no Fifth Amendment privilege.[10] Nonetheless, the custodian will not be compelled to testify as to the contents of the documents if that testimony would incriminate her personally. Because of the personal nature of the privilege, it cannot be asserted by a corporation,

---

10. *Braswell v. United States*, 487 U.S. 99, 108 S.Ct. 2284 (1988).

partnership, or other collective entity. However, business records compiled by a sole proprietor—that is, an individual doing business for herself—are probably protected, even though they would not be if the business were a partnership.

Because the Fifth Amendment only bars the use of compelled self-incriminating testimony, records that government regulations require a business to keep are not protected by the Fifth Amendment and can be used against the reporting individual in a criminal prosecution.[11]

Ethical Consideration

The possibility that a company might have to produce incriminating documents in a criminal investigation provides added impetus for systematically destroying documents pursuant to a document retention policy (which can also protect the company from having to produce damaging documents in civil cases, as discussed in chapter 3). Is it ethical for a company to destroy specific documents because it knows them to be incriminating?

Double Jeopardy

The Double Jeopardy Clause of the Fifth Amendment protects criminal defendants from multiple prosecutions for the same offense. If the defendant is found not guilty, the defendant is cleared of all charges, and the prosecutor may not appeal the verdict. If the defendant is found guilty, however, the defendant can appeal. Double jeopardy does not bar a second prosecution if there was a hung jury in the first proceeding.

There are important limitations on the double jeopardy protection. A single criminal act may result in several statutory violations for which the defendant may be prosecuted even if each prosecution is based on the same set of facts. Additionally, the double jeopardy clause does not protect against prosecutions by different governments (such as state and federal) based on the same underlying facts. Thus two police officers who beat Rodney King in

1991, resulting in rioting in Los Angeles after they were acquitted of state criminal charges in April 1992, could still be tried and convicted in April 1993 of federal charges of violating his civil rights.

Due Process and Voluntary Confessions

When the conduct of law enforcement officials in obtaining a confession is outrageous or shocking, the Due Process Clauses of the Fifth and Fourteenth Amendments bar the government from using the involuntary confession, even if the *Miranda* warnings were given. For example, physical coercion or brutality invalidates a confession. However, the courts have usually held that misleading or false verbal statements that induce the suspect to confess are not grounds for invalidating the confession, unless the statements rise to the level of unduly coercive threats.

A confession elicited through the use of false scientific documents was found invalid in *Florida v. Cayward*.[12] The police in that case intentionally fabricated laboratory reports linking the defendant to the crime and exhibited the reports to the defendant during an interrogation, hoping to induce a confession. The false reports were presented as genuine, and the defendant confessed during the interrogation. A Florida appeals court found that the police tactics violated the defendant's constitutional right to due process of law.

Before a confession of guilt will be admitted into evidence, the trial judge must determine that the confession was voluntarily made, as required by the Due Process Clauses. The Supreme Court has held, however, that the erroneous admission at trial of a coerced confession may not require that the conviction be overturned.[13]

■ Sixth Amendment Protections

The Sixth Amendment grants the criminal defendant a number of procedural protections.

Assistance of Counsel

The defendant in most criminal prosecutions has the right "to have the Assistance of Counsel." This means, first, that the accused has the right to his own attorney. If he cannot afford an attorney, he will be entitled to a court-

---

11. *Shapiro v. United States*, 335 U.S. 1, 68 S.Ct. 1375 (1948).

12. 552 So.2d 971 (Fla. Dist. Ct. App. 1989).
13. *Arizona v. Fulminante*, 499 U.S. 279, 111 S.Ct. 1246 (1991) (harmless error test applies to determine whether conviction must be overturned).

appointed attorney. Second, once an accused is taken into custody, he must be informed of his right to counsel as part of his *Miranda* warnings. Third, the assistance of counsel must be effective, that is, within the range of competence required of attorneys in criminal cases. In practice, counsel is presumed effective and only in outrageous cases is counsel considered ineffective. Fourth, an attorney must be appointed for an appeal of a verdict. The right to a court-appointed attorney for a second appeal, however, has not been granted.

Jury Trial

Most defendants in criminal cases have the right to a jury trial. Jury trials are not required in cases in which authorized punishment for the charged offense is six months or less and also is not required in juvenile proceedings. State court juries consist of 6 to 12 individuals, with a minimum of 6 jurors. Federal courts have 12 jurors. To render a verdict, a federal court jury must be unanimous in its decision. The Supreme Court has ruled that juries of six in state courts must also be unanimous in order to reach a verdict, but it has not ruled on juries of seven or more.

Other Procedural Rights

The Sixth Amendment also guarantees the right to a speedy trial and the right to confront and cross-examine witnesses.

■ Nonconstitutional Protections

In a criminal prosecution, the prosecutor is obligated to show the defendant all evidence that the defendant specifically requests. In addition, certain items must be turned over regardless of whether the defendant requests them. The accused may also have to reveal certain information to the prosecutor, such as prior statements made by witnesses who have testified in a sworn statement.

More requirements to reveal evidence are imposed on the prosecutor than on the defendant. The rationale for this protection is the need to neutralize the natural advantage of the state against the individual defendant.

Attorney-Client Privilege

When criminal charges are brought against a corporate employee, one might ask to whom the attorney-client privilege is applied. It may be unclear whether the client is the employee charged with the offense, the corporation that is paying the lawyer, or both. In general, a client must establish a relationship with the attorney for the attorney-client privilege to apply. Thus if the employee is the client, the employee should obtain an engagement letter from the attorney that expressly states that the employee is the client even if the employer is paying the attorney's fees. (The attorney-client privilege is discussed in chapter 4.)

■ Liability for Criminal Actions

Liability may be imposed on the person who committed the crime, on that person's supervisors as individuals, and on the corporation that employs the person.

Individual Liability

Individuals may commit a criminal act either against a corporation for their own gain, or on behalf of the corporation.

If an officer, director, or employee commits a crime against the corporation, such as theft, embezzlement, or forgery, that person will be prosecuted as an individual. As discussed below, that person's supervisor may also be held responsible.

Officers, directors, or employees who commit crimes while acting in their corporate capacities will also be prosecuted as individuals. Even if the employee was acting in the best interest of the corporation, she is still individually liable for her criminal acts.

> **❝**
> *Even if the employee was acting in the best interest of the corporation, she is still individually liable for her criminal acts.*

Vicarious Liability

Vicarious liability (also called imputed liability) is the imposition of liability on one party for the wrongs of another. As discussed below, under vicarious liability a corporation may be found guilty of a crime committed by an employee of the corporation. Officers, directors, and managers may also be found guilty of a crime committed by employees under their supervision. For a supervisor to be found vicariously liable for the acts of a subordinate, most criminal statutes require proof of some form of wrongful conduct by the supervisor, such as failure to supervise properly.

Sometimes a regulatory statute will combine the elements of both vicarious and strict liability. For example

Ethical Consideration

If a supervisor asks an employee to commit an act that the employee suspects is criminal, the employee should bear two things in mind. First, if there is a criminal prosecution, it is not a valid defense for the employee to state that she was just following the orders of upper-level officers or directors of the corporation. Second, as discussed in chapter 12, an employee cannot be terminated for refusing to commit a criminal act.

the Federal Food, Drug and Cosmetic Act makes it a criminal offense to mislabel or adulterate food, drugs, or cosmetics that are part of interstate commerce. A chief executive officer was held vicariously and strictly liable under this act in *United States v. Park*.[14]

John Park was the chief executive of Acme Markets, Inc., a national retail food chain headquartered in Philadelphia, Pennsylvania. Acme employed 36,000 people and had 874 retail outlets and 16 warehouses. In 1970, the Food and Drug Administration (FDA) informed Park of violations by his company of the Federal Food, Drug and Cosmetic Act, including the presence of rats in the company's Philadelphia warehouse, in which food was stored.

Park was told by members of the company that the appropriate vice president was looking into the matter and was taking corrective action. Park did not investigate the matter further. In 1971, the FDA found that similar conditions existed in the firm's Baltimore warehouse. A letter to Park, dated January 27, 1972, included the following:

We note with much concern that the old and new warehouse areas used for food storage were actively and extensively inhabited by live rodents. . . . We trust this letter will serve to direct your attention to the seriousness of the problem and formally advise you of the urgent need to initiate whatever measures are necessary to prevent recurrence and ensure compliance with the law.

A second inspection was done in March 1972 and on that occasion the inspectors found that there had been improvement in the sanitary conditions, but that there continued to be evidence of rodent activity in the warehouse.

Acme and Park were charged with five counts of violating the Federal Food, Drug and Cosmetic Act by storing food shipped in interstate commerce in a warehouse where it was exposed to rodent contamination. Acme, but not Park, pled guilty to the charges. At trial, Park was convicted on all five counts. He was found guilty under a theory of vicarious liability for the acts or omissions of other corporate employees. Under the statute's strict-liability standard, no proof was required of criminal intent by any member of the corporation.

Impossibility Defense to Strict Liability   The question remains whether Park would be strictly liable if he had done everything possible but was still unable to comply with the FDA standards. In that case, Park may have had available the defense of impossibility.

To establish the impossibility defense, the corporate officer must introduce evidence that he "exercised extraordinary care and still could not prevent violations of the Act. The defense is raised when the defendant introduces a sufficient quantum of evidence as to his exercise of 'extraordinary care' so as to justify placing an additional burden on the government—that of proving beyond a reasonable doubt that the defendant by the use of extraordinary care, was not without the power or capacity to correct or prevent violations of the Act."[15]

Corporate Liability

A corporation can be held liable for criminal offenses committed by its employees if the acts were committed within the scope of their employment and for the benefit of the corporation. This form of vicarious liability is known as *respondeat superior*, which means "let the superior give answer." (The doctrine of *respondeat superior* in civil cases is discussed in chapters 5 and 7.)

There is no current consensus on whether a corporation should be responsible for the actions of all of its employees, or only those of senior corporate officials such as officers and directors or persons linked to the senior officials by authorization.

Federal Courts   The federal courts have held that a corporation is liable for the actions of any of its employees. Thus the actions of middle managers and more sub-

---

14. 421 U.S. 658, 95 S.Ct. 1903 (1975).

15. *United States v. New England Grocers Supply Co.*, 488 F. Supp. 230, 236 (D. Mass. 1980).

ordinate employees in the scope of their employment, as well as those of corporate officials, are attributed to the corporation.

State Courts   Some state courts impose corporate liability even if no manager is involved in the criminal action. In one case, the driver of a school bus owned by a corporation ran over and killed a six-year-old who was crossing in front of the bus. The bus driver, who had just let the child off the bus, could not see the child because mirrors that were required by state statute were missing. The court held that the corporation was criminally liable for homicide by vehicle.[16]

Other state courts, such as the Minnesota Supreme Court, have held that a corporation is not liable merely because an employee committed a crime in furtherance of the corporate business, unless the crime could be attributed to corporate policy or higher management.[17] All state courts impose liability for acts of a high managerial agent.

For example, in a 1985 case[18] the president of defendant Penn Valley Resorts, Edwin Clancy, agreed to provide dinner and an open bar for 60 undergraduate students from the State University of New York at Alfred, New York. Despite the fact that most of the students were not of legal drinking age, many of them were served alcohol.

A 20-year-old minor, William Edward Frazer, Jr., became noticeably intoxicated such that he was staggering, slurred his speech, and had quickly altering moods. Despite protests from his friends, Frazer attempted to drive himself back to the University. In the course of the 45-minute trip back, he caused an automobile accident in which he was killed. Frazer had driven his car into the opposite lane and struck a bridge abutment, causing his vehicle to overturn and become airborne for 75 feet. At the time of death his blood alcohol content was .23; a level of .10 is normally considered sufficient to make a person intoxicated.

The Pennsylvania court held that a corporation can be found liable for a criminal action even if the corporation's board of directors did not condone the action. Furthermore, if the illegal conduct is performed or tolerated by a high managerial agent acting on behalf of the corporation within the scope of his office or employment, the corporation can be held criminally, as well as civilly,

liable. The appellate court found that the defendant corporation was properly convicted of criminal involuntary manslaughter, reckless endangerment, and furnishing liquor to minors and visibly intoxicated persons: "[T]he serving of intoxicating beverages to a minor or visibly intoxicated person alone does not constitute involuntary manslaughter or reckless endangerment. Here, it was the serving of alcohol, coupled with several crucial elements known to Clancy, which established causation, and therefore the offenses."

International Consideration

Many European nations do not recognize corporate criminal liability, because: (1) the corporation does not possess a guilty mind; (2) the corporation is not viewed as the real offender in a crime that is committed; and (3) the corporation is not considered well suited for either punishment or rehabilitation. For example, the German constitution prohibits imposition of criminal liability on corporations. These countries focus instead on identifying and punishing the individuals responsible for the criminal acts.

■ White-Collar Crime

White-collar crime is violation of the law by a corporation or one of its managers. White-collar employees—that is, managers or professionals—may be either the victims or the perpetrators of crime. Most white-collar crime is nonviolent, either committed against a business or the government or committed by a business against a large group of individuals.

Many white-collar criminal statutes do not have a mens rea requirement. It is therefore possible to commit crime in the corporate setting without having the intention of committing the crime.

White-collar criminals are often treated less harshly than perpetrators of violent crimes. Juries and judges are often more sympathetic to white-collar criminals than to other criminals. However, white-collar criminals do receive jail sentences and large fines, especially for violations of environmental statutes and in cases involving what is perceived as extreme greed.

16. *Commonwealth of Pennsylvania v. McIlwain School Bus Lines,* 283 Pa.Super. 1, 423 A.2d 413 (1980).
17. *State v. Christy Pontiac-GMC, Inc.,* 354 N.W.2d 17 (Minn. 1984).
18. *Commonwealth of Pennsylvania v. Penn Valley Resorts, Inc.,* 343 Pa.Super. 387, 494 A.2d 1139 (1985).

There is no exact definition of white-collar crime, but it is generally agreed that the cost of white-collar crime is more than $100 billion a year.

Crime Against the Corporation

Examples of crimes committed by an employee against his employer include theft, embezzlement, fraud, and acceptance of a bribe.

Theft, technically known as *larceny,* is simply the taking of property without the owner's consent. White-collar theft ranges from taking home pens and pencils from the office to stealing money through the company's computer system.

Embezzlement is the taking of money or property that is lawfully in the employee's possession by reason of her employment. For example, a company's treasurer who takes money that belongs to the company by writing checks to dummy accounts is guilty of embezzlement.

Fraud is any deception intended to induce someone to part with property or money. Fraud may involve a false representation of fact, whether by words or by conduct, or concealment of something that should have been disclosed. An example of fraud is the padding of an expense account.

Acceptance of a bribe may also be a crime against the employer. For example, a sales representative cannot legally accept a kickback from a purchaser of his employer's products. Similarly, a purchasing agent for a corporation must not accept a bribe from an outside salesperson.

Ethical Consideration

It is not always clear where the line is drawn between accepting gifts and taking bribes. For instance, if a data processing manager is going to make the decision on the purchase of a mainframe computer, it is unethical and illegal for her to accept a percentage of the sales price of the computer from the seller. Some data processing managers accept expensive meals, sports tickets, and other "perks" from computer salespersons. Is acceptance of such gifts ethical?

Crime by the Corporation

Examples of crimes perpetrated by corporations and their employees include consumer fraud, securities fraud, tax evasion, and environmental pollution.

Corporations can also commit crimes against other corporations. Examples include price fixing (discussed in chapter 18) and misappropriation of trade secrets or violations of copyright or patent laws (discussed in chapter 11).

■ Computer Crime

White-collar crime increasingly involves computers. However, most computer-related crimes are likely to go undetected, because computer offenses generally involve little or no visible physical activity. The computer may be used not only to commit the offense, but also to hide or destroy the evidence. Because most computer crime is perpetrated by insiders, the individuals who are in the best position to discover the crime are often the ones who committed it.

Even if computer crime is detected, it often goes unreported and unpenalized. Most businesses, especially financial institutions, do not want it publicly known that an employee or an outsider used the company's computer system to steal from the company. In some cases the affected company, instead of prosecuting the computer criminal, has hired him as a computer security consultant.

66

In some cases the affected company, instead of prosecuting the computer criminal, has hired him as a computer security consultant.

Even when computer crimes are reported, they are not always prosecuted. Many prosecutors are overworked and understaffed, and they give low priority to nonviolent crimes.

Computer Fraud

Computer fraud is the use of a computer to steal company or government funds. This type of theft generally involves improper or unauthorized access to the computer system and the creation of false data or computer instructions. The automated computer system then generates fraudulent transfers of funds or bogus checks that are cashed by the wrongdoer.

More than 40 different sections of the federal criminal code may apply to thefts by computer, ranging from embezzlement from an Indian tribal organization to wire fraud. The Computer Fraud and Abuse Act broadly addresses the general problem of theft by computer. Most computer-aided thefts can also be prosecuted under traditional state larceny laws.

The Computer Fraud and Abuse Act The Computer Fraud and Abuse Act[19] provides that anyone who accesses a "federal interest computer" without authorization, and alters, damages, or destroys information or prevents authorized use of the computer and causes loss of more than $1,000 is subject to up to five years imprisonment and a fine up to $250,000 or up to twice the amount of the gross gain or loss for the offense. A *federal interest computer* is a computer used by the federal government or by various types of financial institutions, or one of two or more computers used in committing the offense, not all of which are located in the same state.

Since enactment of the Computer Fraud and Abuse Act in 1986, several bills have been introduced to stiffen the penalty provisions. One bill proposed extending the maximum time for imprisonment from five years to twenty years.

In addition, the law does not provide for civil remedies or restitution. Permitting such remedies could result in increased reporting of computer fraud and possibly prevent future crime.

Computer Piracy

Computer piracy is the theft or misuse of computer software. (With the increasing value and decreasing size of computer equipment, the theft of computer hardware is increasing. However, this is larceny, not computer piracy.)

Concerned with the increasing amount of computer software theft, Congress amended the Copyright Act in 1980 to cover computer software. (Copyright law is discussed in chapter 11.) Violations of the Copyright Act normally result in civil sanctions. The act does, however, provide that any person who infringes a copyright willfully and for purpose of commercial advantage or private financial gain may be punished by a maximum of one year's imprisonment, a $25,000 fine, or both.

Most states have made the theft of computer software a crime. For example, New York enacted a computer crime statute in 1986. New York Penal Law sections 156.30 and 156.35 now define six crimes related to computer misuse. Specific protection is given to computer software. The act makes it a felony to duplicate a computer program without authorization either if the software has a value in excess of $2,500 or if the duplication is done in connection with another felony. The legislation also prohibits the possession of unlawfully duplicated materials.

Computer Viruses

A computer virus is a computer program that can replicate itself into other programs without any subsequent instruction, human or mechanical. A computer virus may destroy data, programs, or files, or it may prevent user access to a computer. A computer virus does not have to be destructive. It may be benign and temporary. The virus may act immediately or when a trigger condition is met, such as a certain date of the year.

The proliferation of personal computers has created millions of entry points for viruses. A virus can be concealed in any software and then passed on to other computers through time-sharing services, information services, floppy disks, or other means. The increased linking of computers through networking also increases the vulnerability to a virus.

Although computer viruses were first publicized in 1983, it was in 1988 that government, businesses, and the public generally began to grasp the threat posed by viruses. In a widely publicized incident in 1988, a Cornell graduate student released a virus into the nationwide Internet computer network. In 1990 he became the first person convicted under the Computer Fraud and Abuse Act and faced penalties of up to five years in prison and a $250,000 fine.[20] He was sentenced in May 1990 to three years probation, a $10,000 fine, payment of probation costs, and 400 hours of community service. Experts generally agree that the virus, which clogged computer memory and communications lines, effectively shut down about 6,000 computer systems of various sizes. The program caused no actual damage to any files, although with minor modifications it apparently could have been transformed into a malignant virus which would have destroyed large amounts of data. However, the virus cost many thousands of employee hours to locate and undo. According to the National Center for Computer Crime Data in Los Angeles, estimates of the total cost range from $100,000 to $96 million.

19. 18 U.S.C. § 1030 (1988 & Supp. 1992).

20. *United States v. Morris*, 928 F.2d 504 (2d Cir. 1991), *cert. denied*, _112 S.Ct. 72 (1991).

■ Racketeer Influenced and Corrupt Organizations Act

The Racketeer Influenced and Corrupt Organizations Act (RICO)[21] was originally designed to combat organized crime and provide a mechanism of enforcement against syndicate bosses and masterminds who might otherwise escape liability. Recently, however, the criminal provisions of RICO have been used against classic white-collar crimes.

The RICO statute prohibits: (1) the investment in any enterprise of income derived from racketeering; (2) the acquisition of an interest in an enterprise through a pattern of racketeering activity; (3) participation in an enterprise through a pattern of racketeering activity; and (4) conspiring to engage in any of these activities.

---

21. 18 U.S.C. §§ 1961 *et seq.* (1988 & Supp. 1992).

RICO Requirements

RICO section 1961(4) broadly defines an *enterprise* as "any individual, partnership, corporation, association, or other legal entity, and any union or group of individuals associated in fact although not a legal entity." Racketeering activity is defined to include various state and federal offenses, specifically including mail and wire fraud and fraud in the sale of securities. Consequently, almost any business fraud can serve as the basis for a criminal RICO violation.

In order to demonstrate a pattern of racketeering activity, a plaintiff must show that at least two related acts have occurred within a ten-year period. Two isolated acts are not considered sufficient.

Use of RICO

Use of the RICO statute is particularly effective against groups of traders, brokers, and others who have developed a continuous relationship of passing and trading on

---

Historical Perspective
Adoption of RICO

The presidential campaign of 1968 between Hubert Humphrey and Richard Nixon, while not a particularly close race, was hard fought. One of the key issues in this campaign was law and order. This cause, made popular by political figures like former Alabama governor George Wallace, was championed by the eventual winner, Richard Nixon.

The "law and order" platform appealed to Americans primarily because of the great social upheavals of the 1960s. The war in Vietnam had spawned violence in the streets; college students and other young people were rejecting the ways of their elders; sex was free; drugs were cheap; and the civil rights movement was elevating African Americans and other minorities from the subservient status to which mainstream America had grown accustomed. At least that's how it looked to many middle-class Americans as they read the daily newspapers and watched the evening news on TV. With such images invading their living rooms every night, a cause such as law and order, which promised a return to traditional American values, had obvious appeal.

President Nixon's first target was organized crime, rather than rioters or drug users. This surprised many observers. Nixon, however, felt that "the organized criminal corrupts our government institutions and subverts our democratic processes."[a] He asked Congress to increase its appropriation to fight organized crime from $36 million to $61 million, despite his efforts to shrink the overall federal budget.

The Democrats, not to be outdone, had a proposal of their own for dealing with organized crime. Presented by Senator John McClellan of Arkansas in March 1969, the plan called for strengthening of the investigative function of grand juries, freer use of depositions in criminal trials (which was a limitation on the Sixth Amendment right of confrontation, because a defendant might not be able to cross-examine at trial the person who gave the deposi-

Historical Perspective continued on following page

---

a. "The Pinch of Inflation and Unrest," *Newsweek*, May 5, 1969, 33.

Historical Perspective
Adoption of RICO *continued*

tion), expanded use of immunity to obtain testimony from reluctant witnesses, elimination of certain evidentiary limitations in perjury prosecutions, and an expanded witness-protection program.

In making these proposals, McClellan recounted the common-law history of the various constitutional protections implicated, and asserted that through such mechanisms as the political process and prosecutorial discretion, fundamental rights were not in jeopardy. Nevertheless, several of the proposed changes involved a perception of fundamental rights that differed from that prevalent in the courts.

One interesting comment made by McClellan, which may have foreshadowed the use of organized crime statutes 15 years later, was his comment that

> [i]t is most disturbing, however, to hear, as we have recently from New York Stock Exchange President Robert W. Haack, that there is a question whether or not organized crime may have begun to penetrate securities firms and the stock exchange itself. Apparently, no area of business activity is immune from its grasping claws.[b]

It is not clear what either of these gentlemen meant by the term "organized crime," and indeed, this has been a major stumbling block in efforts to legislate against such activity.

The legislation to which this debate finally gave birth, the Racketeer Influenced and Corrupt Organizations Act of 1970 (RICO), did not define organized crime or the organized criminal. There are constitutional difficulties with criminalizing a status, such as membership in an organization, and with discriminating between different types of defendants, based, for instance, upon their crimes being reported in *Business Week* rather than *Newsweek*. To avoid these problems, RICO is based on a definition of "racketeering activity" rather than of organized crime.

RICO was used, in its early years, primarily in the pursuit of traditional organized criminals, and it was rather effective in this pursuit. Prosecutors and other lawyers eventually realized, however, that other uses

could be made of the statute. To prosecutors, forfeiture provisions and enhanced sentences were attractive. To plaintiff lawyers, treble damages and judicial discretion in defining "racketeering activity" were attractive. Both types of lawyers recognized the possibility that proving the elements of a RICO violation might be easier than proving the elements of serious crimes or torts. Thus, RICO grew quickly during its adolescence, encompassing activities far beyond those originally contemplated by President Nixon or Congress.

An example of activities that have become entangled in the RICO net is the exercise of freedom of the press. An article by Nat Hentoff recounts the story of John Spear, editor of a small weekly newspaper in upstate New York.[c] It seems that Spear's paper advocated the positions of antiabortion groups who were protesting at an abortion clinic. When he criticized police action at a West Hartford demonstration, which he felt was excessive, he was sued by the town under RICO. The underlying racketeering activity alleged was extortion. West Hartford's theory was that by printing such accusations, Spear was attempting to intimidate police and extort improved police behavior at subsequent demonstrations.

Another case that illustrates the uses to which RICO has been put is the criminal prosecution of the investment banking firm Drexel Burnham Lambert Inc. Through the use of RICO forfeiture provisions, which allow for the impounding of ill-gotten gains *before* the trial, federal prosecutors were able to put Drexel Burnham in the position of having to accept a guilty verdict or face the possibility of bankruptcy. Although it is true that most accused criminals must choose between a guilty plea and the possibility of greater punishment if they insist on a trial, prior to RICO that punishment was not imposed before the trial. Drexel Burnham eventually declared bankruptcy anyway, though it seems likely that the fine imposed following Drexel's guilty plea, and more importantly the damage to its reputation due to the securities fraud and RICO allegations, helped make it impossible for Drexel to continue in business.

---

b. John McClellan, "Organized Crime in the United States," *Vital Speeches of the Day,* April 15, 1969, 390.

c. Nat Hentoff, "First Amendment Racketeers," *The Progressive,* February 1, 1990, 12.

inside information. For example, in July 1988 Alfred Elliot was charged with making $680,000 in illegal profits from trading on confidential information he acquired while a partner at a Chicago law firm. Also charged with wire fraud and securities fraud, Elliot was alleged to have engaged in nine incidents between 1984 and 1986 in which he learned of large pending stock acquisitions by clients and invested heavily in the target company. Other similar cases are discussed in chapter 23.

Although RICO is generally given a liberal construction to ensure that Congress's intent is not frustrated by an overly narrow reading of the statute, the reach of the statute is not unlimited, as seen in *Reves v. Ernst & Young*.[22] Purchasers of demand notes from a farmer's cooperative brought a securities fraud and RICO action against the accountants of the cooperative. The United States Supreme Court held that the accountants hired to perform an audit of the cooperative's records did not exert control over the company and did not "participate in operation or management" of the cooperative's affairs. Such a finding of participation would have been necessary to find the accountants liable under RICO for failing to inform the cooperative's board of directors that the cooperative was insolvent.

Reves is an important case for accountants, underwriters, attorneys, and others who work with a company issuing securities. Such persons can no longer be found liable under RICO just because they were involved in the offering process. Instead, some involvement in the management of the issuer of the securities is required.

Penalties Under RICO

Prosecutors have indicated that criminal RICO charges will be used widely in future prosecutions. Persons convicted of criminal RICO violations are subject to a fine and imprisonment for up to 20 years (or life if the violation is based on a racketeering activity for which the maximum penalty includes life imprisonment).

In addition to criminal penalties, the statute grants a private right of action that permits individuals to recover treble damages (that is, three times their actual damages) and also their costs and attorney's fees. The private right of action apparently was intended as a tool against businesses fueled by funds generated through organized crime. The statute contains no such explicit requirement, however, that organized crime be involved, and RICO

has been used in numerous civil suits against legitimate businesses.

■ Other Federal Criminal Laws

A large number of federal regulatory laws provide for criminal as well as civil penalties for their violation. Some of the more important of these are discussed in this section.

Wire and Mail Fraud Acts

Next to RICO, the Wire and Mail Fraud Acts[23] may be the prosecutor's most powerful weapon against the white-collar criminal defendant. Chief Justice Warren Burger characterized the Mail Fraud Act as a "stopgap" provision that criminalizes conduct that a court finds morally reprehensible but that is not mentioned in any other criminal statute.

To establish *mail fraud* or *wire fraud* under the acts, the prosecutor must demonstrate: (1) a scheme intended to defraud or to obtain money or property by fraudulent means; and (2) the use of the mails or of interstate telephone lines in furtherance of the fraudulent scheme. Exactly what constitutes a fraudulent scheme has never been established. It remains a factual question determined on a case-by-case basis. The Supreme Court has broadly construed "fraud" to encompass "everything designed to defraud by representations as to the past or present, or suggestions and promises as to the future."[24] Violations of the acts are punishable by a fine not to exceed $1,000 and a jail sentence not to exceed five years. If the violation affects a financial institution, the violator may be fined up to $1 million or imprisoned up to 30 years, or both.

> 66
>
> *The Supreme Court has broadly construed "fraud" to encompass "everything designed to defraud by representations as to the past or present, or suggestions and promises as to the future."*

---

22. 113 S.Ct. 1163 (1993).

23. 18 U.S.C. § 1343, 1341 (1988 & Supp. 1992).
24. *Durland v. United States*, 161 U.S. 306, 313, 16 S.Ct. 508, 511 (1896).

Federal prosecutions under these acts have involved such diverse activities as defense procurement fraud, insurance fraud, false financial statements fraud, medical advertising fraud, tax fraud, divorce mill fraud, and securities fraud. Indeed, it is rare for a white-collar criminal prosecution to be brought without alleging a violation of the Wire and Mail Fraud Acts.

As the following case demonstrates, the Wire and Mail Fraud Acts can be used to prosecute securities-related activities that may not violate securities laws.

■ **A Case in Point:**   **Summary**

Case 15.5
CARPENTER v. UNITED STATES
Supreme Court of the United States
484 U.S. 19, 108 S.Ct. 316 (1987).

FACTS   R. Foster Winans was a coauthor of an investment advice column called "Heard on the Street" for *The Wall Street Journal*. Due to its perceived quality and integrity, the column had a potential impact on the market prices of the stocks it discussed. Thus, the official policy at the newspaper was that prior to publication the contents of the column were to be kept confidential.

In late 1983, despite this official policy, Winans entered into a scheme with stockbrokers to tell or tip them as to which stocks would be mentioned in his next column. These individuals would then buy the stock and sell it after the stocks had typically risen in price as a result of trading created by the column. Investigations began when correlations occurred between the column and trading in certain brokers' accounts.

ISSUE PRESENTED   Is a conspiracy to trade on a newspaper's confidential information within the reach of the mail and wire fraud statutes?

SUMMARY OF OPINION   The U.S. Supreme Court, in a unanimous decision, upheld Winans's conviction of wire and mail fraud. The Court rejected the defendants' arguments that Winans's conduct in revealing prepublication information was no more than a violation of workplace rules and did not amount to fraudulent activity. The Court reasoned that *The Wall Street Journal*'s confidential business information (its publication schedule and the contents of the advice column) were property rights protected by the wire and mail fraud statutes. As such, *The Wall Street Journal* had a right to decide how to use the information prior to disclosing it to the public. Winans's activity deprived *The Wall Street Journal* of its right to exclusive use of the information.

According to the Court, no monetary loss, such as giving the information to a competitor of *The Wall Street Journal*, was necessary to prove violation of the wire and mail fraud statutes. The requirement under the statutes that the mediums of wire and mail be used to execute the scheme was satisfied, the Court said, by the printing and sending of *The Wall Street Journal* to its customers. Without publication of the advice columns, there would have been no effect on stock prices and therefore no profit from trading on the prepublication information.

The Court, however, was divided on the securities fraud issue and thus the securities law convictions under section 10(b) of the Securities Exchange Act of 1934 were affirmed without opinion. (Securities fraud is discussed in detail in chapter 23.)

RESULT   Winans's conviction of wire and mail fraud was upheld, and David Carpenter, Winans's roommate, was convicted for aiding and abetting.

The Supreme Court in *Carpenter* held that a Wire and Mail Fraud prosecution can be brought in addition to other prosecutions based on the same events. Thus, the defendant may be charged with violation of the securities laws, the bankruptcy laws, the tax laws, or the Truth in Lending Act, as well as for wire or mail fraud.

A prosecutor can choose under which statutes to charge the defendant. This prosecutorial discretion increases the plea-bargaining power of the government. Additionally, by presenting multiple statutory violations to the jury, the prosecutor increases the chances of conviction and the likelihood of a stiffer sentence.

The Wire and Mail Fraud Acts provide the prosecutor with two other important advantages. Under these acts, unlike many others, the prosecutor does not have to establish that the accused's conduct was "willful." A violation of the acts can be established under strict liability. Perhaps most importantly, a wire or mail fraud violation can trigger RICO liability.

False Statements Act

The False Statements Act provides that:

> Whoever, in any manner within the jurisdiction of any department or agency of the United States knowingly and willfully falsifies, conceals or covers up by any trick, scheme, or device a material fact, or makes any false, fictitious or fraudulent statements or representations, or makes or uses any false writing or document knowing the same to contain any false, fictitious or fraudulent statement or entry, shall be fined not more than $10,000 or imprisoned not more than five years, or both.[25]

Although not used as frequently as the Wire and Mail Fraud Acts, the False Statements Act has become an effective tool for criminal prosecutions of business managers who deal dishonestly with governmental administrative agencies. For example, in *United States v. Weatherspoon*[26] an operator of a beauty college who submitted false attendance reports to the Veterans Administration (VA) was found to have violated the Wire and Mail Fraud Acts and the False Statements Act. In order to be eligible for VA financial assistance, both the student and the beauty college had to certify to the VA that the student was attending classes for 30 hours per week. The defendant was convicted of submitting false student enrollment cards and falsifying attendance certificates.

---

25. 18 U.S.C. § 1001 (1988).
26. 581 F.2d 595 (7th Cir. 1978).

The Sherman Act

The antitrust laws are designed to encourage active business competition. (These laws are discussed in detail in chapter 18.)

Criminal prosecutions under the antitrust laws occur most frequently in actions brought under sections 1 and 2 of the Sherman Act. Section 1 of the Sherman Act prohibits, among other things, all conspiracies in restraint of trade, including price fixing. Section 2 prohibits monopolization, that is, the willful acquisition or maintenance of monopoly power coupled with the intent to monopolize.

Penalties Under the Sherman Act   Criminal prosecutions under the Sherman Act are initiated under the direction of the attorney general through the Antitrust Division of the Department of Justice or the appropriate United States attorney. Individuals who violate the act are subject to a statutory maximum of three years in prison and/or a $350,000 fine per violation. Corporations that violate the Sherman Act are subject to a fine of up to $10 million per violation.

Because the Sherman Act contains both criminal and civil sanctions, the government must always determine whether to bring a criminal action, a civil action, or both. In making this determination, the government continues to rely on a report of the United States attorney general issued in 1955, under which the criminal sanction has generally been limited to particularly egregious conduct such as price fixing or group boycotts, or has been applied to individuals previously convicted of an antitrust offense.

Prosecutions   Between 1890 and 1970 no more than a few criminal cases were brought under the Sherman Act. In 1977, in an attempt to put more bite into the criminal sanctions, the Antitrust Division of the Department of Justice published its intention to seek longer sentences for violations of the Sherman Act. Factors that would be more likely to lead to a longer sentence included the amount of commerce involved, the position of the individual in the conspiracy, the existence and degree of predatory or coercive conduct, the duration of participation, and any previous convictions. Cooperation with the government would reduce the sentence.

A dramatic rise in the number of criminal convictions under the antitrust laws occured in the 1980s, with more than 100 criminal convictions requiring imprisonment handed down between 1980 and 1983 alone. Many of the convictions were for bid rigging in highway contracting. The U.S. Sentencing Commission, created in 1984, has promulgated only one federal sentencing guideline for antitrust offenses. It deals with horizontal agreements in restraint of trade (e.g., horizontal price fixing, bid rigging, and market allocation), and guides federal courts in setting penalties up to the statutory maximum. In most cases, first-time offenders sentenced under the federal guideline serve a minimum six- to twelve-month jail sentence. Many defendants in Sherman Act prosecutions plead nolo contendere (no contest) to forestall the use of a guilty verdict in a subsequent civil action.

The Federal Securities Laws

The two main federal securities laws are the Securities Act of 1933[27] (1933 Act) and the Securities Exchange Act of 1934[28] (1934 Act). Both of these statutes were drafted in the wake of the stock market crash of 1929 as a way to restore investor confidence in the nation's securities markets. The Securities and Exchange Commission (SEC) administers both the 1933 Act and the 1934 Act. These acts are discussed more fully in chapters 22 and 23 but are briefly described here.

1933 Act   The 1933 Act covers the initial distribution of a security from the issuer to the public. Unless an exemption applies (see chapter 22), the issuer must file a registration statement with the SEC. To encourage proper disclosure of all information demanded by the statute, section 24 of the act provides for criminal penalties in addition to civil sanctions. Any person or entity that willfully violates the 1933 Act or any regulation promulgated by the SEC is subject to a maximum fine of $10,000 and/or a five-year jail sentence. It is the United States attorney, not the SEC, who decides whether to bring criminal charges.

1934 Act   The 1934 Act focuses on the need for public companies (that is, those with securities trading in the public market) to periodically update disclosures initially made under the 1933 Act. The 1934 Act requires public companies to file annual reports, quarterly reports, and additional reports to reflect any material change in the company, such as a merger or sale of substantially all of its assets. The 1934 Act regulates, among other things, insider transactions, proxy solicitations, tender offers, brokers and dealers, and the securities exchanges. The 1934 Act also contains a general prohibition on securities fraud and on *insider trading,* that is, trading while in possession of material nonpublic information.

The 1934 Act provides for criminal penalties for willful violations of the act or the related SEC rules.

Violators can be punished with a fine not to exceed $1 million and/or a ten-year prison sentence, except that if the violator is a person other than a natural person (e.g., a corporation), a fine up to $2.5 million may be imposed. Violators who prove they had no knowledge of the rule or regulation will not be subject to imprisonment, however. The penalties for insider trading are set forth in chapter 23.

The Foreign Corrupt Practices Act

The Foreign Corrupt Practices Act,[29] as discussed in chapter 3, makes it a crime for any U.S. firm to make payments to a foreign government official in an attempt to influence the actions of the official. The act also requires detailed record-keeping and internal control measures by all public companies, whether international or purely domestic. The penalties for violations of the Foreign Corrupt Practices Act are set forth in chapter 3.

The Environmental Laws

During the past two decades, Congress has passed or significantly modified existing laws to protect the environment (see chapter 16). These laws provide for criminal sanctions against both the corporation and its employees. The Wire and Mail Fraud Acts and the False Statements Act supplement the criminal sanctions included in the environmental statutes.

Two examples of environmental laws that impose criminal sanctions are the Clean Water Act and the Resource Conservation and Recovery Act.

Clean Water Act   The Clean Water Act[30] requires all industrial and municipal entities to obtain a permit from the Environmental Protection Agency (EPA) prior to discharging specified pollutants into a water source. Detailed records of all discharges and periodic testing of sample discharges are required. Criminal penalties under the act vary depending on whether the violation was negligent, knowing, or knowing and endangered others. First-time violators are subject to prison terms ranging from 1 to 15 years, and fines ranging from $2,500 to $100,000 per day. Organizations that knowingly endanger others can be fined up to $1 million. For second and subsequent violations, prison terms and fines are doubled.

Any person who knowingly falsifies any records required to be maintained under the act may be fined

---

27. 15 U.S.C. §§ 77a *et seq.* (1988).
28. 15 U.S.C. §§ 78a *et seq.* (1988).

29. 15 U.S.C. § 78dd-2 (1988).
30. 33 U.S.C. §§ 1351 *et seq.* (1988).

$10,000 and imprisoned for up to two years. Prison terms and fines are also doubled for subsequent violations.

Resource Conservation and Recovery Act   The Resource Conservation and Recovery Act (RCRA) of 1976, as amended in 1984,[31] provides for cradle-to-grave monitoring of hazardous waste material. This statute and the accompanying regulations set out procedures and record-keeping requirements for the transportation, storage, and treatment of hazardous waste. Criminal penalties can be levied both against the corporation and against individual employees who dispose of hazardous waste without the appropriate RCRA permit.

The Tax Laws

Certain violations of the Internal Revenue Code are subject to criminal penalties. The strictest penalties are found in section 7201, which prohibits willful attempts to evade any tax imposed under the code. Anyone convicted under this provision is subject to a fine not to exceed $100,000 ($500,000 for a corporation) plus all costs of the prosecution and/or a prison term not to exceed five years. Section 7206 forbids any false statements in a tax return, punishable with the same fine structure but with a maximum prison sentence of three years. Under section 7207, willful delivery of a fraudulent return to the secretary of the treasury is punishable with up to one year in jail and a fine of $10,000 ($50,000 in the case of a corporation).

A tax fraud prosecution must allege willful misconduct on the part of the accused. Consequently, prosecutors in tax fraud cases often add a mail fraud charge, which can result in a conviction even if willful misconduct is not proved. Moreover, mail fraud, unlike tax fraud, can be the basis for a RICO claim.

The Occupational Safety and Health Act

The Occupational Safety and Health Act (OSHA)[32] applies to all employers engaged in a business affecting interstate commerce. Interstate commerce is defined very loosely, and therefore most employers come under OSHA's umbrella. Certain employers are exempted from having to comply with OSHA, including federal and state governments and employers in industries covered by other safety regulations and statutes.

OSHA Requirements   OSHA requires employers to provide a place of employment free from recognized haz-

---

31. 42 U.S.C. §§ 6901 *et seq.* (1988).
32. 29 U.S.C. § 651 (1988 & Supp. 1992).

ards that are likely to cause death or serious physical harm. Employers are also required to comply with many detailed safety regulations. The Occupational Safety and Health Administration can inspect workplaces for violations of the act and its regulations. Additionally, employers must keep specific records and must keep employees informed of their protections and the employer's obligations under the act and its regulations.

Penalties Under OSHA   Most violations of OSHA are punished by civil penalties. The penalties are mandatory when the employer receives a citation for a serious violation, discretionary when the violation is nonserious. More severe civil penalties (i.e., fines up to $70,000) are imposed for willful or repeated violations. The terms "serious," "nonserious," "willful," and "repeated" are all defined in the act.

Section 666(e) of the act provides for even harsher penalties if the employer commits a willful violation that results in the death of an employee. In this case, the employer may suffer a fine, imprisonment, or both. If the employer had not previously been convicted of a violation, she may be punished by a fine of not more than $10,000 or by imprisonment of up to six months, or both. For a second conviction, the punishment can be a fine of up to $20,000 or imprisonment of up to one year, or both.

The Responsible Manager

Ensuring Criminal Law Compliance

Senior management can implement various actions and procedures to encourage criminal law compliance.

The corporation should develop a code of ethics, as discussed in chapter 1. All criminal acts should be outlawed by the code. The code of ethics should have an enforcement mechanism and should clearly state that violations of the code will result in sanctions such as salary reductions, poor performance ratings, and, in extreme cases, termination of employment.

The code of ethics must be given more than lip service. The corporation should have a procedure to remind all employees about the provisions of the code. Some corporations require that employees sign a yearly statement saying that they have read the code of ethics.

It should be clear throughout the company that ethical behavior is expected. A policy of honesty should be stressed. What top management does when it sees criminal-law-related problems will influence all employees. It is much harder for an employee to justify committing a criminal act against the corporation when he cannot claim that the top management is also guilty of criminal acts. As in the *Park* case, top management may be found vicariously liable for crimes committed by employees under their supervision. Organizations themselves can also be assessed large fines as a result of criminal acts committed by their managers and employees if the acts were committed within the scope of employment and for the benefit of the corporation.

Corporate in-house counsel should be independent. They should not succumb to pressure from division managers to give the go-ahead to an action that counsel believe may violate a criminal statute.

Some courts will excuse a corporation from criminal liability if the corporation shows that it diligently tried to prevent the criminal behavior. Setting up a good reporting structure is one step toward preventing crime.

Outside firms can be hired to audit the corporation's methods of ensuring criminal law compliance. These firms can also make suggestions to improve the corporation's methods.

The corporation should also focus on the continuing education of its employees. All employees need to know the criminal law that affects them. In-house training can keep corporate employees abreast of changes in the criminal law and can help ensure that employees do not forget their criminal law obligations.

Inside Story

Junk-Bond King Pleads Guilty

Public Confession: Milken Pleads Guilty to Six Felony Counts and Issues an Apology [33]

He was almost at the end of a detailed confession when his voice faltered. Michael Milken bent forward, sobbing, as two of his lawyers rushed to support him. Suddenly, under the vast ceiling of Manhattan's largest federal courtroom, the world's once-most-powerful financier, the bigger-than-life commander of the X-shaped trading desk, seemed mortal, even frail.

In contrast, the six felony counts to which Mr. Milken pleaded guilty yesterday after an intense three-year government investigation showed the financier at the height of his power, as founder and head of Drexel Burnham Lambert Inc.'s high-yield junk-bond department. He was able to order the country's largest arbitrager to take illegal stock positions, to conceal the activities of corporate raiders, to create tax losses and gains, and to create artificial prices of junk bonds.

The six felonies, ranging from conspiracy to securities and mail fraud to a tax count, were far from the technical violations of obscure securities laws that many people had come to expect.

Together, they portray a financier with such total power over the junk-bond market Mr. Milken largely created that he seemed to believe himself beyond the reach of law. And, were it not for the unforeseen confession of a co-conspirator, former arbitrager Ivan F. Boesky, he probably would have been.

Four of the six counts directly involved Mr. Boesky, establishing the accuracy of much of what Mr. Boesky told prosecutors at the time of his own plea bargain in 1986. The other two involve David Solomon, the head of a junk-bond mutual fund and a former Drexel client who was granted immunity from prosecution and has been cooperating in the government's investigation of Mr. Milken.

The six crimes show that Mr. Milken:

■ Defrauded investors by unlawfully concealing the fact that hostile suitor Golden Nuggets Inc. had sold its position in the stock of MCA Inc.;

■ Cheated clients of Drexel and Mr. Solomon's investment partnership by falsely reporting to them the prices at which securities had been bought and sold,

33. Laurie P. Cohen, "Public Confession: Milken Pleads Guilty to Six Felony Counts and Issues an Apology," *The Wall Street Journal*, April 25, 1990, A1. Bruce Ingersoll contributed to this article. Reprinted by permission of *The Wall Street Journal*, © 1990 Dow Jones & Company Inc. All Rights Reserved Worldwide.

Inside Story, continued

with Mr. Milken's high-yield department pocketing the difference;

■ Forced an unwilling Fischback Corp. into the hands of corporate raider Victor Posner by having Mr. Boesky take a large and unlawfully secret position in the company's stock;

■ Helped Mr. Solomon evade income taxes by creating losses for him, and then manufactured gains for him the following year;

■ Entered into a criminal conspiracy with Mr. Boesky that included secret record-keeping involving securities that Mr. Boesky held in order to illegally conceal their true owners;

■ Helped Mr. Boesky evade net-capital rules by secretly agreeing to buy stock from him with the understanding it would be bought back later at no loss to Drexel.

While wide-ranging, the counts to which Mr. Milken admitted guilt are a small fraction of the crimes alleged by the government in its 98-count indictment or the even-larger indictment the government said it was prepared to seek as recently as last Friday, when Mr. Milken accepted the offer of a plea agreement. The government said the full sweep of Mr. Milken's allegedly unlawful behavior will be made public in its pre-sentencing memorandum.

Mr. Milken was warned by presiding federal district judge Kimba Wood that the six crimes carry a maximum prison sentence of 28 years. In addition, Mr. Milken agreed to pay a fine of $200 million and $400 million into a fund for restitution as part of his settlement of related Securities and Exchange Commission charges. Judge Wood said Mr. Milken would be sentenced on Oct. 1, after the court has had time to consider sentencing reports from the government and Mr. Milken's response.

"I realize that by my acts I have hurt those who are closest to me," Mr. Milken told the judge as his wife, Lori, his mother, his brother, Lowell, and several former Drexel officials looked on. "I am truly sorry. I thank the court for permitting me to add this apology and for its fairness in handling this complex case." Mrs. Milken wept as her husband acknowledged guilt and apologized.

"I am truly sorry."

–Michael Milken

Judge Wood asked Mr. Milken repeatedly to assure her that he believed himself to be guilty of the crimes alleged, and that he hadn't been pressured into pleading guilty and relinquishing his constitutional right to a jury trial. In each instance, Mr. Milken said that he was guilty and that he hadn't been pressured into settlement. He also said he wasn't taking any drugs, wasn't under the care of a psychiatrist, and was "clear-headed."

Both the chief government prosecutor in the case, John Carroll, and Mr. Milken's principal lawyer, Arthur Liman, emphasized that Mr. Milken would cooperate fully in the government's continuing investigation of wrongdoing in the financial industry. Mr. Carroll said the government would retain considerable leverage over Mr. Milken even though his cooperation will commence only after he is sentenced. The written plea agreement provides that Mr. Milken will speak with federal officials whenever he is asked and will "fully and truthfully disclose all information with respect to Drexel-related activities."

Given his prominence in so many of the last decade's major financial developments, from the rise of junk bonds and the rapid growth of many now-troubled savings and loans to the leveraged buy-out and hostile takeover booms, Mr. Milken could be the most valuable guide to the inner workings of Wall Street the government has ever obtained. If more wrongdoing exists, he is in a good position to know about it. Thus his testimony could trigger a wave of new investigations and pleas.

At the very least, Mr. Milken's agreement is ominous for Mr. Posner, who was named with Mr. Milken as a defendant in the SEC's September 1988 civil complaint. With both Mr. Boesky and Mr. Milken cooperating, Mr. Posner's position would seem greatly weakened.

Robert Morvillo, an attorney for Mr. Posner, said, "The U.S. Attorney's office has not been involved in any way with us for a very long period of time, and we

Inside Story continued on following page

Inside Story, *continued*

are not in the least concerned about the Milken plea because we assume if he tells the truth, Victor Posner will be exonerated."

The government is also known to be investigating some major junk-bond purchasers that were clients of Mr. Milken, such as Columbia Savings & Loan Association and First Executive Corp. Both companies have denied wrongdoing.

As for Mr. Milken's brother Lowell, a defendant in the indictment, the government said it would no longer seek criminal charges against him. This was a crucial aspect of Mr. Milken's decision to plead. In a statement distributed after the proceeding in court, Lowell Milken said, "I can take no satisfaction that the charges against me are being dropped. They never should have been brought in the first place, because I have done nothing wrong."

Attorney General Richard Thornburgh, whose office approved the settlement, characterized Mr. Milken's crimes as "some of the most serious efforts undertaken to manipulate and subvert Wall Street's securities markets." He added that the case sends a strong message about "crime in the suites: Those white-collar criminals are never so powerful or clever that they cannot be caught by diligent and persistent law enforcement efforts."

SEC Chairman Richard Breeden, whose office also settled its case against Mr. Milken, said he was "extremely pleased" by the $600 million settlement, the largest in the SEC's history. While he declined to speculate on where Mr. Milken's cooperation might lead, Mr. Breeden said, "This case clearly does involve some significant ramifications. We do expect the testimony and cooperation we will receive will be valuable." He also noted that by settling the case now, the government will obtain Mr. Milken's cooperation before so much time passes that the statute of limitations might bar additional prosecutions.

> 66
>
> *The case sends a strong message about "crime in the suites: Those white-collar criminals are never so powerful or clever that they cannot be caught by diligent and persistent law enforcement efforts."*
>
> —*U.S. Attorney General*

The settlement of the SEC case was filed in the same courthouse shortly after Mr. Milken's criminal plea. In addition to the $600 million payment, the SEC settlement bars Mr. Milken and his brother from the securities industry for life. Both Milkens signed consent decrees in which they neither admitted nor denied the sweeping allegations in the SEC's suit.

Of the $600 million payment Mr. Milken agreed to, the $200 million that is a fine will go directly to the U.S. Treasury, a sum that comfortably exceeds the amount the government spent pursuing the Milken investigation, the prosecutor, Mr. Carroll, assured Judge Wood. The $400 million portion, to be administered by the SEC, will be available to satisfy claims by investors and others who assert that they have been defrauded by Mr. Milken. Although civil suits have already been filed against Mr. Milken alleging damages far in excess of that amount, his attorney, Mr. Liman, told Judge Wood that he was confident $400 million would be more than adequate, and that anything left over would go to the government.

If nothing else, the hundreds of people packed into the federal courtroom for the criminal plea and many hundreds more surrounding the courthouse in Foley Square were a testament to Mr. Milken's continuing celebrity. Entering the courthouse through the main staircase, Mr. Milken eyed the crowds and television crews gathered for his sentencing, and told U.S. marshals escorting him, "It never ceases to amaze me."

At first, the courtroom had the almost-festive air of a reunion. The courtroom crowd included many long time supporters of Mr. Milken; scores of lawyers who have worked on aspects of the Milken and Drexel cases; a large contingent from the U.S. Attorney's office and the SEC, and dozens of reporters. There were titters when Mr. Milken, whom Drexel paid $550 million in one year alone, was told the court would appoint a lawyer for him if he couldn't afford one. But the mood suddenly turned somber as Mr. Milken acknowledged guilt and began describing his crimes.

During his statement, Mr. Milken defended what will probably be his most enduring legacy, the junk-bond market. Although that market has been in turmoil since last fall, Mr. Milken argued that his admission of guilt is "not a reflection on the underlying soundness and integrity of the segment of the capital markets in which

---

Inside Story, continued

we [Drexel] specialized and which provided capital that enabled hundreds of companies to survive, expand and flourish."

Mr. Liman, commenting after the courtroom proceeding, added that "it is Michael's hope that in the long run, history will see his violations in context and judge him not just on the basis of his lapses, but on the basis of the contributions he made to the economy and to the American people."

[Ed.—In late November 1990, Michael Milken was sentenced to ten years in prison. Following his release in 1993 after only 22 months in prison, Mr. Milken participated as a guest lecturer in corporate finance and financial markets at the University of California-Los Angeles's Anderson Graduate School of Management.[34]]

---

34. "UCLA's Deal with Milken," *The Los Angeles Times,* March 31, 1994, B6.

Key Words and Phrases

actus reus **469**
arrest **478**
burden of proof **472**
computer fraud **489**
computer piracy **490**
consent decree **474**
crime **469**
embezzlement **489**
enterprise **491**
exclusionary rule **478**
federal interest computer **490**
felony **471**
fraud **489**

fruit of the poisonous tree **480**
indictment **474**
information **474**
insider trading **496**
intention to do wrong **469**
larceny **489**
mail fraud **493**
mens rea **469**
misdemeanor **471**
negligence **469**
negligence *per se* **472**
nolo contendere **474**
plea **474**

plea bargaining **474**
preponderance of the evidence **472**
probable cause **478**
recklessness **469**
respondeat superior **487**
strict liability **469**
transactional immunity **474**
use immunity **474**
vicarious liability **486**
white-collar crime **488**
wire fraud **493**

Questions and Case Problems

1. Cronic and two associates were indicted on mail fraud charges involving the transfer of more than $9 million in checks between banks in Tampa, Florida, and Norman, Oklahoma, over a four-month period. Right before the trial was to begin, the attorney for the defendants withdrew. The court-appointed substitute counsel turned out to be an attorney who specialized in real estate and had never argued before a jury.

Once counsel was appointed, the court allowed the attorney only 25 days of pretrial preparation, even though it had taken the government more than four years to investigate the case and review all the documents. Cronic's two codefendants ended up testifying for the government. Cronic was convicted and received a 25-year sentence.

On appeal, Cronic claimed that the conviction cannot stand because he did not have effective assistance of counsel. Is he correct? [*United States v. Cronic*, 466 U.S. 648, 104 S.Ct. 2039 (1984)]

2. All manufacturers of prescription drugs must receive approval from the government for their operations. The police received a tip that Scott Chan was manufacturing prescription drugs without the appropriate governmental clearance in a warehouse located at 4292 Wilkie Way. Without obtaining a search warrant, the police raided the warehouse and found the illegal drug-making apparatus. They then seized all the drugs and relevant business records concerning the manufacturing operation for use as evidence.

At trial, Chan claimed that both the drugs and the business records should be suppressed and not admitted into evidence. Is he correct? On what grounds should he base his argument? Suppose instead that it was agents for the Food and Drug Administration who seized the evidence instead of the police. Does the analysis change? What if Chan lived in the warehouse?

3. Bert's Sporting Goods, Inc., with stores located throughout the state of Lys, sells a wide variety of sporting goods, including guns. Lys Penal Code § 123.45 requires sellers of guns to verify that the purchaser has not committed a felony within the last five years. If the purchaser has committed a felony within the last five years, the seller is not allowed to make the sale. Selling a gun to a recent felon is considered a misdemeanor and is punishable by up to one year in jail and/or a maximum $10,000 fine.

Jim Dandy, who was convicted of a felony under Lys's penal code four years ago, went to purchase a gun at one of the Bert's Sporting Goods stores. Joe Mountain, a salesman at Bert's, sold Dandy the gun without asking for identification or checking to see whether Dandy was a convicted felon.

As a matter of fact, Mountain never checked whether any of the customers to whom he sold guns were felons. Mountain did not know of the Lys law requiring that he check on the customer's prior criminal history. However, Jay Lake, Mountain's supervisor, knew of the law and also knew that Mountain never checked whether a customer was a felon. Bert, the owner of the sporting goods stores, knew about the law but did not know that Mountain did not check on his customers' prior criminal history.

Dandy used the gun in a robbery, and shot two police officers during his getaway. He was never captured. Can Mountain be punished under Lys Penal Code § 123.45? What about Lake? Bert? Bert's Sporting Goods, Inc.? What penalties should be assessed?

4. Assume the same facts as in question 3, except that Dandy had fake identification, so that even if Mountain had checked for prior felony convictions, he would not have found any information listed under the false name Dandy was using. Does your analysis change?

5. Kent Nowlin Construction Co. is a construction company that participates in interstate commerce and is subject to Occupational Safety and Health Act (OSHA) regulations. The company has been cited for willful and repeated violations of various OSHA statutes in the past.

Nowlin has just started construction on a new skyscraper. During construction, an employee operated a crane within ten feet of a high voltage power line in contravention of OSHA and Nowlin's work rules. Three supervisors were aware of the hazards of using the crane near the power line, but allowed it anyway. The crane eventually came in contact with the power line, and caused the electrocution of an employee.

Should the company and the three supervisors be punished for the violations? If the company and/or the supervisors are punished, should civil or criminal penalties be imposed? If criminal penalties are imposed, should they include a jail sentence? [*Kent Nowlin Construction Co. v. Occupational Safety and Health Review Commission*, 648 F.2d 1278 (10th Cir. 1981)]

6. Bermel Enterprises, Inc. is a supplier of computer programming consulting services to the United States government. Alex and Margot Frankel, two Bermel systems analysts, have consistently overstated the time they spend working on the government projects on their time reports. It is these time reports that determine how much money the government pays the company. Additionally, Michelle Laff, a manager at Bermel, has falsified the results of systems tests conducted on the computer systems installed for the government. As a result, it appears that the systems are bug-free when in fact they have many errors.

What criminal charges may the government bring against the employees? Against Larry Bermel, owner of Bermel Enterprises, Inc.? Against Bermel Enterprises, Inc. itself?

7. An Indiana adult bookstore was cited multiple times for violating the state's laws barring the distribution of obscene books and films. The bookstore operator was also charged with violating an Indiana RICO statute by engaging in a pattern of racketeering activity consisting of repeated violations of the obscenity laws. The maximum penalty under the state RICO statute is ten years in prison and a $20,000 fine. The obscenity offense on which the RICO charge is based is a misdemeanor. Should the state RICO statute be used in this context? [*Fort Wayne Books, Inc. v. Indiana*, 489 U.S. 46, 109 S.Ct. 916 (1989)]

8. Several women's health clinics that provide multiple services, including abortions, were the targets of demonstrations by abortion protesters. The clinics brought suit against a coalition of antiabortion groups represented by the protesters. One of the clinics' claims against the protesters was based on the federal RICO statute. Is this an appropriate use of the RICO statute? Does RICO require proof that either the racketeering enterprise or the acts of racketeering were motivated by an economic purpose? [*National Organization for Women v. Scheidler*, 114 S.Ct. 798 (1994)]

9. Many consulting firms try to finish fixed-price projects under the budgeted hours, thus earning more profit. As a result, consultants are often in a hurry.

Speeding tickets can result from the haste to make deadlines, meetings, or planes. Although many consulting firms bill clients for expenses relating to specific projects, it is not legitimate to bill a client for speeding tickets, as the client did not ask the consultant to break the law. As fines for illegal activities are not tax-deductible, the consulting firm cannot write off this expense, either. A common way of passing on the expense is by padding dinner receipts or adding several small amounts to the client's bill, without supplying specific receipts.

If the consultant gets a speeding ticket while on company business, should the consultant absorb the cost herself? Lie to the client? Have the partner on the project reimburse her? What if the consultant is self-employed?

10. Barry Engel was president of Gel Spice Company, which imported, processed, and packaged spices. As president he was responsible for the purchasing and storing of spices in the company's Brooklyn, New York, warehouse. In June 1972, the FDA inspected the Gel Spice warehouse and found widespread rodent infestation. Upon reinspection in August 1972, the FDA found evidence of continuing infestation. Following the two 1972 inspections, the FDA considered a criminal prosecution against Gel Spice. Before referring the case to the Department of Justice, however, an additional inspection was performed. At that July 1973 inspection, no evidence of rodent infestation was found, and the criminal prosecution was dropped. Three years later, in July 1976, the FDA inspected Gel Spice and again found active rodent infestation. Four additional inspections were performed in 1977 to 1979, each of which revealed continuing infestation. Thereafter, the government instituted criminal proceedings against Gel Spice and its president, Barry Engel. Under what theory of criminal liability could Engel be held liable for violating the Food, Drug and Cosmetic Act? Could Engel successfully assert the defense of impossibility? [*United States v. Gel Spice Co.,* 773 F.2d 427 (2d Cir. 1985) *cert. denied,* 474 U.S. 1060, 106 S.Ct. 804 (1986)]

Chapter 16

ENVIRONMENTAL LAW

■ Introduction

Role in Business Management

Since the 1970s, environmental laws have played an increasingly important role in business management. Some industries (such as oil and mining companies, and chemical manufacturing concerns) are well accustomed to intense government regulation of the environmental effects of their operations. In recent years, however, the scope and impact of environmental laws have steadily grown. Today, real estate owners and investors, developers, insurance companies, and financial institutions find that their operations, too, are often affected by laws and regulations intended to protect the environment.

Chapter Summary

This chapter introduces four federal environmental laws that illustrate the importance of environmental regulation for an expanding scope of business activities. It shows how environmental laws may affect the corporate policies and long-term planning of, for example, a manufacturing company, real estate investor, and financing institution. It also discusses the potential liability, under the environmental laws, of individual shareholders, officers, and employees.

Environmental Laws

Environmental law consists of numerous federal, state, and local laws with the common objective of protecting human health and the environment. Although environmental law contributes to the protection of natural resources, it generally does not include wilderness preservation, wildlife protection, coastal zone management, energy conservation, national park designation, and the like. Those laws are commonly referred to as *natural resources laws.* Nor does environmental law cover land use and zoning. Such laws, generally administered by local governments, are commonly referred to as land use laws. They are discussed in chapter 17.

Common-Law Nuisance

Historically, public officials relied primarily on the common-law theory of nuisance (discussed in chapter 7) to control industrial and agricultural activities that interfered with the health or comfort of the community. Thus, industrial odors, noise, smoke, and pollutants of all kinds were the subjects of numerous lawsuits that attempted to balance the legitimate business interests of the polluter with the private interests of the surrounding community. However, the need to file a lawsuit in each case and the complexity of the common law made common-law nuisance a cumbersome way to control environmental pollution in an industrial society. Moreover, a lawsuit could not prevent pollution; it could only provide a remedy after the fact. Today, state and federal regulatory programs have largely replaced common-law nuisance as a means of pollution control.

Statutes

Environmental statutes establish policy, set goals, and authorize the executive branch or one of its administrative agencies to adopt regulations specifying how the law will be implemented. As explained in chapter 4, the statutes and regulations are interpreted and applied in administrative and judicial proceedings. Thus environmental laws consist of the statutes, the regulations, and the administrative and judicial interpretations of their meaning. In addition, the administrative agency often issues policy statements and technical guidance that, while not having the force of law, guide enforcement efforts or provide assistance to the regulated community.

Three Categories   Environmental laws can be divided into three broad categories. The largest category consists of environmental laws that regulate the release of pollu-

tants into the air, water, or ground. These laws usually authorize the government to issue and enforce permits for releases of pollutants. They may also authorize emergency responses and remedial action if, for example, improper waste disposal or accidental chemical spills threaten human health or the environment. Statutes in this category include the Clean Air Act; the Federal Water Pollution Control Act, as amended by the Clean Water Act; the Solid Waste Disposal Act, as amended by the Resource Conservation and Recovery Act; the Comprehensive Environmental Response, Compensation, and Liability Act (CERCLA), as amended by the Superfund Amendments and Reauthorization Act of 1986; and similar state laws. These four pollution-control laws are discussed in this chapter.

A second category includes laws that govern the manufacture, sale, distribution, and use of chemical substances as commercial products. This category includes the Federal Insecticide, Fungicide and Rodenticide Act, which applies to pesticide products, and the Toxic Substances Control Act, which applies to all chemical substances both manufactured in and imported into the United States, excluding certain substances that are regulated under other federal laws. The Safe Drinking Water Act, which governs the quality of drinking water served by public drinking water systems, might also be included in this category.

A third category includes laws that require government decision makers to take into account the effect of

---

In Brief: Major Environmental Legislation

- Clean Air Act
- Clean Water Act
- Resource Conservation and Recovery Act (RCTA)
- Comprehensive Environmental Response, Compensation and Liability Act (CERCLA)
- Federal Insecticide, Fungicide and Rodenticide Act
- Toxic Substances Control Act
- Safe Drinking Water Act
- National Environmental Policy Act (NEPA)

their decisions on the quality of the environment. This category includes the National Environmental Policy Act and the similar laws adopted by most states.

Industry Participation   Companies affected by environmental laws should pay close attention to legislative and regulatory initiatives. Frequently companies can take an active role in shaping such initiatives to protect their interests. Congressional or administrative agency staff may be unaware of how a proposed law or regulation may affect a particular industry. Usually congressional or administrative agency staff welcome constructive industry participation in the law and rule-making process, particularly when a company can propose alternative ways to accomplish the same legislative goals. Environmental laws and regulations are constantly changing as new threats to human health and the environment become apparent, and as new ways are discovered to manage such threats safely and economically. The prudent company anticipates these changes and participates constructively in the legislative and rule-making process.

Popular Initiatives

Sometimes the public grows impatient with the legislative process and takes matters into its own hands through the initiative process. An *initiative* is a law submitted directly to the electorate for approval. If a majority of the voters vote in favor of the initiative, it becomes law without the need for approval by the legislature. For example, in California, citizens were concerned that many commercial products contain substances known to cause cancer. They voted for Proposition 65, which now requires the state to identify all substances known to the state to cause cancer. As of mid-1994, there were approximately 474 toxic chemicals on the California list. Any business that knowingly causes exposure to such substances must provide a warning to the persons exposed unless the exposure presents no significant risk. Also exempted are exposures for which federal warning law governs in a manner that preempts state authority. Many companies, including Gillette Co., the maker of Liquid Paper correction fluid, have reformulated their products rather than label them with cancer warnings. Because California represents 15% of the U.S. market, the law has affected the formulation of products nationwide.

> 66
>
> *Many companies have reformulated their products rather than label them with cancer warnings.*

Ethical Consideration

Environmental laws establish minimum standards to which companies must adhere. However, a company may decide to adopt stricter standards, either because the minimum standards do not sufficiently protect the environment, or because the jurisdiction in which the company operates has not yet established any standards. For example, a company operating in a third-world country may choose to apply the standards that apply to its operations in more developed countries with established pollution prevention programs.

■ Administration of Environmental Laws

All of the federal laws that set national goals and policies for environmental protection are administered by the Environmental Protection Agency (EPA), except for the National Environmental Policy Act, which is administered by the Council on Environmental Quality. State programs administer state laws, and also federal laws with the authorization of the EPA.

The Environmental Protection Agency

The EPA was created in 1970 by an executive order and operates under the supervision of the president. It is not an independent agency and, as of September 1994, does not have cabinet rank. The EPA administrator and assistant administrators are appointed by the president with the advice and consent of the Senate. Several of the assistant administrators are responsible for administering the agency's regulatory programs; others have internal administrative functions. These national program managers share responsibility with the ten regional administrators who head each of the ten EPA regional offices. The national managers at headquarters develop policy and set goals for the regional offices. The regional administrators take responsibility for day-to-day program operation.

State Programs

State environmental laws and programs often predate the comparable federal programs. Moreover, many states have laws that are more stringent and more comprehensive than the federal laws. For example, California's hazardous waste-management laws, water quality control laws, underground tank regulations, and ban on land disposal of certain hazardous wastes all predated and in some cases provided the model for subsequent federal legislation.

Because of the prior existence of state environmental programs, and in order to reduce the burden of administration for the EPA, the EPA may authorize or approve a state program in lieu of the federal program in that state. The EPA does not delegate its federal authority; it merely approves a state program as "equivalent to or more stringent than" the federal program and then refrains from implementing the federal program in that state. However, the EPA generally provides oversight. It retains its enforcement authority and may revoke its authorization if the state program fails to meet federal requirements.

■ Selected Federal Statutes

The National Environmental Policy Act (NEPA), discussed in chapters 6 and 17, is the cornerstone of environmental protection in the United States. Together with its state law counterparts, it affects all business activities that require governmental authorizations, permits, or licenses. The Clean Air Act, the Clean Water Act, and the Resource Conservation and Recovery Act are discussed as examples of environmental statutes that control the release of pollutants into the air, water, and land. The Comprehensive Environmental Response, Compensation, and Liability Act (CERCLA or Superfund) is discussed as an example of a remedial statute with broad application to all kinds of businesses and individuals. More than any other law, CERCLA has made environmental liability a concern of business management and an issue in most business transactions.

> 66
>
> *More than any other law, CERCLA has made environmental liability a concern of business management and an issue in most business transactions.*

The Clean Air Act

The Clean Air Act, as amended by the Clean Air Act of 1990,[1] sets four kinds of air quality goals. First, it requires the EPA to establish *national ambient air quality standards,* that is, to establish the maximum levels of pollutants in the outdoor air that, with adequate margins of safety, are compatible with public health. Standards have been set for six pollutants: (1) particulate matter, (2) sulfur dioxide, (3) ozone, (4) nitrogen dioxide, (5) carbon monoxide, and (6) lead. Every state and locality must seek to achieve and maintain these national air quality standards, which are periodically revised.

Second, the Clean Air Act requires that air quality not be allowed to deteriorate in those areas that already meet the national ambient air quality standards. Third, the act requires the preservation of natural visibility within the major national parks and wilderness areas. Fourth, it requires the EPA to establish emission standards that protect public health, with an ample margin of safety, from hazardous air pollutants.

The national ambient air quality standards are to be achieved through: (1) state implementation plans approved by the EPA; (2) technological controls, including new source performance standards, set by the EPA; and (3) mobile source controls set by the EPA. The *state implementation plans (SIPs)* prescribe emission-control measures for motor vehicles and for stationary sources existing prior to 1970. The SIPs also establish programs for state regulation of the "modification, construction, and operation of any stationary source." The SIPs include special programs for areas in each state that have not yet attained the national ambient air quality standards. For those areas that have attained ambient air quality standards, the SIPs contain a program for prevention of significant deterioration. The SIPs vary considerably in their content and procedures from state to state. In large states like California, the SIPs may be developed and administered by local or regional districts. These districts often promulgate their own rules, which are often, but not always, incorporated into the SIP.

The EPA establishes performance standards for new sources, based on the best control technology available for a category of similar sources. The idea is that by requiring new sources to utilize the best control technology available, the sources of pollution will gradually be

---

1. 42 U.S.C. §§ 7401 *et seq.* (1988 & Supp. 1992).

eliminated. Also, it is hoped that adherance to the performance standards will ensure roughly equal treatment of similar sources throughout the nation. Before construction of major sources of emissions in areas that have achieved national ambient air quality goals is allowed to begin, case-by-case determinations of the best available control technology (BACT) are required. *BACT* is defined as an emission limitation that the permitting authority determines achieves the maximum reduction of pollutants, taking into account energy, environmental, and economic considerations. The permitting authority may consider the cost of the technology only in relation to the reduction of pollutants it achieves. Before construction of major sources of emissions in nonattainment areas, case-by-base determinations of the lowest achievable emission rate (LAER) for the sources are required. New sources include not only new plants but also modifications of existing plants if these cause a significant increase in emissions.

Clean Air Act of 1990   In late 1990, Congress passed a major revision of the Clean Air Act.[2] The amendments provide new deadlines for attaining ambient air quality standards, but also put added pressure on those areas of the country that do not yet meet national ambient air quality standards. If a nonattainment area fails to develop an adequate plan to attain the national standard, the federal government is required to impose penalties, such as bans on construction of new sources of pollution, limits on the use of federal highway funds, limits on drinking water hookups, and the withholding of federal air pollution funds.

The law also requires reductions in vehicle tail-pipe emissions of certain pollutants, the use of reformulated gasoline, and mandates that fleets use clean, low-emission fuels in some nonattainment areas. Major sources of some 200 "hazardous air pollutants" are required to meet new emission limits based on "maximum achievable control technology." Electric power plants must reduce emissions that lead to the formation of acid rain. Finally, the law phases out methylchloroform and chlorofluorocarbons, and places limitations on the production of certain substitute chemicals.[3]

The EPA estimated in 1992 that implementing the legislation would cost the nation approximately $25 billion a year. The law is likely to affect almost every business in the United States. In fact, the 1990 Clean Air Act amendments have been referred to as industrial policy legislation. By affecting land use decisions and transportation changes, as well as imposing emission controls, the bill will determine what areas of the country and what industrial sectors will be able to grow over the next 20 years or more.

The Clean Water Act

The Federal Water Pollution Control Act[4] was adopted in 1972, and was substantially amended by the Clean Water Act of 1977 and by the Water Quality Act of 1987. The original act, as amended, is commonly referred to as the Clean Water Act. The principal goal of the Clean Water Act is to eliminate the discharge of pollutants into the navigable waters of the United States. *Navigable waters* are all "waters of the United States which are used in interstate commerce," including "all freshwater wetlands that are adjacent to all other covered waterways."

The principal regulatory program established by the Clean Water Act is the National Pollutant Discharge Elimination System (NPDES), which requires permits for the discharge of pollutants from any "point source" to navigable waters. EPA regulations establish national *effluent limitations,* which impose increasingly stringent restrictions on pollutant discharges, based on the availability of economic treatment and recycling technologies. More stringent restrictions are imposed on new sources through the setting of "national standards of performance." General and specific industry "pretreatment standards" are set for discharges to publicly owned sewage treatment works (POTWs). The pretreatment standards are designed to ensure the effective operation of the POTW and to avoid the "pass-through" of pollutants. The POTW in turn must comply with its own NPDES permit for the discharge of treated waters. The NPDES program is administered largely through approved state programs. However, the EPA maintains NPDES authority in areas not within the jurisdiction of states housing EPA-approved programs.

The following case addresses the requirement that the EPA establish effluent limitations based on the best available technology economically achievable.

---

2. Pub. L. No. 101-549, 104 Stat. 2399 (1990) (codified in scattered sections 42 U.S.C.).

3. For a discussion of the impact of the act on an industrial company, see Barbara Rosewicz, "Sweeping Change: How Clean-Air Bill Will Force DuPont into Costly Moves," *The Wall Street Journal,* May 25, 1990, A1.

---

4. 33 U.S.C. §§ 1351 *et seq.* (1988 & Supp. 1992).

Economic Perspective
Selling the Right to Pollute

In 1990, Congress amended the Clean Air Act to allow companies that exceed air quality requirements to sell their pollution rights or credit to other companies, particularly public utilities that burn high-sulfur coal to generate power. Under the act, the Environmental Protection Agency set strict spot emissions limits to take effect in 1995, covering 110 of the nation's dirtiest power plants. Stricter advance limits, applicable to 800 plants, will take effect by the year 2000.

Since Congress amended the act, several trades have been privately arranged between utilities. However, the first public auction of emission allowances did not take place until March 1993, when the Chicago Board of Trade offered sulfur dioxide emission allowances issued by the Environmental Protection Agency. Utility companies purchased 95% of the 50,010 emission allowances. Each allowance enables the buyer to discharge one ton of sulfur dioxide. These utilities claim that the allowances will enable them to delay the need to install scrubbers.

At the second annual auction in March 1994, winning bidders paid an average of $159 per credit, up from $156 the year before. By requiring polluters to buy a limited number of permits, the EPA hopes to cut annual sulfur dioxide emissions in half by the year 2000. Sulfur dioxide, a by-product of burning coal, causes acid rain.

The Chicago Board of Trade began trading futures contracts on the pollution permits in 1994. The concept of trading pollution rights has been hailed by utilities and environmentalists as a crucial element in the plan to control acid rain by creating a cost-efficient mechanism to reduce sulfur dioxide emissions by power plants.

Several brokerage firms have formed their own market for selling air pollution credit commodities, challenging the Chicago Board of Trade. A brokered trade in 1994 involving a New Jersey utility and a Connecticut utility was the first interstate trade involving nitrogen oxide credits under the free market system. Nitrogen oxide contributes to smog. Trading in pollution credits, which is favored by economists and some environmentalists, seeks to achieve emissions reductions at the minimum cost by allowing the cleanup to be made wherever it is cheapest.

■ **A Case in Point:**   **Summary**

Case 16.1
NATURAL RESOURCES DEFENSE COUNCIL, INC. v. ENVIRONMENTAL PROTECTION AGENCY
United States Court of Appeals for the Ninth Circuit
863 F.2d 1420 (9th Cir. 1988).

FACTS In 1984, the EPA issued a National Pollutant Discharge Elimination System (NPDES) general permit authorizing the discharge of pollutants from offshore oil and gas drilling operations in the Gulf of Mexico. The Natural Resources Defense Council, Inc. (NRDC) challenged the permit on the ground that it was too lenient. The American Petroleum Institute (API) and other industry representatives challenged the permit on the ground that it was too stringent. The state of Florida claimed that the EPA required state certification for the permit because the permit would allow the discharge of pollutants into Florida's waters.

The NRDC argued that the permit was too lenient because it did not require the use of the best available technology (BAT) for the disposal of wastewater brought to the surface with oil during the drilling operations. The NRDC claimed that it was technically feasible to reinject the wastewater, also known as "produced water," into subsurface geologic formations. By allowing the produced water to be discharged into the ocean, the NRDC argued, the permit violated the Clean Water Act.

Case **16.1** continued on following page

Case **16.1** *continued*

The permit contained a BAT effluent limitation restricting toxic pollutants to 30,000 parts per million (ppm). But the permit allowed the EPA to set "alternative toxicity limitations" if a discharger using toxic drilling fluids could not meet the 30,000 ppm toxicity limitation. The API claimed that the 30,000 ppm toxicity limitation was too stringent. The NRDC claimed that the EPA lacked the authority to set alternative toxicity limitations without discernible standards. The NRDC also claimed that the toxicity limitation was too lenient because it did not limit discharges of cadmium and mercury, which are deemed toxic pollutants. The EPA had merely proposed the use of a "cleaner" drilling fluid to reduce the concentrations of cadmium and mercury in the discharges.

ISSUE PRESENTED   In establishing effluent limitations, how strictly must the EPA adhere to the Clean Water Act's requirement that limitations be based on the "best available technology economically achievable?"

SUMMARY OF OPINION   The U.S. Court of Appeals held that the permit was invalid in two respects: (1) the alternative toxicity limitations were contrary to law because they lacked any discernible standards; and (2) the permit was contrary to law because it did not include toxicity limitations for cadmium and mercury discharges.

The court found that the 30,000 ppm toxicity limitation was not arbitrary or capricious. It deferred to the EPA's scientific determinations and held that the BAT toxicity limitation was within the EPA's discretion. However, the court stated that the EPA's discretion was not unlimited, and found that the alternative toxicity limitations authorized under the permit lacked any specific criteria. The alternative toxicity limitations were not authorized as BAT under the Clean Water Act, as BAT must be established in accordance with technological standards and based on factors specified in the Clean Water Act.

As for the claims relating to the reinjection technique as BAT for produced waters, the court found that the EPA did not act arbitrarily or capriciously by not requiring reinjection. Although the EPA had proposed industrywide BAT standards for offshore drilling, no standards had actually been promulgated. The EPA explained that it required additional information on the feasibility and cost of retrofitting existing offshore facilities before adopting a standard requiring the reinjection technology for existing facilities. Moreover, it would be inconsistent to require the reinjection technique as BAT for the Gulf of Mexico facilities when the national standards did not require it. If the Gulf permit were more stringent than the national standard, antibacksliding rules would prevent the EPA from later amending it to conform to the national standard. On the other hand, the more lenient permit could be modified to incorporate a more stringent national standard if one were later adopted.

The court rejected the EPA's argument that it lacked sufficient economic data to determine whether the reinjection technique should be required as BAT for existing facilities. The Clean Water Act requires BAT to be technologically available and economically achievable, and it must represent a "commitment of the maximum resources economically possible to the ultimate goal of eliminating all polluting discharges." The EPA is not required to calculate BAT costs with precision. It needs only a "rough idea" of the costs industry would incur. However, the court accepted the argument that the EPA was waiting for adoption of the national standard before requiring reinjection as BAT in the permit.

RESULT   The court found the NPDES general permit invalid. Although the EPA may use its discretion in setting effluent limitations to avoid inconsistencies in nationwide industry practices, it is required to set effluent standards based on discernible standards. These standards would require the EPA to establish reasonable, but not necessarily precise, estimates of costs to the industry.

COMMENTS   The EPA's concern about causing inconsistent national practices within an industry is well founded. Compliance with environmental regulations can be a significant cost of doing business. Subjecting competitors to differing regulatory standards could affect competition within the industry. Similar considerations arise when regulating companies that operate in countries with different environmental standards.

The Resource Conservation and Recovery Act

The Solid Waste Disposal Act, as amended by the Resource Conservation and Recovery Act of 1976 and the Hazardous and Solid Waste Amendments of 1984,[5] governs the management of hazardous wastes. The act, known as RCRA, authorizes the EPA to identify and list hazardous wastes, to develop standards for the management of hazardous wastes by generators and transporters of wastes, and to set standards for the construction and operation of hazardous waste treatment, storage, and disposal facilities.

Cradle-to-Grave Responsibility   RCRA imposes "cradle-to-grave" responsibility on generators of hazardous waste. Each generator must obtain an EPA identification number and use a transportation manifest when transporting wastes for treatment or disposal. This allows the EPA to track the transportation, treatment, and disposal of hazardous wastes from the generator's facility to the final disposal site. A manifest is also required to transport hazardous wastes to an authorized storage facility.

Owners and operators of hazardous waste facilities must obtain permits and comply with stringent standards for the construction and operation of their facilities. These standards include maintaining certain liability insurance coverage and providing financial assurances that show the owner/operator has the financial wherewithal to close the facility at the appropriate time and to maintain it properly after closure.

Even though hazardous waste facilities are closely regulated, companies that generate hazardous wastes must carefully select treatment, transportation, and disposal facilities. Liability may be imposed on persons who own or operate the facility or on persons who have used the facility for the storage, treatment, or disposal of wastes. As the following case demonstrates, *persons* include the companies involved and also individual employees, officers, and possibly shareholders who participate in management.

---

5. 42 U.S.C. §§ 6901 *et seq.* (1988 & Supp. 1992).

■   **A Case in Point:**   **In the Language of the Court**

Case 16.2
UNITED STATES v. NORTHEASTERN PHARMACEUTICAL AND CHEMICAL CO.
United States Court of Appeals for the Eighth Circuit
810 F.2d 726 (8th Cir. 1986),
cert. denied, 484 U.S. 848, 108 S.Ct. 146 (1987).

FACTS   Michaels formed Northeastern Pharmaceutical and Chemical Company (NEPACCO) and was a major shareholder and president. The company had a manufacturing plant in Verona, Missouri, and the manufacturing process produced various hazardous and toxic by-products. The by-products were pumped into a holding tank which was periodically emptied by waste haulers.

In 1971, a waste hauler named Mills approached Ray, a chemical plant manager employed by NEPACCO, and proposed disposing of some of

*Case **16.2** continued on following page*

*Case **16.2** continued*

NEPACCO's wastes at a nearby farm. The plant manager, Ray, visited the farm and with the approval of Lee, the vice president and a shareholder of NEPACCO, arranged for disposal of wastes at the Denney farm. Approximately eighty-five 55-gallon drums were dumped into a large trench on the farm. In 1976, NEPACCO was liquidated, and the assets remaining after payment of creditors were distributed to its shareholders.

In 1979, the EPA investigated the site (following an anonymous tip) and discovered dozens of badly deteriorated drums containing hazardous waste buried at the farm. The EPA took remedial action. It then sought to recover its costs under the Resource Conservation and Recovery Act (RCRA) and other statutes.

ISSUE PRESENTED   Can the officers and shareholders of a dissolved chemical company and a transporter of hazardous substances be held liable under RCRA as individuals and be required to pay the costs of remedial action at a hazardous waste disposal site?

OPINION   McMillian, J., writing for the U.S. Court of Appeals:

. . . .

. . . The government argues that the standard of liability under RCRA . . . is strict liability, not negligence, and that liability under RCRA can be imposed even though the acts of disposal occurred before RCRA became effective in 1976. We agree.

. . . .

. . . From the legislative history of the 1984 amendments, it is clear the Congress intended RCRA, as initially enacted and amended, to impose liability without fault or negligence and to apply to the present conditions resulting from past activities. In other words, RCRA, as initially enacted and amended, applies to past non-negligent off-site generators like NEPACCO and to non-negligent past transporters like Mills.

. . . .

. . . The government argues Lee and Michaels are individually liable as "contributors" under RCRA. We agree.

RCRA imposed strict liability upon "any person" who is contributing or who has contributed to the disposal of hazardous substances that may present an imminent and substantial endangerment to health or the environment. As defined by the statute, the term "person" includes both individuals and corporations and does not exclude corporate officers and employees. . . .

. . . .

RESULT   Michaels and Lee, the corporate officers responsible for arranging the disposal of the hazardous substances that presented an imminent and substantial danger to human health and the environment, and Mills, the transporter of the substances, were, among others, strictly liable for reimbursing the EPA's response costs under RCRA.

COMMENTS   The court made clear that under RCRA (as under most environmental laws), "person" includes both corporations and individuals and does not exclude officers and shareholders. Moreover, persons who "contributed" to the improper waste disposal can include persons who had no direct involvement but had the authority to control the corporation's actions and failed to do so.

Questions
1. Could a hauler of waste materials be held liable for having transported substances that were substantially more hazardous than he was led to believe?
2. As NEPACCO's corporate president and major shareholder, Michaels was the individual in charge of and directly responsible for all of NEPACCO's operations, and he had the ultimate authority to control the disposal of NEPACCO's hazardous substances. If he had been aware that hazardous by-products were being dumped at a nearby farm and had voiced strong concerns that were squelched at board meetings, would it still be fair to hold him liable?

Ethical Consideration

Note that Lee's decision to use the Denney farm for disposal occurred in 1971, before the adoption of RCRA in 1976. This case illustrates how important it is for managers to consider not just what the law requires of them at the time, but what future effects their actions might have on the environment. The case also demonstrates that managers should consider doing more than merely complying with existing requirements. Consider the lesson of this case in the context of operations in Third-World countries. Consider also the shortsighted cost analysis by NEPACCO. What may be cost effective in the short term may not be in the long term, particularly where the environment and human health are concerned.

to render them less hazardous. Congress set a timetable for the EPA to implement the land disposal restrictions and to establish appropriate treatment standards for all hazardous wastes. To comply with land disposal requirements, companies that generate hazardous waste may have to make substantial capital investments in treatment systems or may have to incur increased costs for having wastes treated elsewhere prior to disposal.

The 1984 amendments also required generators of hazardous waste to certify that they have a program in place to reduce the quantity and toxicity of their wastes. They must also certify that they are disposing of their wastes in a manner that, to the extent practicable, minimizes future threats to human health and the environment. Many companies are changing their raw materials, changing their production processes, and developing ways to recycle or otherwise use wastes. For some companies, these changes may result in reduced costs of operation over the long term.

Environmental regulatory programs can both increase costs and create opportunities for cost savings. Because the costs of hazardous-waste management can be substantial, the company that develops cost-efficient and forward-looking waste management practices may have a considerable advantage over its less efficient competitors.

New Concepts for Waste Management The original RCRA program was designed to ensure safe storage, treatment, and disposal of hazardous waste. In 1984 Congress adopted new standards for hazardous waste management. For example, it amended RCRA to ban the disposal of hazardous wastes onto land without treatment

66

Environmental regulatory programs can both increase costs and create opportunities for cost savings.

The Federal Superfund Law

The Comprehensive Environmental Response, Compensation, and Liability Act of 1980 (CERCLA), as amended by the Superfund Amendments and Reauthorization Act of 1986,[6] more than any other environmental law, has affected businesses and individuals that do not themselves produce environmental pollutants. CERCLA authorizes the federal government to investigate and take remedial action in response to a release or threatened release of hazardous substances to the environment. CERCLA establishes what is now called the Hazardous Substance Superfund to finance federal response activity. The Superfund was replenished in 1986 with a total of $8.5 billion for a five-year period ending in 1991, and another $5.1 billion for the period commencing in 1991 and ending in September 1994.

How federal Superfund money will be spent is determined in part by the EPA's National Priorities List, which identifies sites that may require remedial action. The sites are listed by the EPA in a rule-making proceeding based on a *hazard ranking score,* which represents the degree of risk that the site presents to the environment and public health.

The EPA may undertake remedial action itself or require responsible persons to do so. If the EPA performs the remedial work, it can recover its costs from the responsible persons. The *responsible persons* include: (1) the present owner or operator of the facility; (2) the owner or operator at the time of disposal of the hazardous substance; (3) any person who arranged for treatment or disposal of hazardous substances at the facility; and (4) any person who transported hazardous substances to and selected the facility.[7]

Liability Provisions   The courts interpret the liability provisions of CERCLA broadly in order to effectuate the remedial policies of the statute. It is now well established in the case law interpreting CERCLA that the present owner of the land can be held liable for the cleanup of hazardous substances disposed of on the land by another person, usually a previous owner or tenant.

Individuals—including shareholders, corporate officers, and employees who have control or authority over the facility or who arrange for the disposal of hazardous substances there—may be personally liable for the costs of response at the facility. For example, in the NEPACCO case discussed earlier, the court also held the

vice-president of NEPACCO liable under CERCLA as a person who arranged for disposal of hazardous substances at the nearby farm facility.

In *United States v. Kayser-Roth Corp.,*[8] a seminal CERCLA case, a parent corporation was held directly liable for response costs as the "owner and operator" of a facility owned and operated by its subsidiary. In this case, the Rhode Island Department of Health and the EPA discovered that the drinking water supplies near Forestdale, Rhode Island, were polluted with a chlorinated solvent called trichloroethylene (TCE). Eventually they traced the TCE to a nearby textile manufacturing facility that had been operated by Stamina Mills, Inc., between 1952 and 1975. Stamina Mills ceased to exist as a corporation in 1977. Pursuant to its CERCLA authority, the EPA conducted remedial activities at the site and then sought to recover its costs from Kayser-Roth Corporation, the former parent company of Stamina Mills. In its decision, the Federal District Court for the District of Rhode Island considered: (1) whether Kayser-Roth itself was an "operator" of the facility under CERCLA by virtue of its control of Stamina Mills's operations; and (2) whether the "corporate veil" of Stamina Mills should be pierced and Kayser-Roth treated as an "owner" of the facility.[9]

The court determined that Kayser-Roth could not be held liable under CERCLA as an "operator" merely because of its stock ownership. However, the court held that Kayser-Roth was liable as an "operator" because of the pervasive control it exercised over Stamina Mills's operations. The court relied on these facts: (1) Kayser-Roth had total monetary control, including control over budgeting and collection of accounts receivable; (2) all contracts with governmental agencies regarding environmental matters had to be funneled through the parent; (3) all real estate transactions, including leases, had to be

---

6. 42 U.S.C. §§ 9601 *et seq.* (1988 & Supp. 1992).

7. 42 U.S.C. § 9607 (1988).

---

8. 724 F.Supp. 15 (D.R.I. 1989), *aff'd*, 910 F.2d 24 (1st Cir. 1990), *cert. denied*, 498 U.S. 1084 (1991).

9. Note that the court's approach to piercing the corporate veil was based on *federal common law* principles, that is, the principles found in cases that the courts have developed for interpreting federal statutes. (This federal common law is to be distinguished from the application of federal law in diversity cases invalidated by *Erie Railroad v. Tompkins*, discussed in chapter 4, which concerned how the federal courts interpret state law.) Under federal common law, courts may give less respect to the corporate form than under the common law of many states (discussed in chapter 20). Federal common law is still developing under CERCLA. Some courts in CERCLA cases have refused to pierce the corporate veil. However, management would be prudent to emphasize corporate separateness in order to protect parent corporations against potential CERCLA liabilities.

approved by the parent; (4) all capital expenditures exceeding $5,000 had to be approved by the parent; and (5) Kayser-Roth personnel were placed in nearly all of Stamina Mills's officer and director positions. The court further determined that the corporate veil of Stamina Mills should be pierced to impose liability on Kayser-Roth as an "owner" under CERCLA. The court reasoned that to allow the parent company to escape liability would frustrate the purpose of the federal statute, which did not place any particular importance on the corporate form. Because of its pervasive control of Stamina Mills, Kayser-Roth was therefore liable as an "owner" under CERCLA.

The following case suggests that both sister and parent corporations can be held liable under CERCLA for the monitoring costs of properties that may potentially have been contaminated by hazardous substances.

■ **A Case in Point:**   **In the Language of the Court**

Case 16.3
LANSFORD-COALDALE JOINT WATER AUTHORITY v. TONOLLI CORP.
United States Court of Appeals for the Third Circuit
4 F.3d 1209 (3d Cir. 1993).

FACTS Lansford-Coaldale Joint Water Authority (Authority) provides public water in Carbon County, Pennsylvania. The Authority's groundwater production and supply wells are adjacent to a site formerly used for lead smelting that is owned by Tonolli Pennsylvania (Tonolli PA). There had been release of hazardous substances on the Tonolli site, and the Authority was concerned that there might be contamination in its wells. After conducting a study, the Authority sued Tonolli PA and its sister corporation Tonolli Canada (a Canadian corporation) and the parent corporation IFIM (a Dutch corporation), alleging common-law claims and a claim for private cost recovery under CERCLA. The Authority alleged that, among other things, the defendants were owners or operators of a company that posed a threat of future contamination to their water supply. Tonolli PA became insolvent, but the proceedings remained against Tonolli Canada and IFIM.

The trial court denied Authority recovery on all claims.

ISSUE PRESENTED Can the sister or parent corporation of a company be held liable for monitoring costs under CERCLA as an "operator" of a site of hazardous substances?

OPINION BECKER, J., writing for the U.S. Court of Appeals:

. . . .

. . . CERCLA authorizes recovery for the costs of "such actions as may be necessary to monitor, assess, and evaluate the release or threat of release of hazardous substances." It is well established that under this provision a plaintiff can recover its monitoring and evaluation costs from a release or threatened release without proving that its property was actually contaminated by the defendant. . . .

. . . .

. . . There is general agreement that under CERCLA "owner" liability and "operator" liability denote two separate concepts and hence require two separate standards for determining whether they apply.

Under CERCLA, a corporation may be held liable as an owner for the actions of its subsidiary corporation in situations in which it is determined that piercing the corporate veil is warranted. Operator liability, in contrast, is

*Case **16.3** continued on following page*

*Case **16.3** continued*

generally reserved for those situations in which a parent or sister corporation is deemed, due to the specifics of its relationship with its affiliated corporation, to have had substantial control over the facility in question. Courts
are divided as to whether operator liability should be predicated on the
actual control one corporation has over the other, or whether the corporation's capacity or authority to control is sufficient.

. . . .

. . . Under the actual control standard, a corporation will only be held
liable for the environmental violations of another corporation when there is
evidence of substantial control exercised by one corporation over the activities of the other. In contrast, under the authority-to-control test, operator liability is imposed as long as one corporation had the capability to control,
even if it was never utilized.

. . . .

We follow the test [that]. . . "to be an operator requires more than merely
complete ownership and the concomitant general authority or ability to control that comes with ownership. At a minimum, it requires actual involvement
in the activities in the subsidiary." Whereas a corporation's "mere oversight"
of the subsidiary or sister corporation's business in a "manner appropriate
and consistent with the investment relationship" does not ordinarily result in
operator liability, a corporation's "actual participation and control" of the
other corporation's decision-making does.

The determination whether a corporation has exerted sufficient control to
warrant imposition of operator liability requires an inherently fact-intensive
study involving consideration of the totality of the circumstances presented.
The factors courts should consider focus on the extent of the corporation's
involvement in the other corporation's day-to-day operations and its policy-
making decisions. . . .

In addition, because the essential focus of the actual control test is the
control of one corporation over another, not only may a parent corporation
be deemed the operator of its subsidiary, but also a corporation may also
be considered the operator of its sister corporation. In other words, the test
is concerned with control rather than ownership and there is no reason not
to hold a corporation liable when it exercises substantial management control over an affiliated corporation.

. . . [T]here are several potentially significant facts that the district court's
findings do not address . . . [Tonolli Canada and Tonolli PA] shared common officers during the period in question. . . . [T]he fact that the same
people served as the president and chief financial officer for the two corporations is not, without more, enough to conclude that one corporation
should be deemed the operator of another. On the other hand, the existence of common high-level officers is troubling and raises serious questions about the independence of the two companies.

. . . .

. . . Given the lack of evidence at trial either way regarding IFIM's liability
. . . [we] remand to the district court. On remand, the district court should
articulate a basis for its judgment in favor of IFIM. . . .

. . . .

RESULT The court affirmed the lower court's judgment in favor of Tonolli Canada and IFIM for the claim based on recovery of securing an alternative water supply and treating the water from its existing wells.

With respect to the Authority's claim for monitoring and evaluation costs, the court held that whether a corporation is liable as an "operator" under CERCLA for the environmental violations of another company, the "actual control" test, rather than "authority-to-control" test applies. The court remanded the case for fact-finding to determine whether the sister and parent corporations could be held liable under CERCLA as "operators" of the site.

Questions

1. In applying the actual control test, would a court be more concerned with the depth or the breadth of control? What if a parent corporation was financially very involved on a day-to-day basis with a subsidiary, but did not concern itself with how it conducted its operations?

2. CERCLA imposes strict liability. Would it be equitable to hold a sister corporation incorporated in Canada liable if the substances were not considered hazardous in Canada?

CERCLA imposes strict liability, meaning that the responsible parties are liable regardless of fault. The law also allows the imposition of joint and several liability, which means that any one responsible party can be held liable for the total amount of response costs and natural resource damages even though others may also be responsible for the release. A responsible party held jointly and severally liable can seek cost recovery or contribution from other responsible parties, provided the other parties are still in existence and able to pay. Many times they are not. Thus, joint and several liability allows the government to select financially sound parties from whom to collect response costs and put the burden of collecting these costs on the selected defendants.

Punitive Damages CERCLA allows recovery for cleanup costs, but under section 107(a) does not allow punitive damages unless recklessness is found. The case of *United States v. Hooker Chemicals & Plastics Corp.*[10] examined the extent to which one company was liable for the adverse effects of chemical dumping. Hooker Chemical Company had used a 16-acre plot of land, the Love Canal site, in the city of Niagara Falls, New York, as a landfill for toxic chemical wastes from Hooker's Niagara Falls plant between 1942 and 1954. There was evidence that some of the containers were not properly sealed. Due to poor drainage and Hooker's dumping practices, the landfill presented serious problems to the surrounding area. The presence of flammable chemicals with flashpoints of less than 100°F led to frequent fires, some with flames as high as 20 feet. After rainstorms, noxious fumes would permeate the neighborhood. Frequent explosions from the site would propel debris for distances as great as two blocks. Children swimming in unfilled parts of the nearby canal reported cases of skin rash.

In 1953 Hooker transferred the site to the city school board to build a school and playground. A year later, an elementary school was built in the central section of the parcel. Even after Hooker learned of the potential hazards of the substances it had dumped, the company did not offer the school board additional information which might have protected the site's users. In 1978, a health emergency was announced when noticeable quantities of chemical residue began seeping into the basements of nearby homes. In 1985 Hooker settled a lawsuit with 1,300 current and former residents of the area for $20 million for personal injury and property damage claims.

The State of New York alleged reckless or wanton disregard for the health and safety of the local residents surrounding the Love Canal site. The district court for the western district of New York found that Hooker Chemical Company's behavior was negligent, but did not rise to the level of recklessness, and therefore punitive damages were not appropriate.

---

10. 850 F. Supp. 993 (W.D.N.Y. 1994).

Defenses   CERCLA provides only three defenses to liability. The defendant must show that the release of hazardous substances was caused solely by: (1) an act of God (that is, an unavoidable natural disaster, such as an earthquake); (2) an act of war; or (3) the act or omission of a third party, provided that certain other requirements are met. To assert the *third-party defense*, a responsible party must show that a third party was not an employee, and had no contractual relationship with the person asserting the defense. If the facility was acquired from the third party, the written instrument of transfer is deemed to create a contractual relationship, unless the purchaser acquired the facility after the hazardous substances were disposed of and without any knowledge or reason to know that hazardous substances had previously been disposed of at the facility. To establish that the purchaser had no reason to know that hazardous substances were disposed of at the facility, the purchaser must show that, prior to the sale, it undertook "all appropriate inquiry into the previous ownership and uses of the property consistent with good commercial or customary practice in an effort to minimize liability."[11]

---

11. 42 U.S.C. § 9601(35)(B) (1988).

Effect on Business Transactions   The average cost of response by the EPA at a Superfund site is estimated at $25 million. Response costs for some sites may be much higher. The magnitude of this liability has caused dramatic changes in the way companies, their lenders, and their investors investigate business transactions involving interests in real property. Many companies engage expert environmental counsel and consultants to assist in what is called the due diligence investigation.

Allocation of the risk of liability under CERCLA and other environmental laws has become a significant issue in the negotiation of agreements and documents relating to business transactions. Buyers, sellers, lenders, and equity investors may be exposed to large CERCLA liabilities. The following case demonstrates the potential exposure of a bank that participates in the day-to-day operational management of a facility.

■   **A Case in Point:**   **Summary**

Case 16.4
UNITED STATES v. MIRABILE
United States District Court for the Eastern District of Pennsylvania
15 Envtl.L.Rep. 20994
(E.D. Pa.1985).

FACTS   American Bank and Trust Company (ABT) held a mortgage on the site of the Turco paint-manufacturing plant. Turco became insolvent and in 1981 ABT foreclosed on the mortgage. ABT was the highest bidder at the sheriff's sale, but it never took title. Four months after the sale, ABT assigned its right to purchase the site to Anna and Thomas Mirabile, who took title through a sheriff's deed. Mellon Bank (through a predecessor) had a financing arrangement with Turco to supply working capital. Mellon Bank held a security interest in the inventory and other assets of Turco at the time of Turco's insolvency. The loan officer in charge of the Turco account was on an advisory board established by the president of Turco to oversee Turco's operations. When Turco began having financial difficulties, a Mellon Bank officer began participating in the management of Turco. Upon Turco's insolvency, Mellon Bank took possession of Turco's inventory. The Small Business Administration (SBA) also made a loan to Turco. The loan was secured by a second-lien security interest in Turco's machinery, equipment, inventory, and accounts receivable, as well as by a second mortgage on the real property. SBA regulations at the time required management assistance to accompany such loans, but no management assistance was ever given. The loan agreement also required Turco to obtain SBA approval prior to execution of certain contracts and placed certain restrictions on Turco's financial dealings.

After the Mirabiles purchased the Turco site, the EPA incurred costs for the removal of hazardous waste from the property. The United States filed an action under CERCLA to recover the EPA's costs from the Mirabiles. The Mirabiles in turn sued ABT and Mellon Bank as third-party defendants. ABT and Mellon then counterclaimed against the United States, alleging that the SBA was also potentially liable. The three lenders each filed a motion to dismiss for failure to state a claim.

ISSUE PRESENTED May secured creditors, including those who foreclosed on the site, who participate in day-to-day operational management of a facility be deemed "owners and operators" of the facility for purposes of CERCLA?

SUMMARY OF OPINION The Federal District Court recognized that the statutory definition of "owner and operator" specifically excludes those who hold a security interest in the facility, provided that they do not participate in management of the facility. The court analyzed how far the holder of a security interest could go in protecting its security interest without becoming "overly entangled" in management of the facility. The court determined that "management of the facility" must involve participation in operational, production, or waste-disposal activities. Involvement in the financial aspects of the business that operates the facility was insufficient to impose liability under CERCLA.

Although ABT held an equitable interest in the facility for four months after its successful bid at the sheriff's sale, ABT did not operate Turco's business, which had ceased operations prior to the sale. Under these circumstances, the court decided that ABT's actions at foreclosure were undertaken merely to protect its security interest. The court therefore granted ABT's motion to dismiss.

The SBA never took legal or equitable title, but its loan agreement did provide for the SBA to become involved in day-to-day management. The court determined, however, that such management did not take place. It therefore also dismissed the SBA from the action.

The court denied Mellon Bank's motion to dismiss, because the bank loan officer who became involved in Turco's day-to-day operations might have been involved in the operational (as opposed to financial) aspects of management. Thus further facts were needed for the court to reach a final disposition of the claim against Mellon Bank.

RESULT ATB and the SBA were found not liable because they had no involvement in the plant's day-to-day affairs. A third creditor, Mellon Bank, sent advisers, one of whom participated in day-to-day nonfinancial matters. The court reserved judgment on this creditor until further facts of Mellon's involvement were disclosed.

COMMENTS The *Mirabile* case stands for the proposition that secured creditors are protected from liability as "owners and operators" of a facility, provided that they do not participate in the day-to-day operation of the company that actually owns or operates the facility. Some degree of involvement in financial management and even the holding of an equitable interest following foreclosure may be protected activities, provided that they are undertaken in an effort to protect the creditor's security interest. However, *United States v. Fleet Factors Corp.*, a case decided by the United States Court of Appeals for the Eleventh Circuit in 1990 and again on remand in 1993 suggests that under a "management participation theory," a secured

*Case **16.4** continued on following page*

*Case **16.4** continued*

lender can be an owner or operator even if it does not participate in the day-to-day operations of the facility.[12]

Although *Fleet Factors* cannot overrule *Mirabile* because the two decisions were rendered in different circuits, it is an important case and has caused great concern within the lending community. The Eleventh Circuit Court stated that there is a level of participation that does not rise to that of active participation in the day-to-day management of a facility that nonetheless can cause a secured lender to be liable for the CERCLA violations of its borrower. According to *Fleet Factors,* if the secured lender's involvement with the facility is sufficiently broad to support the inference that it could affect or control hazardous waste decisions if it so chose, then the lender can be held liable. This holding clearly expands liability beyond the limits of *Mirabile.*

---

12. *United States v. Fleet Factors Corp.*, 901 F.2d 1550 (11th Cir. 1990), *cert. denied*, 498 U.S. 1046, 111 S.Ct. 752 (1991), on remand, 821 F.Supp. 707 (1993).

In the *Mirabile* case, none of the lenders took legal title to the facility. However, as the following case demonstrates, a lender that takes a deed in lieu of (in place of) foreclosure or that actually purchases a facility at the foreclosure sale may be deemed a present owner or operator under CERCLA.

■ **A Case in Point:**   **Summary**

Case 16.5
UNITED STATES v. MARY-LAND BANK & TRUST CO.
United States District Court for the District of Maryland
632 F.Supp. 573 (D.Md. 1986).

FACTS   During the 1970s, Maryland Bank & Trust (MB&T) loaned money to the owners and operators of a garbage and trash business. The loans were secured by a mortgage on land used by the business for garbage and trash disposal. During the early 1970s, the owners allowed the dumping of hazardous wastes on the site, including mercury and organics such as toluene. MB&T foreclosed on the mortgage and in 1982 purchased the land at the foreclosure sale. The EPA later investigated the site and removed more than 200 drums of chemical wastes. The EPA sought to recover its costs from MB&T under CERCLA. MB&T argued that it was a secured creditor, not an "owner and operator," and that even if it were an owner and operator, it was entitled to the third-party defense.

ISSUE PRESENTED   Is a bank that formerly held a mortgage on a parcel of land, and later purchased it at a foreclosure sale and continued to own it for nearly four years, liable under CERCLA for hazardous waste damage caused by the mortgagor and previous operator of the site?

SUMMARY OF OPINION   The Federal District Court held that MB&T was clearly the owner of the facility after 1982, and that it was not necessary for MB&T to have operated the facility. Current ownership of a facility would be sufficient to make MB&T liable under CERCLA. Moreover, the court determined that MB&T was not the holder of a security interest at the time of the EPA cleanup. The security interest, for purposes of CERCLA, terminated at the foreclosure sale. As to the third-party defense, the court determined that more facts were needed to determine whether MB&T had exercised reasonable care with respect to substances at the site and whether it took reasonable precautions at the site after it purchased the property.

RESULT　The bank that formerly held the mortgage on a parcel of land and later purchased the land at a foreclosure sale and continued to use it was required to reimburse the United States approximately $551,714 for the cost of hazardous waste cleanup.

COMMENTS　The *Mirabile* and *Maryland Bank* decisions stake out the ends of a continuum. More court decisions are needed to better describe how far a secured lender can go to protect its security interest. Clearly under the *Maryland Bank* case, purchasing the facility at foreclosure and holding the property for a period of several years will result in liability unless the lender has available the third-party defense. Until clear guidelines are established, any lender considering foreclosure should undertake "all appropriate inquiry" and seek to meet all of the other requirements discussed above for asserting the third-party defense to CERCLA liability. Lenders who take security in personal property may also be at risk. A lender who took possession of personal property and caused a release of hazardous substances on the debtor's real property during the removal and sale of the personal property has been held jointly and severally liable for the costs of cleanup of the debtor's property.

In April 1992, the EPA issued regulations that articulated a lender's scope of liability under CERCLA. Under the regulations, a lender could, without incurring liability, (1) investigate, monitor, or inspect a facility before creating a security interest, (2) engage in workout negotiations and activities, and (3) acquire full title to collateral property through foreclosure, as long as the lender did not participate in management of the facility before foreclosure and tried to divest itself of the property. The EPA regulations, however, were overruled by the U.S. Court of Appeals for the D.C. Circuit.[13] The court concluded that clarification of lender liability must come directly from Congress in the form of an amendment to CERCLA.

Legislation designed to protect secured lenders and persons acting in fiduciary capacities from liability under CERCLA was introduced in Congress in 1993. Legislation has also been introduced in some states to overcome the effect of antideficiency statutes where financial institutions find they have loaned monies for the purchase or improvement of what turns out to be polluted property. *(Antideficiency statutes* prevent the holder of a mortgage or deed of trust secured by real property from

suing the borrower to recover whatever is still owing after a foreclosure sale.)

■ Enforcement of Environmental Laws

Enforcement includes the monitoring of regulated companies' compliance with the environmental laws and the correction or punishment of violations.

Self-Reporting

not a criminal statute.

Many statutes and regulations require regulated companies to report certain facts to the EPA, such as the concentrations and/or the amounts of pollutants discharged from a facility. These reports may indicate a violation and may therefore be the subject of an enforcement action by the agency. There are severe penalties for filing false reports, including criminal sanctions for knowingly providing false information to a government agency.

Agency Inspections

The environmental laws provide broad authority to the administering agencies to conduct on-site inspections of plant facilities and their records. Many laws authorize the

---

13. *Kelley v. Environmental Protection Agency*, 15 F.3d 1100 (D.C. Cir. 1994).

agency to collect samples for analysis. Inspections may be conducted routinely or in response to reports or complaints from neighbors or employees. If criminal violations are suspected, the agency may choose to conduct an inspection under the authority of a search warrant. Violations observed during the inspection may be the subject of civil or criminal enforcement actions.

Enforcement Actions

Because the environmental laws are intended to accomplish such important societal goals, and violations of the laws may cause serious harm or injury, environmental regulatory agencies generally are given strong enforcement powers. For a first violation, the agency might issue a warning and impose a schedule for compliance. If the schedule is not met or the violations are repeated, more aggressive enforcement action will likely follow. Such action may take the form of an administrative order to take specified steps to achieve compliance, or a formal administrative complaint containing an assessment of administrative penalties. The penalties vary, but because they can be assessed for each day of each violation, they can be substantial for repeated, multiple, or long-standing violations.

In more egregious cases, the enforcing agency may initiate a civil lawsuit and/or a criminal prosecution. Courts are authorized in most instances to impose penalties of $25,000 to $50,000 per day of violation and to sentence individuals to jail terms of one or more years. In some cases, the agency may have authority to close down the violator's operations.

Ethical Consideration

Because of the potential for personal liability, a company may face difficult moral choices when confronted with knowledge of a violation that is required by law to be reported. Should the company quietly correct the violation and not report it? Or should the company report the violation and correct it with agency oversight and, possibly, enforcement? A company that fails to report a violation that is later discovered may face more severe penalties and more aggressive enforcement than the company that self-reports.

■ Management of Environmental Compliance

Knowledgeable corporate officials today recognize the need to adopt corporate policies and create management systems to ensure that company operations are protective of human health and the environment. These programs generally include several key elements, discussed in this section.

Corporate Policy

A strong corporate policy of environmental protection, adopted and supported at the highest levels of management, is usually the keystone of an effective program. Mere compliance with environmental laws may not be enough. A practice that is lawful today could nevertheless lead to environmental harm and future liability. For example, underground storage of flammable materials was once considered a sound practice and was actually required by many local fire codes. Little thought was given to the possibility of leaks or spillage around the tanks, with resulting harm to underground water supplies. If the risks had been perceived properly, double containment could have been provided when the tanks were first installed. This lack of foresight caused many companies to incur substantial costs for groundwater restoration.

The corporate policy should require every employee to comply with environmental laws. It should encourage management to consider more stringent measures than those required by law if such measures are necessary to protect human health and the environment. Finally, the policy should encourage a cooperative and constructive relationship with government agency personnel and should support active participation in legislative and administrative rule-making proceedings.

At the Top

A corporation can be held liable for the malfeasance of its employees. In addition, an employee participating in this conduct can be held criminally liable. Therefore, it is necessary for a corporation to conduct an education program designed to make its employees aware of their environmental responsibilities.

Management Organization

Management of environmental compliance requires a well-defined organization with clear responsibilities and reporting relationships. The complex and technical nature of environmental laws and regulations requires a highly trained professional staff with legal and technical expertise.

Periodic Assessment

A program of periodic internal assessments of environmental compliance should be developed to test the effectiveness of the management system, to identify instances of noncompliance, and to ensure that such instances are corrected. It is important in planning the assessment to determine whether the company wishes to maintain the confidentiality of any assessment reports.

Long-Term Strategies

The company should develop strategies for reducing the costs of compliance and the risk of liability over the long term. Corporate strategies might include objectives such as minimizing the amounts and kinds of pollutants produced, developing ways to recycle waste products, and investing in new technologies to render wastes nonhazardous. If hazardous wastes are produced that must be disposed of, the company should have procedures for evaluating and selecting well-managed and well-constructed disposal facilities.

Record Keeping and Accounting

Good record-keeping and cost-accounting systems are also essential. Many environmental laws require certain records to be developed and maintained for specified periods of time. These laws need to be consulted when a company develops a record-retention policy. Because the costs of environmental compliance may be significant and in some circumstances must be separately reported to the Securities and Exchange Commission, cost-accounting procedures need to be developed that allow the company to forecast and report the costs of environmental compliance.

Reporting Policies and Procedures

The company should have policies and procedures for reporting environmental law violations to corporate management and for managing the company's reporting obligations to government agencies.

Agency Inspection Policies and Procedures

Government agencies may undertake inspections with little or no advance notice. The company should be prepared in advance for such an event by having a protocol for handling the inspection. Individuals trained in company protocol should accompany the inspector to ensure that the inspection is properly conducted and within the inspector's authority. The person who accompanies the inspector should prepare a report to management and make sure that any instances of noncompliance identified during the inspection are corrected.

Education and Training

The most essential component of good environmental management is comprehensive education and training. Every employee must know about and understand the company's environmental policy and recognize his responsibilities in carrying it out.

International Consideration

The environmental laws of other nations are generally not as pervasive and do not establish as strict regulatory requirements as those of the United States. However, U.S. and some European environmental laws may serve as models for other nations as they develop regulatory programs to protect their environments. Therefore, forward-looking companies recognize that the global environmental regulation of the future may look very much like the current environmental regulation in the United States and Western Europe.

International Aspects

The National Environmental Policy Act, enacted in 1970, was the first element of the new environmental regulatory regime discussed in this chapter. Other countries, too, have initiated environmental regulatory schemes with environmental policy acts. Central to each of these acts is the requirement that the government expressly consider environmental values in its decision making and that it document this consideration in written environmental impact reports which can be reviewed by the public. These requirements are especially important when the government itself is responsible for major development projects.

A fundamental element of the United States scheme is the policy that the polluter pays. The European Community has also adopted this policy: "The cost of preventing and eliminating nuisances must, as a matter of principle, be borne by the polluter."[14]

66

A fundamental element of the United States scheme is the policy that the polluter pays. The European Community has also adopted this policy.

International Consideration

Environmental concerns are becoming increasingly intertwined with trade regulations. Many environmental activists have argued that the ability of U.S. pesticide manufacturers to ship their products to Third World nations subverts U.S. environmental regulations, because the products often return to the U.S.

In 1987, the Single European Act added environmental provisions to the EC Treaty, and additional provisions were added in the 1992 Treaty on European Union. Community policy on the environment includes the following objectives: preserving, protecting, and improving the quality of the environment; protecting human health; prudent and rational utilization of natural resources; and promoting measures at the international level to deal with regional or worldwide environmental problems.

This concept is also being introduced in Asia. Taiwan, for example, has begun the process of enacting an environmental law modeled, in part, on the United States Superfund statute (CERCLA), with modifications to address the local culture, issues, and concerns.

Where the laws of other nations are closely patterned on United States laws, compliance may be easier for U.S. companies operating in those countries. However, U.S. companies must be careful to note the differences between the United States laws and the laws of their host countries.

Public understanding of the importance of protecting the environment in order to preserve the planet is increasing. There is a growing international recognition of environmental problems such as global warming, ozone depletion, acid rain, and habitat destruction. As nations act individually and together to address these environmental problems, they will develop environmental regulatory schemes that will affect where development can occur and where factories can be constructed; what products can be produced; how these products must be produced, distributed, used, and discarded; and how wastes must be managed and discarded.

66

There is a growing international recognition of environmental problems such as global warming, ozone depletion, acid rain, and habitat destruction.

United Nations Earth Summit In June 1992, national leaders from more than 150 countries met in Rio de Janeiro, Brazil, for the United Nations Earth Summit to discuss serious global challenges to the planet's environment. A focal point for the summit was the biodiversity treaty, which provides for protection of endangered species and their habitats. The United States did not sign the treaty. The political issues surrounding the United States's refusal to sign the biodiversity treaty are the subject of chapter 6's "Inside Story."

Other environmental issues discussed at the summit include global warming and greenhouse gases, and the concept of *sustainable development*. Sustainable development "holds that future prosperity depends on preserving 'natural capital'—air, water, and other ecological treasures—and that doing so will require balancing human activity with nature's ability to renew itself. It also recognizes that growth is necessary to eliminate poverty, which leads to the plunder of resources."[15] Such a concept is politically controversial because it entails

---

14. Objective 17, from "Restatement of the Objectives and Principles of a Community Environment Policy," O. J. Eur. Comm. (No. C 139) (1977).

15. Emily T. Smith, "Growth vs. Environment," *Business Week*, May 11, 1992, 66.

significant changes in national regulatory and economic policies. Also important would be increased cooperation among industrialized and developing nations, the possibility of industrialized nations scaling back their consumption of the world's resources, and the use of new technology to preserve the earth's environment and prevent pollution.

Sustainable development is also controversial among business leaders because two concerns central to the concept—slowing world population growth and fighting poverty in developing nations—are issues that most managers do not see as their concern or problem. Nonetheless, a number of U.S. companies, such as 3M, have set goals to reduce air, water, and solid waste emissions. In the case of 3M, their environmental policies will enable 3M to make and distribute products more efficiently, cutting their costs per unit on most products by 10%.[16]

The Responsible Manager

Managing Risks of Environmental Liability

Several sources of potential environmental liability present risks to the parties in business transactions. In evaluating a company for purposes of acquisition, investment, or financing, a manager must consider that the company's earnings may be affected by the costs of compliance with environmental laws. The value of its equipment assets may be affected by regulatory limitations that make the equipment obsolete. Its ability to expand in existing locations may be impaired as a result of limitations on new sources of air emissions or the availability of nearby waste treatment or disposal facilities. A company's cash flow may be affected by needed capital investments or by increased operating costs necessitated by environmental regulations. Failure to comply with existing regulations may lead to the imposition of substantial penalties, also affecting cash flow. Small companies or companies that are highly leveraged may not be able to meet these additional demands for cash.

Similarly, a small company may not be able to survive the imposition of liability for response costs under CERCLA or similar state laws. A large company with a long history of operations in a number of locations may also have potential liabilities under CERCLA that are not reflected on its balance sheets. Finally, a company's operations or the condition of its properties may present risks of injury to other persons and their property, giving rise to possible tort claims.

The most important element in managing the risk of these potential liabilities is *due diligence*, that is, a systematic process for determining whether property contains or emits hazardous substances and whether the company is in compliance with environmental laws. The object of environmental due-diligence investigations is to identify and characterize the risks associated with the properties and operations involved in the business transaction. In recent years, such investigations have become highly sophisticated undertakings, often requiring the use of technical consultants and legal counsel with special expertise. Although much of the effort is focused on the review of company documents and available public records, it may also involve physical inspections of the properties, including soil and groundwater sampling and analysis. The effort may represent a significant cost of the transaction and may take a much longer time to complete than traditional due-diligence efforts.

The scope of the due-diligence effort will depend on the nature of the assets and the structure of the transaction. For example, if the transaction is a simple purchase and sale of real estate, then the due diligence can be limited to the property to be acquired and its surroundings. However, if the transaction involves the acquisition of a business with a long history of operations in many locations, then the due-diligence investigation must cover not only the current operating locations, but also prior operating locations and the sites used for off-site disposal of wastes. This is particularly true in the case of a merger acquisition, where the surviving company takes over all of the liabilities of the disappearing company.

The parties to the transaction can allocate the identified risks of environmental liability by undertakings of specified obligations, assumptions and retentions of contingent liabilities, adjustments to the purchase price, representations and warranties, indemnifications, and the like. Care must be exercised where risks are identified that are not yet quantifiable. For example, if liability for response costs is accepted in return for a reduction in the purchase price, it should be borne in mind that response costs often exceed by a wide margin the initial estimate provided by a consultant or a government agency.

Under CERCLA, secured lenders, and in some cases equity investors, may be deemed liable for response costs as present operators if they participate in the day-to-day management of the borrower. If a lender takes title at fore-

---

16. *Ibid.*, 74.

closure, it may also be deemed liable for response costs as a present owner. Thus the risk of hazardous-substance releases on the subject property should be carefully evaluated in connection with the loan application. The operations of the borrower should also be carefully reviewed in order to evaluate the risks they present during the life of the loan. If a release of hazardous substances occurs on the property, its value as collateral is impaired. Upon default, the lender may not be able to recover the outstanding amount of the debt. If the lender takes title or is otherwise deemed liable, it may have additional liability for response costs. Some states have adopted *superlien* provisions, which secure recovery of response costs incurred by state agencies. Where a superlien exists, it may take priority over existing security interests.

When an owner leases property, it must take care to evaluate the environmental risks of the tenant operations. Use of the property should be carefully limited to prevent any unauthorized activities. Where the tenant's activities present significant risks, financial assurances in the form of parent corporation guarantees, letters of credit, or per-

formance bonds might be obtained to make sure that any damage caused by the tenant will be remedied. Tenants also should be cautious in taking possession of property formerly occupied by others. Many tenants perform *baseline assessments* to establish the environmental condition of the property at the commencement of the lease and at the termination of the lease. These assessments may provide some protection from liability for conditions caused by prior or succeeding tenants.

The costs of environmental law compliance and the potential environmental liabilities must be carefully evaluated for purposes of Securities and Exchange Commission (SEC) disclosure and reporting requirements. The SEC requires special disclosure of environmental enforcement proceedings and litigation and requires the disclosure of estimated costs of environmental compliance, including capital expenditures and any effects of compliance on earnings and competitive position that may be material. The EPA provides information to the SEC in order to assist the SEC in enforcing these reporting requirements.

Inside Story

Water *Is* a Fighting Word in Texas—The Edwards Aquifer

Oblivious to the battle being fought some 2,000 feet above them, a community of not-so-glamorous creatures abides deep under the Texas Hill Country in the Edwards Aquifer. The aquifer is a unique home for blind catfish, blind salamanders, and the one-inch fountain darter, among others. However, it has recently become a home under siege in a battle that brings into sharp relief the antagonistic concerns of developers, farmers, and endangered species.

The Edwards Aquifer is an expansive underground reservoir that is the lifeblood of farmers, residents, and, of course, the blind salamander. For years, the aquifer has been the exclusive water source for almost 1.5 million people, including the city of San Antonio. The water in the aquifer is so pure that some developers pump water directly from the aquifer into new homes. The aquifer also is the source for central Texas tourist attractions such as the Barton Springs Pool in Austin and San Marcos Springs.

In addition to the developers, there are a number of competing factions who care little if the downstream springs dry up and neither they nor anyone sees a blind salamander again. As might be expected, farmers and ranchers who have relied on the aquifer for generations have been leading the charge against the salamander. Texas still has on the books an old frontier law known as the Right to Free Capture. This law allows any property owner to pump an unlimited amount of water from beneath her land. It is this law that started the controversy over the Edwards Aquifer.

A businessman bought property in San Antonio and built a catfish farm. Once the catfish operation was up and running, he began pumping more than fifty million gallons every day from the aquifer—approximately one-quarter of the daily consumption rate for the city of San Antonio. This use of the aquifer caused Texans to reconsider the continuing practicality of such a law in present-day Texas.

Inside Story, continued

The Sierra Club sued the U.S. Department of the Interior for failing to protect the endangered species contained in the aquifer. Federal District Judge Lucius D. Bunton III heard the case. In response, he ordered the Texas state legislature to come up with a fair plan to regulate use of the aquifer. Judge Bunton also threatened to invoke the Endangered Species Act to force cooperation among the ranchers, developers, legislators, and environmentalists. For example, if the state could not come up with an acceptable plan, the U.S. Fish and Wildlife Service could impose controls on the water without any obligation to consider the effect of the rules on local residents. In times of severe drought, the citizens of San Antonio and others who rely on the aquifer could face a 68% reduction in their water supplies to protect the one-inch fountain darter. Such a reduction would have devastating economic consequences for all of central Texas.

Not everyone felt as strongly about the environment as Judge Bunton and the Sierra Club, however. Texas Agricultural Commissioner Rick Perry represents the farming and ranching interests. He called on Congress in 1993 to overhaul the Endangered Species Act. Noting that environmentalists call the Endangered Species Act the "pit bull of environmental legislation," Perry suggested, "It's time to put a leash on the ESA."

Furthermore, when Interior Secretary Bruce Babbitt supported Judge Bunton's decision (or threat, as it was often characterized), many felt that the federal government was effectively blackmailing the state politicians toward action. Texas state senator Ken Armbrister argued that the ESA was being used in a way that was never intended by Congress. According to Armbrister, "[The ESA is] being used is [sic] a tool of fear, a tool of non-growth, and I don't believe that." Ken Kramer, who heads the Texas chapter of the Sierra Club, did not see it that way. Kramer believes that "It's not a question of people versus critters; it's a question of protecting the ecosystem that is important both to the critters and to people."

In late summer 1993, the Texas state legislature approved and the governor signed SB 1477, creating the Edwards Aquifer Authority, a new regional authority to manage withdrawals from the aquifer and to protect the endangered species that call the aquifer home. Interior Secretary Babbitt lauded the plan and was on hand for the signing.

When the board was finally appointed, but before the new Edwards Aquifer Authority was to be sworn in that September, another problem was discovered. Prior to the creation of the Edwards Aquifer Authority, the Edwards Underground Water District, consisting of an elected board, held responsibility for the aquifer. This board was to be dissolved at the same time the new board was to be sworn in. However, plans were put abruptly on hold when a letter from the Justice Department arrived, pointing out that the replacement of an elected authority with an appointed board violates the Voting Rights Act. This area of central Texas is home to a large Hispanic population. But because none of the bodies responsible for making the appointments to the board has a Hispanic majority among its officials, the influence of Hispanics would be significantly diminished by the new Authority. James P. Turner, acting attorney general for the civil rights division of the Justice Department, has called the new board "legally unenforceable." An appeal may be made to the D.C. Circuit, or the state legislature may ask U.S. Attorney General Janet Reno to review the matter.

The issue remains unresolved in Texas. Although the long-term future is uncertain, for the time being, the ESA still has its teeth and the blind salamander still has its home. What is certain, however, is that this will not be the last debate to pit the interests of humans against those of a less articulate species.

Key Words and Phrases

antideficiency statutes **521**	hazard ranking score **514**	responsible persons **514**
BACT **508**	initiative **506**	state implementation plans (SIPs) **507**
baseline assessments **526**	national ambient air quality	superlien **526**
due diligence **525**	standards **507**	sustainable development **524**
effluent limitations **508**	natural resources laws **505**	third-party defense **518**
environmental law **505**	navigable waters **508**	
federal common law **514**	persons **511**	

Questions and Case Problems

1. Ed Andrews is employed by a company that specializes in commercial and industrial real estate investments. He is responsible for analyzing investment opportunities, making recommendations for investment, and preparing the analysis of risks presented in the prospectus for each property.

(a) How will the environmental laws affect Andrews's analysis of investment opportunities?

(b) What precautions should he take in presenting investment opportunities to the public?

2. George Lu has been named the executive director of a nonprofit association organized to preserve open-space land and ecologically sensitive environments. The association will buy or receive gifts of land and then sell the land to public entities for preservation. The difference between the purchase price and the sale price will be used to finance the association's efforts. One of Lu's first tasks is to develop a protocol and prepare model agreements for making acquisitions.

(a) As a nonprofit organization, does the association have potential liability under the environmental laws?

(b) What procedures should Lu establish to protect the association from potential environmental law liabilities in connection with its acquisitions?

(c) What kinds of contractual arrangements should be considered to protect the association from environmental law liabilities?

[*James Graham Brown Foundation, Inc. v. St. Paul Fire & Marine Ins. Co.*, 814 S.W.2d 273 (Ky. 1991)]

3. ABC Investment Company is considering the leveraged buyout of a small, privately held manufacturing company that has been in operation since the 1930s. ABC is analyzing the cash flow expected from the company's operations over the next five years in order to evaluate the economics of the buyout. To do this, the managers of ABC estimate the future capital and operating expenses of the company. What information should they have to properly estimate future capital and operating costs related to environmental law compliance?

4. Martin Sanchez is a loan officer for a financial institution and is considering whether to finance the leveraged buyout described in question 3 above. The loan would be secured by the real property on which the plant is located, the equipment assets, and all personal property located on the plant premises.

(a) What financial risks do the environmental laws present to the lender?

(b) What steps can the financial institution take to protect the lender against these risks?

(c) If the debtor begins defaulting on its payment obligations, is it wise for the lender to provide management consultation and advice to the borrower?

(d) If the debtor defaults, what steps should the lender take before commencing foreclosure proceedings?

[*Kelley v. Environmental Protection Agency*, 15 F.3d 1100 (D.C. Cir. 1994)]

5. Johanna Landing has been hired by Newco Corporation to identify possible sites for construction of a major new manufacturing facility. Newco's operations will involve the production of substantial quantities of hazardous waste and constitute a major new source of air emissions.

(a) How will these facts affect Landing's consideration of possible construction sites?

(b) How will these facts and the location affect Newco's analysis of its costs of construction and operation?

6. Gregg Entrepreneur is organizing a small company to manufacture a new biotechnology product. Entrepreneur will be a principal shareholder and president of the company. What measures should Entrepreneur take to ensure that his company operates in compliance with environmental laws?

Despite all of the measures Entrepreneur has taken to ensure environmental law compliance, his vice president of operations reports that the production manager has been disposing of wastes into the sewer in violation of national pretreatment standards and that she has been submitting false reports to the publicly owned sewage treatment works (POTW) to cover up the violations. All of the reports have been signed by the vice president of operations, who had no knowledge that they contained false statements. What steps should Entrepreneur take? Should he report the violations to the POTW even if it could result in personal civil or criminal liability? What about the vice president? The production manager? What is Entrepreneur's ethical responsibility? [*United States v. Alley*, 775 F.Supp. 771 (N.D. Ill. 1990)]

7. American Widgets is a manufacturing company that has gained a large share of the international widget market, largely because of high quality and competitive pricing. However, the disposal of the company's wastes has become increasingly expensive. A new ban on land disposal will require that one of the company's largest waste streams be incinerated. Plants of competitors located in Southeast Asia and in South America are subject to increasing environmental regulation modeled after the laws in the United States, but they are not subject to a land disposal ban and will have a significant competitive advantage over plants located in the United States. Jimmy Tsai is considering the possibility of locating a new plant in Southeast Asia. What factors should he take into account? What alternatives are there besides relocation?

8. An enterprising young Texas A&M M.B.A. graduate, Nancy Schmidt, purchased land near Houston from Winetka Development, Inc., for $12 million. Schmidt was speculating that the demands, and consequently the inflated prices, of Houston suburbia would soon reach her property. Within two years, Schmidt formed a joint venture with a developer and broke ground on her subdivision plan, expending $1.4 million on streets, plumbing, and irrigation for the planned championship golf course designed by Arnold Palmer. Much to her chagrin, an Environmental Protection Agency (EPA) investigation identified this parcel of land as a former municipal waste landfill and a source of groundwater pollution. The EPA notified Schmidt and her partner that, as the present owners and operators of the property, pursuant to section 107 of CERCLA they were "potentially responsible parties," jointly and severally liable for all of the costs of cleanup, estimated cleanup costs to be upwards of $29 million.

Who will be liable for the cleanup costs? Is the developer liable? Is it relevant that Schmidt knew or did not know about the landfill prior to the purchase? Does it matter that this was a municipal waste landfill? If a vice president of Winetka Development lied to Schmidt about the prior uses of the land, is Winetka liable for (a) the cleanup costs? (b) the purchase price

and development costs? If a lower-level manager of Winetka is the person who lied to Schmidt, does the analysis change? Does the analysis change if Winetka and all of its employees had not known about the waste? Can Schmidt just give the property back to Winetka in order to free herself from any legal entanglements? [*Tanglewood East Homeowners v. Charles-Thomas, Inc.*, 849 F.2d 1568 (5th Cir. 1988)]

9. You are the CEO of a Brazilian real estate company that owns several hundred thousand acres of rain forest. A representative of a large American hamburger chain approaches you with an offer to buy a portion of the land at a very attractive price. The revenue from the sale of the land would permit your company to undertake a large development project in Rio de Janeiro, which would both provide new jobs and increase the amount of low-cost housing in the city. However, you are aware that the hamburger chain intends to convert the rain forest acreage into grazing lands for cattle. What should you do? Discuss the tradeoffs between environmental preservation and economic development. Describe "sustainable development." How do environmental laws affect national policy with regard to industrial growth and economic development in the United States? Competition in international markets? How do state environmental laws affect competition between states for industrial development?

10. To enforce effluent limitations, the Clean Water Act relies on a permit system, the National Pollutant Discharge Elimination System (NPDES). Between 1981 and 1984, Gwaltney, a meat-packing company, repeatedly violated the conditions of its NPDES permit by exceeding authorized effluent limitations. However, Gwaltney installed new equipment and its last reported violation was in May 1984. In June 1984, the Chesapeake Bay Foundation and the Natural Resources Defense Council filed a citizen's suit against Gwaltney under the Clean Water Act.

Can the plaintiffs bring a suit even though Gwaltney is no longer in violation of the act? Can citizen suits recover for wholly past violations of the act? What if the violations were intermittent? [*Gwaltney of Smithfield, Ltd. v. Chesapeake Bay Found., Inc.*, 484 U.S. 49, 108 S.Ct. 376 (1987)]

Chapter 17

REAL PROPERTY AND LAND USE

■ Introduction

Importance

It is difficult to imagine any business enterprise that does not involve real estate in some manner. From the multinational corporation with retail outlets on several continents to a mail-order business operated out of an apartment, real estate has a strong impact on the functioning of most businesses. Managers need to understand how real estate will affect their own business. Location, the methods used to estimate the useful lives of buildings, the nature of individual real estate markets, the tax consequences of real estate, and the alternatives to owning are just some of the concerns on which managers should focus.

Real estate has a powerful impact on the general economy. It is one of the largest industries in the United States. Much federal legislation is devoted to promoting specific real estate policy goals. The savings and loan crisis of the 1980s arose in substantial part out of defaults on real estate loans. In addition, real estate has the power to evoke strong national sentiment. Many Americans who would not think twice about the large purchase of treasury bills by Japanese banks reacted with emotion when Japanese investors bought a 51% share of the Rockefeller Center in New York City, home of Radio City Music Hall and the Rockettes.

Real estate law finds its roots in both English common law and Spanish civil law. Many of the laws are determined by municipalities, others by the state. In recent years the federal government has played an increasingly active role, through tax policy and environmental regulations that affect the density of real estate development. The federal government is also interested in the safety of real estate (through the Occupational Safety and Health Administration), physical accessibility to commercial facilities (under the Americans with Disabilities Act), foreign investment in U.S. real estate, and the preservation of parklands.

Chapter Summary

This chapter discusses the acquisition of real estate, forms of ownership, and methods of financing. Leasing and lease terms are also discussed. Finally, the chapter outlines governmental regulation of the use of real property by the exercise of police and condemnation powers.

■ Ownership

Ownership of land is transferred by a document known as a *deed,* which is recorded at a public office, typically the office of the county recorder in the county where the real property is located. Any document transferring an interest in real estate, such as a deed or a lease, is called a *conveyance.* The person conveying the property is the *grantor,* and the person to whom the property is conveyed is the *grantee.* Occasionally, but seldom in business, ownership is obtained through an installment sales contract, with the deed to follow when payment for the real estate has been completed. Ownership of property subject to probate is transferred by a court order from the probate court.

In most purchases of real estate, the type of interest conveyed is a *fee simple* interest, that is, absolute ownership of the property. However, many other transactions, such as a lease, convey less than an absolute ownership interest in the property.

When real estate is purchased, the deed conveys the title (that is, the ownership) to the new owner. The various forms of real estate ownership are described below.

Individual Ownership

The simplest type of ownership is that whereby a property is owned by a single individual. From a business perspective, individual ownership is often undesirable because the individual owner may be liable in tort for any accidents occurring on the property. The risk of unlimited personal liability, however, can be covered by insurance.

Tenancy in Common

Tenants in common each own an undivided fractional interest in a parcel of real property. For example, one tenant in common may have a two-thirds interest and another a one-third interest. Two or more persons can hold property as tenants in common. Regardless of the percentage ownership interest, however, each tenant in common has an equal right to possession of the property, and no cotenant has the right of exclusive possession of the property against any other cotenant. However, a cotenant has the right to exclusive possession of the entire property against any third party. Cotenants share the income and burdens of ownership. An action for contribution from the other cotenants is available to a cotenant who has paid more than his share. The interest of a tenant in common is assignable and inheritable without the consent of any other cotenant.

Joint Tenancy

A *joint tenancy* is the ownership of a property in equal shares by two or more persons. The key characteristic of a joint tenancy is the right of survivorship. If a joint tenant dies, her interest passes automatically to the remaining joint tenant or tenants. However, an attempt by a single joint tenant to convey separately her interest in the property will destroy the joint tenancy and convert it to a tenancy in common. Moreover, use of joint tenancy property in a business may also terminate the joint tenancy.[1]

Tenancy by the Entirety

Historically, English common law recognized a special type of co-ownership of real property between husband and wife, called *tenancy by the entirety*. Like joint tenancy, tenancy by the entirety includes a right of survivorship. However, unlike in a joint tenancy, the right of survivorship was historically held to be indestructible by the separate acts of the parties. Consequently, neither spouse could convey an individual interest to a third party and thereby terminate the right of survivorship. Additionally, unlike joint tenancy, where joint tenants have equal rights to possession of the property, tenancy by the entirety entitled only the husband to possession, use, and enjoyment of the property. In effect, he acted as a guardian over the wife's interest.

---

1. *Williams v. Dovell*, 202 Md. 351, 96 A.2d 484 (Md. 1953).

Although many people find the concept incompatible with the status of married women in modern society, approximately 22 states recognize some form of tenancy by the entirety. Although most states have retained the indestructible right of survivorship, the husband and wife are given equal rights to the possession, use, and revenues of the property. Additionally, the modern view is that divorce converts a tenancy by the entirety to a tenancy in common.[2] However, tenancy by the entirety represents an historical anomaly that may not serve a justifiable purpose today. The indestructible right of survivorship can act to the disadvantage of one or both of the spouses. As neither spouse can compel a severance of the property, a deadlock between the spouses may result while both spouses are alive.

> ""
>
> *Although many people find the concept incompatible with the status of married women in modern society, approximately 22 states recognize some form of tenancy by the entirety.*

Community Property

In Arizona, California, Idaho, Louisiana, Nevada, New Mexico, Texas, and Washington, property acquired by either spouse during marriage is considered to be *community property,* that is, each spouse owns an undivided one-half interest in the property. Property acquired prior to the marriage or by gift or inheritance during the marriage is separate property, unless the spouse owning it has converted it to community property. Separate property is converted into community property when one spouse gifts separate property to the other spouse; the parties treat the separate property in such a manner that a presumption of a gift arises; or the separate and common property has been commingled, or mixed together.

Conveyance   Community property cannot be conveyed unless both spouses execute the instrument by which the conveyance is effected. It should be noted, however, that where the instrument is not signed by one of the spouses, but both spouses were present during negotiations and were fully aware of the terms and conditions, the nonsigning spouse may not claim that the transaction is void due to the absence of a signature.[3]

The community property interest of a spouse may be separately willed upon death. In the absence of a will, community property passes to the other spouse.

Divorce   Most of the cases interpreting what is or is not community property arise in the divorce context. The community property laws vary from state to state. For example, in California, if separate property is commingled with community property, all of the commingled property becomes community property. Complicated issues arise, for instance, if one spouse inherits land from his family (which is separate property at the date of inheritance), but subsequently one or both spouses improve or develop the property. In this case, some or all of the inherited property may turn into community property. Among the factors to be considered in determining whether all or part of the property has been transformed from separate to community property are: (1) whether the value of the separate property has increased due to factors other than the inherent investment quality of the property; or (2) whether the party responsible for increasing the value of the property has been compensated, by salary or some other special allocation. Any increase in value resulting from factors other than the inherent investment quality of the property or compensation received by one spouse from development activities undertaken on the property during marriage is community property.

Joint tenancy between spouses and community property are theoretically different, but in the divorce context, courts frequently ignore the differences. In the context of income or estate tax on substantial investments, community property is generally a more desirable form of ownership than joint tenancy.

Trust

Property may be also held in a *trust,* whereby the property is owned and controlled by one person, the *trustee,* for the benefit of another, the *beneficiary.* The duration of the trust, the powers of the trustee and the trustor (the person creating the trust), and the express rights of the beneficiary are set forth in a trust agreement.

General Partnership

When property is held in a *general partnership,* the partners have rights similar to those of cotenants, and each partner is liable for all the debts of the partnership. A general partner has no right to possess partnership property for other than partnership purposes. In addition, she may not assign her individual interest in specific partnership property. On the other hand, a general partner can

---

2. *Markland v. Markland,* 155 Fla. 629, 21 So.2d 145 (Fla. 1945).
3. *Calvin v. Salmon River Sheep Ranch,* 104 Idaho 301, 658 P.2d 972 (Idaho 1983).

convey the entire partnership property to a bona fide purchaser who has no knowledge of any restriction that might exist on the general partner's authority to convey partnership property.

Limited Partnership

Real property may be held in a *limited partnership,* consisting of one or more general partners, who manage the property, and one or more limited partners. The liability of a limited partner is usually restricted to the amount of capital he has contributed to the partnership. The authority of the general partner to convey the property is determined by the limited-partnership agreement and the jurisdiction's limited-partnership law.

Corporate Ownership

A corporation may own real property. Corporate authority to convey the property is governed by the corporation's articles of incorporation and by-laws, as well as the jurisdiction's corporate law.

A business will normally own real estate in the name of the business. Whether that business is organized as a partnership (general or limited) or a corporation will depend on tax, financial, securities, and liability factors. The choice of the proper entity for owning real estate is particularly important at the beginning of an investment or development. It may be difficult to make a change at a later date without adverse tax consequences. The issue of choice of entity is further discussed in chapter 5.

■ Title

A seller of real estate is generally required to convey *marketable title,* that is, a fee simple interest free from defects. Defects of title that make it unmarketable include any "cloud" on the title that would cause the buyer to receive less than a fee simple interest. For example, the existence of a lien on the property would constitute a defect of title sufficient to make the title unmarketable.

The type of interest (usually fee simple) and the quality of title (that is, whether it is marketable) are set forth in a deed executed by the party conveying the property. The type of deed determines the scope of warranties granted.

Types of Deeds

An interest in real property can only be conveyed by a signed deed that specifically describes that interest and is delivered to and accepted by a named grantee. There are three basic types of deeds: grant deeds, quitclaim deeds, and warranty deeds. These differ in the specific warranties they contain.

Grant Deed　A *grant deed* contains implied warranties that the grantor has not previously conveyed the same property or any interest in it to another person, and that the title is marketable. A grant deed also conveys *after-acquired title.* This means that if at the date of execution the grantor does not have title to the real property referred to in the grant deed, but subsequently acquires it, the title will be automatically transferred to the grantee.

Quitclaim Deed　A *quitclaim deed* contains no warranties, and the grantor only conveys whatever right, title, and interest she holds, if any, at the time of execution. A quitclaim deed does not convey after-acquired title.

Warranty Deed　A *warranty deed* contains the implied warranties of a grant deed, and, in addition, the grantor expressly warrants the title to and the quiet possession of the property. Warranty deeds may also contain other express warranties.

■ Recording Acts

Deeds and other instruments of conveyance must be recorded with a public office, where copies will be available to anyone. The documents must be in *recordable form.* The requirements vary from state to state, but typically include legibility and some type of notarization by a notary public. The record in the public office is the principal basis for determining the state of title of real estate, and there is an extensive body of law concerning what and how recording controls that title.

Recording acts are statutes that establish an orderly process by which claims to interests in real property can be recorded. Under most recording acts, the general rule is that "first in time is first in right." This is known as a "race" rule (referring to the race to the recording office).

Another rule is the "notice" rule, whereby a person who has notice that someone else has already bought the property cannot validate his deed by recording it first. A person may have actual, constructive, or inquiry notice of a prior interest. *Actual notice* occurs when the person actually knows of the prior interest. *Constructive notice* is created by the existence of a properly recorded deed. The person is assumed to know of the deed. *Inquiry notice* is imputed when reasonable inquiry would have disclosed the prior interest, for example, if inspection of the property would have revealed that some person other than the grantor was in possession of the property.

In many states, the priority of conflicting interests in real property is determined on a race-notice basis. Under a *race-notice recording act*, priority is determined as follows:

1.   As between two recorded documents, the first to be recorded has priority.

2.   As between a recorded instrument and a preexisting unrecorded instrument, the recorded instrument has priority unless the owner of the recorded interest had notice of the preexisting unrecorded interest.

3.   As between two unrecorded interests, the first in time has priority.

The above rules assume that the purchaser is a bona fide purchaser and that valuable consideration for the interest was paid in good faith, without notice or knowledge of a prior outstanding adverse interest.

Title Insurance

Despite the existence of recording acts, the condition of title to a specific property and the priority of any claims against the property are often difficult to ascertain. In some states, title is searched by attorneys, in others by title abstract companies on which attorneys rely, and in still others by title insurance companies, which may also insure the condition of title or the priority of one's interest. In some states lawyers' opinions are still used rather than title insurance.

Extent of Coverage

A title insurance policy insures against loss as a result of: (1) undisclosed liens or defects in title to the property; or (2) errors in the abstraction of the title, that is, in the summary of the relevant recorded deeds. Generally, the policy limit is the purchase price of the property, or the amount of the *encumbrance,* that is, the claim against the property.

It is obviously important to review a title report or insurance policy carefully before acquiring title to property. The exceptions listed in the report may be defects in title.

As the following case demonstrates, a title company may have a claim against the seller of real property if the seller conveys the property pursuant to a grant deed and it turns out that there is an encumbrance that the title company did not discover.

■   **A Case in Point:**   **Summary**

Case 17.1
FIDELITY NATIONAL TITLE INSURANCE CO. v. MILLER
California Court of Appeal
215 Cal.App.3d 1163, 264
Cal.Rptr. 17 (Cal.Ct.App. 1989).

FACTS   Miller granted his neighbor a *view easement,* that is, an interest in Miller's property that entitled the neighbor to an unobstructed view. The easement was recorded. Miller later contracted to sell the property and disclosed the existence of the view easement to the buyer, Gazzo. A preliminary title report issued by Fidelity National Title Insurance Company failed to disclose the existence of the easement. Gazzo requested that Fidelity investigate the possible existence of the easement. Fidelity assured Gazzo that the easement did not exist and that except for those items set forth in Fidelity's title report, Miller had fee title. Miller executed a grant deed conveying the property to Gazzo.

Gazzo later found out that the easement had in fact been recorded, and he recovered $125,000 from Fidelity for the diminution of the property's value as a result of the easement. Gazzo assigned any claim that he had against Miller to Fidelity, and Fidelity sued Miller for breach of warranty. Fidelity claimed that by executing the grant deed Miller had implicitly warranted that title to the property was being conveyed free of any encumbrances. The trial court granted summary judgment to Miller on the grounds that Fidelity could not acquire rights greater than those of Gazzo, and Gazzo had no claim against Miller, as Miller had expressly disclosed the existence of the easement to Gazzo. Fidelity appealed.

ISSUE PRESENTED   Does the prior disclosure by the seller to the buyer of a recorded encumbrance eliminate the seller's warranty against encumbrances implied in a grant deed?

SUMMARY OF OPINION   The California Court of Appeal ruled that a grant deed implies a warranty that title is being conveyed without encumbrances, unless otherwise expressly restricted. Miller's oral disclosure of the easement to Gazzo was not sufficient to eliminate the implied warranty. A buyer is entitled to rely on the warranty in the deed, even if the encumbrance is otherwise disclosed to the buyer.

RESULT   In finding that many triable factual issues were present, the Court of Appeal reversed the lower court's ruling of summary judgment in favor of Miller.

COMMENTS   In most instances, sellers rely on a title company's title search to determine the state of title. The above case implies that such reliance may not be well founded, especially when the seller knows of the existence of liens or encumbrances, previously recorded or not, that were not uncovered by the title company's search.

Escrow

In addition to issuing title insurance policies, title companies often hold the purchase money in *escrow*, that is, in a special account, until the conditions for the sale have all been met. The money is then paid to the seller. If the sale does not go through, the money is returned to the would-be purchaser. Banks also perform this service, and in some jurisdictions there are separate escrow companies.

The *escrow agent* acts as a neutral stakeholder, allowing the parties to close the transaction without the physical difficulties of passing instruments and funds between the parties. Additionally, it is the duty of the escrow agent to coordinate the closing with the recording of documents, the issuance of title insurance, and other activities that take place concurrently with the closing.

Neutral Party   As a neutral party, the escrow agent is an agent of all parties to the transaction and must follow their specific instructions. Because an escrow agent has a fiduciary duty to all of the parties, it cannot act when the parties have submitted conflicting instructions. Generally, if conflicts between instructions are not resolved by the parties, the escrow agent will go to court for a resolution of the conflict.

■ Brokers

The market for real estate is imperfect, and brokers serve to maintain that market by putting together buyers and sellers. The levels of competence and the areas of expertise of commercial brokers vary greatly. Most brokers

International Consideration

Many countries will not allow foreigners to own land. A foreigner must therefore obtain a long-term lease on the property.

If foreign ownership is permitted, an investor should be cautious when purchasing property abroad. Many countries do not have adequate means for searching the title of property. In addition, many countries allow for *squatter's rights*, whereby ownership of property that is not occupied by its owner for a certain period of time will be transferred to those who have been unlawfully occupying it. Such a transfer is usually not reflected in the official land records.

specialize in a particular market segment, such as raw land, industrial leasing, or office buildings.

Compensation

Brokers are customarily retained by the seller through a listing agreement which, to be enforceable, must be in writing. Generally brokers are compensated by a payment based upon a percentage of the gross selling price (or aggregate rental income). The percentage can vary from 1% to 3% for large commercial properties, to 10% for raw land. To the extent that the buyer's or lessee's broker is compensated, it is usually by sharing the commission paid by the seller.

Listing Agreements

There are several types of listing agreements: open, exclusive, or net.

Open Listing   In an open listing, the listing broker will receive a commission only if she procures a ready, willing, and able buyer. As it is understood that the seller will be contracting with more than one broker, the first broker to procure a buyer is the one who will receive a commission. Because of the uncertainty of earning a commission, even if a buyer is found, it is hard to get a broker to work diligently to sell a commercial property with an open listing.

Exclusive Listing   An exclusive listing grants the broker the right to sell the property, and any sale of the property during the term of the listing will entitle the broker to a commission. If a seller is going to give an exclusive listing, he may wish to restrict from the listing agreement particular buyers with whom the seller has dealt before signing the listing agreement.

Net Listing   A net listing involves a completely different compensation scheme. The broker will receive any sales price in excess of the net listing amount specified by the seller. Net listings are uncommon.

Seller Financing   In commercial transactions, the seller may provide the financing for the buyer. Thus the sale may net very little cash to the seller, and the seller will be unwilling to pay most of it to a broker in the form of a commission. Therefore, the listing agreement may provide that if the seller accepts payment of the purchase price on terms, such as installments, the broker will accept payment of her commission on the same terms.

Regulation of Brokers   In many states, real estate brokers are heavily regulated. They generally require a license to perform brokerage activities, broadly defined as any sale or offer to sell, any purchase or offer to purchase, any solicitation related to the sale of real property or of a business opportunity, and any leases, loans secured by real property, or real property sales contracts. A mere finder, who does nothing more than introduce two parties for a fee, does not need a broker's license. If the person has engaged in brokerage activities without a license, he will not be able to sue successfully to recover his fee.

In many states, real estate brokers must report and keep records of the transactions in which they deal. Brokers may also have to meet continuing education requirements and requirements regarding the particulars of real estate loans.

Agency Relationship

Brokers may also be subject to regulations concerning disclosure of the agency relationship between the broker and the parties to the transaction. As a general rule, a broker may not act for more than one person in a transaction without the knowledge or consent of all parties to the transaction. When a broker acts for both the buyer and the seller, the relationship is characterized as a *dual agency*. In most instances, a dual agent is prohibited from disclosing to the buyer that the seller is willing to sell the property for less than the listing price without the consent of the seller. Similarly, a dual agent may not disclose to the seller that the buyer is willing to pay a price greater than the listing price. Agency issues are discussed further in chapter 5.

■ Acquisitions and Dispositions

Acquisitions and dispositions of real estate interests are contracted for in the same manner as most commercial transactions. To be enforceable, however, a contract for the sale of a real property interest must be in writing. Although standardized contracts are often used in relatively simple transactions, such as the conveyance of a single-family residence or a small commercial property, most large transactions require custom-drafted contracts.

Generally, contracts for the sale of an interest in real property are the result of protracted negotiations between the parties. Besides essential terms such as price, time, and method of payment, common areas of negotiation include types of acceptable financing, the condition of title, closing costs, taxes and compliance with zoning laws, the building code, and environmental regulations. In many purchase and sale agreements, the most heavily negotiated provisions are the seller's representations and warranties concerning the condition of the property.

Representations and Warranties

In the sale of real estate, the seller has a duty to disclose all relevant or material facts regarding the property that would not be readily apparent to the buyer in a diligent inspection of the property. A provision in the contract that the buyer takes the property "as is" does not protect the seller from her obligation to disclose a known material defect.

A skillful buyer will request many representations and warranties from the seller, particularly with respect to environmental issues (discussed in chapter 16). If nothing else, the negotiation of representations and warranties frequently leads to additional disclosures regarding the physical condition of the property.

Environmental Considerations   The buyer should diligently investigate whether there are toxic or hazardous substances on or under the property. Liability under federal and state environmental laws and regulations can be so large as to overshadow any other economic aspect of the property. The buyer should determine the prior uses of the property and look for any indications of underground tanks or other physical evidence that would indicate possible environmental problems.

As the following case illustrates, under the Comprehensive Environmental Response, Compensation, and Liability Act (CERCLA), a past owner at the time of disposal and the current owner of a contaminated facility are both potentially liable for the costs associated with cleaning up such a facility. Under CERCLA, all responsible parties, as defined by statute, are as a group liable for the cleanup costs, and the only issue is division of responsibility.

■ A Case in Point: Summary

Case 17.2
IN RE HEMINGWAY
TRANSPORT, INC.
United States Court of Appeals
for the First Circuit
993 F.2d 915 (1st Cir. 1993),
cert. denied, 114 S.Ct. 303
(1993).

FACTS   In 1980, the Massachusetts Department of Environmental Quality Engineering found 17 corroded drums containing contaminants on a twenty-acre parcel of land. The Department was assured by the previous owners that they would be removed. Several years later the drums were still there. In 1983, Juniper, a local land developer, bought the property, which was in the midst of bankruptcy proceedings. Juniper's representatives conducted an on-site inspection but did not walk through the area in which the drums had been discovered in 1980. In 1985, the EPA discovered additional drums containing various substances considered hazardous under CERCLA in the same area. Juniper was told that it was considered a potentially responsible party under CERCLA and shortly thereafter was required to remove the hazardous substances from the facility at its own expense. Expenses included roughly $30,000 to remove the drums and $54,000 in legal costs. In April 1988, the EPA demanded $2.1 million in CERCLA contributions from Juniper for costs incurred in assessing and evaluating the site. Juniper initiated proceedings against the previous owners for CERCLA response costs already incurred and for future response costs. The bankruptcy court allowed Juniper's claim for the direct cleanup costs but disallowed the legal fees. Juniper appealed.

ISSUE PRESENTED   Can a purchaser of a contaminated property be responsible for the cleanup costs associated with complying with CERCLA?

SUMMARY OF OPINION   Recognizing that the objective of CERCLA is to promote the spontaneous private cleanup of sites contaminated by hazardous substances that jeopardize public health and safety, the U.S. Court of Appeals focused on the fact that all potentially responsible persons—past owners at the time of disposal and present property owners—are strictly liable for all response costs. However, the court also recognized the need for equitable allocation of financial responsibility. The court concluded that Juniper bears the burden of proof that it is entitled to the *innocent landowner defense,* requiring Juniper to prove it (1) acquired the property after the

*Case **17.2** continued on following page*

*Case **17.2** continued*

initial deposit of hazardous substances, (2) had no reason to know that any substances were deposited at the facility at the time of acquisition, and (3) had exercised due care once the presence of the substances had been known.

RESULT   The case was remanded in part to see if the purchaser met the requirements of the innocent landowner defense under CERCLA.

COMMENTS   The second requirement of the innocent landowner defense, namely, that the person had no reason to know of the hazardous waste at the time the property was acquired, is especially hard to satisfy. At a minimum, the law requires extensive due diligence in the form of environmental tests of the water and soil, and research into prior uses of the property and any adjacent property form which waste might have spread.

It is important to remember that past owners at the time of disposal and present owners or operators of a contaminated site are jointly and severally liable for cleanup costs under CERCLA. This means that if the prior owner is insolvent or nonexistent the current owner can be held liable for the entire cleanup.

Due Diligence   From the seller's perspective, the representations and warranties are a potential source of liability. From the buyer's perspective, the representations and warranties are also a means of forcing the seller to disclose information.

However, the buyer should not rely upon the representations and warranties as an alternative to his own careful investigation of the condition of the property. Although the seller is generally required to indemnify the buyer against liability arising from the falseness of any of its representations and warranties, the buyer should not rely on such indemnification, but should conduct his own due diligence.

Tax-Deferred Exchanges

An alternative method of acquiring real property is a *tax-deferred exchange*. Instead of receiving cash, the seller exchanges her property for another piece of property. The capital gains tax owed by the seller may be deferred if the seller is disposing of a property held for investment or for productive use in a trade or business and if the seller is acquiring a property that qualifies under the Internal Revenue Code. Tax-deferred exchanges take many forms. The most common is the three-party exchange, in which the buyer purchases a piece of property designated by the seller and exchanges it for the seller's property.

There are a number of pitfalls in utilizing a tax-deferred exchange. For example, in a three-party exchange, under the environmental laws the buyer may be liable for the cleanup of any toxic or hazardous materials on the property acquired for the purpose of exchange. Changes in tax rates may affect the desirability of a tax-deferred exchange. For example, if the tax rate is likely to increase, it may be better to pay the tax at the time of the transfer of the property rather than at a later date, when the rate may be higher. Because of the complex nature of these exchanges, it is prudent to consult an attorney specializing in tax and real estate issues when acquiring real property through a tax-deferred exchange.

Proposition 13

In 1978, California voters staged what has been described as a "property tax revolt" when they approved Proposition 13. This statewide ballot initiative amended the California State Constitution and limited the rate at which real property is taxed within the state and the rate at which real property assessments are increased. As the following case illustrates, Proposition 13 raised questions of equity and fairness because two very similar pieces of property could have drastically different tax consequences depending on when the property was last transferred.

Historical Perspective

Property Taxes

California Revolts on Revolting Taxes, 1978[a]

The patriots of 1773 protested taxes by dumping British tea into Boston Harbor. The property owners who fought California taxes in 1978 dumped the state's entire fiscal system.

California property taxes had been rising at 20% a year when Howard Jarvis, a 75-year-old retired manufacturer and political gadfly, and Paul Gann, a retired real-estate man, decided to do something about it. Their brainchild was Proposition 13, a voter initiative that would roll taxes back to the level of 1975 assessments and limit future increases to 1% a year. Although the state then had a $5.8 billion surplus in its treasury, in part a legacy from former Gov. Ronald Reagan, the rollback would reduce revenue by $7 billion.

The opposing uproar was led by then Gov. Jerry Brown, who denounced Prop. 13 as a "rip-off" and a "consumer fraud." Despite this, Jarvis and Gann garnered

1.5 million signatures to get their proposal on the ballot and in June [1978] the voters approved it by a resounding 65% majority.

Tax lids were hardly new. New York state has had one since 1884 on property taxes and the Albany legislators have grown adept at circumventing it. Californians proved just as resourceful. Cities made up their losses by jacking fees. San Mateo raised park and recreational fees 50% and increased its transient tax on hotel rooms to 8% from 6%. Downey began charging residents 24 cents a month for sewer services and doubled dog license fees. Sacramento slapped a 5% tax on theater admissions and raised parking meter charges. Gov. Brown vetoed pay raises for state employees. The surplus in the state treasury vanished overnight.

Proposition 13 (plus a 1979 initiative by Paul Gann that put similar handcuffs on state spending) is still law in California. The October [1989] Bay Area earthquake, however, with damage estimated at more than $10 billion, has forced state lawmakers to think again about whether such straitjackets are really a good idea.

a. *The Wall Street Journal*, November 8, 1989. Reprinted by permission of *The Wall Street Journal*, ©1989 Dow Jones & Company, Inc. All Rights Reserved Worldwide.

■

■ A Case in Point:

In the Language of the Court

Case 17.3
NORDLINGER v. HAHN
Supreme Court of the
United States
112 S.Ct. 2326 (1992).

FACTS Proposition 13, embodied in Article XIIIA of the California State Constitution, created an "acquisition value" system of taxation in which property is reassessed to a more current appraised value when there is a change in ownership. Under Proposition 13, the property tax rate is 1% of the assessed value. Unless the property is sold, the assessed value of the property may be increased by no more than 2% per year. Upon sale of the property, however, the new owner's assessed value is the purchase price. Because home prices in most of California soared after the enactment of Proposition 13 in 1978, huge tax disparities were created between property purchased before and after passage of Proposition 13. Owners who have held their property for a number of years might pay only a fraction of the property taxes that newer owners paid, although their properties might be similar. Two types of transfers were exempted from reassessment:

*Case **17.3** continued on following page*

Case **17.3** continued

exchanges of residences by people over the age of 55, and transfers between parents and children.

Stephanie Nordlinger was a Los Angeles apartment renter who purchased a home in Los Angeles County. When she discovered that she was paying property taxes at a rate many times that of her neighbors with similar homes, she filed suit against the county and the tax assessor, claiming that the reassessment scheme violated the Equal Protection Clause of the Fourteenth Amendment of the U.S. Constitution.

The County Superior Court dismissed the claim and the state Court of Appeal affirmed. She appealed to the U.S. Supreme Court.

ISSUE PRESENTED   Does California's Proposition 13, as embodied in the state constitution's acquisition-value assessment scheme, which may result in similar properties being taxed differently, violate the Equal Protection Clause of the Fourteenth Amendment?

OPINION   BLACKMUN, J., writing for the U.S. Supreme Court:

. . . .

The Equal Protection Clause of the Fourteenth Amendment . . . commands that no State shall "deny to any person within its jurisdiction the equal protection of the laws." Of course, most laws differentiate between classes of persons. The Equal Protection Clause does not forbid classifications. It simply keeps governmental decisionmakers from treating differently persons who are in all relevant respects alike.

. . . .

The appropriate standard of review is whether the difference in treatment between newer and older owners rationally furthers a legitimate state interest. . . . This standard is especially deferential in the context of classifications made by complex tax laws. . . .

As between newer and older owners, Article XIIIA does not discriminate with respect to either the tax rate or the annual rate of adjustment in assessments. . . . New owners and old owners are treated differently with respect to one factor only—the basis on which their property is initially assessed. Petitioner's true complaint is that the State has denied her—a new owner—the benefit of the same assessment value that her neighbors—older owners—enjoy. We have no difficulty in ascertaining at least two rational or reasonable considerations of difference or policy that justify denying petitioner the benefits of her neighbors' lower assessments. First, the State has a legitimate interest in local neighborhood preservation, continuity, and stability. The State therefore legitimately can decide to structure its tax system to discourage rapid turnover in ownership of homes and businesses, for example, in order to inhibit displacement of lower income families by the forces of gentrification or of established, "mom-and-pop" businesses by newer chain operations. . . .

Second, the State legitimately can conclude that a new owner at the time of acquiring his property does not have the same reliance interest warranting protection against higher taxes as does an existing owner. The State may deny a new owner at the point of purchase the right to "lock in" to the same assessed value as is enjoyed by an existing owner of comparable property, because an existing owner rationally may be thought to have vested expectations in his property or home that are more deserving of protection than the anticipatory expectations of a new owner at the point of purchase. A new owner has full information about the scope of future tax liability before acquiring the property, and if he thinks the future tax burden is too demanding, he can decide not to complete the purchase at all. By contrast, the existing owner, already saddled with his purchase, does not have the option of deciding not to buy his home if taxes become prohibitively high. . . .

. . . .

Finally, petitioner contends that the unfairness of Article XIIIA is made worse by its exemptions from reassessment for two special classes of new owners: persons aged 55 and older, who exchange principal residences, and children who acquire property from their parents. . . .

The two exemptions at issue here rationally further legitimate purposes. The people of California reasonably could have concluded that older persons in general should not be discouraged from moving to a residence more suitable to their changing family size or income. Similarly, the people of California reasonably could have concluded that the interests of family and neighborhood continuity and stability are furthered by and warrant an exemption for transfers between parents and children. . . .

Petitioner and amici [friends of the court] argue with some appeal that Article XIIIA frustrates the "American dream" of home ownership for many younger and poorer California families. . . .

Time and again, however, this Court has made clear in the rational-basis context that the "Constitution presumes that, absent some reason to infer antipathy, even improvident decisions will eventually be rectified by the democratic process and that judicial intervention is generally unwarranted no matter how unwisely we may think a political branch has acted." Certainly, California's grand experiment appears to vest benefits in a broad, powerful, and entrenched segment of society, and, as the Court of Appeals surmised, ordinary democratic processes may be unlikely to prompt its reconsideration or repeal. Yet many wise and well-intentioned laws suffer from the same malady. Article XIIIA is not palpably arbitrary, and we must decline petitioner's request to upset the will of the people of California.

. . . .

DISSENTING OPINION   STEVENS, J.:

During the two past decades, California property owners have enjoyed extraordinary prosperity. As the State's population has mushroomed, so has the value of its real estate. Between 1976 and 1986 alone, the total assessed value of California property subject to property taxation increased tenfold. Simply put, those who invested in California real estate in the 1970s are among the most fortunate capitalists in the world.

Proposition 13 has provided these successful investors with a tremendous windfall and, in doing so, has created severe inequities in California's property tax scheme.

. . . .

As a result of Proposition 13, . . . [California property owners who bought before enactment of Proposition 13 in 1978, called by Justice Stevens in his dissent "the Squires"], who own 44% of the owner-occupied residences, paid only 25% of the total taxes collected from homeowners in 1989. . . .

*Case **17.3** continued on following page*

*Case **17.3** continued*

. . . .

. . . Similarly situated neighbors have an equal right to share in the benefits of local government. It would obviously be unconstitutional to provide one with more or better fire or police protection than the other; it is just as plainly unconstitutional to require one to pay five times as much in property taxes as the other for the same government services. In my opinion, the severe inequalities created by Proposition 13 are arbitrary and unreasonable and do not rationally further a legitimate state interest.

. . . .

RESULT   The Supreme Court affirmed the lower court's decision and held that the California Constitution Article XIIIA's acquisition-value assessment scheme did not violate the Equal Protection Clause. Petitioner Nordlinger had to pay property taxes many times in excess of some of her neighbors with similar houses.

COMMENTS   Proposition 13 indeed produced many disparate taxes. In the more extreme cases, some homeowners paid 17 times as much in taxes as their neighbors with comparable property, and as much as 500 times as much for vacant land.

In a 1989 West Virginia case, *Allegheny Pittsburgh Coal Co. v. Webster,*[4] the United States Supreme Court held that the disparities of taxation of properties of comparable value violated the Equal Protection Clause and was unconstitutional. A crucial difference between *Allegheny* and *Nordlinger* was the absence in *Allegheny* of a justifiable policy underlying West Virginia's acquisition-value scheme. The Court found in *Allegheny* that the facts precluded any plausible inference that the reason for the unequal assessment practice was to achieve the benefits of an acquisition-value tax scheme. By contrast, Proposition 13, at issue in *Nordlinger*, was enacted with the express objective of achieving the benefits of an acquisition-value assessment system.

Questions
1. The Court in *Nordlinger* states that exempting the transfers of land between parents and children from Proposition 13 furthers the interest of neighborhood stability. Would the result be any different if a piece of property were transferred to an adult child who then subsequently rented the property out, as opposed to living in it?
2. What would be the tax disparity between old and new landowners if land prices plummeted in a certain area? Does an old landowner have the option of paying taxes on the new lower land value, or does the court's argument that the landowner has the expectation of certain values still hold?

---

4. 488 U.S. 336, 109 S.Ct. 633 (1989).

Sale and Leaseback

A sale and leaseback arrangement involves a simultaneous two-step transaction. In the first step, an institutional lender with funds to invest, such as a life insurance company or a pension fund, purchases real property from a corporation. In the second step, or often simultaneously, the property is leased back to the corporation for its use.

The term of the lease is long, often ranging from 20 to 40 years. The tenant may have the option of repurchasing the property at or before the termination date of the lease.

The amount of rent payable is structured so that during the term of the lease, the lessor will recoup the purchase price of the property and realize an acceptable return on its investment. The lessee pays all taxes and maintenance and operating costs.

Advantages to Lessee   The advantage to a corporation of selling and leasing back its real property is that capital funds are obtained at a lower cost and for a longer period than would be available from other sources of financing. A sale and leaseback transaction may also be used to reduce the corporation's debt structure by freeing up cash that would otherwise be tied up in the property. Also, rent is fully tax deductible, whereas only the interest portion of loan payments is deductible.

On the other hand, from the purchaser's point of view, the investment quality of a sale and leaseback transaction depends upon the financial stability of the seller/lessee. Such transactions are usually available only to corporations with strong track records.

Real Estate Investment Trusts (REITs)

Real estate investment trusts, commonly referred to as *REITs,* are a 1960s creation of the Internal Revenue Code and can provide a good tax vehicle for investors seeking to invest in a portfolio of real property. So long as at least 95% of a REIT's net income is distributed to shareholder-beneficiaries, the REIT itself pays no income tax; taxes are paid at the shareholder-beneficiary level only. REITs are limited in the types of operations they may conduct. Ownership concentration is also limited: No five persons can own more than 50% of the REIT's beneficial interests. REITs sell beneficial shares that are traded in the stock markets and permit small investors to invest in a diversified portfolio of real estate, similar to an investment in common stocks through a mutual fund. Although REITs had financial difficulties in the 1970s and 1980s, due to plummeting real estate values and risky development projects, returns on REITs in the first half of the 1990s were generally attractive.

Transactions with Foreigners

Sales of real property interests to foreign persons are regulated by the federal government. Under the Foreign Investment in Real Property Tax Act, the purchaser of a U.S. real property interest from a foreign person is required to withhold 10% of the purchase price to ensure that U.S. capital gains tax is collected on the sale. Additionally, the Agricultural Foreign Investment Disclosure Act requires foreign acquirers of U.S. agricultural land to file an informational report with the U.S. secretary of agriculture.

> 66
>
> *Sales of real property interests to foreign persons are regulated by the federal government.*

Preliminary Agreements

Often, the parties to a real estate transaction are able to reach a general agreement on terms and conditions, but need more time either to negotiate specific representations and warranties or to further investigate the sale. A number of alternatives to the traditional contract for the sale of real property have been developed. Examples of alternative methods of acquiring rights in real estate include option contracts, rights of first refusal, and letters of intent.

Option Contract

In an option contract, the potential buyer pays the seller for the right, but not the obligation, to purchase the property during a given time period. The option gives the buyer time to conduct investigations, determine whether the purchase of the property is economically feasible, and obtain financing. The seller receives payment for taking the property off the market for a specified period of time.

For an option contract to be enforceable, it must be in writing and consideration must be paid to the seller. Additionally, the option contract must state the major terms of the proposed purchase agreement and must specify the manner in which the option may be exercised. It is also advisable to record the option to provide constructive notice to third parties and thereby prevent the sale of the property to a third party before the option has expired.

Right of First Refusal

A *right of first refusal* is the right, conferred by a contract, to purchase the property on the same terms offered by or to a third party. Perhaps its most frequent use is with a tenant of a leasehold interest. The holder of the right of first refusal should require that it be recorded.

A right of first refusal often provides great leverage to the holder. Its very existence can chill the owner's ability to sell the property. Few buyers will want to start investigations and negotiations knowing that they could lose the deal if the party with the right of first refusal exercises his right.

Consequently, it may be advisable to modify the right of first refusal, giving the holder only the right to negotiate the purchase of the property before the seller enters negotiations with another party. This is sometimes called a right of first negotiation. Another method of accommodating the needs of the seller is to provide for a very short time, such as 72 hours, for the holder to exercise her right of first refusal.

Letter of Intent

A letter of intent may create the right to acquire an interest in a specific property. A *letter of intent* sets forth the general terms and conditions of a proposed purchase until a formal acquisition agreement can be signed. Letters of intent are often treated as unenforceable by the parties, but courts have increasingly treated them as enforceable contracts. In one case, the court focused on the conduct of the parties to determine whether an enforceable agreement was intended despite express written statements to the contrary.[5] Consequently, if the parties do not wish to

---

 Ethical Consideration

When properly utilized, letters of intent allow the parties to investigate the proposed transaction to determine whether it is worth pursuing. Although letters of intent are generally not as effective as options or rights of first refusal in removing property from the market, they can create an ethical commitment to consummate the transaction. In some states, the execution of a letter of intent creates an implied covenant of good faith and fair dealing between the parties, requiring good-faith negotiation of a formal acquisition agreement.

---

5. *Computer Systems of America v. International Business Machines Corp.*, 795 F.2d 1086 (1st Cir. 1986).

be bound by their letters of intent, they must make sure that the terms and conditions are not set forth so specifically that a binding legal obligation is created, and they must conduct themselves consistently with the absence of a binding contract (see chapter 8).

■ Financing

Financing the purchase of real estate may involve borrowing funds for a long or short term. The loan is usually secured by a lien on the property, known as a *mortgage* or *deed of trust*. The availability of financing depends on the intrinsic value of the property or on both its value and its potential for the production of income. There are an almost unlimited number of types of financing. Some of the more common forms are discussed in this section.

Permanent Loans

The most common type of real estate loan is the permanent loan. This is usually a long-term loan, repaid over 25 or 30 years.

Fixed-Interest Loans   Traditionally, permanent loans have a fixed interest rate; that is, the rate of interest does not change over the term of the loan. The lender assumes the risk of losing the benefit of any rise in interest rates, and the borrower assumes the risk of losing the benefit of any fall.

In order to benefit from any increases in market interest rates, many lenders reserve the right to call (that is, demand repayment of) fixed-interest loans after a specified period, often after 5, 10, or 15 years. Conversely, to prevent borrowers from refinancing their obligation when market interest rates fall below the fixed interest rate of the loan, some lenders may insert a lock-in clause to prohibit prepayments of principal, or they may impose a penalty, called a *prepayment penalty*, if the loan is paid off early.

Variable-Interest Loans   Variable-interest loans allow lenders to avoid the dilemma of fluctuating interest rates. In a variable-interest loan, the rate of interest is set in relation to a specified standard or base rate. It is often set at a fixed number of percentage points over the *prime rate,* that is, the interest rate offered by major lending institutions to their most creditworthy customers. Over the term of the loan, the interest rate fluctuates with changes in the base rate or index. The interest rate is usually adjusted annually or semiannually. The total amount of the change over the term of the loan is generally subject to some cap or maximum top rate. A floor may also be established to ensure that the interest rate does not fall below a specified percentage.

Points In addition to interest, real estate lenders charge a loan fee, called *points*. The fee is the amount funded, multiplied by a fixed percentage. Each 1% is a point. For example, a 2½-point fee on a $100,000 loan would be $2,500. Points are usually paid at the time the loan is made. The deductibility of points as a payment of interest is determined under the Internal Revenue Code.

Loan-to-Value Ratio The availability of financing for the acquisition of commercial property through the use of a permanent loan is frequently determined by the property's income-producing potential. Permanent loans often have loan-to-value ratios of 60% to 80%; that is, the principal amount of the loan is as much as 60% to 80% of the lender's appraised value of the property.

Appraisal Methods The value of an income-producing property may be appraised by: (1) the cost approach, whereby the construction cost of building a given improvement on the property is added to the value of the unimproved land; (2) the market approach, which looks at the selling prices in recent sales of properties with similar income-producing characteristics; or (3) the income approach, which establishes the present value of the estimated annual cash flow over the anticipated holding period.

It should be borne in mind that the appraisal of property is an inexact science, and it is relatively unregulated by state governments. Because the funds available to a developer, and the financial institution's loan fees, are based upon the property's appraised value, the appraiser may be pressured to inflate its appraisal. Although increased loan fees and increased funds for development may provide short-term benefits, inflated appraisals can have disastrous long-term effects.

The recent savings and loan crisis was in part caused by inflated appraisals that induced savings and loan associations to make reckless loans. The resulting failure of many savings and loans has already cost taxpayers in excess of $300 billion, and could ultimately cost as much as $500 billion. Upon disposal of a failed savings and loan's assets, the government is often able to recoup only a small portion of a property's inflated appraisal value. An article in *The Wall Street Journal* in the spring of 1990 lamented that some of the appraisers responsible for the crisis will have to be relied on in its resolution. The savings and loan crisis is likely to result in the adoption of national standards for appraisals.

Construction Loans

Construction loans generally have a term slightly longer than the estimated construction period. Upon completion of construction, a construction lender may be repaid from either permanent (take-out) financing or interim (gap) financing obtained by the developer. Interim or gap financing is financing that a developer obtains to pay off the construction loan when it becomes due before the permanent financing is available. This financing is provided by someone other than the construction lender and is more long term. A take-out commitment is an agreement by a lender to replace the construction loan with a permanent loan, usually after certain conditions, such as the timely completion of the project, have been met. Prior to negotiating a construction loan, the developer should establish a relationship with a lender willing to make a permanent loan or provide gap financing.

Development Loans

Although developers use construction loans for the acquisition and improvement of commercial properties, they use development loans for the acquisition, subdivision, improvement, and sale of residential properties. Funds are advanced by the lender as development progresses. The lender normally requires that the developer obtain performance bonds and personal guarantees by principals of the developer. Development lenders usually do not require take-out commitments by other lenders because the development loan is repaid upon the sale of building sites. From the lender's perspective, development loans are more risky than construction loans. The ability to pay off the development loan depends on the developer's ability to sell parcels of the development.

Equity Participation by Lender

Many lenders attempt to increase their yield from real estate projects by participating in the *equity*, or ownership, of the property. Such participation can be beneficial to both the lender and the developer. The lender can improve its yield from the project by sharing in the profits as well as receiving interest on its loan. The developers can benefit from the higher loan-to-value ratio, lower interest rates, and slower repayment terms that a participating lender will accept.

Equity participation by lenders is a relatively recent phenomenon. Historically, federal and state statutes prohibited banks and other lenders from owning real estate. In recent years, however, these statutory restraints have been substantially liberalized.

Structure of Participation   The most common form of equity participation by lenders is a *kicker,* that is, the receipt of a percentage of gross or net income in excess of a stipulated base. The lender may, for example, receive a kicker in the amount of a stipulated percentage of income over a break-even point determined by a set formula. Alternatively, the lender may actually purchase an interest in the property or in the entity owning the property.

Wraparound Financing

Occasionally an owner will require financing in addition to an existing loan secured by a deed of trust or mortgage on the property. Unless the second lender is willing to take a position subordinate to the holder of the first loan with respect to rights to the property, the owner will have to obtain a second loan sufficient to satisfy (pay off) the first loan and still provide sufficient funds to meet his financing requirements.

However, it may not be economically attractive to pay off the first loan, because of prepayment penalties or because the interest rate on the first loan may be lower than on a new loan. In such instances, wraparound financing can provide additional funds without requiring the owner to first pay off the original loan.

In a *wraparound financing* transaction the second lender lends the owner the additional funds and agrees to take over the servicing of the first loan. In exchange, the owner executes a deed of trust or mortgage and an all-inclusive note, covering the combined amount of the first and second loans. The new lender benefits because the rate charged on the all-inclusive note is higher than the weighted average interest rates of the first and second loans. The owner benefits because the interest rate on the all-inclusive note is lower than the rate she would have to pay if she paid off the first loan and took out a new loan to cover the entire amount.

Protective Laws

There are laws in every jurisdiction to regulate the conduct of lenders and borrowers, especially in the area of what interest rate can be charged (the usury laws) and the remedies if a borrower fails to pay or is otherwise in default. Both sets of laws are primarily designed to protect individuals more than businesses. Many of the default laws were originated to protect farmers during the Great Depression.

It is worth noting that many of the protective laws apply to all loans, not just to noncommercial loans. However, lenders frequently ask commercial borrowers to waive these protections. Most large lenders use standard documents for loan agreements, although changes are sometimes made. In substantial transactions, it is essential that all documents be reviewed and negotiated by all parties to a transaction.

In recent years, usury laws have tended to disappear, because an out-of-date usury law (for example, limiting the interest rate to 8% when the prevailing rate is 12%) will simply cause loan money to go to a more liberal jurisdiction. There are still states, however, in which the usury laws apply unless the title to the property is held by a corporation. In other states, equity participation by a lender may result in an illegally high interest rate. The penalties for violating the usury laws can be severe, and treble damages are sometimes available. A borrower cannot effectively agree to waive the benefits of a usury law; such a waiver is considered contrary to public policy.

Foreclosure

The legal process in which a mortgagee may have a piece of property put up for sale in the public arena to raise cash in order to pay off a debt due the mortgagee is known as *foreclosure*. The property is sold to the highest bidder; the proceeds are then first used to satisfy the debt obligation (plus interest) of the unpaid mortgage and court costs. Any remainder is given to any other secured creditors holding a mortgage or deed of trust on the property. The mortgagor receives nothing until all creditors with a security interest in the property are paid in full.

The exact details of the foreclosure process differ from state to state. Some states allow *rights of redemption*, which give the mortgagor and certain other categories of interested persons the right to redeem the property within a statutory limited period varying from two months to two years after sale. If payment of the foreclosure amount plus interest is not made by the expiration of the redemption period, the purchaser at the foreclosure sale receives the deed and clear ownership of the land.

■ Commercial Leasing

A commercial lease involves not only a conveyance of an interest in real property from the landlord to the tenant, but also a contract that governs the respective rights and obligations of the parties during the lease term. Because most businesses do not own the premises in which their business operations are conducted, the availability and the terms and conditions of commercial leasing can be crucial factors in determining the success or failure of a business. There are four types of commercial leases: office leases, retail leases, industrial leases, and ground leases.

Office Leases

Most office premises constitute a portion of an office building. Unless the tenant is to occupy a substantial portion of the building, the landlord will ordinarily present a standard lease form used for all of the tenants of the building. The landlord has a significant economic interest in using a standardized form. As the landlord is more interested in obtaining occupants than in obtaining any particular tenant as an occupant, it is often unwilling to negotiate each lease provision separately or permit the tenant to prepare the lease. In a tight market for tenants, however, more negotiation is possible.

Specific provisions of a form office lease, however, may be negotiable. A tenant should try to negotiate modifications to those lease provisions that need to be tailored to that tenant's occupancy. In addition, the money terms of the lease—such as basic and additional rent; responsibility for taxes, operating expenses, and maintenance; and escalation provisions—should be specifically negotiated by the tenant.

Rental Charge   Most office leases set forth the basic rent for the premises, usually in dollars per square foot or per rentable square foot. It is important for the tenant to inquire how the landlord established the rentable square feet in the premises. In some cases, the owner measures from the outside walls, even though the usable space is within the interior walls. The difference may be substantial. In other cases, the landlord includes public areas such as parts of corridors shared with other tenants.

> ❝ *In some cases, the owner measures from the outside walls, even though the usable space is within the interior walls. The difference may be substantial.*

The landlord should be asked to provide detailed plans that clearly indicate the gross rentable space and how much of that space is actually usable. In larger lease transactions, it may be beneficial for the tenant to hire an architect to determine the proportion of rentable square feet to usable space.

Alterations   After the rent has been established, a tenant should determine other costs. If the premises have to be adapted to meet the tenant's needs, the tenant should negotiate what alterations will be acceptable to the landlord and how much of the cost the landlord will credit against the rent.

Such issues are often addressed in a separate agreement, called a *work letter agreement,* attached to the lease. The work letter agreement should describe the alterations, specify the time period for making them, and specify who is to bear the costs. As an incentive to lease the premises, most landlords will provide tenants with either an improvement allowance or an allowance for free rent for a specified period. The amount of such allowances is dictated by the marketplace.

Additional Space   The tenant may be given either an option or a right of first refusal for leasing additional adjoining space.

Assignments and Subleases   An *assignment* of the lease is a permanent transfer of the lease to a third party. The third party acquires the tenant's rights under the lease; however, the tenant remains liable for the rent if the third party defaults unless the lessor has agreed to look only to the third party. A *sublease* is a temporary transfer of the lease to a third party.

If the premises fail to meet the tenant's needs, or if the tenant can no longer afford the lease, it may wish to assign or sublease. Landlords, on the other hand, may be hesitant to grant the right to assign or sublease. In an escalating market, a lease may develop a substantial bonus value if market rents exceed the rent due under the lease. Therefore, the landlord may condition the assignment or subleasing of space on the tenant's paying over any bonus value or splitting it with the landlord. Moreover, landlords are often concerned about the financial wherewithal of any assignees or sublessees. Therefore, most leases require the landlord's written consent for an assignment or a sublease.

Most landlords are willing to provide in the lease that they will not withhold consent unreasonably. However, a landlord may attempt to require a provision stating that it has absolute discretion to grant or withhold consent. In some states, such a provision is considered an unreasonable restraint on the conveyance of a tenant's interest in a commercial lease and is therefore unenforceable.

Retail Leases

In the negotiation of retail leases, the focus is on the operation of the tenant's business. Retail leases frequently contain a percentage rent clause that requires the tenant to pay, in addition to a base monthly rent, a percentage of its gross sales to the landlord. A percentage rent provision provides a hedge against inflation for the landlord, as well as a means for the landlord to participate in a successful tenant's business. In addition, the provision may compensate for a low base rent received from the anchor tenant, that is, a department store or supermarket that determines the economic success of a shopping center.

The definition of gross sales usually covers all sales of merchandise and services for cash or credit. Tenants should try to exclude from the percentage rate provision sources of revenue that do not produce a profit, such as customer services, sales to employees, and carrying charges. The tenant should also require an adjustment to gross sales to allow for bad debts. Although landlords will generally demand the right to audit the tenant's books, the tenant should attempt to limit the frequency of such audits. Some commercial leases have a kick-out clause, which gives the tenant the right to leave if certain gross revenue goals are not met.

Anchor Tenants   A primary concern of most tenants in shopping centers is the identity and longevity of anchor tenants. To protect its economic position, a tenant should strive to build concessions in the lease whereby the lease is terminated or rent is decreased if an anchor tenant leaves and a replacement anchor tenant is not readily found.

Business Hours   For the convenience of customers in all stores in a shopping center, it is generally necessary for stores to maintain similar business hours. Retail leases therefore often require the tenant to maintain the same hours as most stores in the center. However, as not all businesses require the same hours, and the hours of operation of a business may fluctuate due to seasonal variations, a tenant should closely scrutinize any lease provisions concerning hours of operation.

Parking   Tenants should seek commitments from the landlord regarding the availability and configuration of parking. The landlord may consider parking lots as spaces into which to expand. As protection against the loss of parking areas to expansion of the center, the tenant should attempt to negotiate a provision precluding the landlord from reducing the ratio of parking areas to leased space in the center below an agreed minimum. Alternatively, a tenant may be able to negotiate a nonrevocable, nonexclusive easement that provides that the ratio will remain constant if the landlord expands the center.

Landlords often seek to regulate the areas in which employees of tenants are allowed to park. The tenant will want some assurance that any designated employee parking areas will be within a specified distance of its premises and in a safe location.

Exclusivity Clauses   An exclusivity clause limits or prevents the operation of a competing store in the shopping center. It can be both a positive and negative part of the retail lease. Such a clause may provide the tenant with protection against competition. However, competition among tenants is usually important to the viability of a shopping center—many shoppers are attracted to shopping centers because they are able to compare goods and services.

Other Considerations   As in office leases, the ability of a tenant to assign and sublet the premises is important. The tenant will want to preserve flexibility, particularly in the event of a sale of its business. The landlord will want to control the use of the space to monitor the retail mix of the center.

The tenant will often be required either to join a merchant's association, which charges tenants to establish and maintain an advertising fund, or to make payments to a general promotional fund.

Environmental concerns are also significant in retail leases. The existence of a paint store or a dry cleaner as a tenant can impose liability upon the landlord under federal and state environmental laws and regulations.

Industrial Leases

Industrial leases tend to have a three-year term with renewal options. They usually contemplate substantial capital improvements by the tenant in the form of plant and equipment. Industrial leases are almost always *triple net*, which means the tenants pay all taxes, insurance, and maintenance expenses. Additionally, because the industrial use tends to be very site-specific, assignments of industrial leases are usually only allowed upon the sale of a tenant's business, and subleasing is usually strictly prohibited. One of the major considerations in industrial leasing is the financeability of the lease. Some industrial leases contain provisions that allow the tenant to obtain a leasehold mortgage or other security device to secure a lender's interest in the capital improvements that the tenant constructs on the leased premises.

Ground Leases

A ground lease is a very long-term lease, sometimes as long as 99 years. Ground leases are used when a landowner desires to obtain a steady return of income from undeveloped commercial property without the expense of improving or managing the property. Alternatively, a ground lease may be proposed by a tenant that does not wish to invest its own funds in the land but is willing to erect improvements for its own use and at its own risk.

The Internal Revenue Code has helped to increase the use of ground leases as an alternative to sales of real property. If the landowner has a low tax basis in the real property, he would incur a heavy capital gains tax if he were to sell, but not if he leased, the property. The lessee has tax advantages, too: Both the rent paid to the lessor and the depreciation of the building erected by the lessee are deductible expenses.

■ Government Regulation of Land Use

Land use is most heavily regulated at the local level. However, several states regulate at least some aspects of land use on a regional or statewide level. In Florida, the state has preempted the authority of local jurisdictions to regulate land use. The state determines what is permissible in part by deciding what is a sufficient infrastructure. Federal and state laws concerning environmental matters such as air and water quality, and the protection of wetlands and endangered species, can also affect the permitted uses of property.

The discussion that follows first outlines federal and state regulations and then discusses general principles of local land use regulation. Each state has its own scheme for land use regulation at the local level. Local regulatory systems operating under a state's scheme may vary from city to city, although some states require more uniformity than others ("city" is used here to refer to both cities and counties, unless otherwise noted). The specific laws and regulations applicable in each state and local jurisdiction must be consulted in order to understand how land use in that local jurisdiction is regulated.

The National Environmental Policy Act

The National Environmental Policy Act (NEPA)[6] requires all federal agencies to preserve and enhance the environment so that "man and nature can exist in productive harmony, and fulfill the social, economic, and other requirements of present and future generations of Americans." To implement this goal, NEPA requires all

agencies of the federal government to consider the environmental consequences of their actions. In any proposal for legislation or other major federal action that may significantly affect the quality of the environment, the government must include an *environmental impact statement (EIS)*. The EIS considers: (1) the environmental impact of the proposed action; (2) any adverse environmental effects that the proposed action would unavoidably have; (3) alternatives to the proposed action; (4) the relationship between the short-term uses of the environment and the maintenance and enhancement of long-term productivity; and (5) any irretrievable commitments of resources that the proposed action would involve.

EIS Requirement   Some federal actions are "categorically exempt" from the EIS requirement because they do not have any environmental impact. If the action is not categorically exempt, an environmental assessment (EA) is prepared, which identifies any significant impact on the environment. If the EA indicates that the action will not have significant impact on the environment, no EIS is prepared. If there may be significant impact, an EIS is required. In some cases, courts have determined that an EIS may not be required where the agency proposing the action performs an environmental review substantially equivalent to an EIS. Some environmental statutes expressly state that decisions made in accordance with the statute are not subject to the EIS requirement.

State Law Counterparts   Most states have adopted environmental quality laws similar to NEPA, which require state and local agencies to consider the environmental impact of their decisions. The procedures followed are similar to federal procedures but vary from state to state. NEPA and its state law counterparts are enforced mainly through litigation by persons who wish to challenge a government agency decision. NEPA and state law complaints have been used extensively by groups opposing real estate developments and federal leases of public lands for private use. Such litigation can delay projects for many years.

Planning   Planning for compliance with NEPA or its state law counterparts is an important part of planning for any business project that requires state or federal decisions, approvals, or permits. This means not only the preparation of an EIS, if required, but also planning the project to minimize adverse effects on the environment.

The Police Power

The legal basis for land use planning and regulation is the police power. The *police power* is the inherent authority

---

6. 42 U.S.C. §§ 4321 *et seq.* (1988 & Supp. 1992).

of a city or county to protect the health, safety, and welfare of its residents.

The scope of the police power has been given a wider and wider interpretation. Its exercise is no longer limited to addressing immediate threats to the public health and safety such as fires or unsanitary conditions. The Supreme Court has stated:

> The concept of the public welfare is broad and inclusive. . . . The values it represents are spiritual as well as physical, aesthetic as well as monetary. It is within the power of the Legislature to determine that the community should be beautiful as well as healthy, spacious as well as clean, well-balanced as well as carefully patrolled.[7]

Under this broad reading of public welfare, regulations as varied as architectural review, rent control, limitations on condominium conversions, and restrictions on off-site advertising signs have all been upheld as being appropriate uses of a city's police power.

" *"It is within the power of the Legislature to determine that the community should be beautiful as well as healthy, spacious as well as clean, well-balanced as well as carefully patrolled."*

---

7. *Berman v. Parker*, 348 U.S. 26, 33, 75 S.Ct. 98, 102 (1954).

Limits   Although the range of activities a city can engage in is broad, there are limitations to the police power. A land use regulation will be upheld if it is reasonably related to the public welfare, but the city may not act arbitrarily or capriciously in enacting or applying land use regulations. In addition, regulations are sometimes challenged on the ground that they amount to a taking of the property without just compensation, in violation of the Fifth Amendment to the U.S. Constitution (made applicable to the states by the Fourteenth Amendment). The U.S. Supreme Court has stated that a *regulatory taking* (sometimes referred to as inverse condemnation) has occurred if the regulation either: (1) does not substantially advance legitimate state interests, or (2) denies the owner all economically viable use of her land.[8]

In the case that follows, the Supreme Court explored the question of what constitutes a taking requiring just compensation.

---

8. *Agins v. Tiburon*, 447 U.S. 255, 100 S.Ct. 2138 (1980).

■   A Case in Point: **In the Language of the Court**

Case 17.4
PENN CENTRAL TRANSPORTATION CO. v. CITY OF NEW YORK
Supreme Court of the United States
438 U.S. 104, 98 S.Ct. 2646 (1978).

FACTS   New York City's Landmarks Preservation Law was enacted to protect historic landmarks and neighborhoods from alterations. Under the law, an 11-member landmark commission may designate a building or district a landmark. Once the designation is approved, the owner of the landmark is responsible for keeping it in good repair and any exterior alterations require commission approval. The Grand Central Terminal in mid-town Manhattan, New York City, was designated such a landmark site.

Penn Central (owners of the terminal) and UGP Properties entered into an agreement whereby UGP was to construct and lease out a 50-story office building over Grand Central Terminal. UGP would pay Penn Central $1 million per year during construction and then at least $3 million per year for an estimated period of at least 25 years. Penn Central submitted an application for the construction of the 50-story office building over the terminal that met all local zoning requirements, but was subsequently denied permission by the landmark commission. However, Penn Central was granted permission to transfer the right to build a tall building to other parcels in the vicinity.

Penn Central sued the City of New York, claiming that the application of the Landmarks Law had deprived it of its property without just compensation. The trial court granted an injunction, and the New York Court of Appeals reversed, concluding that no taking was involved. Penn Central appealed.

ISSUE PRESENTED May a city as part of a comprehensive program to preserve historic landmarks and districts place restrictions on the development of individual landmarks without effecting a "taking" requiring "just compensation"?

OPINION BRENNAN, J., writing for the U.S. Supreme Court:

. . . .

Over the past 50 years, all 50 States and over 500 municipalities have enacted laws to encourage or require the preservation of buildings and areas with historic or aesthetic importance. These nationwide legislative efforts have been precipitated by two concerns. The first is recognition that, in recent years, large numbers of historic structures, landmarks, and areas have been destroyed without adequate consideration of either the values represented therein or the possibility of preserving the destroyed properties for use in economically productive ways.

The second is a widely shared belief that structures with special historic, cultural, or architectural significance enhance the quality of life for all. Not only do these buildings and their workmanship represent the lessons of the past and embody precious features of our heritage, they serve as examples of quality for today. . . . New York City, responding to similar concerns and acting pursuant to a New York State Enabling Act, adopted its Landmarks Preservation Law in 1965. The city acted from the conviction that "the standing of [New York City] as a world-wide tourist center and world capital of business, culture and government" would be threatened if legislation were not enacted to protect historic landmarks. . . .

. . . While the law does place special restrictions on landmark properties as a necessary feature to the attainment of its larger objectives, the major theme of the law is to ensure the owners of any such properties both a "reasonable return" on their investments and maximum latitude to use their parcels for purposes not inconsistent with the preservation goals.

. . . .

. . . The Terminal . . . is one of New York City's most famous buildings. Opened in 1913, it is regarded not only as providing an ingenious engineering solution to the problems presented by urban railroad stations, but also as a magnificent example of the French beaux-arts style. . . .

. . . .

. . . Stated baldly, appellants' position appears to be that the only means of ensuring that selected owners are not singled out to endure financial hardship for no reason is to hold that any restriction imposed on individual landmarks pursuant to the New York City scheme is a "taking" requiring the payment of "just compensation." Agreement with this argument would, of course, invalidate not just New York City's law, but all comparable landmark legislation in the Nation. We find no merit in it.

*Case **17.4** continued on following page*

*Case **17.4** continued*

. . . .

In any event, appellants' repeated suggestions that they are solely burdened and unbenefited is [sic] factually inaccurate. This contention overlooks the fact that the New York City law applies to vast numbers of structures in the city in addition to the Terminal—all the structures contained in the 31 historic districts and over 400 individual landmarks, many of which are close to the Terminal. . . . [W]e cannot conclude that the owners of the Terminal have in no sense been benefited by the Landmarks Law. . . .

. . . .

. . . We now must consider whether the interference with appellants' property is of such a magnitude that "there must be an exercise of eminent domain and compensation to sustain [it]." That inquiry may be narrowed to the question of the severity of the impact of the law on appellants' parcel, and its resolution in turn requires a careful assessment of the impact of the regulation on the Terminal site.

. . . .

. . . Its designation as a landmark not only permits but contemplates that appellants may continue to use the property precisely as it has been used for the past 65 years: as a railroad terminal containing office space and concessions. So the law does not interfere with what must be regarded as Penn Central's primary expectation concerning the use of the parcel. More importantly, on this record, we must regard the New York City law as permitting Penn Central not only to profit from the Terminal but also to obtain a "reasonable return" on its investment. . . .

. . . .

DISSENTING OPINION   REHNQUIST, J.:

Of the over one million buildings and structures in the city of New York, appellees have singled out 400 for designation as official landmarks. The owner of a building might initially be pleased that his property has been chosen by a distinguished committee of architects, historians, and city planners for such a singular distinction. But he may well discover, as appellant Penn Central Transportation Co. did here, that the landmark designation imposes upon him a substantial cost, with little or no offsetting benefit except for the honor of the designation. The question in this case is whether the cost associated with the city of New York's desire to preserve a limited number of "landmarks" within its borders must be borne by all of its taxpayers or whether it can instead be imposed entirely on the owners of the individual properties.

. . . .

. . . If the cost of preserving Grand Central Terminal were spread evenly across the entire population of the city of New York, the burden per person would be in cents per year—a minor cost appellees would surely concede for the benefit accrued. Instead, however, appellees would impose the entire cost of several million dollars per year on Penn Central. But it is precisely this sort of discrimination that the Fifth Amendment prohibits.

RESULT   The Court affirmed the decision of the lower court. New York City could prevent Penn Central from building an office building above Grand Central Terminal without having to pay Penn Central anything for the restriction on development.

COMMENTS   The Court's decision in this case seemed particularly influenced by the fact the terminal owners were still making a substantial return from their property and that their principal use of the terminal was unaffected.

Questions
1. The landmark law requires the owner to pay for the costs of maintaining the landmark. What happens if the company cannot afford the necessary costs to maintain the property to the extent the law would require?
2. Suppose that a fire caused major damages to a historical landmark and extensive money would be required to restore the property to its original state. Could the owner be required to expend such funds? Could an owner be required to maintain an expensive insurance policy against the property to protect against such occurrences?

In a 1992 case,[9] the United States Supreme Court reviewed a lower court ruling in which a regulation had been found to deny a landowner all economically viable use of his land. In 1986, Lucas paid $975,000 for two residential lots on which he intended to build single-family homes. In 1988, the South Carolina Legislature enacted the Beachfront Management Act, which effectively barred him from erecting any permanent structure on his parcels. Lucas sued, claiming that he was a victim of a taking without just compensation. The state trial court held that his land had been rendered economically useless. The South Carolina Supreme Court reversed the trial court's granting of $1.2 million in compensation, holding that if a regulation is designed to prevent harmful or noxious uses, no compensation is required. The U.S. Supreme Court found that the South Carolina Supreme Court erred in applying this test, and remanded the case. The proper test, according to the U.S. Supreme Court in *Lucas*, is whether the land use regulation permits results that could not have been achieved under state common-law nuisance doctrine. If the regulation does no more than duplicate the result under nuisance law, no compensation is required. If, however, the regulation prohibits activity not prohibited by common-law nuisance and denies an owner economically viable use of her land, compensation may be required. The U.S. Supreme Court in *Lucas* said that in such cases the burden of proof is on the state to show that its regulation is not a taking.

---

9. *Lucas v. South Carolina Coastal Council*, 112 S.Ct. 2886 (1992).

Takings questions also arise when a regulatory agency imposes a condition that must be satisfied before a building permit or other land use approval is granted. This is discussed later in this chapter as part of the discussion of regulatory schemes.

■ Regulatory Schemes

The fundamental components of most land use regulatory schemes are a general plan, a zoning ordinance, and a subdivision ordinance. Some jurisdictions also employ more specialized planning documents, often called specific plans or community plans, which function somewhere between the general plan and the zoning ordinances.

The General Plan

Many cities have a general development plan, known variously as the general plan, city plan, master plan, or comprehensive plan. (All such plans are referred to as the general plan in this chapter.) A *general plan* is a long-range planning document that addresses the physical development and redevelopment of a city. It is comprehensive in that it addresses the entire city and a wide range of concerns, such as housing, natural resources, public facilities, transportation, and the permitted locations for various land uses. It includes goals, objectives, policies, and programs related to these concerns.

The practical effect of the general plan varies from state to state. In some states, a general plan is not required at all. In certain states, the general plan is strictly an advisory document which need not be adhered to when planning decisions are made. In other states, the plan functions as the "constitution" for development and, by law, planning decisions such as zoning, subdivision approval, and road and sewer construction must be consistent with it. Particularly where the general plan has this significance, anyone contemplating development of a specific piece of property should determine what the general plan says about the allowed uses for that property. If development of the type contemplated is not authorized by the general plan, a general plan amendment will be required. The general plan may also be amended to preclude a contemplated development.

The general plan may provide important information about the city's policies regarding growth, where and when public services and facilities will be provided, and whether developers will be expected to provide or pay for needed infrastructure.

Authorization of a type of development in the general plan is not a guarantee that a specific development will be permitted. The development must also be authorized by the zoning ordinance, and other land use approvals could be required.

Other Planning Documents

Some jurisdictions employ other planning documents in addition to the general plan. Called specific plans, special plans, community plans, area plans, and a number of other names, these plans usually encompass just a portion of the city's geographic area. They may focus on areas in particular need of planning, such as a downtown area slated for redevelopment, an environmentally sensitive area, a transportation corridor, or an area facing unusual development pressure. Typically, these plans are more detailed than the general plan.

Zoning

Zoning is the division of a city into districts and the application of specific land use regulations in each district. Zoning regulations are divided into two classes: (1) regulations regarding the structural and architectural design of buildings (such as height or bulk limitations), and (2) regulations regarding the uses, such as commercial or residential, to which buildings within a particular district may be put. These types of regulations are

employed both in traditional zoning systems and in more recently developed approaches to zoning.

Traditional Zoning   Traditional zoning separates different land uses. For example, residential areas are separate from commercial and industrial areas, and residential areas of varying densities are separate. This approach to zoning finds its roots in the earliest land use regulations, which promoted health and safety by separating residences from certain types of manufacturing and service industries. Early zoning also protected property values by preventing apartments from being built near more desirable single-family dwellings.

Planned Unit Development   Although many cities still employ some form of traditional zoning, others have adopted different approaches. For example, under *planned unit development (PUD)* zoning, the land use regulations for a given piece of property reflect the proposed development plans for that property. These plans may include a mixture of uses, such as residential, office, and retail commercial, which could not be accommodated under the separation of uses required by traditional zoning. Residential development may be clustered on a portion of the property, at densities that exceed what would be permitted under traditional zoning, but in such a manner that larger areas of open space are provided. Many feel that this more flexible approach to zoning allows greater creativity and greater sensitivity to environmental and aesthetic concerns.

Zoning Relief   Variances and conditional use permits may create exceptions to a zoning ordinance. A *variance* allows a landowner to construct a structure or carry on an activity not otherwise permitted under the zoning regulations. A variance allows the property owner to use the property in a manner basically consistent with the established regulations, with such minor variations as are necessary to avoid inflicting a unique hardship on that property owner. In some states, variances may be granted to allow uses not authorized by the zoning regulations. In other states, variances are limited to sanctioning deviations from regulations governing physical standards, such as minimum lot size, the maximum number of square feet that may be developed, and off-street parking requirements.

A *conditional use permit* allows uses that are not permitted as a matter of right under the zoning ordinance. The permit imposes conditions to ensure that the use will be appropriate for the particular situation.

Nonconforming Uses   A *nonconforming use* is an existing use that was originally lawful, but that does not comply with a later-enacted zoning ordinance. A zoning ordinance may not compel immediate discontinuance of a nonconforming use (unless it constitutes a public nuisance). A city can require that nonconforming uses be eliminated within a reasonable time or upon application for a building permit to modify the premises.

Subdivision

Frequently, development requires the division of land into separate parcels. This process is known as *subdivision*. It is a necessary step in residential development and often in industrial or commercial development.

The subdivision process allows the city to regulate new development and to limit harm, deterioration of water quality, soil erosion, and building in areas subject to earth movement. The subdivider may also be required to address, for example, the impact of the subdivision on views and other aesthetic concerns, or on traffic circulation.

Subdivision approval frequently requires that the subdivider provide streets, utilities, sewers, drainage facilities, and other infrastructure to serve the subdivision. It may be required to dedicate land for parks, schools, libraries, and fire stations, and to pay "impact fees" to offset the increased burden on public facilities and services resulting from the subdivision. The conditions may include constructing on-site or off-site facilities, or paying fees for purposes as varied as acquiring parkland or providing day-care centers, public art, or low-income housing.

Conditions

Conditions to a land use approval will be upheld if they are reasonably related to the burdens on the community created by the development being approved. Thus, if the development will result in an influx of residents or employees, a fee to fund traffic improvements made necessary by that influx will be upheld. The courts have described the legally required relationship between a condition to an approval and the impacts of the development being approved as a *nexus*. In the absence of the required nexus, the condition may be struck down, as in the case of *Nollan v. California Coastal Commission.*[10]

In 1982, James and Marilyn Nollan sought a permit from the California Coastal Commission to demolish

their existing single-story beachfront house and replace it with a two-story, three-bedroom house approximately three times larger than the existing structure. Public beaches were located within one-half mile to the north and south of the Nollans' property. Finding that the new house would further obstruct the ocean view, increase private use of the beach, and establish a "psychological barrier" to access to the nearby public beaches, the commission approved the construction subject to the condition that the Nollans dedicate an easement for public access across the portion of their property lying between the high water mark and a seawall approximately 10 feet inland. The Nollans challenged this condition.

The U.S. Supreme Court, in a 5-to-4 decision, held that the dedication condition amounted to an unconstitutional taking. Citing its holdings in earlier takings cases, the Court stated that a land use regulation, including a dedication condition, amounts to a taking if it can be shown that the regulation either: (1) does not substantially advance a legitimate governmental interest, or (2) denies an owner economically viable use of his land. The Court found that the regulation failed on the first prong of this test: The condition did not in fact further the governmental interest advanced as its justification.

The Supreme Court elaborated on the lack of connection, or *nexus*, between the identified impacts of the project and the easement condition. The Court concluded it was quite impossible to understand how a requirement that people already on the public beaches be able to walk across the Nollans' property reduced any obstacles to viewing the beach created by the new house. It was also impossible for the Court to understand how it lowered any "psychological barrier" to using the public beaches, or how it helped to remedy any additional congestion on them caused by construction of the Nollans' new house. The Court therefore found that the commission's imposition of the permit condition cannot be treated as an exercise of its land use power for any of these purposes.

The Supreme Court concluded that the condition was not a valid land use regulation, but an "out-and-out plan of extortion." Although the Court recognized California's right to advance its programs and use its power of eminent domain for a "public purpose," the Court concluded by saying that if the government wanted an easement across the Nollans' property, "it must pay for it." The Supreme Court did indicate that a condition that protected the public's ability to see the beach and ocean despite the construction of the Nollans' new house—such as a height limitation, a ban on fences, or even a requirement that the Nollans provide a viewing area for the public—would probably be constitutional.

---

10. 483 U.S. 825, 107 S.Ct. 3141 (1987).

❝
The Supreme Court concluded that the condition was not a valid land use regulation, but an "out-and-out plan of extortion."

The following case addressed a question left open by the Supreme Court in *Nollan,* namely, what is the required degree of connection between the conditions imposed by a city and the projected impact of the proposed development.

■ **A Case in Point:**   **Summary**

Case 17.5
DOLAN v. CITY OF TIGARD
Supreme Court of the
United States
114 S.Ct. 2309 (1994).

FACTS   Florence Dolan, owner of a plumbing and electrical supplies store located on Main Street in the Central Business District in the city of Tigard, Oregon, applied to the city for a permit to redevelop the site. Her proposed plans called for nearly doubling the size of the store to 17,600 square feet, and paving a 39-space parking lot. She also proposed building an additional structure on the site for complementary businesses, and to provide more parking. The proposed expansion and intensified use were consistent with the city's zoning scheme in the Central Business District.

The City Planning Commission granted Dolan's permit application subject to certain conditions imposed by the city's Community Development Code (CDC). The CDC required that new developments facilitate a reduction of congestion in the Central Business District by dedication of land for pedestrian/bicycle pathways intended to encourage alternatives to automobile transportation for short trips. In addition, as part of a drainage plan designed to alleviate flooding that occurs along Fanno Creek, including areas near Dolan's property, the CDC required dedication of sufficient open land area for greenway adjoining and within the floodplain.

Applying the CDC, the City Planning Commission required that Dolan dedicate the portion of her property lying withing the 100-year floodplain for improvement of a storm drainage system along Fanno Creek, and that she dedicate an additional 15-foot strip of land adjacent to the floodplain as a pedestrian/bicycle pathway. The dedication required by the conditions encompassed approximately 7,000 square feet, or roughly 10% of the property.

Dolan challenged the city's dedication requirements, arguing that they constituted an uncompensated taking of her property under the Fifth Amendment, as applied to the states through the Fourteenth Amendment.

ISSUE PRESENTED   What relationship must exist between conditions to a land use approval and the projected impact of a proposed development for the conditions not to constitute an unconstitutional taking of property?

SUMMARY OF OPINION   The U.S. Supreme Court, in a 5-to-4 decision, held that the city had failed to show that there was "rough proportionality" between the conditions imposed on Dolan's permit and the nature and extent of the proposed development's impact. Citing *Nollan,*[11] the Court stated that had the city simply required Dolan to dedicate a strip of land along Fanno Creek for public use, rather than conditioning the grant of a permit to redevelop her property on such a dedication, a taking would have occurred. The Court noted that the purpose of the Takings Clause is to prohibit the

---

11. *Nollan v. California Coastal Commission,* 483 U.S. 825, 107 S.Ct. 3141 (1987).

government from forcing some people alone to bear public burdens which, in all fairness and justice, should be borne by the public as a whole.

In evaluating Dolan's claims, the Court first determined whether the required "essential nexus" existed between the legitimate state interest and the permit condition exacted by the city. The Court found that the essential nexus was present. The prevention of flooding along Fanno Creek and the reduction of traffic congestion in the Central Business District qualify as legitimate public purposes. A nexus existed between preventing flooding along Fanno Creek and limiting development within the creek's 100-year floodplain. Dolan proposed to double the size of her retail store and to pave her now-gravel parking lot, thereby expanding the impervious surface on the property and thus increasing the amount of stormwater runoff into Fanno Creek. Similarly, the Court upheld the city's attempt to reduce traffic congestion by providing for alternate means of transportation for workers and shoppers by requiring a pedestrian/bicycle pathway.

The Court then considered whether the degree of exactions demanded by the city's permit conditions bore the required relationship to the projected impact of Dolan's proposed development. The Court created a test of "rough proportionality" to decide what constitutes a taking. Under this test, while no precise mathematical calculation is required, the city must make some sort of individualized determination that the required dedication is related both in nature and extent to the impact of the proposed development.

Applying this test to Dolan, the court held that requiring her to create a public greenway, as compared with a private greenway, was not justified by the city's interest in flood control. Such an interest could be satisfied equally well by a private greenway, which would give Dolan control over the time in which the public entered the greenway.

With respect to the pedestrian/bicycle pathway, the Court acknowledged that the larger retail sales facility would increase traffic on the streets of the Central Business District by roughly 435 additional trips per day. The Court noted that dedications for streets, sidewalks, and other public ways are generally reasonable exactions to avoid excessive congestion for a proposed property use. But in this case, the Court found that the city had not met its burden of demonstrating that the additional number of vehicle and bicycle trips generated by Dolan's development reasonably relate to the city's requirement for dedication of the pedestrian/bicycle easement. The city had simply found that the creation of the pathway could offset some of the traffic demand and lessen the increase in traffic congestion, but the city failed to make an effort to quantify its findings in support of the dedication for the pedestrian/bicycle pathway beyond the conclusory statement that it could offset some of traffic demand generated.

RESULT The proposed exactions required by Dolan's permit constituted an unconstitutional condition in violation of the Fifth Amendment. The city failed to show rough proportionality, that is, that there had been an individualized determination that the required dedication was related both in nature and extent to the impact of Dolan's proposed development.

COMMENTS In a joint dissent, Justices Stevens, Blackmun and Ginsburg noted that this was "unquestionably an important case." They attacked the decision of the majority, both because it reversed a long-standing presump-

Case **17.5** continued on following page

*Case **17.5** continued*

tion that land-use regulation of commercial space is constitutional, and because it changed the burden in takings cases. These justices argued:

> If the government can demonstrate that the conditions it has imposed in a land-use permit are rational, impartial and conducive to filling the aims of a valid land-use plan, a strong presumption of validity should attach to these conditions. The burden of demonstrating that those conditions have unreasonably impaired the economic value of the proposed improvement belongs squarely on the shoulders of the party challenging the state action's constitutionality. That allocation of burdens has served us well in the past. The Court has stumbled badly today by reversing it.

Vested Development Rights

Until a developer obtains a *vested right*—that is, a fully guaranteed right—to develop a property, the regulations governing that property may be changed. In other words, a developer has no claim to the land use regulations in effect when the property was acquired, when preliminary steps to development were taken, or at any other time prior to the vesting of the right to develop. A change in the land use regulations prior to vesting may thus preclude a proposed development.

In some states, the right to develop vests when substantial work is done and substantial liabilities are incurred in reliance on a building permit. In other states, vesting is tied to obtaining the "last discretionary approval" required for development. States differ on what constitutes the last discretionary approval.

Early Vesting Late vesting of the right to develop leaves a developer vulnerable to loss of time and money should the land use regulations be changed prior to vesting. For this reason, mechanisms to allow early vesting are available in several states. One such mechanism is a development agreement, which is authorized in Arizona, California, Colorado, Florida, Hawaii, and Nevada. The development project is governed by the regulations in effect when the agreement is entered into, and is immune from subsequent changes in the land use regulations.

Environmental Assessment

Some states, before approving a development project, require a detailed evaluation of the effects of the project on the environment. The state may also require a discussion of alternatives to the proposed project and an identification of measures to mitigate adverse environmental effects.

Physical Accessibility to Commercial Facilities

Under the Americans with Disabilities Act (ADA),[12] any new renovations or alterations to commercial facilities must be accessible to disabled persons, including those in wheelchairs. Commercial facilities are defined under the act as all structures except those intended for residential use. However, this accessibility rule applies only to the areas being renovated and requires compliance only to the extent feasible. New construction, on the other hand, is subject to more complex accessibility rules. In building new structures, architects and builders must comply with regulations established by the U.S. attorney general regarding accessibility. In general, new structures must be designed and constructed so that they are "readily accessible to and usable by individuals with disabilities," unless it is structurally impossible to do so. Violation of the physical accessibility rules for renovations and new construction can result in a private lawsuit or action by the U.S. attorney general. Violators may be required to pay damages as well as civil penalties of up to $50,000 for a first violation and $100,000 for subsequent violations.

The ADA also requires minor physical changes to existing workplaces to accommodate disabled workers. For example, the ADA mandates removal of architectural barriers in existing stores, offices, and firms where the removal is "readily achievable." Modifications are readily achievable if they are easy to accomplish and can be done without significant expense. Readily achievable changes might include ramping of a few steps or lowering of a public telephone for wheelchair users, installation of grab bars in rest rooms, raised letters and

---

12. 42 U.S.C. § 12101 *et seq.* (Supp. 1992).

numerals on elevator controls, and rearrangement of office furniture to provide increased accessibility.

The Responsible Manager

Buying and Using Real Estate

The typical manager who does not manage real estate full-time will probably find that there are more laws, administrative regulations, and governmental practices associated with real estate than with many other management activities. The manager will not always be able to rely on common sense in managing real estate, because the laws and administrative practices can impact real estate in surprising ways.

In the acquisition of real estate, for example, the manager should: (1) determine that the property is properly located for his company's operations; (2) decide that the improvements, if already built, comply with applicable building codes and are suitable for the company; (3) determine whether the facility complies with physical accessibility regulations under the Americans with Disabilities Act; (4) determine that previous owners have fully complied with federal, state, and local environmental and hazardous-waste laws and that the company will not be liable under any of those laws; (5) decide whether the company should lease or buy the property; (6) decide, if the property is rental property, for how long and under what terms it should be leased; (7) decide, if the property is for sale, how best to negotiate the purchase contract and finance the purchase; and (8) keep more senior executives and/or the board of directors informed about the manager's actions and decisions throughout the process.

The magnitude of the investment and the permanence of the acquisition render these decisions some of the most important that a manager will make. Although large corporations generally have a department for facilities management, smaller organizations do not. The manager will need to have access to responsible professionals, including knowledgeable commercial/industrial real estate brokers, attorneys who specialize in real estate, environmental consultants, and attorneys specializing in environmental law. If the company is acquiring bare land and building its own improvements, the manager will also need to have available expertise in planning and land use. With the heavy use of outside consultants comes the responsibility of managing the consultants and controlling the costs of the real estate operations.

Similar responsibilities go along with the occupancy of real estate. If a company occupies premises under a full-service lease, which requires the lessor to maintain the property, the tenant's responsibilities may be limited to seeing that the services provided are adequate. Most manufacturing companies, however, do not occupy leased premises on a full-service basis, and this may mean that the management is responsible for continuing maintenance, repairs, and compliance with laws, including environmental laws. In any type of occupancy, management must always plan ahead so that the facilities will continue to be adequate for present and future operations. It is often difficult to anticipate needs, and it is easy to overspend or, conversely, to fail to anticipate a new demand.

Finally, the manager is likely to find that she has less control than she wishes over real estate decisions. For example, building or other occupancy permits may need to be obtained from several agencies, such as building departments and fire departments. Those agencies may not be responsive to the urgent demands of a company, and the official involved may be given a great deal of discretion in both the timing and interpretation of the applicable laws. Delays beyond the company's control frequently try managers' patience and cause inconvenience and downtime. In either the acquisition or disposition phase, a manager would be well advised to allow considerable extra time for delay.

Another Pebble Across an Ocean of Retreat

As the saying goes, the whole is greater than the sum of its parts. This time-worn expression certainly applies to real estate, where local communities often attach sentimental value to land or a building. This sentimentality is frequently difficult to pinpoint, and its value can be distinctly separate from the property's fair market value. The foray by Japanese investors to acquire the famous Pebble Beach Golf Course in Northern California is an excellent case in point.

Nestled along the breathtaking views of the famed 17-Mile Drive lies the exclusive town of Pebble Beach. In addition to its legendary seaside golf course, which has hosted the U.S. Open, this resort on the tip of the Monterey Peninsula is known for picturesque serenity. The rare stands of Monterey pines in the Del Monte Forest create a natural playground for the enormous population of deer which often wander aimlessly across fairways to the chagrin of golfers. Along the coast, not far from the famed Lone Cypress, hundreds of sea lions have made a home of the rocks jutting from the Pacific Ocean. As they lazily soak up the sun and bark at each other, these docile creatures seem oblivious to the sea kayaks that drift slowly by. It is no wonder that residents of Pebble Beach have come to view their peaceful environment as nothing short of sacred.

Minoru Isutani, the owner of the real estate firm Cosmo World, failed to account for this community's ongoing romance with its surroundings when he paid $841 million to buy the Pebble Beach resort from a partnership headed by oilman Marvin Davis in August 1990. To raise the funds necessary to buy Pebble Beach, Isutani sold a large block of membership certificates for his four Japanese golf courses to Itoman, the Osaka trading house made infamous in 1991 for its scandalous activities.[13] Soon after, reports trickled out in the Japanese and U.S. press that Isutani paid such a high price for the Pebble Beach resort because he hoped to sell private Pebble Beach club memberships and use the proceeds to pare down his hefty debt. The price to become a member at the famous course, which had always been open to the public, would not be cheap. Initial reports were that he expected to persuade golf-loving Japanese to pay as much as $740,000 per membership.[14]

However, the gamble proved to be disastrous. If Isutani had done his research, he might have realized that his plan to convert a relatively democratic establishment into a Japanese millionaire's club would prompt an outcry from the concerned citizens of Pebble Beach. Instead, Isutani went forward with the acquisition only to later abandon the membership scheme in the face of implacable local opposition. When this occurred, the Japanese investor was financially ruined, forced to abruptly sell the resort at nearly a $250 million loss.

The new owners—Japanese investors calling themselves the Lone Cypress Co. after the landmark tree along 17-Mile Drive—learned much from Isutani's failed attempt to sell expensive memberships. In addition to lavishing attention and millions of dollars on the Pebble Beach course and The Lodge at Pebble Beach, the owners are doing their best to be good citizens by making generous donations to local charities and keeping officials and homeowners apprised of any developmental plans. The open communication contrasted sharply with the business style of golf course developer Isutani, whose bulldozer approach to land use issues did not sit well with local government officials, residents, or the California Coastal Commission.[15]

Japan Looks Inward[16]

Isutani's experience was merely symptomatic of what had become a trend of retreating Japanese investments.

---

13. "Prosecutors to Probe Isutani's 55 Billion Golf Handicap: Aftermath of Pebble Beach Fiasco Leaves a Question of Fraud," COMLINE Daily News Tokyo Financial Wire, April 8, 1992.

14. Martha Groves, "New Pebble Beach Owners Are Playing Finesse Game," *Los Angeles Times*, May 19, 1992, D1.
15. *Ibid.*
16. The following section draws upon three articles: Ronald E. Yates, "Foreigners' Investment in U.S. Plunges," *Chicago Tribune*, June 10, 1992, C1; John Burgess, "Rush to Buy U.S. Property Slows to a Cautious Walk," *International Herald Tribune*, June 22, 1992; and Arthur M. Louis, "Japanese Dump U.S. Properties," *San Francisco Chronicle*, April 19, 1994, D1.

Inside Story, continued

Japanese investors became seriously interested in American real estate after the Western industrial powers reached an agreement in 1985 to lower the value of the dollar against the yen and European currencies. Although this accord was designed to reduce the U.S. trade deficit, it also made the purchase of U.S. property a much better bargain for those with foreign currency. Japan had accumulated huge supplies of capital through its large trade surpluses and needed to invest it somewhere. The U.S. property market was booming in the mid-1980s and even when investors paid a premium, as many did, the market value often quickly caught up.

Every week, it seemed, newspapers reported high-profile sales of famous American resorts, sports teams, and landmarks. In Hawaii, Japanese agents negotiated purchases of hotels on Waikiki Beach and made offers on private homes in high-value residential neighborhoods. In 1989, Mitsubishi Estate Company attracted nationwide publicity in the United States by paying $846 million for a controlling interest in the firm that owned Rockefeller Center, the coveted Manhattan address that includes the famed Radio City Music Hall. Even cattle ranches were being sold to Japanese investors, who seemed to have endless supplies of money and optimism about the U.S. market.

To some Americans, the buying spree was a troubling sign that Japan was "buying up" their country. The purchases brought home dramatically Japan's emergence as a potent force in the world economy. Real estate purchases became fodder for jokes on TV talk shows and commentary for Congress. In Tokyo, Japanese officials became concerned that the investments would put new strain on trans-Pacific trade relations, and discouraged further purchases of so-called "trophy buildings." When Chicago's Sears Tower, the world's tallest building, went on the market in 1989, the Japanese government was widely reported to have urged Japanese businesses to keep their distance.

Peaking in 1988 at $16.5 billion, the boom in new Japanese real estate investments dropped off precipitously, falling 96% to $705 million in 1993. America, once a powerful magnet for Japanese investors, woke up to a recession-plagued economy at the end of the 1980s. Imploding property values in the U.S., combined with an economic downturn in Japan, caused many Japanese investors like Minoru Isutani to put their U.S.

properties back on the market for a substantial loss. In fact, during 1992 and 1993, the Japanese sold, lost to foreclosure, or restructured $17.6 billion worth (or 23%) of their total U.S. real estate holdings. Approximately another $12 billion worth of Japanese-owned U.S. properties were sold, foreclosed, or restructured in 1994.

In 1991, all foreign investment in the United States plummeted an incredible 66% to $22.6 billion. The dramatic drop from $65.93 billion in 1990 represented the lowest level of foreign investment since 1984. Furthermore, it was the third straight year of decline after foreign investments hit an all-time high of $72.69 billion in 1988. The decreases in 1989 and 1990 were much less—registering 2.1% and 7.4%, respectively.

Although part of this trend can be attributed to the decline in European investments as that continent became preoccupied with its economic unification and investment opportunities in the former communist countries of Eastern Europe, much can also be attributed to rapidly vanishing Japanese investments. In 1990, Japan invested $19.93 billion in the U.S., approximately 65% (nearly $13 billion) of which was in U.S. real estate. Although Japan retained its status in 1991 as the foreign country with the most direct investments in the U.S., it nevertheless reduced its total American investment activity by nearly 75% to $5.07 billion. Consistent with this figure, Japanese real estate investments in 1991 plunged 61%. New Japanese investments in U.S. real estate continued to fall and in 1993 were only $705 million.

The reasons for Japan's reduced presence could be traced to several factors, not the least of which was its weak stock market, which lost almost 50% of its value from 1990 to 1992. In 1991 Japanese property values took a nosedive and bankrupt companies left a record $58 billion in debt. As of 1992, Japan's economy was growing at the sluggish rate of 2.5%; this snail's pace stood in stark contrast to Japan's traditionally robust growth pattern. The cutback in foreign investment was one more sign that the country known as the world's prime source of international capital had switched gears and was looking inward. Japanese foreign investments naturally declined as Japanese firms had less cash to spend on buyouts of American firms, overseas facilities, and the high-profile real estate purchases that dominated the 1980s.

Key Words and Phrases

actual notice **533**
after-acquired title **533**
assignment **547**
beneficiary **532**
community property **532**
conditional use permit **554**
constructive notice **533**
conveyance **531**
deed **531**
deed of trust **544**
dual agency **536**
encumbrance **534**
environmental impact
  statement (EIS) **549**
equity **545**
escrow **535**
escrow agent **535**
fee simple **531**
foreclosure **546**
general partnership **532**
general plan **553**

grant deed **533**
grantee **531**
grantor **531**
innocent landowner defense **537**
inquiry notice **533**
joint tenancy **531**
kicker **546**
letter of intent **544**
limited partnership **533**
marketable title **533**
mortgage **544**
nexus **555**
nonconforming use **554**
planned unit development (PUD) **554**
points **545**
police power **549**
prepayment penalty **544**
prime rate **544**
quitclaim deed **533**
race-notice recording act **534**
real estate investment trust (REIT) **543**

recordable form **533**
recording acts **533**
regulatory taking **550**
right of first refusal **543**
rights of redemption **546**
squatter's rights **535**
subdivision **555**
sublease **547**
tax-deferred exchange **538**
tenancy by the entirety **531**
tenants in common **531**
triple net lease **548**
trust **532**
trustee **532**
variance **554**
vested right **558**
view easement **534**
warranty deed **533**
work letter agreement **547**
wraparound financing **546**
zoning **554**

Questions and Case Problems

1. What does it mean if a state is a race-notice jurisdiction?

2. Ace owns Whiteacre, a 40-acre parcel of unimproved real estate on the outskirts of a burgeoning city in the State of Calvada. In June 1974, the legislature of Calvada approved the construction of a freeway adjacent to Whiteacre. Shortly after the completion of the freeway in 1981, Ace was approached by Greenhorn, who desired to construct an apartment building on Whiteacre. Greenhorn is a licensed general contractor previously employed by several large apartment building developers. Although Greenhorn could not arrange financing to purchase Whiteacre outright, he was able to negotiate a 60-year ground lease from Ace on the express condition that Greenhorn complete construction of the apartment building before July 1, 1983. The lease was duly executed by both Ace and Greenhorn, and a memorandum of the lease was legally recorded.

Greenhorn obtained a $10 million loan at 10% interest that was due and payable on or before July 1, 1983, from Construction Lender. To secure repayment of the construction loan, Greenhorn executed a leasehold mortgage in favor of Construction Lender and legally recorded it.

Concurrently with the funding of the construction loan, Greenhorn obtained a standby commitment from Permanent Lender to advance $10 million at 8% interest contingent upon: (1) the issuance of certificates of occupancy for 80% of the apartment building, and (2) the leasing of 60% of the total rentable space of the apartment building to tenants acceptable

to Permanent Lender. Greenhorn contracted with various subcontractors for the construction of the apartment building. Certificates of occupancy for 80% of the apartment building were issued on or before May 31, 1983. Certificates of occupancy for the remaining units were not obtained until July 3, 1983. The leasing of units was hampered by the availability of apartments at a lower cost in competing complexes. As of May 31, 1983, Permanent Lender had only approved leases for 45% of the rentable space.

Fearful of defaulting on the construction loan, Greenhorn approached both Construction Lender and Permanent Lender and was successful in negotiating a letter of intent between Greenhorn, Construction Lender, and Permanent Lender, whereby it was agreed in principle that the term of the construction note would be extended to December 31, 1983, subject to approval by counsel for both Construction Lender and Permanent Lender. Upon the execution of the letter of intent, the officer of Construction Lender negotiating it exclaimed that he was glad that a definitive agreement had been reached to extend the construction loan. The officer representing Permanent Lender replied that he should receive a memento to mark the importance of the occasion.

Subsequently, the prime interest rate rose from 8% to 13% in a two-month period, the lending policies of Permanent Lender were scrutinized by the federal regulatory authorities, and its reserve requirements were substantially increased. Permanent

Lender, unbeknownst to Greenhorn and Construction Lender, was not in a position to fund the permanent loan because of its increased reserve requirements.

Prior to December 31, 1983, Greenhorn submitted executed leases to Permanent Lender sufficient to meet the 60% lease contingency. The financial condition of the tenants who signed these leases was equal to or greater than that of the tenants previously approved by Permanent Lender. Recognizing the tight position that it was in, Permanent Lender's attorneys uncovered an ancient deed restriction that precluded the sale or lease of Whiteacre or any portion thereof to any person of Chinese descent and refused to approve several leases to individuals with Chinese surnames. Thus, Greenhorn was unable to fulfill the 60% lease contingency prior to December 31, 1983, and Permanent Lender refused to fund the permanent loan.

On January 5, 1984, Construction Lender sent a notice of default to Greenhorn and announced its intent to foreclose the leasehold mortgage.

What are the legal rights and obligations of Ace, Greenhorn, Construction Lender, and Permanent Lender? [*Resolution Trust Corp. v. Mustang Partners*, 946 F.2d 103 (10th Cir. 1991)]

3. The Rocking K Ranch is located in State X, which utilizes a race-notice recording system. Although the ranch had been operated for many years by Abel, record title was actually held by Abel's reclusive uncle, Meier. After a number of years of unexpectedly low cattle prices, Abel encountered severe cash flow difficulties. In an attempt to solve his financial problems, Abel entered into the following transactions:

(a) On January 1, 1994, Abel sold the ranch to Baker for $250,000. Abel delivered a duly executed and acknowledged grant deed to Baker, but the grant deed was not recorded by Baker until September 2, 1994.

(b) On February 1, 1994, Abel leased the ranch to his neighbor, Carter, for a period of five years. Carter immediately removed the fences surrounding the Rocking K and operated both his ranch and the Rocking K as a single outfit.

(c) On February 26, 1994, Abel sold the ranch to Dalton for $250,000, delivering a duly executed and acknowledged quitclaim deed to Dalton. The quitclaim deed was duly recorded by Dalton on March 5, 1994.

(d) Meier died on March 10, 1994, and under the terms of Meier's will, Abel inherited the ranch. A grant deed (the Meier deed) was delivered to Abel by the executor of Meier's estate on August 10, 1994.

(e) On August 25, 1994, with the Meier deed in his back pocket, Abel approached his other neighbor, Everready, offering to sell the ranch to Everready for $240,000. Everready was reluctant to purchase it because he knew that Carter had recently been operating the Rocking K. After talking with Carter and determining that Carter's only interest in the ranch was a leasehold interest, Everready agreed to purchase the ranch from Abel for $220,000. At the consummation of the sale Everready received the Meier deed and a grant deed executed by Abel in favor of Everready. On September 3, 1994, Everready first recorded the Meier deed and then recorded the grant deed executed by Abel.

As of September 4, 1994, who is the lawful owner of the Rocking K Ranch?

4. Patricia and Bobby Star got married in New Mexico in July 1988. They had been living together since 1985. In July 1994 they separated. Before the marriage, in April 1987, they purchased a residence as joint tenants. Patricia made the down payment from her separate funds. The mortgage payments were made out of commingled funds before and after marriage.

In August 1989 Patricia founded XYZ Corporation, a biotechnology firm, with $2,000 that she received as an inheritance from her grandmother. All of the stock of XYZ Corporation was issued in Patricia's name, and Patricia worked full-time for XYZ Corporation. Bobby retained his job with another employer and did not get involved in the operations of XYZ Corporation. Because of limited financial resources, Patricia did not draw a salary from XYZ Corporation until August 1994. In September 1994, XYZ Corporation's first product was approved by the FDA. Shortly thereafter, Patricia sold all of the stock in XYZ Corporation to a large pharmaceutical concern for $30 million. Two days after Patricia's sale of the stock, she filed for dissolution of the marriage.

You are the judge in the Family Law Court. Is the residence that Patricia and Bobby acquired community property or property held in joint tenancy? Would it matter if after marriage they wrote a document stating that they wanted to hold the property as community property? In joint tenancy? Does Bobby have any interest in the proceeds from the sale of the XYZ Corporation stock?

5. David Ross and Chuck McCabe entered into a purchase contract whereby Ross agreed to purchase a 10-acre parcel from McCabe for $3 million. Under the terms of the purchase contract, Ross deposited the purchase contract and $100,000 into an escrow account with Title Company. The purchase contract also provided that the closing was to occur on or before December 31, 1993, and that if McCabe desired to enter into a tax-free exchange, Ross would cooperate in facilitating the exchange at no cost to Ross.

After discussing the transaction with a real estate attorney, McCabe determined that it would be to his advantage to structure the transaction as a three-party exchange. On June 12, 1993, McCabe and Ross entered into a letter of intent outlining the proposed terms of the exchange as follows:

(a) McCabe would attempt to locate an exchange property with a purchase price greater than $2,900,000 on or before September 30, 1994.

(b) Ross would purchase the exchange property through a separate escrow and would exchange that property with McCabe. McCabe further agreed to reimburse Ross to the extent that the purchase price of the exchange property was greater than $2,900,000.

(c) If McCabe did not locate an exchange property on or before September 30, 1994, the purchase price of the 10-acre parcel would be paid by Ross's deposit of the following into escrow: (1) a certified check in the amount of $500,000, (2) a duly executed promissory note in the amount of $2,400,000; and

(3) a deed of trust on the 10-acre parcel in favor of McCabe, securing the payment of the $2,400,000 promissory note.

A formal addendum to the purchase contract, incorporating the terms of the letter of intent, was drafted by McCabe's attorney but never executed by either party.

On September 15, 1994, Ross delivered escrow instructions to Title Company, incorporating the purchase contract by reference, but making no mention of the letter of intent or the addendum. The escrow instructions stated that the purchase price was to be paid by Ross's $100,000 deposit, his delivery of a certified check in the amount of $500,000 and his execution of a $2,400,000 promissory note secured by a deed of trust on the 10-acre parcel. The escrow instructions also fixed the closing date as December 14, 1994.

On September 29, 1994, McCabe called Ross and told him that he had not been able to select a suitable property for the exchange. He requested that David extend McCabe's period for locating an exchange property by ten days. Ross agreed to extend it, but the parties never executed a written agreement to that effect. On October 5, 1994, McCabe located an exchange property. In a letter delivered to Ross on October 6, 1994, McCabe demanded that Ross purchase the exchange property and consummate the three-party exchange in accordance with the terms of the letter of intent.

On December 14, 1994, Ross deposited the certified check, the promissory note, and the deed of trust into escrow and demanded that Title Company close the transaction in accordance with the terms set forth in the purchase contract. Later on the same day, McCabe delivered a letter signed by him demanding that Title Company cancel the escrow.

What are the respective rights and obligations of Ross, McCabe, and Title Company?

6. Developer purchased a 400-acre, unimproved parcel of real property located in Altair City. Developer proposes to construct 450 single-family residences on the parcel. Altair City is concerned that construction of 450 single-family residences will overburden Altair City's streets. Which of the following conditions imposed by Altair City for the issuance of a building permit to Developer would be likely to constitute a taking under the Fifth Amendment to the United States Constitution?

(a) Altair City requires Developer to dedicate 50 of the 400 acres for use as city parks.

(b) Altair City imposes a $2.00 per square foot assessment on each single-family unit constructed by Developer. The fees collected from the assessment accrue to the city's general fund and may or may not be used to finance public transportation projects.

(c) Altair City requires Developer to dedicate 10 acres of the parcel that abut a major thoroughfare for the construction of a park-and-ride lot.

7. William and Jean Hall own and operate a mobile home park in Santa Barbara, California. They provide plots of land on which to install mobile homes. The tenants pay rent for the use of the land and the facilities. The Halls bought the park in 1984. In 1994, the city enacted a rent control ordinance applicable to mobile home parks. The ordinance required park operators to offer their tenants leases of unlimited duration. The leases must also let the tenant terminate at will, whereas the operator can only terminate for cause as narrowly defined by the ordinance. Rent increases are strictly limited by the ordinance.

The Halls consult you, their attorney, about the ordinance. They want to know what they can do about it. What will you tell them? Does it matter that shortly after the ordinance was enacted the resale price of these homes shot up dramatically? [*Hall v. City of Santa Barbara*, 833 F.2d 1270 (9th Cir. 1986), *cert. denied*, 485 U.S. 940, 108 S.Ct. 1120 (1988)]

8. Lucy Dunworth, developer of a shopping mall, entered into an easement and operating agreement with three major department stores. One of the covenants in the agreement was that each occupant promised to operate its store area as a first-class department store under its trade name for a 20-year period. The occupants each purchased their commercial space in fee (that is, they actually purchased the land) from the developer. Kaufman-Straus Co., one of the tenants, sells its place to a discount store two years later. The other two first-class department stores bring an action against the discount store because it is not a first-class operation. What is the result? [*Net Realty Holding Trust v. Franconia Properties, Inc.* 544 F.Supp. 759 (E.D. Va. 1982)]

9. Potential purchasers of a home in a new multi-home development in New Jersey were not told that the development was next to a closed landfill suspected to contain hazardous waste. Promotional items had advertised walks in the woods and "healthy, fresh country air." Did the home builder or the real estate agent have a legal duty to disclose to potential buyers the existence of the landfill? What would good ethics dictate? [*Strawn v. Incollingo,* 638 A.2d 141 (NJ Super Ct App Div. 1994)]

10. Nevada Entertainment applied for a license to operate an adult video store in Henderson, Nevada. Shortly before it filed its application, the town adopted a zoning code limiting adult businesses to Commercial Highway (CH) zones. The town had no CH zones when the new code was adopted. The town told Nevada Entertainment that it could operate an adult business only in a CH zone, and as no zone existed, Nevada Entertainment would have to apply for a zone change or variance, as well as a conditional use permit. Instead, Nevada Entertainment filed a new license application for a general video store rather than an adult video store. The town issued a license and Nevada Entertainment opened an adult video store.

The town then attempted to revoke the store's license because Nevada Entertainment had misrepresented the nature of the business it intended to open. The town council issued an order revoking the license. Nevada Entertainment, rather than appealing the order in state district court, filed an action in federal court challenging the constitutionality of the zoning ordinance. Does Nevada Entertainment have a valid claim against Henderson? What will be the town's defense? [*Nevada Entertainment Indus. v. City of Henderson*, 8 F.3d 1348 (9th Cir. 1993)]

Chapter 18

ANTITRUST LAWS

■ Introduction

Intersection of Political and Economic Theory

The intersection of political and economic theory has produced the antitrust laws. A *trust* is a monopolistic combination of companies. The *antitrust laws* are statutes that prohibit such combinations, and also prohibit other restraints on competition such as price fixing among competitors. The basic principle of the antitrust laws is that the United States economy functions best when firms are free to compete vigorously with one another. A competitive economy allows the consumer to enjoy better goods at lower prices. As economists say, consumer wealth is maximized. In encouraging superior products and services, U.S. antitrust laws may also help the U.S. to compete in a global marketplace. However, if competition is decreased or eliminated by firms seeking jointly or independently to wield monopoly power, consumers suffer and the performance of the economy declines. The antitrust laws seek to identify and forbid anticompetitive practices.

Bright lines which clearly separate lawful from unlawful conduct are rare in this field. The antitrust statutes contain certain very general prohibitions on business conduct. These general prohibitions have little content until courts apply them to the particular facts of each case. A business practice that harms competition in one market setting might not harm competition in another. The courts and agencies that apply antitrust law have to distinguish between the pernicious and the benign.

The first antitrust law, the Sherman Act, was passed by Congress in 1890. It was part of a populist movement to combat the rise of powerful trusts in such basic industries as energy and steel. The Sherman Act's general prohibitions have evolved over the past hundred years through judicial decisions. This rather ad hoc development of the law has led to some seemingly confused results. For example, business practices forbidden by the Sherman Act in the early twentieth century are often permissible in today's changed economic environment.

A century after the Sherman Act was passed, the United States finds itself in the midst of a world economy in which competition in many industries takes place on an international scale and where the United States is no longer the dominant economic power. Many people now think that the antitrust laws hinder, rather than help, the ordinary consumer. A new generation of academics, lawyers, and judges has challenged their predecessors' conclusions that certain business practices or market conditions are anticompetitive. This school of thought, known as the Law and Economics movement, concludes that most anticompetitive practices are defeated by market forces. It questions the efficacy of the government's regulation of commerce and markets, arguing that instead of promoting competition, attempts at regulation often increase the anticompetitive structure of the markets.

As these arguments are made and refined, the evolution of antitrust law continues. To many this evolutionary process is antitrust's greatest strength, the reason it now enters its second century. However, also it makes it difficult to master this field of law.

Chapter Summary

This chapter offers a general overview of the federal antitrust laws, pointing out which aspects are settled and which are not. It begins with a discussion of sections 1 and 2 of the Sherman Act, then discusses the Clayton Act provisions relating to mergers and combinations. It concludes with a discussion of the Robinson-Patman Act's prohibitions on price discrimination.

■ Section 1 of the Sherman Act

Section 1 of the Sherman Act provides that "[e]very contract, combination in the form of trust or otherwise, or conspiracy, in restraint of trade or commerce among the several States, or with foreign nations, is declared to be illegal."[1]

The Sherman Act is enforced in a number of ways. First, violations of section 1 may be prosecuted as felonies. Corporations can be fined up to $10 million for each violation. Individuals can be fined up to $350,000 for each violation, and imprisoned for up to three years. Second, the Justice Department may bring civil actions to enforce the Sherman Act. Third, private plaintiffs, sometimes called private attorneys general, are entitled to recover three times the damages they have sustained as a consequence of the Sherman Act violation. Finally, state attorneys general may bring civil actions for injuries sustained by residents of their respective states. In these *parens patriae actions,* treble damages may also be recovered. (In addition to the federal antitrust laws, there are state antitrust laws giving causes of action both to private persons and to state attorneys general.)

On its face, section 1 appears to prohibit all concerted activity that restrains trade. However, almost every business transaction, even a contract for the purchase of goods or services, restrains trade to a certain extent. A contract, for example, restrains the parties from doing things that would constitute a breach. Read literally, section 1 would outlaw every type of business transaction. In order to avoid an unworkable construction of the Sherman Act, the courts have concluded that section 1 prohibits only those restraints of trade that *unreasonably* restrict competition. This chapter explores in some detail the circumstances under which conduct unreasonably restrains trade.

■ Violation of Section 1

In order for liability to attach under section 1, a plaintiff must demonstrate: (1) that there is a contract, combination, or conspiracy among separate entities; (2) that it unreasonably restrains trade; (3) that it affects interstate or foreign commerce (this requirement is of little practi-

---

1. 15 U.S.C. § 1 (1988 & Supp. 1992).

cal import, as the Supreme Court has interpreted interstate commerce as including virtually all commerce); and (4) that it causes an antitrust injury.

A Contract, Combination, or Conspiracy

Section 1 does not prohibit unilateral activity in restraint of trade. Acting by itself, an individual or firm may take any action, no matter how anticompetitive, and not violate section 1. (However, section 2 of the Sherman Act, discussed later in this chapter, does prohibit some forms of unilateral conduct.)

This threshold requirement of concerted action is one of the most frequently litigated issues in antitrust cases. In 1984 the Supreme Court decided that a parent corporation and its wholly owned subsidiary cannot "agree" within the concerted action requirement of section 1.[2] Whether sister corporations or corporations that are less than wholly owned can impermissibly agree remains an open issue.

Conspiracies, especially illegal conspiracies, are inherently secretive. Most price fixers do not keep minutes of their agreements or send confirming letters. Consequently, requiring direct proof of a conspiracy would likely permit many undesirable activities to escape section 1 liability. On the other hand, because unilateral behavior is not a violation, courts must be careful in relaxing the requirement that conspiracy be proven. The courts have struggled to develop mechanisms that allow lawsuits under section 1 to go forward without direct proof of a conspiracy of agreement while ensuring that only the truly guilty are found guilty.

One such mechanism is the distinction between horizontal and vertical agreements. *Horizontal agreements* are those between firms that directly compete with each other, such as retailers selling the same range of products. *Vertical agreements* are those between firms at different levels of production or distribution, such as a retailer and its supplier.

The judicial characterization of an agreement as horizontal or vertical has dramatic consequences. A horizontal agreement may be proved by *circumstantial evidence,* that is, evidence of the parties' actions from which an agreement may be inferred. A vertical agreement can only be proved by direct evidence that there was an agreement.

Proving a Horizontal Conspiracy Because an agreement among horizontal competitors, such as two automakers, almost invariably reduces interbrand compe-

tition, such agreements are generally disfavored under the antitrust laws.

The classic definition of conspiracy, whether horizontal or vertical, focuses on whether the alleged conspirators had a meeting of the minds in a scheme that violates the law. The courts will not require evidence of an explicit agreement to violate the law. As the Ninth Circuit has stated with respect to a horizontal conspiracy, a "knowing wink can mean more than words."[3]

> **❝**
>
> *As the Ninth Circuit has stated with respect to a horizontal conspiracy, a "knowing wink can mean more than words."*

Plaintiffs often attempt to infer a horizontal conspiracy from evidence of parallel behavior by ostensibly independent firms, for example, that they consistently set prices at the same levels and changed prices at the same times. The problem with this type of evidence (particularly where a homogenous product or service is included) is that it is ambiguous as an indicator of anticompetitive behavior. Parallel pricing of similar products or services can result either from illegal price fixing or from vigorous competition.

The Supreme Court addressed parallel behavior as an indicator of an illegal conspiracy in *Theatre Enterprises, Inc. v. Paramount Film Distributing Corp.*,[4] a horizontal-restraints case. The case involved a suburban Baltimore movie theater which sought to exhibit first-run films from major film distributors. All of the distributors refused the request, and instead continued to distribute first-run films exclusively to downtown theaters. The issue was whether proof of conscious parallel business behavior, without more evidence, supported an inference of conspiracy sufficient to prove a violation of section 1 of the Sherman Act. The Supreme Court found no conspiracy in restraint of trade, because there was no agreement among the distributors to act in concert. Instead, the refusals were made by the distributors individually based on sound economic reasons and in response to the same market conditions.

To infer an agreement or conspiracy from parallel behavior, the courts have required that the plaintiff show

---

2. *Copperweld Corp. v. Independence Tube Corp.*, 467 U.S. 752, 104 S.Ct. 2731 (1984).

3. *Esco Corp. v. United States*, 340 F.2d 1000, 1007 (9th Cir. 1965).
4. 346 U.S. 537, 74 S.Ct. 257 (1954).

additional facts or "plus factors." Under the *Theatre Enterprises* standard, the evidence must tend to exclude the possibility that the defendants were acting independently. Any parallel behavior that would appear to be contrary to the economic interest of the defendants, were they acting independently, would support an inference of conspiracy. On the other hand, if the defendants can produce reasonable business explanations for the behavior, as the movie distributors did in *Theatre Enterprises,* a court will not infer a conspiracy. Other circumstantial evidence of an agreement, such as a meeting between two defendants, would be a plus factor. Increasing prices and persistent profits despite a decline in demand for the good or service would also be plus factors.

Proving a Vertical Conspiracy   Vertical agreements, such as those between an automaker and its local dealers, may reduce *intrabrand competition,* that is, price competition between local dealers selling the same manufacturer's products. But they often enhance *interbrand competition,* that is, competition between dealers selling different manufacturers' products. It is in the best interests of both the automaker and its dealers to provide the most marketable product so as to receive the greatest possible share of available consumer dollars. Courts look more favorably on reductions in intrabrand than interbrand competition.

Since the mid-1980s, the courts have been unwilling to allow proof of vertical conspiracies by circumstantial evidence alone. The Supreme Court has held that firms in a vertical arrangement, unlike competitors, have many legitimate reasons to communicate with each other. Therefore, a plaintiff seeking to prove an unlawful conspiracy must introduce evidence that tends to exclude the possibility that the firms acted independently.[5] Evidence of action that could be either concerted or independent is insufficient to prove a section 1 violation under this test. Since this case, very few plaintiffs lacking direct evidence of a conspiracy have been successful in making out a section 1 claim arising out of a vertical restraint.

Unreasonable Restraint of Trade

There are two ways in which practices may be found to be unreasonable restraints of trade.

Per Se Violations   Some types of activity are considered so inherently anticompetitive that proof of the activity is, in and of itself, sufficient to establish a violation of section 1. If such a per se violation is established, the

---

5. *Monsanto Co. v. Spray-Rite Service Corp.*, 465 U.S. 752, 104 S.Ct. 1464 (1984).

defendant will not be permitted to offer excuses or explanations to avoid liability.

Scholarship, which originated in the Law and Economics movement at the University of Chicago, has argued that very few practices are inherently anticompetitive. As this scholarship has been accepted by many courts, the number of truly per se violations of the antitrust laws has declined.

The Rule of Reason   If the plaintiff has not proven a per se violation, the activity will be evaluated under the *rule of reason.* The objective of this rule is to determine whether, on balance, the activity promotes or restrains competition. In making this determination, the court will consider the structure of the market as well as the defen-

International Consideration

Antitrust laws have potential extraterritorial applications. For example, criminal indictments were brought by the Justice Department against General Electric and De Beers Centenary AG, a South African company, for price fixing in the world market for industrial diamonds. The Justice Department alleged that two executives, one employed by General Electric, a U.S. company, and the other by Diamond Boart, were exchanging prices on a regular basis throughout 1991 and 1992.

General Electric claimed that Diamond Boart was one of its largest customers. Diamond Boart was, however, owned by a Belgian diamond company, Sibeka, which was 20% owned by De Beers. Furthermore, De Beers produced its diamonds through a 50-50 joint venture with Sibeka. The De Beers-Sibeka-Diamond Boart group was therefore not only one of General Electric's customers, but also its largest competitor.

The Justice Department claimed that the price fixing plot was the result of this relationship. Rather than supplying price quotes to customers, General Electric and De Beers were allegedly coordinating their prices. Diamond Boart was allegedly the conduit through which the two countries funneled their price information.

dant's action. The court will then determine whether the activity in question has a procompetitive or anticompetitive effect. Activity that has a net anticompetitive effect is deemed an unreasonable restraint of trade and hence is unlawful.

■ Types of Horizontal Restraints

Unlawful horizontal restraints, that is, restraints between direct competitors, include price fixing, market division, and some kinds of group boycotts. These have traditionally been treated as per se violations of section 1 of the Sherman Act. Trade associations may also be found to be acting unlawfully under the rule of reason in some circumstances.

Horizontal Price Fixing

Horizontal price fixing, such as an agreement between retailers to set a common price for a product, is the classic example of a per se violation of section 1. *Horizontal price fixing* includes: (1) setting prices (including maximum prices); (2) setting the terms of sale, such as customer credit terms; (3) setting the quantity or quality of goods to be manufactured or made available for sale; or (4) bid rigging (agreement between or among competitors to rig contract bids).

The Justice Department views price fixing as "hard crime," to be punished by jail sentences whenever possible, and many executives have been imprisoned for price fixing. Indeed, under the federal sentencing guidelines, some term of confinement is mandatory for individuals convicted of horizontal price fixing, bid rigging, or market allocation agreements; in most cases, first-time offenders serve a minimum six- to twelve-month jail sentence. Multimillion-dollar fines against corporations convicted of price fixing are the rule rather than the exception. But the civil actions, in particular class actions (which inevitably follow criminal prosecutions), have even more drastic financial consequences. Liability for antitrust damages is joint and several among all of the conspirators, so that each conspirator is potentially liable for treble damages for the losses caused by all of the defendants. In one series of cases involving price fixing in the corrugated paper industry, the trial judge estimated the potential treble damages at more than $3.5 billion. Seven defendants settled for more than $24 million each, and ten more settled for between $5 and $20 million. One nonsettling defendant was tried and found liable for $800 million in treble damages but later settled for nearly $50 million while the case was on appeal.

Horizontal Market Division

The Supreme Court considers market divisions so inherently anticompetitive as to constitute per se violations of section 1. *Horizontal market division* can take various forms: Competitors might divide up a market according to class of customer or geographic territory, or they might restrict product output. The Supreme Court has emphasized that horizontal market division by potential as well as actual competitors is per se illegal.[6] As in the following case, market division is prohibited even if it is intended to enable small competitors to compete with larger companies, thereby fostering interbrand competition.

---

6. *Palmer v. BRG of Georgia, Inc.* 498 U.S. 46, 111 S.Ct. 401 (1990).

■ A Case in Point: Summary

Case 18.1
UNITED STATES v. TOPCO ASSOCIATES, INC.
Supreme Court of the
United States
405 U.S. 596, 92 S.Ct. 1126
(1972).

FACTS Topco Associates was a cooperative association of 25 small to medium independent supermarket chains. It was formed to act as a purchasing agent and to develop a marketing program for its members. Each member of the association agreed to sell trademarked Topco brand products only in an assigned area. Exclusive territories were considered necessary to encourage local advertising of the fledgling Topco brand. Members were also prohibited from selling Topco products to other retailers. The United States sued Topco Associates, alleging violation of section 1 of the Sherman Act and seeking injunctive relief.

ISSUE PRESENTED Is an agreement between competitors to divide markets a per se violation of section 1 of the Sherman Act?

Case **18.1** continued on following page

*Case **18.1** continued*

SUMMARY OF OPINION   The U.S. Supreme Court held that because the cooperative's arrangement resulted in a division of the market, it was a per se violation of section 1. Accordingly, it refused to consider business and economic justifications for the arrangement, its impact on the marketplace, or its reasonableness.

RESULT   An agreement between competitors to divide markets is a per se violation of section 1 of the Sherman Act.

COMMENTS   Many scholars have criticized this case because it made it more difficult for the smaller supermarket chains to compete effectively with the national chains. They argue that the Supreme Court improperly focused on the reduction in intrabrand competition (that is, competition between retailers of Topco products) while ignoring the overall gain in interbrand competition (that is, competition between Topco and other brands). Scholars also criticize the Supreme Court for exalting form over substance. Given the small market share of the cooperative members, they could lawfully have merged into one entity to sell the Topco brand, but the Supreme Court prohibited them from forming a cooperative association for the same purpose. (The guidelines for determining market share for deciding which mergers will be permitted are discussed later in this chapter.)

Group Boycotts

It is a fundamental principle that an individual can choose to do business with whomever he wants. Nevertheless, an agreement among competitors to refuse to deal with another competitor—a *group boycott*—has traditionally been treated as a per se violation of section 1. Joint action that eliminates a class of competitors or deprives dealers or distributors of something they need to compete effectively is considered so inherently anticompetitive that no economic motivation for the action may be offered as a defense. For example, manufacturers and distributors of appliances cannot agree among themselves not to sell appliances to certain distributors, or to sell to them only at a higher price. Such an agreement is a per se violation of section 1 even if there is no agreement on the exact price, quantity, or quality of the appliances to be sold.[7]

More recently, however, as in the following case, the Supreme Court has begun to distinguish some forms of group boycotts that it believes are not so inherently anticompetitive as to merit per se treatment.

---

7. *Klor's, Inc. v. Broadway-Hale Stores, Inc.*, 359 U.S. 207, 79 S.Ct. 705 (1959).

■ **A Case in Point:**   **Summary**

Case 18.2
NORTHWEST WHOLESALE STATIONERS, INC. v. PACIFIC STATIONERY AND PRINTING CO.
Supreme Court of the United States
472 U.S. 284, 105 S.Ct. 2613 (1985).

FACTS   Northwest Wholesale Stationers is a purchasing cooperative made up of approximately 100 office supply retailers in the Pacific Northwest states. One of its members, Pacific Stationery and Printing, failed to inform the cooperative of a change in ownership control. This was apparently in violation of the cooperative's bylaws. Pacific was expelled without explanation, notice, or a hearing. Pacific sued the cooperative, alleging that the cooperative's action was a group boycott or concerted refusal to deal and constituted a per se violation of section 1 of the Sherman Act.

ISSUE PRESENTED   Is a refusal to deal a per se violation of section 1 of the Sherman Act?

SUMMARY OF OPINION   The U.S. Supreme Court recognized that in certain cases, where the boycott cuts off competitors from a "supply, facility, or market necessary to enable the boycotted firm to compete," per se treatment is appropriate. However, the Court acknowledged that not all cooperative activity involving a restraint or exclusion is inherently anticompetitive. It held that the cooperative's action could, in some cases, increase economic efficiency and render the market more competitive. Consequently the Court applied the rule of reason. It found no violation.

RESULT   Not all refusals to deal are per se violations. Before determining whether to apply a rule of reason or a per se analysis, the court must make an initial determination, based on market conditions, to ascertain whether anticompetitive effects are likely. The cooperative, Northwest Wholesale Stationers, did not violate section 1 of the Sherman Act.

COMMENTS   In this case, the expelled member had alternative sources of supply which made effective competition possible, and perhaps more likely.

Trade Associations

Trade and professional associations often disseminate information among their members. The Sherman Act requires that the exchange of information be monitored to ensure that it does not facilitate anticompetitive behavior, such as price fixing or market division. Association agreements rarely state goals that violate the Sherman Act, so courts must draw inferences about the probable effects of the information exchanged. The courts will look at the market structure and the type of information exchanged.

A large *cartel,* or group of competitors that agrees to do something, is inherently unstable. Conversely, the fewer the companies that must agree, the more likely they will agree and be able to enforce the agreement. Therefore, the more concentrated the industry, the more closely courts will scrutinize trade association activity.

The type of information exchanged plays an even more critical role in the analysis. For example, a weekly report disseminated by a hardwood manufacturers' trade association listed the names of companies that sold lumber, and the prices at which they sold it. Additionally, monthly reports discussed future price trends and provided future estimates of production. The Supreme Court held that this information violated section 1 of the Sherman Act, as members could utilize the information to police secret agreements setting uniform prices or

terms.[8] Another manufacturers' association disseminated information on average costs and the terms of past transactions. It did not identify individual sellers or buyers, and did not discuss future pricing. The Supreme Court found no violation of section 1.[9]

Information that does not involve prices or terms receives less scrutiny by the courts. Activities such as cooperative industrial research, market surveys, and joint advertising concerning the industry have been upheld. The exchange of information concerning contractors whose payments were two months in arrears was upheld as a reasonable way to help members avoid contractor fraud.[10]

Courts do not look favorably upon attempts at self-regulation by trade and professional associations, particularly where such attempts result in group boycotts. For example, an American Medical Association rule of ethics, which forbade salaried practice and prepaid medical care, was held to violate the Sherman Act.

---

8. *American Column & Lumber Co. v. United States,* 257 U.S. 377, 42 S.Ct. 114 (1921).
9. *Maple Flooring Mfrs. Assn. v. United States,* 268 U.S. 563, 45 S.Ct. 578 (1925).
10. *Cement Mfrs. Protective Assn. v. United States,* 268 U.S. 588, 45 S.Ct. 586 (1925).

More recently the National Football League (NFL), fearing an antitrust challenge, modified its position regarding college players renouncing their college eligibility and applying for the NFL college draft. Whereas in the past only players who had completed four years of college were eligible for the draft, the NFL now allows any player completing three years of college to apply. In a related development, the National Basketball Association has reduced its college draft from ten rounds to two rounds, fearing an antitrust challenge. This is not surprising, given the fact that any college draft is essentially an agreement among competitors to allocate their most important resource—players.

■ Types of Vertical Restraints

Unlawful vertical restraints, that is, restraints between firms at different levels in the chain of distribution, include price fixing, market division, tying arrangements, and some franchise agreements.

Vertical Price Fixing

The Supreme Court has determined that agreements on price between firms at different levels of production or distribution can be as anticompetitive as agreements between direct competitors at the same level of production or distribution. Thus, vertical price fixing, also known as *resale price maintenance (RPM)*, remains, in theory, a per se violation of the Sherman Act. RPM agreements have been challenged by consumers claiming overcharges, by competitors claiming loss of sales, and by dealers or retailers terminated by the manufacturer for offering discounts from list or suggested prices. As is discussed later in this chapter, a competitor cannot successfully bring an action challenging RPM unless it can show antitrust injury.

Resale price maintenance has been unlawful per se since 1911, when the Supreme Court held that an agreement between a drug manufacturer and its distributors setting both wholesale and retail prices violated section 1 of the Sherman Act. Such restrictions impermissibly limited the freedom of choice of other drug distributors and retailers. As a result, society was deprived of the benefits that it would have received from unrestricted distribution of the drugs.[11]

Some academics and jurists have challenged the treatment of resale price maintenance as a per se violation. For example, Robert Bork, a noted legal scholar and Reagan Supreme Court nominee whose appointment was blocked by the Senate, has argued that vertical price restrictions do not limit competition among competitors or give them power to restrict output or to raise prices. Bork contends that vertical price restrictions ensure economic efficiencies and maximize consumer welfare by preventing price competition that forces retailers to cut back on nonprice items such as consumer service. In fact, Bork argues, the prohibition of vertical price restrictions lessens consumer welfare by allowing discount retailers to free-ride on the services provided by other retailers.

Stereo stores provide a classic example of the problem Bork describes. For example, suppose the Esoteric Stereo Store provides its patrons with very sophisticated listening rooms and highly trained salespersons to assist in their stereo selection. Three blocks away is Lou's Discount Appliances, which sells the same stereo equipment at discount prices but does not provide a listening room or knowledgeable salespersons. A consumer might spend hours in the Esoteric Stereo Store listening and learning, then walk three blocks and buy the product from Lou's Discount Appliances. If this becomes a pattern, Esoteric will be forced to cut back its service in order to compete with Lou's prices. High-quality service will be eliminated as a consumer option.

> 66
>
> *A consumer might spend hours in the Esoteric Stereo Store listening and learning, then walk three blocks and buy the product from Lou's Discount Appliances.*

The Supreme Court has so far rejected these arguments and maintained the per se rule against resale price maintenance. It has, however, greatly increased the plaintiff's burden of proof by requiring evidence of an agreement on specific price levels, not merely an agreement to eliminate discounting in general. Many antitrust lawyers believe this change in the analysis has dealt a fatal blow to attempts by terminated discounters to invoke the per se rule in cases alleging resale price maintenance. Very few manufacturers are clumsy enough to insist that their dealers agree on specific price levels.

As noted earlier, the Sherman Act addresses only concerted action. Because unilateral action is not prohibited,

---

11. *Dr. Miles Medical Co. v. John D. Park & Sons Co.*, 220 U.S. 373, 31 S.Ct. 376 (1911).

a manufacturer or distributor can announce list prices to dealers, and the dealers may decide independently to follow those suggestions. Similarly, manufacturers may advertise suggested retail prices. Indeed, a manufacturer may (absent any intent to create or maintain a monopoly) announce that it will terminate any dealer who does not charge its suggested list prices, and then terminate those who do not do so (because the conduct is entirely unilateral).[12] But if the manufacturer or distributor coerces retailers to adhere to its suggested price levels, it will violate the Sherman Act. Any threats of sanctions that interfere with the retailer's freedom to set its own price for the goods or services that it sells will constitute an unreasonable restraint of trade in violation of the Sherman Act. However, the line separating persuasion from coercion is not always clear.

Vertical Market Division

Vertical market division is an arrangement imposed by a manufacturer on its distributors or dealers that limits the freedom of the dealer to market the manufacturer's product. Such an agreement may establish exclusive distributorships, territorial or customer restrictions, location clauses, areas of primary responsibility, and the like. Such practices are not illegal per se. Rather, they are judged under the rule of reason.

The central inquiry is whether the reduction in intrabrand competition is justified by an increase in interbrand competition. The higher the market share of a particular manufacturer's product, the greater the likelihood that a decline in intrabrand competition will violate the rule of reason. For example, suppose Pixel Unlimited controls 80% of the market for high-definition television (HDTV) screens in Atlanta, Georgia, and sells its products through five independent retail outlets. Pixel decides to terminate two dealers, believing that fewer dealers will be better able to compete with non-Pixel HDTV dealers. Although a reduction in the number of Pixel dealers may increase interbrand HDTV competition, that would not offset the decrease in Pixel intrabrand competition. Accordingly, the reduction in the number of Pixel dealers would violate section 1.

Exclusive Distributorships In an *exclusive distributorship* a manufacturer limits itself to a single distributor

in a given territory or, perhaps, line of business. So long as a manufacturer does not have dominant market power, it may allocate different geographic areas to its distributors and refuse to sell to other potential distributors in those areas. Exclusive distributorships have been upheld under the rule of reason where there is some competitive pressure that limits the market power of the retailers holding them. Exclusive automobile dealerships for particular geographic regions are the classic example. This restriction on intrabrand competition is permissible because of the intense interbrand competition among U.S. and foreign automobile manufacturers.

Territorial and Customer Restrictions *Territorial* and *customer restrictions* prevent a dealer or distributor from selling outside a certain territory or to a certain class of customers. For example, a Dow representative selling industrial chemicals might sell only to hardware stores, and only in a specified area. The Supreme Court has held that vertical territorial or customer restrictions are not per se violations of section 1. Such restrictions often increase interbrand competition, thus an accompanying reduction of intrabrand competition may be permissible.

However, a manufacturer cannot disguise an agreement to maintain resale prices as a territorial restriction. A court will look beyond the form of the transaction to the substance and will use the per se rule to strike down what is in reality a vertical price restraint. Similarly, where a number of retailers combine to force a manufacturer to impose an ostensibly vertical agreement on its retailers, the agreement is in reality horizontal and will be deemed a per se violation of section 1.

Dual Distributors A manufacturer that sells its goods both wholesale and at retail is called a *dual distributor.* Early decisions held that such an arrangement was unlikely to create the efficiencies and increased competition created by permissible forms of vertical nonprice agreements. Accordingly, restraints imposed by dual distributors were considered illegal per se. The trend in recent decisions, however, is to analyze such restraints under the rule of reason (so long as they originate with the manufacturer, not the retailers), because they can have beneficial economic effects.

Tying Arrangements

Tying arrangements can be challenged under section 1 of the Sherman Act or section 3 of the Clayton Act. The Clayton Act specifically prohibits tying arrangements in commodities, while the Sherman Act prohibits tying arrangements generally. The legal analysis applied under

---

12. *United States v. Colgate & Co.*, 250 U.S. 300, 39 S.Ct. 465 (1919). However, most businesspeople do not want to terminate dealers who violate the policy. They therefore frequently use termination as a threat to coerce agreement. Once there is agreement, there is a violation.

the two statutes has converged; thus, the following analysis applies to both Clayton Act and Sherman Act claims.

In a *tying arrangement,* the seller will sell product A (the tying, or desired, product) to the customer only if she agrees to purchase product B (the tied product) from the seller. A tying arrangement is a way of forcing a buyer to purchase a product or service it would not buy on the product's or service's own merits.

For example, suppose Metro Cable expands its cable television service into a new town. The public utilities commission grants Metro the exclusive right to provide cable service in the new town. Metro is a subsidiary of Moviemax, a company that provides a cable-television movie channel for subscribers. To improve Moviemax's profit margin, the marketing vice-president decides to require all of Metro's customers to subscribe to Moviemax. In this example, the tying product is the basic cable service. The tied product is the Moviemax television channel.

Tying arrangements unreasonably restrain trade by preventing competitors from selling their goods to customers obliged to buy the tied product. In the Moviemax example, the tying arrangement would make it more difficult for other movie channels, like HBO, to sell their product to cable customers in the new town. Tying arrangements also restrict the freedom of choice of purchasers who are forced to buy the tied product.

Tying arrangements have traditionally been held to be per se violations, provided that: (1) the tying and tied products are separate products; (2) the availability of the tied product is conditioned upon the purchase of the tying product; (3) the party imposing the tie had enough market power in the tying product market to force the purchase of the tied product; and (4) a "not insubstantial" amount of commerce in the tied product is affected.

Separate Products   Whether there are separate products may be difficult to determine. Firms often label or market a combination of goods and services as a single product. The courts attempt to determine whether there are two economically distinct products by determining whether there is a separate demand for them. For example, in one case the Supreme Court found that below-market financing that was provided to buyers of prefabricated metal homes was a separate product from the homes themselves.

Condition of Sale   If the tying product can be purchased on nondiscriminatory terms, without the tied product, there is no tie. It has been suggested that a manufacturer should not make a second product technologically interdependent with the purchased product such that technology, rather than contract terms, forces customers to buy both. To date, however, these technological ties have been found lawful so long as there is not separate demand for the products involved.

Market Power   The nature and extent of the market power required is frequently litigated, as in the case that follows.

■   **A Case in Point:**   **In the Language of the Court**

Case 18.3
**EASTMAN KODAK CO. v.
IMAGE TECHNICAL
SERVICES, INC.**
Supreme Court of the
United States
112 S.Ct. 2072 (1992).

FACTS   After independent service organizations (ISOs) began servicing copying and micrographic (microfilm) equipment manufactured by Eastman Kodak Co., Kodak adopted policies to limit the availability to ISOs of replacement parts for its equipment and to make it more difficult for ISOs to compete with it in servicing such equipment.

The ISOs sued, alleging that Kodak had unlawfully tied the sale of service for its machines to the sale of parts, in violation of section 1 of the Sherman Act, and had unlawfully monopolized and attempted to monopolize the sale of service and parts for such machines, in violation of section 2 of that act. (The section 2 claim is discussed later in this chapter.) The Federal District Court granted summary judgment for Kodak, but the Court of Appeals reversed. Among other things, the appellate court found that respondents had presented sufficient evidence to raise a genuine issue concerning Kodak's market power in the service and parts markets, and rejected Kodak's contention that lack of market power in service and parts must be assumed when such power is absent in the equipment market.

ISSUE PRESENTED Can a defendant's lack of market power in a primary market preclude as a matter of law the possibility of market power in a derivative aftermarket?

OPINION BLACKMUN, J., writing for the U.S. Supreme Court:

. . . .

. . . [Kodak] challenge[s] whether its activities constituted a "tying arrangement" and whether Kodak exercised "appreciable economic power" in the tying market. We consider these issues in turn.

For the respondents to defeat a motion for summary judgment on their claim of a tying arrangement, a reasonable trier of fact must be able to find, first, that service and parts are two distinct products, and, second, that Kodak has tied the sale of the two products.

. . . .

Kodak insists that because there is no demand for parts separate from service, there cannot be separate markets for service and parts. By that logic, we would be forced to conclude that there can never be separate markets, for example, for cameras and film, computers and software, or automobiles and tires. That is an assumption we are unwilling to make.

. . . .

Having found sufficient evidence of a tying arrangement, we consider the other necessary feature of an illegal tying arrangement: appreciable economic power in the tying market. Market power is the power "to force a purchaser to do something that he would not do in a competitive market." . . . The existence of such power ordinarily is inferred from the seller's possession of a predominant share of the market.

Respondents [the ISOs] contend that Kodak has more than sufficient power in the parts market to force unwanted purchases of the tied market, service. . . .

Respondents also allege that Kodak's control over the parts market has excluded service competition, boosted service prices, and forced unwilling consumption of Kodak service. Respondents offer evidence that consumers have switched to Kodak service even though they preferred ISO service, that Kodak service was of higher price and lower quality than the preferred ISO service, and that ISOs were driven out of business by Kodak's policies.

. . . .

Legal presumptions that rest on formalistic distinctions rather than actual market realities are generally disfavored in antitrust law. This Court has preferred to resolve antitrust claims on a case-by-case basis, focusing on the "particular facts disclosed by the record." In determining the existence of market power, and specifically the "responsiveness of the sales of one product to price changes of the other," this Court has examined closely the economic reality of the market at issue.

. . . .

The extent to which one market prevents exploitation of another market depends on the extent to which consumers will change their consumption of one product in response to a price change in another, i.e., the "cross-

Case **18.3** continued on following page

*Case **18.3** continued*

elasticity of demand." Kodak's proposed rule rests on a factual assumption about the cross-elasticity of demand in the equipment and aftermarkets: "If Kodak raised its parts or service prices above competitive levels, potential customers would simply stop buying Kodak equipment. Perhaps Kodak would be able to increase short term profits through such a strategy, but at a devastating cost to its long term interests." Kodak argues that the Court should accept, as a matter of law, this "basic economic reality," that competition in the equipment market necessarily prevents market power in the aftermarkets.

. . . .

Even if Kodak could not raise the price of service and parts one cent without losing equipment sales, that fact would not disprove market power in the aftermarkets. The sales of even a monopolist are reduced when it sells goods at a monopoly price, but the higher price more than compensates for the loss in sales. . . . The fact that the equipment market imposes a restraint on prices in the aftermarkets by no means disproves the existence of power in those markets. Thus, contrary to Kodak's assertion, there is no immutable physical law—no "basic economic reality"—insisting that competition in the equipment market cannot coexist with market power in the aftermarkets.

. . . .

We conclude, then, that Kodak has failed to demonstrate that respondents' inference of market power in the service and parts markets is unreasonable, and that, consequently, Kodak is entitled to summary judgment. It is clearly reasonable to infer that Kodak . . . chose to gain immediate profits by exerting that market power where locked-in customers, high information costs, and discriminatory pricing limited and perhaps eliminated any long-term loss.

. . . .

RESULT   The Supreme Court affirmed the denial of summary judgment on the independent service organizations' section 1 and section 2 Sherman Act claims.

COMMENTS . The Supreme Court in *Kodak* relies heavily on its holding in *Jefferson Parish Hosp. Dist. No. 2 v. Hyde*,[13] in its analysis of tied products and market power in a section 1 violation. The Court in that case determined that the sale of anesthesiological services (the tied product), conditioned on the sale of hospital services (the tying product), did not violate section 1 where the hospital controlled 30% of the relevant hospital services market. The Court held that this was not enough to give the hospital market power. It is noteworthy that four out of the nine justices in *Jefferson Parish Hosp.* voted to eliminate per se treatment of tying arrangements.

Questions
1. What is *cross-elasticity of demand*?
2. Are copier service and copier parts separate markets in the same manner that automobiles and tires are separate markets?

---

13. 466 U.S. 2, 104 S.Ct. 1551 (1984).

Effect on Commerce A "not insubstantial" amount of commerce is affected if more than a trifling dollar amount is involved.

Business Justification Unlike other per se violations, a tying arrangement may be upheld if there is a business justification for it. In a Ninth Circuit decision,[14] Mercedes-Benz's policy of requiring its dealers to sell only factory-made parts was upheld. The court ruled that this tying arrangement was justified by the assurance it provided to Mercedes that service on its automobiles, important in preserving their high-quality image, would not be performed with substandard parts.

Some lower courts have allowed tying arrangements in fledgling industries. For example, one court upheld a tying arrangement whereby purchasers of cable-television satellite antennas were required to purchase service contracts to ensure proper functioning of the antennas.[15]

Thus, although the courts continue to say that tying arrangements are per se illegal, they apply a flexible per se rule that considers market power and business justifications. Tying arrangements are in effect judged under a type of rule of reason.

---

14. *The Mozart Co. v. Mercedes-Benz of North America, Inc.*, 833 F.2d 1342 (9th Cir. 1987), *cert. denied*, 488 U.S. 870, 109 S.Ct. 179 (1988).
15. *United States v. Jerrold Electronics Corp.*, 187 F. Supp. 545 (E.D. Pa. 1960), *aff'd*, 365 U.S. 567, 81 S.Ct. 755 (1961).

Franchise Agreements

A *franchise* is a business relationship in which one party (the franchisor) grants to another party (the franchisee) the right to use the franchisor's name and logo and to distribute the franchisor's products from a specified locale. The franchise agreement may provide that the franchisor will not grant another franchise within a specified distance of the franchisee's business location. To ensure uniformity and quality, the franchisor may impose conditions on the operation of the franchise. For example, a McDonald's hamburger franchisee might be required to have all employees wear an approved uniform and to decorate the restaurant in an approved fashion.

Antitrust issues are raised when a franchisor, in an effort to promote uniformity and name recognition, imposes certain types of limitations on the franchisee. For example, the ice cream manufacturer Baskin Robbins was accused of imposing an illegal tying arrangement when it required all franchisees to buy their ice cream from Baskin Robbins. However, the seller (Baskin Robbins) was held to have no market power over the tying product. Ice cream franchises, like automobile franchises, face intense interbrand competition. No one franchisor has the ability to dominate the market even if it does require all of its franchises to buy its products.

In the following case, the Supreme Court upheld a vertical market division between a franchisor and a franchisee where there was intense interbrand competition that was enhanced by the limitation on intrabrand competition.

■ **A Case in Point:** **Summary**

Case 18.4
CONTINENTAL T.V., INC. v. GTE SYLVANIA INC.
Supreme Court of the United States
433 U.S. 36, 97 S.Ct. 2549 (1977).

FACTS GTE Sylvania manufactured television sets which it sold to Continental T.V., a retail distributor of consumer electronic products. Sylvania adopted a new franchising plan in an attempt to attract more aggressive and competent retailers. Sylvania's plan was designed to increase retailers' margins by reducing intrabrand competition in Sylvania products. To this end, Sylvania limited the number of franchises in each geographical area and allowed franchisees to sell Sylvania products only from specifically franchised locations.

Sylvania's relationship with Continental throve under this new plan until Sylvania terminated Continental for an unauthorized expansion into another market. Continental brought this action alleging that Sylvania's franchising agreement violated section 1 of the Sherman Act.

Case 18.4 continued on following page

*Case **18.4** continued*

ISSUE PRESENTED   Under the rule of reason, can a manufacturer lawfully restrict the number of franchisees in a geographical area?

SUMMARY OF OPINION   The U.S. Supreme Court applied the rule of reason. Sylvania did not hold a large share of the television market. The revised marketing plan had been successful in capturing a greater share of the market. The Supreme Court concluded that the franchising agreement was a reasonable restraint on intrabrand competition designed to improve Sylvania's competitive position in an intensely competitive interbrand market.

RESULT   Sylvania acted lawfully when it terminated Continental for unauthorized expansion into another geographic market.

■ Antitrust Injury

To recover damages, a plaintiff must establish that it sustained an *antitrust injury*, that is, a loss due to a competition-reducing aspect or effect of the defendant's violation of the Sherman Act. A plaintiff may not recover under the antitrust laws for losses that resulted from competition as such.

In the following case, the Supreme Court held that the mere fact that a company instituted a vertical price-fixing scheme was not sufficient to permit a competitor to recover damages under section 1. The prices were not fixed so low as to constitute *predatory pricing,* that is, an attempt to undercut competitors to the point where they lose money and go out of business. The scheme was therefore not anticompetitive.

> **"**
> *A plaintiff may not recover under the antitrust laws for losses that resulted from competition as such.*

■ A Case in Point: Summary

Case 18.5
ATLANTIC RICHFIELD CO. v.
USA PETROLEUM CO.
Supreme Court of the
United States
495 U.S. 328, 110 S.Ct. 1884
(1990).

FACTS   Atlantic Richfield Company (ARCO) is an integrated oil company that markets gasoline in the western United States. It sells gasoline to consumers both directly through its own stations and indirectly through ARCO-brand dealers. USA Petroleum Company is an independent retail marketer of gasoline. Like other independents, it buys gasoline from major petroleum companies for resale under its own brand name. USA Petroleum competes directly with ARCO dealers at the retail level. USA Petroleum's outlets typically are low-overhead, high-volume, discount stations that charge less than stations selling equivalent quality gasoline under major brand names.

In early 1982, ARCO adopted a new marketing strategy to compete more effectively with discount independents. In a highly publicized advertising campaign, it abolished ARCO credit cards, claiming this would result in lower prices. It made available to its dealers and distributors such short-term discounts as "temporary competitive allowances" and "temporary volume allowances" and otherwise reduced dealers' costs.

USA Petroleum claimed that ARCO conspired with retail service stations selling ARCO-brand gasoline to fix prices at below-market levels. It alleged that this was an illegal resale price maintenance scheme whereby the competition that would otherwise exist among ARCO-brand dealers was eliminated by agreement, and the retail price of ARCO-brand gasoline was maintained at artificially low and uncompetitive levels. This allegedly drove many independents in California out of business. USA Petroleum sued ARCO under section 1 of the Sherman Act, alleging that ARCO's vertical maximum-price-fixing scheme constituted an agreement in restraint of trade.

ISSUE PRESENTED Does resale price maintenance give rise to an antitrust injury if the pricing is not predatory? Can a competitor recover damages for its loss without a showing of predatory pricing?

SUMMARY OF OPINION The U.S. Supreme Court held that competitor USA Petroleum could not recover damages for ARCO's resale price maintenance because there was no showing of predatory pricing, that is, pricing below cost designed to drive competitors out of the market. The Court reasoned that when the prices are set under a resale price maintenance program at nonpredatory levels, there can be no anticompetitive effect. Such pricing may reduce the market share of competitors or the price that competitors may charge consumers. Without doubt, those competitors are injured as a result of the practice, but there is nothing anticompetitive about it. Indeed, such a result benefits the consumer. In such a case, the Court held, the competitor may not recover damages under the antitrust laws.

RESULT USA Petroleum was not entitled to recover damages because ARCO's resale price maintenance program did not set prices at a predatory level.

COMMENTS This decision was viewed by some scholars as another victory for the University of Chicago school of economic thought.[16] Charles Rule, a Washington lawyer and former Justice Department antitrust chief, said that the decision is consistent with the Supreme Court's recent approach of viewing the antitrust laws as protecting competition rather than individual competitors.[17] The Supreme Court also expressly stated in its *Atlantic Richfield* opinion that consumers and the manufacturers' own dealers may bring suit to enforce the rule against a vertical maximum-price-fixing scheme if anticompetitive consequences result.

16. Reuben, "High Court Narrows Test for Antitrust," *San Francisco Banner Daily Journal,* May 15, 1990, 1.
17. Stephen Wermiel, "Supreme Court Hardens Stance on Pricing Suits," *The Wall Street Journal,* May 15, 1990, A3.

■ Limitations on Antitrust Enforcement

The courts have limited the private enforcement rights of individual citizens and states by invoking the doctrine of standing. They have also limited the liability of state governments by applying the state-action exemptions.

Standing

To prevent private parties from jumping on the treble-damages bandwagon, the Supreme Court requires that a private plaintiff have standing to sue, that is, that the plaintiff has suffered an injury from the defendant's violation of the antitrust law. For example, a consumer buying goods from an innocent middleman does not have standing to recover from the manufacturer who was a member of a price-fixing cartel.

More complicated standing issues arise where a company alleges that its competitors are violating the antitrust laws. For example, suppose that Connaught Gin complains that its competitor, Profumo Gin, has imposed an illegal exclusive dealing agreement on Connaught's former dealer Liquor World. At first, Connaught's injury appears indirect compared with that of Liquor World. However, the central reason that the antitrust law is concerned with exclusive dealing agreements is their impact on the market opportunities of competitors. Accordingly, Connaught is granted standing because it is deemed to be within the target area of the alleged violation. The courts thus hold substance over form to promote the primary goal of the antitrust laws—fostering competition.

State-Action Exemption

More than 50 years ago the Supreme Court declared that the antitrust laws apply to anticompetitive actions by private parties, not to anticompetitive actions by state legislatures or administrative bodies. Thus, state action is exempt as long as: (1) there is a clear state purpose to displace competition, and (2) the state provides adequate public supervision. For example, the California legislature passed a law designed to limit the production, and consequently raise the price, of raisins. Given that California produced nearly one-half of the world's raisins, the effect of this statute on interstate commerce was substantial. Nevertheless, the Supreme Court enunciated and applied the state-action exemption in this case.[18]

The courts have refused to extend the exemption to local municipalities except in certain limited circumstances. However, Congress did pass the Local Government Antitrust Act of 1984 in response to municipalities' fears of treble damages. This act eliminated all liability for antitrust damages by local governments but preserved equitable remedies such as injunctions. The act extended immunity from damages to all officials or employees acting in an official capacity.

■ Section 2 of the Sherman Act

Section 2 of the Sherman Act provides:

> Every person who shall monopolize, or attempt to monopolize, or combine or conspire with any other person or per-

At the Top

Any communications by a company's employees regarding price fixing, or any director involvement in such activity, may subject the company to potential liability in the form of civil damages and criminal penalties. It is therefore very important that the company maintain an adequate supervisory mechanism.

> sons, to monopolize any part of the trade or commerce among the several States, or with foreign nations, shall be deemed guilty of a felony.[19]

As under section 1 of the Sherman Act, corporations can be fined up to $10 million for each violation, and individuals can be fined up to $350,000 for each violation and imprisoned for up to three years.

A firm that possesses monopoly power is able to set prices at noncompetitive levels, harming both consumers and competitors. Consequently, section 2 condemns actual or attempted monopolization of any market. Unlike section 1, section 2 does not require proof of an agreement or any other collective action.

Section 2 does not, however, prohibit the mere possession of monopoly power. The offense of monopolization has two elements. The plaintiff must first show that the defendant has monopoly power in a relevant market, and then that the defendant willfully acquired or maintained that power through anticompetitive acts. A firm that has monopoly power thrust upon it by circumstances or attains it by superior performance does not violate section 2.

There is thus a status element (the defendant must be an entity with monopoly power) and a conduct element (the defendant must commit anticompetitive acts).

Monopoly Power

Courts define *monopoly power* as the power to control prices or exclude competition in a relevant market. Monopoly power is marked by high profits over an extended period of time and the unavailability of substi-

---

18. *Parker v. Brown,* 317 U.S. 341, 63 S.Ct. 307 (1943).

19. 15 U.S.C. § 2 (1988 & Supp. 1992).

tute goods or services. The determination of whether a particular corporation has monopoly power usually requires complex economic analysis. Presumptions based on market share and other structural characteristics of markets are used to simplify the analysis, but in practice, each case turns on its unique (and usually disputed) facts.

Competition takes place in discrete markets. Therefore, the existence of monopoly power can only be determined once the relevant market for the product is determined. Markets have two components: a product component and a geographic component.

Multiple Brand Product Market   The *multiple brand product market* is made up of product or service offerings by different manufacturers or sellers that are economically interchangeable and may therefore be said to compete. Sometimes it is easy to identify substitutes. No one would deny that Coca-Cola competes against Pepsi. Frequently the question is more complex. Does Coca-Cola compete against Dr. Pepper? Almost certainly. Koala Springs orange and mango juice and mineral water? Maybe. Powdered iced tea? That is hard to say.

These questions are important because the power of a seller to set prices above competitive levels is limited by the ability of purchasers to substitute other types of products. Where purchasers do not want to or are unable to substitute other goods in the face of a price increase, the seller can set prices at monopoly levels. The product market is that collection of goods or services that are substitutes at or near the prevailing prices.

Single Brand Product Market   The Supreme Court in *Eastman Kodak Co. v. Image Technical Services, Inc.* (case 18.3) held that "[b]ecause service and parts for Kodak equipment are not interchangeable with other manufacturers' service and parts, the relevant market from the Kodak-equipment owner's perspective is composed of only those companies that service Kodak machines." Evidence in the case showed that Kodak controlled nearly 100% of the parts market and 80% to 95% of the service market, with no readily available substitutes for Kodak equipment owners. None of Kodak's business justifications for its actions were found by the Court to be sufficient. Thus, in some cases, a single brand of a product or service may constitute a separate market in a section 2 analysis.

Geographic Market   Competition is also affected by geographical restraints on product movement. If a firm in Michigan is the only maker of widgets in the Midwest, it has the potential to exercise monopoly power unless widget makers from other parts of the country can profitably ship their products to that area. Some markets are national or even international in scope, for example, the markets for long-distance telephone service, supercomputer sales, and nuclear power plant design services. Other markets are localized, for example, markets for products that are expensive to transport, such as wet cement. The contours of geographic markets may also be affected by government regulations that confine firms to certain regions.

By defining the geographic market, antitrust courts try to separate firms that affect competition in a given region from those that do not. The geographic market encompasses all firms that compete for sales in a given area at current prices, or would compete in that area if prices rose by a modest amount.

Market Share   Once the relevant market is determined, the plaintiff must show that, within this market, the defendant possessed monopoly power. For example, the Supreme Court has held that monopoly power may be inferred from a firm's predominant share of the market. In determining market share, the initial definition of the relevant market is crucial. For example, Koala Springs soft drinks, made of fruit juices from Australia and mineral water, could be considered part of the market for imported fruit juice. Koala's competitors would include other imported fruit juice sellers like Southern Cross. Koala has a major share of that market. On the other hand, if the market is defined as all fruit juices or all soda, then Koala's market share would be very small. Consequently, how a relevant market is defined often determines whether a particular firm has a dominant share of the market.

In one case, the Supreme Court found that 87% of the market was a predominant share sufficient to create a presumption of monopoly power. As a general proposition, firms with market shares in excess of 60% are especially vulnerable to section 2 litigation. When a single brand of a product or service constitutes the relevant market, market share may be 100%.

Other Factors   Market shares do not, however, conclusively establish monopoly power. Antitrust courts require that the market share be analyzed in the context of other characteristics of the market in question. Courts will thus look at barriers to entry in the industry (including, according to some authorities, initial capital requirements), profit levels, market trends, pricing patterns, product differentiation, economies of scale, and government regulation. Essentially, the court is trying to determine the likelihood that another company will become a viable competitor in the relevant market. The discussion of the breakup of the Bell Telephone System in the "Economic Perspective" of this chapter highlights these issues.

Monopolistic Intent

Once the presence of monopoly power is established, the plaintiff must then prove a *monopolistic intent*. It is possible to prove intent through evidence of statements by the monopolist's executive expressing a desire to eliminate competition. However, hostility between competitors is commonplace and may even be beneficial to vigorous competition. Therefore, the courts often require that monopolistic intent be proved by evidence of conduct (not merely statements) that is inherently anticompetitive.

A defendant may rebut allegations of monopolistic intent by showing that its success in the marketplace is the result of "superior skill, foresight, and industry." A monopoly earned by superior performance is not unlawful. Indeed, the law recognizes that the possibility of attaining such a monopoly may be a powerful incentive to vigorous competition, which benefits consumers. Therefore, a key issue in section 2 litigation is whether the defendant acquired or maintained its monopoly by procompetitive acts or by anticompetitive acts. Anticompetitive acts include predatory pricing and, under certain circumstances, refusal to deal.

> ❝
>
> *A defendant may rebut allegations of monopolistic intent by showing that its success in the marketplace is the result of "superior skill, foresight, and industry."*

Predatory Pricing   The courts have not settled on a single definition of predatory pricing, that is, the attempt to eliminate rivals by undercutting their prices to the point where they lose money and go out of business, so that the monopolist can then raise its prices because it is no longer restrained by competition. The courts have struggled to develop principles that distinguish between such anticompetitive pricing and the procompetitive pricing that occurs when a more efficient firm competes vigorously yet fairly against its rivals. In the latter case, the more efficient firm could undercut its rivals, forcing them out of business, and a lawful monopoly would result.

When prices are above average variable cost but below average total cost and the company has excess capacity, courts will usually find the pricing legal. (Variable cost is the cost of producing the next incremental unit; total cost includes variable cost and fixed costs, like rent and overhead). If a company does not have excess capacity, the legality of the pricing depends on the company's intent; the cases are very fact-specific. Prices below average variable cost are presumptively illegal unless the business can demonstrate that the pricing is an introductory offer or that prices will fall dramatically as the company progresses along the learning curve. At some point, pricing below cost becomes economically irrational unless the predator is anticipating the long-term gains that would result from destroying its rivals.

Some academics have argued that predatory pricing is self-defeating in all but a few market scenarios. Having eliminated its rivals, the predator needs to keep them, and new entrants, out of the market when it raises its prices to recoup its losses. That will be difficult as the high prices—and high profits—can be expected to attract new entrants. Thus predatory pricing is an irrational strategy unless the market, because of barriers to entry or other factors, is structurally conducive to monopolization.

The Supreme Court has accepted this argument. In 1986 the Court rejected a claim brought by United States television manufacturers against their Japanese counterparts. It held that some allegations of predation are inherently implausible because the marketplace cannot be successfully monopolized. In such cases, there is no Sherman Act violation, whatever monopolistic intent the defendant may have had. This has been referred to as the *rule of impossibility.*[20]

Refusal to Deal   As a general proposition, the antitrust laws do not prevent a firm from deciding with whom it will or will not deal. Yet the courts have long recognized that there are circumstances in which a unilateral refusal to deal may allow a firm to acquire or maintain monopoly power. Determining whether a firm has a duty to deal with its rivals is often difficult.

A monopolist has a duty to deal with its rivals when it controls an *essential facility,* that is, some resource necessary to its rivals' survival that they cannot feasibly duplicate. There are four elements a court considers in an essential facility case. First, the court must determine whether the defendant prevents would-be competitors from using the facility. Second, the court must determine

---

20. *See, e.g., Matsushita Electric Industrial Co. v. Zenith Radio Corp.,* 475 U.S. 574, 106 S.Ct. 1348 (1986); *Brooke Group Ltd. v. Brown & Williamson Tobacco Corp.,* 113 S.Ct. 2578 (1993).

whether it is be feasible for the defendant to permit access to the facility by its would-be competitors. Third, the court must determine whether the defendant has monopoly power and control of the facility. Fourth, and most critical, the court must determine whether the competitors are able to duplicate the essential facility. This approach was followed in the AT&T case, which led to the breakup of the Bell Telephone System.

The essential-facility doctrine does not require a firm to share with its competitors resources that are merely useful. It has been held that a company need not share technology that would allow them to compete more effectively, and need not share resources that the competitors could duplicate on their own.

■ Derivative Markets

Ordinarily, section 2 liability is restricted to monopolistic behavior within the specific market in which the firm has monopoly power. However, through leveraging, a firm with monopoly power in one market can use that power to gain an advantage in a separate market. It is clear that when such an advantage amounts to monopoly power in the second market, the firm has violated section 2. (See case 18.3, *Eastman Kodak Co. v. Image Technical Services, Inc.*, for a discussion of derivative aftermarkets.) It is less clear whether a firm can use its monopoly power in one market to gain a competitive advantage, short of actual monopolization, in another market. A federal appeals court explored this issue in another Kodak case, this time involving Kodak's film market.

Kodak had introduced a pocket-sized camera with a new type of film, which was capable of producing photographs that could previously only be taken by much larger cameras. For 18 months after the introduction of the camera system, only Kodak produced the new type of film, which required special photo processing equipment to develop it.

Economic Perspective
The Regulation of Natural Monopolies

In a perfect world, productive efficiency (an equilibrium in which only the lowest-cost producers of goods and services survive) and allocative efficiency (an equilibrium in which scarce societal resources are allocated to the production of various goods and services up to the point where the cost of their product equals the benefit society reaps from their use) would go hand in hand. In the real world, however, this is not always so. For example, the most cost-efficient way to provide telephone connections to homes is to link all of the homes to one central station, using one set of lines. Competition would require duplication of this expensive infrastructure; productive efficiency is best served by a monopoly. But the pricing policy of a monopolist is

not controlled by competition. Consequently, the unregulated price of local telephone service would rise above the socially efficient level, and allocative efficiency would be impaired (see Exhibit 18-a). This can be remedied only by regulation of such industries, which are known as natural monopolies.

For many years, the American Telephone and Telegraph Company (AT&T) enjoyed a regulated monopoly in both local and long-distance telecommunications. The provision of long-distance service is not a natural monopoly, as more than one network of intercity telephone lines can be profitably operated. Nonetheless, there was no competition in long-distance service because AT&T controlled access to the lines to indi-

vidual homes. In 1974, the U.S. government brought an antitrust suit against AT&T, charging monopolization of the telecommunications industry in violation of section 2 of the Sherman Act. The case was decided in 1983.[21] In 1984, AT&T signed a consent decree to enable competition to flourish in the long-distance market. The decree provided for: (1) the breakup of AT&T's monopoly over local service into

---

21. *United States v. American Telephone & Telegraph Co.*, 552 F. Supp. 131 (D.D.C. 1982), *aff'd sub nom.*, *Maryland v. United States,* 460 U. S. 1001, 103 S.Ct. 1240 (1983).

Economic Perspective continued on following page

Economic Perspective

The Regulation of Natural Monopolies, *continued*

EXHIBIT 18-a   Welfare Loss from Monopoly

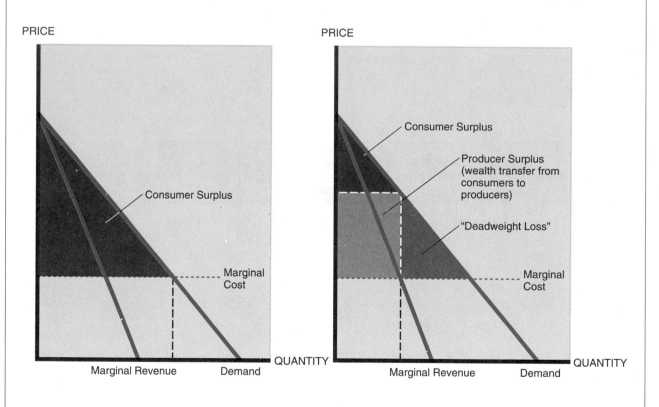

Economic Perspective
The Regulation of Natural Monopolies, *continued*

seven regional telecommunications companies, known as the Baby Bells, and (2) a complex set of rules to ensure that both AT&T and other companies providing long-distance service, such as MCI and Sprint, would have equal access to the local networks. The Baby Bells would, of course, be subject to regulation as each of them would still enjoy a monopoly in the provision of local telephone service.

In the years since the signing of the consent decree, long-distance rates have fallen by 40% in nominal dollars as MCI, Sprint, and other entrants have proven effective competitors to AT&T. In 1994, MCI announced plans to build a local telephone network. Using old telegraph right-of-ways it bought from Western Union in 1990, MCI may eventually provide local service in 200 cities. MCI's plans are barred under current regulations, but its move may speed efforts by regulators to change those laws.[22] Telecommunications regulation is the subject of chapter 19's "Inside Story."

DEFINITION OF TERMS

Consumer Surplus:
The difference between the value of a good to consumers (measured by the price they would be willing to pay for the good) and the price they actually must pay to obtain the good.

Producer Surplus:
The difference between the cost to

producers of producing a good (measured by the minimum price at which they would sell a given quantity of the good) and the price they actually receive in the market.

Total Surplus:
The sum of producer and consumer surplus. Total surplus represents the difference between the cost to society of the inputs used to make a good, including raw materials and labor, and the value of the finished good to society. Total surplus measures the overall increase in societal wealth attributable to production of a good.

Deadweight Loss:
The difference between total surplus in a competitive market and total surplus in a monopolized market.

---

22. Bart Ziegler and Mark Lewyn, "MCI Takes on the Baby Bells—And Everyone Else," *Business Week*, January 17, 1994, 26.

In *Berkey Photo, Inc. v. Eastman Kodak Co.,*[23] Berkey Photo, a seller and processor of film, challenged the introduction of the new camera system. It accused Kodak of attempting to use its monopoly power in the film market to gain leverage in the camera and photo-finishing markets in violation of section 2 of the Sherman Act. In rejecting Berkey's claim, the court concluded that Kodak's invention resulted from its superior business skill, product, and foresight. Thus, the failure to disclose the product innovation prior to introduction of the new product did not constitute willful maintenance of monopoly power in violation of the Sherman Act. However, the court did suggest that the use of monopoly power in one market to leverage monopoly power in another market might violate section 2.

Recent Supreme Court decisions tend to undercut this suggestion, but they do not do so decisively. More specif-

ically, in another case,[24] the Supreme Court held that the plaintiff in every section 2 case involving unilateral conduct must prove a dangerous probability that the defendant's conduct will create or maintain monopoly power in a market. That holding seems to suggest that "leveraging" that only confers a "competitive advantage" in a market cannot violate section 2. On the other hand, there is some language in *Eastman Kodak Co. v. Image Technical Services, Inc.*, that indicates that leveraging monopoly power in one market to create a competitive advantage in another market can be a section 2 violation.

Underlying the decisions under section 2 is the conflict between the goal of preventing anticompetitive behavior and the goal of promoting consumer welfare by encouraging innovation. In certain cases, firms are permitted to adopt practices that, though they might exclude competition, also foster innovation.

---

23. 603 F.2d 263 (2d Cir. 1979), *cert. denied*, 444 U.S. 1093, 100 S.Ct. 1061 (1980).

---

24. *Spectrum Sports, Inc. v. McQuillan*, 113 S.Ct. 884 (1993).

For example, a firm is entitled to introduce technological innovations that adversely affect competitors, even if, in order to do so, it erects barriers to other firms' entry into the market. Consumers pay for such exclusion in the form of higher prices. Nevertheless, the courts and legislators have decided that, as a matter of policy, these higher prices are acceptable as the cost of technological change. If firms were denied the right to act as Kodak did, there would be a disincentive to innovate. Technological innovation, in the long run, increases social welfare.

Other Anticompetitive Acts   Other practices that have been held to indicate the presence of monopolistic intent include the allocation of markets and territories, price fixing, fraudulently obtaining a patent, or engaging in sham litigation against a competitor. Firms can also incur section 2 liability by acquiring or maintaining monopoly power through corporate mergers or acquisitions.

■ Section 7 of the Clayton Act

If a merger or acquisition unreasonably restrains trade, it violates section 1 of the Sherman Act. If it results in monopolization, it violates section 2. These statutes, however, are rarely invoked to challenge mergers. Dissatisfied with the ability of the government to attack mergers under the Sherman Act, Congress amended the Clayton Act in 1950 to prohibit mergers that threatened to harm competition. Section 7 of the Clayton Act provides:

> No person engaged in commerce or in any activity affecting commerce shall acquire, directly or indirectly, the whole or any part of the stock or other share capital and no person subject to the jurisdiction of the Federal Trade Commission shall acquire the whole or any part of the assets of another person engaged also in commerce or in any activity affecting commerce, where in any line of commerce or in any activity affecting commerce in any section of the country, the effect of such acquisition may be substantially to lessen competition, or to tend to create a monopoly.[25]

Two types of mergers are covered by section 7: horizontal mergers between actual or prospective competitors that are likely to reduce competition; and vertical mergers between firms at different points along the chain of distribution. In recent years, challenges to vertical mergers have been rare.

Unlike the Sherman Act, the Clayton Act does not provide criminal sanctions for violations of its terms. The Justice Department, through the courts, and the Federal Trade Commission (FTC), through its own administrative proceedings, may seek: (1) divestiture of acquired stock or assets; (2) sale of particular subsidiaries, divisions, or lines of business; (3) compulsory sale of needed materials to a divested firm; (4) compulsory sharing of technology; or (5) temporary restrictions upon the defendant's own output.

Private parties, such as competitors of the merging firms, may also bring actions for injunctive relief. Recently, however, some courts have come to look with disfavor upon such actions, fearing that they might halt mergers that would actually intensify competition. Firms that are targets of hostile takeovers frequently attempt to use section 7 litigation to prevent the takeover, although recent limitations on antitrust standing—that is, the right to bring such actions—have greatly limited the availability of this tactic.

State attorneys general may also enforce section 7, and they have begun to do so with increasing frequency. For example, the California attorney general challenged the American Stores-Lucky Stores merger after the FTC approved the transaction. If the proposed merger had been completed as planned, the resulting entity would have been the top-volume food retailer in the United States with 600 supermarkets and estimated annual sales exceeding $21 billion. The Supreme Court's decision in the case makes it clear that state law enforcement officials have the power to enforce the federal antitrust laws, if they desire. American Stores was ordered to divest itself of 161 stores.[26] States also may utilize state antitrust laws to challenge proposed mergers.

In contrast to the Sherman Act, which is often enforced by private plaintiffs, the Clayton Act is mainly enforced by the federal agencies. Justice Department or FTC action can delay, if not abort, a corporate merger or acquisition.

❝

Justice Department or FTC action can delay, if not abort, a corporate merger or acquisition.

---

25. 15 U.S.C. § 18 (1988).

26. *California v. American Stores Co.*, 495 U.S. 271, 110 S.Ct. 1853 (1990).

Hart-Scott-Rodino Antitrust Improvements Act

The Hart-Scott-Rodino Antitrust Improvements Act amended section 7 in 1976 to provide a premerger notification procedure whereby the FTC and Justice Department can review the anticompetitive effects of proposed mergers meeting certain size-of-party and size-of-transaction tests. A premerger notification must be filed if one party to the transaction has assets or annual sales of at least $10 million and the other has assets or annual sales of at least $100 million. The transaction must involve a purchase of at least $15 million or 15% of the voting securities of the acquired company.

In general, parties to a merger must give these two agencies 30 days to review their filings, or 15 days in the case of a tender offer. Either period can be extended in the event of a request for additional information by the government. Requests for additional information should be avoided, if possible, because they cause further delays before the merging parties know whether the Justice Department will challenge the proposed merger.

Merger Guidelines

In connection with their enforcement obligations, the Federal Trade Commission and the Justice Department have together developed a series of guidelines as to the kinds of transactions that are likely to be challenged as violative of the Clayton Act.

Under the 1992 merger guidelines, the FTC and Justice Department (the reviewing agencies) seek to determine whether a proposed corporate combination will more likely than not reduce competition, using basically the same analysis as the courts use in applying section 2 of the Sherman Act (discussed earlier in this chapter). The reviewing agency will first determine the relevant geographic and product markets. Then it will calculate the market shares of the companies proposing to merge. Finally, it will determine the effect of the merger on the relevant market.

If the merger appears to increase concentration in the relevant market by a certain amount, the reviewing agency will ordinarily challenge the transaction. However, the question of whether to challenge a combination is left to the discretion of the agency.

As an aid to the interpretation of market data, the Justice Department uses the Herfindahl-Hirschman Index of market concentration (HHI). The HHI is calculated by summing the squares of the individual market shares of all the firms in the market. For example, in a market with four competitors having market shares of 35%, 25%, 25%, and 15%, the HHI is 2,700 ($35^2 + 25^2 + 25^2 + 15^2 = 1,225 + 625 + 625 + 225 = 2,700$).

When the postmerger HHI is less than 1,000, the Justice Department characterizes the market as unconcentrated. In such cases, the department will not challenge the merger or other combination.

Where the postmerger HHI is between 1,000 and 1,800, and the merger will produce an HHI increase of 100 points or more, the 1992 merger guidelines state that the merger will possibly raise significant competitive concerns.

Where the postmerger HHI is above 1,800, the department considers the market to be highly concentrated. In such cases, an increase in the HHI of 100 points or more creates a rebuttable presumption of anticompetitive effects. For example, a merger between firms with market shares of 5% and 10% will result in a 125-point increase in the HHI. Where the increase in the HHI is less than 50 points, Justice Department action is unlikely. Where the increase is between 50 and 100 points, the department will challenge the transaction if it determines, based on a broad-ranging analysis of the market, that the effect of the merger is "substantially to lessen competition." The department will consider such factors as changing market conditions, the relative strength or weakness of the firms in the market, and barriers to entry into the relevant market. It should be noted that even if the Justice Department or the FTC approve the merger, it may still be challenged in court by another party.

■ Litigation Under Section 7

Although the Department of Justice's merger guidelines are of considerable persuasive value, the standards applied by courts differ in several significant respects. Moreover, a court's analysis may vary depending on the type of merger or corporate combination that has been challenged.

Horizontal Mergers

A *horizontal merger* is the combining of two or more competing companies. The first step in determining the lawfulness of such a merger is to identify the relevant product and geographic markets. The same standards discussed in connection with section 2 of the Sherman Act are used.

Once the market is defined, the court will look primarily at three factors: (1) the market shares of the firms involved in the transaction; (2) the level of concentration in the market; and (3) whether the market is structurally conducive to anticompetitive behavior. This analysis is illustrated in the horizontal-merger case that follows.

■ **A Case in Point:**   **In the Language of the Court**

Case 18.6
UNITED STATES v. PHILADELPHIA NATIONAL BANK
Supreme Court of the United States
374 U.S. 321, 83 S.Ct. 1715 (1963).

FACTS   Philadelphia National Bank was the second largest bank in the Philadelphia market, which consisted of 42 commercial banks in the metropolitan area of Philadelphia, Pennsylvania, and its three contiguous counties. Philadelphia National Bank had signed a merger agreement with Girard Bank, the third largest bank in the same market. The United States brought this action to enjoin the merger on the grounds that it would violate section 7 of the Clayton Act.

ISSUE PRESENTED   Does a merger violate section 7 of the Clayton Act when it causes a significant increase in the concentration of firms in a market and results in one firm having an undue share of the market?

OPINION   BRENNAN, J., writing for the U.S. Supreme Court:

. . . .

Having determined the relevant market, we come to the ultimate question under § 7: whether the effect of the merger "may be substantially to lessen competition" in the relevant market.

. . . .

. . . [W]e think that a merger which produces a firm controlling an undue percentage share of the relevant market, and results in a significant increase in the concentration of firms in that market is so inherently likely to lessen competition substantially that it must be enjoined in the absence of evidence clearly showing the merger is not likely to have such anticompetitive effects.

. . . .

The merger of appellees will result in a single bank's controlling at least 30% of the commercial banking business in the four-county Philadelphia metropolitan area. Without attempting to specify the smallest share which would still be considered to threaten undue concentration, we are clear that 30% presents that threat. Further, whereas presently the two largest banks in the area . . . control between them approximately 44% of the area's commercial banking business, the two largest after the merger . . . will control 59%. Plainly, we think, this increase of more than 33% in concentration must be regarded as significant.

. . . .

. . . A fundamental purpose of amending § 7 was to arrest the trend toward concentration, the *tendency* to monopoly, before the consumer's alternatives disappeared through merger, and that purpose would be ill-served if the law stayed its hand until 10, or 20, or 30 more Philadelphia banks were absorbed. This is not a fanciful eventuality, in view of the strong trend toward mergers evident in the area; and we might note also that entry of new competitors into the banking field is far from easy.

So also, we reject the position that commercial banking, because it is subject to a high degree of governmental regulation, or because it deals in the intangibles of credit and services rather than in the manufacture or sale of tangible commodities, is somehow immune from the anticompetitive effects of undue concentration.

. . . .

RESULT   The Court reversed the case and directed the district court to enter judgment enjoining the merger.

COMMENTS   The figure of 30% market share, which the Supreme Court held to be excessive in *Philadelphia National,* has been taken by many lower courts to create a presumption of illegality. However, the Supreme Court has insisted that no single numerical standard can be applied to all markets. In one case the Supreme Court enjoined a merger between competing grocery stores where the acquiring grocery store had a 4.7% market share and the acquired grocery store had a 4.2% market share. The top four firms in the relevant market controlled only 24.4% of the market.[27] (This decision, however, has been relentlessly criticized.) Most courts require that the merging firms have a combined market share of at least 15% to 20% before a section 7 violation will be found.

Questions
1. Is competition likely to be the greatest when there are many sellers, none of which has any significant market share?
2. What could the bank have done to rebut the anticompetitive presumption reflected by the 30% market share figure?

---

27. *United States v. Von's Grocery Co.,* 384 U.S. 270, 86 S.Ct. 1478 (1966).

Even if a merger or combination is determined to be presumptively illegal on the basis of market shares, the defendants may still show that the transaction is not likely to decrease competition. First, if there are no barriers to entry in the relevant market, any transitory increase in concentration will be quickly eroded by the entry of new competitors into the market. Second, if one of the combined firms is failing, the proposed transaction may be the only alternative to that failure. In either of these cases, section 7 liability can be avoided.

Vertical Mergers

A *vertical merger* is the acquisition by one company of another company at a higher or lower level in the chain of production and distribution. For example, the merger of an airplane manufacturer and an airplane engine manufacturer would be a vertical merger. In vertical merger cases, courts tend to focus on whether the merger has

excluded competitors from a significant sector of the market. For example, where competing suppliers were denied access to approximately 25% of the highly concentrated automobile market, section 7 was held to be violated. However, where the market is less concentrated, the courts will analyze the market more thoroughly to determine whether the transaction has any anticompetitive effects.

For example, the U.S. Supreme Court in *Brown Shoe Co. v. United States*[28] pointed to a number of factors that demonstrated the anticompetitive effect of Brown Shoe Company's purchase of retail shoe chain G. R. Kinney Company: (1) an industry trend toward vertical integration; (2) the strength of the parties involved relative to their competitors; (3) the absolute number of shoe sales involved (eight million); and (4) the express purpose of

---

28. 370 U.S. 294, 82 S.Ct. 1502 (1962).

Brown Shoe to restrict competing shoe suppliers from access to the Kinney distribution outlets it sought to control. That decision, however, has been severely criticized, and it is unlikely that the Justice Department would now challenge a proposed merger with market-share effects similar to those in *Brown Shoe*, where only 2% of the nationwide retail shoe market was foreclosed by the merger.

Conglomerate Mergers

In the 1960s and 1970s, many academics and government prosecutors favored expanding section 7 prohibitions to cover mergers that were neither horizontal nor vertical in the traditional sense. The effort to prohibit *conglomerate mergers*—that is, the acquisition of a company by another company in a different line of business—has largely been abandoned. Because the merging companies are in different markets, there is no threat to competition.

One theory advanced during this period has endured, although it has been rarely applied. A merger between firms that are not competitors at the time of the acquisition but that might, absent the merger, have become competitors may be held to violate section 7. This is because potential competition is useful in keeping prices at competitive levels. When prices rise above competitive levels, potential competitors will have an incentive to enter the market and charge competitive prices. When there is no such potential entrant into the market, there is no pressure to keep prices at competitive levels. Monopoly pricing may result.

Consequently, it can be argued that a merger violates section 7 if a plaintiff proves that: (1) the market is highly concentrated; (2) one of the merging firms is an actual, substantial competitor in the market and the other is one of a small number of firms that might have entered the market; (3) entry of that firm *de novo* or anew or by a "toehold" acquisition into the market would be reasonably likely to have procompetitive effects; and (4) entry by that firm absent the merger was likely. A merger does not have to eliminate an actual potential entrant in order to violate section 7. Under this theory it is sufficient if the merger eliminates a perceived potential entrant.

■ The Robinson-Patman Act

Section 2 of the Clayton Act, as amended by the Robinson-Patman Act, prohibits *price discrimination*, that is, selling the same product to different purchasers at different prices. By outlawing price discrimination, the legislators believed that they could protect independent business by preventing the formation of monopolies. It was assumed that price discrimination was the means by which trusts were built, and that discriminatory price concessions were the means by which large retail chains expanded at the expense of smaller independent retailers.

Today, enforcement of the Robinson-Patman Act is a low priority of both the Justice Department and the Federal Trade Commission. However, private enforcement through civil litigation continues.[29]

Elements of a Robinson-Patman Case

In order to establish a case under the Robinson-Patman Act, six elements must be established. First, there must be discrimination in price, that is, a difference in the price at which goods are sold, or in the terms and conditions of sale, or in such items as freight allowances or rebates.

Second, some part of the discrimination must involve sales in interstate commerce, that is, at least one sale must be across state lines or involve the instrumentations of interstate commerce. A seller may discriminate in price as long as no sale across state lines occurs.

Third, the discrimination must involve sales for use, consumption, or resale within the United States.

Fourth, there must be discrimination between different purchasers. In other words, there must be at least two sales.

Fifth, the discrimination must involve sales of tangible commodities of like grade and quality.

Finally, there must be a probable injury to competition. The probable injury to competition is measured at three levels: (1) the seller level, (2) the buyer level, and (3) the customer level.

Defenses

Even if a plaintiff has shown the elements of a Robinson-Patman violation, there are a number of defenses available.

Meeting Competition   Discriminatory prices are not prohibited if the seller acted in "good faith to meet an equally low price of a competitor."[30] As defined by the Federal Trade Commission, good faith is "a flexible and pragmatic, not a technical or doctrinaire, concept. The standard of good faith is simply the standard of the pru-

---

29. See Meyerowitz, "Beware of Price-Discrimination Pitfalls," *Business Marketing*, June 1986, 136.
30. 15 U.S.C. § 13(b) (1988).

dent businessman responding fairly to what he reasonably believes is a situation of competitive necessity."[31]

Cost Justification Price differentials that would be otherwise prohibited by the Robinson-Patman Act are not prohibited if the differentials "make only due allowance for differences in the cost of manufacture, sale or delivery resulting from the differing methods or quantities" in which the goods are sold and delivered.[32] In order to establish this defense, the defendant must show actual cost savings, not merely generalized assertions of cost savings, to justify the price reduction. Defendants may show savings not only in manufacturing costs but also in selling and delivery costs such as costs of billing; credit losses; costs of advertising, promotion, and selling; and freight and delivery charges. The FTC interprets this defense restrictively, and it is expensive to compile the necessary paper trail.

Changing Conditions Section 2(a) does not prohibit price changes

> from time to time where in response to changing conditions affecting the market for or the marketability of the goods concerned such as but not limited to actual or imminent deterioration of perishable goods, obsolescence of seasonal goods, distress sales under court process, or sales in good faith in discontinuance of business in the goods concerned.[33]

In the few cases where this defense has been raised, the issue was whether the price discrimination was a response to one of the conditions listed in the statute. The changing-conditions defense has generally been confined to situations caused by the physical characteristics of the product, such as the perishable nature of fruit. For example, a court permitted price differentials on bananas from a single shipload because they reflected the perishable nature of bananas.

■ International Application of the Antitrust Laws

To avoid antitrust disputes with foreign governments, the U.S. courts will apply the *sovereign immunity* doctrine. This doctrine protects foreign governments from applications of U.S. laws. (The sovereign immunity doctrine is discussed further in chapter 25.) Much litigation turns on

---

31. *Continental Baking Co.*, 63 F.T.C. 2071, 2163 (1963).
32. 15 U.S.C. § 13(a) (1988).
33. 15 U.S.C. § 13(a) (1988).

International Consideration

The Supreme Court has interpreted the Sherman Act to apply extraterritorially where: (1) the intent of parties is to affect commerce within the United States, and (2) their conduct actually affects commerce in the United States. This relatively straightforward statement of the law, however, obscures the complex issues involved in applying the antitrust laws of the United States to activities occurring outside its borders. Because many nations choose to organize their economies in cartels or monopolies, U.S. antitrust laws, firmly committed to fostering competition, often conflict with foreign laws.

whether a foreign firm's anticompetitive activity was directed by its government or if it was merely tolerated. If the foreign government tolerates but does not require the anticompetitive acts, the U.S. antitrust laws apply.

Foreign nations do not always accept the applicability of U.S. antitrust laws under this test. For example, Canada, Australia, and South Africa all enacted laws forbidding their citizens to make available to U.S. courts any documents bearing on the nature and existence of an alleged uranium cartel. This action prevented U.S. courts from gathering the necessary information to ascertain whether an antitrust violation had occurred. (The alleged uranium cartel was one of the defenses Westinghouse Electric Corporation raised in the lawsuit discussed in the "Inside Story" in chapter 9.)

Many countries do not accept treble damages as a remedy. For example, the United Kingdom does not allow any recovery in excess of single damages. Suppose a U.S. court awards a U.S. corporation, USCO, $15 million in damages, after trebling, in a suit against UKCO, a U.K. corporation. When USCO attempts to collect $15 million of UKCO's assets, the U.K. court will treat 2/3 of the $15 million award, or $10 million, as an illegal treble damages award. Thus, USCO will only be able to recover $5 million in the U.K. court. Even when a U.S. court finds a foreign corporation in violation of the antitrust laws, any award of damages is meaningless without foreign enforcement of the award.

As the global economy becomes more of an economic reality, the antitrust analysis of the relevant market will have to take account of foreign goods produced but not sold in the United States. Another issue that must be resolved in the future is how the antitrust laws will apply to U.S. companies purchasing foreign entities that have potentially valuable national security or technology applications in highly concentrated markets.

The Responsible Manager

Avoiding Antitrust Violations

Although it is impossible for a manager to eliminate all possible antitrust violations, there are a number of steps that should be implemented. The underlying purpose of the antitrust statutes is to promote competition. The U.S. economy functions best when firms compete vigorously, but fairly, with one another. However, in antitrust the line between legal and illegal conduct is often blurry. Consequently, there are few rules that a manager can give her employees. Rather, the manager must identify the activities or conditions that most often trigger antitrust liability, such as discussions with competitors, discussions with buyers about their future prices, or activities that may increase concentration in any market that is already highly concentrated.

Discussions among competitors receive the highest degree of antitrust scrutiny. Trade and professional associations are particularly vulnerable. If they disseminate information that identifies parties to individual transactions and the price of even past or current individual transactions, the antitrust laws may be violated. Equally hazardous is the dissemination of information that may result in market division or output restriction. As a general rule, any trade association information concerning prices should be immediately forwarded to in-house or outside counsel to address potential antitrust concerns.

Antitrust scrutiny is also heightened whenever price is discussed, even between manufacturers and retailers. A corporation must make clear to its salespersons that they cannot coerce the retailer regarding the price it charges the end consumer. Such conduct will raise the specter of treble-damages liability.

Finally, antitrust scrutiny is heightened where markets are highly concentrated. The fewer the entities that compete in a particular market, the more likely that agreements among them can be effectuated, and that mergers can lead to unlawful monopolies. Consequently, corporations operating in concentrated markets should be particularly cautious. A manager can receive rough approximations of market concentration from company counsel.

Employees should be encouraged, through an appropriate award system, to inform the manager whenever any of the above "red flags" appear. A manager should not hesitate to seek assistance from counsel in analyzing any activity that might violate the antitrust laws.

Common sense and education are the keys. Actions that don't seem fair usually are not. Continuing education programs will keep corporate employees aware of potential antitrust problems. A manager should always stress that short-term gains through unethical or illegal behavior are always outweighed by longer-term losses, particularly in the area of antitrust with its treble-damages awards.

Political theory also plays a role in antitrust enforcement. Various presidential administrations have either been tough or lenient with regard to enforcement of the antitrust laws.

The code of conduct excerpted in Exhibit 18-1 is an excellent example of the type of information that companies should provide all their employees. However, a code of conduct is not sufficient in itself. It simply provides a solid foundation from which compliance values are imparted to employees on an ongoing basis.

EXHIBIT 18-1 Antitrust and Competition from The Dun & Bradstreet Corporation's Policy of Business Conduct. *Used by permission.*

Dun & Bradstreet will not tolerate any business transaction or activity that violates the letter or spirit of the antitrust and competition laws of any country that apply to the Company's business.

The antitrust and competition laws define acceptable behavior for competing in the marketplace. The general aim of these laws is to promote competition and let businesses compete on the basis of quality, price and service.

U.S. and European Community (EC) law prohibits agreements or actions that might eliminate or discourage competition, bring about a monopoly (in the U.S.) or abuse a dominant market position (in the EC), artificially maintain prices, or otherwise illegally hamper or distort normal commerce.

Individual European countries, Canada, Japan, Australia and a number of other countries have similar laws.

In addition to criminal fines and jail terms, U.S. antitrust violations often allow a private party to recover "treble damages" from the Company. Treble damages are three times the actual money damages. Antitrust lawsuits have frequently resulted in judgments against companies amounting to tens of millions—and on occasion, hundreds of millions—of dollars. Violations of EC competition law are punishable by substantial fines.

The antitrust laws are deliberately broad and general in their language. They contain sweeping provisions against restraints that threaten a competitive business economy, but they provide no definitive list of those activities. This means D&B associates must pay careful attention to possible antitrust implications of the Company's business activities. The Legal Department should be contacted in all cases of doubt.

. . . .

Social Discussions and Company Communications

. . . Any kind of casual understanding between two companies that a business practice adopted by one would be followed by the other may be used in court to prove an illegal agreement.

Even social conversations can be used as evidence that an agreement existed. Memos and other written communications that use casual or inappropriate language might some day be examined by a government agency or opposing lawyers. Using loose language may raise questions about conduct that is entirely legal and may undermine all our efforts to comply with the antitrust and competition laws.

Example: Sales managers of two competing information companies met socially after work. After a few drinks, they agreed that it would be great if they reduced their workload by not chasing after the same customers. The bartender overheard the conversation.

In actuality, neither sales manager stopped selling to particular customers. Later, one company won most of the information business from law firms in the region, while the other company won most of the business from newspapers. This led to an investigation into market allocation of both companies, and the bartender's testimony was used against them.

But aren't my files and memos confidential?

No! Except for certain "privileged" communications with lawyers, all Company documents and computer files, including the most casual note or electronic-mail message, may be disclosed to government enforcement organizations or private parties in lawsuits against the Company. You should also know that stamping documents "restricted" or "confidential" does not protect them from being disclosed in court.

How can I avoid being tripped up by my own memos?

Follow these general guidelines:

Report facts, be concise and objective, and indicate where information came from to establish that there is no cooperation with competitors.

Do not draw legal conclusions.

Avoid expressions that may imply guilt, such as, "Please destroy after reading" or "We stole this customer from Acme Widget Corp."

EXHIBIT 18-1   Antitrust and Competition from The Dun & Bradstreet Corporation's Policy of Business Conduct. *Used by permission, continued.*

Do not refer to "industry policies," "industry price" or similar expressions that imply a common course of action exists even though it does not.

Do not use language that would suggest a false intent to harm competitors, such as, "This new program will 'destroy' the competition" or "establish a dominant position."

Do not overstate your share of the market or refer to a market that is unreasonably narrow in order to make your market share appear larger.

Consult with the Legal Department about when communications with a lawyer can be "privileged."

Questions and Answers

I work in sales and am friendly with a saleswoman from one of our competitors. Our kids are on the same soccer team, so we see each other every week. Last weekend, we talked about a new sales promotion my company is offering. This promotion is no secret; we ran a big advertisement in the trade magazines. Did I do anything wrong?

Yes. You should never discuss price or other terms of sale with competitors under any circumstances. It is too easy for others to misinterpret any conversations you have, however innocent you believe them to be.

My boss asked me how a sales call to a prospective customer went. I mentioned that the customer seemed very interested, but was locked into a three-year contract with one of our competitors that still had two years to go. My boss told me to follow up immediately. I was supposed to convince the customer that no contract was "written in stone" and he shouldn't be so timid about walking away from the other contract. I do not feel comfortable telling the customer what to do about his contract.

You are correct to feel uncomfortable. It is against Company policy to interfere with the contracts of competitors. You might suggest that the customer review his contract to see if he has a right to terminate early, but never advise a customer to violate a contract or offer advice on how to interpret a competitor's contract.

Our main service is so popular that it almost sells itself: We are definitely the industry leaders in this field, and our sales show it. However, some of our other services are a bit stagnant and haven't moved much lately. So, I started to offer the main service only as a partner service to a couple of the slow movers. The customers want the main service so badly they don't seem to care. Isn't this a great idea?

No. If a product with a dominant market share is sold only to customers if they also agree to buy another product, this could be an illegal tying arrangement. While there are exceptions, any such plan should be cleared by your Legal Department.

At a trade association meeting, a few of us from competing companies met for drinks and the talk turned to what we each charge our customers. This seemed wrong but I didn't know how to deal with the situation.

You should say forcefully that you can't participate in price or similar discussions. If the talk continues, walk out and make a show of it (such as spilling your drink) so your protest will be remembered. Discussions like these are frequently used as evidence of illegal agreements, even against people who participated unwillingly but silently.

Inside Story

The Case That Wouldn't Fly—Using Antitrust to Attack Fare Wars[34]

When American Airlines sparked an intense fare war in the summer of 1992, two major competitors alleged that its pricing schemes were illegal because they were aimed at driving them out of business. Continental and Northwest Airlines claimed damages of $500 million each and complained that American was practicing predatory pricing—cutting its fares below costs in order to force its cash-starved competitors to match the cuts and go under.

But the resulting five-week trial in U.S. District Court in Galveston, Texas, showed only how difficult it is to prove predatory pricing and to apply antitrust law rooted in the 19th century to the airline industry in the 1990s.

American Airlines, the nation's largest carrier, held only 20% of the U.S. airline market in early 1992. But in the fiercely competitive airline industry, no carrier can raise prices unless all others follow suit in similar markets. Yet it takes only one carrier to spark a fare war by lowering prices, forcing all others to match or lose critical market share, as consumers view airline seats largely as "commodities" and would rather switch than fight. In the industry, one financial writer noted, empty seats are feared more than discount pricing.

On April 9, 1992, American unveiled a radical new fare structure which included only four pricing levels—first class, unrestricted coach, and two advance-purchase fares aimed at leisure travelers. The coach fares, often forced upon business travelers unable to plan in advance, were usually two or three times the leisure rates. American said its research showed that business travelers were becoming more "elastic"—less likely to fly on high fares. Small business proprietors, who paid for their own tickets, were particularly alienated, American said.

The airline sought to eliminate commonly-granted "corporate discount" fares of as much as 40% by simply publishing a 38%-off coach fare for all takers. An internal American memorandum noted the aim of the reduced business fare was to "make it too costly for competitors to pursue a deep discounting strategy" for corporate passengers by forcing all fares above board. "I couldn't eliminate (discounting) in the industry. The

industry had to do that," American CEO Robert Crandall said.

Crandall said American hoped other airlines would follow suit. Initially, analysts and competitors hailed American's initiative, suggesting the new fares would return profitability to the industry. "The new fare structure will be simpler, fairer and more understandable for our customers and will allow them to fly for less," declared Northwest Airlines CEO John Dasburg.

But Northwest later claimed the fares were doing little to spur leisure travel, a market the company wanted to stimulate. So on May 26, Northwest announced a "Grownups Fly Free" promotion—essentially a half-price fare for an adult-child combination. In usual circumstances, such a move by a national carrier would have forced other airlines to "match" the promotion.

On the next day, however, American struck back. Apparently sensing that its April "value pricing" plan was under attack, American one-upped Northwest by cutting all fares in half, dropping the adult-child restriction. The result was a summer flying frenzy, as all airlines followed suit. It was a boon to hotels, car rental agencies, and tourist resorts across the U.S. "The extraordinary air-fare sale that ended a week ago will create at least 70,000 jobs and stimulate our economy by more than $2.5 billion this summer," Crandall said on June 14. Spurning talk by analysts that the move was "predatory," Crandall said American's pricing was the result of "natural competition."

The consumers' gain was the airline industry's loss, however. Continental and Northwest then went to federal court, claiming American's April pricing and its half-price summer sale amounted to a predatory pricing scheme illegal under antitrust law. American, with more cash, was prepared to lose money simply to drive them under, enabling the carrier to later raise fares and reap monopoly profits, the two competitors said. They each claimed $500 million in damages, making American

---

34. By David N. Danforth. *Used by permission.*

Inside Story continued on following page

Inside Story, continued

liable for $3 billion under treble-damage provisions of the law.

When the case reached the courtroom of Judge Samuel Kent in July 1993, the question at issue was whether American Airlines had the power "to control prices and exclude competition" in 1,000 route markets in the U.S. and 6 hub airports, including its largest at Dallas-Fort Worth and Chicago. Though American had national competitors like Delta and United, it stood to raise fares enough to reap $2.4 billion in profits if Northwest and Continental could be knocked out, an internal Continental analysis showed.

American countersued, claiming the other airlines' losses were the result of mismanagement and high debt. Southwest Airlines, which was not involved in the case, had managed to make money throughout the fare wars, American pointed out. Crandall scoffed at Northwest, writing in a published article that its "new owners were wheeler-dealers who have little experience" in the airline business. He suggested that Northwest's woes resulted from a leveraged buyout which piled $3 billion in debt on the carrier. He also reminded readers that it was Northwest, not American, which initiated the half-price cuts.

Crandall, 57, became a central figure in the suit. His testimony was an anxiously awaited drama which would pit his sharp wit against the most successful trial lawyer in the U.S. Joe Jamail of Houston had coaxed a $10 billion damage award from a jury against Texaco and for Pennzoil eight years earlier in the battle for Getty Oil. He represented Northwest. David Boies was representing Continental. It was Boies who was defending CBS when Gen. William Westmoreland dropped his libel suit against it in exchange for an apology over a series on Vietnam War tactics. If Jamail or Boies, who had opposed each other in Pennzoil-Texaco, could incite the American CEO and inflame his temper, they hoped to show the 9-man, 3-woman Galveston jury that similar scorn had led Crandall to cut fares to punish Northwest.

On the stand, Crandall conceded that American intended to vigorously "defend" its newly introduced pricing scheme. But, he contended, his analysts noted that short-run losses of up to $20 million each month from the reduced business fares—known as "dilution" in the business—would be replaced by "stimulation" as

more of all travelers bought tickets, allowing a profit later. When Jamail suggested that American's 1991 issuance of $1.3 billion in notes amounted to raising a war chest, Crandall countered that his airline needed the money to pay $3.2 billion for gates and planes.

Jamail had difficulty taking advantage of Crandall's public disdain for bankruptcy proceedings, which Crandall felt were unfairly allowing weaker carriers to pick away at his profits by reducing their cost of debt. Jamail confronted Crandall with the CEO's following description of bankrupt airlines: "We vanquished these guys. If they were gone, we wouldn't be shrinking."

"You can vanquish the local football team without getting rid of them," Crandall calmly replied. Crandall also stood by his statement during depositions that "elimination of competition is fine, as long as the objective is to get more money for my company." While he "cared" about job jeopardy for 43,000 Northwest Airlines employees, he cared more about his own 100,000 employees and shareholders, Crandall said.

Crandall had written "kill him" in an internal American memo—a fact which Jamail tried to use to impale the tough-talking CEO. But the move backfired: Crandall had learned that an American chef was serving chicken Kiev rather than chicken cilantro on the Dallas-Boston route. The chef, a good friend, was still alive, though chicken cilantro was back on board, Crandall said.

Perhaps the most damaging evidence against Crandall was barred from the courtroom. When Judge Kent had ruled, in an effort to streamline the trial, that evidence only from 1989 forward could be introduced, he spared jurors a tell-tale taped conversation. Years earlier, ex-Braniff Airways CEO Howard Putnam had taped Crandall in a conversation over the pair's competition out of Dallas.

Crandall: "I think it's dumb as hell, for Christ's sake, to sit here and pound the shit out of each other and neither one of us is making a f—ing dime."

Putnam: "Well. . . ."

Crandall: "I mean, you know goddam, what the f— is the point of it? . . . I have a suggestion for you. Raise your goddam fares 20% and I'll raise mine the next morning."

Putnam: "Robert, we. . . ."

Crandall: "You'll make more money and I will too."

Inside Story, continued

Putnam: "We can't talk about pricing."

Crandall: "Oh, bullshit, Howard. We can talk about any goddam thing we want to talk about."

In 1983, the Justice Department investigated Crandall over the exchange but settled without admission of guilt. Crandall admitted that American was able to raise fares 25% to 40% on competing routes after Braniff went under, but maintained the increases brought fares to a level "just below the industry average."

Northwest and Continental sought to show that American's pricing was below cost. However, their efforts were hampered by a long-running dispute between courts over the definition of "cost." For example, total "variable cost" over all airline seats is much higher than the marginal cost of loading on extra passenger onto a plane with empty seats. The jurisdiction in which Galveston is located also had a unique test which introduced "profit maximizing behavior" as an additional test.

Midway through the trial, the judge admonished both lawyers that the jury was reaching the "saturation point" with technical testimony. But Jamail felt he had gotten the best of Crandall by employing his trademark down-home, folksy style.

The jury took less than three hours to decide a case which had cost American $30 million in legal fees. It first had to consider which market American had attempted to monopolize: hubs, particular routes, or the national market. When jurors quickly concluded that American's large market share didn't necessarily indicate intent to monopolize, the case was over.

The case, Boies later said, was hobbled from the start. It began when Continental and Northwest concluded that discussions between the "big three" carriers—American, Delta and United—were focusing on a joint strategy to penalize weaker carriers. Northwest had just averted bankruptcy, Continental had emerged from two, and TWA was still under Chapter 11 protection.

But Boies' plans to sue under that theory were destroyed by a Supreme Court decision shortly before in an unrelated case that predatory pricing as collusion between several firms would not be a realistic claim.[35] In addition, it would be easier to show predatory behavior with the half-priced fares. But their introduction as a reaction to Northwest's promotion forced the plaintiffs back to the April "value" plan, which was harder to prove since business fares were so high to begin with.

The 19th-century model of monopoly law which conjures images of enormous monopoly behemoths was difficult for the jury to apply to an industry in which a "dominant" share is only 20%.

---

35. *Brooke Group Ltd. v. Brown & Williamson Tobacco Corp.*, 113 S.Ct. 2578 (1993).

Key Words and Phrases

Questions and Case Problems

1. What is prohibited by sections 1 and 2 of the Sherman Act?

2. A manufacturer of electronics in New Orleans, Louisiana, authorized Hayman Electronics and Radio World to sell its products in the New Orleans area. Hayman had been a retailer of these products for several years; Radio World's relationship with the manufacturer was more recent. Hayman complained to the manufacturer that Radio World was price cutting. Hayman requested that the manufacturer terminate Radio World as a retailer. The manufacturer did so. Radio World comes to you, the company attorney, asking you what Radio World can do about the termination. What additional information would you like to know and how will you respond?

3. You work for Lucky Liquor, a manufacturer of liquor. During a marketing meeting, several pricing proposals were made with various arguments to support each proposal.

(a) That the manufacturer should set a minimum price per ounce that the wholesalers can charge.

(b) That the manufacturer should set a maximum price per ounce that the wholesalers can charge.

(c) That the wholesalers can charge any price they want within a certain range; if they charge a higher price, they must give the customer a rebate coupon for the differential.

After the meeting, while sitting in your office, you remember your glorious days in your business-law class at Columbia Business School. You begin to reflect upon the antitrust law regarding price fixing and how it applies to these marketing proposals. What will you tell your fellow marketers regarding the legality of each of these proposals?

4. Randy McConnell, owner of a movie theater in Redmond, a Seattle suburb, wanted to obtain first-run movies from distributors to show in his theater. He approached the eight major movie distributors, who all responded that they restrict first-run movies to the Seattle downtown movie theaters. Suburban theaters can get only the second-run movies. McConnell comes to you, his attorney, wondering whether these theaters have violated any antitrust laws. In the course of the conversation, McConnell also tells you that the downtown theaters pay a relatively high license fee. What will you tell him, and what additional facts would you like to know?

[*Theatre Enterprises, Inc. v. Paramount Film Distributing Corp.*, 346 U.S. 537, 74 S.Ct. 257 (1954)]

5. United States manufacturers want to bring a suit against Japanese manufacturers, alleging a conspiracy to take over the United States automobile industry by exporting low-priced products to the United States while keeping the prices artificially high in Japan. The U.S. manufacturers tell you, their attorney, that the Japanese manufacturers have formed an association in which they discuss market conditions in the United States; potential or actual import restrictions; surcharges; and simplification of export procedures; as well as other topics.

(a) In light of these facts, what are the chances of success-

fully bringing an antitrust suit against these manufacturers? Assume that there are no conflict-of-law or other procedural problems due to the manufacturers' being in another country.

(b) What if, instead of discussing the topics listed above, they discussed the details of individual sales, production, inventories, current price lists, and future price trends?

(c) What if they discussed average costs, freight rates, and terms of past transactions, without identifying buyers or sellers?

[*Matsushita Elec. Indus. Co. v. Zenith Radio Corp.*, 475 U.S. 574, 106 S.Ct. 1348 (1986)]

6. Lillian Alexander worked for Western Propane Company in Colorado. After becoming disgruntled with the company, she left and opened her own propane company, which competed directly with Western Propane. The two companies fought for the same customers. Within two years Alexander's company went from 0% to 25% of the market, and Western Propane's share dropped from 75% to 50%. Alexander comes to you, her attorney, wanting to bring suit against Western Propane for predatory pricing. She tells you that during a recent price war Western Propane priced its product below average total cost. What must you prove to show predatory pricing, and what are your chances of success? [*McGahee v. Northern Propane Gas Co.*, 858 F.2d 1487 (11th Cir. 1988), *cert. denied*, 490 U.S. 1084, 109 S.Ct. 2110 (1989)]

 7. The National Society of Professional Engineers (NSPE), with a membership of 69,000 engineers, adopted a code of ethics that prohibited its members from engaging in competitive bidding. As interpreted by the NSPE's board of ethical review, the rule against competitive bidding barred engineers from submitting any price information to prospective customers and from entering into any discussion of fees until after an engineer is selected for a particular job. When the NSPE's code of ethics was challenged as violating section 1 of the Sherman Act, the NSPE argued that its rule against competitive bidding was reasonable. The NSPE argued that price competition among engineers might adversely affect the quality of engineering, and was accordingly contrary to the public interest.

(a) Should the NSPE's code of ethics be analyzed under the rule of reason, or under the per se rule?

(b) Assuming analysis under the rule of reason, should the code of ethics be held to violate section 1 of the Sherman Act? Make the arguments for and against holding the code of ethics to be illegal price fixing.

[*National Society of Professional Engineers v. United States*, 435 U.S. 679, 98 S.Ct. 1355 (1978)]

 8. The Aspen Skiing Company (Ski Co.) owned three of the four mountain skiing facilities in Aspen, Colorado. The fourth facility was owned by the Aspen Highlands Skiing Corporation (Highlands). Between 1962 and

1977, Ski Co. and Highlands jointly offered a six-day ticket providing skiers with unlimited access to all four facilities. Revenues from the "all-Aspen" ticket, which was very popular with skiers, were divided on the basis of usage. In 1976-1977, Ski Co.'s share of the market for downhill skiing services in Aspen was approximately 80%.

In the late 1970s, Ski Co.'s management came to believe that Ski Co. could expand its market share if it discontinued the all-Aspen ticket. For the 1977-1978 season, Ski Co. refused to market the all-Aspen ticket unless Highlands accepted a fixed share of the revenue, rather than a share based on usage. In 1978-1979, Ski Co. refused to market the all-Aspen ticket unless Highlands accepted an extremely low fixed share of the revenue, which Highlands declined to do. A Ski Co. official admitted that Ski Co. intended to make Highlands an offer that it could not accept. In addition Ski Co. took affirmative steps to make it difficult for Highlands to market its own all-Aspen ticket. This included refusing to sell lift tickets for Ski Co.'s facilities to Highlands and refusing to accept guaranteed Highlands vouchers in exchange for lift tickets to Ski Co.'s facilities.

As a result of these actions, Highlands's share of the market for downhill skiing facilities in Aspen steadily declined, reaching 11% in 1980-1981. In 1979, Highlands sued Ski Co. for monopolization of the downhill skiing market in Aspen.

   (a) What elements are required to prove a charge of monopolization?

   (b) Did Ski Co. enjoy monopoly power in the relevant market?

   (c) Could the all-Aspen ticket be fairly characterized as an essential facility? If so, did Ski Co.'s refusal to provide Highlands with access to the all-Aspen ticket constitute evidence of intent to monopolize?

[*Aspen Skiing Co. v. Aspen Highlands Skiing Corp.,* 472 U.S. 585, 105 S.Ct. 2847 (1985)]

9. Discuss the rules applying to horizontal mergers under section 7 of the Clayton Act. What factors trigger the reporting requirements under the Hart-Scott-Rodino Antitrust Improvements Act of 1976? What tests does the Justice Department use to determine whether it will challenge a proposed merger?

10. Does a decision by the Justice Department not to contest a merger insulate the transaction from attack by private parties or state attorneys general? What standards do courts apply in evaluating a proposed merger?

Chapter 19

CONSUMER PROTECTION

■ Introduction

Role of Consumer Protection Law in Business

Historically, in consumer disputes, consumers had little recourse. The words commonly associated with consumer transactions were *caveat emptor* ("let the buyer beware"). Now many federal and state laws protect consumers from discriminatory credit requirements, unfair and deceptive trade practices and fraud, and unsafe or harmful consumer products. Interestingly, the justification for much of the early congressional action in these areas, including creation of the Federal Trade Commission (FTC) and the Federal Communications Commission (FCC), was antitrust concerns. Congress passed several laws that were intended to protect producers from each other; a side effect was that these same provisions protected the consumers as well. Over time, the responsibility of the FTC, FCC and other federal agencies covered in this chapter evolved to more directly address consumer needs.

Chapter Summary

This chapter examines three primary areas of consumer protection law and the agencies, departments, and commissions that administer and enforce the law's provisions: consumer credit; unfairness, deception, and fraud; and consumer health and safety. The chapter focuses primarily on federal legislation, although numerous state law topics are discussed. In general, consumer protection law at the state level is more stringent than federal law. An overview of the chapter's organization and coverage appears in the following "In Brief."

Commissioners and Appointments

Federal regulatory agencies involved in consumer protection are either independent commissions or executive branch agencies. Independent commissions include the Federal Trade Commission, Federal Communications Commission, Securities and Exchange Commission, Federal Reserve System, and the Consumer Product Safety Commission. The Federal Trade Commission, for example, has five commissioners appointed by the president and confirmed by the Senate for seven-year terms. No more than three of them can be from the same political party. The commissioners vote on decisions by majority vote and issue rules. Executive branch regulatory agencies, on the other hand, are located in cabinet departments. Examples of executive branch regulatory agencies are the Food and Drug Administration (located within the U.S. Department of Health and Human Services), the Office of Interstate Land Sales Registration (U.S. Department of Housing and Urban Development), and the National Highway Traffic Safety Administration (U.S. Department of Transportation).

■ Consumer Credit

At the turn of the century there were general *usury statutes* in most states that applied to lending transactions. These statutes set legal caps on what interest rates lenders could charge. In general, the maximum interest allowed under these laws was 6% to 12%. The result was that many consumers were unable to procure small loans, and an illegal lending market developed which often involved organized crime. In response, Congress made it a federal crime to engage in the *extortionate extension of credit*, defined in the law as the making of a loan for which violence was understood by the parties as likely to occur in the event of nonpayment.

Because credit continues to play an important role in many consumer transactions, a range of consumer protection laws address this area. This chapter discusses federal and state regulation of consumer credit, as well as consumer bankruptcy issues. Business bankruptcy is covered in chapter 24.

■ Federal Law: Consumer Credit Protection Act

Federal consumer credit law can be confusing because of the many acts with similar names. However, these complex acts and regulations are all part of the lengthy Consumer Credit Protection Act (CCPA) which was initially passed by Congress in 1968. Since 1968, several additional acts (or titles) have been added to the original legislation. An overview of the CCPA is provided in the

EXHIBIT 19-1 Consumer Credit Protection Act (CCPA)

Title	Consumer Credit Protection Act[1]
I.	Truth-in-Lending Act (TILA) Chapter 1: General Provisions [omitted] Chapter 2: Credit Transactions Chapter 3: Credit Advertising Chapter 4: Fair Credit Billing Act Chapter 5: Consumer Leasing Act
II.	Extortionate Credit Transactions [discussed above]
III.	Restrictions on Garnishment
IV.	National Commission on Consumer Finance [omitted]
V.	General Provisions [omitted]
VI.	Fair Credit Reporting Act
VII.	Equal Credit Opportunity Act
VIII.	Fair Debt Collection Practices Act
IX.	Electronic Fund Transfer Act

1. 15 U.S.C. §§ 1601 *et seq.* (1988 & Supp. 1992).

In Brief: Consumer Protection Laws and their Administration

Agency, Department or Commission	Consumer Credit	Unfairness, Deception and Fraud	Consumer Health and Safety
Federal Trade Commission Established: 1914 Commissioners: 5 1992 Budget: $71,000,000	Credit Advertising; Fair Credit Reporting Act; Fair Debt Collection Practices Act	Advertising; Sales Practices	
Food and Drug Administration Established: 1930 Commissioners: 2 1992 Budget: $752,000,000		Labeling of Food (except meat, poultry and eggs), Drugs and Cosmetics	Adulterated Food and Cosmetics; Approval of Drugs and Medical Devices
U.S. Department of Agriculture Established: 1862		Labeling of Meat, Poultry and Eggs	Inspection of Meat, Poultry and Egg Processing Facilities
Federal Communications Commission Established: 1934 Commissioners: 7 1992 Budget: $78,000,000		Telemarketing	Broadcast Standards
U.S. Postal Service Est'd: 1775; Reorganized 1970			
U.S. Department of Housing and Urban Development's Office of Interstate Land Sales Registration Established: 1969		Interstate Land Sales	
Securities and Exchange Commission Established: 1934 Commissioners: 5 1992 Budget: $117,000,000		Securities Fraud	
Federal Reserve Board Established: 1913 Governors: 7	Truth in Lending Act (Regulation Z); Consumer Leasing Act (Regulation M); Equal Credit Opportunity Act (Regulation B); Electronic Fund Transfer Act (Regulation E)		
U.S.Department of Transportation's National Highway Traffic Safety Administration (NHTSA) Established: 1970 Administrators: 3			Automobile Safety Standards; Driver Safety
Consumer Product Safety Commission (CPSC) Established: 1972 Commissioners: 5			Consumer Product Safety Act (CPSA); Consumer Product Safety
U.S.Department of Labor	Garnishment of Wages		
State Law, Departments and Commissions	Installment Sales; Loans to Consumers; Uniform Consumer Credit Code (UCCC)	State Labeling Laws; State Deceptive Practices Statutes; Insurance Regulation; Lemon Laws; Uniform Commercial Code (UCC)	State Departments of Consumer Affairs
Other Federal Law	Chapter 13 Consumer Bankruptcy		

table above. Not all titles or provisions of the act are discussed in this chapter; those that are omitted are so noted.

Truth-in-Lending Act

Title I, the Truth-in-Lending Act (TILA), is intended "to assure a meaningful disclosure of credit terms so that the consumer will be able to compare more readily the various credit terms available to him and avoid the uninformed use of credit."[2] In particular, the act makes uniform the actuarial method for determining the rate of charge for consumer credit. But the act is not a usury statute, and nowhere in the act are interest rates set. The TILA applies only to credit transactions (e.g., sales, loans, and leases[3]) between creditors and consumers, not to credit transactions between two consumers. Debtors must be natural persons, so corporations and other entities are not protected by the act.

The TILA also draws a distinction between open-end credit and closed-end credit. The former occurs when the parties intend the creditor to make repeated extensions of credit (e.g., Visa or Mastercard) while the latter involves only one transaction (e.g., a car or house loan). Open-end consumer credit plans must make certain disclosures at three separate times: (1) in an initial disclosure statement when the account is opened, (2) in subsequent periodic billing statements, and (3) annually when a consumer must be notified of her rights under the Fair Credit Billing Act. In general, the required information includes finance and other charges, security interests (collateral), previous balance and credits, identification of transactions, closing date and new balance, and annual percentage rates and period rates.

Closed-end credit plans require disclosure for each transaction of at least the following: identity of creditor, amount financed, finance charge, annual percentage rate, variable rate, payment schedule, total of payments, total sale price, prepayment provisions, late payment fee, security interest, credit insurance, loan assumption policy, and required deposit. Special rules apply for certain residential mortgages and adjustable rate transactions.

---

2. 15 U.S.C. § 1601 (1988).

3. Under federal law, consumer lessees are also protected by the 1976 Consumer Leasing Act, which is chapter 5 of the TILA. The Federal Reserve Board has issued regulations (known collectively as regulation M) to implement the act. Under these regulations, consumer leases are defined to include leases that last more than four months and do not exceed $25,000. The act and accompanying regulations control both advertising and disclosure in connection with these consumer leases.

Federal Reserve Board Regulation Z Congress directed the Federal Reserve Board (FRB) to interpret and enforce the TILA. To that end, the FRB issued regulations, known collectively as *regulation Z*.[4] The FRB has also produced model disclosure forms for use with credit sales and loans. An example of the model form for loans is shown in Exhibit 19-2.

The requirements of regulation Z apply to any transaction (in which both parties are subject to the TILA) that involves an installment contract in which payment is to be made in more than four installments and the credit is primarily for personal, family, or household purposes. The two most important terms in a TILA disclosure statement are the finance charge (interest over the life of the loan expressed as a dollar amount) and the annual percentage rate (APR) (interest expressed as a percentage), both as defined in regulation Z. Typical transactions include car loans, student loans, home improvement loans, and certain real estate loans in which the amount financed is less than $25,000. Regulation Z also contains provisions dealing with disclosure of the terms of any credit or mortgage insurance offered in connection with a loan.

Credit Cards One provision of the TILA limits the liability of credit card holders to $50 per card for unauthorized charges made before a card issuer is notified that the card has been lost or stolen. Once a card issuer has been notified, a card holder incurs no liability from unauthorized use. A credit card company also cannot bill a consumer for unauthorized charges if the card was improperly issued by the card company.

Although regulation Z is usually triggered by credit arrangements in which a finance charge is imposed, the TILA and regulation Z were amended in 1970 to include regulation of both credit cards, such as Visa or Mastercard, which permit deferred payment over a period of time, and so-called charge cards such as American Express, which require payment of the full balance upon receipt of the bill.

Regulation Z also has specific provisions that cover disclosure of information in credit card applications. Information, which must be presented in the form of a table, includes annual fee, annual percentage rates, variable rate information, grace period, minimum finance charge, method of computing balance, cash advance fee, late fee and over limit fee, as well as any fees that vary by state. Any credit card offer or application contains such a table. The FRB model form is shown in Exhibit 19-3 .

---

4. 12 C.F.R. § 226 (1993).

EXHIBIT 19-2   Loan Model Form[5]

ANNUAL PERCENTAGE RATE The cost of your credit as a yearly rate. %	FINANCE CHARGE The dollar amount the credit will cost you. $	Amount Financed The amount of credit provided to you or on your behalf. $	Total of Payments The amount you will have paid after you have made all payments as scheduled. $

You have the right to receive at this time an itemization of the Amount Financed.

☐ I want an Itemization.   ☐ I do not want an itemization.

Your payment schedule will be:

Number of Payments	Amount of Payments	When Payments Are Due

Insurance
Credit life insurance and credit disability insurance are not required to obtain credit, and will not be provided unless you sign and agree to pay the additional cost.

Type	Premium	Signature
Credit Life		I want credit life insurance. _____(signature)
Credit Disability		I want credit disability insurance. _____(signature)
Credit Life and Disability		I want credit life and disability insurance. _____(signature)

You may obtain property insurance from anyone you want that is acceptable to _____(creditor). If you get the insurance from _____ (creditor), you will pay $_____.

Security: You are giving a security interest in:
     ____ the goods or property being purchased.
     ____ (brief description of other property).
Filing fees $_____   Non-filing insurance $_____
Late Charge: If a payment is late, you will be charged $_____/_____% of the payment.

Prepayment: If you pay off early, you
     ____may   ____will not   have to pay a penalty.
     ____may   ____will not   be entitled to a refund of part of the finance charge.
See your contract documents for any additional information about nonpayment, default, any required repayment in full before the scheduled date, and prepayment refunds and penalties.

                                                        _____
e means an estimate

---

5. 12 C.F.R. § 226.18 app. H-2 (1993).

EXHIBIT 19-3 Applications and Solicitations Model Form (Credit Cards)[6]

Annual percentage rate for purchases	_____ %
Variable rate information	Your annual percentage rate may vary. The rate is determined by [*explanation*].
Grace period for repayment of balances for purchases	You have [____ days] [until _____] [not less than _____ days] [between _____ and _____ days] [days on average] to repay your balance [for purchases] before a finance charge on purchases will be imposed. [You have no grace period in which to repay your balance for purchases before a finance charge will be imposed.]
Method of computing the balance for purchases	
Annual fees	[(Annual) [Membership] fee: $_____ per year] [(*type of fee*): $_____ per year] [(*type of fee*): $_____.]
Minimum finance charge	$_____
Transaction fee for purchases	[$____] [____% of _____]
Transaction fee for cash advances, and fees for paying later or exceeding credit limit	Transaction fee for cash advances: [$____] [____% of _____] Late payment fee: [$____] [____% of _____] Over-the-credit-limit fee: $_____

---

6. 12 C.F.R. § 226.5a(b) app. G-10A (1993).

Home Equity Lending Plans   The TILA employs specific protections for consumers who use their home as collateral for a second mortgage or open-end line of credit. Because losing one's home has such significant consequences, Congress felt special disclosure requirements were in order for home equity loans. The TILA provides consumers a *right of recission* (i.e., a right to cancel the contract) whenever their home is used as collateral except for original construction or acquisition. These cancellation rights are generally available for three days if all procedures are properly followed by the lender, three years if they are not. The TILA also mandates disclosure requirements including up-front costs, repayment schedules, and the annual percentage rate and its method of calculation.

Credit Advertising   Chapter 3 of the TILA includes specific provisions that regulate credit advertising. The idea behind these provisions is that consumers equipped with complete and accurate credit information will be able to find the best terms. Regulation Z requires that any advertised specific credit terms must be actually available and that any credit terms (e.g., finance charge or annual percentage rate) mentioned in the advertisement must be explained fully. The FTC enforces the advertising provisions of regulation Z. Unlike the other sections of the TILA, there is no private cause of action for a consumer to sue credit advertisers directly.

Credit Billing: The Fair Credit Billing Act   Chapter 4 of the TILA is also known as the Fair Credit Billing Act. By 1974 Congress had become concerned with the problems consumers were having in getting creditors to respond to their complaints. In response, Congress enacted the Fair Credit Billing Act. The act requires creditors, such as credit card companies, to respond to consumer complaints with an acknowledgment of the complaint, followed by a reasonable investigation to determine whether the complaint is justified. The following case provides an example of the act in practice.

■   **A Case in Point:**   **In the Language of the Court**

Case 19.1
GRAY v. AMERICAN EXPRESS COMPANY
United States Court of Appeals for the District of Columbia
743 F.2d 10 (D.C. Cir. 1984).

FACTS   Gray had been an American Express cardholder since 1964. In 1981, following some complicated billings arising out of deferred travel charges incurred by Gray, disputes arose about the amount due American Express. After considerable correspondence, American Express decided to cancel Gray's card. No notification of this cancellation was communicated to Gray until the night of April 8, 1982, when he offered his American Express card to pay for a wedding anniversary dinner he and his wife had already consumed in a Washington restaurant. The restaurant informed Gray that American Express had refused to accept the charges for the meal and had instructed the restaurant to confiscate and destroy his card. Gray spoke to the American Express employee on the telephone at the restaurant, who informed him, "Your account is canceled as of now."

The billing dispute arose after Gray used his credit card to purchase airline tickets costing $9,312. American Express agreed that Gray could pay for the tickets in 12 equal installments over 12 months. In January and February of 1981, Gray made substantial prepayments of $3,500 and $1,156 respectively. He so advised American Express by letter of February 8, 1981. There was no dispute about these payments, nor about Gray's handling of them. At this point the numbers became confusing because American Express, apparently in error, converted the deferred payment plan to a current charge on the March bill. American Express thereafter began to show Gray as delinquent, due at least in part to the dispute as to how and why the deferred billing had been converted to a current charge.

The district court held that Gray failed to trigger the protection of the act because he neglected to notify American Express in writing within 60 days after he first received an erroneous billing. Gray insisted that his first letter to American Express on April 22, 1981, which was well within the 60-day period set forth in the statute, identified the dispute as it first appeared in the March 1981 billing. According to Gray's complaint, the dispute continued to simmer for over a year because American Express never fulfilled its investigative and other obligations under the act.

ISSUE PRESENTED   Did American Express violate the contract between itself and Gray, known as the "Cardmember Agreement," as well as the Fair Credit Billing Act, when it canceled Gray's American Express card?

OPINION   MIKVA, J., writing for the U.S. Court of Appeals:

. . . .

The District Court made no mention of the April 22, 1981, letter, deeming instead a September, 1981 letter as the first notification from Gray as to the existence of a dispute. We conclude that the District Court erred in overlooking the April letter.

Gray's April 22, 1981, letter complained specifically about the March bill and the miscrediting of the prepayments. Whatever the import and impact of other correspondence and actions of the parties, we hold that, through this earlier letter, Gray triggered the procedural protections of the Act. The letter enabled the card issuer to identify the name and account number, indicated that the cardholder believed that an error existed in a particular amount and set forth the cardholder's reasons why he believed an error had been made.

. . . .

On appeal, American Express also urges that, even if the Act is otherwise pertinent, Gray was bound by the terms of the Cardmember Agreement which empowered American Express to cancel the credit card without notice and without cause. The contract between Gray and American Express provides:

> [W]e can revoke your right to use [the card] at any time. We can do this with or without cause and without giving you notice.

American Express concludes from this language that the cancellation was not of the kind prohibited by the Act, even though the Act regulates other aspects of the relationship between the cardholder and the card issuer. . . . American Express seems to argue that, despite that provision, it can exercise its right to cancellation for cause unrelated to the disputed amount, or for no cause, thus bringing itself out from under the statute. At the very least, the argument is audacious. American Express would restrict the efficacy of the statute to those situations where the parties had not agreed to a "without cause, without notice" cancellation clause, or to those cases where the cardholder can prove that the sole reason for cancellation was the amount in dispute. We doubt that Congress painted with such a faint brush.

The effect of American Express's argument is to allow the equivalent of a "waiver" of coverage of the Act simply by allowing the parties to contract it away. Congress usually is not so tepid in its approach to consumer problems.

*Case **19.1** continued on following page*

*Case **19.1** continued*

. . . .

> Moreover, the consumer-oriented statutes that Congress has enacted in recent years belie the unrestrained reading that American Express gives to the Act in light of its contract. Waiver of statutory rights, particularly by a contract of adhesion, is hardly consistent with the legislature's purpose. The rationale of consumer protection legislation is to even out the inequalities that consumers normally bring to the bargain. To allow such protection to be waived by boiler plate language of the contract puts the legislative process to a foolish and unproductive task. A court ought not impute such nonsense to a Congress intent on correcting abuses in the market place.

. . . .

RESULT   The Fair Credit Billing Act protected cardmember Gray despite the provisions of the Cardmember Agreement which purported to waive the protections of the act. The court remanded the case to the district court for further proceedings consistent with this opinion.

Questions
1. Did American Express act in an ethical manner when it canceled Gray's card?
2. What, if anything, could American Express have done to make the language in its Cardmember Agreement contract enforceable?

Restrictions on Garnishment

Garnishment is the legal procedure by which a creditor may collect a debt by attaching a portion of a debtor's weekly wages. Title III of the CCPA puts limits on the ability of creditors to garnish wages. In particular, the act restricts the amount of a debtor's wages that is available for garnishment to the lesser of either (1) 25% of the "disposable earnings" for that week (defined by the act as the amount remaining after deductions required by law) or (2) the amount by which "disposable earnings" for that week exceed 30 times the current federal minimum hourly wage. The Secretary of Labor enforces the provisions of this title. Some states prohibit garnishment of wages altogether.

Fair Credit Reporting Act

Qualifying for credit is important because of the widespread use of credit in consumer transactions. Nearly everyone over the age of 18 has a credit report on file somewhere. Lenders look to these various reporting agencies for information on an individual's creditworthiness. Because negative information in a credit report can make obtaining credit considerably more difficult, it is helpful for consumers to be able to access these credit reports and correct any false information before it is reported to lenders or shared with any other reporting agency's computer.

A tort law cause of action for defamation may provide a remedy when a reporting agency circulates false information. However, such a claim can be defeated if the person transmitting the information did not know it was false. (Defamation and tort defenses are discussed in chapter 7.)

Congress became concerned about potential injury to consumers through errors in credit reports, and in 1970 passed the Fair Credit Reporting Act (FCRA), which became Title VI of the Consumer Credit Protection Act (CCPA). Under the act, consumers can request all information (except medical information) on themselves, the source of the information, and any recent recipients of a report. The FCRA also gives consumers a right to have corrected copies of their credit reports sent to creditors. The FTC has primary responsibility for the enforcement of the FCRA. An example of how FCRA protects a consumer's credit history is illustrated by the following case.

■ A Case in Point: Summary

Case 19.2
STEVENSON v. TRW, INC.
United States Court of Appeals
for the Fifth Circuit
987 F.2d 288 (5th Cir. 1993).

FACTS   TRW, Inc. is one of the nation's largest credit reporting agencies. Subscribing companies report to TRW both the credit information they obtain when they grant credit to a consumer and the payment history of the consumer. TRW then compiles a credit report on the consumer to distribute to other subscribers from whom the consumer has requested credit.

In late 1988 or early 1989, John M. Stevenson, a 78-year-old real estate and securities investor, began receiving numerous phone calls from bill collectors regarding overdue accounts that were not his. In August 1989, Stevenson wrote TRW and obtained a copy of his credit report. He discovered many errors in the report. Some accounts belonged to another John Stevenson living in Arlington, Texas, and some appeared to belong to his estranged son, John Stevenson, Jr., who had fraudulently obtained some of the disputed accounts by using Stevenson's social security number. In all, Stevenson disputed approximately sixteen accounts, seven inquiries, and much of the identifying information.

On November 1, 1989, TRW began its investigation by sending Consumer Dispute Verification forms (CDV) to the subscribers that had reported the disputed accounts. The CDVs ask subscribers to check whether the information they have about a consumer matches the information in TRW's credit report. Subscribers who receive CDVs typically have 20 to 25 working days to respond. If a subscriber fails to respond or indicates that TRW's account information is incorrect, TRW deletes the disputed information. Stevenson understood from TRW that the entire process should take from three to six weeks.

TRW finally completed its investigation on February 9, 1990. By then, TRW claimed that all disputed accounts containing "negative" credit information had been removed. Inaccurate information, however, either continued to appear on Stevenson's reports or was reentered after TRW had deleted it.

Stevenson filed suit alleging both common-law libel and violations of the Fair Credit Reporting Act (FCRA). The district court awarded Stevenson $1 nominal damages on the libel claim. Although the court found that Stevenson had suffered no out-of-pocket monetary losses, it found that Stevenson had suffered mental anguish and was entitled to actual damages of $30,000 and attorney's fees in the amount of $20,700. Finally, the court awarded Stevenson $100,000 in punitive damages for TRW's willful violations of the FCRA. TRW appealed.

ISSUE PRESENTED   Did TRW violate the Fair Credit Reporting Act (FCRA) in its handling of Stevenson's dispute?

SUMMARY OF OPINION   The U.S. Court of Appeals noted that Congress enacted the FCRA to require that consumer reporting agencies adopt reasonable procedures for meeting the needs of commerce for consumer credit, personnel, insurance, and other information in a manner which is fair and equitable to the consumer, with regard to the confidentiality, accuracy, relevancy, and proper utilization of such information.

Consumers have the right to see their credit information and to dispute the accuracy or completeness of their credit reports. When it receives a complaint, a consumer reporting agency must reinvestigate the disputed information within a reasonable period of time and promptly delete credit

*Case **19.2** continued on following page*

*Case **19.2** continued*

information that has been found to be inaccurate or unverifiable. The parties here stipulated that TRW began its reinvestigation within a reasonable period of time after receiving Stevenson's written dispute. Nevertheless, the court found that TRW had negligently and willfully violated the FCRA by not deleting inaccurate and unverifiable information promptly and by allowing deleted information to reappear.

TRW claimed that it deleted the disputed information as unverifiable if a subscriber did not return a CDV. Yet, some disputed accounts continued to appear on Stevenson's credit report for several weeks. One subscriber returned its CDV by December 4, 1989, indicating that TRW's information was inaccurate, yet the information was not deleted until after February 9, 1990. In addition, a car repossession entry which TRW had deleted in February 1990, reappeared in May 1990. In allowing inaccurate information back onto a credit report after deleting it because it was inaccurate, TRW was negligent.

TRW moved slowly in completing its investigation and was negligent in its compliance with the prompt deletion requirement, the court determined. The record did not reveal, however, any intention by TRW to thwart consciously Stevenson's right to have inaccurate information removed promptly from his report. Thus, the district court erred in finding that TRW's violations were willful.

RESULT   The Court of Appeals affirmed the district court's findings of negligence and the award of actual damages and attorney's fees, but reversed the finding of willfulness on the part of TRW and vacated (set aside) the award of punitive damages.

The Fair Credit Reporting Act also contains restrictions on "investigative consumer reporting" (reports that contain information on character and reputation, not just credit history), including the requirement that in most cases a consumer be notified in writing that such a report may be made.

Equal Credit Opportunity Act

Passed by Congress in 1974, the Equal Credit Opportunity Act (title VII of the CCPA) was originally intended to address the difficulty many women had in obtaining credit, and so prohibited discrimination in the granting of credit on the basis of sex or marital status. The current list of protected categories includes race, color, religion, national origin, sex or marital status, age (except that older applicants may be given favorable treatment), applicants whose income derives from public assistance, and applicants who have exercised in good faith any right under the CCPA.

The Federal Reserve Board has issued regulations (known collectively as regulation B) to implement the

act. Unlike most of the other acts covered so far, the Equal Credit Opportunity Act, as a result of the Women's Business Ownership Act of 1988, applies to business credit as well as consumer credit. In general, the rejection of an application for credit triggers the act and various compliance steps, which include written notification of the reasons for denial. The regulations also establish methods for evaluating the creditworthiness of an applicant.

Ethical Consideration

Is it ethical for a lender to call a friend in the police department to see if a loan applicant has a criminal record? Should the applicant be notified of that investigation?

Fair Debt Collection Practices Act

Prior to enactment of the Fair Debt Collection Practices Act in 1978 (title VIII of the CCPA), the common law was used to protect debtors from outrageous collection practices. For example, if a loan shark broke a debtor's kneecaps, the debtor would have an action for battery. Defamation and invasion of privacy actions were also common.

Since 1978, the Fair Debt Collection Practices Act, which is enforced by the FTC, has regulated "debt collectors" and debt collection practices, and provided a civil remedy for anyone injured by a violation of the statute. The act covers only third-party debt collectors (e.g., collection agencies) or someone pretending to be a third-party collector. First-party debt collectors (e.g., retail store collection departments) are not covered under the act, although the FTC can reach these individuals under its duty to address "unfair and deceptive trade practices" (section 5 of the Federal Trade Commission Act). In general, FTC guidelines require that collectors must tell the truth and not use any deceptive means to collect a debt or locate a debtor. For example, a collector may not give the impression that it is a government agency or credit bureau.

Ethical Consideration

In communicating with a debtor, certain practices are specifically forbidden by the act, including having a debt collector contact a debtor at any time if that debtor is represented by an attorney. What self-imposed limits, if any, might a debt collector adopt and what role should a debtor's personal circumstances (e.g., unemployment or terminal illness) play in how aggressive a debt collector might choose to be?

Electronic Fund Transfer Act

The Electronic Fund Transfer Act (title IX of the CCPA), passed by Congress in 1978, covers debit cards issued by banks for use with automatic teller machines (ATMs) and point-of-sale transactions, as well as preauthorized electronic fund transfers or automatic payments from a consumer's account. As with credit cards, banks are prohibited from sending out debit cards except in response to a consumer's request.

In accordance with the act, the Federal Reserve Board has issued regulations (called collectively regulation E) and model forms for banks to use to satisfy disclosure requirements under the act. In general, the FRB forms ensure disclosure regarding contract terms, potential customer liability for unauthorized use (like credit cards usually limited to no more than $50), and consumer complaint procedures. Banks are also required to issue receipts with every ATM transaction and mail periodic statements showing electronic fund transfer activity on a consumer's account during the period. For preauthorized transfers or automatic payments, banks are required to provide either (1) written or oral notice within two days of the scheduled transaction date that the transaction did or did not occur, or (2) provide a telephone line for consumers to call and ascertain whether the transfer occurred. Most financial institutions have adopted the latter approach.

■ State Law

U-Triple C

All states have statutes regulating consumer credit. Two types of consumer credit transactions are addressed primarily at the state level: installment sales and loans to consumers. These state statutes vary widely, and an attempt to create uniform state laws on consumer credit through adoption of the Uniform Consumer Credit Code (UCCC) has been largely unsuccessful. The UCCC has been adopted by only a handful of states, and in each of those it has been so significantly altered that little uniformity remains. The UCCC is intended to replace a state's consumer credit laws, including those that regulate usury, installment sales, consumer loans, truth-in-lending, and garnishment.

Installment Sales

State installment sales laws set caps on the legal interest rate and permissible charges such as late charges and deferral charges. In addition, the state statutes discuss remedies and attorney's fees, as well as any party's right to assign the sales contract.

Consumer Loans

Most states also have a statute (or several statutes) pertaining to consumer loans. In general, these statutes require compliance with the state's usury statute, although often a lender may be granted an exemption from the usury statute by obtaining a specified license in the state. If a lender is exempted from coverage of the usury laws, it can charge whatever rate of interest the market will bear.

State Credit Card Regulation

State usury statutes are also of concern to the credit card industry. In the early 1980s, in response to New York state's particularly stringent usury statute and credit card fee limits, Citibank moved its entire credit card operations from New York to South Dakota, a state with virtually no credit card regulations. Chase Manhattan Bank and Chemical Bank soon left New York as well, taking with them another 750 jobs.[7] Chase's credit operations remain in Delaware, although recent changes in New York law have persuaded Chemical and another defector, Marine Midland Bank, to return to New York.

San Francisco-based Bank of America, founder of the modern credit card industry, moved all of its credit card operations (and 1,600 jobs) from California to Arizona. Arizona, like South Dakota, has few credit card regulations and lower business costs, including legal costs. Bank of America's move offers significant legal protections because of a 1978 Supreme Court case which held that the rules and regulations in effect in the state where the credit card operation is located apply to all customers, regardless of where they live.[8] A recent private study ranked states by their attractiveness to credit card companies based on regulations and business costs. Among the top ten were South Dakota, Delaware, and Arizona; California ranked 42nd and Massachusetts ranked last.[9]

■ Consumer Bankruptcy: Chapter 13

Chapter 13 (consumer bankruptcy) of the Bankruptcy Code deals with adjustments to the debt of an individual or married couple with regular income. Chapters 7 (liquidation) and 11 (reorganization) of the act are discussed in detail in chapter 24. Although an individual may also be the subject of a chapter 7 liquidation or chapter 11 reor-

ganization, only individuals or small proprietorships are eligible under chapter 13.

Chapter 13 Requirements

Individuals with regular income, including wage earners and individuals engaged in business, may qualify for chapter 13 status if their unsecured debts do not exceed $100,000 and their secured debts do not exceed $350,000. Chapter 13 is similar to a reorganization in that it provides for a plan for repaying creditors.

Chapter 13 plans can be proposed only by debtors and usually are quite simple. The plan ordinarily allows the debtor to retain all of his assets, not just those that would be exempt (exempt property is defined below); but his future disposable income (which would be the debtor's to keep in a chapter 7 or 11 bankruptcy) must be paid to a disbursing trustee for the next three to five years. Creditors holding claims secured by a mortgage, deed of trust, or security interest are entitled to the equivalent of the present value of their lien rights, except that chapter 13 plans cannot modify home mortgage loans unless they provide for payments to cure default. Unlike under chapter 11, creditors do not vote on chapter 13 plans. However, they can object to confirmation if the plan is proposed in bad faith, is not feasible, or offers them less than what they would get in chapter 7 liquidation.

A chapter 13 plan, filed by the debtor, may be either a composition plan or an extension plan. In a *composition plan*, creditors receive a percentage of the indebtedness and the debtor is *discharged* of the remaining obligation, meaning that she is no longer legally liable for that amount. In an *extension plan*, creditors receive the entire indebtedness, but the period for payment is extended beyond the original due date.

After completing all plan payments, the debtor obtains a chapter 13 discharge. An earlier discharge may be granted in hardship cases if the creditors have at least as much as they would have under chapter 7. Apart from the hardship situation, this fresh start (sometimes called *super discharge*) will extinguish otherwise non-dischargeable debts such as claims for fraud, theft, willful and malicious injury, or drunk driving, but not spousal or child support.

Advantages of Chapter 13

Chapter 13 has many advantages for overextended consumers. For example, the filing of a bankruptcy petition stops all creditor collection activity other than the filing of a claim in the bankruptcy proceeding. In addition, unlike in a chapter 7 liquidation, a chapter 13 debtor does

---

7. Robert A. Bennett, "Banks May Shift Units Out of State," *The New York Times*, June 11, 1980, D1.

8. *Marquette National Bank of Minneapolis v. First of Omaha Service Corp.*, 439 U.S. 299, 99 S.Ct. 540 (1978).

9. Carolyn Lochhead, "Credit-Card Issuers Fleeing State, Study Says," *The San Francisco Chronicle*, March 4, 1993, D1.

not surrender any assets. A good faith effort to pay creditors can preserve goodwill and future credit prospects. Unfortunately, chapter 13 debtors are often unable to make the payments outlined in their plan and eventually convert from chapter 13 to chapter 7. After conversion, the debtor's nonexempt property is liquidated and the debtor receives a chapter 7 discharge.

Individual Debtors Under Chapter 7

A chapter 7 liquidation results in the discharge of certain debts. (Chapters 11 and 13 may discharge a portion of a debt through a composition plan, but often plans only modify a repayment schedule.) Certain obligations are nondischargable, including taxes, recent student loans, spousal or child support, fines or penalties, drunk-driving liabilities, or claims arising from fraud, theft, or willful or malicious conduct.

A chapter 7 discharge is not available to debtors who have received a discharge in a bankruptcy filed in the preceding six years. It will also be denied if the debtor has mistreated his creditors or abused the system, such as by fraudulently transferring or concealing property, by destroying or falsifying financial information, or by disobeying lawful court orders. (Unlike in chapter 7, a debtor's prior misconduct or discharge within the past six years will not bar chapter 13 discharge.)

Under chapter 7, individuals are permitted to retain exempt property. *Exempt property*, excluded from the bankruptcy estate, is intended to provide for the individual's future needs and generally includes such things as a homestead, one or more motor vehicles, household or personal items, tools of the debtor's trade, health aids, personal injury awards, alimony or support payments, disability or retirement benefits (including IRAs), life insurance or annuities, and some special deposits or cash. Available exemptions vary from state to state and are usually limited to a maximum dollar amount or by a necessity standard.

The Bankruptcy Code permits debtors to nullify involuntary liens that impair their allowable exemptions. They can even invalidate consensual liens on most household items, tools of the trade, or health aids, unless the secured creditor financed the debtor's purchase of the property or was given possession of it. To take full advantage of the exemptions, debtors often convert assets from nonexempt to exempt forms before filing their bankruptcy cases. However, they must be careful not to take steps that could be considered fraudulent, as fraudulent conduct could jeopardize the right to discharge existing debts.

Ethical Consideration

A manager contemplating personal bankruptcy faces ethical issues when deciding whether to convert nonexempt property to exempt property. For example, buying a large house may be a legal way to make private funds unavailable; but it may be unfair to the creditors who relied on the debtor's general net worth in making an unsecured loan.

Unfairness, Deception, and Fraud

Many regulatory agencies, both federal and state, are involved in the area of unfair and deceptive trade practices and consumer fraud. Among the federal agencies that respond to unfair and deceptive trade practices and consumer fraud are the Federal Trade Commission, the Food and Drug Administration, the Federal Communications Commission, the United States Post Office, the U.S. Department of Housing and Urban Development, and the Securities and Exchange Commission. (Securities fraud is discussed in chapter 23.)

Each of these agencies protects consumers from unfair and deceptive trade practices and fraud in consumer transactions. The areas that these agencies regulate include advertising, packaging and labeling, pricing, warranties, and numerous sales practices. Through government regulation, consumers are shielded from trade practices that are considered unfair, deceptive, or fraudulent. Chapter 6 contains a discussion of how federal agencies function and from where they derive their power.

State attorneys general and state departments of consumer affairs are also involved on the state level in protecting consumers through their administration of various state labeling laws, state warranty provisions (such as "lemon laws"), state deceptive sales practices statutes, and state privacy laws.

Advertising

Consumers are bombarded daily by the competing claims of various advertisers trying to generate new sales. From billboards to television to publications and even the back of grocery receipts, advertisers vie for the consumer's attention. In this competitive environment, companies sometimes make claims that are deceptive or false. Legal solutions to this problem have historically involved three separate approaches: the common law, statutory law, and regulatory law. Regulatory law, enacted and enforced through the Federal Trade Commission (FTC), has proven to be the most effective approach in combating false advertisements.

Common Law

A traditional common-law approach provides two remedies for a consumer who has been misled by false advertising. First, a consumer can sue for breach of contract. In this instance, however, it may be difficult to prove the existence of a contract because advertisements are usually considered by the courts to be only an offer to deal. A consumer might also sue for the tort of deceit. Deceit requires the proof of several elements including knowledge by the seller that the misrepresentation is false. Here, however, the misrepresentation must be one of fact and not opinion, a difficult distinction to make in the context of advertising. (Chapter 8 provides additional coverage of breach of contract. Deceit, also called fraudulent misrepresentation, is discussed in chapter 7.)

Statutory Law

The Uniform Commercial Code and the Lanham Trademark Act are two statutes that may protect consumers from false advertising. Under UCC section 2-313, any statement, sample, or model may constitute an *express warranty* if it is part of the basis of the bargain. Thus, an advertising term may be construed as an express warranty for a product. If the product does not conform to the representation made, the warranty is breached. Express warranties can be disclaimed in a sales contract, however, so the UCC does not generally provide a strong response to false advertising claims. (UCC warranties are discussed in chapter 9.)

A second statute is the Lanham Trademark Act. This act forbids the use of any false "description or representation" in connection with any goods or services and provides a claim for any competitor (rather than consumer) who might be injured by any other competitor's false claims. The purpose of the act is to ensure truthfulness in advertising and eliminate misrepresentations of quality regarding one's own product or the product of a competitor.

For example, the Coca-Cola Company, maker of Minute Maid orange juice, sued Tropicana Products, Inc.

in the early 1980s under the Lanham Trademark Act. At issue was a television commercial in which athlete Bruce Jenner squeezed an orange while saying, "It's pure, pasteurized juice as it comes from the orange," and then pouring the juice into a Tropicana carton. Coca-Cola claimed that commercial was false because it represented that Tropicana contains unprocessed, fresh-squeezed juice when in fact the juice is heated (pasteurized) and sometimes frozen before packaging. The court agreed that the representation was false because it suggested that pasteurized juice comes directly from oranges. The court granted an injunction to prevent Tropicana from continuing to use the advertisement.[10]

Regulatory Law: The FTC

The FTC is charged with preventing unfair and deceptive trade practices, which includes false advertising. Its jurisdiction over advertising, however, was not explicitly established until 1938, when Congress amended the Federal Trade Commission Act and declared "unfair or deceptive acts or [trade] practices" to be unlawful (section 5). One of Congress's primary concerns at the time was injury to consumers through the sale of nonprescription drugs. Today, the FTC's role is much more broad. Among the areas that the FTC has addressed under the Federal Trade Commission Act section 5 are deceptive price and quality claims, and false testimonials and mock-ups.

If the FTC believes a violation of section 5 exists, it will attempt to negotiate a *consent order* with the alleged violator. A consent order is an agreement to stop the activity that the FTC has found illegal. If an agreement cannot be reached, the matter will be heard by an administrative law judge. The judge's decision can be appealed to the full commission, and from the full commission the decision can be appealed to the U.S. Court of Appeals.

Deceptive Price   One example of deceptive pricing practices involves car rental companies. Collision damages waivers (CDW), which release renters from liability for damage to the car, can add up to $14 to the advertised daily rental price of a car. Consumers are enticed by advertisements offering low daily rates, but are then often pressured into buying the additional CDW. In 1989 Illinois prohibited the sale of CDWs, and as a result found that advertised prices began to more accurately reflect the actual cost of car rentals to Illinois consumers.

---

10. *Coca-Cola Co. v. Tropicana Products, Inc.*, 690 F.2d 312 (2d Cir. 1982).

Money collected from CDW sales could no longer be used by car rental companies to maintain artificially low car rental prices. Illinois consumers benefited because they could compare accurate price information and avoid the high pressure sales and scare tactics that had resulted in many consumer complaints in the past. Similar legislation to eliminate CDWs nationwide was introduced in the U.S. House of Representatives but failed to pass.

Deceptive pricing practices also include offers of free merchandise with a purchase or two-for-one deals in which the advertiser recovers the cost of the free merchandise by charging more than the advertiser's regular price for the merchandise bought. Another example of deceptive pricing, *bait and switch advertising*, is regulated by the FTC. An advertiser violates FTC rules if it refuses to show an advertised item, fails to have a reasonable quantity of the item in stock, fails to promise to deliver the item within a reasonable time, or discourages employees from selling the advertised item.

Quality Claims   Advertisements often include quality claims. These quality claims imply that the advertiser has some reasonable basis for making the claim. For example, television and print ads from an October 1990 ad campaign show a Volvo automobile withstanding the impact of a giant-tired "monster truck" named Bear Foot that flattens the rest of a long line of cars. What is not readily apparent from the advertisements is the fact that the Volvo's roof had been reinforced, and some of the other vehicles' supports had been weakened. In response, the Federal Trade Commission required, for the first time, the ad agency—and not just the advertiser—to pay a fine for the deceptive ad. Thus, the car maker and its New York ad firm each agreed to pay a $150,000 penalty, though neither admitted violating laws against false advertising.[11]

Under the FTC's general view, quality claims made without any substantiation are deceptive. On the other hand, obvious exaggerations and vague generalities are considered *puffing,* and are not considered deceptive because they are unlikely to mislead consumers. (Puffing is also covered in chapter 9.) To determine whether an advertiser has made a deceptive quality claim, the FTC must first identify the claim and then determine whether the claim is substantiated.

Testimonials and Mock-ups   Testimonials and endorsements in which the person endorsing a product does not, in fact, use or prefer it have also been determined to be deceptive and therefore violate the FTC act. Additionally, it is deceptive for the endorser to imply falsely that she has superior knowledge or experience.

The misuse of mock-ups is illustrated by the case below.

Ethical Consideration

Is the Volvo ad just an example of puffing? Was Volvo and the ad agency's behavior unethical?

---

11. "F.T.C. Accord on Volvo Ads," *The New York Times,* August 22, 1991, D19.

■   **A Case in Point:**   **In the Language of the Court**

Case 19.3
FEDERAL TRADE COMMISSION v. COLGATE-PALMOLIVE COMPANY
Supreme Court of the United States
380 U.S. 374, 85 S.Ct. 1035 (1965).

FACTS   This case arose out of an attempt by Colgate-Palmolive Company to prove that its shaving cream, "Rapid Shave," outperforms other brands. An advertising agency prepared for Colgate three one-minute television commercials designed to show that Rapid Shave could soften even the toughness of sandpaper. Each of the commercials contained the same "sandpaper test." The announcer informed the audience that, "To prove Rapid Shave's super-moisturizing power, we put it right from the can onto this tough, dry sandpaper. It was apply . . . soak . . . and off in a stroke." While the announcer was speaking, Rapid Shave was applied to a substance that appeared to be sandpaper, and immediately thereafter a razor was shown shaving the substance clean.

*Case **19.3** continued on following page*

*Case **19.3** continued*

The Federal Trade Commission issued a complaint charging that the commercials were false and deceptive. Evidence disclosed that sandpaper of the type depicted in the commercials could not be shaved immediately following the application of Rapid Shave, but required a soaking period of approximately 80 minutes. The evidence also showed that the substance resembling sandpaper was in fact a simulated prop, or "mock-up," made of plexiglass to which sand had been applied.

The FTC, in an opinion dated December 29, 1961, found that because Rapid Shave could not shave sandpaper within the time depicted in the commercials, Colgate-Palmolive had misrepresented the product's moisturizing power. Moreover, the FTC found that the undisclosed use of a plexiglass substitute for sandpaper was an additional material misrepresentation that was a deceptive act separate and distinct from the misrepresentation concerning Rapid Shave's underlying qualities. Even if the sandpaper could be shaved just as depicted in the commercials, the commission found that viewers had been misled into believing they had seen it done with their own eyes.

After a hearing, the commission issued a cease-and-desist order against Colgate-Palmolive that could have been interpreted to forbid all use of undisclosed simulations in television commercials. The court of appeals set aside the order as too broad. Five months later the commission issued a revised order prohibiting Colgate-Palmolive from presenting advertisements depicting a test, experiment, or demonstration represented as actual proof of a product claim, but not in fact constituting actual proof because of the undisclosed use of a prop or mock-up. The court of appeals set aside the revised order, and the FTC petitioned the U.S. Supreme Court for certiorari.

ISSUE PRESENTED   Is it a deceptive trade practice, prohibited by section 5 of the Federal Trade Commission Act, to represent falsely that a televised test, experiment, or demonstration provides a viewer with visual proof of a product claim, regardless of whether the product claim is itself true?

OPINION   WARREN, C.J., writing for the U.S. Supreme Court:

. . . .

According to the Commission, the television commercial in question did not merely tell viewers that the experiment had been or could be performed, but instead told them that they were seeing it for themselves and did not have to take the seller's word for it. This, and not the mere use of a prop, was the misrepresentation found to be a deceptive practice.

. . . .

We are not concerned in this case with the clear misrepresentation in the commercials concerning the speed with which Rapid Shave could shave sandpaper, since the Court of Appeals upheld the Commission's finding on that matter and the respondents have not challenged the finding here. We granted certiorari to consider the Commission's conclusion that even if an advertiser has himself conducted a test, experiment or demonstration which he honestly believes will prove a certain product claim, he may not convey to television viewers the false impression that they are seeing the test, experiment or demonstration for themselves, when they are not because of the undisclosed use of mock-ups.

We accept the Commission's determination that the commercials involved in this case contained three representations to the public: (1) that sandpaper could be shaved by Rapid Shave; (2) that an experiment had been conducted which verified this claim; and (3) that the viewer was seeing this experiment for himself. Respondents admit that the first two representations were made, but deny that the third was. . . .

. . . .

It is generally accepted that it is a deceptive practice to state falsely that a product has received a testimonial from a respected source. In addition, the Commission has consistently acted to prevent sellers from falsely stating that their product claims have been "certified." We find these situations to be indistinguishable from the present case. . . . We find it an immaterial difference that in one case the viewer is told to rely on the word of a celebrity or authority he respects, in another on the word of a testing agency, and in the present case on his own perception of an undisclosed simulation.

. . . .

We agree with the Commission, therefore, that the undisclosed use of plexiglass in the present commercials was a material deceptive practice, independent and separate from the other misrepresentation found. We find unpersuasive respondents' other objections to this conclusion. Respondents claim that it will be impractical to inform the viewing public that it is not seeing an actual test, experiment or demonstration, but we think it inconceivable that the ingenious advertising world will be unable, if it so desires, to conform to the Commission's insistence that the public be not misinformed. If, however, it becomes impossible or impractical to show simulated demonstrations on television in a truthful manner, this indicates that television is not a medium that lends itself to this type of commercial, not that the commercial must survive at all costs.

. . . .

DISSENTING OPINION   HARLAN, J., dissenting in part from the majority opinion:

. . . .

. . . [I]t seems to me that the proper legal test in cases of this kind concerns not what goes on in the broadcasting studio, but whether what is shown on the television screen is an accurate representation of the advertised product and of the claims made for it.

. . . .

RESULT   It is a material deceptive practice to convey to television viewers the false impression that they are seeing an actual test, experiment, or demonstration that proves a product claim when they are not because of the undisclosed use of mock-ups. Accordingly, Colgate-Palmolive's Rapid Shave commercials were deceptive.

COMMENTS   The Supreme Court in this case stated that the FTC's judgment as to what constitutes a deceptive practice is to be accorded great weight by reviewing courts.

*Case **19.3** continued on following page*

*Case **19.3** continued*

Questions
1. Is there a difference between the Rapid Shave commercial and a commercial that extols the goodness of ice cream while showing viewers a picture of a scoop of ice cream that is in fact mashed potatoes? Does it matter if the mashed potato prop is being used to show the ice cream's rich texture?
2. Would it be deceptive for an advertiser to show its product on television if it looks better (e.g., bigger, fluffier, or whiter) on the TV screen than it does in real life?

The FTC has the authority to issue *cease and desist orders* to advertisers who violate section 5 of the Federal Trade Commission Act, such as those advertisers who employ deceptive price or quality claims or false testimonials. In one case, the FTC required the maker of Listerine to cease and desist from making the claim that Listerine prevented colds and sore throats or lessened their severity. Testing performed by the FTC revealed that this claim, which the company had made for more than 50 years, was false. To counteract years of false claims, the FTC required the company to disclose in any future advertisements for Listerine that, contrary to prior advertising, Listerine did not help prevent colds or sore throats or lessen their severity. The order applied to the next ten million dollars of Listerine advertising only.[12]

A cease and desist order instructs advertisers to stop using the methods deemed unfair or deceptive. FTC remedies include: civil damages, affirmative advertising (advertiser required to include specific information), counter or corrective advertising (as with Listerine), and multiple product orders (advertiser required to cease false claims regarding all of its products).

Infomercials

Infomercials, also known as long-form marketing programs or direct response television, are advertisements generally presented in the format of half-hour television talk shows or news programs. Their very format, however, may present problems by blurring the line between advertising and regular television programming.[13] The next trend in infomercials appears to be the "sitcommer-

cial," a full-length show resembling a family sitcom. For example, Bell Atlantic has filmed "The Ringers," a sitcom intended to show off and sell telephone equipment.

Infomercials first became popular in 1984 after the Federal Communications Commission (FCC) deregulated the amount of time that broadcast stations could dedicate to advertisements. As a result, infomercials became a forum for advertising questionable products like cures for baldness and impotence.

Since 1984, consumer advocate groups have lodged numerous complaints alleging deceptive advertising. As a result, the infomercial industry established an internal watchdog agency, the National Infomercial Merchandising Association, in 1990. The association offers guidelines to combat deceptive practices, endorses legitimate infomercial producers, and reports violations to the FTC.

■ Packaging and Labeling

Both the Federal Trade Commission and the Food and Drug Administration (FDA) regulate the packaging and labeling of products. Under the Federal Food, Drug and Cosmetic Act,[14] the FDA regulates the "misbranding" of food, drugs, medical devices, and cosmetics. Numerous state laws, such as California Proposition 65, also deal with information required on product packages and labels. These regulations and laws cover such items as food, drugs, medical devices, cosmetics, clothing, tobacco, and alcohol.

Food, Drugs, Medical Devices, and Cosmetics

Milk producers are permitted by the FDA to stimulate increased milk production in dairy cows with the growth

---

12. *Warner-Lambert Co. v. Federal Trade Commission*, 562 F.2d 749 (D.C. Cir. 1977).
13. *Karen Zagor and Gary Mead*, "Illumination from the Stars: A Look at the New-Found Respectability of So-Called 'InFomercials,'" *Financial Times*, November 5, 1992, 18.

14. 21 U.S.C. §§ 301 *et seq.* (1988 & Supp. 1992).

International Consideration

Manufacturers of goods that are to be exported need to consider foreign labeling requirements such as language translations, country of origin disclosures, and weight conversions.

hormone BST. Also known as BGH or bovine growth hormone, BST (which stands for bovine somatotropin) is a protein hormone created naturally by the pituitary gland of cows. Traces of the hormone occur naturally in milk. Products containing milk from cows injected with BST, however, are not required to show that fact on their labels.

Ethical Consideration

Should hormone use be disclosed to milk consumers? What marketing advantage might be gained from labeling milk produced by cows not injected with BST? Could the milk be labeled "hormone free" when, in fact, trace amounts of the hormone occur naturally in milk?

The FDA has primary responsibility for regulating the packaging and labeling of food (except meat, poultry, and eggs, which are under the jurisdiction of the U.S. Department of Agriculture), drugs, medical devices, and cosmetics. Congress in 1966 passed the Fair Packaging and Labeling Act[15] in response to the surge in prepackaged items available at supermarkets, and the perceived subtle deceptions some manufacturers employed. For example, a survey conducted by the FDA at that time found that food was often packaged in containers three to four times larger than the food product itself. The 1966 act contains both mandatory and discretionary provisions designed to inform the consumer which manufacturer made the product, what is in the package, and how much the package contains.

---

15. 15 U.S.C. §§ 1451 *et seq.* (1988 & Supp. 1992).

In particular, under the act, a food label must contain the name and address of the manufacturer, packer, or distributor; the net quantity on the front panel, placed in a uniform location; and the quantity given in servings with the net quantity of each serving stated and the quantity listed in certain ways, depending on how the product is classified. This last provision requires dual declarations of sizes (e.g., one quart and 32 ounces) and forbids the use of terms such as "jumbo quart" and "super ounce."

Another area of concern for Congress was the proliferation of various package sizes, making price comparison extremely difficult for consumers. For example, a "jumbo" size of one product might contain the same amount as the "large" size of another. Similarly, the terms "small, medium and large" have often been embellished with terms like "ketchup-lover size," "family size," and "fun size." The 1966 act provides authority to add requirements concerning the use of such terms, as well as terms associated with value claims such as "economy size." Many supermarkets now provide unit pricing information so that consumers can more easily compare the prices of competing products.

Nutrition Facts The Nutrition Labeling and Education Act, passed by Congress in 1990, requires mandatory nutrition labeling of almost all foods, a nutrition panel entitled "Nutrition Facts," expanded ingredient labeling requirements, and restrictions on nutrient content claims and health claims.

Under the act, about 90% of processed food must carry nutrition information. Some exceptions include plain coffee and tea, delicatessen items, and bulk food. The "Nutrition Facts" panel, mandated by the act, includes the amount per serving of saturated fat, cholesterol, dietary fiber, sodium, and other nutrients. In addition, these panels provide information on how the food fits into an overall daily diet. Point-of-purchase nutrition information is voluntary under the act for many raw foods including meat, poultry, raw fish, and fresh produce. Such information may be shown, for example, in a poster or chart at a butcher's counter or a produce stand.

The FDA regulation also governs the use of nutrient claims like "light," "fat free" and "low calorie," and provides uniform definitions so that these terms mean the same for any product on which they appear. Because of an exemption the dairy industry won from Congress, however, 2% milk may continue to be labeled "low fat" even though it does not meet the standard FDA definition.

Health claims are also regulated under the act. In particular, claims linking a nutrient or food to the risk of a disease or health-related condition are allowed only under certain circumstances. For example, statements regarding the relationship between calcium and osteoporosis, saturated fat and heart disease, and sodium and hypertension are permitted. Health claims made about dietary supplements are also regulated under the act. Dietary supplements include products such as vitamins, minerals, amino acids, and fatty acids. In general, the act requires that health claims about dietary supplements cannot be misleading, and that claims must be supported by available scientific evidence.

Labeling of medical devices is also under the jurisdiction of the FDA. The application of those labeling requirements is demonstrated in the following case.

■ **A Case in Point:**   **Summary**

Case 19.4
O'GILVIE v. INTERNATIONAL PLAYTEX, INC.
United States Court of Appeals for the Tenth Circuit
821 F.2d 1438 (10th Cir. 1987), *cert. denied*, 486 U.S. 1032, 108 S.Ct. 2014 (1988).

FACTS   Kelly O'Gilvie brought this action, individually and on behalf of the estate of his deceased wife, Betty, against International Playtex, Inc. O'Gilvie alleged that Mrs. O'Gilvie's use of Playtex super-absorbent tampons caused her death from toxic shock syndrome, and he sought damages from Playtex under the Kansas law of strict liability in tort. In answers to special interrogatories, the jury found that Playtex tampons had caused Mrs. O'Gilvie to develop toxic shock syndrome, and that Playtex had failed to adequately warn of the fatal risk of toxic shock from the use of its product. The jury awarded actual damages of $1,525,000, and punitive damages of $10,000,000. After the entry of judgment and apparently in response to the trial court's suggestion, Playtex represented that it was discontinuing the sale of some of its products, instituting a program of alerting the public to the dangers of toxic shock syndrome, and modifying its product warning. The trial court thereupon ordered the punitive damage award reduced to $1,350,000. Both parties appealed.

ISSUE PRESENTED   Was Playtex's warning to tampon consumers of the danger of toxic shock syndrome adequate as a matter of law because it complied with Food and Drug Administration (FDA) regulations?

SUMMARY OF OPINION   Playtex contended that it was entitled to a directed verdict because O'Gilvie presented no evidence that the warning accompanying its super-absorbent tampons was inadequate or that the warning was the cause of Mrs. O'Gilvie's injury. The U.S. Court of Appeals disagreed.

O'Gilvie argued at trial that the warning was inadequate because it did not properly apprise users of the causal connection between toxic shock and the use of tampons, or of the increased risk from the use of super-absorbent tampons. The record contained substantial expert testimony that a causal link exists between toxic shock and the use of super-absorbent tampons such as the Playtex product at issue here. Experts also testified that the warning did not alert buyers to the increased risk from use of high-absorbency tampons, and that simply mentioning an association between toxic shock and tampon use did not adequately alert users to the cause and effect relationship.

The warning accompanying the tampons included the following statement:

Information about TSS [toxic shock syndrome] on the package and in this insert are provided by Playtex in the public interest and in accordance with the Food and Drug Administration (FDA) tampon labeling requirements. TSS is believed to be a recently identified condition caused by a bacteria called staphylococcus aureus. The FDA does not maintain that tampons are the cause of TSS. The FDA recognizes that TSS also occurs among non-users of tampons. If you have any questions about TSS or tampon use, you should check with your doctor.

The district court had instructed the jury as a matter of law that the Playtex package warning was in conformity with FDA regulations, and further instructed:

> If the warning on the product was, at the time of manufacture, in compliance with administrative regulatory safety standards relating to warnings or instructions, then such warning is evidence of due care, and the product shall be deemed not defective by reason of the warning or instructions, unless the plaintiff proves that a reasonably prudent manufacturer could and would have taken additional precautions.

The Court of Appeals' review of the record revealed abundant evidence that Playtex deliberately disregarded studies and medical reports linking high-absorbency tampon fibers with increased risk of toxic shock at a time when other tampon manufacturers were responding to this information by modifying or withdrawing their high-absorbency products. Moreover, there was evidence that Playtex deliberately sought to profit from the situation by advertising the effectiveness of its high-absorbency tampons when it knew other manufacturers were reducing the absorbency of their products due to the evidence of a causal connection between high absorbency and toxic shock. This occurred in the face of Playtex' awareness that its product was far more absorbent than necessary for its intended effectiveness.

The Court of Appeals concluded the trial court had, in reducing the punitive damages award, rewarded Playtex for continuing its tortious conduct long enough to use it as a bargaining chip. The possibility that other potential defendants would be able to reduce their liability for punitive damages in the same way might encourage the very behavior that the punitive award was intended to deter.

Playtex argued that the presence of a warning that complied with FDA requirements precluded, as a matter of law, any finding that Playtex exhibited the reckless indifference necessary to support an award of punitive damages. The Court of Appeals disagreed. It found that compliance with FDA standards was not dispositive under Kansas law if a reasonable manufacturer would have done more. Under the circumstances in this case, compliance with the FDA regulations did not preclude punitive damages when there was evidence sufficient to support a finding of reckless indifference to consumer safety.

RESULT   The $10,000,000 punitive damage award was reinstated.

COMMENTS   The FDA issued new tampon labeling rules in 1989 which standardized absorbency terms like "junior," "regular," "super," and "super plus." This change was important because there is medical evidence of a direct relationship between tampon absorbency and the risk of TSS, with the least absorbent tampons being the safest.

Clothing

The FTC has primary responsibility for regulating the packaging and labeling of commodities other than food, drugs, medical devices, and cosmetics. For example, numerous federal laws regulate the labeling of clothing.

Among these are the Wool Products Labeling Act,[16] the Fur Products Labeling Act,[17] the Flammable Fabrics

---

16. 15 U.S.C. §§ 68 *et seq.* (1988).
17. 15 U.S.C. §§ 69 *et seq.* (1988).

Act,[18] and the Textile Fiber Products Identification Act.[19] Each of these acts is intended to protect distributors and consumers against misbranding and false advertising. Critics of these acts have suggested that the false advertising aspects of each act could have been covered by section 5 of the Federal Trade Commission Act, and that the principal value of these acts has been to protect one producer from another producer's false claims.

Tobacco

Tobacco product packages are required to contain one of several health warnings about the hazards associated with smoking. Such warnings were first required after passage of the Federal Cigarette Labeling and Advertising Act of 1966. In the trial of *Cipollone v. Liggett Group, Inc.*,[20] a jury found that a cigarette manufacturer failed to warn its consumers of the known health risks of smoking prior to 1966, and that this failure caused the plaintiff's lung cancer and death. On appeal, the U.S. Supreme Court ruled that Cipollone's state common-law claims based on failure to warn were preempted by federal law.[21] Increasing evidence of the addictive qualities of nicotine might lead to regulation of cigarettes as a drug. Fierce opposition from the tobacco lobby is expected to any change in the regulation of cigarettes.[22] In 1986, Congress passed the Smokeless Tobacco Health Education Act, which requires similar warnings on packages of smokeless chewing tobacco products.

Alcohol

In 1989 a congressionally mandated warning label began to appear on bottles, cans, and packages of wine, beer, and spirits. It states that alcohol consumption increases the risks of birth defects, says that consuming alcoholic beverages can impair one's ability to drive a car, and cautions against its use with machinery.[23]

The warning label was implemented by the Bureau of Alcohol, Tobacco and Firearms (BATF), a branch of the Treasury Department that also regulates the wine industry. Beyond warning labels, BATF regulates everything that appears on packages of alcoholic beverages. All such products must have certain mandatory information on their labels; wine, which changes with every vintage, has labeling regulations that differ from spirits and beer. BATF receives approximately 4,500 wine label applications per month, many of them identical to the previous year's label. Each wine label must be approved by BATF before it can be used.

BATF regulations attach legal meanings to various statements made on wine labels, including the vintage year, grape variety, producer, and alcohol content. Warnings are also required to alert those who are allergic to sulfites that trace amounts of the substances, which may be used in production as a preservative and which are also produced naturally during fermentation, are contained in the wine.

State Labeling Laws

Many states, through their use of labeling laws, have taken steps to protect consumers from dangerous products. Historically, these laws have sought to protect consumers from risks that involve the danger of imminent bodily harm. Recently, however, some states have enacted more extensive state labeling laws. Most notable among these statutes is California's Safe Drinking Water and Toxic Enforcement Act of 1986, better known as Proposition 65. Proposition 65 provides that "no person . . . shall knowingly and intentionally expose any individual to a chemical known to the state to cause cancer or reproductive toxicity without first giving clear and reasonable warning to such individual."[24]

The law requires the governor to compile a list of the chemicals requiring warnings, and to update the list annually. The current list includes ingredients such as alcohol and saccharin, as well as potential contaminants such as lead and mercury. The labeling requirements apply to manufacturers, producers, packagers, and retail sellers, and may be in the form of product labels, signs at retail outlets, or public advertising. An example of a Proposition 65 warning is: "Warning: This product contains a chemical known to the State of California to cause birth defects or other reproductive harm." The FDA has the authority to issue regulations that would preempt state labeling requirements such as Proposition 65, but the FDA has so far chosen not to do so.

18. 15 U.S.C. §§ 1191 *et seq.* (1988 & Supp. 1992).
19. 15 U.S.C. §§ 70 *et seq.* (1988).
20. 893 F.2d 541 (3d Cir. 1990), *aff'd in part and rev'd in part*, 112 S.Ct. 2608 (1992). See full discussion in chapter 10.
21. *Cipollone v. Liggett Group, Inc.*, 112 S.Ct. 2608 (1992).
22. See generally, Linda Himelstein, Laura Zinn, Maria Mallory, John Carey, Richard S. Dunham, and Joan O'C. Hamilton, "Tobacco—Does It Have a Future," *Business Week* (July 4, 1994).
23. Dan Berger, "Modern Wine Industry Still Fears the 'Feds' But For Labeling Reasons," *Los Angeles Times*, November 24, 1989, H2.

24. Cal. Health & Safety Code § 25,249.6 (Deering 1994).

■ Pricing

Utilities

Price regulation is another form of consumer protection. Various entities, primarily at the state level, are involved in setting rates and price levels for certain commodities. For example, state public utilities commissions often regulate natural monopolies, including local telephone service and other public utilities. (See additional information on natural monopolies and antitrust regulation in chapter 18.) Like public utilities, the insurance industry is heavily regulated on the state level.

Cable Television

In response to consumer complaints, Congress in 1992 passed the Cable Television Consumer Protection Act, which allows local communities to set basic cable rates.

Another provision of the cable regulation law requires cable operators to carry programming that serves the public interest, including all local over-the-air television stations that request to be carried. This rule, known as the must-carry rule, resulted in a July 1993 vote of the Federal Communications Commission to give television stations devoted to 24-hour shopping (home shopping networks) the same right as regular broadcasters to demand that cable television systems carry their programs. In general, cable systems pay to carry particular networks. In the case of the Home Shopping Network, however, the cable operators are paid a portion of the sales generated by the network.

The question presented to the FCC was whether home shopping stations serve the public interest. Having lifted restrictions in 1984 on the amount of advertising a station can carry, the FCC felt unable to make a judgment about the value of one television format over another. One result of the decision, however, is that other cable programmers not covered by the rule, such as C-SPAN, which provides coverage of government proceedings and political events, are being dropped by small cable companies in favor of local broadcast stations and home shopping networks, both of which are subject to the must-carry rule. The situation has prompted critics of the must-carry rule to ask how a home shopping network better serves the public interest than live coverage of Congress.[25]

Drugs and Medical Services

Azidothymide (AZT) is a medicine used for treating complications of AIDS. The Burroughs Wellcome Company has been at the center of a controversy over the price charged for this drug. AZT treatment often costs as much as $6,500 per year, which is prohibitively expensive for many AIDS patients, particularly those with inadequate insurance coverage.

Various national health care reform proposals include provisions that would place legal ceilings on premiums for health benefits packages. Such packages would include coverage for hospitalization, physician visits, prescription drugs, and a range of preventative services.

■ Ethical Consideration

Should free market, competitive forces determine the price of "essential" goods such as pharmaceuticals, or should their prices be regulated? What constitutes "reasonable" profits on a product like AZT?[26]

■ Consumer Warranties

Uniform Commercial Code (UCC) Warranties

State warranty law provides an important basis for many consumer protection claims. In consumer product transactions in which the UCC applies, Article 2 provides a buyer with a remedy for a seller's breach of an express or implied warranty. UCC warranties are discussed in chapter 9.

Magnuson-Moss Warranty Act

In addition to the statutory protections provided by the UCC, the federal government has passed an act that is designed to inform consumers about the products they buy. This law, which applies only when a seller offers a written warranty, is the Magnuson-Moss Warranty Act.[27]

---

25. Edmund L. Andrews, "F.C.C. Lets TV-Shopping Stations Demand Access to Slots on Cable," *The New York Times,* July 3, 1993, A1.

26. For a complete discussion of the AZT controversy, see "Ethics, Pricing and the Pharmaceutical Industry," *Journal of Business Ethics*, August 1992, 617. See also Brian O'Reilly, "The Inside Story of the AIDS Drug," *Fortune*, November 5, 1990, 112.
27. 15 U.S.C. §§ 2301 *et seq.* (1988).

The act does not require any seller to provide a written warranty, but if a seller does offer one, the act requires certain disclosure in connection with that written warranty. In addition, the act restricts disclaimers for implied warranties and permits consumers to sue violators of the Magnuson-Moss Warranty Act and recover damages plus costs, including reasonable attorney's fees.

Disclosure under the act requires a manufacturer or seller, when offering a written warranty on goods costing more than $15, to "fully and conspicuously disclose in simple and understandable language the terms and conditions of the warranty." The FTC has issued various rules relating to this provision, including one that requires consumer notification that some states do not allow certain manufacturer exclusions or limitations.

A manufacturer or seller who offers a written warranty on goods costing more than $10 must also state whether the warranty is full or limited. The act requires that in order for a warranty to be "full" it must meet the following minimum federal standards. First, a full warranty must give the consumer the right to free repair of the product within a reasonable time or, after a reasonable number of failed attempts to fix the product, permit the customer to elect a full refund or replacement. Second, the warrantor may not impose any time limit on the warranty's duration. Lastly, the warrantor may not exclude or limit damages for breach of warranty unless such exclusions are conspicuous on the face of the warranty. Any warranty that does not meet these minimum federal standards must be designated as "limited."

Also under the act, a seller who offers a written warranty may not disclaim *implied warranties*, such as the implied warranty of merchantability. These implied warranties may be limited to the duration of the written warranty, but then the written warranty must be designated as "limited." Still, a seller may disclaim all implied warranties by not offering any written warranty or service contract at all and selling a product "as is."

FTC rules allow a seller to establish an informal dispute resolution procedure, and require consumers to use this procedure before filing a lawsuit under the act. Magnuson-Moss also requires that the warrantor be given an opportunity to remedy its noncompliance before a lawsuit is filed.

State Lemon Laws

A majority of states have laws dealing with warranties on new cars and new mobile homes. These "lemon laws" are designed to protect consumers from defective products that cannot be adequately fixed. The statutes vary considerably from state to state, but there are several common features. In general, a new car must conform to the warranty given by the manufacturer. This means that if, after a reasonable number of attempts (usually four), the manufacturer or dealer is unable to remedy a defect that substantially impairs the value of the car, the car must be replaced or the purchase price refunded. Lemon laws also typically require replacement or refund if a new car has been out of service ("in the shop") for 30 days during the statutory warranty period.

In addition to permitting the revocation of a new car sales contract, state lemon laws are designed (like the Magnuson-Moss Warranty Act) to encourage informal resolution of disputes concerning defective new cars. Lemon laws achieve this objective by requiring that a consumer use a manufacturer's arbitration program before litigating, as long as the manufacturer has established an informal dispute resolution program that complies with FTC regulations. Some states, including New York, have adopted their own standards for these dispute resolution programs.

■ Sales Practices

Many of the laws that are designed to protect consumers from unfair and deceptive trade practices involve disclosure requirements in various sales transactions and regulation of some specific forms of sales practices. Regulations related to sales practices may cover all industries or they may be industry specific, such as the FTC's rules for used cars sellers or state insurance regulations. A number of state and federal agencies currently regulate sales practices, including the FTC, the FCC, the Postal Service, and the Department of Housing and Urban Development.

State Deceptive Practices Statutes

Most state consumer protection laws are directed at deceptive trade practices. Under these laws, sellers are prohibited from providing false or misleading information to consumers. Although there is considerable variation among state laws, they often provide more stringent protections than do federal laws.

Another example involves the autographed sports memorabilia market in California. In response to significant growth and perceived exploitation, California passed legislation regulating the sale of autographed sports memorabilia priced over $50. The law seeks to prevent fraud by requiring dealers to provide a certificate of authenticity. The certificate, which must be in writing and signed by the dealer or his agent, is considered an express warranty that the item sold is authentic. Dealers who fail to comply with the provisions of the new law are subject to civil action by the purchaser for actual damages and attorney's fees, as well as a civil penalty of up to three times the item's price.[28]

State Privacy Laws

A number of states have passed laws that are intended to protect consumer privacy. In 1993, according to the Direct Marketing Association, privacy bills were introduced in 35 states. Among the bills that passed in 1993 was one in Maine that prohibited the sale or rental of lists containing the name, address, and account number of credit card holders without their express written permission. A New York law regulates use of information about videocassette rentals and sales.[29]

 Ethical Consideration

When, if ever, does an advertiser possess too much information about a consumer's preferences and buying habits? What implications might interactive television have for consumer privacy?

UCC Unconscionability Principle

Also on the state level, the UCC protects consumers from unfair sales practices through the unconscionability principle contained in UCC section 2-302. This section prohibits the enforcement of any contracts for the sale of goods that are so unfair and one-sided that they shock the conscience of the court. This provision is discussed in chapter 9.

Door-to Door-Sales

Door-to-door sales are those transactions initiated and concluded at a buyer's home. For a number of reasons, they have invited regulation at both the state and federal level. Door-to-door sales are unique in that individuals may feel more pressured to buy something from someone standing at their door, or they may make a purchase just to get rid of a persistent salesperson. As a result, the FTC has mandated a three-day "cooling-off period," during which a consumer may rescind a door-to-door purchase. Under FTC rules, the seller must also notify a buyer of the right to cancel. Some states offer longer periods during which consumers can cancel a sale.

Referral Sales and Pyramid Sales

A number of states have enacted legislation restricting referral and pyramid sales. In a referral sale, the seller offers the buyer a commission, rebate, or discount for furnishing the seller with a list of additional prospective customers. The discount, however, is usually contingent on the seller actually making later sales to those buyers referred by the original customer.

Pyramid selling involves a scheme where a consumer is recruited as a product "distributor" and receives commissions based on the products she sells and on the recruitment of additional sellers (or even receives commissions on the sales of those she recruits). The problem with both referral and pyramid sales is that unless the buyer or "distributor" becomes involved early in the chain, the supply of prospective recruits is quickly exhausted.

Industry-Specific Sales Practices

Since the early 1980s the FTC has become more involved in regulating the sales practices of specific industries. For example, the FTC in 1985 began to require used car sellers to affix a Buyer's Guide label to the cars that they sell.[30] The Buyer's Guide is intended to disclose to potential buyers information about the car's warranty and any service contract provided by the dealer. If the car is sold without a warranty, the label must state that the car is being sold "as is."

A related and well-developed area of state and federal consumer law concerns restrictions on tampering with car odometers. Congress in 1972 enacted the Motor Vehicle Information and Cost Savings Act,[31] which made it a crime to change car odometers. In its findings, Congress concluded that consumers purchasing a motor vehicle

---

28. Cal. Civ. Code § 1739.7 (Deering 1994).
29. John H. Awerdick, "Marketing Regulation Will Get Tougher," *Direct*, November 1993, 110.
30. 16 C.F.R. § 455 (1993) (Used Motor Vehicle Trade Regulation Rule).
31. 15 U.S.C. § 1901 *et seq.* (1988).

rely heavily on odometer readings as an indication of a car's safety and reliability. Federal odometer regulations issued by the National Highway Traffic Safety Administration require that mileage be disclosed in writing each time a car's title is transferred. The transferor must also certify that, to the best of his knowledge, the odometer reading reflects the actual mileage.

On the state level, industry-specific regulation covers the insurance industry. For example, Metropolitan Life Insurance Co., the nation's largest seller of life insurance, was investigated in 1994 for potentially deceptive insurance sales practices in at least 17 states. State insurance regulators claimed that Metropolitan Life Insurance Co. misrepresented itself in letters sent in 1993 to nurses, disguising the company's life insurance programs as retirement plans. Met Life's lawyers denied that the letters were misleading.[32] State insurance commissioners not only establish regulations regarding the disclosure of information to perspective policyholders, they also set maximum rates within a state.

Telemarketing

Aggressive telemarketing sales practices, particularly the use of autodialers and "900" telephone numbers, have resulted in congressional intervention. For example, in 1991 Congress passed the Telephone Consumer Protection Act (TCPA) of 1991,[33] which directed the FCC to adopt rules and regulations to curb telemarketing abuses. In general, the TCPA prohibits the use of either autodialers or simulated or prerecorded voice messages to deliver calls to emergency telephone lines, health care facilities, radio telephone services, and other services where the called party will incur some charge for the call. The only exception is if the called party has given prior consent to such calls. A second provision prohibits the use of prerecorded messages when calling residential telephone numbers, except with the prior consent of the called party or in the case of an emergency. Enforcement of this second provision, however, was enjoined by a federal court in Oregon on free speech grounds.[34]

In July 1993, the FCC and the FTC adopted final rules regulating the advertising, operation, and billing of "900" numbers. The rules were enacted pursuant to the Telephone Disclosure and Dispute Resolution Act of 1992 (TDDRA),[35] which directed the FTC and the FCC

32. *Los Angeles Times,* January 14, 1994, D3.
33. 47 U.S.C. § 227 (Supp. 1992).
34. *Moser v. Federal Communications Comm'n*, 826 F. Supp. 360 (D. Or. 1993).
35. 15 U.S.C. § 5701 (Supp. 1992).

to issue regulations governing pay-per-call services. Various provisions of the rules require: (1) that 900 calls in excess of two minutes include a preamble disclosing the name of the information provider and a brief description of the service; (2) that any advertisements include the cost of the call adjacent to and in a type size no less than one-half the size of the 900 number; and (3) that the cost per minute and any minimum charges be disclosed to consumers.

Ethical Consideration

Should caller ID be used by telemarketers to identify those individuals who call their 800 or 900 telephone numbers?

Mail Order Sales

Unscrupulous mail order sales practices have led to a high incidence of consumer complaints and resulting state and federal regulation in this area. In general, two practices that have been regulated are processing procedures for mail orders, and the receipt of unsolicited goods. Order processing procedures basically require sellers to respond to consumer orders by shipping merchandise or offering refunds within a reasonable time.

Unsolicited or unordered merchandise sent by the U.S. mail, as provided by the Postal Reorganization Act of 1970, may be kept or disposed of by the recipient without the recipient incurring any obligation to the sender. The United States Postal Service has authority to assess criminal and civil penalties for fraudulent mail schemes that injure consumers. Book and record clubs are generally legal as long as they comply with state law provisions requiring sellers to provide consumers with forms or announcement cards that the consumer may use to instruct the seller not to send the offered merchandise.

Real Estate Sales

A number of state and federal laws protect consumers in real estate transactions. In general, these laws, including the Real Estate Settlement Procedures Act and the Interstate Land Sales Full Disclosure Act, are designed to prevent fraud and require disclosure of certain relevant information. Certain disclosure requirements of the Truth in Lending Act apply to real estate credit transactions as well. In some transactions, real estate buyers have the right to cancel the purchase contract if certain information is not disclosed to them, or if other procedures are not properly followed.

The Real Estate Settlement Procedures Act and revisions made to it in 1976 are designed to assist home buyers by requiring disclosure of any requirements for settlement proceedings, which may include title insurance, taxes, and fees for attorneys, appraisers, and brokers. In general, lenders must give an estimate of settlement costs, identify service providers the applicant is required to use, and provide a statement showing the annual percentage rate for the mortgage.

In the early 1960s Congress became concerned with fraudulent practices used in the sale of subdivided land for investment purposes or for second or retirement homes. Hearings held at that time indicated that many older Americans had invested their savings in new subdivisions, particularly in Florida and the Southwest, in which the lots were unbuildable. Because the lots were often marketed through newspaper advertisements or other interstate means, sales were often finalized before the purchaser had the opportunity to see the property.

To remedy this situation, Congress in 1968 passed the Interstate Land Sales Full Disclosure Act,[36] which is administered by the Secretary of the Department of Housing and Urban Development (HUD). Under the act, the secretary created the Office of Interstate Land Sales Registration, and federal disclosure requirements were imposed on the sale of undeveloped subdivided land. The act gives the secretary of HUD the power to bring suit in federal district court to enjoin sales by developers who have not registered in accordance with the act.

The act was modeled after the Securities Act of 1933 and requires developers to file an initial statement of record with HUD's Office of Interstate Land Sales Registration for approval before the lots can be leased or sold. Only developments of 100 or more lots of unimproved land promoted through a common plan and deemed part of interstate commerce are covered under the act. As discussed in chapter 2, interstate commerce is a very broad concept, and can include almost any otherwise intrastate activity that makes use of the U.S. mail or the telephone.

The act provides both criminal and civil penalties for a land promoter's fraud, misrepresentation, or noncompliance. Purchasers affected by a promoter's wrongdoing have a private cause of action and may cancel the purchase contract.

Consumer Health and Safety

As with unfairness, deception, and fraud, many federal and state regulatory agencies protect consumers' health and safety. Among the federal agencies that work to prevent consumer injury are the Food and Drug Administration, the U.S. Department of Agriculture, the U.S. Department of Transportation's National Highway Traffic Safety Administration, the Federal Communications Commission, and various state and local departments and commissions.

The areas that these agencies regulate include alcohol, tobacco, smoking, gambling, firearms, drugs, medical devices, food, pesticides, automobiles, and broadcasting. Through government regulation consumers are shielded from products or practices that are considered detrimental to health and safety. However, consumer protection law should not be confused with product liability law, discussed in chapter 10. Product liability law provides a common-law remedy enforced by private action, whereas consumer protection law provides a statutory remedy enforced by the government (or in some cases also by private parties).

At the state level, consumer health and safety laws cover a wide variety of areas, such as the availability of alcohol, tobacco, and gambling. State and local provisions also address no-smoking regulations, restaurant inspections, and the competency of professional workers through the granting of various occupational licenses.

Regulating Health and Safety

Alcohol and Tobacco

Regulation of the "vices" alcohol and tobacco (as they relate to consumer health and safety) is achieved, since repeal of the 18th Amendment and the end of Prohibition, primarily at the state and local government levels. States no longer prohibit the use of alcohol and tobacco, but they do regulate access to both by establishing minimum ages for purchase, and enacting laws that limit the hours during which alcohol may be sold at liquor stores, bars, and clubs. In addition, an Indiana law prohibits the sale of alcohol on credit.[37] Although it appeared as of

---

36. 15 U.S.C. §§ 1701 (1988 & Supp. 1992).

37. *Ind. Code Ann.* § 7.1-5-10-12 (Burns 1994).

late-1994 politically unlikely that the FDA would be permitted to assume jurisdiction over cigarettes on the basis that nicotine is a drug, the FDA in early 1994 suggested that it might try to regulate nicotine content in cigarettes unless Congress provided clear guidance otherwise.

Smoking

The regulation of smoking and the recent proliferation of nonsmoking laws, especially in California, has been mostly at the local government level, primarily because of the significant influence of the tobacco industry at the state and federal levels. The passage of many tough local ordinances, banning all smoking in restaurants and offices, was also helped by a 1993 Environmental Protection Agency report that found that second-hand cigarette smoke causes cancer.

Philip Morris, maker of Marlboro cigarettes, sued the City of San Francisco to overturn that city's anti-smoking ordinance. Philip Morris claimed that state workplace safety rules are responsible for regulating the safety of workers, and therefore preempt enforcement of the local smoking regulation. In a 1992 case based on a similar claim, a California judge overturned a San Francisco ordinance regulating the use of video display terminals (VDTs) in private business.[38]

Gambling

Gambling is also a consumer protection issue. Where gambling was once limited to Nevada, it has seen enormous growth in other states, on waterways, and on Native American reservations or reservation-owned property. Highly promoted lotteries in 33 states and the District of Columbia fund public projects from education to environmental preservation. With this expansion, however, has come increased concern that consumers might be deceived by lottery advertisements or become compulsive gamblers, spending beyond their means.

Firearms

The United States Postal Service in 1994 hosted a conference titled "United States Postal Service Symposium on a Growing American Phenomenon: Workplace Violence." Thirty-four postal employees have been murdered by co-workers in the past decade and an additional 26 have been wounded. Advocates of gun control measures have

cited rising workplace violence as one reason for a need to restrict access to firearms. Gun control laws vary from state to state, but a minimum five-working-day national waiting period to purchase a handgun (the so-called Brady bill, named after President Reagan's press secretary, who was shot in an assassination attempt on the president) went into effect in 1993. In 1994, major crime legislation included a ban on the manufacture, future sale, and possession of 19 brands of combat-style assault weapons and their look-alikes.

Ethical Consideration

What can managers do to decrease workplace violence? Would gun control laws help prevent the type of violence that has plagued the U.S. Postal Service over the past decade?

■ Drugs, Medical Devices, and Cosmetics

The Food and Drug Administration (FDA) plays a broad role in consumer protection law. In addition to its involvement in food, drug, medical device, and cosmetic labeling (*misbranding*), the FDA regulates the new drug approval process.

FDA Standards for Drug Approval

The FDA has authority to require that certain drugs be available only by prescription. Thus, if a drug authorized only for prescription use is sold *over-the-counter*, it is misbranded and the FDA will halt its sale. In general, the FDA will require prescription use only when a drug is, for example, toxic, requires a physician's supervision for safe use, or is addictive.

The first step in the approval process for new drugs is their classification by the Drug Enforcement Agency (DEA) into one of five schedules based on potential for abuse and currently accepted medical use. Only Schedule I drugs, those with the highest potential for abuse and no currently accepted medical use, cannot be approved by the FDA.

The drug approval process for non-Schedule I drugs begins with preclinical research (which includes animal

---

38. Eben Shapiro, "Philip Morris Sues City Over No-Smoking Rules," *The Wall Street Journal*, February 2, 1994, B1.

Historical Perspective
Food and Drug Regulation

■ Novel's Ideas Spark Food Law, 1906

Upton Sinclair's novel *The Jungle*, describing filthy conditions in the Chicago meat-packing industry, caused a furor in 1906 and stirred passage of the Pure Food and Drugs Act.[39]

Some business interests opposed the measure, charging it was "socialist interference." The novel's factual base was a 1904 study, financed by the Socialist Party. But some less political groups, including the American Medical Association, had been seeking food industry reform since the turn of the century.

A candy maker who used shredded bone in his coconut bars told government investigators, according to *The Oxford History of the American People* by Samuel Eliot Morison, "It don't hurt the kids; they like it!"

The new law, administered by the Bureau of Chemistry in the Agriculture Department, prohibited adulterated and misbranded food and drugs in interstate and foreign commerce. But penalties weren't clear cut, and courts tended to be lenient with offenders.

The Food and Drug Administration later was established to administer the law, and a number of tougher measures were proposed in 1933. With only lukewarm support from President Franklin D. Roosevelt, however, they failed in Congress.

Then, when 100 people [mostly children] died after taking a new wonder drug [the "elixir of sulfanilamide"], the Food, Drug and Cosmetic Act of 1938 was passed. It was a stronger law and gave the FDA injunctive power, put cosmetics under regulation for the first time and gave the agency authority to set food standards.

■ Thalidomide Tragedy Spurs New Laws, 1962

[T]he thalidomide tragedy of the 1960s, though Americans were spared its worst effects, produced the still-stronger drug-testing laws of 1962.[40]

Thalidomide, developed in Germany, had been hailed as the greatest sleeping pill in history. After it became a bestseller in Germany, Britain and Canada, the century-old William Merrell Co. asked the U.S. Food and Drug Administration in September 1960 for approval to sell it in the U.S. The application, backed by four telephone-book-sized volumes of data, was assigned to Frances Kelsey, a Canadian-born physician and pharmacologist who had just joined the FDA.

Dr. Kelsey thought thalidomide looked "peculiar." For one thing, the sleeping pill didn't make test animals sleepy. Despite constant—and angry—pressure from Merrell, she blocked approval, asking Merrell for more and more data.

Meanwhile, German and other European doctors were puzzling over an epidemic of phocomelia, children born with flipper-like appendages instead of proper arms and legs. In November 1961, Widiking Lenz, a Hamburg pediatrician, discovered the link: Mothers of the deformed babies had been using thalidomide. The drug was withdrawn that month and Merrell dropped its application for FDA approval.

When the thalidomide story hit the U.S., it caused shudders that had seismic effects in Congress. Sen. Estes Kefauver, whose tough drug-regulating bill had been gutted on Capital Hill, now saw it revived, strengthened and sped on its way to President Kennedy's desk. He signed it into law in October 1962, two months after he had awarded Dr. Kelsey the Distinguished Federal Civilian Service Award.

---

39. *The Wall Street Journal*, February 14, 1989. Reprinted by permission of *The Wall Street Journal*, © 1989 Dow Jones & Company, Inc. All Rights Reserved Worldwide.

40. *The Wall Street Journal*, September 6, 1989. Reprinted by permission of *The Wall Street Journal*, © 1989 Dow Jones & Company, Inc. All Rights Reserved Worldwide.

testing) aimed at discovery and identification of drugs that are sufficiently promising to study in humans. The drugmaker then submits this preclinical research, along with a document called "Claimed Exemption for Investigational New Drug," to the FDA. The FDA can then permit or deny continued research. If approved for investigational purposes, a drug will be tested in humans in three separate phases, with FDA review at the end of each phase. This framework is designed to protect the safety of the human subjects used in the study, to develop necessary data on the drug, and to ensure that all studies are done properly. Once all of the testing data are assembled, they are submitted to the FDA, which may approve or deny. Approval is based on a drug safety and effectiveness, may require marketing restrictions, and can be contested by anyone. The FDA must also approve the description of a drug (e.g., labels and package inserts).

Drugs with a high potential for therapeutic gain and no satisfactory alternative may be given priority (expedited) review by the FDA. In addition, such drugs may be available during the investigational stage, to people not within the clinical test group, through "open protocols." For example, people with AIDS may have access to new drugs under investigation if preliminary evidence of effectiveness exists.

Ethical Consideration

Invitro International in 1993 secured U.S. approval for its product Corrositex, the first legal substitute for live rabbits in testing the corrosiveness of chemicals. Invitro's customers are mainly cosmetics and household products companies, such as Helene Curtis and S.C. Johnson, that have stopped using tests on live rabbits.[41] Animal rights activists have praised the company. What ethical concerns are present in product testing? Does the type of product being tested (e.g., food, drugs, or cosmetics) affect these ethical concerns?

41. Nina Munk, "Bunny Money," *Forbes*, December 20, 1993, 212.

■ Food Safety

Product Definition: Food or Drug?

Drugs, as defined by the act, include articles intended for use in the diagnosis, cure, mitigation, treatment, or prevention of disease. Thus many things that are, in fact, food may fit this definition. For example, orange juice may be said to be used to prevent disease. Under the act, "food" is defined as: (1) articles used for food or drink, (2) chewing gum, and (3) articles used for components of either. Because the distinction between drugs and food is important in the application of both the mislabeling and adulteration provisions of the act, as well as the drug approval process, the FDA must categorize each product. In general, the FDA looks to intent to use a product as a drug in determining how to categorize it. Intent may be apparent from the manufacturer's intent or reasons for consumers' use, or derived from labels, promotional material, or advertisement. An example of this analysis is demonstrated by the following case.

■ A Case in Point: Summary

Case 19.5
UNITED STATES v. GENERAL NUTRITION, INC.
United States District Court for the Western District of New York
638 F. Supp. 556 (W.D.N.Y. 1986).

FACTS   General Nutrition, Inc. (GNI) and five individual defendants, including Fenicchia and Copia, were charged in a seven-count indictment with criminal violations of the Food, Drug and Cosmetic Act in connection with the marketing of a substance known as "Gammaprim." Defendant Fenicchia was a manager and store clerk at a GNI retail outlet. Defendant Copia was a store clerk and assistant manager at another GNI outlet. They were charged in connection with undercover purchases of Gammaprim at their respective outlets at which time, it was alleged, they made oral statements concerning the substance, and otherwise connected it to the promotional literature, which constituted a basis for the allegations of misbranding. It was alleged that they caused Gammaprim to be misbranded within the meaning of the act because they played a role in its dispensation without a prescription.

The heart of the matter was the legal distinction between "food" and "drug" on the one hand, and between "over-the-counter" and "prescription" drugs on the other, within the meaning of the act. GNI was a corporation engaged in the production, distribution and sale of nutritional, personal care and related products. The other defendants were officers and employees of GNI. GNI marketed Gammaprim, a substance derived in part from oil of evening primrose.

The indictment charged that Gammaprim was touted as effective in the prevention, mitigation and treatment of certain medical conditions such as hypertension, arthritis, and multiple sclerosis. The indictment alleged that Gammaprim was a drug within the meaning of the act and was therefore misbranded. This misbranding took three different forms, according to the indictment.

First, Gammaprim was misbranded because its label lacked adequate directions for use. Second, it was misbranded because Gammaprim is a drug that "because of its toxicity . . . is not safe, for use except under the supervision of a [doctor] . . ." and must be dispensed by prescription. Third, the defendants violated a provision that drugs coming within the act are misbranded unless they bear the statement "Caution: Federal law prohibits dispensing without a prescription."

ISSUE PRESENTED When does a food become a drug for purposes of the Food, Drug and Cosmetic Act?

SUMMARY OF OPINION The defendants' main arguments in favor of dismissing the indictment were that Gammaprim was improperly classified as a prescription drug. The defendants argued instead that it was a food, or at most an over-the-counter drug, and that the government's failure to adhere to a uniform definition of prohibited conduct under the act implicated the defendants' due process rights. The defendants also claimed the prosecution infringed their First Amendment rights to express opinions regarding Gammaprim's alleged nutritional value. The Federal District Court disagreed.

The Gammaprim label included a listing of contents and the directions "As a food supplement, take up to six capsules per day." The indictment charged that Gammaprim was promoted in the media and elsewhere for its supposed beneficial health effects. For example, it was alleged that Gammaprim was sold in conjunction with certain self-help literature purporting to provide a medical and scientific context to the uses of the substance. Brochures that were part of its integrated distribution program were found, by the court, to constitute drug labeling. Thus Gammaprim was a drug within the meaning of the act.

Moreover, the government asserted that Gammaprim was a prescription drug under the act because collateral measures were necessary to its use. According to the government, collateral measures necessary to the safe use of Gammaprim in the management of hypertension meant all those things that a layperson, because of her lack of education, training, and experience, could not do to safely manage the disease.

The defendants argued that this definition of collateral measures improperly focused on disease rather than the nature of the alleged drug itself. The government, they added, had not pointed out any harmful characteristic of Gammaprim per se. Any number of over-the-counter drugs were labeled

*Case **19.5** continued on following page*

*Case **19.5** continued*

and marketed for diseases commonly considered to require physician diagnosis and management. The defendants asserted that the government's approach to collateral measures was so expansive that it would encompass commonly used substances, both food and drug, that might arguably require physician supervision in relation to certain diseases.

RESULT   The court held that the act provided the defendants with adequate notice of the criminality of the offenses charged. Accordingly, it denied the defendants' motions to dismiss.

COMMENTS   Defendants Fenicchia and Copia's motions to dismiss focused on their relatively low position in the corporate hierarchy (store clerks), the supposed non-commission by them of any criminal acts, or the unreasonableness of expecting anyone in their positions to understand the criminality of such acts. Their respective positions did not excuse their alleged conduct. The act provides that "[a]ny person" who violates the misbranding provisions shall be liable. According to the court, it was unnecessary to go beyond the plain language of the statute: "Any," it said, meant any.

FDA Standards for Food Condemnation

The FDA also protects consumer health and safety through the confiscation of contaminated or adulterated foods. The standards for condemnation are different depending on whether the product is a natural food or contains additives. An *additive* is anything not inherent in the food product, including pesticide residue, unintended environmental contaminants, and unavoidably added substances from packaging. If an additive (in the quantity present in the food product) is injurious to any group in the general population, then the product will be deemed adulterated.

Natural foods are adulterated if they "consist in whole or in part of any filthy, putrid or decomposed substance, or if it is otherwise unfit for food." All foods contain some level of unavoidable natural defects, so the FDA sets minimum tolerance standards for defects that will be tolerated. Articles that exceed those minimum levels are deemed adulterated and seized by the FDA. In some cases a seized product may be rehabilitated by a manufacturer and released by the FDA for sale.

The United States Department of Agriculture also plays a major role in food safety. The Department's primary consumer protection activities all involve food, and include inspecting facilities engaged in the slaughtering or processing of meat, poultry, and egg products; preventing the sale of mislabeled meat or poultry products; and offering producers a voluntary grading program for various agricultural products.

At the Top

A chief executive officer of a food company may be held vicariously and strictly liable for introducing adulterated articles into interstate commerce.[42]

Genetically Engineered Food

Calgene, Inc., a California-based biotech company, has genetically engineered a tomato, which it calls the Flavr Savr, with an "antisense" gene. With antisense technology, genetic engineers use the plant's own genetic design to overcome unwanted traits. In the case of the tomato, a copy of the gene responsible for rotting is cloned and reinserted in reverse order. The two opposites bind to one another, effectively blocking the rot-producing function. As a result, the Flavr Savr is expected to last longer and taste better than conventional tomatoes.

The technology is thought to be less controversial than other genetic engineering techniques, such as introducing genes from one species into another, but the FDA was

---

42. *United States v. Park,* 421 U.S. 658, 95 S.Ct. 1903 (1975).

slow to clear the tomato for consumer sale. Calgene reported a $25 million loss for 1993, and expected the loss for 1994 to be greater, in large part because of the FDA's slow response.[43] Calgene began marketing its genetically engineered Flavr Savr tomato in mid-1994.

Early testing of genetically engineered products in the mid-1980s met with considerable public suspicion. For example, a product called ice-minus, intended to increase strawberries' tolerance to frost, was sprayed on strawberry plants by scientists dressed in space-suit-like protective clothing. Advanced Genetic Sciences, the manufacturer of ice-minus, ultimately received government approval to spray the genetically engineered product on strawberry fields, but fearful public reaction to the televised product tests eventually led to the product's (and later the company's) demise.

Consumers' growing concerns about the environment may, however, lead to greater acceptance of genetically engineered products. For example, genetically engineered pest-resistant plants may reduce the need for chemical pesticides, thereby helping to protect the environment.

■ Pesticides

Under the Food, Drug and Cosmetic Act, the FDA shares with the Environmental Protection Agency (EPA) the responsibility for regulating pesticide residues on food. The EPA registers pesticides and establishes tolerances under the act. The FDA enforces the tolerance levels and deems a food to be adulterated if it does not conform to the pesticide tolerance levels set under the act.

■ Automobiles

Automobile safety has seen enormous gains since Ralph Nader first brought the issue to the nation's attention in the 1960s.[44] Air bags (for the driver and front passenger) and anti-lock brakes have become popular safety features, and are standard equipment on many new cars. Before consumers began to request air bags, many car manufacturers met the legal requirement for passive restraints through the use of automatic seat belts.

In response to consumer-group pressure, the National Highway Traffic Safety Administration (NHTSA) may require automakers to list safety data on new-car window stickers, along with fuel economy data and national origin of parts. Surveys have shown that many consumers want the government to provide more information about crashworthiness by adding data on side impact, offset frontal, and rollover crashes to frontal collision data currently being gathered. For more than 15 years, the New Car Assessment Program has assessed frontal collision safety by crashing cars at 35 MPH, which is one-third more destructive than the 30 MPH crashes vehicles must pass to meet federal safety standards.

The NHTSA, created in 1970, is an agency of the U.S. Department of Transportation. By law, the NHTSA has the power to establish motor vehicle safety standards,[45] establish a National Motor Vehicle Safety Advisory Council, engage in testing and development of motor vehicle safety, prohibit manufacture or importation of substandard vehicles, and develop tire safety.[46] In addition, the NHTSA is charged with developing national standards for driver safety performance, accident reporting, and vehicle registration and inspection. States refusing to comply with established federal standards are denied federal highway funds.[47]

■ Broadcasting

The U.S. attorney general and the chairman of the FCC warned broadcasters in 1994 to voluntarily reduce television violence, or risk having the government step in to regulate it for them. Apart from the issue of whether TV violence merely reflects or actually creates violence in society, this warning to broadcasters brings to light the issue, present in many areas of consumer safety law, of industry self-regulation versus government regulation.

Regulation of broadcasting by the FCC seeks to ensure that broadcast media are competitive and operate for the public's benefit and use. Enforcement of FCC policies is achieved primarily through its ability to withhold license renewals. Licenses cannot be transferred or

---

43. "Business Briefs," *The Wall Street Journal*, February 4, 1994, B2.

44. Ralph Nader, *Unsafe at Any Speed* (1965) (criticizing in particular General Motors Corporation's Corvair model). For a critique of Ralph Nader's consumer activist activities, see Dan Burt, *Abuse of Trust* (1982).

45. Boats are subject to safety regulation under the Federal Boat Safety Act of 1971 (46 U.S.C. §§ 4301 *et seq.* (1988 & Supp. 1992)) and aircraft safety is regulated by the Federal Aviation Act of 1958 (49 U.S.C. §§ 1421 *et seq.* (1988 & Supp. 1992)).

46. Motor Vehicle Safety Act of 1966, 15 U.S.C. §§ 1381 *et seq.* (1988 & Supp. 1992).

47. Highway Safety Act of 1966, 23 U.S.C. §§ 401 *et seq.* (1988 & Supp. 1992).

Ethical Consideration

Adding new safety requirements for automobiles can increase product cost and shut some consumers out of the market. Should individual consumers be allowed to choose whether they are willing to pay for safety features in automobiles?

---

assigned without permission of the FCC and a finding that such a transfer will serve the public interest. The FCC may also affect consumer health and safety through regulating the content of broadcast programming, which may have First Amendment implications.

First Amendment Concerns

George Carlin recorded a 12-minute monologue entitled "Filthy Words" before a live audience in a theater. He began by referring to his thoughts about "the seven words you can't say on the public airwaves." He then proceeded to list those words and repeat them over and over in a variety of colloquial phrases. A radio station broadcast a recording of the "Filthy Words" monologue on a weekday afternoon as part of a program about contemporary society's attitude toward language. The station advised listeners before the broadcast that the piece included language that might be offensive to some listeners.

A few weeks after the broadcast, a man who stated that he heard the broadcast while driving with his young son wrote a letter of complaint to the FCC. In response to the letter, the FCC issued an order condemning the

Ethical Consideration

Does television violence create a violent society? Can content-based regulation of broadcasting protect consumer health and safety? What additional precautions (such as time, place, and manner restrictions), if any, should be taken to protect children?

broadcast as indecent, and threatened to revoke the station's broadcast license if additional complaints were received.

In upholding the FCC's order, the U.S. Supreme Court concluded that of all forms of communication, broadcasting has the most limited First Amendment protection. Among the reasons for the special treatment of indecent broadcasting was, according to the Court, the uniquely pervasive presence that the medium of expression occupies in people's lives. Broadcasts, the Court said, extend into the privacy of the home, and it is impossible to avoid completely those that are patently offensive. Broadcasting, moreover, is uniquely accessible to children.[48]

■ Other Consumer Products: The Consumer Product Safety Commission

Congress created the Consumer Product Safety Commission (CPSC), an independent regulatory agency, in 1972. Among the purposes of the CPSC are protection of the public against unreasonable risks of injury associated with consumer products and assistance to consumers in evaluating the comparative safety of such products. Under the Consumer Product Safety Act[49] (which created the CPSC), the CPSC is authorized to set consumer product safety standards, such as performance or product labeling specifications.

The statute provides a detailed scheme governing the adoption of such a standard. Any interested person may petition the CPSC to adopt a standard, and may resort to judicial remedies if the CPSC denies the petition. The CPSC itself can begin a proceeding to develop such a standard by publishing in the *Federal Register* a notice inviting any person to submit an offer to do the development. Within a specified time limit, the CPSC can then accept such an offer, evaluate the suggestions submitted, and publish a proposed rule. The actual issuance of the final standard is subject to notice and comment by interested persons.

The penalty provisions of the act make it unlawful to manufacture for sale, offer for sale, distribute in commerce, or import into the United States a consumer product that does not conform to an applicable standard. Violators are subject to civil penalties, criminal penalties, injunctive enforcement and seizure, private suits for dam-

---

48. *Federal Communications Commission v. Pacifica Foundation*, 438 U.S. 726, 98 S.Ct. 3026 (1978).
49. 15 U.S.C. §§ 2051 *et seq.* (1988 & Supp. 1992).

ages, and private suits for injunctive relief. This means that if a product cannot be made free of unreasonable risk of personal injury, the CPSC may ban its manufacture, sale, or importation altogether. The supplier of any already distributed products that pose a substantial risk of injury may be compelled by the CPSC to repair, modify, or replace the product, or refund the purchase price.

Before implementing a mandatory safety standard, the CPSC must find that voluntary standards are inadequate. One obvious concern for the commission is that a producer motivated by profits may not be willing or able to self-regulate. Any standards that the CPSC issues must also be reasonably necessary to eliminate an unreasonable risk of injury that the regulated product presents. To determine whether a standard is reasonably necessary, the commission weighs the standard's effectiveness in preventing injury against its effect on the cost of the product.

The CPSC administers several consumer protection acts, including the Flammable Fabrics Act, Federal Hazardous Substances Act,[50] Poison Prevention Packaging Act (child-resistant bottle caps), and the Refrigerator Safety Act. The CPSC currently has no jurisdiction over tobacco products, firearms, pesticides, motor vehicles, food, drugs, medical devices, or cosmet-

ics.[51] These matters are regulated by other entities, such as the FDA, or are unregulated.

In addition to its other duties, the CPSC maintains an Injury Information Clearinghouse to collect and analyze information relating to the causes and prevention of death, injury, and illness associated with consumer products.

Ethical Consideration

Exporting unsafe products to foreign markets raises serious ethical concerns. Should U.S. managers approve the sale of products determined to be hazardous by the CPSC to countries where government regulations are less stringent? Consider the related example of breast implants (regulated by the FDA, not the CPSC). As recently as 1992, three of the four silicone-filled breast implant manufacturers were continuing to export the devices, which were subject to a sales moratorium in the U.S. earlier that year.[52] Also, U.S. tobacco companies have stepped up aggressive marketing of their products abroad as domestic consumption has fallen.

International Consideration

Under Section 2067 of the Consumer Product Safety Act, goods produced in the United States that are manufactured for export only are exempt from compliance with U.S. product safety standards. Goods declared "banned hazardous substances" by the CPSC are also exempt from regulation as long as they are intended for export. Exporters of such goods must, however, file a notifying statement with the CPSC thirty days before shipping the product so that the CPSC can notify the government of the foreign country of the shipment as well as the basis for the applicable U.S. safety standard.

■ State Occupational Licensing

State departments of consumer affairs protect the public by examining and licensing firms and individuals who possess the necessary education and demonstrated skills to perform their services competently. Among the occupations generally regulated are accountants, architects, barbers, contractors, cosmetologists, dentists, dry cleaners, marriage counselors, nurses, pharmacists, physical therapists, physicians, and social workers.[53] State departments of consumer affairs also investigate and resolve consumer complaints, and hold public hearings involving consumer matters.

---

50. A composite of three significant acts: the Hazardous Substances Labeling Act, the Child Protection Act, and the Child Protection and Toy Safety Act.

51. 15 U.S.C. § 2052 (1988).

52. Robert L. Rose, "Breast Implants Still Being Sold Outside U.S.," *The Wall Street Journal*, March 4, 1992, B1.

53. As noted in chapter 8, any person required to be licensed, who is in fact not licensed, cannot enforce a promise to pay relating to unlicensed work.

The Responsible Manager

Complying with Consumer Protection Laws

Managers have a responsibility to make sure that current and potential customers are treated fairly and in a manner that will not subject them to injury, economic or physical. In that regard, managers must take steps to ensure that their company is aware of and in compliance with various federal and state consumer protection regulations.

A manager should maintain open lines of communication with her employees. Employees should be aware of the steps necessary to comply with consumer protection laws. Because both managers and employees can be held legally accountable for their actions (and criminally liable in some cases), specific procedures should be in place to educate others in the company on important consumer law topics.

Managers whose companies extend credit to customers need to be aware that many discriminatory practices in the extension of credit are illegal. In particular, the Equal Credit Opportunity Act covers the following protected categories: race, color, religion, national origin, sex or marital status, age (except that older applicants may be given favorable treatment), and applicants whose income derives from public assistance. Some states also prohibit discrimination in credit based on sexual orientation.

In a competitive marketplace, managers often need to be aggressive in their advertising of products or services. Nonetheless, managers must refrain from making claims that may be deceptive or false. The FTC aggressively pursues companies that make false advertising claims. FTC remedies can include civil damages and corrective advertising campaigns, which can cost companies millions of dollars.

Managers in a manufacturing setting must recognize that product recalls may be necessary to correct a defective product. These recalls may be voluntary, or the government may, under consumer protection laws, order a company to remedy a potentially hazardous situation. Companies have an ethical obligation to issue a warning about a product defect it discovers after its product is sold.

Managers should consider establishing an internal product safety committee to conduct regular product safety inspections. So that the committee can have access to necessary information, production-line employees and others should be empowered to make suggestions on how to improve product safety and thereby protect consumers. Critical also is some form of whistleblower protection for an employee who brings possible consumer protection law violations to the attention of a manager. Concealment or inaction on the part of a manager may subject him to criminal prosecution and a possible jail sentence.

Managers should not be satisfied merely to meet minimum government standards with regard to consumer protection laws. Mere compliance may not be sufficient to release a manager or his company from liability when he has superior product information and should have taken additional precautions.

Managers should embrace the opportunity to self-regulate or, at least, work closely with a regulatory agency to establish industry standards that meet the concerns of both the agency and the company. A good example of a self-regulating industry is the infomercial industry. Faced with possible government regulation, the industry established its own watchdog agency. In doing so it was able to avert government involvement and the possibility of more restrictive regulation.

Inside Story

Regulation of the Information Superhighway

Yield Signs on the Info Interstate—As Regulations Take Shape, It Seems Everyone Must Give a Bit.[54]

Ask Vice-President Al Gore what happens to the U.S. if it doesn't reform its antique telecommunications laws, and he tells a story about the Titanic. More concerned with profit than safety, the ship switched off its wireless after sending the last messages for its passengers. So it didn't receive iceberg warnings that could have prevented the disaster. That led to tough new laws. Now, says Gore, government needs to step in to "not only save lives but utterly change and enrich them."

Gore—and just about everybody else in Washington and in the communications business—views U.S. telecom regulations as dangerously out of date. Cable and telephone companies are forming alliances and invading each other's turf. Long-distance carriers are trying to grab pieces of the local-phone monopolies. It's all part of a frenzied leap toward a nationwide Information Superhighway, a powerful electronic network capable of delivering vast amounts of data and entertainment to businesses and couch potatoes alike, as well as potentially life-saving remote medical diagnosis.

"The telecommunications world as we understood it is gone—shattered," says Jerry Berman, director of the Electronic Frontier Foundation, a Washington advocacy group. James G. Cullen, president of Bell Atlantic Corp., predicts "five years from now, we will not be able to remember which companies were telephone companies and which were cable companies, and, we hope, which were long-distance or wireless."

[Ed.—In February 1994, the proposed merger of Bell Atlantic Corp. and Tele-Communications, Inc. collapsed. The two companies blamed the collapse, at least in part, on the FCC's imposition of a 7% reduction in cable subscriber rates.]

---

54. John Carey and Mark Lewyn, "Yield Signs on the Info Interstate—As Regulations Take Shape, It Seems Everyone Must Give a Bit," *Business Week*, January 24, 1994, 88. Reprinted from January 24, 1994, issue of *Business Week* by special permission, copyright © 1994 by McGraw-Hill, Inc.

So there's broad-based support for a major rewrite of the nation's 60-year-old communications laws. Both Congress and the Administration are hard at work. Pending bills aim to break down outmoded barriers that separate local service from long-distance, telephones from cable TV, and programming owners from delivery systems. And on Jan. 11, [1994] Gore pledged in a speech to the Academy of Television Arts & Sciences in Los Angeles that the Administration would rapidly push through its own sweeping legislation. "This will be the biggest year in telecommunications in decades," says U.S. Representative Rick Boucher (D-Va.), a key player in the rewrite.

Thorny Issues

It could also turn out to be the most contentious—although you would never guess from appearances. Publicly, business interests that had fought bitterly over telecom regulations for decades have lined up together. "Traditional bones of contention aren't being chewed on anymore," says Federal Communications Commission Chairman Reed E. Hundt. To smooth the path to the digital future, local and long-distance carriers and cable companies all agree to support the general principles spelled out in the forthcoming legislation: that the Information Superhighway should continue to be built by private industry with a minimum of government intervention; that existing regulatory restrictions on phone companies be lifted; and that new regulatory policies ensure open access to the data highway—making sure that the new digital networks don't bypass poor and rural America.

But once you get past the generalities and ponder the particulars, you see how thorny the issues remain. In the end, everybody will have to give a little. The local phone companies, for example, agreed to open their networks in exchange for the right to sell now-prohibited services such as entertainment. Cable operators will open theirs in return for the chance to compete in the phone business. And both groups grudgingly agree with public-interest organizations that everyone must have

Inside Story continued on following page

Inside Story, continued

access to the digital cornucopia. Education is another hot issue. On the eve of Gore's speech, Bell Atlantic and Tele-Communications Inc. (TCI) announced that they will pay to wire 26,000 schools.

The bills now before Congress would allow local phone companies to manufacture equipment, provide long-distance services, offer TV programming, and compete with each other. Cable companies would be allowed to offer local and long-distance phone service. The key remaining restriction: barring local phone companies from buying cable operators within their regions, "to ensure that no single giant entity controls access to homes and offices," says Gore.

Even at the Jan. 11 Los Angeles confab, a veritable love-in attended by luminaries including Barry Diller and Michael R. Milken (now an investor in interactive education), the tensions were not far from the surface. Indeed, even comedian Lily Tomlin's onstage appearance with Gore had an edge. Got up as Ernestine the operator, she asked if the new networks will be for everyone or just the "elite." Cable executives were openly leery of even the restrained government role Gore outlined. Said Time Warner Inc. Chairman Gerald A. Levin: "What I worry about is the unintended consequences of this type of legislation." Adds John C. Malone, chairman of TCI: "The government should be mainly a cheerleader."

However, Washington's role will certainly go beyond waving pom-poms. It will have to. Take the concept of open access. Basically, it means that each company's network must be open and accessible in order to create true competition. Anyone who wants to provide a service, such as customized stock listings, over anyone else's highway "should be able to do it just by paying a fair and equitable price to the network provider," says Gore. In addition, Washington wants networks to be linked in such a way that information can flow seamlessly from one to another, creating a true national highway rather than a jumble of private roads. That means mutually compatible equipment and software at the interchanges.

Predators?

The Administration's stance is to leave the details for the FCC and local regulators to work out later. That has some players wary. Cable companies have built their industry on proprietary technology and have no history of either allowing third-party equipment to hook up to their systems or carrying everybody's programming. In a Jan. 6 speech, American Telephone & Telegraph Co. Executive Vice-President Robert M. Kavner likened cable companies to voracious beasts, eager to take advantage of those who offer services on their network. Kavner fears that the cable companies won't open their networks to new AT&T hardware or services.

Another issue that may require more than broad brush strokes from Washington is guaranteeing universal service to prevent creating a class of information have-nots among both the inner-city poor and rural residents. "We have to make sure we don't Balkanize the country," says House telecommunications and finance subcommittee Chairman Edward J. Markey (D-Mass.), co-sponsor of one of the bills in the House.

Everyone favors universal access. But exactly what is it in the multimedia age, and who pays for it? These questions were easy in the good old days. Regulators required long-distance and business customers to subsidize money-losing service to rural and poor customers. But rate subsidies won't work if local calling is opened to competition. New players would skim off the profitable customers. "The objective would be to ensure that companies are not allowed to cherry-pick the system and then leave the telcos with the carcass," says Markey.

Library Dues

Congress and the Administration plan to avoid leaving road-kill on the Information Superhighway through a new scheme of subsidies and a new definition of basic service. The proposed legislation requires that every home and business get a digital line. That way, explains Boucher, "all services will be available in the homes that want them"—or more precisely, to those who can afford to pay for them. But what about socially beneficial services, such as electronic access to libraries, that many people won't be able to afford? The legislation would require each service provider to pay a portion of its revenues into a pool, administered by an FCC-headed federal-state board. The money would subsidize those who can't afford to pay the full cost of whatever is defined as an essential service.

The concept has widespread support from industry. "The private sector is willing to work with the govern-

Inside Story, continued

ment on this," says Suzanne Tichenor, vice-president of the industry-backed Council on Competitiveness. "We recognize we have a social responsibility." But nobody has yet addressed a more fundamental question: Who will pay the cost—perhaps $1,500 per home—to extend the high-speed network to such customers? And what, precisely, will comprise basic service in 2000? "What should be included?" asks Columbia University telecommunications expert Eli M. Noam. "Cellular phones for the poor? Nobody would go for that."

Some industry executives are already concerned about the subsidies. "The government can go too far in insisting on too large a tax to fund access for everyone," says Edward R. McCracken, CEO of Silicon Graphics Inc. Asks AT&T CEO Robert E. Allen: "Why should AT&T long-distance customers be paying for some support for people who otherwise couldn't afford local service?" Allen raises another concern: "Who's going to play God as to who's going to be entitled to universal service and at what price?"

When it comes to crucial particulars like these, the Clinton Administration "has not delivered yet," says Noam. "I'm waiting for them to move beyond generalities." The FCC's Hundt, for instance, declines to specify exactly when and how local phone companies will be allowed to go into long distance. In part, this vagueness is intentional. "Any legislation must have the flexibility to deal with changing technology and market structure," explains a key White House telecom official. Another concern: Writing overly specific rules could touch off a treasure hunt for loopholes. That happened with the 1993 cable reregulation bill. Cable companies obeyed the letter of the law, but flouted its spirit, which was to hold down price increases.

The lack of specifics in the new regulations has both advocacy groups and companies agitating behind the scenes. Consumer groups fear that equating universal access with a digital line into every home misses the point. Nearly every existing phone wire can carry digital signals; what counts is whether the line can support true interactive video, and what services it brings in. Unless everyone gets high-capacity links, frets the EFF's Berman, "we could end up with islands of digital nirvana instead of a national highway."

Worse, these islands might be connected only by one-way bridges. "It's hard to have a true information market when you have a big highway to homes and offices and little roads coming back," says Michael L. Dertouzos, director of Massachusetts Institute of Technology's Laboratory for Computer Science. Such limited-capacity return lines could prevent individuals or small companies from marketing services on the networks. Unless that changes, only the big programmers will get access.

Companies have another set of worries. Timing, for one. H. Laird Walker, US West Inc.'s vice-president for federal relations, wants barriers to come down "yesterday," he says, so that US West can start competing with cable and long-distance operators. Those companies want to wait. John R. Alchin, senior vice-president of cable operator Comcast Corp., argues that phone companies should be kept out of cable in their local area until cable companies win a substantial share of the phone market. AT&T's Allen argues for delaying the Baby Bells' entry into long distance until there's true local competition.

At this point, the Clintonites are being careful to accommodate all views. On Jan. 6, for instance, Commerce Secretary Ronald H. Brown announced the formation of a 27-member advisory council made up of such industry and media bigwigs as MCI Communications Corp. Chairman Bert C. Roberts Jr. and Robert L. Johnson, head of Black Entertainment Television Holdings Inc.

They'll have to work fast, though. Because of the flurry of activity in the industry, including pending megamergers, "it's now or never for legislation," says the EFF's Berman. The House has put the issue on the fast track, with enactment targeted by midyear, before health-care reform dominates the congressional agenda. "I think the bills will be on the President's desk by summer," says Boucher.

A swift overhaul of the 1934 Communications Act would be a momentous achievement. But both the opportunity and the risks are great. That's why Washington must work closely with industry on critical details—while still insisting that broad principles of competition, universal service, and open networks be uncompromised. What lawmakers do will have a profound effect not only on the shape of the highway but

Inside Story continued on following page

Inside Story, continued

on how effectively the U.S. economy uses technology in the new century.

The Players Shaping Telecom Policy

As the debate heats up over how to build the Information Superhighway, Congress and regulators are considering a radical overhaul of the nation's communications policies. Here's where the players stand on the issues:

Washington   Congress and the White House want to open all segments of the communications system to competition, while ensuring that the telephone era policy of universal service—everyone has access—survives. A key issue: What constitutes universal service on the Information Superhighway? Should everyone have access to every information provider?

Local Phone Companies   Bell Atlantic, Ameritech, and others want the right to provide long-distance service and interactive video services. A big question: Who pays for rewiring the homes of low-profit rural and poor customers?

Long Distance Companies   AT&T, MCI, Sprint, and others want to keep local phone companies out of

long distance until there is true competition in local phone markets. But just when is that market considered competitive?

Cable-TV Operators   They want to provide phone service over their lines. But they would like to avoid the common-carrier provisions that apply to local phone companies and mandate equal access to all program suppliers.

Computer and Software Makers   Microsoft, IBM, Apple, AT&T, and others want the new interactive communications systems to be open to various hardware and software suppliers—in contrast to current cable systems.

Media and Entertainment Companies   Television and movie studios want to ensure the widest possible market for their programming.

Public Interest Groups   The Electronic Frontier Foundation and others want to make sure the Information Superhighway is more than a new marketing medium. They seek guaranteed access and lots of bandwidth for electronic town meetings.

Key Words and Phrases

additive   **632**
bait and switch advertising   **615**
caveat emptor   **600**
cease and desist orders   **618**
composition plan   **612**
consent order   **614**
discharged   **612**

exempt property   **613**
express warranty   **614**
extension plan   **612**
extortionate extension of credit   **601**
garnishment   **608**
implied warranties   **624**
misbranding   **628**

over-the-counter   **628**
puffing   **615**
regulation Z   **603**
right of recission   **606**
super discharge   **612**
usury statutes   **601**

Questions and Case Problems

1.   Are airline advertisements showing only one-way fares an example of deceptive pricing techniques when consumers must purchase a round-trip ticket to get the low one-way fare? Should the FTC regulate this practice?

2.   Americans consume an estimated 80 billion aspirin tablets a year, and more than 50 over-the-counter drugs contain aspirin

as the principal active ingredient. Yet aspirin labeling intended for the general public does not discuss its use in arthritis or cardiovascular disease because treatment of these conditions—even with a common over-the-counter drug—has to be medically supervised. The consumer labeling contains only a general warning about excessive or inappropriate use of aspirin, and specifically warns against using aspirin to treat children and teenagers who have chicken pox or the flu because of the risk of Reye's syndrome, a rare but sometimes fatal condition. The FDA in 1993 proposed a new label for aspirin products which would read, "IMPORTANT: See your doctor before taking this product for your heart or for other new uses of aspirin because serious side effects could occur with self treatment." As new uses for old drugs are discovered, how might the FDA respond to protect consumers from possible injury?

3. What role does the Federal Reserve Board play in consumer credit regulation?

4. Rehavem and Eleanor Adiel entered into a contract with Lakeridge Associated, Ltd. to purchase a townhouse to be built by Lakeridge. Thereafter, Lakeridge executed and delivered a mortgage application to Chase Federal Savings & Loan Association. The loan was approved and Lakeridge executed a promissory note payable to Chase. The funds were used by Lakeridge to construct the townhouse. Under the terms of the Adiels' purchase agreement, they were required to also submit a mortgage loan application (for the same amount as the Lakeridge loan) to Chase. The Adiels' application to Chase was for a residential consumer loan. Once approved, the Adiels were to assume the Lakeridge loan. Chase did not provide a truth-in-lending statement in connection with the original loan or when the Adiels assumed the Lakeridge mortgage. Was the original loan a commercial loan or a consumer loan? Does the Truth-in-Lending Act apply to both? Can an argument successfully be made that if Chase was aware of the prearrangement it should have provided truth-in-lending documents with the original loan? [*Adiel v. Chase Federal Savings & Loan Association*, 810 F.2d 1051 (11th Cir. 1987)]

5. You lose your purse or wallet which contains all of your credit cards, checkbook, ATM card, and numerous personal items. You later learn that someone found it and charged several thousand dollars on your credit card before you had the opportunity to notify your credit card companies. This person also found your personal identification number (PIN) and was able to withdraw $400 from your checking account. What are your liabilities to the credit card companies and your bank under the Truth-in-Lending Act and the Electronic Fund Transfer Act? Assume the finder uses your social security number to obtain new credit accounts in your name and then never pays the bills. What are your remedies under the Fair Credit Reporting Act?

6. You have just graduated from college but are unable to find a job. While looking for work, you decide to move back in with your parents. Although your parents are willing to feed and shelter you temporarily, they tell you that your student loans are your own responsibility. After several months of missed loan payments, a friend of yours who went to law school suggests that you file for bankruptcy under chapter 13 and attempt to get your loans discharged under the "hardship" exception, as you are unemployed and have no income. What is the likely result in the bankruptcy court? Is the result different under chapter 7?

7. From 1934 to 1939, Charles of the Ritz Distributors sold more than $1 million worth of its "Rejuvenescence Cream." Advertisements for the cosmetic product typically referred to "a vital organic ingredient" and certain "essences and compounds" that the cream allegedly contained. Users were promised that the cream would restore their youthful appearance, regardless of the condition of their skin. How might the FTC analyze the representations made by Charles of the Ritz? What evidence might the FTC consider to determine whether the advertisements are deceptive? Is it important that consumers actually believe that the product will make them look younger? How might the product's name affect the FTC's analysis? [*Charles of the Ritz Distributors Corp. v. Federal Trade Commission*, 143 F.2d 676 (2d Cir. 1944)]

8. Is it ethical for the U.S. government to provide tobacco subsidies to farmers while promoting health care among its citizens? Should the FDA regulate nicotine as a drug? How is nicotine similar to other substances currently regulated? How is it different?

9. In 1974, a flood, caused by storm-driven waves from the Bering Sea, swept through the city of Nome, Alaska. The floodwaters caused extensive damage to the commercial district of Nome, including the Bering Sea Saloon. The floodwaters burst through the back door of the saloon, resulting in merchandise being thrown to the ground and being exposed to various amounts of seawater and possibly to raw sewage. As a result, the FDA ordered the destruction of 1,638 cases of alcoholic beverages. On what basis can the FDA seize contaminated food or beverages? What criteria does it employ? Might it be possible for the Bering Sea Saloon to recondition the seized articles? [*United States v. 1,638 Cases Of Adulterated Alcoholic Beverages And Other Articles Of Food*, 624 F.2d 900 (9th Cir. 1980)]

10. Your company manufactures recreational all-terrain vehicles (ATVs). The Consumer Product Safety Commission (CPSC) has expressed concern that ATVs may be unnecessarily dangerous. As a result, the CPSC is contemplating regulations regarding the sale and use of ATVs. How might your company respond to the CPSC? In what way might your company work with other ATV manufacturers to avert governmental involvement? What powers does the CPSC have over your business? [*Consumer Federation of America v. Consumer Product Safety Commission*, 990 F.2d 1298 (D.C. Cir 1993)]

UNIT V

OWNERSHIP AND CONTROL

Chapter 20

CORPORATIONS

■ Introduction

Benefits of Incorporation

When a business requires substantial financing or is geared toward large-scale operation, the legal form it most often takes is that of the corporation. A corporation allows an entrepreneur to raise large amounts of capital from a number of shareholders, who are protected from being personally responsible for the corporation's debts by the corporate feature of limited liability. A limited partnership also provides this protection to its limited partners, but the amount of control those partners can exert on the business is sharply curtailed. In contrast, a corporation possesses mechanisms that allow the shareholders a certain degree of control and participation in the governance of the enterprise.

Another central feature of the corporate form is that, subject to restrictions imposed by federal and state securities laws (discussed in chapter 22), a corporation's shares are freely and easily transferable. Although a limited partnership can also be structured so that its shares are freely transferable, such partnerships are taxed as corporations.

A corporation has a more elaborate structure than a limited partnership. Authority is focused in a centralized decision-making body, the board of directors. The shareholders, who are the owners of the enterprise, elect the board of directors. The officers, who are appointed by and serve at the pleasure of the board of directors, act as agents of the corporation, managing its daily operation.

A corporation is an independent legal entity, separate from its owners (the shareholders) and from its managers (the officers and directors). A corporation can own property, enter into contracts, and sue and be sued in its own name.

Chapter Summary

Much of corporate law can be understood as an attempt to describe and define how much participation and control the shareholders should have, as well as whether management has overstepped its broad grant of authority. This chapter focuses on how a corporation is organized, how it raises funds, under what circumstances the corporate form might not provide limited liability for its shareholders, and how control is divided among the shareholders, directors, and officers.

Types of Corporations

There are three broad categories of corporations, which are increasingly treated in different ways under the law. The first is the *close corporation*, defined by statute as a corporation owned by a limited number of shareholders, usually 30, most of whom are actively involved in the management of the corporation. The second is the *privately held corporation*, which may have any number of shareholders, but whose shares are not bought and sold among the general public. The third category is the *publicly held corporation*, which is owned by a large number of shareholders, and whose shares are traded on one of the national stock exchanges or the over-the-counter market NASDAQ, which is operated by the National Association of Securities Dealers.

The primary difference between a close and a nonclose corporation is that the shareholders of a close corporation can directly manage without losing their insulation from personal liability for the corporation's debts. In a nonclose corporation, the power to manage rests with the board of directors. Other differences are discussed later in this chapter.

Incorporation

Incorporation is the process by which a corporation is formed. The corporate statutes of each state set forth the steps that must be taken to establish a corporation in that state. Many states' statutes are based in whole or in part on the Model Business Corporation Act, an annotated uniform statute prepared by academics and practitioners. The state under whose laws a corporation is formed is called the corporation's *corporate domicile*. A corporation is not limited to doing business in its corporate domicile. It can conduct business as a *foreign corporation* in other states. To do so, it may have to file a statement of foreign corporation with the secretary of state and the state taxing authority in each state in which the corporation does business as a foreign corporation.

Where to Incorporate

Corporations can choose to incorporate in any state, not necessarily where their headquarters or most of their business is located. Two important factors frequently affect the decision of where to incorporate: (1) the costs of incorporation in a given state; and (2) the relative advantages and disadvantages of that state's corporation laws. If the corporation is privately held and its business will be conducted largely within one state, incorporation in that state is probably the best choice. However, if the corporation will be large from the outset, or will be engaged in substantial interstate business, then incorporation in a jurisdiction with the most advantageous corporate statutes and case law should be considered.

Corporation laws may be favorable either to management or to the shareholders. Some states, such as Delaware, are known to be pro-management because their statutes and court decisions tend to give control on a wide range of issues to the officers and directors. Other states, such as California, make it difficult for corporate managers to do certain things without the approval and participation of the shareholders. These states are thought of as pro-shareholder.

A discussion of the Delaware statutes helps highlight some of the key corporate governance choices. The power to elect the board of directors is the primary way in which shareholders exercise control, and it is provided for in all jurisdictions. Delaware permits, but does not require, cumulative voting (discussed further below), which allows a minority shareholder greater opportunity to elect someone to the board. Delaware also permits a *staggered* (or *classified*) *board*, whereby directors serve for specified terms, usually three years, with only a fraction of them up for reelection at any one time. A classified board makes it more difficult to replace the entire board at once. In Delaware, classified boards are the norm. Delaware prohibits the removal of directors on a classified board without cause, unless the certificate of incorporation provides otherwise. In addition, as explained further in the next chapter, Delaware permits broad limitations on directors' monetary liability.

> 66
>
> *More than half of the large businesses incorporated in the United States are Delaware corporations.*

More than half of the large businesses incorporated in the United States are Delaware corporations. When deciding whether to incorporate in the local state or Delaware, incorporators must weigh the advantages Delaware law provides for managers against the expense of paying Delaware corporate taxes, the expense of hiring lawyers familiar with Delaware law, and the possibility of having to defend a lawsuit in Delaware. Businesses incorporated in their local state often reincorporate in Delaware once they have grown large enough to justify the effort and expense of reincorporation.

It should be noted that the balance between shareholder and management powers in each state does not remain static. California, a traditionally pro-shareholder state, amended its Corporations Code as of January 1, 1990, to permit publicly held companies to have a staggered board and to make cumulative voting optional. (However, privately held corporations incorporated in California must still have cumulative voting and cannot have a staggered board.) On the other hand, the traditionally pro-management Delaware courts have held that certain decisions affecting the corporation must be made by shareholders, not directors.

How to Incorporate

To create a corporation, one or more incorporators must prepare a document called the *certificate* or *articles of incorporation* (or the *corporate charter*). This document must be filed with the appropriate agent, usually the secretary of state for the jurisdiction that will become the corporate domicile.

The articles of incorporation are generally quite short. For example, the Pennsylvania Business Corporation Law specifies that the articles need only set forth the name of the corporation, the location and mailing address of the corporation's registered office in Pennsylvania, a brief statement of the purpose of the corporation, the term for which the corporation is to exist (which may be perpetual), the total number of shares that the corporation is authorized to issue, the name and mailing address of each of the incorporators, and a statement of the number of shares to be purchased by each.

Section 204 of the Pennsylvania Business Corporation Law, like most modern corporation statutes, goes on to provide that the purpose clause "may consist of or include a statement that the corporation shall have unlimited power to engage in and to do any lawful act concerning any or all lawful business for which corporations may be incorporated under this act." Pennsylvania's corporate law goes on to specify corporate powers, so there is no need to have a long purpose clause in the articles of incorporation. Indeed, to do so invites trouble, because one might inadvertently exclude an activity in which the corporation may later want to engage.

After the articles of incorporation are filed, the incorporators elect a board of directors, either at an organizational meeting or by written consent. The incorporators are exclusively empowered to place the directors in office. The directors then have an organizational meeting at which they adopt *bylaws,* that is, the rules governing the corporation; appoint officers; designate a bank as depository for corporate funds; authorize the sale of stock to the initial shareholders; and determine the consideration to be received in exchange for such shares—cash, other property, or past (but not future) services rendered to the corporation.

Defective Incorporation

Because a corporation does not have a common-law existence, but only a statutory one, any defect in the incorporation process can have the effect of denying corporate status. A business organization that was intended to function as a corporation but has failed to comply with the statutory requirements is in fact a partnership or, if there is only one shareholder, a sole proprietorship. The owners will not enjoy the protection of limited liability, and can be held personally responsible for all debts of the enterprise. However, the courts have developed several doctrines to avoid this result if it would be unfair.

De Jure Corporation   When incorporation has been done correctly, a *de jure* corporation is formed. This means that the entity is a corporation by right, and cannot be challenged. Most jurisdictions will find de jure corporate status so long as the incorporators have substantially complied with the incorporation requirements. For example, substantial compliance will be found even if the incorporators failed to obtain a required signature, or submitted an improper notarization.

De Facto Corporation   If the incorporators cannot show substantial compliance, a court may treat the entity as a *de facto* corporation, that is, as a corporation in fact even though it is not technically a corporation by law. For the court to find a de facto corporation, the incorporators must demonstrate that they were unaware of the defect and that they made a good-faith effort to incorporate correctly. For example, if a clerk for the secretary of state delayed in filing the articles, the business would not be a corporation de jure, but would probably be a corporation de facto.

Corporation by Estoppel An entity that is neither a de jure nor a de facto corporation may be a *corporation by estoppel.* If a third party, in all of its transactions with the enterprise, acts as if it were doing business with a corporation, the third party is prevented or *estopped* from claiming that the enterprise is not a corporation. It is considered unfair to permit the third party to reach shareholders' personal assets when all along it had believed it was dealing with a limited-liability corporation. The court found such a corporation by estoppel in the following case.

■ **A Case in Point:** Summary

Case 20.1
CRANSON v. INTERNATIONAL BUSINESS MACHINE CORP.
Supreme Court of Maryland
234 Md. 477, 200 A.2d 33
(Md.1964).

FACTS In April 1961 Albion C. Cranson was asked to invest in the Real Estate Service Bureau, a new business about to be incorporated. He met with other interested individuals and an attorney, and agreed to purchase stock and become an officer and director of the enterprise. Upon being advised by the attorney that the bureau had been formed under the laws of Maryland, he paid for and received a stock certificate evidencing ownership of shares in the corporation. He was elected president of the corporation, and was shown the corporate seal and minute book.

The new venture was conducted as a corporation. It had corporate bank accounts; auditors maintained corporate books and records; it leased the office where it did business. All of the transactions that Cranson conducted for the corporation, including the dealings with IBM, were made as an officer of the corporation. At no time did he assume any personal obligation or pledge his individual credit to IBM.

Due to an oversight on the part of the attorney, of which Cranson was not aware, the certificate of incorporation, although signed and acknowledged prior to May 1, 1961, was not filed until November 24, 1961. Between May 17 and November 8, the bureau purchased eight typewriters from IBM. Partial payments were made, leaving a balance due of $4,333.40. IBM sued Cranson for the balance due, on the theory that he was a partner in the business conducted by the bureau and as such was personally liable for its debts.

ISSUE PRESENTED Is a person who is an officer, director, and shareholder of a corporation personally liable for debts incurred before the articles of incorporation were filed, if he thought in good faith that the articles had been filed, and a creditor relied on the existence of the corporation when it extended credit?

SUMMARY OF OPINION The Maryland Supreme Court stated that traditionally two doctrines have been used by the courts to clothe an officer of a defectively incorporated association with the corporate attribute of limited liability. The first doctrine, that of de facto corporations, has been applied in cases in which: (1) a state statute authorizes incorporation; (2) the incorporators made an effort in good faith to incorporate under the existing law; and (3) the enterprise actually exercised corporate powers. The second doctrine, that of estoppel, applies if the person seeking to hold the officer personally liable has dealt with the association in such a manner as to recognize and in effect admit its existence as a corporate entity.

IBM contended that the failure of the bureau to file its certificate of incorporation barred any claim to corporate existence. However, the court found

Case 20.1 continued on following page

*Case **20.1** continued*

that IBM, having dealt with the bureau as if it were a corporation and having relied on its credit rather than that of Cranson, was estopped to assert that the bureau was not incorporated at the time the typewriters were purchased.

RESULT   IBM was estopped to deny the corporate existence of the bureau, and Cranson was not liable for the balance due on the typewriters.

International Consideration

Before a business decides to incorporate abroad, its management should consult a lawyer in the country in which the incorporation is to take place, in order to be advised of the country's laws governing tax, labor, and corporate issues. Parties contemplating a partnership or joint venture should note that civil law jurisdictions do not usually recognize "common-law" style partnerships. They instead look through the partnership to the partners, and view the partners as the legal owners.

In Brief: Steps Required to Form a Corporation

- Select a corporate name and agent for service of process.
- File certificate of incorporation (also known as articles of incorporation or charter in some jurisdictions) signed by incorporator(s).
- Sign action by incorporator(s) which:
  - Adopts bylaws
  - Specifies initial directors.
- Obtain written resignation of incorporator(s).
- Hold first directors' meeting or take action by unanimous written consent of the directors. Among other items of business,
  - Ratify acts of incorporator(s)
  - Elect officers
  - Issue stock
  - Authorize corporate bank account.

■ Structural Changes

Both state and federal law establish mechanisms by which the fundamental structure of the corporation can be changed. These changes can range from a reorganization of the enterprise to the end of the corporation as a separate entity. Because structural changes have far-reaching consequences, they cannot be made easily.

State corporation law prohibits certain changes, such as a merger or the sale of substantially all of the corporation's assets, unless they are approved by both the management and the shareholders. Approval by the shareholders usually means approval by a simple majority of the outstanding shares, but the articles of incorporation may require approval by a larger majority, such as two-thirds of the shareholders. Such a requirement for supermajority approval reflects the importance of structural changes.

Merger

A *merger* is the combination of two or more corporations into one. The *disappearing corporation* no longer maintains its separate corporate existence, but becomes part of the *surviving corporation*. The surviving corporation assumes, that is, becomes responsible for, all of the liabilities and debts of the disappearing corporation, and automatically acquires all of its assets, by operation of law. The new corporation may take on the name of one of the parties to the merger, or a new corporate name may be chosen. For example, when Burroughs merged with Sperry Univac, the new corporation was named Unisys.

An agreement of merger, negotiated between the two companies, will specify such crucial matters as who will comprise the management team of the new enterprise. A merger generally cannot occur unless the boards and the shareholders of both companies approve the transaction. Once the requisite approval is given, the agreement of merger is filed with the secretary of state.

In a noncash merger, the shares in the disappearing corporation are automatically converted into shares in the surviving corporation. Shareholders are required to surrender their old stock certificates for new certificates representing the stock of the surviving corporation. If a shareholder does not surrender his old certificate, it is deemed to represent shares of the surviving corporation.

In a cash merger, some shareholders (usually the public shareholders) are required to surrender their shares in the disappearing corporation for cash. They retain no interest in the surviving corporation. Hence such a merger is also called a *freeze-out merger.*

If a proposed merger meets certain size-of-party and size-of-transaction tests, a premerger notification must be filed with the Federal Trade Commission and the Department of Justice. This notification enables the federal agencies to review the anticompetitive effects of the proposed merger before the combination occurs. (Such Hart-Scott-Rodino filings and antitrust in general are covered in chapter 18.)

Ethical Consideration

A freeze-out merger (discussed further in chapter 21) raises issues of fairness to the minority shareholders, who are involuntarily deprived of their ongoing equity interest in the corporation.

Sale of Assets

A company may want to acquire the assets of another company but not its liabilities. To achieve this goal, it can purchase all or most of the other company's assets without merging with the other company. The proceeds of the sale of assets can be distributed to the selling company's shareholders as part of a dissolution of the corporation. Alternatively, the selling company may choose to continue its corporation existence, and invest the proceeds of the sale of assets in a new business.

A sale of all or substantially all of the assets of a corporation must be approved by both the board and the shareholders of the selling company. Most states consider a sale of 50% or more of the assets of a company to be a sale of substantially all of the assets.

Some states do not require that the transaction be approved by the shareholders of the acquiring company,

on the theory that the acquisition of assets is a routine management decision, in which the shareholders should not be involved.

Appraisal Rights

In a merger or a sale of assets, dissenting shareholders—those who voted against the transaction—are frequently granted *appraisal rights*, that is, the right to receive the fair cash value of the shares they were forced to give up as a result of the transaction. This right is only available if the transaction was subject to shareholder approval, and if the dissenting shareholder complies with certain statutory procedures.

For example, minority shareholders of Alabama By-Products Corporation were cashed out at $75.60 pursuant to a merger in 1985. They sought appraisal of their shares pursuant to Section 262 of the Delaware Corporations Code. On August 1, 1990, the *Delaware Court of Chancery* (the trial court in Delaware that hears corporate law cases) issued an opinion that valued the minority's shares in excess of $180 per share, using the discounted future cash flow methodology. The court also awarded the minority shareholders interest on the award of 12½%, or 5% above the 7½% federal discount rate in August 1985. The court rejected the defendants' argument that a lower short-term rate should be used, stating:

> Appraisal cases are akin to wars of attrition, with the dissenting shareholder forced to wait years for a return on his litigation investment. Short-term interest rates would be unfair for such shareholders, and a windfall to the surviving corporation.[1]

■ Ownership Changes

One company may gain control of another by buying a majority of its voting shares, rather than by merging with it or purchasing its assets.

Tender Offers

A *tender offer* is a public offer to all the shareholders of a corporation to buy their shares at a stated price, usually higher than the market price. The party making the offer is called a *bidder*, or sometimes a raider, because of the hostile nature of the bid. The bidder may offer either cash or other securities in exchange for the stock it seeks to

---

1. *Neal v. Alabama By-Products Corporation*, Del. Ch., C.A. No. 8282 (August 1, 1990), *aff'd*, 588 A.2d 255 (Del. 1991).

Historical Perspective

The Origins of the Modern Corporation

The modern corporation is the result of several centuries of political, social, and economic evolution. Universal acceptance of what is now viewed as one of the corporation's key attributes—limited liability for shareholders—was not introduced in the United States until well into the twentieth century.

Origins in England

As with most common-law concepts, the modern corporation has its roots in English medieval society. The ancestor of the corporation was the merchant guild. However, the merchant guilds—comprising members of the same trade or profession—were more akin to trade unions or chambers of commerce than to modern corporations. Each member of the guild was responsible for running his own business, and profits and losses were not shared.

One of the first business entities to be called a corporation was the large trading company. Such companies were given monopolies to engage in commerce in specific regions as trade expanded in the sixteenth and seventeenth centuries. For example, the East India Company was chartered in 1600, and the Hudson Bay Company in 1670. These early corporations were created by the English Crown via royal charter, or by special act of Parliament. They could be chartered for only specific, limited purposes, and it was illegal for the organization to stray from the confines of its charter.

Corporate charters were both expensive and difficult to obtain. They were reserved for large enterprises deemed important to the nation: trading companies; enterprises for the construction of canals and, later, railways; banks; and fire and marine insurance.

Although the chartered corporations played a crucial role in the development of the English economy, the bulk of English commercial activity was not carried on by these corporations, but rather by unincorporated joint stock companies. These companies can be compared to what are currently known as master limited partnerships. They were essentially partnerships with membership shares that were easily transferable. Because they were the predominant vehicle by which large amounts of capital were pooled to undertake business enterprises, the joint stock companies were the true forerunners of the modern corporation. There were more than 1,000 such

organizations in England by 1850, and ownership of shares in some companies was widespread.

The joint stock companies originally did not provide limited liability for their members; each member was held personally liable for the entire debt of the company. In addition, partners were not permitted to sue the firm to redress wrongs committed by its managers.

The owners of joint stock companies sought to limit their liability by adding "Limited" after the company name, and by including in the company's contracts specific clauses that limited the liability of its owners. Although the legal validity of such clauses was questionable, this practice was common. The attempt to limit liability was aided by the difficulty of collecting a damages award from a membership that was constantly changing.

The Companies Act of 1862 abolished the system of exclusive incorporation by royal charter or parliamentary act. It permitted any enterprise to obtain corporate status, so long as it met the requirements set forth in the act. This meant that a simple method of incorporation, with the crucial element of limited liability for shareholders, was now widely available.

Origins in America

After the American Revolution, it was established that each state had the power to create corporations by charter. The state legislatures granted charters more readily than did their English counterpart. However, as in England, the first types of enterprises to receive charters in large numbers were those of importance to the general economy, such as highway and canal building, and banking. As the nation's need to establish its own manufacturing base became obvious, there was a dramatic increase in the number of manufacturing enterprises that were incorporated. From 1783 to the end of the century, charters were given to more than 300 corporations. However, each corporation was permitted to engage in only a specific type of activity, and a monopoly on that activity was often granted.

Favoritism, logrolling, bureaucratic delay, and graft were associated with incorporation by the state legislatures. The growing inability of the legislatures to review carefully the large numbers of requests for incorporation, and the antipathy of competitors and the general public toward the granting of monopolies, fueled significant

Historical Perspective
The Origins of the Modern Corporation, *Continued*

opposition to this system. Many of the states amended their constitutions to prohibit, with certain exceptions, the legislature from chartering corporations.

Instead, incorporation was controlled by the general laws of the state. This meant that instead of facing delay and considerable expense, businesspersons could incorporate their enterprises simply by complying with the formalities established by state statute. This change was gradual; in some states, incorporation through the general laws of the state existed concurrently with incorporation by special act of the legislature.

The state of New York was a leader in enacting general incorporation law. In 1811 its legislature enacted the Act Relative to Incorporations for Manufacturing Purposes, to promote certain types of manufacturing activity. Those engaged in such activity with capital that did not exceed $100,000 were given the power to self-incorporate by signing and filing articles of incorporation. Beginning in 1835, other states followed suit, and self-incorporation became widespread.

---

acquire. The bidder is often a new corporation formed for the purpose of making the offer.

The shareholders are free to reject or accept the tender offer without the approval of the board. If shareholders sell sufficient stock to the bidder, it will acquire control of the *target corporation*. Hence, the term *takeover* is commonly used to describe this transaction.

Because a takeover is almost sure to change substantially the corporate structure of the target, tender offers are the subject of much regulation by federal statutes, as well as by the laws of the individual states.

An example of a takeover that results in a major change in corporate structure is the *second-step back-end merger*, whereby the bidder acquires more than 50% of the shares of a company through a tender offer, and then eliminates the remaining shareholders in a subsequent cash merger. The bidder first replaces the target company's board of directors with its own people. These new board members then approve the merger of the target company into a company owned by the bidder, with the shareholders of the target company receiving cash or securities for their stock. As the majority shareholder of the target company, the bidder can outvote any dissenters and provide the required shareholder approval. The remaining shareholders are thus frozen out of the new company, and the bidder ends up with all the equity interest.

Leveraged Buyouts

Any tender offer can be structured as a *leveraged buyout* (LBO), that is, a stock purchase financed by debt. This debt is often secured by the assets of the target company.

■ Management of the Corporation

Corporate control is apportioned among the directors, officers, and shareholders. The directors are the overall managers and guardians of the shareholders' interests in the corporation. The officers are the day-to-day managers. The shareholders, as the owners of the corporation, do not participate directly in management, but have the final say on the most important decisions.

Directors

Most state statutes provide that the business and the affairs of the corporation shall be managed, and all corporate powers shall be exercised, by or under the direction of the board of directors. The board may delegate the management of the day-to-day operations of the business of the corporation to a management company or to other persons, such as officers. A member of the board may also serve as an officer. Such a person is called an *inside director*. A director who is not also an officer is called an *outside director*. An understanding of the dynamics between the board and the officers is essential to comprehend the workings of a corporation.

> **❝**
> *An understanding of the dynamics between the board and the officers is essential to comprehend the workings of a corporation.*

Officers

The officers appointed by the board of directors are agents of the corporation and have the power to act on its behalf. A corporation will normally have a president, a secretary, a chief financial officer, and other officers as designated in the bylaws or determined by the board. The president, or if there is no president, the chairman of the board, is the general manager and chief executive officer (CEO) of the corporation.

Any number of offices may be held by the same person, unless the articles or bylaws provide otherwise. Officers are chosen by the board and serve at the pleasure of the board. If an officer is terminated in violation of a contract of employment, she cannot sue to get her job back, but she can sue for damages. An officer may resign at any time upon written notice to the corporation. The corporation can sue for damages if an officer's resignation breaches his employment contract.

Shareholders

The shareholders elect the directors. The courts have held that directors have no inherent right to remain in office. In some states, directors can be removed by the shareholders with or without cause at any time. In other states, such as Delaware, a director who is elected to a staggered board (whereby directors serve for designated terms) may not be removed without cause, unless the certificate of incorporation provides otherwise. However, the sharehold-

ers might be able to accomplish the same result by first eliminating the charter or bylaw provision requiring the staggered board, then by voting to remove the directors.

As noted earlier, there are also certain transactions, such as a merger or the sale of substantially all of the corporation's assets, which can be approved only by a vote of the shareholders.

The following case articulates one of the limits on the powers of shareholders.

Ethical Consideration

Directors and officers are allowed to be shareholders in the corporation they manage. In fact, giving the managers an ownership stake is a standard strategy for increasing their motivation. However, a manager's duty is to act in the best interest of all of the shareholders. If there are conflicting interests among the shareholders, a director or officer who is also a shareholder may not place her own interests above those of other shareholders. To do so is both unethical and illegal.

■ A Case in Point: Summary

Case 20.2
McQUADE v. STONEHAM
Court of Appeals of New York
263 N.Y. 323, 189 N.E. 234
(N.Y. 1934).

FACTS   Francis McQuade, manager of the New York Giants baseball team, brought this action to enforce an agreement between himself and two other shareholders of the National Exhibition Company, the owner of the New York Giants. Charles Stoneham (father of Horace Stoneham, who acquired the baseball franchise in 1936 and moved it from New York to San Francisco in 1958) owned a majority of the stock of the company and sold shares to McQuade and to John McGraw. As part of the transaction, these three shareholders each agreed to use his best efforts to continue to keep each of the others as directors and officers of the company at their present salaries. Stoneham and McGraw subsequently failed to use their best efforts to continue to keep McQuade as a director and treasurer of the company. McQuade sued for specific performance of the agreement.

The defendants argued that directors have a duty to act in the interests of the corporation according to their best judgment. Therefore, a contract that compels a director to vote to keep any person in office at a stated salary was, the defendants argued, void because it violated that duty.

ISSUE PRESENTED   Is an agreement between shareholders to keep an officer of the corporation in office enforceable?

SUMMARY OF OPINION The New York Court of Appeals stated that the directors alone are charged with managing the business of the corporation. Shareholders may, of course, combine to elect directors. However, they may not combine to limit the power of directors to manage the business of the corporation. The shareholders may not, by agreement among themselves, control the directors in the exercise of their judgment to appoint officers and fix salaries. Similarly, directors may not, by agreements entered into as shareholders, relinquish their independent judgment.

The court recognized that McQuade had been "shabbily" treated as a purchaser of stock from Stoneham. However, Stoneham and McGraw owed a duty to the corporation and its shareholders, and were under no legal obligation to deal ethically with McQuade if to do so would violate that duty. The court concluded that the contract was void so far as it precluded the board of directors from changing officers, salaries, or policies.

RESULT McQuade could not force the majority shareholders to honor their shareholder agreement to keep him in office at a specified salary. Enforcement of the agreement interfered with the discretion the law gives the directors.

Ethical Consideration

The decision of the court demonstrates how the dictates of ethics on one hand and the need to formulate broad and cohesive legal rules on the other can be in conflict. The court, although recognizing that McQuade had been shabbily treated, felt compelled to subordinate ethical considerations to the broader societal goal of ensuring a consistent system of corporate governance.

■ Actions by Officers

An officer, as an agent of the corporation, may bind the corporation if he has actual or apparent authority to act on its behalf. Even if the officer's actions are not within the scope of his authority, the board of directors may subsequently ratify the officer's actions and thereby bind the corporation.

Actual Authority

Actual authority may be expressly conferred on an officer by the corporation's bylaws, which usually list the officers' positions and describe the powers and duties of each; or by the board, for example, in a resolution authorizing the execution of a particular agreement.

An officer also has implied actual authority by virtue of her position. In particular, corporate presidents are generally viewed as being able to bind the corporation in ordinary business transactions.

Apparent Authority

A third party may in good faith rely on the apparent authority of an officer, based on custom, past conduct, or representations as to the officer's authority.

A plaintiff seeking to enforce an agreement against a corporation has the burden of proving that the officer who entered into the agreement with him had actual or apparent authority to do so. For example, in *Walker v. Carpenter (In Re Westec Corporation)*,[2] Garland Walker was the chief executive and director of Seismic Supply Australia Proprietary, Limited, a wholly owned subsidiary of Westec Corporation. Ernest Hall, the president of Westec, had promised Walker 7,000 shares of Westec stock in exchange for Walker's assistance in acquiring stock of another company for Seismic. The board of directors of Westec did not authorize the issuance of stock to Walker, but did authorize an option for the 7,000 shares.

Walker sued for damages for breach of the alleged contract for the issuance of the 7,000 shares. He argued

---

2. 434 F.2d 195 (5th Cir. 1970).

that Hall, as president, had authority to enter into a contract to issue capital stock. The court held that there was no showing that Hall had actual authority. In fact, the law generally on this point is that the president has no actual authority to enter into a binding contract for the issuance of stock. As to apparent authority, Walker could not show that the board's conduct would have led a reasonably prudent person, using diligence and discretion, to suppose that Hall had the necessary authority to issue stock. Walker, in fact, indicated in his testimony that he knew it was the board's responsibility to issue stock.

■ Actions by the Directors

Many of the recent developments in corporations law have been in the area of mergers and acquisitions, leveraged buyouts, and other forms of alteration in the financial or control structure of the corporation. A central issue that emerges in such cases is who gets to decide on the proposed changes—the board of directors or the shareholders. Theoretically, the board of directors is the guardian of the shareholders' interests, but the interests and obligations of the two groups sometimes conflict.

> 66
> *Theoretically, the board of directors is the guardian of the shareholders' interests, but the interests and obligations of the two groups sometimes conflict.*

For example, a hostile takeover attempt frequently presents a conflict of interest between the shareholders and the board of directors. Sometimes the proposed terms are attractive to the shareholders because the acquiring corporation offers to pay a substantial premium for their stock. However, the board of directors may believe that the acquiring company's plans for the corporation are ultimately destructive, as in the case of a *bust-up takeover*, in which the acquired corporation is taken apart and its assets sold piecemeal. The directors may have legitimate concerns about the effect of such a takeover on the company's employees or on the community where the corporation is located. Such concerns for constituencies other than the shareholders are deemed appropriate by the courts in certain situations, as long as they are rationally related to the interests of the shareholders. Directors and shareholders may disagree as to whether or not this is the case.

A director might oppose a transaction, not only because of its detrimental effects on the corporate constituencies, but also to maintain her own place on the corporation's board. Such attempts to keep one's job are known as *entrenchment*. Entrenchment violates the manager's ethical obligations to put the corporation's interests before his own, and courts have imposed personal liability on directors who opposed a takeover primarily or solely for the purpose of entrenchment.

Conflicts of interest between the shareholders and the board are often complicated by three additional factors. First, the board may be influenced by the officers to keep the existing management in control of the corporation. Officers who sit on the board have a direct say in board decisions, and because such inside directors have two jobs to maintain (officer and director) there is an even greater concern regarding entrenchment. Second, a substantial minority of shareholders may oppose the takeover while the majority supports it. Finally, all or part of the target company's management may be part of the acquiring group. In such a case, the management may end up negotiating with itself unless outside directors are given control of the sale process.

The following case upheld the adoption by a board of directors, without shareholders' approval, of a *poison pill*, that is, a plan that would make any takeover of the company prohibitively expensive.

■ A Case in Point: Summary

Case 20.3
MORAN v. HOUSEHOLD INTERNATIONAL, INC.
Supreme Court of Delaware
500 A.2d 1346 (Del. 1985).

FACTS Household International, Inc. is a diversified holding company with its principal subsidiaries engaged in financial services, transportation, and merchandising. Household owns HFC, National Car Rental, and Vons Grocery.

In August 1984, in response to general concerns that Household might be taken over and busted up, that is, liquidated by the selling of all of its assets, its board of directors adopted a poison pill. This plan, called the Preferred Share Purchase Rights Plan, provided that, under certain triggering circumstances, common shareholders would receive a "right" per every common share. In the event of a merger in which Household was not the surviving corporation, the holder of each common share of Household would have the right to purchase $200 of the common stock of the acquiring company for only $100 per share. If this right were triggered and exercised, it would dilute the value of the stock of the acquiring company, making a takeover prohibitively expensive for the acquiring company.

John Moran was a director of Household and chairman of Dyson-Kissner-Moran (D-K-M), the largest single shareholder of Household. Moran, believing that Household was undervalued, had discussed a leveraged buyout by D-K-M. When Household's directors adopted the poison pill, Moran sued the company, alleging that the directors had no power to adopt such a plan.

ISSUE PRESENTED   May the directors adopt a poison pill plan without shareholder approval?

SUMMARY OF OPINION   The Delaware Supreme Court found that the plan did not usurp the shareholders' ability to receive tender offers, and to sell their shares to a bidder without board approval of the sale. Household's poison pill left "numerous methods to successfully launch a takeover." For example, a bidder could make a tender offer on the condition that the board redeem the rights, that is, buy them back for a nominal sum before they were triggered. A bidder could set a high minimum of shares and rights to be tendered; it could solicit consents to remove the board and replace it with one that would redeem the rights; or it could acquire 50% of the shares and cause Household to self-tender for the rights. In a self-tender, the company would agree to buy back the shareholders' rights for a fair price.

The court also found that the plan did not fundamentally restrict the shareholders' right to conduct a *proxy contest*. In a proxy contest, someone wishing to replace the board with her own candidates must acquire a sufficient number of shareholder votes to do so. Such votes are usually represented by proxies, or limited written powers of attorney entitling the proxy holder to vote the shares owned by the person giving the proxy. The court found that a proxy contest could be won with an insurgent ownership of less than 20% (the threshold for triggering distribution of the rights), and that the key to success in a proxy contest is the merit of the insurgent's arguments, not the size of his holdings.

The court concluded that the decision to adopt the poison pill plan was within the board's authority. Moreover, because the directors "reasonably believed Household was vulnerable to coercive acquisition techniques and adopted a reasonable defensive mechanism to protect itself," the court held that the board had discharged its fiduciary duty appropriately under the business judgment rule. This rule (discussed in chapter 21) protects directors from liability for faulty decisions, unless the plaintiff can show that the directors were uninformed, or acted in bad faith or in a manner they did not honestly believe to be in the best interests of the corporation.

RESULT   A board of directors can adopt a poison pill without shareholder approval.

As of 1994, more than half of the Fortune 500 companies had poison pill plans in effect. Although the Delaware Supreme Court upheld the adoption of such a plan in *Moran*, it reserved judgment on how such a plan would operate in practice. In particular, it left open the question of when directors must redeem the poison pill rights to permit shareholders to tender their shares to a bidder.

The question of whether a board must redeem a pill is fact specific—a court will look at all of the circumstances in making its decision. Certain factors will favor keeping the pill in place; for example, a tender offer that is only slightly above the market price of the stock; an active attempt by the board to solicit other offers; a conscious effort by the board to allow its outside directors, deemed more disinterested, to make the decisions in this area; and the fact that the tender offer is only in its early stages.

A board's action in fending off a takeover attempt may be upheld even if the shareholders might have favored the takeover, as in the following case.

■ **A Case in Point:**   **In the Language of the Court**

Case 20.4
PARAMOUNT COMMUNICATIONS, INC. v. TIME INCORPORATED
Delaware Court of Chancery
Fed. Sec. L. Rep. (CCH)
¶94,514 (Del.Ch. July 14, 1989), *aff'd*, 571 A.2d 1140 (Del. 1990).

FACTS   Time Inc. publishes *Time* and *Sports Illustrated* magazines. A merger was proposed between Time and Warner Communications, Inc., a major entertainment firm with interests in film, video, and music. The merger agreement was subject to approval by the shareholders of Time. Shortly before the Time shareholder vote was to take place, Paramount Communications, Inc., a major U.S. film studio, made a hostile, unsolicited cash tender offer for all Time shares. In response, Time proceeded with its own tender offer to acquire 51% of Warner, to be followed by a back-end, second-step merger of the two companies. This tender offer, which would preclude acceptance of the Paramount tender offer, was not subject to approval by the Time shareholders. Paramount challenged the actions of Time's directors in opposing the Paramount offer.

ISSUE PRESENTED   Does the board of directors have an obligation to permit shareholders to accept a tender offer that is arguably more advantageous than the transaction proposed by the board?

OPINION   ALLEN, Chancellor, writing for the Delaware Court of Chancery:

. . . .

Reasonable persons can and do disagree as to whether it is the better course from the shareholders' point of view collectively to cash out their stake in the company now at this (or a higher) premium cash price. However, there is no persuasive evidence that the board of Time has a corrupt or venal motivation in electing to continue with its long-term plan even in the face of the cost that that course will no doubt entail for the company's shareholders in the short run. In doing so, it is exercising perfectly conventional powers to cause the corporation to buy assets for use in its business. Because of the timing involved, the board has no need here to rely upon a self-created power designed to assure a veto on all changes in control.

The value of a shareholder's investment, over time, rises or falls chiefly because of the skill, judgment and perhaps luck—for it is present in all human affairs—of the management and directors of the enterprise. When they exercise sound or brilliant judgment, shareholders are likely to profit; when they fail to do so, share values likely will fail to appreciate. In either event, the financial vitality of the corporation and the value of the company's shares is in the hands of the directors and managers of the firm. The corporation law does not operate on the theory that directors, in exercising their powers to manage the firm, are obligated to follow the wishes of a majority of shares. In fact, directors, not shareholders, are charged with the duty to manage the firm.

In the decision they have reached here, the Time board may be proven in time to have been brilliantly prescient or dismayingly wrong. In this decision, as in other decisions affecting the financial value of their investment, the shareholders will bear the effects for good or ill. That many, presumably most, shareholders would prefer the board to do otherwise than it has done does not, in the circumstances of a challenge to this type of transaction, in my opinion, afford a basis to interfere with the effectuation of the board's business judgment.

. . . .

RESULT   The Delaware Court of Chancery held that the Time directors did not have a fiduciary obligation to halt the Time-Warner combination to give the Time shareholders an opportunity to accept the all-cash, all-shares tender offer from Paramount. The Delaware Supreme Court affirmed the decision.

COMMENTS   Other aspects of this case, including the duty, if any, of the Time board to auction Time to the highest bidder, are discussed in chapter 21.

Questions

1. Was the Paramount offer coercive?

2. At the time of the Time board's decision, much of Time's stock was held in the hands of short-term arbitrageurs who bought it in the hopes that they could tender into the Paramount offer. Should short-term shareholders be entitled to less protection or deference than those who are in the stock for the long term?

" *"The corporation law does not operate on the theory that directors, in exercising their powers to manage the firm, are obligated to follow the wishes of a majority of shares."*

Before the Delaware Court of Chancery's opinion was issued, Gregg A. Jarrell, past head of the Securities and Exchange Commission's economics unit and now a professor at the University of Rochester, wrote an article about the Paramount and Time-Warner offers.[3] The article attacked what Jarrell viewed as a dangerous "emerging pro-target attitude" in the Delaware courts. His article raised a crucial and controversial issue in the area of takeovers. In evaluating the adequacy of an offer, boards have been allowed to argue that even though the offer is above the current market price, it does not favorably compare with the long-range value of the stock. Jarrell did an analysis, on a present-value basis, in which he concluded that the Paramount deal was better for long-

term value than the alternative that was selected by the Time board.

■ Actions by the Shareholders

Shareholders can act by vote or by written consent. A shareholder who cannot be present at a meeting can vote by *proxy*, that is, by a written authorization for another person to vote on her behalf. Only *shareholders of record*, that is, persons whose names appear on the corporation's shareholder list on a specified date, are entitled to vote.

No action can be taken at a shareholder meeting unless there is a *quorum*; the quorum requirements are set forth in each state's corporate statute. In most jurisdictions, there is no quorum unless the holders of at least 50% of the outstanding shares are present in person or by proxy.

Cumulative Voting

In the election of directors, shareholders can cast one vote per share for each director. A shareholder's total number of votes is thus equal to the number of directors to be elected multiplied by the number of shares owned by the shareholder. Some states permit, and some require,

---

3. Gregg A. Jarrell, "The Paramount Import of Becoming Time-Warner," *The Wall Street Journal,* July 13, 1989, A14.

cumulative voting, whereby each shareholder may cast all of his votes for one nominee, or allocate them among nominees as he sees fit.

In an election permitting cumulative voting, the number of shares, x, required to elect a given number of directors, y, may be calculated by the following formula:

$$x = \frac{y \times z}{1 + d} + 1$$

where z is the total number of shares voting, and d is the total number of directors to be elected.

To illustrate, assume a shareholder wants to elect three directors ($y = 3$) to a board with five members up for election ($d = 5$). There are 100 shares of the corporation outstanding and they are all voted ($z = 100$). Then

$$x = \frac{3 \times 100}{1 + 5} + 1$$

$$= 51$$

With cumulative voting, a shareholder would need 51 shares to elect three directors.

Shareholders' Right of Inspection

Shareholders have a common-law right to inspect the corporate books and records, including the stock register, the minutes of board meetings and shareholder meetings, the bylaws, and books of account. In making the examination, shareholders are permitted the assistance of an accountant, lawyer, or other expert.

The requested inspection must be made: (1) in good faith, (2) at a reasonable time, and (3) for the purpose of advancing a corporate interest or of protecting the rights of its shareholders. Some jurisdictions consider concern about mismanagement a proper purpose; others, not wishing to invite "fishing expeditions," require more than a vague allegation of mismanagement to establish a proper purpose.

> ❝
> *Some jurisdictions consider concern about mismanagement a proper purpose; others, not wishing to invite "fishing expeditions," require more than a vague allegation of mismanagement to establish a proper purpose.*

Some jurisdictions allow inspection of the record of shareholders without requiring a proper purpose, provided the shareholder owns a substantial block of shares. For example, section 1600(a) of the California Corporations Code provides that any 5% shareholder can inspect and copy the record of shareholders' names and addresses and shareholdings during usual business hours upon five business days' written notice. However, a proper purpose is required to inspect minutes and accounting books and records.

Piercing the Corporate Veil

The corporation is built around the central premise of limited liability. Under certain circumstances courts will deny this central premise and hold the shareholders liable for claims against the corporation. A court will *pierce the corporate veil* in this way if necessary to prevent the evasion of statutes, the perpetration of fraud, or other activities against public policy. The need to pierce arises only if the corporation is unable to pay its own debts.

There are two legal approaches to piercing the corporate veil. The *alter ego* theory applies when the owners of a corporation have so mingled their own affairs with those of the corporation that the corporation does not exist as a distinct entity—it is an alter ego (second self) of its owners. The *undercapitalization* theory applies when the corporation is a separate entity, but its lack of adequate capital constitutes a fraud upon the public.

The courts usually apply some combination of these theories. If a court suspects wrongdoing or bad faith on the part of shareholders, it will be more inclined to pierce the corporate veil.

Because a publicly traded corporation generally does not have one controlling shareholder, attempts to pierce the veil of such corporations are rare. Usually the cases involve small, closely held corporations, including subsidiaries of larger corporations.

Alter Ego Theory

There are several factors that a court will consider when deciding whether a corporation is merely the alter ego of a shareholder.

Domination by Shareholder   If an individual or another corporation owning most of the stock of the corporation exerts a great deal of control, such that the standard corporate decision-making mechanisms are not in operation, the courts may find that the corporation has no will of its own.

Commingling of Assets The courts will also examine whether the books and funds of the corporation and of the controlling shareholder have been commingled; for example, whether the shareholder uses company checks to make personal purchases or payments.

Bypassing Formalities If an action that requires approval by the board proceeds without a board meeting being held, or if other procedural rules, such as the requirement of an annual shareholders meeting, are consistently broken, the courts will be inclined to view the corporation as the instrument of the controlling shareholder.

However, recognizing that small businesses are run in a more informal manner than large ones, legislators have created the statutory category of the close corporation, that is, a corporation with a limited number of shareholders, usually 30 or fewer, which is explicitly designated as a close corporation in its charter. Under some close corporation statutes, if a close corporation's shareholders agree not to observe corporate formalities relating to meetings of directors or shareholders in connection with the management of its affairs, the bypassing of these formalities may not be considered a factor tending to establish that the shareholders have personal liability for corporate obligations.

In addition, many statutes permit the management of a close corporation to reside in the shareholders so long as a certain percentage of the shareholders agree to this in writing. Examples of such statutes are section 351 of the Delaware Corporation Law and section 12.37 of the Texas Business Corporation Act.

Undercapitalization Theory

In deciding whether a corporation is undercapitalized, a court will consider whether the founders should have reasonably anticipated that the corporation would be unable to pay the debts or liabilities it would incur. (The amount of capital invested does not have to guarantee business success—if it did, all failed businesses would be deemed undercapitalized.)

For example, assume a new corporation is formed to build airplanes, an activity that requires large expenditures and entails substantial risks of liability for third-party injury. The corporation has only raised $1,000 in capital. It is obvious that the corporation will run out of funds quickly and be unable to pay its bills. It will not have money to buy adequate product liability insurance or to self-insure against claims for injuries caused by defective planes. A court may, because of the undercapitalization, ignore the corporate form and hold the owners of the corporation personally liable for its debts and liabilities.

The above example is an exaggerated case. In reality, it is often difficult for a court to decide how much capital is enough. Two judges examining the same facts may come to different conclusions as to whether the owner should have reasonably anticipated that the corporation would need more capital.

> *Two judges examining the same facts may come to different conclusions as to whether the owner should have reasonably anticipated that the corporation would need more capital.*

Judges may also disagree as to whether undercapitalization alone is sufficient grounds to pierce the corporate veil. In the following case, the majority opinion and the minority dissent reflect two sides of this issue.

■ A Case in Point: In the Language of the Court

Case 20.5
WALKOVSZKY v. CARLTON
Court of Appeals of New York
18 N.Y.2d 414, 276 N.Y.S.2d
585, 223 N.E.2d 6 (N.Y. 1966).

FACTS The plaintiff was severely injured in New York City when he was run down by a taxicab owned by the defendant, Seon Cab Corporation. The individual defendant, Carlton, was a shareholder of ten corporations, including Seon, each of which had two cabs registered in its name. Each cab was covered by only the $10,000 per cab minimum automobile liability insurance required by New York law.

*Case **20.5** continued on following page*

*Case **20.5** continued*

Although seemingly independent of one another, these corporations were, according to the plaintiff, "operated . . . as a single entity, unit and enterprise" with regard to financing, supplies, repairs, employees, and garaging, and all were named as defendants. The plaintiff also asserted that the multiple corporate structure constituted an unlawful attempt "to defraud members of the general public" who might be injured by the cabs. He therefore sought to hold their shareholders personally liable for his injury.

ISSUE PRESENTED   May the corporate veil be pierced solely because the corporation is undercapitalized?

OPINION   FULD, J., writing for the New York Court of Appeals:

. . . .

The law permits the incorporation of a business for the very purpose of enabling its proprietors to escape personal liability but, manifestly, the privilege is not without its limits. Broadly speaking, the courts will disregard the corporate form, or, to use accepted terminology, "pierce the corporate veil," whenever necessary "to prevent fraud or to achieve equity."

. . . .

In the case before us, the plaintiff has explicitly alleged that none of the corporations "had a separate existence of their own." . . . However, it is one thing to assert that a corporation is a fragment of a larger corporate combine which actually conducts the business. It is quite another to claim that the corporation is a "dummy" for its individual stockholders who are in reality carrying on the business in their personal capacities for purely personal rather than corporate ends. Either circumstance would justify treating the corporation as an agent and piercing the corporate veil to reach the principal but a different result would follow in each case. In the first, only a larger corporate entity would be held financially responsible while, in the other, the stockholder would be personally liable.

. . . .

The individual defendant is charged with having "organized, managed, dominated and controlled" a fragmented corporate entity but there are no allegations that he was conducting business in his individual capacity. . . . The corporate form may not be disregarded merely because the assets of the corporation, together with the mandatory insurance coverage of the vehicle which struck the plaintiff, are insufficient to assure him the recovery sought. If Carlton were to be held individually liable on those facts alone, the decision would apply equally to the thousands of cabs which are owned by their individual drivers who conduct their businesses through corporations organized pursuant to [the New York Business Corporation Law] and carry the minimum insurance required. . . . These taxi owner-operators are entitled to form such corporations, and we agree . . . that, if the insurance coverage required by statute "is inadequate for the protection of the public, the remedy lies not with the courts but with the Legislature." It may very well be sound policy to require that certain corporations must take out liability insurance which will afford adequate compensation to their potential tort victims. However, the responsibility for imposing conditions on the privilege of incorporation has been committed by the Constitution to the Legislature and it may not be fairly implied, from any statute, that the Legislature intended, without the slightest discussion or debate, to require of taxi corporations that they carry automobile liability insurance over and above that mandated by the Vehicle and Traffic Law.

. . . .

DISSENTING OPINION KEATING, J.:

. . . .

From their inception these corporations were intentionally undercapitalized for the purpose of avoiding responsibility for acts which were bound to arise as a result of the operation of a large taxi fleet having cars out on the street 24 hours a day and engaged in public transportation. And during the course of the corporations' existence all income was continually drained out of the corporations for the same purpose.

The issue presented by this action is whether the policy of this State, which affords those desiring to engage in a business enterprise the privilege of limited liability through the use of the corporate device, is so strong that it will permit that privilege to continue no matter how much it is abused, no matter how irresponsibly the corporation is operated, no matter what the cost to the public. I do not believe that it is.

[Judge Keating then cited with approval a California Supreme Court case[4] holding that the corporate veil could be pierced based on undercapitalization alone.]

. . . .

What I would merely hold is that a participating shareholder of a corporation vested with a public interest, organized with capital insufficient to meet liabilities which are certain to arise in the ordinary course of the corporation's business, may be held personally responsible for such liabilities. Where corporate income is not sufficient to cover the cost of insurance premiums above the statutory minimum or where initially adequate finances dwindle under the pressure of competition, bad times or extraordinary and unexpected liability, obviously the shareholder will not be held liable.

The only types of corporate enterprises that will be discouraged as a result of a decision allowing the individual shareholder to be sued will be those such as the one in question, designed solely to abuse the corporate privilege at the expense of the public interest.

. . . .

RESULT In New York, the corporate veil may not be pierced solely because the corporation is undercapitalized. Accordingly, plaintiff Walkovszky cannot sue Carlton in his individual capacity.

---

4. *Minton v. Cavaney*, 56 Cal.2d 576, 15 Cal. Rptr. 641, 364 P.2d 473 (Cal. 1961).

*Case **20.5** continued on following page*

*Case **20.5** continued*

COMMENTS In *Walkovszky*, the court rejected the argument that undercapitalization alone constituted fraud. But the court suggested that the plaintiff amend the complaint to allege that the individual defendants were "shuttling . . . personal funds in and out of the corporation 'without regard to formality and to suit their immediate convenience,' " thus stating a valid cause of action under the alter ego theory.

Questions
1. From a public policy standpoint, with which opinion do you agree, the majority or the dissent?
2. Would the result have been different if defendant Carlton's name had been conspicuously displayed on the sides of all of the taxis owned by the various corporations of which Carlton was the sole shareholder, and if Carlton actually serviced, inspected, repaired, and dispatched them?

 ## *Ethical Consideration*

The dissenting opinion highlights the ethical problems created by the majority opinion. If undercapitalization alone is not a basis for piercing the corporate veil, a person can use the corporate form without ensuring that the corporation has sufficient funds to act in a socially responsible manner.

Tort Versus Contract

A tort plaintiff's contact with the corporation (for example, being hit by a taxi) may be completely involuntary. Many courts are therefore more sympathetic to the tort victim who faces an undercapitalized corporate defendant than to a plaintiff seeking to pierce the corporate veil in a breach-of-contract case. Why should someone who voluntarily contracted to provide credit to a weakly capitalized corporation, perhaps charging a premium interest rate in so doing, later be entitled to reach the owner's personal assets? After all, the creditor had, or could have negotiated, access to the corporation's financial statements. Her voluntary decision to do business with the undercapitalized company contrasts quite sharply with the plight of a party who is a victim of a tort committed by an officer or employee of the corporation.

 ## *The Responsible Manager*

Creating and Running a Corporation

Managers associated with a corporation from its inception must make crucial decisions regarding incorporation. The first step is to decide where to incorporate. Because each state's corporations laws create different structures for the internal operation of the enterprise, managers should carefully weigh the alternatives.

To ensure proper incorporation, a manager should obtain competent legal advice. State statutes vary in their requirements for incorporation. As a practical matter, managers should always request that their lawyer send them a certified copy of the articles of incorporation to confirm that the articles were in fact filed with the secretary of state on the specified date.

Even if a corporation is formed in accordance with the appropriate legal requirements, a court may still disregard the corporate form. In some jurisdictions, the corporate veil may be pierced solely because the corporation is undercapitalized. Managers should consult with counsel as to the capital requirements in the jurisdiction of incorporation.

Courts may also pierce the corporate veil if the managers fail to respect the corporate form in their execution of daily activities, or if they commingle personal and corporate funds. Therefore, managers should be certain that in all of their dealings with third parties, the agents of the corporation portray it as a corporation. All firm stationery and agreements should indicate corporate status.

Once the corporation has been established, the managers will oversee the process of capitalization. To decide what percentages of debt and equity are to be used in financing the operation, a manager should have a realistic idea of the existing demand and the distinct markets for both types of financing. In addition, he must be aware of the rates at which the corporation can borrow money, and the terms that debt and equity holders will require. Tax considerations are crucial to this process.

The final capital structure can take a variety of forms, and much creativity can be employed in this area. Managers will often seek assistance from attorneys specializing in finance and tax law, as well as from investment bankers. However, the more a manager understands about capitalization, the better she can utilize the information provided by lawyers and bankers to achieve a suitable capital structure.

The officers of a corporation are empowered by the board to manage the day-to-day operations of the business. They are also agents for the corporation, and must be concerned with the impact of agency law on their actions. First, a manager must be certain that he is acting with actual authority, such as a resolution from the board of directors, passed in a procedurally correct manner, that approves a proposed action. Second, a manager has the power to delegate authority to her subordinates to bind the corporation. Accordingly, the manager should clearly define the scope of employment for all employees of the corporation and clearly indicate to third parties the extent of each employee's authority.

Managers are often inside directors, as well as officers. As board members, they should ensure that the board acts in accordance with the articles of incorporation and the applicable corporate law. Board actions are valid only if the directors act in their collective role, and not in their individual capacity. For example, action can only be taken at a board meeting with the approval of a majority of the board, or by unanimous written consent of the individual directors without a meeting. If the opportunity for a choice exists, the quality of the decisions is enhanced when a meeting is held. A board meeting allows for the free flow and the critical discussion of ideas. Directors have a duty to act in an informed manner. Presentations to the board by lawyers, investment bankers, and the company's officers can be essential for compliance with this duty.

When a corporation is faced with the possibility of a hostile takeover, managers, acting as inside directors, may take such action as installing a poison pill to fend off the takeover. However, such action must be motivated by concern for the corporation and its shareholders as well as for such constituencies as employees. Directors may not use such defensive measures if their primary goal is entrenchment, that is, the desire to remain in power. Managers should develop a plan for responding to takeovers before any actual takeover attempt occurs.

Inside Story

The 3DO Company: A "Virtual" Corporation

Company Background

The 3DO Company was founded by William M. ("Trip") Hawkins in October 1991. 3DO was formed to create a new interactive multimedia platform and to develop technology that could achieve a breakthrough in home audiovisual realism at an affordable price. In addition, the company planned to broadly license the technology to hardware system manufacturers, software title developers, and software publishers. The company targeted its initial product design, the 3DO Interactive Multiplayer, to be the first interactive multimedia product that would appeal to the entire family, bridging the gap between children's video games and adults' home computers. The Multiplayer was designed to run new entertainment, education, and information compact disk (CD) applications developed specifically for the 3DO format, and to also play conventional audio CDs and display photo CDs. The 3DO Multiplayer was not compatible with any other software formats that were cur-

Inside Story continued on following page

Inside Story, continued

rently commercially available. New applications developed for the 3DO format included realistic adventure games, lifelike sports and flight simulations, interactive movies, children's storybooks, education programs, and a variety of information services.

Hawkins graduated from Stanford University's Graduate School of Business in 1978 and became a director of marketing at Apple Computer in 1982. That year, he left Apple and founded Electronic Arts, a game software manufacturer for personal computers and Nintendo and Sega home video game players. By 1991, he had built Electronic Arts into a company with $300 million in sales and a market capitalization of nearly $1 billion. Along the way, Hawkins developed the idea for a company that would compete in the interactive multimedia market, one that at the time had an exciting yet uncertain future. In 1991, he proposed to the board of directors of Electronic Arts that the company set up a subsidiary corporation, which would later be called The 3DO Company, to develop the technology for multimedia products for the whole family. Because Nintendo and Sega were two of Electronic Arts's most important customers for its game software titles, the 3DO concept presented a threat to them and therefore had to be set up as a separate enterprise with Hawkins at its helm.

Hawkins saw a trend in the confluence of computer, communication, and consumer electronics products. As communication lines carried more information, including video images, and as computers became more powerful even as their prices fell, he developed the concept of a technology standard that would allow powerful multimedia players connected to a communication network to download game software titles and other interactive entertainment for the family. A number of large industry players stood to capitalize on these trends, including:

■ Computer companies — Apple Computer, IBM, and Silicon Graphics;

■ Telecommunications companies — AT&T, MCI, and US West;

■ Cable companies — Tele-Communications Inc. (TCI) and Time Warner Cable;

■ Consumer electronics companies — Sony and Matsushita; and

■ Game software companies — Electronic Arts, Nintendo, and Sega.

Hawkins decided that the focus of 3DO should be the development of a technology standard used for multimedia players and game software. The company's target market strategy was typical of other high technology start-ups: Provide the people who were innovators (500,000 consumers) with an exciting new technology, then bring the price/performance parameters down to a level at which the early adopters (several million consumers) would try the product. Continue to focus on value, software availability, and price to convince the interactive system users (approximately 50 million consumer households) who already owned video game consoles or personal computers that they too needed this interactive system. Finally, Hawkins hoped that products would penetrate the mass market, reaching those consumers who have television sets but are not current users of interactive multimedia products (more than 90% of the U.S. population).

The company developed quickly for a new start-up. From the beginning, Hawkins realized the importance of bringing in other partners, such as product suppliers and technology promoters, to share the technological and financial risks. He signed agreements with AT&T to develop the computer graphics integrated circuits (chipset), Matsushita to manufacture the interactive game players, and Time Warner to contribute portions of its media archives and develop interactive software titles; in addition, he signed agreements with a host of software companies to produce the game software titles that would run using 3DO's technology standard, including Electronic Arts. He also brought in venture capital investors Kleiner Perkins Caufield & Byers, which had invested in many successful start-ups and would provide funding to other companies developing software titles for the 3DO platform.

In May 1993, 3DO went public in an initial public offering (IPO) at $15 per share, raising more than $40 million for the development of the technology, working capital needs, and the acquisition of complementary businesses, products, and technologies. For a company with no revenues, and losses totaling more than $13 million in the year and a half since it was founded, the IPO looked a lot like those for biotechnology companies. The total market valuation of 3DO was almost $300 million, and investor interest in the multimedia company was overwhelming—the stock rose quickly to

---

Inside Story, continued

$20 on the first day of trading, and by the next month had risen to more than $25 per share, putting the company's total valuation at more than $450 million.

By October, the stock had reached $48 a share. But seven months later, in May 1994 (one year after the company went public), the stock price fell to below $10 per share. Hurt by slow sales of the Interactive Multiplayer—due in part to its relatively high price and the dearth of software titles to play on the Multiplayer—and increased competition from rivals Sony Corporation, Sega, and Nintendo, 3DO had run into tough times. In June 1994, 3DO sold $36.8 million of stock at $12.375 a share to new Asian investors and its initial equity partners. This capital infusion was necessary to keep 3DO afloat. As of mid-August 1994, the stock traded at $13.50 a share.

The 3DO Company's Business Model

What had investors seen in this company that made it unique from other game software companies? To begin with, most of the company's revenues were expected to come from the technology licenses it granted to others, not from the sale of the game players and software titles that it manufactured. This allowed the company to focus on its core capability, the development of a technology standard around which other multimedia hardware and software companies could coalesce. The 3DO technology license was provided at no cost to the hardware game manufacturers, and by April 1994, Matsushita, AT&T, Sanyo, Toshiba, Samsung, and Goldstar had signed hardware license agreements with 3DO. Software title producers were required to pay a royalty of $3 per copy of a software title to use the 3DO license. By May 1994, the company had shipped more than 550 software development systems to more than 200 licensee companies worldwide. 3DO provided the training and technical support for its standard, but it was not involved in the sales or distribution of any products. In a sense, Hawkins had developed the company into a "virtual corporation." This organizational form was characterized by a web of close relationships among its customers, suppliers, and potential competitors that enabled the company to take advantage of a market opportunity by combining the core capabilities of different companies to bring a new product to market faster than if the company itself had developed all of the capabilities internally.[5] 3DO did not plan to manufacture or market any of the game players or software titles. Rather, it sought to maintain technological leadership and support its licensees.

The 3DO Company went beyond a normal joint venture or strategic alliance. Joint ventures are typically a collection of two or more companies that partner up for a specific project, each holding an ownership stake in the joint venture firm. A strategic alliance is usually a collection of companies that agree on the technical direction of their respective business, without sharing equity ownership in a distinct joint venture. What Hawkins had done was to combine unique features of the joint venture and the strategic alliance. He brought a host of companies from different industries together to agree upon a technical standard, and signed them to contracts as suppliers of computer chips, hardware game players, and game software titles, all of which would run on the 3DO technology standard. Furthermore, he aligned the companies' interests with 3DO's by "allowing" them to take equity stakes in 3DO, and thus shared the financial risk of development with them, while at the same time, giving them a significant opportunity of upside return if the technology became a multimedia standard and gained mass market popularity. To gain credibility in the financial world and ease the transition from a start-up to a public company, Hawkins brought in venture investors such as Kleiner Perkins Caufield & Byers, which had contributed to the development of other successful start-up companies such as Apple Computer and Silicon Graphics.

3DO's strategy and form of business organization brought it and its corporate partners much initial publicity and success. In fact, soon after the IPO, the four corporate partners and the venture capital firm all had large "paper" returns on their initial investments of capital and technology in the company. The large initial invest-

---

5. *See* William H. Davidow and Michael S. Malone, *The Virtual Corporation* (1992), and John A. Byrne, "The Virtual Corporation," *Business Week*, February 8, 1993, 98-103.

Inside Story continued on following page

Inside Story, continued

ment returns for these companies predicted success for 3DO's unique form of business organization and the potential of the interactive multimedia market. Yet 3DO's own interests and the fortunes and future of its alliance partners were intricately intertwined, which brought some problems for the company.

Problems for 3DO

The company is threatened by the conflicts of interest among its corporate partners who have joined a number of alliances that compete with the 3DO technology standard. AT&T formed an alliance with and invested money in the EO Corporation and General Magic to develop personal intelligent communicators that may be applicable to interactive information or video services. Matsushita is also a member of the General Magic alliance. In addition, Time Warner entered into a number of alliances with cable, computer, and communication companies to exploit the growing multimedia market. Furthermore, Electronic Arts's position as a major supplier to Nintendo and Sega, both of which would be affected by 3DO's entry into the interactive multimedia market, put it in a conflicted situation with 3DO. The 3DO organizational structure may bring benefits in product development and the establishment of a technology standard. However, it also carries the burden of conflict and coordination problems.

The company also faces significant competition. Other computer hardware and software, communications, and consumer electronics companies recognized the massive potential of this market and put together their own alliances. In 1993, a myriad of different companies and alliances were announced to develop products for the interactive multimedia market—some complementary to 3DO's technology and others competitive with it. Several large Japanese companies, including Sony Corporation and Fujitsu Limited, have developed video devices that utilize a CD-ROM drive. In addition, several major computer product manufacturers, including Apple Computer Inc., Microsoft Corporation, Silicon Graphics Inc., and Sony Corporation, are developing products to compete directly with the 3DO Interactive Multiplayer. Sega of America created an add-on (Genesis 32X) to soup up its 16-bit cartridge and CD-ROM machines.

Other announced alliances include one between the Microsoft Corporation, the largest software company; Time Warner Inc., the largest entertainment company; and Tele-Communications Inc., the largest cable company, to develop a software standard for interactive television. Microsoft also formed a joint venture with Intel Corporation, the world's largest semiconductor manufacturer, and General Instrument Corporation, the largest maker of set-top control boxes for cable television, to develop a cable converter that would have a built-in personal computer to deliver interactive multimedia products. Time Warner set up a competing alliance to develop an interactive network with a set-top converter developed by Scientific-Atlanta Inc., built by Toshiba, and based on the Mips chip made by Silicon Graphics Inc. Time Warner formed another alliance with Tele-Communications Inc. and Sega of America Inc. to give owners of the Sega Genesis video game machines access to a large library of video games over cable television.

Although these cooperative ventures threaten 3DO, they might also validate its unique business model and the market potential that the company identified. However, it is unclear whether 3DO will be the company to develop the multimedia standard,[6] especially as litigation in the consumer electronics industry has increasingly been used as a competitive tactic both by established companies seeking to protect their existing position in the market and by emerging companies attempting to gain access to the market. Complaints have been filed on a number of grounds, including antitrust, breach of contract, trade secret, patent, copyright, and unfair business practices. If the company is forced to defend itself against claims such as these, it will incur substantial expense and diversion of management attention, and will encounter market confusion and increased reluctance of licensees to commit to the 3DO platform.

---

6. "Home Entertainment: Tripping," *The Economist*, June 12, 1993, 80.

Key Words and Phrases

alter ego theory **658**
appraisal rights **649**
articles of incorporation **646**
bidder **649**
bust-up takeover **654**
bylaws **646**
certificate of incorporation **646**
classified board **645**
close corporation **645**
corporate charter **646**
corporate domicile **645**
corporation by estoppel **647**
cumulative voting **658**
de facto corporation **646**

de jure corporation **646**
Delaware Court of Chancery **649**
disappearing corporation **648**
entrenchment **654**
estopped **647**
foreign corporation **645**
freeze-out merger **649**
incorporation **645**
inside director **651**
leveraged buyout **651**
outside director **651**
pierce the corporate veil **658**
poison pill **654**
privately held corporation **645**

proxy **657**
proxy contest **655**
publicly held corporation **645**
quorum **657**
second-step back-end merger **651**
shareholders of record **657**
staggered board **645**
surviving corporation **648**
takeover **651**
target corporation **651**
tender offer **649**
undercapitalization theory **658**

Questions and Case Problems

1. What are the procedures for incorporation that should be followed to ensure that the corporate form cannot be successfully challenged?

2. Amy Rockwell was a brilliant but penniless electrical engineer. She had designed a new type of cogeneration plant that she believed had great commercial potential. On January 15, she approached Benjamin Furst, a successful and experienced manager in the energy field, with the idea of starting Cogen, Inc., a corporation devoted to building a plant based on this new design. Furst was enthusiastic. On January 28, he enlisted the support of Clyde Pfeffer, a well-known venture capitalist who had retired from venture capital work but was looking to invest the proceeds of his past endeavors. Pfeffer gave the green light on February 16 to establish the new enterprise.

Furst retained the law firm of Fumble & Botchem to handle the details of incorporation. Fumble, one of the partners, drafted the articles of incorporation and filed them with the secretary of state on February 28. He then advised his clients that the articles had been filed. In the filing documents, Fumble was listed as the incorporator. Because of a typographical error, the articles of incorporation filed with the secretary of state referred to the company as Cogene, not Cogen.

Rockwell, Furst, and Pfeffer decided that they would save further expense by completing the incorporation process without any more assistance from Fumble & Botchem. On March 3, they held what they called the meeting of incorporators to elect the directors, and proceeded to elect themselves to the board. As board members, they appointed themselves as the company's officers. They typed up the minutes of this meeting.

On March 4, the daily operations of Cogen, Inc. commenced. In all of their transactions with third parties, the officers represented themselves as doing business for the corporation. One of

these transactions was with Firstloan Bank, which lent the company $5 million. The representations in the loan agreement stated that the corporation had been duly formed, that it existed as a valid corporation under California law, and that the shares of stock owned by the various shareholders had been duly authorized and were fully paid.

On May 5, the corporation began building its cogeneration plant. Three months later, energy prices dropped drastically, and there was no longer a need for a cogeneration facility in that location. The corporation was forced to default on the bank loan. The lawyers for the bank, upon being informed that it would not receive any more loan payments, reviewed the original loan documents, the articles of incorporation, and the minutes of the first meeting of the incorporators. Upon reviewing these documents, they initiated an action directly against the three founders in their individual capacity for liability on the bank loan.

(a) What arguments can the lawyers for the bank make in their effort to hold the founders personally liable for the debt of the corporation? Should their arguments prevail?

(b) What counterarguments can the founders make to avoid such liability?

3. Robert Dexter was the sole force behind In Over Our Heads, Inc., a corporation designed to run a year-round community swimming pool. The enterprise was incorporated in the correct manner in January with Dexter as the manager and the only shareholder. Dexter contributed $100,000 of starting capital, which was just enough to purchase the pool, finance initial advertising, and leave a reserve of $10,000. The corporation had no liability insurance.

On March 10, the pool opened for business. The corporation operated with a profit over the next few months. In June,

Dexter took a two-week vacation to Europe and used a check from the company bank account to purchase his airline ticket. In November, he decided to have the pool repainted. Because business had slowed and the corporation's bank account did not have sufficient funds, Dexter wrote a personal check for this job.

Dexter feared he would not make enough money through the winter to turn a profit, so he decided to take a part-time job as a telephone salesperson for a real estate company. He used the swimming pool's office phone to make his calls, and made a substantial profit.

On February 11, a child drowned in the pool. His parents brought suit for wrongful death against the corporation and against Dexter in his individual capacity as owner. At the time of suit, the corporation had the $10,000 reserve and less than $1,000 in its bank account. Because of these limited funds, the child's parents hoped to recover most of their damages directly from Dexter.

What arguments can be made to hold Dexter liable for any debt of the corporation arising from this death? Should they prevail? How could Dexter have protected himself against such potential liability? Can an owner-manager of a small corporation guarantee that he will not be held liable for the corporation's debts?

4. Teri Simmons, the CEO of Streamline, Inc., a manufacturer and supplier of sports equipment and apparel, was playing golf with Arnold Lowell, whom Simmons was trying to recruit as the company's new vice president of marketing. At the 15th hole Simmons sensed that Lowell was wavering. Not wanting to lose him, she promised Lowell that if he came on board, he would receive a combination of employee stock options, which would vest over a period of five years; in addition, he would receive a certain amount of stock each year for free. To sweeten the pot further, Simmons threw in a cash bonus that would be paid at the end of the year. Lowell accepted the job and began working for Streamline.

One month later, there was a management rift between Simmons and the other directors. The board fired Simmons as CEO. Next they reviewed Lowell's compensation package, and sent him a memo stating that he could stay on at his regular salary, but the company would not honor Simmons's offer for the stock option, the stock bonus, or the cash bonus. Lowell sued to force the company to keep all of these benefits in place.

(a) What legal arguments will the company make to avoid giving these benefits?

(b) Will Lowell be able to retain any of them?

5. Petagogy, Inc. is a large, publicly held biotech corporation that has successfully developed and marketed vaccines for cats, dogs, and other domestic animals. Much of its success is based on the fact that the company possesses trade secrets and proprietary information not in the hands of its competitors. One of these competitors, Catavac, owns 10% of the outstanding shares of Petagogy. On May 28, the managers of Catavac made an official request to review Petagogy's shareholders' list, as well as the company's books and records.

The directors of Petagogy denied these requests and Catavac sued to force compliance. What arguments will the managers on each side make?

On July 26, while the suit was being litigated, the managers of Catavac decided to attempt to take control of the Petagogy board by waging a proxy fight. Petagogy has one million shares outstanding and has a seven-member board. The board is not staggered and shareholders have the right to cumulative voting.

How many more shares, above the 100,000 it already owns, must Catavac win over to its side to gain majority control of the Petagogy board?

6. Three people proposed to incorporate and asked an attorney to assist them. The attorney was instructed to investigate and determine in which state they should incorporate. The attorney made his decision, and the three promoters adopted his plan. The company was incorporated with the three promoters as its only directors.

The attorney's services were performed and expenses were incurred at the request of the three promoters of the corporation, who promised to pay the attorney $1,500 for his services. Could the promoters legally bind the corporation as the corporation's agents? Did the corporation, at the time of its creation, adopt the contract of its promoters? [*Kridelbaugh v. Aldrehn Theatres Co.*, 191 N.W. 803 (Iowa 1923)]

7. Joseph Walker is president of Music City Sawmill Co. and Music City Lumber Company, both Tennessee corporations. On January 27, 1982, Walker allegedly purchased a wheel loader from Thompson & Green Machinery Co. and signed a promissory note on behalf of Sawmill for it. However, on January 27, 1982, Sawmill was not a corporation, a fact unknown to Walker or to Thompson & Green Machinery Co. The company was actually incorporated on January 28, 1982, one day after the sale of the wheel loader.

Sawmill was unable to make its payments, and returned the wheel loader on August 27, 1982. Thompson & Green sold the wheel loader for $15,303, but a balance of $17,925 remained on the note. Thompson & Green then brought suit against Walker to recover the balance. Is Walker liable for the debt? Is Sawmill a de facto corporation? [*Thompson & Green Machinery Co. v. Music City Lumber Co.*, 683 S.W.2d 340 (Tenn. App. 1984)]

8. On March 1, 1983, Widget Company purchased more than 63% of the Bolt Company's common shares from its majority shareholder for $25 per share. Widget agreed that it would pay the same price if it acquired the remaining shares of Bolt stock within one year. Toward the end of the year, Widget decided to acquire the remaining Bolt stock. On March 27, 1984, Widget received an opinion letter from an investment banking firm that a $20 price would be fair to Bolt's minority shareholders. Bolt's investment banking firm advised that its stock was worth $19 to $25 per share, but Widget refused to increase the price.

On July 5, 1984, Bolt was merged into Widget pursuant to a merger plan adopted by Bolt's board and ratified by its shareholders, mainly due to the fact that Widget voted its shares for the plan. The merger cashed out Bolt's minority shareholders at $20 per share. Bolt's shareholders brought suit alleging that the price offered was grossly inadequate, and that Widget unfairly manipulated the timing of the merger to avoid the one-year commitment. Do Bolt's shareholders have an appraisal remedy? [*Rabkin v. Hunt Chemical Corp.*, 498 A.2d 1099 (Del. 1985)]

9. Sullivan purchased an American Football League (AFL) franchise for a professional football team for $25,000. Several months later, he organized a corporation, the American League Professional Football Team of Boston. Sullivan contributed his AFL franchise, and nine other people contributed $25,000. In return, each of the ten investors received 10,000 shares of voting common stock in the corporation. Approximately four months later, the corporation sold 120,000 shares of nonvoting common stock to the public at $5 per share.

In 1975, Sullivan obtained control of all 100,000 voting shares of the corporation. He immediately used his control to vote out the other directors and elect a friendly board. In order to finance the purchase of the voting shares, Sullivan borrowed approximately $5,000,000. As a condition of the loan, Sullivan was to use his best efforts to organize the corporation so that its income could be devoted to the payment of the personal loan, and the assets of the corporation were pledged to secure the loan. In order to accomplish this goal, Sullivan had to eliminate the interests in the nonvoting shares.

In 1976, Sullivan organized a new corporation. The boards of directors of the new and old company executed a merger agreement for the two corporations, providing that after the merger the voting stock of the old corporation would be extinguished and the nonvoting stock would be exchanged for cash at $15 per share.

David Coggins owned ten shares of nonvoting stock in the old corporation. He voted against the merger and brought suit against what he alleged was an unfair and illegal transaction. Was the transaction unfair to the nonvoting shareholders? Should Coggins be able to receive an injunction to stop the merger? [*Coggins v. New England Patriots Football Club*, 492 N.E.2d 1112 (Mass. 1986)]

10. Company A was the target of a hostile tender offer by Company B, which had already acquired sufficient shares to be able to block any merger between the defendant and a third corporation. In order to dilute Company B's "blocking" position, Company A exchanged 75,000 of its unissued shares with the White Knight Corporation in return for the latter's stock. Company A then intended to sell its assets to the White Knight Corporation. Did Company A's actions deprive Company B of its right to assert the voting control it had obtained from its successful tender offer? Did Company B have a legitimate right to control the corporation? [*Condec Corp. v. Lunkenheimer Co.*, 230 A.2d 769 (Del. Ch. 1967)]

Chapter 21

DIRECTORS, OFFICERS, AND CONTROLLING SHAREHOLDERS

■ Introduction

Fiduciary Duties

Directors and officers are agents of the corporation and owe a fiduciary duty to the corporation and its shareholders. They are legally obliged to act primarily for the benefit of the shareholders. Under certain circumstances, a majority or controlling shareholder owes a fiduciary duty to other shareholders. As Judge Cardozo (later a Supreme Court justice) stated, many forms of conduct permissible in the business world for those acting at arm's length are forbidden to those bound by fiduciary ties. A trustee, he said, is held to something stricter than the morals of the marketplace. Not mere honesty, but the "punctilio of honor," is the standard of behavior for fiduciaries, according to Judge Cardozo.[1]

Chapter Summary

This chapter outlines the duties of directors and officers, including the duty of loyalty and the duty of care. A central basis for analyzing director and officer authority and liability, the business judgment rule, is discussed generally and in the context of a decision whether to sell a company. Statutory limitations on directors' liability are also addressed. The chapter discusses the fiduciary duties of officers, especially in the area of corporate opportunities, and the duties of controlling shareholders in a variety of situations, including the sale of a controlling block of stock, freeze-outs, and parent-subsidiary mergers. Finally, the chapter considers the payment of "greenmail" and "hushmail."

---

1. *Meinhard v. Salmon*, 249 N.Y. 458, 464, 164 N.E. 545, 546 (1928). See case 1.1.

■ Duties of Directors

Directors and officers have a duty of loyalty and a duty of care.

Duty of Loyalty

Directors of a corporation have an obligation to act in good faith and in what they believe to be the best interest of the corporation. They must put aside whatever personal interest they may have in a transaction under consideration. This is the *duty of loyalty*.

Duty of Care

Directors also have an obligation to act with the same care that a reasonably prudent person would exercise under similar circumstances. The *duty of care* includes a duty to be informed when making decisions. The directors may rely on information, opinions, reports, financial statements, and other financial data, prepared or presented by officers of the corporation whom the directors believe to be reliable and competent. Directors may also rely on counsel, independent accountants, or other persons as to matters that the directors believe in good faith to be within such person's professional or expert competence.

Director Liability

A director's breach of the duty of care or loyalty can lead to multimillion-dollar liability. For example, the directors of Trans Union Corporation were held liable for $23.5 million—$13.5 million in excess of their liability insurance coverage—because they approved the sale of Trans Union at $55 a share without having first informed themselves of the company's intrinsic value, which was allegedly higher. (The case is discussed later in this chapter; the stock was trading at the time at $37 a share.) Although the purchasers, the Pritzker family, ultimately paid the amount by which the settlement exceeded the directors' insurance coverage, they were not legally obligated to do so.

> **❝**
>
> *A director's breach of the duty of care or loyalty can lead to multimillion-dollar liability.*

In another case, the *Delaware Court of Chancery* (the trial court in Delaware that hears corporate law cases)

held directors personally liable for $6 million, the difference between the amount paid for the shares of United States Sugar in a tender offer and the actual value of the shares. The directors were found to have breached their fiduciary duty by not providing the shareholders with all relevant information concerning the offer and the target company when recommending the offer.

The cost of directors' and officers' insurance, when it is available at all, has skyrocketed. If the directors' liability cannot be covered by insurance, the company often has to pick up the bill under an indemnification agreement with the directors; however, the scope of such agreements is limited by law. For these reasons, some companies are finding it difficult to find qualified individuals willing to serve as directors.

■ The Business Judgment Rule

In cases challenging board decisions, the courts generally defer to the business judgment of the directors, acknowledging that a courtroom is not the appropriate forum to review the soundness of directors' decisions. Courts are ill equipped to second-guess those decisions at a later date. Thus, under the *business judgment rule*, so long as certain standards are met, a court will presume that the directors have acted in good faith and in the honest belief that the action taken was in the best interest of the company. The court will not question whether the action was wise or whether the directors made an error of judgment or a business mistake.

Effect on Directors' Burden of Proof

This presumption under the business judgment rule can only be rebutted (overcome) by a showing by a complaining party that the directors acted in bad faith, engaged in fraudulent conduct, or were grossly negligent in carrying out their duties. Otherwise, the court will presume that the directors satisfied their duties of loyalty and care, and will not require the directors to prove that they acted prudently. On the other hand, if the business judgment rule does not apply to a transaction, the courts generally require the directors to prove that they were not negligent, and that the transaction in question was entered into in good faith and was fair and reasonable to the corporation.

Informed Decision

The business judgment rule is only applicable if the directors make an informed decision. The general corporation law of most jurisdictions authorizes directors to rely on the reports of officers and certain outside experts; however, passive reliance on such reports may result in an insufficiently informed decision, as in the following case.

■ A Case in Point: Summary

Case 21.1
SMITH v. VAN GORKOM
Supreme Court of Delaware
488 A.2d 858 (Del. 1985).

FACTS   Trans Union Corporation was a publicly traded, diversified holding company engaged in the railcar leasing business. Its stock was undervalued, largely due to accumulated investment tax credits. Jerome W. Van Gorkom, the chairman of the board of Trans Union, was reaching retirement age. He asked the chief financial officer, Donald Romans, to work out the per-share price at which a leveraged buyout could be done, given current cash flow. Romans came up with $55, based on debt-servicing requirements. He did not attempt to determine the intrinsic value of the company. Van Gorkom later met with Jay Pritzker and worked out a merger at $55 per share. Trans Union stock was then trading at about $37 per share.

Van Gorkom called a board meeting for September 20, 1980, on one day's notice to approve the merger. All of the directors were familiar with the company's operations as a going concern, but they were not apprised of the merger negotiations before the board meeting on September 20. They were also familiar with the current financial status of the company; a month earlier they had discussed a Boston Consulting Group strategy study. The ten-member board included five outside directors who were CEOs or board members of publicly held companies, and a former dean of the University of Chicago Business School.

Copies of the merger agreement were delivered to the directors, but too late for study before or during the meeting. The meeting began with a 20-minute oral presentation by Chairman Van Gorkom. The chief financial officer then described how he had arrived at the $55 figure. He stated that it was not an indication of a fair price, only a workable number. Trans Union's president stated that he thought the proposed merger was a good deal.

The board approved the merger after a two-hour meeting. Board members later testified that they had insisted that the merger agreement be amended to ensure that the company was free to consider other bids before the closing; however, neither the board minutes nor merger documents reflected this clearly.

Plaintiff Smith sued to challenge the board's action, arguing that the merger price was too low.

The Delaware Court of Chancery held that, given the premium over the market value of Trans Union stock, the business acumen of the board members, and the effect on the merger price of the prospect of other bids, the board was adequately informed and did not act recklessly in approving the Pritzker deal. In making its findings, the court relied in part upon actions taken by the board after the board meeting on September 20, 1980, which were intended to cure defects in the directors' initial level of knowledge.

ISSUE PRESENTED   Were directors who accepted and submitted to the shareholders a proposed cash merger without determining the intrinsic value of the company grossly negligent in failing to inform themselves adequately before making their decision?

SUMMARY OF OPINION   The Delaware Supreme Court reversed the lower court and held that the directors were grossly negligent in failing to reach a properly informed decision. They were not protected by the business judgment rule even though there were no allegations of bad faith, fraud, or conflict of interest. The court found that the directors could not reasonably base their decision on the inadequate information presented to the board. They should have independently valued the company.

The court found that the directors had inadequate information as to: (1) the role of Van Gorkom, Trans Union's chairman and chief executive officer, in initiating the transaction; (2) the basis for the proposed stock purchase price of $55 per share; and most importantly (3) the intrinsic value of Trans Union, as opposed to its current and historical stock price. The court held that in the absence of any apparent crisis or emergency, it was grossly negligent for the directors to approve the merger after a two-hour meeting, with eight of the ten directors having received no prior notice of the proposed merger. The court stated:

> None of the directors, management or outside, were investment bankers or financial analysts. Yet the board did not consider recessing the meeting until a later hour that day (or requesting an extension of Pritzker's Sunday evening deadline) to give it time to elicit more information as to the sufficiency of the offer, either from inside management (in particular Romans) or from Trans Union's own investment banker, Salomon Brothers, whose Chicago specialist in mergers and acquisitions was known to the Board and familiar with Trans Union's affairs.
>
> Thus, the record compels the conclusion that on September 20 the Board lacked valuation information adequate to reach an informed business judgment as to the fairness of $55 per share for sale of the Company.

The court additionally held that the directors' subsequent efforts to find a bidder willing to pay more than Pritzker were inadequate to cure the infirmities of their uninformed exercise of judgment.

The court rejected the directors' argument that they properly relied on the officers' reports presented at the board meeting. The court stated that a pertinent report may be relied on in good faith, but not blindly. In the circumstances, the directors were duty bound to make reasonable inquiry of Van Gorkom, the chief executive officer, and Romans, the chief financial officer. If they had done so, the inadequacy of those officers' reports would have been apparent. Van Gorkom's summary of the terms of the deal was inadequate because he had not reviewed the merger documents and was basically uninformed as to essential terms. Romans's report on price was inadequate because it was not a valuation study, just a cash flow-cash feasibility study.

The court also held that the mere fact that a substantial premium over the market price was being offered did not justify board approval of the merger. According to the court, a premium may be one reason to approve a merger, but sound information as to the company's intrinsic value is required to assess the fairness of an offer. In this case there was no attempt to determine the company's intrinsic value.

RESULT The Delaware Supreme Court found that the Trans Union directors were grossly negligent in making an uninformed decision regarding the proposed merger agreement. The case was remanded to the Delaware Court of Chancery for an evidentiary hearing to determine the fair value of the shares based on Trans Union's intrinsic value on September 20, 1980, the day of the board's meeting in which the Pritzker offer was considered. If

*Case **21.1** continued on following page*

*Case **21.1** continued*

that value was found by the chancellor to be higher than $55 per share, the directors would be liable for the difference.

COMMENTS   *Smith v. Van Gorkom* was one of the most highly debated corporate law cases ever decided. Three years after the decision, one of the key defendants—Trans Union's chief executive officer, Jerome W. Van Gorkom—wrote an article giving the defendants' side of the story. The article makes it clear that the defendants and the Delaware Supreme Court had very different views about what the directors actually did, and what their options really were. In his article Van Gorkom stated that at the September 20 meeting:

> The directors, all broadly experienced executives, realized that an all-cash offer with a premium of almost 50 percent represented an unusual opportunity for the shareholders. They also knew, however, that $55 might not be the highest price obtainable. At the meeting, therefore, there was considerable discussion about seeking an outside "fairness opinion" that might shed further light on the ultimate value of the company.[2]

Furthermore, Van Gorkom explained that:

> Acceptance of the offer was not a decision by the directors that the company should be sold for $55 a share. The acceptance was the only mechanism by which the offer could be preserved for the shareholders. *They* would make the ultimate decision as to the fairness of the price and they would do so only after the free market had had ample time in which to determine if $55 was the top value obtainable. The market's opinion would be definitive and worth infinitely more to the shareholders than any theoretical evaluation opinion that the directors could obtain in 39 hours or even longer. On this reasoning the offer was accepted.

Following the meeting the Trans Union directors hired Salomon Brothers to conduct an intensive search for a higher bidder. In addition, Van Gorkom stated that once the $55 offer became a matter of public knowledge, an auction occurred in the market with Trans Union's stock sometimes selling above $56 on the New York Stock Exchange. After three months of the intensive search and the public auction, no higher bid was ever received. "[T]he market had proven beyond a shadow of a doubt that $55 was the highest price obtainable."

Because of the above factors, Van Gorkom believes that he and the other Trans Union directors wholeheartedly fulfilled their fiduciary obligations. He concludes that their actions clearly should have been protected under the business judgment rule.

Although the holding in *Van Gorkom* seems clear, sometimes boards of directors still do not follow the rules regarding their duties of due care to inform shareholders in the sales of corporations. For example, in the 1993 Delaware Supreme Court case of *Cede & Co. v. Technicolor, Inc.*[3] the court found at least five problems with the Technicolor board's exercise of due care in approving a merger agreement whereby Technicolor was acquired

---

2.   J. W. Van Gorkom, "Van Gorkom's Response: The Defendant's Side of the Trans Union Case," reprinted in *Mergers & Acquisitions*, January/February 1988. Excerpts reprinted by permission.
3.   634 A.2d 345 (Del. 1993).

by MacAndrews & Forbes Group (a company controlled by Ronald O. Perelman).[4]

---

4. The five problems identified by the court were: (1) the agreement was not preceded by a prudent search for alternatives; (2) given the terms of the merger and the circumstances, the directors had no reasonable basis to assume that a better offer from a third party could be expected to be made following the agreement's signing; (3) although the buyer's approach had been discussed with several of the directors before the meeting, most of the directors had little or no knowledge of an impending sale of the company until they arrived at the meeting, and only a few of them had any knowledge of the terms of the sale and of the required side agreements; (4) the intended buyer did, probably, effectively lock up the transaction before the meeting when he acquired rights to buy certain shares from two of the largest shareholders of Technicolor; and (5) the board did not satisfy its obligation to take reasonable steps to be adequately informed before it authorized the execution of the merger agreement.

Written and Reasoned Opinion Many thought that the way to avoid the problems encountered in the *Van Gorkom* case was to hire an investment banker to advise the board before the board takes action. As the directors of SCM Corporation learned in another case, that is sometimes not enough. The opinion must be in writing and be reasoned.

In *Hanson Trust PLC v. ML SCM Acquisition, Inc.*,[5] SCM was the subject of a hostile tender offer by a British conglomerate, Hanson Trust PLC. SCM's board negotiated a friendly management leveraged buyout led by "white knight" Merrill Lynch. As part of this agreement, SCM granted Merrill Lynch an *asset lock-up option* to purchase two divisions of SCM, considered SCM's key assets or *crown jewels*. The option was exercisable if Merrill Lynch were not successful in acquiring control of SCM. A *lock-up option* is a kind of consolation prize for the loser in a bidding war; depending on how it is priced, a lock-up option can have the effect of deterring other bids.

SCM's directors had been orally advised by their investment banker, Goldman Sachs, that the option prices were "within the range of fair value." However, the directors did not inquire what the range of fair value was or how it was calculated. The directors had been advised by preeminent outside counsel that the decision whether to approve the lock-up was within the discretion of the board in exercising its business judgment. Further, white knight Merrill Lynch had represented in negotiations that it would not proceed with its leveraged buyout offer

without the lock-up. Notwithstanding these factors and the directors' own working knowledge of the company, the U.S. Court of Appeals for the Second Circuit held that the SCM directors' "paucity of information" and "their swiftness of decision-making" strongly suggested a breach of the duty of care.

Note that the SCM board did receive a written fairness opinion from an investment banking firm on the overall deal—the sale of SCM to Merrill Lynch. However, it received only an off-the-cuff opinion on the fairness of the prices at which two divisions were to be sold to Merrill Lynch under the lock-up option. Unfortunately for the directors, the banker had not in fact calculated the fair value of the two divisions. In relying on his opinion, therefore, the board was not adequately informed.

Disinterested Decision

Even when the board makes an informed decision, the business judgment rule is not applicable if the directors have a financial or other personal interest in the transaction at issue. For example, if a board of inside directors (that is, directors who are also officers of the corporation) were setting executive compensation, they could be required to prove to a court that the transaction was fair and reasonable. To be disinterested in the transaction normally means that the directors can neither have an interest on either side of the transaction, nor expect to derive any personal financial benefit from the transaction (other than benefits that accrue to all shareholders of the corporation, that are not considered self-dealing).

One or more individual directors may have an interest in the transaction, provided it is approved by a majority of the disinterested directors. However, if the board dele-

---

5. 781 F.2d 264 (2d Cir. 1986).

gates too much of its authority, or is too much influenced by an interested party, then the entire board may be tainted with that individual's personal motivations and lose the protection of the business judgment rule.

In some jurisdictions, a relevant factor in determining whether a board is disinterested is whether the majority of the board consists of outside directors. The fact that outside directors receive directors' fees but not salaries is viewed as heightening the likelihood that the directors were not motivated by personal interest.

The Delaware Supreme Court in *Mills Acquisition Co. v. Macmillan, Inc.*[6] reiterated the duty that corporate directors have to demonstrate their utmost good faith and fairness in transactions in which they possess a financial, business, or other personal interest that is not shared by the corporation or all shareholders generally. For instance, in *Mills* the asset lock-up option granted to a white knight by the target corporation as part of a merger agreement was deemed invalid. The other participant in the auction had indicated its intent to top any offer made by the white knight. Under the agreement between the target and the white knight, target management would receive different consideration from that given the public. Therefore, the lock-up option, which had the effect of terminating any further bidding, did not enhance general shareholder interests. Furthermore, the court held that independent members of the corporation's board of directors should have attempted to negotiate alternative bids for the corporate assets before they granted any bidder a lock-up option intended to end the active auction.

Takeover Defenses   If a hostile raider is successful, it is probably going to replace the company's management and board of directors as its first step after assuming control. A successful defense against the takeover has the effect of preserving the positions of current management and directors. Thus, the directors arguably have a personal interest whenever a board opposes a hostile takeover. However, as in the following case, the courts have applied the business judgment rule to takeover defenses, provided the directors can show that there was a perceived threat to the corporation to which the defense was a reasonable response.

> 66
>
> *The directors arguably have a personal interest whenever a board opposes a hostile takeover.*

---

6.   559 A.2d 1261 (Del. 1989).

■   **A Case in Point:**   **In the Language of the Court**

Case 21.2
UNOCAL CORP. v. MESA PETROLEUM CO.
Supreme Court of Delaware
493 A.2d 946 (Del. 1985).

FACTS   On April 8, 1985, Mesa Petroleum Co., the owner of approximately 13% of oil company Unocal's stock, commenced a two-tier "front loaded" cash tender offer for 64 million shares, or approximately 37%, of Unocal's outstanding stock at a price of $54 per share. Mesa was controlled by T. Boone Pickens. The "back-end" was designed to eliminate the remaining publicly held shares by an exchange of securities purportedly worth $54 per share. However, pursuant to an order entered by the United States District Court for the Central District of California on April 26, 1985, Mesa issued a supplemental proxy statement to Unocal's shareholders disclosing that the securities offered in the second-step merger would be highly subordinated, and that Unocal's capitalization would differ significantly from its present structure. Unocal rather aptly termed such securities "junk bonds."

Various defensive strategies were available to the board if it concluded that Mesa's two-step tender offer was inadequate and should be opposed. One of the devices was a self-tender by Unocal for its own stock. Unocal's vice president of finance and its assistant general counsel made a detailed presentation to the Unocal board of the proposed terms of the exchange offer. A price range between $70 and $80 per share was considered, and ultimately the directors agreed upon $72. The board was also advised about the debt securities that would be issued (the cost of the proposal was estimated to be $6.1 to $6.6 billion), and about the necessity of placing restrictive covenants upon certain corporate activities until the obligations were paid. The board's decisions were made in reliance on the advice of its investment bankers, including the terms and conditions upon which the securities were to be issued. Based upon this advice, and the board's own deliberations, the directors unanimously approved the exchange offer. Their resolution provided that if Mesa acquired 64 million shares of Unocal stock through its own offer, Unocal would buy the remaining 49% of Unocal's outstanding shares for an exchange of debt securities having an aggregate par value of $72 per share. The board resolution also stated that the offer would be subject to conditions described to the board at the meeting, or deemed necessary by Unocal's officers, including the exclusion of Mesa from the proposal.

Legal counsel advised that under Delaware law Mesa could only be excluded for what the directors reasonably believed to be a valid corporate purpose. The directors' discussion centered on the objective of adequately compensating shareholders at the "back-end" of Mesa's proposal, which the latter would finance with "junk bonds." To include Mesa would defeat that goal, because under the proration aspect of the exchange offer, every Mesa share accepted by Unocal would displace one held by another shareholder. Further, if Mesa were permitted to tender to Unocal, the latter would in effect be financing Mesa's own inadequate proposal.

On April 29, 1985, the Delaware Court of Chancery temporarily restrained Unocal from proceeding with the exchange offer unless it included Mesa. The trial court recognized that directors could oppose, and attempt to defeat, a hostile takeover which they considered adverse to the best interests of the corporation. However, the Delaware Court of Chancery decided that in a selective purchase of the company's stock, the corporation bears the burden of showing: (1) a valid corporate purpose, and (2) that the transaction was fair to all of the shareholders, including those excluded. Unocal appealed.

ISSUE PRESENTED   Can a board of directors make a selective stock exchange offer in order to protect a corporation and its shareholders from one of the corporation's own shareholders that is attempting to make a hostile takeover? What standard of judicial review applies to defensive tactics designed to thwart a hostile takeover?

OPINION   MOORE, J., writing for the Delaware Supreme Court:

. . . .

III.

We begin with the basic issue of the power of a board of directors of a Delaware corporation to adopt a defensive measure of this type. . . .

. . . [I]t is now well established that in the acquisition of its shares a Delaware corporation may deal selectively with its stockholders, provided the directors have not acted out of a sole or primary purpose to entrench themselves in office.

. . . .

When a board addresses a pending takeover bid it has an obligation to determine whether the offer is in the best interests of the corporation and its shareholders. In that respect a board's duty is no different from any other responsibility it shoulders, and its decisions should be no less entitled

Case 21.2 continued on following page

Case **21.2** *continued*

to the respect they otherwise would be accorded in the realm of business judgment. There are, however, certain caveats to a proper exercise of this function. Because of the omnipresent specter that a board may be acting primarily in its own interests, rather than those of the corporation and its shareholders, there is an enhanced duty which calls for judicial examination at the threshold before the protections of the business judgment rule may be conferred.

. . . .

. . . [D]irectors must show that they had reasonable grounds for believing that a danger to corporate policy and effectiveness existed because of another person's stock ownership. However, they satisfy that burden "by showing good faith and reasonable investigation. . . ."[7] Furthermore, such proof is materially enhanced, as here, by the approval of a board comprised of a majority of outside independent directors who have acted in accordance with the foregoing standards.

IV.

A.

In the board's exercise of corporate power to forestall a takeover bid our analysis begins with the basic principle that corporate directors have a fiduciary duty to act in the best interests of the corporation's stockholders. As we have noted, their duty of care extends to protecting the corporation and its owners from perceived harm whether a threat originates from third parties or other shareholders. But such powers are not absolute. A corporation does not have unbridled discretion to defeat any perceived threat by any Draconian means available.

The restriction placed upon a selective stock repurchase is that the directors may not have acted solely or primarily out of a desire to perpetuate themselves in office. . . . [This] is designed to ensure that a defensive measure to thwart or impede a takeover is indeed motivated by a good faith concern for the welfare of the corporation and its stockholders, which in all circumstances must be free of any fraud or other misconduct. . . .

B.

A further aspect is the element of balance. If a defensive measure is to come within the ambit of the business judgment rule, it must be reasonable in relation to the threat posed. This entails an analysis by the directors of the nature of the takeover bid and its effect on the corporate enterprise. Examples of such concerns may include: inadequacy of the price offered, nature and timing of the offer, questions of illegality, the impact on "constituencies" other than shareholders (i.e., creditors, customers, employees, and perhaps even the community generally), the risk of nonconsummation, and the quality of securities being offered in the exchange. While not a controlling factor, it also seems to us that a board may reasonably consider the basic stockholder interests at stake, including those of short term speculators, whose actions may have fueled the coercive aspect of the offer at the expense of the long term investor. Here, the threat posed was viewed by the Unocal board as a grossly inadequate two-tier coercive tender offer coupled with the threat of greenmail.

---

7. *Cheff v. Mathes*, 199 A.2d 548, 554-55 (Del. 1964).

. . . .

Thus, we are satisfied that the selective exchange offer is reasonably related to the threats posed. . . . [T]he board's decision to offer what it determined to be the fair value of the corporation to the 49% of its shareholders, who would otherwise be forced to accept highly subordinated "junk bonds," is reasonable and consistent with the directors' duty to ensure that the minority stockholders receive equal value for their shares.

. . . .

V.

Mesa contends that it is unlawful, and the trial court agreed, for a corporation to discriminate in this fashion against one shareholder. . . .

. . . .

[A]s the sophistication of both raiders and targets has developed, a host of . . . defensive measures to counter such ever mounting threats has evolved and received judicial sanction. These include defensive charter amendments and other devices bearing some rather exotic, but apt, names: Crown Jewel, White Knight, Pac Man, and Golden Parachute. Each has highly selective features, the object of which is to deter or defeat the raider.

Thus, while the exchange offer is a form of selective treatment, given the nature of the threat posed here the response is neither unlawful nor unreasonable. If the board of directors is disinterested, has acted in good faith and with due care, its decision in the absence of an abuse of discretion will be upheld as a proper exercise of business judgment.

. . . .

. . . [I]n the face of the destructive threat Mesa's tender offer was perceived to pose, the board had a supervening duty to protect the corporate enterprise, which includes the other shareholders, from threatened harm.

. . . .

VI.

In conclusion, there was directorial power to oppose the Mesa tender offer, and to undertake a selective stock exchange made in good faith and upon a reasonable investigation pursuant to a clear duty to protect the corporate enterprise. Further, the selective stock repurchase plan chosen by Unocal is reasonable in relation to the threat that the board rationally and reasonably believed was posed by Mesa's inadequate and coercive two-tier tender offer. Under those circumstances the board's action is entitled to be measured by the standards of the business judgment rule. Thus, unless it is shown by a preponderance of the evidence that the directors' decisions were primarily based on perpetuating themselves in office, or some other breach of fiduciary duty such as fraud, overreaching, lack of good faith, or being uninformed, a Court will not substitute its judgment for that of the board.

*Case **21.2** continued on following page*

*Case **21.2** continued*

. . . .

RESULT   The board of directors of Unocal could legally make a discriminatory stock repurchase plan available to some of its shareholders in order to protect them and the corporation from a coercive hostile takeover attempt by Mesa Petroleum, one of the other shareholders.

COMMENTS   The strategy used in this case is no longer available because of the SEC's "all holders rule." According to the rule, a selective stock repurchase plan is deemed a tender offer in which all holders of securities of the same class must be allowed to participate. Nonetheless, this case remains key Delaware precedent for the analysis of defensive tactics.

Questions
1. Do you agree with the court that the fact that some members of the board of directors were large shareholders in the corporation should not disqualify them from making a decision regarding a selective stock repurchase plan such as the one found in this case?
2. In the 1990s there have been fewer hostile takeover attempts than there were in the 1980s. Do you think that the laws regarding defensive maneuvers available to boards of directors should, therefore, be tightened to reflect this trend?

■ Directors' Decision About Selling the Company

In deciding whether to sell a company, the courts have held that directors should consider seven key factors: (1) the company's intrinsic value; (2) nonprice considerations; (3) the reliability of officers' reports to the board; (4) the appropriateness of delegating negotiating authority to management; (5) the reliability of experts' reports; (6) the investment banker's fee structure; and (7) the reasonableness of any defensive tactics.

The Company's Intrinsic Value

The ability to make an informed decision as to the acceptability of a proposed buyout price requires knowledge of the company's intrinsic value. Determining intrinsic value entails more than an assessment of the premium of the offering price over the market price per share of the company's stock. When, as in *Van Gorkom,* it is believed that the market has consistently undervalued the company's stock, to evaluate the offered price by comparing it with the market price is "faulty, indeed fallacious."

Thus, the directors must not only assess the adequacy of the premium and how the premium compares with that

paid in other takeovers in the same or similar industries; they must also assess the intrinsic or fair value of the company (or division) as a going concern and on a liquidation basis.

Practitioners have read *Van Gorkom* as virtually mandating participation by an investment banker if directors are to avoid personal liability. However, the *Van Gorkom* court expressly disclaimed such an intention:

> We do not imply that an outside valuation study is essential to support an informed business judgment; nor do we state that fairness opinions by independent investment bankers are required as a matter of law. Often insiders familiar with the business of a going concern are in a better position than are outsiders to gather relevant information; and under appropriate circumstances, such directors may be fully protected in relying in good faith upon the valuation reports of their management.[8]

Hence one commentator's quip that it would be "an overstatement to consider the *Van Gorkom* case as the Investment Bankers' Relief Act of 1985." For all practical purposes, however, directors should look to both internal and external sources for guidance. The most reliable valuation information will consist of financial data

---

8. *Smith v. Van Gorkom*, 488 A.2d 858, 876 (Del. 1985).

supplied by management and evaluated by investment bankers.

The *Hanson Trust* decision makes it clear, however, that the mere presence of investment bankers in the target's boardroom will not shield its directors from personal liability. In that case, Goldman Sachs's oral opinion that the option prices were "within the range of fair value" did not withstand the scrutiny of the Second Circuit on appeal.

Nonprice Considerations

In evaluating a buyout proposal, directors have a fiduciary duty to familiarize themselves with any material nonprice provisions of the proposed agreement. Directors are duty bound to consider separately whether such provisions are in the best interest of the company and its shareholders, or, if not, whether the proposal as a whole, notwithstanding such provisions, is in the best interest of their constituencies.

In *Van Gorkom,* for example, several outside directors maintained that Pritzker's merger proposal was approved with the understanding that "if we got a better deal, we had a right to take it." The directors also asserted that they had "insisted" upon an amendment reserving to Trans Union the right to disclose proprietary information to competing bidders. However, the court found that the merger agreement reserved neither of these rights to Trans Union. In the court's view, the directors had "no rational basis" for asserting that their acceptance of Pritzker's offer was conditioned upon a market test of the offer or that Trans Union had a right to withdraw from the agreement in order to accept a higher bid.

Directors should therefore ensure not only that they correctly understand the nonprice provisions of a proposed merger agreement, but also that the provisions find their way into the definitive agreement. They should verify this by reading the documents prior to execution.

As indicated in *Unocal*, in analyzing a takeover bid and its effect on the corporate enterprise, the board may consider: (1) the adequacy of the price offered; (2) the nature and timing of the offer; (3) questions of legality; (4) the impact on constituencies other than the shareholders, for example, creditors, customers, employees, and perhaps the community generally; (5) the risk of nonconsummation; (6) the quality of the securities being offered in exchange; and (7) the basic shareholder interests at stake.

International Consideration

The laws of Germany and several Scandinavian countries require union and employee representation on the boards of directors of most public corporations. These representatives participate in all of the basic decisions related to investment policy, choice of product and technology, marketing, employee relations, and other matters of managerial concern.

Once the judgment is made that a sale is either unavoidable or in the best interests of the shareholders, directors have a fiduciary duty to obtain the best available price. This rule was first articulated in the following case.

■ **A Case in Point:**   **Summary**

Case 21.3
REVLON, INC. v.
MacANDREWS AND FORBES
HOLDINGS, INC.
Supreme Court of Delaware
506 A.2d 173 (Del. 1986).

FACTS   Revlon, Inc., a manufacturer of cosmetics, was the subject of a hostile takeover attempt by Pantry Pride, Inc., a large food corporation. (The major shareholder in Pantry Pride was MacAndrews and Forbes Holdings, Inc.) After initially resisting the takeover attempt, the Revlon board elected to go forward with a friendly buyout from another company at a lower price than that offered by the hostile bidder. The Revlon board sought to justify the lower price by pointing out the benefits of the friendly buyout for other corporate constituencies, such as the Revlon noteholders. Pantry Pride sued to enjoin this friendly buyout.

Case 21.3 continued on following page

*Case **21.3** continued*

ISSUE PRESENTED   Once the board decides to sell a company, must it try to achieve the best price on behalf of the company's shareholders?

SUMMARY OF OPINION   The Delaware Supreme Court required the Revlon board to seek the highest price for the shareholders. The court defined the duty of the directors as follows:

> The Revlon board's authorization permitting management to negotiate a merger or buyout with a third party was a recognition that the company was for sale. The duty of the board had thus changed from the preservation of Revlon as a corporate entity to the maximization of the company's value at a sale for the stockholders' benefit. . . . The directors' role changed from defenders of the corporate bastion to auctioneers charged with getting the best price for the stockholders at a sale of the company.

RESULT   In order to fulfill their duties as directors, once a board decides to sell a company, it must try to obtain the best available price.

COMMENTS   In *Barkan v. Amsted Industries, Inc.*[9] the Supreme Court of Delaware held that the basic teaching of cases such as *Revlon* is simply that directors of corporations must act in accordance with their fundamental duties of care and loyalty. However, the court ruled that acting in accordance with these duties does not mean that every change of corporate control necessitates an auction. If fairness to shareholders and the minimizing of conflicts of interest can be demonstrated, the added burden of having an auction may not be necessary.

The court in *Barkan* declined making a specific rule for determining when a market test (or "market check") is required. The court simply stated: "[I]t must be clear that the board had sufficient knowledge of relevant markets to form the basis for its belief that it acted in the best interests of the shareholders."[10]

---

9.   567 A.2d 1279 (Del. 1989).
10.   567 A.2d 1279, 1288 (Del. 1989).

It is doubtful that a failure of directors to consider every conceivable alternative would in itself amount to a breach of fiduciary duty. Such a rule would be unduly harsh. In hindsight, a complaining shareholder could almost always conjure up at least one alternative that the directors failed to consider. On the other hand, the failure of a board to consider any alternatives at all, or the unwillingness of a board to negotiate with anyone other than its chosen white knight (or with the initial offeror), would be a breach of fiduciary duty unless there were special circumstances.

The case of *Paramount Communications, Inc. v. Time Inc.*[11] (case 20.4) examined the question of what consti-tutes a change in control triggering the *Revlon* duty to maximize shareholder value. Time had entered into a friendly merger agreement with Warner. Under that agreement, roughly 60% of the stock of the new combined entity—Time-Warner—would be held by former public shareholders of Warner.

The Delaware Supreme Court held that this did not constitute a change in control, because majority control shifted from one "fluid aggregation of unaffiliated shareholders" to another. As a result, the Time board could properly take into account such intangibles as the desire to preserve the Time culture and journalistic integrity in deciding to reject Paramount's hostile tender offer, which was arguably worth more to shareholders than the Time-Warner combination. The court considered this to be a strategic alliance, not a sale of Time to Warner, which

---

11.   571 A.2d 1140 (Del. 1990).

Ethical Consideration

The fight between the management of Revlon and Pantry Pride for control of Revlon was one of the most acrimonious takeover battles on record. After the Delaware Supreme Court's decision, Pantry Pride won control of the company. The exiting CEO of Revlon received more than $15 million in a severance bonus that Revlon was required to pay in the event he was fired or resigned after a change of control in the corporation. Such a severance arrangement, called a golden parachute, is a form of takeover defense that increases the bidder's expense to purchase the target.

Such a bonus may create a conflict of interest for a corporate manager, if he believes that a takeover is not in the shareholders' best interest but knows he will receive a large golden parachute if the takeover is successful.

---

would have triggered the *Revlon* duty to maximize shareholder value.

Relying heavily on this precedent, Paramount entered into a friendly merger agreement with Viacom Inc. in September 1993. When QVC Network, Inc. made a hostile unsolicited offer for Paramount at a price worth $1.3 billion more than what Viacom was offering, the Paramount board refused to negotiate with QVC and instead stood by its merger agreement with Viacom. (The details of the negotiations and board meetings are described in the "Inside Story" at the end of this chapter.) In the following case, the Delaware Supreme Court examined the propriety of the Paramount board's action, especially in light of the fact that Viacom was controlled by a single individual, Sumner Redstone.

■ A Case in Point: In the Language of the Court

Case 21.4
PARAMOUNT COMMUNICATIONS INC. v. QVC NETWORK INC.
Supreme Court of Delaware
637 A.2d 34 (Del. 1994).

FACTS Beginning in the late 1980s, Paramount Communications Inc., which owned and operated a diverse group of entertainment businesses, investigated the possibility of acquiring or merging with other companies in the entertainment, media, or communications industry. Paramount considered such transactions to be desirable, and perhaps necessary, in order to keep pace with competitors in the rapidly evolving field of entertainment and communications.

In April 1993, Martin Davis, chairman and CEO of Paramount, met with Sumner Redstone, CEO, chairman, and majority owner of Viacom, a communications company that included MTV and Showtime Networks. After five months of discussions, they entered into a friendly merger agreement between Paramount and Viacom, along with other related agreements. Under these merger agreements, the Paramount shareholders would receive a combination of stock and cash that was then valued at $69.14 per share. In addition, Paramount amended its poison pill so that it would not be triggered by the Viacom deal.

Viacom and Paramount both made public statements to the effect that outside bids were unwelcome. However, in September 1993, QVC Network

*Case **21.4** continued on following page*

*Case **21.4** continued*

Inc., owner of a television shopping channel, proposed to Davis an acquisition of Paramount by QVC for cash and stock worth approximately $80 per share. In response to the hostile QVC offer, Viacom increased its bid to $80 per share cash at the front end, to be followed by a second-step stock-for-stock merger of equivalent value. In the next two months, QVC and Viacom each continued to enter competing bids. Paramount repeatedly rebuffed QVC, although QVC often submitted offers of higher value than those of Viacom.

QVC then commenced action in the Delaware Court of Chancery, arguing that the Paramount board had put Paramount in the "*Revlon* mode" when it committed to a transaction that would shift control of Paramount from the public shareholders to Redstone.

The Delaware Court of Chancery held that this transaction between Paramount and Viacom clearly had put Paramount in the "*Revlon* mode." Paramount then appealed the decision.

ISSUE PRESENTED   Does a board of directors have an obligation to consider a tender offer from one corporation, although the board has expressed a desire to not receive competing bids because it is engaging in a friendly merger agreement with another corporation?

OPINION   VEASEY, J., writing for the Delaware Supreme Court:

. . . .

II. APPLICABLE PRINCIPLES OF ESTABLISHED DELAWARE LAW

. . . [T]he management of the business and affairs of a Delaware corporation is entrusted to its directors, who are the duly elected and authorized representatives of the stockholders. Under normal circumstances, neither the courts nor the stockholders should interfere with the managerial decisions of the directors. The business judgment rule embodies the deference to which such decisions are entitled.

Nevertheless, there are rare situations which mandate that a court take a more direct and active role in overseeing the decisions made and actions taken by directors. In these situations, a court subjects the directors' conduct to enhanced scrutiny to ensure that it is reasonable. . . . The case at bar implicates two such circumstances: (1) the approval of a transaction resulting in a sale of control, and (2) the adoption of defensive measures in response to a threat to corporate control.

A. The Significance of a Sale or Change of Control

. . . .

In the case before us, the public stockholders (in the aggregate) currently own a majority of Paramount's voting stock. Control of the corporation is not vested in a single person, entity, or group, but vested in the fluid aggregation of unaffiliated stockholders. In the event the Paramount-Viacom transaction is consummated, the public stockholders will receive cash and a minority equity voting position in the surviving corporation. Following such consummation, there will be a controlling stockholder. . . . Irrespective of the present Paramount Board's vision of a long-term strategic alliance with Viacom, the proposed sale of control would provide the new controlling stockholder with the power to alter that vision.

Because of the intended sale of control, the Paramount-Viacom transaction has economic consequences of considerable significance to the Paramount stockholders. Once control has shifted, the current Paramount stockholders will have no leverage in the future to demand another control premium.

. . . .

C. Enhanced Judicial Scrutiny of a Sale or Change of Control Transaction

. . . .

The key features of an enhanced scrutiny test are: (a) a judicial determination regarding the adequacy of the decisionmaking process employed by the directors, including the information on which the directors based their decision; and (b) a judicial examination of the reasonableness of the directors' action in light of the circumstances then existing. The directors have the burden of proving that they were adequately informed and acted reasonably.

. . . .

. . . Accordingly, a court applying enhanced judicial scrutiny should be deciding whether the directors made a reasonable decision, not a perfect decision. If a board selected one of several reasonable alternatives, a court should not second-guess that choice even though it might have decided otherwise or subsequent events may have cast doubt on the board's determination. Thus, courts will not substitute their business judgment for that of the directors, but will determine if the directors' decision was, on balance, within a range of reasonableness.

D. *Revlon* and *Time-Warner* Distinguished

. . . .

In *Revlon*, we reviewed the actions of the board of directors of Revlon, Inc. . . . Based on the facts and circumstances present in *Revlon*, we held that "[t]he directors' role changed from defenders of the corporate bastion to auctioneers charged with getting the best price for the stockholders at a sale of the company. . . ."[12]

. . . .

Under Delaware law there are, generally speaking and without excluding other possibilities, two circumstances which may implicate *Revlon* duties. The first, and clearer one, is when a corporation initiates an active bidding process seeking to sell itself or to effect a business reorganization involving a clear break-up of the company. However, *Revlon* duties may also be triggered where, in response to a bidder's offer, a target abandons its long-term strategy and seeks an alternative transaction involving the breakup of the company.

---

12.   506 A.2d 173, 182 (Del. 1986).

Case **21.4** continued on following page

*Case **21.4** continued*

The Paramount defendants have misread the holding of *Time-Warner*. Contrary to their argument, our decision in *Time-Warner* expressly states that the two general scenarios discussed in the above-quoted paragraph are not the only instances where "*Revlon* duties" may be implicated. The Paramount defendants' argument totally ignores the phrase "without excluding other possibilities. . . ."

. . . .

Accordingly, when a corporation undertakes a transaction which will cause: (a) a change in corporate control; or (b) a break-up of the corporate entity, the directors' obligation is to seek the best value reasonably available to the stockholders. This obligation arises because the effect of the Viacom-Paramount transaction, if consummated, is to shift control of Paramount from the public stockholders to a controlling stockholder, Viacom. Neither *Time-Warner* nor any other decision of this Court holds that a "break-up" of the company is essential to give rise to this obligation where there is a sale of control.

III. BREACH OF FIDUCIARY DUTIES BY PARAMOUNT BOARD

. . . .

A. The Specific Obligations of the Paramount Board

. . . .

Since the Paramount directors had already decided to sell control, they had an obligation to continue their search for the best value reasonably available to the stockholders. This continuing obligation included the responsibility, at the October 24 board meeting and thereafter, to evaluate critically both the QVC tender offers and the Paramount-Viacom transaction to determine if: (a) the QVC tender offer was, or would continue to be, conditional; (b) the QVC tender offer could be improved; (c) the Viacom tender offer or other aspects of the Paramount-Viacom transaction could be improved; (d) each of the respective offers would be reasonably likely to come to closure, and under what circumstances; (e) other material information was reasonably available for consideration by the Paramount directors; (f) there were viable and realistic alternative courses of action; and (g) the timing constraints could be managed so the directors could consider these matters carefully and deliberately.

B. The Breaches of Fiduciary Duty by the Paramount Board

. . . .

Throughout the applicable time period, and especially from the first QVC merger proposal on September 20 through the Paramount Board meeting on November 15, QVC's interest in Paramount provided the opportunity for the Paramount Board to seek significantly higher value for the Paramount stockholders than that being offered by Viacom. QVC persistently demonstrated its intention to meet and exceed the Viacom offers, and frequently expressed its willingness to negotiate possible further increases.

. . . .

When the Paramount directors met on November 15 to consider QVC's increased tender offer, they remained prisoners of their own misconceptions and missed opportunities to eliminate the restrictions they had imposed on themselves. . . . Nevertheless, the Paramount directors remained paralyzed by their uninformed belief that the QVC offer was "illusory." This final opportunity to negotiate on the stockholders' behalf and to fulfill their obligation to seek the best value reasonably available was thereby squandered.

V. CONCLUSION

The realization of the best value reasonably available to the stockholders became the Paramount directors' primary obligation under these facts in light of the change of control. That obligation was not satisfied, and the Paramount Board's process was deficient. The directors' initial hope and expectation for a strategic alliance with Viacom was allowed to dominate their decisionmaking process to the point where the arsenal of defensive measures established at the outset was perpetuated (not modified or eliminated) when the situation was dramatically altered. QVC's unsolicited bid presented the opportunity for significantly greater value for the stockholders and enhanced negotiating leverage for the directors. Rather than seizing those opportunities, the Paramount directors chose to wall themselves off from material information which was reasonably available and to hide behind the defensive measures as a rationalization for refusing to negotiate with QVC or seeking other alternatives. Their view of the strategic alliance likewise became an empty rationalization as the opportunities for higher value for the stockholders continued to develop.

. . . .

RESULT The Paramount board of directors, in order to fulfill its fiduciary duties to its shareholders, must entertain competing merger bids because the board had already agreed to a change in control in the attempted friendly merger deal with Viacom.

COMMENTS The arguably new standards set forth by the Delaware court for the triggering of the *Revlon* duty to maximize shareholder value is troubling for several reasons. First (although the court denies this fact), the decision cannot help but have a chilling effect on strategic acquisitions by Delaware corporations. The court's opinion invites a competing bidder to enter the fray as soon as a target company enters into a strategic merger involving a change of control.

Although a bidder might otherwise be concerned under those facts about tortious interference with contract, the Delaware Supreme Court opinion made it clear that, under Delaware law at least, any contractual limitations on selling a company to someone else must yield to the directors' fiduciary duties. It is ironic in this respect that one of the Paramount directors is Hugh Liedtke, CEO of Pennzoil, who successfully sued Texaco for $3 billion in a case involving Texaco's interference with Pennzoil's contract to acquire Getty Oil. (This case is discussed in the "Inside Story" in chapter 8.)

Second, the Delaware court's decision leaves open the question of what constitutes a change in control. In the 1989 case in which Paramount sought to establish that Time's merger with Warner constituted a change of control, and thus effectively put Time up for sale, the Delaware Supreme

Case 21.4 continued on following page

Case **21.4** continued

Court concluded that there was no change in control even though after the merger approximately 60% of the shares of the combined entity would be owned by former Warner shareholders. The court accepted the argument that, for this purpose at least, public shareholders are fungible.

Questions
1. Why was it relevant that the acquiring company Viacom had such a large shareholder in Redstone?
2. Should the decision in *Paramount v. QVC* be viewed as a retreat by the Delaware Supreme Court from its opinion in *Paramount v. Time*?

Reliability of Officers' Reports

As underscored by *Van Gorkom,* not every statement of an officer can be relied on in good faith, and no statement is entitled to blind reliance. The passivity of the Trans Union directors in *Van Gorkom* unquestionably influenced the court's finding of gross negligence. When the chief financial officer, Romans, told the board that the $55 figure was within a "fair price range" for a leveraged buyout,

> no director sought any further information from Romans. No director asked him why he put $55 at the bottom of his range. No director asked Romans for any details as to his study, the reason why it had been undertaken or its depth. No director asked to see the study; and no director asked Romans whether Trans Union's finance department could do a fairness study within the remaining 36-hour period available under the Pritzker offer. . . . [If he had been asked,] Romans would have presumably . . . informed the Board of his view, and the widespread view of Senior Management, that the timing of the offer was wrong and the offer inadequate.[13]

When the CEO, Van Gorkom, told the board that $55 per share was fair, no questions were asked.

> The Board thereby failed to discover that Van Gorkom had suggested the $55 price to [the bidder] Pritzker and, most crucially, that Van Gorkom had arrived at the $55 figure based on calculations designed solely to determine the feasibility of a leveraged buy-out. No questions were raised either as to the tax implications of a cash-out merger or how the price for the one million share option granted Pritzker was calculated.[14]

Delegation of Negotiating Authority

If members of management are financial participants in the proposed transaction, the delegation of negotiation responsibilities to management or inside directors will expose the board to greater risks of liability. The Second Circuit observed in *Hanson Trust:*

> SCM's board delegated to management broad authority to work directly with Merrill to structure an LBO proposal, and then appears to have swiftly approved management's proposals. Such broad delegations of authority are not uncommon and generally are quite proper as conforming to the way that a Board acts in generating proposals for its own consideration. However, when management has a self-interest in consummating an LBO, standard post hoc review procedures may be insufficient. SCM's management and the Board's advisers presented the various agreements to the SCM directors more or less as faits accompli, which the Board quite hastily approved. In short, the Board appears to have failed to ensure that negotiations for alternative bids were conducted by those whose only loyalty was to the shareholders.[15]

Reliability of Experts' Reports

Two principles regarding the use of experts' reports emerge from the cases. First, a board should engage a reputable investment banking firm, aided if necessary by an outside appraiser, (1) to prepare a valuation study, and (2) to give a written opinion as to the financial fairness of the transaction and of any related purchase of assets or options.

---

13. *Smith v. Van Gorkom,* 488 A.2d 858, 876 (Del. 1985).
14. *Ibid.*

---

15. *Hanson Trust PLC v. ML SCM Acquisition, Inc.,* 781 F.2d 264, 277 (2d Cir. 1986).

Second, directors have a duty to pursue reasonable inquiry and to exercise reasonable oversight in connection with their engagement of investment bankers and other advisors. A conclusory fairness opinion—that is, an opinion that merely states a conclusion without giving the factual grounds for that conclusion—of an investment banker, however expert, is not a sufficient basis for a board decision, particularly if the investment banker's conclusion is questionable in the light of other information known to the directors.

The Second Circuit in *Hanson Trust* contrasted the actions of the SCM directors with what the Delaware Supreme Court referred to as the grossly negligent actions of the directors in *Van Gorkom* and with the commendable actions of the directors in another case, *Treadway Companies, Inc. v. Care Corp.*[16] (Treadway, a New Jersey corporation that operated bowling alleys and motor inns, faced a hostile takeover attempt by Care Corporation, which operated health care and recreational facilities, including bowling alleys.) The Second Circuit stated:

> [T]he SCM directors failed to take many of the affirmative directorial steps that underlie the finding of due care in *Treadway* on which the district court herein relied. In *Treadway,* the directors "armed" their bankers with financial questions to evaluate; they requested balance sheets; they adjourned deliberations for one week to consider the requisitioned advice; and they conditioned approval of the deal on the securing of a fairness opinion from their bankers.

As in the case of officers' reports, blind reliance on the reports of experts creates a risk that the directors will not receive the protection of the business judgment rule.

> " *Blind reliance on the reports of experts creates a risk that the directors will not receive the protection of the business judgment rule.*

Investment Banker's Fee Structure

Another principle, noted in the commentaries but yet to emerge from the case law, is that directors should exercise care to ensure that the terms of the investment banker's compensation do not impair her independence.

Certain compensation schemes are difficult to reconcile with the best interests of the corporation and its shareholders, and should therefore be avoided.

For example, the investment banker may be promised a flat fee if the raider is successful at its initial price or, if a higher price is obtained, a percentage of that price (the percentage fee being larger than the flat fee). In some cases the investment banker is to receive a flat fee plus a percentage of the difference between the bidder's initial price and the price ultimately received by the shareholders. In still others, the investment banker is to receive expenses plus a straight percentage of the sale price. Directors need to recognize that some of these arrangements create a financial incentive for the investment banker to close a transaction at any price, or at a price that is any amount higher (even if by only one cent) than the original offer. The fee structure that is most favorable for the target company is one that gives the investment banker an incentive to obtain a higher price but also an incentive (or at least no disincentive) to resist the hostile takeover.

Defensive Tactics

Issues of management entrenchment arise whenever a target company adopts defensive tactics designed to

---

In Brief: The Business Judgment Rule

The business judgment rule creates a powerful presumption in favor of actions taken by the directors of a corporation. Unless it can be shown there is no rational business purpose for the directors' decision, the courts generally will not overturn such a decision.

In order to invoke the business judgment rule, directors must act with loyalty toward the corporation and must make informed decisions regarding corporate affairs. The business judgment rule does not apply if the directors have an interest in the transaction being acted upon.

In the case of defensive tactics to a hostile takeover, directors are not entitled to the protection of the business judgment rule unless they can demonstrate that the hostile takeover posed a threat to corporate policy and effectiveness, and that their response was reasonable in relation to that threat.

---

16. 638 F.2d 357 (2d Cir. 1980).

thwart a hostile takeover. The courts, as indicated in *Unocal*, case 21.2, generally balance the reasonableness of the defensive tactic against the seriousness of the threat posed by the proposed takeover.

Duty of Directors to Disclose Preliminary Merger Negotiations

Directors can face a difficult decision when deciding when they must disclose an offer to buy the company or the company's participation in merger negotiations. As will be discussed more fully in chapter 23, disclosure can be required even if the parties have not reached an agreement in principle on the price and structure of the transaction. The Supreme Court held in *Basic Inc. v. Levinson*[17] that such "soft information" can be material.

Ethical Consideration

Managers planning a management buyout (MBO) of a company have a real conflict of interest in deciding whether to disclose their offer to the public, because disclosure will often bring forth competing bidders. Prudent directors, like the independent directors of RJR Nabisco when faced with CEO Ross Johnson's bid, will often require public announcement of the bid even if it puts the company "in play."

Statutory Limitations on Directors' Liability

Cases like *Van Gorkom* had a devastating impact on the market for directors' and officers' liability insurance and on the availability of qualified outside directors. In response, Delaware in July 1986, and thereafter most of the other states, adopted legislation to allow shareholders to limit the monetary liability of directors for breaches of the duty of care in any suit brought by the corporation or in a *shareholder derivative suit,* that is, a suit by a share-

---

17.   485 U.S. 224, 108 S.Ct. 978 (1988).

holder on behalf of the corporation. Most such statutes require that the limitation be contained in the original articles of incorporation, or in an amendment approved by a majority of the shareholders.

The statutes do not affect directors' liability for suits brought by third parties; they merely allow the shareholders to agree that under certain circumstances they will not seek monetary recovery against the directors.

The directors' liability for breach of the duty of loyalty may not be limited. Also, most states do not allow officers to be exonerated from liability for breach of the duty of care or the duty of loyalty.

Delaware's Statute

Section 102(b)(7) of the Delaware Corporation Code is an example of a statute that permits a limitation of the directors' liability. Delaware law is especially relevant because many large public companies are incorporated under Delaware law. (As explained in chapter 20, Delaware is considered a desirable jurisdiction because of its liberal, pro-management statutory and case law.)

The Delaware statute permits the certificate of incorporation to include a provision limiting or eliminating the personal liability of directors to the corporation or to its shareholders for monetary damages for breach of fiduciary duty. Such a provision, however, cannot eliminate or limit the liability of a director: (1) for any breach of the directors' duty of loyalty to the corporation or its shareholders, (2) for acts or omissions not in good faith or that involve intentional misconduct or knowing violation of law, (3) for unlawful payments of dividends or stock purchases, or (4) for any transaction for which the director derived an improper personal benefit.

Duties of Officers

Officers, like directors, owe duties of loyalty and care to the corporation and its shareholders. Thus, officers cannot decide to fight a hostile takeover just to keep their jobs.

Officers cannot decide to fight a hostile takeover just to keep their jobs.

Officers must act with the same care that a reasonable person would exercise in similar circumstances. They

Political Perspective

The Pennsylvania Antitakeover Statute

The interest of state legislators—or at least of those persons with enough power to successfully promote legislation—in regulating takeovers and corporate changes of control has resulted in a variety of state statutes designed to challenge the rules of the takeover game. Most of this legislation is the result of antitakeover sentiment. A prime example is Pennsylvania Senate bill 1310, also known as Act 36, which was signed into law by Governor Bob Casey (D) on April 27, 1990.[a] This statute employs a number of state-of-the-art strategies to impede the progress of a corporate raider. An examination of the events surrounding the enactment of this controversial statute highlights the current phase in the ever-changing battle over defining, shaping, and reshaping the law in this area.

Background

The impetus for drafting the statute came from an actual takeover attempt. Armstrong World Industries, Inc., a Fortune 500 company specializing in flooring and furnishings, is headquartered in Lancaster, Pennsylvania. Armstrong was the target of a hostile bid by the Belzberg family, based in Canada. The Belzbergs made an offer to the board of Armstrong to buy the company, but were rejected. Next, the Belzbergs' holding company, First City Financial Corporation, initiated a proxy fight for control of four directors' seats on the board. The shareholders' meeting at which the results of the proxy fight were to be announced was scheduled for April 30.

Noah W. Wenger (R), the state senator from the Lancaster district, introduced a comprehensive antitakeover bill while the Belzbergs and Armstrong were in the midst of their conflict. The bill, drafted in part by the Pennsylvania Chamber of Business and Industry, was designed not only to throw a wrench in the plans of corporate raiders in general, but perhaps also to impede the Belzberg bid in particular. Armstrong downplayed the notion that the company was the force behind the bill, but a company

spokesperson acknowledged that the bill would be "highly beneficial" to the company.

The Statute

The Pennsylvania's antitakeover statute attacks bids for corporate control on three major fronts. First, it requires controlling persons (defined as those who own, or control proxies for, 20% of a company's stock) to disgorge—that is, give back to the company—any profits they make by selling stock of the company. Such disgorgement is required if the stock was acquired within 24 months before or 18 months after becoming a controlling person, and if it was sold within 18 months after becoming a controlling person.

This provision is aimed at those who, after failed takeover attempts, attempt to reap short-term profits by selling acquired stock at a premium. Institutional investors and other shareholders who launch proxy fights for purposes other than gaining control of a majority of the board are exempted from the disgorgement provision. This exemption was a last-minute modification to the bill designed to placate the large institutional investors. These investors did not want to lose a major source of profit simply because they had a large stake in a company and wanted to exert a certain degree of control over its operation.

Second, the statute expands the directors' ability to consider other constituencies when making change-of-control decisions. Subsection (d) of section 511 provides an expansive list of constituencies that a director may consider when exercising his duty to the corporation:

In discharging the duties of their respective positions . . . directors may, in considering the best interests of the corporation, consider to the extent they deem appropriate:

(1) The effects of any action upon *any or all groups affected by such action,* including shareholders, employees, suppliers, customers and creditors of the corporation, and upon communities in which offices or other establishments of the corporation are located.

---

a. The independent sections are codified as 15 Pa. Cons. Stat. Ann. §§ 511, 512, 1721, 2502 (1990) (amended 1990); 15 Pa. Cons. Stat. Ann. §§ 2561-2567, 2571-2574, 2581-2583, 2585-2588 (1990).

Political Perspective
continued on following page

Political Perspective

The Pennsylvania Antitakeover Statute, *Continued*

(2) The short-term and long-term interests of the corporation, including benefits which may accrue to the corporation from its long-term plans and *the possibility that these interests may be best served by the continued independence of the corporation.*

(3) The resources, intent and conduct (past, stated and potential) of person seeking to acquire control of the corporation.

(4) *All other pertinent factors.*

[Italics added.]

The implication is clear. A director's duty when considering a proposal for a change of control is not simply to maximize shareholder value. Under the statute, a director's duty is to consider a broad range of interests, including "all other pertinent factors."

Numerous court decisions have indicated that directors may in some instances consider other constituencies. However, directors could only guess how the interests of other constituencies ranked against the interests of shareholders. The Pennsylvania statute clarified this issue by stating that directors shall not be required to regard any particular corporate interest or the interest of any group as "a dominant or controlling interest or factor."

The drafters' concern for minimizing director liability is evident in subsection (f), which states that there is no heightened duty of directors in a takeover situation. This is in direct contrast with the *Unocal* line of cases from the Delaware courts. (See case 21.2.) In those cases, before the directors could invoke the business judgment rule, they had the burden of proving that they had not breached the duties of care or loyalty. (It is usually the plaintiff who has the burden of proving that the directors breached their duty.)

Third, like some other states' antitakeover statutes, the Pennsylvania law deprives a shareholder of her voting rights when she crosses certain ownership lines, placed at 20%, 33%, and 50% of the company's stock. Her voting rights can be regained only if the majority of shareholders—excluding holders of shares acquired in the previous twelve months—give their approval at a special shareholders' meeting.

The statute also protects the employees of a company that is taken over. Existing labor contracts must be honored, and a successful bidder must pay severance benefits to employees who lose their jobs within two years of the takeover.

Corporations are allowed to opt out of various provisions of the antitakeover statute. The corporation's bylaws could be amended to state that the provisions in question do not apply, provided this was done within 90 days after the statute's enactment. Alternatively, the articles of incorporation could be amended at any time.

Responses

Directly after its enactment, most commentators agreed that the Pennsylvania antitakeover statute was the most stringent passed by any state legislature. It met with some sharp criticism. One of those leading the charge was SEC Chairman Richard Breeden. In a speech to the Council of Institutional Investors, Breeden stated that the statute would "tilt the balance of corporate power in favor of corporate management and against shareholders by protecting decisions of the board of directors from effective challenge by shareholders."

Economists attacked the statute for reducing the value of Pennsylvania corporations. One study by professors from the University of Washington showed that Pennsylvania stocks underperformed the Standard & Poor's 500 by 6.9% in the period from October 1989, when Act 36 was announced, to January 1990, when it passed the Pennsylvania Senate.[b] Another study found a $4 billion drop in the combined market capitalization or value of Pennsylvania companies between the date the act was announced and the date it was signed. The market drop for companies in 25 other states was $6 billion *combined*.[c]

Several leading Pennsylvania corporations chose to opt out of the statute. One such company was Hunt Manufacturing, a leading manufacturer and distributor of office and arts and crafts products. The CEO, Ronald J. Naples, stated on June 26, 1990:

The Board of Directors concluded that both as a matter of principle and as a practical matter, the scope and

b. Vineeta Anand, "Pennsylvania Anti-Takeover Law Slams Stock Prices, Study Finds," *Investors Daily*, October 1, 1990, 31.

c. Jeffrey L. Silberman, "How Do Pennsylvania Directors Spell Relief? Act 36," 17 *Delaware Journal of Corporate Law* 115 (1992).

Political Perspective

The Pennsylvania Antitakeover Statute, *Continued*

uncertain effect of the new Pennsylvania anti-takeover amendments make them undesirable. We believe the company's legitimate interest in controlling its own destiny can be protected in ways more consistent with shareholder rights.

One of Pennsylvania's largest companies, Westinghouse Electric, which had actively promoted the opt-out provisions before the bill was passed, announced on May 31, 1990, that its board of directors had decided to opt out of the statute. As of 1992, more than 66 of the estimated 200 corporations affected by the statute had opted out of at least one of its subchapters.[d]

Two Armstrong shareholders brought suit in federal court on April 27, 1990, against the board of

directors of Armstrong and the Pennsylvania secretary of state. The suit raised broad claims of violation of the U.S. Constitution, but was dismissed by the district court. The U.S. Court of Appeals for the Third Circuit affirmed the district court's decision, concluding that the plaintiffs' claims were not ripe for judicial review.[e] The Belzberg family also filed suit in U.S. district court in Philadelphia, alleging that the law was unconstitutional. The Belzbergs had reason to fight. At the Armstrong annual shareholders' meeting, held just a few days after the legislation was approved, the Belzbergs gained only one seat on the board. *The Wall Street Journal* reported that they subsequently were forced to sell their 11.7% share of Armstrong at a loss.

---
d. *Ibid.*

---
e. *Armstrong World Industries, Inc. v. Adams*, 961 F.2d 405 (3d Cir. 1992).

International Consideration

Because European banks are not subject to the regulatory strictures applicable to U.S. banks, they are much more important institutional investors and exert a more powerful force on how a company is run than comparable U.S. banks. For example, German banks exercise extraordinary control over company access to capital. By law, the banks can represent shareholders who deposit their shares with the banks. Because only the banks are allowed to trade on the floor of the German stock exchanges, and therefore have the best knowledge of stock performance, most shareholders take advantage of this service.

In 1986, German banks held on average proxies for 65% of the shares present at the shareholder meetings at 100 of the largest German companies. For example, at the

1986 shareholder meeting of Siemens, approximately 61% of the outstanding shares were present at the meeting. Of the shares voted, Deutsche Bank voted 18%, Dresdner Bank 11%, and Commerzbank 4%. All banks taken as a group voted approximately 80% of the shares voted at the meeting.[18] Banks are also permitted to purchase directly up to 100% of the shares of a company, although it is considered imprudent for them to invest substantial portions of their capital in any single company.

---
18. Theodor Baums, "Corporate Governance in Germany: The Role of Banks," 40 *The American Journal of Comparative Law* 503, 524 (1992).

must also act in the best interests of the corporation. They can delegate their authority, but they have a duty to oversee their subordinates.

Although most of the cases applying the business judgment rule involve directors, the courts have said that the rule is available to protect officers as well.

Corporate Opportunities

Because officers (and directors and controlling shareholders) owe undivided loyalty to the corporation, they cannot reserve for themselves a corporate opportunity that rightfully belongs to the corporation. For example, suppose a copper-mining corporation is actively looking for mining sites; if an officer of the corporation learns of an attractive site in the course of his business for the corporation, he may not buy it for himself. If he attempted to do so, a shareholder could block the sale or impose a *constructive trust* on any profits he makes from the acquisition, that is, force him to hold such profits for the benefit of the corporation and pay them over to the corporation on request.

The courts have devised several tests for determining whether an opportunity belongs to a corporation. Perhaps the most widely used is the *line-of-business test.* Under this test, if an officer, director, or controlling shareholder learns of an opportunity in the course of her business for the corporation, and if the opportunity is in the corporation's line of business, a court will not permit her to keep the opportunity for herself.

Other courts have considered: (1) whether it would be fair for the fiduciary to keep the opportunity; (2) whether the corporation has an expectancy or interest growing out of an existing right in the opportunity; or (3) whether the interference by the fiduciary will hinder the corporation's purposes. Because different states apply different tests, it is important for a corporate fiduciary to consult local counsel if there is any question of the fiduciary's actions interfering with a corporate opportunity.

The following case set forth the *corporate opportunity doctrine,* whereby a business opportunity cannot legally be taken advantage of by an officer, director, or controlling shareholder if the corporation would be harmed as a result.

■ A Case in Point:	Summary

Case 21.5
GUTH v. LOFT, INC.
Supreme Court of Delaware
5 A.2d 503 (Del. 1939).

FACTS   Loft, Inc. was engaged in the manufacturing and selling of candies, syrups, beverages, and foodstuffs. Charles G. Guth was Loft's president and one of its directors. As part of his official duties as president, Guth was negotiating with Coca-Cola Company for a discount on its purchase of syrup, which greatly exceeded the purchases of some other customers to which a discount had been granted. After a number of conferences, the Coca-Cola Company refused to give a discount. Guth became incensed and contemplated the replacement of the Coca-Cola beverage with some other cola drink, in particular, Pepsi Cola.

The company that compounded and marketed Pepsi Cola was in bankruptcy. Without first offering the opportunity to Loft, Guth entered into an agreement with the party that controlled Pepsi to set up a new corporation to acquire the secret formula and trademark for Pepsi Cola.

A shareholder brought suit, alleging that the shares of this new corporation should belong to Loft and not to Guth.

ISSUE PRESENTED   Did the president of a corporation who acquired for himself an asset that was in the corporation's line of business illegally seize a corporate opportunity?

SUMMARY OF OPINION   The Delaware Court of Chancery imposed a constructive trust on the Pepsi Cola shares bought by Guth and his family business; that is, the court required the shares to be held in trust for the benefit of Loft and its shareholders. The court explained that corporate officers and directors are not permitted to use their position to further their private interests. Although technically not trustees, they stand in a fiduciary relation to the corporation and its shareholders. An officer or director must not only affirmatively protect the interests of the corporation committed to his charge, but also refrain from doing anything that would work injury to the corporation or deprive it of an advantage that his skill might properly bring to it.

The Supreme Court of Delaware affirmed.

RESULT   The president of a corporation who acquires for himself an asset that was in the corporation's line of business has illegally seized a corporate opportunity.

COMMENTS   Although *Guth v. Loft* was decided in 1939, its principles remain applicable today. For example, a Georgia court in *Phoenix Airline Services, Inc. v. Metro Airlines, Inc.*[19] applied the line-of-business test to find that three ex-officers of the Atlanta-based commuter airline Metro Express, Inc. breached their fiduciary duty. They had appropriated for themselves an opportunity to commence commuter service in Memphis that could have been developed by Metro Express's parent corporation. They had developed the idea on company time, using company resources. They formed their company, Phoenix Airline Services, Inc., one day after they resigned from Metro Express; and less than one month later they signed a ten-year contract with Republic to provide commuter services in Memphis. They argued that Metro Express was incorporated solely to provide services from the Atlanta hub and was therefore not interested in the Memphis route; however, the court held that they were estopped (that is, prevented) from making that claim because they had used company time and resources to acquire the opportunity.

---

19.   403 S.E.2d 832 (Ga.Ct.App. 1991).

At the Top

The general rule is that a controlling shareholder may sell her shares at a control premium. However, if there is reason to suspect that a buyer will loot the corporation, the seller will have a duty to investigate the buyer, and may be forced to share her control premium with the minority shareholders.

■ **Duties of Controlling Shareholder**

A shareholder who owns sufficient shares to outvote the other shareholders, and thus to control the corporation, is known as a *controlling shareholder.* Controlling shareholders owe a fiduciary duty to the corporation and to the other shareholders in many situations.

Sale of Control

A controlling interest in a corporation usually commands a higher price per share than a minority interest. Does this control premium belong to the corporation or to the majority shareholder? If it is a corporate asset, it should belong to the corporation. If not, it should belong to the majority shareholder. In *Perlman v. Feldmann*,[20] the controlling shareholder was held to be selling not just its controlling interest but also something that could be characterized as a corporate asset.

As described in *Perlman*, Newport Steel operated mills for the production of steel sheets for sale to manu-

---

20.   219 F.2d 173 (2d Cir. 1955), *cert. denied*, 349 U.S. 952, 75 S.Ct. 880 (1955).

facturers of steel products. C. Russell Feldmann was the chairman of the board of directors and president of the corporation. He was also the controlling shareholder. In August 1950, when the supply of steel was tight due to the Korean War, Feldmann and some other shareholders sold their stock to a syndicate of end users of steel who were interested in securing a source of supply.

Minority shareholders brought a shareholder derivative suit to compel the controlling shareholders to account for, and make restitution of, their gains from the sale. The court held that the consideration received by the defendants included compensation for the sale of a corporate asset, namely the ability of the board to control the allocation of the corporation's product in a time of short supply.

Note that the court did not seek to prohibit majority shareholders from ever selling their shares at a premium:

We do not mean to suggest that a majority stockholder cannot dispose of his controlling block of stock to outsiders

without having to account to his corporation for profits or even never do this with impunity when the buyer is an interested customer, actual or potential, for the corporation's product. But when the sale necessarily results in a sacrifice of this element of corporate good will and consequent unusual profit to the fiduciary who has caused the sacrifice, he should account for his gains. So when a time of market shortage, where a call on a corporation's product commands an unusually large premium, in one form or another, we think it sound law that a fiduciary may not appropriate to himself the value of this premium.

In the following case, the controlling shareholders were held liable for selling what might be best described as the "going public" value of the corporation.

■ **A Case in Point:**   **Summary**

Case 21.6
JONES v.
H. F. AHMANSON & CO.
Supreme Court of California
1 Cal.3d 93, 81 Cal.Rptr. 592,
460 P.2d 464 (Cal. 1969).

FACTS   The shares of the United Savings and Loan Association were not actively traded due to their high book value, the closely held nature of the association, and the failure of its management to provide information to shareholders, brokers, or the public.

In 1958 investor interest in shares of savings and loan associations and holding companies increased. Savings and loan stocks that were publicly marketed enjoyed a steady increase in market price. The controlling shareholders of the United Savings and Loan Association decided to create a mechanism by which the association, too, could attract investor interest. They did not, however, attempt to render the association's shares more readily marketable.

Instead, a holding company, the United Financial Corporation of California, was incorporated in Delaware on May 8, 1959. On May 14, pursuant to a prior agreement, certain association shareholders owning a majority of the association's stock exchanged their shares for those of United Financial.

After the exchange, United Financial held 85% of the association's outstanding stock. The former majority shareholders of the association had become the majority shareholders of United Financial and continued to control the association through the holding company. They did not offer the minority shareholders of the association an opportunity to exchange their shares.

The first public offering of United Financial stock was made in June 1960. An additional public offering in February 1961 included a secondary offering (that is, an offering by selling shareholders) of 600,000 shares. There was active trading in the United Financial shares. Sales of the association shares, however, decreased from 170 shares per year before the formation of United Financial to half that number by 1961. United Financial acquired 90% of the association's shares that were sold.

A shareholder of the association brought suit, on behalf of herself and all other similarly situated minority shareholders, against United Financial and the individuals and corporations that had set up the holding company. The plaintiff contended that the defendants' course of conduct constituted a breach of fiduciary duty owed by the majority shareholders to the minority. She alleged that they used their control of the association for their own advantage and to the detriment of the minority when they created United Financial, made a public market for its shares that rendered the association's stock unmarketable except to United Financial, and then refused either to purchase the minority's association stock at a fair price or to exchange the stock on the same terms afforded to the majority. She further alleged that they created a conflict of interest that might have been avoided had they offered all association shareholders the opportunity to participate in the initial exchange of shares.

ISSUE PRESENTED Did majority shareholders who transferred their shares to a holding corporation, then took it public without allowing the minority to exchange their shares, breach their fiduciary duty to the minority shareholders?

SUMMARY OF OPINION The California Supreme Court began its analysis by stating that the majority shareholders, acting either singly or in concert, have a fiduciary responsibility to the minority and to the corporation. They must use fairly their ability to control the corporation. They may not use it to benefit themselves alone, or in a manner detrimental to the minority. Any use to which they put their power to control the corporation must benefit all shareholders proportionately and must not conflict with the proper conduct of the corporation's business. The court summarized the rule as one of "inherent fairness from the viewpoint of the corporation or those interested therein."

The court noted that there were two other ways the controlling shareholders of the association could have taken advantage of the bull market in savings and loan stock. They could have caused the association to effect a stock split, thereby increasing the number of outstanding shares, or they could have created a holding company and permitted all shareholders to exchange their shares before offering the holding company's shares to the public. Either course would have benefited all of the shareholders alike, although the majority shareholders would have had to relinquish some of their control shares. However, the defendants chose to set up a holding company which they controlled, but did not allow minority shareholders to exchange association shares for shares of the holding company. Moreover, the market created by the defendants for United Financial shares would have been available for association shares had the defendants chosen a stock split of the association's shares.

The court stated that when a controlling shareholder sells or exchanges his shares, the transaction is subject to close scrutiny, particularly if the majority receives a premium over market value for its shares. If the premium constitutes payment for what is properly a corporate asset, all shareholders are entitled to a proportionate share of the premium (citing *Perlman v. Feldmann)*. The defendants' exchange of association stock for United Financial stock was an integral part of a scheme that the defendants could have reasonably foreseen would destroy the potential public market for association stock. The remaining association shareholders would thus be

Case **21.6** continued on following page

Case **21.6** continued

deprived of the opportunity to realize a profit from those intangible characteristics that attach to publicly marketed stock.

RESULT   The majority shareholders who transferred their shares to a holding corporation, then took it public without allowing the minority to exchange their shares, breached their fiduciary duty to the minority shareholders. The minority shareholders were awarded damages that would place them in a position at least as favorable as the majority shareholders created for themselves.

Freeze-outs

The Delaware Supreme Court has held that a majority shareholder may *freeze out* the minority, that is, force the minority to convert their shares into cash, so long as the transaction is fair.[21]

Sometimes a freeze-out is effected by merging a subsidiary into its parent, as in *Rosenblatt v. Getty Oil Co.*[22] In this case, Skelly Oil Company and Mission Corporation merged into Getty Oil Company, which was indirectly the majority shareholder of both Skelly and Mission. All three corporations were in the oil business. At issue was the fairness of the exchange ratio in the merger, that is, the ratio that would be used to convert the minority shareholders' stock into cash.

The Delaware Supreme Court stated that the concept of fairness in parent-subsidiary mergers has two aspects: fair dealing and fair price. Both must be examined together in resolving the ultimate question of entire fairness.

As to fair dealing, a court will look at the timing of the transaction; how it was initiated, structured, negotiated, and disclosed to the board; and how director and shareholder approval was obtained. The court cited a number of factors leading to a conclusion of fair dealing by Getty, including the adversarial nature of the negotiations between the parties to the merger.

Regarding fair price, a court will look at such economic factors as asset value, market value, earnings, and future prospects, and at any other elements that affect the intrinsic value of a company's stock. Both Getty and Skelly believed that the real worth of an oil company is centered in its reserves. Therefore, the court was especially impressed with the fact that they had employed

D & M, a petroleum consulting engineering firm with a worldwide reputation and with nearly 37 years of experience, to estimate Getty's and Skelly's respective oil and natural gas reserves.

The court concluded that Getty had dealt fairly with the Skelly minority shareholders in the merger.

■ Greenmail

While still a senior in college, Saul Steinberg acquired a 3% interest in the O'Sullivan Rubber Company. He demanded that the company diversify into automotive parts. The company refused. Steinberg threatened a proxy fight to replace the existing directors. The company then bought out Steinberg for three times what he had paid for his stock and thereby "helped Saul Steinberg invent greenmail."[23]

> *The company then bought out Steinberg for three times what he had paid for his stock and thereby "helped Saul Steinberg invent greenmail."*

Decades later, in 1984, Steinberg, through a syndicate called MM Acquisition Corporation (MM for Mickey Mouse), took a run at Walt Disney Productions. Within 12 hours of his threatening a cash tender offer for Disney, Steinberg was bought out for $325.4 million, giving him a profit of about $60 million. Some Disney shareholders sued the Disney directors for paying greenmail. Before

21.   *Weinberger v. UOP, Inc.* 457 A.2d 701 (Del. 1983).
22.   493 A.2d 929 (Del. 1985).

23.   Eric Allison, *The Raiders of Wall Street* (1987).

the trial, the plaintiffs sought to impose a constructive trust on the greenmail proceeds received by Steinberg. (A constructive trust is used to make available to their rightful owners any assets misappropriated by a fiduciary.) The trial court imposed constructive trust, and an appellate court affirmed. (In 1989, after three weeks of trial, the case was settled for $89.5 million.) The case presented here addresses the extent to which a shareholder who receives greenmail from a company board of directors is an aider and abettor of that board's breach of duty to the company.

■ **A Case in Point:**   **Summary**

Case 21.7
HECKMANN v. AHMANSON
Court of Appeal of California
168 Cal.App.3d 119,
214 Cal.Rptr. 177
(Cal.Ct.App. 1985).

FACTS In March 1984, a group headed by Saul Steinberg purchased more than two million shares of stock of Walt Disney Productions, the owner of Disneyland. Disney responded by announcing that it would acquire the Arvida Corporation for $200 million in newly issued Disney stock, and it would assume Arvida's $190 million debt. The Steinberg group countered with a shareholder derivative suit in federal court, seeking to block the Arvida transaction. A shareholder derivative suit is a suit brought on behalf of the corporation by one or more of its shareholders. All of the proceeds of such a suit (less expenses) go to the corporation for the benefit of all of its shareholders.

While the shareholder derivative suit was pending, the Steinberg group proceeded to acquire two million additional shares of Disney stock, increasing its ownership position to approximately 12% of the outstanding Disney shares. On June 8, 1984, the Steinberg group advised Disney's directors of its intention to make a tender offer for 49% of the outstanding shares at $67.50 a share, and its intention to later tender for the balance at $72.50 a share.

The Disney directors responded by offering to repurchase all the Disney stock held by the Steinberg group. Disney repurchased that stock for $297.4 million and reimbursed the estimated cost incurred in preparing the tender offer, $28 million, for a total of $325.4 million, or about $77 per share. The Steinberg group garnered a profit of about $60 million. In return, the Steinberg group agreed not to purchase any more Disney stock and to drop the Arvida litigation. It did not actually dismiss the derivative claims, but it agreed not to oppose a motion to dismiss made by Disney.

After the repurchase of the Steinberg group's shares was announced, some Disney shareholders brought an action seeking to rescind Disney's purchase agreement with the Steinberg group. They also sought an accounting and the imposition of a constructive trust upon all funds the Steinberg group received from Disney. At a preliminary hearing, the trial granted a constructive trust. The Steinberg group appealed.

ISSUE PRESENTED Was a shareholder who induced the board of directors to pay greenmail liable as an aider and abettor of the board's breach of its duty to the company? Was the shareholder, who (as part of the greenmail transaction) abandoned a derivative suit against the company, also liable to the other shareholders for breaching his fiduciary duty to them?

SUMMARY OF OPINION The California Court of Appeal found that the plaintiffs had demonstrated a reasonable probability of success at trial, and upheld the trial court's imposition of a constructive trust.

Case 21.7 continued on following page

*Case **21.7** continued*

First, the court found that the plaintiffs had made a sufficient showing of personal interest on the part of the directors to shift the burden onto the board to show that the transaction was fair. The court held that the directors had not sustained that burden merely by making a vague assertion that their objective in repurchasing the stock was to avoid the damage to Disney and its shareholders that would have resulted from the Steinberg tender offer. Thus, the directors were not given the protection of the business judgment rule.

The court further found that the Steinberg group could be held liable as an aider and abettor of the board in its alleged breach of fiduciary duty. The court noted that the Steinberg group knew it was reselling its stock at a price considerably above market value to enable the Disney directors to retain control of the corporation. It also knew or should have known that Disney was borrowing the $325 million purchase price. From its previous dealings with Disney, including the Arvida transaction, it knew that the increased debt load would adversely affect Disney's credit rating and the price of its stock.

Second, the court found that the plaintiff shareholders had adequately demonstrated a breach of the fiduciary duty owed directly by the Steinberg group to the Disney shareholders. When the Steinberg group filed the derivative suit against Disney to block Disney's purchase of Arvida, it assumed a fiduciary duty to the other shareholders. It could not abandon the suit for its own financial advantage. The plaintiff's duty in a derivative action is analogous to the duty of care owed by a volunteer rescuer to the rescuee. The court stated that the members of the Steinberg group "are like the citizens of a town whose volunteer fire department quits fighting the fire and sells its equipment to the arsonist who set it (who obtains the purchase price by setting fire to the building next door)." Thus, the plaintiffs had demonstrated a reasonable probability that the Steinberg group breached its fiduciary duty to the other Disney shareholders by abandoning the Arvida litigation two weeks after it was filed.

RESULT   The shareholder who induced the board to pay greenmail was liable as an aider and abettor of the board's breach of its duty to the company. He was also liable for his breach of fiduciary duty to his fellow shareholders when he abandoned the shareholder derivative suit.

COMMENTS   In another case involving the repurchase of shares at a premium to forestall a takeover attempt, the U.S. District Court for the Southern District of New York found the basis for claiming a similar breach of the directors' fiduciary duty.[24] The plaintiffs had sued to recover $41 million paid to Carl Icahn by tire manufacturer B. F. Goodrich Company when it repurchased one million shares of its stock from Icahn at an above-market price. This transaction resulted in an $8 million loss to Goodrich, with no corresponding benefit to Goodrich shareholders. According to the court, "[t]he only beneficiaries under the repurchase, other than Icahn, were the Goodrich directors, who insured their continued control of the company." Chairman of the Board Ong admitted that the transaction could be characterized as greenmail and that the directors agreed to purchase the shares because they did not wish to have Goodrich put into play for a possible takeover bid. The court held that under New York law the allegation that the

---

24.   *Feinberg Testamentary Trust v. Carter*, 652 F.Supp. 1066 (S.D.N.Y. 1987).

board of directors repurchased stock at a premium over market in an attempt to prevent a hostile takeover stated a claim for breach of fiduciary duty and waste of corporate assets in which the repurchase conferred no benefit on the other shareholders.

66

The court stated that the members of the Steinberg group "are like the citizens of a town whose volunteer fire department quits fighting the fire and sells its equipment to the arsonist who set it (who obtains the purchase price by setting fire to the building next door)."

The payment of greenmail by boards of directors has led to a number of shareholder proposals designed to prohibit the practice. For example, the holders of more than 50% of the outstanding shares of Gillette Company approved the following shareholder resolution in 1988:

RESOLVED, That the stockholders of Gillette Company recommend our Board of Directors take the necessary steps to amend the by-laws as follows:

(a) The Company shall not acquire any of its voting equity securities at a price above the average market price of such securities from any person who is the beneficial owner of more than three percent of the Company's voting equity securities and has been such for less than two years, unless such acquisition is pursuant to the same offer and terms as made to all holders of securities of such class and to all holders of any other class from or into which such securities may be converted.

(b) This provision shall not apply to any acquisition that has been approved by a vote of two-thirds of the shares entitled to vote.

(c) This provision shall not restrict the Company from: (1) reacquiring shares in the open market in transactions in which all shareholders have an equal chance to sell their shares, and in number of shares that do not exceed in any one day the daily average trading volume for the preceding three months; (2) offering to acquire at market price all shares, but no less than all shares, of any shareholder owning less than 100 shares of common stock; or (3) reacquiring shares pursuant to the terms of a stock option plan that has been approved by a vote of a majority of the common shareholders.

Professor Rita Kosnick of Texas A&M University compared 53 companies that paid greenmail with 57 that resisted. She found that the boards that resisted had more outside directors and more directors with executive experience than the boards that paid up.[25]

Hushmail

The Delaware Supreme Court has characterized as *hushmail*—that is, a combination of greenmail and hush money—a repurchase of shares at a premium over market which effectually was an unlawful and secret payment to ensure silence. The term was first used in *Grobow v. Perot*.[26]

General Motors Corporation (GM), one of the Big Three U.S. automobile manufacturers, repurchased certain GM stock and contingent notes owned by H. Ross Perot and his close associates for nearly $745 million. Perot, a U.S. presidential candidate in 1992, himself characterized the price at which his securities were repurchased as being at a "giant premium."

Perot resigned immediately from GM's board. He also resigned as chairman of GM's subsidiary Electronic Data Systems (EDS), of which Perot had been the founder and was the largest shareholder. Perot further agreed: (1) to stop criticizing GM management, in default of which he agreed to pay GM damages of up to $7.5 million; (2) not to purchase GM stock or engage in a proxy contest against the board for five years; and (3) not to compete with EDS for three years or recruit EDS executives for 18 months. The commitment by Perot not to criticize the GM board was later characterized as the "hushmail" feature of the agreement.

The GM repurchase came at a time when GM was experiencing financial difficulty and was engaged in cost cutting. Public reaction to the announcement ranged from mixed to adverse. The repurchase was sharply criticized by industry, including members of GM's management

---

25. Rita Kosnick, "Greenmail: A Study of Board Performance in Corporate Governance," *Administrative Science Quarterly* 32, 163 (1987).
26. 539 A.2d 180 (Del. 1988).

ranks. The criticism focused on the size of the premium over the market price of the repurchased stock and on the hushmail provision. A shareholder suit ensued.

The Delaware Supreme Court found that the plaintiffs' complaints regarding the hushmail provision failed to plead with particularity any facts that would support a conclusion that the primary purpose of the board's payment of the giant premium was to buy Perot's silence. To the contrary, the plaintiffs themselves stated in their complaints two legitimate business purposes for the GM board's decision to sever its relationship with Perot: (1) the board's determination that it would be in GM's best interest to retain control over its wholly owned subsidiary EDS, and (2) the decision to rid itself of the principal cause of the growing internal policy dispute over EDS's management direction. In addition, GM secured significant covenants from Perot besides the hushmail provision: (1) not to compete or hire EDS employees; (2) not to purchase GM stock or engage in proxy contests; and (3) to stay out of GM's and EDS's affairs. Moreover, Perot agreed to pay liquidated damages should he breach his no-criticism covenant. The court found that the plaintiffs' effort to measure the fairness of the premium paid by GM was flawed by their inability to place a dollar value on these promises made by Perot, particularly his covenant not to compete with EDS or attempt to hire away EDS employees.

The court concluded that, although the board of directors might be subject to criticism for the premium paid Perot and his associates for the repurchase of their interest in GM, on the present record the repurchase could only be seen legally as an exercise of business judgment by the General Motors board with which a court may not interfere.

Note that in the spring of 1990, in response to continuing shareholder pressure, General Motors adopted a bylaw prohibiting the payment of greenmail.

The Responsible Manager

Carrying Out Fiduciary Duties

Officers, directors, and controlling shareholders are fiduciaries. They owe their principal—the corporation and its shareholders—undivided loyalty. They must act in good faith. They may not put their own interests before those of the corporation and its shareholders. They cannot, for

example, fight off a hostile takeover just to keep their jobs. They cannot use the company's confidential information for their personal gain.

Officers and directors also owe the corporation and its shareholders a duty of care. They should act with the care a reasonable person would use in the management of her own property. They have a duty to make only informed decisions. They cannot rely blindly on the advice of other people, even experts.

The duty to make informed decisions, which is a part of the duty of care, takes various forms. In the context of takeovers, board members cannot reject an offer without taking sufficient time to analyze its merit. Managers must be able to demonstrate that they made their decisions only after sufficient deliberation and after review of all relevant information. They should consider the possible effects of both the monetary and the nonmonetary aspects of the transaction.

A manager should never sign a document without first reading it. Ideally, each director should read the document the board is asked to approve. If that is not practical, the directors should demand and read a written summary prepared by counsel. They should also make sure that the officers who are authorized to sign the agreement have read it before signing it. (The Delaware Supreme Court in *Van Gorkom* was clearly unimpressed with the CEO's signing of the merger agreement at the opening of the Chicago Lyric Opera without having read it.)

A manager should be informed as to the rules in his jurisdiction regarding the duty of care. Some jurisdictions permit the shareholders to amend the articles of incorporation to relieve directors of any financial liability for violations of the duty of care. But even with such provisions in place, directors must still act in good faith and in what they honestly believe is the best interest of the corporation. Otherwise, they will breach their duty of loyalty. Such a breach can result not only in monetary liability, but can also demoralize the shareholders and employees of the corporation, and make it difficult to maintain a high level of ethical behavior among them.

In a situation involving a potential conflict of interest, a manager should excuse herself and leave the decision to others who do not have a conflict. It is common, for example, to establish special independent committees of the board of directors, either to examine the fairness of a management offer to acquire the company or to review the merits of shareholder litigation against the directors or officers.

A repurchase of stock at a premium from a dissident (or unhappy) shareholder may violate both the directors' duty to the corporation and the shareholder's duty to the other shareholders. Different courts view such repurchases differently, and local counsel should always be consulted. It is often appropriate for the board not only to obtain a written opinion of counsel that such a repurchase is permissible, but also to convene a special independent committee of directors to decide whether the consideration that will be paid for the stock is fair.

Any controlling shareholder engaging in a transaction such as a merger with the company it controls must be able to prove that the transaction is fair both procedurally and substantively. The use of independent committees, advised by independent financial consultants and counsel, helps show procedural fairness, as does a willingness to negotiate the proposed transaction with such a committee on an arm's length basis. Paying a fair price for corporate assets or for shares of a corporation shows substantive fairness. The fairness of a price can be demonstrated by evidence of competing offers or independent appraisals or evaluations. The form of compensation of the appraiser or investment banker should not give that person an interest in the outcome of the appraisal or of the transaction. It is often preferable to pay the appraiser or investment banker a flat fee regardless of whether the deal goes through, rather than an incentive fee based on the value of the deal struck.

Certain acts of directors, officers, and controlling shareholders are both illegal and unethical, such as the seizing of a corporate opportunity by an officer. Other conduct may be legal yet ethically questionable, such as the payment of hushmail or, in some circumstances, greenmail.

Some situations present conflicting ethical concerns. The Delaware Supreme Court has held that the directors must maximize shareholder value, that is, get the best price available, if they decide to sell control of the corporation. Yet a sale to a bust-up artist who will sell the company's assets, or to a union buster, might adversely affect the corporation's other constituencies such as employees, suppliers, and the community in which the corporation does business. A manager should try to select a course of action that protects the corporation's constituencies without sacrificing the shareholders' right to the best price.

A board of directors can use various defensive measures to prevent a hostile takeover, provided the measures are reasonable in relation to the threat posed, and provided the board considers it in the best interests of the company and its constituencies for the company to remain independent. If the management team itself bids for the company, the board may find itself forced to become an auctioneer whose sole goal is to get the best price for the shareholders. Similarly, if the board adopts a strategy resulting in a change of control of a corporation, it cannot use defensive tactics such as no-shop provisions (whereby the board agrees not to solicit other offers) or large asset or stock lock-ups to deter competing bidders. In short, if the board agrees to a change of control, it breaches its fiduciary duties if it makes competing offers impossible by adopting a scorched-earth policy that leaves the successful bidder with a depleted target. Although legal counsel will advise managers and directors in this area, a knowledge of the rules of the game is essential to good management.

Inside Story

Paramount v. QVC—Behind the Scenes

Change in Control Triggers *Revlon* Duties: *Paramount v. QVC*[27]

The hotly contested takeover battle involving Paramount Communications Inc. has spawned litigation in

---

27. Excerpted from Constance E. Bagley, "Change in Control Triggers *Revlon* Duties: *Paramount v. QVC*," 15 *CEB California Business Law Reporter* 236, March 1994. Copyright © 1994 by The Regents of the University of California. All rights reserved. *Reprinted by permission.*

Delaware courts concerning the fiduciary duties of a board of directors in a strategic merger that results in a change of control of one of the companies. On December 9, 1993, the Delaware Supreme Court upheld the Delaware Court of Chancery's decision that the Paramount board breached its duties when it refused to remove its poison pill and other antitakeover devices in the face of a bid by QVC Network, Inc. that was $1.3

Inside Story continued on following page

Inside Story, continued

billion higher than the merger price agreed on by Paramount and Viacom Inc. [See case 21.4.] The court reasoned that because the friendly Paramount-Viacom merger contemplated a change in control, whereby control of Paramount would shift from public shareholders to Mr. Sumner Redstone, CEO, chairman, and majority owner of Viacom, Paramount was in the "*Revlon* mode" and had to maximize shareholder value.

In response to this decision, Paramount abandoned the planned friendly merger with Viacom and put itself up for auction. It dropped its antitakeover devices and agreed to let the shareholders decide which offer to accept.[28] After a series of competing bids by QVC and Viacom, Paramount was acquired by Viacom for approximately $10 billion in cash and securities, or roughly $80.50 a share. This included $107 per share payable in cash to the holders of 50.1% of the shares in the first step tender offer. The remaining 49.9% of Paramount's stock will be acquired for a packet of securities that includes a "collar" or contingent value right. This provides Paramount shareholders some extra compensation if Viacom's stock does not perform well. This feature was important to the Paramount board's decision to recommend the Viacom bid on January 21, 1994.[29]

The Merger Battle

Paramount, a Delaware corporation, is a global producer and distributor of entertainment, with operations in motion pictures, television programming, cable and broadcast home television, home video, theaters, sports and special events. Beginning in 1983, Martin Davis, chairman and CEO of Paramount, led a management team devoted to transforming what was then called Gulf + Western (later renamed Paramount) into a major entertainment and publishing company. To compete in the rapidly evolving global marketplace, Paramount recognized the need to increase its size and financial strength. In pursuit of this goal, Paramount unsuccess-

fully attempted to acquire Time Incorporated in 1989.[30] Between 1989 and the spring of 1993, Paramount considered and evaluated the possibilities of merger with or acquisition of several video media companies, but none of these explorations resulted in a transaction.

On April 20, 1993, Davis met with Redstone, of Viacom, a publicly held corporation operating a diversified communications company whose core businesses include MTV Networks and Showtime Networks. Discussions continued over the course of several months and resulted in execution on September 12, 1993, of a merger agreement between Paramount and Viacom and related agreements (the "original merger agreements").

Two board meetings preceded execution of the original merger agreements. On September 9, 1993, at a regularly scheduled meeting, Davis briefed the Paramount board about the negotiations pending with Viacom and the possibility of a merger. Davis indicated to the board at that point that no matter how the merger was structured, Redstone would be the controlling shareholder of the combined company. On September 12, 1993, at a special meeting, the board of directors approved the original merger agreements. [Ed.—Redstone described the merger as a "marriage made in heaven" that would "never be torn asunder" and stated that only a "nuclear attack" could break up the deal.]

Under those agreements, Paramount agreed to be merged with Viacom in a transaction whereby the Paramount shareholders would receive a combination of stock and cash that was then valued at $69.14 per share. Paramount agreed to amend its poison pill so that it would not be triggered by the Viacom deal. (A poison pill confers rights on all shareholders except the raider to buy stock of the corporation at a discount price in the event an acquirer obtains a specified percentage of the corporation's stock.) The original merger agreements contained a "no-shop" provision prohibiting Paramount from soliciting or considering competing transactions, unless the board, on advice of counsel, determined in

28. See Johnnie L. Roberts and Randall Smith, "Paramount Opts to Put Itself up for Auction," *The Wall Street Journal,* December 15, 1993, A3.

29. See Laura Landro and Johnnie L. Roberts, "Now the Hard Part," *The Wall Street Journal,* February 16, 1994, A1.

30. See *Paramount Communications Inc. v. Time Inc.,* 571 A.2d 1140 (Del. 1990), and Constance E. Bagley, "Paramount-Time Decision Gives Directors Discretion to Set Long Term Corporate Strategies," 11 *CEB California Business Law Reporter* 227, June 1990.

Inside Story, continued

good faith that its fiduciary obligations so required. The agreements also provided a termination fee of $100 million, payable if Paramount terminated the agreements as a result of a competing transaction, the shareholders failed to approve the agreements, or the board recommended a competing transaction. In addition, the agreements provided for a stock option "lock-up" whereby Viacom would be permitted either to exercise an option to acquire 19.9% of Paramount's outstanding common stock at $69.14 per share (the amount of the original Viacom-Paramount deal) or to "put" the option to Paramount and receive cash equal to the profits it would have realized had it exercised the option. The option could be exercised for as little as $1 per share for cash, with the rest payable by means of a subordinated note.

The transaction approved on September 12 would have transferred voting control from the Paramount shareholders to Redstone. It would have vested approximately 70% voting interest in the combined corporation in National Amusements, Incorporated, 91.7% of which is owned by Redstone. Davis would have been the CEO of the merged entity.

At the September 12th meeting, the board of directors met for three hours and considered written materials that included detailed term sheets for the original merger agreements, a business overview of the combined Viacom-Paramount entity, and statements of pro forma revenues, operating cash flow and capitalization of the proposed corporation. These management-prepared documents were presented by Davis, who reviewed the documents with the board and concluded that the merger was consistent with Paramount's long-term strategy and goals for sustained growth. The management documents were accompanied by a fairness opinion rendered by Paramount's financial advisor, Lazard Freres. Although the back-up materials for the Lazard Freres opinion contained a list of six possible acquirers or groups of acquirers of Paramount, the fairness opinion clearly stated that no preagreement "market check" had been undertaken. In addition, it stated that the investment bankers were not asked by the board of directors to solicit third party indications of interest, and that in fact the bankers had not actively sought any such offers. Paramount's counsel, who was also present at the meeting, discussed the board's fiduciary duties and the legal standards governing its decision.

QVC Enters the Fray

Notwithstanding public statements by Viacom and Paramount to the effect that other bids were unwelcome, on September 20, QVC, a nationwide general merchandise retailer that operates one of the leading televised shopping networks in the United States, proposed to Davis an acquisition of Paramount by QVC for cash and stock worth approximately $80 per share. [Ed.—Even before September, Davis allegedly told QVC chairman Barry Diller, "I know you are after my company." Davis testified that he did not intend by this comment to dissuade a hostile bid from Diller.]

On September 27, the Paramount directors met in a special board meeting to discuss QVC's proposal. At that time, Davis indicated that as of Friday, September 24, the QVC proposal had a market value of $83.80 per share, while the Viacom deal had a market value of $65.45. Lazard analyzed the QVC bid and concluded that the QVC $80 merger proposal would provide $63.93 of value per share, while the Viacom merger would yield $59.58 per share. Davis told the board that the original merger agreements prohibited Paramount from entering into discussions with QVC or any other bidder without evidence that the proposal was free of financing contingencies. After discussion with its legal advisors, the board decided to consider QVC's offer once it received satisfactory evidence of financing.

The Paramount board met again on October 11 to consider QVC's proposal in light of documentation delivered on October 5 to Lazard evidencing the fact that QVC did in fact have the financing necessary to consummate its proposed transaction. Although Paramount's board then authorized management to enter into discussions with QVC, Paramount delayed and avoided meaningful discussions with QVC. After being continuously rebuffed by Paramount, QVC on October 21 filed an action to invalidate certain aspects of the original merger agreement, and publicly announced a tender offer for Paramount shares. On October 27, QVC commenced a two-tier front-end offer in which shareholders would receive $80 in cash for 51% of Paramount's outstanding shares, with the balance being acquired in a stock-for-stock second-step merger for a

Inside Story continued on following page

Inside Story, continued

packet of securities valued at approximately $80.71 per share.

In response to QVC's hostile offer, Viacom increased its bid to $80 per share cash at the front end, to be followed by a second-step stock-for-stock merger of equivalent value. This resulted in amended merger agreements entered into on October 24. The amended merger agreements gave Paramount the right to terminate the agreements if the board, in the exercise of its fiduciary duties, when confronted with a competing offer, withdrew its recommendation of the Viacom transaction. It also changed the mix of securities payable at the back end of the Viacom two-step offer.

At another special meeting of the Paramount board, held on October 24, the directors received management-prepared summaries of the amended merger agreements and a one-page overview of the financial terms of the two competing transactions. The board also received the Lazard summary that implied that the blended value of the QVC bid was $68.10, while the blended value of the Viacom bid was $70.75. In addition to the Lazard materials, the board was also presented with a report by Booz Allen and Hamilton (described by Booz Allen as "a first-cut") arguing that the merger with Viacom would create over $3 billion more in incremental shareholder value than a merger with QVC. Based on this information, the board of directors approved the amended merger agreements with Viacom, and recommended the Viacom tender offer to Paramount shareholders.

Viacom commenced its tender offer on October 25, and QVC launched its offer on October 27. QVC tried to continue negotiations with Paramount, but to no avail. On November 6, Viacom unilaterally raised its tender price to $85 cash for 51% of Paramount shares, plus a packet of securities of equivalent value as the second-step merger.

QVC raised its bid to $90 per share on November 12. This bid was rejected at a Paramount board meeting on November 15, following the directors' review of a Paramount document that detailed the "conditions and uncertainties" of QVC's offer without any mention of the financial terms of that offer. One director testified later that this document created a negative impression of the QVC offer from the outset of the meeting, stating: "My reaction was that this was not what I consider a true offer. It was full of contingencies and I would

consider holes in it and I was very . . . by the time I got through reading this I was very negative on the whole subject."

At the November 15 meeting, Lazard submitted a written fairness opinion stating that the proposed Viacom transaction was fair to Paramount shareholders from a financial point of view, even though Lazard had determined that the QVC offer (without the lock-up) was valued at $80.01, while the Viacom offer was valued at $74.29. On this occasion, and for the first time, Lazard questioned the accuracy of the valuation model it had used in previously concluding that the Viacom deal was superior. Based on a qualitative view that the Viacom transaction would provide greater benefit to the shareholders in the long run, the Paramount board determined that the QVC offer was not in the best interests of Paramount and its shareholders.

Based on the information that had been received by the board of directors and the strong pressure from Davis to continue with the Viacom deal, the Delaware Court of Chancery concluded that "although financing concerns were central to the board's rejection of the QVC proposal [at the November 15 meeting], the board did not request that management obtain more information from QVC regarding financing, as it did at its September 27 meeting. Instead, and with this limited data regarding the conditions of QVC's offer, the board simply followed management's lead in rejecting the unwelcome offer."[31]

Although QVC wrote the Paramount board on November 19 and informed them that QVC had obtained full financial commitments evidencing its ability to consummate the transaction, the board failed to obtain additional information necessary to test whether that characterization was correct.

Delaware Supreme Court Opinion

On December 9, 1993, the Delaware Supreme Court upheld the vice chancellor's decision in an order followed by a more detailed written opinion on February 4, 1994. *Paramount Communications Inc. v. QVC Network Inc.*, 637 A.2d 34 (Del. 1994) [case 21.4]. The

---

31. *QVC Network Inc. v. Paramount Communications Inc.*, 635 A.2d 1245 (Del. Ch. 1993).

Inside Story, continued

Delaware Supreme Court stated that the traditional business judgment rule did not apply to the Paramount board's decisions because Paramount's strategic alliance with Viacom was predicated on a sale of control to Redstone. The court stated that the lower court was correct in applying enhanced scrutiny to the decisions of the Paramount directors relating to the QVC tender offers and the Paramount-Viacom transaction.

[Ed.—The court also struck down the no-shop provision and the stock lock-up, which could conceivably have cost QVC an additional $400 million to acquire Paramount. Because the board of Paramount violated its fiduciary duties by agreeing to these provisions, they were invalid and of no effect. As a result, Viacom could not successfully argue that it had a vested contract right to these provisions.]

Key Words and Phrases

asset lock-up option **675**
business judgment rule **671**
constructive trust **694**
controlling shareholder **695**
corporate opportunity doctrine **694**

crown jewels **675**
Delaware Court of Chancery **671**
duty of care **671**
duty of loyalty **671**
freeze out **698**

golden parachute **683**
greenmail **698**
hushmail **701**
line-of-business test **694**
shareholder derivative suit **690**

Questions and Case Problems

1. What are the duties of the board of directors and officers of a corporation?

2. Zapp Corporation is a large, publicly held corporation. The board of directors consists of nine individuals. Three are members of management: Mary Kay Yellow, the CEO; Gordon Green, the CFO; and Collette Gray, the VP of Marketing.

On January 15, these three inside directors announce their intention to attempt a management buyout (MBO) of Zapp. After several discussions between Green and Oliver Oldhouse, Zapp's longtime investment banker, the management team proposes to buy all of Zapp's shares for $72 per share, which is a $12 premium over the current market price of $60. The board is scheduled to meet on February 24 and must approve this transaction if it is to proceed. Yellow establishes a special committee of three outside directors to review the proposal before it reaches the board. Norm Newhouse, an investment banker not affiliated with Zapp, is hired to advise the special committee.

On February 24, at 9 A.M., the special committee meets with Newhouse to assess the MBO proposal. One of the documents they review is a letter from Oldhouse which states that the price offered is fair, but that he has not negotiated the best price, nor has he been given authority to seek other bidders for the company. The entire board meets at 11 A.M. At this meeting, the

special committee reports that it endorses the MBO. The board approves the transaction 9–0. The MBO proceeds and is successfully completed.

Paul Pink, a shareholder in Zapp, is not satisfied with the amount of money he received for his shares, and sues Zapp's board of directors. What arguments will Pink make to win his case? What counterarguments, legal or otherwise, can be made by the directors?

3. The After School Care Corporation owned more than 40 day-care centers specializing in providing care to elementary-aged children in the afternoons. The president of the company, Clark Holmes, received a phone call at work one day from Marney Stein, the owner and sole proprietor of Pro Providers, a firm that owned six nursery schools for children aged two to four. Stein indicated that she wanted to sell Pro Providers for $1 million and asked if After School was interested. Holmes proposed the sale to the After School board of directors. The directors were divided on the issue because they were not certain if branching out into nursery care was a smart move. However, as funds were not available, there was no need at the time to vote on the issue.

Holmes decided that he would try to purchase Pro Providers on his own. After securing a loan, Holmes entered into negotiations with Stein. They agreed on a price of $900,000, and the sale went through. Holmes did not inform the board of his activity until after the sale was completed.

A shareholder sues Holmes, alleging that he is taking for himself a corporate opportunity that belongs to the corporation. What kinds of arguments will the shareholder make? Will she be successful? Will the result be different if Holmes expands one of the Pro Provider nursery schools into a nursery/after-school center?

4. Ann O. Yance owned 15% of Kalas Airlines. Yance was an extremely visible and critical shareholder who attended all of the annual meetings of the company and often made public statements that openly criticized its management. Because Yance was a celebrated stunt pilot, these statements garnered much attention in the press. The board of directors of Kalas repeatedly asked Yance not to make these criticisms publicly, but rather to make them directly to the board. Yance did not comply. However, at a meeting of the board of directors she proposed that the board, acting on behalf of the company, buy back her shares. The price at which Yance was willing to sell was $45 per share, $16 over the market price. The board agreed to the sale on condition that Yance agree not to speak out against the company or buy any more stock in the company for ten years.

What precautions should the board take to protect this transaction against attack from a shareholder of the company? What grounds would a shareholder have to make such an attack? What are the defenses available to the board? Can the behavior of the board or Yance be criticized on ethical grounds?

5. The Engulf Corporation is a large media and entertainment conglomerate with its stock trading on the New York Stock Exchange. Engulf is a major producer of films and videos, and also publishes several magazines. The company has a shareholders' rights plan, that is, a poison pill, which would make any hostile takeover financially prohibitive unless the pill is redeemed by Engulf's board of directors. On January 10 the Megaclout Corporation, in a move designed to gain control of Engulf, announced a tender offer for 51% of Engulf's shares at $140, an $11 premium over the market price.

On January 14, in a board meeting that lasted more than 13 hours, the Engulf board of directors met to consider Megaclout's offer. Engulf's lawyers and investment bankers attended, and they made detailed presentations on the adequacy of the offer. The next day the board officially announced that they believed the Megaclout offer was unacceptable for two reasons. First, the board believed that the long-term value of the Engulf stock ranged from $160 to $170, and thus $140 was financially inadequate. Second, the board claimed that Engulf had a distinct corporate culture which included special ways of doing business, an outstanding record of management-employee relations, and strong support of community projects in the towns in which Engulf businesses were located. Acceptance of Megaclout's tender offer would pose a direct threat to this corporate culture. For these reasons, the board refused to redeem the poison pill.

Megaclout brought suit as a shareholder of Engulf against the Engulf board of directors, demanding that the board redeem the poison pill, which would allow all the shareholders to decide whether they wanted to accept the offer by tendering their shares.

(a) Must the board of directors of Engulf redeem the poison pill at this time?

(b) The board argues that the offer, which is $11 over the market price of the stock, is financially inadequate. Is their argument convincing or not? Why?

(c) Should managers be concerned about corporate constituencies other than shareholders, such as employees or communities in which businesses are located? What if these different concerns conflict?

6. Shlensky was a minority stockholder of Chicago National League Ball Club, Inc., which owned and operated the Chicago Cubs baseball team. The defendants were directors of the club. Shlensky alleged that since night baseball was first played in 1935, every major-league team except the Cubs had scheduled most of its home games at night. This had allegedly been done for the specific purpose of maximizing attendance, thereby maximizing revenue and income.

The Cubs have sustained losses from its direct baseball operations. Shlensky attributes the losses to inadequate attendance at the Cubs' home games, which are played at Wrigley Field. He feels that if the directors continue to refuse to install lights at Wrigley Field and schedule night baseball games, the Cubs will continue to sustain similar losses.

Shlensky further alleges that Philip Wrigley, the president of the corporation, has refused to install lights not, as Wrigley claims, for the welfare of the corporation, but because of his personal opinion that "baseball is a daytime sport." Additionally, Shlensky alleges that the other directors have acquiesced in Wrigley's policy.

In his complaint, Shlensky charges that the directors are acting for reasons contrary to the business interests of the corporation, and that such acts constitute mismanagement and waste of corporate assets. Does the directors' decision fall within the scope of their business judgment? Have the directors failed to exercise reasonable care in the management of the corporation's affairs? [*Shlensky v. Wrigley*, 95 Ill.App.2d 173, 237 N.E.2d 776 (Ill.App.Ct. 1968)]

7. McDonald, a potential buyer of financial institutions, visited Halbert at the Tulane Savings and Loan Association. Halbert was president, manager, and chairman of the board, and, along with his wife, the owner of 53% of the stock of the association. McDonald asked if the association were for sale. Halbert replied that it was not for sale but that he and his wife would sell their controlling stock for $1,548 per share. Halbert did not tell the association's board of directors or its shareholders about McDonald's interest in acquiring the association.

In addition to agreeing to sell his stock, Halbert also agreed to cause the association to withhold the payment of dividends. After Halbert's shares were purchased, Halbert, who had not yet relinquished his corporate offices, helped McDonald solicit the minority shareholders' shares and even advised them that, because McDonald was going to withhold dividends for 10 to 20 years, they ought to take his offer of $300 per share. McDonald bought some of the minority shares at $300 and others for between $611 and $650.

Did Halbert owe the minority shareholders a fiduciary duty? If so, what was his duty in selling his minority stock position? Was his conduct ethical? [*Brown v. Halbert*, 271 Cal.App.2d 252, 76 Cal. Rptr. 781 (1969)]

8. Axton-Fisher Tobacco Corp. had a large inventory of tobacco that had greatly appreciated in value, although investors were unaware of its worth. The company had issued two classes of common stock: Class A and Class B. The controlling shareholder, Transamerica, held mostly Class B stock.

Using its power as controlling shareholder, Transamerica caused Axton-Fisher to redeem the Class A stock, and then caused the distribution of the valuable tobacco inventory to the remaining shareholders as a liquidating distribution. This was obviously a bad outcome for the Class A shareholders.

Management had two other options. First, it could have disclosed the company's true value and the liquidation plan, and could then have given notice of intent to redeem the Class A stock. Second, the managers could have declined to issue a notice of redemption and proceeded with the liquidation.

Did the managers breach their fiduciary duties to the shareholders in the course of action they chose? Which, if any, course of action would not have resulted in a breach of their duties? [*Zahn v. Transamerica*, 162 F.2d 36 (3d Cir. 1947)]

9. Holland had 883,585 shares outstanding, approximately 18.5% of which were owed by Hazelbank, a family holding company. Three of the directors had significant interests in the company: Cheff, the chief executive officer; Mrs. Cheff; and Landwehr. Of the four other directors, only Trenkamp (the general counsel) and one other had interests in the company. All received $300 per diem for monthly board meetings. Cheff received an annual salary of $77,400, and Trenkamp received significant fees as general counsel.

In June 1957, Maremont, an active corporate financier, inquired about merging Holland into one of its companies. When he was rebuffed, he indicated no further interest in Holland. The Holland board investigated and discovered that Maremont had bought 55,000 Holland shares, and that he had the reputation of acquiring and liquidating companies.

In August 1957, Maremont informed Cheff that he owned 100,000 shares and demanded a place on the board. He then indicated that Holland's distribution technique was obsolete and that its products could be sold wholesale through half a dozen salespeople. Consequently, Holland's sales force became fearful of a Maremont acquisition.

Maremont later suggested that Hazelbank either sell its Holland shares or purchase his. In October, Holland's directors considered purchasing Maremont's shares. The board was informed that Mrs. Cheff and Hazelbank were ready to buy the shares if Holland did not, and that to finance the purchase, Holland would have to borrow substantial sums. Nevertheless, the board decided to buy the shares at $14.40 a share, somewhat higher than current market price.

Did the board violate any duty when it decided to purchase Maremont's shares? [*Cheff v. Mathes*, 199 A.2d 548 (Del. 1964)]

10. Missouri Fidelity Union Trust Life Insurance Co. stock was trading at $2.63 per share. Eight directors sold their shares for $7.00 per share, conditioned upon the resignation of 11 of the 15 directors of the corporation, and the provision that five nominees of the buyer be elected as a majority of the executive and investment committees.

Did the directors violate a fiduciary duty by selling corporate control through their directorships? Would the answer be different if the directors had controlled a majority of the voting stock? [*Snyder v. Epstein*, 290 F. Supp. 652 (E.D. Wis. 1968)]

UNIT VI

SECURITIES AND FINANCIAL TRANSACTIONS

Chapter 22

PUBLIC AND PRIVATE OFFERINGS OF SECURITIES

■ Introduction

Raising Capital through Securities Offerings

Most businesses reach a certain point at which the founders' initial capital investment and ongoing bank loans are insufficient for continued growth. At this juncture, the directors and managers of the company must decide whether to rein in the company's growth consistent with its existing capital asset base, or to sell an interest in the company to raise capital for continued expansion. Many companies, especially in high-technology areas like biotechnology and computer electronics, face this decision soon after start-up, and must raise capital from private and public investors to fund their research, product development, and marketing efforts. At first these companies may turn to venture capital or private investment firms, but eventually many will seek to raise capital through an initial public offering of the company's shares. Even those companies that can internally generate the cash flow for growth may decide to sell securities to spread the concentration of risk in the business venture.

For many companies, a public offering of securities might raise capital from a broader spectrum of investors and provide easier opportunities for resale than a private placement. However, some companies seek to avoid the expensive and time-consuming securities registration required in a public offering by qualifying for an exemption from registration. A frequently relied upon exemption is for private offerings. Another exemption facilitates the raising of capital by small businesses. Whether the directors and managers of a company seek an exemption or go through the public offering process, they must understand and comply with securities laws. Penalties for noncompliance include damages, fines, and imprisonment.

Chapter Summary

This chapter discusses the federal statutory scheme that regulates the offer and sale of securities, and provides a list of the more important sections of the securities acts that will be discussed throughout the chapter. It then defines the key terms of *security*, *offer* and *sale*, and illustrates these definitions with three legal cases.

Next, the chapter delves into the public offering process. It covers the registration of securities, the role of an underwriter, the registration statement, and the offering procedure. It also suggests a managerial timeline for a public offering. Following that, the chapter summarizes some key terms of the Securities Act of 1933 that are relevant for a public offering.

The chapter then outlines some of the most relied upon exemptions from registration, including the private-offering and small-business exemptions, and gives a case example of an exemption that was not allowed by the courts. It also provides a table that lists the key elements of certain exemptions.

The chapter goes on to discuss exemptions to secondary offerings, the restrictions on the resale of registered and unregistered securities and foreign offerings under regulation S, and sales to qualified institutional buyers under rule 144A. The periodic reporting and certain other 1934 Act requirements are listed. The chapter then highlights the penalties for violation of the acts. Finally, a flowchart summarizes the requirements of securities registration and exemptions.

■ Federal Statutory Scheme

Regulations governing securities offerings stem from the public and governmental outrage and distrust of the nation's financial markets that followed the stock market crash of 1929. The two principal federal acts that regulate securities transactions and issuers, the Securities Act of 1933 and the Securities Exchange Act of 1934, were adopted during the depths of the Great Depression. These and subsequent acts embodied the belief that investors should be provided with all essential information prior to investing in speculative ventures; that corporate insiders should not be allowed to abuse their position and use nonpublic information concerning their companies to their own financial advantage; and that injured investors should receive adequate relief from common-law actions such as fraud.

The 1933 Act

In adopting the 1933 Act, the United States Congress sought to place the purchaser on the same level as the seller as far as information relating to the offering is concerned. The act requires that promoters of securities offerings register them with the Securities and Exchange Commission (SEC), an agency of the United States federal government, and provide to prospective purchasers material information regarding the issuer and the offering. Congress rejected suggestions that it also regulate the content or quality of securities offerings. As a result,

investors are not protected from making highly speculative or foolish investments. The 1933 Act requires only that they be advised of all material facts before they invest their money.

The "Historical Perspective" later in the chapter recounts the history of securities disclosure and the development of the 1933 Act. The congressional debate between determining the "merit and fairness" of the securities offering and ensuring full disclosure of information provides an interesting background perspective on the current regulations.

The 1934 Act

The 1934 Act sought to build upon the 1933 Act by implementing a policy of continuous disclosure. Companies of a certain size and with a certain number of shareholders, or whose stock is traded on a national securities exchange, are required to file periodic reports with the SEC. The 1934 Act also contains stringent antifraud provisions, and implements filing requirements for insiders dealing in their own company's stock. In addition, the 1934 Act established a framework for the self-regulation of the securities industry under the ultimate supervision of the SEC.

SEC Rules and Regulations

Since Congress adopted the 1933 Act and the 1934 Act, the SEC has used its power as an administrative agency

EXHIBIT 22-1   Important Sections of the 1933 and 1934 Acts

1933 Act

- *Section 2*—defines terms, including security, offer, sale, and underwriter.

- *Sections 3 and 4*—list exempt securities and describe exempt transactions.

- *Section 5*—requires the registration of all securities offered and sold in the U.S. (unless an exemption from registration is available), and the delivery of a prospectus.

- *Sections 6–8 and 10*—outline the general procedures of the registration process and detail the guidelines for the registration statement and the accompanying prospectus.

- *Sections 11 and 12*—describe the penalties, elements of liability, damages, and parties held liable for violation of the 1933 Act.

1934 Act

- *Section 10*—regulates the use of manipulative and deceptive devices in the purchase or sale of securities.

- *Section 12*—lists the reporting requirements for registered public companies.

- *Section 16*—provides the reporting requirements for insiders including directors, officers, and principal shareholders and the limitations on insider transactions.

---

to adopt a number of rules and regulations. The SEC uses these rules and regulations to address some of the ambiguity of the securities acts, make case-specific exemptions, carry out informal discretionary actions, and conduct investigations regarding compliance with the securities acts. For instance, in 1972 the SEC adopted rule 144 to clear the uncertainty in the definition of the term *underwriter*. In 1982, the SEC adopted regulation D with rules that outlined the requirements and limitations for exempt private offerings. Subsequently, it adopted rule 701 to exempt offers and sales of securities pursuant to employee benefit plans. Recently, the SEC revised regulation A to make it easier for small businesses to raise capital without going through a public offering.

All of the securities acts have been amended numerous times since their adoption. Exhibit 22-1 briefly describes the main sections of the two acts. More detailed excerpts from both acts can be found in appendices I and J of this book.

Blue Sky Laws

In addition to the federal securities laws, there are state statutes, called *blue sky laws*. An issuer selling securities must comply not only with the federal securities laws, but also with the securities laws of all of the states in which the securities are offered or sold. In a large public offering to be made on a national basis, this may require complying with the securities registration procedures of

an additional 52 jurisdictions. Fortunately, 36 states, the District of Columbia, and Puerto Rico have adopted the Uniform Securities Act, and thus there is some consistency among state laws. Other states, including New York, California, Illinois, and Ohio, have retained their own version of securities regulatory schemes. However, many of them have adopted simplified procedures applicable to securities offerings registered with the SEC.

The "registration by coordination" procedure makes possible a relatively efficient national offering without sacrificing the regulatory powers and policies of the individual states. Under this procedure, the registration statement filed with the SEC is also filed with the appropriate state securities administrators, together with any other information that may be requested. The registration statement automatically becomes effective at the state level once it becomes effective with the SEC, unless the state administrator issues a stop order based upon failure to comply with state law.

Like the federal statutes, the Uniform Securities Act emphasizes disclosure as the primary means of protecting investors. However, some states authorize the securities administrator to deny a securities selling permit unless she finds that the issuer's plan of business and the proposed issuance of securities are "fair, just, and equitable." Even if the state statute does not state this provision specifically, a state securities commissioner can usually deny registration until he is satisfied that the offering is fair.

International Consideration

On most American stock exchanges, foreign securities are traded in the form of American Depository Receipts (ADRs). The securities themselves are held by a financial institution called a depository, which issues the ADRs traded by foreign investors and handles any foreign exchange transactions. This structure allows the foreign securities to trade at a per-share price level customary in the U.S. market. In addition, it allows investors to trade interests in foreign securities in compliance with U.S. clearance and settlement requirements.

■ Definition of Terms

It is necessary to define three basic terms used in the 1933 Act—security, offer, and sale. Their meanings in a securities law context may be different from their everyday meanings.

"Security"

The term *security* for purposes of the 1933 Act—and most other securities statutes—is much broader than the common conception of the term. Section 2(1) of the 1933 Act defines a security as:

> any note, stock, treasury stock, bond, debenture, evidence of indebtedness, certificate of interest or participation in any profit-sharing agreement, collateral-trust certificate, pre-organization certificate or subscription, transferable share, investment contract, voting-trust certificate, certificate of deposit for a security, fractional undivided interest in oil,

gas, or other mineral rights, any put, call, straddle, option, or privilege on any security, certificate of deposit, or group of index of securities (including any interest therein or based on the value thereof), or any put, call, straddle, option, or privilege entered into on a national securities exchange relating to foreign currency, or, in general, any interest or instrument commonly known as a "security," or any certificate of interest or participation in, temporary or interim certificate for, receipt for, guarantee of, or warrant or right to subscribe to or purchase, any of the foregoing.

Because the term *security* is defined so broadly, the circumstances of a particular transaction must be analyzed to determine whether in fact it involves a security and is subject to regulation.

Certain investments that are commonly agreed to be securities include the stock and bonds of public and private companies. However, some investments, which by their name fall into the definition of securities, are not necessarily considered securities. An example is the stock in a cooperative association owning an apartment building, whereby an occupant of the building owns shares of stock that are inextricably linked to the lease of a particular unit of the building. In *United Housing Foundation v. Forman*,[1] the U.S. Supreme Court held that because the dwelling was used as a place of habitation, the inducement to purchase was solely to acquire living space and not to invest for profit. Consequently, the Court ruled that the shares of stock were not securities under the 1933 Act.

The scope of the law goes further than just the category of commonly agreed upon securities. Under federal law, a type of security—an investment contract—is present if the transaction involves an investment of money in a common enterprise with profits to come solely from the efforts of others. This test was first enunciated in the following case.

---

1. 421 U.S. 837, 95 S.Ct. 2051 (1975).

■ A Case in Point: Summary

Case 22.1
SEC v. W. J. HOWEY CO.
Supreme Court of the
United States
328 U.S. 293, 66 S.Ct. 1100
(1946).

FACTS   The W. J. Howey Company (Howey) owned large tracts of citrus acreage in Lake County, Florida. Expansion of the citrus acreage was financed, in part, by the sale of strips of land bearing citrus trees to persons living in various parts of the United States. Each prospective investor was offered both a land-sale contract and an optional service contract (with a

Case 22.1 continued on following page

Case **22.1** continued

ten-year term) after being told that it was not feasible to invest in a grove unless service arrangements were made. Although investors were free to use any service company, approximately 85% of the acreage sold was serviced by a company affiliated with Howey.

Most of the investors were unskilled in agriculture. The primary motivation for investing was the expectation of substantial profits, projected to be 10% annually over a ten-year period.

ISSUE PRESENTED   Does the offer and sale of parcels of land bearing citrus trees, coupled with optional management contracts pursuant to which the promoter cares for the trees, constitute an investment contract and hence a security under section 2(1) of the 1933 Act?

SUMMARY OF OPINION   The U.S. Supreme Court held that the transactions in this case clearly involved investment contracts as listed in section 2(1). The plan involved a scheme "whereby a person invests his money in a common enterprise and is led to expect profits solely from the efforts of the promoter or a third party." The persons buying the land were not skilled in the cultivation, harvesting, or marketing of citrus fruits, had no intent to occupy the land and develop it for themselves, and were attracted solely by the prospect of a return on their investment.

The Court held that the critical element in the transaction was the large-scale cooperative nature of the enterprise and the managerial efforts of the promoters. The transfer of real property rights was purely incidental. Accordingly, there was no question that an investment contract was involved. The fact that some investors chose not to accept the optional service contract was immaterial, the Court concluded, because the 1933 Act prohibits the offer, as well as the sale, of unregistered, nonexempt securities.

RESULT   Howey had offered and sold securities.

COMMENTS   This case makes it clear that a security can be present even in schemes that are not purely speculative or promotional in nature, and that involve investments in tangible assets having intrinsic value. The Supreme Court shifted the focus in determining whether or not a security was involved from the surface appearance of a transaction to the expectations of the parties. Subsequent cases have expanded the *Howey* test and have held that section 2(1) is not to be read literally, because Congress intended the application of the federal securities laws to turn on the economic realities underlying a transaction, and not on the name attached to it.

Although the *Howey* test required that the investor rely solely on the efforts of others for the expectation of profits, subsequent decisions have established that there can be an investment contract, and thus a security, even if the investor participates in the generation of profits.[2]

An interest in a general partnership is generally not held to be a security, because each partner by law has the right to exercise control in the operation of the partnership. However, the courts have found a general partnership to be an interest in a security if it meets any of the following three tests:

1. The partnership agreement leaves so little power to the partners that the arrangement is tantamount to a limited partnership.

---

2. *SEC v. Glenn W. Turner Enterprises, Inc.*, 474 F.2d 476 (9th Cir. 1973), *cert. denied*, 414 U.S. 821, 94 S.Ct. 117 (1973).

2. The investor is so inexperienced in business affairs that she is incapable of intelligently exercising her partnership powers.

3. The investor is so dependent on the unique management ability of the promoter or manager that he cannot replace the manager or exercise meaningful partnership powers.[3]

A limited partnership interest is almost always held to constitute a security because limited partners, in order to protect their limited liability, are prohibited by law from taking part in the control of the partnership business. An interest in real estate is not in itself considered a security, though it may be a security if combined with a management contract, as in *Howey*.

In recent years there has been a controversy as to whether the sale of an entire business through the sale of its corporate stock involved the sale of a security. Under the sale-of-business doctrine, certain courts held that compliance with federal securities laws was not necessary because the economic reality of the transaction was that a business was being sold, rather than securities. The United States Supreme Court rejected this doctrine in *Landreth Timber Co. v. Landreth*, holding that the sale of a business through a stock transaction is a securities transaction if the stock possesses all of the characteristics traditionally associated with common stock.[4]

Promissory notes and other evidences of indebtedness may or may not constitute a security, depending on the factual context. In the following case the Supreme Court set forth the tests for determining which types of notes are securities.

---

3. The test to determine whether a general partnership constitutes a security was set forth in *Williamson v. Tucker*, 645 F.2d 404 (5th Cir. 1981), *cert. denied*, 454 U.S. 897, 102 S.Ct. 396 (1981), and later applied in *Holden v. Hagopian*, 978 F.2d 1115 (9th Cir. 1992).

4. *Landreth Timber Co. v. Landreth*, 471 U.S. 681, 105 S.Ct. 2297 (1985).

■ **A Case in Point:**   **Summary**

Case 22.2
REVES v. ERNST & YOUNG
Supreme Court of the
United States
494 U.S. 56, 110 S.Ct. 945
(1990).

FACTS Farmers' Cooperative of Arkansas and Oklahoma, Inc. (the Co-op) was an agricultural cooperative of approximately 23,000 members. In order to raise money to support its general business operations, the Co-op sold demand notes, that is, promissory notes payable at any time that the holder of the note requested payment. The notes were not collateralized and were uninsured, and paid a variable rate of interest that was adjusted monthly to keep it higher than the rate paid by local financial institutions. The Co-op offered the notes to both members and nonmembers, marketing the scheme as a safe and secure "investment program."

Despite such assurances, the Co-op filed for bankruptcy, leaving approximately $10 million in demand notes unpaid. A group of holders of the notes sued the Co-op's auditors under section 10(b) of the 1934 Act, claiming that the auditors intentionally failed to follow generally accepted accounting principles in evaluating the financial condition of the Co-op.

The note holders prevailed at the trial level, receiving a $6.1 million judgment. The auditors appealed, claiming that the demand notes were not securities under the 1934 Act. (The definition of "security" under section 3(a)(10) of the 1934 Act is virtually identical to the definition under section 2(1) of the 1933 Act.) The U.S. Court of Appeals for the Eighth Circuit agreed with the auditors, and reversed the trial court's decision. The Eighth Circuit's decision was largely based on the fact that the demand notes did not satisfy the *Howey* test for an investment contract. The note holders appealed.

Case 22.2 continued on following page

*Case **22.2** continued*

ISSUE PRESENTED   Are demand notes issued by a farmers' cooperative to its members securities?

SUMMARY OF OPINION   The U.S. Supreme Court rejected the Eighth Circuit's reasoning and adopted a "family resemblance" test to use in determining whether a promissory note is a security. Under this test, a promissory note is initially presumed to be a security based upon the literal language of the Securities Acts ("The term 'security' means any note. . . ."). This presumption may be rebutted, however, by a showing that the note bears a "strong resemblance" (in terms of four specific factors) to an enumerated category of instruments commonly held not to constitute securities. The four specific factors used in evaluating an instrument are:

(1) the motivations that would prompt a reasonable seller and buyer to enter into the transaction;

(2) the plan of distribution of the instrument;

(3) the reasonable expectations of the investing public; and

(4) whether some factor, such as the existence of another regulatory scheme, significantly reduces the risk of the instrument, thereby rendering application of the federal securities laws unnecessary.

The category of instruments commonly held not to constitute securities includes notes delivered in connection with consumer financing, notes secured by a home mortgage, and short-term notes secured by accounts receivable.

Applying these four factors to the case at hand, the Court observed that:

(1) the Co-op sold the notes in an effort to raise capital for its general business operations, and the purchasers bought them in order to earn a profit in the form of interest;

(2) the notes were distributed to a wide group of people over an extended period;

(3) the notes were characterized to the public as investments, and it is likely that the public perceived them as such; and

(4) there was no risk-reducing factor making application of the federal securities law unnecessary (for example, the notes were not federally insured certificates of deposit).

Because the notes bore no family resemblance to the types of notes commonly held not to constitute securities, and in fact resembled the types of instruments the federal securities laws were designed to regulate, the Court held the notes were securities.

In reaching its decision, the Court expressly rejected the use of the *Howey* test in determining whether or not a note constitutes a security. It stated that the *Howey* test is useful in determining whether an instrument constitutes an investment contract, but is not helpful in determining whether an instrument is a note within the statutory definition of "security."

The Court also expressly rejected the use of an investment-versus-commercial test, which previously had been used by the majority of circuits in determining whether a note constituted a security. Under this test, notes issued in a commercial or consumer context were held not to be securities, but those issued in an investment context were held to be securities.

The Court lastly rejected the auditor's argument that because the notes were demand notes, they fell within the literal terms of section 3(a)(10) of the 1934 Act ("the term 'security'. . . shall not include . . . any note . . . which has a maturity at the time of issuance of not exceeding nine months"). The Court held that a demand note does not necessarily mature in nine months. In light of this patent ambiguity and in light of Congress's broad purposes in enacting the federal securities law, the Court chose not to interpret the exclusion in section 3(a)(10) to cover the Co-op's demand notes.

RESULT   The demand notes issued by the farmers' cooperative to its members were, in fact, securities.

COMMENTS   The holding in *Reves v. Ernst & Young* removed much of the uncertainty regarding the status of promissory notes for securities-law purposes. Prior to this decision, the courts were widely split as to the proper test to use in evaluating promissory notes. Although not a bright-line rule, the common-sense approach adopted by the Supreme Court should make easier the determination of when a particular type of promissory note is or is not a security.

In the following case the U.S. Court of Appeals for the Second Circuit applied the "family resemblance" test from *Reves* to decide whether loan participations were securities.

■ **A Case in Point:**   **In the Language of the Court**

Case 22.3
BANCO ESPAÑOL DE CRÉDITO v. SECURITY PACIFIC NATIONAL BANK
United States Court of Appeals for the Second Circuit
973 F.2d 51 (2d Cir. 1992), *cert. denied*, 113 S.Ct. 2992 (1993).

FACTS   Security Pacific National Bank had extended a line of credit to Integrated Resources under which it obtained short-term loans from the bank. Participations in these loans were sold to various institutional investors under a master agreement containing a disclaimer stating that each investor participated in the loans without relying on Security Pacific. Integrated later defaulted on the loans and declared bankruptcy. Several investors sued Security Pacific, arguing that the loan participations were securities under the 1933 Act, and sought to rescind their purchase agreement.

ISSUE PRESENTED   Are short-term loan participations arranged by a bank securities?

OPINION   ALTIMARI, C.J., writing for the U.S. Court of Appeals:

. . . .

In examining whether the loan participations could be considered "notes" which are also securities, the district court applied the "family resemblance" test set forth by the Supreme Court in *Reves*. Under the family resemblance test, a note is presumed to be a security unless an examination of the note, based on four factors, reveals a strong resemblance between the note and one of a judicially-enumerated list of instruments that are not securities. If the note in question is not sufficiently similar to one of these instruments, a court must then consider, using the same four factors, whether another category of non-security instruments should be added to the list. The four *Reves* factors to be considered in this examination are: (1) the motivations that would prompt a reasonable buyer and seller to enter into the transaction; (2) the plan of distribution of the instrument; (3) the reasonable expectations of the

Case 22.3 continued on following page

Case 22.3 continued

investing public; and (4) whether some factor, such as the existence of another regulatory scheme, significantly reduces the risk of the instrument, thereby rendering application of the securities laws unnecessary.

In addressing the first *Reves* factor, the district court found that Security Pacific was motivated by a desire to increase the lines of credit to Integrated while diversifying Security Pacific's risk; that Integrated was motivated by a need for short-term credit at competitive rates to finance its current operations; and that the purchasers of the loan participations sought a short-term return on excess cash. Based on these findings, the district court concluded that "the overall motivation of the parties was the promotion of commercial purposes" rather than an investment in a business enterprise.

Weighing the second *Reves* factor—the plan of distribution of the instrument—the district court observed that only institutional and corporate entities were solicited and that detailed individualized presentations were made by Security Pacific's sales personnel. The district court therefore concluded that the plan of distribution was "a limited solicitation to sophisticated financial or commercial institutions and not to the general public." We agree.

. . . .

With regard to the third factor—the reasonable perception of the instrument by the investing public—the district court considered the expectation of the sophisticated purchasers who signed [Master Participation Agreements] and determined that these institutions were given ample notice that the instruments were participations in loans and not investments in a business enterprise.

Finally, the district court noted that the Office of the Comptroller of the Currency has issued specific policy guidelines addressing the sale of loan participations. Thus, the fourth factor—the existence of another regulatory scheme—indicated that application of the securities laws was unnecessary.

Thus, under the *Reves* family resemblance analysis, as properly applied by the district court, we hold that the loan participations in the instant case are analogous to the enumerated category of loans issued by banks for commercial purposes and therefore do not satisfy the statutory definition of "notes" which are "securities."

. . . .

RESULT   Because the loan participations did not meet the statutory definition of securities, the plaintiffs could not maintain their action for relief under section 12(2) of the 1933 Act.

COMMENTS   In a strongly worded dissent, Justice Oakes stated that the loan notes differed from traditional loan participations in a number of important ways. First, the participants were motivated by an investment purpose, not a lending transaction. They were in many cases nonfinancial entities acting not as commercial lenders but as investors, and even though there were some banks, they purchased the instruments through their investment and trading departments, not their lending departments. Second, Security Pacific's promotional literature advertised the loan participations as competitive with commercial paper, a recognized security. And third, the loan notes differed from traditional loan participations in the scope of the information available to the purchasers. Thus, according to Justice Oakes, because the loan notes were purchased in investment transactions, they are securities.

Questions
1. If the loan participations had been securities, what type of relief would the plaintiffs have been granted?
2. Did the defendant, Security Pacific, have an ethical obligation to disclose to the investors any adverse facts it knew about Integrated Resources?

"Offer"

Section 2(3) of the 1933 Act defines an *offer* as "every attempt or offer to dispose of, or solicitation of an offer to buy, a security or interest in a security, for value." This definition is much broader than that in contract law. An offer that is unacceptably vague for contract-law purposes may well constitute an offer for federal securities-laws purposes. However, section 2(3) expressly provides that preliminary negotiations or agreements between an issuer and an underwriter or among underwriters do not constitute an offer to sell.

"Sale"

A *sale* is defined by section 2(3) to include "every contract of sale or disposition of a security or interest in a security, for value." The crucial term in this definition is *value*. It has been defined by the courts very broadly; more broadly, for example, than in state corporations statutes, which require that stock can only be issued for "value" in the form of cash, property, or compensation for past services.

■ The Public Offering

Once it is determined that an investment offering does in fact involve a security regulated by the statutes and rules discussed above, the issue of registration must be addressed.

Registration of Securities

Section 5 of the 1933 Act requires the registration of all securities offered and sold in the United States, unless an exemption from registration is available. Section 5 can be summarized as follows.

1. Section 5(a) prohibits the sale of a security before a registration statement has been filed with the SEC. The registration statement consists of filing forms and the *prospectus*, the document that an issuer of securities provides to prospective purchasers. Section 5(c) prohibits the use of any means of interstate commerce to offer to sell or buy any security during this time.

2. During the *quiet period* between the filing of the registration statement and the date the registration statement becomes effective with the SEC, written and oral offers to sell the security may be made, but all written offers must meet the standards required of a prospectus.

3. Once the registration becomes effective with the SEC (referred to as *going effective*), offers and sales of securities may be made. However, section 5(b) continues to require that any written offer or sale of a security be preceded or accompanied by a prospectus meeting the requirements of the 1933 Act.

In general, every public offering of securities must be registered with the SEC. The registration requirement is designed to ensure that certain information is filed with the SEC and distributed to potential investors by means of a prospectus. Unlike certain state securities authorities, the SEC does not have statutory authority to approve or disapprove an offering on its merits. Instead, the registration process is designed to ensure that the information provided to investors is accurate and complete. The general procedures to be followed in the registration process are found in sections 6 and 8 of the 1933 Act.

The registration of a public offering is an expensive and time-consuming affair. The process includes the preparation of the registration statement—that is, the document filed with the SEC—and of the prospectus, which must be included in the registration statement and provided to prospective investors. Securities lawyers, independent accountants, investment bankers, a printer, and an engraver all become involved in the process. The out-of-pocket fees and expenses for an initial public offering, excluding compensation for the investment bankers who underwrite the offering, can easily exceed $600,000. All such fees must be paid by the issuer of the securities (or in the case of offerings by persons other than the issuer, by the seller of the securities).

The Role of the Underwriter

A public offering of securities is typically, though not necessarily, underwritten by one or more broker-dealers or investment banking firms.

Firm-Commitment Underwriting   In a *firm-commitment underwriting*, the underwriters agree to purchase the entire offering, thus effectively shifting the risk of the offering from the issuer to the underwriters. The lead underwriter is responsible for negotiating with the issuer the terms of the offering and compensation, and for putting together an underwriting group. Each member of the underwriting group agrees to purchase a certain number of the securities of the issuer once the offering is declared effective by the SEC.

Such a commitment places the underwriters in a risky position. Therefore, the underwriting agreement between the issuer and the lead underwriter as representative of the underwriting group, and the agreements among the members of the underwriting group, are typically not signed until immediately before the offering is declared effective by the SEC. Until that time, the underwriters and the issuer operate under a letter of intent, which is typically designed not to be an enforceable contract. The price at which the securities will be offered and the underwriters' commission are usually not formally determined until the evening before the offering goes effective.

Once the offering becomes effective, the underwriters attempt to sell the securities that they are obligated to purchase. Most firm underwriting agreements are of short duration. Usually, the sale closes within one week of the day the agreement is signed. As of the closing date, the underwriters are obligated to purchase any securities that remain unsold. The "Inside Story" at the end of this chapter highlights a situation in which a stock offering of British Petroleum by the British government coincided with the October 1987 stock market crash. Weeks in advance of the proposed offering, the U.S. investment banks involved in the deal provided a firm-commitment underwriting to the government. After stock prices plummeted in the market crash, the U.S. underwriters lost up to $500 million from the post-crash offering.

Because a firm-commitment underwriting will provide the issuer with a predetermined amount of money within a specified period, it is attractive to issuers. A firm-commitment underwriting is also attractive to investors because it implies that the underwriters themselves are willing to take a risk on the offering. However, as it does place the members of the underwriting group at risk for the amount of the offering, broker-dealers and investment

bankers will usually only agree to a firm underwriting if they are certain that they will be able to sell the offered securities quickly. Such certainty will depend upon a variety of factors, including the amount of money being sought, the performance and prospects of the company, whether the company is seasoned or relatively new, and the condition of the public securities market.

Best-Efforts Underwriting   In a *best-efforts underwriting*, the underwriters do not agree to purchase the securities being offered. Instead they agree to use their best efforts to find buyers at an agreed-upon price. Best-efforts underwritings are often used for initial public offerings or for companies that are unseasoned.

A best-efforts offering leaves the risks of the offering entirely with the issuer. However, some established, successful companies may prefer a best-efforts offering because the cost of distribution is lower than for a firm-commitment underwriting.

The Registration Statement

Sections 7 and 10 of the 1933 Act, and the rules promulgated by the SEC under the act, contain detailed guidelines as to what must be included in the registration statement and the accompanying prospectus. Regulations C and S-K, adopted by the SEC pursuant to the 1933 Act, list the general information required in connection with most public registrations.[5] In addition, the SEC has issued a variety of forms that list the information required in connection with particular types of transactions.

Forms   Securities offered in an initial public offering are registered in a registration statement meeting the requirements of *form S-1*. The registration statement must include a complete description of the securities being offered, the business of the issuer, the risk factors, the management, and the major shareholders, and must include audited financial statements.

Companies that have been filing periodic reports under the 1934 Act, but that are not so widely followed that the SEC could be confident that information previously filed would be disseminated in the marketplace, file on *form S-2*. Form S-2 allows these companies to present certain information in a streamlined form and to incorporate previous filings by reference, so that investors can obtain more information if desired. This is part of the SEC's integrated disclosure system, which is designed to integrate the reporting requirements under

---

5. 17 CFR § 230.400 *et seq.* (1994); 17 CFR § 229 (1994).

EXHIBIT 22-2 Comparison of Public Offering Requirements

	Form S-1 Offering	**Form SB-1 Offering**	**Form SB-2 Offering**
Amount of offering	No limit.	Up to $10 million in any fiscal year.	No limit.
Type of issuer	Any issuer.	Must be a non-reporting or a transitional small business issuer.	Must be a small business issuer.
Type of offering	No limitations.	No limitations.	No limitations.
Type of disclosure required	S-1 basic registration form for most offerings. S-1 items referenced in regulation S-K.	Offering statement with 3 models: 1) Q&A, form U-7 2) Form 1-A, old form 3) Form SB-2, part I.	Simplified form SB-2. SB-2 items referenced in regulation S-B, a simplified version of regulation S-K.

the 1934 Act with the prospectus requirement under the 1933 Act.

Form S-3 applies to a category of companies that have filed periodic reports under the 1934 Act for at least three years and have a widespread following in the marketplace. For an offering by an issuer of common stock, for example, the issuer can only use form S-3 if the aggregate market value of the voting stock held by nonaffiliates is $150 million or more; or alternatively, if the aggregate market value of the voting stock held by nonaffiliates is $100 million or more, and the issuer has an annual trading volume of 3 million shares or more. (*Affiliates* include officers, directors, and controlling shareholders. The SEC has a rebuttable presumption that any shareholder with 10% of the issuer's stock is an affiliate.)

For companies filing on form S-3, information about the registrant that has been reported in annual and quarterly reports filed under the 1934 Act need not be provided to shareholders in the prospectus, unless there has been a material change in the registrant's affairs or financial statements. However, such reports are incorporated by reference and are deemed a part of the prospectus for liability purposes.

In 1992, the SEC proposed rule changes under its Small Business Initiatives (SBI) that would ease the cost of raising capital for small businesses. It adopted a number of amendments to the 1933 Act registration system that simplified offering methods for small companies by

the adoption of new registration forms, *form SB-1* and *form SB-2*, for *small business issuers*. These issuers are defined as companies with revenues less than $25 million whose market value of publicly held securities (other than those held by affiliates) is less than $25 million. Other aspects of the SBI changes that affect exemptions from registration and reporting requirements will be discussed later in this chapter.

The SEC adopted form SB-1, under which nonreporting and transitional small business issuers can offer up to $10 million annually. Form SB-2 has no limit on the amount of offerings by small business issuers. Both forms can be used for initial and repeat offerings as well as for primary and secondary offerings. In addition, the SB forms reduce the need for audited financial statements compared to what is required under form S-1. Only the last fiscal year's audited balance sheet and the previous two years' audited income statements are required under forms SB-1 and SB-2. Exhibit 22-2 compares some of the requirements of registered offerings on forms S-1, SB-1 and SB-2.

Prospectus The prospectus is the document provided to prospective purchasers of an issuer's securities. It is contained within the registration statement.

The tone of a prospectus frequently strikes nonlawyers as dry, bleak, and confusing. Such a perception arises out of the conflicting purposes of the prospectus. On the one hand, it is a selling document, designed to present the best possible view of the investment and the issuing company. On the other hand, it is a disclosure document, an insurance policy against claims of securities fraud. It is this second function that usually predominates. The prospectus usually contains only provable statements of fact, with numerous disclaimers regarding the future success of the issuer. Businesspeople, accustomed to presenting their company in the best possible light, frequently have difficulty adjusting to the somber tone of the prospectus.

A sample cover page of a prospectus is shown in Exhibit 22-3.

Registration Procedure

The registration statement must be filed with the SEC. Section 8 of the 1933 Act provides that the registration automatically becomes effective on the twentieth day after filing, unless the SEC fixes an earlier date. Most registrants file their registration statement with language stating that it shall not become effective until declared effective by the SEC, so that the staff of the SEC has the necessary time (which usually exceeds the statutory 20-day period) to review the filing.

Each amendment to the registration statement filed prior to the effective date starts the 20-day period running again; however, if the SEC has consented to the amendment, the waiting period may be accelerated. If, on the other hand, the SEC finds that the registration statement is materially defective in some respect, it may, after notice and a hearing, issue a stop order suspending the effectiveness of the offering.

Review   Registration statements received by the SEC are subject to review by the SEC staff. The extent of review is usually affected by the nature of the offering and the number of filings that the SEC is faced with reviewing. In general, all first-time registrants will receive a complete review. Most repeat registrants will receive a more limited review, and some will receive no review.

Comments of the SEC staff are conveyed through a letter of comment, which is either read over the telephone to the issuer's counsel or, less often, mailed to counsel directly. The members of the SEC staff are usually available to discuss these letters of comment either by telephone or in person. Although the comment letters contain only suggestions without force of law, they generally result in the filing of an amendment to the registration statement. Acceding to the staff's reasonable suggestions is less expensive and less time-consuming than fighting

an issue in an administrative hearing and in court. The amended registration statement is usually filed with a letter from counsel answering, item by item, the issues raised by the staff.

Quiet Period   The time between the filing of the registration statement and its becoming effective is called the quiet period because the law severely limits what the issuer and underwriters can say or publish during this time. No sale of securities can occur prior to the effectiveness of the registration statement; however, the underwriters may assemble selling groups, distribute copies of the preliminary prospectus, and even solicit offers to buy the securities. The preliminary prospectus—sometimes referred to as a *red-herring prospectus* because a notice on the cover states in red ink that it is not final and is subject to completion—is an incomplete version of the final prospectus. It sets forth the proposed range for the selling price and omits underwriters except for the lead underwriters, whose names appear on the cover page of the preliminary prospectus.

Selling efforts during the quiet period must be done in strict compliance with the securities laws. Any offers to buy can only be accepted after the registration statement is declared effective by the SEC and only after each prospective investor is provided with a copy of the final prospectus. Notice of a proposed offer is frequently circulated by means of a *tombstone ad*, so named because of its appearance and somewhat somber tone. Exhibit 22-4 depicts a tombstone ad.

Tombstone ads are governed by rule 134 of the 1933 Act. Such ads are not intended to be selling devices but merely a means of identifying the existence of a public offering, and indicating where a prospectus may be obtained. Rule 134 restricts the notice to 14 limited categories of information. If the notice has more, it will be deemed a prospectus and will be required to meet more rigorous information standards.

The information that may be contained in such a notice includes the name of the issuer, the title of the securities, the amount offered, the price of the securities, and similar factual information. This type of advertisement may not solicit offers to buy the securities unless it is preceded or accompanied by a prospectus and unless it contains a statement that no offer to buy the securities can be accepted, and no part of the purchase price can be received, until the registration statement becomes effective.

The issuing company and its underwriter must be careful about the information they release to the public during the quiet period. If an issuer or underwriter conditions the

EXHIBIT 22-3 Prospectus Cover Page

1,900,000 Shares
Common Stock

Of the 1,900,000 shares of Common Stock offered hereby, 950,000 shares are being sold by NetManage, Inc. ("NetManage" or the "Company") and 950,000 shares are being sold by the Selling Stockholders. See "Principal and Selling Stockholders." The Company will not receive any of the proceeds from the sale of shares by the Selling Stockholders. On February 10, 1994, the last reported sale price of the Common Stock was $34.25. The Company's Common Stock is quoted on the NASDAQ National Market System under the symbol NETM. See "Price Range of Common Stock."

The Common Stock offered hereby involves a high degree of risk. See "Risk Factors."

THESE SECURITIES HAVE NOT BEEN APPROVED OR DISAPPROVED BY THE SECURITIES AND EXCHANGE COMMISSION OR ANY STATE SECURITIES COMMISSION NOR HAS THE COMMISSION OR ANY STATE SECURITIES COMMISSION PASSED UPON THE ACCURACY OR ADEQUACY OF THIS PROSPECTUS. ANY REPRESENTATION TO THE CONTRARY IS A CRIMINAL OFFENSE.

	Price to Public	Underwriting Discounts and Commissions	Proceeds to Company(1)	Proceeds to Selling Stockholders
Per Share	$33.00	$1.98	$31.02	$31.02
Total (2)	$62,700,000	$3,762,000	$29,469,000	$29,469,000

(1) Before deducting expenses estimated at $350,000, which are payable by the Company.

(2) The Company has granted to the Underwriters a 30-day option to purchase up to 285,000 additional shares of Common Stock solely to cover over-allotments, if any. See "Underwriting." If such option is exercised in full, the total Price to Public, Underwriting Discounts and Commissions, Proceeds to Company and Proceeds to Selling Stockholders will be $72,105,000, $4,326,300, $38,309,700 and $29,469,000, respectively.

The Common Stock is offered by the Underwriters as stated herein, subject to receipt and acceptance by them and subject to their right to reject any order in whole or in part. It is expected that delivery of such shares will be made through the offices of Robertson, Stephens & Company, L.P. ("Robertson, Stephens & Company"), San Francisco, California on or about February 17, 1994.

Robertson, Stephens & Company   Oppenheimer & Co., Inc.

The date of this Prospectus is February 10, 1994

EXHIBIT 22-4   Tombstone Ad

This announcement is under no circumstances to be construed as an offer to sell or as a solicitation of an offer to buy any of these securities. The offering is made only by the Prospectus.

New Issue   **April 28, 1994**

1,400,000 Ordinary Shares

BELIZE HOLDINGS INC.
(Incorporated under the laws of Belize)

___

Price $16.50 Per Ordinary Share

___

Copies of the Prospectus may be obtained in any State or jurisdiction in which this announcement is circulated from only such of the undersigned or other dealers or brokers as may lawfully offer these securities in such State or jurisdiction.

Merrill Lynch & Co.

Bear, Stearns & Co. Inc.	**CS First Boston**	**Goldman, Sachs & Co.**
Lehman Brothers	**Morgan Stanley & Co.** Incorporated	**N M Rothschild and Smith New Court**
Smith Barney Shearson Inc.	**UBS Securities Inc.**	**S.G.Warburg & Co. Inc.**
Arnhold and S. Bleichroeder, Inc.	**Doley Securities , Inc.**	**Janney Montgomery Scott Inc.**
Monness, Crespi, Hardt & Co., Inc.		**Tucker Anthony** Incorporated

EXHIBIT 22-5   Disclaimer from the MIPS Computer Systems Prospectus

In an article in a securities industry periodical dated December 11, 1989, a representative of Morgan Stanley & Co. Incorporated, one of the underwriters serving as a representative of the U.S. underwriters of this offering, was quoted regarding the offering. The information was solicited by a reporter for the periodical, and the Morgan Stanley representative responded only with information he believed to be contained in the preliminary Prospectus. The following comments included in the article were attributed to the rep: "The Sunnyvale, Calif.-based computer systems manufacturer is expected to price the issue at 14-17. . . . Of the shares offered, one million will be placed in Europe and Japan because the company has a strong business presence overseas and wants a strong base of international shareholders. . . . The issue is expected to do well because MIPS is an industry leader in reduced instruction set computing (RISC). . . . RISC technology can be incorporated in both computer hardware and software and performs microprocessor operations in a significantly quicker and more efficient manner than existing technology. . . . With RISC you get a lot more bang for your buck. It is the new platform for the computer industry. . . . The company is perceived in the industry as a winner because its revenues come not only from the sale of its products but also from licensing arrangements for its technology with the leading computer and semiconductor companies around the world. . . . The company will use the proceeds for working capital and to acquire capital equipment and possibly businesses, products or technologies. The company decided to do the IPO now because it perceived that the market for emerging growth company stock is improving. . . . Morgan was chosen to lead the issue as a result of a mutual courting process." . . . Some of these comments were not contained in the preliminary Prospectus and may be misleading to potential investors. The foregoing comments were not authorized by the Company or any underwriter (including Morgan Stanley), do not represent the views of the Company or any underwriter (including Morgan Stanley), and, to the extent they are inconsistent with or conflict with the information contained in this Prospectus or they relate to information not contained in this Prospectus, are disclaimed by the Company and the underwriters (including Morgan Stanley). Accordingly, prospective investors should not rely on any of these comments or any other information not contained in this Prospectus.

market with a news article or press release about the company and its upcoming offering, the act is referred to as *gun-jumping*. In such circumstances, the company may be in violation of the 1933 Act. Exhibit 22-5 contains excerpts from the prospectus for the public offering of MIPS Computer Systems, Inc. stock on December 21, 1989. Issuance of the disclaimer was necessary to protect the company and its underwriters from a charge of gunjumping, because some of the analyst's published comments were not contained in the preliminary prospectus.

Going Effective   Once a registration statement has been informally cleared by the SEC staff, or the registrant has received notice that the registration statement will not be reviewed, a pre-effective amendment will be filed with the SEC. This is typically accompanied by a request that the waiting period be accelerated so that the registration statement will become effective at a particular date and time. Without the request for acceleration, the registration statement would not become effective until the expiration of an additional 20-day period.

Once an offering is declared effective, sales of the securities may be consummated, provided that each purchaser is given a copy of the final prospectus. Information concerning the price of the securities and underwriting arrangements is filed with the SEC as part of the final prospectus. Supplemental sale literature, which in most cases need not be reviewed by the SEC, may be provided to prospective purchasers. Such sales literature must be preceded or accompanied by the final prospectus.

Exhibit 22-6 suggests a timeline for managers who are considering a public securities offering.

Shelf Registration

Rule 415 under the 1933 Act provides for the *shelf registration* of securities, that is, the registration of a number of securities at one time for issuance later. The securities can then be issued over a period of time, for example, in connection with continuous acquisition programs or employee stock-benefit plans, or at a later date, for example, when interest rates or market conditions are more

EXHIBIT 22-6   Managerial Timeline for a Public Securities Offering

Day 1 - 30	• Decide upon a public offering of securities to raise capital, and choose a securities underwriting firm.
Day 30 - 60	• With the aid of the underwriter, prepare the forms and prospectus for the registration statement.
Day 60 - 90	• File the registration statement with the SEC for review, and submit any amendments to the filing.
Day 90 - 120	• During the quiet period, the underwriter can assemble selling groups, distribute copies of the preliminary prospectus, and solicit offers to sell the securities. The company must not disclose information to the public, except that required in the ordinary course of business.
Day 120 +	• Once the offering is declared effective and the pricing amendment is filed, sales of the company's securities may begin.

favorable to the issuance of securities. Shelf registration can result in reduced legal, accounting, and printing expenses, and increased competition among underwriters. Moreover, the issuer can respond more flexibly to rapidly changing market conditions, by varying the structure and terms of the securities on short notice.

Registration is intended to ensure that current information is available to prospective underwriters and purchasers of securities. Accordingly, shelf registration is restricted to offerings in which the information contained in the registration statement will not become stale or inaccurate after some months or years.

Rule 415 limits the availability of shelf registration to ten types of offerings, which can be broken down into two basic categories: (1) "traditional" shelf offerings, and (2) offerings of securities of certain large, publicly traded companies that are eligible to use short-form registration procedures such as form S-3.

Traditional shelf offerings include securities offered pursuant to employee benefit plans; securities offered or sold pursuant to dividend or interest reinvestment plans; warrants, or rights, or upon conversion of other outstand-

ing securities; mortgage-related securities; and securities issued in connection with business-combination transactions.

With respect to offerings by certain large, publicly traded companies, the SEC has decided that because the market receives a steady stream of high-quality information concerning these issuers, the risks of stale information are minimal.

Reorganizations and Combinations

When securities holders are asked to approve a corporate reorganization or combination—such as a reclassification of securities, a merger involving an exchange of securities, or a transfer of assets of one corporation in exchange for the securities of another—they are in effect faced with an investment decision. In recognition of this fact, the SEC adopted rule 145, which expressly provides that the protections provided by the 1933 Act's registration requirements are applicable to certain types of business reorganizations and combinations. An offer, offer to sell, or sale occurs when a plan of reorganization is submitted

EXHIBIT 22-7 Key Terms of the 1933 Securities Act

Security	Most commonly used criteria under federal law: 1. Investment of money 2. Common enterprise 3. Profits derived "solely" from efforts of others. Section 2(1)
Offer	"Every attempt or offer to dispose of, or solicitation of an offer to buy, a security or interest in a security, for value." Section 2(3)
Sale	"Every contract of sale or disposition of a security or interest in a security, for value." Section 2(3)
Accredited Investor	As defined by rule 501 under Regulation D: 1. National bank, savings and loan, registered broker-dealer, insurance company, investment company, SBIC (small business investment company), employee benefit plan if the investment decision is made by a "plan fiduciary" 2. Charitable organization, corporation, or business trust with total assets greater than $5 million 3. Any director, executive officer, or general partner of the issuer 4. Any natural person with individual income greater than $200,000 in each of the two most recent years or joint income with spouse greater than $300,000 in each of those years with a reasonable expectation of the same income level in the current year 5. Natural person with individual net worth or joint net worth with spouse greater than $1 million at time of purchase 6. Entity owned by any of the above 7. Trust with assets greater than $5 million with purchases directed by a sophisticated investor 8. Private development company (as defined)
Restricted Securities	"Securities issued in a transaction not involving a public offering." Rule 144
Issuer	"Every person who issues or proposes to issue any security," including, for purposes of definition of underwriter, "any person directly or indirectly controlling or controlled by the issuer, or any person under direct or indirect common control with the issuer." Section 2(4)
Affiliate	Any officer, director, or major shareholder (generally presumed to include one holding at least 10% of issuer's stock). Someone who controls, or is controlled by, or co-controls with the issuer. (Rule 144)
Underwriter	"Any person who has purchased from an issuer with a view to, or offers or sells for an issuer in connection with, the distribution of any security." Section 2(11)
"Not an Underwriter"	"Not an underwriter" safe-harbor requirements of rule 144: 1. Adequate public information available 2. Two year holding period (unless affiliate sells unrestricted securities) 3. Sales limitations for any three-month period: the greater of 1% of the outstanding securities of the class, or the average weekly trading volume for the preceding four weeks 4. Must sell through a broker or directly to a market maker 5. Form 144 filing if more than 500 shares or greater than $10,000 aggregate price in three months 6. Must have bona fide intention to sell within a reasonable amount of time after selling
Rule 144(k)	A non-affiliate who has held the security for more than three years may resell without restriction
Rule 144A	A non-affiliate may resell without restriction to a "qualified institutional buyer"

to shareholders for approval. Transactions that fall within the guidelines specified in rule 145 should be registered with the SEC in a combined registration statement and proxy statement on *form S-4*, unless an exemption from registration is available.

Because shareholder approval of mergers and other combinations necessarily involves communications between a corporation and its shareholders, rule 145 also contains specific rules as to whether such communications will not be deemed to be a prospectus or an offer to sell for purposes of the 1933 Act.

Rule 145 also provides that under certain circumstances affiliates of the acquired company, such as officers, directors, or controlling shareholders, are deemed *underwriters*, that is, persons selling securities on behalf of the issuer or a person who controls or is under common control with the issuer. Such affiliates cannot resell their securities without compliance with certain resale restrictions that include limitations on the amount of securities sold in a three-month period.

Secondary Offerings

A principal advantage of registering a securities offering with the SEC and the appropriate state securities authorities is that the securities may be traded relatively freely following the initial public offering. A *secondary offering*, that is, a subsequent offering by a person other than the issuer, must either be registered with the SEC or be exempt from registration. If the secondary offering is of nonrestricted securities and is made by a nonaffiliate, there are no limitations on the size of the offering or the number of offerees.

■ Exemptions for Offerings by the Issuer

In adopting the 1933 Act registration provisions, Congress provided exemptions from registration if there is no practical need for it or if the public benefits from it would be too remote. Exemptions from registration fall into two categories: exempt securities and exempt transactions.

Exempt securities, listed in section 3 of the 1933 Act, include the following.

1. Any security issued or guaranteed by the United States or any state of the United States.

2. Any security issued or guaranteed by any national bank.

3. Any security issued by a charitable organization.

4. Any security that is part of an issue offered and sold only to persons residing within a single state or territory, if the issuer is a resident of the same state or territory. (Note: Even though the intrastate offering exemption is listed under section 3, the SEC treats it like the transactional exemptions under section 4.)

Exempt transactions are described in section 4 of the 1933 Act. They include:

1. "Transactions by any person other than an issuer, underwriter or dealer" (section 4(1)).

2. "Transactions by an issuer not involving any public offering" (section 4(2), the private-offering exemption).

Most state blue sky laws have exemptions from registration that roughly correspond to the federal exemptions.

Private Offerings

Because of the expense and burdens of public offerings, companies trying to raise money usually attempt to qualify for an exemption from registration. The most frequently relied upon is the exemption for private offerings. A *private offering* is a transaction not involving an offer to the public, but rather to selected qualified investors. Private offerings are often referred to as private placements. A private offering can be consummated more quickly and with far less expense than a public offering.

However, because securities offered under the private-offering exemption are unregistered, their subsequent transfer is restricted, and their price will be discounted accordingly. In addition, purchasers of privately offered securities may demand a greater voice in the operation of the business, or sweeteners such as dividend preferences or mandatory redemption privileges, which force the company to repurchase the stock upon the occurrence of certain events.

Under section 4(2), an offering is exempt from registration if it does not involve a "public offering." This term is not defined in the 1933 Act and thus has been the subject of much judicial interpretation. The SEC originally took the position that "under ordinary circumstances an offering to not more than 25 persons is not an offering to a substantial number and presumably does not involve a public offering."[6] This guideline was rejected by the Supreme Court as summarized on the following page.

Regulation D: Safe-Harbor Exemptions

Responding to the need for greater certainty in connection with the private-offering exemption, the SEC adopted reg-

---

6. Securities Act Release No. 285 (1935).

■ **A Case in Point:**   **Summary**

Case 22.4
SEC v. RALSTON PURINA CO.
Supreme Court of the
United States
346 U.S. 119, 73 S.Ct. 981
(1953).

FACTS   Ralston Purina, a feed and cereal company, offered common stock at market prices to the employees of the company. Among those employees responding to the offer were artists, bake shop foremen, chow-loading foremen, clerical assistants, clerks, stenographers, and at least one veterinarian. Between 1947 and 1951, the company sold to 2,000 of its employees a total of $2 million worth of stock. The employees lived in various locations throughout the United States. Ralston Purina took the position that because the stock was offered only to "key employees" of the company, it was a private offering exempt from registration under the 1933 Act.

ISSUE PRESENTED   Does the determination of whether a transaction is a public or private offering depend primarily upon the sophistication of the offerees, rather than upon the number of offerees?

SUMMARY OF OPINION   The U.S. Supreme Court held that the offering was not exempt from registration. The Court stated that absent a showing of special circumstances, employees are indistinguishable from other members of the investing public as far as the securities laws are concerned.

The Supreme Court also rejected a strict numerical test. Instead, the Court held, the critical consideration is whether the class of persons offered the securities needs the protection of the 1933 Act: "An offering to those who are shown to be able to fend for themselves is a transaction not involving any public offering." If, as in the present case, an offering is made to those who are not able to fend for themselves, the transaction is a public offering. The Court noted that an important factor affecting this determination is whether the offerees have access to the same kind of information that the 1933 Act would make available through a registration statement.

RESULT   Ralston Purina's offer of stock to its employees was not exempt from registration.

COMMENTS   The Supreme Court ruling in *Ralston Purina* refocused attention under section 4(2) from a strict numerical test to the sophistication of the offerees. The ruling did little to clarify the private-offering exemption, and reliance on section 4(2) therefore remained an uncertain and somewhat risky proposition.

---

ulation D in 1982. Regulation D offers a safe harbor for those seeking exemption from registration: An issuer that fails to comply with all of the requirements of the applicable rule will not necessarily lose the exemption, because the transaction may still meet the more general conditions of section 4(2).

Regulation D contains three separate exemptions from registration, defined by rules 504, 505, and 506. Rules 501-503 define terms and concepts applicable to one or more of the exemptions.

Accredited Investors   The concept of an *accredited investor*, derived from earlier federal regulations and state securities laws, is based upon the idea that certain investors are so financially sophisticated that they do not need all of the protections afforded by the securities laws. Rule 501 defines an accredited investor as any one of the following:

1.   any national bank;

2.   any corporation, business trust, or charitable organization with total assets in excess of $5 million;

3.   any director, executive officer, or general partner of the issuer;

4.   any natural person who had individual income in excess of $200,000 in each of the two most recent years, or joint income with that person's spouse in excess of $300,000 in each of those years, and who has a reasonable expectation of reaching the same income level in the current year; and

5. any natural person whose individual net worth, or joint net worth with that person's spouse, at the time of the purchase exceeds $1 million.

Integration of Sales If an issuer makes successive sales within a limited period of time, the SEC may *integrate* the successive sales; that is, it may deem them to be part of a single sale. Integrating two or more offerings may increase the number of unaccredited investors beyond acceptable limits, resulting in the loss of a private-offering exemption. The SEC and the courts look at a variety of factors to determine whether offerings should be integrated. If the offerings (1) are part of a single plan of financing, (2) are made at or about the same time, (3) involve the same type of consideration, and (4) are made for the same purpose, then the SEC may recommend an integration of the offerings.

Rule 502(a) provides an integration safe harbor for regulation D offerings. Under rule 502(a), offers and sales made more than six months before the start of a regulation D offering or more than six months after its completion will not be considered part of the regulation D offering, provided that the same issuer makes no offers or sales of a similar class of securities during those six-month periods.

Rule 504 Rule 504 exempts offerings of up to $1 million within a 12-month period. There may be an unlimited number of purchasers under rule 504. Rule 504 is not available to issuers registered under the 1934 Act—known as public companies—or to investment companies like mutual funds. It is also not available to *blank check companies*—those that have no specific business except to locate and acquire a presently unknown business.

Rule 504 restricts the manner of offering the securities (advertising, solicitation, and the like), except in those situations in which the offering is registered in at least one state and a disclosure document is delivered to the purchasers of the securities, before a sale is consummated. The issuer must file with the SEC a notice on form D within 15 days after the first sale of securities.

Rule 505 Rule 505 exempts offerings of up to $5 million within a 12-month period. General solicitations and advertising are not permitted in connection with a rule 505 offering, and the issuer must reasonably believe that there are not more than 35 unaccredited investors. Rule 505 is not available to investment companies. Rule 505 requires that certain specified information be provided to purchasers (unless all are accredited investors). This

information is generally compiled in a private-placement memorandum or offering circular. Rule 505 also requires that purchasers have the opportunity to ask questions and receive answers concerning the terms of the offering. A notice on form D must be filed with the SEC within 15 days of the first sale of securities.

Rule 506 Rule 506 exempts offerings that in the issuer's reasonable belief are limited to no more than 35 unaccredited investors, provided that the issuer reasonably believes immediately prior to making any sale that each unaccredited investor either alone or with her purchaser representative has enough business experience to evaluate the merits and risks of the prospective investment. There can be an unlimited number of accredited investors. However, general solicitations and advertising are not permitted in connection with a rule 506 offering.

Like rule 505, rule 506 requires that certain specified information be provided to purchasers (unless all purchasers are accredited investors), and that purchasers have the opportunity to ask questions and receive answers concerning the terms of the offering. A notice on form D must be filed with the SEC within 15 days of the first sale of securities.

Section 4(6) Exemption

Section 4(6) of the 1933 Act exempts offers and sales by any issuer to an unlimited number of accredited investors, provided that the aggregate offering price does not exceed $5 million and there is no public solicitation or advertising in connection with the offering. The section 4(6) definition of "accredited investor" is almost identical to that of regulation D. The availability of this exemption does not depend upon the use of any type of disclosure document.

Regulation A

The 1992 SEC Small Business Initiatives expanded the previously largely unused regulation A exemption and included the adoption of a "testing the waters" provision, which permits issuers to solicit indications of interest before filing any required disclosure documents.

Size of Offering and Eligible Companies Under the revised regulation A, the amount that can be offered and sold in a 12-month period has been increased to $5 million, of which up to $1.5 million may be sold by the selling security holders. To limit its use to small businesses, only U.S. and Canadian companies that are not required to report under the 1934 Act can qualify to use the revised regulation A.

In addition, the regulation cannot be used by an investment company, a company issuing oil and gas rights, or a "blank check" company. As stated earlier, a blank check company is a development stage company that has no specific business plan or whose business plan is to acquire a presently unknown business.

Under rule 262, the "bad boy" provision, regulation A is unavailable if the issuer or its officers, directors, principal shareholders, or affiliates have been subject to specified proceedings, convictions, injunctions, or disciplinary orders from the SEC or other regulatory agencies arising from the securities business or postal fraud. To disqualify the company from using regulation A, the misconduct must have occurred within five years preceding the filing, or within ten years for officers, directors, and principal shareholders.

"Testing the Waters"   In an innovative step, the SEC permitted regulation A issuers to determine interest in a proposed offering prior to filing an offering statement. The issuer need only to file a solicitation of interest document with the SEC, along with copies of any written or broadcast media ads. There is no prohibition on general solicitation or advertising. Radio and television broadcasts and newspaper ads are permitted to determine investor interest in the offering.

However, no sales may be made or payment received during the test-the-waters period. To move forward, the company must file form 1-A with the SEC, and the regulation A offering statement must be qualified by the SEC. Once the offering statement is filed, testing-the-waters activity ceases. Sales can be made only after the passage of a required 20-day waiting period from the time of the last solicitation of interest.

By late 1993, more than 30 issuers had used the "testing-the-waters" provision for a variety of businesses. Of the 30, only five companies actually proceeded with the regulation A offering. According to an official of the SEC and a number of attorneys, the real success stories were the companies that, after testing the waters and finding them unfavorable, did not spend the considerable amount of money required to do a public offering.[7]

Offerings to Employees

Nonpublic companies that are not registered pursuant to the 1934 Act often face a problem when instituting employee stock plans. If the company relies on rule 504

---

7. "SEC Pleased with SBI, Agency Official Declares," *Securities Regulation and Law Report* (BNA), October 8, 1993, 1341.

it can only issue $1 million in one 12-month period. Because employee offerings are usually continuous, the issuer may face serious integration problems. It is seldom practical to shut a plan down for six months to take advantage of regulation D's integration safe harbor.

In response to these problems, the SEC adopted rule 701 and temporary rules 702T and 703T. Rule 701 exempts offers and sales of securities made: (1) pursuant to a written compensatory benefit plan for employees, directors, general partners, trustees (if the issuer is a business trust), officers, consultants, or advisors; or (2) pursuant to a written contract relating to the compensation of such persons. If the benefit plan is for consultants or advisors, they must render bona fide services not connected with the offer and sale of securities in a capital-raising transaction. Exempt compensatory benefit plans include purchase, savings, option, bonus, stock-appreciation, profit sharing, thrift incentive, and pension plans. The issuer must provide each plan participant with a copy of the plan and each contractor with a copy of his contract, but no other disclosure document is required by rule 701.

Rule 701 applies only to securities offered and sold in an amount not more than the greater of : (1) $500,000, or (2) 15% of the total assets of the issuer, or (3) 15% of the outstanding securities of the class being offered and sold. Moreover, the aggregate offering price of securities subject to outstanding offers made in reliance on rule 701 plus securities sold in the preceding 12 months in reliance on rule 701 may not exceed $5 million.

Rule 701 provides additional integration relief for issuers who sell both under rule 701 and under rules 504 or 505 of regulation D. Offerings under rule 701 are not integrated with those under rules 504 and 505, and vice versa.

Rule 702T requires that a form 701 be filed not later than 30 days after the first sale that brings the aggregate sales under rule 701 above $100,000, and thereafter annually within 30 days following the end of the issuer's fiscal year.

Rule 703T makes rule 701 unavailable to issuers subject to injunctions for failure to file form 701.

The "In Brief" for this chapter summarizes the key elements of certain exemptions from registration discussed in this section.

The Private-Placement Memorandum

The private-placement memorandum is the private-offering counterpart to the prospectus. Like the prospectus, the private-placement memorandum is both a selling document and a disclosure document. The dis-

In Brief: Key Elements of Certain Exemptions from Registration

Type of exemption	Dollar limit of the offering	Limits on the purchasers	Purchaser qualifications	Issuer qualifications
Section 4(2)	No limit	Generally limited to 25 offerees able to understand and bear risk	Offerees and purchasers must have access to information and be sophisticated investors	No limitations
Regulation D[a]				
Rule 504 [b]	Up to $1 million in 12 months	No limit	No requirements	Not a 1934 Act public reporting company nor an investment company
Rule 505	Up to $5 million in 12 months	No limit on the number of accredited investors, but limited to 35 unaccredited investors	No requirements for unaccredited investors	Not an investment company
Rule 506	No limit	No limit on the number of accredited investors, but limited to 35 unaccredited investors	Unaccredited investors must have sufficient experience to evaluate the investment	No limitations

a. All issuers relying on these exemptions are required to file a notice on form D with the SEC within 15 days after the first sale of securities. In addition, solicitations, advertising, and the provision of information during such offerings are limited.

b. This exemption does not depend on the use of any type of disclosure document.

closure function is usually primary, so the memorandum may not be as upbeat as the issuer might like.

The content of the private-placement memorandum is determined by the exemption upon which the issuer relies. For example, rule 502(b) under regulation D provides that if an issuer is selling securities under rule 505 or 506 to any purchaser that is not an accredited investor, certain specified information must be provided to the purchaser. On the other hand, if the issuer is offering securities under rule 504 or only to accredited investors, or in reliance upon the general section 4(2) exemption, the issuer is not required to provide any specific information. State blue sky laws may also influence the content and format of a private-placement memorandum.

Ethical Consideration

Because federal law only requires disclosure of all material information, the responsibility to ensure the quality and content of an offering rests with the managers of the issuing company and with other persons, such as investment bankers and securities lawyers, who are involved in the offering process.

In Brief: Key Elements of Certain Exemptions from Registration, *continued*				
Section 4(6) [a,b]	Up to $5 million	No limit on the number of accredited investors	All purchasers must be accredited—no unaccredited investors allowed	No limitations
Regulation A	$5 million in 12 months, with a maximum of $1.5 million sold by the selling security holders	No limit	No requirements	A U.S. or Canadian company, but not a 1934 Act public reporting company, nor an investment company, nor a blank check company, nor a company issuing oil/gas/mineral rights, nor disqualified under "bad boy" rule 262
Rule 701 [c,d]	The greater of $500,000 or 15% of the total assets of the issuer or 15% of the outstanding securities of the same class, up to a limit of $5 million over 12 months	No limit on the number of employees, directors, officers, advisors, or consultants	Advisory and consulting services must not be connected with the offer and sale of securities in a capital-raising transaction	Not a 1934 Act public reporting company nor an investment company

c. All issuers relying on this exemption must file form 701 with the SEC within 30 days after the sale of more than $100,000 worth of securities, and annually thereafter.

d. Must be pursuant to written compensatory benefit plans or written contracts relating to compensation.

In many circumstances, no private-placement memorandum is technically required. However, an issuer is well advised to create such a document in order to clearly demonstrate the disclosure made to prospective investors. Such disclosure is important to rebut claims of securities fraud, a topic discussed in chapter 23.

■ Exemptions for Secondary Offerings

A principal advantage of registering a securities offering with the SEC and the appropriate state securities authorities is that the securities may be traded relatively freely following the initial public offering. However, securities issued in a private placement cannot be the subject of a *secondary offering*, that is, a subsequent offering by a person other than the issuer, unless they are either registered or exempt from registration. Securities issued in a private placement are thus called *restricted securities*.

Section 4(1) Exemption

Section 4(1) of the 1933 Act provides that "transactions by any person other than an issuer, underwriter, or dealer" are exempt from registration.

Section 2 of the 1933 Act defines an *issuer* as any person "who issues or proposes to issue any security." A *dealer* is defined as "any person who engages either for all or part of his time, directly or indirectly, as agent, broker, or principal, in the business of offering, buying, selling, or otherwise dealing or trading in securities issued by another person."

An *underwriter* is defined as "any person who has purchased from an issuer with a view to, or offers or sells for an issuer in connection with, the distribution of any security." As used in the definition of an underwriter, the term *issuer* includes "any person directly or indirectly controlling or controlled by the issuer, or any person under direct or indirect common control with the issuer." For example, the sale of securities to the public by a controlling shareholder is a transaction involving an underwriter. In this case, the section 4(1) exemption is therefore unavailable.

If the person desiring to sell restricted securities is not an issuer, underwriter or dealer, she may sell the securities without registration under section 4(1). There is no limit to the size of the offering or the number of offerees. Section 4(1) is the exemption most often relied upon by persons who sell securities in the secondary market in an ordinary transaction involving a broker.

Rule 144

Because of the uncertainty in the definition of the term *underwriter*, the SEC adopted rule 144 in 1972. Rule 144 is not meant to be the exclusive means through which restricted securities may be sold, but merely to provide objective criteria for deciding whether a person is an underwriter. Under rule 144, a person is *not an underwriter* if the following conditions are met.

1. Adequate current public information must be available concerning the issuer. This requirement effectively means that the issuer has complied with the reporting requirements imposed by the 1934 Act (discussed later in this chapter).

2. The securities must have been beneficially owned—with all economic rights belonging to the owner—and fully paid for at least two years prior to the date of sale.

3. In any three-month period, the seller must not sell more than the greater of: (i) 1% of the outstanding securities of the class or (ii) the average weekly trading volume in the securities during the four calendar weeks preceding the filing of the notice of sale on form 144.

4. The securities must be sold in "broker's transactions" as defined in the 1933 Act, or directly to a "market-maker," defined in the 1934 Act. Solicitation of offers to buy is not permitted, and no commissions for the sale

may be paid to any person other than the broker who executes the order of sale.

5. If the amount of the securities sold during any three-month period will exceed 500 shares or have an aggregate sale price in excess of $10,000, a notice on form 144 must be filed with the SEC and with the principal stock exchange (if any) on which the securities are traded.

6. The person filing the form 144 must have a bona fide intention to sell the securities within a reasonable time after the filing of the notice.

Rule 144(k) provides that a person who is not an affiliate of the issuer, and has not been an affiliate for three months preceding the sale, may sell restricted securities without regard to items 1, 3, 4, and 5 above if such person has owned the securities for at least three years prior to their sale. This is of particular importance for privately held companies that do not file 1934 Act reports. Affiliates include officers, directors, and major shareholders. The SEC has a rebuttable presumption that anyone owning at least 10% of the issuer's stock is an affiliate.

If the requirements of rule 144 are met, restricted securities may be sold publicly without registration. Usually, restricted securities are identified as such by legends appearing on the face or back of their stock certificates. Accordingly, an opinion from the issuers' attorney may be required before a transfer agent is willing to consummate a transaction involving restricted securities. Certificates issued following a sale pursuant to rule 144 may be issued without restrictive legends.

If an affiliate of the issuer wants to sell stock, he must sell in accordance with rule 144 (except for the two-year holding period requirement which is inapplicable if the securities were acquired in a registered offering) or use another available exemption. The most common is the "section 4(1½)" exemption for private offerings by an affiliate. These offerings could qualify as private placements under section 4(2) if made by the issuer.

■ Rule 144A and Regulation S

In 1990, the SEC adopted two new regulations governing the resale of unregistered securities and the offering of securities outside the United States. The rules were designed to liberalize primary and secondary trading of private-placement securities.

Rule 144A

Rule 144A permits the resale of unregistered securities to qualified institutional buyers—that is, institutional investors holding and managing $100 million or more of securities—if the securities are not of the same class as any securities of the issuer listed on a U.S. securities exchange or quoted on an automated interdealer quotation system (such as NASDAQ). The rule creates a safe harbor for trading unregistered securities that are often issued in private placements and generally subject to rule 144's holding periods. The creation of a secondary market for eligible unregistered securities will increase the liquidity and value of these securities and reduce the private offering discount for them.

Rule 144A works as follows. If a transaction meets the terms of rule 144A, it is deemed not to be a distribution. Therefore, the seller is not an underwriter as defined in the 1933 Act. If the seller is also not an issuer or dealer, she may rely on the section 4(1) exemption for transactions by persons who are not issuers, underwriters, or dealers.

Dealers may also take advantage of rule 144A. Under section 4(3) of the 1933 Act, dealers are entitled to an exemption from registration, unless they are participants in a distribution or in a transaction taking place within a specified period after securities have been offered to the public. If a transaction complies with rule 144A, the dealer will be deemed not to be a participant in a distribution, and the securities will be deemed not to have been offered to the public. Accordingly, the transaction will be exempt from registration.

To handle the expanded market for private placements, the National Association of Securities Dealers established the PORTAL market. The PORTAL market is designed to further increase the liquidity and efficiency of the private-placement market by producing a computerized system for the trading, clearance, and settlement of transactions under rule 144A.

Rule 144A is a nonexclusive exemption. If the requirements of rule 144A cannot be met, the parties to the transaction may still rely on the facts-and-circumstances analysis commonly associated with nonpublic transfers of unregistered stock. For example, the "section 4(1½)" exemption for private resale's of restricted securities may apply.

Regulation S

Regulation S is part of the SEC's expanded international program. It clarifies the general rule that any offer or sale outside the United States is not subject to the federal registration requirements. Transactions meeting the requirements of certain safe harbors for the issuance and resale of securities set forth in regulation S will be deemed to

occur outside the United States. The SEC has long held the view that the section 5 registration requirements do not apply to offers and sales effected in a manner that would result in the securities coming to rest abroad.

All offers and sales of any security under regulation S must be made in *offshore transactions*, defined as those in which no offer is made to a person in the United States and either: (1) at the time the buy order is originated, the buyer is outside the United States, or (2) the transaction is one executed in, on, or through the facilities of a designated offshore securities market. No directed selling efforts may be made in the United States.

Exhibit 22-8 summarizes registration and exemption requirements for securities.

International Consideration

The combination of rule 144A and regulation S should expand the private-placement market by increasing the liquidity of privately placed securities. The clear exemptions from registration and its related expenses, and the development of the PORTAL market, should make the U.S. market more attractive to both U.S. and foreign companies. Regulation S will additionally enable U.S. companies to offer securities abroad with greater certainty that such securities are exempt from registration.

■ Reporting Requirements of Public Companies

The completion of a public offering does not necessarily terminate the issuer's relationship with the SEC. Under section 15(d) of the 1934 Act, a company with registered securities in a public offering must file periodic reports. Usually, under section 12 of the 1934 Act, the company must also register the class of equity securities offered to the public.

Section 12

Under section 12 of the 1934 Act, an issuer engaged in interstate commerce and having total assets exceeding $5 million must register with the SEC each nonexempt class of security that: (1) is listed on a national stock exchange,

EXHIBIT 22-8   An Outline of Registration and Exemption Requirements

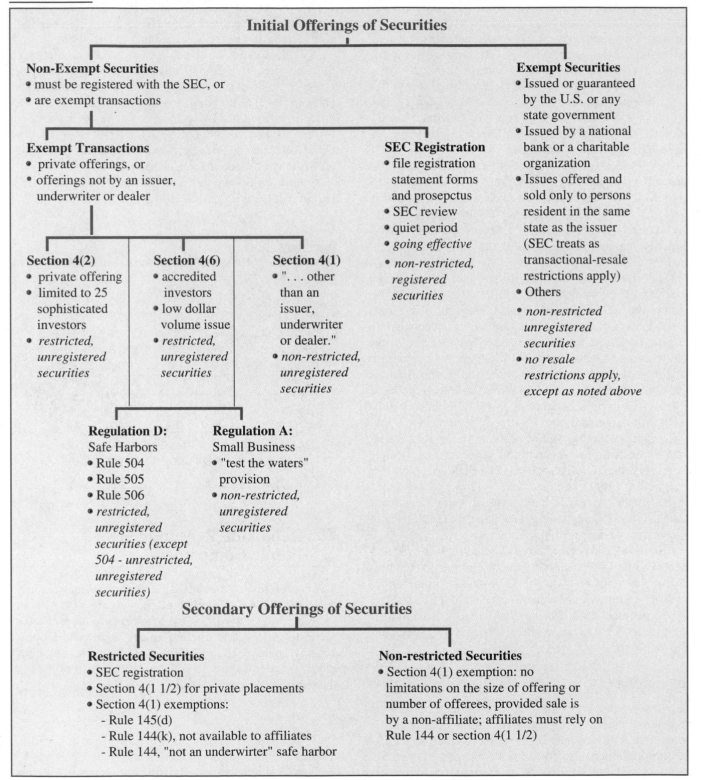

Initial Offerings of Securities

Non-Exempt Securities
- must be registered with the SEC, or
- are exempt transactions

Exempt Securities
- Issued or guaranteed by the U.S. or any state government
- Issued by a national bank or a charitable organization
- Issues offered and sold only to persons resident in the same state as the issuer (SEC treats as transactional-resale restrictions apply)
- Others
  - *non-restricted unregistered securities*
  - *no resale restrictions apply, except as noted above*

Exempt Transactions
- private offerings, or
- offerings not by an issuer, underwriter or dealer

SEC Registration
- file registration statement forms and prosepctus
- SEC review
- quiet period
- *going effective*
- *non-restricted, registered securities*

Section 4(2)
- private offering
- limited to 25 sophisticated investors
- *restricted, unregistered securities*

Section 4(6)
- accredited investors
- low dollar volume issue
- *restricted, unregistered securities*

Section 4(1)
- ". . . other than an issuer, underwriter or dealer."
- *non-restricted, unregistered securities*

Regulation D:
Safe Harbors
- Rule 504
- Rule 505
- Rule 506
- *restricted, unregistered securities (except 504 - unrestricted, unregistered securities)*

Regulation A:
Small Business
- "test the waters" provision
- *non-restricted, unregistered securities*

Secondary Offerings of Securities

Restricted Securities
- SEC registration
- Section 4(1 1/2) for private placements
- Section 4(1) exemptions:
  - Rule 145(d)
  - Rule 144(k), not available to affiliates
  - Rule 144, "not an underwirter" safe harbor

Non-restricted Securities
- Section 4(1) exemption: no limitations on the size of offering or number of offerees, provided sale is by a non-affiliate; affiliates must rely on Rule 144 or section 4(1 1/2)

or (2) is an equity security held of record by at least 500 persons. Registration subjects the issuer to various reporting requirements and to certain rules and regulations concerning proxies, tender offers, insider trading, and so on. A company registered with the SEC under section 12 is commonly referred to as a public or *reporting company*.

Registration under the 1934 Act is intended to supplement the 1933 Act registration and to keep current information concerning the issuer available to the public, enabling investors to make informed decisions about securities purchases. Although registration under the 1934 Act imposes additional burdens on an issuer, some issuers voluntarily register with the SEC in order to receive the protections afforded by the 1934 Act in proxy contests or tender offers, which are attempts to oust the existing management of a company by appealing directly to its shareholders.

The following are some of the significant requirements associated with becoming a registered company under section 12 of the 1934 Act.

■ **10-Q**: An unaudited quarterly statement of operations and financial condition must be filed on form 10-Q with the SEC within 45 days after the end of each fiscal quarter.

■ **10-K**: An annual audited report must be filed on form 10-K with the SEC within 90 days of the end of an issuer's fiscal year.

■ **8-K**: Certain events, including changes in control, acquisitions or dispositions of key assets, and resignation of directors, require a report to be filed on form 8-K with the SEC within 15 days of the event.

Small business issuers that are required to file periodic reports under the 1934 Act can do so with simplified forms under regulation S-B. These abbreviated forms include **10-KSB** for annual reports and **10-QSB** for quarterly reports.

Other Sections of the 1934 Act

Other sections of the 1934 Act regulate such activities as proxy solicitations, insider trading, and tender offers.

Proxy Solicitations   The proxy regulation provisions of section 14 of the 1934 Act apply to all public companies. They govern the solicitation of written powers of attorney, or proxies, that give the proxy holder the right to vote the shares owned by the person who signs the proxy card. Proxy solicitations relate not just to the board of directors, but to shareholder proposals as well. In recent years, proxy proposals have dealt with corporate governance issues such as executive compensation, cumulative voting, repeal of the classified board, recission of poison pill provisions, and confidential voting, and social issues such as doing business in South Africa and China and getting out of the tobacco business.

Insider Trading   Section 16 of the 1934 Act requires that reports be filed with the SEC listing securities holdings of officers, directors, and persons holding more than 10% of the issuer's equity securities, and any changes in such holdings. Form 5 states that these reports must be filed "both initially and on an annual basis." (These reports are described more fully in chapter 23.) Insiders of companies not registered under the 1934 Act need not file regular reports with the SEC.

Tender Offers   Any person making a tender offer to shareholders, in which shareholders are asked to sell their shares to that person, must comply with the tender-offer rules found in section 14 of the 1934 Act. Some rules, such as the requirement that a tender offer be left open for at least 20 business days, apply even if the company is not registered under the 1934 Act, if it has a significant number of shareholders. Other rules, such as the rule giving shareholders the right to withdraw their shares once they are tendered, and the rule requiring proration if the offer is oversubscribed, apply only if the company is registered under the 1934 Act.

Schedule 13D   Under Section 13, any person acquiring at least 5% of the shares of a reporting company must file a schedule 13D within 10 days of that acquisition. The schedule 13D must disclose the number of shares acquired and the intentions of the person acquiring them. Often the person acquiring the shares will state that he is buying the shares for investment purposes only. Sometimes, however, the company suspects an ulterior motive, such as preparation for a hostile takeover attempt. For example, the oil giant Chevron sued Pennzoil in 1989 after Pennzoil acquired more than 5% of the stock of Chevron. It claimed that Pennzoil's schedule 13D statement—that the purchase was for investment purposes only—was not true. The court ruled in favor of Pennzoil. Chevron later reacquired the stock from Pennzoil in exchange for oil assets of Chevron.

■ Violation of the 1933 Act

The penalty for violation of section 5 of the 1933 Act is simple and severe. Section 12(1) provides that, absent an exemption, anyone who offers or sells a security without

Historical Perspective
Securities Disclosure

Although the development of highly centralized and sophisticated financial markets is a relatively recent phenomenon, human greed and credulity are age-old problems. The regulation of securities and securities trading has roots going back to medieval England. As early as 1285, King Edward I issued a proclamation authorizing the Court of Aldermen in the City of London to license certain types of commodities brokers. A number of laws of varying effectiveness were adopted and repealed in the ensuing centuries by the English Parliament, and in 1844 the first identifiable precursor to a modern scheme of securities regulation was adopted. The Companies Act of 1844 contained the world's first modern prospectus requirement, and introduced the principle of compulsory disclosure through the centralized registration of prospectuses. In 1890 Parliament adopted the Directors Liability Act, which subjected corporate directors to personal liability for untrue statements in stock offering prospectuses, even if they had no wrongful intent. The Companies Act of 1900 set forth, among other things, the required contents of a securities prospectus.

The first U.S. laws regulating the sale of securities (*blue sky laws*) began to appear early in the twentieth century. Legend has it that this term first came into use to describe legislation directed at promoters who "would sell building lots in the blue sky in fee simple."[a] Kansas enacted the first effective securities law in 1911, and the trend soon spread to other states. In a series of cases in 1917, the United States Supreme Court held that these statutes did not violate the Fourteenth Amendment and did not unduly burden interstate commerce, and hence were enforceable.[b] Today, every state, plus Puerto Rico and the District of Columbia, has adopted some form of blue sky law.

The stock market crash of 1929 and the Great Depression that followed caused Congress and the public to take a hard look at the U.S. financial markets. Various attempts had been made in the past to regulate the finan-

cial markets on a national scale, but such attempts did not prevent the myriad of abuses and sharp practices that led to the crash and Depression.

In 1933 the American public felt cheated and angry, and Congress was prepared to strike hard at the type of practices that were blamed for robbing countless investors of their hard-earned savings, and plunging the U.S. economy into chaos. According to Representative (later Speaker of the House) Rayburn:

> Millions of citizens have been swindled into exchanging their savings for worthless stocks. The fraudulent promoter has taken an incredible toll from confiding people. . . .
>
> These hired officials of our great corporations who permitted, who promoted, who achieved the extravagant expansion of the financial structure of their respective companies today present a pitiable spectacle. Five years ago they arrogated to themselves the greatest privileges. They scorned the interference of the Government. They dealt with their stockholders in the most arbitrary fashion. They called upon the people to bow down to them as the real rulers of the country. Safe from the pitiless publicity of Government supervision, unrestrained by Federal statute, free from any formal control, these few men, proud, arrogant, and blind, drove the country to financial ruin. Some of them are fugitives from justice in foreign lands; some of them have committed suicide; some of them are under indictment; some of them are in prison; all of them are in terror of the consequences of their own deeds.[c]

The need for federal regulation of the nation's financial and securities' markets was not questioned. Rancorous debate, however, arose over the purposes and scope of the new legislation. Some felt that the federal government should regulate the merits of securities offerings, and that only those offerings that were fair, just, and equitable should be permitted. Representative Mott of Oregon criticized the theory that requiring full disclosure would be enough to protect the investors, without regulation of the merits of offerings:

> This theory ignores entirely the fact that the average investor cannot read and interpret a balance sheet. It ignores

---

a. Louis Loss, *Fundamentals of Securities Regulation* (1988), 8, quoting Thomas Mulvey, "Blue Sky Law," 36 Can.L.T. 37 (1916).
b. *Hall v. Geiger-Jones Co.*, 242 U.S. 539, 37 S.Ct. 217 (1917); *Caldwell v. Sioux Falls Stock Yards Co.*, 242 U.S. 559, 37 S.Ct. 224 (1917); *Merrick v. N. W. Halsey & Co.,* 242 U.S. 568, 37 S.Ct. 227 (1917).

---

c. House Consideration, Amendment and Passage of H.R. 5480, May 5, 1932, 77 Cong. Rec. 2910, 2918 (1933), as reprinted in *Federal Securities Laws Legislative History* 1933–1982 vol. 1 (BNA 1983).

Historical Perspective
Securities Disclosure, *continued*

the fact that he is entirely unfamiliar with securities transactions and with the financial structures of the corporations issuing the paper. It ignores the fact that a balance sheet can be technically accurate and still convey to the untutored investor the idea that an unsound company is sound, and this without the risk of either civil or criminal liability on the part of the seller. And, finally, it completely ignores the most important factor of all: that in most cases the issuers of fraudulent securities cannot respond in a judgment, and that when the defrauded investor finally discovers the fraud his only remedy under this theory is a civil judgment which cannot be collected. . . . I want to make it impossible by law for any financial crook to operate in the United States.[d]

Others, like Representative Rayburn, favored the philosophy underlying the British system, that it was sufficient to require full disclosure:

> What we seek to attain by this enactment is to make available to the prospective purchaser, if he is wise enough to use it, all information that is pertinent, that would put him on notice and on guard, and then let him beware. On the other hand, we demand of the seller that he give full and complete information with reference to the security offered, under penalty of both civil and criminal liability if he evades or

conceals material facts. . . . In this bill we demand not only a new deal, we also demand a square deal.[e]

It was the philosophy of full disclosure that ultimately prevailed. Representative Mapes of Michigan summarized the feelings of Congress in adopting this type of regulatory system:

> The bill is not foolproof. It will not prevent anybody from putting his money into rat holes or into highly speculative ventures if he sees fit to do so, but in the exercise of reasonable care he can go to the Federal Trade Commission [now to the Securities and Exchange Commission] or to the underwriter or the dealer in the securities and find out the facts relating to the business of the corporation issuing the securities, the profits which the dealers are to receive in selling them, and the amount of money that is to go back into the treasury of the corporation after the sale is made—how much of the $100 per share, or whatever amount he pays for his stock, is really going back to the corporation, going into the treasury for the promotion of the business of the corporation.[f]

The 1933 Act remains the cornerstone of the federal regulation of public and private offerings of securities.

---

d. *Ibid.*, 2948.

e. *Ibid.*, 2919.
f. *Ibid.*, 2912.

---

an effective registration statement is liable to the purchaser for recission or damages. In addition, suits can be brought for alleged misrepresentations in offering documents under rule 10b-5 of the 1934 Act, and depending on the circumstances, under sections 11 and 12(2) of the 1933 Act, which are covered in detail in chapter 23.

Elements of Liability

To establish a section 12(1) claim, the plaintiff must show that the defendant sold or offered securities without an effective registration statement through the use of interstate transportation or communication. The plaintiff must also show that she filed suit within one year from the date of the violation. A plaintiff typically satisfies the interstate transportation or communication requirement

by proving that the mails, telephone, or other interstate means were used in the offer or sale to that particular plaintiff.

Section 12(1) imposes a standard of strict liability. That is, the plaintiff need not show that the defendant acted willfully or negligently, only that the defendant committed the act.

Damages

If the plaintiff still owns the securities, he is entitled to rescind his purchase. To rescind, the plaintiff returns the securities, together with any income (such as dividends) he received from them, in exchange for what he paid for the securities, plus interest. If the plaintiff has sold the securities, he is entitled to recover damages—usually the difference between what he paid and what he received for the securities.

Who May Be Sued

The severity of the remedy under section 12(1) has naturally led to a great deal of interest as to just who may be considered to have offered or sold securities within the meaning of the statute. It clearly includes the issuer. But what about others involved in an unregistered securities transaction, such as attorneys, accountants, underwriters, and investment bankers?

Until recently, many courts held that a defendant had seller status under section 12(1) if it engaged in actions that were a substantial factor in bringing about the plaintiff's securities purchase. The Supreme Court rejected the substantial-factor test in the following case.

■ **A Case in Point:**   **In the Language of the Court**

Case 22.5
PINTER v. DAHL
Supreme Court of the
United States
486 U.S. 622, 108 S.Ct. 2063
(1988).

FACTS   Maurice Dahl was a California real estate broker and investor. Dahl purchased unregistered securities in the form of oil and gas interests from B. J. Pinter, an oil and gas producer and registered securities dealer in Texas. Enthusiastic about his investment, Dahl successfully encouraged his friends and family to purchase additional securities from the defendant. When the investment failed, the purchasers sued Pinter for violation of section 12(1) of the Securities Act of 1933.

Pinter claimed that Dahl, who encouraged his friends and family to invest, was a substantial factor in those sales. Pinter therefore contended that Dahl was a seller and should be held liable under section 12(1).

ISSUE PRESENTED   Is a person with no financial interest in an offering of unregistered securities a seller under section 12(1) of the 1933 Act?

OPINION   BLACKMUN, J., writing for the U.S. Supreme Court:

. . . .

In determining whether Dahl may be deemed a "seller" for purposes of 12(1), such that he may be held liable for the sale of unregistered securities to the other investor-respondents, we look first at the language of 12(1). That statute provides, in pertinent part: "Any person who . . . offers or sells a security in violation of the registration requirement of the Securities Act shall be liable to the person purchasing such security from him." This provision defines the class of defendants who may be subject to liability as those who offer or sell unregistered securities. But the Securities Act nowhere delineates who may be regarded as a statutory seller, and the sparse legislative history sheds no light on the issue. The courts, on their part, have not defined the term uniformly.

At the very least, however, the language of 12(1) contemplates a buyer-seller relationship not unlike the traditional contractual privity. Thus, it is settled that 12(1) imposes liability on the owner who passes title, or other interest in the security, to the buyer for value. Dahl, of course, was not a seller in this conventional sense, and therefore may be held liable only if 12(1) liability extends to persons other than the person who passes title.

. . . .

Although we conclude that Congress intended 12(1) liability to extend to those who solicit securities purchases, we share the Court of Appeals' conclusion that Congress did not intend to impose rescission based on strict liability on a person who urges the purchase but whose motivation is solely to benefit the buyer. When a person who urges another to make a securities purchase acts merely to assist the buyer, not only is it uncommon to say that the buyer "purchased" from him, but it is also strained to describe the giving of gratuitous advice, even strongly or enthusiastically, as "soliciting." Section 2(3) defines an offer as a "solicitation of an offer to buy . . . for value." The person who gratuitously urges another to make a particular investment decision is not, in any meaningful sense, requesting value in exchange for his suggestion or seeking the value the titleholders will obtain in exchange for the ultimate sale. The language and purpose of 12(1) suggest that liability extends only to the person who successfully solicits the purchase motivated at least in part by a desire to serve his own financial interests or those of the securities owner. If he had such a motivation, it is fair to say that the buyer "purchased" the security from him and to align him with the owner in a rescission action.

. . . .

We are unable to determine whether Dahl may be held liable as a statutory seller under 12(1). The District Court explicitly found that "Dahl solicited each of the other plaintiffs in connection with the offer, purchase and receipt of their oil and gas interests." We cannot conclude that this finding was clearly erroneous. It is not clear, however, that Dahl had the kind of interest in the sales that make him liable as a statutory seller. We do know that he received no commission from Pinter in connection with the other sales, but this is not conclusive. Typically, a person who solicits the purchase will have sought or received a personal financial benefit from the sale, such as where he "anticipat[es] a share of the profits," or receives a brokerage commission. But a person who solicits the buyer's purchase in order to serve the financial interests of the owner may properly be liable under 12(1) without showing that he expects to participate in the benefits the owner enjoys.

The Court of Appeals apparently concluded that Dahl was motivated entirely by gratuitous desire to share an attractive investment opportunity with his friends and associates. This conclusion, in our view, was premature. The District Court made no findings that focused on whether Dahl urged the other purchases in order to further some financial interest of his own or of Pinter. Accordingly, further findings are necessary to assess Dahl's liability.

RESULT The Supreme Court vacated the judgment of the Court of Appeals and remanded for further proceedings consistent with its opinion.

Questions
1. Do you believe that Dahl was partially responsible for the failure to register the securities? If so, should he have been liable for violating 12(1)?
2. What facts do you need to know to determine whether Dahl was a seller within the meaning of 12(1)?

Who May Sue

Anyone who purchases shares issued in violation of the registration requirements can bring suit. If the securities were sold to a number of persons, then a plaintiff could bring a class action suit, which is filed on behalf of all persons who have allegedly been harmed by the acquisition of the illegally issued securities.

Penalties

In addition to buying back the securities or paying damages, defendants also face criminal penalties for violations of state or federal securities laws that include fines and imprisonment. Under section 24 of the 1933 Act, any person who willfully violates the provisions of the act shall upon conviction be fined not more than $10,000 or imprisoned for up to five years, or both.

The Responsible Manager

Complying with Registration Requirements

Any person offering securities must comply with the registration requirements of the 1933 Act. This includes start-up companies, as well as large, publicly traded companies. The failure to comply gives the purchaser of the security the right to keep the proceeds if the investment is successful, or to return the security to the seller if the investment does not turn out as hoped. Moreover, as was explained in chapter 15, a willful failure to comply is a criminal offense.

The preparation of a private-placement offering memorandum or a prospectus is an involved process that requires an intimate knowledge of the statutory requirements. Managers face considerable liability for incorrect or misleading statements in these documents, as is discussed in chapter 23.

During the waiting period, in particular, managers should work closely with counsel to ensure that there are no gun-jumping problems due to any eagerness on behalf of the underwriter or the company's public relations department. It is very important that the company not issue an abnormal number of press releases or increase the amount of its advertising prior to the registration going effective. In other words, the manager should make sure that the company does not depart from its ordinary routine, and that the company remains quiet.

In addition, a manager should ensure that there are no material misstatements or omissions in any public disclosures (e.g., a 10-K or 10-Q). Once a disclosure is made, even if there were no legal obligation to disclose, the statements contained within it must be truthful, and are subject to securities law.

Managers, particularly those of small firms, should also be familiar with the four-part *Howey* test, and realize that certain contracts that are not normally thought of as securities may run afoul of the 1933 and 1934 acts.

Furthermore, securities held by officers, directors, and other affiliates cannot be freely resold. They must be sold under rule 144, subject to its volume and public information requirements, or in a private offering to sophisticated, eligible buyers. Companies must put legends on affiliates' share certificates, issue stop-transfer orders to the transfer agent, or take such other steps as may be reasonable to ensure compliance with these rules.

Even if a security is exempt from registration, it is not exempt from the antifraud provisions of the 1933 or 1934 acts, discussed in the next chapter.

Inside Story

The British Petroleum Stock Offering

To participate in the British government's share offering of British Petroleum Company plc, a multinational group of investment bankers agreed to a firm-commitment underwriting in which the stock price was set weeks before the bankers actually could sell the stock. In addition, to gain a piece of the multibillion dollar offering, the underwriting banks agreed to an unusual out-clause that gave the British Parliament total control over the transaction.

Before the government's offering came to market, worldwide share prices plummeted in the October 1987 stock market crash. The value of British Petroleum's shares dropped more than 20% from the fixed offer price. The British, European, Canadian, and Japanese underwriters pre-sold portions of their shares of the offering before the market crash and mitigated their losses. However, the U.S. underwriters, which included Goldman Sachs, Morgan Stanley, Salomon Brothers, and Shearson Lehman, were prohibited from pre-selling due to SEC regulations, and faced combined losses of up to $500 million if the offering went to market. Consequently, they argued vociferously for the government to pull or delay the offering.

Despite the underwriters' pleas, the British government did not want to let the underwriters off the hook; such a step would have cost the British taxpayers more

---

Inside Story, continued

than $2 billion in lost proceeds.[8] Many Britons had charged that the banks merely took profits from government privatizations without ever really being at risk, according to attorney Simon MacLachlan of London's Clifford Schance, who observed the events. "Underwriters had to be seen to be taking a loss from time to time."[9]

---

8. Anatole Kaletsky and Richard Tomkins, "Financial Markets in Turmoil; Arguments Are Strong for Lawson to Proceed with Offering," *Financial Times*, October 28, 1987, 2.
9. Sherry R. Sontag, "Can a Market Crash Be an 'Act of God'?; Out-Clauses Revisited," *The National Law Journal*, December 14, 1987, 1.

The U.S. underwriters understood what their firm-commitment underwriting meant. According to Charles S. Whitman III of Davis Polk & Wardell, the New York law firm that represented all four U.S. underwriters involved in the deal, "we made it clear what the contract was. But no one knew what could happen to the market. No one I know is saying it can't happen again."[10]

Although the underwriters could not persuade the British Parliament to let them out of the firm-commitment underwriting agreement, they were successful in persuading the government to cap their losses.

---

10. *Ibid.*

Key Words and Phrases

accredited investor **731**	form SB-2 **723**	reporting company **739**
affiliate **723**	going effective **721**	restricted securities **745**
best-efforts underwriting **722**	gun-jumping **727**	sale **721**
blank check companies **732**	integrate **732**	secondary offering **730**
blue sky laws **714**	issuer **735**	security **715**
dealer **736**	not an underwriter **736**	shelf registration **727**
firm-commitment underwriting **722**	offer **721**	small business issuers **723**
form S-1 **722**	offshore transactions **737**	tombstone ad **724**
form S-2 **722**	private offering **730**	underwriter **736**
form S-3 **723**	prospectus **721**	value **721**
form S-4 **730**	quiet period **721**	
form SB-1 **723**	red-herring prospectus **724**	

Questions and Case Problems

1. Boffo Oil purchased a large section of land near the Mississippi River. Boffo then subdivided the tract into very small parcels and leased the parcels to many investors. The leases included an obligation by Boffo Oil to drill test wells for oil, for which Boffo would be paid a drilling fee. Is it likely that a court would find that Boffo Oil had marketed a security to the lessees?

2. Devour Corporation proposes to issue common stock in exchange for the assets of Quarry Inc. Quarry will first obtain the approval of its shareholders, and then distribute the Devour

common stock to its shareholders. Does Devour have to register the stock that it will give Quarry in exchange for Quarry's assets?

3. Tommy Long owns 5,000 shares of Super Corporation. There are 100,000 shares outstanding, and the stock is actively traded on the New York Stock Exchange. Long is not an issuer, underwriter, or dealer as defined in the Securities Act of 1933. Long publicly purchased the shares on the advice of Mark Fynch. When Long goes to sell these shares, must he register them under the 1933 Act?

4. Ventura Corporation of Denver, Colorado, made a private offering of its common stock on January 1, and additional offerings on March 1, August 1, and November 1. All of the private placements are with the same group of 50 individuals and pension funds. Do these separate private offerings constitute one continuous public offering by Ventura?

5. Susan Newton, 38, founded her own software firm at age 15. She now has a position on the board of directors of EBM Corporation, and owns 15% of its outstanding common stock. Newton grew her firm to $20 million in revenue before it was purchased by EBM for EBM common stock. She no longer is an officer or active in the day-to-day management of her business. She proposes to sell her interest to the public. The stock is actively traded on the American Stock Exchange. Must she register her stock under the 1933 Act?

6. A bitter contest for the control of Piper Aircraft Corp. occurred between Chris-Craft and Bangor Punta. Chris-Craft had made a cash tender offer for Piper Stock. Subsequently, the Piper family negotiated a competing exchange offer of a package of securities from Bangor Punta, under which all Piper shareholders would be entitled to exchange each share of Piper common stock for Bangor Punta securities and cash.

Because the Bangor Punta exchange required a public offering of securities to the Piper shareholders, Bangor Punta prepared to file a registration statement under the 1933 Act. After concluding their negotiations, Bangor Punta and Piper management issued a press release stating that Bangor Punta had agreed to file a registration statement with the SEC covering the proposed exchange offer for any and all remaining outstanding shares of Piper Aircraft, in exchange for Bangor Punta securities to be valued at approximately $80 per Piper share.

Chris-Craft sought a preliminary injunction to prevent Bangor Punta from making the exchange offer, claiming that the press release was gun-jumping under the 1933 Act. Did the press release violate the 1933 Act? [*Chris-Craft Industries, Inc. v. Bangor Punta Corp.*, 426 F.2d 569 (2d Cir. 1970)]

7. Petroleum Management Corporation (PMC) organized a California limited partnership comprising "participants" and "special participants" for the purpose of drilling and operating four wells in Wyoming. PMC and Inter-Tech Resources, Inc. were initially the only "special participants." However, William Doran was later asked and agreed to become a "special participant" in the partnership. In consideration for his partnership share, Doran contributed $125,000 toward the partnership. He paid PMC $25,000 down, and assumed responsibility for the payment of a $113,643 note owed by PMC to Mid-Continent Supply Co.

The Mid-Continent note upon which Doran was primarily liable went into default. Mid-Continent subsequently obtained a state court judgment against Doran, PMC, and the president and vice president of PMC for $50,815.59 plus interest and attorney's fees. Doran then filed suit in federal district court seeking rescission of the contract, based on violations of the 1933 and 1934 acts. Did the transaction come within the exemption from registration found in section 4(2)? [*Doran v. Petroleum Management Corp.*, 545 F.2d 893 (5th Cir. 1977)]

8. Late in 1972, a registration statement was filed for the contemplated public offering of JHIS securities. In January 1973, the registration statement was amended and a preliminary prospectus was filed. The preliminary prospectus was then disseminated to the public by JHIS and the underwriters. During the statutory waiting period, the underwriters orally solicited their customers relating to JHIS. The registration statement became effective in February 1973.

The plaintiff alleged that during January 1973, her husband discussed the proposed JHIS offering with his broker. After receiving a copy of the preliminary prospectus, the plaintiff's husband met with his broker; the plaintiff claims that several misrepresentations about the nature of the offering were made at that time. She also claims that her husband's order for 500 shares was accepted in January, a month before the effective date of the registration statement.

Do the plaintiff and her husband have an adequate claim against the defendants? Was the sale of the securities prior to the effective date a violation of the 1933 Act? [*Wolfson v. Worthley*, Fed. Sec. L. Rep. (CCH) ¶ 96,019 (S.D.N.Y. 1977)]

9. Gearhart is a Texas corporation engaged in the business of oil evaluation. Smith International, which desires to acquire Gearhart, is a Delaware corporation doing business in Texas, and engaged in oil service work there.

Shortly after employing an investment banker, and in connection with their merger discussions, Smith obtained permission from Gearhart to talk with General Electric Venture Capital Corporation (GE) about a block of 3,640,514 Gearhart shares it owned. Discussions of various proposals followed, including the possibility that GE might buy out both companies. However, in October 1983, Smith secretly negotiated a purchase of the GE block at $31 per share. When Gearhart learned of the purchase, it expressed its approval.

Smith filed a schedule 13D disclosure statement just before purchasing the GE shares, stating that its purpose in buying the GE block was acquiring a significant investment in Gearhart and that, if Gearhart's prospects appeared to justify it, "Smith may determine to increase its position in Gearhart." Smith, over the course of the next year continued to purchase more Gearhart shares, and by April 1984 it had obtained more than one-third of Gearhart's outstanding common stock. Gearhart then requested that the court halt Smith's pending tender offer for violating section 13(d) of the 1934 Act. What will Smith have to show in order to prove that it was not in violation of section 13(d)? [*Gearhart Industries v. Smith International,* 741 F.2d 707 (5th Cir. 1984)]

10. Elliott offered conditional sales agreements and beneficial interest agreements, whereby the investor would receive periodic tax-free interest payments up to an annual rate of 15%. These investments were supposed to be secured by municipal and treasury bonds placed in the custody of third parties. There were some shortcomings in Elliott's programs: The interest was not tax-free, and Elliott did not purchase any bonds as collateral.

What type of a claim can the SEC bring against Elliott? Who will prevail? [*SEC v. Elliott*, 953 F.2d 1560 (11th Cir. 1992)]

Chapter 23

SECURITIES FRAUD AND INSIDER TRADING

■ Introduction

Why Special Statutory Provisions Are Needed

The principal antifraud provisions of the federal securities laws are sections 11 and 12 of the Securities Act of 1933 and section 10(b) of the Securities Exchange Act of 1934. These provisions were enacted in part because common-law theories of liability such as fraud and deceit were perceived as inadequate to compensate aggrieved purchasers in the securities markets. The common law, for example, assumed that a typical transaction would involve a face-to-face negotiation between a buyer and a seller. For a buyer to prevail on a claim for fraud, he would therefore have to show that he relied on some misrepresentation made by his seller. In contrast, the securities markets do not conduct their business on the basis of such face-to-face negotiations. Indeed, it is often impossible even to match a particular buyer with a particular seller. The federal securities laws therefore modify and, in some cases, eliminate the common-law requirements such as reliance, in order to take into account the realities of the securities markets.

The fundamental goal of the 1933 Act is to ensure adequate disclosure of material facts to investors. In addition to imposing the various registration requirements discussed in chapter 22, the 1933 Act expressly creates private rights of action for certain violations of its provisions. This means that in addition to public enforcement by the SEC or criminal proceedings by the U.S. Attorney's Office, any investor can bring a private suit for damages.

Section 11 imposes liability upon the securities issuer and various other parties when a registration statement for a registered security is misleading. Section 12(1), discussed in chapter 22, imposes liability upon anyone who offers or sells a security without an effective registration statement (unless an exemption is available). Section 12(2) imposes liability upon anyone who sells a security by means of a misleading prospectus or oral communication.

The 1934 Act was designed to protect investors against manipulation of stock prices. Under section 10(b) and rule 10b-5, promulgated pursuant to the 1934

Act, it is unlawful for any person to use a fraudulent, manipulative, or deceptive device in connection with the purchase or sale of any security. The SEC may order violators to desist, and private parties may sue for damages. Rule 10b-5 also prohibits insider trading, that is, trading securities while in possession of material nonpublic information in violation of a duty to the corporation or its shareholders or others. Section 16(b) of the 1934 Act also regulates trading by insiders. In particular it allows a public corporation to sue for damages if any officer or director of the corporation or any person who owns more than 10% of the corporation's securities engages in short-swing trading, that is, the purchase and sale, or sale and purchase, of securities of the corporation within a six-month period.

Chapter Summary

This chapter discusses the antifraud provisions of the 1933 and 1934 Acts. The discussion of the 1933 Act focuses on section 11, under which issuers are strictly liable for misstatements or omissions in a registration statement, and certain officers, all directors, and accountants and underwriters are liable if they fail to act with due diligence. The chapter explains who may sue, who may be sued, the elements of liability, the available defenses, the calculation of damages, and the guidelines for due diligence. The chapter then discusses section 12(2) of the 1933 Act, which provides a remedy for any person who purchases a registered or unregistered security by means of a misleading prospectus or oral communication. Section 17(a) of the 1933 Act, under which the U.S. government can bring fraud claims, is briefly discussed.

The chapter also discusses the primary antifraud provision in the 1934 Act— section 10(b) and rule 10b-5 adopted thereunder. It sets forth the seven elements necessary in a rule 10b-5 case and the fraud-on-the-market theory of liability. The chapter defines insider trading, and discusses in detail the legal elements of an insider-trading case. Short-swing trading is then defined, and the rules for calculating the recoverable profits are discussed, as well as the requirements for reporting by insiders.

■ Section 11 of the 1933 Act

Section 11 provides a remedy for a person who purchases a security pursuant to a misleading registration statement. The section is the most lengthy and detailed civil-liability provision in the 1933 Act, spelling out who may sue, who may be sued, the elements of the offenses, the permitted defenses, and the damages that may be awarded. Under section 11, a seller of securities is liable for its false statements even if they were not made with intent to defraud.

Who May Sue

Tracing Requirement   Any person who has acquired a registered security may sue under section 11. However, the purchaser must prove that the security at issue was actually one of those sold with the misleading registration statement. Although this requirement does not present a problem for direct purchasers of an initial public offering, open-market purchasers may find it difficult to trace their securities back to a sale made under the defective registration statement.

Class Actions   Plaintiffs in a section 11 case will typically bring a class action, in which the named plaintiffs act on behalf of themselves and "all others similarly situated." The advantage to the plaintiffs (and their attorneys) of proceeding in this manner is that the individual plaintiffs' claims, worth only a few hundred or a few thousand dollars, together amount to millions of dollars. Indeed, these suits are potentially so lucrative that some investors send their monthly brokerage statements to their attorneys as a routine practice, and thus a private enforcement mechanism of sorts is created.

Who May Be Sued

Section 11 lists, and thereby limits, the entities and persons who may be sued: (1) the issuer offering the security; (2) the underwriters; (3) any member of the board of directors at the time of the offering; (4) persons who give their consent to be named in the registration statement as future directors; (5) every person who signed the registration statement—under section 6(a) of the 1933 Act, it must be signed by the issuer, its principal executive officer, its principal financing officer, and its principal accounting officer; and (6) experts who consent to give authority to the "expertized" portion of the registration statement, such as accountants who audit the financial statements contained in it. No person can be named in the registration statement as an expert unless that person has consented in writing to being named.

Plaintiffs often allege that persons or entities other than those specified in section 11 are liable under a theory of secondary liability, such as aiding and abetting or conspiracy. Most (but not all) courts reject such attempts to expand liability under section 11. In 1994, the U.S. Supreme Court held that a private plaintiff may not maintain an aiding and abetting suit under section 10(b).[1] (See case 23.2.)

Controlling Persons   The 1933 Act itself creates an important exception to the tendency of most courts to limit section 11 liability. Section 15 imposes liability on anyone who "controls any person liable under Section 11 or 12." The term "control" is not defined in the 1933 Act. Congress left this issue for the courts to decide:

> It was thought undesirable to attempt to define the term. It would be difficult if not impossible to enumerate or to anticipate the many ways in which actual control may be exerted. A few examples of these methods used are stock ownership, lease, contract, and agency. It is well known that actual control sometimes may be exerted through ownership of much less than a majority of the stock of a corporation either by the ownership of such stock alone or through such ownership in combination with other factors.[2]

Unsurprisingly, the courts do not agree as to when there is *controlling-person liability*. Some courts require that the person must have actually participated in the securities violation. Others will find liability if a person merely possesses the power to control the specific activity that is the basis for the securities violation, regardless of whether that power was exercised, provided that the person did actually exercise some degree of general control or influence over the section 11 defendant.

A controlling person is usually an officer or director of the company. In *Metge v. Baehler*,[3] the plaintiff claimed that the company's bank was a controlling person and therefore liable under the securities laws. The United States Court of Appeals for the Eighth Circuit applied the following test to determine whether Banker's Trust was a controlling person: whether the bank had the power to control the violative conduct and whether it actually exercised control over the company's operations in general. Because it found no actual exercise of control, the court concluded that there was no controlling-person liability.

The case illustrates the flexibility of the securities laws and the creativity of plaintiffs. Had the bank obtained more restrictive covenants in its lending agreements, the court might have found that it was liable as a controlling person even though it did not participate in the specific violations of the securities laws. A lender that overprotects itself via restrictive covenants and control of its borrower may thus create a problem for itself.

Elements of Liability

The elements of a section 11 offense are straightforward. The plaintiff must show that at the time the registration statement became effective it contained a false or misleading statement with respect to a material fact, or that a material fact was omitted from the registration statement.

The Supreme Court has defined a *material fact* as one that a reasonable investor would most likely have considered important in deciding whether to buy or sell—that is, what a reasonable hypothetical investor would have considered important, not necessarily what the actual investor considered important. The Supreme Court has held that an omitted fact is material if there is "a substantial likelihood that the disclosure of the omitted fact would have been viewed by the reasonable investor as

---

1. *Central Bank of Denver v. First Interstate Bank of Denver*, 114 S.Ct. 1439 (1994).
2. H.R. Rep. No. 1383, 73rd Cong., 2d Sess. § 19 at 26 (1934).

3. 762 F.2d 621 (8th Cir. 1985), *cert. denied*, 474 U.S. 1057, 106 S.Ct. 798 (1986).

Ethical Consideration

There is an incentive for plaintiffs to urge the courts to construe broadly the guidelines as to who may be a defendant—particularly when the plaintiff is looking for a "deep pocket" defendant, that is, someone who can pay large damages. A plaintiff has every right to use the securities laws to their fullest extent to redress a wrong covered by one of the statutes. However, some commentators believe that there are plaintiffs who attempt to recover losses beyond the scope of the statutes. Although some claim that plaintiffs cannot be faulted for trying, the better view is that plaintiffs should proceed only if they believe in good faith that the suit is justified, given the legal guidelines. Indeed, rule 11 of the Federal Rules of Civil Procedure, which is designed to deter bad-faith claims, provides for sanctions against an attorney who signs a complaint that the attorney does not reasonably believe has merit.

having significantly altered the 'total mix' of information made available."[4]

The plaintiff does not have to establish that she relied upon the misstatement or omission except in the following instance: A plaintiff who purchases a security on the open market after the issuing company has released its income statements for the year following the registration statement must show that the misrepresentation influenced her decision to buy.

Defenses

Section 11 sets forth several defenses to a claim under its provisions. The defenses of no reliance and no causation focus on the effects of the misstatements on the behavior of investors and the market, while the defense of due diligence looks to the culpability of the defendants.

---

4. *TSC Industries, Inc. v. Northway, Inc.*, 426 U.S. 438, 449, 96 S.Ct. 2126, 2132 (1976).

No Reliance   The defense of no reliance relates to the investor's knowledge. An investor who knows that there was a misstatement or omission cannot claim to have relied on it; he is presumed to have acted despite the misstatement or omission. Thus, if the defendant can establish that the plaintiff knew that a statement was false, or that there was an omission, there is no liability under section 11.

No Causation   The defense of no causation concerns itself with the link between the misstatement and the investor's loss. Even if there was a misstatement or omission of material fact, a defendant will not be liable if it can show that the misstatement or omission did not actually cause the plaintiff to suffer any loss. In other words, the plaintiff may have lost money on a trade, but that loss may not have been due to the defendant's conduct. This showing typically consists of an expert analysis of the various factors that influenced the price movements of the securities in question.

Due Diligence   The defense of due diligence focuses on the behavior of the defendants. It is available to all defendants except the issuing company. A defendant is not liable for a misrepresentation or omission if it acted with *due diligence,* that is, if: (1) it conducted a reasonable investigation, and (2) it reasonably believed (a) that the statements made were true, and (b) that there were no omissions that made those statements misleading. A "reasonable" investigation is what a prudent person managing her own property would conduct.

The primary wrinkle in the due-diligence defense arises in connection with the expertized portions of the registration statement, such as audit reports on the company's financial statements, appraisal reports, or engineering reports. Nonexpert defendants are entitled to rely on the experts. They can establish due diligence by showing that they had no reasonable basis to believe that the experts' reports were misleading and in fact did not believe them to be misleading. Significantly, they need not show that they undertook any investigation of those reports.

The experts are, of course, responsible for their own reports, provided that the reports are identified as having been prepared by them and provided that the experts have given their consent to the use of their reports in the registration statement. The experts are generally not responsible under section 11 for portions of the registration statement other than their reports.

The case that follows is one of the leading section 11 decisions. Its application of the due-diligence standards to the various participants in the offering process remains relevant today.

■ **A Case in Point:**   **Summary**

Case 23.1
ESCOTT v. BARCHRIS
CONSTRUCTION CORP.
United States District Court for
the Southern District of
New York
283 F.Supp. 643 (S.D.N.Y.
1968).

FACTS   BarChris was in the business of building bowling alleys. It obtained capital through a public offering in May 1961. Due to financial problems, the company filed for protection under the Bankruptcy Act in October 1962. A class action followed, alleging section 11 claims against the company, its officers and directors, and its underwriters.

ISSUE PRESENTED   When is the due-diligence defense available to the principal officers or the inside directors of the issuer? May a chief financial officer rely on the audited financial statements if he had reason to believe those statements were incorrect? Have outside directors and underwriters, who relied on the management's statements and made no independent investigation, acted with due diligence?

SUMMARY OF OPINION   The Federal District Court found that both the expertized and nonexpertized portions of the registration statement were misleading. Every defendant raised the defense of due diligence except the issuer, to whom the defense was not available. The court held that the due-diligence standards for nonexperts varied, depending on the nonexpert's degree of involvement, expertise, and access to information.

The court applied the most stringent standards to the company's principal officers and inside directors. It first noted that principal officers and inside directors (directors who are also officers of the corporation) who sign a registration statement have a significant burden. Because of their extensive knowledge of the company's affairs, it is rare that they can successfully establish a due-diligence defense. The court held that the chief financial officer was not entitled to rely on the outside auditors as to the accuracy of the financial statements, because he had reason to believe that those statements were incorrect. The court concluded that the liability of principal officers and inside directors approaches that of the company itself. They cannot escape liability for the nonexpertized portions of the statement even if they did not read the statement, did not understand it, and relied on assistants and lawyers to make adequate disclosures.

Outside directors are held to a lower standard, but they must still do more than read the registration statement and ask questions of management. They must make some independent investigation of the challenged statements to satisfy their due-diligence obligations. The court found that even directors who had joined the issuing company shortly before the registration statement's effective date could not simply ask one or two general questions about the statement and accept the answers at face value. The court did not consider that a prudent person would act in that way concerning "an important matter without any knowledge of the relevant facts, in sole reliance upon representations of persons who are comparative strangers." The court did, however, find that the outside directors were entitled to rely on the auditors as to the expertized portions of the registration statement.

Underwriters are also held to a lower standard than the company's officers. Again, however, they may not simply rely on statements of the company's officers and attorneys. They must verify that which is reasonably verifiable.

RESULT   All the defendants were held liable for the misstatements in the registration statement.

*Case **23.1** continued on following page*

*Case **23.1** continued*

COMMENTS The degree of reliance a participating underwriter may place on a principal underwriter remains unclear. The court in *BarChris* summarily noted that the participating underwriters who relied solely on the primary underwriters did not establish due diligence. An SEC release has since suggested that a participating underwriter has met its due-diligence requirements if it satisfies itself that the managing underwriter has made the kind of investigation the participant would have performed were it the manager.

 Ethical Consideration

Should underwriters be able to escape liability due to the fact that they took management's representations at face value? To what standard should accountants be held: to the standard of their profession or that of a reasonable person?

Exhibit 23-1 provides a long, but useful, list of tasks that should be undertaken by officers, directors, underwriters, and counsel engaged in the offering of securities.

Damages

Section 11 sets forth the damages recoverable for violation of its provisions. If the plaintiff has not sold the securities in question, the recoverable damages are the amount paid for each security minus its value at the time he brings the claim. The value at the time the plaintiff brings the claim is usually the market price, unless the market price has been affected by the misrepresentation or omission. If the securities have been sold before the plaintiff brings the claim, the recoverable damages are the amount paid for the security minus the amount received at sale.

■ Section 12(2) of the 1933 Act

Section 12(2) provides a remedy for any person who purchases a security, registered or unregistered, by means of a misleading prospectus or oral communication. The purchaser may rescind the purchase, or if she has sold the security, she may recover damages—the dif-

ference between what she paid and what she received for the security.

Unlike section 10(b) (discussed later in this chapter), section 12(2) does not require the plaintiff to prove that he relied on the misrepresentation or that the defendant acted with *scienter;* that is, an intent to deceive. On the other hand, section 12(2), unlike section 10(b), applies only to those who offer or sell a security. Under section 12(2) the plaintiff must bring her action within one year from when she discovered or should have discovered the fraud, or three years after the sale, whichever is the shorter.

Who May Be Sued

Section 12(2)'s language relating to who may be liable is identical to that of section 12(1): anyone who "offers or sells" a security by means of a misleading prospectus or oral communication. Accordingly, most courts treat sections 12(1) and 12(2) as the same for the purposes of identifying potential defendants. In *Pinter v. Dahl,* case 22.5, the Supreme Court considered only section 12(1) and declined to extend its holding to section 12(2). Some subsequent cases in the lower courts have, however, applied *Pinter* to section 12(2), holding that only those in privity with the plaintiff or those who solicit the securities sale for financial gain face liability under section 12(2). Those in privity would include underwriters, brokers, and dealers having a direct contractual relationship with the plaintiff.

Elements of Liability

To establish a section 12(2) claim, the plaintiff must prove that: (1) through the mails or other means of interstate commerce, (2) the defendant offered or sold a security, (3) by means of a prospectus or oral communication, (4) which included a material misrepresentation or omission. Materiality under section 12(2) is the same as materiality under section 11.

EXHIBIT 23-1   Due Diligence Checklist

The Product

1. Examine and operate each product, particularly new products, to assess appearance, function, design, etc.
2. Assess the threat of obsolescence for each significant product line.
3. Review new product and service plans and development progress.
4. Compare the product with those of competitors, and assess the threat from new competitors.
5. Perform an analysis of unproven technology, using experts if necessary.

The Industry

1. Estimate the size of the industry, present and projected, in each significant product line, and compare company growth projections with anticipated market size for consistency.
2. Review government and trade reports and trade literature regarding the company's market segments to check for consistency with the representations and unstated premises in the prospectus.
3. Analyze competitors' SEC filings for unanticipated trends or developments.
4. Evaluate the importance of proprietary products, copyrights, and trademarks within the industry.
5. Interview trade association personnel concerning trends of relevance to the prospectus.
6. Assess the effect of macroeconomic trends (for example, interest rate fluctuations, inflation rates, and economic growth rates) on the issuer's prospects for success.
7. Assess the comparative strengths and weaknesses of competitors in terms of the dominant competitive factors in the industry (price, service, performance, etc.).
8. Compare the company's financial performance with that of its competitors.
9. Determine whether research and development (R&D) expenditures are consistent with industry practice.

Marketing and Distribution

1. Evaluate the importance of original equipment manufacturers (OEMs), present and future.
2. Interview principal customers regarding the company's products and services, complaints, anticipated future needs, etc.
3. Analyze each significant contract regarding contingencies, extent of warranties and other service obligations, rights of cancellation, etc. Check contracts with customers for completeness, to determine the existence of side written or oral commitments, or other terms that materially vary company contracts. Evaluate the quality of the backlog.
4. Evaluate the adequacy of the distribution network, the degree of control over distribution, etc.
5. Evaluate the effectiveness of marketing personnel.
6. For new products, estimate the cost of introduction, and determine whether the cost is adequately reflected in cash flow projections.
7. Assess the likelihood of discontinuation of products or services, and whether the prospectus should disclose this information.

Technology

1. Review the company's R&D plans to determine whether any radical changes in product direction are anticipated, and what cost burden will be imposed on the company in coming years.
2. Evaluate the effectiveness of R&D personnel and organization to assess the company's capacity for technological innovation.
3. Evaluate the company's patent position and the enforceability of its technology licenses.
4. Analyze any litigation regarding technology rights.
5. Review royalty contracts for contingencies, etc., and contact the licensees to determine the existence of any agreement or understanding that varies the terms of the contract.
6. Determine, with regard to government contracts, what if any interest the government asserts or may assert in company technology.

Exhibit 23-1 continued on following page

EXHIBIT 23-1　　Due Diligence Checklist, *continued*

Technology

7. Evaluate other professional affiliations of management or R&D personnel (such as academic affiliations) to assess the likelihood of competing claims on company technology.

8. Evaluate the effectiveness of the company's efforts to police its patents, preserve its trade secrets, maintain its copyrights and marks, etc., and assess the company's resources to perform these tasks.

9. Determine whether the company's exports are consistent with export-control laws.

Management

1. Investigate the prior experience of management and directors in the same industry and the same size company, their experience with large firms, etc. Also, investigate backgrounds of officers and directors, standing in the community, reputation in the industry, etc.

2. Evaluate the responsiveness of management to previous auditors' management letters.

3. Assess the effectiveness of management through interviews with outside customers and suppliers, bankers, auditors, etc.

4. Review prior transactions between the company and insiders for fairness, propriety, full disclosure, etc.

5. Determine whether any significant defections from management or the board are imminent, and assess their effect on company competitiveness.

Employees

1. Compare the company's stock option plans, pension plans, salaries, etc., with those of competitors to assess the company's ability to attract and retain skilled employees.

2. Consider whether the public offering is likely to result in loss of key employees to retirement.

3. Review employee contracts for term, unrecorded benefit obligations, contingencies, etc. Interview key employees to determine whether unrecorded written or oral commitments have been made to them.

4. Determine whether compensation obligations have been properly accounted for in the company's books.

5. Assess the adequacy of the labor supply for each operating division.

6. Evaluate the company's labor-relations history, union contracts, prospects of union activity, etc.

Production

1. Assess the ability of production facilities to handle anticipated volumes, and whether the cost of new plant and equipment is consistent with anticipated cash flow.

2. Evaluate product and process obsolescence, and compare production facilities to those of industry competitors to determine future competitiveness, both technical and economic.

3. Inquire into anticipated plant closings as well as plans for new facilities, and consider whether disclosure in the prospectus would be advisable.

4. Evaluate adequacy of management information systems and inventory control programs.

5. Assess the exposure from single-source suppliers, and evaluate the company's contingency plan for responding to an interruption to supplies.

6. Contact major suppliers to determine their satisfaction with the company, and their plans to retire, reduce, or raise the price of, key supplies and components.

Accounting

1. Determine whether intangible expenses, such as R&D expenditures, are being or should be expensed.

2. Analyze company finances, including supporting workpapers where necessary, for prior years.

3. Review budgets and projections in order to determine material changes in the company's financial position, and compare past budgets and projections with actual experience in order to assess the accuracy of management's estimates.

4. Compare the company's revenue-recognition policy and other accounting conventions with those of the industry.

5. Evaluate the effect of customer financing practices on present and future revenues.

6. Evaluate the effect of changes in tax laws, and the company's position with respect to open tax years.

7. Verify that the use of proceeds matches financial needs quantitatively and qualitatively.

EXHIBIT 23-1   Due Diligence Checklist, *continued*

Accounting

8. Determine whether inventory turns are consistent with industry ratios.

9. Assess the accuracy of the inventory reported and the adequacy of the inventory obsolescence reserve, and determine the suitability of the mix of materials inventory.

10. Review aging receivables for consideration of reserve or write-off, and assess the adequacy of the bad debt reserve and other reserves against income.

11. Obtain a report as to the adequacy of the company's accounting controls.

12. Ascertain that the preeffective auditor's "cold comfort" letter is complete.

Legal

1. Identify and assess the effect of new and proposed governmental regulations on operations, expenses, etc.

2. Check title, title insurance, encumbrances, liens, etc. upon company property and equipment.

3. Review incorporation documents, bylaws, and minutes of all shareholder, board, and board committee meetings for several years, both to confirm regularity and to identify events that might require further investigation.

4. Review stock transfer records for regularity, and check for agreements affecting ownership or control of shares.

5. Evaluate pending litigation, review the terms of significant concluded litigation, and investigate the existence of threatened claims or future exposure for statutory or regulatory violations.

6. Determine whether any acquisitions, mergers, reorganizations, etc., are impending or likely, and what effect they will have on the company.

7. Review all press releases, promotional literature, company reports, news accounts, etc., for consistency with the prospectus.

8. Review company banking, leasing, factoring arrangements, etc., and assess the likelihood and effect of disruption or termination.

9. Determine that all insurable risks have been adequately insured against, and that policies do not have material adverse exclusions or omissions.

Derived from Robert Alan Spanner, "Limiting Exposure in the Offering Process," *Review of Securities and Commodities Regulation* (April 8, 1987): 64–66. Copyright © 1987, Standard & Poor's Corporation. Reprinted by permission.

"Prospectus"   A *prospectus* under section 12(2) is "any document which is designed to produce orders for a security, whether or not the document purports on its face to offer the security for sale or otherwise to dispose of it for value." This definition encompasses an advertisement, letter, radio or television communication, or confirmation slip that offers or confirms the sale of any security.

"By Means Of"   The phrase "by means of" simply requires that a communication be intended or perceived as influencing a securities sale. It does not require that the plaintiff actually receive the misleading statement. However, there must be some sort of connection between the misleading statement and the purchase. For example, in one case the defendant's failure to discuss certain financial data during a meeting was not connected with a subsequent sale of securities, because no sale was discussed or contemplated at that meeting. The court found the defendant not liable because the securities were not sold "by means of" an oral communication.

Defense

Section 12(2) provides a defense of reasonable care. A defendant will not be liable for a section 12(2) violation if it can prove that it did not know, and in the exercise of reasonable care could not have known, about the misrepresentations or omissions. In contrast to the due-diligence defense of section 11, the defense of reasonable care is not spelled out in detail. Commentators have suggested that reasonable care may require a defendant to undertake an investigation. In *Sanders v. John Nuveen & Co.*,[5] the United States Court of Appeals for the Seventh Circuit held that there is no difference between the duties imposed on an underwriter by section 11, which requires a reasonable investigation, and section 12(2). An underwriter, the Seventh Circuit held, must look beyond pub-

---

5. 619 F.2d 1222 (7th Cir. 1980), *cert. denied*, 450 U.S. 1005, 101 S.Ct. 1719 (1981).

lished data and undertake some investigation of that part of the data that is verifiable. Because the underwriter in *Sanders* did not examine the issuing company's records, contracts, or tax returns, the underwriter did not act with reasonable care.

■ Section 17(a) of the 1933 Act

Section 17(a) of the 1933 Act prohibits fraud in connection with the sale of securities. It is similar in scope to section 10(b) of the 1934 Act (discussed below), which prohibits fraud in both the sale and the purchase of securities. Unlike section 10(b), section 17(a) does not require proof of scienter or bad intent. Several courts formerly extended a right of action under section 17(a) to private parties; however, most recent decisions reject this extension as inconsistent with the language and purpose of the statute.

■ Section 10(b) of the 1934 Act

Section 10(b) gives the SEC power to prohibit individuals or companies from engaging in securities fraud by authorizing the SEC to prescribe specific rules for the protection of investors.

Rule 10b-5

The SEC promulgated rule 10b-5 as a means to achieve the goals of section 10(b): to encourage disclosure of information relevant to the investing public, to protect investors, and to deter fraud in the securities industry. Rule 10b-5 states:

> It shall be unlawful for any person, directly or indirectly, by the use of any means or instrumentality of interstate commerce, or of the mails, or of any facility of any national securities exchange,
>
> (1) to employ any device, scheme, or artifice to defraud,
>
> (2) to make any untrue statement of a material fact or to omit to state a material fact necessary in order to make the statements made, in the light of the circumstances under which they were made, not misleading, or
>
> (3) to engage in any act, practice, or course of business which operates or would operate as a fraud or deceit upon any person, in connection with the purchase or sale of any security.

The SEC has broad power to investigate apparent violations of rule 10b-5 and to order that the violator stop its wrongful conduct or to recommend criminal prosecution for willful violations.

Since 1946, courts have held that rule 10b-5 also creates an implicit private right of action giving individual investors the right to sue a violator for damages. Although the Supreme Court has lately shown increasing hostility toward implied rights of action under other provisions of the securities laws, most commentators do not expect it to abrogate the right of action under rule 10b-5. The Supreme Court did, however, hold in the following case that a private plaintiff may not maintain an aiding and abetting suit under section 10(b). To prove that a person is an *aider and abettor*, it is necessary to show (1) the existence of a primary violation of section 10(b) or rule 10b-5, (2) the defendant's knowledge of (or recklessness as to) that primary violation, and (3) substantial assistance of the violation by the defendant.

■ A Case in Point: **In the Language of the Court**

Case 23.2
CENTRAL BANK OF DENVER v. FIRST INTERSTATE BANK OF DENVER
Supreme Court of the United States
114 S.Ct. 1439 (1994).

FACTS In 1986 and 1988, the Colorado Springs-Stetson Hills Public Building Authority (Authority) issued a total of $26 million in bonds to finance public improvements at Stetson Hills, a planned residential and commercial development in Colorado Springs. Petitioner Central Bank served as indenture trustee for the bond issues, which means Central Bank had authority to act on behalf of the bondholders.

The bonds were secured by landowner assessment liens, which covered about 250 acres for the 1986 bond issue, and about 272 acres for the 1988 bond issue. The bond covenants required that the land subject to the liens be worth at least 160% of the bonds' outstanding principal and interest. The covenants required AmWest Development, the developer of Stetson Hills, to give Central Bank an annual report containing evidence that the 160% test was met.

In January 1988, AmWest provided Central Bank an updated appraisal of the land securing the 1986 bonds and of the land proposed to secure the 1988 bonds. The 1988 appraisal showed land values almost unchanged from the 1986 appraisal. Soon afterwards, Central Bank received a letter from the senior underwriter for the 1986 bonds. Noting that property values were declining in Colorado Springs, and that Central Bank was operating on an appraisal over 16 months old, the underwriter expressed concern that the 160% test was not being met.

Central Bank asked its in-house appraiser to review the updated 1988 appraisal. The in-house appraiser decided that the values listed in the appraisal appeared optimistic, considering the local real estate market. He suggested that Central Bank retain an outside appraiser to conduct an independent review of the 1988 appraisal. After an exchange of letters between Central Bank and AmWest in early 1988, Central Bank decided to delay independent review of the appraisal until the end of the year, six months after the June 1988 closing on the bond issue. Before the independent review was complete, however, the Authority defaulted on the 1988 bonds.

Respondents First Interstate and Jack Naber had purchased $2.1 million of the 1988 bonds. After the default, the respondents sued the Authority, the 1988 underwriter, a junior underwriter, an AmWest director, and Central Bank for violations of section 10(b) of the Securities Exchange Act of 1934. The complaint alleged that the Authority, the underwriter defendants, and the AmWest director had violated section 10(b). The complaint also alleged that Central Bank was "secondarily liable under section 10(b) for its conduct in aiding and abetting the fraud."

The Federal District Court granted summary judgment to Central Bank. The U.S. Court of Appeals reversed. Central Bank appealed.

ISSUE PRESENTED   Is there a private right of action under section 10(b) against persons who aid and abet a section 10(b) violation?

OPINION   KENNEDY, J., writing for the U.S. Supreme Court:

As we have interpreted it, § 10(b) of the Securities Exchange Act of 1934 imposes private civil liability on those who commit a manipulative or deceptive act in connection with the purchase or sale of securities. In this case, we must answer a question reserved in two earlier decisions: whether private civil liability under § 10(b) extends as well to those who do not engage in the manipulative or deceptive practice but who aid and abet the violation.

. . . .

In our cases addressing § 10(b) and Rule 10b-5, we have confronted two main issues. First, we have determined the scope of conduct prohibited by § 10(b). Second, in cases where the defendant has committed a violation of § 10(b), we have decided questions about the elements of the 10b-5 private liability scheme: for example, whether there is a right to contribution, what the statute of limitations is, whether there is a reliance requirement, and whether there is an in pari delicto defense.

The latter issue, determining the elements of the 10b-5 private liability scheme, has posed difficulty because Congress did not create a private § 10(b) cause of action and had no occasion to provide guidance about the elements of a private liability scheme. We thus have had "to infer how the

*Case **23.2** continued on following page*

Case **23.2** continued

1934 Congress would have addressed the issues had the 10b-5 action been included as an express provision in the 1934 Act."

With respect, however, to the first issue, the scope of conduct prohibited by § 10(b), the text of the statute controls our decision. In § 10(b), Congress prohibited manipulative or deceptive acts in connection with the purchase or sale of securities. It envisioned that the SEC would enforce the statutory prohibition through administrative and injunctive actions. Of course, a private plaintiff now may bring suit against violators of § 10(b). But the private plaintiff may not bring a 10b-5 suit against a defendant for acts not prohibited by the text of § 10(b). To the contrary, our cases considering the scope of conduct prohibited by § 10(b) in private suits have emphasized adherence to the statutory language, "'the starting point in every case involving construction of a statute.'" We have refused to allow 10b-5 challenges to conduct not prohibited by the text of the statute.

. . . .

Our consideration of statutory duties, especially in cases interpreting § 10(b), establishes that the statutory text controls the definition of conduct covered by § 10(b). That bodes ill for respondents, for "the language of Section 10(b) does not in terms mention aiding and abetting." To overcome this problem, respondents and the SEC suggest (or hint at) the novel argument that the use of the phrase "directly or indirectly" in the text of § 10(b) covers aiding and abetting.

The federal courts have not relied on the "directly or indirectly" language when imposing aiding and abetting liability under § 10(b), and with good reason. There is a basic flaw with this interpretation. According to respondents and the SEC, the "directly or indirectly" language shows that "Congress . . . intended to reach all persons who engage, even if only indirectly, in proscribed activities connected with securities transactions." The problem, of course, is that aiding and abetting liability extends beyond persons who engage, even indirectly, in a proscribed activity; aiding and abetting liability reaches persons who do not engage in the proscribed activity but who give a degree of aid to those who do. . . . In short, respondents' interpretation of the "directly or indirectly" language fails to support their suggestion that the text of § 10(b) itself prohibits aiding and abetting.

. . . .

We reach the uncontroversial conclusion, accepted even by those courts recognizing a § 10(b) aiding and abetting cause of action, that the text of the 1934 Act does not itself reach those who aid and abet a § 10(b) violation. Unlike those courts, however, we think that conclusion resolves the case. It is inconsistent with settled methodology in § 10(b) cases to extend liability beyond the scope of conduct prohibited by the statutory text. To be sure, aiding and abetting a wrongdoer ought to be actionable in certain instances. The issue, however, is not whether imposing private civil liability on aiders and abettors is good policy but whether aiding and abetting is covered by the statute.

As in earlier cases considering conduct prohibited by § 10(b), we again conclude that the statute prohibits only the making of a material misstatement (or omission) or the commission of a manipulative act. The proscription does not include giving aid to a person who commits a manipulative or deceptive act. We cannot amend the statute to create liability for acts that are not themselves manipulative or deceptive within the meaning of the statute.

. . . .

Respondents make further arguments for imposition of § 10(b) aiding and abetting liability, none of which leads us to a different answer.

. . . .

Because the text of § 10(b) does not prohibit aiding and abetting, we hold that a private plaintiff may not maintain an aiding and abetting suit under § 10(b). The absence of § 10(b) aiding and abetting liability does not mean that secondary actors in the securities markets are always free from liability under the securities Acts. Any person or entity, including a lawyer, accountant, or bank, who employs a manipulative device or makes a material misstatement (or omission) on which a purchaser or seller of securities relies may be liable as a primary violator under 10b-5, assuming all of the requirements for primary liability under Rule 10b-5 are met.

. . . .

RESULT   Because there is no private aiding and abetting liability under section 10(b), Central Bank could not be held liable as an aider and abettor. The District Court's grant of summary judgment to Central Bank was proper, and the judgment of the Court of Appeals was reversed.

COMMENTS   The Supreme Court noted the vexatious nature of rule 10b-5, and the fact that it requires secondary actors to expend large sums for pretrial defense and the negotiation of settlements. The Court went on to state:

> This uncertainty and excessive litigation can have ripple effects. For example, newer and smaller companies may find it difficult to obtain advice from professionals. A professional may fear that a newer or smaller company may not survive and that business failure would generate securities litigation against the professional, among others. In addition, the increased costs incurred by professionals because of the litigation and settlement costs under 10b-5 may be passed on to their client companies, and in turn incurred by the company's investors, the intended beneficiaries of the statute.

Questions
1. Can the SEC pursue aiders and abettors in civil enforcement actions under section 10(b) and rule 10b-5?
2. Is there still conspiracy liability under rule 10b-5? Should there be?

More suits are brought under rule 10b-5 than under any other provision of securities law, including those, such as sections 11 and 12 of the 1933 Act, that explicitly create private rights of action. Although there is some overlap, rule 10b-5 extends to misconduct not covered by other securities laws. For example, section 11 of the 1933 Act applies only to misleading statements in a registration statement. In contrast, under rule 10b-5, executives could be liable for misleading statements contained in any document—such as a press release, a letter to shareholders, or even a speech to a trade association—as long as the statements were made in a manner reasonably calculated to influence the investing public.

Statute of Limitations   Suits under section 10(b) must be brought within one year of the date the plaintiff discovered or should have discovered the fraud, or within three years of the date of the violation, whichever is shorter.[6]

Elements of a Rule 10b-5 Cause of Action

In order to recover damages from a defendant under rule 10b-5, a plaintiff must show each of the following elements:

1. The defendant used either an instrumentality of interstate commerce or the mails or a facility of a national securities exchange.

2. The defendant made a statement that either misrepresented or omitted a fact.

3. The fact was of material importance.

4. The misrepresentation or omission was made with scienter (culpable state of mind).

5. There was a purchase or sale of securities.

6. The plaintiff acted in reliance either on the defendant's misrepresentation or on the assumption that the market price of the stock accurately reflected its value.

7. The defendant's misrepresentation or omission caused the plaintiff to suffer losses.

---

6. *Lampf, Pleva, Lipkind, Prupis & Petigrow v. Gilbertson*, 501 U.S. 350, 111 S.Ct. 2773 (1991).

Each of these seven elements is described in more detail below.

Interstate Commerce

The requirement that the defendant used interstate commerce, the mails, or a national securities exchange gives Congress the power to regulate the defendant's conduct under the United States Constitution. The requirement is usually easy to satisfy. Use of interstate commerce includes use of a radio broadcast heard in more than one state; use of a newspaper advertisement in a newspaper delivered to more than one state; or use of a telephone wired for interstate calls, even if no interstate calls were actually made. Use of the mails includes sending a letter within a state, because the mail is an instrumentality of interstate commerce. Use of a national securities exchange includes use of any facility of such an exchange.

Misstatement or Omission

A *misstatement* is a misrepresentation of a fact; in other words, a lie. An *omission* is a fact left out of a statement, such that the statement becomes misleading.

Misstatement   In the following case, a company's attempts to dispel rumors were found to misrepresent the facts.

■ A Case in Point: Summary

Case 23.3
SEC v. TEXAS GULF SULPHUR CO.
United States District Court for the Southern District of New York
312 F.Supp. 77 (S.D.N.Y. 1970),
aff'd, 446 F.2d 1301
(2d Cir. 1971),
cert. denied, 404 U.S. 1005,
92 S.Ct. 561 (1971).

FACTS   Texas Gulf Sulphur Company (TGS) drilled a test hole on November 12, 1963, which indicated the possible discovery of copper. TGS did not immediately disclose the results of its drill hole or undertake further drilling because it wanted to acquire property in the surrounding area and did not want to drive up the price of the property.

On April 12, 1964, in response to rumors about the copper discovery, TGS issued a press release. By this time, the company had confirmed the discovery of copper. Preliminary tests indicated that the discovery was significant. The press release, however, minimized the importance of the discovery. It said (in part):

For Immediate Release

TEXAS GULF SULPHUR COMMENT ON TIMMINS, ONTARIO, EXPLORATION

NEW YORK, April 12—The following statement was made today by Dr. Charles F. Fogarty, executive vice president of Texas Gulf Sulphur Company, in regard to the company's drilling operations near Timmins, Ontario, Canada. Dr. Fogarty said:

During the past few days, the exploration activities of Texas Gulf Sulphur in the area of Timmins, Ontario, have been widely reported in the press, coupled with rumors of a substantial copper discovery there. These reports exaggerate the scale of operations, and mention plans and statistics of size and grade of ore that are without factual basis and have evidently originated by speculation of people not connected with TGS.

The facts are as follows. TGS has been exploring in the Timmins area for six years as part of its overall search in Canada and elsewhere for various minerals—lead, copper, zinc, etc. During the course of this work, in Timmins as well as in Eastern Canada, TGS has conducted exploration entirely on its own, without the participation by others. Numerous prospects have been investigated by geophysical means and a large number of selected ones have been core-drilled. These cores are sent to the United States for assay and detailed examination as a matter of routine and on advice of expert Canadian legal counsel. No inferences as to grade can be drawn from this procedure.

Most of the areas drilled in Eastern Canada have revealed either barren pyrite or graphite without value; a few have resulted in discoveries of small or marginal sulphide ore bodies.

Recent drilling on one property near Timmins has led to preliminary indications that more drilling would be required for proper evaluation of this prospect. The drilling done to date has not been conclusive, but the statements made by many outside quarters are unreliable and include information and figures that are not available to TGS.

The work done to date has not been sufficient to reach definite conclusions and any statement as to size and grade of ore would be premature and possibly misleading. When we have progressed to the point where reasonable and logical conclusions can be made, TGS will issue a definite statement to its stockholders and to the public in order to clarify the Timmins project.

The SEC contended that TGS's April 12 release was a misstatement because the impression it left with investors was contrary to the known facts at the time.

ISSUE PRESENTED   Does a press release giving a misleading impression about the results of a drilling operation violate rule 10b-5?

SUMMARY OF OPINION   The Federal District Court acknowledged that the timing of disclosure is a matter for the business judgment of the corporate officers. However, when a company chooses to issue a press release to respond to spreading rumors regarding its activities, it must describe the true picture at the time of the press release. This should include the basic facts known, or which reasonably should be known, to the drafters of the press release. Such facts are necessary to enable the investing public to make a reasonable appraisal of the existing situation.

Because the press release misled reasonable investors to believe either that there was no ore discovery, or that any discovery was not a significant one, TGS violated section 10(b) and rule 10b-5.

RESULT   The defendant TGS violated section 10(b) and rule 10b-5.

COMMENTS   A company may have excellent reasons to attempt to dispel rumors. TGS, for example, had an interest in keeping the find quiet in order to keep down the acquisition costs of land. Or consider a company involved in merger negotiations asked by the press whether there is any reason for unusual trading in its stock. The company may well want to keep the negotiations under wraps for a variety of legitimate reasons. Yet, if it says that it is

Case **23.3** *continued on following page*

Case **23.3** *continued*

unaware of any corporate developments, it runs the risk of rule 10b-5 liability. The SEC has indicated that it considers such a statement in these circumstances to be a violation of rule 10b-5. The Supreme Court addressed this issue in *Basic, Inc. v. Levinson* (case 23.4).

A prediction about the future can be a misstatement, but only if the person making the prediction does not believe it at the time. A prediction is not a guarantee, and it does not become a misstatement simply because the facts do not develop as predicted. For example, in one case the court held that a company president's prediction of growth of 20% to 25% in the next five years was not a misstatement, in spite of facts that indicated that the company's growth would be substantially less than stated. The prediction was merely an overly optimistic view, which appeared to be honestly held.

However, if there is no reasonable basis for a prediction, then it is a misstatement, because the person who made it could not honestly have believed it. In other words, if a company official chooses to see the world through rose-colored glasses, he had better make sure his prescription is accurate. This point was driven home in *Goldman v. Belden*.[7]

The case involved Sykes Datatronics, Inc., a manufacturer of microcomputer systems. After some success with its first product, which resulted in a doubling of sales and earnings per share in its first four years, Sykes introduced its new product, InnVoice, in 1982. InnVoice was a system designed to aid hotels in recording billing information about guests' telephone calls. In its annual report, in a speech to shareholders, and in a quarterly report, company officials stated that Sykes would try to increase growth by 40% to 50%, and expected to be the dominant supplier in the market.

A shareholder sued the company officials under rule 10b-5, alleging that their predictions were misstatements. The plaintiff alleged that the company knew that its product was inferior to competing products, because it was incompatible with the computers that many hotels already had installed, and it could not record international calls as many competing products could. The plaintiff also alleged that the imminent breakup of AT&T (on which Sykes was dependent for a significant amount of business) created major uncertainty for the future marketing of the product.

The United States Court of Appeals for the Second Circuit reasoned that the company's unduly positive predictions could well be misstatements of fact, and that Sykes's management could be liable for intentionally fostering a mistaken belief about the company's earnings prospects. As a result, several officers of Sykes were liable for intentionally misleading investors about the company's earnings prospects. John Sykes, the company's vice-president and director, was held liable for selling his stock at artificially high prices.

Omission   It is clear from the above cases that a company must be careful should it choose to speak. What if it chooses not to speak?

The general rule is that a company has no duty under rule 10b-5 to reveal corporate developments unless it or its insiders trade in its securities, recommend trading to someone else, or disclose the information as a *tip*—that is, a disclosure made to an individual and withheld from the general public. The fact that information is material does not, in itself, give rise to a duty to disclose.[8]

However, once the company has said something about a particular topic, it then has a duty to disclose enough relevant facts so that the statement is not inaccurate, incomplete, or misleading. The statement may be an obligatory one; for example, stock-exchange rules require that issuers promptly reveal material developments unless there is a business reason not to do so, and the securities laws require that certain information be disclosed in registration statements and proxy solicitations. Or the statement may be voluntary; for example, a company may choose to publicize information about favorable new developments or to respond to unfavorable rumors. Whether the statement is obligatory or voluntary, the company's officials must tell the whole truth with respect to that topic, or risk being sued later for a misleading omission.

An omission can occur when a company makes a statement that is true at the time but that becomes misleading in light of later events. If investors are reasonably

---

7. 754 F.2d 1059 (2d Cir. 1985).

8. *Backman v. Polaroid Corp.*, 893 F.2d 1405 (1st Cir. 1990).

relying on the previous statements, the company can be held liable for failing to disclose the new information. For example, a company incurs a duty to update its financial projections when a projection changes or the company discovers that the projection was incorrect from the outset.

There is a duty to disclose the results of product safety tests, if they make previously disclosed test results false. For example, A. H. Robins Company, a pharmaceutical manufacturer, reported in 1970 that its Dalkon Shield intrauterine contraceptive device was safe and effective. In 1972, internal studies indicated that the Dalkon Shield was not as safe or effective as originally reported.[9] The United States Court of Appeals for the Second Circuit held that Robins's omission of the new information rendered its earlier statements misleading. Because investors were still relying on the statement that the Dalkon Shield was safe, the company had a duty to correct that statement once it learned that it was inaccurate.

Ethical Consideration

Even when there is no duty under the securities laws to reveal bad news, there may be an ethical duty to reveal it. For example, a health hazard associated with a product on the market should be disclosed immediately. In some situations there is also a legal duty to disclose bad news, under state and federal laws not explicity dealing with securities.

Statements by Third Parties   Even if the company itself did not publish the misleading projection, or make the statement, or start the rumor, it may nevertheless have a duty to reveal all of the facts regarding the issue. This is the case when the company is so entangled with the third party's statement that the statement can be attributed to the company; the company is then responsible for making sure that the statement is accurate. For example, if a company makes it a practice to review and correct drafts of analysts' forecasts, then the company impliedly represents that the corrected forecast is in accord with the company's

---

9. *Ross v. A. H. Robins Co.*, 607 F.2d 545 (2d Cir. 1979), *cert. denied*, 446 U.S. 946, 100 S.Ct. 2175 (1980).

view, and it has a duty to reveal all facts necessary to ensure that the analyst's report is not misleading.

Similarly, because there is a special relationship between a company and its underwriter or principal market maker, the company will be held liable for misleading statements made by these third parties. Investors are entitled to assume that the company provided the information to its underwriter or principal market maker and would correct any misleading statements.

Material Fact

A buyer or seller of stock cannot win damages just because an executive misrepresented or omitted a fact about her company. The fact must be material. Materiality is judged at the time of the misstatement or omission.

66

A buyer or seller of stock cannot win damages just because an executive misrepresented or omitted a fact about her company. The fact must be material.

The Supreme Court has recognized that for contingent or speculative events, such as negotiations regarding a potential merger, it is difficult to tell whether a reasonable investor would consider the omitted fact material at the time. The Supreme Court has declined to adopt a bright-line rule; materiality is a fact-specific determination. If a misstatement or omission concerns a future event, its materiality will depend upon a balancing of the probability that the event will occur, and the anticipated magnitude of the event in light of the totality of the company activity.

It is not always possible to predict which facts a court will consider material. However, some issues are nearly always considered material, for example, any statements about the earnings, distributions, or assets of a company (unless the misrepresentation concerns a minor amount— if a press release misstates a major corporation's yearly earnings by $100, that is not material).

Materiality is not affected by the intent of the party making the statement. There can be liability even if the manager did not know the omitted or misrepresented fact came within the legal definition of a material fact.

Significant facts about a parent or a subsidiary of a company are usually material. These include the discovery of embezzlement or falsification of financial statements, an impending tender offer, or the loss of a manufacturer's major customer. Other facts that are probably material include inability to obtain supplies, increased costs of supplies, a decision to close a plant, information regarding the outlook in the industry, an intention to market a new product or cease marketing an old one, potential liability for damages in a lawsuit, a major discovery or product development, cost overruns, a change in man-

agement, compensation of corporate officers, and an increase in real estate taxes. As this list illustrates, a material fact is any fact that is likely to affect the market value of the company's stock.

As the following case demonstrates, even "soft"—that is, speculative—information can be deemed material under rule 10b-5.

■ **A Case in Point:**   **In the Language of the Court**

Case 23.4
BASIC INC. v. LEVINSON
Supreme Court of the
United States
485 U.S. 224, 108 S.Ct. 978
(1988).

FACTS In September 1976, officers and directors of Basic Inc. began discussions with representatives of Combustion Engineering, Inc. concerning the possibility of a merger. Basic was a publicly traded company primarily engaged in the business of manufacturing chemical refractories for the steel industry. Combustion produced mostly alumina-based refractories.

Basic made three public statements in 1977 and 1978 denying the existence of ongoing merger negotiations. On December 18, 1978, Basic announced the possibility of a merger.

The plaintiffs had sold their Basic shares after Basic's first public denial of negotiations and before the public announcement of the possibility of a merger. They sued Basic, alleging that its denials violated rule 10b-5.

ISSUE PRESENTED Can even the existence of very preliminary merger negotiations short of an agreement in principle on price and structure be a material fact?

OPINION BLACKMUN, J., writing for the U.S. Supreme Court:

. . . .

Even before this Court's decision in *TSC Industries*, the Second Circuit had explained the role of the materiality requirement of Rule 10b-5, with respect to contingent or speculative information or events, in a manner that gave the term meaning that is independent of other provisions of the Rule. Under such circumstances, materiality "will depend at any time upon a balancing of both the indicated probability that the event will occur and the anticipated magnitude of the event in light of the totality of the company activity." Interestingly, neither the Third Circuit decision adopting the agreement-in-principle test nor petitioners here take issue with this general standard. Rather, they suggest that with respect to preliminary merger discussions, there are good reasons to draw a line at agreement on price and structure.

In a subsequent decision, the late Judge Friendly, writing for a Second Circuit panel, applied the *Texas Gulf Sulphur* probability/magnitude approach in the specific context of preliminary merger negotiations. After acknowledging that materiality is something to be determined on the basis of the particular facts of each case, he stated:

> Since a merger in which it is bought out is the most important event that can occur in a small corporation's life, to wit, its death, we think that inside information, as regards a merger of this sort, can become material at an earlier stage than would be the case as regards lesser transactions—and this even though the mortality rate of merger in such formative stages is doubtless high.

We agree with that analysis.

Whether merger discussions in any particular case are material therefore depends on the facts. Generally, in order to assess the probability that the event will occur, a factfinder will need to look to indicia of interest in the transaction at the highest corporate levels. Without attempting to catalog all such possible factors, we note by way of example that board resolutions, instructions to investment bankers, and actual negotiations between principals or other intermediaries may serve as indicia of interest. To assess the magnitude of the transaction to the issuer of the securities allegedly manipulated, a factfinder will need to consider such facts as the size of the two corporate entities and of the potential premiums over market value. No particular event or factor short of closing the transaction need be either necessary or sufficient by itself to render merger discussions material.

. . . .

RESULT   Because the standard of materiality adopted by the Supreme Court differed from that used by both courts below, the case was remanded (sent back) for further proceedings consistent with the opinion.

COMMENTS   The Supreme Court's advice does not much help executives to predict with certainty whether a fact concerning a future event will be considered material. Most commentators advise that if a company is involved in a speculative matter, aspects of which it wishes to remain private, the only safe way to avoid liability under rule 10b-5 is not to say anything during the early stages of negotiation.

Questions
1. What additional facts do you need to know in order to determine whether the merger discussions were material?
2. Would a reasonable investor have taken the merger into consideration in determining whether to buy or sell his securities?

Silence or a "no comment" statement in response to rumors will not lead to liability if the company has not previously spoken on the subject and insiders are not trading or tipping. However, there is a caveat: A policy of not commenting on rumors must be adhered to in the face of both true and untrue rumors. If the company always says "no comment" when the rumor is true, but provides facts to dispel untrue rumors, then the "no comment" acts as an admission that the rumor is true.

> 66
> *If the company always says "no comment" when the rumor is true, but provides facts to dispel untrue rumors, then the "no comment" acts as an admission that the rumor is true.*

Although keeping silent may be safer under rule 10b-5, in many cases it will be hard to do. If a corporation's stock is traded on rumors of some major development, silence may contribute to disorderly market activity, distrust of company management, and possible abuse by those with access to inside information. Moreover, a blanket "no comment" policy makes it impossible to dispel false but damaging rumors. Once the silence is broken, of course, the company must be exceedingly careful in its statements even as to speculative events.

Bespeaks Caution Doctrine   According to the *bespeaks caution doctrine*, a court may determine that the inclusion of sufficient cautionary statements in a prospectus renders immaterial any misrepresentations and omissions contained therein. The doctrine stands for the proposition that a statement or omission must be considered in context, so that accompanying statements may render it immaterial as a matter of law.

In 1993, Trump Castle Funding issued a prospectus conveying to potential investors the risks inherent in the proposed venture, the financing of the Taj Mahal casino.

The prospectus alerted potential investors that there was a chance that the partnership would be unable to repay the bondholders. The court held that the extensive cautionary statements, tailored to the specific risks involved, negated any potentially misleading effect of the optimistic projections in the prospectus on a reasonable investor. Trump was therefore not liable for violating rule 10b-5.[10]

Not all courts have adopted the bespeaks caution doctrine. In addition, cautionary language may render an alleged omission or misrepresentation immaterial, but only if the cautionary statements are substantive and tailored to specific future projections, estimates, or opinions in the prospectus.

In 1994, the Fifth Circuit stated:

> . . . cautionary language is not necessarily sufficient, in and of itself, to render predictive statements immaterial as a matter of law. . . . The appropriate inquiry is whether, under all the circumstances, the omitted fact or the prediction without a reasonable basis "is one [that] a reasonable investor would consider significant in [making] the decision to invest, such that it alters the total mix of information available about the proposed investment." Inclusion of cautionary language . . . is, of course, relevant to the materiality inquiry. . . . Nevertheless, cautionary language as such is not dispositive of this inquiry.[11]

Scienter

Rule 10b-5 does not impose liability for innocent misstatements or omissions. The misstatements or omissions must be made with scienter, that is, a mental state embracing the intent to deceive, manipulate, or defraud. Intent to deceive means that the defendant says something she believes is untrue which she expects others to rely on, or that she omits a fact that she hopes will cause others to misunderstand what she does say. The Supreme Court has made clear that scienter is more than mere negligence or lack of care.

Recklessness   A majority of jurisdictions have held that recklessness qualifies as scienter. Different jurisdictions define recklessness slightly differently. In some circuits, such as the Seventh (which includes Illinois), a defendant is held to have acted recklessly if he either knew that his statements would probably be misleading, or should have known it because the misleading quality

of the statements was so obvious. In the Second Circuit (which includes New York), recklessness requires a showing that the defendant either knew her statement was misleading or untrue, or was put on notice that it might be, but made the statement anyway without investigating the true facts. In the Ninth Circuit (which includes the West Coast), the definition of recklessness is that the defendant's conduct was an extreme departure from the standards of ordinary care which presented a danger of misleading buyers or sellers that was either known to the defendant or was so obvious that he must have been aware of it.

The officers of a national corporation (which could be sued in any of these jurisdictions) would want to avoid recklessness under all of these definitions. Thus, before making any statement, the officers should investigate what the true facts are, and they should make no statement unless they in good faith believe it to be true. The investigation must be fairly thorough. An officer may be liable for misrepresenting facts that she should have been aware of, even if she was not in fact aware of them. For example, directors may be deemed to have knowledge of facts in the corporate books regardless of whether they have actually examined the books.

Purchase or Sale

Rule 10b-5 requires that the conduct occur "in connection with the purchase or sale of any security." This requirement defines both those who can sue and those who can be sued under rule 10b-5.

The Supreme Court has made it clear that only persons who actually purchase or sell securities can sue under rule 10b-5. A person who has not purchased (or sold) cannot sue on the theory that he would have purchased (or sold) had he known the true facts. Thus, liability under rule 10b-5 does not extend to the whole world of potential investors, but only to those who actually buy or sell stock after a misstatement or omission.

Parties that can be sued under rule 10b-5 are those that make or are responsible for misstatements and omissions in connection with the purchase or sale of securities.

"In Connection With"   Statements are made "in connection with" the purchase or sale of securities if they were made in a manner reasonably calculated to influence the investing public, or if they were of the sort upon which the investing public might reasonably rely.

A company must be careful to monitor its public statements, such as those made in periodic reports, press releases, proxy solicitations, and annual reports. Even when addressing noninvestors such as creditors or labor

---

10. *In re Donald J. Trump Casino Securities Litigation*, 7 F.3d 357 (3d Cir. 1993), *cert. denied*, 114 S.Ct. 1219 (1994). *See also In re Worlds of Wonder Securities Litigation*, 35 F.3d. 1407 (9th Cir. 1994) (adopting bespeaks caution doctrine).

11. *Rubinstein v. Collins*, 20 F.3d 160 (5th Cir. 1994).

union representatives, a manager should exercise caution if the statements can reasonably be expected to reach investors.

Reliance

To establish liability under rule 10b-5, an investor must show that she relied either directly or indirectly on the misrepresentation or omission. If the investor did not rely on the misstatement or omission in deciding to buy or sell stock, then any loss she incurred could not be blamed on the company that made the misrepresentation or omission.

Direct Reliance   A plaintiff may show reliance by showing that he actually read the document, such as a press release or prospectus, that contained the misstatement. In the case of an omission, the Supreme Court has ruled that the plaintiff will be presumed to have relied on the omission, if it was material. That presumption of reliance can be rebutted—that is, shown to be not true—by a showing that the plaintiff would have bought (or sold) the stock even if the omitted fact had been included.

Fraud on the Market   In the securities market, however, direct reliance is rare because transactions are not conducted on a face-to-face basis. The market is interposed between the parties, providing important information to the parties in the form of the market price. As the federal court for the Northern District of Texas said in the LTV Securities Litigation: "The market is acting as the unpaid agent of the investor, informing him that, given all the information available to it, the value of the stock is worth the market price."

The theory underlying this view is known to economists as the *efficient-market theory*. It holds that in an open and developed securities market, the price of a company's stock equals its true value. The market is said to evaluate information efficiently and to incorporate it into the price of a company's securities.

Against this background, the courts have approved the *fraud-on-the-market theory:* If the information available to the market is incorrect, then the market price will not reflect the true value of the stock. Under this theory, an investor who purchases or sells a security is presumed to have relied on the market, which has in turn relied on the misstatement or omission when it set the price of the security. In *Basic Inc. v. Levinson* (case 23.4, discussed above), the Supreme Court affirmed this theory. Quoting one of the earlier lower court decisions, the Supreme Court noted that: "It is hard to imagine that there ever is a buyer or seller who does not rely on market integrity. Who would knowingly roll the dice in a crooked crap game?"

> **"** *"It is hard to imagine that there ever is a buyer or seller who does not rely on market integrity. Who would knowingly roll the dice in a crooked crap game?"*

Thus, plaintiffs do not have to show that they read or heard a defendant's misstatement in order to recover damages from that defendant. Instead, reliance is presumed if the investor shows that the defendant made a public material misrepresentation that would have caused reasonable investors to misjudge the value of the defendant's stock, and that the investor traded shares of the defendant's stock in an open securities market after the misrepresentations were made and before the truth was revealed.

A defendant can rebut the fraud-on-the-market presumption by showing that the plaintiff traded or would have traded despite knowing the statement was false. For example, an insider who is aware of nonpublic information that results in the stock being undervalued, but who sells for other reasons, cannot be said to have relied on the integrity of market price.

Lower courts have declined to apply the fraud-on-the-market presumption in cases in which there is not an efficient, open, and developed market. The courts have identified at least five factors to consider in identifying an efficient market: (1) sufficient weekly trading volume, (2) sufficient reports and analyses by investment professionals, (3) the presence of market makers and arbitrageurs, (4) the existence of issuers eligible to file form S-3 short-form registration statements, and (5) an historical showing of immediate price response to unexpected events or financial releases. In short, for a market to be open and developed, it must have a large number of buyers and sellers, and a relatively high level of trading activity and frequency. It also must be a market that rapidly reflects new information in price.

Truth on the Market   Defendants have also used the efficient-market theory to their advantage. For example, even if the defendant makes the misrepresentation that it is not involved in merger negotiations, if the market makers were privy to the truth, there is no fraud on the market. In the following case, an appellate court found that the market was aware of one set of facts undisclosed by the defendants, but was not aware of another set of undisclosed facts.

■ A Case in Point: Summary

Case 23.5
IN RE APPLE COMPUTER
SECURITIES LITIGATION
United States Court of Appeals
for the Ninth Circuit
886 F.2d 1109 (9th Cir. 1989),
cert. denied, 496 U.S. 943,
110 S.Ct. 3229 (1990).

FACTS   In late 1982 and early 1983, Apple Computer, Inc. made several optimistic public statements concerning its newly developed office computer, the Lisa. For example, in a January 31, 1983, *Business Week* article, Apple's chairman of the board, Steven Jobs, was quoted as saying: "I don't think we will have any problem selling all the Lisa's we can build." In an April 14, 1983, *Wall Street Journal* article, he was quoted as stating: "Lisa is going to be phenomenally successful in the first year out of the chute."

Many of the risks and problems associated with Lisa, however, were widely publicized. The same *Business Week* article quoting Mr. Jobs as saying that Apple would have little trouble selling Lisa also stated: "One indication of how uncertain Apple's prospects are is that expert estimates of how many Lisa's the company will sell are all over the lot—from 2,000 to 30,000." The article also questioned whether vendors would write software to support Lisa, and whether the price tag for Lisa was too high. Similarly the *Wall Street Journal* article in which Mr. Jobs predicted Lisa's great success was captioned: "Some Warm Up to Apple's 'Lisa,' but Eventual Success is Uncertain." The article discussed Lisa's incompatibility with IBM products, the difficulties in attracting software suppliers, and the high price tag.

The Lisa was a commercial failure and was discontinued shortly after its introduction. As a result of this disappointing news, Apple's stock price fell by almost 75%.

The plaintiffs, purchasers of Apple stock, brought a section 10(b) fraud-on-the-market suit against Apple and its officers and directors, alleging that they failed to disclose problems with the Lisa that would have contradicted their earlier, optimistic public statements.

ISSUE PRESENTED   Was there fraud on the market when a manufacturer made optimistic predictions about a new product, even though analysts and others following the company discounted the predictions and publicized the true state of affairs?

SUMMARY OF OPINION   The U.S. Court of Appeals held that in a fraud-on-the-market case a defendant's failure to disclose material information may be excused if that information has been made credibly available to the market by other sources. As the court explained, "individuals who hear [only good news or only bad news] may receive a distorted impression . . ., and thus may have an actionable claim. But the market, and any individual who relies only on the price established by the market, will not be misled."

The press portrayed the Lisa as a risky gamble. At least 20 articles explored the risks Apple was taking. Moreover, many of the optimistic statements challenged by the plaintiffs appeared in those same articles. In the words of the court, "The market could not have been made more aware of Lisa's risks." Therefore the defendants were not liable, as a matter of law, for failing to disclose those risks. Accordingly, the defendants' motion for summary judgment on the claims related to the Lisa was granted.

The court reached a different conclusion with respect to two optimistic statements Apple made concerning Twiggy, the new disk drive to accompany the Lisa computer. In a November 29, 1982, press release, Apple had claimed that Twiggy "represents three years of research and development and has undergone extensive testing and design verification during the past year." The release went on to state that Twiggy "ensures greater integrity of data than the other high density drives by way of a unique, double-sided mechanism designed and manufactured by Apple."

The court concluded that certain technical problems relating to Twiggy had not been revealed to the market. Neither the press nor anyone else disclosed: (1) that the internal tests conducted by Apple indicated that Twiggy was slow and unreliable; (2) that the Apple division responsible for the production of Lisa warned top executives that Twiggy's unreliability could delay the introduction of Lisa by several months; and (3) that Mr. Jobs expressed "virtually zero confidence" in the division that was responsible for the design and development of Twiggy. Accordingly, the court concluded that if Twiggy's technical problems were material facts tending to undermine the optimism of the two statements, the defendants could be liable for failing to reveal those facts. Materiality was thus left as a triable issue of fact, and the defendants' motion for summary judgment on the claims related to Twiggy was denied.

RESULT   The plaintiffs' claims relating to the Lisa computer were dismissed as a matter of law. The claims related to the Twiggy disk drive were not dismissed because they raised questions of fact for a jury to decide. In 1991, after two former executives were found guilty of making "materially misleading statements," Apple agreed to set up a $16 million fund to settle the suit.

COMMENTS   The Ninth Circuit pointed out that a defendant is not relieved of its duty to disclose material information unless that information has been transmitted to the public with a degree of intensity and credibility sufficient to counterbalance any misleading impression created by the defendant. A brief mention of the omitted fact in a few poorly circulated or lightly regarded publications would be insufficient.

Integrated Disclosure   The SEC has adopted at least some of the premises of the efficient-market theory in its disclosure rules. In 1982 the SEC adopted the *integrated disclosure system.* As explained in chapter 22, there are two separate disclosure systems: one under the 1933 Act and one under the 1934 Act. The integrated disclosure system seeks to eliminate duplicative or unnecessary disclosure requirements under the two acts.

Issuers that have been filing periodic reports under the 1934 Act can incorporate certain information from those reports into a registration statement filed under the 1933 Act. The market is deemed to have already absorbed such information in its evaluation of the issuer, so that information can be omitted from the prospectus.

Causation

A plaintiff must prove that the defendant's misstatement or omission caused him to suffer losses. Increasingly this is an economic question—what factors influence the price of a stock in the securities market?

 Ethical Consideration

Managers of companies frequently act as promoters, describing the company's products to the press and the public in an aggressive, upbeat manner. It is reasonable to expect them to engage in a certain amount of puffing and exaggeration. Are these exaggerations ethically justifiable if they do not violate the securities laws?

For example, in a securities case involving Nucorp Energy, investors claimed that a misrepresentation by the company of the value of its oil reserves caused them to suffer losses. The claim was based on the contention that the stock price was maintained at an artificially high level as a result of the misrepresentation. The investors attributed the later drop in the stock price to the revelation of the true facts. At trial, the defendants presented the testimony of an economist that the drop in the price of the stock was not attributable to any misrepresentation of the value of the oil reserves, but rather was caused by a drop in the price of oil. The jury found that the plaintiffs had failed to prove their claim.

As a result of these developments in the area of causation, proponents of the efficient-market theory may be right when they predict that in the future the entire rule 10b-5 case may boil down to one question: Did the misleading statement artificially affect market price?

Fraud-Created-the-Market Theory

In some cases in which the alleged fraud is so pervasive that without it the issuer would not have been able to sell the securities because the information to the market would have shown them to be worthless, the court will dispense with the reliance requirement, and apply a variation of the fraud-on-the-market theory, called the *fraud-created-the-market theory*. Under this theory, the causal connection between the defendant's fraud and the plaintiff's injury is not established by alleging and proving that the fraud affected the market price. Rather, the causal connection is established by alleging and proving that the securities could not have been marketed at any price absent fraud.

The courts are split on when plaintiffs can rely on the fraud-created-the-market-theory. The Seventh Circuit, for example, has rejected the fraud-created-the-market theory[12] on the grounds that the existence of a security does not depend on the adequacy of disclosure. It reasoned that many securities are on the market even though the issuer or a third party has made inaccurate or incomplete disclosures. Therefore, full disclosure of adverse information may lower the price of a security, but it will not exclude the security from being sold on the market.

■ Damages for Violation of Rule 10b-5

The measure of damages in a rule 10b-5 case is typically the out-of-pocket loss, that is, the difference between what the investor paid (or received) and the fair value of the stock on the date of the transaction. Alternately, an investor can elect to rescind the transaction, returning what she received and getting back what she gave. In the

court's discretion, *prejudgment interest*—that is, interest on the amount of the award between the date the securities were purchased and the date of the judgment—may also be awarded. Punitive damages are not available.

In theory, damages must be proven with reasonable certainty. In practice, however, damages are awarded on the basis of expert testimony, which can be highly conjectural. For example, a claim that a company's failure to reveal negative information about its new product artificially inflated the price of its stock is quite difficult to evaluate with any scientific certainty, because even the experts do not agree to what extent any particular piece of information affects the price of a company's securities.

In addition, there can be only estimates for the number of traders who can claim damage. For example, in-and-out traders' trades are included in the total volume of trading, but such traders who buy, then quickly sell, suffer no damage if they sell the securities before the price drop.

Evidence of damages is therefore often presented on the basis of a comparison with industry or market performance, on the assumption that the industry or the market was not subject to the same artificial inflation. This clearly remains a fertile field for argument and future litigation.

■ What Insider Trading Is

Not every instance of trading on inside information constitutes a securities violation. Rather, the term *insider trading* refers to activities that the courts have held to be proscribed by the broad language of rule 10b-5. Because there is no statutory definition of insider trading, the law in this area has developed on a piecemeal basis. This lack of a clear definition has caused enforcement problems for the SEC and federal prosecutors.

In the highly publicized insider-trading cases of the mid-1980s, many defendants attempted to exploit the vagaries of the law, and prosecutors found it difficult to prove the elements of a violation. In the wake of these prosecutions, a general demand arose that Congress codify a precise definition of insider trading.

Various definitions were proposed. The SEC initially sought to define insider trading to include "wrongful trading while in possession of material nonpublic information that was wrongfully obtained or the use of which would be wrongful." It was subsequently suggested that this definition be amended to make the use of inside information unlawful if the person trading knew that the information was wrongfully obtained. However, oppo-

---

12. *Eckstein v. Balcor Film Investors*, 8 F.3d 1121 (7th Cir. 1993), *cert. denied*, 114 S.Ct. 883 (1994).

Economic Perspective
Plaintiffs Consistently Settle for 25% of What They Ask For

Although trial is our paradigm of how civil litigation resolves disputes, in reality only a tiny fraction of litigated cases—perhaps 5% or less—are actually tried to judgment.[13] Most cases are resolved through settlement. Indeed, federal policy (and probably that of most states) favors settlement over trial, to such an extent that it is a "familiar axiom that a bad settlement is almost always better than a good trial."[14]

There is a remarkable dichotomy in our thinking about settlement and trial, however. Trials explicitly aim at substantive accuracy of result. Outcomes are supposed to reflect correct results when the substantive law is applied to the events that actually occurred. The trial is framed as a decision on the merits of the plaintiff's case, and all the actors in the trial—parties, lawyers, judge, jury, and witnesses—operate under rules that are designed to ensure that the end decision is accurate. Although no one argues that trial is a perfect method of achieving accuracy, the

public perception that trials are a "good enough" method, on the average and over time, for disposing of cases accurately on the merits is important for the continued acceptance of litigation as the baseline method of dispute resolution.

When we think about trials we worry about substantive accuracy. We ask whether juries can comprehend complex cases, whether they can be sufficiently unbiased in certain kinds of cases, whether certain types of evidence should be admitted, whether the costs of litigation unduly restrict access to the process, whether discovery should be less adversarial so as to provide more equal access to relevant information.

By contrast, when we talk about settlement, we are not greatly concerned about whether the outcomes are substantively accurate. So long as there is no coercion or hoodwinking, the parties are generally permitted to reach any outcome on which they can agree, without regard to what resolution a judicial decision on the merits might produce.

There are two principal reasons why we do not worry much about the accuracy of settlements. In the first place, trials produce coerced outcomes in the form of a court judgment. Settlements, by contrast, are voluntary resolutions by parties who retain the option of going to trial if they cannot reach agreement. Coerced dispositions must be perceived as substantively accurate for the legal system to retain its credibility and public acceptance. Negotiated outcomes are by definition acceptable to the parties involved.

They are legitimized by the consent of the parties.

Moreover, the available theoretical models of settlement behavior predict that settlement outcomes will approximate trial outcomes. This conclusion is supported by our intuitive feeling that settlements generally reflect the merits, at least in a rough sense. We believe that strong cases are worth more in settlement than weak ones because a plaintiff can hold out on a better offer on the threat of going to trial. If this is true, settlements will be roughly as accurate as trials, and there is no reason to make a special inquiry into their accuracy.

"25 Cents on the Dollar"

Contrary to these accepted assumptions, a significant and identifiable class of settlements is in reality neither voluntary nor accurate. These settlements are not voluntary in that trial is not regarded by parties as a practically available alternative of resolving disputes, and they are not accurate in that the strength of the case on the merits has little or nothing to do with determining the amount of the settlement. To demonstrate the existence of such a class of settlements, Professor Janet Cooper Alexander of the Stanford Law School studied a group of securities class actions alleging fraud in the initial public offerings of computer-related companies in the first six

---

13. This "Economic Perspective" is based on Janet Cooper Alexander's "Do the Merits Matter? A Study of Settlements in Securities Class Actions," 43 *Stanford Law Review* 497 (February 1991). Copyright © 1991 by *Stanford Law Review. Used by permission.* The author is a professor of law at Stanford Law School who examined a group of securities class actions alleging similar claims of fraud in the initial public offerings of computer-related companies.

14. *In re Warner Communications Securities Litigation*, 618 F. Supp. 735, 740 (S.D.N.Y. 1985), *aff'd*, 798 F.2d 35 (2d Cir. 1986).

*Economic Perspective
continued on following page*

Economic Perspective
Plaintiff's Consistently Settle, Continued

months of 1983. These cases presented an unusual opportunity to study a number of contemporaneous cases involving virtually identical claims about very similar companies. According to the general assumption, outcomes should reflect the parties' estimates of differences in the merits. Instead, the cases settled at an apparent "going rate" of approximately one quarter of the potential damages. In other words, a strong case in this group appears to have been worth no more than a weak one. The remarkable similarity of the companies and the claims reduced possible non-merits-related causes of variance in the cases' outcomes. Moreover, because suits were filed against every company in the industry whose stock declined significantly in the months following its initial stock offering, it is likely that the cases included a range of strength on the merits. Nevertheless, the cases settled for approximately one quarter of the potential damages according to the allegations of the complaint. This was true even in one case in which the court had granted partial summary judgment reducing the

recoverable damages by 70%. The strength of the plaintiff's case on the merits was simply not a significant factor in determining the amount of the settlement in these cases.

Professor Alexander argues that a variety of factors decouples the settlement process from expected trial outcomes by denying the parties practical access to an adjudicated resolution. These factors include unusually risk averse defendants, astronomically high potential damages, an hours-based contingency compensation system for plaintiffs' lawyers, agency problems inherent in class actions, and insurance and indemnification rules that make substantial sums of money (not paid directly by the parties) available for negotiated settlements but not for judgments after trial. Because substantive and procedural rules make pretrial adjudication essentially unavailable, and because all participants face these unusually strong incentives to avoid the courtroom, trial becomes virtually unthinkable regardless of the merits of the case. For practical purposes, the merits do not matter.

A settlement process that does not take the merits into account poses a number of disturbing policy implications. Private enforcement of the securities laws through class action litigation is costly, both to the litigants and to the public. If cases are not resolved according to the merits, then we are not receiving the presumed benefits of this costly system of enforcement. A non-merits-based settlement regime also encourages the filing of more and weaker suits, while undercompensating actual victims of securities violations. Instead, we have what amounts to a grotesquely inefficient form of insurance against large stock market losses by giving investors, in effect, a legally mandated "partial put" that entitles them to recover a portion of such losses from issuers. The social value of such a system is questionable at best. Because these cases do not involve purely private disputes, but rather, private enforcement of important public regulatory policies, there is substantial public interest in the accuracy of outcomes.

---

nents feared that the legislative language would be too limiting, and that a statutory definition of insider trading would create loopholes, making enforcement even more difficult.

Unable to agree on a definition, Congress sidestepped the issue. It passed the Insider Trading Sanctions Act of 1984 without including a definition of insider trading. In 1988, Congress unanimously passed a comprehensive bill stiffening the penalties for insider trading, but again failed to include a definition of the offense itself.

If the legislators are unable to agree on a definition of insider trading, investors may well question how they should be expected to know whether their actions constitute prohibited insider trading. The safest course is never to trade while in possession of material inside information; however, such a premise is unduly restrictive. The nature of insider trading can best be understood by examining the purposes underlying the laws that prohibit it.

A fundamental goal of the securities laws in general is the protection of the investing public and the maintenance of fairness in the securities markets. Allowing a party who knows that the market is incorrectly pricing a security to exploit another party's ignorance of that fact is fundamentally unfair. However, the Supreme Court has held that not every trade while in possession of material nonpublic information violates section 10(b). For such a trade to be illegal there must be some breach of a duty by the person trading; or if the person trading is the recipient of a tip—a piece of inside information—there must be a breach of duty by the person who gave the tip. The person giving the tip is known as the *tipper*; the person receiving it is known as the *tippee*.

Corporate officers and directors, for example, have specific legal duties that prohibit them from engaging in insider trading. As corporate fiduciaries, these individuals are required to subordinate their self-interests to the interests of the shareholders, as discussed in chapter 21.

Insider-trading cases focus specifically on the duty to disclose, before trading, material information that is not publicly known (that is, not commonly available to the investing public). An insider must either disclose material nonpublic information in his possession or refrain from trading. The fundamental question in an insider-trading case is whether this obligation should be imposed on a particular trader. Besides officers and directors (who have a clear duty of disclosure), there are other traders who, though not having an independent fiduciary duty to shareholders, should nevertheless be prohibited from trading on inside information. The persons prohibited from such trading—insiders, tippees, and others—are the subject of the following sections.

■ Insiders

An *insider* is a person with access to confidential information and an obligation of disclosure to other traders in the marketplace. Insiders include not only "traditional" insiders—such as officers and directors—but also "temporary" insiders, such as outside counsel and financial consultants.

Traditional Insiders

Traditionally, only persons closely allied with the corporation itself were considered insiders. They are "true" insiders because they acquire information by performing duties within or on behalf of the issuer corporation. Persons or entities traditionally considered insiders include: (1) officers and directors, (2) controlling shareholders, (3) employees, and (4) the corporation itself.

Officers and Directors Officers and directors have a fiduciary obligation of loyalty and care to the corporate shareholders. They also have the greatest access to sensitive information regarding corporate events.

Controlling Shareholders Because of their majority stock ownership, controlling shareholders are generally in a position to control the activities of the corporation. They are therefore likely to be aware of impending corporate events.

Employees As agents or servants of a corporation, employees have a duty of loyalty. They may not personally profit from confidential information that they receive in the course of their employment.

The Corporation Often, a corporation (or other issuer) will engage in the purchase or sale of its own securities. Under these circumstances, the corporation and those acting on its behalf are insiders and must not trade while in possession of material nonpublic information. This was made clear by the Second Circuit in *Texas Gulf Sulphur* (case 23.3), in which a corporation with nonpublic information about its discovery of copper deposits was prohibited from purchasing its own shares on the open market until the true nature of the find was disclosed.

Temporary Insiders

Outside attorneys, accountants, consultants, or investment bankers who are not directly employed by the corporation, but who acquire confidential information through the performance of professional services, are also considered insiders. The Supreme Court extended liability under section 10(b) to such *temporary insiders* in footnote 14 to the *Dirks* case, which is discussed as case 23.6 in the next section.

■ Tippees

Tippees—that is, persons who receive information from a traditional or temporary insider—may also be subject to liability under rule 10b-5, but only if they can be considered derivative insiders. In most cases, a tippee has no independent duty to the shareholders of a corporation, with which she may have little or no connection; a tippee will not be held liable as a *derivative insider* unless the insider's duty of disclosure can somehow be imposed upon the tippee. This rule was established in the following landmark case.

■ **A Case in Point:**   **Summary**

Case 23.6
DIRKS v. SEC
Supreme Court of the
United States
463 U.S 646, 103 S.Ct. 3255
(1983).

FACTS   Raymond Dirks, an officer of a New York broker-dealer firm, specialized in providing investment analysis of insurance company securities to institutional investors. Dirks was contacted by Ronald Secrist, a former employee of Equity Funding of America. Secrist was seeking aid in exposing the fraudulent activities of that corporation. These fraudulent activities had resulted in an overvaluation of Equity Funding's assets. Dirks was thus the potential tippee, with Secrist the tipper. After corroborating Secrist's story, Dirks advised certain clients that they should sell their shares in the company. When the corporate fraud was later revealed, the price of the company's stock went down.

The SEC brought proceedings against Dirks on the theory that he had constructively breached a fiduciary duty. In effect, the SEC maintained that anyone receiving information from an insider stands in the insider's shoes and should be held to the same standards and be subject to the same duties as that insider.

ISSUE PRESENTED   Is a tippee liable absent a violation of fiduciary duty by the tipper?

SUMMARY OF OPINION   The U.S. Supreme Court rejected the argument that anyone receiving information from an insider should be held to the same standards as the insider, holding instead that a tippee is not liable unless he and the tipper join in a co-venture to exploit information. Only in such a case will the fiduciary duty of the tipper be derivatively imposed on the tippee. For the tippee to the liable, therefore, the tipper must have a duty to the corporation not to disclose the information, and must breach this duty by seeking to benefit personally from the disclosure of the information. The benefit sought by the tipper can be either tangible or intangible. Intangible benefits might include an enhanced reputation or the intangible benefit received through the giving of gifts.

In this case, the insider was motivated solely by a desire to expose fraudulent conduct. He did not breach any fiduciary duties because it was in the interests of the corporation that this information be disclosed.

RESULT   Absent a breach of duty on the part of the insider/tipper, no derivative duty could be imposed on Dirks, the tippee. Dirks was not guilty of illegal insider trading.

The requirement that the tipper must be seeking some benefit implies that he must desire that the tippee trade on the information; but it is unclear whether such a showing is necessary. For example, the tipper could derive a benefit merely from impressing the tippee with her access to confidential information. Such a desire could stem from social or career aspirations of the tipper, and could have nothing to do with the stock trading ramifications of the information.

Breach of Fiduciary Duty

In addition to the desire to benefit himself, the tipper must also be acting in breach of a fiduciary duty to the corporation (or to another under the misappropriation theory, discussed later in this chapter) by disclosing the information to the tippee. The information must be non-public at the time it is divulged, and it must be in the interests of the corporation (or the other party in a misappropriation case) to keep the information confidential.

The tippee is liable only if she knew or should have known that the tipper's disclosure of the confidential information constituted a fiduciary breach. If the tippee has reason to know that the insider's disclosure was wrong or against the interest of the corporation, her actual knowledge will be irrelevant.

Remote Tippees

Remote tippees—that is, the tippees of tippees—may be found to have violated section 10(b) and rule 10b-5 even if they are completely unacquainted with and removed from the original insider tipper. However, remote tippees are not liable unless they knew or should have known that the first-tier tipper was breaching a fiduciary duty in passing on the nonpublic information.[15] The phrase "should have known" is key to this formulation. It means that a tippee cannot insulate himself from liability merely by failing to inquire as to the source of the information. If the tippee has reason to suspect that the information was wrongfully acquired, such conscious avoidance of knowledge will not prevent a finding of scienter.

In Brief: Types of Insiders

Traditional Insiders:
- Officers
- Directors
- Controlling shareholders
- Employees
- The corporation (or other issuer)

Temporary Insiders:
- Outside attorneys
- Accountants
- Consultants
- Investment bankers

◼ Other Traders

From time to time, the SEC has unsuccessfully attempted to impose liability on anyone who trades while in possession of material nonpublic information. In *Chiarella v. United States*,[16] the Supreme Court rejected the argument that every trade based on nonpublic material information should be held to violate the securities laws.

---

15. *SEC v. Musella*, 678 F.Supp. 1060 (S.D.N.Y. 1988).
16. 445 U.S. 222, 100 S.Ct. 1108 (1980).

In *Chiarella*, documents relating to a takeover bid containing the coded names of a potential target and takeover company were sent by the takeover company to a financial printer for printing. Chiarella, an employee of the printer hired to reproduce the documents, deciphered the names of these companies and then traded on this information. Chiarella was convicted of insider trading.

The Supreme Court reversed Chiarella's conviction. The Court held that rule 10b-5 does not impose liability in nondisclosure cases unless it can be established that the person involved has an independent duty to disclose. This duty arises only from a relationship of trust and confidence, not from the mere possession of material nonpublic information.

This case might have been decided differently if the jury had been instructed to find liability on the misappropriation theory, discussed below. Under this theory, there is a basis for liability if the trader violated any duty she had to a third party, even if she had no duty to the corporation in whose stock she traded. In *Chiarella,* the argument would be that the defendant violated his duty to his employer, the printing company. The encoding of company names should have been sufficient to put Chiarella on notice that the information was confidential, and his use of the information arguably harmed the printing company's reputation. The SEC did in fact attempt to argue the misappropriation theory against Chiarella, but the Supreme Court, while indicating that the theory might have validity, refused to consider it in this case because it had not been raised at trial.

⬒ *Ethical Consideration*

Even if a defendant such as Chiarella could escape liability, there is an ethical question as to whether he should trade on such information. One's position with respect to the rationale behind the insider-trading laws will influence how one answers that question.

Misappropriation Theory

Under the *misappropriation theory,* there is a rule 10b-5 violation if a person breaches a fiduciary duty to the owner of nonpublic information by trading on that information after misappropriating it for his own use. No independent duty of disclosure is required. Liability is imposed because the trader converted the confidential information to his own use. Application of this theory is demonstrated by the following case.

A Case in Point: **Summary**

Case 23.7
UNITED STATES v. NEWMAN
United States Court of Appeals
for the Second Circuit
664 F.2d 12 (2d Cir. 1981).

FACTS   E. Jacques Courtois, Jr. and Franklin Courtois worked for various New York investment banking firms in the 1970s, including Morgan Stanley and Kuhn Loeb. These individuals misappropriated information entrusted to their employers regarding clients' imminent merger transactions, and tipped James Newman, a broker, who traded on the information. The SEC brought charges against the two investment bankers, alleging that they had breached the trust and confidence placed in them by their employers and indirectly by the employers' corporate clients and the clients' shareholders. The defendants were indicted for violations of section 10(b) and rule 10b-5.

ISSUE PRESENTED   Does an employee violate rule 10b-5 when he misappropriates, for trading purposes, confidential information belonging to his employer?

SUMMARY OF OPINION   Focusing on the bankers' duties to their employer, the U.S. Court of Appeals constructed a "fraud on the source" theory of misappropriation liability. Rejecting the notion that a party could not be criminally liable under rule 10b-5 unless he defrauded a purchaser or seller, the court upheld the defendants' indictments on the ground that they had deceitfully misappropriated confidential information in violation of a fiduciary duty to their employer.

RESULT   Defendants violated rule 10b-5 when they misappropriated, for trading purposes, confidential information belonging to their employer.

Liability under the misappropriation theory requires that the defendant's trading threaten some injury to the defrauded party or the source of information. Actual injury need not be demonstrated. The threatened injury need not be pecuniary; it may be reputational or intangible.

The trader must know that the information utilized was meant to be confidential and that it was not intended to be used for anyone's personal benefit.

The misappropriation theory widens the class of persons who can be found liable for insider trading, but the requirement that there be a fiduciary duty remains a limiting factor. For instance, one who merely overhears a conversation relating to confidential information has no fiduciary duty and therefore no liability. Similarly, one who infers from the movements of corporate executives that an event will likely take place owes no duty to the corporation or its employees. In *U.S. v. Chestman*,[17] the

U.S. Court of Appeals for the Second Circuit held that the nephew-in-law of a controlling shareholder and family patriarch did not violate rule 10b-5 when he passed on inside information to his broker, who traded on the information. The nephew-in-law was not in the inner circle of the family. Although he was married to the sister of one of the patriarch's daughters, the fact of marriage, taken alone, did not create a fiduciary relationship. Although spouses may by their conduct become fiduciaries, the marriage relationship alone does not impose fiduciary status. The court identified certain relationships that are inherently fiduciary: attorney and client, executor and heir, guardian and ward, principal and agent, trustee and trust beneficiary, and senior corporate official and shareholder.

In *Carpenter v. United States*,[18] the Supreme Court justices split 4–4 on whether misappropriation of confi-

---

17. 947 F.2d 551 (2d Cir. 1991), *cert. denied*, 112 S.Ct. 1759 (1992).

18. 484 U.S 19, 108 S.Ct. 816 (1987).

dential corporate information violated section 10(b) when the defendant arguably had no fiduciary duty to the persons with whom he traded. R. Foster Winans, author of *The Wall Street Journal* column entitled "Heard on the Street," was alleged to have misappropriated the content of soon-to-be-published columns, and tipped the information to Peter Brant and Kenneth Felis, two Kidder Peabody brokers, who used the information to make trades based on the anticipated market response to the column's publication. It was known that publication was often followed by active trading of the stock of the companies mentioned in the column.

Winans and his roommate Carpenter were convicted of violating section 10(b) and the federal Wire and Mail Fraud Acts. They appealed. The Supreme Court split 4–4 on the securities-fraud issue, resulting in affirmation, without opinion, of the convictions for securities fraud. Winans argued that he could not be held liable under rule 10b-5 because the only duty he had was to *The Wall Street Journal,* which had no interest in the securities traded. Winans asserted that he had no duty to the victims of the alleged fraud—the persons who traded in the stocks without access to the information Winans was feeding to Brant and Felis. Because the Court split on this question, it did not address the issue of whether Winans's duty to *The Wall Street Journal* was enough to hold him liable for fraud against the persons who actually traded in the stock.

The Supreme Court did, however, address the issues raised under the Wire and Mail Fraud Acts. In a unanimous opinion, the Supreme Court upheld the convictions and expanded the ability to prosecute insider trading under those statutes. The Court held that if confidential information is generated by a business, and if the business has the right to control the use of such information prior to public disclosure, then use of that information to trade can be prohibited under the wire and mail fraud statutes.

The split in the decision of the Supreme Court in *Carpenter v. United States* on the viability of the misappropriation theory has forced the lower courts to decide whether trading on the basis of misappropriated information is a legally sufficient basis for finding a section 10(b) violation. The theory has been accepted in the Second, Third, Seventh, and Ninth Circuits. For example, in *SEC v. Clark*,[19] an executive of an acquiring company who purchased stock in an acquisition target in his wife's maiden name was found liable under section 10(b) under the misappropriation theory.

---

19. 915 F.2d 439 (9th Cir. 1990).

■ RICO

A Wire and Mail Fraud Acts conviction for misappropriation of an employer's confidential information, as happened in the *Carpenter* case, could also, assuming other requirements are met, be the basis for a conviction under the Racketeer Influenced and Corrupt Organizations Act (RICO) (discussed in chapter 15). RICO contains civil enforcement mechanisms that explicitly grant a private right of action with treble damages. It has been used in numerous civil suits against legitimate businesses, as well as organized-crime syndicates in cases involving mail and wire fraud, and fraud in the sale of securities.

■ Enforcement of Insider-Trading Prohibitions

Persons who violate the insider-trading provisions of the federal securities laws are subject to civil enforcement actions by the SEC, private suits for damages, and criminal prosecution. In both government and private actions, the complaining party must demonstrate these five elements: (1) a misstatement or omission of a material fact, (2) scienter, (3) reliance by the injured party, (4) causation, and (5) loss.

Private Actions

In private actions, the plaintiff must have standing to sue; that is, the plaintiff must be an actual purchaser or seller of securities, and her loss must have been proximately caused by the acts of the defendant. A private plaintiff may recover only her actual out-of-pocket damages.

Civil Enforcement

In an SEC civil enforcement action, the defendant may be liable for treble damages and disgorgement of profits, and may be subject to an injunction prohibiting future trading.

Criminal Prosecutions

The SEC itself has no criminal enforcement power. Criminal prosecutions are brought by the Department of Justice through the U.S. Attorney's Office, often upon referral from the SEC. If criminally convicted, a defendant faces a fine of up to $1 million and/or imprisonment for up to ten years for willful violations. Willfulness has been interpreted as awareness by the defendant that he was committing a wrongful act; he need not specifically know that he was violating a statute.

>
>
> *Willfulness has been interpreted as awareness by the defendant that he was committing a wrongful act; he need not specifically know that he was violating a statute.*

International Consideration

The EC Insider Trading Directive requires each member state to enact its own penalties. Many nations with less active trading markets impose civil rather than criminal sanctions. However, since 1993, Britain, France, and Germany have all instituted criminal sanctions against persons engaging in insider trading.

■ The Securities Fraud Enforcement Act

Immediately following the massive insider trading charges against Michael Milken and Drexel Burnham Lambert in the late 1980s (discussed more fully in this chapter's "Inside Story"), Congress passed and President Reagan signed the Insider Trading and Securities Fraud Enforcement Act of 1988. The act raised the maximum penalty for insider trading from five to ten years in prison and increased the likelihood that persons found guilty would actually be incarcerated for some period of time. (Previously, the average sentence for insider trading was under one year, and community service was often ordered in lieu of prison.) In addition, the maximum fine was raised from $100,000 to $1 million.

The legislation also provided strong encouragement to the brokerage industry to police itself. A brokerage house can be fined if it "knew or recklessly disregarded" information that would indicate insider-trading activities on the part of its employees. Intended to force firms to police their employees, to institute compliance systems, and to monitor suspicious activities, the act specifically requires registered brokers and dealers to maintain and enforce reasonably designed written policies and proce-

dures to prevent the misuse of material nonpublic information. The maximum criminal penalty that could be imposed on brokerage firms was raised from $500,000 to $2.5 million.

Although this legislation does not explicitly require it, many commentators have suggested that it is prudent for other companies not in the brokerage business to implement such policies and procedures in light of their potential liability.

Ethical Consideration

A number of brokerage houses have investigated whether any of their employees were involved in insider trading. Most of these firms turned over their trading records to the New York Stock Exchange for computer analysis. Persons suspected of illicit activities could be subject to SEC enforcement actions and criminal prosecutions. Such investigations send a stern message to employees, and encourage ethical behavior and compliance with the insider-trading laws. They also improve the public's perception of the brokerage industry. Managers of such companies must decide how stringently these procedures will be followed.

Bounty Payments

The act provides for bounty payments to individuals whose tips result in insider-trading prosecutions, in a manner similar to that utilized by the Internal Revenue Service in tax cases. These bounties could be as high as 10% of any revenues recovered from a defendant through penalties or settlement. Violators and their firms could also be liable for civil penalties of triple the profit gained or loss avoided as a result of the wrongful trading.

Private Right of Action

The act provides a private right of action for contemporaneous traders, that is, persons who purchased or sold securities of the same class at the same time the insider was trading. The total amount of damages that may be recovered is limited to the amount of the profit gained or loss avoided in the unlawful transaction. Any amounts disgorged pursuant to court order or at the instance of the SEC will offset the amount of recoverable damages by contemporaneous traders. Of significance to potential tippers and tippees is the provision that makes tippers and all direct and remote tippees jointly and severally liable. That means that any individual in the chain can be found liable for all of the profits gained or losses avoided in every transaction within the chain of information.

■ Short-Swing Trading

Section 16(b) of the 1934 Act governs *short-swing trading*—the purchase and sale, or the sale and purchase, by officers, directors, and greater-than-10% shareholders of equity securities of a public company within a six-month period. Unlike section 10(b), which requires scienter (that is, a showing of bad intent), liability is imposed under section 16(b) regardless of the insider's state of mind.

Although the purpose of section 16(b) is to prevent insiders of publicly held companies from exploiting information not generally available to the public in order to secure quick profits, it need not be proven that the insider actually possessed any material nonpublic information at the time he traded in the securities. To establish liability under section 16(b) it is sufficient to prove that an insider purchased and then sold, or sold and then purchased, equity securities within a period of six months.

Section 16(a) of the 1934 Act imposes certain reporting obligations on officers and directors and shareholders owning more than 10% of a public company's equity securities, and section 16(c) prohibits such persons from *selling securities short,* that is, from selling securities they do not yet own.

Definitions

Section 16(b) of the 1934 Act provides that each officer, director, and greater-than-10% shareholder of an issuer that has registered any class of its equity securities under the 1934 Act must surrender to the issuer "any profit realized by him from any purchase and sale, or any sale and purchase, of any equity security of such issuer (other than an exempted security) within any period of less than six months."

Equity Security An *equity security* includes: (1) any stock or similar security; (2) any security that is convertible, with or without consideration, into such a security; (3) any security carrying any warrant or right to subscribe to or purchase such a security; (4) any such warrant or right; and (5) any other security that the SEC deems to be of a similar nature and that, for the protection of investors or in the public interest, the SEC considers appropriate to treat as an equity security. Thus, "equity securities" may include hybrids that are not ordinarily considered equity securities, such as convertible debt securities that have not been registered under the 1934 Act.

Special problems can arise in connection with the grant and exercise of stock options and other derivative securities. A set of complicated rules embodied largely in rule 16b-3 (adopted by the SEC under section 16(b) of the 1934 Act) governs this area. Before becoming an officer or director, a person should consult counsel to avoid inadvertent section 16(b) liability.

Matching The shares that are sold need not be the same shares that were purchased. Any purchase and any sale will incur liability if they occur less than six months apart, regardless of whether the transactions involve the same shares. For example, if on January 1 an officer of XYZ Corporation sold 100 shares of XYZ Corporation common stock which he had held for 10 years, then on February 1 purchased 200 shares of XYZ Corporation common stock at a lower price, he would be liable for the short-swing profits on 100 of the shares. The January 1 sale would be matched with the February 1 purchase, even though the officer had held the securities for ten years before he sold them.

Profit Calculation To calculate the profits recoverable under section 16(b), the sale price is compared with the purchase price. If several purchases and sales occur within a six-month period, the lowest purchase price will be matched with the highest sale price; then the next lowest purchase price with the next highest sale price; and so on, regardless of the order in which the purchases and sales actually occurred. By matching purchases and sales in this manner, the recoverable profit is maximized.

Short-swing profits cannot be offset by trading losses that were incurred in the same period. Thus, there may be recoverable "profits" under section 16(b) even though the officer or director suffered a net loss on the trading transactions.

> *There may be recoverable "profits" under section 16(b) even though the officer or director suffered a net loss on the trading transactions.*

The following example illustrates the "lowest-in, highest-out" matching principle just described. Assume that an officer made purchases and sales, each of 100 shares as follows:

Date	Transaction	Price
Jan. 1	Purchase	$ 9
Jan. 30	Sale	10
Feb. 15	Sale	15
Feb. 28	Purchase	12
March 15	Purchase	6
March 30	Sale	4

These transactions would result in a recoverable short-swing profit of $1,000, calculated as follows. The February 15 sale is matched with the March 15 purchase, for a profit of $15 – $6 = $9 per share, or $900. Then the January 30 sale is matched with the January 1 purchase, for a profit of $10 – $9 = $1 per share, or $100. Even though the March 15 purchase at $6 per share and the subsequent sale at $4 per share resulted in a loss of $2 per share, or $200, that loss will not be taken into account.

The officer would have to surrender $900 + $100 = $1,000, even though he in fact realized only $200 of net profit in his trading transactions (total sales of $2,900 less purchases of $2,700).

Six Months   To result in recoverable short-swing profits, the purchase and sale, or sale and purchase, must have occurred "within any period of less than six months." That period commences on the day on which the first purchase or sale occurred and ends at midnight two days before the corresponding date in the sixth succeeding month. For example, for a transaction on January 1, the six-month period ends at midnight on June 29, two days before July 1.

Officer or Director   An officer or director is subject to liability under section 16(b) even though a purchase or sale may have been made prior to, or subsequent to, the time when the person served as an officer or director. A person may be liable under section 16(b) if she was an officer or director at the time of either the purchase or the sale; it is not necessary that both transactions occur during her tenure.

For example, if an officer purchased 100 shares of XYZ Corporation common stock at $10 per share on January 1, resigned as an officer on February 1, then sold 100 shares of XYZ Corporation common stock at $20 per share on March 1, she would be liable for $1,000 of short-swing profits, because she was an officer when she made the January 1 purchase. Similarly, if a person purchased 100 shares of XYZ Corporation at $10 per share on January 1, then became an officer of XYZ Corporation on February 1, and sold the shares at $20 on March 1, that person would be liable for $1,000 of short-swing profits, because he was an officer at the time of sale. On the other hand, if an officer who had not traded for more than six months before March 1 resigned on March 1, then bought 100 shares of XYZ Corporation at $10 on April 1 and sold them at $20 on April 2, she would not have recoverable profits, because she was not an officer or director at the time of either the purchase or the sale.

Greater-than-10% Shareholder   The rule is different for persons who are not officers or directors but are owners of more than 10% of the issuer's equity securities. Such persons are liable under section 16(b) only if they hold more than 10% of the securities both at the time of the purchase and at the time of the sale. The transaction whereby the person becomes a 10% shareholder does not count.

For example, if a person purchased 10.5% of XYZ Corporation's common stock at $10 on January 1, then sold those shares at $20 on March 1, that person would have no recoverable short-swing profits. However, if the same person had purchased another 2% of XYZ common stock in February, then the February purchase could be matched against the March sale, because the shareholder owned more than 10% of the stock at the time of the February purchase and also at the time of the March sale.

Beneficial Ownership of Shares   Officers, directors, and greater-than-10% shareholders can be liable for purchases and sales of shares they do not own of record, but are deemed to beneficially own. Under section 16(b), a person will be considered the *beneficial owner* of any securities held by his immediate family—his spouse, any minor children, or any other relative living in his household. There is a rebuttable presumption that a person is the beneficial owner of any securities over which she has the practical power to vest title in herself, or from which she receives economic benefits (such as sales proceeds) substantially equal to those of ownership.

Purchases and sales of securities held beneficially by an officer, director, or greater-than-10% shareholder will be attributed to him in determining his liability for short-swing trading. For example, the purchase of securities by an officer's wife could be matched under section 16(b) with the sale of other securities by the officer himself within six months of his wife's purchase, thereby resulting in liability for short-swing profits. Thus, any officer, director, or greater-than-10% shareholder planning a purchase or sale must consider not only his own trading record but also the record of those persons whose securities he is deemed to beneficially own.

Unorthodox Transactions

If a purchase or sale by an officer, director, or greater-than-10% shareholder that would otherwise result in recoverable short-swing profits was involuntary and did not involve the payment of cash, and if there was no possibility of speculative abuse of inside information, then a court may hold that there was an *unorthodox transaction* to which no liability will attach. These situations generally arise in the context of exchanges in mergers and other corporate reorganizations, stock conversions, stock reclassifications, and tender offers in which securities are sold or exchanged for consideration other than cash. On the other hand, in a tender offer or acquisition, an exchange of securities for cash by an officer, director, or greater-than-10% shareholder would almost certainly be deemed a sale for which the person receiving the cash could be liable under section 16(b).

Beneficial-Ownership Reports

Section 16(a) of the 1934 Act requires that officers, directors, and greater-than-10% shareholders of companies that have registered any class of equity securities under the 1934 Act file beneficial-ownership reports with the SEC and with any national securities exchange on which their company's equity securities are listed. Within ten days of becoming an officer or director, a person must file an initial ownership report on form 3, even if she does not beneficially own any securities of the company at that time. In the case of greater-than-10% shareholders, a form 3 must be filed within ten days of the date they acquire their greater-than-10% interest. (In addition, as noted in chapter 22, any person who acquires more than 5% of the voting securities of a public company must file a schedule 13D within ten days of the date he acquires that interest. An amendment to the schedule 13D must be filed promptly after any material change in beneficial ownership or investment purpose.)

Subsequently, an officer, director, or greater-than-10% shareholder must file a form 4 within ten days after the end of each month in which any change in beneficial ownership occurs. In her initial form 4, an officer or director must report all purchases or sales that occurred within the previous six months, even if those transactions were effected before she became an officer or director. A form 5 showing changes in beneficial owner-

ship during the preceding year must be filed annually. However, if there were no changes in beneficial ownership during the year, an officer or director may instead present to the company a certificate stating that there were no reportable events. The company must keep this certificate on file.

A person who ceases to be an officer or director must continue to report any changes in beneficial ownership that occur within six months of the last reportable transaction while the person was an officer or director.

Acquisitions of shares through reinvestment of cash dividends under a qualifying dividend reinvestment plan do not require the filing of a form 4. However, participation in the plan and the ownership of shares under the plan must be disclosed in form 4 reports that are otherwise required to be filed.

The SEC has brought enforcement actions to force executives to file these ownership reports within the required time frame. The SEC also adopted rules that require a corporation to disclose in its proxy statement and in its annual report on form 10-K whether its officers and directors have complied with their section 16(a) reporting obligations.

Prohibition on Selling Short

Section 16(c) of the 1934 Act prohibits officers or directors from selling any of their company's equity securities short, that is, from selling a security that the seller does not own. If the officer or director owns the security he is selling, he must deliver it within twenty days after the sale, or deposit it in the mails or other usual channels of delivery within five days. If he fails to do this, he will be liable under section 16(c) unless: (1) he acted in good faith and was unable to make the delivery or deposit within the specified time, or (2) he acted in good faith and satisfying the time requirements would have caused undue inconvenience or expense.

The Responsible Manager

Preventing Securities Fraud and Insider Trading

Any person involved in a public offering of securities has a legal and ethical duty to ensure that the prospectus contains no misleading statements or omissions. Experts, such as accountants, have a particularly heavy responsibility. The underwriters and outside directors cannot rely passively on the representations of management. Violations of these rules give rise to both civil and criminal liability.

Managers have an obligation not to mislead investors in company public announcements, periodic reports, or speeches. Although a company can remain silent about material developments if neither the company nor insiders are trading, early disclosure is often the better course. This gives all investors equal access to current information about the company. There is a trade-off here, however. Sometimes the company's business or transactions may be in a state of flux. For example, the company might have received an offer to buy the company's assets from an unreliable party who may not have any visible source of financing. It may be worse to get the market's hopes up by disclosing the offer than to wait to see whether in fact the offer is real. Managers, together with their lawyers, must make these judgment calls.

Another reason for early disclosure is to avoid illegal insider trading. A company must make disclosure if it knows its insiders, such as officers or directors, are trading in the company's securities while they are in possession of material nonpublic information.

Each company that takes advantage of the capital markets has a legal and ethical duty to ensure the integrity of those markets. Securities fraud, in any form, erodes investor confidence and makes it more difficult and expensive for honest businesses to raise capital.

Trading by a manager while in possession of material nonpublic information is illegal. It violates the manager's fiduciary duty to subordinate her personal interests to the interests of the corporation and shareholders she serves. A manager is given access to nonpublic information not for her own personal gain but to better enable her to serve her principal—the corporation and its shareholders. Violation of those rules erodes shareholder confidence and erodes the confidence of investors generally in the capital markets. It is also unethical.

A manager cannot give tips to others in exchange for money or even just to enhance his reputation as "someone in the know." He should carefully guard the information given him in confidence by his employer or his client. He must also instill these values in his employees. Everyone, from the person who empties the trash or runs the copy machine to the person who occupies the largest office in the executive suite, must be told to follow these rules or risk dismissal. This edict should be made clear in the corporation's code of ethics and in its personnel manual. All corporations, and especially brokerage firms, without adequate procedures in place to prevent illegal insider trading face potential liability for their insiders' illegal trades.

A company cannot disclose material information only to certain favored analysts. This is unfair to the public investors and can result in liability for the company and for the manager who tips an analyst whose clients then trade based on the tip.

An officer or director of a public company who buys and sells securities within a six-month period has a legal and ethical responsibility to come forward and pay her profits over to the corporation. This is true even if the short-swing trade was inadvertent, as might happen if an officer sold securities, not realizing that her spouse had bought securities less than six months before. A corporation that discovers a short-swing trade must try to persuade the insider to voluntarily turn her profits over to the corporation. If she refuses to do so, the corporation has an obligation to bring suit to recover the profits from the short-swing trading. If a corporation fails to bring suit, any shareholder has the right to sue on behalf of the corporation.

Officers and directors of public companies must report their security holdings and their trades in a timely manner. Disregard of these filing requirements breeds contempt for the law and encourages illegal or unethical behavior by others in the organization.

Each manager has a role to play in preventing securities fraud and insider trading. As with preventing the other types of criminal behavior described in chapter 15, a manager leads by example. If the manager permits his company to engage in unlawful or unethical conduct, he exposes himself and his company to considerable risk of civil and criminal liability. He also is likely to encourage illegal behavior by his subordinates.

Inside Story

1980s Insider Trading Scandals

Inquiries into insider trading tend to focus on high-volume trading that occurs before major corporate announcements. Enforcement agencies generally watch organized trading rings and well-known public figures because of their high profiles. However, ordinary investors and isolated violations are also detected and prosecuted. Surveillance groups monitor daily trading and investigate any suspicious activity. One such group, the American Exchange Stock Watch Group, was instrumental in breaking the "Heard on the Street" case discussed earlier.

Dennis Levine and Ivan Boesky

Prosecutors and enforcement agencies also rely heavily on information gathered from informers and persons already under indictment. For example, the arrest and prosecution of Dennis Levine and Ivan Boesky in 1986 set off the most comprehensive investigation of securities trading practices in the history of federal regulation. Levine, a former managing director of Drexel Burnham Lambert, was initially charged with illegal trading in approximately 54 stocks. An investment banker, Ira B. Sokolow, then pleaded guilty to passing stolen information to Levine. As a result of cooperation by Levine, the SEC was able to bring insider-trading charges against one of Wall Street's richest and most active speculators, Ivan Boesky.

Boesky, the son of an immigrant restaurateur, made his career and fortune as a risk arbitrageur who concentrated on the purchase and sale of stock in target corporations that were the subject of tender offers. Generally the stock of a target corporation will be bought by the acquiring corporation at a premium; thus, people who invest prior to the announcement of the acquisition are in a position to make swift and substantial profits. The SEC alleged that Levine, who worked on mergers and acquisitions, would pass on information to Boesky, who was able to purchase shares in the target prior to public announcement of the impending takeover. It is further believed that Boesky offered Levine a 5% commission for any information leading to an initial stock purchase, and a 1% commission for information pertaining to stocks already owned by Boesky.

In 1985, Levine was alleged to have passed to Boesky information received from Sokolow regarding the merger of Nabisco and R. J. Reynolds. Use of this information resulted in approximately $4 million in profits to Boesky. In all, Boesky was alleged to have made approximately $50 million through these insider-trading activities. Both Levine and Boesky pleaded guilty to criminal charges, and Boesky settled the SEC's civil charges by agreeing to pay $100 million and to cooperate with the government in future prosecutions of others. Both men were sentenced to prison for their actions.

Drexel Burnham Lambert

Approximately two years later, with the cooperation of Ivan Boesky, the SEC brought dramatic charges against Drexel Burnham Lambert and four of its prominent employees, including the head of its junk-bond department, Michael Milken. According to the SEC, Drexel had entered into a secret agreement with Boesky to defraud its clients and drive up the price of target-company stocks. The complaint, filed in September 1988, alleged that Drexel utilized Boesky to engage in *stock parking*—the temporary sale of shares to another entity or individual, intended to hide the true ownership of the shares in order to avoid tax-reporting requirements or the net-margin requirements of the securities laws applicable to brokerage firms. Drexel, which assisted companies interested in acquisitions, was also accused of advising Boesky to purchase massive amounts of shares in certain companies in order to give the appearance of active trading in them and to drive up the takeover price.

In December 1988, Drexel agreed to plead guilty to six felony counts, pay a $680 million fine, and submit to SEC oversight, contingent upon its settlement of civil charges (which occurred in April 1989). As a part of both settlements, Drexel was required to terminate the employment of Michael Milken. (The Milken case is discussed in the "Inside Story" at the end of chapter 15.)

Inside Story continued on following page

Inside Story, continued

Other Boesky-Related Prosecutions

Another prosecution evolving out of the Boesky affair involved Martin A. Siegel, a former managing director of Drexel. Siegel was fingered by Boesky and pleaded guilty in February 1987 to stock parking and tax evasion to the tune of $9 million. In June 1990 he was sentenced to two months in prison; he had faced a possible maximum sentence of ten years. Reuters quoted U.S. District Judge Robert Ward as saying there were three mitigating factors that affected the sentencing decision: Siegel's "cooperation, contrition and candor in a difficult situation."[20]

20. Reuters, "Key Scandal Figure Gets Light Sentence," *San Francisco Chronicle,* June 16, 1990, B1.

Boyd L. Jeffries, founder of the Los Angeles securities firm of Jeffries and Company, was also implicated in the Boesky affair. After pleading guilty to two counts of securities fraud, Jeffries resigned as chairman of his company and agreed to refrain from participating in the securities business for five years.

Key Words and Phrases

aider and abettor **756**
beneficial owner **780**
bespeaks caution doctrine **765**
controlling-person liability **749**
derivative insider **773**
due diligence **750**
efficient-market theory **767**
equity security **779**
fraud-created-the-market theory **770**
fraud-on-the-market theory **767**

insider **773**
insider trading **770**
integrated disclosure system **769**
material fact **749**
misappropriation theory **775**
misstatement **760**
omission **760**
prejudgment interest **770**
prospectus **755**
remote tippees **775**

scienter **752**
selling securities short **779**
short-swing trading **779**
stock parking **783**
temporary insiders **773**
tip **762**
tippee **773**
tipper **773**
unorthodox transaction **781**

Questions and Case Problems

1. During a session with her psychiatrist, Dr. Robert Willis, Joan Weill mentioned in confidence the imminent merger of her husband's company with another. Willis, upon hearing of the merger, communicated the information to Martin Sloate, who traded in the company's securities for his own account and for his customers' accounts.

Did Willis or Sloate engage in illegal insider trading? Does the misappropriation theory apply to Willis? Does it apply to Sloate? Was the conduct of the parties ethical? [*SEC v. Willis,* 777 F. Supp. 1165 (S.D.N.Y. 1991)]

2. In January, Arbor Corporation, a paper company with annual sales of more than $2 billion, issued 4 million registered common shares at an average price of $50 per share. In preparing the registration statement, Charles Controller relied on a report by Acme Appraisers, which stated that the company's woodlands were worth $400 million. Ollie Olson, the company's newly elected outside director (and Controller's brother-in-law) questioned whether the woodland estimate might be too high. Controller reassured him that "if the numbers are good enough for our CPAs, they're good enough for me."

In February, the company discovered that the woodland appraisal was overstated by $150 million. Management and the directors are livid about the error. To add to Arbor's problems, a major competitor shocked the industry by announcing that it will double its paper production capacity. Arbor's stock price is now $20 per share.

Do the shareholders have a basis for a suit? Who can they sue? What problems or defenses will they likely encounter? Assuming that the suit is otherwise successful, how will damages be determined?

3. Duke Distribution, Inc. recently had a public offering of its shares. The company's attorneys, its CPAs, and the underwriter's attorneys worked diligently to meet a tight deadline that management had imposed. Unfortunately, in its haste to meet the deadline, Duke's team failed to include some important information in the registration statement. The registration statement failed to mention that while Duke's inventory-to-sales ratio was constant over the past few years, most competitors' ratios had declined significantly over the same period. It also failed to mention that the company leases warehouses from a partnership consisting of three of its directors. The leases require rent that is about 8% higher than the market rate for equivalent facilities. After the initial public offering, the company engaged in additional transactions with insiders.

Now the economy has softened and competition has increased. The price of Duke stock has fallen from $15 to $10.

Is there a cause of action? Against whom? What are the defenses?

4. Gallop, Inc. is a toy manufacturer specializing in games for boys and girls aged 8 to 12. Gallop had predicted first-quarter earnings of $.20 per share on March 30. On April 15, Gallop received a fax from its key distributor reporting a $10 million claim for personal injury of a nine-year-old child who was allegedly injured by a design defect in Gallop's most popular product line, the Spartan Warriors. Gallop's outside counsel was instructed to prepare a press release describing the claim. Before the press release was sent to the copy center at Gallop's executive office, the vice-president of marketing, one director, and the outside counsel sold all of their Gallop shares at the prevailing market price of $25¼ per share.

Collin Copier, who ran the photocopying machine at Gallop's executive office, saw the draft press release, called his broker, Barbara Broker; told her about the press release; and ordered her to sell the 500 shares of Gallop that Copier had acquired in Gallop's initial public offering. Broker then called her best client, Charleen Client, and suggested that she sell her 100,000 shares of Gallop stock, but did not tell her why. Client agreed, and Broker sold Copier's and Client's stock at $25¼ a share right before the market closed on April 17.

The press release was publicly announced and was reported on the Business Wire after the market closed on April 17. The next day Gallop's stock dropped to $20¾ per share.

A class action suit has been brought, and the SEC has commenced enforcement proceedings. Criminal prosecution is threatened by the U.S. Attorney's Office.

What are the bases on which each proceeding could be brought? Who is potentially liable? For how much?

5. Ann Boland, a freelance writer, called her mother to boast about a press release that she was writing for Empire Corporation. The assignment called for the strictest confidence because it involved the announcement of a takeover.

Later in the day, Ann's mother casually tells her son Tim, a business student, about his sister's press release. She does not mention the name of the takeover target, but she naively provides Tim with enough details that he is almost certain who it is.

Tim calls his rich buddy, Carl Consultant, and tells him the story. They decide to buy options on the target company's stock and to split any profits 50–50. In a week, the two have made a small fortune. Are there any rule 10b-5 violations? If so, who may be required to disgorge profits?

6. Santa Fe Industries, Inc. acquired control of 60% of the stock of Kirby Lumber Corporation, a Delaware corporation. Through additional purchases, Santa Fe increased its control of Kirby stock to 95%. Santa Fe then decided that it wanted to acquire 100% ownership of Kirby.

After obtaining an independent appraisal of Kirby's physical assets, Santa Fe submitted the appraisals, along with additional financial information, to Morgan Stanley to appraise the fair market value of Kirby's stock. Morgan Stanley appraised Kirby's physical assets at $320 million and valued its stock at $125 per share.

Based on Morgan Stanley's findings, Santa Fe decided to enter into a short-form merger with Kirby. In accordance with the short-form merger statute, the minority shareholders were notified the day after the merger became effective and advised of their right to obtain an appraisal in Delaware court if they were dissatisfied with the offer of $150 per share. They were also supplied copies of Morgan Stanley's appraisal concluding that the fair market value of the stock was $125 per share.

The minority shareholders of Kirby objected to the merger, but did not pursue their appraisal remedy. Instead, they filed suit in federal court seeking to enjoin the merger or recover what they viewed was the fair market value of their shares, $772 per share. Their complaint alleged that Santa Fe fraudulently obtained the appraisal report from Morgan Stanley and offered $25 above the appraisal in order to deceive the minority shareholders into believing that their offer was generous. It was further alleged that these acts violated rule 10b-5 because Santa Fe employed a "device, scheme or artifice to defraud."

Did Santa Fe, as a majority shareholder, breach a duty to deal fairly with the minority shareholders? Was Santa Fe's conduct "manipulative or deceptive"? Was it ethical? [*Santa Fe Industries, Inc. v. Green*, 430 U.S. 462, 97 S.Ct. 1292 (1977)]

7. Verifone manufactures and designs products used by retail merchants to automate a variety of transactions, such as authorizing credit card purchases. In 1990, Verifone filed a registration statement and prospectus describing the company's past growth trends in revenues and earnings, including a list of its well-known customers, markets for potential growth, and companies that were considering using its products. The prospectus also contained a section on the risks associated with its stock.

The plaintiffs contended that the discussion of the risks was merely boilerplate, and did not disclose with sufficient detail the risks faced by Verifone shareholders. The plaintiffs further alleged that the company's historic growth trends had ceased, and that the company was "facing a brick wall" in existing markets. Therefore, the plaintiffs alleged, the prospectus was materially misleading.

If the plaintiffs assert the fraud-on-the-market theory, what will they need to show in order to prevail? Will the plaintiffs also have a claim against the underwriters? [*In Re Verifone Securities Litigation*, 784 F. Supp. 1471 (N.D. Cal. 1992), *aff'd*, 11 F.3d 865 (9th Cir. 1993)]

8. Convergent Technologies Inc., a manufacturer of computer workstations, issued stock in a public offering. The prospectus included the following language:

■ The Company is undertaking substantial development, manufacturing and marketing risks;

■ There can be no assurance that the Company will successfully complete the development of its new products or that it will be successful in manufacturing the new products in high volume or marketing the products in the face of intense competition;

■ Lack of availability of components from sole or limited sources would have a temporary adverse effect on the Company by delaying shipments; and

■ While the Company believes that the technical risks in the development of the NGEN [the company's next product] are well controlled, the product cost objectives are very aggressive and there is no assurance that they can be achieved.

In addition, after the offering, Convergent continued to warn investors of the risks posed by the NGEN product line.

When Convergent's stock dropped precipitously after the public offering, plaintiff shareholders sued. Should the plaintiffs' claims be dismissed? On what theory? [*In re Convergent Technologies Securities Litigation*, 948 F.2d 507 (9th Cir. 1991)]

9. National Industries acquired 34% of TSC Industries' voting stock from TSC's founder and principal shareholder and his family. After the sale, the TSC founder resigned from the TSC's board of directors. Subsequently, five National nominees, including National's president and chief executive officer, were placed on TSC's board. Several months later, TSC's board, with the National nominees abstaining, approved a proposal to liquidate and sell all of TSC's assets to National. One month later, the two companies issued a joint proxy statement to their shareholders, recommending approval of the proposal. The proxy solicitation was successful, TSC was liquidated, and the exchange of shares was effected.

A TSC shareholder brought an action against the two companies claiming that their joint proxy statement was materially misleading. The basis of the claim was that the proxy statement omitted material facts relating to the degree of National's con-

trol over TSC. Were the omitted facts material? [*TSC Industries, Inc. v. Northway, Inc.*, 426 U.S. 438, 96 S.Ct. 2126 (1976)]

10. Medtech, Inc. is a Delaware corporation with its principal place of business outside Austin, Texas. The company develops, manufactures, and markets a computer and related software used by hospitals and doctors in conjunction with X-ray machines.

Medtech was founded in 1988 by Hans Joseph, an engineer who was previously the head of Research and Development at Hansen Medical, an American division of Hansen, N.V., a huge Dutch conglomerate with annual sales in excess of $20 billion a year. Hansen Medical is the largest marketer of medical imaging devices in the world. Unlike Medtech, which markets only the computer and related software, Hansen manufactures entire X-ray "suites," which include an X-ray table, a camera, and other related equipment, in addition to the computer and software. Medtech's computer is compatible with Hansen's X-ray suites, as well with as X-ray equipment manufactured by other companies, all of which are much larger than Medtech.

Medtech started on a shoestring. Joseph and two cofounders invested an aggregate of $300,000, which they hoped would be sufficient to allow Joseph to develop a prototype to use to attract venture capital. In order to save cash, Joseph convinced Maggie Lawyer of Lawyer & Counsel to provide legal services in exchange for stock options. Lawyer was also given the title of corporate secretary and a seat on the board of directors.

Due to unexpected delays, it took more than a year to develop the prototype. In late 1989, the basic technology was sufficiently developed to attract a $2 million investment by Texas Ventures (TV), a venture-capital limited partnership put together by First Texas, a regional investment banking firm specializing in emerging high-tech companies. TV received an equity interest and a seat on Medtech's board of directors. Before it made its investment, TV obtained an opinion from John Expert, an expert in medical imaging who was on retainer to First Texas, to the effect that the Medtech prototype was far more advanced than anything on the market and, assuming a production model could be shipped by June 1990, Medtech had an excellent opportunity to capture a significant share of a large market. Expert advised TV that shipment by June 1990 seemed a good bet, given the current state of development.

The production model was completed *not* by June 1990 but in October 1990, when the first customer shipment took place. Even at this later date, though, it was still somewhat ahead of the computers marketed by Medtech's competitors, primarily because of its novel hardware architecture and advanced software, which enabled users to monitor physiological functions better than the software marketed by competitors.

Because of its technological superiority, Medtech's computer was a success. The company was successful in marketing the computer as an add-on to existing X-ray suites, and even to doctors and hospitals that were purchasing new X-ray suites from Hansen and other competitors. Hansen's computer was not quite as good, and Hansen had been advised by its counsel that it could not insist that purchasers buy the entire suite, including the Hansen computer, because of antitrust considerations. However, by offering a discount to purchasers of entire suites, Hansen could effectively offer its computer for a slightly lower price than the Medtech computer. Hansen, of course, had an added advantage because its sales force had first crack at first-time buyers of X-ray suites. Although Hansen's computer, like Medtech's, was compatible with suites made by other companies, Hansen had never marketed its computer separately, as an add-on to existing or new suites made by other manufacturers.

In early 1991, Medtech was able to attract $20 million of additional capital through the sale of preferred stock to other venture capitalists and by entering into an exclusive European distribution agreement with Pierre & Cie., a large French medical equipment company. Jean Pierre, the president of Pierre & Cie., was given a seat on Medtech's board of directors, which now consisted of Joseph; the company's chief financial officer; the TV representative; Maggie Lawyer; Jean Pierre; a prominent Houston surgeon; and an engineering professor from Rice University.

During the fourth quarter of 1991, the company's management, directors, and outside counsel began to consider the possibility of an initial public offering (IPO) of common stock early in the new year. Management knew that in order to remain competitive, the company needed significant new capital to complete the development of the second-generation computer and its related software. The development project, internally code-named Lifesaver, had been under way since early 1991. Substantial progress had been made, but the Lifesaver project was four months behind schedule, primarily due to difficulty in obtaining certain hardware components from outside sources, and unforeseen bugs in the new software. The successful and timely completion of the Lifesaver project was essential to the company's future success because Hansen had released new software for its own computer that had closed the technology gap between Hansen and Medtech. Although the Medtech computer continued to sell well, Medtech was clearly losing market share. The first customer shipment of Lifesaver, originally targeted for year end 1991, was now projected to take place by April 15, 1992.

Medtech retained its regular counsel, Lawyer & Counsel, to represent it with respect to the contemplated IPO. The company also sought the advice of First Texas, which advised that, although it might be somewhat early for a public offering, it might be possible to make an offering late in the first quarter of 1992 if market conditions remained favorable. First Texas indicated that it would very much like to be a managing underwriter of the offering, but that it would be wise for the company to consider a second manager from a prominent national firm with a bigger base of institutional clients and a nationwide retail capacity. After several interviews, Medtech chose Securities Freres, an old-line New York firm, to co-manage the offering and run the books. Securities Freres retained its regular counsel, Smythe and Smythe, to represent the underwriting syndicate.

In mid-December 1991, a meeting was held at Lawyer & Counsel's office in Austin. The meeting was attended by Medtech's senior management and representatives of Lawyer & Counsel, First Texas, Securities Freres, and Smythe and Smythe. The consensus of the meeting was that although Medtech could probably postpone the offering until late 1992, market conditions for an IPO looked extremely favorable early in the year. Securities Freres's chief economist was pessimistic about market conditions remaining strong beyond the first quarter of 1992. The group realized, however, that Medtech had not yet had a profitable quarter, and that the best the company could hope for its 1991 financial statements would be a small loss. Nevertheless, the revenue and earnings trends were highly favorable, and it was possible that the quarter ending December 31, 1991, would be profitable if overseas shipments to Pierre & Cie., currently scheduled for early January, were accelerated to late December. The group decided to meet again in early January.

Just before Christmas, Pierre & Cie. informed management that it had no objection to Medtech's shipping the computers in late December, provided they did not arrive at Pierre's facility in France until the end of January. In late December, the company made a major push to complete the Pierre order before the end of the year. On December 31, the Pierre computers were in shipping crates, ready for pickup by an international carrier at the company's loading docks. Late that afternoon, the carrier called to inform the company that it would be unable to pick up the computers that day, but that if the company brought the computers to a commercial warehouse near the docks, the carrier would load them for shipment to another commercial warehouse in France, where they would be held pending delivery to Pierre at the end of January. Andrea Auditor, a representative of Auditor and Company, Medtech's outside auditor, was present at Medtech's loading dock that afternoon to confirm shipment, and she witnessed the loading of the computers onto a Medtech truck for transport to the warehouse. Auditor also attended the impromptu New Year's/shipment celebration that took place on the Medtech loading dock when, after the last computer was loaded, the company's chief financial officer appeared out of nowhere with a case of champagne and his CD of *The World's Twenty-Four Favorite Christmas Melodies* by Zamfir, Master of the Pan Flute.

Thanks to the efforts of the New Year's celebrants, Medtech enjoyed its first profitable quarter at the end of 1991. The same group that had met in December met again in early January in order to plan the IPO. It was decided to begin the drafting and due-diligence process immediately, with the goal of filing a registration statement by February 14 and going effective on March 12.

The due-diligence and drafting sessions began on January 13, 1992. Representatives of the two managing underwriters and their counsel held three days of meetings with the company's management. During that time, they interviewed the company's directors of finance, engineering, and marketing, in addition to the top corporate executives. Several of the participants took extensive notes. The underwriters did not interview mid- or lower-level engineers who were actually working on the Lifesaver project. Instead, they retained John Expert (the computer expert who was already on retainer to First Texas) to visit the company's facilities, talk to the engineers working on the Lifesaver project, evaluate the development of the project to date, and advise the underwriters concerning the market for both the old computer and the Lifesaver.

During the due-diligence meetings, the underwriters also interviewed Andrea Auditor. Auditor informed the underwriters of the events of December 31, and explained that Medtech's revenue-recognition policy was to record revenue upon passage of title. Pursuant to Medtech's master agreement with Pierre, title passed from Medtech to Pierre upon shipment to Pierre. Auditor explained that the company's decision to recognize the revenue in 1991 was aggressive because the December 31 shipments were to a commercial warehouse, and not technically to Pierre. However, she explained, the company was firmly of the position that questioning the recognition of revenue on that basis would exalt form over substance and, after much soul-searching, her firm had concluded that the company's position was not contrary to generally accepted accounting principles.

In early February, Exton reported his conclusions at a dinner meeting attended by the underwriters and their counsel. Expert spoke informally to those nearest him at the table during dinner, and then formally addressed the group for approximately half an hour after dinner. His presentation was balanced and somewhat heavier on technological details than his audience might have wished. A junior member of the underwriting team from Securities Freres and an associate from Smythe and Smythe took notes intermittently on paper napkins and the back of an envelope, respectively. Two weeks after the meeting, nobody present had any specific recollection of exactly what Expert had said, except that everybody remembered the curious sports metaphor with which Expert summed up his findings: "Medtech's current computer will be dead in the water by mid-summer, but they're on the 90-yard line with the Lifesaver, and if they don't make any errors in the ninth inning, they should be able to finish the race."

During the first two weeks of February, a number of intensive drafting sessions were held at the offices of Lawyer & Counsel. The initial draft of the prospectus, produced by Lawyer at the beginning of these sessions, was a bare-bones document that included a business description, biographical information about the management and the directors, financial information, and so forth. Counsel for the underwriters immediately suggested that the prospectus include a risk-factor section. Lawyer agreed somewhat reluctantly, but stated that the section should be called "Certain Factors," not "Risk Factors," because some of the subjects covered were not necessarily risks. The underwriters and their counsel agreed. The "Certain Factors" section of the prospectus as filed on February 14 was divided into subsections entitled "Short Operating History," "Competition," "Sales to Certain Parties," and "Products Under Development."

The "Short Operating History" section set forth dates for incorporation and first product shipment to customers. It also disclosed that the company had suffered operating losses for all financial reporting periods of its existence except the fourth

quarter of 1991, and stated: "There can be no assurance that the Company will be able to continue to operate at a profit."

The "Competition" section stated that although the company believed it had a superior product to that of its competitors, some competitors had begun shipping second-generation computers and software that included features previously available only from Medtech. Moreover, the section disclosed that Hansen and Medtech's other two largest competitors had greater financial, marketing, and technical resources than Medtech. The section closed with the caveat: "No assurance can be given that the Company will be able to compete successfully against these companies in the future."

The "Sales to Certain Parties" section disclosed that approximately one-third of the company's sales during 1991 were made to Pierre & Cie. pursuant to Pierre's exclusive European distribution agreement. It also disclosed that Pierre & Cie. was the largest stockholder of the company. In addition, it stated that because Pierre could exercise discretion concerning the timing of certain deliveries, there could be no assurance that the company would experience a growth in revenues from quarter to quarter.

The "Products Under Development" section was the subject of a great deal of discussion and debate throughout the drafting sessions. The company and its counsel were adamant that nothing be said concerning the Lifesaver project because any disclosures would give Medtech's competitors information that they could use to compete against Medtech in the marketplace. The underwriters and their counsel believed that because the company's future prospects were largely dependent on the timely and successful introduction of the Lifesaver, something had to be said. After a session that included some raised voices and table pounding, the underwriters and the company agreed to the following disclosure:

> The Company is currently engaged in developing new products, as well as enhancements to its existing products. The developments include improvements in hardware architectures that will improve the performance of the computer, and software enhancements that will enable users to monitor additional physiological functions. Certain of the products under development are scheduled for delivery to customers early in the second quarter of 1992. The future revenues of the Company are dependent, to a large degree, on the successful and timely introduction of products under development. There can be no assurance that there will not be delays in the introduction of products under development. Substantial delays in the introduction of certain of these products could reduce or eliminate the lead time the Company believes it currently enjoys over certain competitive products.

The preliminary prospectus was finalized at an all-hands session on February 13 and filed with the SEC on February 14, 1992. The proposed offering price was set at $12 to $14 per share.

On March 5, 1992, Medtech received a fax from Pierre's chief operating officer in Paris. The fax stated that the computers shipped on December 31 were not functioning correctly, and that if the problems were not corrected within 30 days,

Pierre would return the computers to Medtech and would only accept the anticipated Lifesaver computers as replacements. Medtech informed the underwriters and their counsel about the fax, and explained that the problem had to do with a small adjustment that had to be made on the European version of the software, which was slightly different from the domestic version. The company assured the underwriters that the adjustment could be made easily within the time specified by Pierre, and that, in any event, the Lifesaver version should be ready for shipment in early April. The underwriters' counsel requested that these representations be memorialized in a letter from Medtech to the managing underwriters. The letter was delivered on March 11.

After the market closed on March 11, representatives of the company met with the underwriters at the offices of Securities Freres in New York for the final pricing meeting. The head of Securities Freres's syndicate department reported that the offering was in great demand, and that the stock could easily be sold at or even slightly above the preliminary pricing range of $12 to $14. Knowing that the company would push for a price as high as $18 per share, the underwriters decided to recommend that the stock be priced at $14 and allow themselves to be "talked into" a $15 price. The company insisted that $18 was an appropriate price, given the demand. After much wrangling, the underwriters and the company agreed to a price of $16.50 per share.

The offering went effective on March 12 at $16.50. Shortly after trading opened, demand began to weaken, and the closing price at the end of the day was $15. The stock continued to trade in a range from $14.50 to $16.00 during the next few weeks.

During the week after the offering, the underwriting team put together its file on the offering, monitored the activity of the stock, and kept in close contact with the company. On the advice of Smythe and Smythe, the underwriters drafted a memorandum that summarized the due-diligence effort. Once the final memorandum was completed, reviewed by the senior members of both managing underwriters, and approved by Smythe and Smythe, the underwriters, pursuant to their standard practice, discarded all of their handwritten notes and all drafts of the prospectus. A copy of the final prospectus was annotated to show the source of all material statements of fact and was attached to the due-diligence memorandum. The attorneys from Smythe and Smythe also discarded their notes after creating their own file memorandum. However, nobody informed the Smythe and Smythe junior associate who had taken notes at the dinner meeting with John Expert that it was firm policy to discard notes, and he retained the envelope on which he had scratched his notes of that meeting.

The associate's notes of the dinner meeting consisted of a few words and phrases, not complete thoughts. They included the following entries:

Current "dead in water"

"Lifesaver"—whose life?

ninth inning, if no errors ok

In April, the company announced its operating results for the quarter ended March 31, 1992. The results, which were slightly less positive than had been anticipated by securities analysts, showed that the company had broken even for the quarter. The stock price did not react dramatically to the announcement. During April, the stock continued to trade at the low end of the range at which it traded immediately after the offering.

In May, everything that could go wrong went wrong. The Lifesaver, which had been shipped to two favored customers for initial (or Beta) testing in late April, was not ready for customer shipment. The company believed the problem related to bugs in the software and brought in new engineers to address the problem urgently. At the same time, sales declined on the current computer, primarily because it had lost its competitive advantage, and because rumors had begun to circulate in the marketplace about Medtech's difficulty in completing its second-generation product. Because the company's attention had been concentrated almost exclusively on completing the Lifesaver, the modifications to the Pierre computers were given a low priority, and the French returned the entire shipment. When management saw the company's operating results for April and the first two weeks of May, they realized that some public announcement would be required. On May 19, Maggie Lawyer drafted the following press release:

> Medtech, Inc., a leading manufacturer of computer equipment used in medical imaging, today revised its estimate for the second quarter of 1992 from a projected profit of $.15 per share to a projected loss of $.10 per share. The revised estimate is due primarily to slower than expected sales for the first six weeks of the quarter and the return of $3 million of computers sold to Pierre & Cie. in December 1991.
>
> "We continue to be extremely optimistic about the future," said Hans Joseph, the company's president, "and we still believe we can meet our estimate of having our first profitable full year in 1992. In fact, we will be shipping a large order to Pierre & Cie. early in the next quarter, when we anticipate our next-generation computer will be available for customer shipment."

The press release was issued before the market opened on May 20. On the day of the press release, the price of Medtech's common stock dropped to below $14 per share for the first time since the offering. The stock continued to fall until it hit $11 per share a few days later.

On what basis can investors who bought Medtech stock in the IPO sue for the loss in value of the stock? For example, can the investors sue the issuer on the grounds of a misleading prospectus? What aspects of the prospectus, if any, were misleading? What are the issuer's defenses? What must the investors prove to win their case? Who are the likely defendants? For example, can the investors sue the auditors for misleading financial statements? What defenses are available to them? Who should win?

Analyze whether the conduct of each of the parties was ethical.

Can investors who bought on the open market after the IPO sue? On what theory? Who can be sued and what are their defenses? Who should win?

Chapter 24

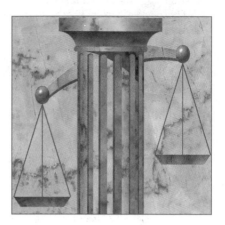

DEBTOR-CREDITOR RELATIONS AND BANKRUPTCY

■ Introduction

Borrowing Money

The reasons for borrowing money, and the uses to which the loan proceeds are applied, are many and varied. A business will generally decide to borrow when it needs funds and believes it is in a position to pay interest for the use of such funds. Although lenders sometimes take equity positions in a borrower, whereby they receive returns based on the profits or losses of the borrower, lenders in a loan transaction are entitled only to interest at a stated rate on the amount borrowed (generally called the *principal*) and the return of the principal at the end of the term.

When a business is in trouble, because of external events or internal miscalculations or misdeeds, it will inevitably run short of cash and fall behind in its payments. Creditors may be temporarily appeased, but those with collateral will ultimately pursue foreclosure, and others will file lawsuits in a race for the remaining assets. Defending against these actions can absorb resources and hamper management's ability to cure the company's underlying ills. Successful collection can cripple or kill the business.

Predatory dismemberment may destroy a company's real economic value. This loss in value will ultimately hurt creditors if there are not enough assets to go around. Even if all debts can be paid, the equity holders in the company will suffer. The collapse of a large enterprise could leave many unemployed and send disruptive waves through related industries.

The legal tools used to stem this potentially destructive tide are found mainly in the Bankruptcy Code (title 11 of the United States Code). Under the U.S. Constitution, Congress is given the power to enact bankruptcy laws. A successful reorganization under chapter 11 of the Bankruptcy Code results in the restructuring of financial relationships among the owners and creditors of a business and, ideally, the preservaton of a viable going concern. Even when reorganization is not possible, the bankruptcy system is designed to realize the maximum value from the available assets, to provide equitable distribution among

790

claimants, and to foster fair and efficient administration through a collective or multiparty process.

Chapter Summary

This chapter categorizes commercial loans according to the type of lender, the purposes to which the loan proceeds will be applied, and whether the loan is secured or unsecured. This discussion is followed by a summary of the typical terms of a loan agreement. Methods for securing a loan under article 9 of the Uniform Commercial Code are discussed, together with a description of the terms of a typical security agreement. Equipment leasing, guaranties, and subordination are addressed. This is followed by a discussion of business bankruptcies under chapter 7 and chapter 11 of the Bankruptcy Code, workouts, and lender liability. (Consumer credit and consumer bankruptcy are covered in chapter 19.)

■ Loans Categorized by Lender

Commercial loans are most commonly made by banks, insurance companies, and purchasers of *commercial paper,* that is, short-term corporate indebtedness. Both banks and insurance companies are highly regulated. Extensive federal and state legislation prescribes the types of entities that may call themselves banks, who may own them, and, once they become banks, what they may or may not do. Similarly, insurance companies are restricted by state legislation in connection with their business of insuring against risk. The regulatory framework within which banks, insurance companies, and other types of lenders operate will affect their sources and availability of funds; these factors in turn will affect the terms on which they will offer to lend money. Banks generally are more flexible in the length of the terms of their loans, the interest-rate formulas, and the mechanics of loan administration. Among insurance companies, medium- to long-term loans at fixed interest rates are more common. Whether it is a bank or an insurance company, a lender may have particular expertise in the industry in which the borrower does business, or in making loans for particular purposes.

■ Loans Categorized by Purpose

A borrower may require funds to meet everyday working capital needs, to finance an acquisition of assets or a business, or to finance a real estate construction project or an engineering project. Under regulations promulgated by the board of governors of the Federal Reserve System,

lenders and borrowers may not enter into transactions whereby secured credit will be used to acquire stock, unless certain requirements are met. Apart from these basic restrictions, and additional restrictions that apply to borrowers in regulated industries, borrowers may borrow money for a wide variety of reasons. These reasons will dictate whether the loan will be a term loan or a revolving loan.

Term Loans

Funds required for a specific purpose, such as an acquisition or a construction project, are generally borrowed in the form of a *term loan.* A specified amount is borrowed, either in a lump sum or in installments. It is to be repaid on a specified date—known as the *maturity date*—or *amortized,* that is, paid off over a period of time. For example, in an acquisition the buyer may be required to pay the purchase price up front and thus will require a lump-sum loan. By contrast, the owner of a construction project will require a loan to be disbursed in installments as scheduled progress payments become due. Amounts repaid under a term loan cannot be reborrowed.

Revolving Loans

A borrower may project her working capital needs for a given period but desire flexibility as to the exact amount of money borrowed at any given time. A *revolving loan* or *revolving line of credit* allows the borrower to borrow whatever sums required, up to a specified maximum amount. The borrower may also reborrow amounts it has repaid (hence the term "revolving"). The lender will require a *commitment fee* as consideration for its promise to keep the commitment available, as it receives no interest on amounts not borrowed.

Secured Loans

In making a loan, the lender relies on the borrower's cash flow, the borrower's assets, or the proceeds of another loan as sources of repayment. If the lender relies solely on the borrower's promise to repay the loan, the lender's recourse for nonpayment is limited to suing the borrower. Moreover, even if he does sue the borrower, he stands in no better position than other general creditors of the borrower, and has no special claim to any specific assets of the borrower as a source of repayment. Because of this risk, lenders are often unwilling to make loans without something more than the borrower's promise of repayment. Lenders usually require *collateral,* that is, property belonging to the borrower that will become the lender's if the loan is not repaid. A loan backed up by collateral is known as a *secured loan.* Unsecured loans, if they are available at all, are priced at a higher rate to reflect the greater credit risk to the lender.

If the borrower fails to repay a secured loan, the lender, in addition to suing for return of the monies lent, may *foreclose* on—that is, take possession of—the collateral, and either sell it to pay off the debt or keep it in satisfaction of the debt. It should be noted that under some *antideficiency* and *one-form-of-action laws*, lenders seeking remedies against real property security may be restricted from suing the borrower personally. In cases in which a lender has recourse to the borrower or to other property of the borrower, and exercises such rights, the lender may be precluded from foreclosing on real estate mortgaged by the borrower. These laws, which date back to the Great Depression, are designed to protect borrowers from forfeiting their properties to overzealous lenders.

Loan Agreements

Given the variety of loans described above, the basic structure of loan agreements is surprisingly standard. Lenders are concerned about the administration of the loan, their ongoing relationship with the borrowers, and the rights they have if the borrowers breach their promises. At times these concerns must be addressed in specially tailored documentation; however, banks generally use a collection of standard forms which are distributed to loan officers along with instructions for their use.

This section discusses the basic features common to all loan agreements.

Parties to the Agreement

The parties to a loan agreement are the lender and the borrower. There may be more than one lender and more than one borrower. If the lender is an insurance company, the loan agreement will be called a *note purchase agreement.*

Lenders   When two or more lenders, usually banks, together make one loan to a borrower, it is called a *syndicated loan.* In a syndicated loan, the lenders enter into concurrent direct obligations with the borrower to make a loan, typically on a pro rata basis. The loan is coordinated by a lead lender who serves as agent for all of the lenders in disbursing the funds, collecting payments of interest and principal, and administering and enforcing the loan.

A *participation loan* is a loan in which the original lender sells shares to other parties, called participants. Each participant acquires an undivided interest in the loan. The sale may be made without the borrower's involvement.

Borrowers   Multiple borrowers are usually related entities, such as a parent corporation and its subsidiaries. It is important to remember that corporate law recognizes each corporation as a separate entity. From the lender's point of view, the parent and its subsidiaries are one economic entity; but from the subsidiaries' point of view, if each subsidiary is jointly and severally liable for the entire debt, its obligation may outweigh the economic benefit it receives from the loan. (To the extent that the loan is used by the parent rather than the subsidiary, the transaction may be invalidated as a fraudulent transfer under state law and the federal Bankruptcy Code, as discussed later in the section titled "Guaranties.")

Additional Parties   In more complicated transactions, additional parties may become involved in the negotiations for a loan, even though they are not parties to the loan agreement. For example, in a leveraged buyout, the acquisition of a company is financed largely by debt secured by its assets. The lender will want assurances from the seller that the assets being sold to the borrower are free and clear of all liens, and this concern may affect the structure of the buyout; or, if the seller is taking a note from the buyer for part of the purchase price, the lender will want to negotiate with the seller an agreement setting forth their relative rights to repayment. In a construction loan, the construction lender will advance sufficient funds to complete the construction project with the expectation of being repaid when a permanent, long-term lender steps in. In such a situation, the construction lender will negotiate with the permanent lender as well as the borrower.

In certain types of project financings, a limited partnership may be formed for the sole purpose of constructing, say, a power plant. The general partner's liability is normally unlimited; however, for tax and other reasons, a lender may agree that it will look only to the partnership's assets for repayment of a loan. In such a case, the lender would need to assure itself that the limited partnership had sufficient resources to repay the loan. Such resources include, for example, fees from the sale of goods or services provided by the enterprise. The nature of the partnership's contracts for the sale of goods or services will therefore be of concern to the lender.

In all of these examples, the lender has a legitimate interest in seeing that the borrower's relationships with third parties will not adversely affect the loan.

Commitment to Make a Loan

A loan agreement may be preceded by a *term sheet,* which is a letter outlining the terms and conditions on which the lender will lend. A commitment to make a loan need not be in writing to be enforceable, but an oral promise may be difficult to enforce, because reasonable people may have honest differences in their recollections of what was said. However, a jury may award damages for breach of an oral loan commitment, as in the following case.

■ A Case in Point:　　　　　Summary

Case 24.1
LANDES CONSTRUCTION CO., INC. v. ROYAL BANK OF CANADA
United States Court of Appeals for the Ninth Circuit
833 F.2d 1365 (9th Cir. 1987).

FACTS　　An officer of the Royal Bank of Canada made an oral promise to lend the Landes Construction Company funds to purchase real property for development. He allegedly said, over dinner, "We are going to lend you $10 million for this project." The bank subsequently maintained that no such commitment had been made, and refused to provide the loan. Landes Construction was unable to obtain alternative financing, and forfeited a $3 million deposit. It sued the bank for breach of contract. Landes Construction presented evidence at trial that it had lost between $29 million and $79.6 million in profits. The jury awarded Landes Construction $18.5 million.

ISSUE PRESENTED　　Is an oral agreement to lend money enforceable?

SUMMARY OF OPINION　　The U.S. Court of Appeals upheld the jury verdict, even though it characterized the trial as "little more than a swearing contest." The jury verdict, it said, was supported by substantial evidence. Neither party disputed that various meetings occurred, that the bank had advanced $3 million, that these funds went to the seller, or that Landes Construction was the buyer named in the purchase agreement. The bank's arguments against the verdict centered on what inferences should be drawn from this evidence. One reasonable inference, the court concluded, was that the bank promised to lend Landes Construction the $10 million for the project. The only possible error of law that the court found was admission of evidence of lost profits. This alleged error, however, was harmless, according to the court.

RESULT　　The jury award of $18.5 million for breach of a promise to lend was valid.

Ethical Consideration

Managers should be careful not to make oral promises that they cannot, or will not, perform. The business environment is always changing, and it is better to qualify one's statements than to make a strong commitment today that may be regretted tomorrow.

Managers should recognize that many types of oral contracts are binding. When there is no independent witness to an oral contract, a contracting party may be tempted to alter her version of the facts, leading to a contest of "your word against mine." This type of behavior is clearly unethical.

In response to cases like *Landes Construction*, state legislatures have proposed, and at least one has adopted, legislation specifically requiring loan commitments that exceed a threshold dollar amount to be in writing in order to be enforceable. Even in the absence of such legislation, a prudent lender will use a written term sheet or commitment letter to specify the terms of a proposed loan, including the amount, the interest rate, fees, and repayment provisions; and to disclaim any obligation to lend until additional investigation is completed, additional terms and conditions are negotiated, and formal documentation is signed.

Description of the Loan

A loan agreement contains the lender's promise to lend a specified amount of money. Frequently this will be the only promise that the lender will make in the loan agreement. The loan agreement also describes the mechanics by which funds will be disbursed, the rate of interest to be charged, the manner of computing such interest, and the repayment terms.

Mechanics of Funding   The funds are usually sent by wire transfer to an account specified by the borrower. If the timing is important, the borrower will want to discuss with the lender the logistical details of the loan agreement, such as the lender's deadline for sending wire transfers. The logistics may become critical if the lender and the borrower are in different time zones, or if there are multiple lenders, as in a syndicated loan.

Interest Rates   Interest rates may be fixed or *floating,* that is, fluctuating throughout the life of the loan according to the interest rate that the lender would pay if it borrowed the funds in order to relend them. Fixed-rate term loans from insurance companies are common; banks generally prefer a floating rate. The floating rate may be pegged to the bank's *prime rate,* that is, the lowest rate of interest at which the bank lends to its most creditworthy customers. (This is also called the *base rate* or *reference rate.*) The floating rate may be expressed either as a percentage of the prime rate (such as 110% of the prime rate) or, more commonly, as the sum of the prime rate and a specified number of percentage points (such as the prime rate plus 10%).

In the following case, the court held that a bank would be liable if it misled a borrower about what the bank's prime rate was.

■ A Case in Point: Summary

Case 24.2
MOROSANI v. FIRST NATIONAL BANK OF ATLANTA
United States Court of Appeals for the Eleventh Circuit
703 F.2d 1220 (11th Cir. 1983).

FACTS   George W. Morosani borrowed money from First National Bank of Atlanta. According to Morosani, the bank agreed to charge interest at a particular percentage above the prime rate, defined as the rate charged to the bank's "best and most creditworthy commercial customers." Morosani claimed that the bank in fact lent to major corporate borrowers at rates below its published prime rate. Morosani sued the bank, alleging that it fraudulently charged him excessive interest on the loan. He sought treble damages under the federal Racketeering Influenced and Corrupt Organizations Act (RICO).

ISSUE PRESENTED   Might a bank that misrepresents its prime rate in selling the interest rate for a loan violate RICO?

SUMMARY OF OPINION   The U.S. Court of Appeals stated that obtaining money by false pretenses "clearly falls within the traditional definition of criminal activity and is specifically prohibited" by RICO when, as in this case, the services of the U.S. Postal Service are used to further the alleged scheme. Accordingly, Morosani could proceed with a RICO suit against the bank.

RESULT   A complaint alleging that a bank had misrepresented its prime rate in selling the interest rate for a loan stated a claim for relief under the Racketeering Influenced and Corrupt Organizations Act.

COMMENTS   *Morosani* was the first of the prime-rate cases to reach an appellate court. In these cases, nonprime borrowers challenged the banks' misleading use of the term "prime rate." Many of the cases were quietly settled out of court; *Morosani* was settled in 1984 for a reported $12.5 million.

In response to such cases, many banks redefined the term "prime rate" in their loan documents. Some substituted the terms "base rate" or "reference rate." Some included in their definition an explicit statement that the prime (or base or reference) rate was not the bank's best or lowest rate.

Alternatively, the floating rate may be pegged to the London Interbank Offered Rate (*LIBOR*) or to the certificate of deposit (*CD*) rate. These rates are based on the theoretical cost that a bank incurs to obtain, for a given period of time, the funds it will lend. To this cost is added a spread (or margin) to arrive at the actual interest rate. Frequently, a loan agreement will offer prime rate, LIBOR, and CD rate options for the borrower to select during the life of the loan.

The LIBOR interest rate is based on the cost of borrowing offshore U.S. dollars in the global interbank market, which nowadays is centered in several locations in addition to London. Deposits made through the interbank offering market are generally for periods of 1, 2, 3, 6, 9, or 12 months, and LIBOR loans are made for corresponding periods. At the end of an interest period, the borrower may elect to roll over the LIBOR loan, that is, to continue it for another interest period; to repay the loan; or to convert it to a loan based on a different interest rate.

The CD rate is based on the average of the bid rates quoted to the bank by dealers in the secondary market for the purchase at face value of certificates of deposit of the bank in a given amount and for a given term. CD-rate loans are commonly available for interest periods of 30, 60, 90, or 180 days.

Computation of Interest   Interest is generally computed on a daily basis according to one of several methods. Under the 365/360 method, the nominal annual interest rate is divided by 360, and the resulting daily rate is then multiplied by the outstanding principal amount and the actual number of days in the payment period. Thus, for a year of 365 or 366 days, the actual rate of interest will be greater than the nominal annual rate.

Under the 365/365 method, the daily rate is determined by dividing the nominal annual interest rate by 365 (or 366, in leap years), then this daily rate is multiplied by the outstanding principal amount and the actual number of days in the payment period.

Under the 360/360 method, it is assumed that all months have 30 days; thus the monthly interest amounts are always the same.

The method used to compute interest is significant when large principal amounts are concerned. It may also be significant if the lender or the loan is subject to state *usury* laws, which limit the maximum rate of interest that may be charged. National banks and other specified classes of lenders are subject to federal legislation that preempts state usury laws; and many states permit higher interest rates for exempt commercial transactions over a given dollar amount. However, unless a state or federal exemption applies, lenders and borrowers should analyze whether a loan is usurious by virtue of its terms and conditions. For example, compensation paid for a loan, such as commitment fees, expenses, and prepayment penalties, may be deemed to constitute interest.

Repayment Terms   A revolving loan may be repaid from time to time at the borrower's discretion, subject to a final maturity date when all sums outstanding become due and payable. In a term loan, the lender may require the entire principal to be repaid in one lump sum upon maturity, or in equal or unequal installments.

Term loan agreements and revolving loan agreements may also require mandatory prepayment when certain events occur. For example, in a receivables and inventory line of credit, a prepayment will be required if the level of receivables and/or inventory supporting the outstanding borrowings drops. Other events that may mandate a prepayment are a sale of assets outside the ordinary course of business, or financial earnings above a specified level.

Asset-Based Loans   In structuring a loan agreement, the fact that a loan is secured or unsecured is not particularly significant, except in certain types of asset-based financing in which the amount lent is determined according to the levels of assets available from time to time. One example of an asset-based loan is a revolving line of credit based on receivables, inventory, or both. Subject to certain criteria as to what inventory or receivables are eligible—that is, acceptable to the lender—the borrower borrows against such assets, and repays such loans on a revolving basis out of collections of the receivables generated from the sale of inventory. Sometimes, payments may be made directly to the lender through such mechanisms as a locked-box or blocked account, which allow the lender to take the outstanding loan repayments out of the proceeds collected, before they are distributed to the borrower.

Representations and Warranties   Before committing to make a loan, a lender will investigate the potential borrower's financial condition and creditworthiness. It will also require the borrower to confirm:

■   The legal status of the borrower, including, in the case of a corporation, its proper incorporation and good standing;

■   That corporate and other actions have authorized the proposed borrowing;

■   That regulatory and other approvals that might be required for the borrowing have been obtained;

■   That there are no court orders or contracts that would be in conflict with the loan agreement;

■   Whether the borrower is involved in any litigation;

■   That the borrower has good and marketable title to all of its assets, including any assets that constitute collateral for the loan;

■   That the loan agreement is legal, valid, and binding; and

■   That no default has occurred or would result from entering into the loan agreement.

The purpose of these representations and warranties is to specify the assumptions upon which the lender is willing to lend. In the negotiation process, the representations and warranties serve as a checklist of major areas of investigation by the lender. They also provide a framework for the borrower to examine its legal and financial position.

Qualifications   Often, a borrower will state that a representation is true to the best of its knowledge. The borrower will want to be held accountable only for what it knows, not for what it does not know. The lender will want the borrower to take steps to ascertain the accuracy of its representations. The risk of a representation proving to be untrue is usually placed on the borrower rather than the lender. Any qualification based on the borrower's knowledge is therefore likely to be phrased in terms of what the borrower either knows or should know after diligent inquiry. It may include a definition of the appropriate standard of diligence.

> *The borrower will want to be held accountable only for what it knows, not for what it does not know. The lender will want the borrower to take steps to ascertain the accuracy of its representations. The risk of a representation proving to be untrue is usually placed on the borrower rather than the lender.*

In the loan agreement, the borrower states that the representations and warranties are true and complete as of the date of the loan agreement. They do not apply prospectively. However, the loan agreement may provide that if advances are to be made, the representations and warranties will be updated as of the time of the advances.

Truthfulness of Representations   Before a disbursement is made under the loan agreement, the lender will require an opinion of counsel and a certification by an independent public accountant, confirming the representations made by the borrower. The lender's obligation to continue to lend will likewise be conditioned upon the continuing truthfulness of the representations in the loan agreement.

Authority to Approve the Loan

The lender will require evidence that the borrower's internal requirements for approving the loan have been met. It may require copies of the relevant corporate resolutions, with a certification by the corporate secretary. It may also require certification of the incumbency of the officers authorized to execute the loan agreement.

Completion of Documents

The loan agreement is typically only one of several documents that must be signed in connection with a loan. The lender will also require a promissory note and, if the loan is secured, a security agreement and financing statements.

Payment of Fees

Some fees, such as commitment fees, must be paid before any funds are disbursed.

Other Conditions

Other conditions may apply in certain circumstances. For example, in the case of a term loan to finance a merger or acquisition, the lender will condition any disbursement on the consummation of such merger or acquisition.

Regulatory approval may be required because of the nature of the borrower's business. In such cases, the particular permits and approvals that must be obtained or issued before the lender is willing to disburse funds will be enumerated.

Lenders are becoming increasingly concerned about the liability they may face when real property held by them, either as security or outright after a foreclosure, is required to comply with environmental cleanup laws. The lender may therefore require an opinion of environmental counsel, an environmental audit by qualified consultants and engineers, and indemnity agreements with the borrower and with any third parties that may be responsible for the environmental condition of the property.

Conditions Precedent

If the basic assumptions and facts upon which the lender has relied change materially after a commitment to lend has been made, the lender will need to reevaluate the loan. It may refuse to advance the funds committed; refuse to advance additional funds if some disbursements have already been made; or accelerate the maturity of the loan. The loan agreement will specify the conditions that must be met before the lender's obligations arise under the agreement. These are known as *conditions precedent*.

Covenants

Covenants are the borrower's promises to the lender that it will or will not take specific actions as long as either a commitment or a loan is outstanding. If a covenant is breached, the lender is free to terminate the loan.

Whereas the lender's obligation is simply to make the loan once the stated conditions are met, the list of obligations imposed upon the borrower can be quite lengthy. The borrower's obligations may also affect nonparties to the loan agreement. For example, the lender may require that the borrower and its subsidiaries maintain a specified net worth, computed on a consolidated basis. Because the subsidiaries are not parties to the loan agreement, that agreement cannot directly impose such an obligation on them. However, the borrower may be required to cause its subsidiaries to comply with the covenant. Such a covenant assumes that the borrower is in a position to influence the nonparties' actions.

Affirmative Covenants *Affirmative covenants* state what the borrower undertakes to do, for example, maintain its corporate existence, pay taxes, maintain insurance, and comply with applicable laws.

The borrower is usually required to keep the lender informed of its financial condition and to submit unaudited financial reports monthly or quarterly, and audited financial reports annually. Financial tests relating to income statement and balance sheet items may be imposed. A catchall covenant will require the borrower to inform the lender of any material adverse change in its operations or financial condition.

Negative Covenants *Negative covenants* state what the borrower undertakes not to do, for example, not to incur additional debt beyond a specified amount, and not to grant liens other than those specifically enumerated or those arising in the ordinary course of business. (A *lien* is a claim on a property that secures a debt owed by the owner of the property.)

Scope Covenants are generally heavily negotiated. Financial covenants, because they are based on projections of future financial results, require flexibility in long-term loans. A covenant will be resisted by the borrower if it is perceived to interfere with the borrower's control and operation of its businesses. A lender sensitive to borrowers' fears of lender control will draft its covenants carefully to impose no more control than is needed to protect the lender's right to be repaid. For example, a provision that effectively gives the lender the right to select the borrower's management may be difficult to justify. Lawsuits, some resulting in multimillion-dollar punitive judgments against unduly interfering lenders, have alerted lenders to the need for caution in drafting and enforcing such provisions.

> *A provision that effectively gives the lender the right to select the borrower's management may be difficult to justify.*

Events of Default

A loan agreement lists the events that will trigger the lender's right to terminate the loan, accelerate the repayment obligations, and, if the loan is secured, take possession of the property securing the loan. These events, known as the *events of default,* may be defined by the parties to the loan agreement, and usually include failure to pay on time any amounts due under the loan agreement; making false or misleading representations or warranties in connection with the loan; or failing to live up to any covenant in the loan agreement. In addition, if the borrower, any subsidiary, or a guarantor enters into bankruptcy, the lender will want to put its obligations on hold while it considers the next course of action.

Some events of default are outside the control of the borrower. For example, if a loan is made to a corporation on the strength of the lender's confidence in a particular individual's management ability, the death of that individual may be included as an event of default. Similarly, involuntary liens or legal judgments against the borrower, while more or less outside of the borrower's control, change the fundamental bases on which a loan was originally made. A loan agreement cannot require the borrower to take or not take actions that are outside of its control. Nevertheless, because the consequences of certain events, regardless of how they are caused, are of concern to the lender, the lender will want to include these events in the default section.

Cross-Default   A *cross-default* provision provides that any breach by the borrower under any other loan agreement constitutes an event of default under this loan agreement. A borrower will want to limit the provision to apply only to a serious breach of a loan agreement covering the loan of an amount greater than a specified minimum. The borrower may also want the lender to agree that the borrower's breach of another agreement will not constitute an event of default under this agreement unless the other lender terminates its loan on account of the breach.

The lender, on the other hand, will want a broad definition of the events of default. It will want the right to join with other creditors to negotiate some form of protection for its position as soon as the borrower's financial condition deteriorates.

Provided the borrower does not seek bankruptcy, the lender and borrower are free to renegotiate the terms and conditions on which the loan will remain outstanding. For example, the lender may agree to continue the loan in exchange for new or additional collateral, new guaranties, or a higher rate of interest. Such negotiations are a practical alternative to the more drastic measure of *calling,* that is, terminating, the loan. (Where the borrower seeks bankruptcy, the lender's efforts to restructure the loan will be subject to the jurisdiction of the bankruptcy court.)

Remedies for Default

The default section sets forth the remedies for default. These remedies are optional for the lender. If the lender *waives* a default—that is, decides not to exercise any of its remedies—it may exact additional consideration from the borrower, in the form of an increase in the interest rate or additional security.

It is prudent to set forth a waiver in writing to avoid any misunderstanding as to the scope of the waiver and the terms and conditions upon which it is being granted, including any additional obligations that the borrower will now be expected to satisfy. In lender-liability lawsuits, express terms in a loan agreement have been found to be superseded by oral or written communications between the lender and the borrower, or by the actions of the borrower or lender. Reducing understandings to writing and avoiding actions that may be inconsistent with the written documents will avoid surprises and failed expectations on both sides.

■ Secured Transactions Under the UCC

The mechanics of taking a security interest in personal property and fixtures, and the consequences of taking such a security interest, are governed by article 9 of the Uniform Commercial Code (UCC), which has been adopted with certain variations in all states. Before article 9 was adopted, such common-law security devices as the pledge, the chattel mortgage, the conditional sale, the trust receipt, and the factor's lien were all governed by different rules. Article 9 of the UCC was intended to provide a unified, comprehensive scheme for all types of *secured transactions,* that is, loans or other transactions secured by collateral put up by the borrower. Article 9 applies "to any transaction (regardless of its form) which is intended to create a security interest in personal property or fixtures including goods, documents, instruments, general intangibles, chattel paper or accounts."

Terminology

Part 1 of article 9 defines terms. In place of the various common-law security devices, the UCC uses the single term *security interest* to signify any interest in personal property or fixtures that are used as collateral to secure payment or the performance of an obligation. The parties to a secured transaction are the *debtor,* that is, the person who owes payment or other performance of the obligation secured, whether or not that person owns or has rights in the collateral; and the *secured party,* that is, the lender, seller, or other person in whose favor there is a security interest. A *security agreement* is an agreement that creates or provides for a security interest.

Formal Requisites

Part 2 of article 9 prescribes the formal requisites for creating an enforceable security interest, and describes the rights of the parties to a security agreement. If the secured party takes possession of the collateral, an oral agreement is sufficient to create a security interest; otherwise a signed security agreement containing a description of the collateral is required. For a security interest to be enforceable, the UCC requires that value has been given in exchange for it, and that the debtor has rights in the collateral. These requirements do not have to be fulfilled in any particular order. When all of the requirements have been met, a security interest is said to have *attached.*

Rights and Remedies

The remainder of article 9 sets forth the rights of the secured party as against other creditors of the debtor; the rules for *perfecting* a security interest, that is, making it valid as against other creditors of the debtor; and the remedies available to a secured party when a debtor defaults.

Scope of Article 9

Article 9 provides a single source of reference for most consensual security interests; but some security interests are outside of its scope. Article 9 does not apply to liens on real property. Various state and federal laws preempt the UCC in the areas of ship mortgages, mechanic's liens, and aircraft liens. Notices of security interests in trademarks are commonly filed in the Patent and Trademark Office, in addition to being perfected as "general intangibles" under the UCC. Article 9 does not apply to security interests subject to a landlord's lien, to a lien given by statute or other rule of law for services or materials, or to a right of setoff. (A right of setoff permits one party to deduct automatically from payments due the other party amounts due the first party.) Security interests in securities are governed by article 8 of the UCC.

The next two sections deal with, respectively, the typical provisions of a security agreement and how a security interest is perfected.

■ Security Agreements

A security agreement identifies the parties and the property to be used as collateral. It may also specify the debtor's obligations and the lender's remedies in case of default.

Parties to the Agreement

Security agreements typically use the UCC terminology to identify the parties. In a loan transaction, the secured party is the lender. The debtor is the borrower, if he owns the collateral or if the owner has authorized him to use the property for collateral. If the third-party owner acts as a guarantor of the borrower's obligation, she may also be referred to as the debtor. (Guaranties are discussed later in this chapter.)

Granting Clause

Unless the security interest is a possessory interest (traditionally called a *pledge*), the security agreement must be signed by the debtor, and must expressly grant a security interest in some specified property. The standard operative words are: "The debtor hereby grants to the secured party a security interest in . . . ." No precise form is required by the UCC; however, the collateral must be described.

Description of the Collateral

The description of the collateral need not be specific, as long as it reasonably identifies what is described. Loans to finance the purchase of specific property, such as an equipment loan, will typically be secured by the property purchased, and the security agreement will contain a specific description of such property.

For example, a working capital loan may be secured by receivables and inventory, with the inventory described as "any and all goods, merchandise, and other personal property, wherever located or in transit, that are held for sale or lease, furnished under any contract of service, or held as raw materials, work in process, supplies, or materials used or consumed in the debtor's business." Frequently, a secured party will take a security interest in all of the assets of the debtor—not only fixed assets, inventory, and receivables, but also trademarks, trade names, goodwill, licenses, books, and records. In such cases the collateral may be described as all tangible and intangible property that, taken together, is intended to preserve the value of the debtor as a going concern.

After-Acquired Property   *After-acquired property* is property that the debtor acquires after the execution of the security agreement. After-acquired assets may be included in the security agreement either in addition to, or as replacements of, currently owned assets. A security interest in after-acquired collateral will attach when the debtor acquires rights in the collateral, assuming that the other prerequisites for attachment have previously been met.

Proceeds   The UCC provides that, unless otherwise agreed, a security agreement gives the secured party a security interest in the proceeds if the collateral is sold, exchanged, collected, or otherwise disposed of. The security interest is equally effective against cash, accounts, or whatever else is received from the transaction. This feature makes a security interest created under article 9 a *floating lien.*

Debtor's Obligations

The debtor is obligated to repay the debt and to pay interest and related fees, charges, and expenses. In addition, the debtor will have nonmonetary obligations, such as obligations to maintain prescribed standards of financial well-being, measured by net worth, cash flow, and debt coverage (the ratio of debt to equity). These obligations are typically set forth in detail in a loan agreement or a promissory note, although occasionally they may be found in a security agreement.

Cross-Collateralization

The collateral for one loan may be used to secure obligations under another loan. This is done by means of a *cross-collateralization* provision—sometimes called a

dragnet clause—in the security agreement. For example, a lender extending an inventory and receivables line of credit to a borrower may insist that the line be secured not only by inventory and receivables, but also by equipment owned by the borrower and already held by the lender as collateral for an equipment loan. Thus if the lender forecloses on the equipment, any proceeds in excess of the amounts owed under the equipment loan will be available to pay down the inventory and receivables line of credit. Likewise, if the equipment loan is cross-collateralized with collateral for the inventory and receivables line of credit, any proceeds realized from foreclosure of the inventory and receivables will be available to pay down the equipment loan.

Remedies for Default

The remedies described in a security agreement track the rights and procedures set forth in article 9. After default, the secured party has the right to take possession of the collateral, without judicial process if this can be done without breach of the peace. The secured party must then dispose of the collateral at a public or private sale. If there is a surplus from the sale of the collateral, the secured party is required to return it to the debtor. If there is a deficiency, the debtor remains liable for that amount. The proceeds from the sale must be applied in this order:

1.   To the reasonable expenses of foreclosure and, if provided for in the agreement, reasonable attorney's fees and legal expenses

2.   To the satisfaction of the obligations secured

3.   To the satisfaction of indebtedness secured by a subordinate security interest, if a written demand for such satisfaction is timely received.

> 66
> *After default, the secured party has the right to take possession of the collateral, without judicial process if this can be done without breach of the peace.*

Although the UCC establishes a framework within which the lender may exercise its remedies, some details must be provided for by contract. For example, the parties may agree to apply the proceeds of a foreclosure sale to attorney's fees and legal expenses, or they may agree that the debtor will assemble the collateral and make it available to the secured party at a designated place. All such provisions are subject to the requirement that the secured party's disposition of the collateral must be commercially reasonable. This term is not defined in the UCC, but it is generally interpreted to require conformity with prevailing standards, and to prevent one party from taking undue advantage of another. However, the secured party and the debtor are free to fashion a mutually acceptable standard of commercial reasonableness, and security agreements typically contain a description of such standards.

■ Perfecting a Security Interest

In order to protect its rights in the collateral, a lender must ensure that its security interest is perfected, that is, valid against other creditors of the debtor and against a trustee in bankruptcy of the debtor. The UCC does not define perfection; instead it describes the situations in which an unperfected security interest will be subordinated to the rights of third parties. For example, a security interest is subordinate to the rights of "a person who becomes a lien creditor before the security interest is perfected." Subordination to lien creditors means in effect that the security interest is not valid against the debtor's trustee in bankruptcy.

Methods of Perfection

Security interests can be perfected by possession of the collateral, by filing a financing statement, or automatically.

By Possession A security interest in letters of credit and advices of credit, goods, instruments (other than certificated securities, which are covered by article 8 of the UCC—see below), money, negotiable documents, or chattel paper is perfected by the secured party's taking possession of the collateral.

By Filing For other types of collateral, perfection is accomplished by filing a financing statement. Standard printed forms, known as UCC-1 forms, are widely available for this purpose.

Automatic Perfection Some security interests require neither possession nor filing for perfection. For example, a *purchase-money security interest* in consumer goods is automatically perfected. Under certain circumstances, a security interest in instruments or negotiable instruments is temporarily perfected without filing or possession. Automatic perfection is of limited duration, however, and

must be followed by possession or filing if perfection is to survive for a longer period.

Uncertificated Securities The once fundamental distinction between possessory and nonpossessory security interests has become blurred by the introduction of uncertificated, or book-entry, securities. In 1967, the United States Treasury Department promulgated procedures for the issuance and maintenance of book-entry Treasury securities, and other agencies, including the Federal National Mortgage Association and the Federal Home Loan Mortgage Corporation, followed suit. These agencies no longer issue securities in certificate form. Even when the securities are in the form of bearer instruments (meaning that they are payable to the holder thereof) or registered instruments (meaning that they are payable to the registered owner), the owners of such securities seldom have possession of the instruments, as the securities are frequently held in brokerage accounts or mutual funds. Article 8 of the UCC, which governs investment securities, was revised in 1977 to provide for the creation and perfection of security interests in certificated and uncertificated securities, and these topics were removed from article 9.

Filing Procedure

The fundamental concept behind perfection by filing is to provide notice "to the world" that assets of one person are subject to the security interest of another. If a security interest is not perfected by possession, the collateral remains in the debtor's possession and control. This occurs, for example, if the collateral is intangible (such as accounts), or if possession by the secured party is impractical (as in the case of inventory). A centralized system gives effective public notice that property in the possession and under the apparent control of the debtor is actually subject to the rights of another. The filing system enables a prospective creditor to determine whether in claiming his rights to such assets he will be competing with other creditors or with a trustee in bankruptcy. It also enables a purchaser of goods to determine whether the seller's creditors have any claims against the goods. (It should be noted that, under certain circumstances, a purchaser of goods is protected from liens on such goods created by the seller; for example, consumers are protected from inventory liens on a seller's goods by UCC section 9-307(1).)

Where to File The proper place to file in order to perfect a security interest is in the office of the secretary of state in the state in which the property is located or, in the case of intangible property, in which the debtor is located. A security interest in collateral closely associated with real property, such as fixtures, growing crops, timber, or minerals, must be filed in the office in which a mortgage on the real estate would be recorded, usually the county recorder's office in the county where the real property is located.

What to File   To perfect a security interest in personal property, a financing statement must be filed. The financing statement merely gives notice that a financing transaction is being or is about to be entered into, without describing the transaction. It need only contain the signatures of the parties to the transaction, their addresses, and a description of the kinds of collateral in which a security interest has been or may be granted. If a financing statement covers crops grown or to be grown, or goods that are or are to become fixtures, the UCC requires also a legal description of the land concerned.

When to File   A financing statement may be filed in advance of the transaction or the security agreement. This is important because, under the UCC, a security interest is perfected when the statement is filed. Thus, the first secured party to file has priority over other parties with security interests in the same debtor's property, unless special priority rules apply, as in the case of purchase-money security interests.

Equipment Leasing

In order to conserve its working capital, a company may desire to lease the equipment it needs, rather than purchase it. Leasing sometimes offers an attractive alternative to borrowing funds to purchase the equipment, because a leasing company may be willing to provide more lenient terms than a bank or other lender. A leasing company may also be willing to accept a greater credit risk than banks, but it will probably charge higher interest rates than a bank to accommodate the greater credit risk involved. A newer enterprise may sometimes be asked for a security deposit or personal guaranty in connection with an equipment lease.

When equipment is leased, three parties are involved: the seller of the equipment, the leasing company, and the user of the equipment. The user determines its needs and negotiates a purchase price for the equipment, then engages a leasing company to purchase the equipment and lease it to the user. The manufacturer or seller of the equipment may lease it to the user, either directly or

through a leasing subsidiary, but third-party leasing companies are more frequently used.

Differences from True Lease

An equipment lease that serves the purpose of financing is known as a *finance lease.* A finance-lease agreement is a lengthy document that differs from a true lease in several ways. It gives the lessor some degree of control over the use, alteration, and location of the equipment. It prohibits major changes in the user's business operations without the consent of the lessor, unless the lessee first repays the lessor in full. The lessee is required to keep the equipment in good repair and to insure it against loss or damage. The lessor is given a security interest in the equipment, and may foreclose and sell the equipment in the event of default by the user.

In addition to the terms of the lease agreement, the rights and remedies of the lessor and lessee are governed by article 9 of the Uniform Commercial Code.

For accounting purposes, a finance lease is treated as a long-term debt of the lessee, who is deemed to own the leased equipment, and may therefore enjoy tax benefits such as depreciation deductions. The lessee may have the right to purchase the equipment at the end of the lease term. In this case, the lease will often provide that the purchase price shall be the fair market value of the equipment at that time.

Guaranties

A *guaranty* is an undertaking by one person, the *guarantor,* to become liable for the obligation of another person, the *primary debtor.* A guaranty allows the party that is to receive payment to look to the guarantor in the event the primary debtor fails to pay. The guarantor can be an individual, a corporation, a partnership, or any other type of entity willing to lend its credit support to another's obligation. The most common form of guaranty is a guaranty that indebtedness or other payment obligations will be paid when due. A less common form is a guaranty that specified nonpayment obligations will be performed; this is sometimes referred to as a guaranty of performance.

In lending transactions, a guaranty is often required when, after completing its credit analysis, the lender determines that the credit of the borrower is not sufficient to support the requested loan. The lender will evaluate the credit of each guarantor, and decide whether to make the loan based on the combined credit of the borrower and the guarantors. Also, a lender may require guaranties from officers, directors, or shareholders of a borrower, especially where the borrower is a closely held corporation. A lender may seek to protect its position under a guaranty by requiring that the guarantor refrain from incurring additional debt or granting liens on her assets.

The type of guaranty and the duties of the guarantor will be determined by the language of the guaranty instrument.

Payment Versus Collection

Under a *guaranty of payment,* the guarantor's obligation to pay the lender is triggered, immediately and automatically, when the primary debtor fails to make a payment when due. In contrast, under a guaranty of collection, the guarantor becomes obliged to pay only after the lender has attempted unsuccessfully to collect the amount due from the primary debtor. With a collection guaranty, the lender will generally have to commence a lawsuit and take other steps to collect a debt before calling on the guarantor to pay (unless the primary debtor is insolvent or is otherwise clearly unable to pay). This condition makes the enforcement of collection guaranties so cumbersome and expensive that lenders almost always require payment guaranties.

Limited Versus Unlimited

The amount of a guarantor's liability under a guaranty may be either limited or unlimited. In the case of a *limited guaranty,* the maximum amount of the guarantor's liability is expressly stated in the guaranty instrument. This maximum liability is usually a specific dollar amount, though it can be based on other criteria, such as a percentage of the primary debtor's total indebtedness to the lender.

Continuing Versus Restricted

A *restricted guaranty* is enforceable only with respect to a specified transaction or series of transactions. A guaranty that covers all future obligations of the primary debtor to the lender is referred to as a *continuing guaranty.* The objective of the continuing guaranty is to make the guarantor liable for any debt incurred at any time by the primary debtor, regardless of whether such debt was contemplated at the time the guaranty was entered into. Lenders naturally favor continuing guaranties over restricted guaranties.

Revocation   In many jurisdictions, a continuing guaranty may be revoked by the guarantor during his lifetime.

The effect of such a revocation is to prevent the guarantor from becoming liable for debts incurred by the primary debtor in connection with transactions not yet entered into. Revocation also results from the death of the guarantor; however, the guarantor's estate will remain liable for debts incurred by the primary debtor prior to the guarantor's death.

Discharging the Guarantor   A lender who makes a guaranteed loan must avoid any actions that would have the effect of discharging the guarantor, such as altering the terms of the agreement between the lender and the primary debtor (for example, increasing the interest rate on the loan or increasing the amount of the scheduled payments); extending the time for payment of the loan or renewing the indebtedness; or releasing or impairing the lender's rights with respect to collateral pledged by the primary debtor. A well-drafted guaranty can alleviate some of these potential pitfalls. However, the best approach is for the lender to obtain the consent of the guarantor before making any material change to the arrangement between the lender and the primary debtor.

Fraudulent Conveyances

A guaranty may be attacked as a fraudulent conveyance under the federal Bankruptcy Code or state fraudulent-transfer statutes. A *fraudulent conveyance* is the direct or indirect transfer of assets to a third party with the intent to or the effect of defrauding creditors by putting the assets out of the creditors' reach. A guaranty may be a fraudulent conveyance if it makes the guarantor's assets unavailable to creditors other than the party receiving the guaranty. For example, if the guarantor did not receive fair value in exchange for giving its guaranty, if the guarantor was insolvent at the time it gave its guaranty, or if the guarantor was rendered insolvent or left with unreasonably small capital as a result of giving its guaranty, the party receiving the guarantee may have an unfair advantage over other creditors of the guarantor. These issues must be carefully examined by the lender before accepting a guaranty.

Upstream Guaranty   An *upstream guaranty* occurs when subsidiaries guarantee the parent company's debt, or pledge their assets as security for the parent's debt. An upstream guaranty may be found fraudulent if the guarantor received none of the loan proceeds, or received an inadequate amount compared to the liability it incurred. Other creditors of the subsidiary (and the creditor's minority shareholders, if the subsidiary is less than wholly owned by the parent) may claim that the lender, as the beneficiary of the guaranty, received an unfair advantage at the other creditors' expense.

Leveraged Buyouts   Leveraged buyouts, in which acquisition of a company is financed largely through debt, may be subject to attack as fraudulent conveyances. For example, if a leveraged buyout is structured so that a newly formed corporation will acquire the stock of the target company using proceeds from a loan, the lender's source of repayment will be dividends paid from the target company to the borrower. In order to ensure that such a source of repayment will be available, the lender may require the target company to give a guaranty, which may or may not be secured by assets of the target company. Alternatively, the lender may require a merger between the target company and the borrower. Such guaranties or mergers will be invalidated if the target company did not receive a reasonably equivalent value, and if the target company was left insolvent, with assets that were unreasonably small in relation to its business, or with insufficient working capital.

■ Subordination

A *debt subordination* is an agreement whereby one or more creditors of a common debtor agree to defer payment of their claims until another creditor of the same debtor is fully paid. The indebtedness that is subordinated under the agreement is referred to as the subordinated or *junior debt*. The indebtedness that benefits from the subordination is called the *senior debt*.

The primary purpose of a debt subordination is to protect the senior creditor in the event of the debtor's insolvency. As long as the debtor is solvent, both the junior debt holder and the senior debt holder can expect to be paid. However, if the debtor becomes insolvent, there will be insufficient assets to satisfy all of its creditors. In such circumstances, creditors can expect to receive only a partial payment on their claims. In subordinating its claim, the holder of the junior debt agrees to yield its right of payment to the senior creditor until the senior creditor has been paid in full.

Corporations frequently use subordinated debt as a means of raising capital. The use of subordinated notes or subordinated debentures (long-term secured bonds) may have certain advantages over equity financing. For example, the interest payable on subordinated debt will be tax-deductible. In addition, the interest rate payable on subordinated debt is often less than the dividend rate that would have to be offered on comparable preferred stock.

Indebtedness to Insiders

When a borrower seeks short-term borrowings from a bank or other commercial lender, the lender will often require that the indebtedness of the borrower to insiders, such as officers, directors, and shareholders, be subordinated. This is especially the case when the borrower is a closely held corporation and the insider debt is significant in relation to the amount of the lender's loans.

Lien Subordination

A *lien subordination* is an agreement between two secured creditors whose respective security interests, liens, or mortgages attach to the same property. The subordinating party agrees that the lien of the other creditor shall have priority notwithstanding the relative priorities that the parties' liens would otherwise have under applicable law. Unlike debt subordination, a lien subordination does not limit the right of the subordinating party to accept payment from the debtor. Instead, the lien subordination has the effect of limiting the subordinating party's recourse to the collateral until the prior secured party's claim has been satisfied.

Equitable Subordination

A creditor's claim may be involuntarily postponed through application of the doctrine of *equitable subordination*. This doctrine was developed in bankruptcy law to prevent one creditor, through fraud or other wrongful conduct, from increasing its recovery at the expense of other creditors of the same debtor. The court will order that the creditor that acted wrongfully shall receive no payment from the debtor until the claims of all other creditors have been fully paid.

■ Business Bankruptcies

This section describes the two major types of business bankruptcies: liquidation under chapter 7, and reorganization under chapter 11. (Adjustments of debts for individuals under chapter 13 are covered in chapter 19.) The pros and cons of filing bankruptcy are discussed, from the points of view of the debtor and the creditors. Out-of-court resolutions, called workouts, are also discussed.

Chapter 7 Liquidations

A bankruptcy case is initiated by filing a petition. The filing of a bankruptcy petition automatically creates a *bankruptcy estate,* which consists of virtually all of the debtor's existing assets. A trustee is appointed to administer the estate. In a chapter 7 bankruptcy, sometimes called a *straight bankruptcy,* the trustee liquidates the estate and distributes the proceeds, first to secured creditors (to the extent of their collateral) and then in a prescribed order and pro rata within each level. The unencumbered funds are applied, first, to pay priority claims such as bankruptcy administrative expenses, wages or benefits up to $2,000 per employee, consumer deposits up to $900, and most unsecured taxes; next, to pay general unsecured creditors (with timely filed claims coming before tardy ones); then to pay noncompensatory fines or penalties; and last to pay legal interest on unsecured claims. In practice, the estate is rarely adequate to pay unsecured creditors even 50 cents on the dollar, and no-asset cases are quite common.

Individual Debtors

Individual debtors normally are *discharged*—that is, relieved—from bankruptcy (also called prepetition) obligations, except for nondischargeable debts such as taxes, recent educational loans, spousal or child support, fines or penalties, drunk-driving liabilities, or claims arising from fraud, theft, or willful and malicious injury. Individual debtors under chapter 7 are discussed more fully in chapter 19.

Nonindividual Debtors

Chapter 7 does not provide a discharge for corporations, partnerships, or similar business entities. Once their assets are sold, these debtors essentially become defunct shells whose unpaid obligations have no significance. Thus, from the vantage point of the debtor firm's management, the only virtue of a liquidation may be that the task of selling property and paying creditors falls to a trustee. The principals of closely held companies are often better advised to avoid bankruptcy and handle these chores themselves. Rather than adhering to the pro rata distribution model, they may wish to "prefer" some creditors by channeling funds first to those who are most likely to pursue them personally (such as holders of guaranties). Also, they may not want to expose earlier transactions (such as preferential payments) to scrutiny by a trustee, who can become a more troublesome foe than any of the company's creditors by invoking the "avoiding powers" discussed below.

Chapter 11 Reorganizations

Chapter 11 is designed for reorganizing troubled businesses, from single-asset limited partnerships to huge publicly held corporations like the oil giant Texaco, the pharmaceutical manufacturer A. H. Robins, the retailer Federated Department Stores, or the building materials supplier Johns-Manville. The treatment of the debtor's creditors and holders of ownership interests, and the future of its business are set forth in a plan developed by one or more of the parties. If the plan meets the statutory requirements and is confirmed by the court, it becomes a master contract that redefines the legal relationships among all who have claims against (or interests in) the debtor, and it binds even those who do not consent to its terms.

The Plan

All plans divide claims and equity interests into separate classes according to their legal attributes. For example, lienholders' claims are classified by collateral and rank (often resulting in one claim per class, because each lien confers distinct rights and usually secures only one claim). Relevant priority claims (such as wages or consumer deposits) are put into discrete classes, separate from general unsecured claims. Holders of preferred shares are grouped separately from common shareholders.

A plan also must prescribe treatment for the claims and interests in each class. Some plans simply extend the time for repaying debts; others reduce the amounts payable. A reduction in the amount payable is known as a *composition.* In many cases, creditors exchange all or part of their claims for preferred or common stock or other ownership interests in the business, thereby diluting or extinguishing the rights of the prebankruptcy shareholders. Sometimes, the entire business will be sold free of claims, with creditors dividing the sale proceeds. A plan can even call for liquidation and distribution comparable to the chapter 7 process.

In addition, the plan must explain the intended means for its execution. Plans often provide for payments from cash on hand, future earnings, asset sales, new capital contributions, or some combination of sources.

Unless they agree otherwise, priority claimants usually are entitled to full payment when the plan becomes effective, except that prepetition unsecured taxes may be paid in installments over six years from the assessment date, with interest at the market rate.

Confirmation

To be confirmed, a plan must meet numerous statutory requirements. Some of the less technical requirements are discussed below.

Feasibility   The plan must be feasible. There is no point in replacing the debtor's existing obligations with a new set of obligations that the debtor cannot meet.

> 66
>
> *The plan must be feasible. There is no point in replacing the debtor's existing obligations with a new set of obligations that the debtor cannot meet.*

Best Interests of Creditors   Unless accepted unanimously, the plan must pass the "best interests of creditors" test. Dissenters must be given a bundle of rights the current value of which is at least as great as the distribution they would receive through a chapter 7 liquidation.

Reorganization Bonus   It should be relatively easy to satisfy the fixed minimum standards for confirmation if the business has significant value as a going concern. In that case, the viability of a plan often turns upon how it proposes to split what might be labeled the "reorganization bonus." This bonus or premium is the difference between the aggregate liquidation value of the assets and the worth of the business as an operating whole. Ordinarily, it must be distributed according to existing priorities. Unless it accepts less favorable treatment, each class of creditor is paid fully before any distribution is made to any junior class. Similarly, creditors are paid in full (with postconfirmation interest) before equity holders receive anything.

Disclosure Statement   Before deciding whether to accept the plan, creditors and shareholders are entitled to receive a disclosure statement that the court has found contains adequate information to enable them to make an informed judgment. This disclosure process largely displaces otherwise applicable laws and regulations governing the issuance and sale of securities, including the requirements of the Securities Act of 1933, described in chapter 22.

Acceptance   A creditor class accepts the plan if the affirmative ballots represent a simple majority and represent two-thirds of the total claim amounts of those voting. An equity class accepts if the favorable ballots represent two-thirds of the voted interests.

Impaired Claims   If a plan impairs any class of claims, then it cannot be confirmed unless at least one impaired class accepts it (excluding favorable votes cast by insiders). Claims are considered *impaired* if the plan does not provide for full cash payment on its effective date, and if it alters the creditors' legal, equitable, or contractual rights in any way (except by curing defaults and reinstating the maturity of the claim).

If the basic requirements discussed above are met and all impaired classes accept the plan, the plan should be confirmed.

Cram-Down Confirmation

Though rejected by a class, the plan can still be confirmed by a *cram down,* that is, confirmed over the objections of creditors. However, a cram down can occur only if the court finds that the plan "does not discriminate unfairly" and that it is "fair and equitable." Although both phrases have technical meanings that are open to interpretation, it is the phrase "fair and equitable" that is more frequently the subject of debate. If the rejecting class consists of secured claims, the plan ordinarily can be found fair and equitable only if creditors will retain their liens until they receive full payment in cash. The cash payment must have a current value at least as great as the value of their liens. For other creditors and equity holders, the plan will be considered fair and equitable only if no class junior to the naysayers will receive anything under the plan, or if the rejecting class is to receive value equivalent to immediate payment in full.

Thus, to cram down a plan that would distribute stock in satisfaction of claims, the proponent must show that the stock will neither overpay nor underpay those who receive it. The value of the stock turns on the going-concern value of the business, which is often a controversial issue. When classes have not accepted a debt-for-stock plan, the confirmation hearing can easily become a battle among expert witnesses arguing over whether higher or lower multiples or multipliers should be used to capitalize the reorganized debtor's expected earnings, which are themselves subject to competing projections.

Plan Negotiations

Because confirmation by cram down is both difficult and uncertain, plan proponents frequently try to draft terms that will encourage broad acceptance. For the first 120 days (or for a longer or shorter time that the court may fix), only the debtor can propose a plan. After this exclusivity period expires, any party may propose a plan. Thus a debtor who does not bargain reasonably may be faced with a competing plan that might be threatened or proposed by a major secured creditor or by the official committee that is appointed in chapter 11 cases to represent the interests of unsecured creditors. Even if the debtor is the only party proposing a plan, an endorsement from the creditors' committee can be essential to obtain the creditor support necessary to achieve confirmation without a cram down. Taken together, these dynamics promote negotiation and accommodation among the interested parties. Most successful plans in large chapter 11 cases reflect such compromises.

Discharge

Just as a discharge under chapter 7 can give individual debtors a fresh start, confirmation under chapter 11 can give reorganized debtors a new financial beginning under the plan. For individual debtors, however, the same debts that would be nondischargeable under chapter 7 are excluded from the chapter 11 discharge. Also, a plan that calls for liquidation and cessation of business will only afford a discharge to individuals who would have been eligible for one in chapter 7. Because entities such as corporations or partnerships are not eligible for a discharge under chapter 7, they will similarly not be discharged under chapter 11 in the event of a liquidation. If the business is rehabilitated, the debtor entity is liable for preconfirmation claims only insofar as they are expressly preserved by the plan. No bankruptcy discharge, whether under chapter 11 or otherwise, protects the debtor's co-obligors, such as guarantors or joint tortfeasors.

International Consideration

Winding-up proceedings in Australia are essentially ex parte: only the creditors appear before the court. As a result, they do not provide debtors the same recourse as U.S. bankruptcy rules. Other countries, such as Germany, do not provide for the complete discharge of debts in bankruptcy, only arrangement for their payment over time.

Other Chapters

In addition to chapter 7 (which includes special subchapters for commodity and stockbroker liquidations), chapter 11 (which includes a subchapter for railroad reorganizations), and chapter 13 (consumer bankruptcy), the Bankruptcy Code contains two chapters that are more limited, and three others of broader significance. Chapter 12, a hybrid of chapters 11 and 13, provides debt adjustment, but not a superdischarge, for family farmers (a technically defined term) whose aggregate debts do not exceed $1.5 million. Chapter 9, largely patterned after chapter 11, provides debt adjustment for municipalities. Chapters 1, 3, and 5 apply to all bankruptcies. These chapters contain important provisions—discussed in the sections that follow—such as the automatic stay, rules for claim allowance and priority, the definition of the bankruptcy estate and framework for its administration, and the trustee's avoiding powers.

Bankruptcy Procedures

Individuals can wipe the slate clean immediately through a chapter 7 liquidation, or obtain a superdischarge by devoting their future earnings to creditors through a chapter 13 plan. Troubled business debtors who file under chapter 11 may be able to preserve value for the benefit of shareholders or other equity interests. Bankruptcy also offers several other advantages for debtors.

Automatic Stay

The most immediate and dramatic advantage of any bankruptcy filing is the *automatic stay,* which instantly suspends most litigation and collection activities against the debtor, its property, or that of the bankruptcy estate. Many debtors file for bankruptcy on the eve of foreclosure to forestall the loss of crucial assets; others file primarily to stave off litigation or collection activities. The latter group includes such notable bankruptcy refugees as Johns-Manville (sued for thousands of asbestos-related injuries), A. H. Robbins (facing claims by thousands of women harmed by an intrauterine device), and Texaco (unable to post a bond while appealing the multibillion dollar judgment against it for interfering with Pennzoil's efforts to acquire Getty Oil).

Though they may feel frustrated, creditors must honor the automatic stay. As the following case demonstrates, failure to do so can be costly.

Historical Perspective
From Mosaic Law to Vulture Capitalists

The principle that debtors should be permitted to discharge certain debts has ancient roots. As early as 1400 B.C., Mosaic law required unconditional forgiveness of debts every seven years to encourage a proper focus on social relationships. The word "bankruptcy" is believed to have evolved from the Latin words "banca" and "rupta," referring to the broken bench or moneychangers' table left behind by failed merchants fleeing from their creditors. In 1542, lawmakers under King Henry VIII passed a Bankruptcy Act to regulate failing English merchants. Over the centuries, strong sanctions for insolvency, including imprisonment, generally made bankruptcy a remedy for creditors rather than a relief for debtors.

The roots of the American bankruptcy system can be traced to the experiences of colonists who were refugees from debtors' prisons in Europe. The drafters of the Constitution, recognizing the importance of debtor relief, gave Congress the exclusive right to establish national bankruptcy laws and thereby override the states' treatment of debtors and creditors. The first bankruptcy enactments, early in the nineteenth century, contained no provisions for voluntary bankruptcy. It was not until 1898, when a severe depression forced many railroads into receivership, that Congress used its bankruptcy power to allow troubled enterprises to reorganize. The Bankruptcy Act of 1898 enabled failing railroads and other businesses to continue operating while reorganizing, generally stripping shareholders of their interests.

Financier J. P. Morgan reorganized so many busted railroads that his work in this area became known as "Morganization." Fifty years after Morgan, the trustee for the estate of Alfred I. du Pont obtained control of the Florida East Coast Railway by holding 56% of its defaulted mortgage bonds. Astute purchases of defaulted rail bonds in the 1940s provided the start for a number of Wall Street fortunes.[a]

In 1978, Congress enacted the Bankruptcy Reform Act, which created the Bankruptcy Code. That legislation, the result of nearly a decade of intensive study and debate about problems in the bankruptcy system and proposed reforms, made sweeping changes in the law, most of them favorable to debtors. It created an independent system of bankruptcy courts in each judicial district, with jurisdiction over controversies pertaining to bankruptcy cases; and it provided for the appointment by the president, with the advice and consent of the Senate, of bankruptcy judges for 14-year terms.

In 1982, a plurality of the Supreme Court ruled that the 1978 Act's grant of jurisdiction to the bankruptcy courts violated the Constitution's requirement for the separation of powers, because it gave broad discretion to Congress to create specialized legislative courts, thereby eroding the domain of the Judicial Branch. Bankruptcy judges appointed under the 1978 Act were not given the life tenure that the Constitution mandates for judges exercising the judicial power of the United States. The Supreme Court stayed the effective date of its decision to permit Congress to enact a bankruptcy system that would pass constitutional muster.[b] However, the stay expired before Congress acted, so the Court's ruling took effect. The Judicial Conference of the United States promulgated an emergency rule for the interim operation of the bankruptcy court system, and all of the districts adopted it.

To cure the problems highlighted by the Supreme Court, Congress passed the Bankruptcy Amendments and Federal Judgeship Act of 1984 (BAFJA). BAFJA vests the district courts with primary bankruptcy jurisdiction; these courts are authorized to refer matters within that jurisdiction to the bankruptcy courts, and all have entered orders of reference to the bankruptcy courts. Bankruptcy judges thus operate today as units of the federal district courts and, as such, are authorized to enter final judgments on core proceedings—that is, proceedings that are an intrinsic part of the bankruptcy procedure, such as confirmation of bankruptcy plans—and in cases arising under the Bankruptcy Code. However, their orders may be appealed to the district courts.[c] In noncore proceedings, unless the parties consent to a final judgment, the bankruptcy judge may submit only proposed findings of fact and conclusions of law. Because of constitutional requirements, the district courts retain the ultimate responsibility for entering dispositive orders in noncore matters.

---

a. Matthew Schifrin, "Enough Already!," *Forbes,* May 28, 1990, 126.

b. *Northern Pipeline Construction Co. v. Marathon Pipe Line Co.,* 458 U.S. 50, 102 S.Ct. 2858 (1982).

c. 28 U.S.C. § 157(b) (1988).

Historical Perspective
From Mosaic Law to Vulture Capitalists, *continued*

In light of the massive defaults on junk bonds in 1989 and the early 1990s, some have questioned whether Congress gave debtors too much relief under the Bankruptcy Code. The lead-in to a *Forbes* article on the subject summarizes the state of affairs as of 1990: "In the old days, a debt was an obligation and bankruptcy was a disgrace. Nowadays bond issuers concoct ever more ways to stiff investors."[d]

In the *Forbes* article, commentator Matthew Schifrin compares the debtor-lenient U.S. system with other Western countries, in which a debtor's property is auctioned off if she can't pay her debts:

> That's why Australian conglomerator Alan Bond is scrambling to save his highly leveraged empire. The bankruptcy laws in Australia have scant provision for reorganization. If you owe and you can't pay, your creditors can liquidate your company.[e]

In the United States, the debtor usually retains control of the enterprise while it is being reorganized.

However, even in the United States, bondholders are fighting back. A new breed, called "vulture capitalists," is beginning to develop. They buy up bonds at depressed prices and then seek to throw out existing management. Or as happened to chapter 11 debtor R. H. Macy & Co. in 1994, a competitor—in this case, Federated Department Stores—can buy up senior debt and promise bondholders more than they might otherwise receive if the debtor stays independent, to force a merger of the two companies as part of the plan of reorganization needed for the debtor to emerge from bankruptcy.[f]

---

f. Patrick M. Reilly and Laura Jereski, "Macy, Federated Reach Accord in Merger Talks," *The Wall Street Journal*, July 15, 1994, A3.

---

d. Matthew Schifrin, "Enough Already!," *Forbes*, May 28, 1990, 126.
e. *Ibid.*, 128.

■ A Case in Point: Summary

Case 24.3
IN RE COMPUTER COMMUNICATIONS, INC.
United States Court of Appeals for the Ninth Circuit
824 F.2d 725 (9th Cir. 1987).

FACTS Codex Corporation, a designer and manufacturer of communications equipment and networks used for transmitting information between complex computer systems, entered into a joint marketing and development agreement in April 1979 with Computer Communications, Inc. (CCI), a manufacturer of computer equipment and software. Under the agreement, Codex agreed to make minimum quarterly purchases of equipment and software from CCI for incorporation in Codex's products. The agreement was amended on November 4, 1980, and its term was extended to four years commencing in April 1979. The amended agreement required CCI to continue to provide technical support and spare parts. On November 6, 1980, two days after the parties executed the amended agreement, CCI filed a petition under chapter 11.

On December 30, 1980, Codex notified CCI that it was terminating the agreement pursuant to a clause in the amended agreement that expressly permitted termination in the event of a filing in bankruptcy. Codex failed to

Case 24.3 continued on following page

*Case **24.3** continued*

make its minimum purchases for the quarter ending December 31, 1980, and failed to make any of its quarterly minimum purchases after that.

CCI filed suit in bankruptcy court on January 30, 1981, alleging that Codex's termination of the agreement violated the automatic-stay provision of the Bankruptcy Code. On February 23, 1981, Codex notified CCI that it was terminating purchases of equipment from CCI pursuant to a clause in the amended agreement that permitted unilateral notice of termination by Codex upon payment of not more than $400,000.

The bankruptcy court held that Codex had willfully violated the automatic stay. The court awarded general damages of $4,750,000 (apparently based on loss of projected profits), plus $250,000 in punitive damages. Codex appealed.

ISSUE PRESENTED   Does unilateral termination of an agreement with a debtor who has filed for bankruptcy violate the automatic-stay provision?

SUMMARY OF OPINION   The U.S. Court of Appeals upheld the award, holding that Codex violated the automatic-stay statute by terminating its contract unilaterally, rather than applying for relief from the bankruptcy court. According to the legislative history, the purpose of the automatic stay is to give the debtor a "breathing spell" from creditors, stop all collection efforts, and permit the debtor to attempt repayment or reorganization.

Codex argued that the contract was not property of the bankrupt estate and was therefore not automatically stayed. The court rejected this argument, finding that the contract did fall within the definition of "property of the estate."

RESULT   Codex violated the automatic stay, and was liable for the debtor's loss of projected profits and for punitive damages.

COMMENTS   This case makes it clear that even if a party to a contract has a unilateral right to terminate it, once the other party is in bankruptcy, the contract cannot be terminated unless the bankruptcy court orders relief from the automatic stay. Willful violations of the automatic stay may also constitute contempt of court and warrant punitive damages.

Ethical Consideration

CCI extended its agreement with Codex only two days before filing for bankruptcy. It seems clear that Codex would not have renewed the agreement if it had known that CCI was going to declare bankruptcy. The managers of CCI locked in a favorable contract by concealing their intentions from Codex. Was the CCI managers' conduct unethical or just good business?

By stopping creditors in their tracks, the stay provides a breathing spell that can enable a chapter 11 debtor to focus on the operation of the business and the reorganization of its financial affairs. The stay is not a permanent shield, however. The court may authorize creditors to resume collection efforts, most often foreclosure on collateral, for cause—that is, if there is inadequate protection of the creditors' property interests, as when the value of collateral declines with use and no replacement security is provided. Relief from the stay will also be granted if the debtor has no equity in property and a stay is not necessary for effective reorganization. Such relief from the automatic stay becomes more likely as time passes without progress toward reorganization. However, the automatic stay is rarely lifted to permit garden-variety litigation against the debtor.

Administration of Claims

Instead of lawsuits, creditors file a relatively simple *proof of claim.* This serves to centralize the administration of most claims in the bankruptcy court, where the process is streamlined. The proof-of-claim requirement in a chapter 11 bankruptcy is deemed satisfied for claims listed in the debtor's schedules as uncontingent and undisputed (unless the creditor wishes to claim more than the debtor acknowledges is due).

Filed claims are deemed valid or "allowed" unless and until someone objects. Except for personal-injury or wrongful-death claims, which are triable to a jury in the district court, disputed claims normally are resolved through a quick hearing before the bankruptcy judge. If resolution would unduly delay administration of the bankruptcy case (such as when a claim is contingent upon a future event), the bankruptcy court will estimate the allowable amount of certain claims.

Some claims are limited in bankruptcy. For example, a landlord's damages claim for termination of a lease cannot exceed rent for the greater of one year or 15% (but not to exceed three years) of the remaining term. Similarly, a terminated employee's damages claim may not exceed one year's compensation. Unless the estate could pay all claims in a liquidation, postpetition interest is allowed only to secured creditors that can recover it from their collateral.

Control

Though handling claims effectively is important, preserving value to pay them is more important. The debtor's track record for good management may be uneven. Nevertheless, based upon the debtor's presumed knowledge of the business, and incentive to save it for the benefit of all concerned, chapter 11 leaves the debtor in possession of the bankruptcy estate. A *debtor in possession* (DIP) has basically the same powers and duties as a trustee. (Because of this general congruity, and unless the context clearly indicates otherwise, references to the DIP below should be understood to apply equally to a duly appointed trustee.)

Under chapter 11, an independent trustee normally will not be appointed to displace the DIP without proof that current management is either dishonest or clearly incompetent. Thus, subject to the constraints discussed below, chapter 11 usually permits the debtor to operate in the ordinary course of business. This, together with the automatic stay and the initial exclusive right to propose a plan, may represent the distressed debtor's best opportunity to exercise control over its fate.

Obtaining Credit

The DIP's first priority often is to stay in business and continue (or resume) providing goods and services to customers at a profit. Yet, as observed at the outset, poor cash flow often paves the way to chapter 11. Although the bankruptcy system does not manufacture money, it may enhance or create some funding possibilities.

> **"**
> *Although the bankruptcy system does not manufacture money, it may enhance or create some funding possibilities.*

Customer's Payments The debtor's liquidity crisis sometimes stems from a secured lender's insistence that all encumbered customer payments be applied to the loan, leaving little or no cash to operate. If a bankruptcy petition is filed, customer payments on prebankruptcy accounts will remain the lender's cash collateral, but the court may authorize the DIP to use the funds if the lender's position is adequately protected. Such protection might be found in surplus collateral that gives the lender an ample equity cushion, or it might be provided by granting the lender a substitute lien on postpetition inventory and receivables. Of course, the court may underestimate the need for protection, and this risk often prods an otherwise recalcitrant lender to negotiate terms for use of its cash collateral.

Extension of Unsecured Credit Filing for reorganization may encourage suppliers (and perhaps other lenders) to extend unsecured credit. During the debtor's prebankruptcy decline, conventional trade terms (such as payment due 30 days after invoice) often become unavailable as the debtor falls behind on accounts payable, and word of its shaky condition spreads. Fearful that they may recover only pennies on the dollar from credit sales if the debtor collapses, vendors typically begin requiring cash on delivery or even in advance. This only aggravates the debtor's problems. Ironically, the same suppliers, particularly those who are sophisticated and who value the debtor's patronage most, may be willing to resume regular credit transactions with the DIP.

Flexibility returns because postpetition debts incurred in the ordinary course of doing business are allowable as administrative expenses, which are accorded priority over virtually all other unsecured claims. Thus, vendors that extend postpetition credit expect full payment on those transactions. In so doing, they may strengthen the debtor's business and promote a greater recovery on their prepetition claims.

Secured Borrowings   The debtor's ability to borrow on a secured basis can be similarly enhanced in a chapter 11 reorganization, mainly because collateral may be more available. For example, assets acquired after the bankruptcy petition is filed (other than those derived directly from prebankruptcy collateral) will not be subject to prepetition security agreements designed to cover such after-acquired property. Therefore, a debtor who can produce inventory or generate accounts receivable after the bankruptcy filing may have enough unencumbered property to support new secured loans. Moreover, if credit is not otherwise available, the court can authorize borrowing that is secured by a priming lien, provided that the preexisting lienholder is adequately protected. A *priming lien* is a lien that is senior to a previously granted security interest. Thus, for example, a first mortgage on raw land might be involuntarily subordinated to a new lien that will secure a DIP-developer's construction financing.

Court Oversight   On occasion, the bankruptcy court's oversight alone may help the debtor arrange new secured loans. By obtaining court approval after giving appropriate notice to other creditors, lenders can virtually immunize their repayment rights and security interests from the attacks by other creditors that sometimes undermine prebankruptcy loans.

Turnover of Debtor's Property

Though usually less expeditious than borrowing, other bankruptcy tools also can help the DIP obtain funds for operations and enhance the value of the estate. Almost anyone can be compelled to turn over property of the estate that could be used by the DIP. Thus, if adequate protection is provided, a lender who has frozen the debtor's deposit accounts at the banking institution or a taxing authority that has seized them may be required to relinquish these funds.

Avoiding Powers

Still more striking is the DIP's ability to invoke the potent *avoiding powers* that trustees can use to invalidate or reverse certain prebankruptcy transactions.

Strong-Arm Clause   Under the *strong-arm clause,* the DIP is granted the rights of a hypothetical creditor who extended credit to the debtor at the time of bankruptcy and who, as a result, either obtained a judicial lien on all property in which the debtor has an interest, or obtained an execution against the debtor that was returned unsatisfied. The DIP also has the rights that a bona fide purchaser of real property from the debtor would have if the transfer was perfected. The DIP has these powers and rights regardless of whether a judgment-lien creditor or a bona fide purchaser actually exists.

Thus, if a deed of trust or mortgage was not properly recorded before bankruptcy, or a security interest in personal property was not duly perfected against third-party claims under applicable law (typically the Uniform Commercial Code), the DIP can establish superior rights to the affected property for the benefit of the estate. This is the case even if the debtor could not have recovered such assets outside of bankruptcy. In addition, the DIP can avoid—that is, invalidate—any transaction that an existing unsecured creditor could invalidate. This might include unauthorized dividends to shareholders, procedurally defective bulk sales, or transfers considered fraudulent as to creditors under nonbankruptcy laws such as a state fraudulent-transfer statute.

The scope of the DIP's strong-arm powers usually depends on state property law, so it may differ from case to case. For example, in many states, the rights of a creditor holding a judicial lien against real property are superior to those of a party with an unrecorded mortgage against the same property. Using the strong-arm powers, a DIP can avoid the unrecorded lien. Similarly, where a judicial creditor's lien would have priority over an unperfected security interest, the DIP may use his hypothetical status to invalidate a security interest that was not perfected by filing or possession, but would otherwise be valid between a debtor and its creditor. If state law permits, the DIP may reverse other transfers of the debtor's property and void otherwise valid obligations of the debtor. Any value the DIP recovers pursuant to the strong-arm clause inures to the benefit of the creditors of the bankruptcy estate.

Fraudulent Transfers   The DIP may invoke the Bankruptcy Code to avoid fraudulent transfers or obligations. In general, these arise from transactions that occured within a year before bankruptcy that: (1) are actually intended to hinder, delay, or defraud creditors, or (2) provide less than reasonably equivalent value in exchange and leave the debtor insolvent or without sufficient capital to engage in business or to pay expected debts. Most states have roughly parallel fraudulent-transfer laws, but the Bankruptcy Code's version may be broader. For example, the state laws may be inapplicable to distressed foreclosure sales that are noncollusive and procedurally proper; bankruptcy law has been applied to invalidate such sales if the proceeds are less than 70% of the collateral's fair market value. Thus, although a good-faith buyer should have a lien for the value given (which is usually the amount of the secured debt), the DIP may be able to reverse the foreclosure and recapture equity.

Preferences   The avoiding power used most extensively is the ability to recover preferences. *Preferences* are transfers to (or for the benefit of) creditors on account of antecedent debts that are made from an insolvent debtor's property within 90 days before bankruptcy and that enable the creditors to receive more than they would through a chapter 7 liquidation. (The preference window is enlarged to a year before bankruptcy if the benefited creditor is an insider—that is, someone in a position to control the debtor's conduct, such as a relative, partner, director, officer, or substantial shareholder.) Preferences are made avoidable in bankruptcy both to discourage creditors from dismembering a troubled business in their race for its assets, and to foster equal distribution among similarly situated claimants. Subject to limited exceptions, the DIP can recover voluntary or involuntary preferential payments and strip away preferential security interests or collection liens, all for the benefit of the bankruptcy estate.

A payment is only a preference if it is for an antecedent, or preexisting, debt. However, to avoid penalizing creditors that continue to deal in a customary fashion with the debtor during its slide into bankruptcy, current payments in the ordinary course of business cannot be recovered as preferences. As the following case demonstrates, it is not always clear whether a payment is for an antecedent debt, or is a current payment in the ordinary course of business.

■ **A Case in Point:**   **In the Language of the Court**

Case 24.4
UNION BANK v. WOLAS
Supreme Court of the
United States
502 U.S. 151, 112 S.Ct. 527
(1991).

FACTS   ZZZZ Best Company, Inc. made two interest payments and paid a loan commitment fee on a long-term debt to Union Bank. Within ninety days, ZZZZ Best Company filed a petition under chapter 7 of the United States Bankruptcy Code. Herbert Wolas was appointed chapter 7 trustee of the company's estate, and filed a complaint against the bank to recover the payments, claiming that they were voidable preferences under 11 U.S.C. § 547(b). The bankruptcy court held that the payments on this long-term debt were made "in the ordinary course of business" under 11 U.S.C. § 547(c)(2) and therefore excepted from the scope of § 547(b). The federal district court agreed with the bankruptcy court, but the court of appeals reversed.

ISSUE PRESENTED   Can payments on long-term debt qualify for the ordinary course of business exception to the trustee's power to avoid preferential transfers?

OPINION   STEVENS, J., writing for the U.S. Supreme Court:

. . . .

III

The Bank and the trustee agree that § 547 is intended to serve two basic policies that are fairly described in the House Committee Report. The Committee explained:

A preference is a transfer that enables a creditor to receive payment of a greater percentage of his claim against the debtor than he would have received if the

Case 24.4 continued on following page

*Case **24.4** continued*

transfer had not been made and he had participated in the distribution of the assets of the bankrupt estate. The purpose of the preference section is two-fold. First, by permitting the trustee to avoid prebankruptcy transfers that occur within a short period before bankruptcy, creditors are discouraged from racing to the courthouse to dismember the debtor during his slide into bankruptcy. The protection thus afforded the debtor often enables him to work his way out of a difficult financial situation through cooperation with all of his creditors. Second, and more important, the preference provisions facilitate the prime bankruptcy policy of equality of distribution among creditors of the debtor. Any creditor that received a greater payment than others of his class is required to disgorge so that all may share equally. The operation of the preference section to deter "the race of diligence" of creditors to dismember the debtor before bankruptcy furthers the second goal of the preference section—that of equality of distribution.

As this comment demonstrates, the two policies are not entirely independent. On the one hand, any exception for a payment on account of an antecedent debt tends to favor the payee over other creditors and therefore may conflict with the policy of equal treatment. On the other hand, the ordinary course of business exception may benefit all creditors by deterring the "race to the courthouse" and enabling the struggling debtor to continue operating its business.

Respondent places primary emphasis, as did the Court of Appeals, on the interest in equal distribution. When a debtor is insolvent, a transfer to one creditor necessarily impairs the claims of the debtor's other unsecured and undersecured creditors. By authorizing the avoidance of such preferential transfers, § 547(b) empowers the trustee to restore equal status to all creditors. Respondent thus contends that the ordinary course of business exception should be limited to short-term debt so the trustee may order that preferential long-term debt payments be returned to the estate to be distributed among all of the creditors.

But the statutory text—which makes no distinction between short-term debt and long-term debt—precludes an analysis that divorces the policy of favoring equal distribution from the policy of discouraging creditors from racing to the courthouse to dismember the debtor. Long-term creditors, as well as trade creditors, may seek a head start in that race. Thus, even if we accept the Court of Appeals' conclusion that the availability of the ordinary business exception to long-term creditors does not directly further the policy of equal treatment, we must recognize that it does further the policy of deterring the race to the courthouse and, as the House Report recognized, may indirectly further the goal of equal distribution as well. Whether Congress has wisely balanced the sometimes conflicting policies underlying § 547 is not a question that we are authorized to decide.

IV

In sum, we hold that payments on long-term debt, as well as payments on short-term debt, may qualify for the ordinary course of business exception to the trustee's power to avoid preferential transfers. We express no opinion, however, on the question whether the Bankruptcy Court correctly concluded that the Debtor's payments of interest and the loan commitment fee qualify for the ordinary course of business exception, § 547(c)(2). In particular, we do not decide whether the loan involved in this case was incurred in the ordinary course of the Debtor's business and of the Bank's business, whether the payments were made in the ordinary course of business, or whether the payments were made according to ordinary business terms. These questions remain open for the Court of Appeals on remand.

The judgment of the Court of Appeals is reversed and the case is remanded for further proceedings consistent with this opinion.

RESULT Payments on long-term debt may qualify for the ordinary course of business exception to the trustee's power to avoid preferential transfers.

Questions
1. Would a policy of encouraging short-term credit transactions enable troubled debtors to regain their financial footing without resorting to bankruptcy?
2. Might the *Wolas* decision increase the availability to debtors of unsecured funds?

Setoff Rights A creditor exercising a setoff right automatically deducts what the debtor owes the creditor from what the creditor owes the debtor. By analogy to the preference provision, creditors who exercise setoff rights within 90 days before bankruptcy can be required to disgorge such offsets to the extent that they decreased their obligations to the debtor within the 90-day period. This provision may deter lenders from setting off against the debtor's bank accounts, as (subject to the automatic stay) their setoff rights normally would otherwise be honored in bankruptcy.

Statutory Liens The DIP can avoid certain statutory liens, including those that first arise upon insolvency or that would not have been enforceable against a bona fide purchaser of the encumbered property when the bankruptcy was filed. This prevents state law from creating hidden priorities that would distort the federal bankruptcy distribution scheme.

Collective Bargaining Agreements The rules for avoiding collective bargaining agreements changed after Frank Lorenzo used chapter 11 to avoid Continental Airlines' collective bargaining agreements. In the early 1980s, when labor rejected his demands for sizable wage concessions, Frank Lorenzo took Continental into a chapter 11 proceeding, and repudiated its collective bargaining agreements. Continental Airlines emerged from bankruptcy a nonunion carrier with a reduced wage structure.

Organized labor protested the use of the Bankruptcy Code by Lorenzo (and, increasingly, others) to break unions. In 1984, Congress responded, amending the Bankruptcy Code so that a debtor no longer has broad discretion to abrogate unilaterally its labor contracts. Instead, a debtor may reject collective bargaining agreements over the objection of its unions only if: (1) it has presented labor with a proposal showing that rejection is economically necessary and fair to the affected parties; (2) it has

bargained to impasse; and (3) the bankruptcy court finds that on balance, fairness clearly favors rejection.

In 1989, with Lorenzo at its helm, Eastern Airlines demanded that its unions agree to reductions in wages and other benefits. Labor refused, and a strike ensued. Within days, Eastern filed a bankruptcy petition for reorganization.

History appeared to be about to repeat itself, but the similarities with the Continental bankruptcy ended there. The consummation of Lorenzo's agreement to sell Eastern Airlines' assets to former baseball commissioner Peter Ueberroth was delayed, if not killed, by the demands of Eastern's unions.

Contracts and Leases

The DIP has the option of assuming or rejecting prebankruptcy *executory contracts*—that is, contracts that have not yet been performed—or unexpired leases. Assumption preserves the debtor's rights and duties under the existing relationship, while rejection terminates them.

If an executory contract or unexpired lease is a valuable asset, the DIP will want to assume it so that it can be preserved for the reorganizing business or sold at a profit. For example, assumption is advantageous when it allows the debtor to sell or buy goods at a favorable price or to lease space or equipment at better-than-market rents. Even a contract or lease in default can be assumed provided the DIP cures and compensates for the breach and gives adequate assurance of future performance. Once assumed, the contract or lease obligations are allowable as administrative expenses, like those arising from other authorized postpetition transactions. Despite contrary contractual restrictions, any assumed contract or lease can be sold and assigned intact if the prospective assignee's future performance is adequately assured.

On the other hand, by rejecting a disadvantageous contract or lease, the DIP can escape burdensome performance obligations. The nondebtor party to the contract or lease will be deemed to have a prepetition damages claim for breach, and thus will be treated like others whose claims arise from prebankruptcy transactions.

However, a debtor may sometimes be prevented from shedding its prebankruptcy obligations, as in the following case.

■ **A Case in Point:**   **Summary**

Case 24.5
PENSION BENEFIT
GUARANTY CORPORATION
v. LTV CORPORATION
Supreme Court of the
United States
496 U.S. 633, 110 S.Ct. 2668
(1990).

FACTS   In July 1986, LTV Corporation and its subsidiaries (collectively, LTV), steel and aerospace companies, filed petitions for reorganization under chapter 11 of the Bankruptcy Code. By the end of 1986, LTV had unfunded pension plan liabilities of almost $2.3 billion. One principal goal of the bankruptcies was to terminate LTV's pension plans, shift responsibility for unfunded liabilities to the federal Pension Benefit Guaranty Corporation (PBGC), and negotiate new pension arrangements with employees. PBGC's funds come from mandatory insurance payments made by employers that maintain ongoing pension plans.

LTV's goal looked reachable. First, when advised that LTV could not fund its pension plans, PBGC determined that the plans' liabilities could increase by as much as $700 million if the plant shutdowns anticipated by LTV occurred and if LTV terminated the plans. Following termination, PBGC was required by ERISA to pay certain benefits that the plans could not cover. Second, LTV settled disputes with the steelworkers. The resulting collective bargaining agreements restored some benefits that neither the terminated pension plans nor PBGC would pay.

The obstacle, which ultimately proved insurmountable, was PBGC's policy against follow-on plans, arrangements that wrap around PBGC's payments to give participants substantially the same benefits they would have received had a pension plan not been terminated. Finding that LTV's new pension benefits constituted an "abusive" follow-on plan, and that LTV's finances had improved, PBGC decided to restore the terminated pension plans and make LTV responsible for funding them.

When LTV refused to comply with the restoration decision, PBGC initiated an enforcement action. The federal district court vacated (that is, voided) the restoration decision, and the court of appeals affirmed. PBGC appealed.

ISSUE PRESENTED   May the PBGC prohibit follow-on plans?

SUMMARY OF OPINION   The U.S. Supreme Court reversed the appeals court decision and held in favor of PBGC. Finding that follow-on plans may lead to more plan terminations and increased PBGC liability, the Supreme Court held that PBGC's anti-follow-on policy and restoration decision were permissible. The premise underlying the PBGC policy is that employee resistance, a significant check on the termination of pension plans, will be greater if a company cannot use a follow-on plan to restore employees to the position they occupied before plan termination. The Supreme Court held this premise to be "eminently reasonable."

RESULT   A reorganizing debtor cannot adopt a plan whereby it would transfer its pension commitments to the federal pension insurance agency, which would pay reduced benefits to be supplemented by the debtor when the debtor's financial situation has improved.

COMMENTS   This case makes it more difficult for struggling companies to reduce debt by foisting pension-plan shortfalls onto the federal pension insurance agency. Hence, bankruptcy may lose its appeal for debtors that seek to reorganize by transferring accrued pension debt, and firms may have a greater incentive to make up pension-plan shortfalls. By upholding the anti-follow-on policy, this case also creates a precedent that could lessen the need for a multibillion dollar U.S. government bailout of the Pension Benefit Guaranty Corporation, which would otherwise be responsible for underfunded pension plans whose termination was made palatable to employees by the adoption of follow-on plans.

Sale of Property

Bankruptcy can facilitate favorable sales of assets other than contracts or leases. For example, if partition or division of property jointly owned by the debtor and another is impractical, and if separate sale of the debtor's undivided interest would yield significantly less for the estate, the DIP can sell both interests and disburse the net proceeds proportionately, as long as the resulting benefit would outweigh the detriment to the other owner. Similarly, the DIP may sell property free and clear of liens or other interests (which normally will be shifted to the proceeds) if the price will exceed all encumbrances, or if the nondebtor's interest is in bona fide dispute. Thus, although the debtor's sale before bankruptcy might be stymied, the DIP can sometimes break the logjam and pass clear title under chapter 11.

This cleansing power of bankruptcy extends beyond specific property. It can be the key to successful reorganization through the sale of the entire business, or through new capital infusions. When a business is troubled and its future is in doubt, potential investors may shy away despite the venture's intrinsic worth. Similarly, the price a prospective going-concern purchaser will pay may be seriously depressed by the fear that acquiring all of the assets will also subject the buyer to the debtor's obligations under doctrines of successor liability (discussed in chapter 7). The same investors or buyers are often less jittery, and hence more willing to recognize the true value of the debtor's business, if the transaction proceeds under a confirmed plan or other court order that quantifies or cuts off preexisting claims. Subject to possible constitutional due-process protections for unknown future claimants, chapter 11 can thus dispel uncertainties that would otherwise prevent the debtor from realizing the equity in its business.

■ Workouts

Because the high transaction costs and the adverse publicity of a chapter 11 bankruptcy can be disadvantageous for debtors and creditors alike, the parties often try to negotiate an out-of-court settlement. Such an agreement, called a *workout*, restructures the debtor's financial affairs in much the same way that a confirmed plan would, but it can bind only those who expressly consent.

The foundation of any successful workout is trust. Creditors will not sign an agreement that leaves the business in the hands of management they consider to be dishonest or incompetent. If the debtor has lost credibility by misleading creditors or evading their reasonable inquiries (a common problem), its management may need to recruit and defer to a turnaround specialist in order to restore confidence. Full disclosure and candor are especially important when creditors are agreeing to accept partial payment in full satisfaction of undisputed debts. The debtor's misrepresentation or concealment of material facts probably would invalidate an otherwise binding release.

> *Full disclosure and candor are especially important when creditors are agreeing to accept partial payment in full satisfaction of undisputed debts.*

Workouts are forged in the shadow of bankruptcy, and the parties measure their concessions against the obvious alternative. The debtor and major creditors may be willing to accept something less than unanimity (for exam-

ple, to preclude dissenters from extorting preferred treatment), but the deal will unravel if there are too many holdouts. When this risk is apparent from the outset, the workout agreement can be drafted in the form of a chapter 11 plan. If necessary, and provided the information disclosed in soliciting assent to the agreement was adequate, the debtor can then file for reorganization and use the prepetition votes to transform the workout into a con-

In Brief: Advantages and Disadvantages of Bankruptcy

Category	Advantages	Disadvantages
Debtors	*Automatic Stay* ■ Instantly suspends most litigation and collection activities against the debtor, its property, or the bankruptcy estate *Control* ■ Debtor retains possession of the bankruptcy estate (unless a trustee is appointed) ■ Chapter 11 permits the debtor to operate in the ordinary course of business *Contracts, Leases, and Property* ■ Debtor in possession (DIP) has option of assuming or rejecting prebankruptcy executory contracts or unexpired leases ■ DIP may (in certain circumstances) sell property free and clear of liens or other interests	*Administrative Costs* ■ Legal and accounting expenses ■ Official creditors' committee fees *Reduction in Autonomy* ■ Creditor ovesight ■ Management's ability to make and implement decisions rapidly and autonomously is curtailed *Stigma of Bankruptcy* ■ Morale or confidence problems among staff, vendors, or customers ■ Customer anxiety regarding future warranty claims or product support
Creditors	*Enhanced Value and Participation* ■ Preserves going-concern value of an insolvent business ■ DIP more accountable due to bankruptcy reporting and notice requirements *Equitable Distribution* ■ When inequitable conduct by any creditor (typically an insider) has prejudiced others, bankruptcy court has authority to subordinate all or part of transgressor's claim to payment of other creditors *Involuntary Petitions* ■ Creditors may file an involuntary petition for relief under chapter 7 or (more rarely) chapter 11, and force the debtor into bankruptcy	*Suspension of Individual Remedies* ■ Automatic stay stalls foreclosure ■ Nondebtor parties to executory contracts and unexpired leases left in limbo *Unequal Effects* ■ Some bankruptcy procedures affect various creditors unequally (e.g., avoiding actions, claim caps, equitable subordination) *Reduced Distribution* ■ Only a small fraction of chapter 11 cases filed result in a successful reorganization. Continued operation results in less funds to distribute at liquidation

firmed plan that binds dissenters. This is called a *prepackaged bankruptcy*.

Regardless of its terms, a workout agreement cannot stop the debtor from taking refuge in chapter 11 if the restructured obligations prove too great. The right to file bankruptcy cannot be waived. Sometimes, however, creditors have strategic reasons to defer the debtor's filing, perhaps to buttress their positions with new guaranties, or to season transfers against the avoiding powers. In any event, if the debtor has broken faith with the workout pact, the court may consider previous creditor concessions in deciding whether to lift the stay, to allow creditors to propose a plan at the outset, to appoint a trustee, or to convert the case to a chapter 7 liquidation.

■ Lender Liability

A series of court decisions has expanded the recoveries available to borrowers against lenders, and as a consequence, lenders have become more aware of the risks of lender liability. The most notable development is not so much the legal theories on which lender-liability claims are based, but rather the frequency with which such claims are being asserted. Some of the theories on which lender-liability claims are based are described in this section.

> 66
>
> *The most notable development is not so much the legal theories on which lender-liability claims are based, but rather the frequency with which such claims are being asserted.*

Breach of Contract

A breach of contract results from a lender's failure to act or to refrain from acting as required by the terms of a loan document or other agreement. Compensatory damages will be awarded to place the borrower in the same position in which it would have been if the lender had properly performed the agreement.

Breach of Duty of Good Faith

Some cases have imposed an implied obligation of good faith and fair dealing on lenders. This duty requires the lender to act reasonably and fairly in dealing with the borrower, and in exercising its rights and remedies under the loan documents and under applicable law.

Where there is a fiduciary relationship between the lender and borrower, or where the parties are of unequal bargaining strength, punitive damages may be recoverable for breach of the implied duty of good faith and fair dealing. For example, the U.S. Court of Appeals for the Sixth Circuit affirmed a judgment of $1.5 million compensatory damages and punitive damages against the Irving Trust Company. The company was found to have breached an implied covenant of good faith and fair dealing when it failed to give notice to the borrower before refusing to make further advances under a discretionary line of credit.[1]

---

1. *K.M.C. Co. v. Irving Trust Co.*, 757 F.2d 752 (6th Cir. 1985).

At the Top

Some large banks have begun to place mandatory arbitration clauses in their loan agreements. These clauses affect the claims a debtor may assert regarding the lender's breach of an implied duty of good faith and fair dealing, and avoid the costs involved with a jury trial.

Fraudulent Misrepresentation

A lender may be liable for making false statements to a borrower if, for example, it represents that it will make a loan facility available to the borrower, when in fact it has decided not to extend any credit to the borrower. If a fiduciary relationship exists between the lender and the borrower, the lender may have an additional duty to disclose information if nondisclosure would result in injury to the borrower. Both compensatory and punitive damages may be recovered for fraudulent misrepresentation.

Economic Duress

Economic duress is the coercion of the borrower, by threatening to do an unlawful act that might injure the borrower's business or property. If the lender pressures the borrower into doing something that the borrower is not required to do under the loan documents, that may result in a finding of economic duress. For example, a threat by the lender to accelerate the loan unless the borrower provides additional collateral may constitute economic duress if there is no default under the loan documents. Compensatory and punitive damages may be recovered for economic duress.

Tortious Interference

The lender was found liable for wrongful or tortious interference with the borrower's corporate governance in the following case, which set a precedent for claims of this kind.

■ **A Case in Point:**   **In the Language of the Court**

Case 24.6
STATE NATIONAL BANK OF EL PASO v. FARAH MANUFACTURING CO.
Court of Appeals of Texas
678 S.W.2d 661 (Tex. App. 1984).

FACTS   The loan agreement between the bank lenders and the borrower, Farah Manufacturing Co. (FMC), contained a clause prohibiting any change in the borrower's management "which any two Banks shall consider, for any reason whatsoever, to be adverse to the interests of the Banks." The lenders threatened to accelerate the loan if a certain individual, of whom the lenders disapproved, was reappointed as chief executive officer of the borrower. In response to this threat, the borrower appointed a series of chief executive officers proposed by the lenders. The financial position of the borrower seriously deteriorated during the tenure of these chief executives.

The borrower sued the lenders for fraud, duress, and tortious interference. In particular, the lenders' threats to accelerate the loan under the management-change clause, in order to influence the choice of managers, was found to be an excessive interference with the borrower's internal affairs. The lenders were found liable for the losses suffered by the borrower while under the bank-imposed management, resulting in a judgment against the banks in excess of $18 million. The banks appealed.

ISSUE PRESENTED   Is a bank that requires the borrower to hire chief executive officers recommended by the bank liable to the borrower for excessive interference with the borrower's internal affairs?

OPINION   SCHULTE, J., writing for the Texas Court of Appeals:

. . . .

Three reasons are asserted by State National in support of its position that FMC has no legal basis for an actionable claim of interference. The first reason states that the lenders were legally justified and privileged to issue warnings based upon the exercise of contractual rights or upon a financial interest. The second states that there is no evidence showing an intent by the lenders to harm FMC.

Interference with another's business relations with a third party is actionable only if the interference is motivated by malice and no useful purpose of the inducing party is subserved. . . .

One is privileged to interfere with a contract between others when he does so in the bona fide exercise of his own rights or when he possesses an equal or superior interest to that of the plaintiff in the subject matter.

. . . [B]usiness relations interference is actionable only if both malice *and* illegal action combine to produce an injury. Malice, in this connection, is not to be understood in its proper sense of ill will against a person, but in its legal sense, as characterizing an unlawful act, done intentionally without just cause or excuse.

In this perspective, that malice constitutes an intentional and unlawful interference, then that is all that must be proven to establish a cause of action to recover actual damages. Actual malice (ill will, spite, evil motive, or purposing the injury of another) need not exist.

. . . To maintain the action for interference with the contract, it must be established that (1) there was a contract subject to interference, (2) the act of interference was willful and intentional, (3) such intentional act was a proximate cause of Plaintiff's damage, and (4) actual damage or loss occurred.

Case 24.6 continued on following page

*Case **24.6** continued*

The proof of these elements establishes a prima facie case of interference. It then becomes incumbent upon the part of the defendant to show that his acts were either justified or privileged. In all cases, the act of interference must be without legal right or justifiable cause on the part of the defendant.

Interference embraces within its scope all intentional invasions of contractual relations, including any act injuring or destroying property and so interfering with the performance of the contract itself, regardless of whether breach of contract is induced. It presupposes knowledge of the plaintiff's interests or, at least of facts that would lead a reasonable man to believe in their existence.

. . . .

. . . Interference requires only that acts be done willfully and intentionally. This does not require that the acts be shown to have been undertaken with an intent to harm.

As its third reason asserted to support the proposition that FMC has no legal basis for an actionable claim of interference, State National argues that there is no evidence of interference with an existing or reasonable probable future contract or business relation. . . .

The central theme of FMC's case is that the lenders interfered with FMC's own business relations and protected rights. Although the lenders may have been acting to exercise legitimate legal rights or to protect justifiable business interests, their conduct failed to comport with the standards of fair play. Upon consideration of the private interests of the parties and of the social utility thereof, the social benefits derived from permitting the lenders' interference are clearly outweighed by the harm to be expected therefrom.

In view of the foregoing principles, the evidence is legally sufficient that the lenders interfered with FMC's business relations, its election of directors and officers and its protected rights. FMC was entitled to have its affairs managed by competent directors and officers who would maintain a high degree of undivided loyalty to the company. . . .

The evidence is factually sufficient that the interference compelled the election of directors and officers whose particular business judgment and inexperience and whose divided loyalty proximately resulted in injury to FMC. The interference by the lenders was done willfully, intentionally and without just cause or excuse. As a matter of law, FMC has established a cause of action for interference. The evidence is legally and factually sufficient to support the jury's finding thereon.

. . . .

RESULT   The Texas Court of Appeals affirmed the judgment. State National Bank of El Paso was liable to the borrower, Farah Manufacturing Co., for excessive interference with the borrower's internal affairs.

Questions
1. Would the result in this case have been the same if FMC had not suffered any actual damage or loss?
2. What is malice?

Intentional Infliction of Emotional Distress

A lender was found liable for intentional infliction of emotional distress when, after deciding not to make any additional advances to the borrower, bank officials publicly ridiculed him, pointing at him, using profanities, and laughing about his financial difficulties. To recover for intentional infliction of emotional distress, the lender's conduct must be extreme and outrageous, and must intentionally or recklessly cause emotional distress to the borrower. Compensatory and punitive damages may be recovered.

Negligence and General Tort Liability

Claims that do not fall into one of the other established categories may be characterized as negligence or general tort liability. Negligence is the failure to exercise reasonable care, resulting in injury to the borrower. General tort liability arises from conduct that intentionally causes injury to a borrower.

Statutory Bases of Liability

A lender may be liable to the borrower if it violates a statutory standard of conduct. For example, the federal Racketeering Influenced and Corrupt Organizations Act (RICO) has been used by private litigants in lender-liability cases. Although RICO was adopted by Congress as a tool for fighting organized crime, the definition of a "pattern of racketeering activity" is arguably broad enough to encompass fraud or misrepresentation by banks or other lenders. The treble damages available under RICO provide an incentive for borrowers to claim RICO violations in their lender-liability suits.

The federal antitying statutes prohibit banks and thrifts from conditioning a loan or other financial service on the borrower's purchase of an unrelated property or service from the lender, or on the borrower's providing to the lender a product or service unrelated to the original loan.

A lender may be subject to penalties for aiding or abetting a borrower in violating federal securities laws if it knew, or should have known, that a violation was taking place, or if it is found to be a controlling person with respect to the borrower.

Under the federal Comprehensive Environmental Response, Compensation and Liability Act (CERCLA, discussed in chapter 16) and state-law counterparts, if the lender falls within the statutory definition of an owner or operator of a site contaminated by hazardous wastes, it may find itself liable for the costs of cleanup.[2]

■ Special Defenses Available to Failed Banks and Savings and Loans

When a bank or savings and loan has failed, and federal banking agencies have taken control, a doctrine called *D'Oench, Duhme*[3] may be used by the FDIC or Resolution Trust Corporation (RTC) to increase the value of the failed institution by easing the federal agencies' ability to collect on loans. In effect, D'Oench, Duhme bars many claims and defenses against conservators and receivers that might have been valid against the failed bank itself. The doctrine (codified as 12 U.S.C. § 1823(e)) bars enforcement of any agreements (or "secret agreements") unless those agreements are in writing, and have been approved contemporaneously by the bank's board or loan committee and recorded in the bank's written records. This recording requirement is justified by the courts because it allows federal and state bank examiners to rely exclusively on the bank's written records in evaluating the worth of the bank's assets.[4] The result of this doctrine is that the federal agencies are usually victorious over borrowers in cases in which a borrower asserts certain common law defenses to escape a loan obligation assumed by the FDIC or RTC. D'Oench, Duhme applies only to banking transactions engaged in by federally insured institutions. It does not apply to nonbanking transactions or to transactions engaged in by a bank's nonbank subsidiaries.

The Responsible Manager

Managing Debtor-Creditor Relations

A responsible manager must understand lender-liability risks. The following steps will help lenders minimize those risks.

---

2. See *United States v. Fleet Factors Corp.,* 901 F.2d 1550 (11th Cir. 1990), as well as the discussion in chapter 16.
3. From the Supreme Court case of the same name, *D'Oench, Duhme & Co. v. FDIC,* 315 U.S. 447, 62 S.Ct. 676 (1942).
4. *Alexandria Assocs. v. Mitchell Co.,* 2 F.3d 598 (5th Cir. 1993).

In negotiating loan terms, the lender should indicate clearly that any commitment must be in writing and approved by the loan committee or other appropriate officials of the lender. The lender's written communications to the borrower should disclaim any commitment if none is intended.

The lender should avoid provisions in loan documents giving it a broad right to control the borrower's management decisions or day-to-day business activities. The lender should refrain from using its financial leverage to influence such activities as the selection of management, the hiring or firing of employees, or the payment of other creditors.

The loan documents should contain a merger clause stating that the written loan documents supersede any prior oral understandings, and that the borrower is not relying on any prior oral promise or representation by the lender. The loan documents should provide that any amendment, modification, or waiver of the terms of such documents or of the rights of the parties must be in writing and signed by both the lender and the borrower.

The lender may ask the borrower to insert in the loan documents a waiver of its right to a jury trial. Juries are often perceived as sympathetic to borrowers; a judge may be less likely to award large compensatory or punitive damages to the borrower.

The lender may want to specify in the loan documents that any legal action by the borrower must be brought in a court in a specific state or city, to avoid the possible disadvantage the lender may have as a defendant in a court in the borrower's home territory.

The lender may want to add an arbitration clause to the loan documents, stating that any disputes arising under the loan documents will be resolved through binding arbitration instead of litigation in a court.

The lender should maintain accurate and complete credit files supporting all of the actions it takes. Virtually all of the documents in the lender's files may be subject to legal discovery; it is wise to assume that any entry in the credit files may someday be read to a judge or jury in a lender-liability case.

The lender should not threaten to take actions that are not yet authorized, or which the lender does not actually intend to take. The lender should give reasonable warning and, if possible, written notice to the borrower before terminating a line of credit, changing an established course of conduct, accelerating a loan, or exercising any remedies.

Except when acting as a trustee or other fiduciary, the lender should refrain from giving any legal, financial, or investment advice to the borrower that might create a fiduciary relationship between the lender and borrower. The lender should be cautious about giving other creditors the financial history of the borrower or opinions as to the borrower's creditworthiness.

In a workout situation, when the borrower is trying to renegotiate a loan she cannot pay, or if it becomes apparent that the borrower may be preparing a lender-liability suit, the lender should consult with legal counsel.

At all times the lender's loan officers should behave professionally, regardless of their level of frustration with the borrower. Any personality conflicts with the borrower should be avoided. If a personality conflict does develop, the matter should be transferred to other loan officers.

It has become fashionable in some circles to view chapter 11 as a strategic option for creative business planning. However, apart from the fresh start granted to individual debtors, the bankruptcy system generally respects a debtor's obligations existing under state or other federal law, and merely provides a forum for dealing fairly, efficiently, and flexibly with the rights of all of the creditors and equity holders. Thus, although insolvency is not a prerequisite for relief, a bankruptcy filing is generally not appropriate unless the business is in serious financial difficulties.

If those difficulties are present, the bankruptcy system can be an effective mechanism for overcoming them while preserving a productive enterprise. Yet for each celebrated success, there are countless failed chapter 11 cases, in which no plan is confirmed and creditors are left with less than they would have received through prompt liquidation. This is partly the price of giving depressed businesses the chance to rebound, but it also reflects fundamental problems.

Many debtors, most of them single-asset or other small businesses, file chapter 11 cases without any realistic prospect for reorganization. In some instances, the principals refuse to recognize and deal with financial ills until the business is too weak to survive. Continuing their ostrichlike pattern, they then file a chapter 11 petition, awash in a sort of terminal euphoria, not recognizing that liquidation is inevitable. Other debtors see the writing on the wall, but file to buy time, hoping for a miracle cure. Still others file merely to postpone the management's impending unemployment.

However, Congress gave creditors the means to protect their interests. If management acts improperly, a trustee can be appointed; if reorganization is improbable, the case can be dismissed or converted to a chapter 7 liquidation. Unfortunately, these remedies are rarely invoked before the creditors' interests are seriously prejudiced. Not surprisingly, individual unsecured creditors tend to be reluctant to throw good money after bad by policing the debtor's conduct. For the same reason (though with less justification), they frequently decline to serve or participate actively on the official creditors' committee, so this watchdog may be somnolent or nonexistent in smaller cases. Thus, unless a secured creditor is motivated to overcome this inertia, a chapter 11 case may have a bleak outcome.

Absent prompting from an interested party, the bankruptcy judge ordinarily will not intervene until the situation becomes egregious, as when the DIP does not comply with the rules, such as those requiring regular financial and tax reporting. Because the court is not well equipped to investigate the progress of each chapter 11 debtor, an abusive case can languish for considerable time before the court itself initiates corrective action.

The effectiveness of the bankruptcy system depends largely upon knowledgeable and responsible conduct by the interested parties. In general, both debtors and creditors benefit by addressing financial problems early, and pursuing a constructive workout. Because the charged emotional climate often makes this difficult, it is important to obtain objective and practical advice from counsel. If a workout is not possible, then before filing for relief under chapter 11, the debtor's management should consider whether a reorganization is plausible. If the case is filed, creditors must recognize that meaningful participation, ideally through the official creditors' committee, is usually necessary to protect their interests.

Inside Story

RJR Nabisco Leveraged Buyout

From time to time, a company may incur long-term indebtedness in the form of bonds. The proceeds of such debt will generally be used for long-term purposes, such as the acquisition of machinery or the construction of a new plant. Bonds are usually negotiable, and are available for purchase and sale by investors in the public market. The company that sells the bonds, called the issuer, will normally sell them to an underwriter who, in turn, markets them to the public.

The agreement governing a bond issue is contained in a written document called an indenture. Like a loan agreement or a note purchase agreement, an indenture contains a description of the terms, or characteristics, of the bond. Such terms include the interest rate; the security, if any, for the bond; and the terms for repayment of the principal and retirement of the bond. In addition, the issuer will make certain representations and warranties about itself, the bonds, and certain promises (or covenants) with respect to what it will or will not do while the bonds are outstanding. Because of the public market that exists for bonds, many of the terms found in indentures have become standardized.

In the past, the standard indenture did not contain protections against changes in corporate structure, such as leveraged buyouts, mergers, or hostile takeovers.

Such events, called event risks, cause the prices of high-grade investments to plummet. For example, in a leveraged buyout (LBO), in which the buyer acquires the stock or assets of a company by borrowing large sums of debt and using little equity, the company's assets must be pledged as security for the debt. Frequently, after the LBO is consummated, the acquired company's assets are sold off to reduce the debt burden.

The case of *Metropolitan Life Insurance Company v. RJR Nabisco, Inc.*[5] arose when two institutional bondholders found themselves holding bonds whose values had allegedly declined after the issuer's LBO. They sued the issuer in the Federal District Court for the Southern District of New York. Even though the indentures did not expressly prohibit an LBO, the bondholders argued that the issuer was required to repurchase the bonds because it had breached an implied covenant of good faith and fair dealing when it entered into the LBO. The court held that, because the

5. 716 F.Supp. 1504 (S.D.N.Y. 1989).

Inside Story continued on following page

Inside Story, continued

written agreement did not contain an express LBO prohibition, to imply a covenant of good faith and fair dealing that prohibited the LBO would add to the indenture a term that was neither bargained for nor contemplated by the parties.

Background

On October 20, 1988, F. Ross Johnson, then the chief executive officer of RJR Nabisco, Inc., proposed a $17 billion leveraged buyout of the company. A bidding war began, and Kohlberg Kravis Roberts and Company (KKR) submitted the successful bid. KKR's proposal called for a $24 billion buyout valued at approximately $109 per share.

Even before the company had accepted KKR's proposal, the bondholders, Metropolitan Life Insurance Company (MetLife) and Jefferson Life Insurance Company, filed suit. They alleged that the company's actions drastically impaired the value of the bonds they held by "misappropriating" the value of those bonds to help finance the acquisition, thereby creating a windfall to the company's shareholders. The plaintiffs argued that the acquisition contradicted the understandings of the market upon which the plaintiffs had relied. They also said that RJR had actively solicited, and had received, investment-grade ratings for their bonds, and because the ratings would be adversely affected by the LBO, the LBO contradicted a basic premise for their investment.

MetLife and Jefferson were sophisticated investors in the bond market, having held approximately $350 million in bonds issued by RJR between July 1975 and July 1988. MetLife had assets exceeding $88 billion and debt holdings exceeding $49 billion. Jefferson had more than $3 billion in total assets and $1.5 billion in debt securities. The court acknowledged that the plaintiffs, like other holders of public bond issues, had acquired the bonds after the indentures had been negotiated and memorialized. Nevertheless, the court noted, the underwriters who ordinarily negotiate the terms of the indentures with the issuers must then sell the bonds, and thus they must negotiate with the interests of the buyers in mind. Moreover, the plaintiffs presumably reviewed the indentures carefully before lending large sums to any company.

The indentures all contained the same basic provisions. None restricted the creation of unsecured debt or the payment of dividends by RJR. All permitted mergers as long as the surviving corporation assumed existing debt. Two of the indentures had previously included restrictions on incurring the type of debt contemplated by the LBO, but these restrictions had been deleted in subsequent negotiations unrelated to the LBO. In one case, MetLife bargained for a guarantee from the parent of RJR's predecessor, R. J. Reynolds, in exchange for its agreement to delete the restrictive covenants. In the other case, MetLife had bargained for a new rate and different maturity in exchange for such deletion.

The Court's Decision

The plaintiffs had argued that the company, explicitly or implicitly, had agreed with the bondholders' premise that the bonds would maintain their investment ratings. However, the court determined that the indentures contained no explicit prohibition against the LBO with KKR, and that they unambiguously permitted the LBO. Because the indentures were unambiguous, the court said, the plaintiffs could not introduce extrinsic evidence—that is, evidence outside of the indenture language—to show that the intention of the parties was to prohibit the LBO. Thus, documents indicating that MetLife had recognized the risk of an LBO to public debt (but had not taken any steps to protect against such risk) were inadmissible as evidence.

The court said that under certain circumstances, courts will consider extrinsic evidence to evaluate the scope of an implied covenant of good faith. However, the court noted that under applicable precedents, a different rule applied in interpreting boilerplate provisions of indentures used in the securities market. The court explained that boilerplate provisions do not result from the relationship of particular borrowers and lenders, and thus do not depend upon the particularized intentions of the parties. Because the efficiency of capital markets relied upon uniform interpretation of indentures, the meaning of boilerplate provisions in such indentures was not subject to case-by-case determination.

The court noted that, even though the plaintiffs had not alleged that an express covenant had been breached, a covenant of good faith and fair dealing could be

---

Inside Story, continued

implied if the "fruits of the agreement" between the parties had been "spoiled." In this analysis, the court determined that the "fruits" guaranteed by the indentures included the periodic and regular payment of interest and the eventual repayment of principal. Yet interest payments had been continuing, and there was no indication that principal would not be paid when due. The court said that a restriction against incurring new debt would be an additional "fruit" or benefit that the parties had not bargained for. The court added that it had no reason to believe that the market, in evaluating bonds, did not discount for the possibility that the issuer might engage in a debt-financed buyout. Thus, the loss in bond value was a market risk that public bondholders accept.

The court noted that the indentures contained provisions for adding new covenants upon the mutual agreement of RJR and the bondholders, and suggested that these provisions could be used to add restrictions against LBO debt. The court acknowledged that huge, sophisticated companies like RJR might not accept such new covenants, but said that multibillion-dollar investors like MetLife and Jefferson presumably had some say in the terms of the investments they make and continue to hold. If the issuers were to need new infusions of capital, for example, the bondholders would have an opportunity to impose new covenants. Because of the plaintiffs' and RJR's relatively equal bargaining positions, the court concluded that the contract between them was not inequitable.

Protecting Against Event Risk

In response to bond purchasers' concern about event risk, underwriters have begun to include new, express covenants. In one recent bond issue, the indenture included a provision granting bondholders the right to sell their bonds back to the issuer under such circumstances. Some lenders have devised debts in which the interest rate is adjusted if the issuer's debt rating is downgraded.

Standard and Poor Corporation responded by introducing a rating system called "event risk covenant rankings." Bonds are ranked on a scale of "E-1, strong protection," to "E-5, insignificant or no protection," based on the degree of covenant protection provided in a bond indenture.

Key Words and Phrases

Questions and Case Problems

1. What is necessary for a perfected security interest in goods?

2. ABC Food Corporation, a food company with annual sales of more than $1 billion, operated a paper division which supplied ABC with packaging for its food products. The management of ABC determined that ABC should concentrate on its core business of manufacturing food products, and recommended to the ABC board of directors that the assets of the paper division be sold.

Newcorp, Inc. is a newly formed corporation with two shareholders who have experience in the timber industry. Those two shareholders also jointly own Lumber Corporation, which operates two lumber mills in the state of Washington. Newcorp was formed specifically to acquire the assets of ABC's paper division.

On February 1, 1993, ABC and Newcorp signed a letter of intent specifying a closing no later than July 1, 1993, subject to Newcorp obtaining satisfactory financing. The letter of intent provided that ABC and Newcorp would enter into a long-term contract whereby Newcorp would supply specified quantities of paper packaging to ABC.

On February 15, 1993, Newcorp approached the Bank of Hope to request a term loan to acquire the assets of ABC's paper division and a revolving line of credit to meet its day-to-day working capital requirements.

On March 31, 1993, the Bank of Hope delivered to Newcorp a letter stating that it would agree to extend a credit facility to Newcorp on the terms and conditions described in a term sheet attached to the letter.

Bank of Hope required, as a condition to its credit facility, that the credit be secured by all fixed and current assets of Newcorp. Carlos Banker, the account officer for the Bank, took all steps necessary to give Bank of Hope a valid first-priority lien on all collateral.

A major source of revenue for Newcorp will be the long-term supply contract with ABC. The Bank of Hope is requiring an assignment of the supply contract. The assignment would prohibit ABC and Newcorp from making any amendments to the contract without the bank's consent.

(a) You are a manager of Newcorp. What objections would you have to such an assignment?

(b) You are a manager of ABC. Any objections?

3. Assume the facts in question 2. One of the terms of the Bank of Hope's loan is a guaranty from each shareholder and from Lumber Corporation.

(a) You are Sylvia Daily, president of Newcorp. As president, you will be involved in the day-to-day operations of Newcorp. What arguments might you make against giving such a guaranty?

(b) You are Joe Moneyman. You own 51% of the stock of Newcorp, and you made loans to Newcorp during the initial stages of its existence. You have since left the running of Newcorp to Sylvia Daily and the other managers of Newcorp. What arguments could you make against giving such a guaranty?

(c) You are the Bank of Hope's attorney. What advice would you give the bank about taking a guaranty from Lumber Corporation?

4. Assume the facts in questions 2 and 3. On June 1, 1993, Revolving Credit Bank takes over the revolving line of credit from Bank of Hope and acquires Bank of Hope's security interest in Newcorp's accounts receivables and inventory. Beginning in early 1994, due to a combination of internal and external conditions, Newcorp's business failed to generate sufficient revenue to meet its debt obligations. The loan agreement between Newcorp and Revolving Credit Bank contains an advance clause, which states that Revolving Credit Bank may, at its discretion, advance up to $2 million based on eligible accounts receivable and inventory. Revolving Credit Bank informed Newcorp that Newcorp has failed to maintain certain financial covenants contained in their credit agreement. Without declaring a default, Revolving Credit Bank required from then on that Newcorp establish a locked-box arrangement with the bank, so that all payments made to Newcorp can be used first to repay any advances outstanding. On March 1, 1994, Newcorp's treasurer called Valerie Lender, Revolving Credit Bank's account officer, and asked for a $350,000 advance to cover checks that would be presented to the bank that day. Revolving Credit Bank refused to lend the full amount requested, but did advance $200,000 to pay certain suppliers.

You represent one of the trade creditors of Newcorp who has not been paid. Do you have any rights against Revolving Credit Bank?

5. Assume the facts in questions 2 through 4. In April 1994, Newcorp began to have difficulty meeting its monthly repayment obligations on the term loan from the Bank of Hope. Although Newcorp never missed a payment, the payments were all a few days late. In May 1994, Carlos Banker called the treasurer at Newcorp, assuring him that the Bank of Hope "would stand by the company" and that Newcorp should do whatever it could to keep the payments current. However, in September 1994, Revolving Credit Bank, concerned about continuing deteriorating conditions, decided to initiate foreclosure proceedings. The Bank of Hope followed suit only when Revolving Credit Bank began such foreclosure proceedings. When the Bank of Hope began foreclosure proceedings against the paper plant, it discovered that the nearby Temecula River was polluted due to waste water discharge from the plant.

(a) You represent Newcorp. What defenses would you raise against Revolving Credit Bank's foreclosure? Against the Bank of Hope's foreclosure?

(b) You represent Revolving Credit Bank. How would you respond to Newcorp's arguments?

(c) You represent the Bank of Hope. How would you respond to Newcorp's arguments? Should the Bank of Hope proceed to foreclose against the plant? Should it require Newcorp to clean up the river? What recourse does the Bank of Hope have against Newcorp if it does not foreclose? Does it have any recourse against any other party?

(d) You are a manager of ABC and hold a junior deed of trust on the property. How would you react to the Bank of Hope's latest action?

(e) Was the Bank of Hope's foreclosure ethical?

6. On September 22, Robert Herriford borrowed $6,500 from Avemco Investment Corp. and executed a promissory note for $9,607.92. The promissory note was secured by an agreement granting Avemco a security interest (or mortgage) in an airplane.

On July 4, Herriford entered into a lease option agreement with the three plaintiffs (Don Brown, Josef Miller, and Allen McAlear) whereby the plaintiffs would pay hourly rentals for the plane and contribute equally toward Herriford's debt retirement with Avemco. Upon full payment of the mortgage on the airplane, the plaintiffs would have an option to purchase one-fourth ownership (each) of the plane for the sum of $1. The plaintiffs became co-insureds with Herriford on the airplane, and copies of the policy were sent to Avemco.

On July 9, the plaintiffs advised Avemco that they had exercised the option with Herriford and tendered to Avemco the $4,859.93 still owed by Herriford. On July 18, Avemco refused the offer and wrote to Herriford announcing that, because of his failure to comply with the note and security agreement, Avemco was accelerating the payments, and the entire balance

of $5,078.97 was due and payable on or before July 28. The additional amount was due to reimburse Avemco for its purchase of "Vender's Single Interest Insurance."

On July 25, plaintiff McAlear advised Avemco that the plaintiffs did not accept Avemco's rejection of the tender, and that the money to retire the debt was available to Avemco at the First Security Bank of Bozeman, upon representation of a satisfaction of the mortgage.

On July 29 or 30, a representative of Avemco used a passkey to start the plane, and flew it to Seattle. Avemco then notified Herriford of the repossession, and demanded payment of $5,578.97 by August 10, or the aircraft would be sold, with the proceeds to be applied first to sale expenses and second to Herriford's account. On September 22, Avemco sold the plane for $7,000.

Assume that Herriford agreed that if he were to lease any of the property covered by the security interest without Avemco's consent, Avemco had the right to accelerate the loan. Avemco could accelerate if Herriford violated a specific provision of the agreement and if it deemed itself insecure. Should Herriford be held to the agreement? Should Avemco be entitled to call the loan because Herriford violated a specific provision of the agreement, or should it also have to show that it was insecure? [*Brown v. Avemco Investment Corp.*, 603 F.2d 1367 (9th Cir. 1979)]

7. On June 29, 1982, Timbers, Ltd. executed a note in the amount of $4,100,000. United Savings Association was the holder of the note, as well as of the security interest created the same day in an apartment project owned by Timbers in Houston, Texas. On March 4, 1985, Timbers filed a voluntary petition under chapter 11 of the Bankruptcy Code.

On March 18, 1985, United Savings Association moved for relief from the automatic stay of enforcement of liens triggered by the petition on the ground that there was lack of "adequate protection" of its interest. At a hearing before the bankruptcy court, it was established that Timbers owed them $4,366,388.77, and the value of the collateral was between $3,650,000 and $4,250,000. United Savings was therefore an undersecured creditor. Timbers had agreed to pay United Savings the postpetition rents from the apartment project, minus operating expenses. United Savings wanted additional compensation. The bankruptcy court agreed, and on April 19, it conditioned continuance of the stay on monthly payments by Timbers on the estimated amount realizable on foreclosure $4,250,000. The court held that postpetition rents could be applied to these payments.

Should an undersecured creditor be entitled to interest on its collateral during the stay to secure adequate protection? [*United Savings Association of Texas v. Timbers of Inwood Forest Associates, Ltd.*, 484 U.S. 365, 108 S.Ct. 626 (1988)]

8. Bill and Bob Green were principal owners of Greenbrook Carpet Company. They attempted to obtain a loan from the bank in order to purchase a controlling block of stock in Lewis Carpet Mills, Inc. The bank refused to make the loan because it considered the Greens's collateral to be inadequate. The bank subsequently agreed to loan $350,000 to Greenbrook in return for a security interest in Greenbrook's inventory. Greenbrook then transferred the loan proceeds to the Greens in return for a note. The Greens used the funds to purchase the Lewis stock, and granted Greenbrook a security interest in that stock. The Greens were not personally liable on the note.

Did the transaction between Greenbrook and the Greens constitute a fraudulent transfer? [*In re Greenbrook Carpet Co.*, 722 F.2d 659 (11th Cir. 1984)]

9. On March 19, Miriam McCannon entered into an agreement with a partnership doing business as the Drake Hotel for the sale of a condominium apartment and of a certain percentage of the common areas in the Drake Hotel.

Pursuant to the agreement, McCannon paid a deposit of $500 toward the purchase price of $17,988. She began living in the apartment in April. However, the bankruptcy court found that "for a variety of reasons, settlement on the property has never taken place."

In November, Drake filed bankruptcy under chapter 11. McCannon filed a complaint in February seeking relief from the automatic stay, and requesting specific performance of the agreement to purchase the apartment.

May the trustee avoid McCannon's interest in the property? [*McCannon v. Marston*, 679 F.2d 13 (3d Cir. 1982)]

10. Brodie Hotel Supply, Inc. sold some restaurant equipment to Standard Management Company, Inc. for use in a restaurant in Anchorage, Alaska. Standard Management went bankrupt. Brodie repossessed the equipment but left it in the restaurant. With the consent of Brodie, James Lyon took possession of the restaurant and began operating it in June. Throughout the summer, Brodie and Lyon negotiated over the price and terms under which Lyon was to purchase the equipment.

In November, Lyon borrowed $17,000 from the National Bank of Alaska and, as security for the loan, which was evidenced by a promissory note, executed a security agreement (or chattel mortgage) covering the restaurant equipment. This equipment consisted of 159 separate types of items, including a refrigerator, a dishwasher, an ice cream cabinet, spoons, and chinaware. The bank assigned its security interest to the Small Business Administration (SBA), represented in this action by the United States. In late November, the bank filed a financing statement, showing the SBA as assignee.

Brodie then delivered to Lyon a bill of sale covering the equipment, and Lyon executed a security agreement (or chattel mortgage) on the equipment, naming Brodie as secured party (or mortgagee). This security interest was given to secure the unpaid purchase price of the equipment.

Which of the parties had priority, under the respective security agreements, to the proceeds of the sale of the restaurant equipment? [*Brodie Hotel Supply v. United States*, 431 F.2d 1316 (9th Cir. 1970)]

Unit VII

International Business

Chapter 25
International Transactions - 832

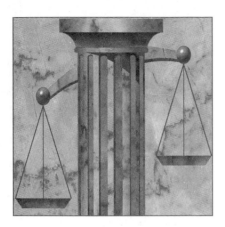

Chapter 25

INTERNATIONAL TRANSACTIONS

■ Introduction

Types of International Business Transactions

International business transactions can be categorized in three groups: (1) sales and leasing of goods, (2) transfers of technology, and (3) equity investments. Many transactions involve more than one of these categories. The issues and practices affecting these transactions are extremely varied due to the different rules applicable to the various types of transactions and the diversity of foreign countries.

Chapter Summary

This chapter discusses buying and selling abroad, focusing primarily on the international sales contract. Leasing, compensation trade, and processing operations are also reviewed. The chapter then discusses international transfers of technology by licensing and international franchising. The discussion of overseas investment covers the need to set investment goals, information dealing with economic and political conditions in the host country, and site options. Finally, the chapter addresses operational concerns and language and cultural considerations. The law governing lawsuits against foreign governments is also considered. The chapter ends with a discussion of United States domestic considerations.

■ Buying and Selling Abroad

The most common form of business across national boundaries is the buying and selling of tangible goods. Importers of foreign products to the United States must be aware of the regulations governing U.S. businesses in addition to U.S. tariff schedules and trade laws, as discussed in chapter 3. Exporters of U.S. products are also affected by the laws (also discussed in chapter 3) that establish what products or information can be exported, the conditions applicable to exports, and the benefits available to certain exporters.

Exporters and importers are also subject to the laws and practices of the foreign country with which they are dealing, as well as those of the international business community as a whole. These laws are often reflected in multilateral and bilateral treaties. By dealing through an agent or distributor with a presence abroad, a U.S. importer or exporter can reduce some of the risk of dealing with nondomestic laws and practices. However, the apportionment of these risks and an understanding of nondomestic rules are still relevant to establishing a good agency or distributorship contract.

■ The International Sales Contract

An international contract, like a domestic one, operates to allocate rights, obligations, and risks. However, in an international context the legal and business practices that are common to the parties may be fewer, the assumptions and expectations may be more divergent, and the risks may be greater. There is, in short, more ground to be covered to ensure a meeting of the minds.

Applicable Law

The substantive terms of a contract are ultimately subject to the laws of a single jurisdiction. Those laws will clarify, modify, or even render voidable the provisions of a contract. If a contract term contradicts mandated legal standards, it can be modified by law to the detriment of one party. If a contract fails to address an element of the business relationship, the applicable law may fill the gap, regardless of the parties' unwritten intentions. Legal terms in one jurisdiction may have different legal effect in another jurisdiction. Therefore, an international business contract must be written with an understanding of the legal framework that governs the enforceability and implementation of its terms.

In most international transactions involving sales, leasing, or the licensing of goods, the parties are free to determine what country's law will govern the implementation of the contract. If the parties fail to address the issue in the contract, and subsequently a dispute arises regarding the implementation or interpretation of the contract, each party may have a different opinion as to which country's courts have jurisdiction to hear the dispute, and which country's laws should be applied to resolving the dispute. (A lawsuit brought in one country may be tried under the law of another country.) To resolve these two issues, the court in which the suit is filed will apply *conflict of laws* principles to determine what country has the most significant relationship to the contract. These principles, sometimes referred to as principles of private international law, vary in some respects from country to country. The process of determining which country's laws to apply can be an extended and costly one. Perhaps more importantly, the contract law of one country may differ from that of another country, so the determination of what country's law is applicable can affect how the dispute will be resolved.

If the parties to an international sales contract are both nationals of countries that are signatories to the United Nations Convention on Contracts for the International Sale of Goods (UNCISG), the rules of that convention may apply. The United States signed the UNCISG which went into effect January 1, 1988. UNCISG rules are also applicable if the country whose law applies (as determined by the contract or by conflict-of-laws principles) is a signatory to UNCISG. The UNCISG rules apply expressly to the formation of the contract and the rights and obligations of the parties to the contract.

The UNCISG does not apply to contracts for the sale of certain types of goods, such as household goods, securities, negotiable instruments, vessels, or aircraft. It also does not apply to sales contracts in which the "preponderant part of the obligation of the party who furnishes the goods consists in the supply of labor or other services." Nor do UNCISG rules apply if the contract expressly disclaims their application.

A corollary treaty to the UNCISG is the 1986 Hague Convention on the Law Applicable to Contracts for the International Sale of Goods. That treaty endorses the freedom of contracting parties to select the law that will govern their contract. If such law is not specified in the contract, parties who are nationals of signatory countries are obliged to apply the laws of the seller's country.

Sometimes, the way a claim is framed may determine whether the choice of law provision in a contract will apply and be honored, as is demonstrated in the following case.

■ **A Case in Point:**   **Summary**

Case 25.1
AROCHEM CORP. v.
WILOMI, INC.
United States Court of Appeals
for the Fifth Circuit
962 F.2d 496 (5th Cir. 1992).

FACTS   On September 1, 1988, Marimpex, Inc., a German oil trader, entered into a charter agreement with Wilomi, Inc., an oil company, for the transport of crude oil from Scotland to the U.S. Gulf Coast aboard Wilomi's tanker. The agreement provided that English law was to govern the agreement's construction and performance.

On September 19, 1988, while the oil was en route, Arochem Corp., an American oil company, purchased it from Marimpex. The ship's destination was changed to Puerto Rico. Upon its arrival, Marimpex informed Wilomi that it was unable to pay for the delivery. Consequently, Wilomi filed lien notices with the U.S. Customs office in Puerto Rico, and commenced an action in the U.S. District Court for the Eastern District of Texas. (A *lien notice* is a written notice that a claim has been placed on property for the payment of a debt.) Arochem was unaware of these actions.

A U.S. marshall *arrested* (seized) the cargo aboard the tanker in Nederland, Texas. Marimpex thereafter paid the amount owed for the freight, and the cargo was released. Arochem then brought suit asking for damages stemming from Wilomi's allegedly wrongful arrest. The federal district court held that American, not English, law governed the dispute.

ISSUE PRESENTED   Should American law or English law govern a suit for wrongful arrest of cargo in the U.S. by a U.S. marshall when the cargo was originally sold under a contract providing for application of English law to which the U.S. plaintiff was not a party?

SUMMARY OF OPINION   The U.S. Court of Appeals began by noting the following facts: The wrongful act claimed in the lawsuit was the arrest of the cargo in Nederland, Texas, after its transshipment. The flag of the ship transporting the cargo at the time of arrest was the American flag. The legal entity claiming injury, Arochem, is a Delaware corporation with a principal place of business in Stamford, Connecticut.

Both American and English courts are equally competent and accessible. The court recognized that the charter agreement was negotiated, drafted, and executed in London, and that the agreement itself provided for English law to govern its construction and performance. This factor was rendered insignificant, however, because plaintiff Arochem was not a party to the charter agreement.

Arochem's claim is for wrongful arrest, and the arrest was administered by a U.S. marshall in a U.S. port. Arochem is a U.S. company, and Wilomi has a place of business and a general agent in the U.S. With these contacts between the transaction and the U.S., it is consistent and rational to apply American law.

Although the contract was formed in England, it is illogical to argue that England has as great an interest as the U.S. does in protecting an American purchaser from an unlawful arrest of cargo on an American vessel in an American port. The Court of Appeals upheld the district court's application of American law.

RESULT   American, not English, law governs the suit for wrongful arrest of cargo.

Dispute Resolution

The choice of a forum and a procedure for resolution of contract disputes is distinct from the choice of substantive law. A party to a contract may be willing to accept the substantive law of the other party's country, but prefer that it be applied by a neutral body according to that body's procedures. If a neutral forum is desired, it is common for the parties to select an international arbitral organization. Arbitration is typically a more flexible, less costly, and speedier method of resolving disputes than court litigation. International arbitral bodies are often more experienced in dealing with international commercial disputes than their judicial counterparts. An added benefit is that arbitral bodies, unlike courts, can keep the nature and the outcome of the dispute confidential.

Commonly selected international arbitral forums include the International Chamber of Commerce (ICC) in Paris, the International Center for the Settlement of Investment Disputes (ICSID), the Arbitration Institution of the Stockholm Chamber of Commerce, and the Arbitration Institute of the Zurich Chamber of Commerce. Each international arbitral body has its own procedural rules. However, internationally accepted arbitration rules, such as those adopted by the United Nations Commission on International Trade Law (UNCITRAL), may also be used in conjunction with the parties' own methods of establishing an arbitral panel. This latter type of arrangement is referred to as ad hoc arbitration.

It is common for the parties to stipulate that an arbitration decision is final and binding, and not subject to review by any courts. Absent such a stipulation, the dispute could be reviewed by a court without reference to the arbitration (a de novo review), rendering the arbitration decision unenforceable. The 1958 United Nations Convention on the Recognition and Enforcement of Foreign Arbitral Awards (often referred to as the New York Convention) has as its purpose "to unify standards by which agreements to arbitrate are observed and arbitral awards are enforced in signatory countries." More than 60 countries, including the United States and most of the major trading nations, are parties to the convention.

Payment

Because the parties to an international sale may not be well known to each other, the buyer may not be willing to pay for the goods before it receives them, and the seller may not be willing to ship the goods before the buyer pays for them. As a result, the most common payment mechanism for international sales transactions is the opening (that is, the establishment) of a documentary credit, commonly known as a *letter of credit (LC)*. The buyer and seller establish by contract the following procedure. The buyer, known as the applicant, will enter into a contract with a bank, known as the issuing bank, which is usually in the buyer's jurisdiction. Pursuant to this contract, the bank will issue a letter of credit in favor of the seller, known as the beneficiary. The LC's terms, which are negotiated between the seller and the buyer, will be the basis of the contract between the issuing bank and the applicant. The LC will provide for payment by the issuing bank to the beneficiary upon presentation by the beneficiary (or its agent or assignee) of specified documents.

The principal document required in an LC transaction involving the sale of goods is a bill of lading. The *bill of lading,* which the carrier (that is, the transporter) of the goods issues to the seller, indicates what goods the carrier has received from the seller, the loading location, the name of the carrying vessel, and the destination. A typical LC requires the beneficiary to present to the issuing bank a *clean bill of lading,* that is, one that has no notations indicating defects or damage to the goods when they were received for transport. When the seller presents the bill of lading (and any other documents specified by the LC), the issuing bank will make the agreed payment. The issuing bank will then give the bill of lading to its customer, the buyer, who will use that document to claim the goods when they arrive.

Additional certification that may be required from the seller as a condition for payment under the LC includes an invoice; a packing list; a certificate of inspection issued by a designated organization, indicating that the quality or condition of the goods at the time of shipment complies with the contract terms; a certificate of origin establishing the origin of the goods for customs purposes; and a certificate of insurance, establishing that the goods are properly insured prior to shipment, in accordance with the sales contract.

A *confirming bank* may be involved in the transaction, that is, a bank located in the seller's jurisdiction that confirms (makes a legal commitment) to the seller that it will honor the terms of the LC issued by the issuing bank. This gives the seller greater comfort by making a more familiar local bank the paying entity.

The seller can use the LC to finance its purchase of products or materials from its supplier. Under this arrangement, commonly known as a *back-to-back letter of credit,* the seller uses the first LC as security for its own issuing bank to issue a second LC in favor of the seller's supplier.

The purpose of documentary credits is to allow the issuing bank to condition payment simply on the presentation of documents, not on the parties' compliance with their sales contract. Article 17 of the Uniform Customs and Practice for Documentary Credits (UCP), written by the International Chamber of Commerce, states:

> Banks assume no liability or responsibility for the form, sufficiency, accuracy, genuineness, falsification or legal effect of any documents, or for the general and/or particular conditions stipulated in the documents or superimposed thereon; nor do they assume any liability or responsibility for the description, quantity, weight, quality, condition, packing, delivery, value or existence of the goods represented by any documents, or for the good faith or acts and/or omissions, solvency, performance or standing of the consignor, the carriers, or the insurers of the goods, or any other person whomsoever.[1]

66

The purpose of documentary credits is to allow the issuing bank to condition payment simply on the presentation of documents, not on the parties' compliance with their sales contract.

Another type of letter of credit that may be presented is an irrevocable letter of credit. An *irrevocable letter of*

---

1. *Uniform Customs and Practice for Documentary Credits*, 1983 Revision, ICC Publication No. 400.

credit cannot be amended or canceled without the consent of the beneficiary and the issuing bank. If the buyer becomes aware of defects in the goods after an irrevocable LC has been issued, its only recourse is to sue the seller for breach of the underlying sales contract.

Two sets of rules can apply to LCs in international sales. The first is article 5 of the Uniform Commercial Code (UCC), which varies slightly from state to state. The second set of rules is set forth in the ICC's UCP, the most recent version of which is contained in a document often cited in bank LC forms as *Uniform Customs and Practice for Documentary Credits*, 1983 Revision, ICC Publication No. 400. There are significant differences between UCC article 5 and the UCP. For example, UCC article 5, as interpreted by most U.S. courts, provides that once established, an LC is irrevocable unless otherwise agreed. The UCP, by its terms, establishes the opposite presumption: An LC is revocable at the issuing bank's option and without prior notice to or agreement of the beneficiary, unless the contract and the LC expressly state that the LC is irrevocable.

The parties can elect to have their LC governed by UCC article 5 or by the UCP. It is essential, then, that parties to an LC know and understand which set of rules they are appending to their contract. These rules, as much as the terms of the underlying sales contract, can determine the outcome of a payment dispute.

The following case demonstrates the application of various sections of the Uniform Commercial Code to a complicated transaction that involved multiple letters of credit issued under UCC article 5, accounts receivable as collateral, and personal guaranties.

■ **A Case in Point:**   **In the Language of the Court**

Case 25.2
BANK OF CHINA v. CHAN
United States Court of Appeals for the Second Circuit
937 F.2d 780 (2d Cir. 1991).

FACTS Three men, Wilson Chang, Wayne Hsueh, and David Chan, formed a company, CH International (CHI), to export semiconductor equipment to China, and to assist China in developing turnkey semiconductor manufacturing operations.

The company began with a $4 million contract with China National Technical Import Corporation and a $2.4 million contract with China Electronics Import and Export Corporation. Both contracts provided that CHI would receive a 15% down payment, secured by a standby letter of credit for the benefit of the buyers if the company failed to deliver, and 75% on delivery. The final 10% was to be paid after the delivery. To secure payment of the 85%, the contract required the purchasers to obtain a master letter of credit for CHI's benefit.

The letters of credit were obtained from the New York branch of the Bank of China, federally chartered in the United States, but wholly owned by the

Chinese government. The letters of credit were issued to protect the Chinese customers' 15% down payment and for the benefit of CHI's American suppliers. The Bank of China's Beijing branch was at the same time providing master letters of credit in favor of the American suppliers, which were to be issued only when the bank's head office in Beijing issued letters of credit for the Chinese customers; otherwise the company would be unable to ship its goods. In sum, there were three types of letters of credit: those in favor of CHI for the payment of the contract price (master letters of credit); those in favor of the Chinese customers to recover their down payment if CHI breached its contract (standby letters of credit); and those in favor of CHI's American suppliers.

Problems developed with at least two of the letters of credit. First, the bank held one letter of credit for $58,000 in CHI's favor for the account of China Electronics Import and Export Corporation that was due to be paid on March 11, 1987. But as of March 30, the New York branch of the bank still had not received the money due the company from the Chinese customer. Second, the bank failed to put a reciprocal condition into another letter of credit issued in favor of another customer—CEDEC—for $194,700. CEDEC drew down (that is, received monies under) the company's letter of credit although the company had no reciprocal letter of credit to guarantee payment. CEDEC did not pay the full amount due under the contract.

Each of the three owners of CHI were required to sign personal guarantees to cover the bank's exposure on the letters of credit. In addition, the bank had a security interest in the accounts receivable due from the Chinese customers. When the business ran into financial problems, the bank was unable to obtain more collateral from the three men. In 1988, it sued appellant Chan for $1 million in principal and interest. Chan defended by arguing that the bank's action was not commercially reasonable within the meaning of article 5 of the UCC. He claimed that the bank intentionally failed to draw down letters of credit, and allowed Chinese customers to receive the goods shipped without paying CHI.

ISSUE PRESENTED   What are the duties of a bank that has issued letters of credit supported by personal guarantees and a security interest in accounts receivable?

OPINION   CARDAMONE, J., writing for the U.S. Court of Appeals:

. . . .

Chan relies on two provisions of the Uniform Commercial Code in arguing that the Bank had a duty to dispose of the master letters of credit in a commercially reasonable manner.

. . . .

The second provision upon which Chan relies falls under Article 9 of the Code that governs secured transactions. NYUCC section 9-504(3) provides in relevant part:

> Disposition of the collateral may be by public or private proceedings and may be made by way of one or more contracts. Sale or other disposition may be as a unit or in parcels and at any time and place and on any terms but every aspect of the disposition including the method, manner, time, place and terms must be commercially reasonable.

Case **25.2** continued on following page

*Case **25.2** continued*

The Bank contends it owed no duty to Chan under this section because when it was handling the letters of credit in favor of the company it was not a creditor that possessed or disposed of collateral within the meaning of section 9-504(3), but was acting solely as CHI's banker.

Section 9-504(1) governs the secured party's disposition of collateral "after default." In this case, some of the allegedly commercially unreasonable acts took place before March 19, 1987—the date the Bank declared the loans in default—while most of them appear to have taken place after that date. After March 19 the Bank stood in the position of a secured creditor whose debtor was in default, and it had effective possession of the collateral securing CHI's loans, that is, the letters of credit that allowed it to collect certain of the company's accounts receivable. The fact that the Bank's roles as creditor and banker converged here does not prevent the application of Article 9, especially when the Bank is, in fact, a secured creditor and the debtor has been declared in default.

With respect to those actions the Bank took before March 19, 1987, the UCC requires a secured party to "use reasonable care in the custody and preservation of collateral in his possession," and the secured party is liable for any loss caused by the failure to use such care. The instant case does not present the ordinary scenario the UCC contemplates, such as the negligent destruction of promissory notes or other collateral. Instead, the facts reveal the unique circumstances of a bank issuing back-to-back letters of credit to both parties to the commercial transaction, and at the same time taking a security interest in the accounts receivable represented by the same letters.

Normally, the purchaser's and the seller's bank would be two different institutions. Here, the Bank was on both sides of the same transaction. However extraordinary the circumstances, there can be no doubt that the Bank was in possession of the collateral and that it is alleged to have taken action impairing the value. Therefore, regardless of whether the Bank's allegedly commercially unreasonable acts took place before or after the date of default, it owed a duty to preserve the value of the accounts receivable by drawing down the master letters of credit when the shipping documents were properly presented to it.

. . . .

RESULT   The bank's handling of the collateral, namely the accounts receivable represented by the letters of credit, was not commercially reasonable. The court remanded the case to the trial court on the issue of whether the presence of commercially unreasonable disposal of the collateral relieved Chan of his obligation on his guaranty.

Questions
1. What were the bank's responsibilities when it issued the letter of credit?
2. Did the bank abuse its power when contracting with Chan?

Branch Offices

U.S. businesses can establish a presence in a foreign country to supervise or manage sales with little or no investment by setting up a liaison, representative, or branch office in the host country. The scope of permissible activities, capital requirements, and tax liabilities of each of these forms of representation varies with the legal scheme of the host jurisdiction.

These types of operations are generally limited to providing services on behalf of a home office. They cannot engage in manufacturing operations.

Typically, the greater the scope of permissible activities, the more stringent the capitalization and taxation rules. In Taiwan, for example, a liaison office may not engage in any business activity, nor may it deliver or accept any goods or cash remuneration. It has, however, no registration or tax obligations. A branch office can perform certain kinds of services, such as import and export, provided it is formally capitalized, registers with local government authorities, and pays income taxes.

■ International Leasing

Under a true lease, the owner of the leased goods expects to recover them at the end of the lease term. Alternatively, leasing may be a method of financing the acquisition of expensive equipment and vehicles such as airplanes, locomotives, and ships. Parties to such a financing lease expect that the lessee will purchase the leased equipment at the end of the lease term, at an agreed-upon residual value. Typical finance-lease transactions range from $100,000 to several million dollars.

There are several advantages of a financing lease over a direct purchase. In a financing lease the owner retains legal title to the goods until the greater part of the purchase price is paid by the lessees. In countries that have an undeveloped law of secured transactions (which establishes creditors' rights to collateral for loans), this alternative offers greater comfort to the owner of the transferred goods.

For foreign banks, leasing offers a way to establish a local presence in countries that may not allow full bank branches. As equipment lessors, banks operate as lenders, factoring in interest charges into the lease payments, while essentially serving a commercial function, the sale of equipment.

In many countries lessors, as owners of the leased goods, can fully depreciate those goods during the lease term, thereby gaining substantial tax benefits. Under many countries' tax laws the lessee is allowed to deduct all or a portion of its lease payments.

Some countries impose restrictions on the purchase of expensive imports, for example, in countries in which foreign-exchange expenditures are carefully monitored. However, lease payments may escape these limitations, either because there is no up-front sale or because the payments can be spread out in acceptable installments. Sometimes the installment payments can even be made from earnings gained from use of the leased goods.

International leasing may be subject to a wide range of relevant foreign laws. Local tax and accounting regulations will determine tax benefits for the owner and user of the leased goods. The creditor's rights, if any, will be determined by local laws. If creditor-debtor laws exist, there may be limitations on the lessor's rights in the event of the lessee's default. Foreign-exchange laws may substantially affect how lease payments are calculated, particularly in countries in which the local currency is not freely convertible or is undergoing high rates of inflation.

Compensation Trade

Compensation trade is a variation on the simple sale or lease transaction. The foreign party transfers use and/or eventual ownership of a good, usually equipment, to the local party, who then repays the foreign party with products produced using the foreign party's equipment. The foreign party may also supply the materials that are processed by the local party using the foreign party's equipment. This is known as a *processing operation*. Both types of transactions are simpler than full-scale equity investments but may still be subject to local foreign-exchange, customs, tax, and creditors'-rights laws.

■ International Transfers of Technology

The transfer of technology across national boundaries involves many of the same legal and commercial issues as the sale of goods: the choice of applicable law, the form of payment, and the method of resolving disputes.

Licensing

Technology is protected by intellectual property laws, which vary from country to country, and are discussed in chapter 11. Generally, technology is transferred pursuant to a licensing agreement whereby the owner of the technology (the licensor) transfers it to the user (the licensee) for manufacturing specified products.

Developing countries encourage the licensing of technology to upgrade local manufacturing capabilities. Their goals can be contradictory, however; although wanting to attract foreign technology, they may also want to limit the licensor's restrictions on the use or confidentiality of that technology. Foreign licensors need to be especially sensitive to the nature of the host country's patent, trademark, copyright, and trade secret laws. An understanding of how these laws are enforced in practice is important.

Because a technology transfer involves intangible property, its dissemination is harder to control than the sale of tangible products. This presents problems for both the licensor and the licensee. The licensee will be concerned with the scope of the rights it has been granted, including whether it has the exclusive right to use the licensed technology.

The licensor, which typically has invested substantial time and money in creating its technology, wants to be certain that the licensee will not disclose or use the technology without the licensor's consent. For technology that the licensor protects as a trade secret, contract provisions requiring confidentiality, and restrictions on the employees who will have access to the technology, are essential. In many developing countries, however, technology licensing laws or administrative policies expressly limit the terms of a license agreement and/or its confidentiality provisions. In some cases these limitations may not be acceptable to a licensor.

If a licensor is also a manufacturer and exporter of products produced by the licensed technology, it will be concerned about the effect of the licensee's prospective sales on the licensor's markets. This issue can be resolved by imposing restrictions on the geographic markets available to the licensee. However, local technology-transfer laws, especially in developing countries, often prohibit certain types of geographic market limitations. In addition, local antitrust laws may be used to challenge such limitations. These issues are all central to the transfer and use of technology, and must be carefully negotiated in the context of local requirements.

The licensing of technology frequently involves the licensing of rights in special types of intellectual property such as copyrights, trademarks, service marks, patents, and trade secrets. The confidentiality of trade secret technology can generally be protected, as between the contract parties, by a well-drafted, enforceable licensing contract. To protect its ownership and use rights in trademarks, service marks, copyrights, and patents as against third parties in foreign countries, the licensor generally must perfect its ownership in compliance with local requirements. Obtaining protection under local patent and trademark laws can be a technical, extended process, but the protection available under those laws is essential to preserving the value of the owner's intellectual property.

International Franchising

An increasingly common category of international licensing is franchising. A typical franchise agreement involves a package of licensed rights, including the right of the franchisee to use the franchisor's trademarks, service marks, patents, and confidential unpatented know-how (including trade secrets). The franchisor may or may not also contribute equity investment; but its major contribution is usually the franchisor's goodwill—the value of the customers' recognition of a popular enterprise. If the franchisor does not properly register its trademarks and service marks locally, it can effectively lose control of its most valuable assets.

The concept of franchising as a method of doing business, and the corresponding rights and obligations between the parties, is still in a state of flux in many countries. Protection of marketing and operations designs, trade dress, quality control systems, and other benchmarks of franchise businesses well understood domestically are often limited or unavailable internationally.

International Intellectual Property Protection

Several multinational treaties seek to harmonize the application of the intellectual-property laws of various jurisdictions. These treaties do not alter the criteria that each jurisdiction applies to determine whether an application for protection merits acceptance; instead, they seek to coordinate the registration and recognition process among signatory countries.

The scope and duration of patent and trademark protection vary from country to country. Many countries have less stringent intellectual property laws than the United States (or their laws are less rigorously enforced). As a result, the production of counterfeit goods that infringe intellectual-property rights is more prevalent in such countries. U.S. trade laws (discussed in chapter 3) may prevent the entry of such counterfeit goods into the United States, but they can only indirectly restrict the production of such goods and their sale in countries other than the United States.

For example, before enactment of new copyright laws in Poland and the Czech Republic, copyright abuse was quite common. Computer software companies, film studios, and clothing manufacturers lost hundreds of millions of dollars because of violations of international copyrights. According to some estimates, recording artists and producers lost approximately $75 million in royalties every year because of copyright piracy in Poland.[2] For example, an estimated 10,000 videocassettes of the film *Jurassic Park* were available in rental stores all over Poland long before the release of the movie by the official distributor.[3]

In many countries, if two entities file for protection of the same patented invention or trademark, protection is granted to the entity that files first. This can be a problem for an inventor or a trademark owner who files for protection in one country, and later discovers that another person has subsequently filed for protection of the same invention or trademark in another country. The International Convention for the Protection of Industrial Property Rights (popularly known as the Paris Convention) seeks to avoid this type of problem by encouraging reciprocal recognition of patents, trademarks, service marks, and similar forms of intellectual property rights among signatory nations, of which there are more than 80, including the United States. Each signatory nation agrees to grant to nationals of other signatory nations a grace period after filing in their home country within which to file corresponding patent or trademark applications in other signatory countries. These grace periods are six months for trademarks and one year for most patents, and give the filers a reasonable time to complete the filing and registration formalities in foreign countries.

The Paris Convention does not alter the substantive requirements of the laws of signatory countries, however, so patent or trademark protection in one signatory country does not necessarily translate into protection in another signatory country.

The Madrid Agreement Concerning the International Registration of Trademarks allows for centralized international registration. The owner of a trademark in its home country can file at the International Bureau of the World Intellectual Property Organization (WIPO) in Geneva for registration of its trademark in those signatory countries that it specifies.

The Pan American Convention recognizes the right of a trademark owner in one signatory country to successfully challenge the registration or use of that same trademark in another country by an entity that knows of the prior existence and use of that trademark in another signatory country. The Berne Convention for the Protection of Literary and Artistic Works and the Universal Copyright Convention extend copyright protection under the respective domestic copyright laws of signatory countries. Bilateral treaties of Friendship, Navigation, and Commerce (FNCs), which exist between the United States and almost 50 foreign countries, and Bilateral Investment Treaties (BITs) may afford further protection to intellectual property rights.

■ Investment Abroad

Prior to World War II, international business in the United States was, for the most part, limited to importing from and exporting to foreign countries. The volume of U.S. investment overseas was relatively small. Only a few large corporations—generally in the oil and mining industries—actually owned assets abroad. Since the war, U.S. foreign investment has increased tremendously. In the period from 1960 to 1970, U.S. private assets abroad increased from $49 billion to $119 billion. By 1980, this figure was $517 billion; in 1987 the figure stood at $1,034 billion, and in 1990 it was $1,254 billion. In other words, between 1960 and 1990 U.S. investment abroad increased 2600% or 26 times. This phenomenon is just one aspect of the globalization of national economies made possible by advances in communications and transportation.

Historically, the bulk of U.S. foreign investment has been concentrated in Western Europe and Canada. U.S. businesses have naturally been attracted by the political stability of these regions. Moreover, cultural affinities, similar business customs and practices, and a familiar linguistic landscape made it relatively easy for U.S. investors to set up active operations in Western Europe and Canada. In the 1970s, 1980s and 1990s, however, the rate of growth of U.S. investment in Asia began to outpace that of investment in Europe. U.S. manufacturers scrambled for new markets and lower production costs, and saw in the developing economies of Asia an opportunity to achieve both.

Investment Goals

A business plan for investing abroad must begin with an assessment of the investor's goals. The attractiveness of a prospective investment in a given host country can vary greatly depending on these goals.

Local Market Penetration Some markets are almost inaccessible, for legal or business reasons, to U.S. manufacturers wishing to sell their products. Developing countries may have shortages of hard currency—that is,

2. Matthew Brzezinski, "Polish Law Takes Aim at Copyright Piracy," *The New York Times*, June 14, 1994, D6.
3. *Ibid.*

convertible foreign exchange—and these shortages may limit their purchase of imports. Applicable laws may restrict imports of certain products, but may grant benefits to foreign investors wishing to manufacture those products locally. To penetrate these types of markets, the only practical approach may be to invest in a manufacturing facility in that country.

Regional Base   U.S. businesses that wish to compete in Europe or Asia, for example, may need to establish manufacturing, marketing, and/or service centers in the relevant region to establish credibility with local customers. U.S. businesses may also need to be on-site to sustain their local sources of supplies for operations elsewhere. Regional bases can reduce transportation costs, help avoid cultural and time-lapse difficulties, and generally help the U.S. business keep in touch with the business pulse of the region.

Cheaper Production Costs   Developing countries typically offer cheaper labor and raw materials than the more industrialized countries. These reduced costs are often the primary reason for U.S. business investment in foreign manufacturing operations. However, as discussed below, the assessment of true production costs is not limited to a line-item comparison of the costs of each element of production. Intangible issues such as labor efficiency, reliability of supplies, local labor-law requirements, and political stability can influence the true costs of production.

Host-Country Conditions

Prospective investors need to consider the economic, political, geographic, legal, and labor conditions in the host country.

Economic Conditions   The economic conditions of the host country are an essential factor in matching a prospective investor's business goals with a desired site. Per capita income, for example, may determine whether a particular country is a realistic market for a particular product, or whether it is a likely source of inexpensive labor. Economic growth trends can suggest a growing consumer market, as well as increasing labor costs. The availability of a readily convertible currency and the nature of the currency-exchange laws will determine whether profits can be easily repatriated (that is, transferred abroad). A high inflation rate may result in local suppliers being reluctant to perform on long-term contracts, or it may make capital and working loans more expensive.

The U.S. Department of Commerce, the U.S. Foreign Commercial Service, and the U.S. Department of State regularly publish reports on the economic condition of various countries. These can offer a good introduction for a prospective foreign investor. The U.S. Foreign Commercial Service has a wide-ranging network of commercial officers stationed at U.S. embassies and consulates throughout the world. They collect and analyze economic data, and are available on-site to U.S. businesses to interpret how that data may be relevant to an investment project.

Political Conditions   Political instability inevitably leads to some degree of economic instability. A prospective foreign investor must look beyond the reasonableness of the contract, the competence of his foreign business counterpart, and the desirability of the site to determine whether the existing government and its policies are aligned with the needs of the project. If such support exists, the investor must assess the likelihood that the government's policies will continue and will not be seriously modified by the political opposition. There may be a risk that the host country's government will expropriate (that is, assume ownership of) a particular industry or project.

One U.S. government agency, the Overseas Private Investment Corporation (OPIC), specializes in providing insurance for eligible U.S. investors against certain defined risks, including political risks such as expropriation. To be eligible for OPIC insurance, an investor must be a U.S. citizen, or a U.S. partnership or corporation substantially owned by U.S. citizens, or a foreign business at least 95% owned by a U.S. citizen or a U.S. partnership or corporation. OPIC insures U.S. investor's interests only in "friendly" countries—that is, those that have investment-protection agreements (FNCs or BITs) with the United States. Coverage is also available for inconvertibility of foreign currency remittances, and losses due to hostile action during civil unrest.[4]

Geographic Conditions   Climatic and geographic conditions can directly affect the production and transportation of products. Severe weather in certain seasons can affect delivery schedules. Location of a manufacturing site and contract commitments for production and shipment should be made with these conditions in mind, as well as with knowledge of the transportation systems and facilities, and other infrastructures that are available.

---

4. OPIC publishes a number of handbooks that describe its programs and services. These are available from the Information Officer, Overseas Private Investment Corporation, 1129 20th Street N.W., Washington, DC 20527.

Economic Perspective
Restructuring of Socialist Economies

As the socialist, centrally-planned economies of Eastern Europe struggled to restructure their domestic economies and integrate them into the world economy, there have been successes as well as reversals. There are no models for the transition from a command economy to a fully functioning market economy, although the experiences in Chile, Taiwan, Korea, and Germany (in 1948) provide some guidelines. In the absence of a model particular to the economies of Eastern Europe, the transformation process is one of experimentation, and proceeds at a slow and uneven pace.

There are three factors to examine in order to evaluate the probability of success of each country in accomplishing a transition to a globally competitive market economy: (1) the political stability of the country; (2) the status and rate of progress on a number of reform issues; and (3) the status and future prospects of the country's political and economic infrastructure.

In terms of political stability, Poland ranks the highest, with Hungary, the Czech Republic, and Slovakia close behind. All republics of the former Yugoslavia, except for Slovenia, and the former Soviet Union are low on the scale.

As far as market reform issues are concerned, Hungary has made the most progress. It has lifted many of its price controls and has made its currency convertible. It has also aggressively pursued reform in such areas as reducing state subsidies, increasing enterprise autonomy, allowing bankruptcies, privatizing state enterprises, and liberalizing for-

eign trade. Poland, the Czech Republic, and the Baltic states are close behind Hungary in progress toward reform. Poland, the Czech Republic, and Russia have gone far in lifting price controls. In addition, Poland has been relatively aggressive in privatizing state enterprises.

Privatization has contributed to the growing private sector within Eastern Europe, but in most countries only to a limited extent and at an enormous cost to jobs. Throughout Eastern Europe, unemployment has been at a record high. Obsolete industries have been shut down, and other firms, attempting to become viable, have greatly reduced their work force. The increasing rate of unemployment in all of Eastern Europe, except in the Czech Republic, has increased resistance to the privatization process.

For these reasons, initial plans for rapid privatization of state holdings were delayed. In Hungary, the first formerly communist state to introduce privatizations, less than half of the economy had been privatized as of 1994. Poland sold only 15% of its industry, failing to meet its target of 33% by 1993. The Czech Republic has had the most successful privatization program; more than half of the country's GNP is produced in the private sector.

By mid-1994, Russia had completed the first stage of its privatization program that began in 1992 with the distribution of vouchers with a face value of 10,000 rubles to all Russian citizens. The vouchers were traded in auctions in exchange for shares in privatized companies. Employees were enticed to trade

vouchers for between 25% and 51% of the shares of their employer company. No restrictions existed on foreign participation in voucher privatization, with the exception of selected companies that were limited to Russian investors. Foreign investors could buy vouchers from individual holders or exchanges, or they could invest in voucher funds specializing in specific industries. Russian voucher auctions have not been popular with all foreign investors, because of uncertainty as to how many shares will be distributed per voucher. Postvoucher privatization will feature simplified cash auctions for 25% to 30% stakes in Russian companies. One of the most important upshots of this second stage of the Russian privatization program will be the appearance of equity markets in the Western sense.

In 1991, municipal property in Eastern Europe was made separate from state-owned property. Local authorities across Eastern Europe now have property rights to the enterprises dealing with municipal services and to some of the commercial enterprises in their municipality. Hence, municipal governments are also privatizing their holdings. Nevertheless, they have also met some resistance due to the prospect of higher unemployment.

The former Soviet Union has encountered the most difficulty in making the transition toward a market economy. It has greater ethnic diversity, greater geographical dis-

Economic Perspective
continued on following page

Economic Perspective
Restructuring of Socialist Economies, *continued*

tances with which to contend, greater diversity of political opinion, and less historical familiarity with the workings of a market economy than Eastern Europe.

In Eastern Europe, political reform came quickly, and the new leaders were able to quickly turn their attention to economic reform. However, political reform occupied center stage in the former Soviet Union to the detriment of economic reform. It has made little progress on economic reform and lacks the physical and economic infrastructure for a competitive market economy.

Nevertheless, the richness of the republics of the former USSR makes them attractive for investors. Many Russian company assets are extremely undervalued, because of the country's double-digit monthly inflation rate. For example, according to CS First Boston Research, shares of Russian oil companies have been valued at the equivalent of 17 cents per barrel, as compared with shares of American oil companies which are priced on the basis of $7 per barrel of proven reserves.

Investing in companies with undervalued assets brought short-

term profits of up to 300% for some foreign investors. For example, the St. Petersburg Telephone Company traded at about $1 per share in December 1993, and six months later sold for around $15. The most popular stocks among foreign investors included Rostelekom, the state telephone company; the GUM Trading House, with its landmark department store across from the Kremlin; and Russian oil companies such as Surgutneftegas and Yuganskneftegas.

The nature, cost, and development status of a prospective site are major considerations. In some countries, such as China and Thailand, foreign investors are not permitted to own land but can, often with the assistance of a local partner, obtain long-term land-use rights. If the capital investment will be large, a foreign investor may want to consider investing only in countries that offer guaranties concerning expropriation, or in friendly developing countries, where U.S. investors are eligible for OPIC insurance.

A country may seek to attract investment to certain areas by offering attractive land-use fees and newly developed infrastructures. China, for example, has named four "special economic zones" and identified fourteen coastal cities that offer special incentives for, and show greater flexibility with, foreign investment projects. The legal, economic, and tax regimes governing these areas are distinctly different from those applicable to other provinces and regions, and as a result, those zones have attracted the vast majority of foreign investment in China since the inception of its economic open-door policy in 1979.

Legal Conditions Local laws can offer predictability and uniformity for prospective business decisions. However, the effectiveness of these laws depends on political conditions and the nature of the legal and admin-

istrative organs that must interpret and enforce them. A developed court system or comparable dispute-resolution forum (such as an established arbitration system) is a significant element, without which there is little leverage to enforce contracts or invoke commercial laws.

Although trade or licensing contracts may allow for choice of the law of a jurisdiction other than the recipient country, in foreign investment projects the laws of the host country will apply. In some instances, however, dispute-resolution procedures may be governed by the rules of a third jurisdiction.

Sources of necessary supplies should be secure, and their transportation and storage not subject to rampant theft. The existence of a reasonably diligent and fair law-enforcement network is a factor to be considered in this regard.

Foreign investors must have a working knowledge of the applicable host-country laws and acceptable forums for dispute resolution, and should obtain professional advice from local attorneys. These professionals can also assist in providing accurate contract translations, where required.

Many countries offer a variety of vehicles for foreign investment. Just as U.S. businesses can choose to operate domestically as a sole proprietorship, a general or limited partnership, or a corporation, foreign investors can select the investment format most appropriate to their project in a foreign country. Each form is subject to its own set of laws, which affect management structure, equity investment requirements, the limitation of investor liabilities, and taxation.

The licensing or contribution of technology by the U.S. business to the foreign business is often a component of an equity investment project. Some countries' investment laws or policies may limit the portion of the foreign party's equity investment that can be attributable to intellectual property—such as patents, trademarks, or know-how—as compared with cash or equipment, for example. Certain restrictions on technology use may be invalid under local technology-licensing laws.

There may be bilateral tax or investment treaties that grant reciprocal rights to businesses from the host and investor countries. These treaties may offer significant benefits, such as avoidance of double taxation (that is, taxation by both the host and investor countries) and guaranties against uncompensated expropriation by the host government.

The U.S. State Department compiles records of ratified treaties and their signatories. A quick review of this information can offer a sense of the relative involvement of various nations in international conventions that affect foreign investment. Attorneys familiar with how these treaties apply locally can best advise investors in a particular jurisdiction.

Labor Conditions A leading reason for investing abroad is to take advantage of relatively low labor costs in a foreign country. The true cost of labor, however, is more than the hourly or daily wage; it includes labor efficiency, trainability, reliability, and adherence to quality-control standards. In addition, the labor and foreign investment laws of some countries, particularly those with socialist economies, require employers to fund a wide range of employee benefits that are not expected by U.S. investors. These benefits include housing, travel, education, and food subsidies, as well as the more common retirement, health insurance, and maternity benefits. Local labor laws can make it difficult to terminate inefficient or redundant workers, thereby reducing the employer's leverage over unsatisfactory employees.

> *Local labor laws can make it difficult to terminate inefficient or redundant workers, thereby reducing the employer's leverage over unsatisfactory employees.*

Financial Issues

An investor in a foreign project needs to consider such financial issues as the capitalization of the project, currency considerations, and taxation.

Project Capitalization Equity investment in foreign countries typically requires availability of capital both for construction costs and for daily operations. The reliability and attractiveness of a host nation in this regard depends on a variety of factors, such as political risk, currency convertibility laws, profit repatriation restrictions, local banking laws and practices, and the enforceability of guaranties or security agreements.

The currency denomination of a foreign investor's equity obligation or of the venture's foreign currency needs can be a principal concern to a U.S. investor in many developing countries. An understanding of local currency controls, financing restrictions, and methods of hedging contract commitments in specified currencies is an integral part of establishing and implementing a successful financial plan. Local financial institutions may be restricted from offering loans in foreign currencies. Conversely, foreign banks may be reluctant to offer a capital loan to a foreign investor if local-currency profits may not be freely convertible for repayment of the loan. Project proceeds, or even project properties, in a foreign country may not offer sufficient security for a loan from a foreign financial institution. The foreign investor may be required to obtain its capital in its own jurisdiction and secure repayment with assets in that jurisdiction.

One method commonly used to secure project financing is for a financial entity to issue a guaranty. If the political or credit risks of a country are perceived to be especially great, an entity in the host country, often an instrumentality of the host-country government, may be called upon to act as the guarantor. Under a guaranty arrangement, a local financial institution guarantees, for the benefit of the project owners, that the lender will be repaid if the project principals are unable to pay, so long as the project contracts have been adhered to by the parties to the project. The choice of law for enforcement of the guaranty may be subject to negotiation. However, the local financial institutions that are authorized to issue guaranties, especially if they involve repayment in hard currencies, may be subject to a variety of local regulations that, if not adhered to, could result in the guaranty being unenforceable.

A *standby letter of credit* is often used to secure financing for construction or similar large projects. Under this arrangement, a financial institution (the issuing bank), often in the host jurisdiction, undertakes at the request of a borrower (the applicant) to pay a sum of money to the entity that has advanced payments for the project (the beneficiary). The issuing bank will pay the money to the beneficiary upon presentation of certain documents specified by the applicant—usually a brief statement, in language agreed upon by the applicant and the beneficiary, that the applicant has failed to adhere to an underlying project contract and that the beneficiary is therefore entitled to payment from the issuing bank.

The effect of this arrangement is similar to that under a guaranty except that the creditor need only present the required documents. Under a guaranty, the creditor would have to establish, possibly through extended litigation or arbitration, that the debtor breached its obligations in the underlying contract. Use of a standby letter of credit is not unusual, but it has its risks, as the following case demonstrates.

■ **A Case in Point:**   **Summary**

Case 25.3
AMERICAN BELL INTERNATIONAL, INC. v. ISLAMIC REPUBLIC OF IRAN
United States District Court for the Southern District of New York
474 F.Supp. 420 (S.D.N.Y. 1979).

FACTS   In the summer of 1978, American Bell International, a subsidiary of American Telephone and Telegraph Company, entered into a $280 million contract with Iran's Ministry of War to provide equipment and consulting services to improve Iran's international communications system. The contract provided for a down payment to Bell of more than $38 million. The Iranian government had the right to demand return of the down payment less reductions attributable to work performed by Bell and accepted by the Iranian government.

To secure the possible repayment of its down payment, Bell was required to obtain a letter of guaranty to be issued by an Iranian bank in favor of the Iranian government. The Iranian bank in turn required Bell to obtain a standby letter of credit issued by Manufacturers Hanover Trust in favor of the Iranian bank (a back-to-back credit). The standby letter of credit provided for payment by Manufacturers to the Iranian bank upon presentation by the Iranian bank of a statement, the precise wording of which was specified in the standby letter of credit. The agreed-upon statement would be to the effect that the Iranian bank had received a payment request from the Iranian government under the letter of guaranty, that the Iranian bank had made such a payment, and that the Iranian bank was claiming payment for an amount due to it by Manufacturers. As the final element of the standby letter of credit transaction, Manufacturers required Bell and its parent corporation, American Telephone and Telegraph Company, to reimburse Manufacturers for all amounts paid by Manufacturers to the Iranian bank pursuant to the standby letter of credit.

In early 1979, the Imperial Government of Iran collapsed and was succeeded by the Islamic Republic. In anticipation of a payment claim by the Iranian government and the Iranian bank, Bell sought a preliminary injunction prohibiting Manufacturers from honoring any demand that the Iranian bank might make for payment under the standby letter of credit. In August 1979 Manufacturers received a demand for payment that complied with the terms of the standby letter of credit, and proposed to make payment. Bell sought to prevent Manufacturers from making payment under the standby letter of credit. Bell argued that the Iranian government had breached the consulting contract, and that the demand on the letter of guaranty and the subsequent demand on the letter of credit reflected "fraud in the transaction," that is, that the Iranian government was seeking fraudulently to regain a portion of the contract deposit.

ISSUE PRESENTED   Does an issuer of a standby letter of credit have an absolute duty to transfer the funds if the demand for payment conforms to the terms of the letter of credit, regardless of the obligations of the parties in the underlying contractual relationship?

SUMMARY OF OPINION   The Federal District Court refused to infer a basis for fraud in the transaction, and rejected Bell's request for a preliminary injunction barring Manufacturers from making payment. The court distinguished between the parties' rights under the underlying contract—including the right to claim damages for breach of that contract—and Manufacturers' obligation under the standby letter of credit to pay the requisite amounts upon its receipt of conforming documents, regardless of whether the Iranian government breached the underlying contract.

The court was unmoved by Bell's claim that it was victimized by unforeseeable political events.

> The Contract with Iran . . . was certain to bring Bell both monetary profit and prestige and good will in the global communications industry. The agreement to indemnify Manufacturers on its Letter of Credit provided the means by which these benefits could be achieved.

> One who reaps the rewards of commercial arrangements must also accept their burdens. One such burden in this case, voluntarily accepted by Bell, was the risk that demand might be made without cause on the funds constituting the down payment. . . . As between two innocents [i.e., Bell and Manufacturers], the party who undertakes by contract the risk of political uncertainty and governmental caprice must bear the consequences when the risk comes home to roost.

RESULT   The court refused to enjoin Manufacturers from making payment under the standby letter of credit.

COMMENTS   *Bell* was one of many cases resulting from the fall of the Imperial Government of Iran and the subsequent demands made by the successor Iranian government for payment under standby letters of credit that had been issued by foreign contractors as security for performance of contracts. Almost uniformly, U.S. courts rejected requests for injunctive relief, holding that the standby letter of credit mechanism should be respected independently of the question of performance in the underlying transaction.

Because U.S. law prohibits U.S. banks from issuing guaranties, the standby letter of credit mechanism is a useful way to provide payment or repayment comfort, especially to a party with superior bargaining power. However, as with letters of credit generally, the applicant should only enter into such arrangements with a clear understanding of how the mechanism works. Because the documentary credit transaction is independent of the underlying contract, applicants should clearly establish what the documentary conditions for payment are, in addition to establishing the terms of the underlying contract.

Currency Considerations   The denomination of the currency required to capitalize a foreign investment project may affect each investor's contribution as currencies appreciate and depreciate against each other. For example, a foreign partner in a joint venture may agree to contribute a specified amount of U.S. dollars over time, with the host-country partner making an equal contribution in local currency; if the local currency depreciates against the U.S. dollar, the foreign partner will end up making a greater than 50% contribution to the joint venture. This problem of unequal contributions may also arise where local law requires foreign-currency capital contributions to be valued at an official exchange rate that does not reflect the local currency's true value. These currency risks can be addressed in careful contract drafting and, where possible, through currency swaps and hedging.

The availability and cost of hard currency can be a major issue in a host country whose currency is not freely convertible. It may be of less concern to a foreign investor who expects to earn hard currency through exports from its foreign project, or is able to use its local-currency profits to purchase local products for sale abroad. This latter arrangement is known as *counter-trade.*

Cash flow hedging methods are increasingly common in countries in which foreign exchange controls remain restrictive. For example, in many Eastern European countries, Western companies with both import and export activities structure import payments to match hard-currency inflows in order to reduce potential exchange-rate losses. If local currencies are being devalued very rapidly, inflows of hard-currency earnings may lag behind import payments to prevent income devaluation. As a currency is devalued, import costs rise. By delaying the conversion of receivables into local currency until imported goods are paid for, companies earn income at at least the same exchange rate used for outflows, reducing potential exchange-rate losses.

Another option open to companies throughout Eastern Europe is to invoice wholesalers and retailers in foreign currency. This is permitted in all of the countries in the region, provided that actual payments are made subject to local foreign-exchange laws—in other words, that bills are paid in local currency.

Taxation   Tax planning is an essential part of any foreign investor's business plan. Careful planning can avoid double taxation and take advantage of local tax benefits. In some host countries it is permissible to negotiate a *gross-up clause* whereby the local partner or licensee is obligated to pay all taxes other than those specifically allocated to the foreign partner. In this way, the foreign party avoids the risk of tax increases or unknown taxes. However, some countries prohibit such shifting of responsibility for the payment of certain taxes and will not recognize gross-up contractual terms.

As of February 1994, the United States had bilateral tax treaties with 52 countries. The treaties seek to avoid double taxation of United States-based businesses and individuals. Some treaties also impose tax ceilings on certain types of income; for example, one treaty imposes a 10% tax ceiling on passive income such as royalties from technology licenses or rental income. Bilateral tax treaties may not affect all of the taxes applicable to a foreign investment project, or the taxation applicable to an individual expatriate employee's income, but where a tax treaty provision is applicable and it offers more favorable tax treatment than the comparable domestic tax rule, the treaty rule will generally apply.

Tax credits may be available to U.S. businesses engaged in foreign projects that are taxed by the host country. Such foreign-tax credits are available for the amount of foreign taxes paid up to a certain limit, which is derived by dividing the foreign-source taxable income by the total taxable income (which includes all foreign- and domestic-source income) and multiplying that fraction by the U.S. tax liability on the total taxable income. Foreign-tax credits for any one year cannot exceed the amount of foreign income taxes that have been paid or accrued, but taxes in excess of the limitation can be carried back two years and forward five years, subject to each year's tax-credit limit.

■ Operational Concerns

A variety of noncommercial issues can affect the desirability of operating a business abroad. These factors include language and cultural customs, ease of communication and transportation, and amenities for expatriate staff.

Language and Cultural Customs

Knowledge of the language of the host country, or the use of competent interpreters, is essential to the success of a business venture abroad. Stories abound concerning the gaffes of U.S. investors who, because of language difficulties or cultural misunderstandings, miscalculated the effect of their business operations, misinterpreted contract negotiations, or simply could not maintain good working relationships with their foreign counterparts. Business skills can be rendered ineffective by the inability to communicate.

Contract terms, both legal and technical, require accurate translation to ensure effective implementation. Product marketing and trademark and trade-name registration require sophisticated language skills and cultural sensitivity to ensure product acceptance in a foreign culture.

The customs of a host country can have a substantial impact on local business operations. A frank and direct management style may be welcomed in some countries; in other countries it may be viewed as arrogant and offensive. Gift giving may be appropriate, even expected, behavior in certain circumstances; in other situations it may be regarded as unethical and possibly illegal.

> *Gift giving may be appropriate, even expected, behavior in certain circumstances; in other situations it may be regarded as unethical and possibly illegal.*

Communications

International, direct-dial phones and fax machines are common business tools in some regions; but many developing countries whose natural resources, labor skills, and markets attract foreign investors do not offer these quick methods of communication. Even postal or courier services may be unreliable. Such deficiencies need to be addressed in contracts that require timely notice or delivery of documents. Expatriate managers without quick access to headquarters may have to be more creative and self-reliant in making decisions than their colleagues in more developed countries.

Transportation

Transportation problems can affect the delivery of raw materials within a host country. Without reliable transportation, products and the people responsible for production cannot effectively reach their destinations. Inadequate port facilities can lead to delayed shipments abroad and lost sales. Inefficient or corrupt customs officials can have the same effect. These concerns must be addressed in contracts that hinge on timely delivery of equipment or products.

Expatriate Amenities

In many developing countries an expatriate manager and staff may be essential. To attract qualified personnel to hardship posts usually requires a compensation package that includes income premiums and benefits. The income-tax laws of the host country may disadvantage expatriate staff, and additional compensation may have to be paid to counteract this disadvantage.

Local managers may resent the higher compensation of their expatriate counterparts; some countries' laws may require that local managers receive compensation comparable to that of their expatriate counterparts.

There can be substantial start-up costs as expatriate personnel acclimatize. On the other hand, some companies have found that an expatriate may eventually become too acclimatized, accepting local practices that may not be consistent with headquarters' or the industry's practices.

Personal safety may be an issue in some countries, effectively precluding assignment of personnel with families, or making it difficult to extend company health and life insurance benefits to expatriate employees.

■ Factors to Consider When Going International

Before expanding into international markets, a firm must take into consideration not only market conditions, but also the legal mores of the foreign country. Some examples of substantive laws that may affect a foreign business are import/export regulations, employment law, tax law, securities law, and antitrust. A company that follows the correct form of doing business, but fails to recognize local law, may reduce its profitability. A company considering foreign investments should therefore carefully analyze the sociopolitical and economic climates of the prospective host country, in addition to obtaining a clear understanding of the legal, regulatory, and administrative regimes, and the future changes that can be anticipated. In other words, an expanding firm should be sensitive to the fact that the variables in international transactions are of a different magnitude and perspective than those involved in carrying on a domestic business.

Before a company conducts business in a foreign country, it should first determine the competition in the region. Market analysis may, however, fail to consider fully the cultural, legal, and political climate that may determine the ultimate costs and returns on investments and assets.

One way in which companies typically expand into the international marketplace is through direct sales to customers. Direct sales pose special problems for the company including, but not limited to, export regulations, international contract law, letters of credit, import regulations, and the use of representatives.

If costs do not justify opening a local office, a firm will often retain a local representative to oversee the sale of its products. However, if the transaction is not correctly structured, the company may find that it has a dependent agent in the foreign country—that it has, under local law, opened an office in the foreign country. Transactions thought to be tax free would, in fact, be subject to corporate tax, and the local agent may have acquired additional rights under local employment law.

Another manner in which a company can conduct business in a foreign country is through the acquisition of an existing company. Such transactions are governed by the laws regulating foreign investment in the country. Tax issues will play a predominant role in the determination of the form of the acquisition and the method of future operation.

A firm might also choose to create an entity distinct from the parent corporation. This entity could be a corporation with 100% foreign ownership, or a joint venture in the form of a corporation or partnership. Local law will define the regulations and restrictions to be imposed on the firm. The investors in many countries may have the flexibility of determining whether the entity is considered a partnership or corporation for United States tax purposes. Other issues to be considered are the requirements for formation, local participation, and administration of the company. The final determination of the most advantageous form should be determined by weighing the company's legal and financial considerations against the substantive law of the country as discussed with local experts.

The main areas of substantive law of concern to foreign companies are exchange controls, taxes, dissolution restrictions, and employee rights. Exchange controls exist to compensate for unstable currencies. They require capitalization, taxes on dividends of subsidiaries, and limitations on foreign exchange.

Tax considerations are also very important when structuring a foreign entity. For example, when a branch office or subsidiary is involved, an American company may, under certain circumstances, have its foreign taxes credited against U.S. taxes. An agreement that creates no tax liability in one country may create full income-tax liability in another. Therefore, any decision to transfer assets or to contract for the purchase, sale, or lease of property with a third party should be evaluated in light of local and U.S. tax laws.

Dissolution restrictions may prevent a company from dissolving (or liquidating the assets of) its foreign entity unless certain conditions are met. Before establishing a foreign entity, the parent company should know what restrictions under local law will preclude the termination or dissolution of the local entity.

If the company employs workers in the foreign country, it must abide by the laws and regulations of that country. Although the laws governing the formation of a business and taxes are dealt with on a rational basis, employment relations may be affected by political pressure. Many governments, in an attempt to protect the workers, have imposed restrictions on the number of foreign workers, or established requirements that a certain percentage of the employees must be nationals. Problems may also arise when the conditions of employment differ from company policy. The company must, however, accept these as a condition of doing business in the foreign country.

A business contemplating doing business abroad must realize that there are major considerations apart from market conditions. The failure to evaluate or understand the legal parameters for doing business in another country can undermine the profitability of the firm. Although compliance with local tax, labor, exchange, and dissolution restrictions might result in smaller profits than the company had envisioned, failure to comply can result in fines, dissolution of the firm, or prison sentences. A company entering a foreign market must therefore develop a sensitivity for the way business is run in a particular country in order to monitor the changes affecting the business.

In Brief: Factors to Consider When Going International

- Market Conditions and Competition
- Legal Mores of Foreign Country
- Substantive Foreign Law, including laws regarding:
    Exchange controls
    Import/Export
    Employment
    Taxes
    Securities
    Antitrust
    Formation, Governance, and Dissolution of Foreign Corporation or Partnership
- Sociopolitical and Economic Climate of Host Country

■ Suing Foreign Governments

Sovereign immunity and the act-of-state doctrine are international legal principles that affect the rights of private commercial parties when a government becomes involved in or interferes with an international commercial transaction.

Sovereign Immunity

Sovereign immunity prevents the courts of one country from hearing suits against the governments of other countries. The rationale underlying this rule is that all sovereign states are equal, and none may subject others to their laws.

However, this rule has been gradually tempered by commercial reality. Because private entities often enter into commercial transactions with foreign governments, it became apparent that allowing a government to have complete immunity from all suits was not desirable. Thus, the concept of absolute immunity yielded to the restrictive theory of sovereign immunity, which allows immunity for a government's public activities but not for its commercial activities.

The Foreign Sovereign Immunities Act of 1977 (FSIA) represents the codification in the United States of the restrictive theory of immunity. The FSIA was designed to eliminate the inconsistencies associated with politically initiated decisions to grant or withhold sovereign immunity in particular cases. It transferred to the courts the power to determine when sovereign immunity applies, "by reference to the nature of the course of conduct or particular transaction or act."

The FSIA is the sole basis for obtaining jurisdiction over a foreign government in United States courts. The FSIA grants a blanket immunity to foreign states except in cases in which: (1) the foreign state expressly or impliedly waives its immunity; (2) the foreign state engages in commercial activities; (3) the foreign state expropriates property in violation of international law (that is, seizes it without proper compensation); (4) property acquired by gift or succession or immovable property located in the United States is in issue; (5) certain noncommercial torts are committed by the foreign state; (6) suit is brought to enforce a maritime lien under admiralty (that is, maritime) law; and (7) in a suit initiated by the foreign state, the defendant wishes to file a counterclaim. The commercial-activity exception is probably the most important.

If the nature of the foreign party to a contract or the subject matter of a contract is not clearly commercial, it may be advisable to establish a waiver of sovereign immunity in the contract.

In the following case, the commercial-activity exception to sovereign immunity was applied to the breach of a contract by an Iraqi commercial bank and by the Iraqi government.

■ **A Case in Point:**   **In the Language of the Court**

Case 25.4
COMMERCIAL BANK OF KUWAIT v. RAFIDAIN BANK
United States Court of Appeals for the Second Circuit
15 F.3d 238 (2d Cir. 1994).

FACTS   The controversy stemmed in part from the situation in the Middle East that began with Iraq's invasion of Kuwait in August 1990 and led to the Gulf War between the U.S. and Iraq. Iraq suspended its payments under various obligations, including those at issue in this litigation.

Rafidain Bank, a commercial bank owned by the Republic of Iraq, entered into several loan agreements and letter of credit transactions involving international banks. The Commercial Bank of Iraq (CBI), the Iraqi equivalent of the Federal Reserve in the United States, guaranteed some of Rafidain's payment obligations to assist Rafidain in obtaining loans. The Commercial Bank of Kuwait (Commercial Kuwait) participated in syndicates formed by lending banks to spread the risks of these transactions with Rafidain. Commercial Kuwait's share of the outstanding payment obligations was approximately $33 million. Commercial Kuwait's allegations were based on CBI's guarantees of Rafidain's obligations and on a letter of credit under which Commercial Kuwait paid approximately $7.4 million. Commercial Kuwait sued Rafidain and CBI (the Iraqi Banks) for intentionally defaulting on their loan obligations. The Iraqi Banks claimed that the U.S. district court had no jurisdiction over them due to sovereign immunity.

ISSUE PRESENTED   Did the Iraqi Banks enjoy sovereign immunity under the Foreign Sovereign Immunities Act (FSIA), thereby depriving the U.S. district court of jurisdiction to determine whether the Iraqi Banks willfully defaulted on their loan agreements?

*Case **25.4** continued on following page*

*Case **25.4** continued*

OPINION   FEINBERG, J., writing for the U.S. Court of Appeals:

. . . .

The Iraqi Banks contend that the district court erred in applying the FSIA's "commercial activity" exception to sovereign immunity, and therefore lacked jurisdiction to consider those counts. The FSIA provides the "sole basis" for obtaining jurisdiction over a foreign sovereign in the United States. Under the FSIA, a "foreign state shall be immune from the jurisdiction of the courts of the United States and of the states" unless one of several statutory exceptions applies. . . .

The "commercial activity" exception to sovereign immunity provides, in relevant part, that a foreign sovereign or its agencies and instrumentalities: shall not be immune from the jurisdiction of the courts of the United States or of the States in any case . . . in which the action is based . . . upon an act outside the territory of the United States in connection with a commercial activity of the foreign sovereign elsewhere and that act causes a direct effect in the United States.

The Supreme Court has recently clarified the "direct effect" language of 1605(a)(2).[5] *Weltover* held that Argentina's unilateral rescheduling of bond payments had a "direct effect" within the meaning of § 1605(a)(2) because New York was the place of payment. Similarly, the agreements at issue . . . require the Iraqi Banks to make payments in U.S. dollars into accounts in New York City. The Iraqi Banks concede that these transactions constitute "commercial activity" under 1603(d). Nevertheless, they argue that the "commercial activity" exception does not apply because the payments were to be made not directly to Commercial but to New York bank accounts held by the lead banks of the various lending syndicates. The Iraqi Banks thus contend that, because the United States is not the place of performance of any contractual obligations owed to this plaintiff, there is no "direct effect in the United States" within the meaning of § 1605(a)(2).

We reject appellants' attempt to limit the Court's opinion in *Weltover*. The "commercial activity" exception of the FSIA withdraws immunity in cases involving essentially private commercial activities of foreign sovereigns that have an impact within the United States. This reflects the "restrictive" theory of sovereign immunity that underlies the FSIA. The focus of § 1605(a)(2) is the activity of the sovereign. If the sovereign's activity is commercial in nature and has a direct effect in the United States, then the jurisdictional nexus is met, no immunity attaches, and a district court has the authority to adjudicate disputes based on that activity.

The failure of the Iraqi Banks to remit funds in New York, as they were contractually bound to do, had a direct effect in the United States under *Weltover*. Furthermore, the requisite "material connection" between Commercial [Kuwait's] cause of action and the "commercial activity" which is the jurisdictional basis is met despite Commercial [Kuwait's] reliance on an agent to collect the sums due. Thus, the district court had jurisdiction to hear Commercial [Kuwait's] claims.

RESULT   The district court had jurisdiction under the "commercial activity" exception to the FSIA. The Iraqi Banks did not enjoy sovereign immunity from any part of this action.

---

5. *Argentina v. Weltover*, 112 S.Ct. 2160 (1992).

Questions

1. Do you agree with the court that the requisite "material connection" between Commercial Kuwait's cause of action and the commercial activity was met?

2. What type of relief should be granted to Commercial Kuwait?

The FSIA is relevant to U.S. companies that do or intend to do business with state-owned or state-managed enterprises, such as those in China and Vietnam. The exception from immunity for the commercial activities of these entities may not always be clear. In addition, if the contract is between a foreign, wholly owned subsidiary of a U.S. company and a foreign state-owned enterprise, the fact that the U.S. parent is affected by a breach of the contract may not give rise to any remedial rights under U.S. law.

Act-of-State Doctrine

The *act-of-state doctrine* applies to the noncommercial acts of a government that affect foreign business interests within that government's territory. The doctrine was most clearly expressed by the U.S. Supreme Court in *Underhill v. Hernandez,*[6] when it stated that "the courts of one country will not sit in judgment on the acts of the government of another, done within its own territory." Pursuant to this doctrine, U.S. courts are extremely reluctant to provide a legal remedy under U.S. law for the public acts of a foreign government. As a result, U.S. businesses generally cannot look to the U.S. courts for protection from or compensation for acts such as expropriation unless there is a bilateral treaty between the United States and the foreign country that specifies the procedural and substantive rights of a U.S. investor in that country. However, OPIC (the Overseas Private Investment Corporation) will insure U.S. businesses against certain host-government acts, such as expropriation or restrictions on the conversion of local currency earnings.

■ U.S. Domestic Considerations

A number of U.S. laws and business practices directly or indirectly affect U.S. investment abroad.

---

6. 168 U.S. 250, 252, 18 S.Ct. 83, 84 (1897).

Trade Laws

If a U.S. investor in a foreign manufacturing facility wishes to market its foreign-manufactured products in the United States, it will face many of the same trade restrictions that are imposed on foreign manufacturers. In addition, if exports to the United States are a primary goal, the U.S. investor abroad should consider the advantages of preferential programs such as the NAFTA and the Caribbean Basin Initiative. (Trade laws are discussed in chapter 3.)

Product Safety Standards

Exports to the United States may have to originate in facilities certified by the U.S. government, or may have to be produced according to U.S. government standards. For example, if pharmaceutical products are manufactured by foreign subsidiaries or joint ventures of U.S. companies for export to the United States, they must be produced in facilities that adhere to the manufacturing practices established by the U.S. Food and Drug Administration (FDA). Airplanes constructed abroad for use in U.S. airspace must be built according to Federal Aviation Administration (FAA) standards in FAA-certified facilities. Investment contracts for such U.S.-export projects need to reflect the production standards required by U.S. law.

Foreign-based U.S. manufacturers, like domestic U.S. manufacturers, need to be aware of U.S. product-liability law (discussed in chapter 10) and of product standards (discussed in chapter 19). Developing countries are increasingly enacting safety standards for manufacturing, and guidelines for manufacturer liability. Events such as the Bhopal disaster in India (discussed in chapter 1) have shown that foreign-based U.S. investors cannot avoid liability solely by compliance with local standards. However, as the case that follows reveals, U.S. procedural law can (although it did not in this instance) insulate a U.S. company from being sued under U.S. law by foreign nationals.

■ **A Case in Point:**   **Summary**

Case 25.5
DOW CHEMICAL CO. v.
ALFARO
Supreme Court of Texas
786 S.W.2d 674 (Tex. 1990).

FACTS Domingo Castro Alfaro, a Costa Rican resident and employee of Standard Fruit Company, and 81 other Costa Rican employees and their wives brought suit against Dow Chemical Company and Shell Oil Company. The employees claimed that while working on a banana plantation in Costa Rica for Standard Fruit Company, they suffered personal injuries as a result of exposure to dibromochloropropane (DBCP). DBCP is a pesticide manufactured by Dow and Shell, which was allegedly furnished to Standard Fruit. Standard Fruit is an American subsidiary of Dole Fresh Fruit Company, headquartered in Boca Raton, Florida. The employees exposed to DBCP allegedly suffered several medical problems, including sterility.

After the U.S. Environmental Protection Agency (EPA) banned DBCP in the United States, Shell and Dow apparently shipped several hundred thousand gallons of the pesticide to Costa Rica for use by Standard Fruit. Alfaro sued Dow and Shell in Texas in April 1984, alleging that their handling of DBCP caused the employees serious personal injuries for which Shell and Dow were liable under the theories of product liability, strict liability and breach of warranty.

The defendants argued that Texas was not a convenient forum in which to litigate this case, under the doctrine of *forum non conveniens.*

ISSUE PRESENTED Does the statutory right to enforce a personal injury or wrongful death claim in the Texas courts preclude a trial court from dismissing the claim on the ground of forum non conveniens?

SUMMARY OF OPINION The Texas Supreme Court began by noting that the law of Texas allows an action to be brought in the courts of one state, even though the injury occurred in another. The court considered the defendants' claim of forum non conveniens in light of the U.S. Court of Appeals decision in *Atchison v. Weeks.*[7] In *Weeks*, the court discussed several of the rationales for the application of forum non conveniens. Among these reasons was the argument that there are many advantages to trying a case where the cause of action arises: the courts of the state in which the cause of action arose can more satisfactorily administer the laws of the state than can the courts of another state, and the expense of a trial would be less at the place of the tort than elsewhere.

In this case, judicial remedies were available in both Texas and Costa Rica. Costa Rica, however, does not allow jury trials. Because Costa Rica also does not allow for deposition of witnesses, it would have been difficult or impossible to depose Dow and Shell officials had the case been tried in Costa Rica.

The court, in light of the statute and the rationale of the *Weeks* decision, determined that although there are some advantages to trying a case where the cause of action arises, the Texas court was the more suitable place to try this case due to the different legal systems and in order to save expenses.

RESULT The plaintiffs can bring their suit against defendants Shell and Dow in the Texas courts even though the harm occurred in Costa Rica.

COMMENTS Both Shell and Dow tried to argue that Texas was an inconvenient forum. It is true that there are advantages to trying a case where the

---
7. 254 F. 513 (5th Cir. 1918).

cause of action arose (e.g., evidence is more accessible). However, with improvements in technology and transportation, most forums today are not inconvenient nor are they cost prohibitive.

Ethical Consideration

Was the conduct of Dow Chemical and Shell Oil ethical when they shipped to Costa Rica an insecticide banned in the U.S.? Was Standard Fruit's use of the U.S.-banned pesticide ethical? Were the defendants arguing inconvenient forum to escape the Texas laws regarding personal injury and wrongful death? If so, is that ethical?

Export Licensing

Foreign investment projects that involve U.S. technology may be subject to licensing and reexport restrictions imposed by the Export Administration Act or the Arms Export Control Act (both discussed in chapter 3). These restrictions can extend to the reexport of products that contain specially licensed technology and to the technical training of foreign technicians in the United States. U.S. investors involved in foreign investment projects with a sensitive technology component must explore these restrictions and obtain an advisory opinion from the relevant U.S. government department.

Restrictions on Corrupt Practices

U.S. law prohibits U.S. businesses from paying or offering anything of value to foreign officials who have discretionary authority for the purpose of inducing such officials to direct business to the U.S. entity. This principle is embodied in the Foreign Corrupt Practices Act of 1977 (discussed in chapter 3).

The Responsible Manager

Managing International Business Transactions

Managing an international business transaction, whether it be a sale, a license of intellectual property, or an equity investment, requires all of the skills needed for a comparable domestic transaction and more. A broad range of foreign and domestic factors—legal, economic, social, and political—affect the transaction. A manager in a multinational business environment must act with these factors in mind, but she cannot suspend the critical approach she would bring to a domestic transaction just because her foreign business counterparts do things differently. A U.S. business organization is subject to the business and ethical expectations of its management, shareholders, and customers. It is also subject to U.S., as well as foreign, laws. The multinational context requires sensitivity, flexibility, and creativity. It also requires a well-prepared checklist of business essentials, and a commitment to the business's traditional standards of performance.

The plan to buy or sell or invest abroad begins with identification of the project goals. Without carefully thought-out project goals, a transnational venture can quickly go wrong. Some goals may be difficult to accomplish, such as repatriating hard-currency earnings from a country with inconvertible currency or strict foreign-exchange laws.

In many countries, a business does not have the freedom to craft a contract within a broad field of permissible business terms. Developing countries, in particular, impose restrictions on certain terms that most U.S. businesses would consider negotiable. The laws of these countries are not, as in the United States, rules that need be consulted only to fine-tune a done deal. They are often intended to establish the very parameters of an acceptable transaction. On the other hand, they often provide incentives for certain types of transactions. Bilateral investment and tax treaties can also offer helpful guidelines as to permissible project terms, incentives, and remedies. Failure to examine the incentives, as well as the restrictions, reflected in treaties and local laws can mean more costly, extended negotiations, or even a less profitable venture.

Early use of professional services, such as those offered by legal counsel, accountants, and banking advisors with experience in the industry and in the appropriate culture, can reduce negotiation costs and the risk of disputes. This is particularly true in the context of international transactions, in which travel costs can substantially increase the cost of negotiations, and the different perspectives (and possibly languages) of the parties can cause misunderstandings and disputes.

Two threshold questions in negotiating any international transaction should be whether there is a choice of applicable law and whether the parties can select the forum for resolving any disputes. Well-drafted contract provisions that address these issues can offer some comfort and can allow the parties to address any substantive disputes without creating additional disputes over procedure.

Arbitration of disputes by a specialized forum may be more efficient and offer more confidentiality than litigation in a public court, but it may not adhere to judicial precedents and may not be easily enforceable. In some countries the judges or arbitrators may favor the local party to the dispute, but a neutral forum in a third country may be impractical for the resolution of modest disputes. The advantages and disadvantages of various options should be considered carefully. The inclination to treat these terms as inconsequential boilerplate should be avoided.

In domestic business transactions in the United States, a variety of vehicles offer some security that each party will perform the contract or will compensate the other party for failure to perform. U.S. laws offer a relatively sophisticated array of contractual and statutory remedies. The laws of foreign countries may offer fewer established options; even where effective remedies are available, as a practical matter, the legal administrative system of the foreign country may not be able to implement them. A discerning manager in an international transaction needs to familiarize himself with both the legal and the practical availability of the remedies for failure to perform.

Managers of international business transactions should be aware of currency exchange and valuation rules. Even in transactions denominated in a single currency, there is usually some risk associated with the changing valuations of the currencies. For example, a U.S. entity that purchases products from abroad and denominates their price in dollars runs the risk that the currency of that foreign country could devalue; the dollar price would then be higher than the local-currency price.

Equity investments abroad carry foreign-exchange risks both in the establishment of formulas and denominations for capital contributions by the respective parties and in the repatriation of profits or royalties. Though a foreign country's currency laws may not impose restric-

tions on repatriation of profits, its tax laws may effectively create such restrictions. An understanding of the tax laws of the foreign country is therefore essential when establishing projections for repatriable earnings from a foreign investment, from a licensing transaction, or even from the sale of products or services abroad.

U.S. laws, ranging from tax and product-liability laws to administrative regulations governing the certification of imported products, need to be considered. Some U.S. laws, such as the Foreign Corrupt Practices Act and the antitrust laws, can affect transactions that occur primarily outside the United States. Legal counsel with experience in international transactions is indispensable.

A manager of an international business transaction is in the unenviable position of having to conform to the sometimes conflicting ethical standards of two or more cultures. For example, in some cultures gift giving—ranging from a token company lapel pin to expensive automobiles—is an expected courtesy. In other cultures (and under the U.S. Foreign Corrupt Practices Act), gift giving, however innocently intended, may be viewed as an impermissible attempt to influence a business decision.

A U.S. business may feel hamstrung by its inability, for legal or ethical reasons, to match a competitor's gift or offer of "training"—in effect an all-expenses-paid vacation abroad—for employees of the foreign counterpart. However, sometimes U.S. business practices are preferred. The existence of certain company policies or U.S. laws can give a manager a face-saving, nonpersonal way to decline to engage in unethical behavior.

The laws of many foreign countries are less developed than those in the United States. As a result, there can be a temptation to accept the "practical" solution rather than the one that is legally sanctioned but rarely followed in local practice. However, as foreign visitors, U.S. companies and their personnel risk being held up as examples of unacceptable behavior if there is a political, and perhaps business, reason for doing so. Though recent events suggest that capitalistic ways are being seen in a less villainous light in many foreign countries, the realities of nationalism and regionalism will remain as a basis for challenging unethical and illegal behavior by U.S. businesses abroad. A discerning manager should have a full appreciation of social customs, applicable laws, and acceptable business practices to make appropriate legal and ethical business decisions in international business transactions.

Inside Story

The Telmex Privatization

Throughout the late 1980s and early 1990s, Mexico's President Carlos Salinas de Gortari carried out a program of privatization of state companies. The privatization program had been started under the administration of Miguel de la Madrid to reduce the budget deficit, increase competitiveness, and expand foreign investment.

The privatization of Telefonos de Mexico (TELMEX) in 1990 attracted much attention because the telephone company is the third largest firm in Mexico and the eighteenth largest national telephone system in the world (based on the number of lines in service at the end of 1988). The privatization was also the largest in Latin American history and one of the five largest in the world.

Before Telmex was opened to bids, the Mexican government reduced the company's debt, streamlined telephone taxes, consolidated labor contracts, and eliminated cross subsidies between local and long-distance calls. These steps increased the company's attractiveness to potential buyers.

The government of Mexico, which had previously owned a majority of the Telmex stock, announced in 1989 its intention to privatize the company. In 1990, it sold 20.4% of the capital stock of Telmex for $1.76 billion to a consortium comprising Grupo Carso de Mexico, Southwestern Bell, and France Telecom. Grupo Carso owns 51% of the shares of the consortium; Southwestern Bell and France Telecom each own 24.5%. This transaction was structured to effectively transfer the control of Telmex to the consortium even though the Mexican government retained a majority of the capital stock.

As consideration for their 20.4% stake and control of the firm, the consortium paid the Mexican government approximately $21.76 per share. Of this amount, $1.74 billion has been paid in cash and $23.6 million is payable by the controlling shareholders jointly before May 1, 1996. The government later sold $3.7 billion in shares to the public in two separate offerings, the only public tenders in the privatization program. A total of 4.4% of the shares were awarded to Telmex workers, while the remainder were floated on the domestic and international securities markets.

In order to ensure the viability of the privatization, the Mexican government granted Telmex some healthy concessions. Competition was barred until 1996. Generous tax breaks for its capital investment in equipment and system expansion were granted. Excise taxes on telephone charges were also removed. In return, Telmex was required to increase the total number of lines by at least 12% annually until January 1995, reduce waiting time for new lines to six months, and replace outmoded exchanges with digital technology.

So far, Telmex's privatization has been successful. Lines per capita increased almost 2%, capital investment was being internally financed, and better technology decreased labor costs. In addition, Telmex became one of the most actively traded companies on the New York Stock Exchange.

The privatization of state-owned companies in Mexico is entering its final phase. As of 1994, the government had sold or dissolved more than 80% of the 1,155 businesses it once ran. The sale of the companies earned the government more than $21 billion, almost all of which went to retire the national debt. As a result of these and other efforts, the Salinas administration was able to slow inflation from more than 150% to below 10% and to open the economy to competition and outside investment.

Key Words and Phrases

act-of-state doctrine **853**
arrested **834**
back-to-back letter of credit **835**
bill of lading **835**
clean bill of lading **835**
compensation trade **839**

confirming bank **835**
conflict of laws **833**
countertrade **848**
forum non conveniens **854**
gross-up clause **848**
irrevocable letter of credit **836**

letter of credit (LC) **835**
lien notice **834**
processing operation **839**
sovereign immunity **850**
standby letter of credit **845**

Questions and Case Problems

1. What factors should a manager take into account when planning to expand operations outside of her home country?

2. Two former football players from the Chicago Winds, a defunct World Football League club, sought payment of their salaries from the club after the franchise was terminated. The original player contracts had obligated the club to secure a "domestic letter of credit" for each player in the amount of his salary. The club obtained the letters of credit, which stated that their purpose was "to guarantee payment for services rendered" by the players to the club. Each letter of credit provided that the issuing bank would pay the player upon presentation of a draft (an order for payment) and an affidavit signed by that player stating that the club had not paid him for a scheduled football game by a certain date. The players were not paid, and they presented their affidavits and draft documents to the bank. The bank refused to pay, on the grounds that the letter of credit was subject, by its terms, to the UCP. Under the UCP, the letter was unilaterally revocable by the bank. Who should prevail? [*Beathard v. Chicago Football Club, Inc.*, 419 F.Supp. 1133 (N.D.Ill. 1976)]

3. The New England Petroleum Corporation (NEPCO), a U.S. corporation, obtained refined oil from its wholly owned Bahamas subsidiary refinery, PETCO. In 1968, PETCO entered into a long-term contract to purchase crude oil from Chevron Oil Trading (COT), a branch of a petroleum company that held 50% of an oil concession in Libya. In 1973, Libya nationalized several foreign-owned oil concessions, including that of the oil company of which COT was a part. As a result, COT terminated its contract with PETCO.

PETCO then entered into a new contract with the National Oil Corporation (NOC), which was wholly owned by the Libyan government. One month after execution of the contract, Libya imposed an oil embargo on the United States, and NOC canceled its contract with PETCO. Three months later, after a dramatic increase in oil prices, PETCO executed a new contract with NOC. NOC allegedly breached that contract.

PETCO's assignee, Carey, brought suit against NOC, seeking to recover damages for NOC's breach of the two contracts. NOC raised the defense of sovereign immunity. Carey claimed that under the Foreign Sovereign Immunities Act (FSIA) there was no sovereign immunity because the breach of contract was an act outside the territory of the United States in connection with a commercial activity that caused a direct effect in the United States. Who should prevail? [*Carey v. National Oil Corp.*, 592 F.2d 673 (2d Cir. 1979)]

4. Optomagic, Inc. is a U.S. corporation that produces optomagic gizmos. Production of optomagic gizmos involves a confidential gizmo-processing technique (which is described in printed Optomagic manuals), labor-intensive processing, and inclusion of an optomagic component for which Optomagic was granted a U.S. patent six months ago. The optomagic component has widespread uses in the space and aviation and medical industries.

Eight months ago, in the Eastern European country of Varoom, there was a relatively peaceful popular uprising that resulted in the removal of the "old guard" leaders, who had favored a strong centrally planned economy. The new provisional government called for free elections in one year, began taking immediate steps to reform the economy, and promised to liberalize foreign-investment laws to attract foreign investment.

Because the government bureaucracy is still in some disarray, it is extremely helpful, as a practical matter, to have close contacts with a government official who can speed the review and approval process for applications for foreign investment. In a recent official tour of the United States, Dr. Leo Baas, the minister of health and welfare of Varoom, visited Optomagic's manufacturing facility in Boston, Massachusetts. Baas is an eminent surgeon and a strong proponent of bringing advanced medical technology to his developing country so that the best medical care can be made available to the public. In addition, he is interested in finding labor-intensive U.S. industries that may be able to produce products in Varoom for export to the more developed countries, so as to earn badly needed foreign exchange for Varoom. Optomagic is very interested in the newly emerging markets of Eastern Europe, and Varoom's in particular. Optomagic would also like to obtain gizmomium, a raw material necessary for the production of optomagic gizmos, which is found in great abundance in the mountains of Varoom, but which, under Varoomian law, is available only to Varoomian enterprises.

Two weeks after his visit to Optomagic, Baas wrote to the chief executive officer of Optomagic to make the following proposal. Baas and a state-owned medical clinic, Varoom Medical, are interested in establishing a joint venture in Varoom with Optomagic. Current Varoomian law limits foreign investment interests in Varoomian enterprises to 50% of the total investment. Baas states that although under local law the Varoomian partners share equal responsibility for the management of the venture, they will in fact defer to Optomagic in all material matters related to the operation of the manufacturing facility. In addition, Baas assures Optomagic that the foreign-investment law is likely to be liberalized within the year. As his investment in the venture, Baas offers to contribute his lease interest in certain property in Varoom, and to ensure that all of the necessary government permits for the construction and licensing of the facility are obtained. Baas expresses his confidence in being able to obtain all of the government approvals for the proposed project because "our government has recently issued a decree emphasizing the national importance of upgrading our health-care industries."

The father of Optomagic's CEO emigrated from Varoom 60 years ago. He is excited about the developments in Varoom and finds Baas to be a delightful, dynamic man. He is convinced that the time to move into Varoom is now, before Optomagic's competitors do.

Your assignment is to put together a business plan for the proposed joint venture, recognizing that it's going to cost something up front but will be worth the expense in the long run. The CEO wants a preliminary report in two weeks to take to the board of directors, which will be considering establishing a wholly owned subsidiary in London to operate prospective sales and manufacturing facilities in Europe. He also wants a comprehensive report to follow in another four weeks.

(a) You have free access to your expert in-house legal counsel, who has experience in international projects. How can you best use her to assist in putting your plan together? What issues of particular importance should be addressed by counsel for inclusion in the preliminary report?

(b) Given the uncertainty in the development of Varoom's foreign investment laws (and its government), what kind of terms or conditions do you think should be included in the contract for the proposed joint venture to protect against unexpected changes in the laws or government policies? What kind of comfort might be obtained from any U.S. government agencies?

5. Assume the facts in question 4. Are there any legal problems with including Baas as an investor in the project? As a paid consultant?

6. Upon further general inquiry on behalf of Optomagic, you learn the following facts in addition to those set forth in question 4. First, Varoom has a patent law and a trademark registration law, but no copyright law. Second, Varoomian law provides that licenses of foreign technology cannot: (1) unreasonably restrict the geographic market for such exports; (2) impose requirements that the Varoom party purchase components or raw materials from the foreign party; or (3) restrict use of the technology by the Varoom licensee beyond a term of ten years without approval from the supervising ministry (which in this case is the Ministry of Health).

What other information do you need to determine how best to protect Optomagic's intellectual-property rights in the proposed venture? Based on what you do know, what steps should be taken to maximize protection of Optomagic's intellectual-property rights? What U.S. laws will apply to the contribution, licensing, or other transfer of optomagic gizmo components by Optomagic to the joint venture?

7. Assume the facts in question 4. Varoom Medical is prepared to invest 600 million baninis (U.S. $1 = 10,000 baninis) over the first five years of the project. Its commitment will be backed by a standby letter of credit to be issued by the National People's Bank of Varoom, a state-owned bank.

(a) What more do you need to know about the proposed capital contribution to be made by Varoom Medical and the standby letter of credit from the bank? Would you impose any additional conditions or requirements on the proposed contribution and the letter of credit?

(b) What do you propose Optomagic contribute as its share of capital to the proposed joint venture?

8. Assume the facts in question 4. You begin to consider the labor force that the joint venture will need. Baas suggests that there be regular technical training visits by the venture technicians to Optomagic's facility in Boston, Massachusetts. Baas also suggests that he can arrange to select the Varoomian technicians for the joint venture. Monthly salaries in Varoom for the types of employees that would be used in the proposed venture are 30% of the salaries of Optomagic's workers in the United States. However, Varoom's labor laws require: (1) payment of housing and health insurance subsidies by all enterprises to their employees, equal to 50% of their salaries; (2) mandatory arbitration with the local labor bureau prior to termination of any employee for any reason; and (3) in the case of foreign-invested enterprises, salaries and benefits to local management that are comparable with those of the expatriate management personnel of the foreign-invested enterprise.

(a) How would you assess the legal and economic advantages and disadvantages of the employees that Baas proposed be hired?

(b) What U.S. laws may apply to the training of joint-venture technicians at Optomagic's facilities?

(c) Would you recommend that resident expatriate management personnel be assigned to the prospective project, or just visiting technicians? Why? What qualities do you think an expatriate employee in Varoom should have?

9. In addition to the facts covered in questions 4 through 8, you learn that the banini is not freely convertible into dollars. The Varoom foreign-exchange and tax laws provide that a

foreign-invested joint venture can repatriate up to 50% of its foreign exchange earnings, subject to a repatriation tax of 15% (in addition to the tax imposed on the joint venture's income). Banini profits can be exchanged only upon prior approval by the supervising ministry (each ministry is allocated a quota of baninis for which it can approve an exchange into foreign currencies). In addition, Varoom's foreign-investment law requires that foreign-invested enterprises export a minimum of 50% of their products.

    (a)   What alternatives exist to repatriating foreign currency earnings in the prospective venture?

    (b)   What U.S. laws, if any, might apply to exports of optomagic gizmos to the U.S. from Varoom?

10.   USCO is a Nevada corporation that manufactures a highly advanced electronic instrument to measure the heat generated by electric motors operating at high speeds. The instrument has a variety of civilian and military applications. Although it can be run with different software packages available in the market, USCO has developed special software that it feels is superior to that of its competitors and that USCO claims gives a more accurate reading on the instrument. The management of USCO is extremely proud of its reputation as the world leader in this type of instrument and vigilantly guards against infringement on its proprietary technology and its tradename. USCO has a number of U.S. patents on both the instrument and the software. In addition, it uses a federal registered trademark on all of its products.

USCO would like to expand the production and sale of the instruments overseas. It is looking at a number of countries in both Europe and the Far East as possible markets, and is considering using one of the following vehicles for its overseas activities: (1) licensing its technology to a foreign entity to produce the products in exchange for a royalty; (2) setting up a branch in the foreign country to produce and sell the products locally; (3) establishing a wholly owned foreign subsidiary to produce and sell the products locally; or (4) establishing a joint venture with a local company to produce and sell the products locally.

USCO wants to protect its market in the U.S. and in certain foreign countries in which it is currently making direct sales. It is also concerned about maintaining the high-quality reputation of its instrument. Therefore, USCO would like to restrict sales of the instrument to the local market and to require that a copy of its software be sold with each sale of the instrument. Regardless of the investment vehicle used, all rights to the software would remain with USCO.

What U.S. laws may have an impact on whether and how USCO expands overseas?

What local foreign laws may have an impact on USCO's decision on the type of vehicle it chooses to conduct its overseas activities and on the country into which it may expand?

APPENDICES

■ Appendix A The Constitution of the United States of America

PREAMBLE

We the People of the United States, in Order to form a more perfect Union, establish Justice, insure domestic Tranquility, provide for the common defence, promote the general Welfare, and secure the Blessings of Liberty to ourselves and our Posterity, do ordain and establish this Constitution for the United States of America.

ARTICLE I

Section 1.   All legislative Powers herein granted shall be vested in a Congress of the United States, which shall consist of a Senate and House of Representatives.

Section 2.   The House of Representatives shall be composed of Members chosen every second Year by the People of the several States, and the Electors in each State shall have the Qualifications requisite for Electors of the most numerous Branch of the State Legislature.

No Person shall be a Representative who shall not have attained to the Age of twenty five Years, and been seven Years a Citizen of the United States, and who shall not, when elected, be an Inhabitant of that State in which he shall be chosen.

Representatives and direct Taxes shall be apportioned among the several States which may be included within this Union, according to their respective Numbers, which shall be determined by adding to the whole Number of free Persons, including those bound to Service for a Term of Years, and excluding Indians not taxed, three fifths of all other Persons. The actual Enumeration shall be made within three Years after the first Meeting of the Congress of the United States, and within every subsequent Term of ten Years, in such Manner as they shall by Law direct. The Number of Representatives shall not exceed one for every thirty Thousand, but each State shall have at Least one Representative; and until such enumeration shall be made, the State of New Hampshire shall be entitled to chuse three, Massachusetts eight, Rhode Island and Providence Plantations one, Connecticut five, New York six, New Jersey four, Pennsylvania eight, Delaware one, Maryland six, Virginia ten, North Carolina five, South Carolina five, and Georgia three.

When vacancies happen in the Representation from any State, the Executive Authority thereof shall issue Writs of Election to fill such Vacancies.

The House of Representatives shall chuse their Speaker and other Officers; and shall have the sole Power of Impeachment.

Section 3.   The Senate of the United States shall be composed of two Senators from each State, chosen by the Legislature thereof, for six Years; and each Senator shall have one Vote.

Immediately after they shall be assembled in Consequence of the first Election, they shall be divided as equally as may be into three Classes. The Seats of the Senators of the first Class shall be vacated at the Expiration of the second Year, of the second Class at the Expiration of the fourth Year, and of the third Class at the Expiration of the sixth Year, so that one third may be chosen every second Year; and if Vacancies happen by Resignation, or otherwise, during the Recess of the Legislature of any State, the

Executive thereof may make temporary Appointments until the next Meeting of the Legislature, which shall then fill such Vacancies.

No Person shall be a Senator who shall not have attained to the Age of thirty Years, and been nine Years a Citizen of the United States, and who shall not, when elected, be an Inhabitant of that State for which he shall be chosen.

The Vice President of the United States shall be President of the Senate, but shall have no Vote, unless they be equally divided.

The Senate shall chuse their other Officers, and also a President pro tempore, in the Absence of the Vice President, or when he shall exercise the Office of President of the United States.

The Senate shall have the sole Power to try all Impeachments. When sitting for that Purpose, they shall be on Oath or Affirmation. When the President of the United States is tried, the Chief Justice shall preside: And no Person shall be convicted without the Concurrence of two thirds of the Members present.

Judgment in Cases of Impeachment shall not extend further than to removal from Office, and disqualification to hold and enjoy any Office of honor, Trust, or Profit under the United States: but the Party convicted shall nevertheless be liable and subject to Indictment, Trial, Judgment, and Punishment, according to Law.

Section 4.   The Times, Places and Manner of holding Elections for Senators and Representatives, shall be prescribed in each State by the Legislature thereof; but the Congress may at any time by Law make or alter such Regulations, except as to the Places of chusing Senators.

The Congress shall assemble at least once in every Year, and such Meeting shall be on the first Monday in December, unless they shall by Law appoint a different Day.

Section 5.   Each House shall be the Judge of the Elections, Returns, and Qualifications of its own Members, and a Majority of each shall constitute a Quorum to do Business; but a smaller Number may adjourn from day to day, and may be authorized to compel the Attendance of absent Members, in such Manner, and under such Penalties as each House may provide.

Each House may determine the Rules of its Proceedings, punish its Members for disorderly Behavior, and, with the Concurrence of two thirds, expel a Member.

Each House shall keep a Journal of its Proceedings, and from time to time publish the same, excepting such Parts as may in their Judgment require Secrecy; and the Yeas and Nays of the Members of either House on any question shall, at the Desire of one fifth of those Present, be entered on the Journal.

Neither House, during the Session of Congress, shall, without the Consent of the other, adjourn for more than three days, nor to any other Place than that in which the two Houses shall be sitting.

Section 6.   The Senators and Representatives shall receive a Compensation for their Services, to be ascertained by Law, and paid out of the Treasury of the United States. They shall in all Cases, except Treason, Felony and Breach of the Peace, be privileged from Arrest during their Attendance at the Session of their respective Houses, and in going to and returning from the same; and for any Speech or Debate in either House, they shall not be questioned in any other Place.

No Senator or Representative shall, during the Time for which he was elected, be appointed to any civil Office under the Authority of the United States, which shall have been created, or the Emoluments whereof shall have been increased during such time; and no Person holding any Office under the United States, shall be a Member of either House during his Continuance in Office.

Section 7.   All Bills for raising Revenue shall originate in the House of Representatives; but the Senate may propose or concur with Amendments as on other Bills.

Every Bill which shall have passed the House of Representatives and the Senate, shall, before it become a Law, be presented to the President of the United States; If he approve he shall sign it, but if not he shall return it, with his Objections to the House in which it shall have originated, who shall enter the Objections at large on their Journal, and proceed to reconsider it. If after such Reconsideration two thirds of that House shall agree to pass the Bill, it shall be sent together with the Objections, to the other House, by which it shall likewise be reconsidered, and if approved by two thirds of that House, it shall become a Law. But in all such Cases the Votes of both Houses shall be determined by Yeas and Nays, and the Names of the Persons voting for and against the Bill shall be entered on the Journal of each House respectively. If any Bill shall not be returned by the President within ten Days (Sundays excepted) after it shall have been presented to him, the Same shall be a Law, in like Manner as if he had signed it, unless the Congress by their Adjournment prevent its Return in which Case it shall not be a Law.

Every Order, Resolution, or Vote, to which the Concurrence of the Senate and House of Representatives may be necessary (except on a question of Adjournment) shall be presented to the President of the United States; and before the Same shall take Effect, shall be approved by him, or being disapproved by him, shall be repassed by two thirds of the Senate and House of Representatives, according to the Rules and Limitations prescribed in the Case of a Bill.

Section 8.   The Congress shall have Power To lay and collect Taxes, Duties, Imposts and Excises, to pay the Debts and provide for the common Defence and general Welfare of the United States; but all Duties, Imposts and Excises shall be uniform throughout the United States;

To borrow Money on the credit of the United States;

To regulate Commerce with foreign Nations, and among the several States, and with the Indian Tribes;

To establish an uniform Rule of Naturalization, and uniform Laws on the subject of Bankruptcies throughout the United States;

To coin Money, regulate the Value thereof, and of foreign Coin, and fix the Standard of Weights and Measures;

To provide for the Punishment of counterfeiting the Securities and current Coin of the United States;

To establish Post Offices and post Roads;

To promote the Progress of Science and useful Arts, by securing for limited Times to Authors and Inventors the exclusive Right to their respective Writings and Discoveries;

To constitute Tribunals inferior to the supreme Court;

To define and punish Piracies and Felonies committed on the high Seas, and Offenses against the Law of Nations;

To declare War, grant Letters of Marque and Reprisal, and make Rules concerning Captures on Land and Water;

To raise and support Armies, but no Appropriation of Money to that Use shall be for a longer Term than two Years;

To provide and maintain a Navy;

To make Rules for the Government and Regulation of the land and naval Forces;

To provide for calling forth the Militia to execute the Laws of the Union, suppress Insurrections and repel Invasions;

To provide for organizing, arming, and disciplining, the Militia, and for governing such Part of them as may be employed in the Service of the United States, reserving to the States respectively, the Appointment of the Officers, and the Authority of training the Militia according to the discipline prescribed by Congress;

To exercise exclusive Legislation in all Cases whatsoever, over such District (not exceeding ten Miles square) as may, by Cession of particular States, and the Acceptance of Congress, become the Seat of the Government of the United States, and to exercise like Authority over all Places purchased by the Consent of the Legislature of the State in which the Same shall be, for the Erection of Forts, Magazines, Arsenals, dock-Yards, and other needful Buildings;—And

To make all Laws which shall be necessary and proper for carrying into Execution the foregoing Powers, and all other Powers vested by this Constitution in the Government of the United States, or in any Department or Officer thereof.

Section 9. The Migration or Importation of such Persons as any of the States now existing shall think proper to admit, shall not be prohibited by the Congress prior to the Year one thousand eight hundred and eight, but a Tax or duty may be imposed on such Importation, not exceeding ten dollars for each Person.

The privilege of the Writ of Habeas Corpus shall not be suspended, unless when in Cases of Rebellion or Invasion the public Safety may require it.

No Bill of Attainder or ex post facto Law shall be passed.

No Capitation, or other direct, Tax shall be laid, unless in Proportion to the Census or Enumeration herein before directed to be taken.

No Tax or Duty shall be laid on Articles exported from any State.

No Preference shall be given by any Regulation of Commerce or Revenue to the Ports of one State over those of another: nor shall Vessels bound to, or from, one State be obliged to enter, clear, or pay Duties in another.

No Money shall be drawn from the Treasury, but in Consequence of Appropriations made by Law; and a regular Statement and Account of the Receipts and Expenditures of all public Money shall be published from time to time.

No Title of Nobility shall be granted by the United States: And no Person holding any Office of Profit or Trust under them, shall, without the Consent of the Congress, accept of any present, Emolument, Office, or Title, of any kind whatever, from any King, Prince, or foreign State.

Section 10. No State shall enter into any Treaty, Alliance, or Confederation; grant Letters of Marque and Reprisal; coin Money; emit Bills of Credit; make any Thing but gold and silver Coin a Tender in Payment of Debts; pass any Bill of Attainder, ex post facto Law, or Law impairing the Obligation of Contracts, or grant any Title of Nobility.

No State shall, without the Consent of the Congress, lay any Imposts or Duties on Imports or Exports, except what may be absolutely necessary for executing its inspection Laws: and the net Produce of all Duties and Imposts, laid by any State on Imports or Exports, shall be for the Use of the Treasury of the United States; and all such Laws shall be subject to the Revision and Controul of the Congress.

No State shall, without the Consent of Congress, lay any Duty of Tonnage, keep Troops, or Ships of War in time of Peace, enter into any Agreement or Compact with another State, or with a foreign Power, or engage in War, unless actually invaded, or in such imminent Danger as will not admit of delay.

ARTICLE II

Section 1. The executive Power shall be vested in a President of the United States of America. He shall hold his Office during the Term of four Years, and, together with the Vice President, chosen for the same Term, be elected, as follows:

Each State shall appoint, in such Manner as the Legislature thereof may direct, a Number of Electors, equal to the whole Number of Senators and Representatives to which the State may be entitled in the Congress; but no Senator or Representative, or Person holding an Office of Trust or Profit under the United States, shall be appointed an Elector.

The Electors shall meet in their respective States, and vote by Ballot for two Persons, of whom one at least shall not be an Inhabitant of the same State with themselves. And they shall make a List of all the Persons voted for, and of the Number of Votes for each; which List they shall sign and certify, and transmit sealed to the Seat of the Government of the United States, directed to the President of the Senate. The President of the Senate shall, in the Presence of the Senate and House of Representatives, open all the Certificates, and the Votes shall then be counted. The Person having the greatest Number of Votes shall be the President, if such Number be a Majority of the whole Number of Electors appointed; and if there be more than one who have such Majority, and have an equal Number of Votes, then the House of Representatives shall immediately chuse by Ballot one of them for President; and if no Person have a Majority, then from the five highest on the List the said House shall in like Manner chuse the President. But in chusing the President, the Votes shall be taken by States, the Representation from each State having one Vote; A quorum for this Purpose shall consist of a Member or Members from two thirds of the States, and a Majority of all the States shall be necessary to a Choice. In every Case, after the Choice of the President, the Person having the greater Number of Votes of the Electors shall be the Vice President. But if there should remain two or more who have equal Votes, the Senate shall chuse from them by Ballot the Vice President.

The Congress may determine the Time of chusing the Electors, and the Day on which they shall give their Votes; which Day shall be the same throughout the United States.

No person except a natural born Citizen, or a Citizen of the United States, at the time of the Adoption of this Constitution, shall be eligible to the Office of President; neither shall any Person be eligible to that Office who shall not have attained to the Age of thirty five Years, and been fourteen Years a Resident within the United States.

In Case of the Removal of the President from Office, or of his Death, Resignation or Inability to discharge the Powers and Duties of the said Office, the same shall devolve on the Vice President, and the Congress may by Law provide for the Case of Removal, Death, Resignation or Inability, both of the President and Vice President, declaring what Officer shall then act as President, and such Officer shall act accordingly, until the Disability be removed, or a President shall be elected.

The President shall, at stated Times, receive for his Services, a Compensation, which shall neither be increased nor diminished during the Period for which he shall have been elected, and he shall not receive within that Period any other Emolument from the United States, or any of them.

Before he enter on the Execution of his Office, he shall take the following Oath or Affirmation: "I do solemnly swear (or affirm) that I will faithfully execute the Office of President of the United States, and will to the best of my Ability, preserve, protect and defend the Constitution of the United States."

Section 2.   The President shall be Commander in Chief of the Army and Navy of the United States, and of the Militia of the several States, when called into the actual Service of the United States; he may require the Opinion, in writing, of the principal Officer in each of the executive Departments, upon any Subject relating to the Duties of their respective Offices, and he shall have Power to grant Reprieves and Pardons for Offenses against the United States, except in Cases of Impeachment.

He shall have Power, by and with the Advice and Consent of the Senate to make Treaties, provided two thirds of the Senators present concur; and he shall nominate, and by and with the Advice and Consent of the Senate, shall appoint Ambassadors, other public Ministers and Consuls, Judges of the supreme Court, and all other Officers of the United States, whose Appointments are not herein otherwise provided for, and which shall be established by Law; but the Congress may by Law vest the Appointment of such inferior Officers, as they think proper, in the President alone, in the Courts of Law, or in the Heads of Departments.

The President shall have Power to fill up all Vacancies that may happen during the Recess of the Senate, by granting Commissions which shall expire at the End of their next Session.

Section 3.   He shall from time to time give to the Congress Information of the State of the Union, and recommend to their Consideration such Measures as he shall judge necessary and expedient; he may, on extraordinary Occasions, convene both Houses, or either of them, and in Case of Disagreement between them, with Respect to the Time of Adjournment, he may adjourn them to such Time as he shall think proper; he shall receive Ambassadors and other public Ministers; he shall take Care that the Laws be faithfully executed, and shall Commission all the Officers of the United States.

Section 4.   The President, Vice President and all civil Officers of the United States, shall be removed from Office on Impeachment for, and Conviction of, Treason, Bribery, or other high Crimes and Misdemeanors.

ARTICLE III

Section 1.   The judicial Power of the United States, shall be vested in one supreme Court, and in such inferior Courts as the Congress may from time to time ordain and establish. The Judges, both of the supreme and inferior Courts, shall hold their Offices during good Behaviour, and shall, at stated Times, receive for their Services a Compensation, which shall not be diminished during their Continuance in Office.

Section 2. The judicial Power shall extend to all Cases, in Law and Equity, arising under this Constitution, the Laws of the United States, and Treaties made, or which shall be made, under their Authority;—to all Cases affecting Ambassadors, other public Ministers and Consuls;—to all Cases of admiralty and maritime Jurisdiction;—to Controversies to which the United States shall be a Party;—to Controversies between two or more States;—between a State and Citizens of another State;—between Citizens of different States;—between Citizens of the same State claiming Lands under Grants of different States, and between a State, or the Citizens thereof, and foreign States, Citizens or Subjects.

In all Cases affecting Ambassadors, other public Ministers and Consuls, and those in which a State shall be a Party, the supreme Court shall have original Jurisdiction. In all the other Cases before mentioned, the supreme Court shall have appellate Jurisdiction, both as to Law and Fact, with such Exceptions, and under such Regulations as the Congress shall make.

The Trial of all Crimes, except in Cases of Impeachment, shall be by Jury; and such Trial shall be held in the State where the said Crimes shall have been committed; but when not committed within any State, the Trial shall be at such Place or Places as the Congress may by Law have directed.

Section 3. Treason against the United States, shall consist only in levying War against them, or, in adhering to their Enemies, giving them Aid and Comfort. No Person shall be convicted of Treason unless on the Testimony of two Witnesses to the same overt Act, or on Confession in open Court.

The Congress shall have Power to declare the Punishment of Treason, but no Attainder of Treason shall work Corruption of Blood, or Forfeiture except during the Life of the Person attainted.

ARTICLE IV

Section 1. Full Faith and Credit shall be given in each State to the public Acts, Records, and judicial Proceedings of every other State. And the Congress may by general Laws prescribe the Manner in which such Acts, Records and Proceedings shall be proved, and the Effect thereof.

Section 2. The Citizens of each State shall be entitled to all Privileges and Immunities of Citizens in the several States.

A Person charged in any State with Treason, Felony, or other Crime, who shall flee from Justice, and be found in another State, shall on Demand of the executive Authority of the State from which he fled, be delivered up, to be removed to the State having Jurisdiction of the Crime.

No Person held to Service or Labour in one State, under the Laws thereof, escaping into another, shall, in Consequence of any Law or Regulation therein, be discharged from such Service or Labour, but shall be delivered up on Claim of the Party to whom such Service or Labour may be due.

Section 3. New States may be admitted by the Congress into this Union; but no new State shall be formed or erected within the Jurisdiction of any other State; nor any State be formed by the Junction of two or more States, or Parts of States, without the Consent of the Legislatures of the States concerned as well as of the Congress.

The Congress shall have Power to dispose of and make all needful Rules and Regulations respecting the Territory or other Property belonging to the United States; and nothing in this Constitution shall be so construed as to Prejudice any Claims of the United States, or of any particular State.

Section 4. The United States shall guarantee to every State in this Union a Republican Form of Government, and shall protect each of them against Invasion; and on Application of the Legislature, or of the Executive (when the Legislature cannot be convened) against domestic Violence.

ARTICLE V

The Congress, whenever two thirds of both Houses shall deem it necessary, shall propose Amendments to this Constitution, or, on the Application of the Legislatures of two thirds of the several States, shall call a Convention for proposing Amendments, which, in either Case, shall be valid to all Intents and Purposes, as part of this Constitution, when ratified by the Legislatures of three fourths of the several States, or by Conventions in three fourths thereof, as the one or the other Mode of Ratification may be proposed by the Congress; Provided that no Amendment which may be made prior to the Year One thousand eight hundred and eight shall in any Manner affect the first and fourth Clauses in the Ninth Section of the first Article; and that no State, without its Consent, shall be deprived of its equal Suffrage in the Senate.

ARTICLE VI

All Debts contracted and Engagements entered into, before the Adoption of this Constitution shall be as valid against the United States under this Constitution, as under the Confederation.

This Constitution, and the Laws of the United States which shall be made in Pursuance thereof; and all Treaties made, or which shall be made, under the Authority of the United States, shall be the supreme Law of the Land; and the Judges in every State shall be bound thereby, any Thing in the Constitution or Laws of any State to the Contrary notwithstanding.

The Senators and Representatives before mentioned, and the Members of the several State Legislatures, and all executive and judicial Officers, both of the United States and of the several States, shall be bound by Oath or Affirmation, to support this Constitution; but no religious Test shall ever be required as a Qualification to any Office or public Trust under the United States.

ARTICLE VII

The Ratification of the Conventions of nine States shall be sufficient for the Establishment of this Constitution between the States so ratifying the Same.

AMENDMENT I [1791]

Congress shall make no law respecting an establishment of religion, or prohibiting the free exercise thereof; or abridging the freedom of speech, or of the press; or the right of the people peaceably to assembly, and to petition the Government for a redress of grievances.

AMENDMENT II [1791]

A well regulated Militia, being necessary to the security of a free State, the right of the people to keep and bear Arms, shall not be infringed.

AMENDMENT III [1791]

No Soldier shall, in time of peace be quartered in any house, without the consent of the Owner, nor in time of war, but in a manner to be prescribed by law.

AMENDMENT IV [1791]

The right of the people to be secure in their persons, houses, papers, and effects, against unreasonable searches and seizures, shall not be violated, and no Warrants shall issue, but upon probable cause, supported by Oath or affirmation, and particularly describing the place to be searched, and the persons or things to be seized.

AMENDMENT V [1791]

No person shall be held to answer for a capital, or otherwise infamous crime, unless on a presentment or indictment of a Grand Jury, except in cases arising in the land or naval forces, or in the Militia, when in actual service in time of War or public danger; nor shall any person be subject for the same offence to be twice put in jeopardy of life or limb; nor shall be compelled in any criminal case to be a witness against himself, nor be deprived of life, liberty, or property, without due process of law; nor shall private property be taken for public use, without just compensation.

AMENDMENT VI [1791]

In all criminal prosecutions, the accused shall enjoy the right to a speedy and public trial, by an impartial jury of the State and district wherein the crime shall have been committed, which district shall have been previously ascertained by law, and to be informed of the nature and cause of the accusation; to be confronted with the witnesses against him; to have compulsory process for obtaining witnesses in his favor, and to have the Assistance of Counsel for his defence.

AMENDMENT VII [1791]

In Suits at common law, where the value in controversy shall exceed twenty dollars, the right of trial by jury shall be preserved, and no fact tried by jury, shall be otherwise re-examined in any Court of the United States, than according to the rules of the common law.

AMENDMENT VIII [1791]

Excessive bail shall not be required, nor excessive fines imposed, nor cruel and unusual punishments inflicted.

AMENDMENT IX [1791]

The enumeration in the Constitution, of certain rights, shall not be construed to deny or disparage others retained by the people.

AMENDMENT X [1791]

The powers not delegated to the United States by the Constitution, nor prohibited by it to the States, are reserved to the States respectively, or to the people.

AMENDMENT XI [1798]

The Judicial power of the United States shall not be construed to extend to any suit in law or equity, commenced or prosecuted against one of the United States by Citizens of another State, or by Citizens or Subjects of any Foreign State.

AMENDMENT XII [1804]

The Electors shall meet in their respective states, and vote by ballot for President and Vice-President, one of whom, at least, shall not be an inhabitant of the same state with themselves; they shall name in their ballots the person voted for as President, and in distinct ballots the person voted for as Vice-President, and they shall make distinct lists of all persons voted for as President, and of all persons voted for as Vice-President, and of the number of votes for each, which lists they shall sign and certify, and transmit sealed to the seat of the government of the United States, directed to the President of the Senate;—The President of the Senate shall, in the presence of the Senate and House of Representatives, open all the certificates and the votes shall then be counted;— The person having the greatest number of votes for President, shall be the President, if such number be a majority of the whole number of Electors appointed; and if no person have such majority, then from the persons having the highest numbers not exceeding three on the list of those voted for as President, the House of Representatives shall choose immediately, by ballot, the President. But in choosing the President, the votes shall be taken by states, the representation from each state having one vote; a quorum for this purpose shall consist of a member or members from two-thirds of the states, and a majority of all states shall be necessary to a choice. And if the House of Representatives shall not choose a President whenever the right of choice shall devolve upon them, before the fourth day of March next following, then the Vice-President shall act as President, as in the case of the death or other constitutional disability of the President.—The person having the greatest number of votes as Vice-President, shall be the Vice-President, if such number be a majority of the whole number of Electors appointed, and if no person have a majority, then from the two highest numbers on the list, the Senate shall choose the Vice-President; a quorum for the purpose shall consist of two-thirds of the whole number of Senators, and a majority of the whole number shall be necessary to a choice. But no person constitutionally ineligible to the office of President shall be eligible to that of Vice-President of the United States.

AMENDMENT XIII [1865]

Section 1.   Neither slavery nor involuntary servitude, except as a punishment for crime whereof the party shall have been duly convicted, shall exist within the United States, or any place subject to their jurisdiction.

Section 2.   Congress shall have power to enforce this article by appropriate legislation.

AMENDMENT XIV [1868]

Section 1.   All persons born or naturalized in the United States, and subject to the jurisdiction thereof, are citizens of the United States and of the State wherein they reside. No State shall make or enforce any law which shall abridge the privileges or immunities of citizens of the United States; nor shall any State deprive any person of life, liberty, or property, without due process of law; nor deny to any person within its jurisdiction the equal protection of the laws.

Section 2.   Representatives shall be apportioned among the several States according to their respective numbers, counting the whole number of persons in each State, excluding Indians not taxed. But when the right to vote at any election for the choice of electors for President and Vice President of the United States, Representatives in Congress, the Executive and Judicial officers of a State, or the members of the Legislature thereof, is denied to any of the male inhabitants of such State, being twenty-one years of age, and citizens of the United States, or in any way abridged, except for participation in rebellion, or other crime, the basis of representation therein shall be reduced in the proportion which the number of such male citizens shall bear to the whole number of male citizens twenty-one years of age in such State.

Section 3.   No person shall be a Senator or Representative in Congress, or elector of President and Vice President, or hold any office, civil or military, under the United States, or under any State, who having previously taken an oath, as a member of Congress, or as an officer of the United States, or as a member of any State legislature, or as an executive or judicial officer of any State, to support the Constitution of the United States, shall have engaged in insurrection or rebellion against the same, or given aid or comfort to the enemies thereof. But Congress may by a vote of two-thirds of each House, remove such disability.

Section 4.   The validity of the public debt of the United States, authorized by law, including debts incurred for payment of pensions and bounties for services in suppressing insurrection or rebellion, shall not be questioned. But neither the United States nor any State shall assume or pay any debt or obligation incurred in aid of insurrection or rebellion against the United States, or any claim for the loss or emancipation of any slave; but all such debts, obligations and claims shall be held illegal and void.

Section 5.   The Congress shall have power to enforce, by appropriate legislation, the provisions of this article.

AMENDMENT XV [1870]

Section 1.   The right of citizens of the United States to vote shall not be denied or abridged by the United States or by any State on account of race, color, or previous condition of servitude.

Section 2.   The Congress shall have power to enforce this article by appropriate legislation.

AMENDMENT XVI [1913]

The Congress shall have power to lay and collect taxes on incomes, from whatever source derived, without apportionment among the several States, and without regard to any census or enumeration.

AMENDMENT XVII [1913]

Section 1.   The Senate of the United States shall be composed of two Senators from each State, elected by the people thereof, for six years; and each Senator shall have one vote. The electors in each State shall have the qualifications requisite for electors of the most numerous branch of the State legislatures.

Section 2.   When vacancies happen in the representation of any State in the Senate, the executive authority of such State shall issue writs of election to fill such vacancies: *Provided*, That the legislature of any State may empower the executive thereof to make temporary appointments until the people fill the vacancies by election as the legislature may direct.

Section 3.   This amendment shall not be so construed as to affect the election or term of any Senator chosen before it becomes valid as part of the Constitution.

AMENDMENT XVIII [1919]

Section 1.   After one year from the ratification of this article the manufacture, sale, or transportation of intoxicating liquors within, the importation thereof into, or the exportation thereof from the United States and all territory subject to the jurisdiction thereof for beverage purposes is hereby prohibited.

Section 2.   The Congress and the several States shall have concurrent power to enforce this article by appropriate legislation.

Section 3.   This article shall be inoperative unless it shall have been ratified as an amendment to the Constitution by the legislatures of the several States, as provided in the Constitution, within seven years from the date of the submission hereof to the States by the Congress.

AMENDMENT XIX [1920]

Section 1.   The right of citizens of the United States to vote shall not be denied or abridged by the United States or by any State on account of sex.

Section 2.   Congress shall have power to enforce this article by appropriate legislation.

AMENDMENT XX [1933]

Section 1.   The terms of the President and Vice President shall end at noon on the 20th day of January, and the terms of Senators and Representatives at noon on the 3d day of January, of the years in which such terms would have ended if this article had not been ratified; and the terms of their successors shall then begin.

Section 2.   The Congress shall assemble at least once in every year, and such meeting shall begin at noon on the 3d day of January, unless they shall by law appoint a different day.

Section 3.   If, at the time fixed for the beginning of the term of the President, the President elect shall have died, the Vice President elect shall become President. If the President shall not have been chosen before the time fixed for the beginning of his term, or if the President elect shall have failed to qualify, then the Vice President elect shall act as President until a President shall have qualified; and the Congress may by law provide for the case wherein neither a President elect nor a Vice President elect shall have qualified, declaring who shall then act as President, or the manner in which one who is to act shall be selected, and such person shall act accordingly until a President or Vice President shall have qualified.

Section 4.   The Congress may by law provide for the case of the death of any of the persons from whom the House of Representatives may choose a President whenever the right of choice shall have devolved upon them, and for the case of the death of any of the persons from whom the Senate may choose a Vice President whenever the right of choice shall have devolved upon them.

Section 5.   Sections 1 and 2 shall take effect on the 15th day of October following the ratification of this article.

Section 6.   This article shall be inoperative unless it shall have been ratified as an amendment to the Constitution by the legislatures of three-fourths of the several States within seven years from the date of its submission.

AMENDMENT XXI [1933]

Section 1.   The eighteenth article of amendment to the Constitution of the United States is hereby repealed.

Section 2.   The transportation or importation into any State, Territory, or possession of the United States for delivery or use therein of intoxicating liquors, in violation of the laws thereof, is hereby prohibited.

Section 3.   This article shall be inoperative unless it shall have been ratified as an amendment to the Constitution by conventions in the several States, as provided in the Constitution, within seven years from the date of the submission hereof to the States by the Congress.

AMENDMENT XXII [1951]

Section 1.   No person shall be elected to the office of the President more than twice, and no person who has held the office of President, or acted as President, for more than two years of a term to which some other person was elected President shall be elected to the office of President more than once. But this Article shall not apply to any person holding the office of President when this Article was proposed by the Congress, and shall not prevent any person who may be holding the office of President, or acting as

President, during the term within which this Article becomes operative from holding the office of President or acting as President during the remainder of such term.

Section 2.   This article shall be inoperative unless it shall have been ratified as an amendment to the Constitution by the legislatures of three-fourths of the several States within seven years from the date of its submission to the States by the Congress.

AMENDMENT XXIII [1961]

Section 1.   The District constituting the seat of Government of the United States shall appoint in such manner as the Congress may direct:

A number of electors of President and Vice President equal to the whole number of Senators and Representatives in Congress to which the District would be entitled if it were a State, but in no event more than the least populous state; they shall be in addition to those appointed by the states, but they shall be considered, for the purposes of the election of President and Vice President, to be electors appointed by a state; and they shall meet in the District and perform such duties as provided by the twelfth article of amendment.

Section 2.   The Congress shall have power to enforce this article by appropriate legislation.

AMENDMENT XXIV [1964]

Section 1.   The right of citizens of the United States to vote in any primary or other election for President or Vice President, for electors for President or Vice President, or for Senator or Representative in Congress, shall not be denied or abridged by the United States, or any State by reason of failure to pay any poll tax or other tax.

Section 2.   The Congress shall have power to enforce this article by appropriate legislation.

AMENDMENT XXV [1967]

Section 1.   In case of the removal of the President from office or of his death or resignation, the Vice President shall become President.

Section 2.   Whenever there is a vacancy in the office of the Vice President, the President shall nominate a Vice President who shall take office upon confirmation by a majority vote of both Houses of Congress.

Section 3.   Whenever the President transmits to the President pro tempore of the Senate and the Speaker of the House of Representatives his written declaration that he is unable to discharge the powers and duties of his office, and until he transmits to them a written declaration to the contrary, such powers and duties shall be discharged by the Vice President as Acting President.

Section 4.   Whenever the Vice President and a majority of either the principal officers of the executive departments or of such other body as Congress may by law provide, transmit to the President pro tempore of the Senate and the Speaker of the House of Representatives their written declaration that the President is unable to discharge the powers and duties of his office, the Vice President shall immediately assume the powers and duties of the office as Acting President.

Thereafter, when the President transmits to the President pro tempore of the Senate and the Speaker of the House of Representatives his written declaration that no inability exists, he shall resume the powers and duties of his office unless the Vice President and a majority of either the principal officers of the executive department or of such other body as Congress may by law provide, transmit within four days to the President pro tempore of the Senate and the Speaker of the House of Representatives their written declaration and the President is unable to discharge the powers and duties of his office. Thereupon Congress shall decide the issue, assembling within forty-eight hours for that purpose if not in session. If the Congress, within twenty-one days after receipt of the latter written declaration, or, if Congress is not in session, within twenty-one days after Congress is required to assemble, determines by two-thirds vote of both Houses that the President is unable to discharge the powers and duties of his office, the Vice President shall continue to discharge the same as Acting President; otherwise, the President shall resume the powers and duties of his office.

AMENDMENT XXVI [1971]

Section 1.   The right of citizens of the United States, who are eighteen years of age or older, to vote shall not be denied or abridged by the United States or by any State on account of age.

Section 2.   The Congress shall have power to enforce this article by appropriate legislation.

AMENDMENT XXVII [1992]

No law, varying the compensation for the services of the Senators and Representatives, shall take effect, until an election of Representatives shall have intervened.

■ Appendix B Title VII of the Civil Rights Act of 1964

Title VII of the Civil Rights Act of 1964—The Employment Discrimination Section

Section 703. Unlawful Employment Practices. (a) It shall be an unlawful employment practice for an employer—

(1) to fail or refuse to hire or to discharge any individual, or otherwise to discriminate against any individual with respect to his compensation, terms, conditions, or privileges of employment, because of such individual's race, color, religion, sex, or national origin; or

(2) to limit, segregate, or classify his employees or applicants for employment in any way which would deprive or tend to deprive any individual of employment opportunities or otherwise adversely affect his status as an employee, because of such individual's race, color, religion, sex, or national origin.

(b) It shall be an unlawful employment practice for an employment agency to fail or refuse to refer for employment, or otherwise to discriminate against, any individual because of his race, color, religion, sex, or national origin, or to classify or refer for employment any individual on the basis or his race, color, religion, sex, or national origin.

(c) It shall be an unlawful employment practice for a labor organization—

(1) to exclude or to expel from its membership, or otherwise to discriminate against, any individual because of his race, color, religion, sex, or national origin;

(2) to limit, segregate, or classify its membership or applicants for membership, or to classify or fail or refuse to refer for employment any individual, in any way which would deprive or tend to deprive any individual of employment opportunities, or would limit such employment opportunities or otherwise adversely affect his status as an employee or as an applicant for employment, because of such individual's race, color, religion, sex, or national origin; or

(3) to cause or attempt to cause an employer to discriminate against an individual in violation of this section.

(d) It shall be an unlawful employment practice for any employer, labor organization, or joint labor-management committee controlling apprenticeship or other training or retraining, including on-the-job training programs to discriminate against any individual because of his race, color, religion, sex, or national origin in admission to, or employment in, any program established to provide apprenticeship or other training.

(e) Notwithstanding any other provision of this subchapter—

(1) it shall not be an unlawful employment practice for an employer to hire and employ employees, for an employment agency to classify, or refer for employment any individual, for a labor organization to classify its membership or to classify or refer for employment any individual, or for an employer, labor organization, or joint labor-management committee controlling apprenticeship or other training or retraining programs to admit or employ any individual in any such program, on the basis of his religion, sex, or national origin in those certain instances where religion, sex, or national origin is a bona fide occupational qualification reasonably necessary to the normal operation of that particular business or enterprise, and

(2) it shall not be an unlawful employment practice for a school, college, university, or other educational institution or institution of learning to hire and employ employees of a particular religion if such school, college, university, or other educational institution or institution of learning is, in whole or in substantial part, owned, supported, controlled, or managed by a particular religion or by a particular religious corporation, association, or society, or if the curriculum of such school, college, university, or other educational institution or institution of learning is directed toward the propagation of a particular religion.

(f) As used in this subchapter, the phrase "unlawful employment practice" shall not be deemed to include any action or measure taken by an employer, labor organization, joint labor-management committee, or employment agency with respect to an individual who is a member of the Communist Party of the United States or of any other organization required to register as a Communist-action or Communist-front organization. . . .

(g) Notwithstanding any other provision of this subchapter, it shall not be an unlawful employment practice for an employer to fail or refuse to hire and employ any individual for any position, for an employer to discharge any individual from any position, or for an employment agency to fail or refuse to refer any individual for employment in any position, or for a labor organization to fail or refuse to refer any individual for employment in any position, if—

(1) the occupancy of such position, or access to the premises in or upon which any part of the duties of such position is performed or is to be performed, is subject to any requirement imposed in the interest of the national security of the United States. . . and

(2) such individual has not fulfilled or has ceased to fulfill that requirement.

(h) Notwithstanding any other provision of this subchapter, it shall not be an unlawful employment practice for an employer to apply different standards of compensation, or different terms, conditions, or privileges of employment pursuant to a bona fide seniority or merit system, or a system which measures earnings by quantity or quality of production or to employees who work in different locations, provided that such differences are not the result of an intention to discriminate because of race, color, religion, sex, or national origin, nor shall it be an unlawful employment practice for an employer to give and act upon the results of any professionally developed ability test provided that such test, its administration or action upon the results is not designed, intended or used to discriminate because of race, color, religion, sex, or national origin. . . .

(j) Nothing contained in this subchapter shall be interpreted to require any employer, employment agency, labor organization, or joint labor-management committee subject to this subchapter to grant preferential treatment to any individual or to any group because of the race, color, religion, sex, or national origin of such individual or group on account of an imbalance which may exist with respect to the total number or percentage of persons of any race, color, religion, sex, or national origin employed by any employer, referred or classified for employment by any employment agency or labor organization, or admitted to, or employed in, any apprenticeship or other training program, in comparison with the total number or percentage of persons of such race, color, religion, sex, or national origin in any community, State, section, or other area, or in the available work force in any community, State, section, or other area.

. . . .

Section 704. Other Unlawful Employment Practices.
(a) It shall be an unlawful employment practice for an employer to discriminate against any of his employees or applicants for employment, for an employment agency, or joint labor-management committee controlling apprenticeship or other training or retraining, including on-the-job training programs, to discriminate against any individual, or for a labor organization to discriminate against any member thereof or applicant for membership, because he has opposed any practice made an unlawful employment practice by this subchapter, or because he has made a charge, testified, assisted, or participated in any manner in an investigation, proceeding, or hearing under this subchapter.

(b) It shall be an unlawful employment practice for an employer, labor organization, employment agency, or joint labor-management committee controlling apprenticeship or other training or retraining, including on-the-job training programs, to print or publish or cause to be printed or published any notice or advertisement relating to employment by such an employer or membership or any classification or referral for employment by such a labor organization, or relating to any classification or referral for employment by such an employment agency, or relating to admission to, or employment in, any program established to provide apprenticeship or other training by such a joint-labor-management committee, indicating any preference, limitation, specification, or discrimination, based on race, color, religion, sex, or national origin, except that such a notice or advertisement may indicate a preference, limitation, specification, or discrimination based on religion, sex or national origin when religion, sex, or national origin is a bona fide occupational qualification for employment.

■ Appendix C Americans with Disabilities Act of 1990 (Excerpts)

Title I—EMPLOYMENT
Sec. 101. Definitions.

As used in this title: . . .

(8) **Qualified individual with a disability.**—The term "qualified individual with a disability" means an individual with a disability who, with or without reasonable accommodation, can perform the essential functions of the employment position that such individual holds or desires. For the purposes of this title, consideration shall be given to the employer's judgment as to what functions of a job are essential, and if an employer has prepared a written description before advertising or interviewing applicants for the job, this description shall be considered evidence of the essential functions of the job.

(9) **Reasonable accommodation.**—The term "reasonable accommodation" may include—

(A) making existing facilities used by employees readily accessible to and usable by individuals with disabilities; and

(B) job restructuring, part-time or modified work schedules, reassignment to a vacant position, acquisition or modification of equipment or devices, appropriate adjustment or modifications of examinations, training materials or policies, the provision of qualified readers or interpreters, and other similar accommodations for individuals with disabilities.

(10) **Undue Hardship.**—

(A) **In general.**—The term "undue hardship" means an action requiring significant difficulty or expense, when considered in light of the factors set forth in subparagraph(B).

(B) **Factors to be considered.**—In determining whether an accommodation would impose an undue hardship on a covered entity, factors to be considered include—

(i) the nature and cost of accommodation needed under this Act;

(ii) the overall financial resources of the facility or facilities involved in the provision of the reasonable accommodation; the number of persons employed at such facility; the effect on expenses and resources, or the impact otherwise of such accommodation upon the operation of the facility;

(iii) the overall financial resources of the covered entity; the overall size of the business of a covered entity with respect to the number of its employees; the number, type, and location of its facilities; and

(iv) the type of operation or operations of the covered entity, including the composition, structure, and functions of the workforce of such entity; the geographic separateness, administrative, or fiscal relationship of the facility or facilities in question to the covered entity.

Sec. 102. Discrimination.

(a) **General Rule.**—No covered entity shall discriminate against a qualified individual with a disability because of the disability of such individual in regard to job application procedures, the hiring, advancement, or discharge of employees, employee compensation, job training, and other terms, conditions, and privileges of employment.

(b) **Construction.**—As used in subsection (a), the term "discriminate" includes—

(1) limiting, segregating, or classifying a job applicant or employee in a way that adversely affects the opportunities or status of such applicant or employee because of the disability of such applicant or employee;

(2) participating in a contractual or other arrangement or relationship that has the effect of subjecting a covered entity's qualified applicant or employee with a disability to the discrimination prohibited by this title (such relationship includes a relationship with an employment or referral agency, labor union, an organization providing fringe benefits to an employee of the covered entity, or an organization providing training and apprenticeship programs);

(3) utilizing standards, criteria, or methods of administration—

(A) that have the effect of discrimination on the basis of disability; or

(B) that perpetuate the discrimination of others who are subject to common administrative control;

(4) excluding or otherwise denying equal jobs or benefits to a qualified individual because of the known disability of an individual with whom the qualified individual is known to have a relationship or association;

(5)(A) not making reasonable accommodations to the known physical or mental limitations of an otherwise qualified individual with a disability who is an applicant or employee, unless such covered entity can demonstrate that the accommodation would impose an undue hardship on the operation of the business of such covered entity; or

(B) denying employment opportunities to a job applicant or employee who is an otherwise qualified individual with a disability, if such denial is based on the need of such covered entity to make reasonable accommodation to the physical or mental impairments of the employee or applicant;

(6) using qualification standards, employment tests or other selection criteria that screen out or tend to screen out an individual with a disability or a class of individuals with disabilities unless the standard, test or other selection criteria, as used by the covered entity, is shown to be job-related for the position in question and is consistent with business necessity; and

(7) failing to select and administer tests concerning employment in the most effective manner to ensure that, when such test is administered to a job applicant or employee who has a disability that impairs sensory, manual, or speaking skills, such test results accurately reflect the skills, aptitude, or whatever other factor of such applicant or employee that such test purports to measure, rather than reflecting the impaired sensory, manual, or speaking skills of such employee or applicant (except where such skills are the factors that the test purports to measure). . . .

Sec. 104. Illegal Use of Drugs and Alcohol. . . .

(b) **Rules of Construction.**—Nothing in subsection (a) shall be construed to exclude as a qualified individual with a disability an individual who—

(1) has successfully completed a supervised drug rehabilitation program and is no longer engaging in the illegal use of drugs, or has otherwise been rehabilitated successfully and is no longer engaging in such use;

(2) is participating in a supervised rehabilitation program and is no longer engaging in such use; or

(3) is erroneously regarded as engaging in such use, but is not engaging in such use; except that it shall not be a violation of this Act for a covered entity to adopt or administer reasonable policies or procedures, including but not limited to drug testing, designed to ensure that an individual described in paragraph (1) or (2) is no longer engaging in the illegal use of drugs. . . .

Sec. 107. Enforcement.

(a) **Powers, Remedies, and Procedures.**—The powers, remedies, and procedures set forth in sections 705, 706, 707, 709, and 710 of the Civil Rights Act of 1964 (42 U.S.C. 2000e-4, 2000e-5, 2000e-6, 2000e-8, and 2000e-9) shall be the powers, remedies, and procedures this title provides to the Commission, to the Attorney General, or to any person alleging discrimination on the basis of disability in violation of any provision of this Act, or regulations promulgated under section 106, concerning employment.

(b) **Coordination.**—The agencies with enforcement authority for actions which allege employment discrimination under this title and under the Rehabilitation Act of 1973 shall develop procedures to ensure that administrative complaints filed under this title and under the Rehabilitation Act of 1973 are dealt with in a manner that avoids duplication of effort and prevents imposition of inconsistent or conflicting standards for the same requirements under this title and the Rehabilitation Act of 1973. The Commission, the Attorney

General, and the Office of Federal Contract Compliance Programs shall establish such coordinating mechanisms (similar to provisions contained in the joint regulations promulgated by the Commission and the Attorney General at part 42 of title 28 and part 1691 of title 29, Code of Federal Regulations, and the Memorandum of Understanding between the Commission and the Office of Federal Contract Compliance Programs dated January 16, 1981 (46 Fed. Reg.

7435, January 23, 1981)) in regulations implementing this title and Rehabilitation Act of 1973 not later than 18 months after the date of enactment of this Act.

Sec. 108. Effective Date.

This title shall become effective 24 months after the date of enactment.

■ Appendix D National Labor Relations Act (Excerpts)

Section 3. National Labor Relations Board. (a) The National labor Relations Board (hereinafter called the "Board") . . . as an agency of the United States, shall consist of five . . . members, appointed by the President by and with advice and consent of the Senate . . . for terms of five years each, . . . The President shall designate one member to serve as Chairman of the Board. Any member of the Board may be removed by the President, upon notice and hearing, for neglect of duty or malfeasance in office, but for no other cause.

Section 7. Rights of Employees. Employees shall have the right to self-organization, to form, join, or assist labor organizations, to bargain collectively through representatives of their own choosing, and to engage in other concerted activities for the purpose of collective bargaining or other mutual aid or protection, and shall also have the right to refrain from any or all of such activities except to the extent that such right may be affected by an agreement requiring membership in a labor organization as a condition of employment as authorized in section 8(a) (3).

Section 8. Unfair Labor Practice. (a) it shall be an unfair labor practice for an employer—

(1) to interfere with, restrain, or coerce employees in the exercise of the rights guaranteed in section 7;

(2) to dominate or interfere with the formation or administration of any labor organization or contribute financial or other support to it: Provide, that subject to rules and regulations made and published by the Board pursuant to section 6, an employer shall not be prohibited from permitting employees to confer with him during working hours without loss of time or pay;

(3) by discrimination in regard to hire or tenure of employment or any term or condition of employment to encourage or discourage membership in any labor organization: Provide, that nothing in this Act . . . shall preclude an employer from making an agreement with a labor organization . . . to require as a condition of employment member-

ship therein . . . Provided further, that no employer shall justify any discrimination against an employee for nonmembership in a labor organization (A) if he has reasonable grounds for believing that such membership was not available to the employee on the same terms and conditions generally applicable to other members, or (B) if he has reasonable grounds for believing that membership was denied or terminated for reasons other than the failure of the employee to tender periodic dues and initiation fees uniformly required as a condition of acquiring or retaining membership;

(4) to discharge or otherwise discriminate against an employee because he has filed charges or given testimony under this Act;

(5) to refuse to bargain collectively with the representatives of his employees, subject to the provisions of section 9(a).

(b) It shall be an unfair labor practice for a labor organization or its agents—

(1) to restrain or coerce (A) employees in the exercise of the rights guaranteed in section 7: Provided, that this paragraph shall not impair the right of a labor organization to prescribe its own rules with respect to the acquisition or retention of membership therein; or (B) an employer in the selection of his representatives for the purposes of collective bargaining or the adjustment of grievances;

(2) to cause or attempt to cause an employer to discriminate against an employee in violation of subsection (a) (3) or to discriminate against an employee with respect to whom membership in such organization has been denied or terminated on some ground other than his failure to tender the periodic dues and the initiation fees uniformly required as a condition of acquiring or retaining membership.

(3) to refuse to bargain collectively with an employer, provided it is the representative of his employees subject to the provisions of section 9 (a).

(4) (i) to engage in, or to induce or encourage any individual employed by any person engaged in commerce or in an

industry affecting commerce to engage in, a strike or a refusal in the course of his employment to use, manufacture, process, transport, or otherwise handle or work on any goods, articles, materials, or commodities or to perform any services; or, (ii) to threaten, coerce, or restrain any person engaged in commerce or in an industry affecting commerce, where in either case an object thereof is:

(A) forcing or requiring any employer or self-employed person to join any labor or employer organization or to enter into any agreement which is prohibited by section 8 (e);

(B) forcing or requiring any person to cease using, selling, handling, transporting, or otherwise dealing in the products of any other producer, processor, or manufacturer, or to cease doing business with any other person, or forcing or requiring any other employer to recognize or bargain with a labor organization as the representative of his employees unless such labor organization has been certified as the rep- resentative of such employees. . . . Provided, that nothing contained in this clause (B) shall be construed to make unlawful, where not otherwise unlawful, any primary strike or primary picketing;

(C) forcing or requiring any employer to recognize or bar- gain with a particular labor organization as the representa- tive of his employees if another labor organization has been certified as the representative of such employees. . . .

(D) forcing or requiring any employer to assign particular work to employees in a particular labor organization or in a particular trade, craft, or class. . . .

Provided, that nothing contained in this subsection (b) shall be construed to make unlawful a refusal by any person to enter upon the premises of any employer (other than his own employer), if the employees of such employer are engaged in a strike ratified or approved by a representative of such employees whom such employer is required to rec- ognize under this Act: Provided further, that for the purpos- es of this paragraph (4) only, nothing contained in such paragraph shall be construed to prohibit publicity, other than picketing, for the purpose of truthfully advising the public, including consumers and members of a labor organization, that a product or products are produced by an employer with whom the labor organization has a primary dispute and are distributed by another employer, as long as such publicity does not have an effect of inducing any individual employed by any person other than the primary employer in the course of his employment to pick up, deliver, or transport any goods, or not to perform any services, at the establishment of the employer engaged in such distribution;

(5) to require of employees covered by an agreement autho- rized under subsection (a) (3) the payment, as a condition precedent to becoming a member of such organization, of a fee in an amount which the Board finds excessive or dis- criminatory. . . .

(6) to cause or attempt to cause an employer to pay or deliver or agree to pay or deliver any money or other thing

of value, in the nature of an exaction, for services which are not performed or not to be performed; and

(7) to picket or cause to be picketed, or threaten to picket or cause to be picketed, any employer where an object thereof is forcing or requiring an employer to recognize or bargain with a labor organization as the representative of his employees, or forcing or requiring the employees of an employer to accept or select such labor organization as their collective bargaining representative, unless such labor orga- nization is currently certified as the representative of such employees:

(A) where the employer has lawfully recognized in accor- dance with this Act any other labor organization and a ques- tion concerning representation may not appropriately be raised under section 9(c) of this Act.

(B) where within the preceding 12 months a valid election under section 9(c) of this Act has been conducted, or

(C) where such picketing has been conducted without a peti- tion under section 9(c) being filed within a reasonable peri- od of time not to exceed 30 days from the commencement of such picketing: Provided, that when such a petition has been filed the Board shall forthwith, without regard to the provisions of section 9(c) (1) or the absence of a showing of a substantial interest on the part of the labor organization, direct an election in such units as the Board finds to be appropriate and shall certify the results thereof: Provided further, that nothing in this subparagraph (C) shall be con- strued to prohibit any picketing or other publicity for the purpose of truthfully advising the public (including con- sumers) that an employer does not employ members of, or have a contract with, a labor organization, unless an effect of such picketing is to induce any individual employed by any other person in the course of his employment, not to pick up, deliver or transport any goods or not to perform any services.

Nothing in this paragraph (7) shall be construed to permit any act which would otherwise be an unfair labor practice under this section 8(b).

(c) The expressing of any views, argument, or opinion, or the dissemination thereof, whether in written, printed, graphic, or visual form, shall not constitute or be evidence of an unfair labor practice under any of the provisions of this Act, if such expression contains no threat of reprisal or force or promise of benefit.

(d) For the purposes of this section, to bargain collectively is the performance of the mutual obligation of the employer and the representative of the employees to meet at reason- able times and confer in good faith with respect to wages, hours, and other terms and conditions of employment, or the negotiation of an agreement, or any question arising there- under, and the execution of a written contract incorporating any agreement reached if requested by either party, but such obligation does not compel either party to agree to a propos- al or require the making of a concession: Provided, that where there is in effect a collective bargaining contract covering employees in an industry affecting commerce, the duty to bargain collectively shall also mean that no party to such contract shall terminate or modify such contract, unless the party desiring such termination or modification—

(1) serves a written notice upon the other party to the contract of the proposed termination or modification 60 days prior to the expiration date thereof, or in the event such contract contains no expiration date, 60 days prior to the time it is proposed to make such termination or modification;

(2) offers to meet and confer with the other party for the purpose of negotiating a new contract or a contract containing the proposed modifications;

(3) notifies the Federal Mediation and Conciliation Service within 30 days after such notice of the existence of a dispute . . .

(4) continues in full force and effect, without resorting to strike or lockout, all the terms and conditions of the existing contract for a period of 60 days after such notice is given or until the expiration date of such contract, whichever occurs later.

(e) it shall be an unfair labor practice for any labor organization and any employer to enter into any contract or agreement, express or implied, whereby such employer ceases or refrains or agrees to cease or refrain from handling, using, selling, transporting, or otherwise dealing in any of the products of any other employer, or to cease doing business with any other person, . . . Provided, that nothing in this subsection (e) shall apply to an agreement between a labor organization and an employer in the construction industry relating to the contracting or subcontracting of work to be done at the site. . . .

Section 9. Representatives and Elections. (a) Representatives designated or selected for the purposes of collective bargaining by the majority of the employees in a unit appropriate for such purposes, shall be the exclusive representatives of all the employees in such unit for the purposes of collective bargaining in respect to rates of pay, wages, hours of employment, or other conditions of employment: Provided, that any individual employee or a group of employees shall have the right at any time to present grievances to their employer and to have such grievance adjusted, without the intervention of the bargaining representative, as long as the adjustment is not inconsistent with the terms of a collective bargaining contract or agreement then in effect: Provided further, that the bargaining representative has been given opportunity to be present at such adjustment.

(b) The Board shall decide in each case whether, in order to assure to employees the fullest freedom in exercising the rights guaranteed by this Act, the unit appropriate for the purposes of collective bargaining shall be the employer unit, craft unit, plant unit, or subdivision thereof: Provided, that the Board shall not (1) decide that any unit is appropriate for such purposes if such unit includes both professional employees and employees who are not professional employees unless a majority of such professional employees vote for inclusion in such unit; or (2) decide that any craft unit is inappropriate for such purposes on the ground that a different unit has been established by a prior Board determination, unless a majority of the employees in the proposed craft unit vote against separate representation or (3) decide that any unit is appropriate for such purposes, if it includes, together with other employees, any individual employed as a guard to enforce against employees and other persons, rules to protect property of the employer or to protect the safety of persons on the employer's premises; but no labor organization shall be certified as the representative of employees in a bargaining unit of guards if such organization admits to membership, or is affiliated directly or indirectly with an organization which admits to membership, employees other than guards.

(c) (1) Wherever a petition shall have been filed, in accordance with such regulations as may be prescribed by the Board—

(A) by an employee or group of employees or any individual or labor organization acting in their behalf alleging that a substantial number of employees (i) wish to be represented for collective bargaining and that their employer declines to recognize their representative as the representative defined in section 9(a), or (ii) assert that the individual or labor organization, which has been certified or is being currently recognized by their employer as the bargaining representative as defined in section 9(a); or

(B) by an employer, alleging that one or more individuals or labor organizations have presented to him a claim to be recognized as the representative defined in section 9(a);

the Board shall investigate such petition and if it has reasonable cause to believe that a question of representation affecting commerce exists shall provide for an appropriate hearing upon due notice. Such hearing may be conducted by an officer or employee of the regional office, who shall not make any recommendations with respect thereto. If the Board finds upon the record of such hearing that such a question of representative exists, it shall direct an election by secret ballot and shall certify the results thereof.

(2) In determining whether or not a question of representation affecting commerce exists, the same regulations and rules of decision shall apply irrespective of the identity of the persons filing the petition or the kind of relief sought and in no case shall the Board deny a labor organization a place on the ballot by reason of an order with respect to such labor organization or its predecessor not issued in conformity with section 10(c).

(3) No election shall be directed in any bargaining unit or any subdivision within which, in the preceding twelve-month period, a valid election shall have been held. Employees engaged in an economic strike who are not entitled to reinstatement shall be eligible to vote under such reg-

ulations as the Board shall find are consistent with the purposes and provisions of this Act in any election conducted within twelve months after the commencement of the strike. In any election where none of the choices on the ballot receives a majority, a run-off shall be conducted, the ballot providing for a selection between the two choices receiving the largest and second largest number of valid votes cast in the election.

(4) Nothing in this section shall be construed to prohibit the waiving of hearings by stipulation for the purpose of a consent election in conformity with regulations and rules of decision of the Board.

(5) In determining whether a unit is appropriate for the purposes specified in subsection (b) the extent to which the employees have organized shall not be controlling.

(d) Whenever an order of the Board made pursuant to section 10(c) is based in whole or in part upon facts certified following an investigation pursuant to subsection (c) of this section and there is a petition for the enforcement or review of such order, such certification and the record of such investigation shall be included in the transcript of the entire record required to be filed under section 10(c) or 10(f), and thereupon the decree of the court enforcing modifying, or setting aside in whole or in part the order of the Board shall be made and entered upon the pleadings, testimony, and the proceedings set forth in such transcript.

(e)(1) Upon the filing with the Board, by 30 per centum or more of the employees in a bargaining unit covered by an agreement between their employer and a labor organization made pursuant to section 8(a)(3), of a petition alleging they desire that such authority be rescinded, the Board shall take a secret ballot of the employees in such unit, and shall certify the results thereof to such labor organization and to the employer.

(2) No election shall be conducted pursuant to this subsection in any bargaining unit or any subdivision within which, in the preceding twelve month period, a valid election shall have been held.

Section 19. Individuals with Religious Convictions. Any employee who is a member of and adheres to established and traditional tenets or teachings of a bona fide religion, body, or sect which has historically held conscientious objections to joining or financially supporting labor organizations shall not be required to join or financially support any labor organization as a condition of employment; except that such employee may be required in a contract between such employee's employer and a labor organization in lieu of periodic dues and initiation fees, to pay sums equal to such dues and initiation fees to a nonreligious, nonlabor organization charitable fund exempt from taxation under section 501(c) (3) of title 26 of the Internal Revenue Code.

■ Appendix E Sherman Antitrust Act (Excerpts)

The Sherman Antitrust Act (1890, as amended)

Section 1.   Every contract, combination in the form of trust or otherwise, or conspiracy, in restraint of trade or commerce among the several States, or with foreign nations, is hereby declared to be illegal. Every person who shall make any contract or engage in any such combination or conspiracy shall be deemed guilty of a felony, and, on conviction thereof, shall be punished by fine not exceeding $10,000,000 if a corporation, or, if any other person, $350,000 or by imprisonment not exceeding three years, or by both said punishments in the discretion of the court.

Section 2.   Every person who shall monopolize, or attempt to monopolize, or conspire with any other person or persons, to monopolize any part of the trade or commerce among the several States, or with foreign nations, shall be deemed guilty of a felony, and, on conviction thereof, shall be punished by fine not exceeding $10,000,000 if a corporation, or, if any other person, $350,000 or by imprisonment not exceeding three years, or by both said punishments, in the discretion of the court.

■ Appendix F Clayton Act of 1914 (Excerpts)

Section 3.   That it shall be unlawful for any person engaged in commerce, in the course of such commerce, to lease or make a sale or contract for sale of goods, wares, merchandise, machinery, supplies, or other commodities,

whether patented or unpatented, for use, consumption, or resale within the United States or . . . other place under the jurisdiction of the United States, or fix a price charged therefor, or discount from, or rebate upon, such price, on the condition, agreement, or understanding that the lessee or purchaser thereof shall not use or deal in the goods, wares, merchandise, machinery, supplies, or other commodities of a competitor or competitors of the lessor or seller, where the effect of such lease, sale, or contract for sale or such condition, agreement, or understanding may be to substantially lessen competition to tend to create a monopoly in any line of commerce.

Section 4. That any person who shall be injured in his business or property by reason of anything forbidden in the antitrust laws may sue therefor in any district court of the United States in the district in which the defendant resides or is found, or has an agent, without respect to the amount in controversy, and shall recover threefold the damages by him sustained, and the cost of suit, including a reasonable attorney's fee.

Section 4A. Whenever the United States is hereafter injured in its business or property by reason of anything forbidden in the antitrust laws it may sue therefor in the United States district court for the district in which the defendant resides or is found or has an agent, without respect to the amount in controversy, and shall recover actual damages by it sustained and the cost of suit.

Section 4B. Any action to enforce any cause of action under sections 4 or 4A shall be forever barred unless commenced within four years after the cause of action accrued. No cause of action barred under existing law on the effective date of this act shall be revived by this Act.

Section 6. That the labor of a human being is not a commodity or article of commerce. Nothing contained in the antitrust laws shall be construed to forbid the existence and operation of labor, agricultural or horticultural organizations, instituted for the purposes of mutual help, and not having capital stock or conducted for profit, or to forbid or restrain individual members of such organizations from lawfully carrying out the legitimate objects thereof; nor shall such organizations or the members thereof, be held or construed to be illegal combinations or conspiracies in restraint of trade, under the antitrust laws.

Section 7. That no person engaged in commerce shall acquire, directly or indirectly, the whole or any part of the stock or other share capital and no corporation subject to the jurisdiction of the Federal Trade Commission shall acquire the whole or any part of the assets of another corporation engaged also in commerce, where in any line of commerce in any section of the country, the effect of such acquisition may be substantially to lessen competition, or to tend to create a monopoly.

No person shall acquire, directly or indirectly, the whole or any part of the stock or other share capital and no corporation subject to the jurisdiction of the Federal Trade Commission shall acquire the whole or any part of the assets of one or more corporations engaged in commerce, where in any line of commerce in any section of the country, the effect of such acquisition, of such stocks or assets, or of the use of such stock by the voting or granting of proxies or otherwise, may be substantially to lessen competition, or to tend to create a monopoly.

This section shall not apply to persons purchasing such stock solely for investment and not using the same by voting or otherwise to bring about, or in attempting to bring about, the substantial lessening of competition . . .

Section 8. . . . No person shall, at the same time, serve as a director or officer in any two or more corporations (other than banks, banking associations, and trust companies) that are—

(A) engaged in whole or in part in commerce; and

(B) by virtue of their business and location of operation, competitors, so that the elimination of competition by agreement between them would constitute a violation of any of the antitrust laws; if each of the corporations has capital, surplus, and undivided profits aggregating more than $10,000,000 as adjusted pursuant to paragraph (5) of this subsection.

■ Appendix G Federal Trade Commission Act of 1914 (Excerpts)

Unfair Methods of Competition Prohibited

Section 5.—Unfair methods of competition unlawful; prevention by Commission—declaration. Declaration of unlawfulness; power to prohibit unfair practices.

(a) (1) Unfair methods of competition in or affecting commerce, and unfair or deceptive acts or practices in or affecting commerce, are declared unlawful . . .

(b) Any person, partnership, or corporation who violates an order of the Commission to cease and desist after it has become final, and while such order is in effect, shall forfeit and pay to the United States a civil penalty of not more than $5,000 for each violation, which shall accrue to the United States and may be recovered in a civil action brought by the Attorney General of the United States. Each separate violation of such an order shall be a separate offense, except that in the case of a violation through continuing failure or neglect to obey a final order of the Commission each day of continuance of such failure or neglect shall be deemed a separate offense.

■ Appendix H Robinson-Patman Act (Excerpts)

Price Discrimination; Cost Justification; Changing Conditions

Section 2—Discrimination in price, services, or facilities.

(a) Price; Selection of Customers.

It shall be unlawful for any person engaged in commerce, in the course of such commerce, either directly or indirectly, to discriminate in price between different purchases of commodities of like grade and quality, where either or any of the purchases involved in such discrimination are in commerce, where such commodities are sold for use, consumption, or resale within the United States or any Territory thereof or the District of Columbia or any insular possession or other place under the jurisdiction of the United States, and where the effect of such discrimination may be substantially to lessen competition or tend to create a monopoly in any line of commerce, or to injure, destroy, or prevent competition with any person who either grants or knowingly receives the benefit of such discrimination, or with customers of either of them; *Provided,* That nothing herein contained shall prevent differentials which make only due allowance for differences in the cost of manufacture, sale, or delivery resulting from the differing methods or quantities in which such commodities are to such purchasers sold or delivered: *Provided, however,* That the Federal Trade Commission may, after due investigation and hearing to all interested parties, fix and establish quantity limits, and revise the same as it finds necessary as to particular commodities or classes of commodities, where it finds that available purchasers in greater quantities are so few as to render differentials on account thereof unjustly discriminatory or promotive of monopoly in any line of commerce; and the foregoing shall then not be construed to permit differentials based on differences in quantities greater than those so fixed and established: *And provided further,* That nothing herein contained shall prevent persons engaged in selling goods, wares, or merchandise in commerce from selecting their own customers in bona fide transactions and not in restraint of trade: *And provided further,* That nothing herein contained shall prevent price changes from time to time where in response to changing conditions affecting the market for or the marketability of the goods concerned, such as but not limited to actual or imminent deterioration of perishable goods, obsolescence of seasonal goods, distress sales under court process, or sales in good faith in discontinuance of business in the goods concerned.

Meeting Competition

(b) Burden of rebutting prima-facie case of discrimination.

Upon proof being made, at any hearing on a complaint under this section, that there has been discrimination in price or services or facilities furnished, the burden of rebutting the prima-facie case thus made by showing justification shall be upon the person charged with a violation of this sec-

tion, and unless justification shall be affirmatively shown, the Commission is authorized to issue an order terminating the discrimination: *Provided, however,* That nothing herein contained shall prevent a seller rebutting the prima-facie case thus made by showing that his lower price or the furnishing of services or facilities to any purchaser or purchasers was made in good faith to meet an equally low price of a competitor, or the services or facilities furnished by a competitor.

Brokerage Payments

(c) Payment or acceptance of commission, brokerage or other compensation.

It shall be unlawful for any person engaged in commerce, in the course of such commerce, to pay or grant, or to receive or accept, anything of value as a commission, brokerage, or other compensation, or any allowance or discount in lieu thereof, except for services rendered in connection with the sale or purchase of goods, wares, or merchandise, either to the other party to such transaction or to an agent, representative, or other intermediary therein where such intermediary is acting in fact for or in behalf, or is subject to the direct or indirect control, of any party to such transaction other than the person by whom such compensation is so granted or paid.

Promotional Allowances

(d) Payment for services or facilities for processing or sale.

It shall be unlawful for any person engaged in commerce to pay or contract for the payment of anything of value to or for the benefit of a customer of such person in the course of such commerce as compensation or in consideration for any services or facilities furnished by or through such customer in connection with the processing, handling, sale or offering for sale of any products or commodities manufactured, sold, or offered for sale by such person, unless such payment of consideration is available on proportionally equal terms to all other customers competing in the distribution of such products or commodities.

Promotional Services

(e) Furnishing services or facilities for processing, handling, etc.

It shall be unlawful for any person to discriminate in favor of one purchaser against another purchaser or purchasers of a commodity bought for resale, with or without processing, or by contracting to furnish or furnishing, or by contributing to the furnishing of, any services or facilities connected with the processing, handling, sale, or offering for sale of such commodity so purchased upon terms not accorded to all purchasers on proportionally equal terms.

Buyer Discrimination

(f) Knowingly inducing or receiving discriminatory price.

It shall be unlawful for any person engaged in commerce, in

the course of such commerce, knowingly to induce or receive a discrimination in price which is prohibited by this section.

Predatory Practices

Section 3—Discrimination in rebates, discounts, or advertising service charges; underselling in particular localities; penalties. It shall be unlawful for any person engaged in commerce, in the course of such commerce, to be a party to, or assist in, any transaction of sale, or contract to sell, which discriminates to his knowledge against competitors of the purchaser, in that, any discount, rebate, allowance, or advertising service charge is granted to the purchaser over and above any discount, rebate, allowance, or advertising service charge available at the time of such transaction to said competitors in respect of a sale of goods of like grade, quality, and quantity; to sell, or contract to sell, goods in any part of the United States at prices lower than those exacted by said person elsewhere in the United States for the purpose of destroying competition, or eliminating a competitor in such part of the United States; or, to sell, or contract to sell, goods at unreasonably lower prices for the purpose of destroying competition or eliminating a competitor.

Any person violating any of the provisions of this section shall, upon conviction thereof, be fined not more than $5,000 or imprisoned not more than one year, or both.

■ Appendix 1 Securities Act of 1933 as amended. (Excerpts)

. . .

Prohibitions Relating to Interstate Commerce and the Mails

Sec. 5. (a) Unless a registration statement is in effect as to a security, it shall be unlawful for any person, directly or indirectly—

(1) to make use of any means or instruments of transportation or communication in interstate commerce or of the mails to sell such security through the use or medium of any prospectus or otherwise; or

(2) to carry or cause to be carried through the mails or in interstate commerce, by any means or instruments of transportation, any such security for the purpose of sale or for delivery after sale.

[Prospectus Requirements]

(b) It shall be unlawful for any person, directly or indirectly—

(1) to make use of any means or instruments of transportation or communication in interstate commerce or of the mails to carry or transmit any prospectus relating to any security with respect to which a registration statement has been filed under this title, unless such prospectus meets the requirements of section 10, or

(2) to carry or to cause to be carried through the mails or in interstate commerce any such security for the purpose of sale or for delivery after sale, unless accompanied or preceded by a prospectus that meets the requirements of subsection (a) of section 10.

[Prohibition Against Offers Prior to Registration]

(c) It shall be unlawful for any person, directly or indirectly, to make use of any means or instruments of transportation or communication in interstate commerce or of the mails to offer to sell or offer to buy through the use or medium of any prospectus or otherwise any security, unless a registration statement has been filed as to such security, or while the registration statement is the subject of a refusal order or stop order or (prior to the effective date of the registration statement) any public proceeding or examination under section 8.

Civil Liabilities on Account of False Registration Statement

Sec. 11. (a) In case any part of the registration statement, when such part became effective, contained an untrue statement of a material fact or omitted to state a material fact required to be stated therein or necessary to make the statements therein not misleading, any person acquiring such security (unless it is proved that at the time of such acquisition he knew of such untruth or omission) may, either at law or in equity, in any court of competent jurisdiction, sue—

[Signers of Registration Statement]

(1) every person who signed the registration statement;

[Directors and Partners]

(2) every person who was a director of (or person performing similar functions), or partner in, the issuer at the time of the filing of the part of the registration statement with respect to which his liability is asserted;

[Persons Named as Being, or About to Become, Directors or Partners]

(3) every person who, with his consent, is named in the registration statement as being or about to become a director, person performing similar functions, or partner;

[Accountants, Engineers, Appraisers, and Other Professional Persons]

(4) every accountant engineer, or appraiser, or any person whose profession gives authority to a statement made by him, who has with his consent been named as having prepared or certified any part of the registration statement, or as having prepared or certified any report or valuation which is used in connection with the registration statement, with respect to the statement in such registration statement, report, or valuation, which purports to have been prepared or certified by him;

[Underwriters]

(5) every underwriter with respect to such security.

[Purchase after Publication of Earning Statement]

If such person acquired the security after the issuer has made generally available to its security holders an earning statement covering a period of at least twelve months beginning after the effective date of the registration statement, then the right of recovery under this subsection shall be conditioned on proof that such person acquired the securities relying on such untrue statement in the registration statement or relying upon the registration statement and not knowing of such omission, but such reliance may be established without proof of the reading of the registration statement by such person.

[Defenses of Persons Other than Issuer]

(b) Notwithstanding the provisions of subsection (a) no person, other than the issuer, shall be liable as provided therein who shall sustain the burden of proof—

[Resignation before Effective Date]

(1) that before the effective date of the part of the registration statement with respect to which his liability is asserted (A) he had resigned from or had taken such steps as are permitted by law to resign from, or ceased or refused to act in, every office, capacity or relationship in which he was described in the registration statement as acting or agreeing to act, and (B) he had advised the Commission and the issuer in writing, that he had taken such action and that he would not be responsible for such part of the registration statement; or

[Statements Becoming Effective without Defendants Knowledge]

(2) that if such part of the registration statement became effective without his knowledge, upon becoming aware of such fact he forthwith acted and advised the Commission, in accordance with paragraph (1), and, in addition, gave reasonable public notice that such part of the registration statement had become effective without his knowledge; or

[Belief on Reasonable Grounds that Statements Were True]

(3) that (A) as regards any part of the registration statement not purporting to be made on the authority of an expert, and not purporting to be a copy of or extract from a report or valuation of an expert and not purporting to be made on the authority of a public official document or statement, he had, after reasonable investigation, reasonable ground to believe and did believe, at the time such part of the registration statement became effective, that the statements therein were true and that there was no omission to state a material fact required to be stated therein or necessary to make the statements therein not misleading; and

[Statement Made on Authority of Defendant as Expert]

(B) as regards any part of the registration statement purporting to be made upon his authority as an expert or purporting to be a copy of or extract from a report or valuation of himself as an expert, (i) he had, after reasonable investigation, reasonable ground to believe and did believe, at the time such part of the registration statement became effective, that the statements therein were true and that there was no omission to state a material fact required to be stated therein or necessary to make the statements therein not misleading, or (ii) such part of the registration statement did not fairly represent his statement as an expert or was not a fair copy of or extract from his report or valuation as an expert; and

[Statement Made on Authority of Expert Other than Defendant]

(C) as regards any part of the registration statement purporting to be made on the authority of an expert (other than himself) or purporting to be a copy of or extract from a report or valuation of an expert (other than himself), he had no reasonable ground to believe and did not believe, at the time such part of the registration statement became effective, that the statements therein were untrue or that there was an omission to state a material fact required to be stated therein or necessary to make the statements therein not misleading, or that such part of the registration statement did not fairly represent the statement of the expert or was not a fair copy of or extract from the report or valuation of the expert; and

[Statement Made by Official Person; Copy of Public Official Document]

(D) as regards any part of the registration statement purporting to be a statement made by an official person or purporting to be a copy of or extract from a public official document, he had no reasonable ground to believe and did not believe, at the time such part of the registration statement became effective, that the statements therein were untrue, or that there was an omission to state a material fact required to be stated therein or necessary to make the statements therein not misleading, or that such part of the registration statement did not fairly represent the statement made by the official person or was not a fair copy of or extract from the public official document.

["Reasonable" Investigation and "Reasonable" Grounds for Belief]

(c) In determining, for the purpose of paragraph (3) of subsection (b) of this section, what constitutes reasonable investigation and reasonable ground for belief, the standard of reasonableness shall be that required of a prudent man in the management of his own property.

[Person Becoming Underwriter after Effectiveness of Registration Statement]

(d) If any person becomes an underwriter with respect to the security after the part of the registration statement with respect to which his liability is asserted has become effective, then for the purposes of paragraph (3) of subsection (b) of this section such part of the registration statement shall be considered as having become effective with respect to such person as of the time when he became an underwriter.

[Amount of Damages; Bond for Costs of Suit]

(e) The suit authorized under subsection (a) may be to recover such damages as shall represent the difference between the amount paid for the security (not exceeding the price at which the security was offered to the public) and (1) the value thereof as of the time such suit was brought, or (2) the price at which such security shall have been disposed of in the market before suit, or (3) the price at which such security shall have been disposed of after suit but before judgment if such damages shall be less than the damages representing the difference between the amount paid for the security (not exceeding the price at which the security was offered to the public) and the value thereof as of the time such suit was brought: Provided, That if the defendant proves that any portion or all of such damages represents other than the depreciation in value of such security resulting from such part of the registration statement, with respect to which his liability is asserted, not being true or omitting to state a material fact required to be stated therein or necessary to make the statements therein not misleading, such portion of or all such damages shall not be recoverable. In no event shall any underwriter (unless such underwriter shall have knowingly received from the issuer for acting as an underwriter some benefit, directly or indirectly in which all other underwriters similarly situated did not share in proportion to their respective interests in the underwriting) be liable in any suit or as a consequence of suits authorized under subsection (a) for damages in excess of the total price at which the securities underwritten by him and distributed to the public were offered to the public. In any suit under this or any other section of this title the court may, in its discretion, require an undertaking for the payment of the costs of such suit, including reasonable attorney's fees, and if judgment shall be rendered against a party litigant, upon the motion of the other party litigant, such costs may be assessed in favor of such party litigant (whether or not such undertaking has been required) if the court believes the suit or the defense to have been without merit, in an amount sufficient to reimburse him for the reasonable expenses incurred by him, in connection with such suit, such costs to be taxed in the manner usually provided for taxing of costs in the court in which the suit was heard.

[Joint and Several Liability]

(f) All or any one or more of the persons specified in subsection (a) shall be jointly and severally liable, and every person who becomes liable to make any payment under this section may recover contribution as in cases of contract from any person who, if sued separately, would have been liable to make the same payment, unless the person who had become liable was, and the other was not, guilty of fraudulent misrepresentation.

[Limitation on Amount of Damages]

(g) In no case shall the amount recoverable under this section exceed the price at which the security was offered to the public.

Civil Liabilities Arising in Connection with Prospectuses and Communications

Sec. 12. Any person who—

(1) offers or sells a security in violation of section 5, or

Offers or Sells by Use of Interstate Communications or Transportation

(2) offers or sells a security (whether or not exempted by the provisions of section 3, other than paragraph (2) of subsection (a) thereof), by the use of any means or instruments of transportation or communication in interstate commerce or of the mails, by means of a prospectus or oral communication, which includes an untrue statement of a material fact or omits to state a material fact necessary in order to make the statements, in the light of the circumstances under which they were made, not misleading (the purchaser not knowing of such untruth or omission), and who shall not sustain the burden of proof that he did not know, and in the exercise of reasonable care could not have known, of such untruth or omission, shall be liable to the person purchasing such security from him, who may sue either at law or in equity in any court of competent jurisdiction, to recover the consideration paid for such security with interest thereon, less the amount of any income received thereon, upon the tender of such security, or for damages if he no longer owns the security.

■ Appendix J Securities Exchange Act of 1934 as amended. (Excerpts)

. . .

Regulation of the Use of Manipulative and Deceptive Devices

Sec. 10. It shall be unlawful for any person, directly or indirectly, by the use of any means or instrumentality of interstate commerce or of the mails, or of any facility of any national securities exchange—

. . .

[Use or Employment of Manipulative or Deceptive Devices]

(b) To use or employ, in connection with the purchase or sale of any security registered on a national securities exchange or any security not so registered, any manipulative or deceptive device or contrivance in contravention of such rules and regulations as the commission may prescribe as necessary or appropriate in the public interest or for the protection of investors.

. . .

[Directors, Officers, and Principal Stockholders]

Sec. 16. (a) Every person who is directly or indirectly the beneficial owner of more than 10 per centum of any class of any equity security (other than exempted security) which is registered pursuant to section 12 of this title, or who is a director or an officer of the issuer of such security, shall file, at the time of the registration of such security on a national securities exchange or by the effective date of a registration statement filed pursuant to section 12(g) of this title, or within ten days after he becomes such beneficial owner, director, or officer, a statement with the Commission (and, if such security is registered on a national securities exchange, also with the exchange) of the amount of all equity securities of such issuer of which he is the beneficial owner, and within ten days after the close of each calendar month thereafter, if there has been a change in such ownership during such month, shall file with the Commission (and if such security is registered on a national securities exchange, shall also file with the exchange), a statement indicating his ownership at the close of the calendar month and such changes in his ownership as have occurred during such calendar month.

[Profits Realized from Purchase and Sales within Period of Less than Six Months]

(b) For the purpose of preventing the unfair use of information which may have been obtained by such beneficial owner, director, or officer by reason of his relationship to the issuer, any profit realized by him from any purchase and sale, or any sale and purchase, of any equity security of such issuer (other than an exempted security) within any period of less than six months, unless such security was acquired in good faith in connection with a debt previously contracted, shall inure to and be recoverable by the issuer, irrespective of any intention on the part of such beneficial owner, director, or officer in entering into such transaction of holding the security purchased or of not repurchasing the security sold for a period exceeding six months. Suit to recover such profit may be instituted at law or in equity in any court of competent jurisdiction by the issuer, or by the owner of any security of the issuer in the name and in behalf of the issuer if the issuer shall fail or refuse to bring such suit within sixty days after request or shall fail diligently to prosecute the same thereafter; but no such suit shall be brought more than two years after the date such profit was realized. This subsection shall not be construed to cover any transaction where such beneficial owner was not such both at the time of the purchase and sale, or the sale and purchase, of the security involved, or any transaction or transactions which the Commission by rules and regulations may exempt as not comprehended within the purpose of this subsection.

■ Appendix K Rule 10b-5 from Code of Federal Regulations

§ 240.10b-5 Employment of manipulative and deceptive devices.

It shall be unlawful for any person, directly or indirectly, by the use of any means or instrumentality of interstate commerce, or of the mails or of any facility of any national securities exchange,

(a) To employ any device, scheme, or artifice to defraud,

(b) To make any untrue statement of a material fact or to omit to state a material fact necessary in order to make the statements made, in the light of the circumstances under which they were made, not misleading, or

(c) To engage in any act, practice, or course of business which operates or would operate as a fraud or deceit upon any person, in connection with the purchase or sale of any security.

(Sec. 10; 48 Stat. 891; 15 U.S.C. 78j)

[13 FR 8183, Dec. 22, 1948, as amended at 16 FR 7928, Aug. 11, 1951]

■ Appendix L Rule 14e-3 from Code of Federal Regulations

§ 240.14e-3 Transactions in securities on the basis of material, nonpublic information in the context of tender offers.

(a) If any person has taken a substantial step or steps to commence, or has commenced, a tender offer (the "offering person"), it shall constitute a fraudulent, deceptive or manipulative act or practice within the meaning of section 14(e) of the Act for any other person who is in possession of material information relating to such tender offer which information he knows or has reason to know is nonpublic and which he knows or has reason to know has been acquired directly or indirectly from:

(1) The offering person,

(2) The issuer of the securities sought or to be sought by such tender offer, or

(3) Any officer, director, partner or employee or any other person acting on behalf of the offering person or such issuer, to purchase or sell or cause to be purchased or sold any of such securities or any securities convertible into or exchangeable for any such securities or any option or right to obtain or dispose of any of the foregoing securities, unless within a reasonable time prior to any purchase or sale such information and its source are publicly disclosed by press release or otherwise.

(b) A person other than a natural person shall not violate paragraph (a) of this section if such person shows that:

(1) The individual(s) making the investment decision on behalf of such person to purchase or sell any security described in paragraph (a) of this section or to cause any such security to be purchased or sold by or on behalf of others did not know the material, nonpublic information; and

(2) Such person had implemented one or a combination of policies and procedures, reasonable under the circumstances, taking into consideration the nature of the person's business, to ensure that individual(s) making investment decision(s) would not violate paragraph (a) of this section, which policies and procedures may include, but are not limited to, (i) those which restrict any purchase, sale and causing any purchase and sale of any such security or (ii) those which prevent such individual(s) from knowing such information.

(c) Notwithstanding anything in paragraph (a) of this section to contrary, the following transactions shall not be violations of paragraph (a) of this section:

(1) Purchase(s) of any security described in paragraph (a) of this section by a broker or by another agent on behalf of an offering person; or

(2) Sale(s) by any person of any security described in paragraph (a) of this section to the offering person.

(d)(1) As a means reasonably designed to prevent fraudulent, deceptive or manipulative acts or practices within the meaning of section 14(e) of the Act, it shall be unlawful for any person described in paragraph (d)(2)) of this section to communicate material, nonpublic information relating to a tender offer to any other person under circumstances in which it is reasonably foreseeable that such communication is likely to result in a violation of this section *except* that this paragraph shall not apply to a communication made in good faith.

(i) To the officers, directors, partners or employees of the offering person, to its advisors or to other persons, involved in the planning, financing, preparation or execution of such tender offer;

(ii) To the issuer whose securities are sought or to be sought by such tender offer, to its officers, directors, partners, employees or advisors or to other persons, involved in the planning, financing, preparation or execution of the activities of the issuer with respect to such tender offer; or

(iii) To any person pursuant to a requirement of any statute or rule or regulation promulgated thereunder.

(2) The persons referred to in paragraph (d)(1) of this section are;

(i) The offering person or its officers, directors, partners, employees or advisors;

(ii) The issuer of the securities sought or to be sought by such tender offer or its officers, directors, partners, employees or advisors;

(iii) Anyone acting on behalf of the persons in paragraph (d)(2)(i) of this section or the issuer or persons in paragraph (d)(2)(ii) of this section; and

(iv) Any person in possession of material information relating to a tender offer which information he knows or has reason to know is nonpublic and which he knows or has reason to know has been acquired directly or indirectly from any of the above.

[46 FR 60418, Sept. 12, 1980]

GLOSSARY

A

ABANDONMENT (OF A TRADEMARK) The failure to use a mark after acquiring legal protection may result in the loss of rights, and such loss is known as abandonment.

ABSOLUTE PRIVILEGE In defamation cases, the right by the defendant to publish with impunity a statement known by the defendant to be false.

ACCEPTANCE An agreement to the amount offered for certain services or products. Acceptance may be verbal, written or implied by action.

ACCREDITED INVESTOR Certain investors who are so financially sophisticated that they do not need all of the protections afforded by the securities laws.

ACT-OF-STATE DOCTRINE The doctrine which states that the courts of one country will not sit in judgment on the acts of the government of another, done within its own territory.

ACTIONABLE Behavior that is the basis for a claim.

ACTUAL (COMPENSATORY) DAMAGES The amount required to repair or to replace an item or the decrease in market value caused by tortious conduct. Actual damages restore the injured party to the position he was in prior to the injury.

ACTUAL AUTHORITY The express or implied power of an agent to act for and bind a principal to agreements entered into by an agent.

ACTUAL CAUSE Proof that but for a defendant's negligent conduct a plaintiff would not have been harmed.

ACTUAL INTENT The subjective desire to cause the consequences of an act, or the belief that the consequences are substantially certain to result from it.

ACTUAL MALICE A statement made with the knowledge that it is false or with a reckless disregard for the truth.

ACTUAL NOTICE Concerning claims on title, actual notice refers to a claimant actually knowing of a prior interest to the real property.

ACTUS REUS (guilty deed) A crime; an act done with criminal intent.

AD VALOREM (according to value) TARIFF An importer must pay a percentage of the value of the imported merchandise.

ADDITIVE Anything not inherent in a food product, including pesticide residues, unintended environmental contaminants, and unavoidably added substances from packaging.

ADHESION CONTRACT An unfair type of contract by which sellers offer goods or services on a take it or leave it basis with no chance for consumers to negotiate for goods except by agreeing to the terms on said contract.

ADMINISTRATIVE LAW JUDGE The presiding official at an administrative proceeding who has the power to issue an order resolving the legal disputes.

ADVERSE POSSESSION Ownership of property that is not occupied by its owner for a certain period of time may be transferred to those who have been unlawfully occupying it and exercising rights of ownership. Such a transfer is usually not reflected in the official land records. Also called squatter's rights.

AFFIDAVIT A written or printed declaration or statement of facts, made voluntarily, and confirmed by the oath or affirmation of the party making it, taken before a person having authority to administer such oath or affirmation.

AFFILIATE Any person who controls an issuer of securities, or is controlled by the issuer, or is under common control. Includes officers, directors, and major shareholders of a corporation.

AFFIRMATIVE COVENANT The borrower's promise of what it undertakes to do under the loan agreement.

AFFIRMATIVE DEFENSE The admission in an Answer to Complaint that defendant has acted as plaintiff alleges, but denies that defendant's conduct was the real or legal cause of harm to plaintiff.

AFTER-ACQUIRED PROPERTY The property a debtor acquires after the execution of a security agreement.

AFTER-ACQUIRED TITLE If at the date of execution of a grant deed the grantor does not have title to the real property referred to in the grant deed, but subsequently acquires it, such after-acquired title is deemed automatically transferred to the grantee.

AGENCY A relationship in which one person, the agent, acts for or represents another person, the principal.

AGENT A person who manages a task delegated by another, the principal, and exercises whatever discretion is given to the agent by the principal.

AIDER AND ABETTOR A person with knowledge of (or recklessness as to) a primary violation who provides substantial assistance to the primary violation.

ALTER EGO THEORY When owners have so mingled their own affairs with those of a corporation that the corporation does not exist as distinct entity—it is an alter ego (second self) of its owners.

AMORTIZE To pay over a period of time.

ANSWER The instrument by which defendant admits or denies the various allegations stated in the complaint against the defendant.

ANTIDEFICIENCY STATUTE A statute which prevents the holder of a mortgage or deed of trust secured by real property from suing the borrower to recover whatever is still owing after a foreclosure sale.

ANTITRUST INJURY The damages sustained by a plaintiff to an antitrust suit as a result of the anticompetitive aspect of a Sherman Act violation.

ANTITRUST LAWS The laws which seek to identify and forbid business practices that are anticompetitive.

APPARENT AUTHORITY A principal, by words or actions, causes a third party to reasonably believe that an agent has authority to act for or bind the principal.

APPELLANT The person who is appealing a judgment or seeking a writ of certiorari. Also called a petitioner.

APPELLATE JURISDICTION The power of the Supreme Court and other courts of appeal to decide cases which have been tried in a lower court and appealed.

APPELLEE The party in a case against whom an appeal is taken; that is, the party who has an interest adverse to setting aside or reversing the judgment. Also called respondent.

APPRAISAL RIGHTS In a merger or sale of assets, shareholders who voted against the transaction have appraisal rights, that is, the right to receive the fair cash value of the shares they were forced to give up as a result of the transaction.

APPROPRIATION OF A PERSON'S NAME OR LIKENESS Unauthorized use of a person's name or likeness for financial gain.

ARREST To deprive a person of his liberty by legal authority. Taking, under real or assumed authority, custody of another for the purpose of holding or detaining him to answer a criminal charge or civil demand.

ARTICLES OF INCORPORATION The basic document filed with the appropriate governmental agency upon the incorporation of a business. The contents are prescribed in the general incorporation statutes but generally include the name, purpose, agent for service of process, authorized number of shares, and classes of stock of a corporation. It is executed by the incorporator(s). Also called the charter.

ASSAULT An intent to create a well-grounded apprehension of an immediate harmful or offensive contact. Generally, assault also requires some act, like a threatening gesture, and the ability immediately to follow through with the battery.

ASSET LOCK-UP OPTION A lock-up option relating to assets.

ASSIGNMENT The subleasing by a tenant of all or a portion of rented premises.

ASSUMPTION OF RISK The expressed or implied consent by plaintiff to defendant to take the chance of injury from a known and appreciated risk.

AT-WILL CONTRACT An employment agreement of indefinite duration.

ATTACH If the three basic prerequisites of a security interest exist (agreement, value, and collateral), the security interest becomes enforceable between the parties and is said to attach. Also called attachment.

ATTORNEY-CLIENT PRIVILEGE The common-law rule that a court cannot force the disclosure of confidential communications between client and client's attorney.

ATTRACTIVE NUISANCE RULE The duty imposed on landowner for liability for physical injury to children trespassers caused by artificial conditions on the land.

AUTHORITATIVE DECISION A court decision that must be followed regardless of its persuasive power, by virtue of relationship between the court that made decision and the court to which decision is cited.

AUTOMATIC CONVERSION The exchange of preferred stock for common stock which is triggered by specified events at a specified ratio.

AUTOMATIC STAY Feature of bankruptcy filing which instantly suspends most litigation and collection activities against the debtor, its property, or that of the bankruptcy estate.

AVOIDING POWERS The powers trustees can use to invalidate or reverse certain prebankruptcy transactions.

B

BACK-TO-BACK LETTER OF CREDIT A seller uses a letter of credit to finance its purchase of products or materials from its supplier.

BACT (best available control technology) An emission limitation which the permitting authority determines achieves the maximum reduction of pollutants, taking into account energy, environmental, and economic considerations.

BAIT AND SWITCH ADVERTISING An area of deceptive pricing in which an advertiser refuses to show an advertised item, fails to have a reasonable quantity of the item in stock, fails to promise to deliver the item within a reasonable time, or discourages employees from selling the item.

BANKRUPTCY ESTATE Virtually all of a debtor's existing assets, less exempt property.

BASE RATE The lowest rate of interest offered by major lending institutions to their most creditworthy customers. Base rate or reference rate is preferable to prime rate in describing the rate charged the lender's most creditworthy customers because it does not imply that it is the lowest rate charged any customer.

BASELINE ASSESSMENT The appraisal performed by tenant which establish the environmental condition of leased property at the commencement and termination of the lease.

BATTERY The intentional, non-consensual harmful or offensive contact with an individual's body or with those things in contact with or closely connected with it.

BENEFICIAL OWNER A person is considered to be a beneficial owner of any securities held by his immediate family, spouse, any minor children or any other relative living in his household.

BENEFICIARY An individual who is benefited by a trust or a will.

BESPEAKS CAUTION DOCTRINE A doctrine whereby a court may determine that the inclusion of sufficient cautionary statements in a prospectus or other document renders immaterial any misrepresentations and omissions contained therein.

BEST-EFFORTS UNDERWRITING An agreement among underwriters of an offering to use their best efforts to find buyers at an agreed upon price.

BFOQ DEFENSE Civil Rights Act of 1964 provision which states that it is not an unlawful employment practice for an employer to hire and employ an individual on the basis of his or her religion, sex or national origin where religion, sex or national origin is a bona fide occupational qualification reasonably necessary to the normal operation of that particular business or enterprise.

BID RIGGING An agreement between or among competitors to rig contract bids.

BIDDER The party who makes a tender offer.

BILATERAL CONTRACT A promise given in exchange for another promise.

BILL OF ATTAINDER A law enacted to punish individuals or an easily ascertainable member of a group. Prohibited by Article I, section 9, of the U.S. Constitution.

BILL OF LADING The document carrier issues to seller which indicates what goods the carrier has received from the seller, the loading location, the names of the carrying vessel, and the destination.

BLANK CHECK COMPANY A development-stage company that has no specific business plan or whose business plan is to acquire a presently unknown business.

BLUE-SKY LAWS A popular name for the state statutes which regulate and supervise offerings and sales of securities; protect citizen-investors from investing in fraudulent companies.

BOILERPLATE Standardized.

BOND The most common type of debt security. A debt security indicates that a corporation has incurred a debt by borrowing money from the holder of the document.

BOUND TARIFFS The GATT principle which holds that each time tariffs are reduced, they may not be raised again.

BREAK-UP FEE An amount agreed to in merger agreement to be paid to a suitor company if the agreement with the target company is not consummated through no fault of the suitor company.

BURDEN OF PROOF The requirement of prosecutor in a criminal case to establish a defendant's guilt beyond a reasonable doubt.

BUSINESS JUDGMENT RULE In a case challenging a board decision, this rule holds that as long as directors have acted in good faith and in the honest belief that the action they've taken was in the best interest of the company, a court will not question whether the directors' action was wise or whether they made an error of judgment or a business mistake.

BUST-UP TAKEOVER In a bust-up takeover, the corporation, upon acquisition, is taken apart and its assets sold.

BYLAWS The internal rules governing a corporation.

C

C CORPORATION A business organization which is taxed at both the entity level and the owner level.

CALL A LOAN To terminate a loan.

CAPACITY The ability (requisite presence of mind) to enter into a binding contract.

CARTEL A group of competitors which agrees to set prices.

CAVEAT EMPTOR (let the buyer beware) This maxim summarizes the rule that a purchaser must examine, judge, and test for himself. It does not apply where strict liability, warranty, or other consumer protection laws protect consumer-buyers.

CD Certificate of deposit.

CEASE AND DESIST ORDER An order of an administrative agency or court prohibiting a person or business firm from continuing a particular course of conduct.

CERTIFICATE OF INCORPORATION The basic document filed with the appropriate governmental agency upon the incorporation of a business. The contents are prescribed in the general incorporation statutes but generally include the name, purpose, agent for service of process, authorized number of shares, and classes of stock of a corporation. It is executed by the incorporator(s). Also called the charter.

CERTIFICATION MARK A mark placed on a product or used in connection with a service that indicates that the product or service in question has met the standards of safety or quality that have been created and advertised by the certifier.

CERTIORARI A writ of common-law origin issued by a superior to an inferior court requiring the latter to produce a certified record of a particular case tried in the inferior court. The U.S. Supreme Court uses the writ as a discretionary device to choose the cases it wishes to hear.

CHECK KITING The issuing of checks from bank accounts with nonexisting fund to cover overdrafts created at other bank accounts.

CHOICE OF FORUM CLAUSE The clause in a contract wherein the parties agree in advance in which jurisdiction a dispute arising out of their agreement is to be litigated.

CIRCUMSTANTIAL EVIDENCE The indirect (not based on personal knowledge or observation) evidence of certain facts which taken alone do not prove a particular conclusion, but if taken as a whole, give a trier of fact a reasonable basis for asserting a certain conclusion is true.

CLAIMS (under patent law) The description of those elements of an invention which will be protected by the patent.

CLASS ACTION SUIT A suit filed on behalf of all persons who have allegedly been harmed by a defendant's conduct.

CLASSIFIED (or STAGGERED) BOARD A board on which directors serve for specified terms, usually three years, with only a fraction of them up for reelection at any one time.

CLEAN BILL OF LADING Bill of lading that has no notations indicating defects or damage to the goods when they were received for transport.

CLIFF VESTING A common vesting schedule which provides that if a person granted stock options leaves in the first year of employment, she forfeits all of her rights to any stock.

CLOSE CORPORATION A corporation owned by a limited number of shareholders, usually 30, most of whom are actively involved in the management of the corporation.

CODIFY To collect and arrange items, such as statutes or regulations, systematically.

COLLATERAL The property belonging to a borrower that will become the lender's if the loan is not repaid.

COMMERCIAL IMPOSSIBILITY An excuse for nonperformance of a contract because of dramatic changes in circumstances or the relative benefits and burdens of the contract to each party.

COMMERCIAL PAPER Short-term corporate indebtedness.

COMMITMENT FEE The fee payable to a lender in connection with a revolving loan as consideration for its promise to keep the commitment available, as it receives no interest on amounts not borrowed.

COMMON LAW The legal rules made by judges when they decide a case in which no constitution, statute, or regulation resolves the dispute.

COMMON MARKET The customs union in which there are no tariffs on trade among its members, and a single set of tariffs applies to goods imported from outside the union.

COMMON STOCK Stock that subjects all the shareholders to the same rights and restrictions.

COMMUNITY PROPERTY The property acquired during marriage with assets earned by either spouse during the marriage.

COMPARATIVE FAULT The liability of an injured party because of misuse or abuse of manufacturer's product.

COMPARATIVE NEGLIGENCE The doctrine by which courts decide amount of award to be given a plaintiff based on the amount (percentage) of negligence plaintiff demonstrated when injured by defendant.

COMPENSATION TRADE An international transaction in which a foreign party transfers use and/or eventual ownership of a good, usually equipment, to the local party, who then repays the foreign party with products produced using the foreign party's equipment.

COMPENSATORY (ACTUAL) DAMAGES The amount required to repair or to replace an item or the decrease in market value caused by tortious conduct. Compensatory damages restore the injured party to the position he was in prior to the injury.

COMPENSATORY JUSTICE Aims at compensating people for the harm done by another.

COMPLAINT The statement of plaintiff's grievance that makes allegations of the particular facts giving rise to dispute, and states the legal reason why plaintiff is entitled to a remedy, the request for relief, the explanation why the court applied to has jurisdiction over the dispute and whether plaintiff requests a jury trial.

COMPOSITION PLAN An agreement between an insolvent debtor and his creditors whereby the creditors agree to accept a sooner payment of less than the whole amount in satisfaction of the whole amount.

COMPUTER FRAUD The unauthorized access to a computer used by the federal government, or by various types of financial institutions with the intent to alter, damage, destroy information or prevent authorized use of the such computers.

COMPUTER PIRACY The theft or misuse of computer software or hardware.

CONCERTED ACTIVITY (NLRA) The exercise by employees of their rights to band together for mutual aid and protection that is engaged in with or on the authority of other employees, and not solely by and on behalf of one employee.

CONDITION PRECEDENT A condition that must be met

before the lender's obligations arise under a loan agreement.

CONDITION SUBSEQUENT In contracts, a provision giving one party the right to divest himself of liability and obligation to perform further if the other party fails to meet the condition.

CONDITIONAL MFN (Most Favored Nation) The limitation on trade benefits to GATT members who refuse to accede to the codes created at the Tokyo Round of Multilateral Trade Negotiations regarding nontariff barriers.

CONDITIONAL USE PERMIT A method of relief from the strict terms of a zoning ordinance which provides for other uses for real property that are not permitted as a matter of right, but for which a use permit must be obtained.

CONDITIONS CONCURRENT Conditions that are mutually dependent and are to be performed at the same time or simultaneously.

CONFIRMING BANK A bank located in the seller's jurisdiction that makes a legal commitment to the seller that it will honor the terms of the letter of credit issued by the issuing bank.

CONFLICT OF LAW RULES In international contracts, conflict of law refers to a dispute regarding which country's courts have jurisdiction to hear the contract dispute and which country's laws should be applied to resolving the dispute.

CONGLOMERATE MERGER A combination of firms which were not competitors at the time of the acquisition, but which may, absent the merger, have become competitors.

CONSENT ORDER A judgment entered by the consent of the parties whereby the defendant agrees to stop the alleged illegal activity without admitting guilt or wrongdoing. An agreement by a defendant to cease activities asserted as illegal by government. Also called consent decree.

CONSEQUENTIAL DAMAGES Compensation for losses that occur as a foreseeable result of a breach of contract. Actual damages represent the damage, loss or injury that flows directly and immediately from the act of the other party; in contrast, consequential damages refer to damage, loss or injury flowing from some of the consequences or results of such act.

CONSIDERATION A thing of value (money, services, an object, a promise, forbearance or giving up the right to do something) exchanged in a contract.

CONSTRUCTION (of a statute) Interpretation.

CONSTRUCTIVE NOTICE Notice attributed by the existence of a properly recorded deed.

CONSTRUCTIVE TRUST A trust imposed on profits derived from a corporate opportunity taken by an officer, director or controlling shareholder for personal gain when corporate opportunity was discovered during the course of business for the corporation.

CONTINUING GUARANTY A guaranty which covers all future obligations of the primary debtor to the lender.

CONTRIBUTION The doctrine which provides for the distribution of loss among several defendants by requiring each to pay its proportionate share to one who has discharged the joint liability of the group.

CONTRIBUTORY INFRINGEMENT One party knowingly sells an item which has one specific use which will result in the infringement of another patent.

CONTRIBUTORY NEGLIGENCE Plaintiff was negligent in some manner when injured by defendant.

CONTROLLING SHAREHOLDER A shareholder who owns sufficient shares to outvote the other shareholders, and thus to control the corporation.

CONTROLLING-PERSON LIABILITY A person (or other entity), usually an officer or director of a company, responsible and liable for a securities violation.

CONVERSION The exercise of dominion and control over the personal property, rather than the real property (land), of another. Term includes any unauthorized act which deprives an owner of his personal property permanently or for an indefinite time.

CONVERTIBLE DEBT INSTRUMENT The document which permits conversion of debt principal into stock.

CONVERTIBLE PREFERRED STOCK Preferred stock that may be converted into common stock at a specified exchange ratio.

CONVEYANCE An instrument transferring an interest in real estate, such as a deed or lease.

COPYRIGHT The legal right to prevent others from copying the expression embodied in a protected work.

CORPORATE CHARTER The document issued by a state agency or authority granting a corporation legal existence and the right to function as a corporation.

CORPORATE DOMICILE The state under whose laws a corporation is formed.

CORPORATE OPPORTUNITY DOCTRINE The doctrine which holds that a business opportunity cannot legally be taken advantage of by an officer, director, or controlling shareholder if the corporation would be harmed as a result.

CORPORATION An organization authorized by state law to act as a legal entity distinct from its owners.

CORPORATION BY ESTOPPEL When a third party, in all its transactions with an enterprise, acts as if it were doing business with a corporation, the third party is prevented or estopped from claiming that the enterprise is not a corporation.

COUNTERCLAIM A legal claim by defendant in opposition to or deduction from claim of plaintiff.

COUNTEROFFER A new offer by the initial offeree which rejects and modifies the terms originally proposed by the offeror.

COUNTERTRADE A foreign investor uses its local currency profits to purchase local products for sale abroad.

COUNTERVAILING DUTY LAW The law which provides that if a U. S. industry is materially injured by imports of a product benefiting from a foreign subsidy, an import duty that offsets the amount of the benefit must be imposed on those imports.

COUNTERVAILING SUBSIDY The benefits provided by a government to stimulate exports.

COVENANT The borrower's promise to the lender that it will or will not take specific actions as long as either a commitment or a loan is outstanding.

COVENANT NOT TO COMPETE An agreement, generally part of a contract of employment or a contract to sell a business, in which the covenantor agrees for a specific period of time and within a particular area to refrain from competition with the convenantee.

COVER In the case of a seller failing to make delivery of goods, cover refers to buyer's legal remedy of buying the goods elsewhere and recovering the cost of the substitute goods.

CRAM DOWN A bankruptcy relief plan confirmed over the objections of creditors.

CREDITOR BENEFICIARY Third party to a contract which the promisee enters into in order to discharge a duty to said third party.

CRIME An offense against the public at large; an act that violates the duties owed to the community, for which the offender must make satisfaction to the public.

CROSS-COLLATERALIZATION The collateral for one loan is used to secure obligations under another loan.

CROSS-DEFAULT Any breach by the borrower under any other loan agreement will constitute an event of default under the subject loan agreement.

CROSS-ELASTICITY OF DEMAND The extent to which consumers will change their consumption of one product in response to a price change in another.

CROWN JEWELS The most valuable assets or divisions of a target company in a takeover battle.

CUMULATIVE VOTING The process by which a shareholder can (and, in some states, must) cast all her votes for one nominee or allocate them among nominees as she sees fit.

CUSTOMER RESTRICTIONS Restrictions which prevent a dealer or distributor from selling to a certain class of customer. Also called territorial restrictions.

CUSTOMS VALUATION The value assigned to imported article by the U.S. Customs Service.

D

D'OENCH, DUHME **DOCTRINE** A doctrine that bars many claims and defenses against conservators and receivers that might have been valid against the failed bank or savings and loan itself. It bars enforcement of agreements unless those agreements are in writing and have been approved contempora-

neously by the bank's board or loan committee and recorded in the bank's written records.

DE FACTO (in fact) CORPORATION When incorporators cannot show substantial compliance with incorporation requirements, a court may find a corporation is a de facto corporation or corporation in fact even though it is not technically a corporation by law, if the incorporators demonstrate that they were unaware of the defect and that they made a good faith effort to incorporate correctly.

DE JURE (by law) CORPORATION When incorporators have substantially complied with incorporation requirements, the entity is a de jure corporation or a corporation by right.

DE NOVO (new) PROCEEDING An administrative agency's decision is appealed and case goes to court to be litigated from the beginning.

DEALER (1933 Act) Any person who engages either for all or part of his time, directly or indirectly, as agent, broker, or principal, in the business of offering, buying, selling, or otherwise dealing or trading in securities issued by another person.

DEBT SECURITIES The documents indicating that a corporation has incurred a debt by borrowing money from the holder of the document.

DEBT SUBORDINATION An agreement whereby one or more creditors of a common debtor agree to defer payment of their claims until another creditor of the same debtor is fully paid.

DEBTOR (under the UCC) The person who owes payment or other performance of the obligation secured, whether or not that person owns or has rights in the collateral.

DEBTOR IN POSSESSION Under a chapter 11 bankruptcy, debtor may, for the benefit of all concerned, be left in possession of the bankruptcy estate.

DEED An instrument transferring an interest in real estate which is recorded at a public office where title documents are filed.

DEED OF TRUST A loan to buy real property secured by a lien on the real property. Also called a mortgage.

DEFAMATION The intentional communication to a third party of an untrue statement of fact that injures the plaintiff's reputation or good name, by exposing her to hatred, ridicule or contempt.

DEFAULT JUDGMENT A judgment that may be entered in favor of the plaintiff if the defendant does not file an answer within the time required.

DEFENDANT The person defending or denying; the party against whom relief or recovery is sought in an action or suit. The accused in a criminal case.

DELAWARE COURT OF CHANCERY The trial court in Delaware that hears corporate law cases.

DEMAND RIGHTS An investor's right to require an issuer to register a stated portion of the investor's shares in a public offering.

DEONTOLOGICAL THEORY An ethical theory which focuses on the motivation behind an action rather than the consequences of an action.

DEPOSITION The written or oral questioning of any person who may have helpful information about the facts of a case.

DERIVATIVE INSIDER A person, such as a tippee, upon whom the insider's duty of disclosure is imposed.

DESCRIPTIVE MARK The identifying marks which directly describe (size, color, use of) the goods sold under the mark.

DESIGN DEFECT A type of product defect that occurs when the product is manufactured according to specifications, but its inadequate design or poor choice of materials causes it to be defective.

DESIGN PATENT A patent which protects any novel, original, and ornamental design for an article of manufacture.

DETOUR A temporary turning aside from a usual or regular route, course or procedure, or from a task or employment. To be distinguished from a frolic, which is outside of an agent's scope of employment.

DIRECT INFRINGEMENT The making, use, or sale of any patented invention within the United States during the term of the patent.

DIRECTED VERDICT After the presentation of evidence in a trial before jury, either party may assert that other side has not produced enough evidence to support the legal claim or defense alleged. The moving party then requests that the judge take the case away from the jury and direct that a verdict be entered in favor of the moving party.

DISAPPEARING CORPORATION In a corporate merger, the corporation that no longer maintains its separate corporate existence is the disappearing corporation.

DISCHARGE Relieve.

DISCLOSURE OF PRIOR ART A part of patent application that discusses pre-existing art that relates to a claimed invention.

DISCOVERY OF INJURY STATUTES Statutes that provide that the statute of limitations does not begin to run until the person discovers the injury.

DISCOVERY RULE The statute of limitations period does not accrue until the injured party discovers or, by using reasonable diligence, should have discovered the injury.

DISCOVERY The process through which parties to a lawsuit collect evidence to support their claims.

DISPARAGEMENT Untrue statements derogatory to the quality or ownership of a plaintiff's goods or services, that the defendant knows are false, or to the truth of which the defendant is consciously indifferent.

DISPARATE IMPACT The systematic exclusion of women or ethnic groups from employment through testing and other selection procedures.

DISPARATE TREATMENT Intentional discrimination against a person by employer by denying person employment or a benefit or privilege of employment because of race, religion, sex, or national origin.

DISSOLUTION The designation of the point in time when partners no longer carry on their business together.

DISTRIBUTIVE JUSTICE A theory of justice that looks to how the burden and benefits of a particular situation of a system are distributed.

DIVERSITY JURISDICTION The power of U. S. District Courts to decide lawsuits between citizens of two different states when amount in controversy, exclusive of interest and all costs, exceeds $50,000.

DOCTRINE OF EQUIVALENTS The doctrine that holds that a direct infringement of a patent has occurred when a patent is not literally copied, but is replicated to the extent that the infringer has created a product or process that works in substantially the same way and accomplishes substantially the same result as the patented invention.

DOCTRINE OF SELF-PUBLICATION A defamatory communication by an employer to an employee may constitute publication if the employer could foresee that the employee would be required to repeat the communication, for instance, to a prospective employer.

DONEE BENEFICIARY Third party to a contract to whom promisee does not owe an obligation, but rather wishes to confer a gift or a right of performance.

DOUBLE JEOPARDY Fifth Amendment guarantee that protects against a second prosecution for the same offense after acquittal or conviction, and against multiple punishments for the same offense.

DRAM SHOP ACT A statute that makes a tavern liable for damage or injury caused by a drunk driver who was served drinks even though visibly intoxicated.

DUAL AGENCY In a real estate transaction, a broker acts for both the buyer and the seller.

DUAL DISTRIBUTOR A manufacturer that sells its goods wholesale and at retail itself.

DUE DILIGENCE The identification and characterization of risks associated with property and operations involved in various business transactions. A defendant in a securities violation case concerning a registration statement who (1) conducted a reasonable investigation, and (2) reasonably believed that (a) the statements made were true, and (b) that there were no omissions that made those statements misleading has exercised due diligence.

DUMPING When imported products are sold in the U. S. below the current selling price in the exporter's home market or below the exporter's cost of production, they are said to be dumped.

DURESS Coercion. A contract is voidable if one party was forced to enter into the agreement through duress.

DUTIABLE Import articles subject to required payment.

DUTY (1) The obligation to act as a reasonably prudent person would act under the circumstances to prevent an unreasonable risk of harm to others. (2) The required payment on imports.

DUTY OF CARE The fiduciary duty of agents, officers, and directors to act with the same care that a reasonably prudent person would exercise under similar circumstances. Sometimes expressed as the duty to use the same level of care a reasonably prudent person would use in the conduct of her own affairs.

DUTY OF LOYALTY The fiduciary duty of agents, officers, and directors to act in good faith and in what they believe to be the best interest of the principal or the corporation.

E

ECONOMIC DURESS The coercion of the borrower, threatening to do an unlawful act that might injure the borrower's business or property.

ECONOMIC STRIKE A union strikes employers when they are unable to extract acceptable terms and conditions of employment through collective bargaining.

EFFICIENT-MARKET THEORY The theory which holds that in an open and developed securities market, the price of a company's stock equals its true value.

EFFLUENT LIMITATIONS The regulations designed to impose increasingly stringent limitations on pollutant discharges based on the availability of economic treatment and recycling technologies.

EMBEZZLEMENT The acquisition by an employee of money or property by reason of some office or position, which money or property the employee takes for personal use.

EMINENT DOMAIN The power of state and federal governments to take private property for government uses for which property owners are entitled to just compensation.

EMPLOYER One who employs the services of others; one for whom employees work, and who pays their wages or salaries.

ENCUMBRANCE A claim against real property.

ENTERPRISE Any individual, partnership, corporation, association, or other legal entity, and any union or group of individuals associated in fact although not a legal entity.

ENTRENCHMENT Entrenchment occurs when a director opposes a transaction in order to maintain a place on the corporation's board.

ENVIRONMENTAL LAWS The numerous federal, state, and local laws with the common objective of protecting human health and the environment.

EQUAL DIGNITIES RULE Under this rule if an agent acts on behalf of another (his principal) in signing an agreement of the type that must under the statute of frauds be in writing, the authority of the agent to act on behalf of the principal must also be in writing.

EQUITABLE RELIEF An injunction issued by the court to prohibit defendant from continuing in a certain course of activity or to require defendant to perform a certain activity.

EQUITABLE SUBORDINATION The doctrine which prevents one creditor, through fraud or other wrongful conduct, from increasing its recovery at the expense of other creditors of the same debtor.

EQUITY CAPITAL The cash or property contributed to an enterprise in exchange for an ownership interest.

EQUITY SECURITY (section 16(b)) An equity security includes: (1) any stock or similar security; (2) any security that is convertible, with or without consideration, into such a security; (3) any security carrying any warrant or right to purchase such a security; (4) any such warrant or right; and (5) any other security which the SEC deems to be of a similar nature and which, for the protection of investors or in the public interest, the SEC considers appropriate to treat as an equity security.

EQUITY The value of real property which exceeds the liens against it.

***ERIE* DOCTRINE** In an action in federal court, except as to matters governed by the U.S. Constitution and acts of Congress, the law to be applied in any case is the law of the state in which the federal court is situated.

ESCROW AGENT A neutral stake holder who facilitates the transfer of real property between interested parties.

ESCROW The system by which a neutral stake holder (escrow agent) allows parties to a real property transaction to fulfill the various conditions of the closing of the transaction without the physical difficulties of passing instruments and funds between the parties.

ESSENTIAL FACILITY Some resource necessary to a company's rival's survival that they cannot economically or feasibly duplicate.

ESTOPPED A defendant is legally barred from alleging or denying a certain fact when the defendant's words and/or actions have been to the contrary.

EVENT RISKS Changes in the structure of a corporation such as leveraged buyouts, mergers, or hostile takeovers that affect the credit rating or riskiness of outstanding debt.

EVENTS OF DEFAULT The events contained in a loan agreement that will trigger the lender's right to terminate the loan, accelerate the repayment obligations, and, if the loan is secured, take possession of the property securing the loan.

EX POST FACTO LAWS (after the fact) The laws prohibited by the U.S. Constitution which punish actions that were not illegal when performed.

EXCLUSIONARY RULE The evidence obtained in a warrantless search cannot be introduced into evidence at trial against a defendant.

EXCLUSIVE DEALERSHIP An agreement in which a manufacturer limits itself to a single dealer in a given territory. Also called exclusive distributorship.

EXECUTIVE PRIVILEGE The type of immunity granted

the president against the forced disclosure of presidential communications made in the exercise of executive power.

EXECUTORY CONTRACT Contracts that have not yet been performed.

EXEMPLARY DAMAGES Damages awarded to a plaintiff over and above what will fairly compensate her for her loss. They are intended to punish the defendant and deter others from engaging in similar conduct. Also called punitive damages.

EXEMPT PROPERTY Excluded from a bankruptcy estate, and intended to provide for the individual's future needs. Generally includes a homestead, motor vehicles, household or personal items, tools of the debtor's trade, health aids, personal injury awards, alimony or support payments, disability or retirement benefits (including IRAs), life insurance or annuities, and some special deposits of cash.

EXHAUSTION OF ADMINISTRATIVE REMEDIES A court will not entertain an appeal from the administrative process until an agency has had a chance to act and all possible avenues of relief before the agency have been fully pursued.

EXIT VEHICLE A way for investors to get their money back without liquidating a company, for example, through acquisition by a larger company or through an initial public offering of the company's securities.

EXPECTATION DAMAGES In the case of breach of contract, expectation damages refers to remuneration that puts a plaintiff into the cash position the plaintiff would have been in if the contract had been fulfilled.

EXPRESS WARRANTY An explicit promise to guarantee by the seller that the goods purchased by a buyer will have certain qualities.

EXTENSION PLAN A plan by which creditors are repaid the entire indebtedness, but the period for payment is extended beyond the original due date.

EXTORTIONATE EXTENSION OF CREDIT Making a loan for which violence is understood by the parties as likely to occur in the event of nonpayment.

F

FAILURE TO WARN Failure of a product to carry adequate warnings of the risks involved in the normal use of the product.

FAIR TRADE LAW A federal law providing for temporary relief to domestic industries seriously injured by increasing imports, regardless of whether unfair practices are involved.

FAIR USE DOCTRINE The doctrine that protects from liability a defendant who has infringed a copyright owner's exclusive rights when countervailing public policies predominate. Activities such as literary criticism, social comment, news reporting, educational activities, scholarship, or research are traditional fair use domains.

FALSE IMPRISONMENT The confinement of an individual without that individual's consent and without lawful authority.

FAST TRACK AUTHORITY This law allowed the president to negotiate trade agreements and submit them for up or down consideration by Congress. Trade agreements negotiated pursuant to fast track authority can be voted down by Congress but cannot be amended by Congress.

FEDERAL COMMON LAW The judicial interpretations of federal statutes and administrative regulations.

FEDERAL INTEREST COMPUTER A computer used by the federal government or by various types of financial institutions, or a computer which is one of two or more computers used in committing the offense, not all of which are located in the same state.

FEDERAL QUESTION When a dispute concerns federal law, namely, a legal right arising under the U.S. Constitution, a federal statute, an administrative regulation issued by a federal government agency, federal common law, or a treaty of the United States, it is said to be a federal question.

FEE SIMPLE Title to property that grants owner full right of disposition during his lifetime and may be passed on to owner's heirs and assigns forever.

FELONY An offense punishable by death or prison term exceeding one year.

FETAL PROTECTION POLICY A company policy that bars a woman from certain jobs unless her inability to bear children is medically documented.

FIDUCIARY A person having a duty to act primarily for the benefit of another in matters connected with undertaking fiduciary responsibilities.

FIDUCIARY DUTY A trustee's obligation to act for the benefit of trustor.

FIDUCIARY OUT The allowance in a merger agreement for directors of target company to remain faithful to their fiduciary duties to their shareholders (for example, by recommending other unsolicited offers) even after signing an agreement with a suitor company.

FILE-WRAPPER ESTOPPEL The doctrine which prevents a patent owner involved in infringement from introducing any evidence at odds with the information contained in the owner's application on file with the United States Patent and Trademark Office.

FINANCE LEASE An equipment lease which serves the purpose of financing.

FIRM OFFER (under the UCC) An offer signed by a merchant that indicates that the offer will be kept open is not revocable, for lack of consideration, during the time stated, or for a reasonable period of time if none is stated, but in no event longer than three months.

FIRM-COMMITMENT UNDERWRITING An agreement among underwriters of an offering to purchase the entire offering, thus effectively shifting the risk of the offering from the issuer to the underwriters.

FIXTURES (under the UCC) The items of personal property

that are attached to real property and that cannot be removed without substantial damage to the item.

FICTITIOUS BUSINESS NAME A name of a business that is other than the name of the owner and must be registered with the state.

FLOAT The difference between the amount of funds credited to a bank account and the amount of funds actually collected for that account.

FLOATING INTEREST RATE An interest rate which fluctuates throughout the life of the loan according to the interest rate that the lender would pay if it borrowed the funds in order to relend them.

FLOATING LIEN In a security interest, if the collateral is sold, exchanged, collected, or otherwise disposed of, the security interest is equally effective against cash, account, or whatever else is received from the transaction.

FORECLOSE To take possession of the collateral and either sell it to pay off the debt or keep it in satisfaction of the debt.

FOREIGN CORPORATION A corporation doing business in one state though chartered or incorporated in another state is a foreign corporation as to the first state.

FOREIGN TRADE ZONE The special areas within or adjacent to U.S. ports of entry, where import duties on merchandise normally due upon entry into the U.S. are not due until the merchandise is withdrawn from the zone.

FORGOTTEN FOUNDER A problem that can arise when several persons work together on an informal basis with a common business objective, and then one leaves. The person who left—the forgotten founder—may have ownership rights in the enterprise.

FORUM SHOPPING A party to a lawsuit attempts to have a case tried in a particular court or jurisdiction where party feels the most favorable judgment or verdict will be received.

FRANCHISE A business relationship in which one party (the franchisor) grants to another party (the franchisee) the right to use the franchisor's name and logo and to distribute the franchisor's products from a specified locale.

FRAUD Any intentional deception that has the purpose of inducing another in reliance upon the deception to part with some property or money. Fraud may involve false representations of fact, whether by words or conduct, false allegations, omission, or concealment of something that should have been disclosed.

FRAUD IN THE FACTUM A type of fraud that occurs when a party is persuaded to sign one document thinking that it is another.

FRAUD IN THE INDUCEMENT A type of fraud that occurs when a party makes a false statement to persuade the other party to enter into an agreement.

FRAUD ON THE MARKET The theory that holds that if the information available to the market is incorrect, then the market price will not reflect the true value of the stock.

FRAUD-CREATED-THE-MARKET THEORY A theory accepted by some courts whereby a plaintiff need not prove reliance in securities fraud cases when the alleged fraud is so pervasive that without it the issuer would not have been able to sell the securities because the information would have shown them to be worthless.

FRAUDULENT CONVEYANCE The direct or indirect transfer of assets to a third party with actual intent to defraud or have inadequate consideration in circumstances when the transferor is insolvent.

FRAUDULENT MISREPRESENTATION Deceit; intentionally misleading by making material misrepresentations of fact that the plaintiff relied upon which cause injury to the plaintiff.

FREEZE-OUT A majority shareholder may force the minority shareholders to convert their shares into cash, so long as the transaction is fair.

FROLIC An activity by an employee which is entirely outside the employer's purpose. To be distinguished from a detour, which is within the scope of employment.

FRUIT OF THE POISONOUS TREE Evidence acquired directly or indirectly as a result of an illegal search or arrest.

FULL WARRANTY The warranty which gives the consumer the right to free repair or replacement of a defective product.

G

GARNISHMENT The legal procedure by which a creditor may collect a debt by attaching a portion of a debtor's weekly wages.

GENERAL PARTNERSHIP A form of business organization between two or more persons in which the partners share in the profits or losses of a common business enterprise.

GENERAL PLAN A long-range planning document which addresses the physical development and redevelopment of a city.

GENERAL RELEASE An agreement by person engaging in a dangerous activity to assume all risks and hold party offering access to said dangerous activity free of all liability.

GEOGRAPHIC MARKET All firms that compete for sales in a given area at current prices, or would compete in that area if prices rose by a modest amount.

GOING EFFECTIVE Culmination of the securities registration process with the Securities and Exchange Commission. Sales can be legally consummated as of this date and time.

GOLDEN PARACHUTE A termination agreement which gives extra salary and other benefits to an executive upon a corporate change in control.

GOODS (under the UCC) All things (including specially manufactured goods) which are movable at the time of identification to the contract for sale.

GOVERNMENT-CONTRACTOR DEFENSE The limited

immunity available for manufacturers who produce products to the specifications of government contracts.

GRANT DEED A deed that contains implied warranties that the grantor has not previously conveyed the same property or any interest in it to another person and that the title is marketable.

GRANTEE A person to whom real property is conveyed.

GRANTOR A person conveying his real property.

GREENMAIL Payment by a target company to buy back shares owned by potential acquirer at a premium over market. The acquirer in exchange agrees not to pursue its hostile takeover bid.

GROSS-UP CLAUSE The clause in foreign investment contracts by which local partner or licensee is obligated to pay all taxes other than those specifically allocated to the foreign partner.

GROUP BOYCOTT An agreement among competitors to refuse to deal with another competitor. Group boycotts violate antitrust law.

GUARANTOR The person who becomes liable for the obligation of another person.

GUARANTY An undertaking by one person to become liable for the obligation of another person.

GUARANTY OF PAYMENT A provision that holds guarantor's obligation to pay the lender is triggered, immediately and automatically, if the primary debtor fails to make a payment when due.

GUARDIAN AD LITEM (guardian for the suit) A person authorized to bring suit for a minor.

GUN-JUMPING A violation of the securities laws that occurs when an issuer or underwriter conditions the market with a news article, press release, or speech about a company engaged in the registration of its securities.

H

HAZARD RANKING SCORE The EPA ranking which represents the risks presented by certain sites to the environment and public health.

HORIZONTAL AGREEMENT A conspiracy agreement between firms that compete with each other on the same level of production or distribution.

HORIZONTAL MARKET DIVISION An agreement among competitors to divide a market according to class of customer or geographic territory; it violates antitrust law.

HORIZONTAL MERGER A corporate combination of actual or prospective competitors.

HORIZONTAL PRICE FIXING An agreement between competitors at the same level of distribution to set a common price for a product. Horizontal price fixing violates antitrust law.

HOSTILE ENVIRONMENT HARASSMENT The creation of a hostile working environment, such as continually subjecting an employee to ridicule and racial slurs, or unwanted sexual advances.

HOSTILE TAKEOVER A transaction in which a third party, called a raider, seeks to obtain control of a company, called the target, over the objections of its management.

HUSHMAIL A repurchase of shares at a premium over market to ensure silence from a shareholder who has been critical of management.

I

IDENTIFICATION TO THE CONTRACT The particular goods for sale under a contract.

ILLEGAL CONTRACT A contract is illegal if its formation or performance is expressly forbidden by a civil or criminal statute, or if a penalty is imposed for doing the act agreed upon.

ILLUSORY PROMISE A promise which does not in fact confer any benefit on the promisor or subject the promisee to any detriment.

IMPAIRED CLAIM A claim is considered impaired if the bankruptcy relief plan does not provide for full cash payment on its effective date and it alters the creditors' legal, equitable, or contractual rights in any way (except by curing defaults and reinstating the maturity of the claim).

IMPLIED CONTRACT An employment contract implied from such facts as long-term employment; receipt of raises, bonuses and promotions; and assurance from management that the employee was doing a good job, that the employee would not be terminated except for good cause.

IMPLIED COVENANT OF GOOD FAITH AND FAIR DEALING An implied covenant in every contract that imposes on each party a duty not to do anything that will deprive the other party of the benefits of the agreement.

IMPLIED INTENT If a person does not intend a particular consequence of an act, but knew that the consequence of the act was certain, or substantially certain, and does the act anyway, intent to cause the consequence is implied.

IMPLIED WARRANTY OF FITNESS FOR A PARTICULAR PURPOSE The warranty whereby goods involving the following elements are judged guaranteed: (1) the buyer must have a particular purpose for the goods, (2) the seller must have known or have had reason to know of that purpose, (3) the seller must have known or had reason to know that the buyer was relying on the seller's expertise, and (4) the buyer must have relied upon the seller.

IMPLIED WARRANTY OF MERCHANTABILITY The warranty by which all goods sold by merchants in the normal course of business must meet following criteria (1) pass without objection in the trade under the contract description; (2) be fit for the ordinary purposes for which such goods are used; (3) be within the variations permitted by the agreement, of even kind, quality and quantity within each unit and among all units involved; (4) be adequately contained, packaged, and labeled as the agreement may require; and (5) conform to the promises or affirmations of fact made on the container or label, if any.

IMPROPER MEANS (UTSA) Deceitful actions through which party obtains trade secrets of another.

IN BANC (EN BANC) HEARING A hearing at which all the judges of a court of appeals sit together to hear and decide a particularly important or close case.

IN PERSONAM JURISDICTION Personal jurisdiction based upon the residence or activities of the person being sued. It is the power which a court has over the defendant herself, in contrast to the court's power over the defendant's interest in property (quasi in rem jurisdiction) or power over the property itself (in rem jurisdiction).

IN REM JURISDICTION Jurisdiction based upon the location of property at issue in the lawsuit.

INCORPORATION The process by which a corporation is formed.

INDEMNIFICATION The doctrine that allows a defendant to recover its individual loss from a co-defendant whose relative blame is greater or who has contractually agreed to assume liability.

INDENTURE The agreement governing a bond issue.

INDEPENDENT CONTRACTOR A person is deemed to be an independent contractor only if the employer neither exercises control over the means of performing the work nor the end result of that work.

INDICTMENT Formal charges filed by a grand jury.

INDIRECT INFRINGEMENT One party's active inducement of another party to infringe a patent.

INFORMAL DISCRETIONARY ACTION The administrative agencies' decision-making process for repetitive actions that are inappropriate to litigate in courts.

INFORMATION The formal charges filed with the court in a criminal case.

INHERENTLY DISTINCTIVE MARK Inherently distinctive marks (often called strong marks) are identifying marks that need no proof of distinctiveness.

INITIATIVE A formal petition generated by a certain percentage of the electorate to introduce legislative change.

INJUNCTION A remedy granted by the court that requires defendant to perform or cease from performing some activity.

INJURIOUS FALSEHOOD False statements knowingly made that lead to economic loss for a plaintiff.

INQUIRY NOTICE Notice attributed when reasonable inquiry would have disclosed an adverse interest, for example, if inspection of a property would have revealed that some person other than the grantor was in possession or owned the property.

INSIDE DIRECTOR A member of a board who is also an officer.

INSIDER A person with access to confidential information

and an obligation of disclosure to other traders in the marketplace.

INSIDER TRADING Trading securities while in possession of material nonpublic information, in violation of a duty to the corporation or its shareholders or others.

INTEGRATED DISCLOSURE SYSTEM The system that seeks to eliminate duplicative or unnecessary disclosure requirements under the 1933 and 1934 Acts.

INTEGRATED SALES When an issuer makes successive sales of securities within a limited period of time, the SEC may integrate the successive sales; that is, it may deem them to be part of a single sale for purposes of deciding whether there was an exemption from registration.

INTEGRATION OF OFFERING Where an issuer makes successive offerings of securities within a limited period of time, the SEC may integrate the successive offerings; that is, it may deem them to be part of a single offering.

INTELLECTUAL PROPERTY Any product or result of a mental process that is given legal protection against unauthorized use.

INTENT The actual, subjective desire to cause the consequences of an act, or the belief that the consequences are substantially certain to result from it.

INTENT TO BE BOUND The oral or written statement regarding intention of parties to enter into a contract.

INTENTION TO DO WRONG Subjective intent or desire to do wrong or intent to take action substantially certain to cause a wrong to occur.

INTENTIONAL INFLICTION OF EMOTIONAL DISTRESS Outrageous conduct by the individual inflicting the distress; intention to cause, or reckless disregard of the probability of causing, emotional distress; severe emotional suffering; and actual and proximate (or legal) causation of the emotional distress.

INTERBRAND COMPETITION The price competition between a company and its local dealers.

INTERFERENCE WITH CONTRACTUAL RELATIONS A defendant intentionally induces another to breach a contract with a plaintiff.

INTERFERENCE WITH PROSPECTIVE BUSINESS ADVANTAGE Intentional interference by the defendant with business relationship the plaintiff seeks to develop, which interference causes loss to the plaintiff.

INTERLOCUTORY Something intervening between the commencement and the end of a suit which decides some point or matter, but is not a final decision regarding the whole controversy.

INTERROGATORY The written question to the parties to a lawsuit and their attorneys.

INTRABRAND COMPETITION The price competition among the different dealers of the same company.

INTRUSION Objectionable prying, such as eavesdropping or unauthorized rifling through files. It includes the act of wrongfully entering upon or taking possession of property of another.

INVASION OF PRIVACY Prying or intrusion that would be objectionable or offensive to a reasonable person, including eavesdropping, rifling through files one has no authorization to see, public disclosure of private facts, or unauthorized use of an individual's picture in an advertisement or article with which that person has no connection.

INVESTORS Persons putting up cash or property in exchange for an equity interest in an enterprise.

INVITEE A business visitor who enters a premises for the purposes of the possessor's business.

INVOLUNTARY REDEMPTION RIGHTS The permission of a corporation, at its option, to redeem the shares for a specified price either after a given period of time or on the occurrence of a certain event.

IRREBUTTABLE PRESUMPTION A presumption that cannot be disputed even through the introduction of contrary evidence.

IRREVOCABLE LETTER OF CREDIT A letter of credit which cannot be amended or canceled without the consent of the seller and the issuing bank.

ISSUER A company that offers or sells.

J

JOIN In cases where more than one defendant is liable for damages, named defendant(s) may ask the court to join or add other defendants.

JOINT AND SEVERAL LIABILITY The doctrine whereby a plaintiff may collect the entire judgment from any single defendant, regardless of the degree of that defendant's fault, in a case where the court determines that multiple defendants are at fault.

JOINT TENANCY A specialized form of co-ownership involving real property owned in equal shares by two or more persons who have a right of survivorship if one joint tenant dies.

JOINT VENTURE A one-time group of two or more persons in a single specific business enterprise or transaction.

JUDGMENT N.O.V. (non obstante veredicto, not withstanding the verdict) The motion by attorney for the losing party that reverses the jury verdict on the grounds that the evidence of the prevailing party was so weak that no reasonable jury could have resolved the dispute in that party's favor.

JUDICIAL REVIEW The power of federal courts to review acts of the legislative and executive branches of government to determine whether they violate the Constitution.

JUNIOR DEBT Indebtedness that is subordinated under a debt subordination agreement.

JUNK BOND A form of high yield, high risk unsecured corporate indebtedness that is not investment grade.

JURISTIC PERSONALITY The characteristic of a business entity, such as a corporation, whereby the entity is treated as a legal entity separate from its owners.

K

KANTIAN THEORY An ethical theory that looks to the form of an action, rather than the intended result, in examining the ethical worth.

KICKER A percentage of gross or net income in a real estate transaction payable to lender.

KNOW-HOW Detailed information on how to make or do something.

L

LAESIO ENORMIS A doctrine developed from language in the Code of Justinian that provided a remedy for those who sold land at less than half its just price.

LARCENY Theft. The taking of property without the owner's consent.

LETTER OF CREDIT (LC) A payment mechanism for international sales transactions that a bank in the buyer's jurisdiction uses to mange the transaction between the buyer and the seller.

LETTER OF INTENT An instrument entered into by the parties to a real estate transaction for the purpose of setting forth the general terms and conditions of a purchase and sale agreement until a formal legal commitment can be made through the execution of a formal acquisition agreement.

LEVERAGED BUYOUT (LBO) A takeover financed with loans secured by the acquired company's assets, in which groups of investors, including management, use borrowed money along with some of their own money to buy back the company's stock from its current shareholders.

LIBEL A written communication to a third part by a defendant of an untrue statement of fact that injures a plaintiff's reputation.

LIBOR London Interbank Offered Rate.

LICENSEE Anyone who is privileged to enter upon land of another because the possessor has given expressed or implied consent.

LIEN A claim on a property that secures a debt owed by the owner of the property.

LIEN SUBORDINATION An agreement between two secured creditors whose respective security interest, liens, or mortgages attach to the same property. The subordinating party agrees that the lien of the other creditor shall have priority notwithstanding the relative priorities that the parties' liens would otherwise have under applicable law.

LIMITED GUARANTY A guaranty in which the maximum amount of the guarantor's liability is expressly stated in the guaranty instrument.

LIMITED LIABILITY COMPANY A form of business entity authorized by state law that is taxed like a limited partnership and provides its members with limited liability, but like a corporation gives its members the right to participate in management without incurring unlimited liability.

LIMITED PARTNERS The participants in a limited partnership whose liability for partnership business is limited to their capital contribution.

LIMITED PARTNERSHIP A form of business organization in which limited partners must refrain from actively participating in the management of the partnership but are liable for the debts of the partnership only up to the amount they personally contributed to the partnership.

LIMITED WARRANTY The warranty that limits the remedies available to the consumer for a defective product.

LINE-OF-BUSINESS TEST If an officer, director, or controlling shareholder learns of an opportunity in the course of business for the corporation, and if the opportunity is in the corporation's line of business, a court will not permit that person to keep the opportunity for personal gain.

LIQUIDATED DAMAGES The amount of money stipulated in a contract to be paid to non-breaching party should one of the parties breach the agreement.

LOCK-UP OPTION An option to buy assets or stock of a target company; it is exercisable only if the recipient of the option is unsuccessful in acquiring control of the target company. Depending on how it is priced, a lock-up option can have the effect of deterring other bids.

LONG-ARM STATUTE A state statute that subjects an out-of-state defendant to jurisdiction when the defendant is doing business or commits a civil wrong in the state.

LOOK-AND-FEEL TEST A copyrightable work is arguably infringed by another work even if the subsequent work does not copy any individual element of the original work, if an ordinary observer would regard the subsequent work as a copy of the original work's look or feel.

M

MAIL FRAUD A scheme intended to defraud or to obtain money or property by fraudulent means through use of the mails.

MALPRACTICE A claim of professional negligence.

MANUFACTURING DEFECT A flaw in a product that occurs during production, such as a failure to meet the design specifications.

MARKET-SHARE LIABILITY The liability for damages caused by a manufacturer's products assessed based on a manufacturer's national market share.

MARKETABLE TITLE Title to property that is fee simple and is free of liens or encumbrances.

MARSHALING ASSETS Partnership creditors have first priority to partnership assets and stand in front of creditors of individual partners themselves.

MASTER LIMITED PARTNERSHIP An entity structured as a limited partnership that has readily transferable limited partnership interests that are traded on a national securities exchange.

MATERIAL FACT A fact that a reasonable investor would most likely have considered important in deciding whether to buy or sell his stock.

MATURITY DATE The date a term loan becomes due and payable.

MENS REA (state of mind) In the committing of a crime, this refers to criminal intent.

MERCHANT (under the UCC) A person who deals in goods of the kind or otherwise by his occupation holds himself out as having knowledge of skill peculiar to the practices or goods involved in the transaction.

MERGER AGREEMENT An agreement between two companies to combine those companies into one.

MERGER DOCTRINE If an idea and its expression are inseparable, the merger doctrine dictates that the expression is not copyrightable.

MINIMUM CONTACTS As long as the person has sufficient minimum contacts with a state, such that it is fair to require her to appear in a court of that state, the state has personal jurisdiction over that person.

MISAPPROPRIATION (OF A TRADE SECRET) Learning through improper means and use of the trade secret of another.

MISAPPROPRIATION THEORY The theory that holds that a securities violation occurs when a person breaches a fiduciary duty to the owner of nonpublic information by trading on that information after misappropriating it for his own use.

MISBRANDING False or misleading labeling; prohibited by federal and state statutes. Includes claiming unsubstantiated medicinal benefits for a food, inadequate labeling for a drug, or selling over-the-counter a drug for which a prescription is required.

MISDEMEANOR An offense lower than a felony, punishable by fine or imprisonment (not in a penitentiary).

MISSTATEMENT (rule 10b-5) A misrepresentation of a fact; a lie.

MITIGATION OF DAMAGES After a breach of contract, the non-breaching party has a duty to take any reasonable actions that will lessen the amount of the damages.

MONOPOLISTIC INTENT The maintenance or acquisition of monopoly power through anticompetitive acts.

MONOPOLY POWER The power to control market prices or exclude competition in the relevant market.

MORTGAGE A loan to buy real property secured by a lien on the real property. Also called deed of trust.

MOST FAVORED NATION The principle which holds that each member country of the General Agreement on Tariffs and

Trade (GATT) must accord to all other GATT members tariff treatment no less favorable than it provides to any other country.

MOTION TO DISMISS The formal request that court terminate lawsuit on the ground that plaintiff's claim is technically inadequate.

MUTUALITY OF OBLIGATION Both parties in a bilateral contract are obligated to perform their side of the bargain.

N

NATIONAL AMBIENT AIR QUALITY STANDARDS The permissible levels of pollutants in the ambient or outdoor air that, with adequate margins of safety, are required to protect public health; stated in Clean Air Act.

NATIONAL TREATMENT The GATT principle which holds that GATT members must not discriminate against imported products in favor of domestically produced products.

NATURAL RESOURCE LAW The laws which govern wilderness protection, wildlife protection, coastal zone management, energy conservation and national park designation.

NAVIGABLE WATERS The waters of the United States and the territorial seas, as well as lakes and streams that are not in fact usable for purposes of navigation.

NEGATIVE CONVENANT The borrower's promise of what it undertakes not to do under the loan agreement.

NEGLIGENCE A breach of the requirement that a person act with the care a reasonable person would use in the same circumstances.

NEGLIGENCE PER SE Violation of a statute that shifts the burden to the defendant to prove the defendant was not negligent once the plaintiff shows the defendant violated a statute and the violation caused an injury.

NEGLIGENT-HIRING THEORY An employer is negligent if the employer hires an employee who endangers the health and safety of other employees.

NEUTRAL GATE SYSTEM In a secondary boycott situation, the union may picket only at the gate reserved for the employees and vendors of the primary employer that is physically separated from the gate to be used by all other persons.

NEXUS The legally required relationship between a condition to a land-use approval and the impacts of the development being approved.

NOLO CONTENDERE (I will not contest it) A plea that means accused does not contest the charges.

NON OBSTANTE VEREDICTO (notwithstanding the verdict) Immediately after the jury has rendered its verdict and the jury has been excused from the courtroom, the attorney for the losing party may make a motion for judgment notwithstanding the verdict. Such a judgment, also known as a judgment n.o.v., reverses the jury verdict on the ground that the evidence of the prevailing party was so weak that no reasonable jury could have resolved the dispute in that party's favor.

NONCONFORMING USE The existing use of land that was lawful, but that does not comply with a later-enacted zoning ordinance.

NOTE PURCHASE AGREEMENT The title of loan agreement when the lender is an insurance company.

NOVATION The method of contract modification by which original contract is canceled and a new one is written with perhaps only one change.

NUISANCE A thing or activity that unreasonably and substantially interferes with an owner's use and enjoyment of owner's property.

O

OBVIOUS RISK If the use of a product carries an obvious risk, the manufacturer will not be held liable for injuries that result from ignoring the risk.

OFFER (contracts) A proposal to enter into a contract. Proposal may be verbal, written or implied by action.

OFFER (1933 Act) Every attempt or offer to dispose of, or solicitation of an offer to buy, a security or interest in a security, for value.

OFFEREE A person to whom an offer is made.

OFFEROR A person making an offer.

OFFSHORE TRANSACTION A security transaction in which no offer is made to a person in the United States and either: (1) at the time the buy order is originated, the buyer is outside the United States; or (2) the transaction is one executed in, on, or through the facilities of a designated offshore securities market.

OMISSION (rule 10b-5) A company or its managers fail to tell the whole truth about a fact to the investing public, and what the company does say makes it likely that reasonable investors will take away an impression contrary to the true facts.

ONE-FORM-OF-ACTION LAWS Statutes that restrict lenders seeking remedies against real property security from suing the borrower personally. If a lender has recourse to the borrower or to other property of the borrower, and exercises such rights, the lender may be precluded from foreclosing on real estate mortgaged by the borrower. Also referred to as anti-deficiency laws.

OPPRESSION An inequality of bargaining power that results in no real negotiation and an absence of meaningful choice for one party to the contract.

OPTION CONTRACT A contract in which the offeror promises to hold an offer open for a certain amount of time.

ORGANIZATIONAL STRIKE An unlawful strike whose purpose is to organize employees.

ORIGINAL JURISDICTION The power of Supreme Court to take cognizance of a cause at its inception, try it, and pass judgment upon the law and facts. Distinguished from appellate jurisdiction.

OUTPUT CONTRACT A contract under which a buyer promises to buy all of the products that the seller produces.

OUTSIDE DIRECTOR A member of a board who is not also an officer.

OVER-THE-COUNTER A drug for which a prescription is not required.

P

PARENS PATRIAE (parent of the country) ACTION Antitrust suits brought by state attorneys general for injuries sustained by residents of their respective states.

PAROL EVIDENCE RULE If there is a written contract that the parties intended would encompass their entire agreement, parol evidence of prior or contemporaneous statements will not be permitted to vary or alter the terms of the contract.

PARTICIPATION LOAN A loan in which the original lender sells shares to other parties, called participants.

PASS-THROUGH ENTITY A business organization that is not a separate taxpayer, and all of its income and losses are passed through and taxed to its owner. An S Corporation is a pass-through entity.

PASSIVE INVESTOR An investor in a business who does not materially participate in that business.

PASSIVE-LOSS LIMITATIONS The rule enacted by the Tax Reform Act of 1986 under which only owners who materially participate in a business may deduct losses against their other income.

PATENT A government-granted right to exclude others from making, using, or selling within the government's jurisdiction an invention that is the subject of the patent.

PATTERN An involvement in racketeering activity demonstrated by at least two such acts occurring within a ten-year period.

PATTERN BARGAINING In collective bargaining, a technique of matching agreements within an industry.

PER SE VIOLATION A violation without proof of anything more.

PERFECTION (under the UCC) In connection with security interests, perfection refers to making the security interest valid as against other creditors of the debtor.

PERSON (under environmental law) A party who has contributed to imminent and substantial endangerment to human health or the environment and therefore is required in a civil action to take remedial action. Person in this sense includes companies, individual employees, officers, and possibly shareholders.

PERSONAL JURISDICTION The power of state court to hear (decide) a civil case based upon residence or location of activities of the person being sued or upon the location of property at issue in lawsuit.

PERSUASIVE DECISION A well-reasoned court decision that another court, not bound by the first decision, would, when confronted with a similar dispute, probably follow.

PETITIONER The person who is appealing a judgment or seeking a writ of certiorari; also called appellant.

PIERCING THE CORPORATE VEIL When courts deny limited liability to a corporation and hold shareholders personally responsible for claims against the corporation, the court has pierced the corporate veil.

PIGGYBACK RIGHTS An investor's right to request registration of that investor's shares in a public offering initiated by the company.

PLACEMENT AGENT A broker-dealer who distributes the private placement memorandum to suitable persons and assists in private placement of securities.

PLAINTIFF A person who brings an action; the party who complains or sues in a civil action and is so named on the record. The prosecution in a criminal case (i.e., the state or the United States in a federal case).

PLANNED UNIT DEVELOPMENT (PUD) The land use regulations for a given piece of property that reflect the proposed development plans for that property. PUD allows for mixture of uses for property not possible under traditional zoning regulations.

PLEA BARGAINING The process by which the prosecutor agrees to reduce the charges in exchange for a guilty plea from the accused.

PLEA The response by a defendant in criminal case of guilty, not guilty, or nolo contendere.

PLEADINGS The formal allegations by the parties to a lawsuit of their respective claims and defenses.

PLEDGE A type of security interest whereby the creditor or secured party takes possession of the collateral owned by the debtor.

POINTS A one-time charge to a borrower buying real property (in addition to interest) computed by a lender by multiplying the amount funded by a fixed percentage.

POISON PILL A plan that would make any takeover of a corporation prohibitively expensive.

POLICE POWER The general power granted state and city governments to protect the health, safety, welfare, or morals of its residents.

POLITICAL QUESTION A conflict that should be decided by one of the political branches of government or by the electorate. A court will refuse to decide questions of a purely political character.

POWER OF ATTORNEY A written instrument that authorizes a person, called an attorney-in-fact (who need not be a lawyer), to sign documents or perform certain specific acts on behalf of another person.

PRE-PACKAGED BANKRUPTCY A workout plan

approved by key creditors and the debtor before the debtor files bankruptcy; it becomes the plan of reorganization in a chapter 11 bankruptcy.

PRECONTRACTUAL LIABILITY The claims by the disappointed party if contract negotiations fail before a contract has been signed.

PREDATORY PRICING The act of pricing below the producer's actual cost with the intent of driving other competitors out of the market, thus enabling the person engaging in predatory pricing to raise prices later.

PREEMPT A federal law takes precedence when state law conflicts with federal law.

PREEMPTION DEFENSE The immunity granted manufacturers if they meet minimum standards of conduct under certain regulatory schemes.

PREFERENCES Transfers to (or for the benefit of) creditors on account of antecedent debts that are made from an insolvent debtor's property within 90 days before bankruptcy and that enable the creditors to receive more than they would through a chapter 7 liquidation.

PREFERRED RETURN The legal right to have distributions made to the person entitled to a preferred return before any distributions are made to any other equity holder.

PREFERRED STOCK Stock which has priority over common stock in the payment of dividends (and in the distribution of assets if the corporation is dissolved).

PREJUDGMENT INTEREST The interest on the amount of an award from the date of the injury to the date of judgment.

PRENUPTIAL AGREEMENT An agreement entered into before marriage which sets forth the manner in which the parties' assets will be distributed, and the support to which each party will be entitled, in the event the parties get divorced.

PREPAYMENT PENALTY A clause whereby a lender imposes a penalty if the loan is paid off early.

PREPONDERANCE OF THE EVIDENCE The evidence offered in a civil trial which is more convincing than the evidence presented in opposition to it.

PRICE AMENDMENT Information concerning the price of securities and underwriting arrangement filed with the SEC once the registration statement has been informally cleared by the SEC staff, or the registrant receives notice that the registration statement will not be reviewed.

PRICE ANTIDILUTION A provision which prevents a corporation from diluting their interests by simply issuing shares of common stock at a price below the conversion price.

PRICE DISCRIMINATION Sellers charge different prices to purchasers in interstate sales for commodities of like grade and quality.

PRICE FIXING The cooperative setting of price levels or ranges by competing firms.

PRIMA FACIE (on its face) A fact considered true until evidence is produced to the contrary.

PRIMARY DEBTOR The person with an obligation for which the guarantor becomes liable.

PRIMARY EMPLOYER (NLRA) In a secondary boycott situation, the employer with whom union has a dispute.

PRIME RATE The lowest rate of interest offered by major lending institutions to their most creditworthy customers. Better practice dictates using the terms base rate or reference rate because sometimes lenders offer a loan below prime.

PRIMING LIEN A lien that is senior to a previously granted security interest.

PRINCIPAL (OF A LOAN) The amount borrowed.

PRINCIPAL A person who delegates a portion of her tasks to another person who represents the principal as an agent.

PRIOR ART Developments or pre-existing art which relates to a claimed invention.

PRIOR RESTRAINTS Prohibitions barring speech before it occurs.

PRIVATE NUISANCE Interference with a person's use and enjoyment of his land and water.

PRIVATE OFFERING An offering to selected individuals or entities who have the ability to evaluate and bear the risk of the investment; that is, they have the ability to fend for themselves.

PRIVATE PLACEMENT MEMORANDUM A booklet offered by entrepreneurs seeking financing from private individual investors that furnishes all information about themselves and their enterprise.

PRIVATELY HELD CORPORATION A corporation whose shares are not bought and sold among the general public.

PRIVITY OF CONTRACT The necessity for a person injured by a product to be in a contractual relationship with the seller of the product in order for the injured person to recover damages.

PROBABLE CAUSE As applied to an arrest or a search warrant, probable cause is defined as a reasonable belief that the suspect has committed a crime or is about to commit a crime. Mere suspicion or belief, unsupported by facts or circumstances, is insufficient.

PROCEDURAL DUE PROCESS The parties whose rights are to be affected are entitled to be heard and, in order that they may enjoy that right, they must be notified.

PROCEDURAL OBLIGATIONS The rules that define the manner in which rights and duties are enforced.

PROCESSING OPERATION In a compensation trade arrangement, a processing operation refers to the foreign party supplying the materials that are processed by the local party using the foreign party's equipment.

PRODUCT MARKET A product or service offering made by different manufacturers or sellers that are economically interchangeable and may therefore be said to compete.

PRODUCT LIABILITY The liability of a manufacturer or seller of a product that because of a defect, causes injury to a purchaser, user, or bystander.

PROFESSIONAL CORPORATION An organization of professionals (e.g., doctors, lawyers, or architects) authorized by state law to act as a legal entity distinct from its owners.

PROMISEE In contract law, the promisee is the person to whom the promise (contract) was made.

PROMISOR In contract law, the promisor is the person who made the promise.

PROMISSORY ESTOPPEL A promise that the promisor should reasonably expect to induce action or forbearance on the part of the promisee or a third person and that does induce such action or forbearance is binding if injustice can be avoided only by enforcement of the promise.

PROOF OF CLAIM A claim filed by creditors on uncontingent and undisputed debt.

PROSPECTUS (1933 Act) Any document that is designed to produce orders for a security, whether or not the document purports on its face to offer the security for sale or otherwise to dispose of it for value. The descriptive document that an issuer of securities provides to prospective purchasers.

PROTECTED EXPRESSION The part of a work that is subject to copyright protection.

PROXIMATE CAUSE A specific negligent act that leads to an injury, without which no injury would have occurred.

PROXY A written authorization by a shareholder to another person to vote on the shareholder's behalf.

PUBLIC DISCLOSURE OF PRIVATE FACTS The publication of a private fact that is not newsworthy. The matter must be private, such that a reasonable person would find publication objectionable. Unlike in a defamation case, truth is not a defense.

PUBLIC FIGURES Individuals, who, by reason of their achievements or the vigor and success with which they seek the public's attention, are injected into the public eye.

PUBLIC NUISANCE Unreasonable and substantial interference with the public health, safety, peace, comfort, convenience, or utilization of land.

PUBLIC POLICY EXCEPTION An employer is prohibited from discharging an employee for a reason that violates public policy.

PUBLICATION Communication to a third party.

PUBLICLY HELD CORPORATION A corporation whose shares are traded on one of the national stock exchanges or the over-the-counter market.

PUFFING The expression of opinion by a seller regarding goods; not a warranty.

PUNITIVE DAMAGES Damages awarded to a plaintiff over and above what will fairly compensate her for her loss. They are intended to punish the defendant and deter others from engaging in similar conduct. Also called exemplary damages.

PURE COMPARATIVE NEGLIGENCE A tort system in which the plaintiff may recover for the part of the injury due to the defendant's negligence, even though the plaintiff was the more negligent party.

Q

QUALIFIED PRIVILEGE In defamation cases, the right by a defendant to make statements to (1) protect one's own personal interests, (2) protect business interests, such as statements to a prospective employer, or (3) provide information for the public interest, such as credit reports.

QUANTUM MERUIT A basis for equitable relief by a court when there was no contract between the parties, but one party has received a benefit for which he has not paid.

QUASH To declare invalid.

QUID-PRO-QUO (what for what) HARASSMENT The specific, job-related adverse action, such as denial of a promotion, in retaliation for a worker's refusal to respond to a worker's or supervisor's sexual advances.

QUIET PERIOD (1933 Act) The time between filing of securities registration statement and the date the registration statement becomes effective with the SEC.

QUITCLAIM DEED A deed which contains no warranties, and the grantor conveys only any right, title and interest held by the grantor, if any, at the time of execution.

QUORUM The holders of more than 50% of the outstanding shares of a corporation.

R

RACE NORMING OF EMPLOYMENT TESTS A device designed to ensure that a minimum number of minorities and women are in an application pool by adjusting the scores or using different cutoff scores for employment related tests on the basis of race, color, religion, sex, or national origin.

RACE-NOTICE RECORDING ACT Under a race-notice recording act, priority of conflicting interests in real property is determined as follows:

1. As between two recorded documents, the first to be recorded has priority.

2. As between a recorded instrument and a preexisting unrecorded instrument, the recorded instrument has priority unless the owner of the recorded interest had notice of the preexisting unrecorded interest.

3. As between two unrecorded interests, the first in time has priority.

RACKETEERING ACTIVITY The state and federal offenses engineered by syndicate bosses, including mail and wire fraud and fraud in the sale of securities.

RAIDER In a hostile takeover, a third party who seeks to obtain control of a corporation, called the target, over the objections of its management.

RATIFICATION A principal affirms through words or actions a prior act of an agent which did not bind the principal.

RAWLSIAN MORAL THEORY A deontological line of thought that aims to maximize the utility of the worst off person in society.

RECKLESSNESS In the criminal context, conscious disregard of a substantial risk that an individual's actions would result in the harm prohibited by a statute.

RECOGNITIONAL STRIKE An unlawful strike whose purpose is to force an employer to recognize the union as the collective bargaining agent for certain of its employees.

RECOGNIZED HAZARD (OSHA) Workplace conditions that are obviously dangerous or are considered by the employer or other employers in the industry to be hazardous.

RECORD The oral and written evidence presented at an administrative hearing.

RECORDABLE FORM The requirements established by the state regarding how title to real estate is filed and recorded. Requirements generally include legibility and notarization.

RECORDING ACTS An orderly process by which claims to interests in real property can be recorded as part of the public record.

RED-HERRING PROSPECTUS Preliminary prospectus; incomplete version of the final prospectus.

REDEMPTION The buying back of shares by a corporation from a shareholder.

REFERENCE RATE The lowest rate of interest offered by major lending institutions to their most creditworthy customers. Reference rate or base rate is preferable to prime rate in describing the rate charged the lender's most creditworthy customers because it does not imply that it is the lowest rate charged any customer.

REGISTERED MASK WORK Highly detailed transparencies which represent the topological layout of semiconductor chips.

REGISTRATION RIGHTS An investor's right to require a company to register under applicable federal and state securities laws the shares of common stock into which the preferred stock is convertible.

REGULATION Z Regulations issued by the Federal Reserve Board to interpret and enforce the federal Truth-in-Lending Act.

REGULATIONS The rules of order prescribed by superior or competent authority relating to action of those under its control.

REGULATORY NEGOTIATIONS A style of administrative rulemaking in which representatives of major groups convene with an administrative agency and work out a compromise through negotiation on the substance of new regulations.

REGULATORY TAKING The unlawful taking of private real property by the federal government for a public use without just compensation.

RELIANCE DAMAGES The awards made to a plaintiff for any expenditures made in reliance on a contract that was subsequently breached.

REMAND The power of a court of appeal to send a case back to a lower court for reconsideration.

REMOTE TIPPEE Tippees of tippees other than the original tippee.

REPORTER The published volumes of case decisions by a particular court or group of courts.

REPORTING COMPANY A company registered under section 12 of the 1934 Act which subjects issuers to various reporting requirements and to certain rules and regulations concerning proxies, tender offers, and insider trading.

REPRESENTATION ELECTION (NLRA) An election among employees to decide whether or not they want a union to represent them for collective bargaining.

REQUESTS FOR PRODUCTION OF DOCUMENTS Requests for documents such as medical records and personal files to be produced as part of the discovery process before a trial.

REQUIREMENTS CONTRACT A contract under which the buyer agrees to buy all of a specified commodity the buyer needs from the seller and the seller agrees to provide that amount.

RES IPSA LOQUITUR (the thing speaks for itself) The doctrine that allows a plaintiff to prove breach and causation indirectly.

RESALE PRICE MAINTENANCE (RPM) An agreement on price between firms at different levels of production or distribution that violates antitrust law.

RESCIND Void or make ineffective.

RESPONDEAT SUPERIOR (let the master answer) The doctrine under which an employer may be held vicariously or secondarily liable for the negligent or intentional conduct of the employee that is committed in the scope of the employee's employment.

RESPONDENT The party in a case against whom an appeal is taken; that is, the party who has an interest adverse to setting aside or reversing the judgment.

RESTATEMENT A former common-law rule codified and collected into formal written law.

RESTITUTION An award made to a plaintiff of a benefit improperly obtained by the defendant.

RESTRICTED GUARANTY A guaranty in which the guarantor's liability is enforceable only with respect to a specified transaction or series of transactions.

RESTRICTED SECURITIES Securities issued in a private placement; they cannot be resold or transferred unless they are either registered or exempt from registration. The most common exemption is pursuant to Securities and Exchange Commission rule 144.

RETRIBUTIVE JUSTICE A theory which states that every crime demands payment in the form of punishment.

REVERSIBILITY A theory which looks to whether one would want a rule applied to one's self.

REVIVAL STATUTES State and federal statutes which allow plaintiffs to file lawsuits which have been barred by the running of the statute of limitations.

REVOKE To annul an offer by recission.

REVOLVING LINE OF CREDIT A line of credit that allows a borrower to borrow whatever sums it requires up to a specified maximum amount and reborrow amounts it has repaid.

REVOLVING LOAN A loan that allows a borrower to borrow whatever sums it requires up to a specified maximum amount and reborrow amounts it has repaid.

RIGHT OF FIRST REFUSAL A contract that provides the holder with the right to purchase property on the same terms and conditions offered by or to a third party.

RIGHT OF REDEMPTION Gives the mortgagor or the debtor under a deed of trust, and certain other categories of interested persons, the right to redeem foreclosed property within a statutory limited period.

RIGHT OF RESCISSION A right to cancel a contract.

RIPENESS A court will not hear agency cases until they are ripe for decision, i.e., after a rule is adopted but before the agency seeks to apply it to a particular case.

RULE OF IMPOSSIBILITY The rule under which claims of predation are rejected because the marketplace in question cannot be successfully monopolized.

RULE OF REASON The rule that takes into account a defendant's actions as well as the structure of the market to determine whether an activity promotes or restrains competition.

RULES The legislative enactments which serve as general principles and guidelines for sensitive issues not governed by law.

RUNAWAY SHOP An illegal attempt by an employer to escape its collective-bargaining obligation by shutting down a unionized operation and moving the functions of that former operation to a nearby site.

S

S CORPORATION A business organization which is taxed only at the owner level.

SALE (1933 Act) Every contract of sale or disposition of a security or interest in a security, for value.

SCIENTER An intent to deceive.

SEC FORMS Regulations adopted by the Securities and Exchange Commission that specify what information must be provided the public. Examples include form S-1 for a prospectus for an initial public offering and form 10-K for an annual report of a publicly traded company, containing audited annual financial statements.

SECOND-STEP, BACK-END MERGER The second step in a corporate takeover whereby the shareholders who did not tender their shares receive cash or securities in a subsequent merger.

SECONDARY BOYCOTT A strike against an employer with whom a union has no quarrel in order to encourage it to stop doing business with an employer with whom it does have a dispute.

SECONDARY MEANING A descriptive trademark becomes protectable by acquiring secondary meaning, or sufficient consumer recognition through sufficient use and/or advertising of the goods under the mark.

SECONDARY OFFERING A securities offering by a person other than the issuer.

SECURED LOAN A loan backed up by collateral.

SECURED PARTY (under the UCC) The lender, seller, or other person in whose favor there is a security interest.

SECURED TRANSACTION A loan or other transaction secured by collateral put up by the borrower.

SECURITY (1933 Act) Any note, stock, treasury stock, bond, debenture, evidence of indebtedness, certificate of interest or participation in any profit-sharing agreement, collateral trust certificate, pre-organization certificate or subscription, transferable share, investment contract, voting-trust certificate, certificate of deposit for a security, fractional undivided interest in oil, gas, or other mineral rights, any put, call, straddle, option, or privilege on any security, certificate of deposit, or group or index of securities (including any interest therein or based on the value thereof, or any put, call, straddle, option, or privilege entered into on a national securities exchange relating to foreign currency, or, in general, any interest or instrument commonly known as a "security," or any certificate of interest or participation in, temporary or interim certificate for, receipt for, guarantee, of, or warrant or right to subscribe to or purchase, any of the foregoing.

SECURITY AGREEMENT (under the UCC) An agreement which creates or provides for a security interest.

SECURITY INTEREST (under the UCC) Any interest in personal property or fixtures which is used as collateral to secure payment or the performance of an obligation.

SELF-FINANCING Generating capital by carefully managing a company's own funds.

SELLING SHORT The sale of securities the seller does not yet own.

SENIOR DEBT Indebtedness that benefits from a debt subordination agreement.

SEPARATION OF POWERS The distinct authority of governance granted the three branches of U.S. government—judicial, executive and legislative—by the U.S. Constitution.

SEQUESTRATION ORDER A governmental order that requires spending levels to be reduced below the levels provided in the budget.

SERVICE MARK A legally protected identifying mark connected with services.

SETTLE When parties to a lawsuit go over claims and ascertain and agree upon the balance due one another prior to taking case to trial, they have settled the lawsuit.

SHAREHOLDER A holder of equity securities of a corporation. Also called stockholder.

SHAREHOLDER DERIVATIVE SUIT A lawsuit brought

against directors or officers of a corporation by a shareholder on behalf of the corporation.

SHAREHOLDER OF RECORD The persons whose names appear on a corporation's shareholder list on a specified date who are entitled to vote.

SHELF REGISTRATION The registration of a number of securities at one time for issuance later.

SHORT-SWING TRADING The purchase and sale or sale and purchase by an officer, director or greater than 10% shareholders of securities of a public company within a six-month period.

SHOWING OF INTEREST A sufficient number of employees who express interest in a representation election.

SLANDER A spoken communication to a third party by a defendant of an untrue statement of fact that injures a plaintiff's reputation.

SLANDER PER SE Words that are slanderous in and of themselves. Only statements that a person has committed a serious crime, has a loathsome disease, is guilty of sexual misconduct, or is not fit to conduct business are slanderous per se.

SMALL BUSINESS ISSUERS Companies with revenues less than $25 million whose market value of publicly held securities (other than those held by affiliates) is less than $25 million.

SOLE PROPRIETORSHIP One person owns all the assets of the business, has complete control of the business, and is solely liable for all the debts of the business.

SOVEREIGN IMMUNITY The doctrine that prevents the courts of one country from hearing suits against the governments of other countries. This Supreme Court doctrine protects from antitrust law enforcement those foreign governments that act anticompetitively and firms required by foreign governments to act anticompetitively.

SPECIFIC PERFORMANCE A court order to a breaching party to complete the contract as promised.

SPECIFICATIONS The description of an invention in its best mode and the manner and process of making and using the invention so that a person skilled in the relevant field may make and use the invention.

SQUATTER'S RIGHTS Ownership of property that is not occupied by its owner for a certain period of time may be transferred to those who have been unlawfully occupying it and exercising rights of ownership. Such a transfer is usually not reflected in the official land records. Also called adverse possession.

STAGGERED (or CLASSIFIED) BOARD A board on which directors serve for specified terms, usually three years, with only a fraction of them up for reelection at any one time.

STANDBY LETTER OF CREDIT A method of securing financing for large projects in which an issuing bank in the host jurisdiction undertakes at the request of the borrower to pay a sum of money to the entity that has advanced payments for the project. The issuing bank will pay the money to the entity upon presentation of certain documents specified by the borrower, usually a brief statement, in language agreed upon by the borrower and the entity, that the borrower has failed to adhere to an underlying project contract and that the entity is entitled to payment from the issuing bank.

STANDING A party to a lawsuit has standing if the person seeking relief is the proper party to advance the litigation, has a personal interest in the outcome of the suit, and will benefit from a favorable ruling.

STARE DECISIS (to abide by) The doctrine which holds that once a court resolves a particular issue, other courts addressing a similar legal problem generally follow the initial court's decision.

STATE IMPLEMENTATION PLANS (SIPs) The prescribed emission control measures for stationary sources existing prior to 1970 and on the use of motor vehicles as necessary to achieve national ambient air quality standards.

STATE-OF-THE-ART-DEFENSE A defense against claims based upon a manufacturer's compliance with the best available technology (which may or may not be synonymous with the custom and practice of the industry).

STATUTE OF FRAUDS A statute which requires that certain contracts, such as contracts conveying an interest in real property, must be in writing to be enforceable in a court.

STATUTE OF LIMITATIONS A time limit, defined by the statute, within which a lawsuit must be brought.

STATUTE OF REPOSE A time limit that cuts off the right to assert a cause of action after a specified period of time.

STATUTORY BAR An inventor is denied patent protection in the event that prior to one year before the inventor's filing, the invention was patented or described in a printed publication in the United States or a foreign country or publicly used or sold in the United States.

STOCK LOCK-UP OPTION A lock-up option relating to stock.

STOCK PARKING The temporary sale of shares to another entity or individual to avoid tax reporting requirements or the net margin requirements of the securities laws applicable to brokerage firms.

STOCKHOLDER A holder of equity securities of a corporation. Also called shareholder.

STRAIGHT BANKRUPTCY A bankruptcy in which the trustee liquidates the estate and distributes the proceeds first to secured creditors (to the extent of their collateral) and then in a prescribed order, pro rata within each level.

STRATEGIC ALLIANCE A source of financing by which a collaborative arrangement is entered into between an established company that has complementary business needs or objectives to another company.

STRICT LIABILITY The concept that sellers are liable for all hazardous products that unduly threaten consumers' personal safety. Strict liability is imposed in two circumstances: (1)

strict liability in product liability cases; and (2) traditional strict liability for abnormally dangerous activities.

STRONG ARM CLAUSE The clause which grants a debtor in possession the rights of a hypothetical creditor who extended credit to the debtor at the time of bankruptcy and who, as a result, either obtained a judicial lien on all property in which the debtor has an interest or obtained an execution against the debtor that was returned unsatisfied.

STRUCTURAL ANTIDILUTION A provision that adjusts the conversion ratio at which convertible preferred shares may be exchanged for shares of common stock, if the total number of shares of common stock is increased, for example, by a stock split.

SUBDIVISION A division of land into separate parcels for development purposes.

SUBJECT MATTER JURISDICTION The specific types of cases enumerated under Article III of the U.S. Constitution to be decided by the Supreme Court and lower courts established by Congress.

SUBLEASE An act by a tenant of renting out all or a portion of property the tenant has rented from a landlord.

SUBORDINATED DEBT INSTRUMENT The document that provides that a holder's right to repayment is subordinate to that of other creditors of a corporation.

SUBSTANTIAL EVIDENCE STANDARD Under this standard, the courts defer to agency factual determinations in formal adjudications even if the record would support other factual conclusions.

SUBSTANTIAL TRANSFORMATION An article exported from its country of origin is changed into a new article of commerce in a different country.

SUBSTANTIVE DUE PROCESS The Constitutional guarantee that no person shall be arbitrarily deprived of life, liberty or property; the essence of substantive due process is protection from arbitrary and unreasonable action.

SUBSTANTIVE LEGAL OBLIGATIONS The legal rules that define the rights and duties of the agency and of persons dealing with it.

SUCCESSOR LIABILITY Individuals or entities who acquire an interest in a business or in real property may be held liable for personal injury or property or environmental damage resulting from acts of the predecessor entity or previous owner.

SUMMARY JUDGMENT A procedural device available for disposition of a controversy without trial. A judge will grant summary judgment only if all of the written evidence before the court clearly establishes that there are no disputed issues of material fact and the party who requested the summary judgment is entitled to prevail as a matter of law.

SUMMONS The official notice to a defendant that a lawsuit is pending against the defendant in a particular court.

SUPER 301 A provision of the Omnibus Trade Act of 1988, requiring that a list be drawn up of the foreign governments whose practices pose the most significant barriers to U.S. exports, and that section 301 investigations be commenced immediately with respect to these practices.

SUPER DISCHARGE A type of discharge available under chapter 13 that extinguishes otherwise nondischargeable debts such as claims for fraud, theft, willful and malicious injury, or drunk driving, but not spousal or child support.

SUPERLIEN An instrument that secures recovery of response costs incurred by state agencies.

SUPERVISOR (NLRA) Anyone possessing specified personnel functions if the exercise of that authority is not of a merely routine or clerical nature, but requires the use of independent judgment.

SURPRISE The extent to which the supposedly agreed upon terms of the bargain are hidden in a densely printed form drafted by the party seeking to enforce the disputed terms.

SURVIVING CORPORATION In a corporate merger, the corporation that maintains its corporate existence is the surviving corporation.

SUSTAINABLE DEVELOPMENT A theory that holds that future prosperity depends on preserving natural capital—air, water, and other ecological resources.

SYNDICATED LOAN In a syndicated loan, the lenders enter into concurrent direct obligations with the borrower to make a loan, typically on a pro rata basis. The loan is coordinated by a lead lender that serves as agent for all of the lenders in disbursing the funds, collecting payments of interest and principal, and administering and enforcing the loan.

T

TAKEOVER A bidder acquires sufficient stock from a corporation's shareholders to obtain control of the corporation.

TARGET CORPORATION A corporation that is the subject of a tender offer.

TARIFF CLASSIFICATION The tariff on articles imported to the U.S. is determined by their description on the Harmonized Tariff Schedule.

TAX BASIS The amount of cash or the fair market value of property exchanged for another asset, such as a general partnership interest.

TAX-DEFERRED EXCHANGE The transfer of real property for an alternative piece of real property which transfer is subject to certain restrictions.

TELEOLOGICAL THEORY An ethical theory concerned with the consequences of something. The good of an action is to be judged by the effect of the action on others.

TEMPORARY INSIDERS Outside attorneys, accountants, or investment bankers who are not directly employed by a corporation, but who acquire confidential information through performance of professional services.

TENANTS IN COMMON The individuals who own undivided interests in a parcel of real property.

TENDER OFFER A public offer to all of the shareholders of a corporation to buy their shares at a stated price, usually higher than the market price.

TERM LOAN A loan for a specified amount, either in a lump sum or in installments to be repaid on a specified maturity date or paid off over a period of time.

TERM SHEET A letter that outlines the terms and conditions on which a lender will lend.

TERMINATION The point after the dissolution of a partnership when all the partnership affairs are wound up and partners' authority to act for the partnership is completely extinguished.

TERRITORIAL RESTRICTIONS Restrictions which prevent a dealer or distributor from selling outside a certain territory. Also called customer restrictions.

THIRD-PARTY BENEFICIARY One who does not give consideration for a promise yet has legal rights to enforce the contract. A person is a third-party beneficiary with legal rights when the contracting parties intend to benefit that person.

TIP A disclosure made to an individual and withheld from the general public.

TIPPEE A person who receives inside information.

TIPPER A person who gives inside information.

TOMBSTONE AD A newspaper advertisement surrounded by bold black lines identifying the existence of a public offering and indicating where a prospectus may be obtained.

TORT A civil wrong resulting in injury to a person or a person's property.

TOXIC TORT Any wrongful injury that is caused by exposure to a harmful, hazardous, or poisonous substance.

TRADE NAME A trade name or a corporate name identifies and symbolizes a business as a whole, as opposed to a trademark, which is used to identify and distinguish the various products and services sold by the business.

TRADE SECRET Information that derives independent economic value from not being generally known and that is subject to reasonable efforts to maintain its secrecy.

TRADEMARK A word or symbol used on goods or with services that indicates their origin.

TRANSACTION VALUE The price of an imported article indicated on a sales invoice.

TRANSACTIONAL IMMUNITY The prohibition from prosecution granted a witness that relates to any matter discussed in that person's testimony.

TRESPASS TO LAND The intentional, negligent, or ultrahazardous invasion of property (below the surface or in the airspace above) without consent of the owner.

TRESPASS TO PERSONAL PROPERTY When personal property is interfered with but not taken, destroyed, or substantially altered (i.e., not converted), there is said to be a trespass to personal property.

TRIPLE NET LEASE A type of industrial lease that requires the tenant to pay all taxes, insurance, and maintenance expenses.

TRUST (1) A combination of competitors who act together to fix prices thereby stifling competition. (2) A manner of holding property which is controlled by a trustee for the benefit of a beneficiary.

TRUSTEE An individual who controls property held in trust for the benefit of a beneficiary.

TYING ARRANGEMENT A business arrangement whereby a seller will only sell product A (the tying or desired product) to the customer if the customer agrees to purchases product B (the tied product) from the seller.

U

ULTRAHAZARDOUS ACTIVITY Activity which is so dangerous that no amount of care could protect others from the risk of harm.

UNAVOIDABLY UNSAFE PRODUCT A product such as a vaccine that is generally beneficial but is known to have harmful side effects in some cases.

UNCONSCIONABLE A contract term that is oppressive or fundamentally unfair.

UNDERCAPITALIZATION THEORY A corporation is a separate entity, but its lack of adequate capital constitutes a fraud upon the public.

UNDERWRITER (1933 Act) Any person who has purchased from an issuer with a view to, or offers or sells for an issuer in connection with, the distribution of any security.

UNDISCLOSED PRINCIPAL A third party to an agreement does not know or have reason to know of a principal's identity or existence.

UNDUE BURDEN Under the U.S. Constitution, a regulation creates an undue burden when the regulatory burden on interstate commerce outweighs the state's interest in the legislation.

UNENFORCEABLE CONTRACT A contract having no legal effect or force in a court action. A contract is unenforceable if it is: (1) illegal, or (2) unconscionable. A contract is also unenforceable if some public policy interest dictates that the agreement should not be upheld, regardless of the desire of one or more of the parties.

UNFAIR LABOR PRACTICE STRIKE A union strikes an employer for the employer's failure to bargain in good faith.

UNFAIR LABOR PRACTICES (NLRA) Unlawful misconduct by an employer to employees.

UNILATERAL CONTRACT A promise given in exchange for an act.

UNION AUTHORIZATION CARDS Generally, these cards contain a statement that the individual signing it wishes to be represented for purposes of collective bargaining by a certain union.

UNION SECURITY CLAUSE The clause in a collective bargaining contract under which employees in a particular unit are required, after a certain period of time, to become members of a union as a condition of employment.

UNJUST ENRICHMENT The unfair appropriation of the benefits of negotiation of contracts for the party's own use.

UNORTHODOX TRANSACTION The purchase or sale by an officer, director, or greater than 10% shareholder that would otherwise result in recoverable short-swing profits but is involuntary and does not involve the payment of cash, and there is no possibility of speculative abuse of insider information.

UNREASONABLE PER SE Unreasonable no matter what the circumstances.

UPSTREAM GUARANTY A guaranty whereby subsidiaries guarantee the parent corporation's debt, or pledge their assets as security for the parent corporation's debt.

USE IMMUNITY The prohibition of the testimony of a witness from being used in any way in connection with the case in which that person is testifying.

USEFUL ARTICLE DOCTRINE The doctrine that holds that copyrightable pictorial, graphic, and sculptural works shall include works of artistic craftsmanship insofar as their form but not their mechanical or utilitarian aspects are concerned.

USURY Charging an amount of interest on a loan that is in excess of the maximum specified by applicable law.

USURY STATUTES State statutes that set legal caps on what interest rates lenders may charge.

UTILITARIANISM A major teleological system that stands for the proposition that the ideal is to maximize the total benefit for everyone involved.

UTILITY PATENT A patent that protects any novel, useful and nonobvious process, machine, manufacture or composition of matter, or any novel, useful and nonobvious improvement of such process, machine, manufacture or composition of matter.

V

VACATE The power of a court of appeal to nullify a previous court's ruling.

VALUE Cash, property, or compensation for past services.

VARIANCE A method of relief from the strict terms of a zoning ordinance that allows a landowner to construct a structure or carry on an activity not otherwise permitted under zoning regulations.

VENTURE CAPITAL Money managed by professional investors for investment in new enterprises.

VENUE The particular county, or geographical area, in which a court with jurisdiction may hear and determine a case.

VERTICAL AGREEMENT A conspiracy agreement between firms that operate at different levels of production or distribution.

VERTICAL MARKET DIVISION An agreement between a company and a dealer or distributor that prevents the dealer or the distributor from selling outside a certain territory or to a certain class of customer.

VERTICAL MERGER A combination between firms at different points along the chain of distribution.

VESTED RIGHT The right of a developer to develop property sometimes, but not always, obtained when a building permit is issued, substantial work is done, and substantial liabilities are incurred in reliance of that permit.

VICARIOUS LIABILITY The imposition of criminal liability on a defendant for the wrong acts of its agents. Also called imputed liability.

VIEW EASEMENT An interest in property owned by another by which an easement holder is guaranteed that a landowner will not obstruct the holder's view by making changes to said property.

VOIDABLE Unenforceable.

VOIR DIRE Questioning of potential jurors to determine possible bias.

VOLUNTARY CONVERSION The exchange by a holder of preferred stock for common stock on the occurrence of certain events.

VOLUNTARY REDEMPTION RIGHTS The requirement of a corporation to redeem an investor's shares for cash at a specified price, provided that the corporation is not prohibited by law from buying back stock or making distributions to its shareholders.

W

WAIVE To refrain from exercising certain rights.

WARRANT A right, for a given period of time, to purchase a stated amount of a security (frequently, stock) at a stated price (often equal to the fair market value when the warrant is issued, permitting its holder to benefit from any increase in values of the securities).

WARRANTY DEED A warranty deed is similar to a grant deed. In addition to the implied warranties contained in a grant deed, the grantor of a warranty deed also expressly warrants the title to and the quiet possession of the property to grantee.

WHITE-COLLAR CRIME The violations of the law by corporations or their agents.

WINDING UP The process of settling partnership affairs after dissolution.

WIRE FRAUD A scheme intended to defraud or to obtain money or property by fraudulent means through use of telephone systems.

WORK LETTER AGREEMENT An agreement between a tenant and a landlord, often an exhibit to a lease, that covers issues regarding tenant's improvements to rented space.

WORK-PRODUCT RULE The common-law rule that the court cannot force disclosure of the private memoranda and personal thoughts of an attorney made while preparing a case for trial.

WORKOUT An out-of-court settlement between debtors and

creditors that restructures the debtor's financial affairs in much the same way that a confirmed plan would, but it can bind only those who expressly consent.

WRAP-AROUND FINANCING The transaction in which a new lender lends the owner of mortgaged real property additional funds and agrees to take over the servicing of the first loan. In exchange, the owner executes a deed of trust or mortgage and an all-inclusive note, covering the combined amount of the first and new loans.

WRIT An order in writing issued under seal in the name of a court or judicial officer commanding the person to whom it is directed to perform or refrain from performing an act specified therein.

WRIT OF CERTIORARI An order written by the U.S. Supreme Court when it decides to hear a case, ordering the lower court to certify the record of proceedings below and send it up to the U.S. Supreme Court.

WRONGFUL DISCHARGE An employee termination without good cause.

Z

ZONE OF DANGER The area in which an individual is physically close enough to a victim of an accident to also be in personal danger.

ZONING The division of a city into districts and the application of specific land use regulations in each district.

INDEX